Lecture Notes in Computer Science 12825

More information about this subseries at http://www.springer.com/series/7410

Tal Malkin · Chris Peikert (Eds.)

Advances in Cryptology – CRYPTO 2021

41st Annual International Cryptology Conference, CRYPTO 2021
Virtual Event, August 16–20, 2021
Proceedings, Part I

Springer

Editors
Tal Malkin 🆔
Columbia University
New York City, NY, USA

Chris Peikert 🆔
University of Michigan
Ann Arbor, MI, USA

ISSN 0302-9743   ISSN 1611-3349   (electronic)
Lecture Notes in Computer Science
ISBN 978-3-030-84241-3   ISBN 978-3-030-84242-0   (eBook)
https://doi.org/10.1007/978-3-030-84242-0

LNCS Sublibrary: SL4 – Security and Cryptology

This Springer imprint is published by the registered company Springer Nature Switzerland AG
The registered company address is: Gewerbestrasse 11, 6330 Cham, Switzerland

Preface

The 41st International Cryptology Conference (Crypto 2021), sponsored by the International Association of Cryptologic Research (IACR), was held during August 16–20, 2021. Due to the ongoing COVID-19 pandemic, and for the second consecutive year, Crypto was held as an online-only virtual conference, instead of at its usual venue of the University of California, Santa Barbara. In addition, six affiliated workshop events took place during the days immediately prior to the conference.

The Crypto conference continues its substantial growth pattern: this year's offering received a record-high 430 submissions for consideration, of which 103 (also a record) were accepted to appear in the program. The two program chairs were not allowed to submit a paper, and Program Committee (PC) members were limited to two submissions each. Review and extensive discussion occurred from late February through mid-May, in a double-blind, two-stage process that included an author rebuttal phase (following the initial reviews) and extensive discussion by reviewers. We thank the 58-person PC and the 390 external reviewers for their efforts to ensure that, during the continuing COVID-19 pandemic and unusual work and life circumstances, we nevertheless were able to perform a high-quality review process.

The PC selected four papers to receive recognition via awards, along with invitations to the Journal of Cryptology, via a voting-based process that took into account conflicts of interest (the program chairs did not vote).

- The Best Paper Award went to "On the Possibility of Basing Cryptography on $\mathrm{EXP} \neq \mathrm{BPP}$" by Yanyi Liu and Rafael Pass.
- The Best Paper by Early Career Researchers Award, along with an Honorable Mention for Best Paper, went to "Linear Cryptanalysis of FF3-1 and FEA" by Tim Beyne.
- Honorable Mentions for Best Paper also went to "Efficient Key Recovery for all HFE Signature Variants" by Chengdong Tao, Albrecht Petzoldt, and Jintai Ding; and "Three Halves Make a Whole? Beating the Half-Gates Lower Bound for Garbled Circuits" by Mike Rosulek and Lawrence Roy.

In addition to the regular program, Crypto 2021 included two invited talks, by Vanessa Teague on "Which e-voting problems do we need to solve?" and Jens Groth on "A world of SNARKs." The conference also carried forward the long-standing tradition of having a rump session, organized in a virtual format.

The chairs would also like to thank the many other people whose hard work helped ensure that Crypto 2021 was a success:

- Vladimir Kolesnikov (Georgia Institute of Technology)—Crypto 2021 general chair.
- Daniele Micciancio (University of California, San Diego), Thomas Ristenpart (Cornell Tech), Yevgeniy Dodis (New York University), and Thomas Shrimpton (University of Florida)—Crypto 2021 Advisory Committee.

- Carmit Hazay (Bar Ilan University)—Crypto 2021 workshop chair.
- Bertram Poettering and Antigoni Polychroniadou—Crypto 2021 rump session chairs.
- Kevin McCurley, for his critical assistance in setting up and managing the HotCRP paper submission and review system, conference website, and other technology.
- Kevin McCurley, Kay McKelly, and members of the IACR's emergency pandemic team for their work in designing and running the virtual format.
- Anna Kramer and her colleagues at Springer.

July 2021   Tal Malkin
                                                                         Chris Peikert

Organization

General Chair

Vladimir Kolesnikov   Georgia Institute of Technology, USA

Program Committee Chairs

Tal Malkin   Columbia University, USA
Chris Peikert   University of Michigan and Algorand, Inc., USA

Program Committee

Abhi Shelat   Northeastern University, USA
Andrej Bogdanov   Chinese University of Hong Kong, Hong Kong
Antigoni Polychroniadou   JP Morgan AI Research, USA
Brice Minaud   Inria and École Normale Supérieure, France
Chaya Ganesh   Indian Institute of Science, India
Chris Peikert   University of Michigan and Algorand, Inc., USA
Claudio Orlandi   Aarhus University, Denmark
Daniele Venturi   Sapienza University of Rome, Italy
David Cash   University of Chicago, USA
David Wu   University of Virginia, USA
Dennis Hofheinz   ETH Zurich, Switzerland
Divesh Aggarwal   National University of Singapore, Singapore
Dominique Unruh   University of Tartu, Estonia
Elena Andreeva   Technical University of Vienna, Austria
Elena Kirshanova   Immanuel Kant Baltic Federal University, Russia
Fabrice Benhamouda   Algorand Foundation, USA
Fang Song   Portland State University, USA
Frederik Vercauteren   KU Leuven, Belgium
Ghada Almashaqbeh   University of Connecticut, USA
Itai Dinur   Ben-Gurion University, Israel
Jean-Pierre Tillich   Inria, France
Jeremiah Blocki   Purdue University, USA
John Schanck   University of Waterloo, Canada
Jonathan Bootle   IBM Research, Switzerland
Joseph Jaeger   University of Washington, USA
Junqing Gong   East China Normal University, China
Lisa Kohl   CWI Amsterdam, The Netherlands
Manoj Prabhakaran   IIT Bombay, India
Marcel Keller   CSIRO's Data61, Australia
Mariana Raykova   Google, USA

Mike Rosulek	Oregon State University, USA
Mor Weiss	Bar-Ilan University, Israel
Muthuramakrishnan Venkitasubramaniam	University of Rochester, USA
Ni Trieu	Arizona State University, USA
Nir Bitansky	Tel Aviv University, Israel
Nuttapong Attrapadung	AIST, Japan
Omer Paneth	Tel Aviv University, Israel
Paul Grubbs	NYU, Cornell Tech and University of Michigan, USA
Peihan Miao	University of Illinois at Chicago, USA
Peter Schwabe	Max Planck Institute for Security and Privacy, Germany, and Radboud University, The Netherlands
Ran Canetti	BU, USA, and Tel Aviv University, Israel
Romain Gay	IBM Research, Switzerland
Ron Steinfeld	Monash University, Australia
Rosario Gennaro	City University of New York, USA
Ryo Nishimaki	NTT Secure Platform Laboratories, Japan
Sandro Coretti	IOHK, Switzerland
Sikhar Patranabis	Visa Research, USA
Sina Shiehian	UC Berkeley and Stony Brook University, USA
Siyao Guo	NYU Shanghai, China
Stanislaw Jarecki	University of California, Irvine, USA
Tal Malkin	Columbia University, USA
Tarik Moataz	Aroki Systems, USA
Thomas Peters	UC Louvain, Belgium
Thomas Peyrin	Nanyang Technological University, Singapore
Tianren Liu	University of Washington, USA
Viet Tung Hoang	Florida State University, USA
Xavier Bonnetain	University of Waterloo, Canada
Yu Yu	Shanghai Jiao Tong University, China

Additional Reviewers

Aaram Yun	Akshayaram Srinivasan
Aarushi Goel	Akshima
Aayush Jain	Alain Passelègue
Abhishek Jain	Alex Bienstock
Adrien Benamira	Alex Lombardi
Agnes Kiss	Alexander Golovnev
Aishwarya Thiruvengadam	Alexander Hoover
Ajith Suresh	Alexander May
Akin Ünal	Alexandre Wallet
Akinori Kawachi	Alexandru Cojocaru
Akira Takahashi	Alice Pellet-Mary
Akshay Degwekar	Alin Tomescu

Amin Sakzad
Amit Singh Bhati
Amitabh Trehan
Amos Beimel
Anat Paskin-Cherniavsky
Anca Nitulescu
André Chailloux
Andre Esser
André Schrottenloher
Andrea Coladangelo
Andreas Hülsing
Antonin Leroux
Antonio Florez-Gutierrez
Archita Agarwal
Ariel Hamlin
Arka Rai Choudhuri
Arnab Roy
Ashrujit Ghoshal
Ashutosh Kumar
Ashwin Jha
Atsushi Takayasu
Aurore Guillevic
Avijit Dutta
Avishay Yanay
Baiyu Li
Balazs Udvarhelyi
Balthazar Bauer
Bart Mennink
Ben Smith
Benjamin Diamond
Benjamin Fuller
Benny Applebaum
Benoît Cogliati
Benoit Libert
Bertram Poettering
Binyi Chen
Bo-Yin Yang
Bogdan Ursu
Bruno Freitas dos Santos
Bryan Parno
Byeonghak Lee
Carl Bootland
Carles Padro
Carmit Hazay
Carsten Baum
Cecilia Boschini

Chan Nam Ngo
Charles Momin
Charlotte Bonte
Chen Qian
Chen-Da Liu-Zhang
Chenkai Weng
Chethan Kamath
Chris Brzuska
Christian Badertscher
Christian Janson
Christian Majenz
Christian Matt
Christina Boura
Christof Paar
Christoph Egger
Cody Freitag
Dahmun Goudarzi
Dakshita Khurana
Damian Vizar
Damiano Abram
Damien Stehlé
Damien Vergnaud
Daniel Escudero
Daniel Jost
Daniel Masny
Daniel Tschudi
Daniel Wichs
Dario Catalano
Dario Fiore
David Gerault
David Heath
Debbie Leung
Dean Doron
Debapriya Basu Roy
Dima Kogan
Dimitrios Papadopoulos
Divya Gupta
Divya Ravi
Dominique Schröder
Eduardo Soria-Vazquez
Eldon Chung
Emmanuela Orsini
Eran Lambooij
Eran Omri
Eshan Chattopadhyay
Estuardo Alpirez Bock

Evgenios Kornaropoulos
Eysa Lee
Fabio Banfi
Felix Engelmann
Felix Günther
Ferdinand Sibleyras
Fermi Ma
Fernando Virdia
Francesco Berti
François-Xavier Standaert
Fuyuki Kitagawa
Gaëtan Cassiers
Gaëtan Leurent
Gayathri Annapurna Garimella
Geoffroy Couteau
Georg Fuchsbauer
Ghous Amjad
Gildas Avoine
Giorgos Panagiotakos
Giorgos Zirdelis
Giulio Malavolta
Guy Rothblum
Hamidreza Khoshakhlagh
Hamza Abusalah
Hanjun Li
Hannah Davis
Haoyang Wang
Hart Montgomery
Henry Corrigan-Gibbs
Hila Dahari
Huijia Lin
Ian McQuoid
Ignacio Cascudo
Igors Stepanovs
Ilan Komargodski
Ilia Iliashenko
Ingrid Verbauwhede
Itamar Levi
Ittai Abraham
Ivan Damgård
Jack Doerner
Jacob Schuldt
James Bartusek
Jan Czajkowski
Jan-Pieter D'Anvers
Jaspal Singh

Jean Paul Degabriele
Jesper Buus Nielsen
Jesús-Javier Chi-Domínguez
Ji Luo
Jian Guo
Jiaxin Pan
Jiayu Xu
Joanne Adams-Woodage
João Ribeiro
Joël Alwen
Julia Hesse
Julia Len
Julian Loss
Junichi Tomida
Justin Holmgren
Justin Thaler
Kai-Min Chung
Katerina Sotiraki
Katharina Boudgoust
Kathrin Hövelmanns
Katsuyuki Takashima
Kazuhiko Minematsu
Keita Xagawa
Kevin Yeo
Kewen Wu
Khoa Nguyen
Koji Nuida
Kristina Hostáková
Laasya Bangalore
Lars Knudsen
Lawrence Roy
Lejla Batina
Lennart Braun
Léo Colisson
Leo de Castro
Léo Ducas
Léo Perrin
Lin Lyu
Ling Song
Luca De Feo
Luca Nizzardo
Lucjan Hanzlik
Luisa Siniscalchi
Łukasz Chmielewski
Maciej Obremski
Madalina Bolboceanu

Mahimna Kelkar
Maria Eichlseder
María Naya-Plasencia
Marilyn George
Marios Georgiou
Mark Abspoel
Mark Simkin
Mark Zhandry
Markulf Kohlweiss
Marshall Ball
Marta Mularczyk
Martin Albrecht
Martin Hirt
Mary Wooters
Masayuki Abe
Matteo Campanelli
Matthias Fitzi
Mia Filic
Michael Reichle
Michael Rosenberg
Michael Walter
Michele Orru
Miguel Ambrona
Mingyuan Wang
Miran Kim
Miruna Rosca
Miyako Ohkubo
Mohammad Hajiabadi
Mohammad Hossein Faghihi Sereshgi
Monosij Maitra
Morgan Shirley
Mridul Nandi
Muhammed F. Esgin
Mustafa Khairallah
Naomi Ephraim
Nathan Manohar
Naty Peter
Navid Alamati
Ngoc Khanh Nguyen
Nicholas Spooner
Nicholas-Philip Brandt
Nico Döttling
Nicolas Resch
Nicolas Sendrier
Nikolaos Makriyannis
Nikolas Melissaris

Nils Fleischhacker
Nina Bindel
Nirvan Tyagi
Niv Gilboa
Noah Stephens-Davidowitz
Olivier Blazy
Olivier Bronchain
Omri Shmueli
Orfeas Stefanos Thyfronitis Litos
Orr Dunkelman
Oxana Poburinnaya
Patrick Derbez
Patrick Longa
Patrick Towa
Paul Rösler
Paul Zimmermann
Peter Gazi
Peter Rindal
Philippe Langevin
Pierre Briaud
Pierre Meyer
Pierrick Gaudry
Pierrick Mèaux
Po-Chu Hsu
Prabhanjan Ananth
Prashant Vasudeval
Pratik Sarkar
Pratik Soni
Pratyay Mukherjee
Pratyush Mishra
Qian Li
Qiang Tang
Qipeng Liu
Quan Quan Tan
Rachit Garg
Radu Titiu
Rajeev Raghunath
Rajendra Kumar
Ran Cohen
Raymond K. Zhao
Riad Wahby
Rishab Goyal
Rishabh Bhadauria
Rishiraj Bhattacharyya
Ritam Bhaumik
Robi Pedersen

Rohit Chatterjee
Rolando La Placa
Roman Langrehr
Rongmao Chen
Rupeng Yang
Ruth Ng
Saba Eskandarian
Sabine Oechsner
Sahar Mazloom
Saikrishna Badrinarayanan
Sam Kim
Samir Hodzic
Sanjam Garg
Sayandeep Saha
Schuyler Rosefield
Semyon Novoselov
Serge Fehr
Shai Halevi
Shashank Agrawal
Sherman S. M. Chow
Shi Bai
Shifeng Sun
Shivam Bhasin
Shota Yamada
Shuai Han
Shuichi Katsumata
Siang Meng Sim
Somitra Sanadhya
Sonia Belaïd
Sophia Yakoubov
Srinivas Vivek
Srinivasan Raghuraman
Sruthi Sekar
Stefano Tessaro
Steve Lu
Steven Galbraith
Stjepan Picek
Sumegha Garg
Susumu Kiyoshima
Sven Maier
Takahiro Matsuda
Takashi Yamakawa
Tal Moran
Tamer Mour
Thom Wiggers

Thomas Agrikola
Thomas Attema
Thomas Debris-Alazard
Thomas Decru
Tiancheng Xie
Tim Beyne
Titouan Tanguy
Tommaso Gagliardoni
Varun Maram
Vassilis Zikas
Venkata Koppula
Vincent Zucca
Virginie Lallemand
Ward Beullens
Wei Dai
Willy Quach
Wouter Castryck
Xiao Liang
Xiao Wang
Xiong Fan
Yael Kalai
Yan Bo Ti
Yann Rotella
Yannick Seurin
Yaobin Shen
Yashvanth Kondi
Yfke Dulek
Yiannis Tselekounis
Yifan Song
Yilei Chen
Yixin Shen
Yongsoo Song
Yu Long Chen
Yu Sa
Yue Guo
Yuncong Hu
Yupeng Zhang
Yuriy Polyakov
Yuval Ishai
Zahra Jafargholi
Zeyong Li
Zhengfeng Ji
Zichen Gui
Zuoxia Yu
Zvika Brakerski

Contents – Part I

Invited Talk

Which E-Voting Problems Do We Need to Solve? 3
   Vanessa Teague

Award Papers

On the Possibility of Basing Cryptography on $EXP \neq BPP$ 11
   Yanyi Liu and Rafael Pass

Linear Cryptanalysis of FF3-1 and FEA 41
   Tim Beyne

Efficient Key Recovery for All HFE Signature Variants 70
   Chengdong Tao, Albrecht Petzoldt, and Jintai Ding

Three Halves Make a Whole? Beating the Half-Gates Lower Bound
for Garbled Circuits 94
   Mike Rosulek and Lawrence Roy

Signatures

Threshold Schnorr with Stateless Deterministic Signing from Standard
Assumptions 127
   *François Garillot, Yashvanth Kondi, Payman Mohassel,
   and Valeria Nikolaenko*

Two-Round Trip Schnorr Multi-signatures via Delinearized Witnesses 157
   Handan Kılınç Alper and Jeffrey Burdges

MuSig2: Simple Two-Round Schnorr Multi-signatures 189
   Jonas Nick, Tim Ruffing, and Yannick Seurin

Tighter Security for Schnorr Identification and Signatures:
A High-Moment Forking Lemma for Σ-Protocols 222
   Lior Rotem and Gil Segev

DualRing: Generic Construction of Ring Signatures
with Efficient Instantiations 251
   *Tsz Hon Yuen, Muhammed F. Esgin, Joseph K. Liu, Man Ho Au,
   and Zhimin Ding*

Compact Ring Signatures from Learning with Errors   282
    Rohit Chatterjee, Sanjam Garg, Mohammad Hajiabadi,
    Dakshita Khurana, Xiao Liang, Giulio Malavolta, Omkant Pandey,
    and Sina Shiehian

Quantum Cryptography

A Black-Box Approach to Post-Quantum Zero-Knowledge in Constant
Rounds   315
    Nai-Hui Chia, Kai-Min Chung, and Takashi Yamakawa

On the Concurrent Composition of Quantum Zero-Knowledge   346
    Prabhanjan Ananth, Kai-Min Chung, and Rolando L. La Placa

Multi-theorem Designated-Verifier NIZK for QMA   375
    Omri Shmueli

On the Round Complexity of Secure Quantum Computation   406
    James Bartusek, Andrea Coladangelo, Dakshita Khurana,
    and Fermi Ma

Round Efficient Secure Multiparty Quantum Computation with Identifiable
Abort.   436
    Bar Alon, Hao Chung, Kai-Min Chung, Mi-Ying Huang, Yi Lee,
    and Yu-Ching Shen

One-Way Functions Imply Secure Computation in a Quantum World   467
    James Bartusek, Andrea Coladangelo, Dakshita Khurana,
    and Fermi Ma

Impossibility of Quantum Virtual Black-Box Obfuscation
of Classical Circuits   497
    Gorjan Alagic, Zvika Brakerski, Yfke Dulek, and Christian Schaffner

New Approaches for Quantum Copy-Protection   526
    Scott Aaronson, Jiahui Liu, Qipeng Liu, Mark Zhandry,
    and Ruizhe Zhang

Hidden Cosets and Applications to Unclonable Cryptography   556
    Andrea Coladangelo, Jiahui Liu, Qipeng Liu, and Mark Zhandry

On Tight Quantum Security of HMAC and NMAC in the Quantum
Random Oracle Model.   585
    Akinori Hosoyamada and Tetsu Iwata

Quantum Collision Attacks on Reduced SHA-256 and SHA-512   616
    Akinori Hosoyamada and Yu Sasaki

Succinct Arguments

Halo Infinite: Proof-Carrying Data from Additive Polynomial
Commitments   649
   Dan Boneh, Justin Drake, Ben Fisch, and Ariel Gabizon

Proof-Carrying Data Without Succinct Arguments   681
   Benedikt Bünz, Alessandro Chiesa, William Lin, Pratyush Mishra,
   and Nicholas Spooner

Subquadratic SNARGs in the Random Oracle Model   711
   Alessandro Chiesa and Eylon Yogev

Sumcheck Arguments and Their Applications   742
   Jonathan Bootle, Alessandro Chiesa, and Katerina Sotiraki

An Algebraic Framework for Universal and Updatable SNARKs   774
   Carla Ràfols and Arantxa Zapico

Author Index   805

Invited Talk

Invited Talk

Which E-Voting Problems Do We Need to Solve?

Vanessa Teague[1,2]($\boxtimes$)

[1] Thinking Cybersecurity Pty. Ltd., Melbourne, Australia
vanessa.teague@anu.edu.au
[2] The Australian National University, Canberra, Australia

Secure e-voting sounds like a cryptography problem. There are private inputs, complex computations to be done on them, things to be verified, and authorities to be partially trusted. The cryptography literature is full of mathematically beautiful schemes for efficiently running electronic elections under various trust models and with various verifiability and privacy properties.

But nearly thirty years after the first voting-specific cryptography papers were written, some parts of the problem are solved while others seem as unachievable as ever. The more we learn about voting as a practical problem in security, the harder it seems.

First, we discovered that there are specific properties just for voting: *receipt freeness* [BT94]—the impossibility of proving your inputs even if you want to—is different from privacy, and necessary to avoid vote-buying and coercion. *Forced-randomisation* is a specific attack that makes sense in some voting systems, and could have a political impact if deployed against politically-biased classes of voters. Elections also need *public verifiability*, in which not only the participants, but any observer, can verify the accuracy of the computation without trusting authorities. Voting is not just a class of specific functions to be computed by (standard) MPC.

Second, decades after Ken Thompson's "Reflections on Trusting Trust" Turing Award lecture, we are still not good at checking what a computer is actually doing (oddly enough). For voting, this really matters: can we run a trustworthy electoral process using an unscrutinisable voting device? (Honestly, I wonder why this doesn't matter more in other contexts too.) There are surprising and clever techniques for allowing real humans to challenge and verify computations done by a computer [Ben06, RBH+09, AN06]. There is useful work on formalising the process in which a human can verify an electronic computation [KZZ17]. However, they are both practically and intellectually difficult for even the most diligent real human. Most practical systems use something simpler such as code voting, which has much stronger trust assumptions but is much easier to use—some even have multiple steps to allow voters to signal whether their verification succeeded [ZCC+13]. Also, important practical studies [KHRV19] demonstrate that the accuracy of fraud detection is much higher for simple schemes that people can easily understand. Nevertheless *cast-as-intended verification*, in which a voter verifies that their electronic vote matches their intention, is probably the hardest part of the voting problem. People do not even check plain-paper printouts well enough to give decent confidence [BMM+20]. Cryptographic veri-

T. Malkin and C. Peikert (Eds.): CRYPTO 2021, LNCS 12825, pp. 3–7, 2021.
https://doi.org/10.1007/978-3-030-84242-0_1

fication is harder—if people are deliberately deceived in their verification instructions, or just confused, then their verification is unsound. So practical, usable, cast-as-intended verification is likely to remain an active area of research.

Third, incentives really matter: not only, "Who has an incentive to conduct a challenge properly?" but also, "Which administrator has an incentive to implement a truly transparent and verifiable election system, when they are more likely to keep their job by sweeping problems under the rug?" In the vVote end-to-end verifiable pollsite voting project I worked on [CRST15], the electoral authorities in Victoria were reluctant to give voters any cast-as-intended verification instructions at all —the cast-as-intended protocol existed, but it only slowed the process down and ran the risk of exposing problems in a system that would otherwise be trusted. Unless this incentive is reversed, by requiring election outcomes to be supported by evidence, this behaviour will not change.

Fourth, there is no particular correlation between trustworthiness and trust, for electronic processes. Many criticisms of end-to-end verifiability in the research literature highlight the problem that people may not trust something they do not understand. That is a valid criticism and a genuine problem, but so is the opposite problem: too much trust in things that do not deserve it. Arguably the long US history of trusting the untrustworthy, particularly paperless DREs (direct-recording electronic voting machines), has caused a situation in which trust has completely broken down due to a historical lack of evidence supporting election results. Although most US jurisdictions have now returned to using paper, trust has not returned as quickly as improved processes. A little bit of healthy skepticism—and quicker scrapping of untrustworthy machines—might have been a better way of building long-term trust.

Fifth (at last we get to something related to cryptography), precise security definitions and implementation correctness really matter. The two cryptographic errors in the Swisspost/iVote/Scytl e-voting system [HLPT20] were misalignments of a primitive's properties with its protocol assumptions. In the case of the shuffle proof, a trapdoor commitment scheme was used in a protocol that was proven secure only under the assumption that the trapdoor was not known to the prover. In the case of the noninteractive ZKPs for equality of discrete logs, the problem was adaptive vs static security—a statically secure primitive was used in a protocol in which the adversary could adapt the input. It might be tempting to dismiss these errors as a consequence of inadequately reviewed software, and hence irrelevant to the research community, but the same problem had been identified earlier in Helios (by its designers: [BPW12]). The Civitas system [CCM08], based on Juels, Catalano and Jakobsson [JCJ10], had an equivalent problem: the use of plaintext equivalence tests (with distributed trust) in a context where Plaintext Equivalence proofs (with public verifiability) were required [MPT20]. There is no mistake in the JCJ proof, nor is there a mistake in the security proof of the PETs they refer to, but there is a misalignment between the property that is proven of the primitive, and the property that is assumed by the protocol proof. This misalignment breaks the main security goals of the system, as well as several followup works. It is hard to see how formal methods—even very sophisticated ones—could catch this kind of problem without a human looking very closely. Of course, this could happen in any system (not just in voting), but it is frightening how long things that completely undermined the core security properties went undetected, even in good quality systems that had been open for years. It is hard to see how a system based on cryptography alone could be robust against these kinds of mistakes.

Sixth, every democratic country is different (which is lucky for some of us). In Australia, participation is compulsory; in Switzerland, it is important to maintain privacy over who participated. Some countries take the secret ballot very seriously, others not so much. Some countries have a tolerable public key infrastructure, others don't. And elections may consist of numerous referenda very frequently, detailed preferences to be expressed every few years, or something else. A technical solution that works well in one country may not even meet the basic requirements elsewhere.

It is humbling that probably the best advance in recent times has come not from cryptography but from statistics—Risk Limiting Audits (RLAs) [LS12] use random sampling of paper ballots to guarantee an upper bound on the probability of accepting a wrong election result (this probability is called the *risk limit*). Ballots keep being sampled until either the risk limit is reached or the administrators decide to conduct a full hand count. The precise statistics are no easier for ordinary people to understand than cryptography is, but a lot of people see value in randomly selecting some ballots and observing the error rate. However, there are serious details related to cryptography here too. For example, random ballot samples require publicly verifiable pseudorandom number generation—if it is predictable, the audit is completely meaningless. This is a problem cryptographers can help with: the idea of an RLA as a publicly-verifiable computational process has yet to be adequately formalised and proven secure.

There is Practical Progress in (Some Parts of) the World

The Swiss Internet Voting Rethink. I would not say that the Swiss Internet voting *system* is a great example, but that the Swiss Federal Chancellery's *process* of engaging a large number of experts in an open, public analysis in order to help rewrite their regulations, is a great example other countries could follow.[1] I have no idea what their conclusion will be. Perhaps Internet voting will be discontinued, or further restricted, or replaced with verifiable pollsite e-voting. Perhaps Swiss Internet voting will remain in a perpetual state of experimentation, analysis and limited trust (perhaps that would be a fine outcome), but the decision will be based on evidence.

Open Source Commercial Projects such as Microsoft's ElectionGuard and VotingWorks. Do not underestimate the impact of a supported, open,

---

[1] CoI statement: I have received money from this process. Nevertheless the fact that they pay people like us to help them improve their legislation indicates that they are making decisions in a better way than most other authorities.

library that everyone can easily use. The ideas have been in the literature for a long time, but they are being produced for the first time in a way that administrators can easily buy and incorporate into transparent elections. These projects focus on the pollsite e-voting case where there are good practical solutions.

Research Challenges for Cryptographers

We do not have an end-to-end verifiable system with receipt freeness for remote voting, even one 'usable' to the standards appropriate for the IACR. Cast-as-intended verification can use a Benaloh-challenge (like Helios) or plain ciphertext-opening (like the Estonian e-voting system). Coercion-resistance can be achieved with JCJ-style fake-able voting tokens. However, we still don't have a good solution that provides both cast-as-intended verification and receipt freeness in a remote setting, except with the introduction of some much stronger trust assumptions. Nor can we add privacy from the client without greatly complicating the voting process. The fact that we haven't even solved this problem, in principle, for highly sophisticated users, shows how far we have to go to make online voting practical, without substantially stronger trust assumptions than I would want in my democracy.

I think the interesting practical research advances are to be made in paper-based cast-as-intended verification enhanced with some cryptography to allow voters to verify what happened to the paper after they submitted it, either in a polling place or by post. There are some interesting early designs in this space, but anyone who can design a system with three or more of: privacy from the voting device, usable verification, receipt freeness, and intuitive public verifiability (to a reasonable risk-limit), will make a substantial contribution to democracy.

Acknowledgement. I would like to thank all my coauthors over the years for making voting research so interesting and rewarding.

References

[AN06] Adida, B., Neff, C.A.: Ballot casting assurance. Proc. Electron. Voting Technol. Workshop (EVT) **6**, 7 (2006)

[Ben06] Benaloh, J.: Simple verifiable elections. EVT **6**, 1–10 (2006)

[BMM+20] Bernhard, M., et al.: Can voters detect malicious manipulation of ballot marking devices? In: 2020 IEEE Symposium on Security and Privacy (SP), pp. 679–694. IEEE (2020)

[BPW12] Bernhard, D., Pereira, O., Warinschi, B.: How not to prove yourself: pitfalls of the fiat-shamir heuristic and applications to helios. In: Wang, X., Sako, K. (eds.) ASIACRYPT 2012. LNCS, vol. 7658, pp. 626–643. Springer, Heidelberg (2012). https://doi.org/10.1007/978-3-642-34961-4_38

[BT94] Benaloh, J., Tuinstra, D.: Receipt-free secret-ballot elections. In: Proceedings of the Twenty-Sixth Annual ACM Symposium on Theory of Computing, pp. 544–553 (1994)

[CCM08] Clarkson, M.R., Chong, S., Myers, A.C.: Civitas: toward a secure voting system. In: 2008 IEEE Symposium on Security and Privacy (sp 2008), pp. 354–368. IEEE (2008)

[CRST15] Culnane, C., Ryan, P.Y.A., Schneider, S., Teague, V.: vVote: a verifiable voting system. ACM Trans. Inf. Syst. Secur. (TISSEC) **18**(1), 1–30 (2015)

[HLPT20] Haines, T., Lewis, S.J., Pereira, O., Teague, V.: How not to prove your election outcome. In: 2020 IEEE Symposium on Security and Privacy (SP), pp. 644–660. IEEE (2020)

[JCJ10] Juels, A., Catalano, D., Jakobsson, M.: Coercion-resistant electronic elections. In: Chaum, D., et al. (eds.) Towards Trustworthy Elections. LNCS, vol. 6000, pp. 37–63. Springer, Heidelberg (2010). https://doi.org/10.1007/978-3-642-12980-3_2

[KHRV19] Kulyk, O., Henzel, J., Renaud, K., Volkamer, M.: Comparing challenge-based and code-based internet voting verification implementations. In: Lamas, D., Loizides, F., Nacke, L., Petrie, H., Winckler, M., Zaphiris, P. (eds.) INTERACT 2019. LNCS, vol. 11746, pp. 519–538. Springer, Cham (2019). https://doi.org/10.1007/978-3-030-29381-9_32

[KZZ17] Kiayias, A., Zacharias, T., Zhang, B.: Ceremonies for end-to-end verifiable elections. In: Fehr, S. (ed.) PKC 2017. LNCS, vol. 10175, pp. 305–334. Springer, Heidelberg (2017). https://doi.org/10.1007/978-3-662-54388-7_11

[LS12]   Lindeman, M., Stark, P.B.: A gentle introduction to risk-limiting audits. IEEE Secur. Priv. **10**(5), 42–49 (2012)

[MPT20] McMurtry, E., Pereira, O., Teague, V.: When is a test not a proof? In: Chen, L., Li, N., Liang, K., Schneider, S. (eds.) ESORICS 2020. LNCS, vol. 12309, pp. 23–41. Springer, Cham (2020). https://doi.org/10.1007/978-3-030-59013-0_2

[RBH+09] Ryan, P.Y.A., Bismark, D., Heather, J., Schneider, S., Xia, Z.: Prêt à voter: a voter-verifiable voting system. IEEE Trans. Inf. Forensics Secur. **4**(4), 662–673 (2009)

[ZCC+13] Zagórski, F., Carback, R.T., Chaum, D., Clark, J., Essex, A., Vora, P.L.: Remotegrity: design and use of an end-to-end verifiable remote voting system. In: Jacobson, M., Locasto, M., Mohassel, P., Safavi-Naini, R. (eds.) ACNS 2013. LNCS, vol. 7954, pp. 441–457. Springer, Heidelberg (2013). https://doi.org/10.1007/978-3-642-38980-1_28

Award Papers

Award Papers

On the Possibility of Basing Cryptography on EXP ≠ BPP

Yanyi Liu[1(✉)] and Rafael Pass[2]

[1] Cornell University, Ithaca, USA
yl2866@cornell.edu
[2] Cornell Tech, New York, USA
rafael@cs.cornell.edu

Abstract. Liu and Pass (FOCS'20) recently demonstrated an equivalence between the existence of one-way functions (OWFs) and mild average-case hardness of the time-bounded Kolmogorov complexity problem. In this work, we establish a similar equivalence but to a different form of time-bounded Kolmogorov Complexity—namely, Levin's notion of Kolmogorov Complexity—whose hardness is closely related to the problem of whether $\mathsf{EXP} \neq \mathsf{BPP}$. In more detail, let $Kt(x)$ denote the Levin-Kolmogorov Complexity of the string x; that is, $Kt(x) = \min_{\Pi \in \{0,1\}^*, t \in \mathbb{N}} \{|\Pi| + \lceil \log t \rceil : U(\Pi, 1^t) = x\}$, where U is a universal Turing machine, and $U(\Pi, 1^t)$ denotes the output of the program Π after t steps, and let MKtP denote the language of pairs (x, k) having the property that $Kt(x) \leq k$. We demonstrate that:

- $\mathsf{MKtP} \notin \mathsf{Heur}_{\mathsf{neg}}\mathsf{BPP}$ (i.e., MKtP is infinitely-often *two-sided error* mildly average-case hard) iff infinitely-often OWFs exist.
- $\mathsf{MKtP} \notin \mathsf{Avg}_{\mathsf{neg}}\mathsf{BPP}$ (i.e., MKtP is infinitely-often *errorless* mildly average-case hard) iff $\mathsf{EXP} \neq \mathsf{BPP}$.

Thus, the only "gap" towards getting (infinitely-often) OWFs from the assumption that $\mathsf{EXP} \neq \mathsf{BPP}$ is the seemingly "minor" technical gap between two-sided error and errorless average-case hardness of the MKtP problem.

As a corollary of this result, we additionally demonstrate that any reduction from errorless to two-sided error average-case hardness for MKtP implies (unconditionally) that $\mathsf{NP} \neq \mathsf{P}$.

We finally consider other alternative notions of Kolmogorov complexity—including space-bounded Kolmogorov complexity and conditional Kolmogorov complexity—and show how average-case hardness of problems related to them characterize log-space computable OWFs, or OWFs in NC^0.

R. Pass—Supported in part by NSF Award SATC-1704788, NSF Award RI-1703846, AFOSR Award FA9550-18-1-0267, and a JP Morgan Faculty Award. This material is based upon work supported by DARPA under Agreement No. HR00110C0086. Any opinions, findings and conclusions or recommendations expressed in this material are those of the author(s) and do not necessarily reflect the views of the United States Government or DARPA.

T. Malkin and C. Peikert (Eds.): CRYPTO 2021, LNCS 12825, pp. 11–40, 2021.
https://doi.org/10.1007/978-3-030-84242-0_2

1   Introduction

A *one-way function* [DH76] (OWF) is a function f that can be efficiently computed (in polynomial time), yet no probabilistic polynomial-time (PPT) algorithm can invert f with inverse polynomial probability for infinitely many input lengths n. Whether one-way functions exist is unequivocally the most important open problem in Cryptography (and arguably the most important open problem in the theory of computation, see e.g., [Lev03]): OWFs are both necessary [IL89] and sufficient for many of the most central cryptographic primitives and protocols (e.g., pseudorandom generators [BM88, HILL99], pseudorandom functions [GGM84], private-key encryption [GM84], digital signatures [Rom90], commitment schemes [Nao91], identification protocols [FS90], coin-flipping protocols [Blu82], and more). These primitives and protocols are often referred to as *private-key primitives*, or "Minicrypt" primitives [Imp95] as they exclude the notable task of public-key encryption [DH76, RSA83]. Additionally, as observed by Impagliazzo [Gur89, Imp95], the existence of a OWF is equivalent to the existence of polynomial-time method for sampling hard *solved* instances for an NP language (i.e., hard instances together with their witnesses).

While many candidate constructions of OWFs are known—most notably based on factoring [RSA83], the discrete logarithm problem [DH76], or the hardness of lattice problems [Ajt96]—the question of whether OWFs can be based on some "standard" complexity-theoretic assumption is mostly wide open. Indeed, a central open problem, originating in the seminal work of Diffie and Hellman [DH76] is whether the existence of OWFs can be based on the assumptions that $NP \neq P$ or $NP \neq BPP$. Arguably, this is the most important open problem in the foundations of Cryptography. So far, however, most results in the literature have been negative. Notably, starting with the work by Brassard [Bra83] in 1983, a long sequence of works have shown various types of black-box separations between *restricted* types of OWF (e.g., one-way permutations) and NP-hardness (see e.g., [Bra83, BT03, AGGM06, GWXY10, Liv10, HMX10, BB15]). We emphasize, however, that these results only show limited separations: they either consider restricted types of one-way functions, or restricted classes of black-box reductions.[1]

In this work, our goal is to address an even more basic (and ambitious) problem: can we base Cryptography on the "super-weak" assumption that $EXP \neq BPP$:

Can the existence of OWFs be based on the assumption that $EXP \neq BPP$?

While we (obviously) are not able to provide a full positive answer to this problem (which as we shall see later on, would imply that $NP \neq P$), we are able to show that the task of basing OWFs on the assumption that $EXP \neq BPP$ boils

---

[1] We highlight that a recent result by Pass and Venkitasubramaniam [PV20] takes a step towards a positive results, showing that to prove the existence of OWFs from average-case hardness of NP, it suffices to prove that average-case hardness of TFNP (rather than NP) implies the existence of OWFs.

down to (more precisely, is equivalent to) a seemingly minor technical problem regarding different notions of average-case w.r.t. Levin's notion of Kolmogorov Complexity [Lev73]. Towards explaining our main result, let us first review some recent connections between Cryptography and Kolmogorov Complexity.

1.1 Connections Between OWFs and Kolmogorov Complexity

What makes the string 12121212121212121 less random than 6048485066 8340357492? The notion of *Kolmogorov complexity* (*K*-complexity), introduced by Solomonoff [Sol64], Kolmogorov [Kol68] and Chaitin [Cha69], provides an elegant method for measuring the amount of "randomness" in individual strings: The *K*-complexity of a string is the length of the shortest program (to be run on some fixed universal Turing machine U) that outputs the string x. From a computational point of view, however, this notion is unappealing as there is no efficiency requirement on the program. The notion of $t(\cdot)$-*time-bounded Kolmogorov Complexity* (K^t-*complexity*) overcomes this issue: $K^t(x)$ is defined as the length of the shortest program that outputs the string x within time $t(|x|)$. As surveyed by Trakhtenbrot [Tra84], the problem of efficiently determining the K^t-complexity for $t(n) = \mathsf{poly}(n)$ predates the theory of NP-completeness and was studied in the Soviet Union since the 60s as a candidate for a problem that requires "brute-force search". The modern complexity-theoretic study of this problem goes back to Sipser [Sip83], Ko [Ko86] and Hartmanis [Har83].

A very recent result by Liu and Pass [LP20] shows that "mild" average-case hardness[2] of the time-bounded Kolmogorov complexity problem (when the time-bound is some polynomial) is *equivalent* to the existence of OWFs. While the time-bounded Kolmogorov complexity problem is in NP (when the time-bound is a polynomial), it is not known whether this problem is average-case complete for NP, thus their result falls short of basing OWFs on the assumption that NP is average-case hard (i.e., that there exists some problem in NP that is average-case hard w.r.t. some sampleable distribution over instances).

In this work, we will extend their work to consider other variants of the notion of "resource-bounded" Kolmogorov complexity [Kol68]. The central advantage of doing so will be that we will be able to base OWFs on the average-case hardness of some problem that is average-case complete for EXP! The only reason that this result falls short of basing OWF on EXP $\neq$ BPP is that the notion of average-case hardness in the EXP-completeness result is slightly different from the notion of average-case hardness for the "OWF-completeness" result. However, "morally", this result can be interpreted as an indication that the existence of OWFs is equivalent to EXP $\neq$ BPP.

---

[2] By "mild" average-case hardness, we here mean that no PPT algorithm is able to solve the problem with probability $1 - \frac{1}{p(n)}$ on inputs of length n, for all polynomials $p(\cdot)$

1.2   Characterizing Average-Case Hardness of Levin-Kolmogorov Complexity

While the definition of time-bounded Kolmogorov complexity, K^t, is simple and clean, as noted by Leonid Levin [Lev73] in 1973, an annoying aspect of this notion is that it needs to be parametrized by the time-bound t. To overcome this issue, Levin proposed an elegant "non-parametrized" version of Kolmogorov complexity that directly incorporates the running time as a *cost*. To capture the idea that polynomial-time computations are "cheap", Levin's definition only charges logarithmically for running time. More precisely, let the Levin-Kolmogorov Complexity of the string, $Kt(x)$, be defined as follows:

$$Kt(x) = \min_{\Pi \in \{0,1\}^*, t \in \mathbb{N}} \{|\Pi| + \lceil \log t \rceil : U(\Pi, 1^t) = x\},$$

where U is a universal Turing machine, and we let $U(\Pi, 1^t)$ denote the output of the program Π after t steps. Note that, just like the standard notion of Kolmogorov complexity, $Kt(x)$ is bounded by $|x| + O(1)$—we can simply consider a program that has the string x hard-coded and directly halts.

Let MKtP denote the decisional Levin-Kolmogorov complexity problem; namely, the language of pairs (x, k) where $k \in \{0,1\}^{\lceil \log |x| \rceil}$ having the property that $Kt(x) \leq k$. MKtP is no longer seems to be in NP, as there may be strings x that can be described by a short program Π (with description size e.g., $n/10$) but a "largish" running time (e.g., $2^{n/10}$); the resulting string x thus would have small Kt-complexity ($n/5$), yet verifying that the witness program Π indeed outputs x would require executing it which would take exponential time. In fact, Allender et al. [ABK+06] show that MKtP actually is EXP-complete w.r.t. P/poly reductions; in other words, MKtP $\in$ P/poly if and only if EXP $\subseteq$ P/poly.

We will be studying (mild) average-case hardness of the MKtP problem, and consider two standard (see e.g. [BT08]) notions of average-case tractability for a language L with respect to the uniform distribution over instances:

- **2-sided error average-case heuristics:** We say that $L \in \mathsf{Heur_{neg}BPP}$ if for every polynomial $p(\cdot)$, there exists some PPT heuristic $\mathcal{H}$ that decides L (w.r.t. uniform n-bit strings) with probability $1 - \frac{1}{p(n)}$.
- **errorless average-case heuristics:** We say that $L \in \mathsf{Avg_{neg}BPP}$ if for every polynomial $p(\cdot)$, there exists some PPT heuristic $\mathcal{H}$ such that (a) for every instance x, with probability 0.9, $\mathcal{H}(x)$ either outputs $L(x)$ or $\bot$, and (b), $\mathcal{H}(x)$ outputs $\bot$ with probability at most $\frac{1}{p(n)}$ given uniform n-bits strings x.

In other words, the difference between an errorless and a 2-sided error heuristic $\mathcal{H}$ is that an errorless heuristic needs to (with probability 0.9 over its own randomness but not the instance x) output either $\bot$ (for "I don't know") or the correct answer $L(x)$, whereas a 2-sided error heuristic may simply make mistakes without "knowing it".

To better understand the class $\mathsf{Avg_{neg}BPP}$, it may be useful to compare it to the class $\mathsf{Avg_{neg}P}$ (languages solvable by deterministic errorless heuristics): $L \in$

$\mathsf{Avg_{neg}P}$ if for every polynomial $p(\cdot)$, there exists some deterministic polynomial-time heuristic $\mathcal{H}$ such that (a) for every input x, $\mathcal{H}(x)$ outputs either $L(x)$ or $\bot$, and (b) the probability over uniform n-bit inputs x that $\mathcal{H}$ outputs $\bot$ is bounded by $\frac{1}{p(n)}$. In other words, the *only* way an errorless heuristic may make a "mistake" is by saying $\bot$ ("I don't know"); if it ever outputs a non-$\bot$ response, this response needs to be correct. (Compare this to a 2-sided error heuristic that only makes mistakes with a small probability, but we do not know when they happen). $\mathsf{Avg_{neg}BPP}$ is simply the natural "BPP-analog" of $\mathsf{Avg_{neg}P}$ where the heuristic is allowed to be randomized.

2-Sided Error Average-Case Hardness of MKtP and OWFs. Our first main result shows that the characterization of [LP20] can be extended to work also w.r.t. MKtP. More precisely,

Theorem 1. MKtP $\notin$ Heur$_{\mathsf{neg}}$BPP *iff infinitely-often OWFs exist.*

We highlight that whereas [LP20] characterized "standard" OWF, the above theorem only characterizes *infinitely-often* OWFs—i.e., functions that are hard to invert for infinitely many inputs lengths (as opposed to all input lengths). The reason for this is that [LP20] considered an "almost-everywhere" notion of average-case hardness of K^t, whereas the statement MKtP $\notin$ Heur$_{\mathsf{neg}}$BPP only considers an infinitely-often notion of average-case hardness. (As we demonstrate in the full paper, we can also obtain a characterization of standard "almost-everywhere" OWFs by assuming that MKtP is "almost-everywhere" mildly average-case hard, but for simplicity, in the main body of the paper, we focus our attention on the more standard complexity-theoretic setting of infinitely-often hardness).

On a high-level, the proof of Theorem 1 follows the same structure as the characterization of [LP20]. The key obstacle to deal with is that since MKtP is not known to be in NP, there may not exists some polynomial time-bound that bounds the running-time of a program Π that "witnesses" the Kt-complexity of a string x; this is a serious issue as the OWF construction in [LP20] requires knowing such a running-time bound (and indeed, the running-time of the OWF depends on it). To overcome this issue, we rely on a new insight about Levin-Kolmogorov Complexity.

We say that the program Π is a Kt-*witness* for the string x if Π generates x within t steps while minimizing $|\Pi| + \log t$ among all other programs (i.e., Π is a witness for the Kt-complexity of x). The crucial observation (see Fact 31) is that for every $0 < \varepsilon < 1$, except for an ε fraction of n-bit strings x, x has a Kt-witness Π that runs in time $O(\frac{1}{\varepsilon})$. That is, "most" strings have a Kt-witness that has a "short" running time. To see this, recall that as mentioned above, for every string x, $Kt(x) \leq |x| + O(1)$; thus, every string $x \in \{0,1\}^n$ with a Kt-witnesses Π with running time exceeding $O(\frac{1}{\varepsilon})$, must satisfy that $|\Pi| + \log O(\frac{1}{\varepsilon}) \leq Kt(x) \leq n + O(1)$, so $|\Pi| \leq n + O(1) - \log(\frac{O(1)}{\varepsilon}) = n + O(1) + \log \varepsilon$. Since the length of Π is bounded by $n + O(1) + \log \varepsilon$, it follows that we can have at most $O(\varepsilon)2^n$ strings x where the Kt-witness for x has a "long" running time.

We can next use this observation to consider a more computationally tractable version of Kt-complexity where we cut off the machine's running time after $\frac{1}{\varepsilon}$ steps (where ε is selected as an appropriate polynomial), and next follow a similar paradigm as in [LP20].

Errorless Average-Case Hardness of MKtP and EXP $\neq$ BPP. We next show how to extend the result of Allender et al. [ABK+06] to show that MKtP is not just EXP-complete in the worst-case, but also EXP-average-case complete; furthermore, we are able to show completeness w.r.t. BPP (as opposed to P/poly) reductions. We highlight, however, that completeness is shown in a "non-black-box" way (whereas [ABK+06] present a P/poly truthtable reduction). By non-black-box we here mean that we are not able to show how to use any algorithm that solves MKtP (on average) as an oracle (i.e., as a black-box) to decide EXP (in probabilistic polynomial time); rather, we directly show that if MKtP $\in$ Avg$_{neg}$BPP, then EXP $\subseteq$ BPP.[3]

Theorem 2. MKtP $\notin$ Avg$_{neg}$BPP *iff* EXP $\neq$ BPP.

Theorem 2 follows a similar structure as the EXP-completeness results of [ABK+06]. Roughly speaking, Allender et al. observe that by the result of Nisan and Wigderson [NW94], the assumption that EXP $\not\subseteq$ P/poly implies the existence of a (subexponential-time computable) pseudorandom generator that fools polynomial-size circuits. But using a Kt-oracle, it is easy to break the PRG (as outputs of the PRG have small Kt-complexity since its running time is "small"). We first observe that the same approach can be extended to show that MKtP is (errorless) average-case hard w.r.t. polynomial-size circuits (under the assumption that EXP $\not\subseteq$ P/poly). We next show that if we instead rely on a PRG construction of Impagliazzo and Wigderson [IW98], it suffices to rely on the assumption that EXP $\neq$ BPP to show average-case hardness of MKtP w.r.t. PPT algorithms.

Interpreting the Combination of Theorem 1 and Theorem 2. By combining Theorem 1 and Theorem 2, we get that the only "gap" towards getting (infinitely-often) one-way functions from the assumption that EXP $\neq$ BPP is the seemingly "minor" technical gap between two-sided error and errorless average-case hardness of the MKtP problem (i.e., proving MKtP $\notin$ Avg$_{neg}$BPP $\Longrightarrow$ MKtP $\notin$ Heur$_{neg}$BPP). Furthermore, note that this "gap" *fully characterizes* the possibility of basing (infinitely-often) OWFs on the assumption that EXP $\neq$ BPP: Any proof that EXP $\neq$ BPP implies infinitely-often OWFs also shows the implication MKtP $\notin$ Avg$_{neg}$BPP $\Longrightarrow$ MKtP $\notin$ Heur$_{neg}$BPP.

As a corollary of Theorem 1 and Theorem 2, we next demonstrate that the implication MKtP $\notin$ Avg$_{neg}$BPP $\Longrightarrow$ MKtP $\notin$ Heur$_{neg}$BPP implies that NP $\neq$ P (in fact, even average-case hardness of NP).

Theorem 3. *If* MKtP $\notin$ Avg$_{neg}$BPP $\Longrightarrow$ MKtP $\notin$ Heur$_{neg}$BPP, *then* NP $\neq$ P.

---

[3] This non-black box aspect of our results stems from its use of [IW98].

This results can be interpreted in two ways. The pessimistic way is that closing this gap between 2-sided error, and errorless, heuristics will be very hard. The optimistic way, however, is to view it as a new and algorithmic approach towards proving that NP ≠ P: To demonstrate that NP ≠ P, it suffices to demonstrate that MKtP can be solved by an errorless heuristic, given access to a two-sided error heuristic for the same problem.

1.3   Space-Bounded Notions of Kolmogorov Complexity

We additionally consider other alternative notions of resource-bounded Kolmogorov complexity. In more detail, we consider a space-bounded notion of Kolmogorov complexity K^s and a space-bounded notion of *conditional* Kolmogorov complexity, and show that these notions, respectively, characterize log-space computable one-way functions, or one-way functions in NC^0.

Characterizing OWFs in Log-Space. The s-space bounded Kolmogorov complexity, $K^s(x)$, of a string $x \in \{0,1\}^*$ is defined as

$$K^s(x) = \min_{\Pi \in \{0,1\}^*} \{|\Pi| : \forall i \in [|x|], U(\Pi(i), 1^{2^{s(|x|)}}) = x_i$$

$$\text{and } \Pi(i) \text{ uses at most } s(|x|) \text{ space}\}$$

(Since we will be limiting the amount of space, we consider a notion of Kolmogorov complexity where the program Π needs to output just bit x_i of the string x, given the index i as input.) Given some function $s(\cdot)$, define MKSP[s] analogously to MKtP. We will be interested in the regime where $s(n) = O(\log n)$. Using a proof that closely follows [LP20] (and observing that the components needed in this proof can be computed in log space), we obtain the following characterization of log-space computable OWFs.

Theorem 4. *Infinitely-often one-way functions in log-space exist if and only if* MKSP[$O(\log n)$] ∉ Heur$_{neg}$BPP.

(We can also get a characterization of "standard" (i.e., almost-everywhere) OWFs in log-space if we assume that MKSP[s] is almost-everywhere average-case hard; see the full paper for more details.)

   We remark that by the results of [AIK06], the existence of a log-space computable OWF implies a OWF that is uniform NC^0 computable; in fact, as observed by [RS21] (see Remark 31), by a slight tweak of the construction of [AIK06], one actually gets a OWF that is *log-space* uniform NC^0 computable. In other words, the existence of log-space computable OWFs is equivalent to the existence of log-space uniform NC^0-computable OWFs. Theorem 4 thus also characterizes OWFs computable in log-space uniform NC^0.[4]

Characterizing OWF in Uniform NC^0. We finally turn to consider the question of characterizing OWF in just uniform (as opposed to log-space uniform)

---

[4] We remark that this observation was added after becoming aware of [RS21].

NC^0. To do this, we consider generalization of space-bounded Kolmogorov complexity which considers a *conditional* notion of Kolmogorov complexity.

The *conditional Kolmogorov complexity* [ZL70, Lev73, Tra84, LM91] of a string x given the string str is the length of the shortest program Π that given the "auxiliary input" str outputs x. We here consider a variant of MKSP[s], which considers conditional Kolmogorov complexity instead of the (unconditional) version, and where the "auxiliary input" str is generated by some deterministic polynomial-time machine F. More precisely, given some Turing machine F, define the F-conditional $s(\cdot)$-space bounded Kolmogorov complexity, $cK^{F,s}(x)$, as follows:

$$cK^{F,s}(x) = \min_{\Pi \in \{0,1\}^*} \{|\Pi| : \forall i \in [|x|], U(\Pi(i, \text{str}), 1^{2^{s(|x|)}}) = x_i$$

$$\text{and } \Pi(i, \text{str}) \text{ uses at most } s(|x|) \text{ space}\}$$

where str $= F(1^{|x|})$. We next define a decisional version, McKSP[F, s], analogously to MKSP[s], and get the following theorem by appropriately generalizing the proof of Theorem 4 and leveraging the result of [AIK06]:

Theorem 5. *Infinitely-often OWFs in uniform* NC^0 *exist iff there exists some polynomial-time Turing machine F such that* McKSP[$F, O(\log n)$] $\notin$ Heur$_{\text{neg}}$BPP.

(As before, we can also get a characterization of "standard" (i.e., almost-everywhere) OWFs in uniform NC^0 if we assume that McKSP is almost-everywhere average-case hard; see the full paper for more details.)

1.4   Concurrent Works

A concurrent and independent work by Hanlin and Santhanam [RS21] presents related but orthogonal characterizations of MKtP and OWFs in NC$_0$. W.r.t., MKtP, both works essentially show an equivalence between mild average-case hardness of MKtP and the existence of OWFs; we next show that errorless average-case hardness of MKtP is equivalent to EXP $\neq$ BPP, whereas they instead consider an incomparable notion of two-sided error hardness with a "tiny" error and show that such average-case hardness of MKtP w.r.t. non-uniform polynomial-time adversaries is equivalent to the assumption that EXP $\notin$ P/poly. W.r.t. OWF in NC$_0$, [RS21] shows that, surprisingly, an alternative notion of time-bounded Kolmogorov complexity, KT, [ABK+06] which *charges* for running-time (as opposed to bounding it) characterizes OWFs in log-space uniform NC^0. In contrast, we present a characterization in terms of space-bounded Kolmogorov complexity (and also of uniform NC^0-computable OWFs).

Resource bounded notions of *conditional* Kolmogorov complexity are useful also in other (related) contexts. In a companion paper to the current work [LP21a], we rely on a notion of time-bounded conditional Kolmogorov complexity to characterize OWFs; the advantage of using this notion is that [LP21a] shows that the time-bounded conditional Kolmogorov complexity problem, McKTP, is NP-complete. Taken together, the current work and [LP21a], demonstrate that the existence of OWFs can be characterized through the average-case hardness of (essentially) EXP-complete (this work) and NP-complete [LP21a] languages.

We additionally note the concurrent and independent work of [ACM+21] which bases OWFs on average-case hardness of different conditional Kolmogorov complexity style problem. Their conditional Kolmogorov complexity problem—which they show is NP-complete—instead considers a conditional variant of the KT notion of [ABK+06, ACM+21], however, they only show a one-directional implication between average-case hardness of their problem and OWFs (and only a weak converse in the other direction).

1.5   Outline

In this extended abstract, we provide the formalizations and proofs of Theorems 1, 2, 3 and 4. We refer the reader to the full version [LP21b] for the remaining content.

2   Preliminaries

We assume familiarity with basic concepts and computational classes such as Turing machines, polynomial-time algorithms, probabilistic polynomial-time (PPT) algorithms, NP, EXP, BPP, log-space (or alternatively L), and P/poly. In this work, following [AIK06], we mostly consider *polynomial-time uniform* versions of NC^0 and L/poly: we let *uniform* NC^0 be the class of functions[5] that admit polynomial-time uniform NC^0 circuits, and *uniform* L/poly be the class of functions computed by log-space Turing machines with a polynomial-time computable advice. A function μ is said to be *negligible* if for every polynomial $p(\cdot)$ there exists some n_0 such that for all $n > n_0$, $\mu(n) \leq \frac{1}{p(n)}$. A *probability ensemble* is a sequence of random variables $A = \{A_n\}_{n \in \mathbb{N}}$. We let $\mathcal{U}_n$ denote the uniform distribution over $\{0, 1\}^n$. Given a string x, we let $[x]_j$ denote the first j bits of x.

2.1   One-Way Functions

We recall the definition of one-way functions [DH76]. Roughly speaking, a function f is one-way if it is polynomial-time computable, but hard to invert for PPT attackers. The standard cryptographic definition of a one-way function (see e.g., [Gol01]) requires that for every PPT attacker A, there exists some negligible function $\mu(\cdot)$ such that A only succeeds in inverting the function with probability $\mu(n)$ for *all* input lengths n. (That is, hardness holds "almost-everywhere".) We will also consider a weaker notion of an *infinitely-often* one-way function [OW93], which only requires that the success probability is bounded by $\mu(n)$ for *infinitely many* inputs lengths n. (That is, hardness only holds "infinitely-often".)

---

[5] We abuse the notation and say that a function f is in a class $\mathcal{C}$ if each bit on the output of f is computable in $\mathcal{C}$.

Definition 1. *Let* $f : \{0,1\}^* \rightarrow \{0,1\}^*$ *be a polynomial-time computable function.* f *is said to be a* one-way function (OWF) *if for every* PPT *algorithm* $\mathcal{A}$, *there exists a negligible function* μ *such that for all* $n \in \mathbb{N}$,

$$\Pr[x \leftarrow \{0,1\}^n; y = f(x) : A(1^n, y) \in f^{-1}(f(x))] \leq \mu(n)$$

f *is said to be an* infinitely-often one-way function (ioOWF) *if the above condition holds for infinitely many* $n \in \mathbb{N}$ *(as opposed to all).*

We may also consider a weaker notion of a *weak one-way function* [Yao82], where we only require all PPT attackers to fail with probability noticeably bounded away from 1:

Definition 2. *Let* $f : \{0,1\}^* \rightarrow \{0,1\}^*$ *be a polynomial-time computable function.* f *is said to be a* α-weak one-way function (α-weak OWF) *if for every* PPT *algorithm* $\mathcal{A}$, *for all sufficiently large* $n \in N$,

$$\Pr[x \leftarrow \{0,1\}^n; y = f(x) : A(1^n, y) \in f^{-1}(f(x))] < 1 - \alpha(n)$$

We say that f *is simply a* weak one-way function (weak OWF) *if there exists some polynomial* $q > 0$ *such that* f *is a* $\frac{1}{q(\cdot)}$*-weak OWF.* f *is said to be an* weak infinitely-often one-way function (weak ioOWF) *if the above condition holds for infinitely many* $n \in \mathbb{N}$ *(as opposed to all).*

Yao's hardness amplification theorem [Yao82] shows that any weak (io) OWF can be turned into a "strong" (io) OWF.

Theorem 6 ([Yao82]). *Assume there exists a weak one-way function (resp. infinitely-often one-way function). Then there exists a one-way functions (resp. infinitely-often one-way function).*

We observe that Yao's construction remains in log-space (resp uniform L/poly) if the weak one-way function it takes is in log-space (resp uniform L/poly) [AIK06, Gol01].

2.2   Levin's Notion of Kolmogorov Complexity

Let U be some fixed Universal Turing machine that can emulate any Turing machine M with polynomial overhead. Given a description $\Pi \in \{0,1\}^*$ which encodes a pair (M, w) where M is a (single-tape) Turing machine and $w \in \{0,1\}^*$ is an input, let $U(\Pi, 1^t)$ denote the output of $M(w)$ when emulated on U for t steps. Note that (by assumption that U only has polynomial overhead) $U(\Pi, 1^t)$ can be computed in time $\mathsf{poly}(|\Pi|, t)$. We turn to defining Levin's notion of Kolmogorov complexity [Lev73]:

$$Kt(x) = \min_{\Pi \in \{0,1\}^*, t \in \mathbb{N}} \{|\Pi| + \lceil \log t \rceil : U(\Pi, 1^t) = x\}.$$

Its decisional variant, the Minimum Kt Complexity Problem MKtP, is defined as follows:

- Input: A string $x \in \{0, 1\}^n$ and a size parameter $k \in \{0, 1\}^{\lceil \log n \rceil}$.
- Decide: Does (x, k) satisfy $Kt(x) \leq k$?

As is well known, we can always produce a string by hardwiring the string in (the tape of) a machine that does nothing and just halts, which yields the following central fact about (Levin)-Kolmogorov complexity.

Fact 21 ([Sip96]). *There exists a constant c such that for every $x \in \{0, 1\}^*$ it holds that $Kt(x) \leq |x| + c$.*

2.3   Average-Case Complexity

We will consider average-case complexity of languages L with respect to the *uniform* distribution of instances. Let $\mathsf{Heur_{neg}BPP}$ denote the class of languages that can be decided by PPT heuristics that only make mistakes on a inverse polynomial fraction of instances. More formally:

Definition 3 ($\mathsf{Heur_{neg}BPP}$). *For a decision problem $L \subset \{0, 1\}^*$, we say that $L \in \mathsf{Heur_{neg}BPP}$ if for all polynomial $p(\cdot)$, there exists a probabilistic polynomial-time heuristic $\mathcal{H}$, such that for all sufficiently large n,*

$$\Pr[x \leftarrow \{0, 1\}^n : \mathcal{H}(x) = L(x)] \geq 1 - \frac{1}{p(n)}.$$

We will refer to languages in $\mathsf{Heur_{neg}BPP}$ as languages that admit *2-sided error* heuristics. We will also consider a more restrictive type of *errorless* heuristics $\mathcal{H}$: for every instance x, with probability 0.9 (over the randomness of only $\mathcal{H}$), $\mathcal{H}(x)$ either outputs $L(x)$ or $\perp$ (for 'I don't know'). More formally,

Definition 4 ($\mathsf{Avg_{neg}BPP}$). *For a decision problem $L \subset \{0, 1\}^*$, we say that $L \in \mathsf{Avg_{neg}BPP}$ if for all polynomial $p(\cdot)$, there exists a probabilistic polynomial-time heuristic $\mathcal{H}$, such that for all sufficiently large n, for every $x \in \{0, 1\}^n$,*[6]

$$\Pr[\mathcal{H}(x) \in \{L(x), \perp\}] \geq 0.9,$$

and

$$\Pr[x \leftarrow \{0, 1\}^n : \mathcal{H}(x) = \perp] \leq \frac{1}{p(n)}.$$

We will refer to languages in $\mathsf{Avg_{neg}BPP}$ as languages that admit *errorless* heuristics. As explained in the introduction, to better understand the class $\mathsf{Avg_{neg}BPP}$, it may be useful to compare it to the class $\mathsf{Avg_{neg}P}$ (languages solvable by *deterministic* errorless heuristics): $L \in \mathsf{Avg_{neg}P}$ if for every polynomial $p(\cdot)$, there exists some deterministic polynomial-time heuristic $\mathcal{H}$ such that (a) for every input x, $\mathcal{H}(x)$ outputs either $L(x)$ or $\perp$, and (b) the probability over uniform n-bit inputs x that $\mathcal{H}$ outputs $\perp$ is bounded by $\frac{1}{p(n)}$. In other words, the *only* way

---

[6]   We remark that the constant 0.9 can be made arbitrarily small—any constants bounded away from $\frac{2}{3}$ works as we can amplify it using a standard Chernoff-type argument.

an errorless heuristic may make a "mistake" is by saying $\perp$ ("I don't know"), whereas for a 2-sided error heuristic we do not know when mistakes happen. $\mathsf{Avg_{neg}BPP}$ is simply the natural "BPP-analog" of $\mathsf{Avg_{neg}P}$ where the heuristic is allowed to be randomized.

2.4 Computational Indistinguishability

We recall the definition of (computational) indistinguishability [GM84] along with its infinitely-often variant.

Definition 5. *Two ensembles* $\{A_n\}_{n\in\mathbb{N}}$ *and* $\{B_n\}_{n\in\mathbb{N}}$ *are said to be* $\varepsilon(\cdot)$-*indistinguishable, if for every* PPT *machine* D *(the "distinguisher") whose running time is polynomial in the length of its first input, there exists some* $n_0 \in \mathbb{N}$ *so that for every* $n \geq n_0$:

$$|\Pr[D(1^n, A_n) = 1] - \Pr[D(1^n, B_n) = 1]| < \varepsilon(n)$$

We say that $\{A_n\}_{n\in\mathbb{N}}$ *and* $\{B_n\}_{n\in\mathbb{N}}$ *are infinitely-often* $\varepsilon(\cdot)$-*indistinguishable (io-ε-indistinguishable) if the above condition holds for infinitely many* $n \in \mathbb{N}$ *(as opposed to all sufficiently large ones).*

2.5 Pseudorandom Generators

We recall the standard definition of pseudodrandom generators (PRGs) and its infinitely-often variant.

Definition 6. *Let* $g : \{0,1\}^n \rightarrow \{0,1\}^{m(n)}$ *be a polynomial-time computable function.* g *is said to be a* $\varepsilon(\cdot)$-*pseudorandom generator (ε-PRG) if for any* PPT *algorithm* $\mathcal{A}$ *(whose running time is polynomial in the length of its first input), for all sufficiently large* n,

$$|\Pr[x \leftarrow \{0,1\}^n : \mathcal{A}(1^n, g(x)) = 1] - \Pr[y \leftarrow \{0,1\}^{m(n)} : \mathcal{A}(1^n, y) = 1]| < \varepsilon(n).$$

g *is said to be an infinitely-often* $\varepsilon(\cdot)$-*pseudorandom generator (io-ε-PRG) if the above condition holds for infinitely many* $n \in \mathbb{N}$ *(as opposed to all).*

Although the standard cryptographic definition of a PRG g requires that g runs in polynomial time, when used for the other purposes (e.g., for derandomizing BPP), we allow the PRG g to have an exponential running time [TV02]. We refer to such PRGs (resp ioPRGs) as *inefficient* PRGs (resp *inefficient* ioPRGs).

2.6 Conditionally Entropy-Preserving PRGs

Liu and Pass [LP20] introduced variant of a PRG referred to as an *entropy-preserving* pseudorandom generator (EP-PRG). Roughly speaking, an EP-PRG is a pseudorandom generator that expands n-bits to $n + O(\log n)$ bits, having the property that the output of the PRG is not only pseudorandom, but also preserves the entropy of the input (i.e., the seed): The Shannon-entropy of the output is $n - O(\log n)$. [LP20] did not manage to construct an EP-PRG from OWFs, but rather constructed a relaxed form of an EP-PRG, called a *conditionally-secure* entropy-preserving PRG (condEP-PRG), which relaxes both the pseudorandomness, and entropy-preserving properties of the PRG, to hold only conditioned on some event E. We will here consider also an infinitely-often variant:

Definition 7. *An efficiently computable function* $G : \{0,1\}^n \to \{0,1\}^{n+\gamma \log n}$ *is a* $\mu(\cdot)$-*conditionally secure entropy-preserving pseudorandom generator* (μ-condEP-PRG) *if there exist a sequence of events* $= \{E_n\}_{n\in\mathbb{N}}$ *and a constant* α *(referred to as the* entropy-loss constant*) such that the following conditions hold:*

- **(pseudorandomness):** $\{G(\mathcal{U}_n \mid E_n)\}_{n\in\mathbb{N}}$ *and* $\{\mathcal{U}_{n+\gamma \log n}\}_{n\in\mathbb{N}}$ *are* $\mu(n)$-*indistinguishable;*
- **(entropy-preserving):** *For all sufficiently large* $n \in \mathbb{N}$, $H(G(\mathcal{U}_n \mid E_n)) \geq n - \alpha \log n$.

G is referred to as an $\mu(\cdot)$-*conditionally secure entropy-preserving infinitely-often pseudorandom generator* (μ-condEP-ioPRG) *if it satisfies the above definition except that we replace* $\mu(n)$-*indistinguishability with io-*$\mu(n)$-*indistinguishability.*

We say that G has *rate-1 efficiency* if its running time on inputs of length n is bounded by $n + O(n^\varepsilon)$ for some constant $\varepsilon < 1$. We recall that the existence of rate-1 efficient condEP-PRGs can be based on the existence of OWFs, and that the same theorem holds in the infinitely-often setting.

Theorem 7 ([LP20]). *Assume that OWFs (resp. ioOWFs) exist. Then, for every* $\gamma > 1$, *there exists a rate-1 efficient* μ-*condEP-PRG (resp.* μ-*condEP-ioPRG)* $G_\gamma : \{0,1\}^n \to \{0,1\}^{n+\gamma \log n}$, *where* $\mu = \frac{1}{n^2}$.

3   2-Sided Error Average-Case Hardness of MKtP and OWFs

In this section, we prove our main characterization of OWFs through 2-sided error average-case hardness of MKtP.

Theorem 8. MKtP $\notin$ Heur$_{\mathrm{neg}}$BPP *iff infinitely-often OWFs exist.*

We remark that in the full paper [LP21b], we also characterize "standard" (as opposed to infinitely-often) OWFs through (almost-everywhere) mild average-case hardness of MKtP.

Theorem 8 follows directly from Theorem 9 (which is proven in Sect. 3.1) and Theorem 10 (which is proven in Sect. 3.2).

3.1   OWFs from Two-Sided Error Avg-Case Hardness of MKtP

In this section, we show that if weak ioOWFs do not exists, then we can compute the Kt-complexity of random strings with high probability (and thus MKtP is in $\mathsf{Heur_{neg}BPP}$). On a high-level, we will be using the same proof approach as in [LP20]. One immediate obstacle to relying on the proof in [LP20] is that it relies on the fact that the program Π (which we refer to as the "witness") that certifies the time-bounded Kolmogorov complexity K^t of a string x, has some a-priori *polynomial* running time, namely $t(\cdot)$; this polynomial bound gets translated into the running time of the constructed OWF. Unfortunately, this fact no longer holds when it comes to Kt-complexity: We say that the program Π is a Kt-*witness* for the string x if Π generates x within t steps while minimizing $|\Pi| + \log t$ among all other programs (i.e., Π is a witness for the Kt-complexity of x). Note that given a Kt-witness of a string x, there is no a-priori polynomial time-bound on the running time of Π, since only the *logarithm* of the running time gets included in the complexity measure. For instance, it could be that the Kt-witness is a program Π of length $n/10$ that requires running time $2^{n/10}$, for a total Kt-complexity of $n/5$. Nevertheless, the crucial observation we make is that *for most strings* x, the running-time of the Kt-witness actually is small: For every $0 < \varepsilon < 1$, except for an ε fraction of n-bit strings x, x has a Kt-witness Π that runs in time $O(\frac{1}{\varepsilon})$.

More formally:

Fact 31. *For all $n \in \mathbb{N}$, $0 < \varepsilon < 1$, there exists $1 - \varepsilon$ fraction of strings $x \in \{0,1\}^n$ such that there exist a Turing machine Π_x and a running time parameter t_x satisfying $U(\Pi_x, 1^{t_x}) = x$, $|\Pi_x| + \lceil \log t_x \rceil = Kt(x)$, and $t_x \le 2^c/\varepsilon$ (where c is as in Fact 21).*

Proof: Consider some $n \in \mathbb{N}$, $0 < \varepsilon < 1$, and some set $S \subset \{0,1\}^n$ such that $|S| > \varepsilon 2^n$. For any string $x \in \{0,1\}^n$, let (Π_x, t_x) be a pair of strings such that $U(\Pi_x, 1^{t_x}) = x$ and $|\Pi_x| + \lceil \log t_x \rceil = Kt(x)$; that is, (Π_x, t_x) is the optimal compression for x. Note that for any $x \in \{0,1\}^n$, such (Π_x, t_x) always exists due to Fact 21.[7] Let c be the constant from Fact 21.

We assume for contradiction that for any $x \in S$, $t_x > 2^c/\varepsilon$. Note that by Fact 21, it holds that $Kt(x) \le |x| + c$. Thus, $|\Pi_x| = Kt(x) - \lceil \log t_x \rceil \le n + c - \lceil \log 2^c/\varepsilon \rceil \le n - \log 1/\varepsilon$. Consider the set $Z = \{\Pi_x : x \in S\}$ of all (descriptions of) Turing machines Π_x. Since $|\Pi_x| \le n - \log 1/\varepsilon$, it follows that $|Z| \le 2^{n - \log 1/\varepsilon} = \varepsilon 2^n$. However, for each machine Π in Z, it could produce only a single string in S. So $|Z| \ge |S| > \varepsilon 2^n$, which is a contradiction. ∎

We now show how to adapt the proof in [LP20] by relying on the above fact.

Theorem 9. *If MKtP $\notin \mathsf{Heur_{neg}BPP}$, then there exists a weak ioOWF (and thus also an ioOWF).*

---

[7] We note that the choice of (Π_x, t_x) for some x is not unique. Our argument holds if any such (Π_x, t_x) is chosen.

Proof: We start with the assumption that $\mathsf{MKtP} \notin \mathsf{Heur_{neg}BPP}$; that is, there exists a polynomial $p(\cdot)$ such that for all PPT heuristics $\mathcal{H}'$ and infinitely many n,

$$\Pr[x \leftarrow \{0,1\}^n, k \leftarrow \{0,1\}^{\lceil \log n \rceil} : \mathcal{H}'(x,k) = \mathsf{MKtP}(x,k)] < 1 - \frac{1}{p(n)}.$$

Let c be the constant from Fact 21. Consider the function $f :$ $\{0,1\}^{n+c+\lceil \log(n+c) \rceil} \to \{0,1\}^*$, which given an input $\ell || \Pi'$ where $|\ell| = \lceil \log(n + c) \rceil$ and $|\Pi'| = n + c$, outputs $\ell + \lceil \log t \rceil || U(\Pi, 1^t)$ where Π is the ℓ-bit prefix of Π', t is the (smallest) integer $\leq 2^{c+2}p(n)$ such that Π (when interpreted as a Turing machine) halts in step t. (If Π does not halt in $2^{c+2}p(n)$ steps, f picks $t = 2^{c+2}p(n)$.) That is,

$$f(\ell || \Pi') = \ell + \lceil \log t \rceil || U(\Pi, 1^t).$$

Observe that f is only defined over some input lengths, but by an easy padding trick, it can be transformed into a function f' defined over all input lengths, such that if f is (weakly) one-way (over the restricted input lengths), then f' will be (weakly) one-way (over all input lengths): $f'(x')$ simply truncates its input x' (as little as possible) so that the (truncated) input x now becomes of length $m = n + c + \lceil \log(n + c) \rceil$ for some n and outputs $f(x)$.

We now show that f is a $\frac{1}{q(\cdot)}$-weak ioOWF where $q(n) = 2^{2c+4}np(n)^2$, which concludes the proof of the theorem. Assume for contradiction that f is not a $\frac{1}{q(\cdot)}$-weak ioOWF; that is, there exists some PPT attacker $\mathcal{A}$ that inverts f with probability at least $1 - \frac{1}{q(n)} \leq 1 - \frac{1}{q(m)}$ for all sufficiently large input lengths $m = n + c + \lceil \log(n + c) \rceil$. We first claim that we can use $\mathcal{A}$ to construct a PPT heuristic $\mathcal{H}^*$ such that

$$\Pr[x \leftarrow \{0,1\}^n : \mathcal{H}^*(x) = Kt(x)] \geq 1 - \frac{1}{p(n)}.$$

If this is true, consider the heuristic $\mathcal{H}$ which given a string $x \in \{0,1\}^n$ and a size parameter $k \in \{0,1\}^{\lceil \log n \rceil}$, outputs 1 if $\mathcal{H}^*(x) \leq k$, and outputs 0 otherwise. Note that if $\mathcal{H}^*$ succeeds on some string x, $\mathcal{H}$ will also succeed. Thus,

$$\Pr[x \leftarrow \{0,1\}^n, k \leftarrow \{0,1\}^{\lceil \log n \rceil} : \mathcal{H}(x,k) = \mathsf{MKtP}(x,k)] \geq 1 - \frac{1}{p(n)},$$

which is a contradiction.

It remains to construct the heuristic $\mathcal{H}^*$ that computes $Kt(x)$ with high probability over random inputs $x \in \{0,1\}^n$, using $\mathcal{A}$. By an averaging argument, except for a fraction $\frac{1}{2p(n)}$ of random tapes r for $\mathcal{A}$, the *deterministic* machine $\mathcal{A}_r$ (i.e., machine $\mathcal{A}$ with randomness fixed to r) fails to invert f with probability at most $\frac{2p(n)}{q(n)}$. Consider some such "good" randomness r for which $\mathcal{A}_r$ succeeds to invert f with probability $1 - \frac{2p(n)}{q(n)}$.

On input $x \in \{0,1\}^n$, our heuristic $\mathcal{H}_r^*$ runs $\mathcal{A}_r(i||x)$ for all $i \in [n+c]$ where i is represented as a $\lceil \log(n + c) \rceil$-bit string, and outputs the smallest

i where the inversion on $(i||x)$ succeeds. Let $\varepsilon = \frac{1}{4p(n)}$, and S be the set of strings $x \in \{0,1\}^n$ for which $\mathcal{H}_r^*(x)$ fails to compute $Kt(x)$ and x satisfies the requirements in Fact 31. Note that the probability that a random $x \in \{0,1\}^n$ does not satisfy the requirements in Fact 31 is at most ε. Thus, $\mathcal{H}_r^*$ fails with probability at most (by a union bound)

$$\mathsf{fail}_r \leq \varepsilon + \frac{|S|}{2^n}.$$

Consider any string $x \in S$ and let $w = Kt(x)$ be its Kt-complexity. Note that x satisfies the requirements in Fact 31; that is, there exist a Turing machine Π_x and a running time parameter t_x such that $U(\Pi_x, 1^{t_x}) = x$, $|\Pi_x| + \lceil \log t_x \rceil = Kt(x)$, and $t_x \leq 2^c/\varepsilon = 2^{c+2}p(n)$. By Fact 21, we have that $|\Pi_x| \leq w \leq n + c$. Thus, for all strings $(\ell||\Pi') \in \{0,1\}^{n+c+\lceil \log(n+c) \rceil}$ such that $\ell = |\Pi_x|$, $[\Pi']_{|\ell|} = \Pi_x$, it holds that $f(\ell||\Pi') = (w||x)$. Since $\mathcal{H}_r^*(x)$ fails to compute $Kt(x)$, $\mathcal{A}_r$ must fail to invert $(w||x)$. But, since $|\Pi_x| \leq n + c$, the output $(w||x)$ is sampled with probability at least

$$\frac{1}{n+c} \cdot \frac{1}{2^{|\Pi_x|}} \geq \frac{1}{n+c} \frac{1}{2^{n+c}} \geq \frac{1}{n2^{2c+1}} \cdot \frac{1}{2^n}$$

in the one-way function experiment, so $\mathcal{A}_r$ must fail with probability at least

$$|S| \cdot \frac{1}{n2^{2c+1}} \cdot \frac{1}{2^n} = \frac{1}{n2^{2c+1}} \cdot \frac{|S|}{2^n} \geq \frac{\mathsf{fail}_r - \varepsilon}{n2^{2c+1}}$$

which by assumption (that $\mathcal{A}_r$ is a good inverter) is at most that $\frac{2p(n)}{q(n)}$. We thus conclude that

$$\mathsf{fail}_r \leq \frac{2^{2c+2}np(n)}{q(n)} + \varepsilon.$$

Finally, by a union bound, we have that $\mathcal{H}^*$ (using a uniform random tape r) fails in computing Kt with probability at most

$$\frac{1}{2p(n)} + \frac{2^{2c+2}np(n)}{q(n)} + \varepsilon = \frac{1}{2p(n)} + \frac{2^{2c+2}np(n)}{2^{2c+4}np(n)^2} + \frac{1}{4p(n)} = \frac{1}{p(n)}.$$

Thus, $\mathcal{H}^*$ computes Kt with probability $1 - \frac{1}{p(n)}$ for all sufficiently large $n \in \mathbb{N}$, which is a contradiction. ∎

3.2   Two-Sided Error Avg-Case Hardness of MKtP from ioOWFs

In this section, we will prove the following theorem:

Theorem 10. *If ioOWFs exist, then* MKtP $\notin$ Heur$_{\mathsf{neg}}$BPP.

Proof: The theorem follows immediately from Theorem 7 and Theorem 11 that will be stated and proved below. ∎

Recall that Theorem 7 shows that ioOWFs imply the existence of rate-1 efficient condEP-ioPRGs. Theorem 11 below will show that the existence of rate-1 efficient condEP-ioPRGs implies that MKtP $\notin$ Heur$_{\text{neg}}$BPP. We remark that the proof of this theorem closely follows the proof in [LP20] and relying with only relatively minor modifications to observe that the properties used of the time-bounded Kolmogorov complexity function actually also hold for K^t—namely that random strings have "high" K^t-complexity, whereas outputs of a PRG have "low" K^t-complexity.[8]

Theorem 11. *Assume that for some $\gamma \geq 4$, there exists a rate-1 efficient μ-condEP-ioPRG $G : \{0,1\}^n \to \{0,1\}^{n+\gamma \log n}$ where $\mu(n) = 1/n^2$. Then, MKtP $\notin$* Heur$_{\text{neg}}$BPP.

Proof: Let $G : \{0,1\}^n \to \{0,1\}^{m(n)}$ where $m(n) = n + \gamma \log n$ be a rate-1 efficient $\frac{1}{n^2}$-condEP-ioPRG with entropy loss constant α. Let $p(n) = 2n^{2(\alpha+\gamma+2)}$. We assume for contradiction that MKtP $\in$ Heur$_{\text{neg}}$BPP; that is, there exists some PPT $\mathcal{H}$ that decides MKtP with probability at least $1 - \frac{1}{p(m')}$ where $m'(m) = m + \lceil \log m \rceil$ (on input length m') for all sufficiently large n, $m(n)$, and $m'(m)$. Recall that G is associated with a sequence of events $\{E_n\}_{n \in \mathbb{N}}$.

We show that $\mathcal{H}$ can be used to break the condEP-ioPRG G. Towards this, recall that a random string has high Kt-complexity with high probability: for $m = m(n)$, we have,

$$\Pr_{x \in \{0,1\}^m}[Kt(x) > m - \frac{\gamma}{2}\log n] \geq \frac{2^m - 2^{m - \frac{\gamma}{2}\log n}}{2^m} = 1 - \frac{1}{n^{\gamma/2}}, \quad (1)$$

since the total number of Turing machines with length smaller than $m - \frac{\gamma}{2}\log n$ is only $2^{m - \frac{\gamma}{2}\log n}$. However, any string output by G, must have "low" Kt complexity: For every sufficiently large $n, m = m(n)$, we have that,

$$\Pr_{z \in \{0,1\}^n}[Kt(G(z)) > m - \frac{\gamma}{2}\log n] = 0, \quad (2)$$

since $G(z)$ can be represented by combining a seed z of length n with the code of G (of constant length), and the running time of $G(z)$ is bounded by $1.1n$ for all sufficiently large n (since G is rate-1 efficient), so $Kt(G(z)) = n + O(1) + \lceil \log(1.1n) \rceil = (m - \gamma \log n) + O(1) + \lceil \log(1.1n) \rceil \leq m - \gamma/2 \log n$ for sufficiently large n (since recall that $\gamma \geq 4$).

Based on these observations, we now construct a PPT distinguisher $\mathcal{A}$ breaking G. On input $1^n, x$, where $x \in \{0,1\}^{m(n)}$, $\mathcal{A}(1^n, x)$ lets $k = m - \frac{\gamma}{2}\log n$ and outputs 1 if $\mathcal{H}(x, k)$ outputs 1 and 0 otherwise. Consider some sufficiently large n, $m(n)$, and $m'(n)$. The following two claims conclude that $\mathcal{A}$ distinguishes $\mathcal{U}_{m(n)}$ and $G(\mathcal{U}_n \mid E_n)$ with probability at least $\frac{1}{n^2}$.

---

[8] There are also some other minor differences due to the fact that the proof in [LP20] considered the hardness of *computing* (or approximating) K^t, whereas we here consider a *decisional* problem with a random threshold k, but the proof in [LP20] extends in a relatively straightforward way to deal also with decisional problems with a random threshold k.

Claim 1. $\mathcal{A}(1^n, \mathcal{U}_m)$ *outputs 0 with probability at least* $1 - \frac{2}{n^{\gamma/2}}$.

Proof: Note that $\mathcal{A}(1^n, x)$ will output 0 if x is a string with Kt-complexity larger than $m - \gamma/2 \log n$ and $\mathcal{H}$ succeeds on input (x, k). Thus,

$$
\begin{aligned}
&\Pr[\mathcal{A}(1^n, x) = 0] \\
&\geq \Pr[Kt(x) > m - \gamma/2 \log n \wedge \mathcal{H} \text{ succeeds on } (x, k)] \\
&\geq 1 - \Pr[Kt(x) \leq m - \gamma/2 \log n] - \Pr[\mathcal{H} \text{ fails on } (x, k)] \\
&\geq 1 - \frac{1}{n^{\gamma/2}} - \frac{1}{p(m')} \\
&\geq 1 - \frac{2}{n^{\gamma/2}}.
\end{aligned}
$$

where the probability is over a random $x \leftarrow \mathcal{U}_m$, $k \leftarrow \lceil \log m \rceil$ and the randomness of $\mathcal{A}$ and $\mathcal{H}$. ∎

Claim 2. $\mathcal{A}(1^n, G(\mathcal{U}_n \mid E_n))$ *outputs 0 with probability at most* $1 - \frac{1}{n} + \frac{2}{n^2}$

Proof: Recall that by assumption, $\mathcal{H}(x, k)$ fails to decide whether $(x, k) \in \mathsf{MKtP}$ for a random $x \in \{0, 1\}^m$, $k \in \{0, 1\}^{\lceil \log m \rceil}$ with probability at most $\frac{1}{p(m')}$ (where $m' = m + \lceil \log m \rceil$). By an averaging argument, for at least a $1 - \frac{1}{n^2}$ fraction of random tapes r for $\mathcal{H}$, the deterministic machine $\mathcal{H}_r$ fails to decide MKtP with probability at most $\frac{n^2}{p(m')}$. Fix some "good" randomness r such that $\mathcal{H}_r$ decides MKtP with probability at least $1 - \frac{n^2}{p(m')}$. We next analyze the success probability of $\mathcal{A}_r$. Assume for contradiction that $\mathcal{A}_r$ outputs 1 with probability at least $1 - \frac{1}{n} + \frac{1}{n^{\alpha+\gamma}}$ on input $G(\mathcal{U}_n \mid E_n)$. Recall that (1) the entropy of $G(\mathcal{U}_n \mid E_n)$ is at least $n - \alpha \log n$ and (2) the quantity $- \log \Pr[G(\mathcal{U}_n \mid E_n) = y]$ is upper bounded by n for all $y \in G(\mathcal{U}_n \mid E_n)$. By an averaging argument, with probability at least $\frac{1}{n}$, a random $y \in G(\mathcal{U}_n \mid E_n)$ will satisfy

$$
- \log \Pr[G(\mathcal{U}_n \mid E_n) = y] \geq (n - \alpha \log n) - 1.
$$

We refer to an output y satisfying the above condition as being "good" and other y's as being "bad". Let $S = \{y \in G(\mathcal{U}_n \mid E_n) : \mathcal{A}_r(1^n, y) = 0 \wedge y \text{ is good}\}$, and let $S' = \{y \in G(\mathcal{U}_n \mid E_n) : \mathcal{A}_r(1^n, y) = 0 \wedge y \text{ is bad}\}$. Since

$$
\Pr[\mathcal{A}_r(1^n, G(\mathcal{U}_n \mid E_n)) = 0] = \Pr[G(\mathcal{U}_n \mid E_n) \in S] + \Pr[G(\mathcal{U}_n \mid E_n) \in S'],
$$

and $\Pr[G(\mathcal{U}_n \mid E_n) \in S']$ is at most the probability that $G(\mathcal{U}_n \mid E_n)$ is "bad" (which as argued above is at most $1 - \frac{1}{n}$), we have that

$$
\Pr[G(\mathcal{U}_n \mid E_n) \in S] \geq \left(1 - \frac{1}{n} + \frac{1}{n^{\alpha+\gamma}}\right) - \left(1 - \frac{1}{n}\right) = \frac{1}{n^{\alpha+\gamma}}.
$$

Furthermore, since for every $y \in S$, $\Pr[G(\mathcal{U}_n \mid E_n) = y] \leq 2^{-n+\alpha \log n+1}$, we also have,

$$
\Pr[G(\mathcal{U}_n \mid E_n) \in S] \leq |S| 2^{-n+\alpha \log n+1}
$$

So,

$$|S| \geq \frac{2^{n-\alpha \log n - 1}}{n^{\alpha+\gamma}} = 2^{n-(2\alpha+\gamma)\log n - 1}$$

However, for any $y \in G(\mathcal{U}_n \mid E_n)$, if $\mathcal{A}_r(1^n, y)$ outputs 0, then by Eq. 2, $Kt(y) \leq m - \gamma/2 \log n = k$, so $\mathcal{H}_r$ fails to decide MKtP on input (y, k).

Thus, the probability that $\mathcal{H}_r$ fails (to decide MKtP) on a random input $(y, k) \in \{0, 1\}^{m'}$ is at least

$$|S|/2^{m'} = \frac{2^{n-(2\alpha+\gamma)\log n - 1}}{2^{n+\gamma \log n + \lceil \log m \rceil}} \geq \frac{2^{-(2\alpha+2\gamma)\log n - 1}}{2^{\lceil \log m \rceil}} \geq 2^{-2(\alpha+\gamma+1)\log n - 1} = \frac{1}{2n^{2(\alpha+\gamma+1)}}$$

which contradicts the fact that $\mathcal{H}_r$ fails to decide MKtP with probability at most $\frac{n^2}{p(m')} < \frac{1}{2n^{2(\alpha+\gamma+1)}}$ (since $n < m'$).

We conclude that for every good randomness r, $\mathcal{A}_r$ outputs 0 with probability at most $1 - \frac{1}{n} + \frac{1}{n^{\alpha+\gamma}}$. Finally, by union bound (and since a random tape is bad with probability $\leq \frac{1}{n^2}$), we have that the probability that $\mathcal{A}(G(\mathcal{U}_n \mid E_n))$ outputs 1 is at most

$$\frac{1}{n^2} + \left(1 - \frac{1}{n} + \frac{1}{n^{\alpha+\gamma}}\right) \leq 1 - \frac{1}{n} + \frac{2}{n^2},$$

since $\gamma \geq 2$.   ∎

We conclude, recalling that $\gamma \geq 4$, that $\mathcal{A}$ distinguishes $\mathcal{U}_m$ and $G(\mathcal{U}_n \mid E_n)$ with probability of at least

$$\left(1 - \frac{2}{n^{\gamma/2}}\right) - \left(1 - \frac{1}{n} + \frac{2}{n^2}\right) \geq \left(1 - \frac{2}{n^2}\right) - \left(1 - \frac{1}{n} + \frac{2}{n^2}\right) = \frac{1}{n} - \frac{4}{n^2} \geq \frac{1}{n^2}$$

for all sufficiently large $n \in \mathbb{N}$.   ∎

4   Errorless Avg-Case Hardness of MKtP and EXP $\neq$ BPP

In this section, we will prove the following theorem:

Theorem 12. EXP $\neq$ BPP *if and only if* MKtP $\notin$ Avg$_{\text{neg}}$BPP.

Roughly speaking, the above theorem is proved in two steps:

- We first observe that, assuming EXP $\neq$ BPP, there exists an (inefficient, infinitely-often) pseudorandom generator [IW98] that maps a n^ε-bit seed to a n-bit string in time $O(2^{n^\gamma})$ (for some $0 < \varepsilon, \gamma < 1$).
- We will next show that an errorless heuristic for MKtP can be used to break such PRGs (since the Kt-complexity of the output of the PRG is at most $n^\varepsilon + n^\gamma + O(1) \leq n - 1$), which is a contradiction and concludes the proof.

Recall that Impagliazzo and Wigderson [IW98] showed that BPP can be derandomized (on average) in subexponential time by assuming EXP $\neq$ BPP. The central technical contribution in their work can be stated as proving the existence of an inefficient PRG assuming EXP $\neq BPP$:

Theorem 13 (implicit in [IW98], explicitly stated in e.g., [TV02, Theorem 3.9]). *Assume that* $\mathsf{EXP} \neq \mathsf{BPP}$. *Then, for all* $\varepsilon > 0$, *there exists an inefficient io-$\frac{1}{10}$-PRG* $G : \{0,1\}^{n^\varepsilon} \to \{0,1\}^n$ *that runs in time* $2^{O(n^\varepsilon)}$.

We note that the proof in [IW98], is non black-box. In particular, it does not show how to solve EXP in probabilistic polynomial-time having black-box access to an attacker that breaks the PRG.

It remains to show that if there exists an (inefficient) ioPRG $G : \{0,1\}^{n^\varepsilon} \to \{0,1\}^n$ with running time $O(2^{n^\gamma})$ (for some $0 < \varepsilon, \gamma < 1$), then $\mathsf{MKtP} \notin \mathsf{Avg}_{\mathsf{neg}}\mathsf{BPP}$. We recall that a string's Kt-complexity is the minimal sum of (1) the description length of a Turing machine that prints the string and (2) the logarithm of its running time. Note that the output of G could be printed by a machine with the code of G (of constant length) and the seed (of length n^ε) hardwired in it within $O(2^{n^\gamma})$ time. Thus, strings output by G have Kt-complexity less than or equal to $O(1) + n^\varepsilon + n^\gamma \leq n - 1$. On the other hand, random strings have high Kt-complexity (e.g., $> n - 1$) with high probability (e.g., $\geq \frac{1}{2}$). It follows that an errorless heuristic for MKtP can be used to break G. Let us highlight why it is important that we have an *errorless* heuristic (as opposed to a 2-sided error heuristic): while a 2-sided error heuristic would still work well on random strings, we do not have any guarantees on its success probability given pseudorandom strings (as they are sparse); an errorless heuristics, however, will either correctly decide those strings, or output $\perp$ (in which case, we can also guess that the string is pseudorandom).

We proceed to a formal statement of the theorem, and its proof.

Theorem 14. *Assume that there exist constants* $0 < \varepsilon, \gamma < 1$ *and an inefficient io-$\frac{1}{10}$-PRG* $G : \{0,1\}^{n^\varepsilon} \to \{0,1\}^n$ *with running time* $O(2^{n^\gamma})$. *Then,* $\mathsf{MKtP} \notin \mathsf{Avg}_{\mathsf{neg}}\mathsf{BPP}$.

Proof: We assume for contradiction that $\mathsf{MKtP} \in \mathsf{Avg}_{\mathsf{neg}}\mathsf{BPP}$, which in turn implies that there exists an errorless PPT heuristic $\mathcal{H}$ such that for all sufficiently large n, every $x \in \{0,1\}^n$ and $k \in \{0,1\}^{\lceil \log n \rceil}$,

$$\Pr[\mathcal{H}(x,k) \in \{\mathsf{MKtP}(x,k), \perp\}] \geq 0.9, \tag{3}$$

and

$$\Pr[x \leftarrow \{0,1\}^n, k \leftarrow \{0,1\}^{\lceil \log n \rceil} : \mathcal{H}(x,k) = \perp] \leq \frac{1}{2n^2}.$$

Fix some sufficiently large n, and let $k = n - 1$. It follows by an averaging argument that

$$\Pr[x \leftarrow \{0,1\}^n : \mathcal{H}(x, n-1) = \perp] \leq \frac{1}{2n^2} \cdot 2^{\lceil \log n \rceil} \leq \frac{1}{n}. \tag{4}$$

We next show that we can use $\mathcal{H}$ to break the PRG G. On input $x \in \{0,1\}^n$, our distinguisher $\mathcal{A}(1^{n^\varepsilon}, x)$ outputs 1 if $\mathcal{H}(x, n-1) = 1$ or $\mathcal{H}(x, n-1) = \perp$. $\mathcal{A}$ outputs 0 if and only if $\mathcal{H}(x, n-1) = 0$. The following two claims conclude that $\mathcal{A}$ distinguishes $\mathcal{U}_n$ and $G(\mathcal{U}_{n^\varepsilon})$ with probability at least 0.2.

Claim 1. $\mathcal{A}(1^{n^\varepsilon}, \mathcal{U}_n)$ will output 0 with probability at least $0.4 - \frac{1}{n}$.

Proof: Note that the probability that a random string $x \in \{0,1\}^n$ is of Kt-complexity at most $n-1$ is at most $\frac{2^{n-1}}{2^n} = \frac{1}{2}$ (since the total number of machines with description length $\leq n-1$ is 2^{n-1}). And the probability that $\mathcal{H}(x, n-1)$ outputs $\bot$ is at most $\frac{1}{n}$ (over random $x \in \{0,1\}^n$) by Eq. 4. In addition, the probability that $\mathcal{H}(x, n-1)$ fails to output either $\mathsf{MKtP}(x, n-1)$ or $\bot$ is at most 0.1 by Eq. 3. Thus, by a union bound,

$$\begin{aligned}
&\Pr[\mathcal{A}(1^{n^\varepsilon}, \mathcal{U}_n) = 0] \\
&\geq 1 - \Pr[Kt(\mathcal{U}_n) \leq n-1] - \Pr[\mathcal{H}(\mathcal{U}_n, n-1) = \bot] - \Pr[\mathcal{H}(\mathcal{U}_n, n-1) \text{ fails}] \\
&\geq 1 - \frac{1}{2} - \frac{1}{n} - 0.1 \\
&= 0.4 - \frac{1}{n}.
\end{aligned}$$

∎

Claim 2. $\mathcal{A}(1^{n^\varepsilon}, G(\mathcal{U}_{n^\varepsilon}))$ will output 0 with probability at most 0.1.

Proof. We first show that for all $z \in \{0,1\}^{n^\varepsilon}$, $Kt(G(z)) \leq n^\varepsilon + n^\gamma + O(1) \leq n - 1 = s$. Note that the string $G(z)$ could be produced by a machine with the code of G (of length $O(1)$) and the seed z (of length n^ε) in time $O(2^{n^\gamma})$ (which adds $\log O(2^{n^\gamma}) = n^\gamma + O(1)$ to its Kt-complexity). In addition, recall that $\mathcal{H}$ is a probabilistic errorless heuristics. Thus, $\mathcal{H}(G(z), n-1)$ will output 0 with probability at most 0.1 (by Eq. 3), and the claim follows. ∎

This conclude the proof of Theorem 14. ∎

We are now ready to conclude the proof of Theorem 12.

Proof (of Theorem 12): We show each direction separately:

- To show that $\mathsf{EXP} \neq \mathsf{BPP} \implies \mathsf{MKtP} \notin \mathsf{Avg}_{\mathrm{neg}}\mathsf{BPP}$, assume that $\mathsf{EXP} \neq \mathsf{BPP}$ and let $\varepsilon = \frac{1}{3}$, and $\gamma = \frac{1}{2}$. By Theorem 13, there exists an io-$\frac{1}{10}$-PRG $G : \{0,1\}^{n^\varepsilon} \to \{0,1\}^n$ with running time $2^{O(n^\varepsilon)} \leq O(2^{n^\gamma})$. We conclude by Theorem 14 that $\mathsf{MKtP} \notin \mathsf{Avg}_{\mathrm{neg}}\mathsf{BPP}$.
- To show that $\mathsf{MKtP} \notin \mathsf{Avg}_{\mathrm{neg}}\mathsf{BPP} \implies \mathsf{EXP} \neq \mathsf{BPP}$, assume that $\mathsf{MKtP} \notin \mathsf{Avg}_{\mathrm{neg}}\mathsf{BPP}$; this trivially implies that $\mathsf{MKtP} \notin \mathsf{BPP}$. We observe that $\mathsf{MKtP} \in \mathsf{EXP}$ as by Fact 21, $Kt(x) \leq |x| + O(1)$ and thus the running-time for a Kt-witness, Π, for x is bounded by $2^{|x|+O(1)}$. Thus, $\mathsf{EXP} \not\subseteq \mathsf{BPP}$, which in particular means that $\mathsf{EXP} \neq \mathsf{BPP}$.

∎

5 On the Implication MKtP $\not\in$ Avg$_{\text{neg}}$BPP $\implies$ MKtP $\not\in$ Heur$_{\text{neg}}$BPP

Recall that in Theorem 12, we showed that if one assumes an (extremely) weak lowerbound (namely, EXP $\neq$ BPP), then the problem MKtP is hard on average for errorless heuristics. Furthermore, in Theorem 9, we showed that if the problem MKtP is hard-on-average for 2-sided error heuristics that only make a small number of mistakes, then (infinitely-often) one-way functions exist. Combining the two theorems together, we have that the implication MKtP $\not\in$ Avg$_{\text{neg}}$BPP $\implies$ MKtP $\not\in$ Heur$_{\text{neg}}$BPP fully characterizes when we can base the existence of (infinitely-often) one-way functions on EXP $\neq$ BPP. Formally,

Theorem 15. MKtP $\not\in$ Avg$_{\text{neg}}$BPP $\Rightarrow$ MKtP $\not\in$ Heur$_{\text{neg}}$BPP *holds iff* EXP $\neq$ BPP $\Rightarrow$ *the existence of ioOWFs.*

Proof: The proof immediately follows from Theorem 12 and Theorem 9.   ∎

Perhaps surprisingly, we observe that the implication itself (without any assumptions) implies that NP $\neq$ P. The pessimistic way to interpret this is that closing the gap between 2-sided error, and errorless, heuristics will be very hard (as it requires proving that NP $\neq$ P). The optimistic way to interpret it, however, is as a new and algorithmic approach towards proving that NP $\neq$ P: To demonstrate that NP $\neq$ P, it suffices to demonstrate that MKtP can be solved by an errorless heuristic, given access to a two-sided error heuristic for the same problem. (As we shall point out shortly, this approach also does not "overshoot" the NP vs P problem by too much: any proof of the existence of infinitely often one-way functions, needs to show this implication.)

Theorem 16. *If it holds that* MKtP $\not\in$ Avg$_{\text{neg}}$BPP $\Rightarrow$ MKtP $\not\in$ Heur$_{\text{neg}}$BPP, *then* NP $\neq$ P.

Proof: Assume for contradiction that MKtP $\not\in$ Avg$_{\text{neg}}$BPP $\Rightarrow$ MKtP $\not\in$ Heur$_{\text{neg}}$BPP holds, yet NP = P. Recall that BPP $\subseteq$ NP^{NP} [Sip83,Lau83], so it follows that P = BPP, and thus by the time-hierarchy Theorem [HS65], EXP $\neq$ BPP. Then, by Theorem 12, MKtP $\not\in$ Avg$_{\text{neg}}$BPP. It follows from our assumption that MKtP $\not\in$ Avg$_{\text{neg}}$BPP $\Rightarrow$ MKtP $\not\in$ Heur$_{\text{neg}}$BPP and from Theorem 15 that ioOWFs exist, which contradicts the assumption that NP = P.   ∎

We remark that the above theorem could be strengthened to show even that NP is average-case hard (w.r.t. deterministic errorless heuristics), since Buhrman, Fortnow, and Pavan [BFP03] have showed that unless this is the case, P = BPP, which suffices to complete the rest of the proof.

Finally, we remark that the implication MKtP $\not\in$ Avg$_{\text{neg}}$BPP $\Rightarrow$ MKtP $\not\in$ Heur$_{\text{neg}}$BPP must be true if infinitely-often one-way functions exist since by Theorem 10, the existence of ioOWFs implies MKtP $\not\in$ Heur$_{\text{neg}}$BPP, which in turn implies that the implication trivially holds.

6   Characterizing Cryptography in Log-Space

In this section, we show how to characterize the existence of OWFs that are computable in log-space through a notion of resource-bounded Kolmogorov complexity. In more detail, we will consider an appropriate notion of *space-bounded* Kolmogorov complexity.

6.1   Space-Bounded Kolmogorov Complexity

We consider a space-bounded variant of Kolmogorov complexity [Kol68]. We here let U be a fixed universal Turing machine that emulates any Turing machine with polynomial overhead in time and *constant multiplicative overhead in space*. The s-space bounded Kolmogorov complexity, $K^s(x)$, of a string $x \in \{0,1\}^*$ is defined as

$$K^s(x) = \min_{\Pi \in \{0,1\}^*} \{|\Pi| : \forall i \in [|x|], U(\Pi(i), 1^{2^{s(|x|)}}) = x_i \text{ and } \Pi(i) \text{ uses at most } s(|x|) \text{ space}\}$$

where $\Pi(i)$ denotes $M(w,i)$ and $\Pi = (M,w)$. Its decisional variant, the minimum K^s-complexity problem MKSP[s], for some function s, is defined as follows:

– Input: A string $x \in \{0,1\}^n$ and a size parameter $k \in \{0,1\}^{\lceil \log n \rceil}$.
– Decide: Does (x,k) satisfy $K^s(x) \leq k$?

Whenever the space-bound is logarithmic or more, $K^s(x) \leq |x| + O(1)$.

Fact 61. *There exists a constant c such that for every $s(n) \geq \log n$ and every $x \in \{0,1\}^*$, $K^s(x) \leq |x| + c$.*

Proof: Consider a machine $\Pi_x = (M,x)$ where M is a Turing machine (of constant size) such that $M(y,i)$ outputs y_i for any string y and any index i. It follows that for all $i \in [|x|]$, $\Pi_x(i) = M(x,i)$ will output x_i using at most $\log n$ space. Note that Π_x can be encoded in $|x| + c$ bits, and the fact follows.   ∎

6.2   The Characterization

We are now ready to state the main theorem of this section:

Theorem 17. *The following are equivalent:*

(a) The existence of infinitely-often one-way functions computable in log-space.
(b) The existence of a constant $\delta \geq 1$ such that MKSP[$\delta \log(n)$] $\notin$ Heur$_{neg}$BPP.
(c) For all $\delta \geq 1$, MKSP[$\delta \log(n)$] $\notin$ Heur$_{neg}$BPP.

Proof:

(b) $\Longrightarrow$ **(a)** follows from Theorem 18, which will be proven in Sect. 6.3;

(a) $\implies$ (c) follows from Theorem 19 and Theorem 20, which will be proven in Sect. 6.4;

(c) $\implies$ (b) trivially follows.

∎

We remark that by the results of [AIK06], the existence of a log-space computable OWF implies a OWF that is uniform NC^0 computable; in fact, as observed by [RS21] (see Remark 31), by a slight tweak of the construction of [AIK06], one actually gets a OWF that is *log-space* uniform NC^0 computable. In other words, the existence of log-space computable OWFs is equivalent to the existence of log-space uniform NC^0-computable OWFs. Theorem 4 thus also characterizes OWFs computable in log-space uniform NC^0.[9]

6.3 Log-Space Computable ioOWFs from Avg-Case Hardness of MKSP[$O(\log n)$)]

We here show how to get a log-space computable OWF assuming $\mathsf{MKSP}[O(\log n))] \notin \mathsf{Heur_{neg}BPP}$. The proof very closely follows [LP20], while making minor adjustments to account for log-space computability.

Theorem 18. *If there exists a constant $\delta \geq 1$ such that $\mathsf{MKSP}[\delta \log n] \notin \mathsf{Heur_{neg}BPP}$, then there exists a weak ioOWF (and thus also a ioOWF) that is computable in log-space.*

Proof: Assume that there exists some constant $\delta \geq 1$ such that $\mathsf{MKSP}[\delta \log n] \notin \mathsf{Heur_{neg}BPP}$; that is, there exists a polynomial $p(\cdot)$ such that for all PPT heuristics $\mathcal{H}'$ and infinitely many n,

$$\Pr[x \leftarrow \{0,1\}^n, k \leftarrow \{0,1\}^{\lceil \log n \rceil} : \mathcal{H}'(x,k) = \mathsf{MKSP}[s](x,k)] < 1 - \frac{1}{p(n)},$$

where $s(n) = \delta \log n$. Let c be the constant from Fact 61. Consider the function $f : \{0,1\}^{n+c+\lceil \log(n+c) \rceil} \rightarrow \{0,1\}^{\lceil \log n \rceil + n}$, which given an input $\ell || \Pi'$ where $|\ell| = \lceil \log(n + c) \rceil$ and $|\Pi'| = n + c$, outputs $\ell || U(\Pi(1), 1^t) || \ldots || U(\Pi(n), 1^t)$ where Π is the ℓ-bit prefix of Π' and $t = 2^{s(n)}$. Furthermore, f will just abort if in the execution of $\Pi(i)$, the program consumes more than $s(n)$ bits of memory. That is,

$$f(\ell || \Pi') = \ell || U(\Pi(1), 1^t) || U(\Pi(2), 1^t) || \ldots || U(\Pi(n), 1^t).$$

Note that f is computable in log-space (since the universal Turing machine U is assumed to have constant multiplicative overhead in terms of space). Observe that f is only defined over some input lengths, but by the same padding trick as in the proof of Theorem 9, it can be transformed into a function f' defined over all input lengths that preserves weak onewayness of f.

---

[9] This observation was added after becoming aware of [RS21].

We now show that f is a $\frac{1}{q(\cdot)}$-weak ioOWF function where $q(n) = 2^{2c+3}np(n)^2$, which concludes the proof of the theorem. This claim essentially follows from the proof [LP20]; we provide a formal proof here for the reader's convenience.

Assume for contradiction that f is not a $\frac{1}{q(\cdot)}$-weak ioOWF; that is, there exists some PPT attacker $\mathcal{A}$ that inverts f with probability at least $1 - \frac{1}{q(n)} \leq 1 - \frac{1}{q(m)}$ for all sufficiently large $m = n + c + \lceil \log(n+c) \rceil$. We first claim that we can use $\mathcal{A}$ to construct a PPT heuristic $\mathcal{H}^*$ such that

$$\Pr[x \leftarrow \{0,1\}^n : \mathcal{H}^*(x) = K^s(x)] \geq 1 - \frac{1}{p(n)}.$$

If this is true, consider the heuristic $\mathcal{H}$ which given a string $x \in \{0,1\}^n$ and a size parameter $k \in \{0,1\}^{\lceil \log n \rceil}$, outputs 1 if $\mathcal{H}^*(x) \leq k$, and outputs 0 otherwise. Note that if $\mathcal{H}^*$ succeeds on some string x, $\mathcal{H}$ will also succeed. Thus,

$$\Pr[x \leftarrow \{0,1\}^n, k \leftarrow \{0,1\}^{\lceil \log n \rceil} : \mathcal{H}(x,k) = \mathsf{MKSP}[s](x,k)] \geq 1 - \frac{1}{p(n)},$$

which is a contradiction.

It remains to construct the heuristic $\mathcal{H}^*$ that computes $K^s(x)$ with high probability over random inputs $x \in \{0,1\}^n$, using $\mathcal{A}$. By an averaging argument, except for a fraction $\frac{1}{2p(n)}$ of random tapes r for $\mathcal{A}$, the *deterministic* machine $\mathcal{A}_r$ (i.e., machine $\mathcal{A}$ with randomness fixed to r) fails to invert f with probability at most $\frac{2p(n)}{q(n)}$. Consider some such "good" randomness r for which $\mathcal{A}_r$ succeeds to invert f with probability $1 - \frac{2p(n)}{q(n)}$.

On input $x \in \{0,1\}^n$, our heuristic $\mathcal{H}_r^*$ runs $\mathcal{A}_r(i||x)$ for all $i \in [n+c]$ where i is represented as a $\lceil \log(n+c) \rceil$-bit string, and outputs the smallest i where the inversion on $(i||x)$ succeeds; that is, the inverter $\mathcal{A}_r(i||x)$ outputs a program Π that prints each bit of x within $s(n)$ space. Let S be the set of strings $x \in \{0,1\}^n$ for which $\mathcal{H}_r^*(x)$ fails to compute $K^s(x)$. Thus, $\mathcal{H}_r^*$ fails with probability at most

$$\mathsf{fail}_r \leq \frac{|S|}{2^n}.$$

Consider any string $x \in S$ and let $w = K^s(x)$ be its K^s-complexity. It follows that there exists a Turing machine Π_x such that $|\Pi_x| = w$ and $\Pi_x(i)$ outputs x_i in space $s(n)$ (for all $i \in [n]$). Since $\mathcal{H}_r^*(x)$ fails to compute $K^s(x)$, $\mathcal{A}_r$ must fail to invert $(w||x)$. But, since $|\Pi_x| \leq w \leq n + c$, the output $(w||x)$ is sampled with probability at least

$$\frac{1}{n+c} \cdot \frac{1}{2^w} \geq \frac{1}{n+c} \frac{1}{2^{n+c}} \geq \frac{1}{n 2^{2c+1}} \cdot \frac{1}{2^n}$$

in the one-way function experiment, so $\mathcal{A}_r$ must fail with probability at least

$$|S| \cdot \frac{1}{n 2^{2c+1}} \cdot \frac{1}{2^n} = \frac{1}{n 2^{2c+1}} \cdot \frac{|S|}{2^n} \geq \frac{\mathsf{fail}_r}{n 2^{2c+1}}$$

which by assumption (that $\mathcal{A}_r$ is a good inverter) is at most that $\frac{2p(n)}{q(n)}$. We thus conclude that

$$\mathsf{fail}_r \leq \frac{2^{2c+2}np(n)}{q(n)}$$

Finally, by a union bound, we have that $\mathcal{H}^*$ (using a uniform random tape r) fails in computing K^s with probability at most

$$\frac{1}{2p(n)} + \frac{2^{2c+2}np(n)}{q(n)} = \frac{1}{2p(n)} + \frac{2^{2c+2}np(n)}{2^{2c+3}np(n)^2} = \frac{1}{p(n)}.$$

Thus, $\mathcal{H}^*$ computes K^s with probability $1 - \frac{1}{p(n)}$ for all sufficiently large $n \in \mathbb{N}$. ∎

6.4 Average-Case Hardness of MKSP$[O(\log n)]$ from ioOWFs in Log-Space

To show that MKSP$[O(\log n)]$ is average-case hard for PPT heuristics, we first build a condEP-ioPRG G that is computable in log-space from a log-space computable ioOWF. Then, we will show that a heuristic for MKSP$[O(\log n)]$ can be used to break G.

Recall that Liu and Pass [LP20] constructed a condEP-PRG G from a standard OWF. At a high level, their construction follows the construction of a PRG from a *regular* OWF [GKL93], which applies universal hash functions (parameterized according to the regularity of the OWF) to both the input and the output of the OWF to extract the randomness in the input and the output, and finally outputs several Goldreich-Levin hardcore bits (to make the PRG stretch its input). When the regularity of the function is unknown, a random guess of the regularity is sampled (and the universal hash functions are thus paramemterized by this guess). They prove that the construction is both entropy-preserving and pseudorandom *conditioned on* the event that the guess matches the regularity of the function (on the input string). We observe that this construction is computable in log-space if the OWF is log-space computable since both the universal hash functions and Goldreich-Levin hardcore bits can be implemented in log-space [AIK06]. In addition, by a padding argument, we can transform any PRG that is computable in $O(\log n)$ space into a PRG computable in $\log(n)$ space.

Theorem 19 (essentially implicit in [LP20], relying on observations from [AIK06]). *Assume the existence of an ioOWF that is computable in log-space. Then, for every $\gamma > 1$, there exists a μ-condEP-ioPRG $G_\gamma : \{0,1\}^n \to \{0,1\}^{m(n)=n+\gamma \log n}$ that is computable in space $\log(m(n))$, where $\mu = \frac{1}{n^2}$.*

We next show that a heuristic for MKSP$[O(\log n)]$ can distinguish the output of a condEP-ioPRG G from a random string. The proof follows the structure of the proof in [LP20] and Theorem 11 (relying on the observations that (a) random strings have high K^s-complexity, whereas (b) outputs of the PRGs have small K^s-complexity, where $s(n) = O(\log n)$).

Theorem 20. *Assume that for some $\gamma \geq 4$, there exists a μ-condEP-ioPRG $G : \{0,1\}^n \rightarrow \{0,1\}^{m(n)=n+\gamma \log n}$ that is computable in space $\log(m(n))$, where $\mu(n) = 1/n^2$. Then, for all $\delta \geq 1$, MKSP$[\delta \log n] \notin$ Heur$_{neg}$BPP.*

Proof: Let $G : \{0,1\}^n \rightarrow \{0,1\}^{m(n)}$ where $m(n) = n + \gamma \log n$ be a $\frac{1}{n^2}$-condEP-ioPRG, computable in space $\log(m(n))$, with entropy loss constant α. Let $p(n) = 2n^{2(\alpha+\gamma+2)}$. Consider any $\delta \geq 1$ and function $s(n) = \delta \log(n)$. Assume for contradiction that MKSP$[s] \in$ Heur$_{neg}$BPP; that is, there exists some PPT $\mathcal{H}$ that decides MKSP$[s]$ with probability at least $1 - \frac{1}{p(m')}$ where $m'(m) = m + \lceil \log m \rceil$ (on input length m') for all sufficiently large n, $m(n)$, and $m'(m)$. Recall that G is associated with a sequence of events $\{E_n\}_{n \in \mathbb{N}}$.

We next show that $\mathcal{H}$ can be used to break the condEP-ioPRG G. Towards this, recall that a random string has high K^s-complexity with high probability: for $m = m(n)$, we have,

$$\Pr_{x \in \{0,1\}^m}[K^s(x) > m - \frac{\gamma}{2} \log n] \geq \frac{2^m - 2^{m - \frac{\gamma}{2} \log n}}{2^m} = 1 - \frac{1}{n^{\gamma/2}}, \quad (5)$$

since the total number of Turing machines with length smaller than $m - \frac{\gamma}{2} \log n$ is only $2^{m - \frac{\gamma}{2} \log n}$. However, any string output by G, must have "low" K^s complexity: For every sufficiently large n, $m = m(n)$, we have that,

$$\Pr_{z \in \{0,1\}^n}[K^s(G(z)) > m - \frac{\gamma}{2} \log n] = 0, \quad (6)$$

since $G(z)$ can be represented by combining a seed z of length n with the code of G (of constant length), and the space of $G(z)$ is bounded by $\log(m(n)) \leq s(m)$ for all sufficiently large n.

Based on these observations, we now construct a PPT distinguisher $\mathcal{A}$ breaking G. On input $1^n, x$, where $x \in \{0,1\}^{m(n)}$, $\mathcal{A}(1^n, x)$ lets $k = m - \frac{\gamma}{2} \log n$ and outputs 1 if $\mathcal{H}(x, k)$ outputs 1 and 0 otherwise. It follows from Claim 1 and Claim 2 (by replacing Kt-complexity with K^s-complexity, MKtP with MKSP$[s]$) in the proof of Theorem 11 that $\mathcal{A}$ distinguishes $\mathcal{U}_{m(n)}$ and $G(\mathcal{U}_n \mid E_n)$ with probability at least $\frac{1}{n^2}$, which concludes the proof. ∎

Acknowledgments. We are very grateful to Salil Vadhan for helpful discussions about the PRG construction of [IW98]. The first author also wishes to thank Hanlin Ren for helpful discussions about Levin's notion of Kolmogorov Complexity.

References

[ABK+06] Allender, E., Buhrman, H., Koucký, M., Van Melkebeek, D., Ronneburger, D.: Power from random strings. SIAM J. Comput. **35**(6), 1467–1493 (2006)

[ACM+21] Allender, E., Cheraghchi, M., Myrisiotis, D., Tirumala, H., Volkovich, I.: One-way functions and a conditional variant of MKTP (2021). Manuscript

[AGGM06] Akavia, A., Goldreich, O., Goldwasser, S., Moshkovitz, D.: On basing one-way functions on NP-hardness. In: STOC 2006, pp. 701–710 (2006)

[AIK06]   Applebaum, B., Ishai, Y., Kushilevitz, E.: Cryptography in nc^0. SIAM J. Comput. **36**(4), 845–888 (2006)

[Ajt96]   Ajtai, M.: Generating hard instances of lattice problems (extended abstract). In: Miller, G.L. (ed.) Proceedings of the 28th Annual ACM Symposium on the Theory of Computing, Philadelphia, Pennsylvania, USA, 22–24 May 1996, pp. 99–108. ACM (1996)

[BB15]   Bogdanov, A., Brzuska, C.: On basing size-verifiable one-way functions on NP-hardness. In: Dodis, Y., Nielsen, J.B. (eds.) TCC 2015. LNCS, vol. 9014, pp. 1–6. Springer, Heidelberg (2015). https://doi.org/10.1007/978-3-662-46494-6_1

[BFP03]   Buhrman, H., Fortnow, L., Pavan, A.: Some results on derandomization. In: Alt, H., Habib, M. (eds.) STACS 2003. LNCS, vol. 2607, pp. 212–222. Springer, Heidelberg (2003). https://doi.org/10.1007/3-540-36494-3_20

[Blu82]   Blum, M.: Coin flipping by telephone - a protocol for solving impossible problems. In: 24th IEEE Computer Society International Conference, COMPCON 1982, Digest of Papers, San Francisco, California, USA, 22–25 February 1982, pp. 133–137. IEEE Computer Society (1982)

[BM88]   Babai, L., Moran, S.: Arthur-Merlin games: a randomized proof system, and a hierarchy of complexity classes. J. Comput. Syst. Sci. **36**(2), 254–276 (1988)

[Bra83]   Brassard, G.: Relativized cryptography. IEEE Trans. Inf. Theor. **29**(6), 877–893 (1983)

[BT03]   Bogdanov, A., Trevisan, L.: On worst-case to average-case reductions for NP problems. In: FOCS 2003, pp. 308–317 (2003)

[BT08]   Bogdanov, A., Trevisan, L.: Average-case complexity (2008). Manuscript. http://arxiv.org/abs/cs.CC/0606037

[Cha69]   Chaitin, G.J.: On the simplicity and speed of programs for computing infinite sets of natural numbers. J. ACM **16**(3), 407–422 (1969)

[DH76]   Diffie, W., Hellman, M.: New directions in cryptography. IEEE Trans. Inf. Theor. **22**(6), 644–654 (1976)

[FS90]   Feige, U., Shamir, A.: Witness indistinguishable and witness hiding protocols. In: STOC 1990, pp. 416–426 (1990)

[GGM84]   Goldreich, O., Goldwasser, S., Micali, S.: On the cryptographic applications of random functions (extended abstract). In: Blakley, G.R., Chaum, D. (eds.) CRYPTO 1984. LNCS, vol. 196, pp. 276–288. Springer, Heidelberg (1985). https://doi.org/10.1007/3-540-39568-7_22

[GKL93]   Goldreich, O., Krawczyk, H., Luby, M.: On the existence of pseudorandom generators. SIAM J. Comput. **22**(6), 1163–1175 (1993)

[GM84]   Goldwasser, S., Micali, S.: Probabilistic encryption. J. Comput. Syst. Sci. **28**(2), 270–299 (1984)

[Gol01]   Goldreich, O.: Foundations of Cryptography – Basic Tools. Cambridge University Press (2001)

[Gur89]   Gurevich, Yuri: The challenger-solver game: variations on the theme of P = ?NP. In: Logic in Computer Science Column. The Bulletin of EATCS (1989)

[GWXY10] Gordon, S.D., Wee, H., Xiao, D., Yerukhimovich, A.: On the round complexity of zero-knowledge proofs based on one-way permutations. In: Abdalla, M., Barreto, P.S.L.M. (eds.) LATINCRYPT 2010. LNCS, vol. 6212, pp. 189–204. Springer, Heidelberg (2010). https://doi.org/10.1007/978-3-642-14712-8_12

[Har83] Hartmanis, J.: Generalized Kolmogorov complexity and the structure of feasible computations. In: 24th Annual Symposium on Foundations of Computer Science, SFCS 1983, November 1983, pp. 439–445 (1993)

[HILL99] Håstad, J., Impagliazzo, R., Levin, L.A., Luby, M.: A pseudorandom generator from any one-way function. SIAM J. Comput. **28**(4), 1364–1396 (1999)

[HMX10] Haitner, I., Mahmoody, M., Xiao, D.: A new sampling protocol and applications to basing cryptographic primitives on the hardness of NP. In: IEEE Conference on Computational Complexity, pp. 76–87 (2010)

[HS65] Hartmanis, J., Stearns, R.E.: On the computational complexity of algorithms. Trans. Am. Math. Soc. **117**, 285–306 (1965)

[IL89] Impagliazzo, R., Luby, M.: One-way functions are essential for complexity based cryptography (extended abstract). In: 30th Annual Symposium on Foundations of Computer Science, Research Triangle Park, North Carolina, USA, 30 October–1 November 1989, pp. 230–235 (1989)

[Imp95] Impagliazzo, R.: A personal view of average-case complexity. In: Structure in Complexity Theory 1995, pp. 134–147 (1995)

[IW98] Impagliazzo, R., Wigderson, A.: Randomness vs. time: de-randomization under a uniform assumption. In: Proceedings 39th Annual Symposium on Foundations of Computer Science (Cat. No. 98CB36280), pp. 734–743. IEEE (1998)

[Ko86] Ko, K.-I.: On the notion of infinite pseudorandom sequences. Theor. Comput. Sci. **48**(3), 9–33 (1986)

[Kol68] Kolmogorov, A.N.: Three approaches to the quantitative definition of information. Int. J. Comput. Math. **2**(1–4), 157–168 (1968)

[Lau83] Lautemann, C.: BPP and the polynomial hierarchy. Inf. Process. Lett. **17**(4), 215–217 (1983)

[Lev73] Levin, L.A.: Universal search problems (Russian). Probl. Inf. Transm. **9**(3), 265–266 (1973). Translated into English by B.A. Trakhtenbrot in [Tra84]

[Lev03] Levin, L.A.: The tale of one-way functions. Probl. Inf. Transm. **39**(1), 92–103 (2003)

[Liv10] Livne, N.: On the construction of one-way functions from average case hardness. In: ICS, pp. 301–309. Citeseer (2010)

[LM91] Longpré, L., Mocas, S.: Symmetry of information and one-way functions. In: Hsu, W.-L., Lee, R.C.T. (eds.) ISA 1991. LNCS, vol. 557, pp. 308–315. Springer, Heidelberg (1991). https://doi.org/10.1007/3-540-54945-5_75

[LP20] Liu, Y., Pass, R.: On one-way functions and kolmogorov complexity. In: 61st IEEE Annual Symposium on Foundations of Computer Science, FOCS 2020, Durham, NC, USA, 16–19 November 2020, pp. 1243–1254. IEEE (2020)

[LP21a] Liu, Y., Pass, R.: On one-way functions from NP-complete problems. Electron. Colloquium Comput. Complex. **28**, 59 (2021)

[LP21b] Liu, Y., Pass, R.: On the possibility of basing cryptography on $ \exp \neq \bpp$. Electron. Colloquium Comput. Complex. **28**, 56 (2021). Kindly check and confrim that Ref. [LP21b] is correct. Amend if necessary

[Nao91] Naor, M.: Bit commitment using pseudorandomness. J. Cryptol. **4**(2), 151–158 (1991)

[NW94] Nisan, N., Wigderson, A.: Hardness vs randomness. J. Comput. Syst. Sci. **49**(2), 149–167 (1994)

[OW93] Ostrovsky, R., Wigderson, A.: One-way fuctions are essential for non-trivial zero-knowledge. In: ISTCS, pp. 3–17 (1993)

[PV20]   Pass, R., Venkitasubramaniam, M.: Is it easier to prove theorems that are guaranteed to be true? In: 2020 IEEE 61st Annual Symposium on Foundations of Computer Science (FOCS), pp. 1255–1267. IEEE (2020)

[Rom90] Rompel, J.: One-way functions are necessary and sufficient for secure signatures. In: STOC, pp. 387–394 (1990)

[RS21]   Ren, H., Santhanam, R.: Hardness of KT characterizes parallel cryptography. Electron. Colloquium Comput. Complex. 28, 57 (2021)

[RSA83] Rivest, R.L., Shamir, A., Adleman, L.M.: A method for obtaining digital signatures and public-key cryptosystems (reprint). Commun. ACM 26(1), 96–99 (1983)

[Sip83] Sipser, M.: A complexity theoretic approach to randomness. In: Proceedings of the 15th Annual ACM Symposium on Theory of Computing, Boston, Massachusetts, USA, 25–27 April 1983, pp. 330–335. ACM (1983)

[Sip96] Sipser, M.: Introduction to the theory of computation. ACM SIGACT News 27(1), 27–29 (1996)

[Sol64] Solomonoff, R.J.: A formal theory of inductive inference. Part i. Inf. Control 7(1), 1–22 (1964)

[Tra84] Trakhtenbrot, B.A.: A survey of Russian approaches to perebor (brute-force searches) algorithms. Ann. Hist. Comput. 6(4), 384–400 (1984)

[TV02]   Trevisan, L., Vadhan, S.: Pseudorandomness and average-case complexity via uniform reductions. In: Proceedings 17th IEEE Annual Conference on Computational Complexity, p. 0129. IEEE Computer Society (2002)

[Yao82] Yao, A.C.-C.: Theory and applications of trapdoor functions (extended abstract). In: 23rd Annual Symposium on Foundations of Computer Science, Chicago, Illinois, USA, 3–5 November 1982, pp. 80–91 (1982)

[ZL70]   Zvonkin, A.K., Levin, L.A.: The complexity of finite objects and the development of the concepts of information and randomness by means of the theory of algorithms. Russ. Math. Surv. 25(6), 83–124 (1970)

Linear Cryptanalysis of FF3-1 and FEA

Tim Beyne[(⊠)]

imec-COSIC, KU Leuven, Leuven, Belgium
`tim.beyne@esat.kuleuven.be`

Abstract. Improved attacks on generic small-domain Feistel ciphers with alternating round tweaks are obtained using linear cryptanalysis. This results in practical distinguishing and message-recovery attacks on the United States format-preserving encryption standard FF3-1 and the South-Korean standards FEA-1 and FEA-2. The data complexity of the proposed attacks on FF3-1 and FEA-1 is $\widetilde{\mathcal{O}}(N^{r/2-1.5})$, where N^2 is the domain size and r is the number of rounds. For example, FF3-1 with $N = 10^3$ can be distinguished from an ideal tweakable block cipher with advantage $\geq 1/10$ using 2^{23} encryption queries. Recovering the left half of a message with similar advantage requires 2^{24} data. The analysis of FF3-1 serves as an interesting real-world application of (generalized) linear cryptanalysis over the group $\mathbb{Z}/N\mathbb{Z}$.

Keywords: Linear cryptanalysis · FF3-1 · FEA-1 · FEA-2 · Format-preserving encryption

1 Introduction

Format-preserving encryption enables the encryption of plaintext with a specific format, while ensuring that the ciphertext has the same format. For example, in some applications it is convenient to be able to encrypt nine-digit integers (such as social security numbers) to nine-digit integers.

Several generic techniques such as cycle walking [5,7] can be used to transform (tweakable) block ciphers into format-preserving ciphers. However, these techniques are inefficient when there is a significant size difference between the domain of the underlying block cipher and the target domain. Consequently, a number of dedicated constructions based on small-domain tweakable Feistel ciphers were introduced. The best known examples are the United States standards FF1 and FF3-1 [12] (NIST SP800-38G rev. 1). The South-Korean standards FEA-1 and FEA-2 [16] (TTAK.KO-12.0275) follow a similar design but with lighter round functions.

Small-domain Feistel ciphers are known to be vulnerable to a number of generic attacks. In a series of papers, Patarin [18–20] analyzed the security of r-round Feistel ciphers with uniform random round functions. In particular, Patarin [20, Sect. 8] describes a distinguisher with data and time complexity $\widetilde{\mathcal{O}}(N^{r-4})$ for Feistel ciphers with domain size N^2. At CCS 2016, Bellare, Hoang

ⓒ International Association for Cryptologic Research 2021
T. Malkin and C. Peikert (Eds.): CRYPTO 2021, LNCS 12825, pp. 41–69, 2021.
https://doi.org/10.1007/978-3-030-84242-0_3

and Tessaro [4] presented a message-recovery attack with a data complexity of $\widetilde{\mathcal{O}}(N^{r-2})$ or $\widetilde{\mathcal{O}}(N^{r-3})$ (to recover the left half of the message) queries. Subsequent improvements were obtained by Hoang, Tessaro and Trieu [15].

The applicability of these attacks to FF3 in part motivated the US National Institute of Standards and Technology (NIST) to revise the FF3 standard [12]. In particular, the revised standard FF3-1 includes the requirement that the domain size must be at least one million, *i.e.* $N \geq 10^3$. Furthermore, the revision decreased the size of the tweak from 64 to 56 bits. This change was introduced to prevent a powerful slide-type attack presented by Durak and Vaudenay [11] at CRYPTO 2017 that was subsequently improved by Hoang *et al.* [14] and Amon *et al.* [1]. These attacks were the consequence of a weakness in the tweak-schedule of FF3 that is resolved by the changes in FF3-1.

Recently, Dunkelman *et al.* [10] have proposed new distinguishers for FEA, FF1 and FF3-1. The data complexity of these attacks is $\widetilde{\mathcal{O}}(N^{r-4})$, which is comparable to the attack of Patarin [20]. The time complexity is $\widetilde{\mathcal{O}}(N^{r-3})$.

Contribution. This paper develops new distinguishing and message-recovery attacks on small-domain Feistel ciphers with alternating round tweaks. The attacks are based on linear cryptanalysis, but go beyond standard methods in several ways. In particular, the role of the tweak input is analyzed, properties of small uniform random functions are exploited, and for FF3-1 a generalization of linear cryptanalysis to the group $\mathbb{Z}/N\mathbb{Z}$ is used. Furthermore, the principle behind the message-recovery attacks is novel.

If the round tweaks alternate between two values, as in FEA-1 and FF3-1, the data and time complexity of these attacks is $\widetilde{\mathcal{O}}(N^{r/2-1.5})$. For FEA-2, which has a different tweak schedule, distinguishing and message-recovery respectively require $\widetilde{\mathcal{O}}(N^{r/3-1.5})$ and $\widetilde{\mathcal{O}}(N^{r/3-0.5})$ data and time. The new attacks are not applicable to FF1. For many instances of FF3-1, FEA-1 and FEA-2, the data and time complexity are well within the reach of real-world adversaries.

The proposed distinguishers only need weak access to the block cipher: it is sufficient to have ciphertext-only access to encryptions of an arbitrary constant message under many half-constant tweaks. In fact, access to the complete ciphertext is not necessary. The message-recovery attacks follow the security model introduced by Bellare *et al.* [4]. Specifically, given the encryption (with FF3-1 or FEA-1) of a secret message and a known message with the same right-hand side under $\widetilde{\mathcal{O}}(N^{r/2-1.5})$ tweaks, the attack recovers the left half of the secret message. With $\widetilde{\mathcal{O}}(N^{r/2-0.5})$ queries, full messages can also be recovered. For FEA-1, the message-recovery attack can be used to set up a key-recovery attack. If q is the concrete data cost of the left-half message-recovery attack, then the key-recovery attack requires less than $16\lceil 8/\log_2 N \rceil q + 8q$ data and time equivalent to at most $2^{69}/N + 16\lceil 8/\log_2 N \rceil q + 8q$ evaluations of FEA-1.

Table 1 summarizes the cost of the main attacks from the literature and some of the new attacks proposed in this paper. In addition, the bottom part of the table reports concrete costs for the smallest instances of FEA-1, FEA-2 ($N = 16$) and FF3-1 ($N = 10^3$). Detailed cost-estimates for previous attacks on the same instances are not always available, but the improvement is substantial. For example, the attacks on FF3-1 with $N = 10^3$ require data and time comparable to previous attacks for $N = 2^5$ [4,15] that led to the requirement $N \geq 10^3$. The numbers in Table 1 have been experimentally verified by performing each attack many times. Source code to reproduce this is provided as supplementary material[1]. Further experiments and cost calculations are given in the indicated sections.

As with previous attacks on tweakable small-domain Feistel ciphers, the maximum value of N for which the attacks are applicable is typically determined by the tweak length rather than by the length of the key. For FEA-1 and FEA-2 the main interest of these attacks is for small N, so the tweak is long enough for most practical purposes. For FF3-1, the upper bounds are similar to those for previous attacks: naive estimates are $N < 2^{19}$ for distinguishing and right-half message-recovery and $N < 2^{12}$ for left-half recovery. The latter bound is quite close to the required $N \geq 10^3$ for FF3-1, However, as discussed in Sect. 5, it is not a hard limit.

Early Notification. Prior to the submission of this paper, both NIST (for FF3-1) and ETRI (for FEA-1 and FEA-2) were notified about these results. Both parties have acknowledged the attacks and have indicated their intention to revise their standards. Modifying the tweak schedule seems to be the most promising approach to thwart the attacks.

Organization. After revisiting the overall structure of FEA-1, FEA-2 and FF3-1 in Sect. 2, the basic idea behind the attacks is introduced in Sect. 3. It is shown that there exists a linear trail through FEA-1 (and similarly for FEA-2) with high correlation. The novelty of this trail is the fact that it requires considering the tweak as a proper part of the input of the cipher, and its reliance on the properties of small random functions. An analogous $\mathbb{Z}/N\mathbb{Z}$-linear trail is then obtained for FF3-1. This result is an application of a generalization of linear cryptanalysis to other finite Abelian groups [3,6].

Section 4 combines the linear approximations identified in Sect. 3 to obtain multidimensional linear approximations. These approximations are subsequently used to construct a χ^2-distinguisher. The formalism of (generalized) multidimensional linear cryptanalysis is applied to justify the attack and to obtain initial estimates of the data complexity. Finally, Sect. 5 shows how the χ^2-distinguisher can be turned into a message-recovery attack. Each attack comes with a detailed analysis of the advantage and data complexity, and an experimental verification of the theoretical analysis.

2 Preliminaries

The attacks in this paper are applicable to tweakable small-domain Feistel ciphers with alternating round tweaks. The South-Korean format-preserving encryption standards FEA-1 and FEA-2 [16] and the NIST standard FF3-1 [12] all follow such a design.

---

[1] https://homes.esat.kuleuven.be/~tbeyne/fpe.

Table 1. Summary of attacks on FEA-1, FEA-2 and FF3-1. The costs in the top half of the table are up to polylogarithmic factors in N (all of which are small in practice). Time is expressed in encryption operations. Memory requirements are small for all attacks. All of the message-recovery attacks listed in this table recover the left half of a message.

		Data	Time	Advantage	Reference
		N^{r-4}	N^{r-3}	Constant	[10]
		N^{r-4}	N^{r-4}	Constant	[20]
	Distinguisher	$N^{r/2-1}$	$N^{r/2-1}$	Constant	Sect. 3[a]
		$N^{r/2-1.5}$	$N^{r/2-1.5}$	Constant	Sect. 4[a]
Generic		$N^{r/3-1}$	$N^{r/3-1}$	Constant	Sect. 3[b]
		$N^{r/3-1.5}$	$N^{r/3-1.5}$	Constant	Sect. 4[b]
		N^{r-3}	N^{r-3}	Constant	[4,15]
	Message recovery	$N^{r/2-1.5}$	$N^{r/2-1.5}$	Constant	Sect. 5[a]
		$N^{r/3-0.5}$	$N^{r/3-0.5}$	Constant	Sect. 5[b]
FEA-1		2^{22}	2^{22}	0.1	Sect. 3
$N = 16, r = 12$	Distinguisher	2^{17}	2^{17}	0.1	Sect. 4
		2^{22}	2^{22}	0.6	Sect. 4
	Message recovery	2^{17}	2^{17}	0.1	Sect. 5
		2^{24}	2^{24}	0.6	Sect. 5
FEA-2		2^{20}	2^{20}	0.1	Sect. 3
$N = 16, r = 18$	Distinguisher	2^{17}	2^{17}	0.1	Sect. 4
		2^{21}	2^{21}	0.6	Sect. 4
FF3-1		2^{29}	2^{29}	0.1	Sect. 3
$N = 10^3, r = 8$	Distinguisher	2^{23}	2^{23}	0.1	Sect. 4
		2^{26}	2^{26}	0.6	Sect. 4
	Message recovery	2^{24}	2^{24}	0.1	Sect. 5
		2^{27}	2^{27}	0.6	Sect. 5

[a] Assuming the round tweaks alternate between two values, as in FEA-1 and FF3-1.
[b] Assuming the round tweaks alternate between three values, as in FEA-2.

Figure 1 depicts two rounds of the overall structure of FEA-1 and FF3-1. For simplicity, it will be assumed that both branches have the same size. In both designs, the tweak is divided into two equal halves, which will be denoted by T_L and T_R for convenience. A crucial property that will be exploited by the new attacks is that the round tweak alternates between T_L and T_R. The round functions $F_1, F_2, \ldots$ can nevertheless be arbitrary.

As shown in Fig. 1a, FEA-1 is a regular Feistel cipher over $\mathbb{F}_2^m \oplus \mathbb{F}_2^m$ with $m = \log_2 N$, where $\oplus$ denotes the direct sum. For 128 bit keys, it has a total of 12 rounds. The tweaks T_L and T_R consist of $64 - m$ bits. The round functions F_i are truncations of a two-round SHARK-like construction [21], but can be considered to be uniform random functions for all attacks discussed in this paper except for the key-recovery attack in Sect. 6. The necessary details of the round function will be reproduced in Sect. 6.

The design of FEA-2 is very similar to that of FEA-1. The main difference is that it uses three distinct round tweaks (repeating with period three), one of which is constant. In addition, for FEA-2, both tweaks have a length of 64 bits and the number of rounds is 18 for 128 bit keys.

FF3-1 is an eight-round Feistel cipher over $\mathbb{Z}/N\mathbb{Z} \oplus \mathbb{Z}/N\mathbb{Z}$. The round functions $F_1, F_2, \ldots$ are defined as truncations of the AES with the round tweak and a unique round counter as the input; the details are not important for this work as these functions will be modelled as uniform random. The tweaks T_L and T_R are bitstrings of length 28.

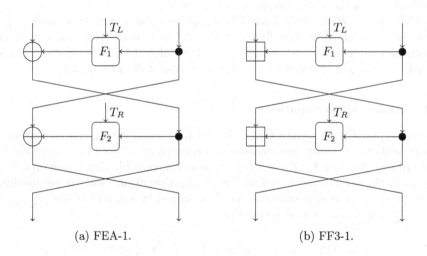

(a) FEA-1.   (b) FF3-1.

Fig. 1. Two rounds of a tweakable Feistel cipher with alternating round tweaks.

Sections 3 and 4 introduce distinguishers for full-round FEA-1, FEA-2 and FF3-1. The *advantage* of a distinguisher is equal to the difference between its success-probability P_S and false-positive rate P_F and provides a convenient measure for its statistical quality. The distinguishers discussed in Sects. 3 and 4 allow for a trade-off between success-probability and false-positive rate. Since they are ultimately simple hypothesis tests, the trade-off is determined by the choice of some threshold parameter t. The advantage that will be considered in this paper is thus the maximum achievable advantage for some value of t:

$$\mathsf{Adv} = \max_t \; |P_{\mathsf{S}}(t) - P_{\mathsf{F}}(t)|.$$

For message-recovery attacks, it is also meaningful to define a similar measure of quality. Given a list of possible messages, one is interested in narrowing it down to some fraction P_{F} with a given probability P_{S}. Clearly, P_{F} and P_{S} are dependent quantities. The advantage of a message-recovery attack will be defined as the maximum achievable value of $|P_{\mathsf{S}} - P_{\mathsf{F}}|$ for a given amount of data. This corresponds to the notion of key-recovery advantage that is often used in linear and differential cryptanalysis [22]. For the attacks in this paper, it also coincides with the message-recovery advantage defined by Bellare $et\ al.$ [4].

Concepts related to linear and multidimensional linear cryptanalysis will be introduced in Sects. 3 and 4 respectively.

3   Linear Distinguishers

In this section, linear distinguishers for FEA-1, FEA-2 and FF3-1 are introduced. Section 3.1 summarizes the main concepts from linear cryptanalysis, but some familiarity with these ideas is necessarily assumed.

Since the attacks on FEA-1 and FEA-2 are based on ordinary $\mathbb{F}_2$-linear cryptanalysis, these are described first in Sect. 3.2. Section 3.3 then transfers these results to Feistel ciphers defined over $\mathbb{Z}/N\mathbb{Z}$. Finally, the data complexity of the attacks is analyzed in detail and verified experimentally in Sect. 3.4.

3.1   Linear Approximations

Linear cryptanalysis was introduced by Matsui [17] and is based on probabilistic linear relations or *linear approximations*, a concept introduced by Tardy-Corfdir and Gilbert [23]. Let $F : \mathbb{F}_2^n \to \mathbb{F}_2^m$ be a function, possibly depending on a key. Linear distinguishers are based on linear approximations with large absolute correlation. A linear approximation for F is defined by a pair of masks $(u_1, u_2) \in \mathbb{F}_2^m \oplus \mathbb{F}_2^n$ and its *correlation* is equal to

$$C_{u_1,u_2}^F = 2\Pr\left[u_1^\top F(\boldsymbol{x}) = u_2^\top \boldsymbol{x}\right] - 1 = \frac{1}{2^n} \sum_{\boldsymbol{x} \in \mathbb{F}_2^n} (-1)^{u_1^\top F(\boldsymbol{x}) + u_2^\top \boldsymbol{x}},$$

where the probability is over a uniform random $\boldsymbol{x}$ on $\mathbb{F}_2^n$. If $u_1 \neq 0$, then the correlation for a uniform random function is concentrated around zero with a standard deviation of $2^{-n/2}$. A more detailed result is given in Theorem 3.1 in Sect. 3.2 below. Hence, if the correlation c is significantly larger than $2^{-n/2}$, a distinguisher is obtained by estimating the correlation using $q = \Theta(1/c^2)$ queries and comparing the result to some threshold t. As discussed in Sect. 3.2 below, this description is somewhat simplified since the correlation is usually key-dependent.

For FF3-1, $\mathbb{F}_2$-linear approximations are inconvenient because the FF3-1 Feistel structure operates on the ring $\mathbb{Z}/N\mathbb{Z} \oplus \mathbb{Z}/N\mathbb{Z}$. Instead, Sect. 3.3 will rely on a generalization of linear cryptanalysis to arbitrary finite Abelian groups. Such a generalization was first proposed by Baignères, Stern and Vaudenay [3]. A more general perspective that includes the multidimensional case (which will be used in Sect. 4) was introduced in [6].

Let $F : G \to H$ be a function between finite Abelian groups G and H. A linear approximation corresponds to a pair of *group characters* (ψ_1, ψ_2) of H and G respectively. A group character ψ_1 is a group homomorphism $\psi_1 : H \to \mathbb{C}^\times$. The characters of H themselves also form a group of order $|H|$ under pointwise multiplication. The correlation of the linear approximation (ψ_1, ψ_2) is equal to

$$C^F_{\psi_1,\psi_2} = \frac{1}{|G|} \sum_{x \in G} \overline{\psi_1(F(x))}\psi_2(x) \, .$$

In the above, $\overline{\psi_1}$ denotes the complex-conjugate of ψ_1. For $H = \mathbb{F}_2^m$, every character ψ_1 corresponds to a vector $u \in \mathbb{F}_2^m$ such that $\psi_1(x) = (-1)^{u^\top x}$. If $H = \mathbb{Z}/N\mathbb{Z}$, then for each character ψ_1, there exists a non-negative integer $k < N$ such that $\psi_1(x) = \exp(2\pi\sqrt{-1}\,kx/N)$. This essentially covers all cases, since any finite Abelian group is a direct sum of cyclic groups. An important property of group characters is that they are orthogonal functions. That is,

$$\sum_{x \in G} \overline{\chi(x)}\psi(x) = \begin{cases} |G| & \text{if } \chi = \psi, \\ 0 & \text{otherwise.} \end{cases}$$

for any two characters χ and ψ of G. Additional background on group characters and Fourier analysis may be found in [24].

For a sequence of functions $F_1, \ldots, F_l$, the *piling-up principle* can be used to estimate the correlation of linear approximations over the composition $F = F_l \circ \cdots \circ F_1$. The idea is that, for an approximation with characters (ψ_1, ψ_{l+1}), there may exist a dominant sequence of approximations $(\psi_1, \psi_2), \ldots, (\psi_l, \psi_{l+1})$ such that

$$C^F_{\psi_1,\psi_{l+1}} \approx \prod_{i=1}^{l} C^{F_i}_{\psi_i,\psi_{i+1}} \, .$$

The sequence of approximations $(\psi_1, \psi_2), \ldots, (\psi_l, \psi_{l+1})$ is called a *trail* and the right-hand side of the above equation is called the correlation of the trail. The sum of the correlations of all trails over $F_l \circ \cdots \circ F_1$ equals the correlation of the approximation (ψ_1, ψ_{l+1}) of F [8].

3.2   FEA-1 and FEA-2

At first sight, both FEA-1 and FEA-2 seem to be robust against linear cryptanalysis, especially when their round functions $F_1, F_2, \ldots$ are replaced by uniform

random functions. The key observation behind the attacks in this paper is that
this is not the case when (part of) the tweak is considered as a proper part of
the input.

Figure 2 shows linear trails over two rounds of FEA-1 and three rounds of
FEA-2[2]. In these trails, the tweak T_L is an arbitrary constant and T_R is considered to be a variable part of the input. Note that the tweak T_R is not active, so
it need not be known to perform the attack. The idea behind these trails is that
the absolute correlation of a linear approximation over round function F_i (chosen uniformly at random) exceeds $1/\sqrt{N} = 2^{-m/2}$ with fairly large probability.
This becomes meaningful when the tweak is included in the input, because the
domain of the function which maps the tweak and the plaintext to the ciphertext
is large. Indeed, the correlation of linear approximations over a random function
with the same input size (including T_R of length $64 - m$) as FEA-1 is centered
around zero with a standard deviation of $2^{-32-m/2}$. More specifically, we have
the following result.

Theorem 3.1 (Daemen and Rijmen [9]). *Let c denote the correlation of
a nontrivial linear approximation for a uniform random function $\mathbb{F}_2^n \to \mathbb{F}_2^m$.
The random variable $2^{n-1}(c + 1)$ is binomially distributed with mean 2^{n-1} and
variance 2^{n-2}. In particular[3], as $n \to \infty$, the distribution of $2^{n/2}c$ converges to
the standard normal distribution $\mathcal{N}(0, 1)$.*

Let $r \geq 2$ be an even integer. By the piling-up principle, the correlation of the
r-round trail from Fig. 2a is equal to $c = \prod_{i=1}^{r/2} c_i$, where $c_i \sim \mathcal{N}(0, 1/N)$ holds
asymptotically due to Theorem 3.1. The random variables c_i will be assumed to
be independent, which follows for instance from the strong assumption that the
round functions $F_1, F_3 \ldots F_{r-1}$ are independent. One can verify that the other
trails through FEA-1 and FF3-1 have negligible correlation.

As mentioned above, the data complexity of a constant-advantage linear
distinguisher based on an approximation with correlation c is $\Theta(1/c^2)$. In this
case, the correlation varies strongly with the key so this result can not be applied
directly to estimate the data complexity. A commonly used heuristic estimate is
given by $1/\mathbb{E}c^2$, where $\mathbb{E}c^2$ is the average squared trail correlation for a uniform
random key. For FEA-1, this yields $1/\mathbb{E}c^2 = N^{r/2}$. The data complexity is
analyzed in considerably more detail in Sect. 3.4.

For FEA-2 with r divisible by three, the expected squared correlation of each
trail is equal to $N^{-2r/3}$. However, the number of trails for a given choice of input
and output masks is $(N-1)^{r/3-1}$. Recall that the correlation of a linear approximation is equal to the sum of the correlations over all possible trails. Hence,
since the trails in Fig. 2b are indeed dominant, the sum c of the correlations of
these trails is a good estimate for the correlation of the corresponding approximation. Since the covariance between the correlations of distinct trails is zero
for independent uniform random round functions, it follows that

$$1/\mathbb{E}c^2 = N^{2r/3}/(N-1)^{r/3-1} \sim N^{r/3+1}.$$

---

[2] I thank Dongyoung Roh for bringing the trails with $u \neq v$ to my attention.

[3] This result is a useful approximation even when n is small (for example, when $n \geq 8$).

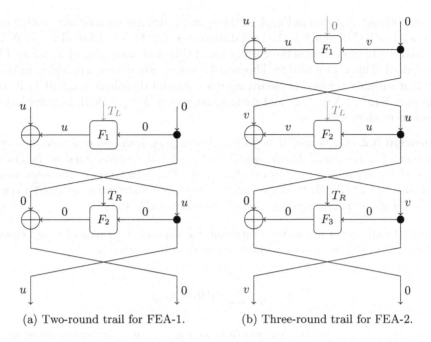

(a) Two-round trail for FEA-1.   (b) Three-round trail for FEA-2.

Fig. 2. Linear trails for FEA-1 and FEA-2. The tweak T_R is considered part of the input and the value of T_L should be fixed.

The fact that the covariance terms are zero is somewhat nontrivial, but it can be easily deduced from the definition of correlation for a uniform random function. Neglecting the covariance between the correlation of different trails is, in general, inaccurate. Finally, note that any other trail through FEA-2 necessarily has a much smaller average squared correlation.

Before continuing with the analysis of FF3-1, a simple but significant improvement to the correlation of the aforementioned linear approximation should be pointed out. If the right part of the plaintext is fixed to an arbitrary constant, then after two rounds the left branch of the state is equal to the left part of the plaintext up to addition by some constant. Consequently, the first two rounds can be effectively skipped. This decreases the data complexity by a factor N to $N^{r/2-1}$ for FEA-1. By fixing both halves of the plaintext, the first three rounds of FEA-2 can similarly be avoided. In addition, since the input mask is then no longer fixed, the number of trails within one approximation increases to $(N-1)^{r/3}$. Hence, the resulting data complexity estimate becomes $N^{r/3-1}$. A more detailed estimate of the data complexity will be given in Sect. 3.4.

3.3 FF3-1

The analysis of FF3-1 proceeds analogously to that of FEA-1, but with linear cryptanalysis over the additive group $\mathbb{Z}/N\mathbb{Z}$ rather than $\mathbb{F}_2^m$. An iterative two-round trail is shown in Fig. 3. In the figure, ψ denotes an arbitrary nontrivial character of $\mathbb{Z}/N\mathbb{Z}$ and $\mathbb{1}$ is the trivial character, *i.e.* $\mathbb{1}(x) = 1$ for all $x \in \mathbb{Z}/N\mathbb{Z}$.

In order to characterize the correlation of this trail, an analog of Theorem 3.1 is required. This is provided by Theorem 3.2 below. Recall that a complex-valued random variable z has a standard complex normal distribution $\mathcal{CN}(0,1)$ if its real part $\Re\{z\} \sim \mathcal{N}(0, 1/2)$ and its imaginary part $\Im\{z\} \sim \mathcal{N}(0, 1/2)$ are independent random variables.

Theorem 3.2. *Let G and H be finite Abelian groups and let c denote the correlation of a nontrivial linear approximation for a uniform random function $G \to H$ corresponding to non-real characters. The correlation c has mean zero and variance $1/|G|$. Furthermore, as $|G| \to \infty$, the distribution of $\sqrt{|G|}\,c$ converges to the standard complex normal distribution $\mathcal{CN}(0,1)$.*

Proof. Recall that a linear approximation corresponds to a pair of group characters $(\overline{\psi_1}, \psi_2)$. The random variable c can then be written as

$$c = \frac{1}{|G|} \sum_{i=1}^{|G|} \psi_1(\boldsymbol{y}_i)\psi_2(x_i),$$

where $x_1, \ldots, x_{|G|}$ are the elements of G and $\boldsymbol{y}_1, \ldots, \boldsymbol{y}_{|G|}$ are independent uniform random variables on H. The mean of c is zero, since $\mathbb{E}\psi_1(\boldsymbol{y}_i) = 0$ by the orthogonality relations for group characters. In addition, it follows from $\mathbb{E}|\psi_1(\boldsymbol{y}_i)|^2 = 1$ that $\mathbb{E}|c|^2 = 1/|G|$. Finally, the convergence to a normal distribution follows from the central limit theorem for the sum of independent identically distributed random variables. $\qquad\square$

By Theorem 3.2, the average squared correlation of the r-round trail from Fig. 3 is equal to $N^{-r/2}$. As in the case of FEA-1, the right part of the plaintext can be fixed in order to obtain a trail with average squared correlation $N^{1-r/2}$. This gives a corresponding data complexity estimate of $N^{r/2-1}$.

3.4   Cost Analysis and Experimental Verification

As mentioned in Sects. 3.2 and 3.3 above, the data complexity of a distinguisher based on a linear approximation with correlation c is roughly $1/|c|^2$. By *heuristically* plugging in the average squared trail correlation, the approximation $1/\mathbb{E}|c|^2$ was obtained. This resulted in an estimated data complexity of $N^{r/2-1}$ for FEA-1 and FF3-1 and $N^{r/3-1}$ for FEA-2. This section analyzes the data complexity in more detail, along with the advantage achieved by the distinguisher. Broadly speaking, the detailed analysis confirms the heuristic estimates from Sects. 3.2 and 3.3.

The distinguisher performs a hypothesis test, with null-hypothesis that the data comes from an ideal tweakable block cipher and alternative hypothesis that the data comes from the real cipher. If the absolute value of the estimated correlation exceeds a predetermined threshold, then the null-hypothesis is rejected.

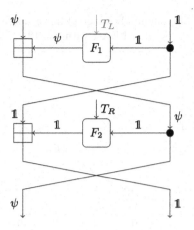

Fig. 3. Iterative two-round trail for FF3-1. The tweak T_L is fixed.

Like any hypothesis test, linear distinguishers allow for a trade-off between success probability P_S and false-positive rate P_F. Both probabilities are determined by the threshold parameter t. The distinguisher is successful if the estimated correlation exceeds $t\sqrt{q}$ when interacting with the true block cipher after q queries. If the estimated correlation exceeds this threshold for an ideal tweakable block cipher, then a false-positive occurs. Note that $P_S(t)$ and $P_F(t)$ are key-averaged quantities.

Figure 4 depicts the estimates of the maximum advantage $\max_t |P_S(t) - P_F(t)|$ which are derived below. Importantly, for large N, the curve is essentially independent of N. This will be shown below. The red dots correspond to experimental verifications of the estimates for full-round instances of FEA-1, FEA-2 and FF3-1. Each point corresponds to 1024 (FEA-1 and FF3-1) or 512 (FEA-2) evaluations of the distinguisher. For FF3-1, the experiments were performed for $N = 100 < 1000$ to limit the computational cost. The verification of the more efficient χ^2-distinguishers in Sect. 4 will be performed for $N = 1000$.

The false-positive rate is easily computed. Assume the correlation is estimated using q independent queries. If the input space is sufficiently large[4], then by Theorems 3.1 and 3.2 the variance of the ideal correlation is negligible. Hence, if the number of queries q is moderately large, then the estimated correlation $\widehat{c}_{\text{ideal}}$ is approximately distributed as $\mathcal{N}(0, 1/q)$ for FEA-1 and FEA-2 or $\mathcal{CN}(0, 1/q)$ for FF3-1. The false-positive rate is then

$$P_F(t) = \Pr\left[|\widehat{c}_{\text{ideal}}| \geq t/\sqrt{q}\right] \approx 1 - \chi_\nu(\sqrt{\nu}t),$$

where χ_ν is the cumulative distribution function of the χ-distribution with ν degrees of freedom. For FEA-1 and FEA-2, $\nu = 1$ since c is real. For FF3-1, $\nu = 2$.

---

[4] Relative compared to the required number of queries q.

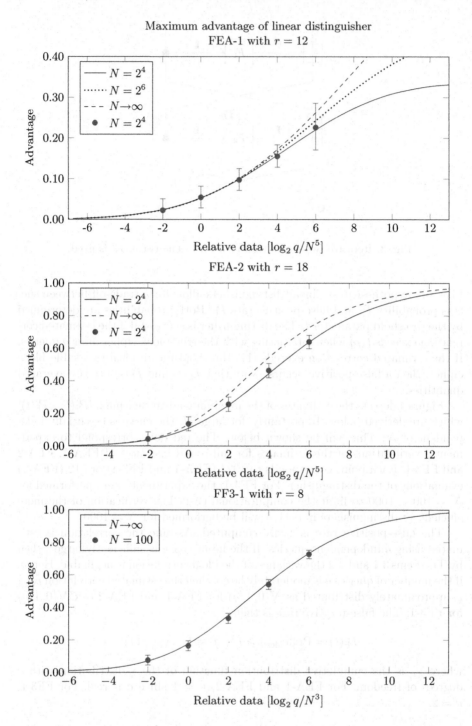

Fig. 4. Theoretical and experimentally observed maximum advantage of the linear distinguishers for full-round FEA-1, FEA-2 and FF3-1. The error bars correspond to 95% Clopper-Pearson confidence intervals. (Color figure online)

The calculation of the success rate P_S is more complicated, because the absolute correlation $|c_{real}|$ is not as strongly concentrated around its mean. Let $\hat{c}_{real}$ denote the estimated correlation for a particular choice of the key. If the underlying correlation for this key is equal to c_{real}, then $\hat{c}_{real}$ is approximately distributed as $\mathcal{N}(c_{real}, 1/q)$ for FEA-1 and FEA-2 or $\mathcal{CN}(c_{real}, 1/q)$ for FF3-1 if q is large enough and $c_{real}^2 \ll 1$. The average success probability can be approximated as

$$P_S(t) \approx \underset{c_{real}}{\mathbb{E}} \Pr\left[|z_\nu - c_{real}\sqrt{q}| \geq t\right]$$

where c_{real} is the trail correlation assuming uniform random round functions and z_ν a standard (complex if $\nu = 2$) normal random variable. To compute the average with respect to c_{real}, a Monte-Carlo approach was used. The implementation is provided as supplementary material. Importantly, the success probability curve (and consequently the maximum advantage) has essentially the same shape for all sufficiently large values of N. Indeed, by Theorems 3.1 and 3.2, the distribution of the round correlations converges to a (complex) normal distribution for large N. Hence, for $q_0 = 1/\mathbb{E}|c_{real}|^2$, the distribution of $c_{real}\sqrt{q_0}$ will be approximately the same for all large values of N. Consequently, the success probability curves tend to a constant function of q/q_0.

4 χ^2 Distinguishers

This section introduces additional distinguishers on FEA-1, FEA-2 and FF3-1, based on Pearson's χ^2-test for goodness-of-fit between distributions. Vaudenay [25] proposed χ^2-distinguishers as a method for distinguishing non-uniform distributions in cryptanalysis when precise knowledge about these distributions is lacking.

The distinguishers in Sect. 3 are based on individual linear approximations. A natural improvement to these attacks is to exploit all approximations simultaneously. Multidimensional linear cryptanalysis provides a convenient framework to describe such attacks.

As shown in Sect. 4.2 below, the existence of a multidimensional linear approximation implies that a particular probability distribution related to the ciphertext is highly non-uniform. Pearson's χ^2-test can then be used to verify this property, resulting in a distinguisher.

Sections 4.1 and 4.2 explain the distinguisher in detail. The data complexity is estimated and experimentally verified in Sect. 4.3.

4.1   Multidimensional Linear Approximations

A multidimensional $\mathbb{F}_2$-linear approximation can be defined as a collection of linear approximations such that the set of pairs of input and output masks is a vector space [13]. This generalizes to arbitrary groups, by requiring that the set of pairs of input and output characters is a group under pointwise multiplication. A general description of this approach can be found in [6].

To obtain a uniform description of the attacks on FEA-1, FEA-2 and FF3-1, denote the half-domain by $\mathcal{D}$ and the space of tweaks T_R by $\mathcal{T}$. The ciphertext space is then $H = \mathcal{D} \oplus \mathcal{D}$. The input space G is either $\mathcal{D} \oplus \mathcal{T}$ or $\mathcal{T}$, depending on whether or not the left half of the plaintext is kept fixed (the right half always is).

Any character ψ of $H \oplus G$ uniquely determines a linear approximation of the cipher. Specifically, the restriction of ψ to H corresponds to the output character of the approximation, and the restriction to G corresponds to the complex conjugate of the input character. The need for complex conjugation is due to technical reasons. Let Z^0 be the set of all such characters ψ corresponding to the linear approximations that were investigated in Sect. 3. The choice of notation for Z^0 will be motivated in Sect. 4.2. Concretely, with $\widehat{\mathcal{D}}$ the group of characters of the domain, let

$$
Z^0 = \begin{cases} \left\{ \psi : (y_L, y_R, x_L, T_R) \mapsto \overline{\chi(x_L)}\chi(y_L) \mid \chi \in \widehat{\mathcal{D}} \right\} & \text{for FEA-1 and FF3-1,} \\ \left\{ \psi : (y_L, y_R, T_R) \mapsto \chi(y_L) \mid \chi \in \widehat{\mathcal{D}} \right\} & \text{for FEA-2.} \end{cases}
$$

Note that for all three ciphers, Z^0 is a group under pointwise multiplication of functions. Hence, the collection of these approximations is a multidimensional linear approximation. Finally, let $c : Z^0 \to \mathbb{C}$ be a function that assigns to a group character $\psi \in Z^0$ the correlation $c(\psi)$ of the corresponding linear approximation.

The data complexity of an optimal distinguisher based on a multidimensional linear approximation is inversely proportional to the capacity of the approximation [2], which is defined as the quantity

$$
\sum_{\psi \neq \mathbb{1}} |c(\psi)|^2,
$$

where the sum is over all nontrivial characters in Z^0. However, as pointed out in Sect. 3, the correlations $c(\psi)$ are heavily key-dependent and this will affect the optimal data complexity. Nevertheless, by linearity of expectation, it is easy to compute the key-averaged capacity:

$$
\mathbb{E} \sum_{\psi \neq \mathbb{1}} |c(\psi)|^2 \approx \begin{cases} N^{2-r/2} & \text{for FEA-1 and FF3-1,} \\ N^{2-r/3} & \text{for FEA-2.} \end{cases}
$$

The above calculation suggests a data complexity of $N^{r/2-2}$ for FEA-1 and FF3-1 and $N^{r/3-2}$ for FEA-2. However, as will be shown below, this is somewhat optimistic because the result that relates the capacity to the data complexity of an optimal distinguisher assumes that the correlations $c(\psi)$ are known exactly.

The multidimensional linear approximation can be turned into a distinguisher by directly estimating the capacity. It will be shown in Sect. 4.3 that the data complexity of this approach can be heuristically estimated as $\sqrt{N}/\sum_{\psi \neq \mathbb{1}} \mathbb{E}|c(\psi)|^2$. However, there exists an equivalent but more direct distinguisher in terms of Pearson's χ^2-statistic.

4.2   Distinguisher Based on Pearson's χ^2 Statistic

The relation between χ^2-distinguishers and multidimensional linear approximations is due to the link between correlations and the Fourier transformation of
the probability distribution of the active parts of the input and output state. In
particular, the existence of a strong multidimensional approximation can be used
to show that a distribution related to the approximations is highly non-uniform.

Pearson's χ^2-statistic will be used as a measure of goodness-of-fit between
an estimated (empirical) probability distribution $\widehat{p} : S \to [0, 1]$ and the uniform
distribution on S. For this particular case, the χ^2-statistic with q samples satisfies

$$\chi^2/q = M \, \|\widehat{p} - \mathbb{1}/M\|_2^2,$$

where $\| \cdot \|_2$ is the Euclidean norm, $M = |S|$ and $\mathbb{1}(x) = 1$ for all $x \in S$. The
χ^2-distinguisher succeeds in identifying the real cipher when the χ^2-statistic
exceeds some threshold. Indeed, as $q \to \infty$, the estimated distribution $\widehat{p}$ tends
to the true distribution p and χ^2/q tends to $M \, \|p - \mathbb{1}/M\|_2^2$. In particular, if the
tested distribution is uniform, then χ^2/q tends to zero as $q \to \infty$. Statistical
aspects will be discussed in Sect. 4.3.

The link between multidimensional linear approximations and probability
distributions is provided by the following result, which generalizes a classical
result for G and H vector spaces over $\mathbb{F}_2$ [3,13]. Below, this result will be used
to show that the existence of large correlations leads to highly non-uniform
distributions.

Theorem 4.1. *Let $F : G \to H$ be a function between finite Abelian groups G
and H. Let Z be a subgroup of the group $H \oplus G$ and let Z^0 be the group of
characters of $H \oplus G$ with kernel Z. If $\boldsymbol{x}$ is a uniform random variable on G,
then*

$$\Pr\left[(F(\boldsymbol{x}), \boldsymbol{x}) \equiv z \bmod Z\right] = \frac{1}{|Z^0|} \sum_{\psi \in Z^0} C^F_{\psi_H, \overline{\psi}_G} \, \psi(z),$$

where ψ_H is the restriction of ψ to H and ψ_G similarly for G.

Proof. The result is a straightforward consequence of the coordinate-free characterization of multidimensional linear approximations given in [6]. For the sake
of completeness, a self-contained proof is given here. Let $S = \{(F(x), x) \mid x \in G\}$
be the graph of F. By the definition of correlation given in Sect. 3.1,

$$C^F_{\psi_H, \overline{\psi}_G} = \frac{1}{|G|} \sum_{z' \in S} \overline{\psi(z')}.$$

It follows that for any $z \in H \oplus G$,

$$\sum_{\psi \in Z^0} C^F_{\psi_H, \overline{\psi}_G} \, \psi(z) = \frac{1}{|G|} \sum_{z' \in S} \sum_{\psi \in Z^0} \overline{\psi(z')} \psi(z) = \frac{1}{|G|} \sum_{z' \in S} \sum_{\psi \in Z^0} \psi(z - z').$$

If $z - z' \in Z$, then $\psi(z - z') = 1$ by the definition of Z^0. If $z - z' \notin Z$, then there exists some character $\chi \in Z^0$ such that $\chi(z - z') \neq 1$. However, since Z^0 is a group under pointwise multiplication, we have

$$\sum_{\psi \in Z^0} \psi(z - z') = \chi(z - z') \sum_{\psi \in Z^0} \psi(z - z').$$

It follows that

$$\sum_{\psi \in Z^0} \psi(z - z') = \begin{cases} |Z^0| & \text{if } z - z' \in Z \\ 0 & \text{otherwise.} \end{cases}$$

Since $z - z' \in Z$ is equivalent to $z \equiv z' \bmod Z$, the above implies that

$$\sum_{\psi \in Z^0} C^F_{\psi_H, \overline{\psi}_G} \psi(z) = |Z^0| \Pr\left[(F(\boldsymbol{x}), \boldsymbol{x}) \equiv z \bmod Z\right].$$

Dividing both sides by $|Z^0|$ gives the result.   □

Theorem 4.1 can be applied to the multidimensional linear approximations that were discussed in Sect. 4.1. For FEA-1 and FEA-2, Z can be taken as the orthogonal complement of the $\mathbb{F}_2$-vector space consisting of the masks in the multidimensional linear approximation. For both FEA-1 and FF3-1, the right half of the plaintext is fixed and reduction modulo Z corresponds to taking the difference of the left half of the ciphertext and the plaintext. More explicitly, if $\mathcal{D}$ is the half-domain of the cipher and $\mathcal{T}$ the space of half-tweaks T_R, then $H = \mathcal{D} \oplus \mathcal{D}$, $G = \mathcal{D} \oplus \mathcal{T}$ and

$$Z = \{(y_L, y_R, x_L, T_R) \in \mathcal{D} \oplus \mathcal{D} \oplus \mathcal{D} \oplus \mathcal{T} \mid y_L - x_L = 0\}.$$

For FEA-2, the full plaintext will be fixed, so $G = \mathcal{T}$. Consequently, reduction modulo Z will amount to truncating the ciphertext to its left half.

As in Sect. 4.1, let $c(\psi)$ denote the correlation of the approximation corresponding to $\psi \in Z^0$. For all three ciphers, Theorem 4.1 then shows that

$$\Pr\left[(F(\boldsymbol{x}), \boldsymbol{x}) \equiv z \bmod Z\right] = \frac{1}{|Z^0|} \sum_{\psi \in Z^0} c(\psi)\psi(z),$$

where $\boldsymbol{x}$ is uniform random on the input domain (which includes half of the tweak) and F is the mapping to the ciphertext. In fact, the right hand side above is the inverse Fourier transformation of the function $\psi \mapsto c(\psi)$ [24].

A χ^2-distinguisher can now be set up based on the non-uniformity of $(F(\boldsymbol{x}), \boldsymbol{x})$ modulo Z. Denote the probability mass functions of this random variable by $p(z)$ and denote the size of its domain by $M = |G|/|Z| = |Z^0|$. As the number of queries q increases, the empirical distribution approaches p and the χ^2/q statistic approaches the value

$$M \|p - \mathbb{1}/M\|_2^2 = \|c - \delta_{\mathbb{1}}\|_2^2 = \sum_{\psi \neq \mathbb{1}} |c(\psi)|^2. \tag{†}$$

The first equality above follows from the fact that characters are orthogonal functions (as noted in Sect. 3.1) and is also known as Parseval's theorem [24]. This shows that the χ^2-statistic can be interpreted as an alternative method to estimate the sum of the squared correlations $|c(\psi)|^2$ for $\psi \in Z^0$ with $\psi \neq \mathbb{1}$. As discussed in the next section, this result suggests that the data complexity of the χ^2-distinguisher can be heuristically estimated as $\sqrt{M}/\sum_{\psi \neq \mathbb{1}} \mathbb{E}|c(\psi)|^2$ with $c(\psi)$ the correlation $c(\psi)$ for a uniform random key and $M = N$ for the choices of Z discussed above.

Using the estimates of $\sum_{\psi \neq \mathbb{1}} \mathbb{E}|c(\psi)|^2$ from Sect. 4.1, the data complexity of the χ^2-distinguishers for r-round FEA-1 and FF3-1 can be estimated as $N^{r/2-1.5}$. For FEA-2, the data complexity estimate becomes $N^{r/3-1.5}$. This is a significant improvement over the linear attacks from Sect. 3. Furthermore, by considering smaller choices of the group Z, it is still possible to set up χ^2-distinguishers even if only part of the ciphertext is available.

4.3   Cost Analysis and Experimental Verification

As in Sect. 4.2, consider the χ^2-statistic for the empirical probability distribution of $(F(x), x)$ modulo Z, where x is a uniform random input (consisting of the tweak T_R and possibly the right half of the plaintext). Before going into detailed calculations of the advantage of the distinguisher, the heuristic estimate that was used in the previous section will be derived.

Let χ^2_{ideal} be the χ^2-statistic when the true distribution is uniform random. This is a good model for the distribution that would be observed for an ideal tweakable block cipher. Likewise, denote the χ^2-statistic for the real cipher by χ^2_{real}. It is well known that χ^2_{ideal} follows a χ^2 distribution with $N-1$ degrees of freedom when the number of queries q is sufficiently large. Hence, $\mathbb{E}\chi^2_{\text{ideal}} = N-1$. For χ^2_{real}, taking the Fourier transformation (as in †) yields

$$\mathbb{E}\chi^2_{\text{real}} = q \sum_{\psi \neq \mathbb{1}} \mathbb{E}\,|\hat{c}(\psi)|^2$$

where the average is taken with respect to a uniform random key and the random empirical correlations $\hat{c}(\psi)$ based on q samples. The expected value of $|\hat{c}(\psi)|^2$ for a fixed key is approximately equal to $|c(\psi)|^2 + 1/q$ when $|c(\psi)|^2$ is negligible compared to one. For a uniform random key, the true correlation $c(\psi)$ is itself a random variable and hence

$$\mathbb{E}\chi^2_{\text{real}} \approx N - 1 + q \sum_{\psi \neq \mathbb{1}} \mathbb{E}\,|c(\psi)|^2 \approx \mathbb{E}\chi^2_{\text{ideal}} + q \sum_{\psi \neq \mathbb{1}} \mathbb{E}\,|c(\psi)|^2 \,.$$

To obtain a low false-positive rate, the decision threshold t should be larger than the standard deviation of χ^2_{ideal}. That is, $t \geq \sqrt{2(N-1)}$. Hence, a constant advantage can be expected when $\mathbb{E}\chi^2_{\text{real}} - \mathbb{E}\chi^2_{\text{ideal}} \gg \sqrt{N}$. That is,

$$q \gg \sqrt{N}/\sum_{\psi \neq \mathbb{1}} \mathbb{E}|c(\psi)|^2 \,.$$

Since the main purpose of this section is to obtain accurate estimates of the advantage for concrete values of N, the above heuristic reasoning will not be formalized here.

It is relatively easy to estimate the average false-positive rate $P_F(t)$ of the χ^2-distinguisher. Indeed, as mentioned above, the statistic χ^2_{ideal} follows a χ^2 distribution with $N - 1$ degrees of freedom when the number of queries q is sufficiently large. Consequently,

$$P_F(t) = \Pr\left[\chi^2_{\text{ideal}} \geq t\right] \approx 1 - \chi^2_{N-1}(t).$$

The average success-probability $P_S(t)$ is significantly harder to compute. If χ^2_{real} denotes the χ^2-statistic for a random sample and a random key, then

$$P_S(t) = \Pr\left[\chi^2_{\text{real}} \geq t\right].$$

To accurately estimate this probability, a Monte-Carlo approach was used to sample from χ^2_{real}. Sampling from the correlation distribution can be done efficiently, provided that the piling-up approximation is used. A detailed exposition of the sampling strategy is beyond the goals of this paper, but an implementation is provided as supplementary material.

Figure 5 shows the estimated maximum achievable advantage for the χ^2-distinguishers for full-round FEA-1 and FEA-2 with $N = 16$ and FF3-1 with $N = 1000$. The red dots correspond to experimental verifications of the advantage by performing each attack 512 times. These figures confirm the rough data complexity estimate of $N^{r/2-1.5}$.

5   Message Recovery Attacks

In this section, it is shown how the χ^2-distinguishers from Sect. 4 can be turned into message-recovery attacks. These attacks should be situated in the message-recovery security model of Bellare *et al.* [4]. Informally, this model assumes that the adversary is allowed to (non-adaptively) query the encryption of many *distinct* tweak-message pairs related to a secret message. The distinctness requirement is sufficient to ensure that a trivial guessing attack cannot achieve a nontrivial advantage.

Section 5.1 shows how the left-half of a message encrypted using FEA-1 or FF3-1 can be recovered. The assumptions of the attack are very similar to previous work: the attacker is given the encryption of a target message and a second message with the same right half under many tweaks. Contrary to previous work [4,15], it is not necessary that both messages are encrypted under exactly the same set of tweaks. Instead, part of each tweak (T_L) must be constant. The data complexity of the attack is computed and experimentally verified in Sect. 5.2.

With more data, it is also possible to recover the right half of messages. This is discussed in Sect. 5.3. When combined with the left-half recovery attack, this results in recovery of entire messages. The same idea is used to extend the attacks to FEA-2.

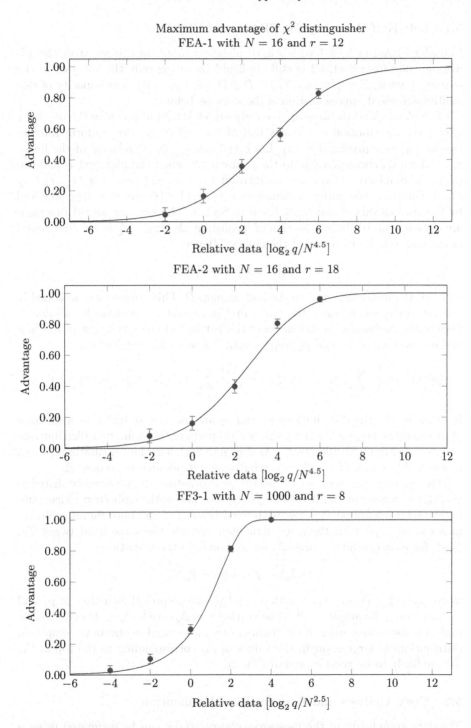

Fig. 5. Theoretical and experimental maximum advantage of the χ^2-distinguishers for full-round FEA-1, FEA-2 and FF3-1. The error bars correspond to 95% Clopper-Pearson confidence intervals. (Color figure online)

5.1 Left-Half Recovery for FEA-1 and FF3-1

Consider FEA-1 or FF3-1 with a fixed plaintext input. In this scenario, the χ^2-distinguisher from Sect. 4.2 is still applicable by using only the left part of the output. That is, $Z = \{(y_L, y_R, T_R) \in \mathcal{D} \oplus \mathcal{D} \oplus \mathcal{T} \mid y_L = 0\}$. The capacity of this multidimensional approximation is the same as before.

The idea behind the message-recovery attack is that a change in the plaintext affects the distribution of the left half of the ciphertext (for uniform random tweaks T_R) in a predictable way. Let $c_1(\psi)$ denote the correlation of the linear approximation corresponding to the character ψ when the plaintext is fixed to (x_L, x_R). Similarly, denote the correlation for a second plaintext (x'_L, x_R) by $c_2(\psi)$. Following the piling-up principle, $c_1(\psi)$ and $c_2(\psi)$ are well-approximated by the correlations of the trails given in Sect. 3. The two considered functions are the same up to the subtraction of a constant $\Delta = x_L - x'_L$ in the first round of the trail (the third round of the cipher). Hence,

$$c_2(\psi) \approx \psi_{\mathcal{D}}(\Delta)c_1(\psi)$$

with $\psi_{\mathcal{D}}$ the restriction of ψ to the half-domain $\mathcal{D}$. This approximation is highly accurate in practice, since the trails in Fig. 2a and 3 are strongly dominant. Denote the probability distribution of the left half of the ciphertext in the first and second case by p_1 and p_2 respectively. Theorem 4.1 implies that

$$p_2(y_L) = \frac{1}{N} \sum_{\psi \in Z^0} c_2(\psi)\psi(y_L) \approx \frac{\psi_{\mathcal{D}}(\Delta)}{N} \sum_{\psi \in Z^0} c_1(\psi)\psi(y_L) = p_1(y_L + \Delta).$$

In other words, the distributions p_1 and p_2 are (nearly) shifted over a distance Δ. It should be emphasized that this is a property of the ciphertext distributions and *not* of individual ciphertexts. As shown in Sect. 4.2, the distributions p_1 and p_2 are highly non-uniform. This is what makes it possible to recover Δ.

The message-recovery attack begins by estimating the probability distribution (for uniform random tweaks T_R) of the left half of the ciphertext twice: once for the secret plaintext (x_L, x_R) with fixed tweak T_L, and once for an arbitrary message (x'_L, x_R) with the same right half and for the same fixed tweak T_L. Next, for each candidate value Δ_{g} for Δ, compute the statistic

$$r(\Delta_{\mathrm{g}}) = qN/4 \, \|\widehat{p}_1 - \widehat{p}_{\mathrm{g}}\|_2^2,$$

where $\widehat{p}_{\mathrm{g}}(y_L) = \widehat{p}_2(y_L - \Delta_{\mathrm{g}})$ with $\widehat{p}_1$ and $\widehat{p}_2$ the empirical estimates of p_1 and p_2 based on $q/2$ samples each. The statistics $r(\Delta_{\mathrm{g}})$ with $\Delta_{\mathrm{g}} \in \mathcal{D}$ can then be ranked in ascending order. If the number of samples used to obtain the empirical distributions is large enough, the values of Δ_{g} corresponding to the top of the list are likely to be good candidates for Δ.

5.2 Cost Analysis and Experimental Verification

The data complexity of the message-recovery attack can be estimated using a heuristic argument similar to the one that was used for the χ^2-distinguisher in

Sect. 4.2. For a random sample, the statistic $r(\Delta_{\mathbf{g}})$ satisfies

$$r(\Delta_{\mathbf{g}}) = \frac{q}{4} \sum_{\psi \neq 1} |\widehat{c}_1(\psi) - \overline{\psi_{\mathcal{D}}(\Delta_{\mathbf{g}})}\widehat{c}_2(\psi)|^2,$$

where $\widehat{c}_1(\psi)$ and $\widehat{c}_2(\psi)$ are the empirical correlations and the sum is over all nontrivial $\psi \in Z^0$. When the fixed-key correlation $|c_i(\psi)|^2$ is small, averaging over the sample gives $\mathbb{E}|\widehat{c}_i(\psi)|^2 \approx |c_i(\psi)|^2 + 2/q$. Hence, the average of $r(\Delta_{\mathbf{g}})$ over the sample and over a uniform random key is equal to

$$\mathbb{E}\, r(\Delta_{\mathbf{g}}) = \frac{q}{4} \sum_{\psi \neq 1} \mathbb{E}\left(|\widehat{c}_1(\psi)|^2 + |\widehat{c}_2(\psi)|^2 - 2\Re\left\{ \overline{\psi_{\mathcal{D}}(\Delta_{\mathbf{g}})}\, \overline{\widehat{c}_1(\psi)}\widehat{c}_2(\psi)\right\}\right)$$

$$\approx \frac{q}{4} \sum_{\psi \neq 1} \left(\frac{4}{q} + \mathbb{E}|c_1(\psi)|^2 + \mathbb{E}|c_2(\psi)|^2\right) - \frac{q}{2}\Re\left\{ \sum_{\psi \neq 1} \overline{\psi_{\mathcal{D}}(\Delta_{\mathbf{g}})}\, \mathbb{E}\overline{c_1(\psi)}c_2(\psi)\right\}$$

$$\approx N - 1 + \frac{q}{2} \sum_{\psi \neq 1} \mathbb{E}|c_1(\psi)|^2 - \frac{q}{2} \sum_{\psi \neq 1} \Re\{\psi_{\mathcal{D}}(\Delta - \Delta_{\mathbf{g}})\}\, \mathbb{E}|c_1(\psi)|^2.$$

where the third step follows from $c_2(\psi) \approx \psi_{\mathcal{D}}(\Delta)c_1(\psi)$. In fact, $\mathbb{E}|c_1(\psi)|^2$ is nearly constant in ψ. If $\Delta_{\mathbf{g}} \neq \Delta$, then $\sum_{\psi \neq 1} \psi_{\mathcal{D}}(\Delta - \Delta_{\mathbf{g}}) = -1$ and it follows that

$$\mathbb{E}\, r(\Delta_{\mathbf{g}}) - \mathbb{E}\, r(\Delta) \approx q \sum_{\psi \neq 1} \mathbb{E}|c_1(\psi)|^2.$$

In particular, if $q \gg \sqrt{N}/\sum_{\psi \neq 1} \mathbb{E}|c_1(\psi)|^2$, then $\mathbb{E}\, r(\Delta_{\mathbf{g}}) - \mathbb{E}\, r(\Delta) \gg \sqrt{N}$. This is sufficient to obtain a constant advantage since the standard deviation of $r(\Delta_{\mathbf{g}})$ is of the order $\sqrt{N}$. This can be motivated by noting that, for a uniform output distribution, the distribution of $r(\Delta_{\mathbf{g}})$ would be asymptotically χ^2 with $N - 1$ degrees of freedom. Hence, $\widetilde{\mathcal{O}}(N^{r/2-1.5})$ data should suffice to obtain a constant message-recovery advantage.

No attempt will be made here to make the above argument rigorous. Instead, accurate estimates of the message-recovery advantage for specific values of N can be computed using a Monte-Carlo approach. The main ingredient is a method to sample from the correlation distributions, which is identical to the one used for the calculations in Sect. 4.3. Results for full-round FEA-1 with $N = 16$ and FF3-1 with $N = 1000$ are shown in Fig. 6, along with experimental estimates of the advantage.

Observe that for FF3-1 with $q = 4 \times \lfloor 2N^{2.5} \rceil \approx 2^{28}$, the theoretical advantage is an overestimate. This is due to the fact that only 2^{28} data is available for a fixed choice of the plaintext and tweak T_L. Once the variations in the ideal distribution (which was assumed to be uniform in the analysis) are of the same order as the sampling error, the advantage begins to flatten off. However, this does not imply that the advantage of the FF3-1 message-recovery attack cannot be made close to one. Indeed, one can simply perform the attack for a different choice of T_L. Of course, for even larger N, the maximum advantage that can be achieved using one choice of T_L decreases and the attack eventually becomes infeasible. Based on the estimated data complexity of the attack and Fig. 6, this is expected to occur for $N > 2^{12}$. The right-half recovery attack from Sect. 5.3 avoids this problem and can be used for all $N < 2^{19}$, but it has a higher overall data complexity.

5.3   Right-Half Recovery and Application to FEA-2

The left-half recovery attack on FEA-1 and FF3-1 could also be applied for two messages (x_L, x_R) and (x'_L, x'_R) with $x_R \neq x'_R$. However, the recovered difference would then be $\Delta = x_L - x'_L + F_1(x_R) - F_1(x'_R)$. If $x_L - x'_L$ is known, then the adversary can recover Δ to obtain the difference $F_1(x_R) - F_1(x'_R)$. This is useful because it leads to a right-half recovery attack. In addition, the output differences will be directly used in the key-recovery attack on FEA-1 that is described in Sect. 6. It is also possible to apply the same attack with a different choice of Z that includes the left half of the plaintext. In this case, the recovered difference would simply be $F_1(x_R) - F_1(x'_R)$ due to reduction modulo Z. The main advantage of this approach is that it increases the amount of available data per choice of the right half by a factor of N. This extends the reach of the attack to $N < 2^{19}$, compared to $N < 2^{12}$ for left-half recovery.

The right-half can be recovered by guessing x'_R until the recovered difference is zero. This does not violate the distinctness requirement of the message-recovery framework, since the tweaks T_R and the left halves of the guessed messages can be different from those of the secret message. The attack proceeds by computing the statistics $r(0)$ from Sect. 5.1 with $\widehat{p}_1$ the empirical distribution for the secret message and $\widehat{p}_2$ the empirical distribution with right-half guess x'_R. If these statistics are ranked in ascending order, the values of x'_R corresponding to the top of the list are the most promising candidates for x_R. By the analysis in Sect. 5.2, this attack requires $\widetilde{\mathcal{O}}(N^{r/2-0.5})$ data. A simulation of the maximum advantage is shown in the bottom of Fig. 6, along with experimental results. Note that the error bars are wider than for the left-half recovery experiments because each data point was estimated using only 40 runs of the attack (to limit the time complexity of the experiment).

The same idea as above can be used to extend the message-recovery attack to FEA-2. For example, consider left-half recovery. In this case, the adversary queries the encryption of the secret message (x_L, x_R) under many tweaks with constant T_L. In addition, for each guess of x'_L, similar queries are made for (x'_L, x_R). The same process as above can be used to identify the values of x_L for which

$$F_2(x_L + F_1(x_R)) + x_R = F_2(x'_L + F_1(x_R)) + x_R.$$

However, there is an additional issue that must be addressed: since the approximation shown in Fig. 2b does not have equal input and output masks, the effect of changing the plaintext input on the correlations is more complicated. Nevertheless, one can still use the same approach (with roughly the same data complexity) to check for equality between the two output distributions.

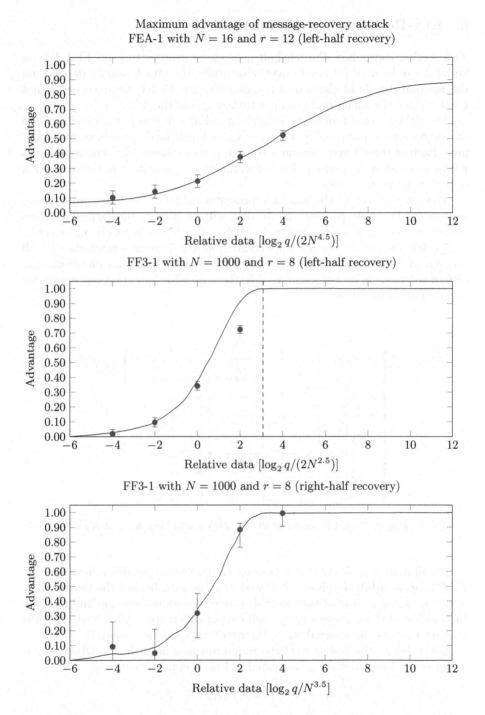

Fig. 6. Theoretical and experimental maximum advantage of the message-recovery attacks for full-round FEA-1 and FF3-1. The error bars correspond to 95% Clopper-Pearson confidence intervals. The dashed vertical line corresponds to a data complexity of 2×2^{28}.

6   Key-Recovery Attack on FEA-1

This section shows how the left-half message-recovery attack on FEA-1 from Sect. 5.1 can be used for key-recovery. Naturally, the attack heavily depends on the internal details of the round function F_1. For FF3-1, key-recovery is not feasible since the round functions are truncations of the AES.

The FEA-1 round function is illustrated in Fig. 7. It consists of two iterations of a key-addition layer, an S-box layer and a linear layer with branch number nine. Each of these layers acts on a state in a vector space $\mathbb{F}_{2^8}^8$. The round keys will be denoted by K_a and K_b. The round function F_1 is defined as the truncation of this structure to m bits.

The exact choice of the matrix representation M of the linear layer is not important. The only property of M that will be used is the fact that it has branch number nine (equivalently, is MDS). The S-box is based on inversion in $\mathbb{F}_{2^8}$, but the details are not important. However, it is important that for all nonzero Δ_1 and Δ_2, the equation $S(x + \Delta_1) = S(x) + \Delta_2$ has either no, two or four solutions in x. For each $\Delta_1 \neq 0$, the case with four solutions occurs for exactly one choice of Δ_2.

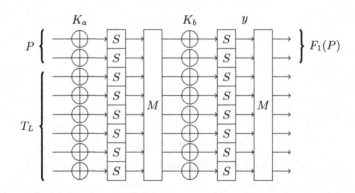

Fig. 7. Round function of FEA-1 with round keys K_a and K_b.

Recall from Sect. 5.3 that it is possible to recover output differences $F_1(P) + F_1(P')$ for an arbitrary choice of P and P'. The idea behind the key-recovery attack is to guess parts of the internal state of the round function and to check the validity of these guesses using such output differences. After recovering the relevant parts of the internal state, the round keys can be recovered.

Let x denote the first byte of the round function input $P\|T_L$. Observe that byte i of the internal state y (indicated in Fig. 7) can be written as

$$y_i = S(\gamma_i + M_{i,1} S(K_{a,1} + x)),$$

where $\gamma_1, \ldots, \gamma_8 \in \mathbb{F}_{2^8}$ are constants depending on the round keys K_a and K_b (but not on the first byte $K_{a,1}$) and on the tweak T_L. Importantly, $\gamma_1, \ldots, \gamma_8$ do not depend on x. Specifically,

$$\gamma_i = K_{b,i} + \sum_{j=2}^{8} M_{i,j} S([P\|T_L]_j + K_{a,j}).$$

In Sect. 6.1, it will be shown how $K_{a,1}$ and γ_i can be recovered using a limited number of output differences. Section 6.2 then shows how the entire round keys K_a and K_b can be extracted from these constants and a few additional output differences.

6.1   Recovering $K_{a,1}$ and the Internal Constants γ_i

It is clear from Fig. 7 that the output difference is a linear function of the difference between the internal states y and y' (corresponding to two inputs x and x'). Furthermore, since M is an invertible matrix, this function is of rank m. Hence, $y + y'$ can take $2^{64-m} = 2^{64}/N$ possible values. By computing an echelon form for the linear function that maps $y + y'$ to the output difference, these candidate solutions can easily be enumerated. For each guess of $y + y'$, one obtains the values

$$y_i + y_i' = S(\gamma_i + M_{i,1} S(K_{a,1} + x)) + S(\gamma_i + M_{i,1} S(K_{a,1} + x')).$$

For each $i = 1, \ldots, 8$, one can determine the set of possible input differences $S(K_{a,1} + x) + S(K_{a,1} + x')$ that can lead to the known difference $y_i + y_i' \neq 0$. Due to the properties of S, there are 127 possible input differences. Hence, each i reduces the number of candidate differences by a factor $127/255 < 1/2$. It follows that the difference $S(K_{a,1} + x) + S(K_{a,1} + x')$ can be uniquely determined. However, since the difference $x + x'$ is known, two candidates for $K_{a,1}$ can be computed from the difference equation. The case with four solutions is unlikely to occur and does not significantly affect the overall time and data complexity of the attack.

Once $K_{a,1}$ has been determined (as one of two possible values), the constants γ_i can also be obtained by solving a difference equation. In particular, since the case with four solutions is rare, one usually ends up with two candidates for each γ_i. To check the validity of these candidates, additional output differences will be used. To save data, one of x or x' can be reused. For each of the 2^9 candidate values, the expected output difference should then be computed and compared to the observed difference. This requires roughly 2^{12} S-box evaluations. If the candidate values are wrong, the output difference will match in roughly $1/N$ of the cases. Hence, the computational cost is dominated by the calculation of the expected output difference for the first pair.

The total number of candidates for the difference $y + y'$, the internal constants and the first byte of K_a is $2^{64+9}/N = 2^{73}/N$. Hence, $\lceil 73/m - 1 \rceil$ pairs are sufficient to obtain a unique solution. For $m = 4$, the number of available input differences is too small to obtain a unique candidate. However, this is not a major issue since the time complexity of the round key recovery procedure described in Sect. 6.2 is small enough that it can be repeated several times.

The data complexity of the above process is $(\lceil 73/m - 1 \rceil + 1)q/2$ queries, where q is the data complexity of the left-half message-recovery attack. This comes with an equal computational cost, measured in FEA-1 evaluations. The remaining computational cost is dominated by $2^{64+12}/N$ S-box evaluations. Since the cipher contains 12×16 S-boxes, one can conservatively estimate that this takes less time than $2^{68}/N$ evaluations of full-round FEA-1.

6.2 Recovering the Round Keys

Once the constants $\gamma_1, \ldots, \gamma_8$ have been recovered, obtaining the round keys K_a and K_b is relatively easy. In particular, recall that

$$\gamma_i = K_{b,i} + \sum_{j=2}^{8} M_{i,j} S([P\|T_L]_j + K_{a,j}).$$

Suppose $P\|T_L$ and $P'\|T_L'$ differ only in byte $j \in \{2, \ldots, 8\}$ and let γ_i' be the new value of γ_i for input $P'\|T_L'$. It is easy to see that

$$\gamma_i + \gamma_i' = M_{i,j} S([P\|T_L]_j + K_{a,j}) + M_{i,j} S([P'\|T_L']_j + K_{a,j}).$$

Hence, after guessing $K_{a,j}$, one can compute the new constants γ_i' and the expected output differences for pairs with tweak T_L'. To obtain a unique (up to a constant) candidate for $K_{a,j}$, a total of $\lceil 8/m \rceil$ differences are sufficient. Recovering all of the bytes of K_a thus requires $7 \times \lceil 8/m \rceil$ differences. Once K_a is recovered, K_b can be computed directly.

To conclude, the data complexity of this step is $7q/2 \times (\lceil 8/m \rceil + 1)$ with q the data complexity of the left-half message-recovery attack. A few additional pairs will be required to filter spurious candidates for $K_{a,j}$, or if no unique solution for the constants $\gamma_1, \ldots, \gamma_8$ was obtained in the first step of the attack ($m = 4$). The time complexity, excluding the time required for message-recovery, is negligible compared to that of the first step.

6.3 Recovering All Round Keys

By the results in Sects. 6.1 and 6.2, the round keys K_a and K_b of the first round function can be recovered using at most $\lceil 73/m - 1 \rceil + 7 \lceil 8/m \rceil \leq 16 \lceil 8/m \rceil$ evaluations of the left-half message-recovery attack and additional time equivalent to at most $2^{68}/N$ FEA-1 evaluations. If q is the amount of data required for the left-half recovery attack, this amounts to a total of less than $8 \lceil 8/m \rceil q + 4q$ queries. However, the FEA-1 key-schedule is a Lai-Massey structure that generates two round keys per iteration. Hence, the remaining round keys can not be obtained by iterating the key-schedule without knowing the round keys for the second round. To obtain these keys, it suffices to perform the same key-recovery attack on F_2. Hence, the total cost is less than $16 \lceil 8/\log_2 N \rceil q + 8q$ data for left-half recoveries and additional time equivalent to less than $2^{69}/N$ evaluations of FEA-1.

7 Conclusion

It was shown that the format-preserving encryption standards FF3-1, FEA-1 and FEA-2 are all vulnerable to linear cryptanalysis. More generally, the analysis in this paper is applicable to any small-domain Feistel cipher with alternating round tweaks.

The attacks rely on the ability to vary the tweaks in even-numbered rounds (FF3-1 and FEA-1) or rounds numbered by a multiple of three (FEA-2), while keeping the tweaks in the other rounds fixed. Combined with the observation that the variance of the correlation of a nontrivial linear approximation over a small random function is quite large, this results in strong linear trails through the cipher. The analysis of FF3-1 is also of theoretical interest as an application of the theory of linear cryptanalysis over the group $\mathbb{Z}/N\mathbb{Z}$.

The data requirements of the basic linear distinguishers were reduced using multidimensional linear cryptanalysis. Based on the same principle, efficient message-recovery attacks were obtained. For FEA-1, the message-recovery attack was in turn extended to a key-recovery attack.

For many instances of FF3-1, FEA-1 and FEA-2, the data requirements of the new attacks are small enough to be a practical concern for users of these standards.

Acknowledgments. I thank Dongyoung Roh (ETRI) and Morris Dworkin (NIST) for useful comments on an early draft of this work, and Vincent Rijmen for proofreading the paper. The author is supported by a PhD Fellowship from the Research Foundation – Flanders (FWO).

References

1. Amon, O., Dunkelman, O., Keller, N., Ronen, E., Shamir, A.: Three third generation attacks on the format preserving encryption scheme FF3. Cryptology ePrint Archive, Report 2021/335 (2021). https://eprint.iacr.org/2021/335
2. Baignères, T., Junod, P., Vaudenay, S.: How far can we go beyond linear cryptanalysis? In: Lee, P.J. (ed.) ASIACRYPT 2004. LNCS, vol. 3329, pp. 432–450. Springer, Heidelberg (2004). https://doi.org/10.1007/978-3-540-30539-2_31
3. Baignères, T., Stern, J., Vaudenay, S.: Linear cryptanalysis of non binary ciphers. In: Adams, C., Miri, A., Wiener, M. (eds.) SAC 2007. LNCS, vol. 4876, pp. 184–211. Springer, Heidelberg (2007). https://doi.org/10.1007/978-3-540-77360-3_13
4. Bellare, M., Hoang, V.T., Tessaro, S.: Message-recovery attacks on Feistel-based format preserving encryption. In: Weippl, E.R., Katzenbeisser, S., Kruegel, C., Myers, A.C., Halevi, S. (eds.) Proceedings of the 2016 ACM SIGSAC Conference on Computer and Communications Security, Vienna, Austria, 24–28 October 2016, pp. 444–455. ACM (2016). https://doi.org/10.1145/2976749.2978390
5. Bellare, M., Ristenpart, T., Rogaway, P., Stegers, T.: Format-preserving encryption. In: Jacobson, M.J., Rijmen, V., Safavi-Naini, R. (eds.) SAC 2009. LNCS, vol. 5867, pp. 295–312. Springer, Heidelberg (2009). https://doi.org/10.1007/978-3-642-05445-7_19
6. Beyne, T.: Linear Cryptanalysis in the Weak Key Model. Master's thesis, KU Leuven (2019). https://homes.esat.kuleuven.be/~tbeyne/masterthesis/thesis.pdf

7. Black, J., Rogaway, P.: Ciphers with arbitrary finite domains. In: Preneel, B. (ed.) CT-RSA 2002. LNCS, vol. 2271, pp. 114–130. Springer, Heidelberg (2002). https://doi.org/10.1007/3-540-45760-7_9

8. Daemen, J., Govaerts, R., Vandewalle, J.: Correlation matrices. In: Preneel, B. (ed.) FSE 1994. LNCS, vol. 1008, pp. 275–285. Springer, Heidelberg (1995). https://doi.org/10.1007/3-540-60590-8_21

9. Daemen, J., Rijmen, V.: Probability distributions of correlation and differentials in block ciphers. J. Math. Cryptol. 1(3), 221–242 (2007)

10. Dunkelman, O., Kumar, A., Lambooij, E., Sanadhya, S.K.: Cryptanalysis of Feistel-based format-preserving encryption. Cryptology ePrint Archive, Report 2020/1311 (2020). https://eprint.iacr.org/2020/1311

11. Durak, F.B., Vaudenay, S.: Breaking the FF3 format-preserving encryption standard over small domains. In: Katz, J., Shacham, H. (eds.) CRYPTO 2017. LNCS, vol. 10402, pp. 679–707. Springer, Cham (2017). https://doi.org/10.1007/978-3-319-63715-0_23

12. Dworkin, M.: Recommendation for block cipher modes of operation: methods for format-preserving encryption. NIST Special Publication 800 38Gr1 (February 2019). https://doi.org/10.6028/NIST.SP.800-38Gr1-draft

13. Hermelin, M., Cho, J.Y., Nyberg, K.: Multidimensional linear cryptanalysis of reduced round serpent. In: Mu, Y., Susilo, W., Seberry, J. (eds.) ACISP 2008. LNCS, vol. 5107, pp. 203–215. Springer, Heidelberg (2008). https://doi.org/10.1007/978-3-540-70500-0_15

14. Hoang, V.T., Miller, D., Trieu, N.: Attacks only get better: how to break ff3 on large domains. In: Ishai, Y., Rijmen, V. (eds.) EUROCRYPT 2019. LNCS, vol. 11477, pp. 85–116. Springer, Cham (2019). https://doi.org/10.1007/978-3-030-17656-3_4

15. Hoang, V.T., Tessaro, S., Trieu, N.: The curse of small domains: new attacks on format-preserving encryption. In: Shacham, H., Boldyreva, A. (eds.) CRYPTO 2018. LNCS, vol. 10991, pp. 221–251. Springer, Cham (2018). https://doi.org/10.1007/978-3-319-96884-1_8

16. Lee, J.-K., Koo, B., Roh, D., Kim, W.-H., Kwon, D.: Format-preserving encryption algorithms using families of tweakable blockciphers. In: Lee, J., Kim, J. (eds.) ICISC 2014. LNCS, vol. 8949, pp. 132–159. Springer, Cham (2015). https://doi.org/10.1007/978-3-319-15943-0_9

17. Matsui, M.: Linear cryptanalysis method for DES cipher. In: Helleseth, T. (ed.) EUROCRYPT 1993. LNCS, vol. 765, pp. 386–397. Springer, Heidelberg (1994). https://doi.org/10.1007/3-540-48285-7_33

18. Patarin, J.: New results on pseudorandom permutation generators based on the DES scheme. In: Feigenbaum, J. (ed.) CRYPTO 1991. LNCS, vol. 576, pp. 301–312. Springer, Heidelberg (1992). https://doi.org/10.1007/3-540-46766-1_25

19. Patarin, J.: Generic attacks on Feistel schemes. In: Boyd, C. (ed.) ASIACRYPT 2001. LNCS, vol. 2248, pp. 222–238. Springer, Heidelberg (2001). https://doi.org/10.1007/3-540-45682-1_14

20. Patarin, J.: Security of random Feistel schemes with 5 or more rounds. In: Franklin, M. (ed.) CRYPTO 2004. LNCS, vol. 3152, pp. 106–122. Springer, Heidelberg (2004). https://doi.org/10.1007/978-3-540-28628-8_7

21. Rijmen, V., Daemen, J., Preneel, B., Bosselaers, A., De Win, E.: The cipher SHARK. In: Gollmann, D. (ed.) FSE 1996. LNCS, vol. 1039, pp. 99–111. Springer, Heidelberg (1996). https://doi.org/10.1007/3-540-60865-6_47

22. Selçuk, A.A.: On probability of success in linear and differential cryptanalysis. J. Cryptol. 21(1), 131–147 (2008). https://doi.org/10.1007/s00145-007-9013-7

23. Tardy-Corfdir, A., Gilbert, H.: A known plaintext attack of FEAL-4 and FEAL-6. In: Feigenbaum, J. (ed.) CRYPTO 1991. LNCS, vol. 576, pp. 172–182. Springer, Heidelberg (1992). https://doi.org/10.1007/3-540-46766-1_12
24. Terras, A.: Fourier Analysis on Finite Groups and Applications. Cambridge University Press (1999)
25. Vaudenay, S.: An experiment on DES statistical cryptanalysis. In: Gong, L., Stern, J. (eds.) ACM CCS 96, pp. 139–147. ACM Press (March 1996). https://doi.org/10.1145/238168.238206

Efficient Key Recovery for All HFE Signature Variants

Chengdong Tao[2], Albrecht Petzoldt[3], and Jintai Ding[1,2(✉)]

[1] Yau Mathematical Center, Tsinghua University, Beijing, China
[2] Ding Lab, Beijing Institute of Mathematical Science and Applications, Beijing, China
[3] FAU Erlangen-Nuremberg, Nuremberg, Germany

Abstract. The HFE cryptosystem is one of the most popular multivariate schemes. Especially in the area of digital signatures, the HFEv-variant offers short signatures and high performance. Recently, an instance of the HFEv- signature scheme called GeMSS was selected as one of the alternative candidates for signature schemes in the third round of the NIST Post-Quantum Crypto (PQC) Standardization Project.

In this paper, we propose a new key recovery attack on the HFEv-signature scheme. Our attack shows that both the Minus and the Vinegar modification do not enhance the security of the basic HFE scheme significantly. This shows that it is very difficult to build a secure and efficient signature scheme on the basis of HFE. In particular, we use our attack to show that the proposed parameters of the GeMSS scheme are not as secure as claimed.

Keywords: Multivariate cryptography · HFEv- · Key recovery · MinRank · NIST standardization process

1 Introduction

Cryptographic techniques such as encryption and digital signatures are an indispensable part of modern communication systems. However, the currently used schemes RSA and ECDSA become insecure as soon as large quantum computers arrive. Due to recent progress in the development of such computers, there is an urgent need for alternatives to these classical schemes which are resistant against attacks with quantum computers. These are known as post-quantum cryptosystems [4,6].

One of the main candidates for such schemes are multivariate public key crypto- systems [15]. Especially in the area of digital signatures, there exist many promising multivariate schemes. In fact, the multivariate signature scheme Rainbow is among the three signature schemes in the third round of the NIST standardization process of post-quantum cryptosystems [8]. Another multivariate signature scheme, GeMMS, is one of the alternative candidates. GeMMS is a special instance of the well known HFEv- signature scheme, which was first

© International Association for Cryptologic Research 2021
T. Malkin and C. Peikert (Eds.): CRYPTO 2021, LNCS 12825, pp. 70–93, 2021.
https://doi.org/10.1007/978-3-030-84242-0_4

proposed by Patarin et al. in [26]. The principle idea of HFEv- is to combine the Minus and the Vinegar modifications with the HFE cryptosystem of [25]. Since the resulting multivariate quadratic system contains more variables than equations, HFEv- can only be used for digital signatures.

Attacks Against HFEv- and Related Work. There exist many attack methods on HFEv-, such as the direct attack [9,27], the distinguishing attack [13], the differential attack [7], and the MinRank attack [13]. The most studied attack against HFEv- is the MinRank attack, which was first proposed by Kipnis and Shamir in [23]. Later, many variants of this technique have been proposed to increase its efficiency. The most prominent examples of this are the minors modeling of Bettale, Faugére and Perret [3] as well as the support minors modelling of Bardet, Bros, Cabarcas, Gaborit, Perlner, Smith-Tone, Tillich and Verbel [1]. Another recent paper closely related to our work is that of Beullens [2]. The main difference to our paper is that Beullens studies MinRank type attacks against SingleField schemes such as Rainbow, while we are interested in applying this attack to BigField schemes.

In this paper, we mainly consider the MinRank attack using minors modeling as a reference. According to [3], the complexity of this attack is given as

$$
\mathcal{O}\left(\binom{n+d+a+v+1}{d+a+v+1}^{\omega}\right),
$$

where n is the degree of the field extension, $d = \lceil \log_q(D) \rceil$, where D is the degree bound on the HFE central polynomial, a is the number of Minus equations, v is the number of Vinegar variables and $2 < \omega \le 3$ is the linear algebra constant. More information about the different strategies to solve the MinRank problem can be found in Sect. 3.2.

Our Contribution. In this paper, we present an improved MinRank type key recovery attack on the HFEv- signature scheme. The complexity of our new attack on HFEv- using minors modeling is

$$
\mathcal{O}\left(\binom{n+d+v+1}{d+1}^{\omega}\right).
$$

This shows that the Minus modification does not enhance the security of HFE type cryptosystems, while the Vinegar modification increases the complexity of our attack only by a polynomial factor. This shows that the currently used techniques are insufficient to transform HFE into a secure signature scheme. In particular, we use our attack to show that the parameters of GeMSS which were submitted to the NIST Post-Quantum Crypto Standardization Project are not as secure as claimed.

The remainder of this paper is organized as follows. Section 2 gives a short introduction into multivariate cryptography and introduces the HFEv- signature scheme, while Sect. 3 repeats some cryptanalytic concepts used in the further parts of the paper. In Sect. 4 we present our attack against the HFEv- signature scheme and analyze its complexity. Section 5 discusses a possible speed up of our attack by solving the MinRank problem using the support minors modeling and Sect. 6 analyzes the importance of our attack on the NIST alternative candidate GeMMS. Finally, Sect. 7 concludes the paper.

2 Multivariate Cryptography

The public key of a multivariate public key cryptosystem is a system of quadratic polynomials in several variables over a finite field $\mathbb{F}_q$ of q elements, i.e.

$$p^{(1)}(x_1, \ldots, x_n) = \sum_{1 \leq i \leq j \leq n} \alpha_{ij}^{(1)} x_i x_j + \sum_{1 \leq i \leq n} \beta_i^{(1)} x_i + \gamma^{(1)},$$

$$\vdots$$

$$p^{(m)}(x_1, \ldots, x_n) = \sum_{1 \leq i \leq j \leq n} \alpha_{ij}^{(m)} x_i x_j + \sum_{1 \leq i \leq n} \beta_i^{(m)} x_i + \gamma^{(m)}.$$

The problem of inverting such a system is known as the MQ problem and was proven to be NP hard [20].

In order to construct a digital signature scheme on the basis of the MQ problem, one starts with an easily invertible quadratic map $\mathcal{F} : \mathbb{F}_q^n \to \mathbb{F}_q^m$ (central map). To hide the structure of this map in the public key, one combines $\mathcal{F}$ with two randomly chosen invertible affine maps $\mathcal{T} : \mathbb{F}_q^m \to \mathbb{F}_q^m$ and $\mathcal{S} : \mathbb{F}_q^n \to \mathbb{F}_q^n$. The public key of a multivariate signature scheme is therefore given as

$$\mathcal{P} = \mathcal{T} \circ \mathcal{F} \circ \mathcal{S} : \mathbb{F}_q^n \to \mathbb{F}_q^m,$$

the private key of the scheme consists of the three maps $\mathcal{T}$, $\mathcal{F}$ and $\mathcal{S}$.

In order to generate a signature for a document $d \in \{0,1\}^*$, the owner of the private key performs the following steps.

1. Use a hash function $\mathcal{H}$ to compute the hash value $\mathbf{h} = \mathcal{H}(d) \in \mathbb{F}_q^m$.
2. Compute $\mathbf{x} = \mathcal{T}^{-1}(\mathbf{h}) \in \mathbb{F}_q^m$.
3. Find a pre-image $\mathbf{y} \in \mathbb{F}_q^n$ of $\mathbf{x}$ under the central map $\mathcal{F}$.
4. Compute the signature $\mathbf{z} \in \mathbb{F}_q^n$ of the document d as $\mathbf{z} = \mathcal{S}^{-1}(\mathbf{y})$.

To check the correctness of a message/signature pair $(d, \mathbf{z})$, one simply computes $\mathbf{h} = \mathcal{H}(d)$ and $\mathbf{h}' = \mathcal{P}(\mathbf{z})$. The signature is accepted, if and only if $\mathbf{h} = \mathbf{h}'$ holds. The process of signature generation and verification is illustrated by Fig. 1.

2.1 The HFEv- Signature Scheme

The HFEv- signature scheme is an example of a multivariate BigField scheme. In such a scheme, the central map $\mathcal{F}$ is a univariate map over a degree n extension

Signature Generation

$$d \in \{0,1\}^{\star} \xrightarrow{\;\mathcal{H}\;} \mathbf{h} \in \mathbb{F}^m \xrightarrow{\;\mathcal{T}^{-1}\;} \mathbf{x} \in \mathbb{F}^m \xrightarrow{\;\mathcal{F}^{-1}\;} \mathbf{y} \in \mathbb{F}^n \xrightarrow{\;\mathcal{S}^{-1}\;} \mathbf{z} \in \mathbb{F}^n$$

$$\mathcal{P}$$

Signature Verification

Fig. 1. Signature generation and verification process for multivariate signature schemes

field $\mathbb{F}_{q^n}$ of $\mathbb{F}_q$. Using an isomorphism ϕ between the field $\mathbb{F}_{q^n}$ and the vector space $\mathbb{F}_q^n$, we can transform the univariate polynomial map $\mathcal{F}$ into a quadratic map $\bar{\mathcal{F}} = \phi \circ \mathcal{F} \circ \phi^{-1}$ over the vector space $\mathbb{F}_q^n$ (see Fig. 2).

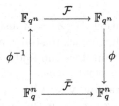

Fig. 2. Construction of the central map for multivariate BigField schemes

The HFEv- signature scheme uses three integer parameters D, a and v. The three algorithms for key generation, signature generation and signature verification can be described as follows.

Key Generation. In order to generate a key pair for the HFEv- signature scheme, one randomly generates a polynomial (the central map) of the form

$$\mathcal{F}(X, x_{n+1}, \ldots, x_{n+v}) = \sum_{\substack{i,j \in \mathbb{N} \\ q^i + q^j \le D}} \alpha_{ij} X^{q^i + q^j} + \sum_{\substack{i \in \mathbb{N} \\ q^i \le D}} \beta_i(x_{n+1}, \ldots, x_{n+v}) X^{q^i}$$

$$+ \gamma(x_{n+1}, \ldots, x_{n+v}).$$

So, $\mathcal{F}$ is a map from $\mathbb{F}_{q^n} \times \mathbb{F}_q^v$ to $\mathbb{F}_{q^n}$, where the $\alpha_{i,j}$ are randomly chosen elements of the field $\mathbb{F}_{q^n}$, the $\beta_i : \mathbb{F}_q^v \to \mathbb{F}_{q^n}$ are linear maps from the vector space $\mathbb{F}_q^v$ to the field $\mathbb{F}_{q^n}$ and $\gamma : \mathbb{F}_q^v \to \mathbb{F}_{q^n}$ is a quadratic map in the Vinegar variables $x_{n+1}, x_{n+2}, \ldots, x_{n+v}$.

Due to the special structure of it, the central map $\mathcal{F}$ corresponds to a quadratic map $\bar{\mathcal{F}} = \phi \circ \mathcal{F} \circ \phi^{-1} : \mathbb{F}_q^{n+v} \to \mathbb{F}_q^n$. Furthermore, in order to hide the structure of the central map $\mathcal{F}$ in the public key, one randomly chooses two affine transformations $\mathcal{T} : \mathbb{F}_q^n \to \mathbb{F}_q^{n-a}$ and $\mathcal{S} : \mathbb{F}_q^{n+v} \to \mathbb{F}_q^{n+v}$ of maximal rank.

Therefore, the public key of the scheme is the quadratic map

$$\mathcal{P} = \mathcal{T} \circ \bar{\mathcal{F}} \circ \mathcal{S} = \mathcal{T} \circ \phi \circ \mathcal{F} \circ (\phi^{-1} \times id_v) \circ \mathcal{S} : \mathbb{F}_q^{n+v} \to \mathbb{F}_q^{n-a}.$$

The *private key* of the HFEv- scheme consists of the three maps $\mathcal{T}$, $\mathcal{F}$ and $\mathcal{S}$, the *public key* is given by $\mathcal{P}$.

Signature Generation. Let $d \in \{0,1\}^*$ be a document to be signed. The process of signature generation works as follows:

1. Use a hash function $\mathcal{H} : \{0,1\}^* \to \mathbb{F}_q^{n-a}$ to compute the hash value $\mathbf{h} = (h_1, \ldots, h_{n-a}) \in \mathbb{F}_q^{n-a}$ of the document d.
2. Compute a pre-image $\mathbf{x} \in \mathbb{F}_q^n$ of $\mathbf{h}$ under the affine transformation $\mathcal{T} : \mathbb{F}_q^n \to \mathbb{F}_q^{n-a}$ and lift it to the extension field, obtaining $X = \phi^{-1}(\mathbf{x}) \in \mathbb{F}_{q^n}$.
3. Choose random values for the Vinegar variables $(y_{n+1}, \ldots, y_{n+v}) \in \mathbb{F}_q^v$ and substitute them into the central map $\mathcal{F}$ to obtain a univariate polynomial map $\mathcal{F}_V(Z) : \mathbb{F}_{q^n} \to \mathbb{F}_{q^n}$.
4. Find a solution to the equation $\mathcal{F}_V(Z) = X$ using Berlekamps algorithm. If this equation has no solution, go back to step 2, and randomly choose another vector $(y_{n+1}, \ldots, y_{n+v}) \in \mathbb{F}_q^v$ until we can find a solution. Let $Y \in \mathbb{F}_{q^n}$ be one of the solutions and set $\mathbf{y}' = \phi(Y) = (y_1, \cdots, y_n) \in \mathbb{F}_q^n$. Append the Vinegar variables of step 2 to it, obtaining $\mathbf{y} = (\mathbf{y}', y_{n+1}, \cdots, y_{n+v}) \in \mathbb{F}_q^{n+v}$.
5. Compute $\mathbf{z} = \mathcal{S}^{-1}(\mathbf{y})$. Then $\mathbf{z} \in \mathbb{F}_q^{n+v}$ is the signature of the document d.

Signature Verification. To check if $\mathbf{z} \in \mathbb{F}_q^{n+v}$ is indeed a valid signature for the document $d \in \{0,1\}^*$, the receiver simply computes

- $\mathbf{h} = \mathcal{H}(d) \in \mathbb{F}_q^{n-a}$ and
- $\mathbf{h}' = \mathcal{P}(\mathbf{z})$.

If $\mathbf{h}' = \mathbf{h}$ holds, the signature is accepted, otherwise it is rejected.

Efficiency. The most costly step during the signature generation of HFEv- is the solution of the polynomial equation $\mathcal{F}_V(Z) = X$ by Berlekamps algorithm. The complexity of this algorithm is given as

$$O(D^\omega + Dn(log(D)log(log(D))log(q))),$$

(see [15]) where D is the degree of the HFE polynomial, n is the degree of the extension field $\mathbb{F}_{q^n}$ and q is the cardinality of the base field.

A higher value of D therefore slows down the signature generation process of HFEv- drastically.

One important strategy for the design of HFE based signature schemes was therefore to choose D small and to compensate for this fact by increasing a and v.

2.2   Previous Attacks on HFE

Historically, the most efficient attacks against signature schemes of the HFE type are the direct and the MinRank attack. With regard to the direct attack, it was discovered that the public systems of HFE and its variants can be solved much more efficiently than random systems. This phenomenon was analyzed in a series of papers [11,12,16]. The authors of these papers found that the degree of regularity of a public HFEv- system is bounded from above by

$$\begin{cases} \frac{(q-1)(d+v+a-1)}{2} + 2 & \text{if } q \text{ is even and } d+a \text{ is odd}, \\ \frac{(q-1)(d+v+a)}{2} + 2 & \text{otherwise}. \end{cases}$$

Regarding attacks of the MinRank type, many researchers considered the so called min-Q-rank of the HFE system, which can be seen as the rank of the quadratic form $\mathcal{P}$ lifted to the extension field $\mathbb{F}_{q^n}$. Similar to the degree of regularity, the min-Q-rank of the HFE system is bounded by the HFE parameters.

However, in our attack, we don't consider the min-Q-rank of the HFE system, but perform a MinRank attack over the base field $\mathbb{F}_q$. While it is clear that the complexity of a direct attack on a system of the HFE type is exponential in d, a and v [10], our attack shows that this is not the case for MinRank. We take a closer look at the MinRank problem and different strategies to solve it in Sect. 3.2.

3   Preliminaries

For simplification, in the following sections of this paper, we assume that $\mathcal{T}$ and $\mathcal{S}$ are linear transformations and q is an odd prime. Our attack method can be easily extended to the case of affine maps $\mathcal{T}$ and $\mathcal{S}$ and even characteristic.

3.1   Equivalent Keys

An important notion in this paper is that of equivalent keys. For a multivariate public key cryptosystem, the concept of equivalent keys is defined as follows.

Definition 1. *Let $((\mathcal{T},\mathcal{F},\mathcal{S}),\mathcal{P})$ be a key pair of a multivariate public key crypto- system. A tuple $(\mathcal{T}',\mathcal{F}',\mathcal{S}')$ is called an equivalent private key if and only if*

$$\mathcal{P} = \mathcal{T} \circ \mathcal{F} \circ \mathcal{S} = \mathcal{T}' \circ \mathcal{F}' \circ \mathcal{S}'$$

and $\mathcal{F}'$ is a valid central map of the cryptosystem, i.e. $\mathcal{F}'$ has the same algebraic structure as $\mathcal{F}$.

We have

Theorem 1 (Theorem 4.13 in [28]). *Let $\mathcal{P}$ be a public key of the HFEv-scheme over $\mathbb{F}_q$. Let v be the number of Vinegar variables, a be the number of Minus equations and n be the degree of the field extension. Then there exist*

$$nq^{a+2n+vn}(q^n - 1)^2 \prod_{i=0}^{v-1}(q^v - q^i) \prod_{i=n-a-1}^{n-1}(q^n - q^i)$$

equivalent private keys for the public key $\mathcal{P}$.

Given an HFEv- public key $\mathcal{P}$, our attack finds one of the equivalent private keys.

3.2 The MinRank Problem

The search version of the MinRank problem is defined as follows.

Definition 2 (MinRank problem). *Given a positive number r and n_x matrices $M_1, M_2, \ldots, M_{n_x}$ with m rows and n columns over a field $\mathbb{F}_q$, find a nonzero vector $(x_1, x_2, \ldots, x_{n_x}) \in \mathbb{F}_q^{n_x}$, such that the linear combination $M = \sum_{i=1}^{n_x} x_i M_i$ has rank at most r.*

The MinRank problem is an NP-complete problem [5]. The main methods for solving the MinRank problem are linear algebra search [21], Kipnis-Shamir modeling [23], minors modeling [19] and support minors modeling [1].

In this paper, we mostly consider the minors modeling of the MinRank attack. The main idea of this modeling is that the $r + 1$ minors of the low rank matrix M are all zero. Since there are $\binom{n}{r+1}$ minors and n_x variables $x_1, \ldots, x_{n_x}$, this gives us a highly overdetermined system of equations of degree $r + 1$, which can be solved by e.g. Gröbner basis techniques. The complexity of this process can be estimated as

$$\text{complexity}_{\text{minors modelling}} = \mathcal{O}\left(\binom{n+r+1}{r+1}^{\omega}\right),$$

where, for previous attacks against HFEv-, r was given as $d + v + a$. We show, how this value can be dropped to d.

In Sect. 5 of this paper we show how our attack might be speed up using the support minors modeling approach. However, since we don't have a full theoretical understanding of the outcome of our experiments yet, we leave a complete analysis of our attack using support minors modeling as a future work.

3.3 Matrix Representation of HFEv- Keys

Similar to [3], we represent the HFEv- central map in matrix form.

Proposition 1. *Let*

$$
F^{*0} = \begin{pmatrix}
\alpha_{00} & \alpha_{01} & \cdots & \alpha_{0,n-1} & \gamma_{00} & \gamma_{01} & \cdots & \gamma_{0,v-1} \\
\alpha_{10} & \alpha_{11} & \cdots & \alpha_{1,n-1} & \gamma_{10} & \gamma_{11} & \cdots & \gamma_{1,v-1} \\
\vdots & \vdots & \ddots & \vdots & \vdots & \vdots & \ddots & \vdots \\
\alpha_{n-1,0} & \alpha_{n-1,1} & \cdots & \alpha_{n-1,n-1} & \gamma_{n-1,0} & \gamma_{n-1,1} & \cdots & \gamma_{n-1,v-1} \\
\beta_{00} & \beta_{01} & \cdots & \beta_{0,n-1} & \delta_{00} & \delta_{01} & \cdots & \delta_{0,v-1} \\
\beta_{10} & \beta_{11} & \cdots & \beta_{1,n-1} & \delta_{10} & \delta_{11} & \cdots & \delta_{1,v-1} \\
\vdots & \vdots & \ddots & \vdots & \vdots & \vdots & \ddots & \vdots \\
\beta_{v-1,0} & \beta_{v-1,1} & \cdots & \beta_{v-1,n-1} & \delta_{v-1,0} & \delta_{v-1,1} & \cdots & \delta_{v-1,v-1}
\end{pmatrix}
$$

be an $(n+v) \times (n+v)$ *matrix over the field* $\mathbb{F}_{q^n}$ *and*

$$
F(X, x_1, \ldots, x_v) = (X, X^q, \ldots, X^{q^{n-1}}, x_1, \ldots, x_v) F^{*0} (X, X^q, \ldots, X^{q^{n-1}}, x_1, \ldots, x_v)^t
$$

be a polynomial in the quotient ring $\mathbb{F}_{q^n}[X, x_1, \ldots, x_v]/\langle x_1^q - x_1, \ldots, x_v^q - x_v \rangle$. *Then we have for all* $0 \le k < n$

$$
F^{q^k}(X, x_1, \ldots, x_v) = (X, X^q, \ldots, X^{q^{n-1}}, x_1, \ldots, x_v) F^{*k} (X, X^q, \ldots, X^{q^{n-1}}, x_1, \ldots, x_v)^t,
$$

where $F^{*k} \in \mathcal{M}_{(n+v) \times (n+v)}(\mathbb{F}_{q^n})$, *the* (i, j)*-th entry of* F^{*k} *is* $\alpha_{i-k,j-k}^{q^k}$ *for all* $0 \le i, j, k < n$, *the* $(i, n+j)$*-th entry of* F^{*k} *is* $\gamma_{j-k,i}^{q^k}$ *for all* $0 \le j, k < n$, $0 \le i < v$, *the* $(n+i, j)$*-th entry of* F^{*k} *is* $\beta_{i,j-k}^{q^k}$ *for all* $0 \le i < v, 0 \le j, k < n$, *and the* $(n+i, n+j)$*-th entry is* $\delta_{ij}^{q^k}$ *for all* $0 \le i < v, 0 \le j < v, 0 \le k < n$.

Proof. If $k = 0$, we have obviously $F^{q^k}(X, x_1, \cdots, x_v) = F(X, x_1, \cdots, x_v)$. Now we consider the case of $1 \le k < n$. Since $x_i^{q^k} = x_i$ for all $1 \le i \le v$, we have

$$
\begin{aligned}
F^{q^k} &= \sum_{i=0}^{n-1} \sum_{j=0}^{n-1} \alpha_{ij}^{q^k} X^{q^{i+k}+q^{j+k}} + \sum_{i=0}^{v-1} \sum_{j=0}^{n-1} (\beta_{ij}^{q^k} + \gamma_{ji}^{q^k}) x_i X^{q^{j+k}} + \sum_{i=0}^{v-1} \sum_{j=0}^{v-1} \delta_{ij}^{q^k} x_i x_j \\
&= \sum_{i=k}^{n-1+k} \sum_{j=k}^{n-1+k} \alpha_{i-k,j-k}^{q^k} X^{q^i+q^j} + \sum_{i=0}^{v-1} \sum_{j=k}^{n-1+k} (\beta_{i,j-k}^{q^k} + \gamma_{j-k,i}^{q^k}) x_i X^{q^j} + \sum_{i=0}^{v-1} \sum_{j=0}^{v-1} \delta_{ij}^{q^k} x_i x_j
\end{aligned}
$$

Then it can be divided as follows

$$
\begin{aligned}
F^{q^k} = &\sum_{i=k}^{n-1} \left(\sum_{j=k}^{n-1+k} \alpha_{i-k,j-k}^{q^k} X^{q^i+q^j} \right) + \sum_{i=n}^{n-1+k} \left(\sum_{j=k}^{n-1+k} \alpha_{i-k,j-k}^{q^k} X^{q^i+q^j} \right) \\
&+ \sum_{i=0}^{v-1} \sum_{j=k}^{n-1} (\beta_{i,j-k}^{q^k} + \gamma_{j-k,i}^{q^k}) x_i X^{q^j} + \sum_{i=0}^{v-1} \sum_{j=n}^{n-1+k} (\beta_{i,j-k}^{q^k} + \gamma_{j-k,i}^{q^k}) x_i X^{q^j} + \sum_{i=0}^{v-1} \sum_{j=0}^{v-1} \delta_{ij}^{q^k} x_i x_j.
\end{aligned}
$$

That is

$$
\begin{aligned}
F^{q^k} = &\sum_{i=k}^{n-1} \left(\sum_{j=k}^{n-1} \alpha_{i-k,j-k}^{q^k} X^{q^i+q^j} + \sum_{j=n}^{n-1+k} \alpha_{i-k,j-k}^{q^k} X^{q^i+q^j} \right) \\
&+ \sum_{i=n}^{n-1+k} \left(\sum_{j=k}^{n-1} \alpha_{i-k,j-k}^{q^k} X^{q^i+q^j} + \sum_{j=n}^{n-1+k} \alpha_{i-k,j-k}^{q^k} X^{q^i+q^j} \right) \\
&+ \sum_{i=0}^{v-1} \sum_{j=k}^{n-1} (\beta_{i,j-k}^{q^k} + \gamma_{j-k,i}^{q^k}) x_i X^{q^j} + \sum_{i=0}^{v-1} \sum_{j=n}^{n-1+k} (\beta_{i,j-k}^{q^k} + \gamma_{j-k,i}^{q^k}) x_i X^{q^j} + \sum_{i=0}^{v-1} \sum_{j=0}^{v-1} \delta_{ij}^{q^k} x_i x_j.
\end{aligned}
$$

Thus we have

$$
\begin{aligned}
F^{q^k} &= \sum_{i=k}^{n-1}\left(\sum_{j=k}^{n-1}\alpha_{i-k,j-k}^{q^k}X^{q^i+q^j}+\sum_{j=0}^{k-1}\alpha_{i-k,j-k+n}^{q^k}X^{q^i+q^{j+n}}\right)\\
&+\sum_{i=0}^{k-1}\left(\sum_{j=k}^{n-1}\alpha_{i-k+n,j-k}^{q^k}X^{q^{i+n}+q^j}+\sum_{j=0}^{k-1}\alpha_{i-k+n,j-k+n}^{q^k}X^{q^{i+n}+q^{j+n}}\right)\\
&+\sum_{i=0}^{v-1}\sum_{j=k}^{n-1}(\beta_{i,j-k}^{q^k}+\gamma_{j-k,i}^{q^k})x_i X^{q^j}+\sum_{i=0}^{v-1}\sum_{j=0}^{k-1}(\beta_{i,j-k+n}^{q^k}+\gamma_{j-k+n,i}^{q^k})x_i X^{q^{j+n}}+\sum_{i=0}^{v-1}\sum_{j=0}^{v-1}\delta_{ij}^{q^k}x_i x_j.
\end{aligned}
$$

Since $X^{q^n}=X$ we obtain by reducing the index of coefficients modulo n

$$
\begin{aligned}
F^{q^k} &= \sum_{i=k}^{n-1}\left(\sum_{j=k}^{n-1}\alpha_{i-k,j-k}^{q^k}X^{q^i+q^j}+\sum_{j=0}^{k-1}\alpha_{i-k,j-k}^{q^k}X^{q^i+q^j}\right)\\
&+\sum_{i=0}^{k-1}\left(\sum_{j=k}^{n-1}\alpha_{i-k,j-k}^{q^k}X^{q^i+q^j}+\sum_{j=0}^{k-1}\alpha_{i-k,j-k}^{q^k}X^{q^i+q^j}\right)\\
&+\sum_{i=0}^{v-1}\sum_{j=k}^{n-1}(\beta_{i,j-k}^{q^k}+\gamma_{j-k,i}^{q^k})x_i X^{q^j}+\sum_{i=0}^{v-1}\sum_{j=0}^{k-1}(\beta_{i,j-k}^{q^k}+\gamma_{j-k,i}^{q^k})x_i X^{q^j}+\sum_{i=0}^{v-1}\sum_{j=0}^{v-1}\delta_{ij}^{q^k}x_i x_j.
\end{aligned}
$$

Grouping the sums back together, we get

$$
\begin{aligned}
F^{q^k} &= \sum_{i=0}^{n-1}\sum_{j=0}^{n-1}a_{i-k,j-k}^{q^k}X^{q^i+q^j}+\sum_{i=0}^{v-1}\sum_{j=0}^{n-1}(\beta_{i,j-k}^{q^k}+\gamma_{j-k,i}^{q^k})x_i X^{q^j}+\sum_{i=0}^{v-1}\sum_{j=0}^{v-1}\delta_{ij}^{q^k}x_i x_j\\
&= (X,X^q,\cdots,X^{q^{n-1}},x_1,\cdots,x_v)F^{*k}(X,X^q,\cdots,X^{q^{n-1}},x_1,\cdots,x_v)^t,
\end{aligned}
$$

where $F^{*k}\in\mathcal{M}_{(n+v)\times(n+v)}(\mathbb{F}_{q^n})$, the (i,j)-th entry of F^{*k} is $\alpha_{i-k,j-k}^{q^k}$ for all $0\le i,j,k<n$, the $(i,n+j)$-th entry of F^{*k} is $\gamma_{j-k,i}^{q^k}$ for all $0\le j,k<n,0\le i<v$, the $(n+i,j)$-th entry of F^{*k} is $\beta_{i,j-k}^{q^k}$ for all $0\le i<v,0\le j,k<n$, and the $(n+i,n+j)$-th entry is $\delta_{ij}^{q^k}$ for all $0\le i<v,0\le j<v,0\le k<n$. $\square$

Proposition 2 (Proposition 2.1 in [3]). *Let $(\theta_1,\theta_2,\cdots,\theta_n)\in\mathbb{F}_{q^n}^n$ be a vector basis of $\mathbb{F}_{q^n}$ over $\mathbb{F}_q$ and*

$$
M=\begin{pmatrix}
\theta_1 & \theta_1^q & \cdots & \theta_1^{q^{n-1}}\\
\theta_2 & \theta_2^q & \cdots & \theta_2^{q^{n-1}}\\
\vdots & \vdots & \ddots & \vdots\\
\theta_n & \theta_n^q & \cdots & \theta_n^{q^{n-1}}
\end{pmatrix}
$$

be the matrix whose columns are the Frobenius powers of the basis elements. We can express the morphism $\phi:\mathbb{F}_{q^n}\to\mathbb{F}_q^n$ as

$$
V\mapsto(V,V^q,\cdots,V^{q^{n-1}})M^{-1}.
$$

Its inverse $\phi^{-1}:\mathbb{F}_q^n\to\mathbb{F}_{q^n}$ is given as

$$
(v_1,v_2,\cdots,v_n)\mapsto V,
$$

where V is the first component of the vector $(v_1, v_2, \cdots, v_n)M$. More generally, we have

$$(v_1, v_2, \cdots, v_n) \cdot M = (V, V^q, \cdots, V^{q^{n-1}}).$$

In this paper, we choose

$$M = \begin{pmatrix} 1 & 1 & \cdots & 1 \\ \theta & \theta^q & \cdots & \theta^{q^{n-1}} \\ \vdots & \vdots & \ddots & \vdots \\ \theta^{n-1} & (\theta^{n-1})^q & \cdots & (\theta^{n-1})^{q^{n-1}} \end{pmatrix}, \tag{1}$$

where θ is a generator of $\mathbb{F}_{q^n}$. Define

$$\widetilde{M} = \begin{pmatrix} M & 0 \\ 0 & I_v \end{pmatrix} \in \mathcal{M}_{(n+v)\times(n+v)}(\mathbb{F}_{q^n}), \tag{2}$$

where I_v is the $v \times v$ identity matrix. According to Proposition 2, we have

$$(v_1, v_2, \cdots, v_n, x_1, \cdots, x_v) \cdot \widetilde{M} = (V, V^q, \cdots, V^{q^{n-1}}, x_1, \cdots, x_v),$$

where $v_i, x_j \in \mathbb{F}_q, 1 \leq i \leq n, 1 \leq j \leq v$ and $V \in \mathbb{F}_{q^n}$.

Proposition 3. *Let $p_i \in \mathbb{F}_q[x_1, x_2, \cdots, x_{n+v}]$ be the public key polynomials of HFEv- and P_i be the matrix representing the quadratic form of p_i, $0 \leq i < n-a$. Let the central map of HFEv- be*

$$F = (X, X^q, \cdots, X^{q^{n-1}}, x_1, \cdots, x_v)F^{*0}(X, X^q, \cdots, X^{q^{n-1}}, x_1, \cdots, x_v)^t,$$

where $F^{*0} \in \mathcal{M}_{(n+v)\times(n+v)}(\mathbb{F}_{q^n})$. Let $S \in \mathcal{M}_{(n+v)\times(n+v)}(\mathbb{F}_q)$ and $T \in \mathcal{M}_{n\times(n-a)}(\mathbb{F}_q)$ be the matrices representing the linear parts of S and T. Then

$$\left(\widetilde{M}^{-1}S^{-1}P_0(S^{-1})^t(\widetilde{M}^{-1})^t, \cdots, \widetilde{M}^{-1}S^{-1}P_{n-a-1}(S^{-1})^t(\widetilde{M}^{-1})^t\right)$$
$$= \left(F^{*0}, \cdots, F^{*n-1}\right) M^{-1}T \tag{3}$$

Proof. Similar to Lemma 2 in [3].

Denote $U = \widetilde{M}^{-1}S^{-1} \in \mathcal{M}_{(n+v)\times(n+v)}(\mathbb{F}_{q^n})$ and $W = M^{-1}T \in \mathcal{M}_{n\times(n-a)}(\mathbb{F}_{q^n})$, then Eq. (3) can be rewritten as

$$(UP_0U^t, \cdots, UP_{n-a-1}U^t) = \left(F^{*0}, \cdots, F^{*n-1}\right) W. \tag{4}$$

4   Our Key Recovery Attack on HFEv-

In this section we describe our key recovery attack on the HFEv- signature scheme. Our attack is very much motivated by the basic idea that the best attack on any cryptosystem should make full use of information available for attack. In this sense, our attack follows a current trend in the cryptanalysis of multivariate schemes, namely to utilize information provided by certain rows of the public matrices (see also [1,2]).

Let q, n, v, D, a be the parameters of HFEv- and denote $d = \lceil \log_q(D) \rceil$. In this paper, we assume that $0 \leq a < n - 2d - 1$. Note that this condition is fulfilled for all practical parameter sets for HFEv-.[1]

Our attack consists of two steps. In the first step, we recover an equivalent linear transformation S by solving a MinRank problem over the base field $\mathbb{F}_q$. In the second step, we use this equivalent linear map to recover equivalent maps $\mathcal{F}$ and $\mathcal{T}$. By doing so, we obtain an equivalent HFEv- private key which allows us to generate signatures for arbitrary messages.

4.1   Recovering an Equivalent Linear Transformation S

In this subsection, we will present our technique of finding an equivalent map S. We first show that the right hand side of (4) is a matrix of rank $\leq d$ and then show how to recover S by solving a MinRank problem.

Proposition 4. *Let $F^{*0}, \cdots, F^{*n-1}$ and $W = [w_{ij}]$ be the matrices of Eq. (4) and $\mathbf{a}_i$ be the first row of matrix F^{*i} ($i = 0, 1, \ldots, n - 1$). Let Q be the matrix given as $Q = W^t \cdot \begin{pmatrix} \mathbf{a}_0 \\ \vdots \\ \mathbf{a}_{n-1} \end{pmatrix}$. Then the rank of Q is at most $d = \lceil \log_q(D) \rceil$.*

Proof. We have

$$Q = \begin{pmatrix} w_{11}\mathbf{a}_0 + w_{21}\mathbf{a}_1 + \cdots + w_{n1}\mathbf{a}_{n-1} \\ w_{12}\mathbf{a}_0 + w_{22}\mathbf{a}_1 + \cdots + w_{n2}\mathbf{a}_{n-1} \\ \cdots \\ w_{1,n-a}\mathbf{a}_0 + w_{2,n-a}\mathbf{a}_1 + \cdots + w_{n,n-a}\mathbf{a}_{n-1} \end{pmatrix} = W^t \cdot \begin{pmatrix} \mathbf{a}_0 \\ \mathbf{a}_1 \\ \cdots \\ \mathbf{a}_{n-1} \end{pmatrix}$$

Due to the construction of the matrices $F^{*i}(i = 0, 1, \ldots, n - 1)$, we have

$$\begin{pmatrix} \mathbf{a}_0 \\ \mathbf{a}_1 \\ \cdots \\ \mathbf{a}_{n-1} \end{pmatrix} = \begin{pmatrix} A_1 \\ 0 \\ A_2 \end{pmatrix},$$

---

[1] Indeed, $a \geq n - 2d + 1$ implies that the number $n - a$ of equations in the public system is bounded from above by $2d + 1$. Defending the scheme against brute force attacks would therefore require a high value of d which would make the scheme completely impractical.

where A_1 is an $1 \times (n+v)$ matrix and A_2 is a $(d-1) \times (n+v)$ matrix. That is, this matrix has only d non-zero rows, therefore its rank is at most d. Therefore the rank of Q is at most d. □

Theorem 2. *Let $P_0, P_1, \ldots, P_{n-a-1}$ and U be the matrices of Eq. (4), the vector $\mathbf{u} = (u_0, u_1, \cdots, u_{n+v-1})$ be the first row of U and $\mathbf{b}_i = (u_0, u_1, \ldots, u_{n+v-1})P_i$, $(i = 0, 1, \ldots, n-a)$. Define $Z \in \mathcal{M}_{(n-a) \times (n+v)}(\mathbb{F}_{q^n})$ as the matrix whose row vectors are the $\mathbf{b}_i$. Then the rank of Z is at most d.*

Proof. From Eq. (4) and Proposition 4, we know that the rank of ZU^t is not more than d. Thus the rank of Z is at most d. □

Proposition 5. *Let $A = [a_{ij}]$ be an $n \times m$ matrix over $\mathbb{F}_q$, $B = M^{-1}A = [b_{ij}] \in \mathcal{M}_{n \times m}(\mathbb{F}_{q^n})$. Then*

$$b_{ij} = b_{i-1,j}^q, \quad \text{for all } i, j, \text{ with } 0 \leq i < n, 0 \leq j < m.$$

That is, each row is obtained from the previous one using a Frobenius application. Therefore, the whole matrix B is completely defined by any of its rows.

Proof. Let $(\varepsilon_1, \varepsilon_2, \cdots, \varepsilon_n)$ be a dual basis of $(\theta_1, \theta_2, \cdots, \theta_n)$ of $\mathbb{F}_{q^n}$ over $\mathbb{F}_q$, then we have

$$M^{-1} = \begin{pmatrix} \varepsilon_1 & \varepsilon_2 & \cdots \varepsilon_n \\ \varepsilon_1^q & \varepsilon_2^q & \cdots \varepsilon_n^q \\ \vdots & \vdots & \ddots \vdots \\ \varepsilon_1^{q^{n-1}} & \varepsilon_2^{q^{n-1}} & \cdots \varepsilon_n^{q^{n-1}} \end{pmatrix}.$$

Thus $b_{ij} = \sum_{k=0}^{n-1} a_{kj} \varepsilon_{k+1}^{q^i}$ for all $i, j, 0 \leq i < n, 0 \leq j < m$. Since $a_{ij}^q = a_{ij}$ and the linearity of Frobenius, we have

$$b_{i-1,j}^q = \left(\sum_{k=0}^{n-1} a_{kj} \varepsilon_{k+1}^{q^{i-1}} \right)^q = \sum_{k=0}^{n-1} a_{kj}^q (\varepsilon_{k+1}^{q^{i-1}})^q = \sum_{k=0}^{n-1} a_{kj} \varepsilon_{k+1}^{q^i} = b_{ij}$$

for all $i, j, 0 < i \leq n, 0 \leq j < m$. □

Proposition 5 implies that we only need to find one row of matrix $U = \widetilde{M}^{-1}S^{-1}$ to recover the first n rows of U. Let $u_0, u_1, \cdots, u_{n+v-1}$ be the first row of U. We assume that $u_0, u_1, \cdots, u_{n+v-1}$ are unknowns. Since we need to find only one of the equivalent HFEv- private keys, we can fix $u_0 = 1$ [22]. Since the rank of Z is at most d, we can find the u_i $(i = 1, \ldots, n+v-1)$ by solving a MinRank Problem over the base field. This can be done by using any of the methods presented in Sect. 3. Our method to recover S can be summarized as shown in Algorithm 1.

Algorithm 1. Recovering an Equivalent Linear Transformation S

Input: HFEv- parameters (q, n, v, D, a), matrices $(P_0, \cdots, P_{n-a-1})$ representing the quadratic forms of the public key polynomials, matrix $\widetilde{M}$ (see Eq. (2)).

Output: Equivalent linear transformation S.

1. Set $\mathbf{b}_i = (1, u_1, \cdots, u_{n+v-1})P_i$, $0 \leq i < n - a$, where $(u_1, \cdots, u_{n+v-1})$ are unknowns.

2. Construct a matrix Z whose row vectors are $\mathbf{b}_i$, $0 \leq i < n - a$. According to Theorem 2, the rank of Z is at most d.

3. Solve the MinRank Problem with matrix Z using one of the methods described in Section 3. Denote the solution by $u_0, u_1, \cdots, u_{n+v-1}$.

4. Set $U = \begin{pmatrix} u_0 & u_1 & \cdots & u_{n+v-1} \\ u_0^q & u_1^q & \cdots & u_{n+v-1}^q \\ \vdots & \vdots & \ddots & \vdots \\ u_0^{q^{n-1}} & u_1^{q^{n-1}} & \cdots & u_{n+v-1}^{q^{n-1}} \\ r_{00} & r_{01} & \cdots & r_{0,n+v-1} \\ \vdots & \vdots & \ddots & \vdots \\ r_{v-1,0} & r_{v-1,1} & \cdots & r_{v-1,n+v-1} \end{pmatrix}$, where $r_{ij}, 0 \leq i < v, 0 \leq j < n + v$

   are randomly chosen from the finite field $\mathbb{F}_q$ such that U is invertible.

5. Compute $S' = (\widetilde{M}U)^{-1}$.

6. Return S'.

4.2   Recovering Equivalent Maps $\mathcal{F}$ and $\mathcal{T}$

In this subsection we show how, having found an equivalent linear transformation $\mathcal{S}$, we can recover equivalent maps $\mathcal{F}$ and $\mathcal{T}$ by solving several systems of (non)linear equations.

Proposition 6. *Let (q, n, v, D, a) be the parameters of HFEv-, P_i $(0 \leq i < n - a)$, $M, U, W, F^{*j} (0 \leq j < n)$ be the matrices of Eq. (4). We set $d = \lceil \log_2 D \rceil$. Assume that U is known, then F^{*0} can be recovered by solving a linear system with $n - a - 1$ variables, $(d + a) \cdot (n + v)$ additional linear equations in at most $d + v$ variables, and $\binom{v+1}{2}$ univariate polynomial equations of degree q^d.*

Proof. From Eq. (4) we know that $W = M^{-1}T \in \mathcal{M}_{n \times (n-a)}(\mathbb{F}_{q^n})$. Let $W = \begin{pmatrix} W_1 \\ W_2 \end{pmatrix}$, where $W_1 \in \mathcal{M}_{a \times (n-a)}(\mathbb{F}_{q^n})$ and $W_2 \in \mathcal{M}_{(n-a) \times (n-a)}(\mathbb{F}_{q^n})$. Since M is invertible and the entries of T are randomly chosen from $\mathbb{F}_q$, the probability of W_2 being singular is $1 - \prod\limits_{i=1}^{n-a} (1 - \frac{1}{q^i})$. According to Theorem 1, there are at least q^n equivalent maps T, thus the probability that all matrices W_2 associated to the equivalent maps T are singular is approximately $(1 - \prod\limits_{i=1}^{n-a} (1 - \frac{1}{q^i}))^{q^n}$. Therefore we find an invertible matrix W_2 with overwhelming probability. We multiply both sides of Eq. (4) by W_2^{-1}, obtaining

$$\left(U P_0 U^t, \cdots, U P_{n-a-1} U^t \right) W_2^{-1} = \left(F^{*0}, \cdots, F^{*n-1} \right) \begin{pmatrix} W_1 W_2^{-1} \\ I_{n-a} \end{pmatrix}, \qquad (5)$$

where I_{n-a} is the $(n-a) \times (n-a)$ identity matrix. Let $(\widetilde{w}_0, \widetilde{w}_1, \ldots, \widetilde{w}_{n-a-1})$ be the first column of W_2^{-1} and $(\widetilde{l}_0, \widetilde{l}_1, \ldots, \widetilde{l}_{a-1}, 1, 0, \ldots, 0)$ be the first column of $\begin{pmatrix} W_1 W_2^{-1} \\ I_{n-a} \end{pmatrix}$, then Eq. (5) yields

$$\sum_{k=0}^{n-a-1} \widetilde{w}_k U P_k U^t = \sum_{i=0}^{a-1} \widetilde{l}_i F^{*k} + F^{*a}.$$

We multiply both sides by $\widetilde{l}_0^{-1}$, obtaining

$$\sum_{k=0}^{n-a-1} \widetilde{l}_0^{-1} \widetilde{w}_k U P_k U^t = F^{*0} + \sum_{i=1}^{a-1} \widetilde{l}_0^{-1} \widetilde{l}_i F^{*i} + \widetilde{l}_0^{-1} F^{*a}.$$

Denoting $w_k = \widetilde{l}_0^{-1} \widetilde{w}_k, (k = 0, 1, \cdots, n-a-1)$, and $l_i = \widetilde{l}_0^{-1} \widetilde{l}_i, (i = 1, 2, \cdots, a-1)$, $l_a = \widetilde{l}_0^{-1}$ yields

$$\sum_{k=0}^{n-a-1} w_k U P_k U^t = \sum_{i=1}^{a} l_i F^{*i} + F^{*0}. \qquad (6)$$

Note that $\sum_{i=1}^{a} l_i F^{*i} + F^{*0} = \begin{pmatrix} F_0' & 0 & F_1' \\ 0 & 0 & 0 \\ F_1'^t & 0 & F_2' \end{pmatrix} \in \mathcal{M}_{(n+v) \times (n+v)}(\mathbb{F}_{q^n})$, where $F_0' = [f_{ij}']$ is a $(d+a) \times (d+a)$ diagonal band symmetric matrix of width $2d-1$, that is $f_{ij}' = 0$, if $|i-j| \geq d$, $F_1' \in \mathcal{M}_{(d+a) \times v}(\mathbb{F}_{q^n})$, $F_1'^t \in \mathcal{M}_{v \times (d+a)}(\mathbb{F}_{q^n})$ is the transpose of F_1', $F_2' \in \mathcal{M}_{v \times v}(\mathbb{F}_{q^n})$ is a symmetric matrix .

Assume that $w_0, w_1, \ldots, w_{n-a-1}$ are unknowns. Since we need to find only one of the equivalent HFEv- private keys, we can fix $w_0 = 1$ [28]. Due to the fact that U is known and the special structure of the matrix $\sum_{i=1}^{a} l_i F^{*i} + F^{*0}$, we obtain from Eq. (6) $d(n - a - d)$ linear equations in the $n - a - 1$ variables $w_1, w_2, \cdots, w_{n-a-1}$. Since $0 < a < n - 2d - 1$, we have $d(n-a-d) \geq n - a - 1$. Therefore, by solving these linear equations, we get a solution $(w_0', w_1', w_2', \cdots, w_{n-a-1}')$ with $w_0' = 1$. Thus Eq. (6) can be rewritten as

$$\sum_{k=0}^{n-a-1} w_k' U P_k U^t = \sum_{i=1}^{a} l_i F^{*i} + F^{*0}. \qquad (7)$$

Now we will find $l_1, \cdots, l_a$ and F^{*0} from Eq. (7). We know that F^{*0} has the form

$$F^{*0} = \begin{pmatrix} F_0 & 0 & F_1 \\ 0 & 0 & 0 \\ F_1^t & 0 & F_2 \end{pmatrix},$$

where $F_0 = [\alpha_{ij}] \in \mathcal{M}_{d \times d}(\mathbb{F}_{q^n})$ is a symmetric matrix, $F_1 = [\gamma_{ij}] \in \mathcal{M}_{d \times v}(\mathbb{F}_{q^n})$, $F_1^t \in \mathcal{M}_{v \times d}(\mathbb{F}_{q^n})$ is the transpose of F_1 and $F_2 = [\delta_{ij}] \in \mathcal{M}_{v \times v}(\mathbb{F}_{q^n})$ is a symmetric matrix . According to Proposition 1 we can represent F^{*k} ($1 \leq k \leq n-1$) by the entries of F^{*0}.

Assume that $l_1, \ldots, l_a$, α_{ij} ($0 \leq i \leq j < d$), γ_{ij} ($0 \leq i < d, 0 \leq j < v$), δ_{ij} ($0 \leq i \leq j < v$) are unknowns. Then we can recover F^{*0} as follows.

- From the first row of matrix Eq. (7), we can find a linear system in the variables α_{0j} ($0 \leq j < d$) and γ_{0j} ($0 \leq j < v$) of the form

$$\alpha_{00} + \theta_{00} = 0, \cdots, \alpha_{0,d-1} + \theta_{0,d-1} = 0, \gamma_{00} + \theta_{0,d} = 0, \cdots, \gamma_{0,v-1} + \theta_{0,d+v-1} = 0.$$

  Thus we can obtain the first row of F^{*0} by solving this linear system.
- Once the first row of F^{*0} is known, we can obtain from the second row of matrix Eq. (7) a linear system in the variables l_1 and α_{1j} ($1 \leq j < d$) and γ_{1j} ($0 \leq j < v$). By solving this linear system we can obtain the second row of F^{*0} and l_1.
- Similarly, if $a \leq d$, we can obtain $l_1, \cdots, l_a$, F_0 and F_1 using the first d rows of matrix Eq. (7). If $a > d$, we can obtain $l_1, \cdots, l_d$, F_0 and F_1 by using the first d rows of matrix Eq. (7) and l_{d+k} ($1 \leq k \leq a - d$) by using the $(d+k)$-th row of matrix Eq. (7). Thus we obtain $l_1, \cdots, l_a$, F_0 and F_1.
- Once $l_1, \cdots, l_a$, F_0 and F_1 are known, we get from the last v rows of matrix Eq. (7), $\binom{v+1}{2}$ univariate polynomial equations of the form

$$\sum_{k=0}^{d} \lambda_{ijk} \delta_{ij}^{q^k} + \eta_{ij} = 0,$$

  where $\lambda_{ijk}, \eta_{ij} \in \mathbb{F}_{q^n}, 0 \leq i \leq j < v$. Solving these equations we obtain δ_{ij} and then recover F^{*0}.
- Once F^{*0} is known, we can obtain an equivalent central map as

$$F'(X, x_1, \ldots, x_v)$$
$$= (X, X^q, \cdots, X^{q^{n-1}}, x_1, \cdots, x_v) F^{*0}(X, X^q, \cdots, X^{q^{n-1}}, x_1, \cdots, x_v)^t.$$

$\square$

Proposition 7. *Let (q, n, v, D, a) be the parameters of HFEv-, P_i ($0 \leq i < n-a$), S, T, M, F^{*j} ($0 \leq j < n$) be the matrices of Eq. (3). Assume that $S, P_i (0 \leq i < n-a), M, F^{*j}(0 \leq j < n)$ are known, then T can be recovered by solving $n-a$ linear systems in n variables.*

Proof. Equation (3) can be rewritten as

$$(P_0, \cdots, P_{n-a}) = (SMF^{*0}M^t S^t, \cdots, SMF^{*n-1}M^t S^t) M^{-1}T. \qquad (8)$$

Let $(t_{1k}, t_{2k}, \cdots, t_{nk})$ be the entries of the k-th ($k = 1, 2, \cdots, n-a$) column of T. Since S, P_i ($0 \leq i < n-a$), $M, F^{*j}(0 \leq j < n)$ are known, we obtain from Eq. (8) a linear system with $\frac{n(n+1)}{2}$ equations in the n variables $(t_{1k}, t_{2k}, \cdots, t_{nk})$ for all ($k = 1, 2, \cdots, n-a$). We can recover T by solving $(n-a)$ of these linear systems. $\square$

The process of recovering the maps $\mathcal{F}$ and $\mathcal{T}$ of our equivalent HFEv- key is summarized in Algorithm 2 .

Algorithm 2. Recovering Equivalent Maps $\mathcal{F}$ and $\mathcal{T}$

Input: HFEv- parameters (q, n, v, D, a), Frobenius matrix M (see (1)), matrices $(P_0, \cdots, P_{n-a-1})$ representing the quadratic forms of the public key polynomials, recovered linear map S.

Output: Equivalent private maps F and T.

1. Let $w_0, w_1, \cdots, w_{n-a-1}$ be unknowns and $w_0 = 1$. Get a linear system with $d(n - d - a)$ equations in the $n - a - 1$ variables $w_i, (1 \le i < n - a - 1)$ from matrix Eq. (6). as shown in the proof of Proposition 6. By solving this linear system we obtain a solution $w'_0, w'_1, \cdots, w'_{n-a-1}$ with $w'_0 = 1$.
2. Let $l_1, \cdots, l_a$ and the nonzero entries of F^{*0} be unknowns in matrix Eq. (7). We get $(d+a) \cdot (n+v)$ bilinear equations from the first $d+a$ rows of matrix Eq. (7) and $\binom{v+1}{2}$ univariate polynomial equations from the last v rows of matrix Eq. (7). By solving these linear systems and univariate polynomial equations we recover F^{*0} (see Proposition 6). Then we can obtain an equivalent central map as

$$F' = (X, X^q, \cdots, X^{q^{n-1}}, x_1, \cdots, x_v) F^{*0} (X, X^q, \cdots, X^{q^{n-1}}, x_1, \cdots, x_v)^t.$$

3. Compute F^{*k} $1 \le k < n$ according to Proposition 1.
4. Let $(t_{1k}, t_{2k}, \cdots, t_{nk})$ be the (unknown) entries of the k-th $(k = 1, 2, \cdots, n - r)$ column of T. Get $n - r$ linear systems from matrix Eq. (8) as shown in Proposition 7. By solving these linear systems we can recover an equivalent map T.
5. Return F', T.

4.3   Complexity of the Attack

The most complex step of our attack is step 3 of Algorithm 1. That is the step of solving the MinRank problem on the matrix Z, which has rank at most d. For this step, we can use the methods discussed in Sect. 3.2, in particular the minors modeling or the support minors modeling.

If we solve the MinRank problem using minors modeling, the degree of regularity of solving the public system using the F4 algorithm is given as $d + 1$ (c.f. [3]). Therefore, the complexity of our attack using minors modeling is

$$\mathcal{O}\left(\binom{n + v + d + 1}{d + 1}^{\omega} \right),$$

where $2 < \omega \le 3$ is the linear algebra constant.

4.4 Discussion

The complexity of our attack is independent of the number a of Minus Equations and polynomial both in the parameter n and the number v of Vinegar variables. So, for a fixed parameter D, we obtain a polynomial time attack on all HFE signature variants. Therefore, the only way of enhancing the security of the HFEv- scheme is by increasing the parameter d (i.e. the degree D of the HFE polynomial). However, during the signature generation process, we have to invert the HFE polynomial using for example Berlekamps algorithm. Since the complexity of this algorithm grows with D^ω or $2^{d\omega}$, this slows down the scheme drastically.

Our attack therefore raises the question if it is possible at all to construct a secure and efficient signature scheme on the basis of the HFE cryptosystem. An alternative might be to use polynomials of degree >2 (see for example [24]).

5 Possible Speed up Using Support Minus Modeling

In [1] Bardet et al. proposed a new modeling for the MinRank attack called support minors modeling. The main idea of this modeling is to write the low rank matrix M as a product $M = AC$, where A is an $m \times r$ matrix and C is an $r \times n$ matrix. For $i = 1, 2, \ldots, m$ we define matrices of the form $\widetilde{C_i} = \begin{pmatrix} \mathbf{r}_i \\ C \end{pmatrix}$, where $\mathbf{r}_i$ is the i-th row of M. Since $\mathbf{r}_i$ lies in the space spanned by the rows of C, the rank of the matrix $\widetilde{C_i}$ $(i = 1, 2, \ldots, m)$ is at most r. This implies that all $(r+1) \times (r+1)$ minors of the matrices $\widetilde{C_i}$ $(i = 1, 2, \ldots, m)$ are 0. We view the $r \times r$ minors of the matrix C as new variables which are called kernel variables and are denoted as $y_1, y_2, \ldots, y_{n_y}$, where $n_y = \binom{n}{r}$. The $(r+1) \times (r+1)$ minors of the matrices $\widetilde{C_i}$ are therefore given as bilinear equations in the variables $x_1, \ldots, x_{n_x}$ and $y_1, \ldots, y_{n_y}$. Altogether, we obtain $m\binom{n}{r+1}$ of these bilinear equations. The total number of monomials of degree 2 in these bilinear equations is at most $n_x \binom{n}{r}$. If

$$m\binom{n}{r+1} \geq n_x \binom{n}{r} - 1,$$

holds, we can solve this system of bilinear equations using relinearization.

In practical applications, we can assume that C has the form (I_r, C_0), where I_r is an $r \times r$ identity matrix and C_0 is an $r \times (n-r)$ matrix. Moreover, instead of using all $r \times r$ minors of the matrix C as variables, we choose a positive integer $n' \leq n$ such that

$$m\binom{n'}{r+1} \geq n_x \binom{n'}{r} - 1 \tag{9}$$

holds and restrict the computation of minors to the first n' rows of the matrices $\tilde{C}_i$.

If the MinRank problem has only one solution, the resulting linear system is sparse, and we can solve it using the Wiedemann algorithm. The complexity of solving this linear system is

$$\mathcal{O}\left(\left(n_x\binom{n'}{r}\right)^2 \cdot n_x(r+1)\right)$$

field operations. If the MinRank problem has no unique solution and $\mathbb{F}_q$ is a small finite field, we can guess the values of some variables such that the resulting linear system has a unique solution, and then solve it using the Wiedemann algorithm. Otherwise, we solve the bilinear system using a Gröbner basis algorithm such as F_4 or F_5 [17].

When applying the support minors modeling to our attack, we obtain an over-determined bilinear system of $n_x + n_y$ variables and $\frac{(n_x+n_y)(n_x+n_y+1)}{2}$ equations, where $n_x = n + v$ and $n_y = \binom{n'}{d}$, $n' = \lceil\frac{(n-a)(d+1)}{n+v}\rceil + d + 1$, $n' < 2d + 2$. This bilinear system has at least n solutions. In fact, if $(u_0, u_1, \ldots, u_{n+v-1})$ is a solution of this bilinear system, $(u_0^{q^{i-1}}, u_1^{q^{i-1}}, \ldots, u_{n+v-1}^{q^{i-1}})$ for all $1 \leq i \leq n$ are also solutions of the bilinear system (see [22] for more details). Therefore, we don't longer have a unique solution as in the case of e.g. Rainbow, which makes the use of the Wiedemann algorithm inefficient. Thus we use a Gröbner basis technique such as the F_4 or F_5 algorithm to solve the system instead of using the relinearization method and Wiedemann.

To estimate the complexity of our attack using the support minors modeling, we carried out a large number of experiments using the F_4 algorithm included in MAGMA. For these experiments, we created HFEv- public keys over base fields of size $q \in \{2, 3, 5, 7\}$ using the HFEv- parameters $n \in \{20, 30, 40\}$, $a \in \{0, 2, 4\}$, $v \in \{0, 2, 4, 6\}$ and $d \in \{4, 5, 6\}$. We applied our attack on these instances solving the MinRank problem for the matrix Z with target rank d using the support minors modeling. The resulting bilinear system was solved using the F_4 algorithm included in MAGMA. We found that, independently of the HFEv- parameters used in the experiments, the first degree fall occurs at degree 3. Therefore we come up with the following

Conjecture: Independently of the HFEv- parameters, the bilinear systems obtained by our attack and the support minors modeling, can be solved at degree 3.

However, so far, we do not have theoretical arguments for the correctness of our conjecture and therefore leave a proof of the conjecture as future work.

Since the total number of monomials in the bilinear system generated by the support minors modeling is $n_x n_y + n_x + n_y + 1$, the total number of monomials of degree at most 3 is given as $\mathcal{O}(n_x^2 n_y + n_x n_y^2)$. Thus, assuming the correctness of our conjecture, the complexity of our attack on HFEv- using support minors modeling is $\mathcal{O}\left(n_x^2 n_y + n_x n_y^2\right)^\omega$ or $\mathcal{O}\left((n+v)^2\binom{2d+2}{d} + (n+v)\binom{2d+2}{d}^2\right)^\omega$. Here, $2 < \omega \leq 3$ is again the linear algebra constant. However we note again that this formula only holds assuming the correctness of our conjecture about the first fall degree.

6   Application to GeMSS

GeMSS is an HFEv- type signature scheme which is one of the alternative candidates in the third round of the NIST Post Quantum Crypto Standardization Project [8]. The attack complexity on GeMSS using our key recovery attack method can be estimated as shown in Table 1. The table shows:

Table 1. Complexity of our Attack on GeMMS (# of gates)

NIST security category		parameters (q, n, v, D, a)	required security level	our attack using	
				minors modeling	support minors modeling
I	GeMSS128	(2,174,12,513,12)	143	139	118
	BlueGeMSS128	(2,175,14,129,13)		119	99
	RedGeMSS128	(2,177,15,17,15)		86	72
II	GeMSS192	(2,265,20,513,22)	207	154	120
	BlueGeMSS192	(2,265,23,129,22)		132	101
	RedGeMSS192	(2,266,25,17,23)		95	75
III	GeMSS256	(2,354,33,513,30)	272	166	121
	BlueGeMSS256	(2,358,32,129,34)		141	103
	RedGeMSS256	(2,358,35,17,34)		101	76

1. Especially for the higher security categories (NIST category II and III), the proposed parameters for GeMMS don't reach the required security levels.
2. Speeding up the signature generation process of GeMSS by decreasing D while increasing a and v is, with regard to the security of the scheme, not possible. This forbids the GeMSS variants BlueGeMMS and RedGeMMS.
3. In order to meet NIST security level III (272 gates), we would need an HFE parameter d of at least 20, which corresponds to a degree D of the HFE polynomial of at least $2^{19} + 1 = 524.289$. This would lead to a slow down of the signature generation process by a factor of $1.4 \cdot 10^7$. Therefore, the techniques used in GeMMS don't suffice to reach high levels of security while keeping the scheme efficient.

7   Conclusion

In this paper we proposed a new key recovery attack on the HFEv- signature scheme. While most of the cryptanalysts tried to attack the HFEv- scheme by solving a MinRank attack over the extension field $\mathbb{F}_{q^n}$, our attack works completely over the base field. The complexity of the attack is exponential in the parameter $d = \lceil \log_q(D) \rceil$, but polynomial in n. Therefore, the complexity of our attack behaves asymptotically exactly as the complexity of the signing process of HFEv-. Our attack shows that the Minus modifications does not enhance the security of the HFEv- scheme, while the Vinegar modification only adds a polynomial factor. Therefore, in order to meet the NIST security requirements, a very large value of D is needed. However, this makes the signature generation process of HFEv- very inefficient. We therefore conclude that the currently existing techniques are not sufficient to transform the HFE scheme into a secure and efficient signature scheme.

Acknowledgements. Parts of the work were done while the third author was at Cincinnati. We thank CCB Fintech Co. Ltd for partially sponsoring the work of the first and the last author with No. KT2000040. Furthermore we thank NFS for partially sponsoring this work and the anonymous reviewers of CRYPTO 2021 for their valuable comments which helped to improve the paper.

A Example of the Attack

To illustrate our new attack method, we present a complete key recovery for a toy example of the HFEv- scheme over a small field. Let the parameters of our HFEv-instance be $(q, n, v, D, a) = (7, 7, 2, 14, 2)$. Then we have $d = \lceil \log_q(D) \rceil = 2$. We construct the degree n extension field $\mathbb{F}_{q^n} = \mathbb{F}_q[x]/\langle x^7 + 6x + 4 \rangle$. Let θ be a primitive root of the irreducible polynomial $p(x) = x^7 + 6x + 4$.

We randomly generate central map $F = \theta^{176932} X^{14} + \theta^{461287} X^8 + \theta^{199902} X^2 + (\theta^{270502} x_1 + \theta^{358630} x_2) X + (\theta^{65557} x_1 + \theta^{2597} x_2) X^7 + \theta^{811326} x_1^2 + \theta^{14415} x_1 x_2 + \theta^{151050} x_2^2$. The linear transformations $\mathcal{S}$ and $\mathcal{T}$ are given by the matrices

$$
S = \begin{pmatrix}
3 & 1 & 1 & 6 & 4 & 2 & 0 & 1 & 6 \\
6 & 2 & 4 & 5 & 3 & 3 & 2 & 6 & 0 \\
6 & 1 & 3 & 4 & 4 & 2 & 4 & 5 & 3 \\
0 & 1 & 4 & 6 & 4 & 2 & 2 & 3 & 1 \\
2 & 0 & 0 & 5 & 2 & 4 & 2 & 1 & 3 \\
0 & 5 & 1 & 2 & 4 & 2 & 1 & 4 & 3 \\
3 & 3 & 5 & 0 & 2 & 6 & 4 & 6 & 6 \\
5 & 2 & 0 & 2 & 5 & 6 & 3 & 1 & 2 \\
6 & 2 & 5 & 5 & 5 & 4 & 3 & 6 & 1
\end{pmatrix}
\quad \text{and} \quad
T = \begin{pmatrix}
1 & 4 & 4 & 6 & 5 \\
0 & 6 & 5 & 3 & 2 \\
0 & 2 & 0 & 2 & 2 \\
1 & 3 & 1 & 0 & 1 \\
2 & 4 & 2 & 5 & 3 \\
3 & 4 & 1 & 0 & 6 \\
6 & 5 & 6 & 5 & 0
\end{pmatrix}.
$$

We compute the public key as $\mathcal{P} = \mathcal{T} \circ \mathcal{F} \circ \mathcal{S}$. The quadratic forms representing the public key polynomials are given as

$$
P_0 = \begin{pmatrix}
1 & 2 & 0 & 3 & 3 & 6 & 1 & 3 & 3 \\
2 & 6 & 0 & 4 & 4 & 3 & 4 & 4 & 3 \\
0 & 0 & 3 & 5 & 4 & 4 & 4 & 5 & 3 \\
3 & 4 & 5 & 2 & 1 & 1 & 3 & 2 & 1 \\
3 & 4 & 4 & 1 & 0 & 2 & 1 & 6 & 2 \\
6 & 3 & 4 & 1 & 2 & 5 & 0 & 5 & 1 \\
1 & 4 & 4 & 3 & 1 & 0 & 6 & 0 & 0 \\
3 & 4 & 5 & 2 & 6 & 5 & 0 & 3 & 2 \\
3 & 3 & 3 & 1 & 2 & 1 & 0 & 2 & 1
\end{pmatrix},
P_1 = \begin{pmatrix}
4 & 0 & 3 & 3 & 5 & 6 & 6 & 3 & 2 \\
0 & 3 & 0 & 6 & 1 & 1 & 0 & 4 & 4 \\
3 & 0 & 3 & 3 & 5 & 4 & 5 & 5 & 4 \\
3 & 6 & 3 & 1 & 6 & 6 & 2 & 3 & 5 \\
5 & 1 & 5 & 6 & 1 & 6 & 3 & 6 & 4 \\
6 & 1 & 4 & 6 & 6 & 5 & 3 & 3 & 1 \\
6 & 0 & 5 & 2 & 3 & 3 & 0 & 0 & 5 \\
3 & 4 & 5 & 3 & 6 & 3 & 0 & 2 & 1 \\
2 & 4 & 4 & 5 & 4 & 1 & 5 & 1 & 6
\end{pmatrix},
P_2 = \begin{pmatrix}
3 & 2 & 6 & 4 & 5 & 2 & 6 & 6 & 2 \\
2 & 5 & 1 & 0 & 6 & 4 & 1 & 5 & 4 \\
6 & 1 & 6 & 0 & 0 & 5 & 0 & 3 & 3 \\
4 & 0 & 0 & 5 & 5 & 5 & 5 & 2 & 2 \\
5 & 6 & 0 & 5 & 1 & 2 & 1 & 6 & 0 \\
2 & 4 & 5 & 5 & 2 & 4 & 1 & 5 & 0 \\
6 & 1 & 0 & 5 & 1 & 1 & 4 & 4 & 5 \\
6 & 5 & 3 & 2 & 6 & 5 & 4 & 4 & 4 \\
2 & 4 & 3 & 2 & 0 & 0 & 5 & 4 & 0
\end{pmatrix},
$$

$$
P_3 = \begin{pmatrix}
2 & 6 & 4 & 5 & 4 & 1 & 6 & 0 & 1 \\
6 & 6 & 6 & 1 & 2 & 1 & 0 & 6 & 3 \\
4 & 6 & 2 & 6 & 1 & 5 & 0 & 4 & 6 \\
5 & 1 & 6 & 0 & 0 & 0 & 0 & 3 & 5 \\
4 & 2 & 1 & 0 & 6 & 1 & 6 & 0 & 4 \\
1 & 1 & 5 & 0 & 1 & 2 & 6 & 3 & 5 \\
6 & 0 & 0 & 0 & 6 & 6 & 5 & 6 & 1 \\
0 & 6 & 4 & 3 & 0 & 3 & 6 & 2 & 0 \\
1 & 3 & 6 & 5 & 4 & 5 & 1 & 0 & 1
\end{pmatrix}
P_4 = \begin{pmatrix}
3 & 0 & 5 & 4 & 5 & 6 & 0 & 5 & 2 \\
0 & 3 & 0 & 3 & 3 & 5 & 4 & 2 & 2 \\
5 & 0 & 4 & 2 & 4 & 6 & 1 & 1 & 3 \\
4 & 3 & 2 & 3 & 4 & 3 & 2 & 6 & 1 \\
5 & 3 & 4 & 4 & 1 & 2 & 3 & 3 & 6 \\
6 & 5 & 6 & 3 & 2 & 4 & 0 & 0 & 2 \\
0 & 4 & 1 & 2 & 3 & 0 & 6 & 5 & 1 \\
5 & 2 & 1 & 6 & 3 & 0 & 5 & 5 & 0 \\
2 & 2 & 3 & 1 & 6 & 2 & 1 & 0 & 3
\end{pmatrix},
$$

$$\text{Let } M = \begin{pmatrix} 1 & 1 & 1 & 1 & 1 & 1 & 1 \\ \theta & \theta^7 & \theta^{49} & \theta^{343} & \theta^{2401} & \theta^{16807} & \theta^{117649} \\ \theta^2 & \theta^{14} & \theta^{98} & \theta^{686} & \theta^{4802} & \theta^{33614} & \theta^{235298} \\ \theta^3 & \theta^{21} & \theta^{147} & \theta^{1029} & \theta^{7203} & \theta^{50421} & \theta^{352947} \\ \theta^4 & \theta^{28} & \theta^{196} & \theta^{1372} & \theta^{9604} & \theta^{67228} & \theta^{470596} \\ \theta^5 & \theta^{35} & \theta^{245} & \theta^{1715} & \theta^{12005} & \theta^{84035} & \theta^{588245} \\ \theta^6 & \theta^{42} & \theta^{294} & \theta^{2058} & \theta^{14406} & \theta^{100842} & \theta^{705894} \end{pmatrix} \text{ and } \widetilde{M} = \begin{pmatrix} M & 0 \\ 0 & I_v \end{pmatrix} \text{ In the following}$$

we demonstrate our method to recover the private key from $\mathcal{P}$.

A.1 Recovering $\mathcal{S}$

Let the first row of matrix $U = \widetilde{M}^{-1} S^{-1}$ be $(u_0, u_1, \cdots, u_{n+v-1})$. Fix $u_0 = 1$ and let $u_1, \cdots, u_{n+v-1}$ be unknowns. Set $\mathbf{b}_i = (1, u_1, \cdots, u_{n+v-1}) P_i, i = 0, 1, \cdots, n - a - 1$. Let $\mathbf{b}_i$ be the i-th row of the matrix Z. Then the rank of Z is 2. This implies that all minors of order 3 are 0. Solving the MinRank Problem for matrix Z gives us a solution $\mathbf{u} = (1, \theta^{2689}, \theta^{240750}, \theta^{393451}, \theta^{682468}, \theta^{184068}, \theta^{218176}, \theta^{85224}, \theta^{760002})$. Then we have

$$U = \begin{pmatrix} 1 & \theta^{2689} & \theta^{240750} & \theta^{393451} & \theta^{682468} & \theta^{184068} & \theta^{218176} & \theta^{85224} & \theta^{760002} \\ 1 & \theta^{18823} & \theta^{38166} & \theta^{283531} & \theta^{659566} & \theta^{464934} & \theta^{703690} & \theta^{596568} & \theta^{378762} \\ 1 & \theta^{131761} & \theta^{267162} & \theta^{337633} & \theta^{499252} & \theta^{783912} & \theta^{808120} & \theta^{58266} & \theta^{180708} \\ 1 & \theta^{98785} & \theta^{223050} & \theta^{716347} & \theta^{200596} & \theta^{546132} & \theta^{715588} & \theta^{407862} & \theta^{441414} \\ 1 & \theta^{691495} & \theta^{737808} & \theta^{73177} & \theta^{580630} & \theta^{528756} & \theta^{67864} & \theta^{384408} & \theta^{619272} \\ 1 & \theta^{722755} & \theta^{223404} & \theta^{512239} & \theta^{770242} & \theta^{407124} & \theta^{475048} & \theta^{220230} & \theta^{217194} \\ 1 & \theta^{118033} & \theta^{740286} & \theta^{291505} & \theta^{450442} & \theta^{379242} & \theta^{31168} & \theta^{718068} & \theta^{696816} \\ 1 & 5 & 1 & 0 & 1 & 3 & 0 & 3 & 2 \\ 4 & 6 & 1 & 5 & 4 & 5 & 5 & 6 & 6 \end{pmatrix},$$

where the last v rows of U are randomly chosen from $\mathbb{F}_q$, such that U is invertible. Thus we can recover an equivalent linear transformation $\mathcal{S}$ as

$$S' = U^{-1}\widetilde{M}^{-1} = \begin{pmatrix} 0 & 1 & 1 & 2 & 3 & 6 & 6 & 0 & 6 \\ 1 & 4 & 5 & 3 & 1 & 6 & 0 & 4 & 6 \\ 4 & 5 & 3 & 1 & 5 & 6 & 0 & 6 & 4 \\ 5 & 0 & 1 & 2 & 5 & 6 & 0 & 2 & 0 \\ 2 & 3 & 1 & 3 & 5 & 6 & 0 & 3 & 1 \\ 1 & 6 & 5 & 0 & 4 & 1 & 0 & 4 & 1 \\ 0 & 4 & 6 & 4 & 2 & 2 & 0 & 6 & 2 \\ 2 & 1 & 5 & 2 & 5 & 1 & 2 & 1 & 2 \\ 6 & 0 & 2 & 6 & 4 & 6 & 1 & 5 & 6 \end{pmatrix}.$$

Recovering $\mathcal{F}$ and $\mathcal{T}$. Step 1. Once $\mathcal{S}$ is known, let $w_0, w_1, \cdots, w_{n-a-1}$ be unknowns and $w_0 = 1$. We generate a linear system with $d(n - d - a)$ equations in the $n-a-1$ variables $w_i, (1 \le i < n-a-1)$ using the matrix Eq. (6). By solving this linear system we obtain a solution $(1, \theta^{558954}, \theta^{326166}, \theta^{142979}, \theta^{806014})$.

Step 2. Let $l_1, \cdots, l_a$ and the nonzero entries of F^{*0} be variables in matrix Eq. (7). By using the first $d + a$ rows of matrix Eq. (7) we get $(d + a) \cdot (n + v)$ bilinear equations as follows:

$$\begin{pmatrix} \alpha_{00}+\theta^{599798} & \alpha_{01}+\theta^{499519} & 0 & 0 & 0\ 0\ 0 & \gamma_{00}+\theta^{424284} & \gamma_{01}+\theta^{665059} \\ \alpha_{10}+\theta^{499519} & \alpha_{00}^7 l_1+\alpha_{11}+\theta^{381840} & \alpha_{01}^7 l_1+\theta^{349085} & 0 & 0\ 0\ 0 & \gamma_{00}^7 l_1+\gamma_{10}+\theta^{228693} & \gamma_{01}^7 l_1+\gamma_{11}+\theta^{396254} \\ 0 & \alpha_{10}^7 l_1+\theta^{349085} & \alpha_{00}^{49} l_2+\alpha_{11}^7 l_1+\theta^{622586} & \alpha_{01}^{49} l_2+\theta^{524551}\ 0\ 0\ 0 & \gamma_{00}^{49} l_2+\gamma_{10}^7 l_1+\theta^{475138} & \gamma_{01}^{49} l_2+\gamma_{11}^7 l_1+\theta^{2659} \\ 0 & 0 & \alpha_{10}^{49} l_2+\theta^{524551} & \alpha_{11}^{49} l_2+\theta^{32832}\ 0\ 0\ 0 & \gamma_{10}^{49} l_2+\theta^{9738} & \gamma_{11}^{49} l_2+\theta^{392135} \end{pmatrix}$$
$$= 0_{(d+a)\times(n+v)}.$$

From the first row, we obtain $\alpha_{00} = \theta^{188027}, \alpha_{01} = \theta^{87748}, \gamma_{00} = \theta^{12513}, \gamma_{01} = \theta^{253288}$. Once α_{00}, α_{01} are known, we get from the second row $\alpha_{10} = \theta^{87748}, \alpha_{11} = \theta^{10485}, \gamma_{10} = \theta^{581451}, \gamma_{11} = \theta^{606062}, l_1 = \theta^{146620}$. From the third row we can obtain $l_2 = \theta^{754380}$.

Once l_1, l_2 are known, we get from the last v rows of matrix Eq. (7), $\binom{v+1}{2}$ univariate polynomial equations as follows:

$$\theta^{754380}\delta_{00}^{49} + \theta^{146620}\delta_{00}^{7} + \delta_{00} + \theta^{81317} = 0,$$
$$\theta^{754380}\delta_{01}^{49} + \theta^{146620}\delta_{01}^{7} + \delta_{01} + \theta^{689914} = 0,$$
$$\theta^{754380}\delta_{11}^{49} + \theta^{146620}\delta_{11}^{7} + \delta_{11} + \theta^{162754} = 0.$$

Each of these equations has 49 solutions. We choose one of them as the value of δ_{ij}. Thus we have $\delta_{00} = \theta^{27191}, \delta_{01} = \delta_{10} = \theta^{19044}, \delta_{11} = \theta^{9718}$ and

$$F^{*0} = \begin{pmatrix} \theta^{188027} & \theta^{87748} & 0 & 0 & 0 & 0 & 0 & \theta^{12513} & \theta^{253288} \\ \theta^{87748} & \theta^{10485} & 0 & 0 & 0 & 0 & 0 & \theta^{581451} & \theta^{606062} \\ 0 & 0 & 0 & 0 & 0 & 0 & 0 & 0 & 0 \\ 0 & 0 & 0 & 0 & 0 & 0 & 0 & 0 & 0 \\ 0 & 0 & 0 & 0 & 0 & 0 & 0 & 0 & 0 \\ 0 & 0 & 0 & 0 & 0 & 0 & 0 & 0 & 0 \\ 0 & 0 & 0 & 0 & 0 & 0 & 0 & 0 & 0 \\ \theta^{12513} & \theta^{581451} & 0 & 0 & 0 & 0 & 0 & \theta^{27191} & \theta^{19044} \\ \theta^{253288} & \theta^{606062} & 0 & 0 & 0 & 0 & 0 & \theta^{19044} & \theta^{9718} \end{pmatrix}$$

Therefore we get an equivalent central map as $F' = \theta^{10485}X^{14} + \theta^{362262}X^8 + \theta^{188027}X^2 + (\theta^{287027}x_1 + \theta^{527802}x_2)X + (\theta^{32423}x_1 + \theta^{57034}x_2)X^7 + \theta^{27191}x_1^2 + \theta^{293558}x_1x_2 + \theta^{9718}x_2^2$ for F.

Let $(t_{1k}, t_{2k}, \cdots, t_{nk})$ be entries of the k-th $(k = 1, 2, \cdots, n - a)$ column of T. Get $n - a$ linear systems from matrix Eq. (8) as shown by Proposition 7. By solving these linear systems we can recover a equivalent key of T as follows

$$T' = \begin{pmatrix} 1 & 1 & 6 & 0 & 5 \\ 3 & 3 & 2 & 0 & 2 \\ 1 & 3 & 2 & 5 & 6 \\ 6 & 6 & 6 & 0 & 2 \\ 2 & 2 & 3 & 3 & 6 \\ 2 & 2 & 1 & 0 & 5 \\ 0 & 5 & 1 & 3 & 0 \end{pmatrix}.$$

It is easy to check that $\mathcal{P} = \mathcal{T} \circ \mathcal{F} \circ \mathcal{S} = \mathcal{T}' \circ \mathcal{F}' \circ \mathcal{S}'$. Therefore the adversary can use the three maps $\mathcal{T}', \mathcal{F}'$ and $\mathcal{S}'$ to forge signatures for arbitrary messages.

References

1. Bardet, M., et al.: Improvements of algebraic attacks for solving the rank decoding and MinRank problems. In: Moriai, S., Wang, H. (eds.) ASIACRYPT 2020. LNCS, vol. 12491, pp. 507–536. Springer, Cham (2020). https://doi.org/10.1007/978-3-030-64837-4_17

2. Beullens, W.: Improved Attacks on UOV and Rainbow. IACR eprint 2020/1343 (2020)

3. Bettale, L., Faugere, J.C., Perret, L.: Cryptanalysis of HFE, multi-HFE and variants for odd and even characteristic. Des. Codes Crypt. **69**(1), 1–52 (2013). https://doi.org/10.1007/s10623-012-9617-2

4. Bernstein, D., Buchmann, J., Dahmen, E. (eds.): Post Quantum Cryptography. Springer, Berlin (2009). https://doi.org/10.1007/978-3-540-88702-7_1

5. Buss, J.F., Frandsen, G.S., Shallit, J.O.: The computational complexity of some problems of linear algebra. J. Comput. Syst. Sci. **58**(3), 572–596 (1999)

6. Campagna, M., Chen, K., Dagdelen, Ö., Ding, J., Ferrick, J.K., Gisin, N., et al.: Quantum safe cryptography and security. ETSI White paper 8. https://www.etsi.org/images/files/ETSIWhitePapers/QuantumSafeWhitepaper.pdf (2015)

7. Cartor, R., Gipson, R., Smith-Tone, D., Vates, J.: On the differential security of the HFEv- signature primitive. In: Takagi, T. (ed.) PQCrypto 2016. LNCS, vol. 9606, pp. 162–181. Springer, Cham (2016). https://doi.org/10.1007/978-3-319-29360-8_11

8. Casanova, A., Faugere, J.C., Macario Rat, G., Patarin, J., Perret, L., Ryckegem, J.: GeMSS: a great multivariate short signature (2019). Submission to NIST PQC competition Round-3

9. Courtois, N.T., Daum, M., Felke, P.: On the security of HFE, HFEv- and quartz. In: Desmedt, Y.G. (ed.) PKC 2003. LNCS, vol. 2567, pp. 337–350. Springer, Heidelberg (2003). https://doi.org/10.1007/3-540-36288-6_25

10. Ding, J., Clough, C., Araujo, R.: Inverting square systems algebraically is exponential. Finite Fields Appl. **26**, 32–46 (2014)

11. Ding, J., Hodges, T.J.: Inverting HFE systems is quasi-polynomial for all fields. In: Rogaway, P. (ed.) CRYPTO 2011. LNCS, vol. 6841, pp. 724–742. Springer, Heidelberg (2011). https://doi.org/10.1007/978-3-642-22792-9_41

12. Ding, J., Kleinjung, T.: Degree of regularity for HFE Minus (HFE-). J. Math Ind. **4**, 97–104 (2012)

13. Ding, J., Perlner, R., Petzoldt, A., Smith-Tone, D.: Improved cryptanalysis of HFEv- via projection. In: Lange, T., Steinwandt, R. (eds.) PQCrypto 2018. LNCS, vol. 10786, pp. 375–395. Springer, Cham (2018). https://doi.org/10.1007/978-3-319-79063-3_18

14. Ding, J., Petzoldt, A.: Current state of multivariate cryptography. IEEE Secur. Priv. **15**(4), 28–36 (2017)

15. Ding, J., Petzoldt, A., Schmidt, D.S.: Multivariate Public Key Cryptosystems. AIS, vol. 80. Springer, New York (2020). https://doi.org/10.1007/978-1-0716-0987-3. ISBN 978-1-0716-0985-9

16. Ding, J., Yang, B.-Y.: Degree of regularity for HFEv and HFEv-. In: Gaborit, P. (ed.) PQCrypto 2013. LNCS, vol. 7932, pp. 52–66. Springer, Heidelberg (2013). https://doi.org/10.1007/978-3-642-38616-9_4

17. Faugère, J.C.: A new efficient algorithm for computing Gröbner bases (F4). J. Pure Appl. Algebra **139**(1–3), 61–88 (1999)

18. Faugère, J.C., El Din, M.S., Spaenlehauer, P.J.: Computing loci of rank defects of linear matrices using Gröbner bases and applications to cryptology. In: Proceedings of the International Symposium on Symbolic and Algebraic Computation, pp. 257–264 (2010)

19. Gaborit, P., Ruatta, O., Schrek, J.: On the complexity of the rank syndrome decoding problem. IEEE Trans. Inf. Theor. **62**(2), 1006–1019 (2016)

20. Garey, M.R., Johnson, D.S.: Computers and Intractability: A Guide to the Theory of NP-Completeness. W.H. Freeman and Company, New York (1979)

21. Goubin, L., Courtois, N.T.: Cryptanalysis of the TTM cryptosystem. In: Okamoto, T. (ed.) ASIACRYPT 2000. LNCS, vol. 1976, pp. 44–57. Springer, Heidelberg (2000). https://doi.org/10.1007/3-540-44448-3_4

22. Jiang, X., Ding, J., Hu, L.: Kipnis-shamir attack on HFE revisited. In: Pei, D., Yung, M., Lin, D., Wu, C. (eds.) Inscrypt 2007. LNCS, vol. 4990, pp. 399–411. Springer, Heidelberg (2008). https://doi.org/10.1007/978-3-540-79499-8_31

23. Kipnis, A., Shamir, A.: Cryptanalysis of the HFE public key cryptosystem by relinearization. In: Wiener, M. (ed.) CRYPTO 1999. LNCS, vol. 1666, pp. 19–30. Springer, Heidelberg (1999). https://doi.org/10.1007/3-540-48405-1_2

24. Macario-Rat, G., Patarin, J.: Ariadne Thread and Salt: New Multivariate Cryptographic Schemes with Public Keys in Degree 3. https://eprint.iacr.org/2021/084.pdf

25. Patarin, J.: Hidden fields equations (HFE) and isomorphisms of polynomials (IP): two new families of asymmetric algorithms. In: Maurer, U. (ed.) EUROCRYPT 1996. LNCS, vol. 1070, pp. 33–48. Springer, Heidelberg (1996). https://doi.org/10.1007/3-540-68339-9_4

26. Patarin, J., Courtois, N., Goubin, L.: QUARTZ, 128-bit long digital signatures. In: Naccache, D. (ed.) CT-RSA 2001. LNCS, vol. 2020, pp. 282–297. Springer, Heidelberg (2001). https://doi.org/10.1007/3-540-45353-9_21

27. Petzoldt, A., Chen, M.-S., Yang, B.-Y., Tao, C., Ding, J.: Design principles for HFEv- based multivariate signature schemes. In: Iwata, T., Cheon, J.H. (eds.) ASIACRYPT 2015. LNCS, vol. 9452, pp. 311–334. Springer, Heidelberg (2015). https://doi.org/10.1007/978-3-662-48797-6_14

28. Wolf, C., Preneel, B.: Equivalent keys in multivariate quadratic public key systems. J. Math. Cryptology **4**(4), 375–415 (2011)

Three Halves Make a Whole? Beating the Half-Gates Lower Bound for Garbled Circuits

Mike Rosulek$^{(\boxtimes)}$ and Lawrence Roy

Oregon State University, Corvallis, USA
{rosulekm,royl}@oregonstate.edu

Abstract. We describe a garbling scheme for boolean circuits, in which XOR gates are free and AND gates require communication of $1.5\kappa + 5$ bits. This improves over the state-of-the-art "half-gates" scheme of Zahur, Rosulek, and Evans (Eurocrypt 2015), in which XOR gates are free and AND gates cost 2κ bits. The half-gates paper proved a lower bound of 2κ bits per AND gate, in a model that captured all known garbling techniques at the time. We bypass this lower bound with a novel technique that we call **slicing and dicing**, which involves slicing wire labels in half and operating separately on those halves. Ours is the first to bypass the lower bound while being fully compatible with free-XOR, making it a drop-in replacement for half-gates. Our construction is proven secure from a similar assumption to prior free-XOR garbling (circular correlation-robust hash), and uses only slightly more computation than half-gates.

1 Introduction

Garbled circuits (GC) were introduced by Yao in the 1980s [Yao82] in one of the first secure two-party computation protocols. They remain the leading technique for constant-round two-party computation. Garbled circuits exclusively use extremely efficient symmetric-key operations (*e.g.*, a few calls to AES per gate of the circuit), making communication rather than computation the bottleneck in realistic deployments—the parties must exchange $O(\kappa)$ bits per gate. For that reason, most improvements to garbled circuits have focused heavily on reducing their concrete size [BMR90,NPS99,KS08,PSSW09,KMR14,GLNP15]. The current state of the art for garbled (boolean) circuits is the *half-gates* construction of Zahur, Rosulek, and Evans [ZRE15]. In the half-gates scheme, AND gates are garbled with size 2κ bits, while XOR gates are free, requiring no communication.

The half-gates paper also establishes a lower bound for the size of garbled circuits. Specifically, the authors define a model of **linear garbling**—which captured all known techniques at the time—and proved that a garbled AND gate

First author partially supported by NSF award #1617197. Second author supported by a DoE CSGF Fellowship.

T. Malkin and C. Peikert (Eds.): CRYPTO 2021, LNCS 12825, pp. 94–124, 2021.
https://doi.org/10.1007/978-3-030-84242-0_5

in this model requires 2κ bits. Thus, half-gates is optimal among linear garbling schemes. In response, there has been a line of work focused on finding ways around the lower bound. Several works [KKS16, BMR16, WmM17] were successful in constructing an AND gate using only κ bits, using techniques outside of the linear-garbling model. However, these constructions work *only for a single AND gate in isolation,* so they do not result in any improvement to half-gates for garbling general circuits.[1] Garbling an entire *arbitrary circuit* with less than 2κ bits per AND-gate remained an open problem. We discuss the linear garbling lower bound and different paths around it later in Sect. 7.

1.1 Our Results

We show a garbling scheme for general boolean circuits, in which XOR gates are free and AND gates cost only $1.5\kappa + 5$ bits. This is the first scheme to successfully bypass the linear-garbling lower bound for all AND gates in a circuit, not just a single isolated AND gate. For the typical case of $\kappa = 128$ this is a concrete reduction of 23% in the size of garbled circuits relative to half-gates. Our construction compares to half-gates along other dimensions as follows:

- **Hardness assumption:** All free-XOR-based garbling schemes require a function H with output length κ and satisfying a *circular correlation-robust* property. In short, this means that terms of the form $H(X \oplus \Delta)$ and $H(X \oplus \Delta) \oplus \Delta$ are indistinguishable from random, for adversarially chosen X and global, secret Δ. Our construction requires a slight generalization. First, we require H that gives outputs of length $\kappa/2$. Second, the secret Δ is split into two halves $\Delta = \Delta_L \| \Delta_R$, and we require terms like $H(X \oplus \Delta) \oplus \Delta_L$, $H(X \oplus \Delta) \oplus \Delta_L \oplus \Delta_R$, etc. to be indistinguishable from random.
- **Computation:** Our scheme requires 50% more calls to H per AND gate than half-gates (6 vs 4 for the garbler, and 3 vs 2 for the evaluators). Similar to other work, we can instantiate the necessary H using just 1 call to AES with a key that is fixed for the entire circuit. As a result, the computational cost of our scheme is comparable to prior work.

  Additionally, since we require H with only $\kappa/2$ bits of output, certain queries to H for different AND-gates can be combined into a single query to a κ-bit-output function. The effect of this optimization depends on the circuit topology but in some cases our construction can have identical or better computation to half-gates (see Sect. 6.2).

We bypass the [ZRE15] lower bound by using two techniques that are outside of its linear-garbling model. We refer to the techniques collectively as **slicing-and-dicing.**

- **Slicing:** In our construction the evaluator **slices wire labels** into halves, and uses (*possibly different!*) linear combinations to compute each half. We stress

---

[1] These constructions require the input labels to have a certain correlation that they do not guarantee for the gate's output labels.

that this does not halve the security—the hash H is still given the whole wire label with κ bits of entropy. To the best of our knowledge, this technique is novel in garbled circuits. As we demonstrate in detail later, introducing more linear combinations for the evaluator increases the linear-algebraic dimension in which the scheme operates, in a way that lets us exploit more linear-algebraic structures that prior schemes could not exploit.

– **Dicing:** The evaluator first decrypts a constant-size ciphertext containing "**control bits**", which determine the linear combinations (of input label [halves], gate ciphertexts, and H-outputs) he/she will use to compute the output label [halves]. The control bits are chosen randomly by the garbler (*i.e.*, by tossing "dice") in a particular way. Randomized control bits are outside of the linear garbling model, which requires the evaluator's linear combinations to be *fixed*. This technique first appeared in [KKS16].

We also describe a variant of our scheme that can garble *any* kind of gate (*e.g.*, XOR gates, even constant-output gates) for $1.5\kappa + 10$ bits, in a way that hides the gate's truth table from the evaluator. This improves on the state of the art for *gate-hiding* garbling, due to Rosulek [Ros17], in which each gate is garbled for $2\kappa + 8$ bits, and constant-output gates are not supported. Additionally, our gate-hiding construction is fully compatible with free-XOR, meaning that the circuit can contain both "public" XOR gates (evaluator knows that this gate is an XOR) and "private" XOR gates (only the garbler knows that this gate is an XOR), with the public ones being free.

1.2 Related Work

The garbled circuits technique was first introduced by Yao [Yao82], although the first complete description and security proof for Yao's protocol was given much later [LP09]. Bellare, Hoang, and Rogaway [BHR12] promoted garbled circuits from a *technique* to well-defined cryptographic *primitive* with standardized security properties, which they dubbed a **garbling scheme.** In this work, we use their framework to formally express our schemes and prove security.

The garbling scheme formalization captures many techniques, but in this work we focus on "practical" GC techniques built from symmetric-key tools (PRFs, hash functions, but not homomorphic encryption or obfuscation). In the realm of practical garbling, there have been many quantitative and qualitative improvements over the years, especially focused on reducing the size of garbled circuits. These works are showcased in Fig. 1. Of particular note are the Free-XOR technique of Kolesnikov and Schneider [KS08] and the half-gates construction [ZRE15], mentioned above. Free-XOR allows XOR gates in the circuit to be garbled with no communication, and our construction inherits this technique to achieve the same feature. The free-XOR technique requires a cryptographic hash with a property called circular correlation-resistance [CKKZ12]. As mentioned above, the half-gates paper introduced a lower bound for garbling, which several works have bypassed in some limited manner. We discuss the lower bound and these related works in more detail in Sect. 7.

scheme	GC size (κ bits / gate)		calls to H per gate				assump.
			garbler		evaluator		
	AND	XOR	AND	XOR	AND	XOR	
unoptimized textbook Yao	8	8	4	4	2.5	2.5	PRF
Yao + point-permute [BMR90]	4	4	4	4	1	1	PRF
$4 \rightarrow 3$ row reduction [NPS99]	3	3	4	4	1	1	PRF
$4 \rightarrow 2$ row reduction [PSSW09]	2	2	4	4	1	1	PRF
free-XOR [KS08]	3	0	4	0	1	0	CCR
fleXOR [KMR14]	2	$\{0,1,2\}$	4	$\{0,2,4\}$	1	$\{0,1,2\}$	CCR
half-gates [ZRE15]	2	0	4	0	2	0	CCR
[GLNP15]	2	1	4	3	2	1.5	PRF
ours	**1.5**	**0**	≤ 6	0	≤ 3	0	CCR

Fig. 1. Comparison of efficient garbling schemes. Gate size ignores small constant additive term (*i.e.*, "2" means $2\kappa + O(1)$ bits per gate). CCR = circular correlation robust hash function.

scheme	GC size (κ bits/gate)	calls to H per gate		supported gates	assump.
		garbler	evaluator		
Yao + point-permute [BMR90]	4	4	1	all	PRF
$4 \rightarrow 3$ row reduction [NPS99]	3	4	1	all	PRF
[KKS16]	2	3	1	symmetric	CCR
[WmM17]	2	3	1	symmetric	CCR
[Ros17]	2	4	1	non-const	PRF
ours	**1.5**	≤ 6	≤ 3	all	CCR

Fig. 2. Comparison of **gate-hiding** garbling schemes, where the garbled circuit leaks only the topology of the circuit and not the type of each gate. Gate size ignores small constant additive term (*i.e.*, "2" means $2\kappa + O(1)$ bits per gate). CCR = circular correlation robust hash function. "Symmetric" means all gates g with $g(0,1) = g(1,0)$. "Non-const" means all gates g except $g(a,b) = 0$ and $g(a,b) = 1$.

Several garbling schemes are tailored to support both AND and XOR gates while hiding the type of gate from the evaluator [KKS16, WmM17, Ros17]. These works are compared in Fig. 2. They differ in the exact class of boolean gates they can support—all gates, all symmetric gates (satisfying $g(0,1) = g(1,0)$), or all non-constant gates.

2 Preliminaries

2.1 Circuits

We represent a circuit $f = (\mathsf{inputs}, \mathsf{outputs}, \mathsf{in}, \mathsf{leak}, \mathsf{eval})$ by choosing a topological order of the $|f|$ inputs and gates in the circuit. Let inputs be the number of inputs in the circuit, which we require to come first in the ordering. Each gate is then labeled by its index in the order. For every gate index g in the circuit, its two input indices[2] are $\text{in}_1(g)$ and $\text{in}_2(g)$, where $\text{in}_i(g) < g$. Each gate can be evaluated using a function $\text{eval}(g)\colon \{0,1\}^2 \to \{0,1\}$. Finally, the outputs are a subset of the indices $\text{outputs} \subseteq [1, |f|]$.

Garbling only hides only partial information about the circuit. What is revealed is contained in the "leakage function" $\Phi(f)$. Sometimes two gates in a circuit may both be e.g. XOR-gates, but one will publicly be XOR while the operation performed by the other gate will be hidden. To support this, each gate is associated with some leakage $\text{leak}(g)$. Gates with different leakages may compute the same function, but have different rules about how much information is revealed. We then define $\Phi(f)$ to be $(\text{inputs}, \text{outputs}, \text{in}, \text{leak})$, containing the circuit topology and partial information about the gates' truth tables.

2.2 Garbling Schemes

We use a slightly modified version of the garbling definitions of [BHR12].

Definition 1. *A* garbling scheme *consists of four algorithms:*

- $(F, e, d) \leftarrow \text{Garble}(1^\kappa, f)$.
- $X := \text{Encode}(e, x)$. *(deterministic)*
- $Y := \text{Eval}(F, X)$. *(deterministic)*
- $y := \text{Decode}(d, Y)$. *(deterministic)*

such that the following conditions hold.

Correctness: *For any circuit f and input x, if $(F, e, d) \leftarrow \text{Garble}(1^\kappa, f)$ then $f(x) = \text{Decode}(d, \text{Eval}(\text{Encode}(e, x)))$ holds with all but negligible probability.*

Privacy with respect to leakage Φ: *There must be a simulator S such that for any circuit f and input x the following distributions are indistinguishable.*

$(F, e, d) \leftarrow \text{Garble}(1^\kappa, f)$
$X := \text{Encode}(e, x)$
return (F, X, d)

$(F, X, d) \leftarrow S(1^\kappa, \Phi(f), f(x))$
return (F, X, d)

Obliviousness w.r.t. leakage Φ: *There must be a simulator S such that for any circuit f and input x the following distributions are indistinguishable.*

$(F, e, d) \leftarrow \text{Garble}(1^\kappa, f)$
$X := \text{Encode}(e, x)$
return (F, X)

$(F, X) \leftarrow S(1^\kappa, \Phi(f))$
return (F, X)

---

[2] We assume that all gates take two inputs. NOT gates can be merged into downstream gates—e.g. if x goes into a NOT gate, and then into an AND gate with another input y, this is equivalent to a single $\bar{x} \wedge y$ gate.

Authenticity: *For any circuit f and input x, no PPT adversary $\mathcal{A}$ can make the following distribution output* TRUE *with non-negligible probability.*

$$
\begin{array}{|l|}
\hline
(F, e, d) \leftarrow \mathsf{Garble}(1^\kappa, f) \\
X := \mathsf{Encode}(e, x) \\
Y \leftarrow \mathcal{A}(F, d, X) \\
\text{return } \mathsf{Decode}(d, Y) \notin \{f(x), \bot\} \\
\hline
\end{array}
$$

The definitions differ from [BHR12] in two ways. First, we change correctness to allow a negligible failure probability.[3] Secondly, we strengthen the authenticity property by giving d to the adversary. This stronger property is easy to achieve by simply changing what one takes as garbled output Y.

2.3 Circular Correlation Robust Hashes

Our construction requires a hash function H with a property called *circular correlation robustness (CCR)*. A comprehensive treatment of this property is presented in [CKKZ12, GKWY20].

The relevant definition of [GKWY20] is *tweakable CCR* (TCCR). For a hash function H, define a related oracle $\mathcal{O}_\Delta(X, \tau, b) = H(X \oplus \Delta, \tau) \oplus b\Delta$. Then H is a TCCR if $\mathcal{O}_\Delta$ is indistinguishable from a random oracle, provided that the distinguisher never repeats a (X, τ) pair in calls to the oracle.

We modify their definition in several important ways:

- We require H to have different input and output lengths. In the original definition, the adversary used the argument $b \in \{0, 1\}$ to determine whether Δ was XOR'ed with the output of H. We generalize so that the adversary can choose a linear function of (the bits of) Δ that will be XOR'ed with the output of H. Our construction ultimately needs only 4 linear functions reflecting our slicing of wire labels in half: $L_{a,b}(\Delta_L \| \Delta_R) = a\Delta_L \oplus b\Delta_R$, for $a, b \in \{0, 1\}$.
- [GKWY20] observe that a "full" TCCR is stronger than what is needed for garbled circuits. In order to construct a TCCR that uses only one call to an ideal permutation, they prove TCCR security against adversaries that query only on *"naturally derived"* keys. It is somewhat cumbersome to generalize *"naturally derived"* keys to our setting, where the values are sliced into pieces. We instead relax TCCR so that H is drawn from a *family* of hashes, and the adversary only receives the description of H after making all of its oracle queries. This relaxation suffices for garbled circuits (the garbler chooses H and reveals it only in the garbled circuit description, after all queries to H have been made), and simplifies both our definition and our proof.

---

[3] Most garbling schemes actually do not have perfect correctness. If an output wire has labels W_0, W_1, then d will contain both $H(W_0)$ and $H(W_1)$. Correctness is violated if $H(W_0) = H(W_1)$.

Definition 2. *A family of hash functions* $\mathcal{H}$, *where each* $H \in \mathcal{H}$ *maps* $\{0,1\}^n \times \mathcal{T} \rightarrow \{0,1\}^m$ *for some set of tweaks* $\mathcal{T}$, *is* **randomized tweakable circular correlation robust (RTCCR)** *for a set of linear functions* $\mathcal{L}$ *from* $\{0,1\}^n$ *to* $\{0,1\}^m$ *if, for any PPTs* $\mathcal{A}_1, \mathcal{A}_2$ *that never repeat an oracle query to* $\mathcal{O}_{H,\Delta}$ *on the same* (X, τ),

$$\left| \Pr_{H,\Delta} \left[v \leftarrow \mathcal{A}_1^{H,\mathcal{O}_{H,\Delta}}; \mathcal{A}_2(v, H) = 1 \right] - \Pr_{H,R} \left[v \leftarrow \mathcal{A}_1^{H,R}; \mathcal{A}_2(v, H) = 1 \right] \right|$$

is negligible, where R *is a random oracle and* $\mathcal{O}_{H,\Delta}$ *is defined as*

$$\begin{array}{|l|}\hline \mathcal{O}_{H,\Delta}(X \in \{0,1\}^n, \tau \in \mathcal{T}, L \in \mathcal{L}): \\ \text{return } H(X \oplus \Delta, \tau) \oplus L(\Delta) \\ \hline \end{array}$$

In the full version we show that if $F_k(X)$ is both a (plain) CCR hash for $\mathcal{L}$ when k is fixed and a PRF when k is random, and $\{(X, \tau) \mapsto X \oplus U(\tau) \mid U \in \mathcal{U}\}$ is a universal hash family,[4] then $\{(X, \tau) \mapsto F_k(X \oplus U(\tau)) \mid k \in \{0,1\}^\kappa, U \in \mathcal{U}\}$ is a secure RTCCR hash family for $\mathcal{L}$.

For our recommended instantiation, let σ be a simple function of the form $\sigma(X_L \| X_R) = \alpha X_L \| \alpha X_R$, where α is any fixed element in $GF(2^{\kappa/2}) \setminus GF(2^2)$. Then $\mathsf{AES}_k(X) \oplus \sigma(X)$ is both a PRF for random k, and a CCR for any fixed k (modelling AES_k as an ideal permutation). Hence we get an RTCCR of the form:

$$(X, \tau) \mapsto \mathsf{AES}_k \left(X \oplus U(\tau) \right) \oplus \sigma(X \oplus U(\tau))$$

U can likewise be a simple function, e.g., when $|\tau| \leq \kappa/2$ then we can use $U(\tau) = u_1 \tau \| u_2 \tau$ where u_1, u_2 are random elements of $GF(2^{\kappa/2})$.

3   A Linear-Algebraic View of Garbling Schemes

In this section we present a linear-algebraic perspective of garbling schemes, which is necessary to understand our construction and its novelty. This perspective is inspired by the presentation of Rosulek [Ros17], where the evaluator's behavior (in each of the 4 different gate-input combinations) defines a set of linear equations that the garbler must satisfy, and we rearrange those equations to isolate the values that are outside of the garbler's control.

3.1   The Basic Linear Perspective

Throughout this section, we consider an AND gate whose input wires have labels (A_0, A_1) and (B_0, B_1). We will always consider the free-XOR setting [KS08], where all wires have labels that xor to a common global Δ; i.e., $A_0 \oplus A_1 = B_0 \oplus B_1 = \Delta$. Our view of garbling will always start with the circuit evaluator's

---

[4] Equivalently, $\mathcal{U}$ is $2^{-\kappa}$-almost-XOR-universal (AXU).

perspective; hence we consider the subscripts to be public. In other words, if the evaluator holds A_i, then he knows the value i. In some works these subscripts are called "color bits" or "permute bits." The garbler secretly knows which of $\{A_0, A_1\}$ represent true and which of $\{B_0, B_1\}$ represent true.

Let's take an example of a textbook Yao garbled gate, using the point-permute technique. The garbled gate consists of 4 ciphertexts $G_{00}, \ldots, G_{11}$. When the evaluator has input labels A_i, B_j, he computes the output label by decrypting the (i, j)'th ciphertext, as $H(A_i, B_j) \oplus G_{ij}.$[5] In order to correspond to an AND gate, this evaluation expression must result in some label C (which could be either C_0 or C_1) representing (false) in 3 cases and $C \oplus \Delta$ (true) in the other. Suppose (A_1, B_0) is the case corresponding to inputs (true,true), then the garbler needs to arrange for:

$$C = H(A_0, B_0) \oplus G_{00} \qquad\qquad C \oplus \Delta = H(A_1, B_0) \oplus G_{10}$$
$$C = H(A_0, B_1) \oplus G_{01} \qquad\qquad C = H(A_1, B_1) \oplus G_{11}$$

We can rearrange these equations as follows:

$$\begin{bmatrix} 1 & 1 & 0 & 0 & 0 \\ 1 & 0 & 1 & 0 & 0 \\ 1 & 0 & 0 & 1 & 0 \\ 1 & 0 & 0 & 0 & 1 \end{bmatrix} \begin{bmatrix} C \\ G_{00} \\ G_{01} \\ G_{10} \\ G_{11} \end{bmatrix} = \begin{bmatrix} 1 & 0 & 0 & 0 \\ 0 & 1 & 0 & 0 \\ 0 & 0 & 1 & 0 \\ 0 & 0 & 0 & 1 \end{bmatrix} \begin{bmatrix} H(A_0, B_0) \\ H(A_0, B_1) \\ H(A_1, B_0) \\ H(A_1, B_1) \end{bmatrix} \oplus \underbrace{\begin{bmatrix} 0 \\ 0 \\ 1 \\ 0 \end{bmatrix}}_{t} \Delta$$

In this equation, values that the garbler **cannot control** are on the right, and the results of the garbling process (gate ciphertexts and output labels) are on the left. The vector marked t is the truth table of the gate (when inputs are ordered by color bits), and known only to the garbler.

In order for the scheme to work, for all possible values on the right-hand side (including all choices of secret t!) the garbler must be able to solve for the variables on the left-hand side. In this case the left-hand side is under-determined so solving is easy. The garbler can simply choose random C and move it to the right-hand side. Then the matrix remaining on the left-hand side is an invertible identity matrix. Multiplying by the inverse solves for the desired values. Clearly this can be done for any t, meaning that this approach works to garble any gate (not just AND gates).

3.2   Row-Reduction Techniques

Row reduction refers to any technique to reduce the size of the garbled gate below 4 ciphertexts. The simplest method works by removing the ciphertext G_{00}, and simply having the evaluator take $H(A_0, B_0)$ as the output label when he has inputs A_0, B_0.

---

[5] For now, assume H is a random oracle. We ignore including the gate ID as an additional argument to H.

$$
\begin{array}{l}
C = H(A_0, B_0) \\
C = H(A_0, B_1) \oplus G_{01} \\
C \oplus \Delta = H(A_1, B_0) \oplus G_{10} \\
C = H(A_1, B_1) \oplus G_{11}
\end{array}
\Rightarrow
\begin{bmatrix}
1\,0\,0\,0 \\
1\,1\,0\,0 \\
1\,0\,1\,0 \\
1\,0\,0\,1
\end{bmatrix}
\begin{bmatrix}
C \\
G_{01} \\
G_{10} \\
G_{11}
\end{bmatrix}
=
\begin{bmatrix}
1\,0\,0\,0 \\
0\,1\,0\,0 \\
0\,0\,1\,0 \\
0\,0\,0\,1
\end{bmatrix}
\begin{bmatrix}
H(A_0, B_0) \\
H(A_0, B_1) \\
H(A_1, B_0) \\
H(A_1, B_1)
\end{bmatrix}
\oplus
\underbrace{
\begin{bmatrix}
0 \\
0 \\
1 \\
0
\end{bmatrix}
}_{t}
\Delta
$$

The matrix on the left is now a square matrix, and invertible. Thus for any choice of t, the garbler can solve for C and the G_{ij} values by multiplying by the inverse matrix.

3.3   Half-Gates

The previous example shows that decreasing the size of the garbled gate from 4 to 3 causes the matrix on the left to change from size 4×5 to 4×4. Reducing the garbled gate further (from 3 ciphertexts to 2) would cause the matrix to be 4×3, and the system of linear equations would be overdetermined! So how does the half-gates garbling scheme [ZRE15] actually achieve a 2-ciphertext AND gate?

Let us recall the gate-evaluation algorithm for the half-gates scheme, which is considerably different from all previous schemes. On inputs A_i, B_j the evaluator computes the output label as $H(A_i) \oplus H(B_j) \oplus i \cdot G_0 \oplus j(G_1 \oplus A_i)$, where G_0, G_1 are the two gate ciphertexts.

Suppose as before that A_1 and B_0 correspond to true. Then the garbler must arrange for the following to be true:

$$
\begin{array}{rl}
C = & H(A_0) \oplus H(B_0) \\
C = & H(A_0) \oplus H(B_1) \qquad\qquad \oplus G_1 \oplus A_0 \\
C \oplus \Delta = & H(A_1) \oplus H(B_0) \oplus G_0 \\
C = & H(A_1) \oplus H(B_1) \oplus G_0 \oplus G_1 \oplus \underbrace{(A_0 \oplus \Delta)}_{A_1}
\end{array}
$$

Rearranging in our usual way, we get:

$$
\begin{bmatrix}
1\,0\,0 \\
1\,0\,1 \\
1\,1\,0 \\
1\,1\,1
\end{bmatrix}
\begin{bmatrix}
C \\
G_0 \\
G_1
\end{bmatrix}
=
\left(
\begin{bmatrix}
1\,0\,1\,0\,0\,0 \\
1\,0\,0\,1\,1\,0 \\
0\,1\,1\,0\,0\,0 \\
0\,1\,0\,1\,1\,1
\end{bmatrix}
\oplus
\underbrace{
\begin{bmatrix}
0 \cdots\cdots 0 & 0 \\
\vdots \qquad \vdots & 0 \\
\vdots \qquad \vdots & 1 \\
0 \cdots\cdots 0 & 0
\end{bmatrix}
}_{t}
\right)
\begin{bmatrix}
H(A_0) \\
H(A_1) \\
H(B_0) \\
H(B_1) \\
A_0 \\
\Delta
\end{bmatrix}
$$

Note that Δ is used both in the truth table adjustment (t) and in the usual operations of the evaluator (implicitly, in the one case where he includes $A_1 = A_0 \oplus \Delta$ in the linear combination).

As promised, the matrix on the left is only 4×3. We cannot solve for the left-hand side by inverting this matrix as in the previous cases. Instead, the garbler takes advantage of the fact that the **matrices on both sides have the same**

column space. Specifically, the columns on the left span the space of all even-parity vectors. For any choice of t containing just a single 1 (corresponding to the truth table of an AND gate), every column on the right also has even parity! Concretely, suppose the evaluator solved the first three rows of this system of linear equalities (which is possible since the first three rows on the left form an invertible matrix), then the fourth row would automatically be in equality since on both sides it is the sum of the first 3 rows.[6] One can see that this technique works only for gates whose truth table has odd parity (e.g., AND gates).

Half-gates was the first garbling scheme to structure its oracle queries as $H(A_i)$ and $H(B_j)$, instead of $H(A_i, B_j)$. Our linear-algebraic perspective highlights the importance of this change. For a 2-ciphertext AND gate, the matrix on the left will be 4×3, so the matrix on the right must have rank 3. An expression like $H(A_i, B_j)$ can be used by the evaluator in only one combination of inputs, leading to an identity matrix minor that has rank 4. By contrast, each $H(A_i)$ and $H(B_j)$ term is used for two input combinations, so the corresponding matrix can have rank 3.

Our linear algebraic perspective confirms and provides an explanation for a prior finding of Carmer and Rosulek [CR16]. They used a SAT solver to show that no garbling scheme (in the linear model of the half-gates paper) could achieve a 2-ciphertext AND gate, when the evaluator makes only one query to H. This reiterates the importance of half gates using $H(A), H(B)$ oracle queries to achieve a 2-ciphertext AND gate.

4 High-Level Overview of Our Scheme

In the previous section, we saw that it was important that the evaluator used oracle queries like $H(A_i)$ and $H(B_j)$ in the half-gates scheme. For every term of the form $H(A_i)$ there are two gate-input combinations in which the evaluator uses this term. This property led to a desirable redundancy in the matrix that relates H-queries to input combinations. Redundancies in this matrix lead to smaller garbled gates. We push this idea further using several key observations.

4.1 Observation #1: Get the Most Out of the Oracle Queries

$H(A_i)$ and $H(B_j)$ are not the only oracle queries that can be made in two different gate-input combinations. We can also ask the evaluator to query $H(A_i \oplus B_j)$. Because of the free-XOR constraint, $A_0 \oplus B_0 = A_1 \oplus B_1$, and $A_0 \oplus B_1 = A_1 \oplus B_0$. This means that the following oracle queries can be made for each gate-input combination:

	$H(A_0)$	$H(A_1)$	$H(B_0)$	$H(B_1)$	$H(A_0 \oplus B_0)$	$H(A_0 \oplus B_1)$
gate input (0,0)	✓		✓		✓	
gate input (0,1)	✓			✓		✓
gate input (1,0)		✓	✓			✓
gate input (1,1)		✓		✓	✓	

$$(1)$$

---

[6] More generally, multiplying by a **left-inverse** of the matrix on the left-hand side "just works," as in the case where the matrix on the left-hand side is invertible.

Can we use queries of this form to introduce even more redundancy in the relevant matrices?

4.2 Observation #2: Increase Dimension by Slicing Wire Labels

Our linear-algebraic perspective of garbling includes only 4 linear equations, corresponding to the 4 different gate-inputs. Having only 4 linear equations makes it difficult to take advantage of any new structure introduced by observation #1. Our second observation, and perhaps the key to our entire approach, is to **split each wire label into a left and right half,** and let the evaluator compute the two halves (of the output label) with different linear combinations. This results in 8 linear equations in our linear-algebraic perspective—2 equations for each of the 4 gate-input combinations.

Consider the following proposal,

	$H(A_0)$	$H(A_1)$	$H(B_0)$	$H(B_1)$	$H(A_0 \oplus B_0)$	$H(A_0 \oplus B_1)$
(0,0) left	✓				✓	
(0,0) right			✓		✓	
(0,1) left	✓					✓
(0,1) right				✓		✓
(1,0) left		✓				✓
(1,0) right			✓			✓
(1,1) left		✓			✓	
(1,1) right				✓	✓	

$$(2)$$

For example, on gate-input (0,0) the evaluator will compute the left half of the output label as $H(A_0) \oplus H(A_0 \oplus B_0) \oplus \cdots$ (plus other terms, involving gate ciphertexts and input labels). There are several important features of this table to note:

- $H(\cdot)$ is used in a linear equation to compute half of an output label, therefore $H(\cdot)$ is a function with $\kappa/2$ bits of output. Three of these half-sized hash functions are combined to encrypt the gate output.[7] However, we still will use the *entire* input wire labels as input to H—using wire-label halves as input to H would cut the effective security parameter in half.
- For an evaluator with gate-input (0,0), the values $H(A_1)$, $H(B_1)$, and $H(A_0 \oplus B_1)$ are all jointly indistinguishable from random. With that in mind, consider the linear combinations for any other gate-input. For example, in the (1,0) case the evaluator will compute the output as

$$\text{left} = H(A_1) \oplus H(A_0 \oplus B_1) \oplus \cdots$$
$$\text{right} = H(B_0) \oplus H(A_0 \oplus B_1) \oplus \cdots$$

---

[7] Hence the title: "Three Halves Make a Whole".

Because $H(A_1)$ and $H(A_0 \oplus B_1)$ are pseudorandom, this makes both of these outputs *jointly* pseudorandom. The entire output of the (1,0) case is pseudorandom from the perspective of the evaluator in the (0,0) case. This is a necessary condition, since sometimes the (0,0) and (1,0) cases give different outputs. This pattern holds with respect to any pair of two gate-inputs.

– If we interpret Eq. 2 as a matrix ($\checkmark$=1, empty cell=0), we see that it has rank 5. This suggests that the garbling process can result in only 5 output values, where in this case each of these values is $\kappa/2$ bits. Two of the values are the halves of the output wire label C, leaving 3 values to comprise the garbled gate ciphertexts. In other words, we are on our way to a garbled gate with only $3\kappa/2$ bits, if only we can get all of the relevant linear equations to cooperate.

4.3 Observation #3: Randomize and Hide the Evaluator's Coefficients

Let us apply our observations so far to our linear perspective of Sect. 3. Since wire labels are divided into halves, we use notation like A_{0R} to denote the right half of A_0. Note that the free-XOR constraint applies independently to the wire label halves; *i.e.*, $A_{1R} = A_{0R} \oplus \Delta_R$ and so on.

The evaluator computes each half of the output label separately, using a linear combination of available information: oracle responses, gate ciphertexts, and the 4 (!) halves of the input labels. If we account for all 8 of the evaluator's linear equations, while using the oracle-query structure suggested in Eq. 2, we obtain the following system:

$$
\begin{bmatrix}
1 & 0 & ? & ? & ? \\
0 & 1 & ? & ? & ? \\
1 & 0 & ? & ? & ? \\
0 & 1 & ? & ? & ? \\
1 & 0 & ? & ? & ? \\
0 & 1 & ? & ? & ? \\
1 & 0 & ? & ? & ? \\
0 & 1 & ? & ? & ?
\end{bmatrix}
\begin{bmatrix}
C_L \\ C_R \\ G_0 \\ G_1 \\ G_2
\end{bmatrix}
=
\left(
\begin{bmatrix}
1 & 0 & 0 & 0 & 1 & 0 & ? & ? & ? & ? & ? & ? \\
0 & 0 & 1 & 0 & 1 & 0 & ? & ? & ? & ? & ? & ? \\
1 & 0 & 0 & 0 & 0 & 1 & ? & ? & ? & ? & ? & ? \\
0 & 0 & 0 & 1 & 0 & 1 & ? & ? & ? & ? & ? & ? \\
0 & 1 & 0 & 0 & 0 & 1 & ? & ? & ? & ? & ? & ? \\
0 & 0 & 1 & 0 & 0 & 1 & ? & ? & ? & ? & ? & ? \\
0 & 1 & 0 & 0 & 1 & 0 & ? & ? & ? & ? & ? & ? \\
0 & 0 & 0 & 1 & 1 & 0 & ? & ? & ? & ? & ? & ?
\end{bmatrix}
\oplus
\underbrace{
\begin{bmatrix}
0 & \cdots & 0 & 0 & 0 \\
\vdots & & \vdots & 0 & 0 \\
\vdots & & \vdots & 0 & 0 \\
\vdots & & \vdots & 0 & 0 \\
\vdots & & \vdots & 1 & 0 \\
\vdots & & \vdots & 0 & 1 \\
\vdots & & \vdots & 0 & 0 \\
0 & \cdots & 0 & 0 & 0
\end{bmatrix}
}_{t}
\right)
\begin{bmatrix}
H(A_0) \\ H(A_1) \\ H(B_0) \\ H(B_1) \\ H(A_0 \oplus B_0) \\ H(A_0 \oplus B_1) \\ A_{0L} \\ A_{0R} \\ B_{0L} \\ B_{0R} \\ \Delta_L \\ \Delta_R
\end{bmatrix}
\tag{3}
$$

The first row represents the evaluator's linear equation to compute the *left half* C_L of the output label on input A_0, B_0, etc. Note that the truth table t now consists of 2×2 identity blocks and 2×2 zero-blocks.

For everything to work correctly, we need to replace the "?" entries, so that for every choice of t, the matrices on both sides have the same column space.

– The columns on the right-hand side (representing the H outputs) already span a space of dimension 5, so there is no choice but to extend the left-hand side matrix to a basis of that space.

- The "?" entries on the right are subject to other constraints, so that they reflect what an evaluator can actually do in each input combination. For example, on input A_0, B_1, the evaluator cannot include B_{0R} in its linear combination, it can only include $B_{1R} = B_{0R} \oplus \Delta_R$. Note that the matrix is written in terms of B_0 only.

Unfortunately, it is not possible to complete the right-hand-side matrix subject to these constraints. **For every t, there is a valid way to replace the "?" entries,** but there is no one way that works for *all* t.

To get around this problem, we **randomize and encrypt the entries of the matrix**. To the best of our knowledge, the technique first appeared in the garbling scheme of [KKS16], and was also used in [WmM17, Ros17]. The garbler will complete the matrices so that the system of equations can be solved (*i.e.*, the column spaces coincide). This causes the matrix entries to now depend on the garbler's secret t. Next, the garbler will **encrypt these matrix entries**, so that when the evaluator has input A_i, B_j, he can decrypt *only those matrix entries needed for that particular input combination*—not the entire matrix. For example, the evaluator can use A_0, B_0 to decrypt the top two rows of the matrix—just enough to determine the coefficients of the linear combinations computing the output label. Unlike other schemes, there is a step of indirection (decrypting this additional ciphertext) before the evaluator determines which linear combinations to apply—the linear combination does not depend solely on the color bits of the input labels. We call the contents of these ciphertexts **control bits**, which tell the evaluator what linear combination to apply. The control bits are of small constant size, so encrypting them adds only a constant number of bits to the garbling scheme.

The garbler completes the missing entries in the matrix by drawing them randomly from a *distribution* over matrices. The distribution depends on t, as we mentioned—however, it can be arranged that **each marginal view of the matrix is independent of t.** Since the evaluator sees only such a marginal view, not the entire matrix, the value of t is hidden.

5   Details: Slicing and Dicing

5.1   Choosing the Matrices

Let us begin by filling out the question marks in Eq. 3. We rewrite this equation using block matrices, and we group related parts together.

$$V \begin{bmatrix} C \\ \vec{G} \end{bmatrix} = M\vec{H} \oplus (R \oplus [0 \cdots 0|t]) \begin{bmatrix} A_0 \\ B_0 \\ \Delta \end{bmatrix} \tag{4}$$

Here C, A_0, B_0, and Δ are two-element (column) vectors representing the two halves of these wire labels; $\vec{G}$ is the vector of gate ciphertexts; and

$\vec{H} = \begin{bmatrix} H(A_0) & H(A_1) & H(B_0) & H(B_1) & H(A_0 \oplus B_0) & H(A_0 \oplus B_1) \end{bmatrix}^{\top}$ is the vector of H-outputs. t is the 8×2 truth table matrix, which contains a 2×2 identity matrix block for each case of the gate that should output true. We have already filled out M—it is the portion of the right-hand side matrix in Eq. 3 with no question marks, that operates on the hash outputs $\vec{H}$. R is called the **control matrix** because it determines which pieces of input labels are added to the output.

Choosing V. Recall that the matrices on both sides of the equation must have the same column space, and that M already spans this 5-dimensional space. Call this common column space the *gate space* $\mathcal{G}$. Then

$$\mathcal{G} = \text{colspace}\,(V) = \text{colspace}\,(M) \supseteq \text{colspace}\,(R \oplus [0 \cdots 0 | t]).$$

It will be more convenient to represent $\mathcal{G}$ using linear constraints, rather than as the span of the columns of M. We use a matrix K as a basis for the cokernel of M, so that any vector v is in $\mathcal{G}$ if and only if $Kv = 0$. Then V must satisfy $rank(V) = 5$ and $KV = 0$.

Any K and V satisfying these constraints will suffice, and we will use the following:

$$K = \begin{bmatrix} 1 & 0 & 1 & 0 & 1 & 0 & 1 & 0 \\ 0 & 1 & 0 & 1 & 0 & 1 & 0 & 1 \\ 0 & 0 & 0 & 1 & 1 & 0 & 1 & 1 \end{bmatrix} \qquad V = \begin{bmatrix} 1 & 0 & 0 & 0 & 0 \\ 0 & 1 & 0 & 0 & 0 \\ 1 & 0 & 0 & 0 & 1 \\ 0 & 1 & 0 & 1 & 1 \\ 1 & 0 & 1 & 0 & 1 \\ 0 & 1 & 0 & 0 & 1 \\ 1 & 0 & 1 & 0 & 0 \\ 0 & 1 & 0 & 1 & 0 \end{bmatrix}$$

Note that the columns of V corresponding to the gate ciphertexts (the 3 rightmost columns) are the same as the columns in M corresponding to hash outputs $H(A_1), H(B_1), H(A_0 \oplus B_1)$, so they are clearly in the column space of M.

Constraints on Choosing R. It remains to see how we choose the control matrix R. Using our new notation, colspace $(R \oplus [0 \cdots 0 | t]) \subseteq \mathcal{G}$ is equivalent to $KR = K[0 \cdots 0 | t]$, so we must choose R to match Kt. Because t is composed of 2×2 zero or identity blocks, we can deduce:

$$KR = K[0 \cdots 0 | t] = \begin{bmatrix} 0 & 0 & 0 & 0 & p & 0 \\ 0 & 0 & 0 & 0 & 0 & p \\ 0 & 0 & 0 & 0 & a & b \end{bmatrix} \tag{5}$$

for some $a, b \in \{0, 1\}$, where p is the parity of the truth table. In our main construction, $p = 1$ since it only considers garbling AND gates. However, the bits a, b reveal more than the parity of the gate—they leak the position of the "1" in the truth table. Since R must depend on these a, b bits, we resort to randomizing the control matrix R to hide a, b.

We also need the control matrix to reflect linear combinations that the evaluator can actually do with the available wire labels. The linear constraints are expressed in terms of A_0, B_0, and Δ, but when the evaluator has wire label, say, A_1, he can either include it in the linear combination (adding both A_0 and Δ) or not (adding neither A_0 nor Δ)—he cannot include only one of A_0, Δ in the linear combination. This means that R must decompose into 2×2 matrices in the following way:

$$R = \begin{bmatrix} R_{00A} & R_{00B} & 0 \\ R_{01A} & R_{01B} & R_{01B} \\ R_{10A} & R_{10B} & R_{10A} \\ R_{11A} & R_{11B} & R_{11A} \oplus R_{11B} \end{bmatrix} \tag{6}$$

When the evaluator holds input labels A_i, B_j, the submatrix $R_{ij} = \begin{bmatrix} R_{ijA} & R_{ijB} \end{bmatrix}$ is enough to completely determine which linear combination should be applied. We call R_{ij} the **marginal view** for that input combination. We will randomize the choice of R, subject to the constraints listed above, so that any single marginal view leaks nothing about t. That is, we want to find a distribution $\mathcal{R}(t)$ such that when $R \leftarrow \mathcal{R}(t)$, $KR = K[0 \cdots 0|t]$ with probability 1, yet for every $i, j \in \{0,1\}$, if $t \leftarrow T$ and $R \leftarrow \mathcal{R}(t)$ then t and R_{ij} are independently distributed.

Basic Approach to the Distribution $\mathcal{R}(t)$: We must choose R to match the p, a, b bits defined above (which depend on the truth table t). Suppose we have a distribution $\mathcal{R}_0$ with the following properties:

- If $R_\$ \leftarrow \mathcal{R}_0$ then $KR_\$ = 0$
- For all $i, j \in \{0,1\}$, if $R_\$ \leftarrow \mathcal{R}_0$ then $(R_\$)_{ij}$ (the marginal view) is uniform

and we also have fixed matrices R_p, R_a, R_b such that:

$$KR_p = \begin{bmatrix} 0\,0 & 0\,0 & 1\,0 \\ 0\,0 & 0\,0 & 0\,1 \\ 0\,0 & 0\,0 & 0\,0 \end{bmatrix} \quad KR_a = \begin{bmatrix} 0\,0 & 0\,0 & 0\,0 \\ 0\,0 & 0\,0 & 0\,0 \\ 0\,0 & 0\,0 & 1\,0 \end{bmatrix} \quad KR_b = \begin{bmatrix} 0\,0 & 0\,0 & 0\,0 \\ 0\,0 & 0\,0 & 0\,0 \\ 0\,0 & 0\,0 & 0\,1 \end{bmatrix}, \tag{7}$$

Define $\mathcal{R}(t)$ to first sample $R_\$ \leftarrow \mathcal{R}_0$ and output $R = pR_p \oplus aR_a \oplus bR_b \oplus R_\$$. The result R will always satisfy the condition of Eq. 5. The randomness in $R_\$$ also causes marginal views of R_{ij} to be uniform and therefore hide p, a, b. Concrete values for R_p, R_a, R_b are given in Figs. 3 and 4, as part of a different construction.

If $\mathcal{R}_0$ is the *uniform distribution* over all matrices satisfying $KR = 0$, then the garbler must encrypt the full marginal views R_{ij} at 8 bits per view. A more thoughtful choice of distribution will allow the garbler to convey R_{ij} marginal views with fewer bits.

Compressing the Marginal Views: Each marginal view R_{ij} is a 2×4 matrix. We can "compress" these if we manage to restrict all R_{ij} to some linear subspace $S = \text{span}\{S_1, S_2, \ldots, S_d\}$ of 2×4 matrices (presumably with dimension $d < 8$), while still maintaining the other properties needed.

$$S_1 = \begin{bmatrix} 1 & 1 & 1 & 0 \\ 1 & 0 & 0 & 1 \end{bmatrix} \qquad S_2 = \begin{bmatrix} 1 & 0 & 0 & 1 \\ 0 & 1 & 1 & 1 \end{bmatrix}$$

$$\bar{R}_a = \begin{bmatrix} 0 & 0 \\ 1 & 1 \\ 0 & 1 \\ 1 & 0 \end{bmatrix} \qquad \bar{R}_b = \begin{bmatrix} 0 & 0 \\ 1 & 0 \\ 1 & 1 \\ 0 & 1 \end{bmatrix} \qquad \bar{R}_\$ \leftarrow \mathrm{span} \left\{ \begin{bmatrix} 1 & 0 \\ 1 & 0 \\ 1 & 0 \\ 1 & 0 \end{bmatrix} , \begin{bmatrix} 0 & 1 \\ 0 & 1 \\ 0 & 1 \\ 0 & 1 \end{bmatrix} \right\}$$

$$R_a = \begin{bmatrix} 0 & 0 & 0 & 0 & 0 & 0 \\ 0 & 0 & 0 & 0 & 0 & 0 \\ 0 & 1 & 1 & 1 & 1 & 1 \\ 1 & 1 & 1 & 0 & 1 & 0 \\ 1 & 0 & 0 & 1 & 1 & 0 \\ 0 & 1 & 1 & 1 & 0 & 1 \\ 1 & 1 & 1 & 0 & 0 & 1 \\ 1 & 0 & 0 & 1 & 1 & 1 \end{bmatrix} \quad R_b = \begin{bmatrix} 0 & 0 & 0 & 0 & 0 & 0 \\ 0 & 0 & 0 & 0 & 0 & 0 \\ 1 & 1 & 1 & 0 & 1 & 0 \\ 1 & 0 & 0 & 1 & 0 & 1 \\ 0 & 1 & 1 & 1 & 0 & 1 \\ 1 & 1 & 1 & 0 & 1 & 1 \\ 1 & 0 & 0 & 1 & 1 & 1 \\ 0 & 1 & 1 & 1 & 1 & 0 \end{bmatrix} \quad R_\$ \leftarrow \mathrm{span} \left\{ \begin{bmatrix} 1 & 1 & 1 & 0 & 0 & 0 \\ 1 & 0 & 0 & 1 & 0 & 0 \\ 1 & 1 & 1 & 0 & 1 & 0 \\ 1 & 0 & 0 & 1 & 0 & 1 \\ 1 & 1 & 1 & 0 & 1 & 1 \\ 1 & 0 & 0 & 1 & 1 & 0 \\ 1 & 1 & 1 & 0 & 0 & 1 \\ 1 & 0 & 0 & 1 & 1 & 1 \end{bmatrix} , \begin{bmatrix} 1 & 0 & 0 & 1 & 0 & 0 \\ 0 & 1 & 1 & 1 & 0 & 0 \\ 1 & 0 & 0 & 1 & 0 & 1 \\ 0 & 1 & 1 & 1 & 1 & 1 \\ 1 & 0 & 0 & 1 & 1 & 0 \\ 0 & 1 & 1 & 1 & 0 & 1 \\ 1 & 0 & 0 & 1 & 1 & 1 \\ 0 & 1 & 1 & 1 & 1 & 0 \end{bmatrix} \right\}$$

Fig. 3. Control matrices for even-parity gates. The top row contains the two basis matrices for S. The bottom row shows the full control matrices (R_p is not needed for even-parity gates). The middle row shows the "compressed" representation of the control matrices, in terms of the basis $\{S_1, S_2\}$ (*i.e.*, each row expresses which linear combination of S_1, S_2 appears in the corresponding blocks of the control matrix). The reader can verify that (1) each row in $\bar{R}_\$$ is individually uniform; (2) $K R_\$ = 0$; and (3) Eq. 7 holds.

$$S_1 = \begin{bmatrix} 1 & 1 & 1 & 0 \\ 1 & 0 & 0 & 1 \end{bmatrix} \quad S_2 = \begin{bmatrix} 1 & 0 & 0 & 1 \\ 0 & 1 & 1 & 1 \end{bmatrix} \quad S_3 = \begin{bmatrix} 0 & 0 & 1 & 0 \\ 0 & 0 & 0 & 0 \end{bmatrix} \quad S_4 = \begin{bmatrix} 0 & 0 & 0 & 0 \\ 0 & 1 & 0 & 0 \end{bmatrix}$$

$$\bar{R}_p = \begin{bmatrix} 0 & 0 & 1 & 1 \\ 0 & 0 & 1 & 0 \\ 0 & 0 & 0 & 1 \\ 0 & 0 & 0 & 0 \end{bmatrix} \qquad \bar{R}_\$ \leftarrow \mathrm{span} \left\{ \begin{bmatrix} 0 & 0 & 1 & 0 \\ 1 & 1 & 1 & 0 \\ 0 & 1 & 1 & 0 \\ 1 & 0 & 1 & 0 \end{bmatrix} , \begin{bmatrix} 0 & 0 & 0 & 1 \\ 1 & 0 & 0 & 1 \\ 1 & 1 & 0 & 1 \\ 0 & 1 & 0 & 1 \end{bmatrix} , \ldots \right\}$$

$$R_p = \begin{bmatrix} 0 & 0 & 1 & 0 & 0 & 0 \\ 0 & 1 & 0 & 0 & 0 & 0 \\ 0 & 0 & 1 & 0 & 1 & 0 \\ 0 & 0 & 0 & 0 & 0 & 0 \\ 0 & 0 & 0 & 0 & 0 & 0 \\ 0 & 1 & 0 & 0 & 0 & 1 \\ 0 & 0 & 0 & 0 & 0 & 0 \\ 0 & 0 & 0 & 0 & 0 & 0 \end{bmatrix} \quad R_\$ \leftarrow \mathrm{span} \left\{ \begin{bmatrix} 0 & 0 & 1 & 0 & 0 & 0 \\ 0 & 0 & 0 & 0 & 0 & 0 \\ 0 & 1 & 0 & 1 & 0 & 1 \\ 1 & 1 & 1 & 0 & 1 & 0 \\ 1 & 0 & 1 & 1 & 1 & 0 \\ 0 & 1 & 1 & 1 & 0 & 1 \\ 1 & 1 & 0 & 0 & 1 & 1 \\ 1 & 0 & 0 & 1 & 1 & 1 \end{bmatrix} , \begin{bmatrix} 0 & 0 & 0 & 0 & 0 & 0 \\ 0 & 1 & 0 & 0 & 0 & 0 \\ 1 & 1 & 0 & 1 & 0 & 0 \\ 1 & 1 & 0 & 1 & 0 & 1 \\ 0 & 1 & 1 & 1 & 0 & 1 \\ 1 & 0 & 1 & 0 & 1 & 0 \\ 1 & 0 & 0 & 1 & 1 & 1 \\ 0 & 0 & 1 & 1 & 1 & 1 \end{bmatrix} , \ldots \right\}$$

Fig. 4. Control matrices for gate-hiding garbling. The top row contains the basis matrices for S. The basis of Fig. 3 is a subset of this basis, so we can use the same R_a and R_b as Fig. 3. The distributions on $\bar{R}_\$$ and $R_\$$ also include the matrices from Fig. 3 (omitted with "..." here). The middle row gives the control matrices in terms of the new basis, while the bottom row shows them directly. The reader may verify that (1) each row of $\bar{R}_\$$ is individually uniform; (2) $K R_\$ = 0$; and (3) Eq. 7 holds.

Let $\bar{R}_{ij}$ denote the representation of R_{ij} with respect to the basis S—i.e., a vector of length d. Then the garbler can encrypt only the $\bar{R}_{ij}$'s to convey the marginal views of R. The choice of the subspace S depends on the class of truth tables that need to be hidden.

Parity-Leaking Gates: We performed an exhaustive computer search of low dimensional subspaces to determine how to pick the basis S for different types of gates. For even-parity gates (e.g. XOR or constant gates) we found a 2-dimensional subspace that works. Details of the $\mathcal{R}(t)$ distribution are given in Fig. 3. For odd-parity gates (like AND, OR) we simply use the even-parity distribution and add a public constant R_p (from Fig. 4) to the result. This approach works when the parity of the gate is public, since the evaluator must know to add R_p when decoding the description of their marginal view R_{ij}.

The construction for odd-parity gates is our primary construction, which would be used in most applications of garbling (in combination with free XOR gates).

Parity-Hiding Gates: To make the garbling scheme gate-hiding, we also need to hide the parity of the truth table. In other words, the distribution on $R_\$$ must be random enough to mask the presence (or absence) of a matrix R_p as in Eq. 7. The R_p in Fig. 4 is not in the subspace S of control matrices in Fig. 3. Hence, to support parity-hiding we have had to extend that subspace with two additional basis elements (the basis matrices S_1, S_2 are as in the parity-leaking case). Our parity-hiding gates require 4 (compressed) control bits per gate-input combination, corresponding to the 4-dimensional basis S. See Fig. 4 for details.

5.2 Garbling the Control Bits

So far we have glossed over the details of how the control bits actually get encrypted and sent to the evaluator. We know that there will be some $4 \times d$ ($d = 2$ for parity-leaking gates and $d = 4$ for parity hiding gates) matrix $\bar{R}$, and that the evaluator should only get to see a single row $\bar{R}_{ij}$ of $\bar{R}$ telling them what linear combination of $S_1, \ldots, S_d$ to use as control bits. The garbler can easily encrypt these values so that on input A_i, B_j the evaluator can decrypt only $\bar{R}_{ij}$.

In order to reuse the calls to H that the evaluator already uses, it turns out that we can use our new garbling construction to *garble the control bits as well.* At first it looks like this would just give infinite recursion, as if we used something like Eq. 4 to garble the control bits then that garbling would need its own control bits, which would need to be garbled, and so on. In reality, the compressed control bits actually have a structure that allows us to garble them without recursive control bits.

Conceptually, we can treat the bits of $\bar{R}$ as wire labels and slice them as we do regular wire labels. Collect the bits from odd and even-indexed positions of $\bar{R}_{ij}$ into numbers $\bar{r}_{ijL}$ and $\bar{r}_{ijR} \in GF(2^{d/2})$, respectively. Define the vector

$$\vec{r} = \begin{bmatrix} \bar{r}_{00L} & \bar{r}_{00R} & \bar{r}_{01L} & \bar{r}_{01R} & \bar{r}_{10L} & \bar{r}_{10R} & \bar{r}_{11L} & \bar{r}_{11R} \end{bmatrix}^\top$$

We observed that for both our parity-leaking and parity-hiding constructions, this vector is always in the gate subspace $\mathcal{G}$—i.e., that $K\vec{r} = 0$. Looking at Fig. 3, the reader can check that this holds for any possible $\vec{r}$ (which in this case is the same as $\bar{R}$ read in row-major order). And similarly for Fig. 4; this time the test for $\bar{R}$ is equivalent to checking its two 4×2 blocks individually.

Since the control bits, when expressed as $\vec{r}$, are always in the gate subspace $\mathcal{G}$, they can be garbled without needing their own control bits. The garbler can compute a constant-size ciphertext $\vec{z}$ such that:

$$V\vec{z} \oplus M \, \mathrm{lsb}_{\frac{d}{2}}(\vec{H}) = \vec{r}, \tag{8}$$

where $V, M, \vec{H}$ are as in Eq. 4. Here we assume that every hash has been extended by an extra $d/2$ bits (or more realistically given that block ciphers have a fixed size, each wire label slice has been shrunk by $d/2$ bits to make room), and that these extra bit can be extracted with $\mathrm{lsb}_{\frac{d}{2}}$. The remainder of the hash vector, $\mathrm{msb}_{\frac{\kappa}{2}}(\vec{H})$, is used for garbling the wire labels themselves. By the same reasoning as for usual garbling, when the evaluator has input labels A_i, B_j, he can learn only the $\vec{r}_{ij}$ portions of $\vec{r}$.

We can combine Eqs. 4 and 8 into a single system, allowing the whole gate to be garbled at once.

$$V\left(\vec{z} \,\middle\|\, \begin{bmatrix} C \\ \vec{G} \end{bmatrix}\right) \oplus M\vec{H} = \vec{r} \,\middle\|\, \left((R \oplus [0 \cdots 0|t]) \begin{bmatrix} A_0 \\ B_0 \\ \Delta \end{bmatrix}\right), \tag{9}$$

where $\|$ denotes element wise concatenation, so e.g. the bits of $\bar{r}_{00L} \in GF(2^{d/2})$ get concatenated with some $x \in GF(2^{\kappa/2})$ to get a value in $GF(2^{(\kappa+d)/2})$. We write the bits in little endian order, so $\mathrm{lsb}_{\frac{d}{2}}(\vec{H}) \,\|\, \mathrm{msb}_{\frac{\kappa}{2}}(\vec{H}) = \vec{H}$.

5.3 The Construction

We can now describe our garbling scheme formally. All of our different types of gates are compatible, so we describe a single unified scheme. The circuit has a leak function that indicates what information about each gate is public (which affects the cost of garbling each gate):

- EVEN: even-parity gate
- ODD: odd-parity gate
- XOR: free XOR gate
- NONE: no leakage (gate-hiding)

Because we need different control matrices depending on what kind of gate is being garbled, we use the notation $\mathcal{R}(L, t)$, for $L \in \{\text{EVEN}, \text{ODD}, \text{NONE}\}$ to denote the appropriate distribution over control matrices. For EVEN/ODD gates, the distribution is as in Fig. 3 (with R_p added in the case of ODD), and for NONE the distribution is as in Fig. 4.

Our garbling scheme is shown in Figs. 5 and 6. The garbler associates the kth wire in the circuit with a wire label W_k (and its opposite label $W_k \oplus \Delta$) and

---

SampleR(t, leak):
 $R \leftarrow \mathcal{R}(\text{leak}, t)$
 for $i, j \in \{0, 1\}$:
  find coeffs c s.t. $R_{ij} = \bigoplus_k c_k S_k(\text{leak})$
  $\bar{r}_{ijL} := c_1 \| \cdots \| c_{d-1}$ // odd positions
  $\bar{r}_{ijR} := c_2 \| \cdots \| c_d$ // even positions
 $\vec{r} = \begin{bmatrix} \bar{r}_{00L} \ \bar{r}_{00R} \ \bar{r}_{01L} \ \bar{r}_{01R} \ \bar{r}_{10L} \ \bar{r}_{10R} \ \bar{r}_{11L} \ \bar{r}_{11R} \end{bmatrix}^T$
 if leak = ODD:
  $R := R \oplus R_p(\text{ODD})$
 return $R, \vec{r}$

Encode$((\Delta, W, \pi), x)$:
 for $k = 1$ to inputs:
  $E_k := W_k \oplus (x_k \oplus \pi_k)\Delta$
 return E

DecodeR$(\vec{r}, \text{leak}, i, j)$:
 $\begin{bmatrix} c_1 \| \cdots \| c_{d-1} \\ c_2 \| \cdots \| c_d \end{bmatrix} := \vec{r}$
 $R_{ij} := \bigoplus_k c_k S_k(\text{leak})$
 if leak = ODD:
  $R_{ij} := R_{ij} \oplus (R_p(\text{ODD}))_{ij}$
 return R_{ij}

Decode$((\Phi, D), E)$:
 (inputs, outputs, in, leak) $:= \Phi$
 $y :=$ empty list
 for $k \in$ outputs:
  if $\exists j. \, D_k^j = H'(E_k, k)$:
   append j to y
  else: abort
 return y

Fig. 5. Our garbling scheme (continued in Fig. 6).

a point-and-permute bit π_k. W_k is the label with color bit $\text{lsb}(W_k) = 0$ (visible to the evaluator). The label $W_k \oplus \pi_k \Delta$ is the wire label representing false on that wire. Equivalently, W_k is the wire label representing logical value π_k.

For each non-free gate, the garbler first samples a control matrix R and encodes its marginal views (i.e., expresses each view in terms of the basis $\{S_j\}_j$). We have factored out this sampling procedure into a helper function SampleR, along with a corresponding decoding function DecodeR used by the evaluator to reconstruct its marginal view of the control matrix. One thing to note about SampleR is that in the case of a ODD gate, the control matrices include the term R_p, but R_p is not in the subspace spanned by the basis $\{S_j\}_j$. The compressed representation of each marginal view excludes the contribution of R_p, but in these cases it is publicly known that the evaluator should compensate by manually adding R_p.

For each gate k, we have a master evaluation equation in the style of Eq. 9. This equation expresses constraints that must be true about that gate, but the garbler is interested in computing garbled gate ciphertexts $\vec{G}_k$, control bit ciphertexts $\vec{z}_k$, and output wire label that satisfy the constraints. As previously discussed, we can solve for these values by multipying both sides by V^{-1}, a left inverse of V. One possible choice of V^{-1} is given below:

$$V^{-1} = \begin{bmatrix} 1 & 0 & 0 & 0 & 0 & 0 & 0 & 0 \\ 0 & 1 & 0 & 0 & 0 & 0 & 0 & 0 \\ 1 & 1 & 0 & 0 & 1 & 1 & 0 & 0 \\ 1 & 1 & 1 & 0 & 0 & 0 & 0 & 0 \\ 0 & 0 & 0 & 0 & 1 & 0 & 1 & 0 \end{bmatrix} \tag{10}$$

The queries to hash function H include tweaks based on the gate ID, for domain separation. Finally, for each output wire, the garbler computes hashes

$\mathsf{Garble}(1^\kappa, f)$:

$\quad (\mathsf{inputs}, \mathsf{outputs}, \mathsf{in}, \mathsf{leak}, \mathsf{eval}) := f$

$\quad H \leftarrow \mathcal{H}$

$\quad \Delta \leftarrow \begin{bmatrix} 1 \parallel \mathrm{GF}(2^{\kappa/2 - 1}) \\ \mathrm{GF}(2^{\kappa/2}) \end{bmatrix}$

$\quad \text{for } k = 1 \text{ to inputs:}$

$\qquad W_k \leftarrow \begin{bmatrix} 0 \parallel \mathrm{GF}(2^{\kappa/2 - 1}) \\ \mathrm{GF}(2^{\kappa/2}) \end{bmatrix}$

$\qquad \pi_k \leftarrow \{0, 1\}$

$\quad \text{for } k = \mathsf{inputs} + 1 \text{ to } |f|:$

$\qquad A_0, B_0 := W_{\mathsf{in}_1(k)}, W_{\mathsf{in}_2(k)}$

$\qquad \pi_A, \pi_B := \pi_{\mathsf{in}_1(k)}, \pi_{\mathsf{in}_2(k)}$

$\qquad \text{if } \mathsf{leak}(k) = \mathsf{XOR}:$

$\qquad\quad W_k := A_0 \oplus B_0$

$\qquad\quad \pi_k := \pi_A \oplus \pi_B$

$\qquad\quad \text{continue}$

$\qquad g := \mathsf{eval}(k)$

$\qquad t := \begin{bmatrix} g(\pi_A, \pi_B) \ g(\pi_A, 1 - \pi_B) \ g(1 - \pi_A, \pi_B) \ g(1 - \pi_A, 1 - \pi_B) \end{bmatrix}^\top$

$\qquad R, \vec{r} := \mathsf{SampleR}(t, \mathsf{leak}(k))$

$$\vec{z}_k \parallel \begin{bmatrix} C \\ \vec{G}_k \end{bmatrix} := V^{-1} \left(\vec{r} \parallel (R \oplus [0 \cdots 0|t]) \begin{bmatrix} A_0 \\ B_0 \\ \Delta \end{bmatrix} \right) \oplus V^{-1} M \begin{bmatrix} H(A_0, 3k - 3) \\ H(A_0 \oplus \Delta, 3k - 3) \\ H(B_0, 3k - 2) \\ H(B_0 \oplus \Delta, 3k - 2) \\ H(A_0 \oplus B_0, 3k - 1) \\ H(A_0 \oplus B_0 \oplus \Delta, 3k - 1) \end{bmatrix}$$

$\qquad \pi_k := \mathsf{lsb}(C)$

$\qquad W_k := C \oplus \pi_k \Delta$

$\quad \text{for } k \in \mathsf{outputs}, j \in \{0, 1\}:$

$\qquad D_k^j := H'(W_k \oplus (j \oplus \pi_k)\Delta, k)$

$\quad \text{return } F = (\Phi(f), H, \vec{G}, \vec{z}), \ e = (\Delta, W, \pi), \ d = (\Phi(f), D)$

$\mathsf{Eval}(F = (\Phi, H, \vec{G}, \vec{z}), E)$:

$\quad (\mathsf{inputs}, \mathsf{outputs}, \mathsf{in}, \mathsf{leak}) := \Phi$

$\quad \text{for } k = \mathsf{inputs} + 1 \text{ to } |\Phi|:$

$\qquad A, B := E_{\mathsf{in}_1(k)}, E_{\mathsf{in}_2(k)}$

$\qquad i, j := \mathsf{lsb}(A), \mathsf{lsb}(B)$

$\qquad \text{if } \mathsf{leak}(k) = \mathsf{XOR}:$

$\qquad\quad E_k := A \oplus B$

$\qquad \text{else}$

$\qquad\quad \vec{r} \parallel X_{ij} := V_{ij} \left(\vec{z}_k \parallel \begin{bmatrix} 0 \\ \vec{G}_k \end{bmatrix} \right) \oplus \begin{bmatrix} 1 & 0 & 1 \\ 0 & 1 & 1 \end{bmatrix} \begin{bmatrix} H(A, 3k - 3) \\ H(B, 3k - 2) \\ H(A \oplus B, 3k - 1) \end{bmatrix}$

$\qquad\quad R_{ij} := \mathsf{DecodeR}(\vec{r}, \mathsf{leak}, i, j)$

$\qquad\quad E_k := X_{ij} \oplus R_{ij} \begin{bmatrix} A \\ B \end{bmatrix}$

$\quad \text{return } E$

Fig. 6. Our garbling scheme (continued from Fig. 5). V^{-1} is a left inverse of V.

of the wire labels, which will be used in Decode to authenticate labels and determine their logical value (true or false). These hashes need κ bits for authenticity, so they are computed using another hash function $H'(E, k)$ with output length κ instead $\frac{\kappa + d}{2}$. It is simplest to set $H'(E, k) = \mathrm{msb}_{\frac{\kappa}{2}}(H(E, 3|f| + 2k)) \parallel \mathrm{msb}_{\frac{\kappa}{2}}(H(E, 3|f| + 2k + 1))$, which puts together κ bits from two evaluations of H, while avoiding any overlaps in tweaks.

The evaluator follows a similar process. Starting with the input wire labels E, it evaluates the garbled circuit one gate at a time. The invariant is that on wire k, the evaluator will hold the "active" wire label $E_k = W_k \oplus (x_k \oplus \pi_k)\Delta$, where x_k is the logical value on that wire, for the given circuit input. If A, B are the active wire labels on the input wires of this gate, then the evaluator computes terms of the form $H(A), H(B), H(A \oplus B)$ and evaluates the gate according to Eq. 9. The evaluator only knows enough for two rows of Eq. 9, depending on the color bits $i = \mathrm{lsb}(A)$, $j = \mathrm{lsb}(B)$, so we let V_{ij} be the corresponding pair of rows from V. It only evaluates the gate partially at first, in order to find the encoded control bits so that it can decode them with DecodeR and use them to finally compute the output wire label.

5.4   Security Proof

Theorem 3. *Let $\mathcal{H}$ be a family of hash functions, with output length $(\kappa + d)/2$ bits, that is RTCCR for $\mathcal{L} = \{L_{ab}(\Delta_L \| \Delta_R) = 0^{d/2} \| a\Delta_L \oplus b\Delta_R \mid a, b, \in \{0, 1\}\}$. Then our construction (Figs. 5 and 6) is a secure garbling scheme.*

Proof. We need to prove four properties of the construction.

Correctness: We need to prove an invariant: $E_k = W_k \oplus (x_k \oplus \pi_k)\Delta$ for all k, if x_k is the plaintext value on that wire. Encode chooses the inputs in this way, so at least it's true for $k \leq$ inputs, and it is trivially maintained for free-XOR gates. For any $v \in \mathrm{colspace}(V) = \mathcal{G}$, we have $VV^{-1}v = v$, as there exists some u such that $v = Vu$ and $VV^{-1}Vu = Vu = v$ because V^{-1} is a left inverse of V. In Sect. 5.1 we showed that $\mathrm{colspace}(M) = \mathcal{G}$, $\mathrm{colspace}(R \oplus [0 \cdots 0|t]) \subseteq \mathcal{G}$, and $\vec{r} \in \mathcal{G}$, so after multiplying both sides of garbler's equation by V on the left, the VV^{-1}s will cancel, and taking a two-row piece of this equation gives the evaluator's equation. In this equation, X_{ij} is the two rows of

$$\vec{X} = C \oplus (R \oplus [0 \cdots 0|t]) \begin{bmatrix} A_0 \\ B_0 \\ \Delta \end{bmatrix}, \tag{11}$$

corresponding to the evaluation case i, j. The structure of R (see Eq. 6) implies that the evaluator's row pair of $R[A_0^\top \ B_0^\top \ \Delta^\top]^\top$ will be $R_{ij}[A^\top \ B^\top]^\top$. Therefore

$$E_k = X_{ij} \oplus R \begin{bmatrix} A \\ B \end{bmatrix} = C \oplus t_{ij}\Delta = W_k \oplus (\mathrm{eval}(k)(\pi_A \oplus i, \pi_B \oplus j) \oplus \pi_k)\Delta,$$

which maintains this invariant because

$$i = \mathrm{lsb}(E_{\mathrm{in}_1(k)}) = \mathrm{lsb}\big(W_{\mathrm{in}_1(k)} \oplus (x_{\mathrm{in}_1(k)} \oplus \pi_{\mathrm{in}_1(k)})\Delta\big) = x_{\mathrm{in}_1(k)} \oplus \pi_{\mathrm{in}_1(k)},$$

$Hybrid1(1^\kappa, f, x)$:
(inputs, outputs, in, leak, eval) := f
$H \leftarrow \mathcal{H}$
$\Delta \leftarrow \begin{bmatrix} 1 \parallel \mathrm{GF}(2^{\kappa/2-1}) \\ \mathrm{GF}(2^{\kappa/2}) \end{bmatrix}$
for $k = 1$ to inputs:
    $E_k \leftarrow \mathrm{GF}(2^{\kappa/2})^2$
for $k = $ inputs $+ 1$ to $|f|$:
    $A, B := E_{\mathsf{in}_1(k)}, E_{\mathsf{in}_2(k)}$
    $i, j := \mathsf{lsb}(A), \mathsf{lsb}(B)$
    $x_A, x_B := x_{\mathsf{in}_1(k)}, x_{\mathsf{in}_2(k)}$
    if $\mathsf{leak}(k) = $ XOR:
        $E_k := A \oplus B$
        $x_k := x_A \oplus x_B$
        continue
    $g := \mathsf{eval}(k)$
    $x_k := g(x_A, x_B)$

$\mathcal{S}_{\mathrm{priv}}(1^\kappa, \Phi, x)$:
(inputs, outputs, in, leak) := Φ
$(F, E) \leftarrow \mathcal{S}_{\mathrm{obliv}}(1^\kappa, \Phi)$
$E' := \mathsf{Eval}(F, E)$
for $k \in $ outputs:
    $D_k^{x_k} := H'(E'_k, k)$
    $D_k^{1-x_k} \leftarrow \mathrm{GF}(2^\kappa)$
return $F, E, (\Phi, D)$

$t := \begin{bmatrix} g(x_A \oplus i, x_B \oplus j) \\ g(x_A \oplus i, x_B \oplus j \oplus 1) \\ g(x_A \oplus i \oplus 1, x_B \oplus j) \\ g(x_A \oplus i \oplus 1, x_B \oplus j \oplus 1) \end{bmatrix}$
$R, \vec{r} := \mathsf{SampleR}(t, \mathsf{leak}(k))$

$\mathcal{S}_{\mathrm{obliv}}(1^\kappa, \Phi)$:
(inputs, outputs, in, leak) := Φ
$H \leftarrow \mathcal{H}$
for $k = 1$ to inputs:
    $E_k \leftarrow \mathrm{GF}(2^{\kappa/2})^2$
for $k = $ inputs $+ 1$ to $|\Phi|$:
    if $\mathsf{leak}(k) = $ XOR: continue
    $\vec{G}_k \leftarrow \mathrm{GF}(2^{\kappa/2})^3$
    $\vec{z}_k \leftarrow \mathrm{GF}(2^{d(\mathsf{leak}(k))/2})^5$
return $(\Phi, H, \vec{G}, \vec{z}), E$

$R' := R \begin{bmatrix} 1 & 0 & 0 & 0 & i & 0 \\ 0 & 1 & 0 & 0 & 0 & i \\ 0 & 0 & 1 & 0 & j & 0 \\ 0 & 0 & 0 & 1 & 0 & j \\ 0 & 0 & 0 & 0 & 1 & 0 \\ 0 & 0 & 0 & 0 & 0 & 1 \end{bmatrix}$

$\vec{H}_0 := \begin{bmatrix} H(A, 3k-3) \\ H(B, 3k-2) \\ H(A \oplus B, 3k-1) \end{bmatrix}$

$\vec{H}_\Delta := \begin{bmatrix} H(A \oplus \Delta, 3k-3) \\ H(B \oplus \Delta, 3k-2) \\ H(A \oplus B \oplus \Delta, 3k-1) \end{bmatrix}$

$(\vec{z}_k)_{\mathrm{bot}} \parallel \vec{G}_k := V_{\mathrm{gate}}^{-1}\left(\vec{r} \parallel (R' \oplus [0 \cdots 0 | t]) \begin{bmatrix} A \\ B \\ \Delta \end{bmatrix}\right)$

$\oplus\, V_{\mathrm{gate}}^{-1}(M_0 \vec{H}_0 \oplus M_\Delta \vec{H}_\Delta)$

$E_k := V_{ij} \begin{bmatrix} 0 \\ \vec{G}_k \end{bmatrix} \oplus \begin{bmatrix} 1 & 0 & 1 \\ 0 & 1 & 1 \end{bmatrix} \mathsf{msb}_{\frac{\kappa}{2}}(\vec{H}_0) \oplus R_{ij} \begin{bmatrix} A \\ B \end{bmatrix}$

$(\vec{z}_k)_{\mathrm{top}} := V_{ij} \begin{bmatrix} 0 \\ (\vec{z}_k)_{\mathrm{bot}} \end{bmatrix} \oplus \begin{bmatrix} 1 & 0 & 1 \\ 0 & 1 & 1 \end{bmatrix} \mathsf{lsb}_{\frac{d}{2}}(\vec{H}_0) \oplus \vec{r}_{ij}$

for $k \in $ outputs, $j \in \{0, 1\}$:
    $D_k^j := H'(E_k \oplus (j \oplus x_k)\Delta, k)$
return $(\Phi(f), \vec{G}, \vec{z}), E, (\Phi(f), D)$

Fig. 7. Left: simulators for privacy and obliviousness. Right: a hybrid for privacy.

and similarly for j. Finally, Decode will correctly find that $D_k^{x_k} = H'(W_k \oplus (x_k \oplus \pi_k)\Delta, k) = H'(E_k, k)$, assuming that $D_k^{x_k} \neq D_k^{1-x_k}$, which has only negligible probability of failing. Therefore it gives the correct result.

Privacy: We need to prove that generating $(\Phi, \vec{G}, \vec{z}), E, (\Phi, D)$ with Garble and Encode is indistinguishable from the output of $\mathcal{S}_{\mathrm{priv}}$. We give a sequence of intermediate hybrids, going from the real garbler to the simulator.

Hybrid 1: This hybrid switches from the garbler's perspective to the evaluator's perspective when garbling the circuit. Instead of keeping track of the "zero" wire label W_k for every gate, we keep track of the "active" wire label E_k, and rewrite the garbling procedure in terms of the "active" labels. This basically involves a change of variable names throughout the garbling algorithm. The changes are extensive, and given in detail in Fig. 7:

- Replace point-and-permute bits π_k with the equivalent expression $x_k \oplus \mathrm{lsb}(E_k)$.
- Write the control matrix part of the garbling equation in terms of active wire labels $A = E_{\mathrm{in}_1(k)}$ and $B = E_{\mathrm{in}_2(k)}$ instead of A_0 and B_0.

$$\text{replace } R \times \begin{bmatrix} A_0 \\ B_0 \\ \Delta \end{bmatrix} \text{ with equivalent } R' \times \begin{bmatrix} A \\ B \\ \Delta \end{bmatrix}.$$

where a change of basis has been applied to R, that expresses A_0 as the appropriate linear combination of A and Δ, and expresses B_0 in terms of B and Δ.

- Partition $\vec{H}$ into two pieces:

$$\vec{H}_0 = [H(A)\ H(B)\ H(A \oplus B)]^\top$$
$$\vec{H}_\Delta = [H(A \oplus \Delta)\ H(B \oplus \Delta)\ H(A \oplus B \oplus \Delta)]^\top$$

where again A and B are the active wire labels. Similarly partition the matrix M into M_0 and M_Δ, and replace $M \times \vec{H}$ with $(M_0 \vec{H}_0 \oplus M_\Delta \vec{H}_\Delta)$.

- Note that the matrix V^{-1} has 5 rows, where the first 2 correspond to slices of the output label and the last 3 correspond to the gate ciphertexts. Denote this division of V^{-1} by V^{-1}_{label} and V^{-1}_{gate}. Instead of multiplying on the left by V^{-1} to solve for the output label and gate ciphertexts, we now multiply on the left by V^{-1}_{gate} to solve for only the gate ciphertexts. We then evaluate those gate ciphertexts with A and B to learn the (active) output label E_k. This different approach has the same result by the correctness of the scheme. We can similarly partition the control bit ciphertexts $\vec{z}_k = [(\vec{z}_k)_{\mathrm{top}}\ (\vec{z}_k)_{\mathrm{bot}}]$, use V^{-1}_{gate} to compute $(\vec{z}_k)_{\mathrm{bot}}$, and then use the evaluator's computation to solve for $(\vec{z}_k)_{\mathrm{top}}$. Solving for $(\vec{z}_k)_{\mathrm{top}}$ is simplified by the first two columns of V_{ij} being the identity matrix. In this case, we solve for the missing positions using knowledge of the compressed control bits $\bar{r}_{ij}$.

All of the changes are simple variable substitutions or basis changes in the linear algebra, so this hybrid is distributed identically to the real garbling.

Hybrid 2: In this hybrid, we apply the RTCCR property of H to all oracle queries of the form $H(\cdot \oplus \Delta)$. We must show that Δ is used in a way that can be achieved by calling the oracle from the RTCCR security game.

We focus on the term

$$V^{-1}_{\mathrm{gate}} M \vec{H} = V^{-1}_{\mathrm{gate}}(M_0 \vec{H}_0 \oplus M_\Delta \vec{H}_\Delta)$$

First, consider the expression $V^{-1} \times M$, and recall that M is written in terms of the zero-labels A_0, B_0. Using the V^{-1} given in Eq. 10 , we can compute:

$$
V^{-1}M = \begin{bmatrix} 1 & 0 & 0 & 0 & 1 & 0 \\ 0 & 0 & 1 & 0 & 1 & 0 \\ 1 & 1 & 0 & 0 & 0 & 0 \\ 0 & 0 & 1 & 1 & 0 & 0 \\ 0 & 0 & 0 & 0 & 1 & 1 \end{bmatrix} \tag{12}
$$

Thus $V_{\text{gate}}^{-1} \times M$ will consist of the bottom three rows of Eq. 12.

Recall that the columns of M correspond to oracle queries $H(A_0), H(A_0 \oplus \Delta), H(B_0), H(B_0 \oplus \Delta), H(A \oplus B), H(A \oplus B \oplus \Delta)$, in that order. In the current hybrid M is partitioned into M_0 (corresponding to H-queries on active labels) and M_Δ (corresponding to the other queries). In other words, M_Δ will consist of exactly one of rows $\{1, 2\}$, exactly one of rows $\{3, 4\}$, and exactly one of rows $\{5, 6\}$ from M. In all cases, the result of $V_{\text{gate}}^{-1}M_\Delta$ (i.e., the bottom 3 rows of $V^{-1}M_\Delta$) is the 3×3 identity matrix!

This means we can rewrite the hybrid in the following way:

$$
(\vec{z}_k)_{\text{bot}} \,\big\|\, \vec{G}_k := V_{\text{gate}}^{-1} \left(\vec{r} \,\big\|\, (R' \oplus [0 \cdots 0 \mid t]) \begin{bmatrix} A \\ B \\ \Delta \end{bmatrix} \right) \oplus V_{\text{gate}}^{-1}(M_0 \vec{H}_0 \oplus M_\Delta \vec{H}_\Delta)
$$

$$
= \vec{H}_\Delta \oplus [\text{linear combinations of } \Delta] \oplus \cdots
$$

Since all the H-queries in $\vec{H}_\Delta$ include a Δ term, we can compute this expression with 3 suitable calls to the RTCCR oracle.[8] Finally, $D_k^{1-x_k} = H'(E_k \oplus \Delta, k)$ also uses Δ, and will become two calls to the RTCCR oracle. These transformations successfully moves all references to Δ into the RTCCR oracle.

Applying RTCCR security, it has negligible effect to replace the results of these H-queries with uniformly random values. This has the effect of making the entire expression uniform, i.e.:

$$
(\vec{z}_k)_{\text{bot}} \,\big\|\, \vec{G}_k \leftarrow GF(2^{(\kappa+d)/2})^3
$$

Also, $D_k^{1-x_k}$ is now sampled uniformly at random in $GF(2^\kappa)$.

Hybrid 3: After making the previous change, the only place that R is used is when we use the marginal views R_{ij} and $\vec{r}_{ij}$ to solve for the output label and for the missing pieces of the control bit ciphertexts. In Sect. 5.1 we specifically chose $\mathcal{R}$ so that this marginal views is uniform for all t and all i, j. Therefore instead of doing $R, \vec{r} \leftarrow \mathsf{SampleR}(t, \mathsf{leak}(k))$, we can simply choose uniform $\vec{r}_{ij}$ and use $\mathsf{DecodeR}$ to reconstruct R_{ij}. The change has no effect on the overall view of the adversary.

Note that after making this change, the control-bit ciphertexts $(\vec{z}_k)_{\text{top}}$ become uniform since $\vec{r}_{ij}$ acts as a one-time pad.

---

[8] Note also that the calls to H have globally distinct tweaks.

Hybrid 4: As a result of the previous change, the hybrid no longer uses t. Additionally, t was the only place where the plaintext values x_k were used, other than in the computation of D. But D only uses plaintext values for the circuit's output wires. In other words, the entire hybrid can be computed knowing only the circuit output $f(x)$. Additionally, all garbled gate ciphertexts and control bit ciphertexts are chosen uniformly, and the active wire labels on output wires are determined by the scheme's evaluation procedure. Hence, the hybrid exactly matches what happens in S_{priv}.

Obliviousness: Notice that S_{priv} calls S_{obliv} to generate (F, E), then samples some more random bits for decoding and returns it all. Therefore, any adversary for obliviousness could be turned into one for privacy by only looking at (F, E) and ignoring the rest.

Authenticity: The first two steps of the authenticity distribution are exactly the same as the real privacy distribution, so we can swap them for the simulated distribution S_{priv} in a hybrid. Then to break authenticity the adversary must cause Decode to choose $j = 1 - x_k$ for at least one output k, as otherwise it will either produce the correct answer or abort. But $D_k^{1-x_k}$ is fresh uniform randomness, so the probability that $D_k^{1-x_k} = H'(E_k, k)$ is $2^{-\kappa}$.

5.5   Discussion

Concrete Costs. The garbler makes 6 calls to H per non-free gate, while the evaluator makes 3 calls to H per non-free gate.

Each non-free garbled gate consists of gate ciphertexts $\vec{G}$ and encrypted control bits $\vec{z}$. There are 3 gate ciphertexts, each being $\kappa/2$ bits long. The encrypted control bits are a vector of length 5, where each component of the vector has length $d/2$ (where d is the dimension of the control matrix subspace). For the standard (parity-leaking) instantiation of our scheme, $d = 2$ and we get that the total size of a garbled gate is $1.5\kappa + 5$ bits. For the gate-hiding instantiation, $d = 4$ and we get a size of $1.5\kappa + 10$ bits.

Comparison to Half-Gates. We assume that calls to H are the computational bottleneck, in any implementation of both our scheme and in half-gates [ZRE15]. The following analysis therefore ignores the cost of xor'ing wire labels and bit-fiddling related to color bits and control bits.

In the time it takes to call H 12 times, half-gates generates 3 gates and sends 6κ bits (4 calls to H and 2κ bits per gate), while our scheme generates 2 gates and sends 3κ bits (6 calls to H and 1.5κ bits per gate). Thus, a CPU-bound implementation of our scheme will produce garbled output at half the rate of half-gates. We evaluated the optimized half-gates garbling algorithm from the ABY3 library [MR18], and found it capable of generating garbled output at a rate of ~850 Mbyte/s on single core of a i7-7500U laptop processor running at 3.5 GHz. Thus, we conservatively estimate that a comparable implementation of our scheme could generate garbled output at ~400 Mbyte/s = 3.2 Gbit/s. This rate would still leave our scheme network-bound in most situations and applications of garbled circuits. When both half-gates and our scheme are network bound, our scheme is expected to take $\sim25\%$ less time by virtue of reducing communication by 25%.

6   Optimizations

6.1   Optimizing Control Bit Encryptions

In our scheme the control bit encryptions $\vec{z}$ is a vector of length 5, where the components in that vector are each a single bit (in the case of parity-leaking gates) or 2 bits (in the case of parity-hiding gates). These ciphertexts therefore contribute 5 or 10 bits to the size of each garbled gate.

We remark that it is possible to use ideas of garbled row reduction [NPS99, PSSW09] to reduce $\vec{z}$ to a length-3 vector. This will result in these ciphertexts contributing 3 or 6 bits to the garbled gate. Such an optimization may be convenient in parity-hiding case, where the change from 10 to 6 bits allows these control bit ciphertexts to fit in a single byte.

Recall that in the security proof, we partition the control bit ciphertexts $\vec{z}$ into $(\vec{z})_{\mathsf{top}}$ (2 components) and $(\vec{z})_{\mathsf{bot}}$ (3 components). Our idea to reduce their size is to simply fix $(\vec{z})_{\mathsf{top}}$ to zeroes, so that these components do not need to be explicitly included in the garbled gate. The evaluator can act exactly as before, taking the missing values from $\vec{z}$ to be zeroes. The garbler must sample the control matrix subject to it causing $(\vec{z})_{\mathsf{top}} = 0$.

A drawback to this optimization is that it significantly complicates the security proof (and hence why we only sketch it here). When we apply the security of RTCCR in the security proof, the hybrid acts as follows:

1. It uses the $d/2$ least significant bits of the H-outputs to determine how the control bits are going to be "masked".
2. Based on these masks, it chooses a consistent control matrix R that causes the first two components of $\vec{z}$ to be 0.
3. The choice of R determines which linear combinations of wire label slices (including slices of Δ) are applied.

So the reduction to RTCCR security must first read the low bits of several $H(\cdot \oplus \Delta)$ queries before it decides which linear combination of Δ should be XOR'ed with the remaining output of H. Of course the RTCCR oracle requires the choice of linear combination to be provided when H is called. It is indeed possible to formally account for this, but only by modeling the two parts of H's output (for masking wire label slices and for masking control bits) as separate hash functions for the purposes of the security proof.

6.2   Optimizing Computation

Our construction requires a RTCCR function H with output length $(\kappa + d)/2$. We propose an efficient instantiation of H which naturally results in κ-bit output, which is then truncated to $(\kappa + d)/2$. The hash produces nearly twice as many bits as needed, raising the question of whether we are "wasting" these extra bits. In fact, if we reduce the security parameter slightly so that H is derived from a $(\kappa + d)$-bit primitive, we can use these extra bits to reduce the computation cost.

Suppose H' is a [RT]CCR with $(\kappa + d)$ bits of output. Then define

$$H(X, \tau) = \begin{cases} \text{first half of } H'(X, \frac{\tau}{2}) & \tau \text{ even} \\ \text{second half of } H'(X, \frac{\tau-1}{2}) & \tau \text{ odd} \end{cases}$$

Clearly H is also a [RT]CCR with $(\kappa + d)/2$ bits of output. How can we use this H to reduce the total number of calls to the underlying H'?

When a wire with labels $(A, A \oplus \Delta)$ is used as input to an AND gate, our scheme makes calls of the form $H(A, j), H(A \oplus \Delta, j)$ where j is the ID of that AND gate. Let us slightly change how the tweaks are used. Suppose this wire with label $(A, A \oplus \Delta)$ is used as input in n different AND gates. Then those gates should make calls of the form $H(A, 0 \| i), H(A, 1 \| i), \ldots, H(A, n - 1 \| i)$, where i is now the index of *the wire whose labels are* $(A, A \oplus \Delta)$. When H is defined as above, these queries can be computed with only $\lceil n/2 \rceil$ queries to H'.

Note that both the garbler and evaluator can take advantage of this optimization, with the garbler always requiring exactly twice as many calls to H' (if in some scenario the evaluator needs $H'(X)$ then the garbler will need $H'(X)$ and $H'(X \oplus \Delta)$). Our AND gates require calls to H of the form $H(A), H(B), H(A \oplus B)$, and so far we have discussed optimizing only the $H(A)$ and $H(B)$ queries. Similar logic can be applied to the queries of the form $H(A \oplus B)$; for example, if a circuit contains gates $a \wedge b$ and $(a \oplus b) \wedge c$, then both of those AND gates will require $H(A \oplus B)$ terms that can be optimized in this way.

circuit	baseline	optimized	improvement	half-gates [ZRE15]
64-bit adder	6.00	6.00	0%	4.00
64-bit division	6.00	5.75	4.1%	4.00
64-bit multiplication	6.00	4.99	16.8%	4.00
AES-128	6.00	4.31	28.2%	4.00
SHA-256	6.00	5.77	3.8%	4.00
Keccak f	6.00	4.00	33.3%	4.00

Fig. 8. Number of calls to κ-bit H' RTCCR function (per AND gate) to garble each circuit, with and without the optimization of Sect. 6.2. Evaluating the garbled circuit costs exactly half this number of calls to H'.

We explored the effect of this optimization for a selection of circuits.[9] The results are shown in Fig. 8. The improvement ranges from 0% to 33.3%. As a

---

[9] Circuits were obtained from https://homes.esat.kuleuven.be/~nsmart/MPC/.

reference, our baseline construction requires 6 calls to $((\kappa + d)/2$-bit output) H to garble an AND gate, while half-gates requires 4 calls (to a κ-bit function). Interestingly, in the Keccak f-function every wire used as input to an *even number* of AND gates, so that our optimized scheme has the same computation cost as half-gates (4 calls to H' per AND gate). In principle, this optimization can result in as few as 3 calls to H' per AND gate,[10] but typical circuits do not appear to be nearly so favorable.

7 The Linear Garbling Lower Bound

In [ZRE15], the authors present a lower bound for garbled AND gates in a model that they call **linear garbling.** The linear garbling model considers schemes with the following properties:

- Wire labels have an associated *color bit* which must be $\{0, 1\}$.
- To evaluate the garbled gate, the evaluator makes a sequence of calls to a random oracle (that depend only on the input wire labels), and then outputs some linear combination of input labels, gate ciphertexts, and random oracle outputs. The linear combination must depend only on the color bits of the input labels.

The bound of [ZRE15] considers only linear combinations over the field $GF(2^\kappa)$, and it is unclear to what extent the results generalize to other fields.

Several works have bypassed this lower bound, and we summarize them below. All of these works show how to garble an AND gate for $\kappa + O(1)$ bits, but only a single AND gate in isolation. These constructions all require the input wire labels to satisfy a certain structure, but do not guarantee that the output labels also satisfy that structure.

- Kempka, Kikuchi, and Suzuki [KKS16] and Wang and Malluhi [WmM17] both use a technique of randomizing the control bits. The evaluator decrypts a constant-size ciphertext to determine which linear combination to apply. This approach is outside of the linear garbling model, which requires that the linear combination depend only on the color bits. These works also add wire labels in $\mathbb{Z}_{2^\kappa}$ rather than XOR them (as in $GF(2^\kappa)$). Apart from these similarities, the two approaches are quite different.
- Ball, Malkin, and Rosulek [BMR16] deviate from the linear garbling model by letting each wire label have a color "trit" from $\mathbb{Z}_3$ instead of a color bit from $\mathbb{Z}_2$. There is no further "indirection" of the evaluator's linear combination—it depends only on the colors of the input labels. They also perform some linear combinations on wire labels over a field of characteristic 3.

As described earlier, we bypass the lower bound by adopting the control-bit randomization technique of [KKS16] but also introducing the wire-label-slicing technique.

---

[10] This can happen, *e.g.*, when for every $a \wedge b$ gate there is a corresponding $a \vee b = \overline{a} \wedge \overline{b}$ gate.

8 Open Problems

We conclude by listing several open problems suggested by our work.

Optimality. Is 1.5κ bits optimal for garbled AND gates in a more inclusive model than the one in [ZRE15]? A natural model that excludes "heavy machinery" like fully homomorphic encryption is Minicrypt, in which all parties are computationally unbounded but have bounded access to a random oracle. Conversely, can one do better—say, $4\kappa/3$ bits per AND gate? Does it help to sacrifice compatibility with free-XOR? In our construction, free-XOR seems crucial.

Computation Cost. In Sect. 6.2 we described how to reduce the number of queries to an underlying κ-bit primitive, with an optimization that depends on topology of the circuit. Is there a way to reduce the computation cost of our scheme (measured in number of calls to, say, a κ-bit ideal permutation), for *all* circuits?

In the best case, we can garble a circuit for only 3 (amortized) calls per AND gate, whereas all prior schemes require 4. Setting aside garbled circuit size and free-XOR compatibility, is there any scheme that can garble arbitrary circuits for less than 4 (amortized) calls to a κ-bit primitive per AND gate?

Hardness Assumption. Free-XOR garbling requires some kind of circular correlation robust assumption (see [CKKZ12] for a formal statement). The state-of-the-art garbling scheme based on the minimal assumption of PRF is due to Gueron *et al.* [GLNP15], where AND gates cost 2κ and XOR gates cost κ bits. Can our new techniques be used to improve on garbling from the PRF assumption, or alternatively can the optimality of [GLNP15] be proven? Again, our construction seems to rely heavily on the free-XOR structure of wire labels, which (apparently) makes circular correlation robustness necessary.

Privacy-Free Garbling. Frederiksen *et al.* [FNO15] introduced *privacy-free* garbled circuits, in which only the authenticity property is required of the garbling scheme. The state-of-the-art privacy-free scheme is due to [ZRE15], where XOR gates are free and AND gates cost κ bits. Can our new techniques lead to a privacy-free garbling scheme with less than κ bits per AND gate (with or without free-XOR)?

Simpler Description. Is there a way to describe our construction as the clean composition of simpler components, similar to how the half-gates construction is described in terms of simpler "half gate" objects? The challenge in our scheme is the way in which left-slices and right-slices of the wire labels are used together.

References

BHR12. Bellare, M., Hoang, V.T., Rogaway, P.: Foundations of garbled circuits. In: Yu, T., Danezis, G., Gligor, V.D. (eds.) ACM CCS 2012, pp. 784–796. ACM Press, October 2012

BMR90. Beaver, D., Micali, S., Rogaway, P.: The round complexity of secure protocols (extended abstract). In: 22nd ACM STOC, pp. 503–513. ACM Press, May 1990

BMR16. Ball, M., Malkin, T., Rosulek, M.: Garbling gadgets for Boolean and arithmetic circuits. In: Weippl, E.R., Katzenbeisser, S., Kruegel, C., Myers, A.C., Halevi, S. (eds.) ACM CCS 2016, pp. 565–577. ACM Press, October 2016

CKKZ12. Choi, S.G., Katz, J., Kumaresan, R., Zhou, H.-S.: On the security of the "Free-XOR" technique. In: Cramer, R. (ed.) TCC 2012. LNCS, vol. 7194, pp. 39–53. Springer, Heidelberg (2012). https://doi.org/10.1007/978-3-642-28914-9_3

CR16. Carmer, B., Rosulek, M.: Linicrypt: a model for practical cryptography. In: Robshaw, M., Katz, J. (eds.) CRYPTO 2016. LNCS, vol. 9816, pp. 416–445. Springer, Heidelberg (2016)

FNO15. Frederiksen, T.K., Nielsen, J.B., Orlandi, C.: Privacy-free garbled circuits with applications to efficient zero-knowledge. In: Oswald, E., Fischlin, M. (eds.) EUROCRYPT 2015. LNCS, vol. 9057, pp. 191–219. Springer, Heidelberg (2015)

GKWY20. Guo, C., Katz, J., Wang, X., Yu, Y.: Efficient and secure multiparty computation from fixed-key block ciphers. In: 2020 IEEE Symposium on Security and Privacy, pp. 825–841. IEEE Computer Society Press, May 2020

GLNP15. Gueron, S., Lindell, Y., Nof, A., Pinkas, B.: Fast garbling of circuits under standard assumptions. In: Ray, I., Li, N., Kruegel, C. (eds.) ACM CCS 2015, pp. 567–578. ACM Press, October 2015

KKS16. Kempka, C., Kikuchi, R., Suzuki, K.: How to circumvent the two-ciphertext lower bound for linear garbling schemes. In: Cheon, J.H., Takagi, T. (eds.) ASIACRYPT 2016. LNCS, vol. 10032, pp. 967–997. Springer, Heidelberg (2016). https://doi.org/10.1007/978-3-662-53890-6_32

KMR14. Kolesnikov, V., Mohassel, P., Rosulek, M.: FleXOR: flexible garbling for XOR gates that beats free-XOR. In: Garay, J.A., Gennaro, R. (eds.) CRYPTO 2014. LNCS, vol. 8617, pp. 440–457. Springer, Heidelberg (2014)

KS08. Kolesnikov, V., Schneider, T.: Improved garbled circuit: free XOR gates and applications. In: Aceto, L., Damgård, I., Goldberg, L.A., Halldórsson, M.M., Ingólfsdóttir, A., Walukiewicz, I. (eds.) ICALP 2008. LNCS, vol. 5126, pp. 486–498. Springer, Heidelberg (2008). https://doi.org/10.1007/978-3-540-70583-3_40

LP09. Lindell, Y., Pinkas, B.: A proof of security of Yao's protocol for two-party computation. J. Cryptol. 22(2), 161–188 (2009)

MR18. Mohassel, P., Rindal, P.: ABY^3: a mixed protocol framework for machine learning. In: Lie, D., Mannan, M., Backes, M., Wang, X. (eds.) ACM CCS 2018, pp. 35–52. ACM Press, October 2018

NPS99. Naor, M., Pinkas, B., Sumner, R.: Privacy preserving auctions and mechanism design. In: Proceedings of the 1st ACM Conference on Electronic Commerce, New York, NY, USA, pp. 129–139. ACM (1999)

PSSW09. Pinkas, B., Schneider, T., Smart, N.P., Williams, S.C.: Secure two-party computation is practical. In: Matsui, M. (ed.) ASIACRYPT 2009. LNCS, vol. 5912, pp. 250–267. Springer, Heidelberg (2009)

Ros17. Rosulek, M.: Improvements for gate-hiding garbled circuits. In: Patra, A., Smart, N.P. (eds.) INDOCRYPT 2017. LNCS, vol. 10698, pp. 325–345. Springer, Heidelberg (2017)

WmM17. Wang, Y., Malluhi, Q.M.: Reducing garbled circuit size while preserving circuit gate privacy. Cryptology ePrint Archive, Report 2017/041 (2017). https://eprint.iacr.org/2017/041

Yao82. Yao, A.C.-C.: Protocols for secure computations (extended abstract). In: 23rd FOCS, pp. 160–164. IEEE Computer Society Press, November 1982

ZRE15. Zahur, S., Rosulek, M., Evans, D.: Two halves make a whole-reducing data transfer in garbled circuits using half gates. In: Oswald, E., Fischlin, M. (eds.) EUROCRYPT 2015. Part II, LNCS, vol. 9057, pp. 220–250. Springer, Heidelberg (2015)

Signatures

Threshold Schnorr with Stateless Deterministic Signing from Standard Assumptions

François Garillot[1], Yashvanth Kondi[2(✉)], Payman Mohassel[3], and Valeria Nikolaenko[1]

[1] Novi/Facebook, Palo Alto, USA
`francois@garillot.net, valerini@fb.com`
[2] Northeastern University, Boston, USA
`ykondi@ccs.neu.edu`
[3] Facebook, Palo Alto, USA
`paymanm@fb.com`

Abstract. Schnorr's signature scheme permits an elegant threshold signing protocol due to its linear signing equation. However each new signature consumes fresh randomness, which can be a major attack vector in practice. Sources of randomness in deployments are frequently either unreliable, or require *state continuity*, i.e. reliable fresh state resilient to rollbacks. State continuity is a notoriously difficult guarantee to achieve in practice, due to system crashes caused by software errors, malicious actors, or power supply interruptions (Parno et al., S&P '11). This is a non-issue for Schnorr variants such as EdDSA, which is specified to derive nonces deterministically as a function of the message and the secret key. However, it is challenging to translate these benefits to the threshold setting, specifically to construct a threshold Schnorr scheme where signing neither requires parties to consume fresh randomness nor update long-term secret state.

In this work, we construct a dishonest majority threshold Schnorr protocol that enables such stateless deterministic nonce derivation using standardized block ciphers. Our core technical ingredients are new tools for the zero-knowledge from garbled circuits (ZKGC) paradigm to aid in verifying correct nonce derivation:
- A mechanism based on UC Commitments that allows a prover to commit once to a witness, and prove an unbounded number of statements online with only cheap symmetric key operations.
- A garbling gadget to translate intermediate garbled circuit wire labels to arithmetic encodings.

A proof per our scheme requires only a small constant number of exponentiations.

1 Introduction

The Schnorr signature scheme [Sch91] is a simple discrete logarithm based construction where the public key is of the form $X = x \cdot G$, and to sign a message m

Yashvanth Kondi did part of this work during an internship at Novi/Facebook.

T. Malkin and C. Peikert (Eds.): CRYPTO 2021, LNCS 12825, pp. 127–156, 2021.
https://doi.org/10.1007/978-3-030-84242-0_6

the signer provides $R = r \cdot G$ and the linear combination $\sigma = xe + r$ where e is derived by hashing X, R, m (or just R, m as in the original specification). This relation can easily be verified in the exponent as $\sigma \cdot G = e \cdot X + R$. Assuming an ideal hash function (modelled as a random oracle) unforgeability is rooted in the hardness of the discrete logarithm problem. The signatures themselves embody a zero-knowledge property: assuming that the r values are uniformly chosen, the σ values reveal *no information* about x.

1.1 Practical Concerns: Determinism and Statelessness

The fact that r values are chosen uniformly upon every invocation permits many useful theoretical properties, among them a clean proof [PS96]. However, the necessity of fresh randomness introduces a new attack vector in practice: the assumption that a consistent source of entropy will be available for use has repeatedly turned out to be ill-founded.

As an example, the public cloud is a context in which access to good entropy and a well-seeded PRNG is particularly difficult. Indeed, deploying an application on cloud infrastructure delivers the convenience of modern enterprise-grade offerings, yielding significant benefits in uptime, availability, APIs, threat detection, load balancing, storage, and more. Yet this choice often entails that a user application will run as a guest in a virtualized environment of some kind. Existing literature shows that such guests have a lower rate of acquiring entropy [KASN15], that their PRNG behaves deterministically on boot and reset [EZJ+14], and that they show coupled entropy in multi-tenancy situations [KC12], including in containers [Bay14]. This can have disastrous consequences, as even a small amount of bias in r values across many Schnorr signatures can be leveraged to completely break the scheme [HS01].

The idea of deterministically deriving r values from randomness established during key generation has correspondingly gained traction [MNPV99, KW03, KL17]. The widely used EdDSA signature scheme [BDL+12] derives its nonces as $r = H(H(k), m)$ where k is sampled during key generation and m is the message to be signed. Assuming k has enough entropy and that H produces pseudorandom outputs, the r values will be pseudorandomly determined for each m, leading to signatures that are essentially as secure as the original Schnorr algorithm that consumes fresh randomness for each r. In this work, we aim to translate the benefits of deterministic signing to the threshold signature setting. In particular, we study *deterministic threshold Schnorr* as the problem of designing a decentralized protocol to produce Schnorr signatures where each party's signing algorithm is deterministic.

State Continuity is Non-trivial. Folklore would suggest that the problem at hand is simple: first design a randomized protocol (of which many exist for threshold Schnorr) and then simply 'compress' the random tape by using a PRG/block cipher invoked with a fresh counter each time new randomness is needed. However this approach fundamentally assumes *state continuity* [PLD+11], i.e. that the state of the device running the protocol can be reliably updated and read on demand. However as Parno et al. [PLD+11] first pointed out, even secure hardened devices with strong isolation guarantees can not take this property for granted. In particular, malicious attackers or even natural circumstances such as software errors or power interruptions may induce a device to turn off and roll back to a 'last known safe' state upon restart. While such a state may be entirely consistent in every detectable way, it could be stale, leading to randomness reuse in the PRG context. We stress that reliably storing long-term secrets is significantly easier than for instance updating a counter every time a signature is produced.

Why Not Solve This at the Systems Level? While state continuity in general has been studied as a systems problem, we argue here that incorporating resiliency to state resets in cryptographic protocol design has both qualitative and quantitative advantages:

- **Qualitative:** Systems-level solutions depend on context, and consequently hinge on specific assumptions such as trusted hardware [PLD+11,SP16], a number of helper nodes with uncorrelated failures [BCLK17,MAK+17], or a trusted server [vDRSD07]. In contrast, a cryptographic protocol in the standard model offers provable security and strong composition guarantees without resorting to context-specific physical assumptions.
- **Quantitative:** Deployment of a protocol that relies on state continuity will require the expending of resources on establishing context-specific solutions to this problem for each new environment; acquiring such dedicated hardware is expensive. Moreover it is unclear that the best systems solution in every environment will be more efficient than a canonical stateless cryptographic protocol. Consider two-party distributed signing: it defeats the purpose to incorporate extra parties/servers for state continuity, and solutions that rely on monotonic counters maintained on special purpose hardware such as Intel SGX or Trusted Platform Modules suffer other issues inherent to these platforms. Matetic et al. [MAK+17] showed that the upper limit on the number of writes to such protected counters (due to non-volatile memory wearing out) can be exhausted in a few days of continuous use. Moreover maintaining and reading from such memory is slow; Strackx and Piessens [SP16] report a 95 ms latency, and Brandenburger et al. [BCLK17] report a 60 ms latency in incrementing an SGX Trusted Monotonic Counter. In summary, dedicated hardware for state continuity is expensive, slow, and comes with limited lifespan. The protocols we construct in this work are expected to run significantly faster on commodity hardware (order of 10 ms) - well within the performance envelope of trusted hardware solutions due to their latency.

We therefore incorporate *statelessness* into the problem statement, to mean that security must hold even when devices are arbitrarily crashed (even in the middle of a protocol) and restored with only their long-term secrets.

1.2   Why Is Stateless Deterministic Threshold Signing Challenging?

Schnorr signatures permit a very elegant multiparty variant [SS01,GJKR07] as signatures are simply linear combinations of secret values. Most natural secret sharing schemes permit linear combinations "for free", with the result that threshold Schnorr in different settings has essentially reduced to the task of establishing $x \cdot G$ and $r \cdot G$ such that x, r are random and secret-shared among parties.

The instructions for each of the parties in the classic threshold Schnorr protocols [SS01,GJKR07] looks very much like the regular signing algorithm. We give a brief sketch of how the semi-honest two party version works, which is sufficient to understand the challenges we address in the rest of our exposition. The description is from the point of view of party P_b for $b \in \{0, 1\}$.

1. **Key generation**: P_b samples $\mathsf{sk}_b \leftarrow \mathbb{Z}_q$ and sets $\mathsf{pk}_b = \mathsf{sk}_b \cdot G$. It then sends pk_b to P_{1-b} and waits for pk_{1-b}. The shared public key is set to $\mathsf{pk} = \mathsf{pk}_0 + \mathsf{pk}_1$
2. **Given message m to sign**:
    (a) P_b samples $r_b \leftarrow \mathbb{Z}_q$ and sets $R_b = r_b \cdot G$. It then sends R_b to P_{1-b} and waits for R_{1-b}. The signing nonce is computed by both as $R = R_0 + R_1$
    (b) P_b computes $e = H(\mathsf{pk}, R, m)$ and sets $\sigma_b = \mathsf{sk}_b \cdot e + r_b$. It then sends σ_b to P_{1-b} and waits for σ_{1-b}. Finally $(R, \sigma = \sigma_0 + \sigma_1)$ is a signature on m

The above protocol can be made secure against an active adversary with an extra commitment round [NKDM03], however this will not be important for our discussion. An immediate observation is that instead of having P_b sample a fresh r_b for each message, one could adopt the EdDSA approach and have P_b sample k_b during key generation and instead compute $r_b = H(H(k_b), m)$. This does in fact yield a deterministic threshold signing protocol, with security against at least passive corruption. However, as previously noted by Maxwell et al. [MPSW19], a malicious adversary will be able to completely break such a system. The attack is as follows: a malicious P_1 can first run the honest signing procedure for message m with the correct r_1 (as per Step 2a), and subsequently ask to sign the same m but use a different $r_1' \neq r_1$ this time. The honest P_0 follows the protocol specification and unfortunately uses the same r_0 value in both executions, as it is derived as a function of m, k_0, both of which are independent of r_1. Consequently, $R = (r_0 + r_1)G$ and $R' = (r_0 + r_1')G$ are the nonces derived for each execution, which induce unequal challenges $e = H(..R)$ and $e' = H(..R')$. The honest party therefore gives P_1 the values $\sigma_0 = \mathsf{sk}_0 e + r_0$ and $\sigma_0' = \mathsf{sk}_0 e' + r_0$ in different executions, which jointly reveal its secret key share sk_0.

Going forward, we follow the natural template for threshold Schnorr set by previous works [NKDM03,SS01,GJKR07], and investigate how to enforce that parties indeed derive their nonces deterministically by following the protocol.

1.3   Desiderata

There are many possible ways to enforce deterministic nonce derivation, and so we first highlight the constraints of our context in order to inform our choice of technology.

- **Standard assumptions.** This is a subtle but important constraint. As with any safety critical application, we would like to avoid new and insufficiently vetted assumptions in our protocol. However even more important than protocol security (which is only relevant when parties in the system are corrupt) is the security of artefacts exposed to the outside world, i.e. the signature. In particular, we wish to be very conservative in instantiating the PRF that is used to derive nonces; Schnorr signatures are known to be extremely sensitive to nonce bias [HS01, TTA18], meaning that the slightest weakness discovered in the PRF could lead to attackers retrieving entire signing keys using previously published signatures.

- **Lightweight computation.** We want our schemes to be as widely applicable as possible, and consequently we do not want to make use of heavy cryptography. In the case of decentralized cryptocurrency wallets where one or more signing party is likely to be a weak device (e.g. low budget smartphone, or Hardware Security Module) both computation cost and memory consumption must be minimized. On the other end of the spectrum for threshold signing at an institutional level with powerful hardware, lightweight signing is conducive to high throughput.
- **Round efficiency.** As much as possible we would like to avoid compromising on round efficiency in our endeavour to make signing deterministic and stateless. In particular ordinary threshold Schnorr signing [NKDM03, SS01, GJKR07] requires only three rounds, and we would like to match this efficiency.

We therefore formulate a more precise problem statement,

How can we construct a lightweight threshold signing protocol for Schnorr signatures where parties do not consume fresh randomness or update state after the initial key generation? Moreover nonce derivation must strictly use standardized primitives (e.g. AES, SHA).

To be clear, our focus is on the 'online' signing operations; we do not worry about optimizing the efficiency of the distributed key generation, which is one-time.

1.4   This Work

In this work, we construct an efficient zero-knowledge proof system for proving correct nonce derivation that makes use of only cheap symmetric key cryptography and a small constant number of exponentiations when invoked, and does not require updating long-term state.

Our proof system is in the Zero-knowledge from Garbled Circuits (ZKGC) paradigm of Jawurek et al. [JKO13], and the techniques that we develop improve the ZKGC paradigm even outside of the stateless deterministic setting.

General ZKGC Bottlenecks. The efficiency of the ZKGC paradigm is rooted in the fact that the prover and verifier pay at most three AES invocations per AND gate in the circuit, when instantiated with the privacy-free variant of Half-Gates [ZRE15]. However especially for small circuits such as AES, SHA, etc., the bottleneck usually lies in logistics for the witness (i.e. input to the circuit). In particular:

- **Input Encoding:** Transferring wire labels for a $|q|$-bit input requires $|q|$ Oblivious Transfers, which means $O(\kappa)$ public key operations per invocation even with OT Extension, for κ bits of computational security.
- **Binding Composite Statements:** The state of the art technique [CGM16] to tie statements about an order q elliptic curve group elements to a Boolean circuit involves the garbling of an additional private circuit to multiply a $|q|$-bit value with an s-bit statistical MAC. While the cost of these $\tilde{O}(s \cdot |q|)$ extra gates may disappear as the circuit size grows, it incurs high concrete cost relative to common ciphers that have compact Boolean circuit representations. Consider the parameter regime relevant here, a 256-bit curve and 60 bits of statistical security: the cost of garbling with privacy ($2\times$ the per-gate cost of privacy-free [ZRE15]) the corresponding 32k gate multiplication circuit for the MAC[1] is considerably more expensive than privacy-free garbling of the circuit for the relation itself: nearly an order of magnitude more than AES-128 (7k gates [AMM+]) and even $3\times$ that of SHA-256 (22k gates [CGGN17]).

We develop novel techniques to address both of these problems in this work, which we briefly describe below.

Commit Once, Prove Many Statements. As the use of $O(\kappa)$ public key operations used for input encoding in garbled circuit based protocols is a difficult foundational issue, we relax the problem to fit our setting more closely. In particular, it is sufficient for a party to commit to a nonce derivation key k once during distributed key generation, and subsequently prove an unbounded number of statements (i.e. PRF evaluations) online. This gives us a more targeted problem statement:

> How can we enable the prover to commit to its witness w once, and prove an unbounded number of statements x such that $R(x, w) = 1$ with only symmetric key operations per instance in the ZKGC paradigm?

This problem reduces to the task of constructing a variant of Committed OT, where an OT receiver commits to a choice bit once and subsequently receives one out of two messages for an unbounded number of message pairs sent by the sender. Importantly, after the sender has sent a message pair, the sender should be able to reveal the pair at a later point without changing the messages or learning the receiver's choice bit. We devise a novel method that makes non-blackbox use of any Universally Composable (UC) commitment [Can01] in the one-time preprocessing model to solve this problem. Roughly, each OT in the canonical instantiation of input encoding is replaced by a pair of UC commitments. This is substantially more computationally efficient, as we summarize below in Table 1.

On a Macbook Pro 2017 laptop (i7-7700HQ CPU, 2.80 GHz) running OpenSSL 1.1.1f: a single AES-128 invocation takes $0.07\,\mu s$, SHA-512 takes $0.3\,\mu s$, and a Curve25519 exponentiation takes $59.8\,\mu s$. This data in combination with Table 1 suggests that our technique for preprocessing Committed OT can perform input encoding an order of magnitude faster than using the fastest plain OT.

---

[1] Calculated with Karatsuba's multiplication algorithm per Table 6.7 in [CCD+20].

Table 1. Cost per bit of the witness (send+receive+open), per instance not including preprocessing. Parameters: 128 bits of computational security, 60 bits of statistical security. Estimated runtime with AES for F, SHA-512 for CRHF, and Curve25519 for exponentiations.

Scheme	Comp.	Comm. (bits)	Estd. runtime
OT [CO15]	5 exponentiations	1152	$299\,\mu s$
This work	$240 \cdot F + 31 \cdot CRHF$	5120	$26.1\,\mu s$

Beyond Stateless Deterministic Signing. This pattern of proving an unbounded number of statements about the same private input is not unique to threshold signing. Consider the example of distributed symmetric key encryption [AMMR18]: Servers A and B (one of which may be malicious) hold keys k_A, k_B respectively, and comprise one endpoint of a secure channel. Ciphertexts on this channel are of the form $(r, m \oplus F_{k_A}(r) \oplus F_{k_B}(r))$, and so encryption/decryption requires the servers to reveal $F_{k_A}(r), F_{k_B}(r)$ and prove correct evaluation.

Intuition. Recall that a UC commitment scheme must be 'straight-line extractable', i.e. there must exist an extractor algorithm Ext, which when given a commitment C to message m and a trapdoor ek should efficiently output m. Our insight is to run Ext to implement the committed OT receiver, even though its utility in the context of the UC commitment is simply as a 'proof artefact' which is never executed in a real protocol. Roughly, we generate a pair of commitment keys ck_0, ck_1 for the OT sender during the preprocessing phase, and give the trapdoor ek_b corresponding to ck_b to the OT receiver, where b is the choice bit. To send a message pair (m_0, m_1) the sender commits to m_0 using ck_0 and m_1 using ck_1, of which the receiver retrieves m_b by invoking Ext with ek_b. In order to 'open' its messages, the sender simply runs the decommitment phase of the UC commitment scheme. The novelty in this approach lies in our use of the extraction trapdoor ek, which is an object that only appears in the security proof of a UC commitment (but not in the 'real' world), to construct a concrete protocol. The real-world OT receiver essentially runs the simulator of the UC commitment scheme.

Exponentiation Garbling Gadget. We design a gadget to garble the exponentiation function $f_G(x) = x \cdot G$ at very low cost. The gadget takes as input a standard Yao's garbled circuit style encoding of a bit string x (i.e. keys $(k_i^{x_i})_{i \in [|x|]}$), and outputs a convenient algebraic encoding of this value $Z = (ax + b) \cdot G$ for some secret $a, b \in \mathbb{Z}_q^*$.

A similar effect is achieved by Chase et al. [CGM16] by garbling an explicit multiplication circuit. However our gadget is drastically more efficient, as summarized below in Table 2.

This leads to significant savings, as stated earlier the MAC computation alone would have dominated bandwidth cost.

Table 2. Cost to apply algebraic MAC $z = ax + b$ to a secret x encoded in a garbled circuit. Concrete costs are given for $|q| = 256$, $s = 60$, and $\kappa = 128$, with the HalfGates [ZRE15] garbling scheme. KDF is the cipher used for garbling.

Scheme	Asymptotic Comm.	Concrete Comm.	Calls to KDF
[CGM16]	$\tilde{O}(s \cdot |q| \cdot \kappa)$	1024 KB	64000
Our gadget	$O(|q| \cdot \kappa)$	8.2 KB	1024

Beyond Stateless Deterministic Signing. This gadget cuts down the heavy MAC computation in [CGM16] by a factor of 125, and therefore is useful for composite statements where the Boolean circuit size for the non-algebraic component is smaller or comparable in size to $\tilde{O}(s \cdot |q|)$. Concretely bandwidth savings can range from $\sim 90\%$ for AES-128, to $\sim 70\%$ for SHA-256. The latter translates significant bandwidth savings in the context of proving knowledge of an ECDSA signature [CGM16].

Intuition. The gadget is inspired by the Oblivious Linear Evaluation technique of Gilboa [Gil99]. The ciphertexts are structured so that the evaluator always decrypts $z_i = b_i + \mathbf{x}_i \cdot \mathbf{u}_i \cdot a$ on wire i, where a and $b = \sum_i b_i$ are the garbler's MAC keys and $x = \langle \mathbf{u}, \mathbf{x} \rangle$. Adding up $z = \sum_i z_i$ yields $z = ax + b$, which is the desired arithmetic encoding, and allows for easy exponentiation outside the garbled circuit. This self-contained gadget can be expressed as a garbling scheme and proven secure as such.

We are therefore able to construct a highly efficient zero-knowledge proof system, where a prover commits to a some nonce derivation key k during key generation, and subsequently proves correct nonce derivation, i.e. $R = \mathsf{F}_k(m) \cdot G$ for an unbounded number of messages m that are signed online. Simply augmenting the semi-honest threshold signing protocol sketched earlier with this zero-knowledge proof yields an n-party stateless deterministic threshold signing protocol that is secure against $n - 1$ malicious corruptions.

2   Related Work

Resettable Zero-Knowledge (rZK). The notion of rZK introduced by Canetti et al. [CGGM00] allows an adversarial verifier to arbitrarily reset a prover, and requires zero-knowledge to hold even in the absence of fresh randomness for the prover upon being reset. This achieves stateless determinism as we require, and indeed the attacks discovered by Canetti et al. on canonical protocols when confronted with such an adversary are of the same flavour as the one in Sect. 1.2. However the adversarial model that we consider in this work is weaker for two reasons: one is that the prover and verifier are allowed a one-time reset-free interactive setup phase, and the other is that in case an abort is induced at any point no further interaction will occur. Therefore rZK protocols would be overkill for our setting.

MuSig-DN. The closest work to ours is the very recent work of Nick et al. [NRSW20], in which the authors construct a two-round multisignature scheme called MuSig-DN which enforces deterministic nonces with security against $n-1$ out of n malicious corruptions. Their protocol achieves stateless deterministic signing for Schnorr signatures, however their approach diverges from ours in two significant ways:

- The security of the PRF they use for nonce derivation is based on the Decisional Diffie-Hellman assumption over a carefully chosen custom elliptic curve that supports efficient proofs. While this offers a nice tradeoff between the efficiency of proving statements about arithmetization-friendly primitives and plausibility of assumptions, the assumption is not exactly the same as DDH over a standardized curve.
- They opt for a SNARK-based approach (specifically Bulletproofs [BBB+18]), which is very communication efficient (around a kilobyte for a proof) but computation intensive; they report 943 ms on commodity hardware for a single execution.

In contrast, our dishonest majority protocol occupies a different point on the spectrum: it supports standardized ciphers for nonce derivation, and is computationally very light at the expense of higher bandwidth.

Threshold EdDSA. Due to the fact that the EdDSA signing algorithm derives r as a non-linear function of some preprocessed seed, securely computing EdDSA in a threshold setting exactly as per its specification is quite challenging. Current implementations of threshold EdDSA either require elaborate (randomized) MPC protocols [BST21] or abandon deterministic nonce derivation altogether and simply implement randomized threshold Schnorr over the correct curve [LPR19]. As an example, the Unbound library [LPR19] drops the determinism requirement with the justification that a nonce jointly sampled in a multiparty protocol will be uniformly random if even one of the parties uses good randomness. However this does not protect a device using bad randomness from a malicious adversary controlling a party in the system. Moreover we contend that in practice it is common for all parties in the system to be using similar implementations, hence inducing correlated randomness-related vulnerabilities. Additionally faults/bugs may occur at the system or hardware levels, which further motivates the need for threshold signing protocols that do not assume that *any* party in the system has reliable randomness.

In this work we are not concerned with *exactly* computing the correct EdDSA signing equation in a distributed setting, as this will likely require expensive MPC [BST21]. Instead we would like to construct a threshold Schnorr protocol that embodies the spirit of deterministic nonce derivation; in particular our primary goal is to construct a multiparty protocol to compute Schnorr signatures where *each participant* runs a deterministic and stateless signing algorithm. Also note that the work of Bonte et al. [BST21] is in the incomparable honest majority setting, and highly interactive.

3 Our Techniques

The task at hand can be roughly characterized as follows: parties in the system first sample some state during a "key generation" phase. When given a message to sign later, they must securely derive the signing material from the joint state they sampled earlier. Moreover, this derivation must be deterministic and should not create new state, i.e. signing material for each message must only rely on the key generation state and the message itself. The template of sampling a PRF key during key generation and applying this PRF on the message to be signed to derive signing material works well in the semi-honest setting as discussed, but falls apart when adversaries deviate from the protocol.

The canonical method to upgrade a semi-honest protocol to malicious security without an honest majority is for parties to commit to some initial randomness, and subsequently prove that they computed each message honestly relative to the committed randomness [GMW87]. What this entails for threshold Schnorr is for parties to commit to a PRF key during distributed key generation, and when signing a message, prove that the discrete log of their claimed nonce is indeed the result of applying the PRF on the public message using the committed key. In particular for some public $x, R_i, \mathsf{Commit}(k_i)$, party P_i must prove that $\mathsf{F}_{k_i}(x) \cdot G = R_i$ where F is a PRF. We encapsulate this mechanism in the functionality $\mathcal{F}_{\mathsf{F} \cdot \mathsf{G}}$ later in this paper.

3.1 What Existing Proof Technologies Suit Our Task?

As per our desiderata that we set in Sect. 1.3, we wish to prioritize *standard assumptions*, *light computation*, and *retaining round efficiency*. We examine the different proof technologies available to us with this lens, as follows:

SNARK-Based. The recent progress in succinct proof systems [BFS20, BCR+19, BBB+18, Gro16] provides a tempting avenue to explore, as a SNARK attesting to the correctness of nonce generation yields a conceptually simple approach. We highlight here that we wish to rely on standard assumptions, the implication being that we would like to use a time-tested and vetted, preferably standardized PRF. While there has been tremendous progress in constructing SNARK/STARK-friendly ciphers [BSGL20], efficiently proving statements involving more traditional non-algebraic ciphers (such as SHA/AES) has remained elusive using any SNARK technology. For instance the fastest such succinct proof system at present (Spartan [Set20]) would require over 100 ms to prove a *single* AES computation ($\approx 2^{14}$ R1CS constraints [Kos]) on a modern laptop as per their implementation.

Generic MPC. Advances in generic MPC [KRRW18, HSS17, KPR18] have brought the secure computation of sophisticated cryptographic functions into the realm of practicality. However they are all inherently interactive and randomized (with many being heavily reliant on preprocessing), posing fresh challenges in the deterministic/stateless setting. Additionally even the most advanced constant round techniques [KRRW18, HSS17] require several rounds of interaction, marking a departure from conventional threshold Schnorr which needs only three rounds.

Zero-Knowledge for Composite Statements. Chase et al. [CGM16] construct two protocols in the ZKGC paradigm [JKO13] that bind algebraic and non-algebraic bitwise encodings of the same value, so that the algebraic encoding may be used for efficient sigma protocols while the non-algebraic encoding can be used to evaluate a garbled circuit. Roughly, the two methods are as follows, with the following tradeoffs:

1. *Homomorphic bitwise commitments to the witness*: This method produces smaller proofs, and is even extended to the MPC-in-the-head setting by Backes et al. [BHH+19]. However this fundamentally requires exponentiations for each bit of the input, i.e. $O(|q|)$ asymptotically and hundreds concretely for our parameter range, which would require many tens of milliseconds at least to compute on commodity hardware. We therefore do not pursue this line further.

2. *Algebraic MAC applied to the witness*: This method produces larger proofs, as the MAC is computed by garbling an $\tilde{O}(s \cdot |q|)$ circuit. However this avoids public key operations (besides OT) and presents a promising direction to investigate.

Equipped with an understanding of the landscape of proof systems, we expand on the results that we summarized in Sect. 1.4.

4   Organization

We first establish the technical background in Sect. 5. We then expand on our solutions to the gaps that we identified in Sect. 1.4: Sect. 6 details the garbling gadget for exponentiation, and Sect. 7 elaborates on how to construct Committed OT from UC Commitments. Section 8 shows how to combine these ideas to build a nonce verifying mechanism, and finally Sect. 9 constructs an n-party protocol resilient to $n - 1$ corruptions based on this mechanism.

5   Preliminaries

Security Model. We construct and prove our protocols secure in the Universal Composability framework of Canetti [Can01]. We assume synchronous networks, with well-defined upper bounds on adversarial message delay.

Standard Helper Functionalities. We make use of the standard notion of choose all-but-one OT $\mathcal{F}_{\binom{\ell}{\ell-1}\mathsf{OT}}$.

5.1   Garbling Schemes and Zero-Knowledge

We first recall the syntax of garbled circuits, in the language of Bellare et al. [BHR12]. A garbling scheme $\mathcal{G}$ comprises: a garbling algorithm Gb that on

input a circuit C produces a garbled circuit $\tilde{C}$ along with encoding information
en and decoding information de. The encoding algorithm En maps an input x
to a garbled input $\tilde{X}$ relative to en. The evaluation algorithm Ev then evaluates $\tilde{C}, \tilde{X}$ to produce a garbled output $\tilde{Y}$, which is then decoded by De using
de to a clear output y. The verification algorithm Ve given $\tilde{C}$, en validates their
well-formedness, and extracts the decoding information de if they are so.

For the purpose of the paper, we will assume that $\mathcal{G}$ is *projective* [BHR12], i.e.
garbled input $\tilde{X} = (\text{en}_{i,x_i})_{i \in [|x|]}$. We require the garbling scheme to be privacy-
free [FNO15], i.e. satisfy two main security properties:

- **Authenticity**[2]: let $\tilde{C}$, en, de $\leftarrow$ Gb$(C, 1^\kappa)$ and $\tilde{X} \leftarrow$ En(x, en), and $\hat{y} \neq C(x)$
  for an adversarially chosen $C, x, \hat{y}$. It should be computationally infeasible for
  any PPT adversary $\mathcal{A}(\tilde{C}, \tilde{X})$ to output $\hat{Z}$ such that De(de, $\hat{Z}$) $= \hat{y}$.
- **Verifiability**: given $\tilde{C}$, en, the algorithm Ve produces decoding information
  de if $\tilde{C}$ is well-formed (i.e. a legitimate output of Gb). Alternatively if $\tilde{C}$ is
  malformed, Ve outputs $\perp$ with certainty.

Additionally we need 'Uniqueness', i.e. that if $C(x) = C(x')$, then
Ev$(\tilde{C}, \text{En}(\text{en}, x)) = $ Ev$(\tilde{C}, \text{En}(\text{en}, x'))$ for any valid $\tilde{C}$, en. We defer formal definitions to the full version.

Committed Oblivious Transfer. Committed Oblivious Transfer (COT) offers
the same interface as regular OT, but it also allows a 'reveal' phase where the
both the sender's messages are revealed to the receiver, while the receiver's choice
bit stays hidden. We encapsulate this notion (along with additional bookkeping
to account for statelessness) in functionality $\mathcal{F}^*_{\text{COT}}$. Additionally in order to facilitate a round compression optimization in the higher level protocol, $\mathcal{F}^*_{\text{COT}}$ lets
the sender lock its messages with a 'key', and reveals these messages upon the
receiver presenting the key. As this is a straightforward reproduction of previous
work, we defer the formalism to the full version.

Zero-Knowledge from Garbled Circuits. We are now ready to recall a
description of the original ZKGC protocol [JKO13]. The prover P holds a private
witness x (of which the ith bit is x_i), such that $C(x) = 1$ for some public circuit C.

1. The verifier V garbles the verification circuit, $\tilde{C}$, en, de $\leftarrow$ Gb$(C, 1^\kappa)$. Both
   parties engage in $|x|$ parallel executions of Committed Oblivious Transfer,
   with the following inputs in the ith instance: V plays the sender, and inputs
   en$_{i,0}$, en$_{i,1}$ as its two messages. P plays the receiver, and inputs x_i as its choice
   bit in order to receive en$_{i,x_i}$.

---

[2] This is slightly weaker than the standard notion of authenticity [BHR12], which
requires that *any* output other than $C(x)$ is hard to forge. It is sufficient for ZKGC
if it is hard to forge an output only for any $\hat{y} \neq C(x)$ specified before $\tilde{C}, \tilde{X}$ are
generated. Our gadget achieves this weaker notion, however it can easily be upgraded
to the stronger notion if required by executing the gadget twice with independent
randomness, and checking that they decode to the same output.

2. P assembles $\tilde{X} = (\mathsf{en}_{i,x_i})_{i \in [|x|]}$ locally. V sends $\tilde{C}$ to P, who then computes $\tilde{Y} \leftarrow \mathsf{Ev}(\tilde{C}, \tilde{X})$, and sends $\mathsf{Commit}(\tilde{Y})$ to V.

3. V opens its randomness from all the COTs to reveal en in its entirety

4. P checks $\mathsf{Ve}(\tilde{C}, \mathsf{en}) = 1$, and if satisfied decommits $\mathsf{Commit}(\tilde{Y})$. V accepts iff $\mathsf{De}(\tilde{Y}, \mathsf{de}) = 1$

Intuitively the above protocol is sound due to authenticity of the garbling scheme: a malicious P^* who inputs x' such that $C(x') \neq 1$ to the OT will receive $\tilde{X}'$ such that $\mathsf{De}(\mathsf{Ev}(\tilde{C}, \tilde{X}'), \mathsf{de}) = 0$, and so to make V accept P^* will have to forge a valid $\tilde{Y}$ that is not the outcome of 'honest' garbled evaluation. Zero-knowledge comes from the verifiability and unique evaluation properties of the garbling scheme: an incorrect garbled circuit $\tilde{C}^*$ will be rejected in step 4 by P (who has not sent any useful information to V yet), and conditioned on $\tilde{C}$ being a valid garbled circuit, the uniqueness property hides which input was used to arrive at the output.

Extensions to ZKGC. The work of Chase et al. [CGM16] examines how to integrate proofs of algebraic statements into the garbled circuit based zero-knowledge framework, in order to prove composite statements. Roughly, their technique has P commit to a MAC of the witness $z = ax + b$ (computed via the garbled circuit/OT) along with $\tilde{Y}$ using a homomorphic commitment scheme. Once V reveals the randomness of the circuit, a, b become public and P leverages the homomorphism of the commitment in order to prove additional algebraic statements about the witness via Sigma protocols, such as the relation between x, z.

Subsequently Ganesh et al. [GKPS18] showed how to compress the original [JKO13] protocol to three rounds using a conditional disclosure of secrets technique, essentially by having V encrypt the OT randomness necessary for step 4 using the correct $\tilde{Y}$.

6 Exponentiation Garbling Gadget

In this section, we give our new garbling gadget that translates a standard Yao-style representation of a binary string (i.e. with wire labels) to an algebraic encoding of the same value in the target elliptic curve group. As we intend to compose this gadget with the Half Gates garbling scheme [ZRE15] we give the construction and proof assuming FreeXOR style keys [KS08]. Consequently we prove security assuming a correlation robust hash function (strictly weaker than circular correlation robustness [CKKZ12] as needed by FreeXOR/HalfGates). Note that this structure is not required by our scheme, and security can easily by proven assuming just PRFs if desired.

Algorithm 6.1. $\mathcal{G}_{\mathsf{exp}}$. Privacy-free Exponentiation Garbling Gadget

This scheme allows to garble the gadget $f : \{0,1\}^\eta \mapsto \mathbb{G}$, in particular $f(x) = \langle \mathbf{u}, \mathbf{x} \rangle \cdot G$ where $\mathbf{u} \in (\mathbb{Z}_q^*)^\eta$ is a public vector of group elements, the vector $\mathbf{x}$ is a length η bit string, and $G \in \mathbb{G}$ generates an elliptic curve group $\mathbb{G}$. Note that the garbled output is encoded arithmetically, and as such can not be composed with (i.e. fed as input to) a standard binary circuit garbling scheme. All algorithms make use of the key derivation function KDF.

$\mathsf{Gb}(1^\kappa, g)$:.

1. Sample $\Delta \leftarrow \{0,1\}^\kappa$ and $a \leftarrow \mathbb{Z}_q^*$
2. For each $i \in [\eta]$,
   - (a) Sample $k_i \leftarrow \{0,1\}^\kappa$
   - (b) Compute $b_i = \mathsf{KDF}(i, k_i)$
   - (c) Set $\tilde{C}_i = \mathsf{KDF}(i, k_i \oplus \Delta) - (b_i + \mathbf{u}_i \cdot a)$
3. Set $b = \sum_{i \in [\eta]} b_i$ and $B = b \cdot G$
4. Compute encoding information $\mathsf{en} = \left[\Delta, \{k_i\}_{i \in [\eta]} \right]$
5. The decoding information is $\mathsf{de} = (a, B)$
6. Output $\tilde{C}, \mathsf{en}, \mathsf{de}$

$\mathsf{En}(\mathsf{en}, x)$:.

1. Parse $\left[\Delta, \{k_i\}_{i \in [\eta]} \right]$ from en, and for each $i \in [\eta]$: set $X_i = k_i \oplus x_i \cdot \Delta$
2. Output $\tilde{X} = \{(x_i, X_i)\}_{i \in [\eta]}$

$\mathsf{Ev}(\tilde{C}, \tilde{X})$:.

1. Parse $\{(x_i, X_i)\}_{i \in [\eta]}$ from $\tilde{X}$
2. For each $i \in [\eta]$: Compute $z_i = \mathsf{KDF}(i, X_i) - x_i \cdot \tilde{C}_i$
3. Compute $z = \sum_{i \in [\eta]} z_i$, and output $\tilde{Z} = z \cdot G$

$\mathsf{De}(\mathsf{de}, \tilde{Z})$: Parse (a, B) from de and output $(\tilde{Z} - B)/a$

We first give the exact definition required of KDF in order to secure the garbling scheme. Informally, KDF is correlation robust if $\mathsf{KDF}(x \oplus \Delta)$ appears random even under adversarial choice of x when Δ is chosen uniformly and hidden from the adversary.

Definition 6.2. (Correlation Robust Hash Function). Let the security parameter κ determine a κ-bit prime q, and be an implicit parameter in the following stateful oracles $\mathcal{O}_{\mathsf{KDF}}$ and $\mathcal{O}_R$ defined as follows:

- $\mathcal{O}_{\mathsf{KDF}}(i, x)$: Upon first invocation, sample $\Delta \leftarrow \{0,1\}^\kappa$. Return $\mathsf{KDF}(i, x \oplus \Delta)$
- $\mathcal{O}_R(i, x)$: If not previously queried on x, sample $F(i, x) \leftarrow \mathbb{Z}_q$. Return $F(i, x)$.

A hash function KDF is correlation robust if $\mathcal{O}_{\mathsf{KDF}}$ and $\mathcal{O}_R$ are computationally indistinguishable to any PPT adversary with unrestricted oracle access.

Theorem 6.3. Assuming KDF is a correlation robust hash function, $\mathcal{G}_{\mathsf{exp}}$ is a privacy-free garbling scheme for the function $f_\mathbf{u}(\mathbf{x}) = \langle \mathbf{u}, \mathbf{x} \rangle \cdot G$.

Proof. **Correctness.** Observe that for each $i \in [\eta]$ the evaluator computes

$$z_i = \mathsf{KDF}(i, X_i) - x_i \cdot \tilde{C}_i$$

Substituting $\tilde{C}_i = \mathsf{KDF}(i, k_i \oplus \Delta) - (b_i + \mathbf{u}_i \cdot a)$ and $X_i = k_i \oplus x_i \cdot \Delta$ into the above equation, we obtain:

$$z_i = \mathsf{KDF}(i, k_i \oplus x_i \cdot \Delta) - x_i \cdot (\mathsf{KDF}(i, k_i \oplus \Delta) - (b_i + \mathbf{u}_i \cdot a))$$

The above expression therefore simplifies to two cases:

$$z_i = \begin{cases} \mathsf{KDF}(i, k_i) \text{ when } x_i = 0 \\ b_i + \mathbf{u}_i \cdot a \text{ when } x_i = 1 \end{cases}$$

Since $\mathsf{KDF}(i, k_i) = b_i$, we can simplify the above to $z_i = b_i + x_i \cdot \mathbf{u}_i \cdot a$. We therefore have that $z = \sum_{i \in [\eta]} z_i = \sum_{i \in [\eta]} (b_i + x_i \cdot \mathbf{u}_i \cdot a) = b + a \cdot \langle \mathbf{u}, \mathbf{x} \rangle$, and therefore $\tilde{Z} = z \cdot G = B + a \cdot \langle \mathbf{u}, \mathbf{x} \rangle \cdot G$. Decoding by $(\tilde{Z} - B)/a$ yields $\langle \mathbf{u}, \mathbf{x} \rangle \cdot G$.

Verifiablity. Revealing en allows each b_i to be computed and $\tilde{C}_i$ to be decrypted, and clearly if every $\tilde{C}_i = \mathsf{KDF}(i, k_i \oplus \Delta) - (b_i + \mathbf{u}_i \cdot a)$ for the same value of a, the values $\tilde{C}, \tilde{X}$ will always evaluate consistently for all inputs.

Authenticity. We prove that the encoded output is unforgeable (i.e. authentic) via hybrid experiments. Recall that the experiment for authenticity of a garbling scheme works as follows: the adversary $\mathcal{A}$ sends a circuit f and input x to the challenger, which then responds with $\tilde{C}, \tilde{X}$ where $\tilde{C}, \mathsf{en}, \mathsf{de} \leftarrow \mathsf{Gb}(f)$ and $\tilde{X} = \mathsf{En}(\mathsf{en}, x)$. If $\mathcal{A}$ is able to produce valid garbled output $\hat{Z}$ such that $\mathsf{De}(\mathsf{de}, \hat{Z}) \neq f(x)$ then the adversary wins.

Hybrid $\mathcal{H}_1$. We first define a hybrid experiment $\mathcal{H}_1$ that changes the way $\tilde{C}, \tilde{X}$ is computed. In particular, $\tilde{C}, \tilde{X}$ are jointly produced using f, x rather than by separate garbling and encoding procedures, as detailed below:

1. Sample $\Delta \leftarrow \{0,1\}^\kappa$ and $a \leftarrow \mathbb{Z}_q^*$
2. For each $i \in [\eta]$,
   (a) Sample $k_i \leftarrow \{0,1\}^\kappa$
   (b) If $\mathbf{x}_i = 0$ then
      i. Compute $b_i = \mathsf{KDF}(i, k_i)$
      ii. Set $\tilde{C}_i = \mathsf{KDF}(i, k_i \oplus \Delta) - (b_i + \mathbf{u}_i \cdot a)$
   (c) Otherwise
      i. Compute $b_i = \mathsf{KDF}(i, k_i \oplus \Delta)$
      ii. Set $\tilde{C}_i = \mathsf{KDF}(i, k_i) - (b_i + \mathbf{u}_i \cdot a)$
3. Set $b = \sum_{i \in [\eta]} b_i$ and $B = b \cdot G$
4. Compute $\tilde{X} = \{k_i\}_{i \in [\eta]}$
5. The decoding information is $\mathsf{de} = (a, B)$
6. Output $\tilde{C}, \tilde{X}, \mathsf{de}$

The distribution of $\tilde{C}, \tilde{X}$ in this hybrid experiment is identical to the real experiment. Observe that the only change is that the 'active' key (i.e. key seen by the evaluator) on the ith wire is defined to be k_i in $\mathcal{H}_1$, whereas in the real experiment the active key is $k_i \oplus x_i \cdot \Delta$. As the inactive key in both experiments is simply the active key $\oplus \Delta$, this is merely a syntactic change. Therefore we have that for all adversaries $\mathcal{A}$, functions and inputs $f_{\mathbf{u}}, \mathbf{x}$ and any string $\hat{Z}$:

$$\Pr\left[\hat{Z} \leftarrow \mathcal{A}(\tilde{C}, \tilde{X}) : (\tilde{C}, \text{en}, \text{de}) \leftarrow \text{Gb}(f_{\mathbf{u}}), \tilde{X} \leftarrow \text{En}(\text{en}, \mathbf{x})\right]$$
$$= \Pr\left[\hat{Z} \leftarrow \mathcal{A}(\tilde{C}, \tilde{X}) : (\tilde{C}, \tilde{X}, \text{de}) \leftarrow \mathcal{H}_1(f_{\mathbf{u}}, \mathbf{x})\right] \tag{1}$$

Hybrid $\mathcal{H}_2$. In this hybrid experiment, the inactive key is changed from $k_i \oplus \Delta$ to a uniformly random value. In particular, the code for this hybrid experiment is identical to the last except for the following two changes:

	Experiment $\mathcal{H}_1$	Experiment $\mathcal{H}_2$
Step 2(b)ii	$\tilde{C}_i = \text{KDF}(i, k_i \oplus \Delta) - (b_i + \mathbf{u}_i \cdot a)$	$\tilde{C}_i \leftarrow \mathbb{Z}_q$
Step 2(c)i	$b_i = \text{KDF}(i, k_i \oplus \Delta)$	$b_i \leftarrow \mathbb{Z}_q$

A distinguisher for the values $(\tilde{C}, \tilde{X})$ produced by $\mathcal{H}_1$ and $\mathcal{H}_2$ immediately yields a distinguisher for the correlation robustness property of KDF. The reduction simply runs the code of $\mathcal{H}_1$, and in place of using KDF in Step 2(b)ii and Step 2(c)i, it queries the challenge oracle $\mathcal{O}$ with the same arguments. In the case that $\mathcal{O} = \mathcal{O}_{\text{KDF}} = \text{KDF}$ this exactly produces the distribution per $\mathcal{H}_1$, and in the case $\mathcal{O} = \mathcal{O}_R$ (i.e. truly random function) the distribution per $\mathcal{H}_2$ is exactly produced, resulting in a lossless reduction to the correlation robustness property of KDF. We therefore have that there is a negligible function negl such that for all PPT adversaries $\mathcal{A}$ and $\hat{Z} \in \mathbb{G}$:

$$\left| \begin{array}{l} \Pr[\hat{Z} \leftarrow \mathcal{A}(\tilde{C}, \tilde{X}) : (\tilde{C}, \tilde{X}, \text{de}) \leftarrow \mathcal{H}_2(f_{\mathbf{u}}, \mathbf{x})] \\ - \Pr[\hat{Z} \leftarrow \mathcal{A}(\tilde{C}, \tilde{X}) : (\tilde{C}, \tilde{X}, \text{de}) \leftarrow \mathcal{H}_1(f_{\mathbf{u}}, \mathbf{x})] \end{array} \right| \leq \text{negl}(\kappa) \tag{2}$$

Hybrid $\mathcal{H}_3$. This hybrid experiment is the same as the last, with the exception that $\tilde{C}_i \leftarrow \mathbb{Z}_q$ for each $i \in [\eta]$. This differs from Step 2(c)ii, which computes $\tilde{C}_i = \text{KDF}(i, k_i) - (b_i + \mathbf{u}_i \cdot a)$ when $\mathbf{x}_i = 1$. However in $\mathcal{H}_2$ when $\mathbf{x}_i = 1$ the value b_i is sampled uniformly from $\mathbb{Z}_q$ and never exposed anywhere else in $\tilde{C}, \tilde{X}$ anyway, effectively acting as a one-time pad. Therefore the distribution of $\tilde{C}, \tilde{X}$ remains unchanged from $\mathcal{H}_2$. In particular,

$$\Pr\left[\text{De}(\text{de}, \hat{Z}) = Y : \hat{Z} \leftarrow \mathcal{A}(\tilde{C}, \tilde{X}), (\tilde{C}, \tilde{X}, \text{de}) \leftarrow \mathcal{H}_2(f_{\mathbf{u}}, \mathbf{x})\right]$$
$$= \Pr\left[\text{De}(\text{de}, \hat{Z}) = Y : \hat{Z} \leftarrow \mathcal{A}(\tilde{C}, \tilde{X}), (\tilde{C}, \tilde{X}, \text{de}) \leftarrow \mathcal{H}_3(f_{\mathbf{u}}, \mathbf{x})\right] \tag{3}$$

Hybrid $\mathcal{H}_4$. This experiment is the same as the last, except that the definition of the decoding information $\text{de} = (a, B)$ is postponed to after $\tilde{C}, \tilde{X}$ are defined. This induces no change in the distribution of $\tilde{C}, \tilde{X}$ as in $\mathcal{H}_3$ they are computed independently of a, B. The value a is derived the same way (uniformly sampled from $\mathbb{Z}_q^*$), whereas now B is computed as $B = Z - a \cdot Y$ where $Y = f_{\mathbf{u}}(\mathbf{x})$ and

$Z = \mathsf{Ev}(\tilde{C}, \tilde{X})$. The distribution of (a, B) is unchanged from $\mathcal{H}_3$, note that by definition $\mathsf{De}(\mathsf{de}, \mathsf{Ev}(\tilde{C}, \tilde{X})) = f_\mathbf{u}(\mathbf{x})$ in both experiments. Therefore:

$$\Pr\left[\mathsf{De}(\mathsf{de}, \hat{Z}) = Y : \hat{Z} \leftarrow \mathcal{A}(\tilde{C}, \tilde{X}), \ (\tilde{C}, \tilde{X}, \mathsf{de}) \leftarrow \mathcal{H}_3(f_\mathbf{u}, \mathbf{x})\right]$$
$$= \Pr\left[\mathsf{De}(\mathsf{de}, \hat{Z}) = Y : \hat{Z} \leftarrow \mathcal{A}(\tilde{C}, \tilde{X}), \ (\tilde{C}, \tilde{X}, \mathsf{de}) \leftarrow \mathcal{H}_4(f_\mathbf{u}, \mathbf{x})\right] \quad (4)$$

We can now bound the probability that an adversary is able to forge an output: consider any $\hat{Y} \in \mathbb{G}$ such that $\hat{Y} \neq Y$. In order to induce $\mathsf{De}(\mathsf{de}, \hat{Z}) = \hat{Y}$, the adversary $\mathcal{A}(\tilde{C}, \tilde{X})$ must output $\hat{Z}$ such that $\hat{Z} - Z = a(\hat{Y} - Y)$. As $\hat{Y} - Y \neq 0$ and a is sampled uniformly from $\mathbb{Z}_q^*$ only after $\hat{Z}, Z, \hat{Y}, Y$ have already been defined, the probability that this relation is satisfied is exactly $1/(q-1)$.

More precisely, for any $f_\mathbf{u}, \mathbf{x} \in \{0,1\}^\eta$, $\hat{Y} \in \mathbb{G}$ such that $\hat{Y} \neq f_\mathbf{u}(\mathbf{x})$ and unbounded adversary $\mathcal{A}$,

$$\Pr\left[\mathsf{De}(\mathsf{de}, \hat{Z}) = \hat{Y} : \hat{Z} \leftarrow \mathcal{A}(\tilde{C}, \tilde{X}), \ (\tilde{C}, \tilde{X}, \mathsf{de}) \leftarrow \mathcal{H}_4(f_\mathbf{u}, \mathbf{x})\right] = 1/(q-1) \quad (5)$$

For our choice of parameters, we have $1/(q-1) \leq 2^{-\kappa}$ which is negligible in κ. Combining Eqs. 1–5 we conclude that the following probability is negligible for any $f_\mathbf{u}, \mathbf{x} \in \{0,1\}^\eta$, $\hat{Y} \in \mathbb{G}$ such that $\hat{Y} \neq f_\mathbf{u}(\mathbf{x})$ and PPT adversary $\mathcal{A}$:

$$\Pr\left[\mathsf{De}(\mathsf{de}, \hat{Z}) = \hat{Y} : \hat{Z} \leftarrow \mathcal{A}(\tilde{C}, \tilde{X}), (\tilde{C}, \mathsf{en}, \mathsf{de}) \leftarrow \mathsf{Gb}(f_\mathbf{u}), \tilde{X} \leftarrow \mathsf{En}(\mathsf{en}, \mathbf{x})\right]$$

The garbling scheme $\mathcal{G}_{\mathsf{exp}}$ is therefore correct, verifiable, and authentic.

□

7   Committed OT from UC Commitments

In this section, we give the details of our approach to constructing our committed OT from UC commitments. Recall that we need an OT protocol where the receiver commits to its choice bits during an offline phase, and the sender is able to send (and subsequently open) message pairs relative to the same choice bit. This is because the receiver's choice bits will correspond to the prover's witness (i.e. the PRF key for nonce derivation) which can be committed once during key generation; signing corresponds to proving different statements about the same witness.

Why Is This Challenging? Consider the following simple attempt at instantiating this object: during the preprocessing phase, the sender samples two PRF keys k_0, k_1, of which the receiver obtains k_b via OT. In order to transmit a message pair m_0, m_1 online, assuming some public instance-specific information x, the sender computes $c_0 = \mathsf{F}_{k_0}(x) \oplus m_0$, $c_1 = \mathsf{F}_{k_1}(x) \oplus m_1$ and sends them to the receiver, who is able to decrypt m_b. In order to 'open' the messages, the sender gives $\mathsf{F}_{k_0}(x), \mathsf{F}_{k_1}(x)$ to the receiver, who then obtains m_{1-b}. While this protects the sender against a malicious receiver, the flaw lies in that it doesn't bind the sender to any particular message pair m_0, m_1. For instance during the opening phase, the sender could provide $F_{k_0}(x), r^*$ (for some $r^* \neq F_{k_1}(x)$). If the receiver's choice bit was 0, it does not notice this deviation and outputs $m_1^* = c_1 \oplus r^*$, as opposed to $m_1 = c_1 \oplus F_{k_1}(x)$ which would have been the output if the receiver's choice bit was 1. Inconsistencies of this flavour propagate upwards to induce selective failure attacks in the ZKGC protocol. We leave the exact attack implicit. This issue is easily solved by using a PRF which allows outputs to be efficiently verified such as a Verifiable Random Function [MRV99]. However to the best of our knowledge, all such known primitives require public key operations, which would defeat the purpose of having moved the OTs offline.

To recap our idea: assume that $\mathcal{C}$ is a commitment scheme that permits *straight-line extraction*. In particular there exists an extractor which, given a commitment and an extraction key ek (corresponding to the commitment key ck), outputs the committed message. This is a property that is conducive to arguing security under concurrent composition [Can01]. However in the 'real' protocol no party has ek; the receiver has a verification key vk which it uses to validate openings to commitments, but the existence of ek is only required for the proof. We will characterize the commitment scheme as a collection of concrete algorithms (rather than working in an $\mathcal{F}_{\mathsf{Commit}}$ hybrid model) and so in principle the trapdoor ek can created by a generic setup functionality and given to the receiver. We use such a commitment scheme to realize the notion of committed OT that we need as follows: create two pairs of keys $(\mathsf{ck}_0, \mathsf{vk}_0, \mathsf{ek}_0)$ and $(\mathsf{ck}_1, \mathsf{vk}_1, \mathsf{ek}_1)$, and provide sender S with both $\mathsf{ck}_0, \mathsf{ck}_1$ and receiver R with $\mathsf{ek}_b, \mathsf{vk}_{1-b}$. In order to send a message pair m_0, m_1, S commits to m_0 using ck_0 and m_1 using ck_1. Then R is able to extract m_b using ek_b immediately. Subsequently when it's time to reveal both messages, S provides decommitment information for m_0, m_1, and R uses vk_{1-b} to validate m_{1-b}.

In more detail, the commitment scheme $\mathcal{C}$ comprises the following algorithms:

- One-time setup:
    - $\mathsf{Gen\text{-}ck}(1^\kappa; \rho^S) \mapsto \mathsf{ck}$. Samples the committer's key with randomness ρ^S.
    - $\mathsf{Gen\text{-}vk}(\mathsf{ck}; \rho^R) \mapsto \mathsf{vk}$. Samples the receiver's verification key using ck with randomness ρ^R.
    - $\mathsf{Gen\text{-}ek}(\mathsf{ck}) \mapsto \mathsf{ek}$. Determines the extraction key given ck.
    - $\mathsf{Gen\text{-}td}(\mathsf{vk}) \mapsto \mathsf{td}$. Determines the trapdoor for equivocation given vk.
- Per message with index ind:
    - $\mathsf{Commit}(\mathsf{ck}, \mathsf{ind}, m) \mapsto C, \delta$. Produces commitment C and decommitment information δ for message m and index ind.
    - $\mathsf{DecomVrfy}(\mathsf{vk}, \mathsf{ind}, C, \delta, m) \mapsto \{0, 1\}$. Commitment verification by R.
    - $\mathsf{Ext}(\mathsf{ek}, \mathsf{ind}, C) \mapsto m \cup \{\bot\}$. Extracts the committed message from C.
    - $\mathcal{S}_{\mathsf{Com}, R^*}(\mathsf{td})$. A simulator that produces and equivocates commitments.

Rather than enumerating a series of definitions that the scheme must satisfy, we use the above interface to construct a protocol, and require that the protocol must UC-realize our commitment functionality. The structure of the commitment functionality $\mathcal{F}_{\mathsf{Com}}$ and the protocol π_{Com} and Simulator $\mathcal{S}_{\mathsf{Com}}$ are straightforward in their usage of $\mathcal{C}$. Protocol π_{Com} makes use of a helper functionality

$\mathcal{F}_{\mathsf{Com}}^{\mathsf{setup}}$ which simply runs the one-time setup algorithms. We defer the formal details to the full version.

Commitment schemes that are of interest to us allow protocol π_{Com} to be simulated by simulator $\mathcal{S}_{\mathsf{Com}}$ with respect to functionality $\mathcal{F}_{\mathsf{Com}}$. Also note that by virtue of the definition, commitment is inherently stateless; no state has to be maintained across commitment instances that use different ind values.

Definition 7.1. A commitment scheme $\mathcal{C}$ is a **preprocessable UC commitment** if protocol $\pi_{\mathsf{Com}}[\mathcal{C}]$ can be simulated by $\mathcal{S}_{\mathsf{Com}}[\mathcal{C}]$ with respect to functionality $\mathcal{F}_{\mathsf{Com}}$ in the UC experiment where an adversary statically corrupts up to one party, in the $\mathcal{F}_{\mathsf{Com}}^{\mathsf{setup}}$-hybrid model.

We stress that while we refer to $\mathcal{C}$ as the preprocessable UC commitment scheme, the actual protocol for the UC experiment is $\pi_{\mathsf{Com}}[\mathcal{C}]$, which is merely a wrapper for the algorithms specified by $\mathcal{C}$.

Instantiating $\mathcal{F}_{\mathsf{Com}}$. Efficiently instantiating the UC commitment functionality (of which $\mathcal{F}_{\mathsf{Com}}$ is a relaxation) has been studied extensively in the literature [DN02, Lin11, CJS14]. However the subset of such works most relevant here are those that operate in the offline-online paradigm, where expensive message-independent public key operations are pushed to an offline phase and (de)committments online only require cheap symmetric key operations. Such protocols have been constructed in a line of works [DDGN14, GIKW14, CDD+15, FJNT16] where a number of oblivious transfers are performed offline to establish correlations, and (de)committing online derives security from the fact that the receiver knows some subset (but not all) of the sender's secrets. Some of these works [CDD+15, FJNT16] are quite practical; their technique is roughly to have the sender commit to a message by first encoding it using an error correcting code, then producing additive shares of each component of the resulting codeword, and finally sending the receiver each additive share encrypted by a pseudorandom one-time pad derived by extending a corresponding PRG seed. The receiver has some subset of these seeds (chosen via OT offline) and obtains the corresponding shares of the codeword. The committed message stays hidden as the receiver is missing one additive share of each component. To decommit, the sender reveals the entire codeword and its shares, and the receiver checks consistency with the shares it already knows. Soundness comes from the property that changing the committed message requires changing so many components of the codeword that the receiver will detect such a change with overwhelming probability. The trapdoor for extraction is the entire set of PRG seeds that are used to encrypt the codeword components. As the sender must encrypt a value that is close to a codeword using these seeds, the extractor is able to decrypt and decode the near-codeword to retrieve the committed message. Extraction is possible as the simulator knows all PRG seeds, and the sender must have encrypted a value sufficiently close to a real codeword in order to have a non-negligible chance of the receiver accepting it later.

Cascudo et al. [CDD+15] report a concretely efficient instantiation of this idea by using binary BCH codes. However existing constructions are designed to amortize the cost of (de)committing large numbers of messages, and as such they are heavily reliant on maintaining state for the PRG. It is feasible to modify their constructions to be stateless by the standard method of replacing the PRG with a PRF, but the resulting cost per instance would save little compared to exponentiation; for instance the protocol of Frederiksen et al. [FJNT16] would require over 800 PRF invocations per instance at a 40 bit security level. While this cost disappears over many simultaneous instances in their setting, we unfortunately can not amortize our costs as independent instances must not share state.

Our Technique. Our commitment scheme essentially implements the same high-level idea, but with a repetition code. The sender S has ℓ PRF keys $k_1, \cdots, k_\ell$, of which the receiver R is given a random subset of $\ell-1$ (say all but $i \in [\ell]$). In order to commit to a message μ for index ind, S sends $\mathsf{F}_{k_1}(\mathsf{ind}) \oplus \cdots \oplus \mathsf{F}_{k_\ell}(\mathsf{ind}) \oplus \mu$ to the receiver. In order to decommit, S reveals μ and $\mathsf{F}_{k_1}(\mathsf{ind}), \cdots, \mathsf{F}_{k_\ell}(\mathsf{ind})$, given which R computes $\mathsf{F}_{k_i}^* = \mu \bigoplus_{j \in [\ell] \setminus i} \mathsf{F}_{k_j}(\mathsf{ind})$ and verifies that it matches F_{k_i} claimed by S. Intuitively, S has to guess exactly which key R is missing in order to fool it. This has soundness error $1/\ell$, however simply repeating this procedure sufficiently many times in parallel (with independent keys) boosts the protocol to have negligible soundness error. This description omits some details, such as how the repetitions are bound together, and optimizing communication, so we describe the commitment scheme itself in terms of the language we laid out earlier.

Algorithm 7.2. $\mathcal{C}$. Commitment scheme

This set of algorithms instantiates a commitment scheme $\mathcal{C}$. The security parameter κ fixes statistical security parameter s and integers ℓ and r such that $\mathsf{r} \log_2(\ell) = s$. The (de)commitment protocols make use of a random oracle RO for equivocation, but notably the extractor does not observe queries to the RO (meaning that it can be run without a backdoor for RO). The protocols additionally use a collision resistant hash function CRHF.

$\mathsf{Gen\text{-}ck}(1^\kappa; \rho^S)$:.
1. For each $j \in [\mathsf{r}]$ and $l \in [\ell]$, sample $k_{j,l} \leftarrow \{0,1\}^\kappa$
2. Sample $k^* \leftarrow \{0,1\}^\kappa$
3. Output $\mathsf{ck} = k^*, \{k_{j,l}\}_{j \in [\mathsf{r}], l \in [\ell]}$

$\mathsf{Gen\text{-}vk}(\mathsf{ck}; \rho^R)$:.

1. Parse $\{k_{j,l}\}_{j \in [\mathsf{r}], l \in [\ell]}$ from ck, and for each $j \in [\mathsf{r}]$, sample integer $i_j \leftarrow [\ell]$
2. Output $\mathsf{vk} = \left\{ (k_{j,l})_{l \in [\ell] \setminus i_j} \right\}_{j \in [\mathsf{r}]}$

$\mathsf{Gen\text{-}ek}(\mathsf{ck})$: Output ck
$\mathsf{Gen\text{-}td}(\mathsf{vk})$: Output $\{i_j\}_{j \in [\ell]}$
$\mathsf{Commit}^{\mathsf{RO}}(\mathsf{ck}, \mathsf{ind}, m)$:.

1. Compute $\mu = \mathsf{F}_{k^*}(\mathsf{ind})$, and for each $j \in [\mathsf{r}]$ set $\mathsf{ct}_j = \mu \bigoplus_{l \in [\ell]} \mathsf{F}_{k_{j,l}}(\mathsf{ind})$

2. Set $\mathsf{ct} = \{\mathsf{ct}_j\}_{j \in [r]}$, $\mathsf{h} = \mathsf{RO}(\mu)$, $\xi = \mu \oplus m$

3. Set $\delta = \mathsf{CRHF}\left(\{\mathsf{F}_{k_{j,l}}(\mathsf{ind})\}_{j \in [r], l \in [\ell]}\right)$, and output $\mathsf{C} = (\mathsf{ct}, \mathsf{h}, \xi), \delta$

$\mathsf{DecomVrfy}(\mathsf{vk}, \mathsf{ind}, \mathsf{C}, \delta, m)$:.

1. Parse $\{i_j\}_{j \in [\ell]} = \mathsf{vk}$, and $\mathsf{ct}, \mathsf{h}, \xi$ from C

2. Compute $\mu = m \oplus \xi$ and verify $\mathsf{RO}(\mu) \overset{?}{=} \mathsf{h}$

3. For each $j \in [r]$ compute $\mathsf{F}^*_{j,k_{i_j}} = \mu \oplus \mathsf{ct}_j \bigoplus_{l \in [\ell] \setminus i_j} \mathsf{F}_{k_{j,l}}(\mathsf{ind})$

4. For each $j \in [r]$, set $\mathsf{F}[j,l] = \mathsf{F}_{k_{j,l}}(\mathsf{ind})$ for $l \in [\ell] \setminus i_j$ and $\mathsf{F}[j, i_j] = \mu \oplus \mathsf{ct}_j \bigoplus_{l \in [\ell] \setminus i_j} \mathsf{F}_{k_{j,l}}(\mathsf{ind})$

5. Verify $\delta \overset{?}{=} \mathsf{CRHF}\left(\{\mathsf{F}[j,l]\}_{j \in [r], l \in [\ell]}\right)$

$\mathsf{Ext}(\mathsf{ek}, \mathsf{ind}, \mathsf{C})$:.

1. Parse $\{k_{j,l}\}_{j \in [r], l \in [\ell]}$ from ck, and $\mathsf{ct}, \mathsf{h}, \xi$ from C

2. For each $j \in [r]$, compute $\mu^*_j = \mathsf{ct}_j \bigoplus_{l \in [\ell]} \mathsf{F}_{k_{j,l}}(\mathsf{ind})$

3. If $\exists j \in [r]$ such that $\mathsf{RO}(\mu^*_j) = \mathsf{h}$, then output $m = \mu^*_j \oplus \xi$

4. If no such μ^*_j exists, then output $\perp$

$\mathcal{S}_{\mathsf{Com}, \mathsf{R}^*}(\mathsf{td})$: Postponed to full version as it is straightforward.

We postpone the theorem and proof to the full version.

How to Implement the Setup? Observe that the structure of the verification key is to choose all but one out of the ℓ keys in each of the r batches. This is directly achieved by r invocations of $\mathcal{F}_{\binom{\ell}{\ell-1}\mathsf{OT}}$.

Efficiency. A commitment to a message m (assume $|m| = \kappa$) is of size $(r + 3) \cdot \kappa$ bits, and in terms of computation requires $r \cdot \ell$ PRF evaluations and hashing a $r \cdot \ell \cdot \kappa$ bit message via CRHF. Decommitment requires the same effort.

Parameters. Looking ahead, we will introduce a privacy amplifying optimization in the ZKGC protocol so that for s bits of statistical security, the receiver's security in the Committed OT protocol it uses (and therefore soundness of the Commitment scheme under the hood) need only achieve $s/2$ bits of statistical security. We therefore calibrate our parameters here appropriately. A reasonable instantiation of parameters would be $\ell = 4$, $s = 30$, $\kappa = 128$, and $r = 15$ (i.e. a 30-bit statistical soundness level) with AES-128 as the PRF, and SHA-512 as the CRHF and RO. This means that a single commitment to a 128-bit message requires 288 bytes (32 bytes to decommit), 60 AES-128 evaluations, and hashing a 0.96 kilobyte message via SHA-512. The work done by R in verifying a commitment is almost the same. Looking ahead, we will use a pair of these commitments to replace a single OT instance, providing a significant improvement in computation time.

7.1 Committed OT from Preprocessable UC Commitments

Using commitment scheme $\mathcal{C}$, we now have an clean template for a protocol to build committed OT. We first define a helper functionality $\mathcal{F}_{\text{COT}}^{\text{setup}}$ to handle the preprocessing stage. Intuitively, $\mathcal{F}_{\text{COT}}^{\text{setup}}$ samples two commitment keys ck_0, ck_1 for the sender and corresponding verification and extraction keys $\text{vk}_0, \text{vk}_1, \text{ek}_0, \text{ek}_1$, and gives $\text{vk}_0, \text{vk}_1, \text{ek}_b$ to the receiver upon its choice of bit b. The formalism is straightforward and so we postpone it to the full version. Unfortunately it is unclear how to generically construct $\mathcal{F}_{\text{COT}}^{\text{setup}}$ using the commitment scheme, but for our specific case we can construct a custom protocol based on the same Bellare-Micali construction that we used for $\mathcal{F}_{\binom{\ell}{\ell-1}\text{OT}}$. We give the exact construction in the full version.

Protocol 7.3. $\pi_{\text{COT}}[\mathcal{C}]$. **Committed Oblivious Transfer**

This protocol is run between a sender S and a receiver R, and is parameterized by a commitment scheme $\mathcal{C}$. This protocol makes use of the ideal oracle $\mathcal{F}_{\text{COT}}^{\text{setup}}$ and random oracle $\text{RO} : \{0,1\}^* \mapsto \{0,1\}^{4\kappa}$.

Setup: R has private input $b \in \{0,1\}$
1. S and R send (sid, init) to $\mathcal{F}_{\text{COT}}^{\text{setup}}$
2. R additionally sends (choose, b) to $\mathcal{F}_{\text{COT}}^{\text{setup}}$, and receives $(sid, \text{keys}, \text{ek}_b, \text{vk}_0, \text{vk}_1)$ in response.
3. S receives $(sid, \text{ck-keys}, \text{ck}_0, \text{ck}_1)$ from $\mathcal{F}_{\text{COT}}^{\text{setup}}$

Transfer: S has private inputs m_0, m_1, key, and ind is public input.

1. S computes $\mathsf{C}_0, \delta_0 = \text{Commit}(\text{ck}_0, \text{ind}, m_0)$ and $\mathsf{C}_1, \delta_1 = \text{Commit}(\text{ck}_1, \text{ind}, m_1)$
2. S encrypts the decommitment information with key as $\nu = \text{RO}(\text{key}) \oplus (m_0, \delta_0, m_1, \delta_1)$
3. S sends $\mathsf{C}_0, \mathsf{C}_1, \nu$ to R
4. R outputs $m_b = \text{Ext}(\text{ek}_b, \text{ind}, \mathsf{C}_b)$

Reveal: R does the following with inputs ind and key:

1. R computes $(m_0, \delta_0, m_1, \delta_1) = \text{RO}(\text{key}) \oplus \nu$
2. R outputs
   $\text{DecomVrfy}(\text{vk}_0, \text{ind}, \mathsf{C}_0, \delta_0, m_0) \wedge \text{DecomVrfy}(\text{vk}_1, \text{ind}, \mathsf{C}_1, \delta_1, m_1)$

Theorem 7.4. Assuming $\mathcal{C}$ is a preprocessable UC commitment (Definition 7.1), protocol π_{COT} UC-realizes $\mathcal{F}_{\text{COT}}^*$ in the presence of an adversary corrupting up to one party, in the $\mathcal{F}_{\text{COT}}^{\text{setup}}$-hybrid random oracle model.

The theorem directly follows from the definition of preprocessable UC commitments, and the fact that encryptions with the random oracle carry no information until the correct pre-image is queried.

Efficiency. There are three components to analyze: the setup, transfer, and reveal phases.

Setup. We do not analyze the exact cost of setup, beyond that it requires $O(\ell r \kappa / \log \kappa)$ curve multiplications, and as many field elements transmitted.

Transfer and Reveal. This is the important metric, as the transfer and reveal phases are executed when a message has to be signed. A transfer consists of two independent instances of preprocessable UC commitments for S, of which R simply receives one and runs Ext on the other. A reveal requires no work for S, and two decommitment verifications for R. In our specific instantiation, the work done by S when committing and R when verifying is roughly the same. Additionally R can reuse the work of Ext in verifying a commitment. Based on Sect. 7, the work done by each party in total for a transfer and reveal of a message pair is 120 AES invocations, and hashing a 1.92 KB message via SHA-512. The bandwidth consumed is two UC commitments and their decommitments, so 0.64 KB. Note that these parameters are for a 30-bit statistical security level, which is inadequate by itself, but will be sufficient in the ZKGC context due to a privacy amplifying technique.

8 Provable Nonce Derivation

In order to clarify the target, we give the ideal functionality $\mathcal{F}_{\mathsf{F}\cdot\mathbb{G}}$ for proving deterministic nonce derivation, with a conditional disclosure property woven in.

Functionality 8.1. $\mathcal{F}_{\mathsf{F}\cdot\mathbb{G}}$. Deterministic Nonce Derivation

This functionality is accessed by a prover P and a verifier V, and is parameterized by the keyed function $\mathsf{F} : \{0,1\}^\kappa \times \{0,1\}^\kappa \mapsto \mathbb{Z}_q$, and the group $(\mathbb{G}, G, q)$. In principle, the public instance $x = (m, R_m^*)$ for which the prover has witness $w = k$ satisfies relation $f(x, w)$ only when $R_m^* = \mathsf{F}_k(m) \cdot G$. All messages are adversarially delayed.

Key Generation: This phase is run exactly once for each sid. Any requests to the functionality with an sid for which Key Generation has not yet been run are ignored.

1. Wait to receive $(sid, \texttt{input-key}, k)$ from P.
2. If $k \in \{0,1\}^\kappa$, then store $(sid, \texttt{key}, k)$ and send $(sid, \texttt{initialized})$ to V.

Verify Nonce: Upon receiving $(sid, \texttt{verify-nonce}, m, R_m^*)$ from P and $(sid, \texttt{verify-nonce}, m, R_m^*, z)$ from V, if $(sid, \texttt{key}, k)$ exists in memory, $m \in \{0,1\}^\kappa$, and $R_m^* \in \mathbb{G}$ then:

1. Compute $r_m = \mathsf{F}_k(m)$ and $R_m = r_m \cdot G$.
2. If $R_m^* \stackrel{?}{=} R_m$ then send $(sid, \texttt{secret}, m, z)$ to P and then $(sid, \texttt{verified}, m, R_m^*)$ to V. Otherwise send $(sid, \texttt{fail}, m, R_m^*)$ to V.

This is essentially a specific instantiation of the standard zero-knowledge functionality, with the exception that the prover commits its witness w first, and subsequently multiple statements x are supplied to the functionality, which verifies that $R(x, w) = 1$. This is directly achieved by replacing the committed OT functionality used by ZKGC with $\mathcal{F}_{COT}^*$ which allows the receiver to commit to a choice bit and subsequently receive/open multiple message pairs independently without ever revealing the choice bit. Note that the circuit to be garbled $(C(k, x) = F_k(x) \cdot G)$ is supported by HalfGates with our garbling gadget. Finally, the disclosure of the secret z conditioned on the validity of the statement/witness is the same as the technique introduced by Ganesh et al. [GKPS18]. We give the explicit protocol in the full version.

8.1   A Privacy Amplifying Optimization

While the ZKGC protocol makes only oracle use of $\mathcal{F}_{COT}^*$, we can make an instantiation-specific optimization which will likely apply to any similarly structured instantiation, where the receiver only has statistical security inherited from statistical soundness of the decommitment/reveal phase. Currently, a naive instantiation would protect each choice bit of the receiver's (and hence private witness bit) with s bits of statistical security, i.e. there is at most a 2^{-s} probability of an adversary subverting the reveal phase by opening its message to a different one than committed earlier. As each instance of protocol π_{COT} makes use of independent randomness, the probability that a malicious sender is able to subvert the reveal phases of a *pair* of commitments is 2^{-2s}. Therefore if we are willing to tolerate one bit of leakage, we can in some sense consider the soundness of the reveal phase to be doubled.

Plugging the Leak. The prover samples a random bit $r \leftarrow \{0, 1\}$ during the one-time key setup phase. Now instead of directly using its witness bits $\mathbf{x}_i$ as the choice bit to the ith instance of $\mathcal{F}_{COT}^*$, the prover instead uses $\mathbf{x}'_i = \mathbf{x}_i \oplus r$ as the choice bit to the ith instance. Finally the prover also inputs r as the choice bit to the $|\mathbf{x}| + 1^{th}$ instance of $\mathcal{F}_{COT}^*$. When the time comes to evaluate a circuit $C(\mathbf{x})$, the prover and verifier instead use the circuit $C'(\mathbf{x}', r) = C(\mathbf{x}'_1 \oplus r || \mathbf{x}'_1 \oplus r || \cdots || \mathbf{x}'_{|\mathbf{x}|} \oplus r)$ to cancel out the effect of r. Since XOR gates come for free in a garbled circuit [KS08], this adds essentially no overhead beyond the single extra instance of $\mathcal{F}_{COT}^*$ for r. Now the input to C' can tolerate a single bit of leakage; any one bit leaked from $\mathbf{x}' || r$ is perfectly independent of $\mathbf{x}$.

Security. This clearly does not harm security against a corrupt prover, as the encoded input $\mathbf{x}' || r$ supplied to $\mathcal{F}_{COT}^*$ unambiguously specify its candidate witness $\mathbf{x}$ just as earlier. As for when simulating for a corrupt verifier, in case one of the extractors for a π_{COT} instance i reports an extraction error for the key $k_{i,b}$ corresponding to bit b (this happens with probability 2^{-s}, but recall that the target security level is $2s$ bits) the simulator tosses a coin b'. If $b' = b$, then the simulator aborts the protocol (corresponding to a cheat being caught in the real protocol). Otherwise, the simulator simply runs the honest prover's protocol for the ith bit going forward, effectively setting $\mathbf{x}'_i = \neg b$. The subtle point is that failing to extract $k_{i,b}$ does not hamper the simulator's ability to extract garbled circuits' embedded decoding information in the future: in case $i = |\mathbf{x}| + 1$, the value compromised is r, which does not influence any output wires anyway. In case $i \leq |\mathbf{x}|$, the simulator still obtains $k_{i,\neg b}$ by running the honest prover's code, and the availability of both keys on the r wire allow for the retrieval of both keys for $\mathbf{x}_i$ as $\mathbf{x}'_i \oplus 0$ and $\mathbf{x}'_i \oplus 1$ (i.e. substituting both values of r). We defer a more formal proof to the full version of this paper.

Therefore in order to achieve $s' = 60$ bits of statistical security for ZKGC, one can parameterize the underlying OT protocol with $s = 30$ bits of soundness and remove the resulting leakage as described above.

8.2   Estimated Efficiency

We give estimates for an Ed25519 [BDL+12] style configuration. In particular, we assume a 256-bit curve, with SHA-512 as the PRF used to derive nonces just as in the EdDSA specification. SHA-512 has 58k AND gates [AMM+]. The nonce derivation key is 128 bits.

- **Garbled Circuit.** We can use a privacy-free garbled circuit in this context [FNO15], as the evaluator knows the entire input. In particular we can use the privacy-free variant of the Half Gates garbling scheme [ZRE15] which produces only one 128-bit ciphertext per AND gate. Each ciphertext is computed with two AES-128 invocations, and evaluated with one. The exponentiation gadget produces one 256-bit ciphertext for each output wire of the Boolean circuit. Consequently in the course of a single proof, V garbles the circuit (116k AES invocations), and P evaluates and verifies it (116k AES invocations). The bandwidth consumed is 928 KB to transmit the garbled circuit $\tilde{C}$ and ciphertexts **ct**.
- $\mathcal{F}^*_{\mathsf{COT}}$. As discussed in Sect. 7.1, a single transfer and reveal instance costs 120 AES invocations and hashing a 1.92 KB message via SHA-512 to compute, and 0.64 KB in bandwidth. A single proof here requires 128 concurrent transfers and reveals via $\mathcal{F}^*_{\mathsf{COT}}$, bringing the computation cost to 16k AES invocations and hashing a 245 KB message via SHA-512 for each P and V, and 81.92 KB of bandwidth consumption.

Overall Burden. In summary, P and V have roughly the same workload, dominated by 132k AES invocations and hashing a 245 KB message. Each party additionally performs up to three curve multiplications, 256 additions in $\mathbb{Z}_q$, at little overhead. Bandwidth for $(|\tilde{C}| + |\mathbf{ct}| + |\mathcal{F}^*_{\mathsf{COT}}|)$ is 1.01 MB. Given the cost breakup above, it is evident that the logistics for input encoding and exponentiation are no longer the bottleneck, and the cost of proving correctness of a derived nonce is now essentially the cost of evaluating the garbled circuit of the PRF (usually in the order of milliseconds [GLNP15, HK20]) used for nonce derivation. Our figures are derived assuming SHA-512 is used for this task as it is the same hash function used by Ed25519, however it is likely that exploring standardized ciphers with smaller circuits such as AES will lead to substantial efficiency improvements.

9 Multiparty Dishonest Majority Threshold Signing

With the most complex component of stateless deterministic threshold signing - verifiable nonce derivation - instantiated, we are equipped to construct a clean multiparty signing protocol. The outline is as follows:

- **Setup:** All parties run canonical distributed key generation [Ped91] to obtain additive shares sk_i of a secret key sk (for public pk), and every pair of parties initializes an instance of $\mathcal{F}_{\mathsf{F.G}}$ to commit to a nonce derivation key k_i. Note that we do not explicitly enforce any consistency across parties. Each party also samples a key k_* to derive randomness online.
- **Signing m:** Each party P_i derives its nonce $R_{m,i} = \mathsf{F}_{k_i}(m)$ and sends it to all other parties. Consistency is verified by standard echo-broadcast in parallel with the next round. Every party derives its local random tape going forward by applying F_{k_*} on the digest of the view from the first round, i.e. $v = \mathsf{CRHF}(R_{m,0}||R_{m,1}||,\cdots||R_{m,n})$. Each party P_i sets $(z_{i,j})_{j\in[n]\setminus i} = \mathsf{F}_{k_*}(j||v)$ and instructs $\mathcal{F}_{\mathsf{F.G}}$ to deliver $z_{i,j}$ to P_j only if $R_{m,j}$ is the correct nonce. Finally each P_i sets the nonce to be $R_m = \sum_i R_{m,i}$ and computes its signature share

$$\sigma_i = (\mathsf{sk}_i \cdot H(\mathsf{pk}, R_m, m) + r_{m,i}) + \sum_{j\in[n]\setminus i} (z_{i,j} - z_{j,i})$$

and sends it to all parties. The signature is then computed as $\sigma = \sum_i \sigma_i$.

Intuitively, P_i's share adds the mask $z_{i,j}$ to its contribution, and P_j's share removes this mask by subtracting $z_{i,j}$. Note that this is possible only if P_j obtained $z_{i,j}$ from $\mathcal{F}_{\mathsf{F.G}}$ by having sent the correct $R_{m,j}$. Adding up all parties' σ_is cancels out the z values (if everyone is honest), and what remains is simply $\mathsf{sk}\cdot H(\mathsf{pk}, R_m, m) + r$ which is a valid signature on m. We give the formal functionality, and full threshold signing protocol and proof in the full version.

9.1 Efficiency

The protocol is essentially a thin wrapper on top of $\mathcal{F}_{\mathsf{F.G}}$, and consequently the cost is dominated by running $\mathcal{F}_{\mathsf{F.G}}$ between every pair of parties. Every pair of parties P_i, P_j shares two instantiations of $\mathcal{F}_{\mathsf{F.G}}$, one in which P_i plays the prover and P_j the verifier, and another with the roles reversed. However by the structure of our protocol $\pi_{\mathsf{F.G}}$, instantiating $\mathcal{F}_{\mathsf{F.G}}$ in both directions induces little computational overhead on top of a single instantiation: while the verifier garbles the circuit the prover sits idle, and while the prover evaluates the garbled circuit the verifier has nothing to do. This means that when P_i is working as the verifier in one instance of $\mathcal{F}_{\mathsf{F.G}}$ with P_j, it will be idling in its role as the prover in the other instance of $\mathcal{F}_{\mathsf{F.G}}$ with P_j, and vice versa.

For this reason, we expect a two-party instantiation of $\pi_{n,\mathsf{Sign}}$ to run in the order of milliseconds just as a single instance of $\pi_{\mathsf{F.G}}$, and bandwidth stays at roughly 1.01 MB transmitted per party. This cost is multiplied by n for an n party instantiation.

References

[AMM+]   Archer, D., Abril, V.A., Maene, P., Mertens, N., Sijacic, D., Smart, N.:
Bristol fashion MPC circuits. https://homes.esat.kuleuven.be/~nsmart/
MPC/. Accessed 24 Feb 2021

[AMMR18] Agrawal, S., Mohassel, P., Mukherjee, P., Rindal, P.: DiSE: distributed
symmetric-key encryption. In: ACM CCS 2018. ACM Press (2018)

[Bay14]   Bayer, J.: Challenges With Randomness In Multi-tenant Linux Container
Platforms (2014)

[BBB+18] Bünz, B., Bootle, J., Boneh, D., Poelstra, A., Wuille, P., Maxwell, G.:
Bulletproofs: short proofs for confidential transactions and more. In: 2018
IEEE S&P (2018)

[BCLK17] Brandenburger, M., Cachin, C., Lorenz, M., Kapitza, R.: Rollback and
forking detection for trusted execution environments using lightweight col-
lective memory. In: DSN 2017 (2017)

[BCR+19] Ben-Sasson, E., Chiesa, A., Riabzev, M., Spooner, N., Virza, M., Ward,
N.P.: Aurora: transparent succinct arguments for R1CS. In: Ishai, Y., Rij-
men, V. (eds.) EUROCRYPT 2019, Part I. LNCS, vol. 11476, pp. 103–128.
Springer, Cham (2019). https://doi.org/10.1007/978-3-030-17653-2_4

[BDL+12] Bernstein, D.J., Duif, N., Lange, T., Schwabe, P., Yang, B.-Y.: High-speed
high-security signatures. J. Cryptogr. Eng. 2, 77–89 (2012). https://doi.
org/10.1007/s13389-012-0027-1

[BFS20]   Bünz, B., Fisch, B., Szepieniec, A.: Transparent SNARKs from DARK
compilers. In: Canteaut, A., Ishai, Y. (eds.) EUROCRYPT 2020. LNCS,
vol. 12105, pp. 677–706. Springer, Cham (2020). https://doi.org/10.1007/
978-3-030-45721-1_24

[BHH+19] Backes, M., Hanzlik, L., Herzberg, A., Kate, A., Pryvalov, I.: Efficient
non-interactive zero-knowledge proofs in cross-domains without trusted
setup. In: Lin, D., Sako, K. (eds.) PKC 2019, Part I. LNCS, vol. 11442,
pp. 286–313. Springer, Cham (2019). https://doi.org/10.1007/978-3-030-
17253-4_10

[BHR12]   Bellare, M., Hoang, V.T., Rogaway, P.: Foundations of garbled circuits.
In: ACM CCS 2012 (2012)

[BSGL20] Ben-Sasson, E., Goldberg, L., Levit, D.: Stark friendly hash – survey and
recommendation. IACR Cryptol. ePrint Arch. 2020:948 (2020)

[BST21]   Bonte, C., Smart, N.P., Tanguy, T.: Thresholdizing HashEdDSA: MPC to
the rescue. Int. J. Inf. Secur. 1–16 (2021). https://doi.org/10.1007/s10207-
021-00539-6

[Can01]   Canetti, R.: Universally composable security: a new paradigm for cryptographic protocols. In: 42nd FOCS (2001)

[CCD+20] Chen, M., et al.: Multiparty generation of an RSA modulus. In: Micciancio,
D., Ristenpart, T. (eds.) CRYPTO 2020. LNCS, vol. 12172, pp. 64–93.
Springer, Cham (2020). https://doi.org/10.1007/978-3-030-56877-1_3

[CDD+15] Cascudo, I., Damgård, I., David, B., Giacomelli, I., Nielsen, J.B., Trifiletti, R.: Additively homomorphic UC commitments with optimal amortized overhead. In: Katz, J. (ed.) PKC 2015. LNCS, vol. 9020, pp.
495–515. Springer, Heidelberg (2015). https://doi.org/10.1007/978-3-662-
46447-2_22

[CGGM00] Canetti, R., Goldreich, O., Goldwasser, S., Micali, S.: Resettable zero-
knowledge (extended abstract). In: 32nd ACM STOC, pp. 235–244. ACM
Press, May 2000

[CGGN17] Campanelli, M., Gennaro, R., Goldfeder, S., Nizzardo, L.: Zero-knowledge contingent payments revisited: attacks and payments for services. In: ACM CCS 2017 (2017)

[CGM16] Chase, M., Ganesh, C., Mohassel, P.: Efficient zero-knowledge proof of algebraic and non-algebraic statements with applications to privacy preserving credentials. In: Robshaw, M., Katz, J. (eds.) CRYPTO 2016, Part III. LNCS, vol. 9816, pp. 499–530. Springer, Heidelberg (2016). https://doi.org/10.1007/978-3-662-53015-3_18

[CJS14] Canetti, R., Jain, A., Scafuro, A.: Practical UC security with a global random oracle. In: ACM CCS 2014 (2014)

[CKKZ12] Choi, S.G., Katz, J., Kumaresan, R., Zhou, H.-S.: On the security of the "free-XOR" technique. In: Cramer, R. (ed.) TCC 2012. LNCS, vol. 7194, pp. 39–53. Springer, Heidelberg (2012). https://doi.org/10.1007/978-3-642-28914-9_3

[CO15] Chou, T., Orlandi, C.: The simplest protocol for oblivious transfer. In: Lauter, K., Rodríguez-Henríquez, F. (eds.) LATINCRYPT 2015. LNCS, vol. 9230, pp. 40–58. Springer, Cham (2015). https://doi.org/10.1007/978-3-319-22174-8_3

[DDGN14] Damgård, I., David, B., Giacomelli, I., Nielsen, J.B.: Compact VSS and efficient homomorphic UC commitments. In: Sarkar, P., Iwata, T. (eds.) ASIACRYPT 2014, Part II. LNCS, vol. 8874, pp. 213–232. Springer, Heidelberg (2014). https://doi.org/10.1007/978-3-662-45608-8_12

[DN02] Damgård, I., Nielsen, J.B.: Perfect hiding and perfect binding universally composable commitment schemes with constant expansion factor. In: Yung, M. (ed.) CRYPTO 2002. LNCS, vol. 2442, pp. 581–596. Springer, Heidelberg (2002). https://doi.org/10.1007/3-540-45708-9_37

[EZJ+14] Everspaugh, A., Zhai, Y., Jellinek, R., Ristenpart, T., Swift, M.: Not-so-random numbers in virtualized Linux and the Whirlwind RNG. In: 2014 IEEE Symposium on Security and Privacy, pp. 559–574. IEEE, May 2014

[FJNT16] Frederiksen, T.K., Jakobsen, T.P., Nielsen, J.B., Trifiletti, R.: On the complexity of additively homomorphic UC commitments. In: Kushilevitz, E., Malkin, T. (eds.) TCC 2016, Part I. LNCS, vol. 9562, pp. 542–565. Springer, Heidelberg (2016). https://doi.org/10.1007/978-3-662-49096-9_23

[FNO15] Frederiksen, T.K., Nielsen, J.B., Orlandi, C.: Privacy-free garbled circuits with applications to efficient zero-knowledge. In: Oswald, E., Fischlin, M. (eds.) EUROCRYPT 2015, Part II. LNCS, vol. 9057, pp. 191–219. Springer, Heidelberg (2015). https://doi.org/10.1007/978-3-662-46803-6_7

[GIKW14] Garay, J.A., Ishai, Y., Kumaresan, R., Wee, H.: On the complexity of UC commitments. In: Nguyen, P.Q., Oswald, E. (eds.) EUROCRYPT 2014. LNCS, vol. 8441, pp. 677–694. Springer, Heidelberg (2014). https://doi.org/10.1007/978-3-642-55220-5_37

[Gil99] Gilboa, N.: Two party RSA key generation. In: Wiener, M. (ed.) CRYPTO 1999. LNCS, vol. 1666, pp. 116–129. Springer, Heidelberg (1999). https://doi.org/10.1007/3-540-48405-1_8

[GJKR07] Gennaro, R., Jarecki, S., Krawczyk, H., Rabin, T.: Secure distributed key generation for discrete-log based cryptosystems. J. Cryptol. 20(1), 51–83 (2006). https://doi.org/10.1007/s00145-006-0347-3

[GKPS18] Ganesh, C., Kondi, Y., Patra, A., Sarkar, P.: Efficient adaptively secure zero-knowledge from garbled circuits. In: Abdalla, M., Dahab, R. (eds.) PKC 2018, Part II. LNCS, vol. 10770, pp. 499–529. Springer, Cham (2018). https://doi.org/10.1007/978-3-319-76581-5_17

[GLNP15] Gueron, S., Lindell, Y., Nof, A., Pinkas, B.: Fast garbling of circuits under standard assumptions. In: Ray, I., Li, N., Kruegel, C. (eds.) ACM CCS 2015, pp. 567–578. ACM Press, October 2015

[GMW87] Goldreich, O., Micali, S., Wigderson, A.: How to play any mental game or a completeness theorem for protocols with honest majority. In: 19th ACM STOC (1987)

[Gro16] Groth, J.: On the size of pairing-based non-interactive arguments. In: Fischlin, M., Coron, J.-S. (eds.) EUROCRYPT 2016, Part II. LNCS, vol. 9666, pp. 305–326. Springer, Heidelberg (2016). https://doi.org/10.1007/978-3-662-49896-5_11

[HK20] Heath, D., Kolesnikov, V.: Stacked garbling for disjunctive zero-knowledge proofs. In: Canteaut, A., Ishai, Y. (eds.) EUROCRYPT 2020, Part III. LNCS, vol. 12107, pp. 569–598. Springer, Cham (2020). https://doi.org/10.1007/978-3-030-45727-3_19

[HS01] Howgrave-Graham, N., Smart, N.P.: Lattice attacks on digital signature schemes. Des. Codes Cryptogr. **23**(3), 283–290 (2001)

[HSS17] Hazay, C., Scholl, P., Soria-Vazquez, E.: Low cost constant round MPC combining BMR and oblivious transfer. In: Takagi, T., Peyrin, T. (eds.) ASIACRYPT 2017, Part I. LNCS, vol. 10624, pp. 598–628. Springer, Cham (2017). https://doi.org/10.1007/978-3-319-70694-8_21

[JKO13] Jawurek, M., Kerschbaum, F., Orlandi, C.: Zero-knowledge using garbled circuits: how to prove non-algebraic statements efficiently. In: ACM CCS 2013 (2013)

[KASN15] Kumari, R., Alimomeni, M., Safavi-Naini, R.: Performance analysis of Linux RNG in virtualized environments. In: ACM Workshop on Cloud Computing Security Workshop - CCSW 2015, New York, USA (2015)

[KC12] Kerrigan, B., Chen, Yu.: A study of entropy sources in cloud computers: random number generation on cloud hosts. In: Kotenko, I., Skormin, V. (eds.) MMM-ACNS 2012. LNCS, vol. 7531, pp. 286–298. Springer, Heidelberg (2012). https://doi.org/10.1007/978-3-642-33704-8_24

[KL17] Khovratovich, D., Law, J.: BIP32-Ed25519: hierarchical deterministic keys over a non-linear keyspace. In: 2017 IEEE European Symposium on Security and Privacy Workshops (EuroS&PW), pp. 27–31. IEEE, April 2017

[Kos] Kosba, A.: xJsnark

[KPR18] Keller, M., Pastro, V., Rotaru, D.: Overdrive: making SPDZ great again. In: Nielsen, J.B., Rijmen, V. (eds.) EUROCRYPT 2018, Part III. LNCS, vol. 10822, pp. 158–189. Springer, Cham (2018). https://doi.org/10.1007/978-3-319-78372-7_6

[KRRW18] Katz, J., Ranellucci, S., Rosulek, M., Wang, X.: Optimizing authenticated garbling for faster secure two-party computation. In: Shacham, H., Boldyreva, A. (eds.) CRYPTO 2018, Part III. LNCS, vol. 10993, pp. 365–391. Springer, Cham (2018). https://doi.org/10.1007/978-3-319-96878-0_13

[KS08] Kolesnikov, V., Schneider, T.: Improved garbled circuit: free XOR gates and applications. In: Aceto, L., Damgård, I., Goldberg, L.A., Halldórsson, M.M., Ingólfsdóttir, A., Walukiewicz, I. (eds.) ICALP 2008, Part II. LNCS, vol. 5126, pp. 486–498. Springer, Heidelberg (2008). https://doi.org/10.1007/978-3-540-70583-3_40

[KW03]   Katz, J., Wang, N.: Efficiency improvements for signature schemes with tight security reductions. In: ACM CCS 2003 (2003)

[Lin11]   Lindell, Y.: Highly-efficient universally-composable commitments based on the DDH assumption. In: Paterson, K.G. (ed.) EUROCRYPT 2011. LNCS, vol. 6632, pp. 446–466. Springer, Heidelberg (2011). https://doi.org/10. 1007/978-3-642-20465-4_25

[LPR19]   Lindell, Y., Peer, G., Ranellucci, S.: Unbound blockchain-crypto-MPC library. White Paper (2019)

[MAK+17] Matetic, S., et al.: ROTE: rollback protection for trusted execution. In: USENIX Security 2017 (2017)

[MNPV99] M'Raïhi, D., Naccache, D., Pointcheval, D., Vaudenay, S.: Computational alternatives to random number generators. In: Tavares, S., Meijer, H. (eds.) SAC 1998. LNCS, vol. 1556, pp. 72–80. Springer, Heidelberg (1999). https://doi.org/10.1007/3-540-48892-8_6

[MPSW19] Maxwell, G., Poelstra, A., Seurin, Y., Wuille, P.: Simple Schnorr multi-signatures with applications to bitcoin. Des. Codes Crypt. **87**(9), 2139–2164 (2019)

[MRV99]   Micali, S., Rabin, M.O., Vadhan, S.P.: Verifiable random functions. In: 40th FOCS (1999)

[NKDM03] Nicolosi, A., Krohn, M.N., Dodis, Y., Mazières, D.: Proactive two-party signatures for user authentication. In: NDSS 2003 (2003)

[NRSW20] Nick, J., Ruffing, T., Seurin, Y., Wuille, P.: MuSig-DN: schnorr multi-signatures with verifiably deterministic nonces. In: ACM CCS 2020 (2020)

[Ped91]   Pedersen, T.P.: A threshold cryptosystem without a trusted party. In: Davies, D.W. (ed.) EUROCRYPT 1991. LNCS, vol. 547, pp. 522–526. Springer, Heidelberg (1991). https://doi.org/10.1007/3-540-46416-6_47

[PLD+11] Parno, B., Lorch, J.R., Douceur, J.R., Mickens, J.W., McCune, J.M.: Memoir: practical state continuity for protected modules. In: 2011 IEEE S&P (2011)

[PS96]   Pointcheval, D., Stern, J.: Security proofs for signature schemes. In: Maurer, U. (ed.) EUROCRYPT 1996. LNCS, vol. 1070, pp. 387–398. Springer, Heidelberg (1996). https://doi.org/10.1007/3-540-68339-9_33

[Sch91]   Schnorr, C.P.: Efficient signature generation by smart cards. J. Cryptol. **4**(3), 161–174 (1991). https://doi.org/10.1007/BF00196725

[Set20]   Setty, S.: Spartan: efficient and general-purpose zkSNARKs without trusted setup. In: Micciancio, D., Ristenpart, T. (eds.) CRYPTO 2020. LNCS, vol. 12172, pp. 704–737. Springer, Cham (2020). https://doi.org/ 10.1007/978-3-030-56877-1_25

[SP16]   Strackx, R., Piessens, F.: Ariadne: a minimal approach to state continuity. In: USENIX Security 2016 (2016)

[SS01]   Stinson, D.R., Strobl, R.: Provably secure distributed schnorr signatures and a (t, n) threshold scheme for implicit certificates. In: Varadharajan, V., Mu, Y. (eds.) ACISP 2001. LNCS, vol. 2119, pp. 417–434. Springer, Heidelberg (2001). https://doi.org/10.1007/3-540-47719-5_33

[TTA18]   Takahashi, A., Tibouchi, M., Abe, M.: New Bleichenbacher records: fault attacks on qDSA signatures. IACR TCHES **2018**, 331–371 (2018)

[vDRSD07] van Dijk, M., Rhodes, J., Sarmenta, L.F.G., Devadas, S.: Offline untrusted storage with immediate detection of forking and replay attacks. In: ACM STC 2007 (2007)

[ZRE15]   Zahur, S., Rosulek, M., Evans, D.: Two halves make a whole. In: Oswald, E., Fischlin, M. (eds.) EUROCRYPT 2015, Part II. LNCS, vol. 9057, pp. 220–250. Springer, Heidelberg (2015). https://doi.org/10.1007/978-3-662-46803-6_8

Two-Round Trip Schnorr
Multi-signatures via Delinearized
Witnesses

Handan Kılınç Alper[✉] and Jeffrey Burdges

Web3 Foundation, Zug, Switzerland
handan@web3.foundation

Abstract. We construct a two-round Schnorr-based signature scheme
(DWMS) by delinearizing two pre-commitments supplied by each signer.
DWMS is a secure signature scheme in the algebraic group model (AGM)
and the random oracle model (ROM) under the assumption of the hardness of the one-more discrete logarithm problem and the 2-entwined sum
problem that we introduce in this paper. Our new *m-entwined sum* problem tweaks the k-sum problem in a scalar field using the associated group.
We prove the hardness of our new problem in the AGM assuming the
hardness of the discrete logarithm problem in the associated group. We
believe that our new problem simplifies the security proofs of multi-
signature schemes that use the delinearization of commitments.

1 Introduction

A multi-signature scheme is a signature scheme that allows multiple parties
collaboratively to sign a message so that the final signature can be verified with
the public keys of the signers by a user. The trivial solution for this is that
each entity signs the data individually and provides it to the user. However,
this is not a space and time-efficient solution since the user needs to verify each
signature separately and keep a larger amount of signatures. Hence, we require
more elegant multi-signature schemes which save time and space on the user and
the signer side.

To this end, multi-signature schemes [3,6,9,15,17–19,22] have been studied
for a long time. Increased operational security demands have driven a growth
spurt in multi-signer implementations in recent years especially for Schnorr-
based multi-signature schemes [2,9–11,17,24]. At their core, any multi-signature
scheme should protect each honest signer who participates against forgeries by
an adversary who controls all the other signers and interacts extensively with
our one honest signer. Yet in [11], Drijvers, et al. broke all previously known
Schnorr-based two-round multi-signature protocols [3,18,19,26], using the trau-
matic ROS [8] or k-SUM attack [27] that break blind Schnorr signatures [23,25].
In short, these attacks are executed by the adversary who engages in enough parallel signing sessions to reply with appropriate witnesses against honest witnesses

© International Association for Cryptologic Research 2021
T. Malkin and C. Peikert (Eds.): CRYPTO 2021, LNCS 12825, pp. 157–188, 2021.
https://doi.org/10.1007/978-3-030-84242-0_7

in the first round of each session. Then, the linear combination of signatures in each session constitutes a forgery.

In this paper, we propose a simple and lightweight two-round Schnorr-based multi-signature protocol that we call delinearized witness multi-signatures (DWMS) and prove its security. We call the linear combination of the witnesses with random oracle outputs delinearization. The reason of this naming is that the coefficients of the linear combinations are random and cannot be known by the adversary before the adversary selects its own witnesses. The security of DWMS is based on the hardness assumptions of entwined sum problem that we define and one more discrete logarithm (OMDL) problem [5,7]. In more detail, our contributions in this paper are as follows:

- We define a new computationally hard problem that we called m-entwined sum problem. We show that this problem is hard as long as $m > 1$ and the discrete logarithm is hard in the algebraic group model (AGM) [12] and the random oracle model (ROM). Thanks to this problem, we prove the security of our signature scheme without any complicated linear algebra analysis. Thus, we avoid possible mistakes in the proof. We believe that our new problem improves and simplifies the security proof of multi-signature [20] and threshold signature schemes [16] based delinearization of witnesses as ours. Beyond the simplified proof, we wonder if it is possible to improve Clause Schnorr-based blind signature [13] invoking the m-entwined sum problem instead of the modified-ROS problem [13] which does not have any extensive cryptanalysis yet.
- We construct our new protocol DWMS which consists of two-rounds: first, all signers generate two witnesses and propose two pre-commitment of them in the prime-order group, and second, after obtaining all pre-commitments, all signers compute the Schnorr commitment by delinearizing these pre-commitment with a random oracle and produce their signature share using their portion of the combined witnesses. As we mentioned above, most of the two-round Schnorr-based multi-signature schemes can be broken by solving the k-sum problem with respect to the session witnesses. Similarly, our new protocol DWMS can be broken by solving more complex k-sum problem that we call the m-entwined sum problem. Since we show that the m-entwined sum problem is hard when $m > 1$, DWMS is not vulnerable to this attack as long as the number of witnesses is at least two. After making sure that the 2-entwined sum problem is hard, we prove the security of DWMS in the plain public-key model [3], in the AGM and the ROM under the assumption that the OMDL problem and the 2-entwined sum problem is hard.

We note that DWMS is implemented in the cryptographic library 'schnor-rkel/sr25519' [1] and it is used by substrate based blockchains since January 2020 as an option for multi-signatures.

1.1 Related Work

Insecure Multi-signatures: Drijvers et al. [11] invalidated the security of some Schnorr-based two-round multi-signature schemes [3,18,19,26] by showing an attack based on the k-sum problem [27]. The key observation that Drijvers et al. [11] made was that a multi-signature participant choosing her signature randomness (nonce) after other participants could launch a parallel attack by initiating multiple concurrent signature sessions (say k of them) and let the honest participants commit to their randomness across all those sessions before choosing its own randomness for these sessions. It could then choose her randomness so that the hash on the sum of session randomness across the k sessions equals the sum of hashes on each individual session randomness, thereby helping it to derive a multi-signature session on a message of its own choice. They also noted a subtle flaw in the security proofs of these schemes, where the reduction to DL (or ODML depending on the scheme) on rewinding the multi-signature forger was inadvertently giving two signatures of the honest signer on the same randomness and two different challenges to the forger, thereby letting the latter potentially derive the honest signer's secret key. Note, all the earlier multi-signature schemes used different techniques: BCJ1, BCJ2 [2,3] used a multiplicatively homomorphic equivocal commitment scheme to prove security under the DL assumption, MWLD [18] used Okamoto signatures [22] and the double-hashing technique to prove security under the DL assumption and MuSig [19] used regular Schnorr signatures and proved security under the OMDL assumption, but all of them crucially relied on the rewinding of the multi-signature forger to derive its security. Thus, mBCJ [11] ruled out the possibility of the existence of secure two-round multi-signatures based on Schnorr signatures via an impossibility result that formalized the above inconsistency in the proof to construct a meta-reduction (which now simulated the multi-signature forger for the DL/OMDL reduction) to solve the OMDL problem itself.

A recent work of Bellare et al. [4] introduced a new problem called the Multi-Base Discrete Log (MBDL) problem that enables the security of several schemes including Schnorr signatures, Okamoto signatures, Bellare-Neven multi-signatures, and other Schnorr based ring and threshold signatures to be proved using a non-rewinding reduction.

Random Inhomogeneities in a Overdetermined Solvable System of Linear Equations (ROS): Earlier blind signatures constructed from Schnorr signatures [25] were shown to be insecure via a k-SUM attack [27]. The security of these blind signatures had been proven under the ROS assumption which was shown to be false as Wagner's (sub-exponential) algorithm on the k-SUM problem was used to break the ROS problem. Fuchsbauer et al. [14] was able to overcome this attack and constructed a two-round blind signature scheme that is proved secure under a (new) modified-ROS assumption that does not seem to fall prey to a k-SUM attack. Recently, Benhamouda et al. [8] find an algorithm that solves the ROS problem in polynomial time for large enough dimensions.

Table 1. Review of the efficiency and security of existing Schnorr-based multi-signature schemes with n-signers. Optim. is the optimized DWMS where signers are organised in a tree structure: i.e., each multi-signature round takes 2-sub-rounds: parent-children communication only [11]. $\mathbb{G}$ is the prime p order group that the schemes work. $k$exp shows k-exponentiation in $\mathbb{G}$. NIZK is non-interactive zero knowledge and NIZK proof and NIZK verify corresponds to the number of exp in order to execute the prove and verify algorithm. pk is the individual public key and PK is the aggregated public key.

Protocol	Sign		Verify	Domain			Security
				pk	signature	PK	
mBCJ [11]	5exp		6exp	$\mathbb{G} \times \mathbb{Z}_p^2$	$\mathbb{G}^2 \times \mathbb{Z}_p^3$	$\mathbb{G}$	DL, ROM
MuSig-DN [21]	NIZK proof + n NIZK verification		2exp	$\mathbb{G}$	$\mathbb{G} \times \mathbb{Z}_p$ or $\mathbb{Z}_p \times \mathbb{Z}_p$	$\mathbb{G}$	DL, DDH, ZK, PRF, ROM
Musig2 $v = 4$ [20]	7exp		2exp	$\mathbb{G}$	$\mathbb{G} \times \mathbb{Z}_p$ or $\mathbb{Z}_p \times \mathbb{Z}_p$	$\mathbb{G}$	$4q_s$-OMDL, ROM
Musig2 $v = 2$ [20]	3exp		2exp	$\mathbb{G}$	$\mathbb{G} \times \mathbb{Z}_p$ or $\mathbb{Z}_p \times \mathbb{Z}_p$	$\mathbb{G}$	$2q_s$-OMDL, AGM, ROM
Ours (DWMS $m = 2$)	(Worst Case)	$(2n + 2)$exp	2exp	$\mathbb{G}$	$\mathbb{G} \times \mathbb{Z}_p$ or $\mathbb{Z}_p \times \mathbb{Z}_p$	$\mathbb{G}$	q_s-OMDL, 2-entwined sum, AGM, ROM
	(Optim.)	$(2n+2)$exp by the root, 2exp by others					

Secure 2-Round Schnorr-Based Multi-signatures: We compare the existing 2-round Schnorr-based Multi-Signatures in Table 1. We note that we do not give the key aggregation operations in Table 1 to obtain the aggregated public key PK because this is necessary step for all multi-signature protocols. Some of them [11] first verifies the proof of knowledge of each public key with two-exponentiation and then obtains the aggregated public key and some of them [20, 21] including DWMS delinearize each public key by one exponentiation and then obtain the aggregated public key.

mBCJ [11] is one of the few existing two-round Schnorr-based signature schemes. mBCJ is more efficient in terms of signing operations than DWMS, but DWMS is more efficient in terms of verification operations and has also shorter signature size (See Table 1). mBCJ's first round messages can be spread by aggregating. Thus, the signers use the network bandwidth more efficiently. One advantage of mBCJ over DWMS is that it is secure in the random oracle model while DWMS is secure in AGM and the random oracle model.

Aside from mBCJ, MuSig-DN [21] is another Schnorr multi-signature protocol which provides deterministic witnesses, a nice property previously unavailable in a Schnorr multi-signature. It achieves determinism using several novel bulletproof optimizations which require a suitable group for an efficient instantiation. In MuSig-DN, the first round messages require only 1124 bytes per signer, but their participant-only benchmarks show 0.9 s proving times.

In DWMS, all signers incur a per signer cost of only 64 bytes and only two scalar multiplications in a prime order-elliptic curve group. Besides, DWMS asks no special features of the underlying group as MuSig-DN.

FROST [16] is a recent Schnorr-based threshold signature scheme that uses the delinearization of witnesses in the first round similar to DWMS. However, the security proof of FROST applies an ad-hoc heuristic that resembles a Fiat-Shamir transform which adds an additional round the FROST. Therefore, the proven FROST and the original FROST protocol are different. We hope that the hardness of our new problem 'the m-entwined sum problem' or its extensions improve the security proof of FROST.

There exists also simultaneous and independent protocol MuSig2 [20] which applies a similar idea as our DWMS protocol. DWMS's pre-commitments that signers send in the first round are delinearized first and then aggregated while Musig2's pre-commitments can be aggregated before delinearizing the pre-commitments. Therefore, the first round messages in Musig2 can be spread by aggregating. Thus, signers use the network bandwidth more efficiently. Besides, the signers in DWMS exponentiate each pre-commitment by a random oracle output for the delinearization while signers in Musig2 exponentiate only the summation of pre-commitments by a random oracle output. As a result of this, Musig2 is more efficient in terms of signing operations than DWMS (See Table 1). MuSig2 is secure in AGM with two pre-commitments as DWMS. They also show that its security with four pre-commitments without AGM. They deal with the case, where we need the hardness of the 2-entwined sum problem in our security proof in AGM, inside their signature proof with complex linear algebra analysis. It makes the proof much longer and hard to follow and verify. This also shows the ease that the m-entwined sum problem provides.

2   Preliminaries

2.1   Notations

We denote by $\mathbb{G}$ a prime p-order group. For the sake of representation, we consider *additive operation* in $\mathbb{G}$ in this paper. The notations with capital letters represent the elements of $\mathbb{G}$ and with small letters represent the elements in the scalar field $\mathbb{Z}_p$. The addition and multiplication operation between elements of $\mathbb{Z}_p$ is always in   mod p even though we do not specifically write it.

We use superscript (i) on any notation where $i \in \mathbb{N}$ to distinguish values generated in a session i e.g., $X^{(i)}$.

We use bold style for the vectors. If elements of the vector are from $\mathbb{G}$ then we represent the vector with the capital bold letter e.g. $\boldsymbol{V}$. If they are from $\mathbb{Z}_p$ then we represent the vector with the small bold letter e.g. $\boldsymbol{v}$.

2.2   Security Definitions

Multi-signature Schemes: We describe the multi-signature scheme and the security model that we consider for DWMS.

Definition 1 (Multi-Signature Scheme). *Multi-signature scheme with the security parameter λ consists of the following algorithms.*

- ParamGen$(\lambda) \rightarrow par$: *It generates the parameters of the signature scheme par with respect to the security parameter λ.*

- KeyGen(par) → (sk, pk): *It generates a secret/public key pair* (sk, pk) *with the input par.*
- Sign(par, sk, msg) → σ: *It is an interactive algorithm which is run between other signers to sign a message $msg \in \mathcal{M}$ where $\mathcal{M}$ is the message space.*
- KeyAg(par, $\{pk_i\}_{i=1}^n$) → PK: *It receives public key pk_i of each signer and generates the aggregated public key PK.*
- Verify(par, PK, σ, msg) → 1/0: *It verifies whether the signature σ is signed by the parties with public key pk_i for the message msg.*

We consider the plain public-key model [3] for the security of our multi-signature scheme as described below. In this model, KeyVerify(par, pk_i) outputs always 1.

Definition 2 (Multi-Signature Security in the Plain Public-key Model [3]). *The challenger generates the parameters par with ParamGen(λ) and generates a secret/public key pair* (sk, pk) *and gives par, pk to the adversary $\mathcal{A}$. $\mathcal{A}$ has access to the signing oracle Σ which returns Sign(par, sk, msg) given input msg by $\mathcal{A}$.*

In the end, $\mathcal{A}$ outputs a signature σ^*, message $msg^* \in \mathcal{M}$ and $PK = \{pk_1, pk_2, \ldots, pk_n\}$. $\mathcal{A}$ wins if

- *the public key given by the challenger is in PK i.e., $pk \in PK$,*
- *$\mathcal{A}$ never queries with the input msg^* to the signing oracle Σ before,*
- *the signature is valid i.e., Verify(par, PK, σ, msg) → 1 where KeyAg(par, PK) → PK.*

We say that a multi-signature scheme is secure in the plain public-key model if for all probabilistic polynomial time (PPT) adversary $\mathcal{A}$ with q_s-signing oracle queries, the probability of winning the above game is ϵ which is negligible in terms of λ.

There is also a weaker security definition called the knowledge of secret key (KOSK) model where the adversary outputs its secret keys in the end of the game.

Algebraic Group Model (AGM). The AGM is a model between the standard model and the generic group model, i.e., the security in the standard model implies security in the AGM and the security in the AGM implies the security in the GGM [12]. In short, the AGM is a computational model that considers only algebraic algorithms (corresponds to the adversaries in the security proofs) as described below. As in the standard model, it is possible to have security proofs with reductions [12].

Definition 3 (Algebraic Adversary). *Let $\mathbb{G}$ be a group with order p and P be the element of $\mathbb{G}$. Informally, we call an algorithm $\mathcal{A}$ is algebraic if it fulfills the following requirement: whenever $\mathcal{A}$ outputs $Z \in \mathbb{G}$, "representation" $\mathbf{z} = (z_1, \ldots, z_t) \in \mathbb{Z}_p^t$ such that $Z = \mathbf{z} \cdot \mathbf{L} = \sum_{i=1}^t z_i L_i$ where $\mathbf{L} = (L_1, \ldots, L_t)$ is the vector in $\mathbb{G}^t$ and each element of $\mathbf{L}$ is a group element that $\mathcal{A}$ has seen during its execution so far.*

Now, we give the OMDL problem [5,7] since DWMS's security relies on the hardness of the OMDL problem.

Definition 4 (n-OMDL Problem [5,7]). *Given a prime p-order group $\mathbb{G}$ generated by P, and random $Y_1, Y_2, \ldots, Y_{n+1} \in \mathbb{G}$ and a discrete logarithm oracle* DLOracle *which returns discrete logarithm of any given input in $\mathbb{G}$, if a PPT adversary $\mathcal{A}$ outputs the discrete logarithms of $Y_1, Y_2, \ldots, Y_{n+1}$ with the access of at most n-times to the* DLOracle, *then $\mathcal{A}$ solves the n-OMDL problem. We say that n-OMDL problem is hard in $\mathbb{G}$, if for all PPT adversaries, the probability of solving the n-OMDL problem is ϵ_{omdl} which is negligible in terms of the security parameter.*

2.3 Multi-signature Schemes vs. the k-Sum Problem

In this section, we show an example attack to one of the broken schemes in [11] to explain why a solution of the k-sum problem helps an adversary to break some multi-signature schemes. This section will make more clear the necessity of defining a new k-sum-like problem for our new scheme DWMS and proving its hardness.

Definition 5 (k-sum Problem). *Given k-lists $\mathsf{L}_1, \mathsf{L}_2, \ldots, \mathsf{L}_k$ of size s_L where each elements of L_i is from $\mathbb{Z}_p$, the problem requires to find $x_1, x_2, \ldots, x_k$ where $x_i \in \mathsf{L}_i$ such that $x_1 + x_2 + \ldots + x_k \equiv 0 \mod p$.*

Wagner [27] described an algorithm which solves the k-sum problem within $O(k2^{n/(1+\log n)})$ when $s_L = 2^{n/(1+\log n)}$ where n is the bit length of the elements in lists. Benhamouda et al. [8] recently showed that with the list of dimensions $s_L = k > \log p$, the ROS-problem can be solved in polynomial time. Recall that the ROS problem is a generalization of the k-sum problem. Solving the ROS problem is sufficient to break security of the schemes [3,18,19,26].

Drijvers et al. [11] showed an attack on many two-round Schnorr-based multi-signatures [3,18,19,26] based on a solution of the k-sum problem. We next show the attack on CoSi [26] described in [11] to illustrate the relation between the k-sum problem and multi-signature schemes. The other attacks on other schemes [3,18,19] can be found in [11].

CoSi Protocol [26]: CoSi works in a prime p-order group $\mathbb{G}$ with the hash function $H : \{0,1\}^* \to \mathbb{Z}_p$. Public parameters are the group structure $(\mathbb{G}, P, p)$ where P is a generator of $\mathbb{G}$. Normally, each public key of the signers are associated with the proof-of-knowledge of the secret key to prevent the rogue key attacks. We omit this part in the description of the protocol because the attack is still applicable even if the public keys are generated as described in the protocol.

Key Generation: Each signer generates a random private key x and computes the public key $X = xP$.

Signing: Each signer i does the following to sign a message msg with public keys $\mathcal{PK} = \{X_1, X_2, \ldots, X_n\}$:

- **[Round 1:]** Each signer i picks $r_i \in \mathbb{Z}_p$ and computes $T_i = r_i P$. Then, each publishes the witness T_i.
- **[Round 2:]** After receiving all witnesses, each signer i aggregates all witnesses and obtains $T = \sum_{j=1}^{n} T_j$ and computes the partial signature $s_i = r_i + cx_i$ where $c = H(T, msg)$. In the end, each publishes s_i.

The signature of the message msg is $\sigma = (c, s)$ where $s = \sum_{j=1}^{n} s_j$.

Key Aggregation: Given list of public keys $\mathcal{PK} = \{X_1, X_2, \ldots, X_n\}$, the aggregated public key is $X = \sum_{j=1}^{n} X_j$.

Verification: The verification algorithm outputs 1 if $c = H(sP - cX, msg)$. Otherwise, it outputs 0.

Now, we explain the k-sum attack on the CoSi protocol described in [11].

The k-sum Attack on CoSi [11]: For simplicity, we describe the attack with one honest party having the public key X_1 and one adversary having the public key X_2 and we let $\mathcal{PK} = \{X_1, X_2\}$. In a nutshell, the adversary aims in this attack to find an appropriate adversarial witnesses for each parallel session that is started with an honest party such that the linear combination of the honest partial signatures lets the adversary obtain a forgery. It consists of the following steps:

1. The adversary starts q_s concurrent session for an arbitrary message(s) $msg^{(i)}$ with an honest signer and obtains q_s-witnesses $T_1^{(1)}, T_1^{(2)}, \ldots, T_1^{(q_s)}$ of the honest signer for each session $i \in [1, q_s]$. Now, the adversary needs to select corresponding witnesses for each session. For this selection, it continues with the next step.
2. The adversary creates $q_s + 1$ lists of size s_L. It creates the first q_s list L_i as follows: picks a random element $r_2^{(i)} \in \mathbb{Z}_p$ and lets $T_2^{(i)} = r_2^{(i)} P$ as a possible adversarial witness against the honest witness $T_1^{(i)}$, computes $c^{(i)} = H(\sum T_1^{(i)} + T_2^{(i)}, msg^{(i)})$ and adds $c^{(i)}$ to the list L_i. The adversary repeats this process s_L times until the size of L_i is s_L. It creates the last list L_{q_s+1} differently. For each element of L_{q_s+1}, it picks a message msg^* and adds $-H(\sum_i^{q_s} T_1^{(i)}, msg^*)$ to L_{q_s+1}. The adversary repeats this process s_L times until the size of L_{q_s+1} is s_L.
3. Adversary finds elements $c^{(i)}$ in each list L_i such that $c^{(1)} + c^{(2)} + \ldots c^{(q_s)} + c^{(q_s+1)} = 0$ as in the k-sum problem (Definition 5) i.e.,

$$c^{(1)} + c^{(2)} + \ldots + c^{(q_s)} = H(\sum_{i=1}^{q_s} T_1^{(i)}, msg^*) \tag{1}$$

Then the adversary gets the corresponding adversarial witness $T_2^{(i)}$ that was selected in step 2 for each found element $c^{(i)}$ for $i \in [1, q_s]$. In the end, it responds with $T_2^{(1)}, T_2^{(2)}, \ldots, T_2^{(q_s)}$ respectively to each q_s session that was initiated in the beginning and receives partial signatures for all sessions $s_1^{(1)}, \ldots, s_{q_s}^{(q_s)}$ where $s_1^{(i)} = r_1^{(i)} + x_1 c^{(i)}$ and $c^{(i)} = H(T_1^{(i)} + T_2^{(i)}, msg^{(i)})$. Thus, all sessions end.

This step of the attack is equivalent to solving the k-sum problem [27] with the lists $\mathsf{L}_1, \mathsf{L}_2, \ldots, \mathsf{L}_{q_s+1}$ where $k = q_s + 1$.

4. Now, the adversary outputs (c^*, s^*), as a forgery of the message msg^* signed by $\mathcal{PK}$ where

$$s^* = \sum_{i=1}^{q_s} s_1^{(i)} + x_2 c^*$$

and $c^* = H(\sum_{i=1}^{q_s} T_1^{(i)}, msg^*)$. This is a valid forgery because

$$s^* P - c^* X = (\sum_{i=1}^{q_s} s_1^{(i)})P + c^* x_2 P - c^*(X_1 + X_2)$$

$$= (\sum_{i=1}^{q_s} T_1^{(i)} + c^{(i)} X_1) - c^* X_1 \tag{2}$$

$$= \sum_{i=1}^{q_s} T_1^{(i)} \tag{3}$$

We obtain Eq. (3) by using Eq. (1) that the adversary obtained in the third step.

The main reason for the above attack comes from the fact that the adversary selects its witnesses after seeing the honest witnesses. Therefore, three-round Schnorr-based multi-signatures are not vulnerable to this type of attack because the adversary has to commit its witness in the first round before seeing the honest witness. Existing two-round multi-signature protocols overcome this issue in different ways. Witnesses in mBCJ [11] are generated with different group elements for each message. This makes the adversary's job hard to generate compatible list L_{q_s+1}. In Musig-DN [21], the witnesses are generated deterministically so that the adversary cannot choose an appropriate witness as in the above attack. We consider a different solution. We observe that the independence of the last list L_{q_s+1} from the selection of the adversarial witnesses is causing to apply this attack. Therefore, we decide to solve the issue by preventing this independence in our scheme. Accordingly, we solve this problem in our scheme by delinearizing each witness by a corresponding random value generated with the adversarial and honest witnesses. We will explain this in the next sections in more detail.

3   Delinearized Witness Multi-signature (DWMS)

We give our two-round delinearized witness multi-signature (DWMS) protocol that replaces the witness sharing and combination steps in multi-signer Schnorr protocol with a delinearization phase inspired by the delinearization defense [6] against rogue key attacks. The DWMS protocol works in prime p-order group $\mathbb{G}$ with the functions $H : \{0,1\}^* \times \mathbb{G} \times \mathbb{G} \to \mathbb{Z}_p$, $H_1 : \{0,1\}^* \times \mathbb{G}^{mn} \times \mathbb{N} \times \mathbb{N} \to \mathbb{Z}_p$ and $H_2 : \mathbb{G}^n \times \mathbb{G} \to \mathbb{Z}_p$ where $n \geq 1$ is the number of signers and m is a parameter.

Public Parameter Generation (ParamGen(λ)). Given λ, ParamGen generates a prime p order group $\mathbb{G}$ and a generator $P \in \mathbb{G}$. In the end, it outputs $par = (\mathbb{G}, P, p)$.

Key Generation (KeyGen(par) $\to$ (sk, pk)). Each signer generates a random private key $x \in \mathbb{Z}_q$ and computes the public key $X = xP$.

Signing (Sign(par, x_i, msg) $\to \sigma$). It consists of two rounds where in the first round signers exchange their pre-commitments and in the second round signers generate their signature by delinearizing their pre-commitments.

- **[Round 1]:** Each signer i with the secret key $x_i \in \{x_1, x_2, \ldots, x_n\}$ generates random witnesses $r_{i1}, r_{i2}, \ldots, r_{im} \in \mathbb{Z}_p$ and computes the pre-commitments $T_{i1} = r_{i1}P, T_{i2} = r_{i2}P, \ldots, T_{im} = r_{im}P$ and broadcasts $(T_{i1}, T_{i2}, \ldots, T_{im})$ together with their public key $X_i{}^1$. This round ends when each signer i receives all pre-commitments. Let $\mathcal{PK} = \{X_1, \ldots, X_n\}$ be the multi-set of all public keys involved in the session.
- **[Round 2]:** On receiving $(T_{j1}, T_{j2}, \ldots, T_{jm})$ from the co-signers, each signer i sets the list of public keys $\mathcal{PK} = \{X_1, X_2, \ldots, X_n\}$, it computes the delinearization parameter of each key $X_j \in \mathcal{PK}$: $a_j = H_2(\mathcal{PK}, X_j)$ and finds the aggregated public key $X = \sum_{j=1}^{n} a_j X_j$. This step is necessary to prevent rogue-key attacks. It lets the session identifier be

$$\mathsf{SID} = (\mathcal{PK}, msg, \{T_{1j}\}_{j=1}^m, \ldots, \{T_{nj}\}_{j=1}^m).$$

Then, it computes delinearization scalars for each pre-commitments T_{uj} where $u \in \{1, 2, \ldots, n\}$ and $j \in \{1, 2, \ldots, m\}$ which are

$$\alpha_{ij} = H_1(\mathsf{SID}, i, j)$$

and computes the individual delinearized commitment of each signer u:

$$T_u = \sum_{j=1}^{m} \alpha_{uj} T_{uj}, \text{for } u \in [1, n]$$

---

[1] There can be a specified structure (e.g., tree structure [11]) between parties for more efficient communication.

Signer i further computes $T = \sum_{u=1}^{n} T_u$ and $c = H(msg, X, T)$ and the signature

$$s_i = (\sum_{j=1}^{m} \alpha_{ij} r_{ij}) + c a_i x_i$$

and broadcasts s_i as its signature.

On receiving other signatures s_j's from the co-signers, signer can compute $s = \sum_{j=1}^{n} s_i$. The multi-signature on message msg under the aggregated public key X is $\sigma = (c, s)$. We remark that the signature is the same as the Schnorr signature.

Key Aggregation ($\mathsf{KeyAg}(par, \mathcal{PK})$). It outputs the aggregated public key $X = \sum_{i=1}^{n} a_i X_i$ where $a_i = H_2(\mathcal{PK}, X_i)$

Verification ($\mathsf{Verify}(par, X, \sigma, msg)$). It accepts the signature if c equals to $H(msg, X, sP - cX)$ as in the standard Schnorr signature scheme.

Network and Computation Optimization: In the worst case, each signer sends the first round messages (m-exponentiations) to all other signers, each signer computes T (mn-exponentiation) and sends the partial signature to all other signers. So, the communication complexity is $O(n^2)$ and computation complexity is $O(n)$ i.e., the number of exponentiations made by each signer is $mn + m$. We can optimize this with the tree based network topology suggested in [11]. The leaf nodes start the protocol by sending their pre-commitments to their parents. When a party P_i receives pre-commitments from its children, it relays them and its own pre-commitments $T_{i1}, \ldots, T_{im}$ to its parent. In the end, the root node receives all of them. Then, the root node computes $T = \sum_{u=1}^{n} T_u$ and sends T to its children so that the leaf nodes receives them. Finally, each leaf node gives its partial signature to its parent to be added parent's partial signature and the root node obtains the multi-signature. The communication complexity is $O(n)$ and the computation complexity is $O(n)$ ($mn + m$-exponentiations) for the root node and $O(1)$ (m-exponentiations) for the other parties. The computation can be distributed among other nodes where each node computes m-exponentiation by additional 2-sub-rounds. In this case, the root node should send the pre-commitments to the children so that the computation of T can be done from leaves to root by aggregation.

We prove in Sect. 5 the security of DWMS when $m = 2$. However, we show below that it is not secure when $m = 1$ by solving a k-sum problem. Then, we discuss whether such an attack is possible when $m > 1$ to illustrate a relation between our new problem 'the m-entwined sum problem' and these attacks in DWMS.

Forgery Attack When $m = 1$: For simplicity, we describe the attack with one honest party with the public key X_1 and one adversary with the public key X_2 and we let $\mathcal{PK} = \{X_1, X_2\}$, $a_1 = H_2(\mathcal{PK}, X_1)$ and $a_2 = H_2(\mathcal{PK}, X_2)$, the aggregated key $X = a_1 X_1 + a_2 X_2$. As in the CoSi attack in Sect. 2.3, the adversary wants to find adversarial witnesses for each parallel session to obtain a forgery with the linear combinations of honest partial signatures. It consists of the following steps:

1. The adversary starts q_s-concurrent session for an arbitrary message(s) $msg^{(i)}$ with an honest signer and obtain q_s-pre-commitments $T_{11}^{(1)}, T_{11}^{(2)}, \ldots, T_{11}^{(q_s)}$ of the honest signer for each session $i \in [1, q_s]$. Now, the adversary needs to select the corresponding witnesses for each session. For this selection, it continues with the next step.

2. The adversary creates $q_s + 1$ lists of size s_L. It creates the first q_s list L_i as follows: picks a random element $r_{21}^{(i)} \in \mathbb{Z}_p$ and lets $T_{21}^{(i)} = r_{21}^{(i)} P$ as a possible adversarial pre-commitments against the honest pre-commitment $T_{11}^{(i)}$, computes the corresponding $\alpha_{21}^{(i)}$ and $c^{(i)}$ as in the second round of DWMS and adds $\frac{c^{(i)}}{\alpha_{11}^{(i)}}$ to the list L_i. The adversary repeats this process s_L times until the size of L_i is s_L. It creates the last list L_{q_s+1} differently. For each element of L_{q_s+1}, it picks randomly an element $\beta' \in \mathbb{Z}_p$ and a forgery message msg^* and adds $-\frac{H(msg^*, X, \beta' \sum_{i=1}^{q_s} T_{11}^{(i)})}{\beta'}$ to L_{q_s+1}. We note that selecting β' is necessary to populate L_{q_s+1} with random elements if the forgery msg^* is fixed. The adversary repeats this process s_L times until the size of L_{q_s+1} is s_L.

3. The adversary finds elements $v^{(i)}$ in each list L_i such that $v^{(1)} + v^{(2)} + \ldots v^{(q_s)} + v^{(q_s+1)} = 0$ i.e.,

$$\frac{c^{(1)}}{\alpha_{11}^{(1)}} + \frac{c^{(2)}}{\alpha_{11}^{(2)}} + \ldots + \frac{c^{(q_s)}}{\alpha_{11}^{(q_s)}} = \frac{H(msg^*, X, \beta' \sum_{i=1}^{q_s} T_{11}^{(i)})}{\beta'} \tag{4}$$

Then the adversary gets the corresponding adversarial pre-commitment $T_{21}^{(i)}$ that was selected in step 2 for each found element $v^{(i)}$ for $i \in [1, q_s]$. In the end, it responds with $T_{21}^{(1)}, T_{21}^{(2)}, \ldots, T_{21}^{(q_s)}$ respectively to each q_s session that is initiated in the beginning and receives partial signatures $s_1^{(1)}, \ldots, s_1^{(q_s)}$ where $s_1^{(i)} = \alpha_{11}^{(i)} r_{11}^{(i)} + x_1 a_1 c^{(i)}$ and $c^{(i)} = H(msg^{(i)}, X, \alpha_{11}^{(i)} T_{11}^{(i)} + \alpha_{21}^{(i)} T_{21}^{(i)})$. Thus, all sessions end.

This step of the attack is equivalent to solving the k-sum problem [27] with the lists $\mathsf{L}_1, \mathsf{L}_2, \ldots, \mathsf{L}_{q_s+1}$ where $k = q_s + 1$.

4. Now, the adversary outputs (c^*, s^*), as a forgery of the message msg^* signed by $\mathcal{PK}$ where

$$s^* = \beta'(\frac{s_1^{(1)}}{\alpha_{11}^{(1)}} + \frac{s_1^{(2)}}{\alpha_{11}^{(2)}} + \ldots + \frac{s_1^{(q_s)}}{\alpha_{11}^{(q_s)}}) + c^* a_2 x_2$$

and $c^* = H(msg^*, X, T^*)$ where $T^* = \beta' \sum_{i=1}^{q_s} T_{11}^{(i)}$.. This is a valid forgery because $c^* = H(msg^*, X, T^*)$ and

$$s^*P - c^*X = (\beta'(\frac{s_1^{(1)}}{\alpha_{11}^{(1)}} + \frac{s_1^{(2)}}{\alpha_{11}^{(2)}} + \ldots + \frac{s_1^{(q_s)}}{\alpha_{11}^{(q_s)}}) + c^*a_2x_2)P - (c^*a_1X_1 - c^*a_2X_2)$$

$$= \beta'(T_{11}^{(1)} + T_{11}^{(2)} + \ldots + T_{11}^{(q_s)}) + (\beta' \sum_{i=1}^{q_s} \frac{x_1a_1c^{(i)}}{\alpha_{11}^{(i)}})P - c^*a_1X_1 \tag{5}$$

$$= T^* \tag{6}$$

We obtain Eq. (6) from Eq. (5) by using Eq. (4) that the adversary obtained in the third step.

The adversary's attack described above is equivalent to finding a message msg^*, a vector $\boldsymbol{\beta} = (\beta^{(1)}, \ldots, \beta^{(q_s)})$ and $T_{21}^{(1)}, T_{21}^{(2)}, \ldots, T_{21}^{(q_s)}$ such that $c^* = \sum \beta^{(i)}c^{(i)} = H(msg^*, X, \sum_{i=1}^{q_s} \beta^{(i)}\alpha_{11}^{(i)}T_{11}^{(i)})$. In this case, the forgery $\sigma^* = (c^*, s^*)$ of msg^* is a valid signature signed by X_1 and X_2 where $s^* = \sum_{i=1}^{q_s} \beta^{(i)}s_1^{(i)} + c^*a_2x_2$. So, in the attack that we describe, $\boldsymbol{\beta} = (\frac{\beta'}{\alpha_{11}^{(1)}}, \frac{\beta'}{\alpha_{11}^{(2)}}, \ldots, \frac{\beta'}{\alpha_{11}^{(q_s)}})$.

Is a Similar Attack Possible When $m > 1$?: Now, we informally discuss whether an adversary can do the similar attack when $m > 1$. We believe that these discussions give a motivation for our new problem 'the m-entwined sum problem' which we introduce in the next section.

The question we should examine is after initiating q_s parallel sessions with an honest signer and receiving honest pre-commitments $\boldsymbol{T_h^{(i)}} = (T_{11}^{(i)}, T_{12}^{(i)}, \ldots, T_{1m}^{(i)})$ for each session $i \in [1, q_s]$ whether the adversary can find a message msg^*, a vector $\boldsymbol{\beta} = (\beta^{(1)}, \ldots, \beta^{(q_s)})$ and $(T_{21}^{(1)}, \ldots, T_{2m}^{(1)}), \ldots, (T_{21}^{(q_s)}, \ldots, T_{2m}^{(q_s)})$ such that

$$c^* = \sum \beta^{(i)}c^{(i)} = H(msg^*, X, \sum_{i=1}^{q_s} \beta^{(i)}(\sum_{j=1}^{m} \alpha_{1j}^{(i)}T_{1j}^{(i)})). \tag{7}$$

In this case, the forgery $\sigma^* = (c^*, s^*)$ of msg^* is a valid signature signed by X_1 and X_2 where $s^* = \sum_{i=1}^{q_s} \beta^{(i)}s_1^{(i)} + c^*a_2x_2$ and $s_1^{(i)} = (\sum_{i=1}^{m} \alpha_{1j}^{(i)}r_{1j}^{(i)}) + c^{(i)}a_1x_1$.

In Definition 8, we formalize this attack as a new problem and prove its hardness when $m > 1$ in the AGM. We show that an algebraic adversary (Definition 3) cannot find $\boldsymbol{\beta} \in \mathbb{Z}_p^{q_s+1}$ and $\boldsymbol{T_{\mathcal{A}}^{(i)}}$ for $i \in [1, q_s]$ satisfying Eq. (7) except with the negligible probability as long as the discrete logarithm problem is hard and $m > 1$.

In the next section, we have a break on DWMS and introduce the simple m-entwined sum and the m-entwined sum problem and show their hardness. We later prove the security of DWMS when $m > 1$ under the assumption that the q_s-OMDL and the m-entwined sum problems are hard.

4   Entwined Sum Problem

In this section, we introduce our new k-sum [27] like problem 'the entwined sum problem' and show its hardness in AGM. Before giving the problem, we introduce a version of the discrete logarithm problem (the DLR problem) that we use in the hardness proof of our entwined sum problem. DLR is equivalent to the discrete logarithm problem. We employ DLR because it is a more flexible variant of the discrete logarithm problem in which an adversary finding any new relationship among group elements interests us.

Definition 6 (Discrete Logarithm Relation (DLR) problem). *Given prime p-order group* $\mathbb{G}$ *generated by* P *and random* $X_i \in \mathbb{G}$ *for* $i \in \{1, 2, \ldots, k\}$ *with* $k \geq 1$ *then find* $y_0, y_1, \ldots, y_k \in \mathbb{Z}_p$ *such that* $y_0 P + \sum_{i=1}^{k} y_i X_i = 0$ *where not all* y_i *'s are 0.*

Proposition 1. *The discrete logarithm (DLOG) problem in the group structure* $(\mathbb{G}, P, p)$ *is equivalent to the DLR problem in the same group structure.*

Proof. It is clear that if DLOG problem is easy then DLR is easy. Now, we show that if DLR is easy then DLOG is easy. Let X denote our DLOG challenge over prime p order group $\mathbb{G}$ generated by P. We compute the Pedersen commitment $X_i = a_i X + b_i P$ for random $a_i, b_i \in \mathbb{Z}_p$ for $i \in \{1, 2, \ldots, k\}$ and give $X_1, X_2, \ldots, X_k, (\mathbb{G}, P, p)$ to the DLR solver. In the end, the DLR solver outputs a DLR solution $y_0, y_1, y_2, \ldots, y_k \in \mathbb{Z}_p$ such that $y_0 P + \sum_{i=1}^{k} y_i X_i = y_0 P + \sum_{i=1}^{k} y_i (a_i X + b_i P) = 0$. It follows that $X = \frac{-(y_0 + \sum_i y_i b_i)}{\sum_i y_i a_i} P$, as desired. We remark that $\sum_i y_i a_i \neq 0$ except with probability $\frac{1}{p}$ because these Pedersen commitments X_i's are perfectly hiding.

We first introduce a simple version of our problem that we call 'the simple m-entwined sum problem'. Then, we extend the simple version and give the m-entwined sum problem. The simple m-entwined sum problem has fewer variables. When we introduce the m-entwined sum problem, we show its hardness based on the results in the proof of the simple m-entwined sum problem so that we avoid dealing with more variables that may complicate the proof.

The classical k-sum problem [27] works in the field $\mathbb{Z}_p$ (See Definition 5). Differently, an attacker in our problem works not only in the field $\mathbb{Z}_p$ but also in its associated group $\mathbb{G}$. This difference makes our problem hard as long as the DLR problem is hard in the AGM.

Definition 7 (Simple m-entwined sum Problem). *The challenger generates a prime p order group* $\mathbb{G}$ *with the security parameter* λ *and selects a generator* $P \in \mathbb{G}$. *As an input, the challenger supplies the group description* $(p, \mathbb{G}, P)$ *and vectors* $\boldsymbol{T_h^{(1)}}, \boldsymbol{T_h^{(2)}}, \ldots, \boldsymbol{T_h^{(q_s)}} \in \mathbb{G}^m$ *to the the adversary* $\mathcal{A}$ *where* $\boldsymbol{T_h^{(i)}} = (T_{11}^{(i)}, T_{12}^{(i)}, \ldots, T_{1m}^{(i)})$. $\mathcal{A}$ *has access to the random oracles* $H, H' : \Omega \times \mathbb{G} \to \mathbb{Z}_p$ *and* $H_1 : \Omega \times \mathbb{G}^m \times \mathbb{N} \to \mathbb{Z}_p$ *where* Ω *is an arbitrary set.*

In the end, the adversary outputs the following vectors $\boldsymbol{\beta} = (\beta^{(0)},$ $\beta^{(1)}, \ldots, \beta^{(q_s)}) \in \mathbb{Z}_p^{q_s+1}$, $\mathcal{T}_{\text{out}} = (\mu^{(1)}, \mu^{(2)}, \ldots, \mu^{(q_s)}) \in \Omega^{q_s}$ *and* $\omega^* \in \Omega$. *If the following holds, then the adversary wins the simple entwined sum game:*

$$\sum_{u=1}^{q_s} \beta^{(u)} H'(\mu^{(u)}, T_h^{(u)}) = H(\omega^*, \beta^{(0)} P + \sum_{u=1}^{q_s} \beta^{(u)} T_h^{(u)}) \tag{8}$$

where

$$T_h^{(u)} = \sum_{j=1}^{m} \alpha_{1j}^{(u)} T_{1j}^{(u)} \text{ and } \alpha_{1j}^{(u)} = H_1(\mu^{(u)}, \boldsymbol{T_h^{(u)}}, j) \tag{9}$$

We call that the simple m-entwined sum problem is hard in $\mathbb{G}$, *if for all PPT adversaries who access the random oracles* H, H' *and* H_1 *at most* $q_h, q_{h'}, q_{h_1}$- *times respectively, the probability of solving the above problem is* ϵ_{eSum} *which is negligible in terms of* λ.

We named our problem *entwined* because the adversary should satisfy the same linear relationship in $\mathbb{Z}_p$ (see the left hand side of Eq. 8) and in $\mathbb{G}$ (see the right hand side of Eq. 8). Both linear relationships in $\mathbb{Z}_p$ and in $\mathbb{G}$ are constructed with respect to the challenges and adversarial outputs. We note that if the simple m-entwined sum was not a hard problem then an adversary could obtain adversarial witnesses that satisfy the Eq. 7 and construct a forgery in DWMS.

We prove that the simple m-entwined sum problem when $m > 1$ is hard under the assumption that DLR problem is hard. Our hardness proof is based on the lemma (Lemma 1) that for any choice of $W \in \mathbb{G}$ as an input to the right hand side random oracle input of Eq. 8, the adversary can obtain only one possible solution $(\boldsymbol{\beta}, \mathcal{T}_{\text{out}})$ and vice versa. This fact makes the adversary's job hard to solve the problem.

Theorem 1. *Assume that there exits a PPT,* **algebraic** *adversary* $\mathcal{A}$ *that solves the simple m-entwined sum problem for* $m > 1$ *with probability* ϵ_{eSum} *in the group structure* $(\mathbb{G}, P, p)$ *with* $q_h \geq q_{h'}$ *and* q_{h_1} *random oracle queries. Then, there exists a PPT adversary* $\mathcal{B}$ *that solves the DLR problem in the group structure* $(\mathbb{G}, P, p)$ *with probability* $\epsilon_{dlr} \geq \epsilon_{eSum} - \frac{q_h}{p} - \frac{q_{h_1}}{\sqrt{p}p^{m-2}}$.

Proof. We construct an adversary $\mathcal{B}$ which simulates the simple m-entwined sum problem against an *algebraic* adversary $\mathcal{A}$. We denote by $\Pr[eSum \rightarrow 1] = \epsilon_{eSum}$ the probability that $\mathcal{A}$ solves the simple m-entwined sum problem. The DLR challenger gives the group $(\mathbb{G}, P, p)$, the challenges $T_{11}^{(1)}, \ldots, T_{1m}^{(1)}, T_{11}^{(2)}, \ldots, T_{1m}^{(2)}, \ldots, T_{11}^{(q_s)}, \ldots, T_{1m}^{(q_s)} \in \mathbb{G}$ to $\mathcal{B}$. $\mathcal{B}$ forwards them to $\mathcal{A}$ as m-entwined sum challenges. $\mathcal{B}$ simulates the random oracles H, H' and H_1 against $\mathcal{A}$ as a usual random oracle. We let

$$\boldsymbol{T_{\text{inp}}} = (P, T_{11}^{(1)}, \ldots, T_{1m}^{(1)}, \ldots, T_{11}^{(q_s)}, \ldots, T_{1m}^{(q_s)})$$

which is the vector including the group elements given to $\mathcal{A}$ during the simulation and we also let $\boldsymbol{T_h^{(i)}} = (T_{11}^{(i)}, T_{12}^{(i)}, \ldots, T_{1m}^{(i)})$.

Whenever $\mathcal{A}$ queries the oracle H, H' or H_1 with an input including a group element $Y \in \mathbb{G}$, it gives the representation of it $\boldsymbol{z} = (z_0, z_{11}^{(1)}, z_{12}^{(1)}, \ldots, z_{1m}^{(1)}, \ldots, z_{11}^{(q_s)}, z_{12}^{(q_s)}, \ldots, z_{1m}^{(q_s)}) \in \mathbb{Z}_p^{mq_s+1}$ such that $\boldsymbol{z} \cdot \boldsymbol{T}_{\mathsf{inp}} = Y$ because $\mathcal{A}$ is algebraic (Definition 3) and $\boldsymbol{T}_{\mathsf{inp}}$ are the group elements that $\mathcal{A}$ has seen. If $\mathcal{A}$ gives two different representation of an element $Y \in \mathbb{G}$ which are $\boldsymbol{z} \in \mathbb{Z}_p^{mq_s+1}$ and $\hat{\boldsymbol{z}} \in \mathbb{Z}_p^{mq_s+1}$ such that $\boldsymbol{z} \neq \hat{\boldsymbol{z}}$, $\mathcal{B}$ gives the vector $\boldsymbol{v} = \boldsymbol{z} - \hat{\boldsymbol{z}}$ to the DLR challenger as a solution and ends the simulation against $\mathcal{A}$. We remark that $\boldsymbol{v} \cdot \boldsymbol{T}_{\mathsf{inp}} = 0$ so it is a valid solution to the DLR problem. Otherwise, in the end, $\mathcal{A}$ outputs $\boldsymbol{\beta} = (\beta^{(0)}, \beta^{(1)}, \beta^{(2)}, \ldots, \beta^{(q_s)})$, ω^* and $\mathcal{T}_{\mathsf{out}} = (\mu^{(1)}, \mu^{(2)}, \ldots, \mu^{(q_s)})$ as a solution of the simple entwined sum problem which satisfies the below equation and the simulation against $\mathcal{A}$ ends.

$$\sum_{u=1}^{q_s} \beta^{(u)} H'(\mu^{(u)}, T_h^{(u)}) = H(\omega^*, \beta^{(0)} P + \sum_{u=1}^{(q_s)} \beta^{(u)} T_h^{(u)}) \tag{10}$$

Then, $\mathcal{B}$ computes $W = \beta^{(0)} P + \sum_{u=1}^{(q_s)} \beta^{(u)} T_h^{(u)}$. By using the fact that $T_h^{(u)} = \sum_{j=1}^m \alpha_{1j}^{(u)} T_{1j}^{(u)}$ (See Eq. 9), $\mathcal{B}$ reorganizes W and obtains $W = \beta^{(0)} P + \sum_{u=1}^{q_s} \sum_{j=1}^m \beta^{(u)} \alpha_{1j}^{(u)} T_{1j}^{(u)}$. Thus, $\mathcal{B}$ obtains a representation $\boldsymbol{b} = (\beta^{(0)}, b_{11}^{(1)}, \ldots, b_{1m}^{(1)}, \ldots, b_{11}^{(q_s)}, \ldots, b_{1m}^{(q_s)})$ of W in terms of $\boldsymbol{T}_{\mathsf{inp}}$ where $b_{1j}^{(u)} = \beta^{(u)} \alpha_{1j}^{(u)}$ i.e. $W = \boldsymbol{b} \cdot \boldsymbol{T}_{\mathsf{inp}}$. Then, $\mathcal{B}$ checks the oracle queries of H with $(., W)$. We remark that there should be such query, otherwise $\mathcal{A}$ cannot check the correctness of its solution. When $\mathcal{A}$ queries $(., W)$ to H, it gives a representation $\boldsymbol{a} = (a, a_{11}^{(1)}, \ldots, a_{1m}^{(1)}, \ldots, a_{11}^{(q_s)}, \ldots, a_{1m}^{(q_s)})$ of W such that $W = \boldsymbol{a} \cdot \boldsymbol{T}_{\mathsf{inp}}$. If $\boldsymbol{b} \neq \boldsymbol{a}$, then $\mathcal{B}$ finds a solution of the DLR problem which is $\boldsymbol{b} - \boldsymbol{a}$ and wins. Otherwise, $\mathcal{B}$ aborts.

So, the success probability of $\mathcal{B}$ is

$$\epsilon_{dlr} = \Pr[\mathcal{A} \text{ wins}] - \Pr[\mathcal{A} \text{ wins} | \boldsymbol{a} = \boldsymbol{b}]$$

Next, we find $\Pr[\mathcal{A} \text{ wins} | \boldsymbol{a} = \boldsymbol{b}]$. We distinguish the session indexes i where $\beta^{(i)} \neq 0$. For this, we define an index set $\mathcal{I} = \{i : \beta^{(i)} \neq 0, i \in [1, q_s]\}$ which includes the session indexes of non-zero elements of the vector $\boldsymbol{\beta}$. We note that $\mu^{(j)} \in \mathcal{T}_{\mathsf{out}}$ where $j \notin \mathcal{I}$ does not play any role in the correctness of the m-entwined sum solution because $\beta^{(j)} = 0$. Therefore, we consider $\mathcal{T}_{\mathsf{out}} = \{\mu^{(j)}\}_{i \in \mathcal{I}}$ in the rest of the proof.

We call that $\hat{\mu} \in \Omega$ is an ith potential session where $i \in \mathcal{I}$, for all $1 \leq j \leq m$ if $(\hat{\mu}, T_h^{(i)}, j)$ is queried to the random oracle H_1. In other words, $\hat{\mu} \in \Omega$ is the ith potential session, if $\mathcal{A}$ obtained all $\hat{\alpha}_{1j}^{(i)} = H_1(\hat{\mu}, T_h^{(i)}, j)$ values to be able to compute $\hat{T}_h^{(i)} = \sum_{j=1}^m \hat{\alpha}_{1j}^{(i)} T_{1j}^{(i)}$. We denote by $\mathbb{O}_{H_1}^{(i)}$ the set of ith potential sessions.

We define a function $\phi : \mathbb{Z}_p^{q_s+1} \times (\times_{i \in \mathcal{I}} \mathbb{O}_{H_1}^{(i)}) \rightarrow \mathbb{Z}_p^{q_s+1}$. Given input $\hat{\boldsymbol{\beta}} = (\hat{\beta}^{(0)}, \hat{\beta}^{(1)}, \ldots, \hat{\beta}^{(q_s)}) \in \mathbb{Z}_p^{q_s+1}$ and $\mathcal{T}_{\mathsf{out}} = \{\hat{\mu}^{(i)}\}_{i \in \mathcal{I}} \in (\times_{i \in \mathcal{I}} \mathbb{O}_{H_1}^{(i)})$, we define the function ϕ as $\phi(\hat{\beta}, \hat{T_{\mathsf{out}}}) = \boldsymbol{y}$ where $\boldsymbol{y} = (y^{(0)}, y_{11}^{(1)}, \dots, y_{1m}^{(1)}, \dots, y_{11}^{(q_s)}, \dots, y_{1m}^{(q_s)})$

$$\phi(\hat{\beta}, \hat{T_{\mathsf{out}}}) = \boldsymbol{y} = \begin{cases} y^{(0)} = \beta^{(0)} \\ y_{1j}^{(i)} = \hat{\beta}^{(i)} \hat{\alpha}_{1j}^{(i)} & \text{if } i \in \mathcal{I} \\ y_{1j}^{(i)} = 0 & \text{otherwise} \end{cases} \tag{11}$$

We remark that $(\beta, T_{\mathsf{out}})$ provided by $\mathcal{A}$ as a solution to the simple m-entwined sum problem satisfies $\phi(\beta, T_{\mathsf{out}}) = \boldsymbol{b}$.

Lemma 1. ϕ *is an injective function for $m > 1$ except with the probability less than $\frac{q_{h_1}}{\sqrt{p}p^{m-2}}$.*

Proof. Let's assume that ϕ is not injective. Then, there exists $(\tilde{\beta}, \tilde{T_{\mathsf{out}}}) \neq (\hat{\beta}, \hat{T_{\mathsf{out}}})$ such that $\phi(\tilde{\beta}, \tilde{T_{\mathsf{out}}}) = \phi(\hat{\beta}, \hat{T_{\mathsf{out}}}) = \boldsymbol{y} \in \mathbb{Z}_p^{q_s+1}$. In this case, $\tilde{\beta}^{(i)} \tilde{\alpha}_{1j}^{(i)} = y_{1j}^{(i)}$ and $\hat{\beta}^{(i)} \hat{\alpha}_{1j}^{(i)} = y_{1j}^{(i)}$ for all $i \in \mathcal{I}$ and $1 \leq j \leq m$ which implies that

$$\frac{\tilde{\alpha}_{11}^{(i)}}{\hat{\alpha}_{11}^{(i)}} = \dots = \frac{\tilde{\alpha}_{1m}^{(i)}}{\hat{\alpha}_{1m}^{(i)}} \tag{12}$$

So, if ϕ is not injective, there should exist two different potential sessions $\hat{\mu}^{(i)}$ and $\tilde{\mu}^{(i)}$ in a potential session set $\mathbb{O}_{H_1}^{(i)}$ satisfies Eq. (12). The probability that it happens is for $m > 1$, given that $|\mathbb{O}_{H_1}^{(i)}| \leq q_{h_1}$

$$\Pr\left[\frac{\alpha_{11}^{(i)}}{\hat{\alpha}_{11}^{(1)}} = \dots = \frac{\alpha_{1m}^{(i)}}{\hat{\alpha}_{1m}^{(1)}} \right] \leq \frac{q_{h_1}}{\sqrt{p}p^{m-2}}$$

$\square$

As a result of the lemma, for each representation $\boldsymbol{c} \in \mathbb{Z}_p^{mq_s+1}$ of W such that $W = \boldsymbol{c} \cdot \boldsymbol{T_{\mathsf{inp}}}$, $\mathcal{A}$ can have only one possible $(\tilde{\beta}, \tilde{T_{\mathsf{out}}})$ except with the probability $\frac{q_{h_1}}{\sqrt{p}p^{m-2}}$ that satisfies $W = \tilde{\beta}^{(0)} P + \sum_{u=1}^{(q_s)} \tilde{\beta}^{(u)} \sum_{j=1}^{m} \tilde{\alpha}_{1j}^{(u)} T_{1j}^{(u)}$ because $\phi(\tilde{\beta}, \tilde{T_{\mathsf{out}}}) = \boldsymbol{c}$ is injective. So, when $\mathcal{A}$ queries $(., W)$ to the oracle H and gives its representation $\boldsymbol{a}$, it can have only one appropriate $(\beta, T_{\mathsf{out}})$. Therefore, if $\mathcal{A}$ finds a solution with respect to the representation $\boldsymbol{a}$, in other words, if $\boldsymbol{a} = \boldsymbol{b}$, the probability that $\mathcal{A}$ satisfies Eq. (10) with only one possible β, T_{out} for $W \in \mathbb{G}$ is $\frac{q_h}{p}$. The reason of this is that the left hand side of the Eq. 8 is fixed when $\mathcal{A}$ gives the representation $\boldsymbol{a}$ because ϕ is injective. Since the probability that the fixed left hand side equals to $H(\bar{\omega}, W)$ for $\bar{\omega} \in \Omega$ is $\frac{1}{p}$, the adversary's success probability to win when $\boldsymbol{a} = \boldsymbol{b}$ is $\frac{q_h}{p}$.

As a result of this, $\epsilon_{dlr} \geq \epsilon_{eSum} - \frac{q_h}{p} - \frac{q_{h_1}}{\sqrt{p}p^{m-2}}$ which implies that ϵ_{eSum} is negligible in terms of λ.

$\square$

We next give the m-entwined sum problem which is a version of the simple m-entwined sum problem with one more variable.

Definition 8 (m-entwined sum problem). *It is the same as the simple m-entwined sum problem in Definition 7 except that the challenger gives additionally $Y \in \mathbb{G}^n$ to the adversary and the adversary additionally outputs $v \in \mathbb{Z}_p$. Adversary wins the m-entwined sum game if*

$$\sum_{u=1}^{q_s} \beta^{(u)} H'(\mu^{(u)}, T^{(u)}) = H(\omega^*, \underline{v}\underline{Y} + \beta^{(0)} P + \sum_{u=1}^{(q_s)} \beta^{(u)} T_h^{(i)}) \tag{13}$$

We call that the m-entwined sum problem is hard in $\mathbb{G}$, if for all PPT adversaries who access the random oracles H, H' and H_1 at most $q_h, q_{h_1'} q_{h_1}$-times respectively, the probability of solving above problem is ϵ_{eSum} which is negligible in terms of λ.

Theorem 2. *If the simple m-entwined sum problem is hard then the m-entwined sum problem is hard.*

Proof. We construct an adversary $\mathcal{B}$ that breaks the simple m-entwined sum problem given that there is another adversary $\mathcal{A}$ that breaks the m-entwined sum problem. The simulation against $\mathcal{A}$ is trivial. $\mathcal{B}$ receives the simple m-entwined sum challenges $(p, \mathbb{G}, P)$ and vectors $T_h^{(1)}, T_h^{(2)}, \ldots, T_h^{(q_s)} \in \mathbb{G}^m$. Then, $\mathcal{B}$ picks randomly $y \in \mathbb{Z}_p$ and sends the simple m-entwined sum challenges and *additionally* $Y = yP$ to $\mathcal{A}$. Whenever $\mathcal{A}$ queries any random oracle with an input, $\mathcal{B}$ queries the same to the corresponding simple m-entwined sum oracle and forwards the answer to $\mathcal{A}$. In the end, $\mathcal{A}$ outputs a solution $\beta, \mathcal{T}_{out}$ and ω^*, v. $\mathcal{B}$ lets $\beta = \beta^{(0)} + vy$ and sends $\bar{\beta} = (\beta, \beta^{(1)}, \ldots, \beta^{(q_s)})$ and the same $\mathcal{T}_{out}, \omega^*$ that $\mathcal{A}$ outputted as a solution of the m-entwined sum problem. The simulation against $\mathcal{A}$ is perfect. Therefore, the probability that $\mathcal{B}$ wins the simple m-entwined sum problem is the same as the probability that $\mathcal{A}$ wins the m-entwined sum problem. Since we know that $\mathcal{B}$'s success probability is negligible, the success probability of $\mathcal{A}$ is negligible in the m-entwined sum problem.   □

5   Security Proof of DWMS

In the next theorem, we prove that DWMS is a secure multi-signature scheme in the ROM and the AGM.

Theorem 3. *Suppose there exists a PPT **algebraic** adversary $\mathcal{A}$ in the AGM against DWMS with parameters $(\mathbb{G}, P, p)$ and $m > 1$ who accesses random oracles H, H_1, H_2 at most q_h, q_{h_1}, q_{h_2} times respectively and breaks the security of DWMS in the plain public-key model (Definition 2) with probability ϵ. Then, under the 2-entwined sum assumption, there exists a PPT reduction $\mathcal{R}$ that solves the q_s-OMDL problem with probability $\epsilon_{omdl} \geq \epsilon - \frac{2q_s - 2q_{h_1} - q_{h_2} + q_s q_{h_1}}{p} - \frac{q_{h_2}}{\sqrt{p}} - \frac{q_s}{p^2} - \epsilon_{eSum}$ where $\epsilon_{eSum} \leq \epsilon_{dlr} + \frac{q_h}{p} + \frac{q_{h_1}}{\sqrt{p}}$.*

Before giving the proof, we give the main ideas about how to construct a reduction that solves the OMDL problem given that an adversary outputs a forgery in DWMS. The q_s-OMDL challenger gives $q_s + 1$ challenges. The reduction selects the last challenge as its public key. In each signing query, the reduction sends a random linear combination of the first q_s OMDL challenges as pre-commitments. Since the reduction does not know its secret key and the discrete logarithm of pre-commitments, it obtains the partial signature while simulating round 2 of DWMS from the DLOracle. Thus, the reduction obtains a linear equation with $q_s + 1$ unknowns (discrete logarithm of the OMDL challenges) in each signing session simulation. After at most q_s signing oracle calls, $\mathcal{A}$ outputs a forgery. Since we are in the AGM, $\mathcal{A}$ gives the representation of each group element during the simulation. From these representations, the reduction obtains $q_s + 1^{th}$ linear equation with the $q_s + 1$ unknowns which are the discrete logarithm of the OMDL challenges. If the last linear equation obtained from the forgery is not linearly dependent on other equations obtained from DLOracle, then the reduction solves the linear system of equations and obtains the discrete logarithm of the OMDL challenges. If it is linearly dependent, it means that the adversary obtained the forgery with a linear combination of the partial signatures generated in each signing session so the forgery does not give any new information and OMDL challenges cannot be found. During the proof, we see that if it is the case, the adversary actually solves the 2-entwined sum problem which can happen with negligible probability. Therefore, the reduction obtains the OMDL solution by solving $q_s + 1$ linear equations as long as the 2-entwined sum problem is hard.

Proof. We will show that given a forger $\mathcal{A}$ on the multi-signature scheme DWMS, there exists a reduction $\mathcal{R}$ that can solve the q_s-OMDL problem under the entwined sum assumption. We will use the following three notations for the adversary in the proof: $\mathcal{A}$ is an abbreviated notation that we will use often in the text description. A more formal and expanded notation is $\mathcal{A}^{H,H_1,H_2,\Sigma_1,\Sigma_2}(X_1, par; \rho)$, which accesses various oracles (all explained later) H, H_1, H_2, Σ_1 and Σ_2 that are simulated by the reduction $\mathcal{R}$ and receives the two inputs, namely X_1 - the honest signer's public key, *par*- the parameters of the multi-signature scheme and ρ - any random coins, provided by the reduction.

The formal security definition for multi-signatures is defined in Definition 2 and we denote it as **Game 0**. The challenger (simulated by the reduction $\mathcal{R}$) publishes the public parameters using the ParamGen algorithm and shares the honest signer's public key generated using the key generation algorithm KeyGen with the adversary. The reduction also provides any random coins ρ used by the adversary. Thereafter, the reduction simulates the random oracles H, H_1, H_2 for the adversary. The reduction also simulates the honest signer for the adversary using two oracles Σ_1 and Σ_2 that execute the two rounds of the Sign algorithm. The adversary can make up to q_s queries to Oracles Σ_1 and Σ_2. The adversary's challenge is to output a tuple $(\mathcal{PK}^*, msg^*, \sigma^*)$, such that the honest signer's public key X_1 is part of the multiset $\mathcal{PK}^*$, and the message msg^* was never queried to Oracle Σ_1 and the signature σ^* verifies for $(\mathcal{PK}^*, msg^*)$ while making fewer than q_h, q_{h_1}, q_{h_2} queries to the random oracles H, H_1, H_2, respectively and q_s queries to oracles Σ_1 and Σ_2.

The oracles that $\mathcal{A}$ can access are in more detail as follows in **Game 0**:

Oracle H, H_1, H_2: The reduction simulates a perfect random oracle by responding with a random group element from $\mathbb{Z}_p$ for each previously unseen query.

Oracle Σ_1: The reduction maintains a counter ℓ to track each query made by the adversary. We use the notation superscript $^{(\ell)}$ to distinguish the values specific to ℓ^{th} signature query. The reduction simulates a perfect response to a signature initiation query msg from the adversary by generating randomly chosen witnesses $r_{11}^{(\ell)}, r_{12}^{(\ell)}$. It stores all responses in a list L_{Σ_1}. In more detail, Σ_1 in **Game 0** is as follows:

$\Sigma_1(\mathsf{msg}^{(\ell)})$ in Game 0

1: $\ell := \ell + 1$
2: $r_{11}^{(\ell)}, r_{12}^{(\ell)} \leftarrow_R \mathbb{Z}_p, T_{11}^{(\ell)} = r_{11}^{(\ell)} P, T_{12}^{(\ell)} = r_{12}^{(\ell)} P$
3: $\mathsf{L}_{\Sigma_1} := \mathsf{L}_{\Sigma_1} \cup \{msg, T_{11}^{(\ell)}, T_{12}^{(\ell)}, r_{11}^{(\ell)}, r_{12}^{(\ell)}\}$
4: **return** $(msg^{(\ell)}, T_{11}^{(\ell)}, T_{12}^{(\ell)})$

Oracle Σ_2: The reduction simulates a perfect response to the ℓth signature query from the adversary by retrieving witnesses $r_{11}^{(\ell)}$ and $r_{12}^{(\ell)}$ from List L_{Σ_1} and using the pre-commitments of other session participants to derive a signature contribution. It stores all necessary elements related to the session in List L_{Σ_2}. In more detail, Σ_2 in **Game 0** is as described below:

$\Sigma_2(\mathcal{PK}^{(\ell)}, \mathsf{msg}^{(\ell)}, (\mathbf{T}_{i1}^{(\ell)}, \mathbf{T}_{i2}^{(\ell)})_{i \in [1,n]})$ in Game 0

---

if $(msg, T_{11}^{(\ell)}, T_{12}^{(\ell)}, ., .) \notin \mathsf{L}_{\Sigma_1}$ or $|\mathcal{PK}^{(\ell)}| \neq n - 1$ **then return** 0
retrieve $(r_{11}^{(\ell)}, r_{12}^{(\ell)})$ from L_{Σ_1}
$\mathsf{SID} = (\mathcal{PK}^{(\ell)}, msg^{(\ell)}, \{T_{11}^{(\ell)}, T_{12}^{(\ell)}\}, \ldots, \{T_{n1}^{(\ell)}, T_{n2}^{(\ell)}\})$
$\alpha_{i1}^{(\ell)} \leftarrow H_1(\mathsf{SID}, i, 1), \alpha_{i2}^{(\ell)} \leftarrow H_1(\mathsf{SID}, i, 2), \forall i \in [1, n]$
$T_h^{(\ell)} = \alpha_{11}^{(\ell)} T_{11}^{(\ell)} + \alpha_{12}^{(\ell)} T_{12}^{(\ell)}$
$T_i^{(\ell)} = (\alpha_{i1}^{(\ell)} T_{i1}^{(\ell)} + \alpha_{i2}^{(\ell)} T_{i2}^{(\ell)}), \forall i \in [2, n]$
$T^{(\ell)} = T_h^{(\ell)} + \sum_{i=2}^n T_i^{(\ell)}$
$\mathcal{PK}^{(\ell)} := \mathcal{PK}^{(\ell)} \cup \{X_1\}$
$X^{(\ell)} \leftarrow \mathsf{KeyAgg}(par, \mathcal{PK})$
$a_1^{(\ell)} = H_2(\mathcal{PK}^{(\ell)}, X_1)$
$c^{(\ell)} \leftarrow H(msg^{(\ell)}, X^{(\ell)}, T^{(\ell)})$
$s_1^{(\ell)} = \alpha_{11}^{(\ell)} r_{11}^{(\ell)} + \alpha_{12}^{(\ell)} r_{12}^{(\ell)} + c^{(\ell)} a_1^{(\ell)} x_1$
$\mathsf{L}_{\Sigma_2} := \mathsf{L}_{\Sigma_2} \cup \{\ell, \mathsf{SID}, (T^{(\ell)}, s_1^{(\ell)}, c^{(\ell)}), r_{11}^{(\ell)}, r_{12}^{(\ell)}, \alpha_{11}^{(\ell)}, \alpha_{12}^{(\ell)}\}$
return $s_1^{(\ell)}$

Remember that $\mathcal{A}$ is an algebraic adversary (See Definition 3). Therefore, whenever it queries to oracles with a group element $Z \in \mathbb{G}$, it also gives the representation of them $z \in \mathbb{Z}_p^{|V|}$ such that $Z = z.V$ in terms of the group elements that it has seen so far which we denote in vector V. For the sake of the presentation, we do not specify the representation vector of each group element in the oracle descriptions.

In the end, we define the **Game 0** which is equivalent to the game in Definition 2 as follows:

Game 0
$par = (\mathbb{G}, P, p) \leftarrow \mathsf{ParamGen}(\lambda)$
$(x_1, X_1) \leftarrow \mathsf{KeyGen}(par)$
$\ell := 0$
$(\mathcal{PK}^*, msg^*, \sigma^* = (s^*, c^*)) \leftarrow \mathcal{A}^{H, H_1, H_2, \Sigma_1, \Sigma_2}(X_1, par; \rho)$
return $(X_1 \in \mathcal{PK}^* \wedge msg^* \notin \mathsf{L}_{\Sigma_2} \wedge \mathsf{Verify}(par, \mathcal{PK}^*, msg^*, \sigma^*))$

The adversary is said to succeed in **Game 0** if **Game 0** returns 1 and thus the success probability of the adversary, $\epsilon = \Pr[\mathbf{Game\,0} \rightarrow 1]$.

In the following, we will show how the reduction $\mathcal{R}$ solves the q_s-OMDL problem given a multi-signature adversary $\mathcal{A}$ against the DWMS scheme. To simplify the presentation of the proof, we define a sequence of security games: **Game 1**, ..., **Game 9**, each game differing *slightly* from the previous one. We relate the probability of the output being 1 in any two consecutive games, and finally show that probability of solving the q_s-OMDL problem is close to the probability of the output being 1 in **Game 9**.

*In **Game 1**,* the reduction $\mathcal{R}$ uses its OMDL challenge $\{Y_1, \ldots, Y_{q_s+1}\}$ to derive the honest signer's public key as well as the pre-commitments in the simulation of Oracle Σ_1. $\mathcal{R}$ sets its public key X_1 as Y_{q_s+1}. The details of **Game 1** is given below. The gray color lines are the same as **Game 0**.

Game 1
$(Y_1, Y_2, \ldots, Y_{q_s}, Y_{q_s+1}) \leftarrow \mathsf{OMDL\text{-}Game}$
$X_1 := Y_{q_s+1}$
$\ell := 0$
$(\mathcal{PK}^*, msg^*, \sigma^* = (s^*, c^*)) \leftarrow \mathcal{A}^{H, H_1, H_2, \Sigma_1, \Sigma_2}(X_1, par; \rho)$
$\mathbf{return}(\mathsf{pk} \in \mathcal{PK}^* \wedge msg^* \notin \mathsf{L}_{\Sigma_2} \wedge \mathsf{Verify}(\mathcal{PK}^*, msg^*, \sigma^*))$

We also change the way of generating pre-commitments in Σ_1 **Game 1**. Instead of generating fresh witnesses r_{11}, r_{12} to generate the honest signer's pre-commitments in Oracle Σ_1, $\mathcal{R}$ uses the first q_s OMDL challenges as follows: $T_{11} = \sum_{j=1}^{q_s} \eta_{1j} Y_j, T_{12} = \sum_{j=1}^{q_s} \eta_{2j} Y_j$ for randomly chosen $\{\eta_{1j}, \eta_{2j}\}_{j \in [1, q_s]}$ from $\mathbb{Z}_p$. In more detail, the oracle Σ_1 in **Game 1** is modified as below:

$\mathcal{R}$ also modifies the oracle Σ_2 in **Game 1** because the discrete logarithms of the OMDL challenges are not known to the reduction $\mathcal{R}$. So, it uses the available DL oracle from the OMDL problem, to which it can make up to q_s queries, to simulate Oracle Σ_2. The reduction queries to the DL oracle on $T_h^{(\ell)} + c^{(\ell)} a_1^{(\ell)} Y_{q_s+1} = \alpha_{11}^{(\ell)}(\sum_{j=1}^{q_s} \eta_{1j}^{(\ell)} Y_j) + \alpha_{12}^{(\ell)}(\sum_{j=1}^{q_s} \eta_{2j}^{(\ell)} Y_j) + c^{(\ell)} a_1^{(\ell)} Y_{q_s+1}$ to generate

---

$\Sigma_1(\text{msg}^{(\ell)})$ in Game 1

1: $\ell := \ell + 1$
2: $\eta_{ij}^{(\ell)} \leftarrow_R \mathbb{Z}_p, \forall i \in [1,2], \forall j \in [1,q_s]$
3: $T_{11}^{(\ell)} = \sum_{j=1}^{q_s} \eta_{1j}^{(\ell)} Y_j, T_{12}^{(\ell)} = \sum_{j=1}^{q_s} \eta_{2j}^{(\ell)} Y_j$
4: $\mathsf{L}_{\Sigma_1} := \mathsf{L}_{\Sigma_1} \cup \{\text{msg}^{(\ell)}, T_{11}^{(\ell)}, T_{12}^{(\ell)}, \{\eta_{1j}^{(\ell)}\}_{j\in[1,q_s]}, \{\eta_{2j}^{(\ell)}\}_{j\in[1,q_s]}\}$
5: **return** $(\text{msg}^{(\ell)}, T_{11}^{(\ell)}, T_{12}^{(\ell)})$

$\Sigma_2(\mathcal{PK}, \text{msg}, (\mathbf{T}_{i1}^{(\ell)}, \mathbf{T}_{i2}^{(\ell)})_{i\in[1,n]})$ in Game 1

if $(\text{msg}, T_{11}^{(\ell)}, T_{12}^{(\ell)}) \notin \mathsf{L}_{\Sigma_1}$ or $|\mathcal{PK}^{(\ell)}| \neq n-1$ then return 0
retrieve $(\{\eta_{1j}^{(\ell)}\}_{j\in[1,q_s]}, \{\eta_{2j}^{(\ell)}\}_{j\in[1,q_s]})$ **from** L_{Σ_1}
$\mathsf{SID}^{(\ell)} = (\mathcal{PK}^{(\ell)}, \text{msg}^{(\ell)}, \{T_{11}^{(\ell)}, T_{12}^{(\ell)}\}, \ldots, \{T_{n1}^{(\ell)}, T_{n2}^{(\ell)}\})$
$\alpha_{i1}^{(\ell)} \leftarrow H_1(\mathsf{SID}, i, 1), \alpha_{i2}^{(\ell)} \leftarrow H_1(\mathsf{SID}, i, 2), \forall i \in [1,n]$
$T_h^{(\ell)} = \alpha_{11}^{(\ell)} T_{11}^{(\ell)} + \alpha_{12}^{(\ell)} T_{12}^{(\ell)}$
$T_i^{(\ell)} = (\alpha_{i1}^{(\ell)} T_{i1}^{(\ell)} + \alpha_{i2}^{(\ell)} T_{i2}^{(\ell)}), \forall i \in [2,n]$
$T^{(\ell)} = T_h^{(\ell)} + \sum_{i=2}^{n} T_i^{(\ell)}$
$\mathcal{PK}^{(\ell)} := \mathcal{PK}^{(\ell)} \cup \{X_1\}$
$X^{(\ell)} \leftarrow \mathsf{KeyGen}(par, \mathcal{PK}^{(\ell)})$
$a_1^{(\ell)} = H_2(\mathcal{PK}^{(\ell)}, X_1)$
$c^{(\ell)} \leftarrow H(\text{msg}^{(\ell)}, X^{(\ell)}, T^{(\ell)})$
$s_1^{(\ell)} \leftarrow \mathsf{DLOracle}(T_h^{(\ell)} + c^{(\ell)} a_1^{(\ell)} Y_{q_s+1})$
$\mathsf{L}_{\Sigma_2} := \mathsf{L}_{\Sigma_2} \cup \{\ell, \mathsf{SID}^{(\ell)}, (T^{(\ell)}, s_1^{(\ell)}, c^{(\ell)}), \{\eta_{1j}^{(\ell)}\}_{j\in[1,q_s]}, \{\eta_{2j}^{(\ell)}\}_{j\in[1,q_s]}, \alpha_{11}^{(\ell)}, \alpha_{12}^{(\ell)}\}$
return $s_1^{(\ell)}$

---

the honest signer's signature towards the multi-signature. The details of Σ_2 is below. The different lines from the Σ_2 of the previous game are in color black.

Since all η_{ij}'s are uniformly distributed in $\mathbb{Z}_p$ and Y_i's are randomly chosen elements in $\mathbb{G}$ (received as part of the OMDL challenge), both $T_{11} = \sum_{j=1}^{q_s} \beta_{1j} Y_j$ and $T_{12} = \sum_{j=1}^{q_s} \beta_{2j} Y_j\}$ are uniformly distributed over $\mathbb{G}$ as in Game 1. So, **Game 0** and **Game 1** are identical. Therefore $\Pr[\textbf{Game 0}] = \Pr[\textbf{Game 1}]$.

Remember that, given the signing counter equals to ℓ, when $\mathcal{A}$ outputs a group element $B \in \mathbb{G}$ with its representation vector $\boldsymbol{b} = (b_0, b_{11}^{(1)}, b_{12}^{(1)}, \ldots, b_{12}^{(\ell)}, b_{12}^{(\ell)}, b_{q_s+1}) \in \mathbb{Z}_p^{2\ell+2}$ in terms of the group elements $\boldsymbol{V} = (P, T_{11}^{(1)}, T_{12}^{(1)}, \ldots, T_{11}^{(\ell)}, T_{12}^{(\ell)}, Y_{q_s+1})$ that it has seen so far. In the rest of the proof, we consider another representation of $Z \in \mathbb{G}$ in terms of vector $\boldsymbol{Y} = (P, Y_1, Y_2, \ldots, Y_{q_s+1})$ whenever $\mathcal{A}$ gives a representation of Z. Since all group elements that $\mathcal{A}$ sees are the linear combinations of $Y_1, Y_2, \ldots, Y_{q_s}$, the another representation of Z in terms $\boldsymbol{Y}$ is as follows:

$$B = b_0 P + b_{11}^{(1)} T_{11}^{(1)} + b_{12}^{(1)} T_{12}^{(1)} + \dots + b_{11}^{(\ell)} T_{11}^{(\ell)} + b_{12}^{(\ell)} T_{12}^{(\ell)} + b_{q_s+1} Y_{q_s+1}$$

$$= b_0 P + b_{11}^{(1)} \sum_{j=1}^{q_s} \eta_{1j}^{(1)} Y_j + b_{12}^{(1)} \sum_{j=1}^{q_s} \eta_{2j}^{(1)} Y_j + \dots + b_{11}^{(\ell)} \sum_{j=1}^{q_s} \eta_{1j}^{(\ell)} Y_j + b_{12}^{(\ell)} \sum_{j=1}^{q_s} \eta_{2j}^{(\ell)} Y_j + b_{q_s+1} Y_{q_s+1}$$

$$= b_0 P + \sum_{j=1}^{q_s} \underbrace{(\sum_{i=1}^{\ell} b_{11}^{(i)} \eta_{1j}^{(i)} + b_{12}^{(i)} \eta_{2j}^{(i)})}_{b_j} Y_j + b_{q_s+1} Y_{q_s+1} = b_0 P + \sum_{i=1}^{q_s+1} b_j Y_j \tag{14}$$

In Game 2, $\mathcal{R}$ works as in the previous game except that it outputs abort if H_1 ever outputs 0. Since H_1 is a random oracle, the probability of aborting in **Game 2** is $\frac{q_{h_1}}{p}$. From the difference lemma, $\Pr[\text{Output}(\textbf{Game 2}) = 1] \geq \Pr[\text{Output}(\textbf{Game 1}) = 1] - \frac{q_{h_1}}{p}$.

In Game 3, $\mathcal{R}$ works as in the previous game except that it outputs abort if $\alpha_{11}^{(i)} T_{11}^{(i)} + \alpha_{11}^{(i)} T_{11}^{(i)} = 0$ for a session i. Remark that $\alpha_{11}^{(i)} T_{11}^{(i)} + \alpha_{12}^{(i)} T_{12}^{(i)} = (\alpha_{11}^{(i)} (\sum_{j=1}^{q_s} \eta_{1j}^{(i)} y_j) + \alpha_{12}^{(i)} (\sum_{j=1}^{q_s} \eta_{2j}^{(i)} y_j)) P = \tau^{(i)} P$. Therefore, if $\alpha_{11}^{(i)} T_{11}^{(i)} + \alpha_{12}^{(i)} T_{12}^{(i)} = 0$ for a session i, it means that either $T_{11}^{(i)} = T_{12}^{(i)} = 0$ or $\alpha_{11}^{(i)} (\sum_{j=1}^{q_s} \eta_{1j}^{(i)} y_j) = -\alpha_{12}^{(i)} (\sum_{j=1}^{q_s} \eta_{2j}^{(i)} y_j)$ given that $T_{11}^{(i)} \neq 0, T_{12}^{(i)} \neq 0$. Therefore, the probability of this event for a session i is $(1 - (1 - \frac{1}{p^2})^{q_s}) + (1 - (1 - \frac{q_{h_1}}{p})^{q_s}) \leq (1 - (1 - \frac{q_s}{p^2})) + (1 - (1 - \frac{q_{h_1} q_s}{p})) = \frac{q_s}{p^2} + \frac{q_{h_1} q_s}{p} 2$. From the difference lemma, $\Pr[\text{Output}(\textbf{Game 3}) = 1] \geq \Pr[\text{Output}(\textbf{Game 2}) = 1] - \frac{q_s q_{h_1}}{p} - \frac{q_s}{p^2}$.

In Game 4, $\mathcal{R}$ works as in the previous game except that it also generates a matrix M of size $\ell \leq q_s$ after receiving the forgery and it aborts the game if the rank of M is not ℓ. In more details, $\mathcal{R}$ obtains $\{\eta_{1j}^{(i)}\}_{j \in [1, q_s]}, \{\eta_{2j}^{(i)}\}_{j \in [1, q_s]}, \alpha_{11}^{(i)}, \alpha_{12}^{(i)}, a_1^{(i)}, c^{(i)}$ from $\mathsf{L}_{\Sigma_2}[i]$ for all $i \in [1, \ell]$. Then, $\mathcal{R}$ constructs a matrix M of size $(\ell \times q_s + 1)$ as below:

$$M = \begin{bmatrix} \alpha_{11}^{(1)} \eta_{11}^{(1)} + \alpha_{12}^{(1)} \eta_{21}^{(1)} & \dots & \alpha_{11}^{(1)} \eta_{1q_s}^{(1)} + \alpha_{12}^{(1)} \eta_{2q_s}^{(1)} & a_1^{(1)} c^{(1)} \\ \alpha_{11}^{(2)} \eta_{11}^{(2)} + \alpha_{12}^{(2)} \eta_{21}^{(2)} & \dots & \alpha_{11}^{(2)} \eta_{1q_s}^{(2)} + \alpha_{12}^{(2)} \eta_{2q_s}^{(2)} & a_1^{(2)} c^{(2)} \\ \vdots & \dots & \vdots & \vdots \\ \alpha_{11}^{(\ell)} \eta_{11}^{(\ell)} + \alpha_{12}^{(\ell)} \eta_{21}^{(\ell)} & \dots & \alpha_{11}^{(q_s)} \eta_{1q_s}^{(\ell)} + \alpha_{12}^{(\ell)} \eta_{2q_s}^{(\ell)} & a_1^{(\ell)} c^{(\ell)} \end{bmatrix}$$

After the construction of M, if the rank of M is not ℓ, $\mathcal{R}$ aborts. Clearly, the only difference of **Game 4** from **Game 3** is aborting when the rank of M is not ℓ. Therefore, we analyse the probability of abort in **Game 4**.

We assume next that the q_s-OMDL challenger never selects $y_i = 0$. If there was $y_i = 0$, $\mathcal{R}$ wins the q_s-OMDL game without the forgery by $\mathcal{A}$ i.e., $\mathcal{R}$ knows the discrete logarithm of $Y_i = 0$ and receives discrete logarithm of rest of the challenges from the DL- oracle.

---

[2] Remark that $\alpha_{11}^{(i)} = H_1(\text{SID}^{(i)}, 1, 1), \alpha_{12}^{(i)} = H_1(\text{SID}^{(i)}, 1, 2)$. So, the probability of having $\alpha_{11}^{(i)} (\sum_{j=1}^{q_s} \eta_{1j}^{(i)} y_j) = -\alpha_{12}^{(i)} (\sum_{j=1}^{q_s} \eta_{2j}^{(i)} y_j)$ given that $T_{11}^{(i)} \neq 0, T_{11}^{(i)} \neq 0$ is not a collision probability.

We first consider the case where $\ell < q_s$. We remark that given that $y_1 \neq 0$, $T_{11}^{(i)}$ and $T_{12}^{(i)}$ are uniformly random even if we fix $\eta_{1j}^{(i)}, \eta_{2j}^{(i)}$ for $j > 1$ (i.e., fix all $\eta_{1j}^{(i)}, \eta_{2j}^{(i)}$'s except $\eta_{11}^{(i)}, \eta_{21}^{(i)}$) and all $y_1, y_2, \ldots, y_\ell$. values. Therefore, conditioned on $T_{11}^{(i)}, T_{12}^{(i)}$ and $y_1 \neq 0$, all $\eta_{1j}^{(i)}, \eta_{2j}^{(i)}$-values for $\mathbf{j} > \mathbf{1}$ are independent and uniformly distributed i.e.,

$$\Pr\left[\eta_{1j}^{(i)}, \eta_{2j}^{(i)}, \forall j > 1 | T_{11}^{(i)}, T_{12}^{(i)}\right] = \frac{\Pr\left[T_{11}^{(i)}, T_{12}^{(i)} | \eta_{1j}^{(i)}, \eta_{2j}^{(i)}, \forall j > 1\right] \Pr\left[\eta_{1j}^{(i)}, \eta_{2j}^{(i)}, \forall j > 1\right]}{\Pr\left[T_{11}^{(i)}, T_{12}^{(i)}\right]}$$

$$= \frac{\frac{1}{p^2} \frac{1}{p^{2q_s - 2}}}{\frac{1}{p^2}} = \frac{1}{p^{2q_s - 2}}$$

We remark that we can say only $\eta_{1j}^{(i)}, \eta_{2j}^{(i)}$ values for $\mathbf{j} > \mathbf{1}$ are independent and uniformly distributed because $\Pr\left[\eta_{1j}^{(i)}, \eta_{2j}^{(i)}, \forall j \geq 1 | T_{11}^{(i)}, T_{12}^{(i)}\right] = \frac{\frac{1}{p^{q_s}}}{\frac{1}{p}} = \frac{1}{p^{2q_s - 2}} \neq \frac{1}{p^{2q_s}}$. Therefore, all column vectors from 2nd column vector to the q_s^{th} column vector are uniformly random and independent random variables given that α-values are not 0 (See **Game 2**). In other words, we have a random submatrix $\bar{M}$ of size $(\ell \times q_s - 1)$ which is M without the first and the last column. It is a known fact that random $\bar{M}$'s rank is ℓ except with the probability $\frac{\ell}{p}$ where $\ell \leq q_s - 1$ (See Appendix A). Therefore, the rank of M is $\ell \leq q_s - 1$ except with the probability $\frac{\ell}{p}$ because the rank of a matrix is defined as the maximum number of linearly independent columns (or rows) and the columns of $\bar{M}$ are also M's columns. Remember that the rank of M is at most ℓ. In other words, $\Pr[\text{RANK}(M) < \ell | \ell < q_s] \leq \frac{\ell}{p} \leq \frac{q_s - 1}{p}$.

Now, we assume that $\ell = q_s$. In this case, $\bar{M}$ without the first and last column of M consists of independent and random column vectors because of the same reasoning as above. Let's define a vector $\boldsymbol{\tau} = (\tau^{(1)}, \tau^{(2)}, \ldots, \tau^{(q_s)}) \in \mathbb{Z}_p^{q_s}$ where $\tau^{(i)} P = \alpha_{11}^{(i)} T_{11}^{(i)} + \alpha_{11}^{(i)} T_{11}^{(i)} = (\alpha_{11}^{(i)} (\sum_{j=1}^{q_s} \eta_{1j}^{(i)} y_j) + \alpha_{12}^{(i)} (\sum_{j=1}^{q_s} \eta_{2j}^{(i)} y_j)) P$. Remember that $\boldsymbol{\tau}$ is a non-zero vector i.e., $\boldsymbol{\tau} \neq \mathbf{0}$ because of **Game 3**.

We can write the first column of M as a linear combination of $\boldsymbol{\tau}$ and the column vectors of $\bar{M}$ i.e.,

$$\alpha_{11}^{(i)} \eta_{11}^{(i)} + \alpha_{12}^{(i)} \eta_{21}^{(i)} = \frac{-1}{y_1} \tau^{(i)} - \sum_{j=2}^{q_s} \frac{y_j}{y_1} (\alpha_{11}^{(i)} \eta_{1j}^{(i)} + \alpha_{12}^{(i)} \eta_{2j}^{(i)}) \tag{15}$$

since $\frac{1}{y_1} \neq 0$ and $y_1 \neq 0$. Next, we prove a lemma that implies that if $\boldsymbol{\tau}$ and the column vectors of $\bar{M}$ are linearly independent, then the first column vector and the column vectors of $\bar{M}$ (i.e., the first q_s columns of M) are linearly independent.

Lemma 2. *Assume that there exist vectors $\boldsymbol{v_1}, \boldsymbol{v_2}, \boldsymbol{v_3}, \ldots, \boldsymbol{v_{q_s}}$ in $\mathbb{Z}_p^{q_s}$ and another vector $\boldsymbol{v_1'} \in \mathbb{Z}_p^{q_s}$ such that $\boldsymbol{v_1'} = \sum_{j=1}^{q_s} \lambda_j \boldsymbol{v_j}$ where $\lambda_j \in \mathbb{Z}_p \setminus \{0\}$. If $\boldsymbol{v_1}, \boldsymbol{v_2}, \boldsymbol{v_3}, \ldots, \boldsymbol{v_{q_s}}$ are linearly independent, then $\boldsymbol{v_1'}, \boldsymbol{v_2}, \boldsymbol{v_3}, \ldots, \boldsymbol{v_{q_s}}$ are linearly independent,*

Proof. Assume that it is not the case to prove by contradiction i.e., $v_1', v_2, v_3, \ldots, v_{q_s}$ are not linearly independent while $v_1, v_2, v_3, \ldots, v_{q_s}$ are linearly independent. In this case, there exists a non-zero vector $\theta = (\theta_2, \theta_3, \ldots, \theta_{q_s}) \in \mathbb{Z}_p^{q_s-1}$ such that $v_1' = \sum_{i=2}^{q_s} \theta_i v_j$. We also know that $v_1' = \sum_{j=1}^{q_s} \lambda_j v_j$. These two imply that $v_1 = \sum_{j=2}^{q_s} \frac{\theta_j - \lambda_j}{\lambda_1} v_j$ which is a contradiction with the linear independence of $v_1, v_2, v_3, \ldots, v_{q_s}$. Remark that not all $\frac{\theta_j - \lambda_j}{\lambda_1} = 0$ because $v_1 \neq 0$ due to the fact that $v_1, v_2, v_3, \ldots, v_{q_s}$ are linearly independent. $\square$

Lemma 2 shows that if we show τ and the column vectors of $\bar{M}$ are linearly independent, then the first column vector and the column vectors of $\bar{M}$ are linearly independent because of Eq. (15). Next, we show another lemma to relate the linear independence of τ and the column vectors of $\bar{M}$.

Lemma 3. *Given a fixed vector $\tau \in \mathbb{Z}_p^{q_s}$ where $\tau \neq 0$ and uniformly and independently chosen vectors $v_2, v_3, \ldots, v_{q_s}$ in $\mathbb{Z}_p^{q_s}$, τ and $v_2, v_3, \ldots, v_{q_s}$ are linearly independent except with the probability $\frac{q_s}{p}$.*

Proof. τ and $v_2, v_3, \ldots, v_{q_s}$ are linearly dependent if either

1. $v_2, v_3, \ldots, v_{q_s}$ are linearly dependent or
2. τ and $v_2, v_3, \ldots, v_{q_s}$ are linearly dependent given that $v_2, v_3, \ldots, v_{q_s}$ are linearly independent.

The probability of condition 1 is $1 - \frac{q_s-1}{p}$ since $v_2, v_3, \ldots, v_{q_s}$ are randomly and independently selected (See Appendix A). Therefore, they span a random vector space $\mathcal{V}$ with the size p^{q_s-1} except with the probability $\frac{q_s-1}{p}$.

If condition 2 does not hold, it means that τ is not in the vector space $\mathcal{V}$. Since $\mathcal{V}$ is a random vector space of size p^{q_s-1}, the probability that a fixed τ is not in it is $\frac{p^{q_s} - p^{q_s-1}}{p^{q_s}} = 1 - \frac{1}{p}$. So, condition 2 holds with the probability $\frac{1}{p}$.

Hence, the probability that they are linearly dependent is $\frac{q_s-1}{p} + \frac{1}{p} = \frac{q_s}{p}$. $\square$

When $\mathcal{A}$ gives a forgery, we set the first q_s columns of M and we fix τ. Thanks to Lemma 3, fixed τ and independent and random column vectors of $\bar{M}$ are linearly independent except with the probability $\frac{q_s}{p}$. By applying Lemma 2 thanks to the Eq. (15), we conclude that the first q_s columns of M (equivalently the first column of M and the column vectors of $\bar{M}$) are linearly independent. It means that the rank of M is q_s except with the probability $\frac{q_s}{p}$. In other words, $\Pr[\text{RANK}(M) < \ell | \ell = q_s] \leq \frac{q_s}{p}$.

As a result, the rank of M is ℓ except with the probability

$$\Pr[\text{RANK}(M) < \ell] = \Pr[\text{RANK}(M) < \ell | \ell < q_s] + \Pr[\text{RANK}(M) < \ell | \ell = q_s]$$
$$\leq \frac{q_s - 1}{p} + \frac{q_s}{p}$$

By the difference lemma, $\Pr[\text{Output}(\textbf{Game 4}) = 1] \geq \Pr[\text{Output}(\textbf{Game 3}) = 1] - \frac{2q_s-1}{p}$.

In **Game 5**, the reduction simulates all the oracles as in the previous game except H_2. $\mathcal{R}$ defines a map map_{key} from $\mathbb{Z}_p \to \mathbb{Z}_p^*$. When $(\mathcal{PK}, X_i) \in \mathbb{Z}_p^{n'} \times \mathbb{Z}_p$ is queried to H_2 and $X_i \in \mathcal{PK}$, $\mathcal{R}$ finds the aggregated public key which is $X \leftarrow$ $\mathsf{KeyAgg}(par, \mathcal{PK})$ i.e., $X = \sum_{X_i \in \mathcal{PK}} H_2(\mathcal{PK}, X_i) X_i$. Then, it checks whether X is mapped to a set in map_{key}. If it is not mapped, it lets $\mathsf{map}_{key}(X) = \mathcal{PK}$. Otherwise, it checks whether $\mathsf{map}_{key}(X) = \mathcal{PK}$. If $\mathsf{map}_{key}(X) \neq \mathcal{PK}$, $\mathcal{R}$ aborts. When $\mathcal{A}$ first time queries with a list of $\mathcal{PK}$ to H_2, it actually commits $\mathcal{PK}$ to X without knowing it. Therefore, the probability that an aggregated public key maps to two list of public key sets $\mathcal{PK}, \mathcal{PK}'$ is $\frac{b}{p} \leq \frac{q_{h_2}}{p}$ where b is the number of elements that is mapped. By the difference lemma, $\Pr[\mathrm{Output}(\mathbf{Game\,5}) = 1] \geq \Pr[\mathrm{Output}(\mathbf{Game\,4}) = 1] - \frac{q_{h_2}}{p}$.

In **Game 6**, the reduction simulates all the oracles as in the previous game except H_1. $\mathcal{R}$ defines a map map_{commit} from $\mathbb{Z}_p \to \{0,1\}^*$. In this game, we call (SID, i, j) is a legit input for H_1 if $\mathsf{SID} = (\mathcal{PK}, msg, \{T_{11}, T_{12}\}, \dots, \{T_{n1}, T_{n2}\}) \in \mathbb{G}^n \times \{0,1\}^* \times \mathbb{G}^{2n}$, $(msg, T_{11}, T_{12}) \in \mathsf{list}_{\Sigma_1}$, $1 \leq i \leq n$ and $1 \leq j \leq 2$. In short, (SID, i, j) is legit if SID is a valid session id for the second round of the signing the message msg by Σ_2. When legit (SID, i, j) is queried to H_1, $\mathcal{R}$ finds the commitment $T = \sum_{i=1}^n \alpha_{i1} T_{i1} + \alpha_{i2} T_{i2}$ where $\alpha_{ij} = H_1(\mathsf{SID}, i, j)$. Then, it checks whether T is mapped to a value in map_{commit}. If it is not mapped, it lets $\mathsf{map}_{commit}(T) = \mathsf{SID}$. Otherwise, it checks whether $\mathsf{map}_{commit}(T) = \mathsf{SID}$. If $\mathsf{map}_{commit}(T) \neq \mathsf{SID}$, $\mathcal{R}$ aborts. Similarly to **Game 5**, when $\mathcal{A}$ first time queries with legit SID to H_1, it actually commits SID to the value T without knowing it. Therefore, the probability that T maps to two session ids $\mathsf{SID}, \mathsf{SID}'$ is $\frac{b}{p} \leq \frac{q_{h_1}}{p}$ where b is the number of elements that is mapped. By the difference lemma, $\Pr[\mathrm{Output}(\mathbf{Game\,6}) = 1] \geq \Pr[\mathrm{Output}(\mathbf{Game\,5}) = 1] - \frac{q_{h_1}}{p}$.

In **Game 7**, the reduction simulates all the oracles as in the previous game except H_2. When the adversary queries with $\mathcal{PK} = \{X_1, X_2, \dots, X_n\}$ and $X_j \in \mathbb{G}$ with the representation vectors of each group element in $\mathcal{PK}$, $\mathcal{R}$ obtains the representation $\boldsymbol{x_i} \in \mathbb{Z}_p^{|\boldsymbol{Y}|}$ of the each group element $X_i \in \mathcal{PK}$ in terms of $\boldsymbol{Y}$. If $Y_{q_s+1}, X_j \in \mathcal{PK}$ (the valid key aggregation input), the reduction simulates H_2 as follows: We assume that $X_1 = Y_{q_s+1}$ without loss of generality and there exists a key database DB_{key} which stores the aggregated key and its representation. $\mathcal{R}$ computes $X \leftarrow \mathsf{KeyAgg}(par, \mathcal{PK})$ and if $\mathsf{DB}_{key}[X]$ is empty, it does the following: $\mathcal{R}$ first obtains the representation of adversarial aggregated key $\tilde{X} = \sum_{i=2}^n a_i X_i$ which is $\tilde{z} = \sum_{i=2}^n a_i \boldsymbol{x_i}$ in terms of $\boldsymbol{Y}$. Then, it lets $z = \tilde{z} + (0, 0, \dots, 0, a_1)$ be the representation of the aggregated public key of $\mathcal{PK}$ (i.e., $X = \mathsf{KeyAgg}(par, \mathcal{PK}) = \tilde{X} + a_1 Y_{q_s+1})$ in terms of $\boldsymbol{Y}$ where $(0, 0, \dots, 0, a_1)$ is a representation $a_1 Y_{q_s+1}$. If $\tilde{z}_{q_s+1} = -a_1$, $\mathcal{R}$ aborts and the simulation ends. If it is not the case, $\mathcal{R}$ stores z to the valid key database $\mathsf{DB}_{key}[X] = z$. We remark that $\tilde{z}_{q_s+1} = \sum_{i=2}^n a_i \boldsymbol{x_i}[q_s + 1]$ is random because $\mathcal{R}$ does this check when $\mathcal{A}$ queries first time with the valid key aggregation input $\mathcal{PK}, X_j$ and its representations to H_2. In other words, $\mathcal{R}$ does this check when $\mathcal{A}$ does not know $a_1, a_2, \dots, a_n$. The later queries of the same input with different representation of keys are not considered in this check. Since a_1 is the random oracle output and $\tilde{z}_{q_s+1}$

is random, the probability that $a_1 = -\tilde{z}_{q_s+1}$ less than or equal to $\frac{1}{\sqrt{p}}$. By the difference lemma, $\Pr[\text{Output}(\mathbf{Game\,7}) = 1] \geq \Pr[\text{Output}(\mathbf{Game\,6}) = 1] - \frac{q_{h_2}}{\sqrt{p}}$.

In **Game 8**, the reduction simulates all the oracles as in the previous game. Differently, after receiving the forgery, it constructs a new matrix M' by adding a new row $\boldsymbol{v} = (t_1 + c^* z_1, t_2 + c^* z_2, \ldots, t_{q_s+1} + c^* z_{q_s+1})$ to M and it aborts the game if the rank of the new matrix M' is less than $\ell + 1$. Here, $\boldsymbol{t} = (t_0, t_1, \ldots, t_{q_s+1})$ is the representation of $T^* = s^* P - c^* X^*$ where $X^* = \mathsf{KeyAgg}(par, \mathcal{PK}^*)$ is the aggregated public key of the forgery. The vector $\boldsymbol{z} = (z_0, z_1, z_2, \ldots, z_{q_s+1})$ is $\mathsf{DB}_{key}[X^*]$ which is a representation of X^* as defined in **Game 7**.

$\mathcal{R}$ can obtain the representation $\boldsymbol{t}$ by checking the H-oracle queries with the input $(msg^*, X^*, s^* P - c^* P)$ where $\boldsymbol{t}$ must be given. We remark that $\mathcal{A}$ has to query with the input $(msg^*, X^*, s^* P - c^* P)$ to output c^* as a part of the forgery. $\mathsf{DB}_{key}[X^*]$ cannot be null because $\mathcal{A}$ needs the aggregated public key for the forgery. We remark that $s^* P - c^* X^* = \boldsymbol{t} \cdot \boldsymbol{Y}$ and $c^* X^* = c^*(\boldsymbol{z} \cdot \boldsymbol{Y})$

$$
\mathsf{M}' = \begin{bmatrix}
\alpha_{11}^{(1)} \eta_{11}^{(1)} + \alpha_{12}^{(1)} \eta_{21}^{(1)} & \cdots & \alpha_{11}^{(1)} \eta_{1q_s}^{(1)} + \alpha_{12}^{(1)} \eta_{2q_s}^{(1)} & a_1^{(1)} c^{(1)} \\
\vdots & \cdots & \vdots & \vdots \\
\alpha_{11}^{(\ell)} \eta_{11}^{(\ell)} + \alpha_{12}^{(\ell)} \eta_{21}^{(\ell)} & \cdots & \alpha_{11}^{(\ell)} \eta_{1q_s}^{(\ell)} + \alpha_{12}^{(\ell)} \eta_{2q_s}^{(\ell)} & a_1^{(\ell)} c^{(\ell)} \\
t_1 + c^* z_1 & \cdots & t_{q_s} + c^* z_{q_s} & t_{q_s+1} + c^* z_{q_s+1}
\end{bmatrix}
$$

Let's assume that the rank of M' is less than $\ell + 1$ to analyse the probability that it happens. We show next that if it happens, $\mathcal{A}$ solves the 2-entwined sum problem (Definition 8) with the challenges $(p, \mathbb{G}, P)$, $\boldsymbol{T_h^{(i)}} = (T_{11}^{(i)}, T_{12}^{(i)})$ for $i \in [1, \ell]$ and $Y = Y_{q_s+1}$, the random oracles $\bar{H} : (\{0,1\}^* \times \mathbb{G}) \times \mathbb{G} \to \mathbb{Z}_p$, $\bar{H}' : (\mathbb{G}^n \times \{0,1\}^* \times \mathbb{G}^{2n}) \times \mathbb{G} \to \mathbb{Z}_p$ and $\bar{H}_1 : (\mathbb{G}^n \times \{0,1\}^* \times \mathbb{G}^{2n}) \times \mathbb{G}^2 \times \mathbb{N} \to \mathbb{Z}_p$ for $n \geq 1$. The random oracles $\bar{H}, \bar{H}', \bar{H}_1$ are defined as follows where each stores their responses in the database $\mathsf{DB}_{\bar{H}}, \mathsf{DB}_{\bar{H}'}$ and $\mathsf{DB}_{\bar{H}_1}$, respectively:

$\bar{H}(\omega, T)$:
input: $\omega = (msg, X) \in \{0,1\}^* \times \mathbb{G}$ and $\boldsymbol{t} = (t_0, t_1, t_2, \ldots, t_{q_s+1})$ which is the representation of T
if $(\omega, W) \notin \mathsf{DB}_{\bar{H}}$:
    if $\mathsf{DB}_{key}[X] \neq$ null :
        $\boldsymbol{z} \leftarrow \mathsf{DB}_{key}[X]$
        $\rho_1 \leftarrow z_{q_s+1}$
        $\rho_2 \leftarrow t_{q_s+1}$
        $\mathsf{DB}_{\bar{H}}[(\omega, T)] \leftarrow \rho_1 H(\omega, T) + \rho_2$
    else:
        $\mathsf{DB}_{\bar{H}}[(\omega, T)] \leftarrow_\$ \mathbb{Z}_p$
return $\mathsf{DB}_{\bar{H}}[(\omega, T)]$

$\bar{H}$ is a random oracle because H is a random oracle and ρ_1 is not 0 in this game (See **Game 7**).

$\bar{H}'(\mu, T_h)$:

input: $\mu = (\mathcal{PK}, msg, \{T_{11}, T_{12}\}, \ldots, \{T_{n1}, T_{n2}\}) \in \mathbb{G}^n \times \{0,1\}^* \times \mathbb{G}^{2n}$

if $(\mu, T_h) \notin \mathsf{DB}_{\bar{H}'}$:

    $\alpha_{11} \leftarrow H_1(\mu, 1, 1), \alpha_{12} \leftarrow H_1(\mu, 1, 2)$

    if $T_h = \sum_{j=1}^{2} \alpha_{1j} T_{1j}$:

        $\alpha_{i1}^{(\ell)} \leftarrow H_1(\mu, i, 1), \alpha_{i2}^{(\ell)} \leftarrow H_1(\mu, i, 2), \forall i \in [2, n]$

        $T = T_h + \sum_{i=2}^{n} (\alpha_{i1}^{(\ell)} T_{i1} + \alpha_{i2}^{(\ell)} T_{i2})$

        $X \leftarrow \mathsf{KeyAgg}(par, \mathcal{PK})$

        $a_1 \leftarrow H_2(\mathcal{PK}, X_1)$

        $c = H(msg, X, T)$

        $\mathsf{DB}_{\bar{H}'}[(\mu, T_h)] \leftarrow a_1 c$

    else: $\mathsf{DB}_{\bar{H}'}[(\mu, T_h)] \leftarrow_{\$} \mathbb{Z}_p$

return $\mathsf{DB}_{\bar{H}'}[(\mu, T_h)]$

$\bar{H}'$ is a random oracle because H_1, H_2 and H are random oracles and also there exists no $\mathcal{PK} \neq \mathcal{PK}'$ that aggregates to same X (See **Game 5**) and there exists no $\mu \neq \mu'$ that maps to same T (See **Game 6**).

$\bar{H}_1(\mu, T, j)$:

input: $\mu = (\mathcal{PK}, msg, \{T_{11}, T_{12}\}, \ldots, \{T_{n1}, T_{n2}\}) \in \mathbb{G}^n \times \{0,1\}^* \times \mathbb{G}^{2n}$

if $(\mu, T, j) \notin \mathsf{DB}_{\bar{H}_1}$

    if $T = \{T_{11}, T_{12}\}$

        $\mathsf{DB}_{\bar{H}_1}[(\mu, T, j)] \leftarrow H_1(\mu, 1, j)$

    else: $\mathsf{DB}_{\bar{H}_1}[(\mu, T, j)] \leftarrow \mathbb{Z}_p$

else: $\mathsf{DB}_{\bar{H}_1}[(\mu, T, j)] \leftarrow \mathbb{Z}_p$

return $\mathsf{DB}_{\bar{H}_1}[(\mu, T, j)]$

$\bar{H}_1$ is a random oracle because H_1 is a random oracle.

Now, we show why $\mathsf{Rank}(\mathsf{M}') < \ell$ implies that $\mathcal{A}$ finds a 2-entwined sum solution: We remark that the rank of M' must be ℓ if it is less than $\ell+1$ thanks to **Game 4**. Therefore, if the last row of M' is linearly dependent, then there exists a **unique** vector $\boldsymbol{\beta} = (\beta^{(1)}, \beta^{(2)}, \ldots, \beta^{(\ell)})$ such that $t_j + c^* z_j = \sum_{i=1}^{\ell} \beta^{(i)}(\alpha_{11}^{(i)} \eta_{1j}^{(i)} + \alpha_{12}^{(i)} \eta_{2j}^{(i)})$ for $j \in [1, q_s]$ and $t_{q_s+1} + c^* z_{q_s+1} = \sum_{i=1}^{\ell} \beta^{(i)} a_1^{(i)} c^{(i)}$. We remark that in this case $s^* = t^* + c^* (\sum_{i=2}^{n} a_i^* x_i + a_1^* y_{q_s+1}) = t_0 + (\sum_{i=1}^{q_s+1} t_i y_i) + c^* z_0 + c^* (\sum_{i=1}^{q_s+1} z_i y_i) = t_0 + c^* z_0 + \sum_{i=1}^{q_s} \beta^{(i)} s^{(i)}$ as in the m-entwined sum attack that we show in Sect. 3. Accordingly, if we reorganize $T^* = s^* P - c^* X$, we obtain the following:

$$T^* = (t_0 + \sum_{j=1}^{q_s+1} y_j t_j)P$$

$$= t_0 P + (\sum_{j=1}^{q_s} y_j (\sum_{i=1}^{\ell} \beta^{(i)}(\alpha_{11}^{(i)}\eta_{1j}^{(i)} + \alpha_{12}^{(i)}\eta_{2j}) - c^* z_j))P + t_{q_s+1}Y_{q_s+1}$$

$$= t_0 P + \sum_{i=1}^{\ell} \beta^{(i)}(\alpha_{11}^{(i)}T_{11}^{(i)} + \alpha_{12}^{(i)}T_{12}^{(i)}) - \sum_{j=1}^{q_s} c^* z_j Y_j + t_{q_s+1}Y_{q_s+1} \qquad (16)$$

$$= (t_0 - c^*(\sum_{i=2}^{n} a_i x_i - z_0))P + \sum_{i=1}^{\ell} \beta^{(i)}T_h^{(i)} + (t_{q_s+1} - c^*(a_1^* - z_{q_s+1}))Y_{q_s+1}$$
$$(17)$$

$$= \beta^{(0)}P + \sum_{i=1}^{\ell} \beta^{(i)}T_h^{(i)} + vY_{q_s+1} \qquad (18)$$

We obtain from Eq. (16) to Eq. (17) by using the fact that $\sum_{j=1}^{q_s} c^* z_j Y_j = c^*(X^* - z_{q_s+1}Y_{q_s+1} - z_0 P) = c^*((\sum_{i=2}^{n} a_i^* x_i)P + a_1^* Y_{q_s+1} - z_{q_s+1}Y_{q_s+1} - z_0 P)$. Since the forgery is a valid signature, $c^* = H(msg^*, X^*, T^*)$. c^* satisfies the following because $\text{RANK}(\mathbf{M}') = \ell$ that

$$z_{q_s+1}c^* + t_{q_s+1} = \sum_{i=1}^{\ell} \beta^{(i)}a_1^{(i)}c^{(i)}.$$

These imply that

$$\bar{H}(msg^*, X^*, T^*) = \sum_{i=1}^{\ell} \beta^{(i)}\bar{H}'(SID^{(i)}, T_h^{(i)})$$

Therefore, if the rank of $\mathbf{M}'$ is ℓ, it means that $\mathcal{A}$ generates the forgery by solving 2-entwined sum problem with the solution $\beta = (\beta^{(0)}, \beta^{(1)}, \dots, \beta^{(\ell)})$, $\mathcal{T}_{\text{out}} = (SID^{(1)}, SID^{(2)}, \dots, SID^{(\ell)})$, $\omega = (msg^*, X^*)$ and v. We remark that the adversary knows the solution β because $\beta^{(0)} = t_0 - c^*(\sum_{i=2}^{n} a_i x_i - z_0)$ and for $i \in [1, \ell]$, $\beta^{(i)} = \frac{t_{11}^{(i)} + z_{11}^{(i)}}{\alpha_{11}^{(i)}} = \frac{t_{12}^{(i)} + z_{12}^{(i)}}{\alpha_{12}^{(i)}}$ (See Eq. (14)), $v = t_{q_s+1} - c^*(a_1^* - z_{q_s+1})$ which are generated by the parameters selected by the adversary.

Since the probability of having 2-entwined sum problem solution is ϵ_{eSum}, the probability that the rank of $\mathbf{M}'$ is ℓ is ϵ_{eSum}. Therefore, $\Pr[\mathbf{Game\ 8} = 1] \geq \Pr[\mathbf{Game\ 7} = 1] - \epsilon_{eSum}$.

In Game 9, $\mathcal{R}$ obtains the OMDL solution by solving a linear system of equations. If $\ell < q_s$, $\mathcal{R}$ can make $q_s - \ell$ more DL-query. So, it queries $Y_{\ell+1}, Y_{\ell+2}, \dots, Y_{q_s}$ to the DL-oracle and obtain $y_{\ell+1}, y_{\ell+2}, \dots, y_{q_s}$. Now, it needs to learn the DL of $Y_1, Y_2, \dots, Y_\ell, Y_{q_s+1}$.

Given that $s^* = t^* + c^*(a_1 y_{q_s+1} + \sum_{i=2}^{n} a_i x_i) = t_0 + \sum_{j=1}^{q_s+1} t_j y_j + c^*(z_0 + \sum_{j=1}^{q_s+1} z_j y_j) = t_0 + c^* z_0 + \sum_{j=1}^{q_s+1}(t_j + c^* z_j)y_j$, $\mathcal{R}$ obtains a linear equation with

$\ell + 1$ unknowns $y_1, y_2, \ldots, y_\ell, y_{q_s+1}$ i.e., $\bar{s} = s^* - t_0 - c^* z_0 - \sum_{j=\ell+1,\text{if } \ell<q_s}^{q_s}(t_j + z_j)y_j = \sum_{j=1}^{\ell}(t_j + c^* z_j)y_j + (t_{q_s+1} + c^* z_{q_s+1})y_{q_s+1}$ Similarly, given that for $u \in [1, \ell]$, $s_1^{(u)} = \sum_{i=1}^{q_s} y_i(\alpha_{11}^{(u)}\eta_{1i}^{(u)} + \alpha_{12}^{(u)}\eta_{2i}^{(u)}) + c^{(u)}a_1^{(u)}y_{q_s+1}$ $\mathcal{R}$ also obtains ℓ-more linear equations such that $\bar{s}_1^{(u)} = s_1^{(u)} - \sum_{j=\ell+1,\text{if } \ell<q_s}^{q_s}(\alpha_{11}^{(u)}\eta_{1j}^{(u)} + \alpha_{12}^{(u)}\eta_{2j}^{(u)})y_j = \sum_{j=1}^{\ell}(\alpha_{11}^{(u)}\eta_{1j}^{(u)} + \alpha_{12}^{(u)}\eta_{2j}^{(u)})y_j + c^{(u)}a_1^{(u)}y_{q_s+1}$.

In the end, $\mathcal{R}$ obtains a unique solution $y_1, y_2, \ldots, y_\ell, y_{q_s+1}$ by solving the following linear equation system $\mathsf{M}'\boldsymbol{y} = \bar{\boldsymbol{s}}$ where $\boldsymbol{y} = (y_1, y_2, \ldots, y_\ell, y_{q_s+1})$ and $\bar{\boldsymbol{s}} = (\bar{s}_1^{(1)}, \bar{s}_1^{(2)}, \ldots, \bar{s}_1^{(\ell)}, \bar{s})$

We remark that matrix of the linear system of equations is M' without columns $\ell+1, \ell+2, \ldots, q_s$. Therefore, its rank is $\ell+1$ which is the reason of the unique solution. Hence, $\Pr[\mathbf{Game\ 9} = 1] = \Pr[\mathbf{Game\ 8} = 1] = \epsilon_{omdl}$.

$\square$

6   Conclusion

In this paper, we introduce our new Schnorr-based two-round multi-signature scheme DWMS. Our protocol is one of the few provably secure protocols among the existing secure Schnorr-based two-round multi-signature schemes [11,20,21]. Drawing upon the lessons learned from the k-sum attack [11], we proved the security of our scheme with special care. We introduced the m-entwined sum problem that simplifies the security proof of DWMS. We showed that the m-entwined sum problem is hard in the AGM as long as the DLOG problem is hard. We believe that the m-entwined sum problem shows a way to improve and simplify the security proofs which require excluding a specific relationship between the group and the field in the ROM. As future work, it would be interesting to show the hardness of the m-entwined sum problem in the standard model.

Acknowledgement. We thank Raghav Bhaskar and Alistair Stewart for their extensive advise and extremely insightful conversations throughout the effort. We warmly thank Michele Orrù for his helpful conversations, especially around understanding the algebraic group models.

A   Rank of a Random Matrix

Assume that we have a random matrix M of size $(\ell \times \ell')$. Given that $\ell \leq \ell'$, the rank of M can be at most ℓ.

Let's define another event E_i where the first i row vectors of M are linearly independent. In this case, $\Pr[E_1] = 1 - \frac{1}{p^\ell}$ which is the probability that a random vector equals to $\mathbf{0}$ (vector consisting of 0). In this case,

$$\Pr[E_\ell] = \Pr[E_\ell | E_{\ell-1}] \Pr[E_{\ell-1}] + \underbrace{\Pr[E_\ell | \neg E_{\ell-1}] \Pr[\neg E_{\ell-1}]}_{0}$$

$$= \Pr[E_1] \prod_{k=2}^{\ell} \underbrace{\Pr[E_k | E_{k-1}]}_{(1 - \frac{p^{k-1}}{p^\ell})}$$

$$= \prod_{k=1}^{\ell}(1 - \frac{p^{k-1}}{p^\ell}) \le \prod_{k=1}^{\ell}(1 - \frac{p^{k-1}}{p^\ell}) \le (1 - \frac{1}{p})^\ell \le 1 - \frac{\ell}{p}$$

So, the probability of M's rank is less than ℓ is at most $\frac{\ell}{p}$.

References

1. Schnorrkel library, January 2020. https://github.com/w3f/schnorrkel/commit/fa6c35f832

2. Bagherzandi, A., Cheon, J.-H., Jarecki, S.: Multisignatures secure under the discrete logarithm assumption and a generalized forking lemma. In: Proceedings of the 15th ACM Conference on Computer and Communications Security, pp. 449–458 (2008)

3. Bagherzandi, A., Jarecki, S.: Multisignatures using proofs of secret key possession, as secure as the Diffie-Hellman problem. In: Ostrovsky, R., De Prisco, R., Visconti, I. (eds.) SCN 2008. LNCS, vol. 5229, pp. 218–235. Springer, Heidelberg (2008). https://doi.org/10.1007/978-3-540-85855-3_15

4. Bellare, M., Dai, W.: The multi-base discrete logarithm problem: Concrete security improvements for Schnorr identification, signatures and multi-signatures. IACR Cryptology ePrint Archive 2020:416 (2020)

5. Bellare, N., Pointcheval, S.: The one-more-RSA-inversion problems and the security of Chaum's blind signature scheme. J. Cryptol. **16**(3), 185–215 (2003). https://doi.org/10.1007/s00145-002-0120-1

6. Bellare, M., Neven, G.: Multi-signatures in the plain public-key model and a general forking lemma. In: Proceedings of the 13th ACM Conference on Computer and Communications Security, pp. 390–399 (2006)

7. Bellare, M., Palacio, A.: GQ and Schnorr identification schemes: proofs of security against impersonation under active and concurrent attacks. In: Yung, M. (ed.) CRYPTO 2002. LNCS, vol. 2442, pp. 162–177. Springer, Heidelberg (2002). https://doi.org/10.1007/3-540-45708-9_11

8. Benhamouda, F., Lepoint, T., Orrù, M., Raykova, M.: On the (in)security of ROS. Cryptology ePrint Archive, Report 2020/945 (2020). https://eprint.iacr.org/2020/945

9. Boldyreva, A.: Threshold signatures, multisignatures and blind signatures based on the gap-Diffie-Hellman-group signature scheme. In: Desmedt, Y.G. (ed.) PKC 2003. LNCS, vol. 2567, pp. 31–46. Springer, Heidelberg (2003). https://doi.org/10.1007/3-540-36288-6_3

10. Boneh, D., Drijvers, M., Neven, G.: Compact multi-signatures for smaller blockchains. In: Peyrin, T., Galbraith, S. (eds.) ASIACRYPT 2018. LNCS, vol. 11273, pp. 435–464. Springer, Cham (2018). https://doi.org/10.1007/978-3-030-03329-3_15

11. Drijvers, M., et al.: On the security of two-round multi-signatures. In: 2019 IEEE Symposium on Security and Privacy (SP), pp. 1084–1101. IEEE (2019)
12. Fuchsbauer, G., Kiltz, E., Loss, J.: The algebraic group model and its applications. In: Shacham, H., Boldyreva, A. (eds.) CRYPTO 2018. LNCS, vol. 10992, pp. 33–62. Springer, Cham (2018). https://doi.org/10.1007/978-3-319-96881-0_2
13. Fuchsbauer, G., Plouviez, A., Seurin, Y.: Blind Schnorr signatures in the algebraic group model. Cryptology ePrint Archive, Report 2019/877 (2019). https://eprint.iacr.org/2019/877
14. Fuchsbauer, G., Plouviez, A., Seurin, Y.: Blind Schnorr signatures and signed ElGamal encryption in the algebraic group model. In: Canteaut, A., Ishai, Y. (eds.) EUROCRYPT 2020. LNCS, vol. 12106, pp. 63–95. Springer, Cham (2020). https://doi.org/10.1007/978-3-030-45724-2_3
15. Itakura, K., Nakamura, K.: A public-key cryptosystem suitable for digital multisignatures. NEC Res. Dev. **71**, 1–8 (1983)
16. Komlo, C., Goldberg, I.: FROST: flexible round-optimized Schnorr threshold signatures (2020)
17. Lu, S., Ostrovsky, R., Sahai, A., Shacham, H., Waters, B.: Sequential aggregate signatures and multisignatures without random oracles. In: Vaudenay, S. (ed.) EUROCRYPT 2006. LNCS, vol. 4004, pp. 465–485. Springer, Heidelberg (2006). https://doi.org/10.1007/11761679_28
18. Ma, C., Weng, J., Li, Y., Deng, R.: Efficient discrete logarithm based multisignature scheme in the plain public key model. Des. Codes Crypt. **54**(2), 121–133 (2010). https://doi.org/10.1007/s10623-009-9313-z
19. Maxwell, G., Poelstra, A., Seurin, Y., Wuille, P.: Simple Schnorr multi-signatures with applications to bitcoin. Des. Codes Crypt. **87**(9), 2139–2164 (2019). https://doi.org/10.1007/s10623-019-00608-x
20. Nick, J., Ruffing, T., Seurin, Y.: MuSig2: simple two-round Schnorr multi-signatures. Cryptology ePrint Archive, Report 2020/1261 (2020). https://eprint.iacr.org/2020/1261
21. Nick, J., Ruffing, T., Seurin, Y., Wuille, P.: MuSig-DN: Schnorr multi-signatures with verifiably deterministic nonces. Cryptology ePrint Archive, Report 2020/1057 (2020). https://eprint.iacr.org/2020/1057
22. Ohta, K., Okamoto, T.: A digital multisignature scheme based on the Fiat-Shamir scheme. In: Imai, H., Rivest, R.L., Matsumoto, T. (eds.) ASIACRYPT 1991. LNCS, vol. 739, pp. 139–148. Springer, Heidelberg (1993). https://doi.org/10.1007/3-540-57332-1_11
23. Pointcheval, D., Stern, J.: Security arguments for digital signatures and blind linsignatures. J. Cryptol. **13**, 361–396 (2000)
24. Ristenpart, T., Yilek, S.: The power of proofs-of-possession: securing multiparty signatures against rogue-key attacks. In: Naor, M. (ed.) EUROCRYPT 2007. LNCS, vol. 4515, pp. 228–245. Springer, Heidelberg (2007). https://doi.org/10.1007/978-3-540-72540-4_13
25. Schnorr, C.P.: Security of blind discrete log signatures against interactive attacks. In: Qing, S., Okamoto, T., Zhou, J. (eds.) ICICS 2001. LNCS, vol. 2229, pp. 1–12. Springer, Heidelberg (2001). https://doi.org/10.1007/3-540-45600-7_1
26. Syta, E., et al.: Keeping authorities "honest or bust" with decentralized witness cosigning. In: 2016 IEEE Symposium on Security and Privacy (SP), pp. 526–545. IEEE (2016)
27. Wagner, D.: A generalized birthday problem. In: Yung, M. (ed.) CRYPTO 2002. LNCS, vol. 2442, pp. 288–304. Springer, Heidelberg (2002). https://doi.org/10.1007/3-540-45708-9_19

MuSig2: Simple Two-Round Schnorr Multi-signatures

Jonas Nick[1]([✉]), Tim Ruffing[1], and Yannick Seurin[2]

[1] Blockstream, Victoria, Canada
[2] ANSSI, Paris, France

Abstract. Multi-signatures enable a group of signers to produce a joint signature on a joint message. Recently, Drijvers *et al.* (S&P'19) showed that all thus far proposed two-round multi-signature schemes in the pure DL setting (without pairings) are insecure under concurrent signing sessions. While Drijvers *et al.* proposed a secure two-round scheme, this efficiency in terms of rounds comes with the price of having signatures that are more than twice as large as Schnorr signatures, which are becoming popular in cryptographic systems due to their practicality (e.g., they will likely be adopted in Bitcoin). If one needs a multi-signature scheme that can be used as a drop-in replacement for Schnorr signatures, then one is forced to resort either to a three-round scheme or to sequential signing sessions, both of which are undesirable options in practice.

In this work, we propose MuSig2, a simple and highly practical two-round multi-signature scheme. This is the first scheme that simultaneously *i)* is secure under concurrent signing sessions, *ii)* supports key aggregation, *iii)* outputs ordinary Schnorr signatures, *iv)* needs only two communication rounds, and *v)* has similar signer complexity as ordinary Schnorr signatures. Furthermore, it is the first multi-signature scheme in the pure DL setting that supports preprocessing of all but one rounds, effectively enabling a non-interactive signing process without forgoing security under concurrent sessions. We prove the security of MuSig2 in the random oracle model, and the security of a more efficient variant in the combination of the random oracle and the algebraic group model. Both our proofs rely on a weaker variant of the OMDL assumption.

1 Introduction

Multi-signature schemes [17] enable a group of signers (each possessing an own secret/public key pair) to run an interactive protocol to produce a single signature σ on a message m. A recent spark of interest in multi-signatures is motivated by the idea of using them as a drop-in replacement for ordinary (single-signer) signatures in applications such as cryptocurrencies that support signatures already. For example the Bitcoin community, awaiting the adoption of Schnorr signatures [32] as proposed in BIP 340 [38], is seeking for practical multi-signature schemes which are *fully compatible* with Schnorr signatures: multi-signatures produced by a group of signers should just be ordinary Schnorr signatures and

© International Association for Cryptologic Research 2021
T. Malkin and C. Peikert (Eds.): CRYPTO 2021, LNCS 12825, pp. 189–221, 2021.
https://doi.org/10.1007/978-3-030-84242-0_8

should be verifiable like Schnorr signatures, i.e., they can be verified using the ordinary Schnorr verification algorithm given only a single *aggregate public key* that can be computed from the set of public keys of the signers and serves as a compact representation of it.

This provides a number of benefits that reach beyond simple compatibility with an upcoming system: Most importantly, multi-signatures enjoy the efficiency of Schnorr signatures, which are very compact and cheap to store on the blockchain. Moreover, if multi-signatures can be verified like ordinary Schnorr signatures, the additional complexity introduced by multi-signatures remains on the side of the signers and is not exposed to verifiers who need not be concerned with multi-signatures at all and can simply run Schnorr signature verification. Verifiers, who are just given the signature and the aggregate public key, in fact do not even learn whether the signature was created by a single signer or by a group of signers (or equivalently, whether the public key is an aggregation of multiple keys), which is advantageous for the privacy of users.

Multi-signatures Based on Schnorr Signatures. A number of modern and practical proposals [2,4,11,20,22,28,29,36] for multi-signature schemes are based on Schnorr signatures. The Schnorr signature scheme [32] relies on a cyclic group $\mathbb{G}$ of prime order p, a generator g of $\mathbb{G}$, and a hash function H. A secret/public key pair is a pair $(x, X) \in \{0, \ldots, p-1\} \times \mathbb{G}$ where $X = g^x$. To sign a message m, the signer draws a random integer r in $\mathbb{Z}_p$, computes a nonce $R = g^r$, the challenge $c = H(X, R, m)$, and $s = r + cx$. The signature is the pair (R, s), and its validity can be checked by verifying whether $g^s = RX^c$.

The naive way to design a multi-signature scheme fully compatible with Schnorr signatures would be as follows. Say a group of n signers want to sign a message m, and let $L = \{X_1 = g^{x_1}, \ldots, X_n = g^{x_n}\}$ be the multiset[1] of all their public keys. Each signer randomly generates and communicates to others a nonce $R_i = g^{r_i}$; then, each of them computes $R = \prod_{i=1}^{n} R_i$, $c = H(\widetilde{X}, R, m)$ where $\widetilde{X} = \prod_{i=1}^{n} X_i$ is the product of individual public keys, and a partial signature $s_i = r_i + cx_i$; partial signatures are then combined into a single signature (R, s) where $s = \sum_{i=1}^{n} s_i \bmod p$. The validity of a signature (R, s) on message m for public keys $\{X_1, \ldots, X_n\}$ is equivalent to $g^s = R\widetilde{X}^c$ where $\widetilde{X} = \prod_{i=1}^{n} X_i$ and $c = H(\widetilde{X}, R, m)$. Note that this is exactly the verification equation for an ordinary key-prefixed Schnorr signature with respect to the aggregate public key $\widetilde{X}$. However, as already pointed out many times [16,19,23,24], this simplistic protocol is vulnerable to a rogue-key attack where a corrupted signer sets its public key to $X_1 = g^{x_1}(\prod_{i=2}^{n} X_i)^{-1}$, allowing him to produce signatures for public keys $\{X_1, \ldots, X_n\}$ by himself.

One way to generically prevent rogue-key attacks is to require that users prove possession of the secret key, e.g., by attaching a zero-knowledge proof of knowledge to their public keys [9,31]. However, this makes key management cumbersome, complicates implementations, and is not compatible with existing and widely used key serialization formats.

---

[1] Since we do not impose any constraint on the key setup, the adversary can choose corrupted public keys arbitrarily and duplicate public keys can appear in L.

The MuSig Scheme. A more direct defense against rogue-key attacks proposed by Bellare and Neven [4] is to work in the *plain public-key model*, where public keys can be aggregated without the need to check their validity. To date, the only multi-signature scheme provably secure in this model and fully compatible with Schnorr signatures is MuSig (and the variant MuSig-DN [28]) by Maxwell *et al.* [22], independently proven secure by Boneh, Drijvers, and Neven [9].

In order to overcome rogue-key attacks in the plain public-key model, MuSig computes partial signatures s_i with respect to "signer-dependent" challenges $c_i = \mathsf{H}_{\mathrm{agg}}(L, X_i) \cdot \mathsf{H}_{\mathrm{sig}}(\widetilde{X}, R, m)$, where $\widetilde{X}$ is the *aggregate public key* corresponding to the multiset of public keys $L = \{X_1, \ldots, X_n\}$. It is defined as $\widetilde{X} = \prod_{i=1}^{n} X_i^{a_i}$ where $a_i = \mathsf{H}_{\mathrm{agg}}(L, X_i)$ (note that the a_i's only depend on the public keys of the signers). This way, the verification equation of a signature (R, s) on message m for public keys $L = \{X_1, \ldots, X_n\}$ becomes $g^s = R \prod_{i=1}^{n} X_i^{a_i c} = R\widetilde{X}^c$, where $c = \mathsf{H}_{\mathrm{sig}}(\widetilde{X}, R, m)$. This recovers the key aggregation property enjoyed by the naive scheme, albeit with respect to a more complex aggregate key $\widetilde{X} = \prod_{i=1}^{n} X_i^{a_i}$.

In order to be able to simulate an honest signer in a run of the signing protocol via the standard way of programming the random oracle $\mathsf{H}_{\mathrm{sig}}$, MuSig has an initial commitment round (like the scheme by Bellare and Neven [4]) where each signer commits to its share R_i before receiving the shares of other signers.

As a result, the signing protocol of MuSig requires three communication rounds, and only the initial commitment round can be preprocessed without knowing the message to be signed [26].

Two-Round Schemes. Following the scheme by Bellare and Neven [4], in which signing requires three rounds of interaction, multiple attempts to reduce this number to two rounds [2,4,22,36] were foiled by Drijvers *et al.*. [11]. In their pivotal work, they show that all thus far proposed two-round schemes in the pure DL setting (without pairings) cannot be proven secure and are vulnerable to attacks with subexponential complexity when the adversary is allowed to engage in an arbitrary number of concurrent sessions (*concurrent security*), as required by the standard definition of unforgeability.

If one prefers a scheme in the pure DL setting with fewer communication rounds, only two options remain, and none of them is fully satisfactory. The first option is the mBCJ scheme by Drijvers *et al.* [11], a repaired variant of the scheme by Bagherzandi, Cheon, and Jarecki [2]. While mBCJ needs only two rounds, it does not output ordinary Schnorr signatures and is thus not suitable as a drop-in replacement for Schnorr signatures, e.g., in cryptocurrencies whose validation rules support Schnorr signatures (such as proposed for Bitcoin). The second option is MuSig-DN (MuSig with Deterministic Nonces) [28], which however relies on heavy zero-knowledge proofs to prove a deterministic derivation of the nonce to all cosigners. This increases the complexity of the implementation significantly and makes MuSig-DN, even though it needs only two rounds, in fact less efficient than three-round MuSig in common settings. Moreover, in neither of these two-round schemes is it possible to reduce the rounds further by preprocessing the first round without knowledge of the message to be signed.

1.1   Our Contribution

We propose a novel and simple two-round variant of the MuSig scheme that we call MuSig2. In particular, we remove the preliminary commitment phase, so that signers start right away by sending nonces. However, to obtain a scheme secure under concurrent sessions, each signer i sends a list of $\nu \geq 2$ nonces $R_{i,1}, \ldots, R_{i,\nu}$ (instead of a single nonce R_i), and effectively uses a linear combination $\hat{R}_i = \prod_{j=1}^{\nu} R_{i,j}^{b^{j-1}}$ of these ν nonces, where b is derived via a hash function.

MuSig2 is the first multi-signature scheme that simultaneously $i)$ is secure under concurrent signing sessions, $ii)$ supports key aggregation, $iii)$ outputs ordinary Schnorr signatures, $iv)$ needs only two communication rounds, and $v)$ has similar signer complexity as ordinary Schnorr signatures. Furthermore, it is the first scheme in the pure DL setting that supports preprocessing of all but one rounds, effectively enabling non-interactive signing without forgoing security under concurrent sessions. MuSig-DN [28], which relies on rather complex and expensive zero-knowledge proofs (proving time ≈ 1 s), only enjoys the first four properties and does not allow preprocessing of the first round without knowledge of the message.

In comparison to other multi-signature schemes based on Schnorr signatures, the price we pay for saving a round is a stronger cryptographic assumption: instead of the DL assumption, we rely on the *algebraic one-more discrete logarithm* (AOMDL) assumption, a weaker and falsifiable variant of the one-more discrete logarithm (OMDL) assumption [3,5], which states that it is hard to find the discrete logarithm of $q + 1$ group elements by making at most q queries to an oracle solving the DL problem.

We give two independent security proofs which reduce the security of MuSig2 to the AOMDL assumption. Our first proof relies on the random oracle model (ROM), and applies to MuSig2 with $\nu = 4$ nonces. Our second proof additionally assumes the algebraic group model (AGM) [12], and for this ROM+AGM proof, $\nu = 2$ nonces are sufficient.

Assuming a group element is as large as a collision-resistant hash of a group element, the overhead for every MuSig2 signer as compared to normal three-round MuSig is broadcasting $\nu - 2$ group elements as well as $\nu - 1$ exponentiations plus one multi-exponentiation of size $\nu - 1$. As a result, for the optimal choice of $\nu = 2$, the computational overhead of a signing session of MuSig2 is just two exponentiations as compared to the state-of-the-art scheme MuSig. This makes MuSig2 highly practical.

A further optimized variant of MuSig2, which we call MuSig2* and discuss in the full version [27], reduces the size of the multi-exponentiation in the key aggregation algorithm from n to $n - 1$.

1.2   Concurrent Work

Concurrently to our work, two other works rely on a similar idea of using a linear combination of multiple nonces in order to remove a communication round while achieving security under concurrent sessions.

FROST. Komlo and Goldberg [18] use this idea for their FROST scheme in the context of the more general setting of threshold signatures: in a "t-of-n" threshold signature scheme, any subset of size t of some set of n signers can create a signature. By setting $t = n$ (as supported in FROST), it is possible to obtain a multi-signature scheme as a special case. In comparison, the scope of our work is restricted to only "n-of-n" multi-signatures, which enables us to optimize for this case and achieve properties which, in the pure DL setting, are unique to multi-signatures, namely non-interactive key generation as well as non-interactive public key aggregation, two features not offered by FROST.

A major difference between our work and their work is the cryptographic model. The FROST security proof relies on a non-standard heuristic which models the hash function (a public primitive) used for deriving the coefficients for the linear combination as a one-time VRF (a primitive with a secret key) in the security proof. This treatment requires an additional communication round in FROST preprocessing stage and to disallow concurrent sessions in this stage, resulting in a modified scheme FROST-Interactive. As a consequence, the FROST-Interactive scheme that is proven secure is in fact a three-round scheme and as such differs significantly from the two-round FROST scheme that is recommended for deployment. Komlo and Goldberg [18] show that the security of FROST-Interactive is implied by the DL assumption. In contrast, our MuSig2 proofs use the well-established ROM (or alternatively, AGM+ROM) to model the hash function as a random oracle and rely on a falsifiable and weaker variant of the OMDL assumption.

DWMS. Again concurrently, Alper and Burdges [1] use the idea of a linear combination of multiple nonces to obtain a two-round multi-signature scheme DWMS, which resembles MuSig2 closely but lacks several optimizations present in MuSig2. Concretely, DWMS does not aggregate the first-round messages of all signers, an optimization which saves bandwidth and ensures that each signer needs to perform only a constant number of exponentiations. Moreover, DWMS does not make use of the optimizations of setting the coefficient of one nonce to the constant 1, which saves one more exponentiation per signer when aggregating nonces, as well as setting the coefficient of one public key to the constant 1, which saves one exponentiation when aggregating keys (see the variant MuSig2* of our scheme in the full version [27]).

In terms of provable security, Alper and Burdges [1] provide a proof only in the combination of ROM+AGM, whereas we additionally provide a proof that does not rely on the AGM.

2   Technical Overview

2.1   The Challenge of Constructing Two-Round Schemes

Already an obsolete preliminary version [21] of the MuSig paper [22] proposed a two-round variant of MuSig in which the initial commitment round is omitted. We call this scheme InsecureMuSig in the following. Maxwell *et al.* [21] claimed concurrent security under the OMDL assumption but their proof turned out be flawed: it fails to cover a subtle problem in the simulation of the signing oracle, which in fact had been described (and correctly sidestepped by restricting concurrency) already 15 years earlier in a work on two-party Schnorr signatures by Nicolosi *et al.* [29].

Drijvers *et al.* [11] rediscovered the flaw in the security proof of InsecureMuSig and show that similar flaws appear also in the proofs of the other two-round DL-based multi-signature schemes by Bagherzandi *et al.* [2] and Ma *et al.* [20].[2] Moreover, they show through a meta-reduction that the concurrent security of these schemes cannot be reduced to the DL or OMDL problem using an algebraic black-box reduction (assuming the OMDL problem is hard).[3] In addition to the meta-reduction, Drijvers *et al.* [11] also gave a concrete attack of subexponential complexity based on Wagner's algorithm [37] for solving the Generalized Birthday Problem [37], which has led to similar attacks on Schnorr blind signatures [33]. Their attack breaks InsecureMuSig and the other aforementioned multi-signature schemes and inherently exploits the ability to run multiple sessions concurrently. Recently, Benhamouda *et al.* [7] gave a novel, simple, and very efficient attack of polynomial complexity, which confirms and extends these negative results.

A Concrete Attack. We outline the attack by Drijvers *et al.* [11] in order to provide an intuition for how we can overcome their negative results. The attack relies on Wagner's algorithm for solving the Generalized Birthday Problem [37], which can be defined as follows for the purpose of this paper: Given a constant value $t \in \mathbb{Z}_p$, an integer $k_{\max}$, and access to random oracle H mapping onto $\mathbb{Z}_p$, find a set $\{q_1, \ldots, q_{k_{\max}}\}$ of $k_{\max}$ queries such that $\sum_{k=1}^{k_{\max}} H(q_k) = t$. While for $k_{\max} \leq 2$, the complexity of this problem is the same as finding a preimage ($k_{\max} = 1$) or a collision ($k_{\max} = 2$) in the random oracle, the problem becomes, maybe surprisingly, easy for large $k_{\max}$. In particular, Wagner [37] gives a subexponential algorithm assuming that $k_{\max}$ is not bounded.

The attack proceeds as follows. The adversary opens $k_{\max}$ concurrent signing sessions, in which it plays the role of the signer with public key $X_2 = g^{x_2}$, and receives $k_{\max}$ nonces $R_1^{(1)}, \ldots, R_1^{(k_{\max})}$ from the honest signer with public key $X_1 = g^{x_1}$. Let $\widetilde{X} = X_1^{a_1} X_2^{a_2}$ be the corresponding aggregate public key. Given a forgery target message m^*, the adversary computes $R^* = \prod_{k=1}^{k_{\max}} R_1^{(k)}$ and uses Wagner's algorithm to find nonces $R_2^{(k)}$ to reply with such that

$$\sum_{k=1}^{k_{\max}} \underbrace{\mathsf{H}_{\mathrm{sig}}(\widetilde{X}, R_1^{(k)} R_2^{(k)}, m^{(k)})}_{=:\, c^{(k)}} = \underbrace{\mathsf{H}_{\mathrm{sig}}(\widetilde{X}, R^*, m^*)}_{=:\, c^*}. \tag{1}$$

---

[2] Remarkably, both Maxwell *et al.* [21] and Drijvers *et al.* [11] were apparently unaware of the much earlier work by Nicolosi *et al.* [29].

[3] We refer the interested reader to the full version [27] for a high-level explanation of why the meta-reduction cannot be adapted to work with our scheme.

Having received $R_2^{(k)}$, the honest signer will reply with partial signatures $s_1^{(k)} = r_1^{(k)} + c^{(k)} \cdot a_1 x_1$. Let $r^* = \sum_{k=1}^{k_{\max}} r_1^{(k)} = \log_g(R^*)$. The adversary is able to obtain

$$s_1^* = \sum_{k=1}^{k_{\max}} s_1^{(k)} = \sum_{k=1}^{k_{\max}} r_1^{(k)} + \left(\sum_{k=1}^{k_{\max}} c^{(k)} \right) \cdot a_1 x_1 = r^* + c^* \cdot a_1 x_1,$$

where the last equality follows from Eq. (1). The adversary can further complete s_1^* to the full value

$$s^* = s_1^* + c^* \cdot a_2 x_2 = r^* + c^* \cdot (a_1 x_1 + a_2 x_2).$$

In other words, (R^*, s^*) is a valid forgery on message m^* with signature hash $c^* = \mathsf{H}_{\mathsf{sig}}(\widetilde{X}, R^*, m^*)$. In this example, the forgery is valid for the aggregate public key $\widetilde{X}$, which is the result of aggregating public keys X_1 and X_2. It is however straightforward to adapt the attack to produce a forgery under a different aggregate public key as long as it is the result of aggregating the honest signer's public key X_1 with any multiset of adversarial public keys.

The complexity of this attack is dominated by the complexity of Wagner's algorithm, which is $O(k_{\max} \, 2^{\log_2(p)/(1+\lfloor(\log_2(k_{\max}))\rfloor)})$. While this is superpolynomial, the attack is practical for common parameters and moderately large numbers $k_{\max}$ of sessions. For example, for a group size of $p \approx 2^{256}$ as common for elliptic curves, a value of $k_{\max} = 128$ brings the complexity of the attack down to approximately 2^{39} operations, which is practical even on off-the-shelf hardware. If the attacker is able to open more sessions concurrently, the improved polynomial-time attack by Benhamouda et al. [7] assumes $k_{\max} > \log_2 p$ sessions, but then has complexity $O(k_{\max} \log_2 p)$ and a negligible running time in practice.

2.2 Our Solution

The attack by Drijvers et al. (and similarly the attack by Benhamouda et al.) relies on the ability to control the signature hash by controlling the aggregate nonce $R_1^{(k)} R_2^{(k)}$ (on the LHS of Eq. (1)) in the first round of each of the concurrent signing sessions. Since all signers must know the aggregate nonce at the end of the first round, it seems hard to prevent the adversary from being able to control the aggregate nonce on the LHS without adding a preliminary commitment round. Our high-level idea to solve this problem and to foil the attacks is to accept that the adversary can control the LHS of the equation but prevent it from controlling the RHS instead.

The main novelty in our work is to let every signer i send a list of $\nu \geq 2$ nonces $R_{i,1}, \ldots, R_{i,\nu}$ and let it effectively use a random linear combination $\hat{R}_i = \prod_{j=1}^{\nu} R_{i,j}^{b^{j-1}}$ of those nonces in lieu of the former single nonce R_i. The scalar b is derived via a hash function $\mathsf{H}_{\mathsf{non}}$ (modeled as a random oracle) applied the nonces of all signers, i.e., $b = \mathsf{H}_{\mathsf{non}}(\widetilde{X}, (\prod_{i=1}^{n} R_{i,1}, \ldots, \prod_{i=1}^{n} R_{i,\nu}), m)$.

As a result, whenever the adversary tries different values for R_2, the coefficient b changes, and so does the honest signer's effective nonce $\hat{R}_1 = \prod_{j=1}^{\nu} R_{1,j}^{b^{j-1}}$.

This ensures that the sum of the honest signer's effective nonces taken over all open sessions, i.e., value $R^* = \prod_{k=1}^{k_{\max}} \hat{R}_1^{(k)}$ in the RHS of Eq. (1), is no longer a constant value. Without a constant RHS, the adversary lacks an essential prerequisite in the definition of the Generalized Birthday Problem and Wagner's algorithm is not applicable.

With this idea in mind, it is tempting to fall back to only a single nonce ($\nu = 1$) but instead rely just on the coefficient b such that $\hat{R}_1 = R_1^b$. However, then the adversary can effectively eliminate b by redefining $R^* = \prod_{k=1}^{k_{\max}} R_1^{(k)}$ (which is independent of all $b^{(k)}$) and considering the equation

$$\sum_{k=1}^{k_{\max}} \frac{\mathsf{H}_{\mathrm{sig}}(\widetilde{X}, (R_1^{(k)} R_2^{(k)})^{b^{(k)}}, m^{(k)})}{b^{(k)}} = \mathsf{H}_{\mathrm{sig}}(\widetilde{X}, R^*, m^*)$$

instead of Eq. (1) in order to perform the attack.

2.3 Proving Security

Before we describe how to prove MuSig2 secure, we first take a step back to InsecureMuSig in order to understand the flaw in its purported security proof. Then, we explain how the usage of more than once nonce in MuSig2 enables us to fix that flaw.

The Difficulty of Simulating Signatures. Following the textbook security proof of Schnorr signatures, a natural but necessarily flawed approach to reduce the security of InsecureMuSig[4] to the DL problem in the ROM will be to let the reduction announce the challenge group element X_1 as the public key of the honest signer and fork the execution of the adversary in order to extract the discrete logarithm of X_1 from the two forgeries output by the adversary in its two executions (using the Forking Lemma [4,30]).

The insurmountable difficulty for the reduction in this approach is to simulate the honest signer in signing sessions without knowledge of the secret key of the honest signer. From the perspective of the reduction, simply omitting the preliminary commitment phase enables the adversary to know the combined nonce R before the reduction learns it, which prevents the reduction from simulating the signing oracle using the standard technique of programming the random oracle on the signature challenge $\mathsf{H}_{\mathrm{sig}}(\widetilde{X}, R, m)$. In more details, observe that in InsecureMuSig, an adversary (controlling public key X_2) can impose the value of $R = R_1 R_2$ used in signing sessions since it can choose R_2 after having received R_1 from the honest signer (with public key $X_1 = g^{x_1}$). This forbids the textbook way of simulating the honest signer in the ROM without knowing x_1 by randomly drawing s_1 and c, computing $R_1 = g^{s_1}(X_1)^{-a_1 c}$, and programming $\mathsf{H}_{\mathrm{sig}}(\widetilde{X}, R, m) = c$, since the adversary might have made the random oracle query $\mathsf{H}_{\mathrm{sig}}(\widetilde{X}, R, m)$ *before* making the corresponding signing query.

---

[4] Observe that InsecureMuSig is identical to an imaginary MuSig2 with a just a single nonce, i.e., $\nu = 1$.

The Flawed Security Proof of InsecureMuSig. The hope of Maxwell *et al.* [21] was to rely on the stronger OMDL assumption instead of the DL assumption in order to solve this problem without a commitment round. The DL oracle in the formulation of the OMDL problem enables the reduction to answer a signing query by obtaining the partial signature s_1 of the honest signer via a DL oracle query for the discrete logarithm of $R_1(X_1)^{a_1 c}$. The reduction does not generate the nonce R_1 of the honest signer randomly, but instead sets it to a DL challenge freshly drawn from the OMDL problem at the start of each signing session. As in the standard security proof of Schnorr signatures, the reduction forks the adversary and extracts the discrete logarithm x_1 of the first DL challenge X_1 from the forgeries that the adversary outputs in its different executions. This allows computing the discrete logarithm of each challenge R_1 from s_1 as $r_1 = s_1 - a_1 c x_1$.

With the adversary opening q_s signing sessions, if the reduction was not flawed, it would return the DL of $q_s + 1$ challenge elements (including the DL challenge X_1 used as public key of the honest signer) using only q_s DL oracle calls, i.e., the reduction would solve the OMDL problem.

This simulation technique however fails in a subtle way when combined with the Forking Lemma, since the adversary might be forked in the middle of a signing session, when it has received R_1 but has not returned R_2 to the reduction yet. This can be seen as follows. Assume that the adversary sends a different value R_2 and R_2' in the two executions after the fork, resulting in different signature hashes c and c' respectively. This implies that in order to correctly simulate the signing oracle in the forked execution, the reduction needs *two* queries to the DL oracle, both of which are related to the same single challenge R_1. Since the answer of the first DL oracle query will already be enough to compute the discrete logarithm of R_1 later on, the second query does not provide any additional useful information to the reduction (neither about the discrete logarithm of R_1 nor about the discrete logarithm of another DL challenge) and is thus wasted. As a result, the reduction forgoes any hope to solve the OMDL problem when making the second query.[5]

How Multiple Nonces in MuSig2 *Help the Reduction.* With MuSig2 however, the reduction can handle this situation. Now assume $\nu = 2$, i.e., the reduction will obtain two (instead of one) group elements $R_{1,1}, R_{1,2}$ as DL challenges from the OMDL challenger during the first round of each signing session. This will allow the reduction to make two DL queries per signing session, and thus be able to simulate signatures even if the adversary forces different signature hashes $c \neq c'$ in the two executions.

The natural question is how the reduction ensures that it is able to answer both DL challenges $R_{1,1}, R_{1,2}$ for each signing session. MuSig2 solves this by having signers effectively use the linear combination $\hat{R}_1 = R_{1,1} R_{1,2}^b$ as nonce where $b = \mathsf{H}_{\mathrm{non}}(\widetilde{X}, (\prod_{i=1}^{n} R_{i,1}, \prod_{i=1}^{n} R_{i,2}), m)$. As a result, the reduction is able to program the $\mathsf{H}_{\mathrm{non}}$ and $\mathsf{H}_{\mathrm{sig}}$ such that whenever the adversary gives a different

---

[5] This is exactly the issue which had been observed earlier by Nicolisi *et al.* [29], and which is exploited in the meta-reduction by Drijvers *et al.* [11].

response to a signing query in the second execution such that $c \neq c'$, then also b and b' differ between the two executions. Consequently, the two DL queries made by the reduction will be answered with some s_1 and s_1' that give rise to two linear independent equations $s_1 = r_{1,1} + br_{1,2} + a_1cx_1$ and $s_1' = r_{1,1} + b'r_{1,2} + a_1c'x_1$. After the reduction has extracted x_1 from the forgeries output by the adversary in the two executions, it can solve those equations for the unknowns $r_{1,1}$ and $r_{1,2}$, the discrete logarithms of the DL challenges $R_{1,1}$ and $R_{1,2}$.

Similarly, in the case that $c = c'$, the reduction ensures that $b = b'$ and therefore needs only one DL query to simulate the honest signer in both executions. Thus, it can use the free DL query to obtain a second linear independent equation.

Note that for this simulation technique, it is not important how the adversary controls the signature hashes c and c'. So far we only considered the case that the adversary influences c and c' by choosing its nonces depending on the honest signer's nonce. The reduction works equally for an adversary which controls the signature hash computed as $\mathsf{H}_{\mathrm{sig}}(\widetilde{X}, R, m)$ not by influencing R but instead by being able to choose the message m or the set of signers L (and thus the aggregate public key $\widetilde{X}$) only in the second round of the signing protocol, i.e., after having seen the honest signer's nonce. This explains why our scheme enables preprocessing and broadcasting the nonces (the first round) without having determined the message and the set of signers. This is in contrast to existing schemes, which are vulnerable to essentially the same attack as explained above if the adversary is given the ability to select the message or the set of signers after having seen the honest signer's nonce [26].

So far we discussed only how the reduction is able to handle two different executions of the adversary (due to a single fork). However, since our reduction needs to fork the adversary twice to support key aggregation, it needs to handle four possible executions of the adversary. As a consequence, it will need four DL queries as well as $\nu = 4$ nonces.

2.4 A More Efficient Solution in the Algebraic Group Model

In the algebraic group model (AGM) [12], the adversary is assumed to be algebraic, i.e., whenever it outputs a group element, it outputs a representation of this group element in the base formed by all group elements it has received so far. While the AGM is idealized, it is a strictly weaker model than the generic group model (GGM) [34], i.e., security proofs in the AGM carry over to the GGM but the AGM imposes fewer restrictions on the adversary. Security proofs in the AGM work via reductions to hard problems (similar to the standard model) because computational problems such as DL and OMDL are not information-theoretically hard in the AGM (as opposed to the GGM). In the AGM, Schnorr signatures (and related schemes such Schnorr blind signatures [10]) can be proven secure using a straight-line reduction without forking the execution of the adversary [13].

The main technical reason why our ROM proof works only for MuSig2 with as many as $\nu = 4$ nonces is that our reduction needs to handle four executions of the adversary due to two applications of the Forking Lemma. Since this fundamental reason for requiring $\nu = 4$ in the plain ROM simply disappears in the AGM, we are able to prove MuSig2 with $\nu = 2$ nonces secure in the combination ROM+AGM.

Due to space limitations, our results in the AGM+ROM can be found in the full version of the paper [27].

2.5 Algebraic OMDL: A Falsifiable Variant of OMDL

A cryptographic assumption is algorithmically *falsifiable* if it can be decided in p.p.t. whether a given algorithm breaks it.[6] While this is true for most standard assumptions such as the RSA assumption or the DL assumption, it is notably not true for the OMDL assumption, where the OMDL challenger needs to provide the adversary with a DL oracle that cannot be implemented in p.p.t. (unless the DL problem is easy, but then the OMDL assumption does not hold anyway).

While we believe that the OMDL has withstood the test of time, it is still desirable to avoid non-falsifiable assumptions whenever possible. We observe that the DL oracle can be in fact implemented in p.p.t. when the solving algorithm is required to be algebraic. In the context of OMDL, this translates to the requirement that whenever the adversary queries the discrete logarithm of a group element via the DL oracle, it outputs a representation of this group element in the basis formed by the generator and all DL challenges it has received thus far (which together constitute all group elements it has received thus far). As a result we obtain a falsifiable variant of the OMDL assumption that we call the *algebraic OMDL* (AOMDL) assumption. Since every algebraic algorithm is also a normal algorithm, the AOMDL assumption is immediately implied by the well-established OMDL assumption.

Since our reductions in both the ROM and in the AGM+ROM are algebraic in this sense, we can rely on the falsifiable AOMDL assumption. We would like to stress that being algebraic here refers to a property of the reduction, which acts as the algorithm solving (A)OMDL, and our reductions are algebraic independent of whether the unforgeability adversary, to which the reduction has access internally, is algebraic. As such, the use of the AOMDL assumption is independent and orthogonal of our use of the AGM as described in the previous subsection. In particular we can rely on the AOMDL assumption even in our ROM-only proof.

We believe that the AOMDL problem is helpful beyond the scope of this paper, as it turns out that essentially all security proofs in the literature use the OMDL problem in an algebraic and thus falsifiable fashion [e.g., 5,6,13,29]. We do not claim that our observation about algebraic algorithms is a deep insight—in fact implementing the DL oracle is straight-forward given an algebraic solving algorithm—we simply believe it is useful for the evaluation of security results.

---

[6] Note that there are multiple different formal definitions of falsifiability in the literature. In this work we work with the commonly used definition by Gentry and Wichs [14,15] which unlike the definition by Naor [25] allows for interactive assumptions.

Game AOMDL$_{\mathsf{GrGen}}^{\mathcal{A}}(\lambda)$ Oracle CH()   Oracle DLOG$_g(X, (\alpha, (\beta_i)_{1 \le i \le c}))$

$(\mathbb{G}, p, g) \leftarrow \mathsf{GrGen}(1^\lambda)$ $c := c + 1$ $/\!/ \; X = g^\alpha \prod_{i=1}^{c} X_i^{\beta_i}$ for $X_i = g^{x_i}$

$c := 0; \; q := 0$ $x_c \leftarrow\!\!\text{\$} \, \mathbb{Z}_p$ $q := q + 1$

$\vec{y} \leftarrow \mathcal{A}^{\text{CH},\text{DLOG}_g}(\mathbb{G}, p, g)$ $X := g^{x_c}$ **return** $\alpha + \sum_{i=1}^{c} \beta_i x_i$

$\vec{x} := (x_1, \ldots, x_c)$ **return** X **return** $\log_g(X)$

return $(\vec{y} = \vec{x} \; \wedge \; q < c)$

Fig. 1. The algebraic OMDL problem. The changes from the OMDL problem to the algebraic OMDL problem are in gray.

3 Preliminaries

The security parameter is denoted λ. A *group description* is a triple $(\mathbb{G}, p, g)$ where $\mathbb{G}$ is a cyclic group of order p and g is a generator of $\mathbb{G}$. A (prime-order) *group generation algorithm* is an algorithm GrGen which on input 1^λ returns a group description $(\mathbb{G}, p, g)$ where p is a λ-bit prime. The group $\mathbb{G}$ is denoted multiplicatively, and we conflate group elements and their encoding when given as input to hash functions. Given an element $X \in \mathbb{G}$, we let $\log_g(X)$ denote the discrete logarithm of X in base g, i.e., the unique $x \in \mathbb{Z}_p$ such that $X = g^x$.

Algebraic OMDL Problem. We introduce the *algebraic OMDL (AOMDL)* problem, which is at least as hard as the standard one-more discrete logarithm (OMDL) problem [3,5].

Definition 1 (AOMDL Problem). *Let* GrGen *be a group generation algorithm, and let game* AOMDL$_{\mathsf{GrGen}}^{\mathcal{A}}$ *be as defined in Fig. 1. The algebraic one-more discrete logarithm (AOMDL) problem is hard for* GrGen *if for any p.p.t. algorithm* $\mathcal{A}$,

$$\mathsf{Adv}_{\mathcal{A},\mathsf{GrGen}}^{\mathsf{AOMDL}}(\lambda) := \Pr\left[\mathsf{AOMDL}_{\mathsf{GrGen}}^{\mathcal{A}}(\lambda) = \mathbf{true}\right] = \mathsf{negl}(\lambda).$$

We highlight the changes from the standard OMDL problem to the AOMDL problem in gray in Fig. 1. Since every algorithm solving AOMDL can be turned into an algorithm solving OMDL by dropping the representation from the DLOG$_g$ oracle queries, the AOMDL problem is hard for some GrGen if the OMDL problem is hard for GrGen.

It is immediate that the entire AOMDL$_{\mathsf{GrGen}}^{\mathcal{A}}$ game runs in p.p.t. whenever $\mathcal{A}$ runs in p.p.t., i.e., the assumption that the AOMDL problem is hard is falsifiable as defined for instance by Gentry and Wichs [14].

3.1   Syntax and Security Definition of Multi-signature Schemes

To keep the notation simple, we make a few simplifying assumptions. In particular, we restrict our syntax and security model to two-round signing algorithms, and in order to model that the first round can be preprocessed without having determined a message to be signed or the public keys of all signers, and without accessing the secret key, those inputs are given only to the second round of the signing algorithm.

Syntax. A two-round multi-signature scheme Σ with key aggregation consists of algorithms (Setup, KeyGen, KeyAgg, (Sign, SignAgg, Sign′, SignAgg′, Sign″), Ver) as follows. System-wide parameters *par* are generated by the setup algorithm Setup taking as input the security parameter. For notational simplicity, we assume that *par* is given as implicit input to all other algorithms. The randomized key generation algorithm takes no input and returns a secret/public key pair $(sk, pk) \leftarrow_{\$} \mathsf{KeyGen}()$. The deterministic key aggregation algorithm KeyAgg takes a multiset of public keys $L = \{pk_1, \ldots, pk_n\}$ and returns an aggregate public key $\widetilde{pk} := \mathsf{KeyAgg}(pk_1, \ldots, pk_n)$.

The interactive signature algorithm (Sign, SignAgg, Sign′, SignAgg′, Sign″) is run by each signer i and proceeds in a sequence of two communication rounds. Sign does not take explicit inputs and returns a signer's first-round output out_i and some first-round secret state $state_i$. SignAgg is a deterministic algorithm that aggregates the first-round outputs $(out_1, \ldots, out_n)$ from all signers into a single first-round output out to be broadcast to all signers. Similarly, Sign′ takes the first-round secret state $state_i$ of signer i, the aggregate first-round output out, the secret key sk_i of signer i, a message m to sign, public keys $(pk_2, \ldots, pk_n)$ of all cosigners, and returns this signer's second-round output out_i' and some second-round secret state $state_i'$, and SignAgg′ is a deterministic algorithm that aggregates the second-round outputs $(out_1', \ldots, out_n')$ from all signers into a single second-round output out' to be broadcast to all signers. Finally, Sign″ takes the second-round secret state $state_i'$ of signer i and the aggregate second-round output out' and outputs a signature σ.

The purpose of the aggregation algorithms SignAgg and SignAgg′ is to enable savings in the broadcast communication in both signing rounds: An *aggregator node* [18,35], which will be untrusted in our security model and can for instance be one of the signers, can collect the outputs of all signers in both rounds, aggregate the outputs using SignAgg and SignAgg′, respectively, and broadcast only the aggregate output back to all signers. This optimization is entirely optional. If it is not desired, each signer can simply broadcast its outputs directly to all signers, which then all run SignAgg and SignAgg′ by themselves.

The deterministic verification algorithm Ver takes an aggregate public key $\widetilde{pk}$, a message m, and a signature σ, and returns true iff σ is valid for $\widetilde{pk}$ and m.

Security. Our security model is the same as in previous works on multi-signatures for multi-signatures with key aggregation [9,11,22] and requires that it is infeasible to forge multi-signatures involving at least one honest signer. As in previous work [4,8,23], we assume without loss of generality that there is a single honest public key (representing a honest signer) and that the adversary has corrupted all other public keys (representing possible cosigners), choosing corrupted public keys arbitrarily and potentially as a function of the honest signer's public key.

The security game $\text{EUF-CMA}_\Sigma^{\mathcal{A}}$ is defined as follows. A key pair (sk_1, pk_1) is generated for the honest signer and the adversary $\mathcal{A}$ is given pk_1. The adversary can engage in any number of (concurrent) signing sessions with the honest signer. Formally, $\mathcal{A}$ has access to oracles SIGN, SIGN$'$, and SIGN$''$ implementing the three steps Sign, Sign$'$, and Sign$''$ of the signing algorithm with the honest signer's secret key. This in particular means that the adversary can pass the same L, containing pk_1 multiple times, and the same m to multiple SIGN$'$ calls, effectively obtaining a signing session in which the honest signer participates multiple times.

Note that oracles SIGN$'$ and SIGN$''$ expect as input aggregate values out and out', purported to be the aggregation of all signers' outputs from the respective previous round. This leaves the task performed by the algorithms SignAgg and SignAgg$'$ to the adversary and models that the aggregator node (if present) is untrusted. We omit explicit oracles for SignAgg and SignAgg$'$. This is without loss of generality because these algorithms do not take secret inputs and can be run by the adversary locally.

Eventually, the adversary returns a multiset $L = \{pk_1, \ldots, pk_n\}$ of public keys, a message m, and a signature σ. The game returns `true` (representing a win of $\mathcal{A}$) if $pk_1 \in L$, the forgery is valid, i.e., $\text{Ver}(\text{KeyAgg}(L), m, \sigma) = \text{true}$, and the adversary never made a SIGN$'$ query for multiset L and message m.

Definition 2 (EUF-CMA). *Given a multi-signature scheme with key aggregation* $\Sigma = (\text{Setup}, \text{KeyGen}, \text{KeyAgg}, (\text{Sign}, \text{SignAgg}, \text{Sign}', \text{SignAgg}', \text{Sign}''), \text{Ver})$, *let game* $\text{EUF-CMA}_\Sigma^{\mathcal{A}}$ *be as defined above. Then* Σ *is existentially unforgeable under chosen-message attacks (EUF-CMA) if for any p.p.t. adversary* $\mathcal{A}$,

$$\text{Adv}_{\mathcal{A},\Sigma}^{\text{EUF-CMA}}(\lambda) := \Pr\left[\text{EUF-CMA}_\Sigma^{\mathcal{A}}(\lambda) = \text{true}\right] = \text{negl}(\lambda).$$

Our security model is based on the model by Bellare and Neven [4] which was proposed in the context of multi-signatures *without key aggregation*. Even though this security model has been used previously for multi-signatures with key aggregation [9,11,22], one may wonder if it is at all suitable in this context. We argue in the full version [27] that it is indeed suitable.

4 The Multi-signature Scheme MuSig2

Our new multi-signature scheme MuSig2 is parameterized by a group generation algorithm GrGen and by an integer ν, which specifies the number of nonces sent by each signer. The scheme is defined in Fig. 2. Note that verification is exactly the same as for ordinary key-prefixed Schnorr signatures with respect to the aggregate public key $\widetilde{X}$.

Setup(1^λ)

$(\mathbb{G}, p, g) \leftarrow \mathsf{GrGen}(1^\lambda)$
Select three hash functions
$\quad \mathsf{H_{agg}, H_{non}, H_{sig}} : \{0,1\}^* \to \mathbb{Z}_p$
$par := ((\mathbb{G}, p, g), \mathsf{H_{agg}, H_{non}, H_{sig}})$
return par

KeyGen()

$x \leftarrow_\$ \mathbb{Z}_p \; ; \; X := g^x$
$sk := x \; ; \; pk := X$
return (sk, pk)

MuSigCoef(L, X_i)

---

return $\mathsf{H_{agg}}(L, X_i)$

KeyAgg(L)

$\{X_1, \ldots, X_n\} := L$
for $i := 1 \ldots n$ **do**
$\quad a_i := \mathsf{MuSigCoef}(L, X_i)$
return $\widetilde{X} := \prod_{i=1}^n X_i^{a_i}$

Ver($\widetilde{pk}, m, \sigma$)

$\widetilde{X} := \widetilde{pk} \; ; \; (R, s) := \sigma$
$c := \mathsf{H_{sig}}(\widetilde{X}, R, m)$
return $(g^s = R\widetilde{X}^c)$

Sign()

// Local signer has index 1.
for $j := 1 \ldots \nu$ **do**
$\quad r_{1,j} \leftarrow_\$ \mathbb{Z}_p \; ; \; R_{1,j} := g^{r_{1,j}}$
$out_1 := (R_{1,1}, \ldots, R_{1,\nu})$
$state_1 := (r_{1,1}, \ldots, r_{1,\nu})$
return $(out_1, state_1)$

SignAgg($out_1, \ldots, out_n$)

---

for $i := 1 \ldots n$ **do**
$\quad (R_{i,1}, \ldots, R_{i,\nu}) := out_i$
for $j := 1 \ldots \nu$ **do**
$\quad R_j := \prod_{i=1}^n R_{i,j}$
return $out := (R_1, \ldots, R_\nu)$

Sign'($state_1, out, sk_1, m, (pk_2, \ldots, pk_n)$)

// Sign' must be called at most once per $state_1$.
$(r_{1,1}, \ldots, r_{1,\nu}) := state_1$
$x_1 := sk_1 \; ; \; X_1 := g^{x_1}$
$(R_{1,1}, \ldots, R_{1,\nu}) := (g^{r_{1,1}}, \ldots, g^{r_{1,\nu}})$
$(X_2, \ldots, X_n) := (pk_2, \ldots, pk_n)$
$L := \{X_1, \ldots, X_n\}$
$a_1 := \mathsf{MuSigCoef}(L, X_1)$
$\widetilde{X} := \mathsf{KeyAgg}(L)$
$(R_1, \ldots, R_\nu) := out$
$b := \mathsf{H_{non}}(\widetilde{X}, (R_1, \ldots, R_\nu), m)$
$R := \prod_{j=1}^\nu R_j^{b^{j-1}}$
$c := \mathsf{H_{sig}}(\widetilde{X}, R, m)$
$s_1 := ca_1 x_1 + \sum_{i=1}^\nu r_{1,j} b^{j-1} \bmod p$
$state_1' := R \; ; \; out_1' := s_1$
return $(state_1', out_1')$

SignAgg'($out_1', \ldots, out_n'$)

$(s_1, \ldots, s_n) := (out_1', \ldots, out_n')$
$s := \sum_{i=1}^n s_i \bmod p$
return $out' := s$

Sign''($state_1', out'$)

$R := state_1' \; ; \; s := out'$
return $\sigma := (R, s)$

Fig. 2. The multi-signature scheme $\mathsf{MuSig2}[\mathsf{GrGen}, \nu]$. Public parameters par returned by Setup are implicitly given as input to all other algorithms. We use a helper algorithm MuSigCoef as a wrapper for $\mathsf{H_{agg}}$ to make the description of the scheme more modular, which will help us describe a variant $\mathsf{MuSig2}^*$ of the scheme with optimized key aggregation (see the full version [27]).

Implementers should be aware that derandomizing techniques often applied to the signing algorithm of single-signer signatures are in general not secure in the case of multi-signatures, and that care has to be taken when implementing the stateful signing algorithm of MuSig2. We discuss these issues as well as further practical considerations and optimizations in the full version [27].

5   Security of MuSig2 in the ROM

In this section, we establish the security of MuSig2 with $\nu = 4$ nonces in the random oracle model.

Theorem 1. *Let* GrGen *be a group generation algorithm for which the AOMDL problem is hard. Then the multi-signature scheme* MuSig2[GrGen, $\nu = 4$] *is EUF-CMA in the random oracle model for* $\mathsf{H_{agg}}$, $\mathsf{H_{non}}$, $\mathsf{H_{sig}} : \{0,1\}^* \to \mathbb{Z}_p$.

Precisely, for any adversary $\mathcal{A}$ against MuSig2[GrGen, $\nu = 4$] *running in time at most t, making at most q_s* SIGN *queries and at most q_h queries to each random oracle, and such that the size of L in any signing session and in the forgery is at most N, there exists an algorithm $\mathcal{D}$ taking as input group parameters $(\mathbb{G}, p, g) \leftarrow$ GrGen(1^λ), running in time at most*

$$t' = 4(t + Nq + 6q)t_{\exp} + O(qN),$$

where $q = 2q_h + q_s + 1$ and $t_{\exp}$ is the time of an exponentiation in $\mathbb{G}$, making at most $4q_s$ DLOG$_g$ *queries, and solving the AOMDL problem with an advantage*

$$\mathsf{Adv}^{\mathsf{AOMDL}}_{\mathcal{D},\mathsf{GrGen}}(\lambda) \geq (\mathsf{Adv}^{\mathsf{EUF\text{-}CMA}}_{\mathcal{A},\mathsf{MuSig2[GrGen},\nu=4]}(\lambda))^4/q^3 - (32q^2 + 22)/2^\lambda.$$

Before proving the theorem, we start with an informal explanation of the key techniques used in the proof. Let us recall the security game defined in Sect. 3.1, adapting the notation to our setting. Group parameters $(\mathbb{G}, p, g)$ and a key pair (x^*, X^*) for the honest signer are generated. The target public key X^* is given as input to the adversary $\mathcal{A}$. Then, the adversary can engage in protocol executions with the honest signer by providing a message m to sign and a multiset L of public keys involved in the signing process where X^* occurs at least once, and simulating all signers except one instance of X^*.

The Double-Forking Technique. This technique is already used by Maxwell *et al.* in the security proof for MuSig [22]. We are repeating the idea below with slightly modified notation.

The first difficulty is to extract the discrete logarithm x^* of the challenge public key X^*. The standard technique for this would be to "fork" two executions of the adversary in order to obtain two valid forgeries (R, s) and (R', s') for the same multiset of public keys $L = \{X_1, \ldots, X_n\}$ with $X^* \in L$ and the same message m such that $R = R'$, $\mathsf{H_{sig}}(\widetilde{X}, R, m)$ was programmed in both executions to some common value h_{sig}, $\mathsf{H_{agg}}(L, X_i)$ was programmed in both executions to the same value a_i for each i such that $X_i \neq X^*$, and $\mathsf{H_{agg}}(L, X^*)$ was programmed to two distinct values h_{agg} and h'_{agg} in the two executions, implying that

$$g^s = R(X^*)^{n^* h_{\mathrm{agg}} h_{\mathrm{sig}}} \prod_{\substack{i \in \{1,\ldots,n\} \\ X_i \neq X^*}} X_i^{a_i h_{\mathrm{sig}}}, \quad g^{s'} = R(X^*)^{n^* h'_{\mathrm{agg}} h_{\mathrm{sig}}} \prod_{\substack{i \in \{1,\ldots,n\} \\ X_i \neq X^*}} X_i^{a_i h_{\mathrm{sig}}},$$

where n^* is the number of times X^* appears in L. This would allow to compute the discrete logarithm of X^* by dividing the two equations above.

However, simply forking the executions with respect to the answer to the query $\mathsf{H}_{\mathrm{agg}}(L, X^*)$ does not work: indeed, at this moment, the relevant query $\mathsf{H}_{\mathrm{sig}}(\widetilde{X}, R, m)$ might not have been made yet by the adversary,[7] and there is no guarantee that the adversary will ever make this same query again in the second execution, let alone return a forgery corresponding to the same $\mathsf{H}_{\mathrm{sig}}$ query. In order to remedy this situation, we fork the execution of the adversary *twice*: once on the answer to the query $\mathsf{H}_{\mathrm{sig}}(\widetilde{X}, R, m)$, which allows us to retrieve the discrete logarithm of the aggregate public key $\widetilde{X}$ with respect to which the adversary returns a forgery, and on the answer to $\mathsf{H}_{\mathrm{agg}}(L, X^*)$, which allows us to retrieve the discrete logarithm of X^*.

As in Bellare and Neven [4], our technical tool to handle forking of the adversary is a "generalized Forking Lemma" which extends Pointcheval and Stern's Forking Lemma [30] and which does not mention signatures nor adversaries and only deals with the outputs of an algorithm $\mathcal{A}$ run twice on related inputs.

However, the generalized Forking Lemma of Bellare and Neven [4] is not general enough for our setting, and we rely on the following variant.

Lemma 1. *Fix integers q and m. Let $\mathcal{A}$ be a randomized algorithm which takes as input a main input inp generated by some probabilistic algorithm $\mathsf{InpGen}()$, elements $h_1, \ldots, h_q$ from some sampleable set H, elements $v_1, \ldots, v_m$ from some sampleable set V, and random coins from some sampleable set R, and returns either a distinguished failure symbol $\perp$, or a tuple (i, j, out), where $i \in \{1, \ldots, q\}$, $j \in \{0, \ldots, m\}$, and out is some side output. The accepting probability of $\mathcal{A}$, denoted $acc(\mathcal{A})$, is defined as the probability, over $inp \leftarrow \mathsf{InpGen}()$, $h_1, \ldots, h_q \leftarrow_\$ H$, $v_1, \ldots, v_m \leftarrow_\$ V$, and the random coins of $\mathcal{A}$, that $\mathcal{A}$ returns a non-$\perp$ output. Consider algorithm $\mathsf{Fork}^{\mathcal{A}}$, taking as input inp and $v_1, v'_1, \ldots, v_m, v'_m \in V$, described in Fig. 3. Let frk be the probability (over $inp \leftarrow \mathsf{InpGen}()$, $v_1, v'_1, \ldots, v_m, v'_m \leftarrow_\$ V$, and the random coins of $\mathsf{Fork}^{\mathcal{A}}$) that $\mathsf{Fork}^{\mathcal{A}}$ returns a non-$\perp$ output. Then*

$$frk \geq acc(\mathcal{A}) \left(\frac{acc(\mathcal{A})}{q} - \frac{1}{|H|} \right).$$

Since the proof of the lemma is very similar to the one of [4, Lemma 1], it is deferred to the full version [27].

---

[7] In fact, it is easy to see that the adversary can only guess the value of the aggregate public key $\widetilde{X}$ corresponding to L at random before making the relevant queries $\mathsf{H}_{\mathrm{agg}}(L, X_i)$ for $X_i \in L$, so that the query $\mathsf{H}_{\mathrm{sig}}(\widetilde{X}, R, m)$ can only come after the relevant queries $\mathsf{H}_{\mathrm{agg}}(L, X_i)$ except with negligible probability.

Fork$^{\mathcal{A}}(inp, v_1, v_1', \ldots, v_m, v_m')$

$\rho \leftarrow_\$ R \mathbin{/\!\!/}$ pick random coins for $\mathcal{A}$

$h_1, \ldots, h_q \leftarrow_\$ H$

$\alpha := \mathcal{A}(inp, (h_1, \ldots, h_q), (v_1, \ldots, v_m); \rho)$

if $\alpha = \perp$ **thenreturn** $\perp$

$(i, j, out) := \alpha$

$h_i', \ldots, h_q' \leftarrow_\$ H$

$\alpha' := \mathcal{A}(inp, (h_1, \ldots, h_{i-1}, h_i', \ldots, h_q'), (v_1, \ldots, v_j, v_{j+1}', \ldots, v_m'); \rho)$

if $\alpha' = \perp$ **thenreturn** $\perp$

$(i', j', out') := \alpha'$

if $i \neq i' \vee h_i = h_i'$ **thenreturn** $\perp$

return (i, out, out')

Fig. 3. The "forking" algorithm Fork$^{\mathcal{A}}$ built from $\mathcal{A}$.

Simulating the Honest Signer. For now, consider the scheme with $\nu = 1$. (We will illustrate the problem of this choice further down in this section.) The adversary has access to an interactive signing oracle, which enables it to open sessions with the honest signer. The signing oracle consists of three sub-oracles SIGN, SIGN', and SIGN'' but note that we can without loss of generality ignore SIGN'', which computes the final signature $s = \sum_{i=1}^{n} s_i \bmod p$, because it does not depend on secret state and thus the adversary can simply simulate it locally.

The reduction's strategy for simulating the signing oracle is to use the DL oracle available in the formulation of the AOMDL problem as follows. Whenever the adversary starts the k-th signing session by querying SIGN, the reduction uses a fresh DL challenge $R_{1,1}$ from the AOMDL challenge oracle and returns it as its nonce to the adversary. At any later time the adversary queries SIGN' with session counter k, a nonce R (purported to be obtained as $R = \prod_{i=1}^{n} R_{i,1}$), a message m to sign, and $n-1$ public keys $X_2, \ldots, X_n$. The reduction then sets $L = \{X_1 = X^*, X_2, \ldots, X_n\}$, computes $\widetilde{X}$ and $c = \mathsf{H}_{\mathsf{sig}}(\widetilde{X}, R, m)$, and uses the DL oracle in the formulation of the AOMDL problem to compute s_1 as

$$s_1 = \mathrm{DLOG}_g(R_{1,1}(X^*)^{ca_1}, \ldots),$$

where the required algebraic representation of $R_{1,1}(X^*)^{ca_1}$ is omitted in this informal description and can be computed naturally by the reduction. The reduction then returns s_1 to the adversary. Since a fresh DL challenge is used as $R_{1,1}$ in each signing query, the reduction will be able to compute its discrete logarithm $r_{1,1}$ once x^* has been retrieved via $r_{1,1} = ca_1 x^* - s_1$.

Leveraging Two or More Nonces. The main obstacle in the proof and the novelty in this work is to handle adversaries whose behavior follows this pattern:

The adversary initiates a signing session by querying the oracle SIGN to obtain $R_{1,1}$, then makes a query $H_{sig}(\tilde{X}, R, m)$, for which it will output a forgery later, and only then continues the signing session with a query to SIGN$'$ with arguments $m, R, (X_2, \ldots, X_n)$. Our goal is to fork the execution of the adversary at the H_{sig} query. But then, the adversary may make SIGN$'$ queries with different arguments $m, R, (X_2, \ldots, X_n)$, and $m', R', (X'_2, \ldots, X'_{n'})$ in the two executions. In that case, this results in different signature hashes $c \neq c'$ and requires the reduction simulating the honest signer to make two DL oracle queries in order to answer the SIGN$'$ query. Consequently, the reduction will lose the AOMDL game because it had only requested the single AOMDL challenge $R_{1,1}$.

This is exactly where $\nu \geq 2$ nonces will come to the rescue. Now assume $\nu = 2$, i.e., the reduction will obtain two (instead of one) group elements $R_{1,1}, R_{1,2}$ as challenges from the AOMDL challenger. This will allow the reduction to make two DL queries. In order to answer SIGN$'$, the reduction follows the MuSig2 scheme by computing $\tilde{X}$ from the public keys, and b by hashing $\tilde{X}$, m and all R values of the signing session with H_{non}. The reduction then aggregates the nonces of the honest signer into its effective nonce $\hat{R}_1 = R_{1,1}R_{1,2}^b$, queries the signature hash c and replies to the adversary with $s_1 = \text{DLOG}_g(\hat{R}_1(X^*)^{a_1 c}, \ldots)$.

Now since the reduction has obtained two AOMDL challenges, it can make a second DLOG_g query to compute $s'_1 = \text{DLOG}_g(\hat{R}'_1(X^*)^{a'_1 c'}, \ldots)$ and answer the SIGN$'$ query in the second execution. Moreover, to ensure that the AOMDL challenge responses $r_{1,1}$ and $r_{1,2}$ can be computed after extracting x^*, the reduction programs H_{non} to give different responses in each execution after a fork. Let us assume for now that the signing session was started with a SIGN query after the H_{agg} fork. We can distinguish the following two cases depending on when H_{non} is queried with the inputs corresponding to the signing session:

H_{non} **is queried after the** H_{sig} **fork.** Regardless of what values the adversary sends in SIGN$'$, hashing with H_{non} ensures that with overwhelming probability the second execution will use a value b' that is different from b in the first execution. In order to answer the SIGN$'$ queries, the reduction uses DLOG_g to compute s_1 and s'_1 resulting in a system of linear equations

$$r_{1,1} + br_{1,2} = s_1 - a_1 cx^* \bmod p$$
$$r_{1,1} + b'r_{1,2} = s'_1 - a'_1 c' x^* \bmod p$$

with unknowns $r_{1,1}$ and $r_{1,2}$. As the system is linearly independent (as $b \neq b'$) the reduction can solve it and forward the solutions to the AOMDL challenger.

H_{non} **is queried before the** H_{sig} **fork.** This implies that b in the first execution is equal to b' in the second execution and requires the reduction to ensure that a'_1 and c' are identical in both executions. Then the input to the DLOG_g query is also identical and the reduction can simply cache and reuse the result of the DLOG_g query from the first execution to save the DLOG_g query in the second execution. (Without this caching, the reduction would waste a second DLOG_g query to compute $s'_1 = s_1$, which it knows already, and then would not have a second, linearly independent equation that allows solving for $r_{1,1}$ and $r_{1,2}$.)

The value a_1 is equal to a_1' because the inputs of $\mathsf{H}_{\mathrm{non}}$ contain $\widetilde{X}$ which implies that the corresponding $\mathsf{H}_{\mathrm{agg}}$ happened before $\mathsf{H}_{\mathrm{non}}$ and therefore before the fork. Similarly, $\mathsf{H}_{\mathrm{sig}}$ requires the aggregate nonce R of the signing session and therefore $\mathsf{H}_{\mathrm{non}}$ must be queried before the corresponding $\mathsf{H}_{\mathrm{sig}}$. In order to argue that $c = c'$, observe that from the inputs (and output) of a $\mathsf{H}_{\mathrm{non}}$ query it is possible to compute the inputs of the $\mathsf{H}_{\mathrm{sig}}$ query. Therefore, the reduction can make such an internal $\mathsf{H}_{\mathrm{sig}}$ query for every $\mathsf{H}_{\mathrm{non}}$ query it receives. This $\mathsf{H}_{\mathrm{sig}}$ query is before the fork point implying $c = c'$ as desired. (The reduction does not need to handle the case that this $\mathsf{H}_{\mathrm{sig}}$ query *is* the fork point, because then the values L and m of forgery were queried in a signing session and thus the forgery is invalid.) Now the reduction has a DLOG_g query left to compute the discrete logarithm of $R_{1,1}$, which enables to compute the discrete logarithm of $R_{1,2}$ after x^* has been extracted.

More generally, if the signing session can be started before the $\mathsf{H}_{\mathrm{agg}}$ fork, the reduction may have to provide different signatures in all *four* executions. To answer the signature queries nonetheless, the reduction requires four DL queries and therefore requires MuSig2 with $\nu = 4$ nonces. Similar to the above, whenever $\mathsf{H}_{\mathrm{non}}$ is queried after the $\mathsf{H}_{\mathrm{sig}}$ fork, the reduction ends up with up to four equations, which are constructed to be linearly independent with high probability. Whenever $\mathsf{H}_{\mathrm{non}}$ is queried before the $\mathsf{H}_{\mathrm{sig}}$ fork, the DLOG_g queries in the corresponding executions will be identical and the result can be cached and reused. The DLOG_g queries saved due to caching can then be used to complete the linear system to $\nu = 4$ linearly independent equations, and the reduction can solve for the unknowns $r_{1,1}, \ldots, r_{1,4}$.

5.1 Security Proof

Proof Overview. We first construct a "wrapping" algorithm $\mathcal{B}$ which essentially runs the adversary $\mathcal{A}$ and returns a forgery together with some information about the adversary execution, unless some bad events happen. Algorithm $\mathcal{B}$ simulates the random oracles $\mathsf{H}_{\mathrm{agg}}$, $\mathsf{H}_{\mathrm{non}}$, and $\mathsf{H}_{\mathrm{sig}}$ uniformly at random and the signing oracle by obtaining ν DL challenges from the AOMDL challenge oracle for each SIGN query and by making a single query to the DL oracle for each SIGN$'$ query. Then, we use $\mathcal{B}$ to construct an algorithm $\mathcal{C}$ which runs the forking algorithm Fork$^{\mathcal{B}}$ as defined in Sect. 3 (where the fork is w.r.t. the answer to the $\mathsf{H}_{\mathrm{sig}}$ query related to the forgery), allowing it to return a multiset of public keys L together with the discrete logarithm of the corresponding aggregate public key. Finally, we use $\mathcal{C}$ to construct an algorithm $\mathcal{D}$ computing the DL of the public key of the honest signer by running Fork$^{\mathcal{C}}$ (where the fork is now w.r.t. the answer to the $\mathsf{H}_{\mathrm{agg}}$ query related to the forgery). Throughout the proof, the reader might find helpful to refer to Fig. 4 which illustrates the inner working of $\mathcal{D}$.

Due to $\mathcal{D}$ and $\mathcal{C}$ carefully relaying DL challenges, it is ensured that the $\nu \geq 4$ DL challenges that $\mathcal{B}$ obtains in each SIGN query are identical across all

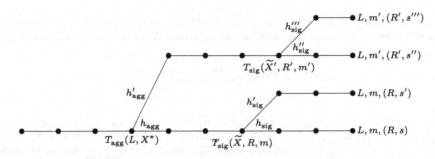

Fig. 4. A possible execution of algorithm $\mathcal{D}$. Each path from left to right represents an execution of the adversary $\mathcal{A}$. Each vertex symbolizes a call to random oracles H_{agg} and H_{sig}, and the edge originating from this vertex symbolizes the response used for the query. Leaves symbolize the forgery returned by the adversary.

executions of $\mathcal{B}$. Since $\mathcal{D}$ (via $\mathcal{C}$ and $\mathcal{B}$) obtains $1 + \nu q_s$ DL challenges (one for the public key of the honest signer and ν for each of the q_s signing sessions) and solves all of these challenges using at most νq_s queries to the DL oracle (one for each of the q_s signing session in at most $4 \leq \nu$ executions due to double-forking), algorithm $\mathcal{D}$ solves the AOMDL problem.

Normalizing Assumptions and Conventions. Let a (t, q_s, q_h, N)-adversary be an adversary running in time at most t, making at most q_s SIGN queries, at most q_h queries to each random oracle, and such that $|L|$ in any signing session and in the forgery is at most N.

In all the following, we assume that the adversary only makes "well-formed" random oracles queries, meaning that $X^* \in L$ and $X \in L$ for any query $\mathsf{H}_{\text{agg}}(L, X)$. This is without loss of generality, since "ill-formed" queries are irrelevant and could simply be answered uniformly at random in the simulation.

We further assume without loss of generality that the adversary makes exactly q_h queries to each random oracle and exactly q_s queries to the SIGN oracle, and that the adversary closes every signing session, i.e., for every SIGN query it will also make a corresponding SIGN′ query at some point. This is without loss of generality because remaining queries can be emulated after the adversary has terminated (in the case of SIGN′ queries using a set of public keys and a message m which are different from the adversary's forgery to make sure not to invalidate a valid forgery).

We ignore the SIGN″ oracle in the simulation. This is without loss of generality because it does not depend on secret state and thus the adversary can simply simulate it locally.

Lemma 2. *Given some integer ν, let $\mathcal{A}$ be a (t, q_s, q_h, N)-adversary in the random oracle model against the multi-signature scheme $\mathsf{MuSig2}[\mathsf{GrGen}, \nu]$, and let $q = 2q_h + q_s + 1$. Then there exists an algorithm $\mathcal{B}$ that takes as input group parameters $(\mathbb{G}, p, g) \leftarrow \mathsf{GrGen}(1^\lambda)$, uniformly random group elements $X^*, U_1, \ldots, U_{\nu q_s} \in \mathbb{G}$, and uniformly random scalars $h_{\text{agg},1}, \ldots, h_{\text{agg},q}$,*

$h_{\mathrm{non},1}, \ldots, h_{\mathrm{non},q}, h_{\mathrm{sig},1}, \ldots, h_{\mathrm{sig},q} \in \mathbb{Z}_p$, *makes at most* q_s *queries to a discrete logarithm oracle* DLOG_g, *and with accepting probability (as defined in Lemma 1)*

$$acc(\mathcal{B}) \geq \mathsf{Adv}_{\mathcal{A},\mathsf{MuSig2}[\mathsf{GrGen},\nu]}^{\mathsf{EUF\text{-}CMA}}(\lambda) - \frac{4q^2}{2^\lambda}$$

outputs a tuple $(i_{\mathrm{agg}}, j_{\mathrm{agg}}, i_{\mathrm{sig}}, j_{\mathrm{sig}}, L, R, s, \vec{a})$ *where* $i_{\mathrm{agg}}, i_{\mathrm{sig}} \in \{1, \ldots, q\}$, j_{agg}, $j_{\mathrm{sig}} \in \{0, \ldots, q\}$, $L = \{X_1, \ldots, X_n\}$ *is a multiset of public keys such that* $X^* \in L$, $\vec{a} = (a_1, \ldots, a_n) \in \mathbb{Z}_p^n$ *is a tuple of scalars such that* $a_i = h_{\mathrm{agg},i_{\mathrm{agg}}}$ *for any* i *such that* $X_i = X^*$, *and*

$$g^s = R \prod_{i=1}^n X_i^{a_i h_{\mathrm{sig},i_{\mathrm{sig}}}}. \tag{2}$$

Proof. We construct algorithm $\mathcal{B}$ as follows. It initializes three empty sets T_{agg}, T_{non} and T_{sig} for storing key-value pairs (k,v), which we write in assignment form "$T(k) := v$" for a set T. The sets represent tables for storing programmed values for respectively $\mathsf{H}_{\mathrm{agg}}$, $\mathsf{H}_{\mathrm{non}}$ and $\mathsf{H}_{\mathrm{sig}}$. It also initializes four counters $ctrh_{\mathrm{agg}}$, $ctrh_{\mathrm{non}}$, $ctrh_{\mathrm{sig}}$, and $ctrs$ (initially zero), an empty set S for keeping track of open signing sessions, an empty set Q for keeping track of completed signing sessions, an empty set K for keeping track of aggregate keys resulting from queries to $\mathsf{H}_{\mathrm{agg}}$, and two flags $\mathsf{BadOrder}$ and $\mathsf{KeyColl}$ (initially $\mathtt{false}$) that will help keep track of bad events. Then, it picks random coins ρ_A, runs the adversary $\mathcal{A}$ on $(\mathbb{G}, p, g)$ and public key X^* as input and answers its queries as follows.

- *Hash query* $\mathsf{H}_{\mathrm{agg}}(L, X)$: (Recall that by assumption, $X^* \in L$ and $X \in L$.) If $T_{\mathrm{agg}}(L, X)$ is undefined, then $\mathcal{B}$ increments $ctrh_{\mathrm{agg}}$, randomly assigns $T_{\mathrm{agg}}(L, X') \leftarrow_\$ \mathbb{Z}_p$ for all $X' \in L \setminus \{X^*\}$, and assigns $T_{\mathrm{agg}}(L, X^*) := h_{\mathrm{agg},ctrh_{\mathrm{agg}}}$. Then, $\mathcal{B}$ computes the aggregate key corresponding to L, namely $\widetilde{X} := \prod_{i=1}^n X_i^{a_i}$ where $\{X_1, \ldots, X_n\} := L$ and $a_i := T_{\mathrm{agg}}(L, X_i)$. If $\widetilde{X}$ is equal to the first argument of some defined entry in T_{sig} (i.e., there exists R and m such that $T_{\mathrm{sig}}(\widetilde{X}, R, m) \neq \bot$), then $\mathcal{B}$ sets $\mathsf{BadOrder} := \mathtt{true}$. If $\widetilde{X} \in K$, then $\mathcal{B}$ sets $\mathsf{KeyColl} := \mathtt{true}$, otherwise it sets $K := K \cup \{\widetilde{X}\}$. Finally, it returns $T_{\mathrm{agg}}(L, X)$.
- *Hash query* $\mathsf{H}_{\mathrm{non}}(\widetilde{X}, (R_1, \ldots, R_\nu), m)$: If $T_{\mathrm{non}}(\widetilde{X}, (R_1, \ldots, R_\nu), m)$ is undefined, then $\mathcal{B}$ increments $ctrh_{\mathrm{non}}$ and assigns $T_{\mathrm{non}}(\widetilde{X}, (R_1, \ldots, R_\nu), m) := h_{\mathrm{non},ctrh_{\mathrm{non}}}$. Then $\mathcal{B}$ sets $b := T_{\mathrm{non}}(\widetilde{X}, (R_1, \ldots, R_\nu), m)$ and computes $R := \prod_{j=1}^\nu R_j^{b^{j-1}}$. If $T_{\mathrm{sig}}(\widetilde{X}, R, m)$ is undefined, then $\mathcal{B}$ makes an internal query to $\mathsf{H}_{\mathrm{sig}}(\widetilde{X}, R, m)$. Finally, it returns b.
- *Hash query* $\mathsf{H}_{\mathrm{sig}}(\widetilde{X}, R, m)$: If $T_{\mathrm{sig}}(\widetilde{X}, R, m)$ is undefined, then $\mathcal{B}$ increments $ctrh_{\mathrm{sig}}$ and assigns $T_{\mathrm{sig}}(\widetilde{X}, R, m) := h_{\mathrm{sig},ctrh_{\mathrm{sig}}}$. Then, it returns $T_{\mathrm{sig}}(\widetilde{X}, R, m)$.
- *Signing query* $\mathrm{SIGN}()$: $\mathcal{B}$ increments $ctrs$, adds $ctrs$ to S, lets $\hat{k} := \nu(ctrs - 1) + 1$ and sends $(R_{1,1} := U_{\hat{k}}, \ldots, R_{1,\nu} := U_{\hat{k}+\nu-1})$ to the adversary.
- *Signing query* $\mathrm{SIGN}'(k, out, m, (pk_2, \ldots, pk_n))$: If $k \notin S$ then the signing query is answered with $\bot$. Otherwise, $\mathcal{B}$ removes k from S. Let $k' := \nu(k - 1) + 1$

and $R_{1,1} := U_{k'}, \ldots, R_{1,\nu} := U_{k'+\nu-1}$. Let $X_i := pk_i$ for each $i \in \{2, \ldots, n\}$ and let $L := \{X_1 = X^*, X_2, \ldots, X_n\}$. If $T_{\text{agg}}(L, X^*)$ is undefined, $\mathcal{B}$ makes an internal query to $\mathsf{H}_{\text{agg}}(L, X^*)$ which ensures that $T_{\text{agg}}(L, X_i)$ is defined for each $i \in \{1, \ldots, n\}$. It sets $a_i := T_{\text{agg}}(L, X_i)$, computes $\widetilde{X} := \prod_{i=1}^{n} X_i^{a_i}$, and sets $Q := Q \cup \{(L, m)\}$. Then $\mathcal{B}$ sets $(R_1, \ldots, R_\nu) := out$. If $T_{\text{non}}(\widetilde{X}, (R_1, \ldots, R_\nu), m)$ is undefined, then $\mathcal{B}$ makes an internal query to $\mathsf{H}_{\text{non}}(\widetilde{X}, (R_1, \ldots, R_\nu), m)$. It sets $b := T_{\text{non}}(\widetilde{X}, (R_1, \ldots, R_\nu), m)$, aggregates the nonces as $R := \prod_{j=1}^{\nu} R_j^{b^{j-1}}$,[8] and sets $c := T_{\text{sig}}(\widetilde{X}, R, m)$, where $T_{\text{sig}}(\widetilde{X}, R, m)$ is defined due to the internal H_{sig} query when handling the internal H_{non} query. Then, $\mathcal{B}$ computes the honest signer's effective nonce $\hat{R}_1 := \prod_{j=1}^{\nu} R_{1,j}^{b^{j-1}}$. It sets $\alpha := 0$ and $(\beta_i)_{1 \le i \le \hat{k}} := (a_1 c, 0, \ldots, 0, \beta_{k'} = b^0 = 1, \ldots, \beta_{k'+\nu-1} = b^{\nu-1}, 0, \ldots, 0)$ for $\hat{k} := \nu(ctrs - 1) + 1$, and obtains $s_1 := \mathrm{DLOG}_g(\hat{R}_1(X^*)^{a_1 c}, (\alpha, (\beta_i)_{1 \le i \le \hat{k}}))$ by querying the DL oracle. Finally, $\mathcal{B}$ returns s_1.

If $\mathcal{A}$ returns $\bot$ or if $\mathsf{BadOrder} = \mathtt{true}$ or $\mathsf{KeyColl} = \mathtt{true}$ at the end of the game, then $\mathcal{B}$ outputs $\bot$. Otherwise, let $(L, m, (R, s))$ denote the output of the adversary, where (R, s) is a purported forgery for a public key multiset L such that $X^* \in L$ and a message m. Then, $\mathcal{B}$ parses L as $\{X_1 = X^*, \ldots, X_n\}$ and checks the validity of the forgery as follows. If $T_{\text{agg}}(L, X^*)$ is undefined, it makes an internal query to $\mathsf{H}_{\text{agg}}(L, X^*)$ which ensures that $T_{\text{agg}}(L, X_i)$ is defined for each $i \in \{1, \ldots, n\}$, sets $a_i := T_{\text{agg}}(L, X_i)$, and computes $\widetilde{X} := \prod_{i=1}^{n} X_i^{a_i}$. If $T_{\text{sig}}(\widetilde{X}, R, m)$ is undefined, it makes an internal query to $\mathsf{H}_{\text{sig}}(\widetilde{X}, R, m)$ and lets $c := T_{\text{sig}}(\widetilde{X}, R, m)$. If $g^s \ne R\widetilde{X}^c$, i.e., the forgery is not a valid signature, or if $(L, m) \in Q$, i.e., the forgery is invalid because the adversary made a SIGN' query for L and m, $\mathcal{B}$ outputs $\bot$. Otherwise, it takes the following additional steps. Let

- i_{agg} be the index such that $T_{\text{agg}}(L, X^*) = h_{\text{agg}, i_{\text{agg}}}$,
- j_{agg} be the value of $ctrh_{\text{non}}$ at the moment $T_{\text{agg}}(L, X^*)$ is assigned,
- i_{sig} be the index such that $T_{\text{sig}}(\widetilde{X}, R, m) = h_{\text{sig}, i_{\text{sig}}}$,
- j_{sig} be the value of $ctrh_{\text{non}}$ at the moment $T_{\text{sig}}(\widetilde{X}, R, m)$ is assigned.

Then $\mathcal{B}$ returns $(i_{\text{agg}}, j_{\text{agg}}, i_{\text{sig}}, j_{\text{sig}}, L, R, s, \vec{a})$, where $\vec{a} = (a_1, \ldots, a_n)$. By construction, $a_i = h_{\text{agg}, i_{\text{agg}}}$ for each i such that $X_i = X^*$, and the validity of the forgery implies Equation (2).

H_{agg} is called at most q_h times by the adversary, at most once per SIGN' query, and at most once when verifying the forgery, hence at most $q_h + q_s + 1$ times in total. Similarly, H_{non} is called at most q_h times by the adversary and at most once per SIGN' query, hence at most $q_h + q_s$ times in total. Finally, H_{sig} is called at most q_h times by the adversary, at most once per H_{non} query, and at most once when verifying the forgery, hence at most $2q_h + q_s + 1$ times in total. Hence, each random oracle is called at most $q = 2q_h + q_s + 1$ times in total.

---

[8] This computation can be saved by caching the result when handling the internal H_{non} query.

We now lower bound the accepting probability of $\mathcal{B}$. Since $h_{\text{agg},1}, \ldots, h_{\text{agg},q}$, $h_{\text{non},1}, \ldots, h_{\text{non},q}$ and $h_{\text{sig},1}, \ldots, h_{\text{sig},q}$ are uniformly random, $\mathcal{B}$ perfectly simulates the security experiment to the adversary. Moreover, when the adversary eventually returns a forgery, $\mathcal{B}$ returns a non-$\bot$ output unless BadOrder or KeyColl is set to true. Hence, by the union bound,

$$acc(\mathcal{B}) \geq \mathsf{Adv}^{\mathsf{EUF\text{-}CMA}}_{\mathcal{A},\mathsf{MuSig2}[\mathsf{GrGen},\nu]}(\lambda) - \Pr[\mathsf{BadOrder}] - \Pr[\mathsf{KeyColl}].$$

It remains to upper bound $\Pr[\mathsf{BadOrder}]$ and $\Pr[\mathsf{KeyColl}]$. Note that for any query $\mathsf{H}_{\text{agg}}(L', X')$, either $T_{\text{agg}}(L', X')$ is already defined, in which case H_{agg} returns immediately and neither BadOrder nor KeyColl can be set to true, or $T_{\text{agg}}(L', X')$ is undefined, in which case $T_{\text{agg}}(L', X'')$ is undefined for every $X'' \in L'$ since all these table values are set at the same time when the first query $\mathsf{H}_{\text{agg}}(L', *)$ happens. In the latter case, the corresponding aggregate key is

$$\widetilde{X}' = (X^*)^{n^* h_{\text{agg},i}} \cdot Z$$

where $n^* \geq 1$ is the number of times X^* appears in L' and $h_{\text{agg},i}$ (where i is the value of ctrh_{agg} when $T_{\text{agg}}(L', X^*)$ is set) is uniformly random in $\mathbb{Z}_p$ and independent of Z which accounts for public keys different from X^* in L'. Hence, $\widetilde{X}'$ is uniformly random in $\mathbb{G}$ of size $p \geq 2^{\lambda-1}$. Since there are always at most q defined entries in T_{sig} and at most q queries to H_{agg}, BadOrder is set to true with probability at most $q^2/2^{\lambda-1}$. Similarly, the size of K is always at most q (since at most one element is added per H_{agg} query), hence KeyColl is set to true with probability at most $q^2/2^{\lambda-1}$. Combining all of the above, we obtain

$$acc(\mathcal{B}) \geq \mathsf{Adv}^{\mathsf{EUF\text{-}CMA}}_{\mathcal{A},\mathsf{MuSig2}[\mathsf{GrGen},\nu]}(\lambda) - \frac{4q^2}{2^\lambda}.$$

$\square$

Using $\mathcal{B}$, we now construct an algorithm $\mathcal{C}$ which returns a multiset of public keys L together with the discrete logarithm of the corresponding aggregate key.

Lemma 3. *Given some integer ν, let $\mathcal{A}$ be a (t, q_s, q_h, N)-adversary in the random oracle model against the multi-signature scheme* $\mathsf{MuSig2}[\mathsf{GrGen}, \nu]$ *and let* $q = 2q_h + q_s + 1$. *Then there exists an algorithm $\mathcal{C}$ that takes as input group parameters* $(\mathbb{G}, p, g) \leftarrow \mathsf{GrGen}(1^\lambda)$, *uniformly random group elements* $X^*, U_1, \ldots, U_{\nu q_s} \in \mathbb{G}$, *and uniformly random scalars* $h_{\text{agg},1}, \ldots, h_{\text{agg},q}$, $h_{\text{non},1}, h'_{\text{non},1}, \ldots, h_{\text{non},q}, h'_{\text{non},q} \in \mathbb{Z}_p$, *makes at most $2q_s$ queries to a discrete logarithm oracle* DLOG_g, *and with accepting probability (as defined in Lemma 1)*

$$acc(\mathcal{C}) \geq \frac{(\mathsf{Adv}^{\mathsf{EUF\text{-}CMA}}_{\mathcal{A},\mathsf{MuSig2}[\mathsf{GrGen},\nu]}(\lambda))^2}{q} - \frac{2(4q+1)}{2^\lambda}$$

outputs a tuple $(i_{\text{agg}}, j_{\text{agg}}, L, \vec{a}, \tilde{x})$ *where* $i_{\text{agg}} \in \{1, \ldots, q\}$, $j_{\text{agg}} \in \{0, \ldots, q\}$, $L = \{X_1, \ldots, X_n\}$ *is a multiset of public keys such that* $X^* \in L$, $\vec{a} = (a_1, \ldots, a_n) \in \mathbb{Z}_p^n$ *is a tuple of scalars such that* $a_i = h_{\text{agg},i_{\text{agg}}}$ *for any i such that $X_i = X^*$, and $\tilde{x}$ is the discrete logarithm of* $\widetilde{X} = \prod_{i=1}^n X_i^{a_i}$ *in base g.*

Proof. Algorithm $\mathcal{C}$ runs $\mathsf{Fork}^{\mathcal{B}}$ with $\mathcal{B}$ as defined in Lemma 2 and takes additional steps as described below. The mapping with notation of our Forking Lemma (Lemma 1) is as follows:

- $(\mathbb{G}, p, g)$, X^*, $U_1, \ldots, U_{\nu q_s}$, and $h_{\mathrm{agg},1}, \ldots, h_{\mathrm{agg},q}$ play the role of *inp*,
- $h_{\mathrm{non},1}, h'_{\mathrm{non},1}, \ldots, h_{\mathrm{non},q}, h'_{\mathrm{non},q}$ play the role of $v_1, v'_1, \ldots, v_m, v'_m$,
- $h_{\mathrm{sig},1}, \ldots, h_{\mathrm{sig},q}$ play the role of $h_1, \ldots, h_q$,
- $(i_{\mathrm{sig}}, j_{\mathrm{sig}})$ play the role of (i, j),
- $(i_{\mathrm{agg}}, j_{\mathrm{agg}}, L, R, s, \vec{a})$ play the role of *out*.

In more details, $\mathcal{C}$ picks random coins ρ_B and uniformly random scalars $h_{\mathrm{sig},1}, \ldots,$ $h_{\mathrm{sig},q} \in \mathbb{Z}_p$, and runs algorithm $\mathcal{B}$ on coins ρ_B, group description $(\mathbb{G}, p, g)$, group elements $X^*, U_1, \ldots, U_{\nu q_s} \in \mathbb{G}$, and scalars $h_{\mathrm{agg},1}, \ldots, h_{\mathrm{agg},q}, h_{\mathrm{non},1}, \ldots, h_{\mathrm{non},q},$ $h_{\mathrm{sig},1}, \ldots, h_{\mathrm{sig},q} \in \mathbb{Z}_p$. Recall that scalars $h_{\mathrm{agg},1}, \ldots, h_{\mathrm{agg},q}$ and $h_{\mathrm{non},1}, h'_{\mathrm{non},1}, \ldots,$ $, h_{\mathrm{non},q}, h'_{\mathrm{non},q}$ are part of the *input* of $\mathcal{C}$ and the former will be the same in both runs of $\mathcal{B}$. All DLOG_g oracle queries made by $\mathcal{B}$ are relayed by $\mathcal{C}$ to its own DLOG_g oracle. If $\mathcal{B}$ returns $\bot$, $\mathcal{C}$ returns $\bot$ as well. Otherwise, if $\mathcal{B}$ returns a tuple $(i_{\mathrm{agg}}, j_{\mathrm{agg}}, i_{\mathrm{sig}}, j_{\mathrm{sig}}, L, R, s, \vec{a})$, where $L = \{X_1, \ldots, X_n\}$ and $\vec{a} = (a_1, \ldots, a_n)$, $\mathcal{C}$ picks uniformly random scalars $h'_{\mathrm{sig},i_{\mathrm{sig}}}, \ldots, h'_{\mathrm{sig},q} \in \mathbb{Z}_p$ and runs $\mathcal{B}$ again with the same random coins ρ_B on input

$$(\mathbb{G}, p, g), X^*, U_1, \ldots, U_{\nu q_s},$$
$$h_{\mathrm{agg},1}, \ldots, h_{\mathrm{agg},q},$$
$$h_{\mathrm{non},1}, \ldots, h_{\mathrm{non},j_{\mathrm{sig}}}, h'_{\mathrm{non},j_{\mathrm{sig}}+1}, \ldots, h'_{\mathrm{non},q},$$
$$h_{\mathrm{sig},1}, \ldots, h_{\mathrm{sig},i_{\mathrm{sig}}-1}, h'_{\mathrm{sig},i_{\mathrm{sig}}}, \ldots, h'_{\mathrm{sig},q}.$$

Again, all DLOG_g oracle queries made by $\mathcal{B}$ are relayed by $\mathcal{C}$ to its own DLOG_g oracle. If $\mathcal{B}$ returns $\bot$ in this second run, $\mathcal{C}$ returns $\bot$ as well. If $\mathcal{B}$ returns a second tuple $(i'_{\mathrm{agg}}, j'_{\mathrm{agg}}, i'_{\mathrm{sig}}, j'_{\mathrm{sig}}, L', R', s', \vec{a}')$, where $L' = \{X'_1, \ldots, X'_{n'}\}$ and $\vec{a}' = (a'_1, \ldots, a'_{n'})$, $\mathcal{C}$ proceeds as follows. Let $\widetilde{X} = \prod_{i=1}^{n} X_i^{a_i}$ and $\widetilde{X}' = \prod_{i=1}^{n'} (X'_i)^{a'_i}$ denote the aggregate public keys from the two forgeries. If $i_{\mathrm{sig}} \neq i'_{\mathrm{sig}}$, or $i_{\mathrm{sig}} = i'_{\mathrm{sig}}$ and $h_{\mathrm{sig},i_{\mathrm{sig}}} = h'_{\mathrm{sig},i_{\mathrm{sig}}}$, then $\mathcal{C}$ returns $\bot$. Otherwise, if $i_{\mathrm{sig}} = i'_{\mathrm{sig}}$ and $h_{\mathrm{sig},i_{\mathrm{sig}}} \neq h'_{\mathrm{sig},i_{\mathrm{sig}}}$, we will prove shortly that

$$i_{\mathrm{agg}} = i'_{\mathrm{agg}}, \ j_{\mathrm{agg}} = j'_{\mathrm{agg}}, \ L = L', \ R = R', \text{ and } \vec{a} = \vec{a}', \tag{3}$$

which implies in particular that $\widetilde{X} = \widetilde{X}'$. By Lemma 2, the two outputs returned by $\mathcal{B}$ are such that

$$g^s = R\widetilde{X}^{h_{\mathrm{sig},i_{\mathrm{sig}}}} \quad \text{and} \quad g^{s'} = R'(\widetilde{X}')^{h'_{\mathrm{sig},i_{\mathrm{sig}}}} = R\widetilde{X}^{h'_{\mathrm{sig},i_{\mathrm{sig}}}},$$

which allows $\mathcal{C}$ to compute the discrete logarithm of $\widetilde{X}$ as

$$\tilde{x} := (s - s')(h_{\mathrm{sig},i_{\mathrm{sig}}} - h'_{\mathrm{sig},i_{\mathrm{sig}}})^{-1} \bmod p.$$

Then $\mathcal{C}$ returns $(i_{\mathrm{agg}}, j_{\mathrm{agg}}, L, \vec{a}, \tilde{x})$.

$\mathcal{C}$ returns a non-$\perp$ output if $\mathsf{Fork}^{\mathcal{B}}$ does, so that by Lemmas 1 and 2, and letting $\varepsilon = \mathsf{Adv}^{\mathsf{EUF\text{-}CMA}}_{\mathcal{A},\mathsf{MuSig2[GrGen},\nu]}(\lambda)$, $\mathcal{C}$'s accepting probability satisfies

$$
\begin{aligned}
acc(\mathcal{C}) \geq acc(\mathcal{B})\left(\frac{acc(\mathcal{B})}{q} - \frac{1}{p}\right) &\geq \frac{(\varepsilon - 4q^2/2^\lambda)^2}{q} - \frac{\varepsilon - 4q^2/2^\lambda}{2^{\lambda-1}} \\
&= \frac{\varepsilon^2}{q} - \frac{2\varepsilon(4q+1)}{2^\lambda} + \frac{8q^2(2q+1)}{2^{2\lambda}} \\
&\geq \frac{\varepsilon^2}{q} - \frac{2(4q+1)}{2^\lambda}.
\end{aligned}
$$

It remains to prove the equalities of Eq. (3). In $\mathcal{B}$'s first execution, $h_{\mathrm{sig},i_{\mathrm{sig}}}$ is assigned to $T_{\mathrm{sig}}(\widetilde{X}, R, m)$, while is $\mathcal{B}$'s second execution, $h'_{\mathrm{sig},i_{\mathrm{sig}}}$ is assigned to $T_{\mathrm{sig}}(\widetilde{X}', R', m')$. Note that these two assignments can happen either because of a direct query to $\mathsf{H}_{\mathrm{sig}}$ by the adversary, during a query to $\mathsf{H}_{\mathrm{non}}$, during a $\textsc{Sign}'$ query, or during the final verification of the validity of the forgery. Up to these two assignments, the two executions are identical since $\mathcal{B}$ runs $\mathcal{A}$ on the same random coins and input, uses the same values $h_{\mathrm{agg},1}, \ldots, h_{\mathrm{agg},q}$ for $T_{\mathrm{agg}}(\cdot, X^*)$ assignments, the same values $h_{\mathrm{sig},1}, \ldots, h_{\mathrm{sig},i_{\mathrm{sig}}-1}$ for T_{sig} assignments, and the same values $h_{\mathrm{non},1}, \ldots, h_{\mathrm{non},j_{\mathrm{sig}}}$ for T_{non} assignments, $T_{\mathrm{agg}}(\cdot, X \neq X^*)$ assignments, and DL oracle outputs s_1 in $\textsc{Sign}'$ queries. Since both executions are identical up to the two assignments $T_{\mathrm{sig}}(\widetilde{X}, R, m) := h_{\mathrm{sig},i_{\mathrm{sig}}}$ and $T_{\mathrm{sig}}(\widetilde{X}', R', m') := h'_{\mathrm{sig},i_{\mathrm{sig}}}$, the arguments of the two assignments must be the same, which in particular implies that $R = R'$ and $\widetilde{X} = \widetilde{X}'$. Assume that $L \neq L'$. Then, since $\widetilde{X} = \widetilde{X}'$, this would mean that $\mathsf{KeyColl}$ is set to true in both executions, a contradiction since $\mathcal{B}$ returns a non-$\perp$ output in both executions. Hence, $L = L'$. Since in both executions of $\mathcal{B}$, $\mathsf{BadOrder}$ is not set to true, assignments $T_{\mathrm{agg}}(L, X^*) := h_{\mathrm{agg},i_{\mathrm{agg}}}$ and $T_{\mathrm{agg}}(L', X^*) := h_{\mathrm{agg},i'_{\mathrm{agg}}}$ necessarily happened *before* the fork. This implies that $i_{\mathrm{agg}} = i'_{\mathrm{agg}}$, $j_{\mathrm{agg}} = j'_{\mathrm{agg}}$, and $\vec{a} = \vec{a}'$. □

We are now ready to prove Theorem 1 by constructing from $\mathcal{C}$ an algorithm $\mathcal{D}$ solving the AOMDL problem.

Proof of Theorem 1. Fix some integer $\nu \geq 4$.[9] Algorithm $\mathcal{D}$ runs $\mathsf{Fork}^{\mathcal{C}}$ with $\mathcal{C}$ as defined in Lemma 3 and takes additional steps as described below. The mapping with the notation in our Forking Lemma (Lemma 1) is as follows:

- $(\mathbb{G}, p, g)$, X^*, $U_1, \ldots, U_{\nu q_s}$ play the role of inp,
- $(h_{\mathrm{non},1}, h'_{\mathrm{non},1})$, $(h''_{\mathrm{non},1}, h'''_{\mathrm{non},1})$, $\ldots$, $(h_{\mathrm{non},q}, h'_{\mathrm{non},q})$, $(h''_{\mathrm{non},q}, h'''_{\mathrm{non},q})$ play the role of $v_1, v'_1, \ldots, v_m, v'_m$,
- $h_{\mathrm{agg},1}, \ldots, h_{\mathrm{agg},q}$ play the role of $h_1, \ldots, h_q$,
- $(i_{\mathrm{agg}}, j_{\mathrm{agg}})$ play the role of (i, j),
- $(L, \vec{a}, \tilde{x})$ play the role of out.

---

[9] Theorem 1 states the security of MuSig2 only for $\nu = 4$, because there is no reason to use more than four nonces in practice. The proof works for any $\nu \geq 4$.

In more details, algorithm $\mathcal{D}$ makes $\nu q_s + 1$ queries to its challenge oracle $X^*, U_1, \ldots, U_{\nu q_s} \leftarrow \text{CH}()$, picks random coins ρ_C and scalars $h_{\text{agg},1}, \ldots, h_{\text{agg},q}$, $h_{\text{non},1}, h'_{\text{non},1}, \ldots, h_{\text{non},q}, h'_{\text{non},q} \in \mathbb{Z}_p$, and runs $\mathcal{C}$ on coins ρ_C, group description $(\mathbb{G}, p, g)$, group elements $X^*, U_1, \ldots, U_{\nu q_s} \in \mathbb{Z}_p$, and scalars $h_{\text{agg},1}, \ldots, h_{\text{agg},q}$, $h_{\text{non},1}, h'_{\text{non},1}, \ldots, h_{\text{non},q}, h'_{\text{non},q} \in \mathbb{Z}_p$. It relays all DLOG_g oracle queries made by $\mathcal{C}$ to its own DLOG_g oracle, caching pairs of group elements and responses to avoid making multiple queries for the same group element. If $\mathcal{C}$ returns $\perp$, $\mathcal{D}$ returns $\perp$ as well. Otherwise, if $\mathcal{C}$ returns a tuple $(i_{\text{agg}}, j_{\text{agg}}, L, \vec{a}, \tilde{x})$, $\mathcal{D}$ picks uniformly random scalars $h'_{\text{agg},i_{\text{agg}}}, \ldots, h'_{\text{agg},q} \in \mathbb{Z}_p$ and $h''_{\text{non},j_{\text{agg}}+1}, h'''_{\text{non},j_{\text{agg}}+1}, \ldots, h''_{\text{non},q}, h'''_{\text{non},q} \in \mathbb{Z}_p$, and runs $\mathcal{C}$ again with the same random coins ρ_C on input $X^*, U_1, \ldots, U_{\nu q_s}$,

$$h_{\text{agg},1}, \ldots, h_{\text{agg},i_{\text{agg}}-1}, h'_{\text{agg},i_{\text{agg}}}, \ldots, h'_{\text{agg},q}, \text{ and}$$

$$h_{\text{non},1}, h'_{\text{non},1} \ldots, h_{\text{non},j_{\text{agg}}}, h'_{\text{non},j_{\text{agg}}}, h''_{\text{non},j_{\text{agg}}+1}, h'''_{\text{non},j_{\text{agg}}+1}, \ldots, h''_{\text{non},q}, h'''_{\text{non},q}.$$

It relays all DLOG_g oracle queries made by $\mathcal{C}$ to its own DLOG_g oracle after looking them up in its cache to avoid making duplicate queries. If $\mathcal{C}$ returns $\perp$ in this second run, $\mathcal{D}$ returns $\perp$ as well. If $\mathcal{C}$ returns a second tuple $(i'_{\text{agg}}, j'_{\text{agg}}, L', \vec{a}', \tilde{x}')$, $\mathcal{D}$ proceeds as follows. Let $L = \{X_1, \ldots, X_n\}$, $\vec{a} = (a_1, \ldots, a_n)$, $L' = \{X'_1, \ldots, X'_{n'}\}$, and $\vec{a}' = (a'_1, \ldots, a'_n)$. Let n^* be the number of times X^* appears in L. If $i_{\text{agg}} \neq i'_{\text{agg}}$, or $i_{\text{agg}} = i'_{\text{agg}}$ and $h_{\text{agg},i_{\text{agg}}} = h'_{\text{agg},i_{\text{agg}}}$, $\mathcal{D}$ returns $\perp$. Otherwise, if $i_{\text{agg}} = i'_{\text{agg}}$ and $h_{\text{agg},i_{\text{agg}}} \neq h'_{\text{agg},i_{\text{agg}}}$, then we will show below that

$$L = L' \text{ and } a_i = a'_i \text{ for each } i \text{ such that } X_i \neq X^*. \tag{4}$$

By Lemma 3, we have that

$$g^{\tilde{x}} = \prod_{i=1}^{n} X_i^{a_i} = (X^*)^{n^* h_{\text{agg},i_{\text{agg}}}} \prod_{\substack{i \in \{1, \ldots, n\} \\ X_i \neq X^*}} X_i^{a_i},$$

$$g^{\tilde{x}'} = \prod_{i=1}^{n} X_i^{a'_i} = (X^*)^{n^* h'_{\text{agg},i_{\text{agg}}}} \prod_{\substack{i \in \{1, \ldots, n\} \\ X_i \neq X^*}} X_i^{a_i}.$$

Thus, $\mathcal{D}$ can compute the discrete logarithm of X^* as

$$x^* := (\tilde{x} - \tilde{x}')(n^*)^{-1}(h_{\text{agg},i_{\text{agg}}} - h'_{\text{agg},i_{\text{agg}}})^{-1} \bmod p.$$

We will now prove the equalities in Eq. (4). In the two executions of $\mathcal{B}$ run within the first execution of $\mathcal{C}$, $h_{\text{agg},i_{\text{agg}}}$ is assigned to $T_{\text{agg}}(L, X^*)$, while in the two executions of $\mathcal{B}$ run within the second execution of $\mathcal{C}$, $h'_{\text{agg},i_{\text{agg}}}$ is assigned to $T_{\text{agg}}(L', X^*)$. Note that these two assignments can happen either because of a direct query $\text{H}_{\text{agg}}(L, X)$ made by the adversary for some key $X \in L$ (not necessarily X^*), during a signing query, or during the final verification of the validity of the forgery. Up to these two assignments, the four executions of $\mathcal{A}$ are identical since $\mathcal{B}$ runs $\mathcal{A}$ on the same random coins and the same input, uses the same values $h_{\mathrm{agg},1},\ldots,h_{\mathrm{agg},i_{\mathrm{agg}}-1}$ for $T_{\mathrm{agg}}(\cdot,X^*)$ assignments, the same values $h_{\mathrm{sig},1},\ldots,h_{\mathrm{sig},q}$ for T_{sig} assignments, the same values $h_{\mathrm{non},1},\ldots,h_{\mathrm{non},j_{\mathrm{agg}}}$ for T_{non} assignments, $T_{\mathrm{agg}}(\cdot,X\neq X^*)$ assignments, and the DL oracle outputs s_1 in SIGN$'$ queries (note that this relies on the fact that in the four executions of $\mathcal{B}$, BadOrder is not set to true). Since the four executions of $\mathcal{B}$ are identical up to the assignments $T_{\mathrm{agg}}(L,X^*):=h_{\mathrm{agg},i_{\mathrm{agg}}}$ and $T_{\mathrm{agg}}(L',X^*):=h'_{\mathrm{agg},i_{\mathrm{agg}}}$, the arguments of these two assignments must be the same, which implies that $L=L'$. Besides, all values $T_{\mathrm{agg}}(L,X)$ for $X\in L\setminus\{X^*\}$ are chosen uniformly at random by $\mathcal{B}$ using the same coins in the four executions, which implies that $a_i=a_i'$ for each i such that $X_i\neq X^*$. This shows the equalities in Eq. (4).

Recall that $\mathcal{D}$ internally ran four executions of $\mathcal{B}$ (throughout forking in Fork$^{\mathcal{B}}$ and in Fork$^{\mathcal{C}}$). Consider a SIGN query handled by $\mathcal{B}$, and let i be the index such that the group elements $U_i,\ldots,U_{i+\nu-1}$ queried by $\mathcal{D}$ to CH were assigned to $R_{1,1},\ldots R_{1,\nu}$ by $\mathcal{B}$ when handling this query. In the corresponding SIGN$'$ query, algorithm $\mathcal{B}$ has computed a_1, b and c and has queried the DL oracle with

$$s_1:=\mathrm{DLOG}_g\left(\left(\prod_{j=1}^{\nu}R_{1,j}^{b^{j-1}}\right)(X^*)^{a_1 c},\ldots\right) \tag{5}$$

(and the appropriate algebraic representation, which we do not repeat here). Note that all four executions of $\mathcal{B}$ have been passed the same group elements $U_i,\ldots,U_{i+\nu-1}$ as input to be used in SIGN queries. However, when handling the corresponding SIGN$'$ queries, $\mathcal{B}$ may have made different queries to the DL oracle in the four executions.[10]

Algorithm $\mathcal{D}$ initializes a flag LinDep representing a bad event and attempts to deduce the discrete logarithm of all challenges which were used in each SIGN query in all four executions of $\mathcal{B}$ as follows.

For each SIGN$'(k,\ldots)$ query with session index k, algorithm $\mathcal{D}$ proceeds to build a system of ν linear equations with unknowns $r_1,\ldots,r_\nu$, the discrete logarithms of $R_{1,1},\ldots,R_{1,\nu}$. Let P_k be the partition of the four executions of $\mathcal{B}$ such that two executions are in the same component if they were identical up to assignment of the T_{non} entry accessed by the SIGN$'(k,\ldots)$ query handler when defining $b:=T_{\mathrm{non}}(\widetilde{X},(R_1,\ldots,R_\nu),m)$.[11] Consider the variables b,a_1,c,s_1 in the SIGN$'(k,\ldots)$ query handler within all executions within some component $\ell\in P_k$. We will show below that all executions in component $\ell\in P_k$ assign identical values $b^{(\ell)},a_1^{(\ell)},c^{(\ell)},s_1^{(\ell)}$ to these variables. As a consequence, all executions in component ℓ pass identical group elements as inputs to their DL oracles in the

---

[10] For example, the adversary may have replied with different L, m or R values in different executions, or algorithm $\mathcal{B}$ may have received different "h_{non}" values.

[11] For example, all four executions (as visualized in Fig. 4) are in the same component if the corresponding T_{non} value was set before the $\mathsf{H}_{\mathrm{agg}}$ fork point, and two executions in the same branch of the $\mathsf{H}_{\mathrm{agg}}$ fork are in the same component if the T_{non} value was set before the $\mathsf{H}_{\mathrm{sig}}$ fork point.

SIGN$'(k, \ldots)$ query handler (see Eq. (5)). Thus, due to the caching of DL oracle replies in $\mathcal{D}$, algorithm $\mathcal{D}$ has used only $|P_k|$ DL queries to its own DL oracle to answer the DL oracle queries originating by all four executions of $\mathcal{B}$. Then $\mathcal{D}$ has a system of $|P_k| \leq 4 \leq \nu$ linear equations

$$\sum_{j=1}^{\nu} (b^{(\ell)})^{j-1} r_j = s_1^{(\ell)} - a_1^{(\ell)} c^{(\ell)} x^*, \quad \ell \in \{1, \ldots, |P_k|\} \tag{6}$$

with unknowns $r_1, \ldots, r_\nu$. If the values $b^{(\ell)}$ for $\ell \in \{1, \ldots, |P_k|\}$ are not pairwise distinct, then $\mathcal{D}$ sets LinDep := true and returns $\bot$.

Otherwise, $\mathcal{D}$ completes the linear system with $\nu - |P_k|$ remaining DL queries as follows. For each $\ell \in \{|P_k|+1, \ldots, \nu\}$, it picks a value $b^{(\ell)}$ from $\mathbb{Z}_p$ such that $b^{(\ell)} \neq b^{(\ell')}$ for all $\ell' < \ell$ and obtains the additional equations

$$\sum_{j=1}^{\nu} (b^{(\ell)})^{j-1} r_j = \mathrm{DLOG}_g \left(\prod_{j=1}^{\nu} (R_{1,j})^{(b^{(\ell)})^{j-1}}, \left(\alpha^{(\ell)}, (\beta_i^{(\ell)})_{1 \leq i \leq \nu q_s + 1} \right) \right), \tag{7}$$

$\ell \in \{|P|+1, \ldots, \nu\}$, computing the algebraic representations of the queried group elements appropriately as $\alpha^{(\ell)} := 0$ and $(\beta_i^{(\ell)})_{1 \leq i \leq \nu q_s + 1} := (0, \ldots, 0, \beta_{\nu(k-1)} = (b^{(\ell)})^0 = 1, \ldots, \beta_{\nu k - 1} = (b^{(\ell)})^{\nu-1}, 0, \ldots, 0)$.

The coefficient matrix

$$B = \begin{pmatrix} 1 & (b^{(1)})^1 & \cdots & (b^{(1)})^{\nu-1} \\ 1 & (b^{(2)})^1 & \cdots & (b^{(2)})^{\nu-1} \\ \vdots & \vdots & \ddots & \vdots \\ 1 & (b^{(\nu)})^1 & \cdots & (b^{(\nu)})^{\nu-1} \end{pmatrix}$$

of the complete linear system (Eqs. (6) and (7)) is a square Vandermonde matrix with pairwise distinct $b^{(\ell)}$ values, and thus has full rank ν. At this stage, $\mathcal{D}$ has a system of ν linear independent equations with ν unknowns. Because the system is consistent by construction, it has a unique solution $r_1, \ldots, r_\nu$, which is computed and output by $\mathcal{D}$.

It remains to show that if for some given SIGN$'(k, \ldots)$ query, two executions of $\mathcal{B}$ are in the same component of P_k, then

$$b = b', \quad a_1 = a_1', \quad c = c', \quad \text{and} \quad s_1 = s_1', \tag{8}$$

where here and in the following, non-primed and primed terms are the values used in the SIGN$'$ query in the respective execution. By definition, the executions were identical up to the assignments of $T_{\mathrm{non}}(\widetilde{X}, (R_1, \ldots, R_\nu), m)$ and $T_{\mathrm{non}}(\widetilde{X}', (R_1', \ldots, R_\nu'), m')$, which implies that $\widetilde{X} = \widetilde{X}'$, $(R_1, \ldots, R_\nu) = (R_1', \ldots, R_\nu')$, $m = m'$, and $T_{\mathrm{non}}(\widetilde{X}, (R_1, \ldots, R_\nu), m) = T_{\mathrm{non}}(\widetilde{X}', (R_1', \ldots, R_\nu'), m')$. The equality $b = b'$ follows immediately.

To prove $c = c'$, note that previous equalities imply that $\prod_{j=1}^{\nu} R_j^{b^{j-1}} = \prod_{j=1}^{\nu} (R_j')^{(b')^{j-1}}$, i.e. $R = R'$. Hence, c and c' were defined using the same table entry $T_{\text{sig}}(\widetilde{X}, R, m)$ in both executions. If entry $T_{\text{sig}}(\widetilde{X}, R, m)$ had already been set when $T_{\text{non}}(\widetilde{X}, (R_1, \ldots, R_\nu), m)$ was set, then $c = c'$ due to the executions being identical. Otherwise, if the value $T_{\text{sig}}(\widetilde{X}, R, m)$ had not already been set when $T_{\text{non}}(\widetilde{X}, (R_1, \ldots, R_\nu), m)$ was set, then the internal H_{sig} query in the H_{non} query handler set $T_{\text{sig}}(\widetilde{X}, R, m)$ exactly when the query $H_{\text{non}}(\widetilde{X}, (R_1, \ldots, R_\nu), m)$ was handled. Since $\mathcal{B}$ did not receive a forgery which is invalid due to the values m and L from the forgery having been queried in a SIGN' query, the internal H_{sig} query was not the H_{sig} fork point. Therefore, both executions are still identical when $T_{\text{sig}}(\widetilde{X}, R, m)$ is set, which implies that $c = c'$.

To prove $a_1 = a_1'$ we first note that in the first execution, $H_{\text{agg}}(L, X^*)$ was set before $T_{\text{sig}}(\widetilde{X}, R, m)$ (as otherwise $\mathcal{B}$ would have set BadOrder := true), hence before $T_{\text{non}}(\widetilde{X}, (R_1, \ldots, R_\nu), m)$ since as proved above $T_{\text{sig}}(\widetilde{X}, R, m)$ was set before or at the same time as $T_{\text{non}}(\widetilde{X}, (R_1, \ldots, R_\nu), m)$. Similarly, in the second execution, $H_{\text{agg}}(L', X^*)$ was set before $T_{\text{non}}(\widetilde{X}, (R_1, \ldots, R_\nu), m)$. Because both executions are identical up to the assignment of $T_{\text{non}}(\widetilde{X}, (R_1, \ldots, R_\nu), m)$, $H_{\text{agg}}(L, X^*)$ and $H_{\text{agg}}(L', X^*)$ were set in *both* executions. Assume that $L \neq L'$. Then $\text{KeyAgg}(L) = \widetilde{X} = \widetilde{X}' = \text{KeyAgg}(L')$, a contradiction since $\mathcal{B}$ has not set KeyColl := true in either of the executions. This implies that a_1 and a_1' were defined using the same table entry $H_{\text{agg}}(L, X^*)$ which was set when executions were identical, hence $a_1 = a_1'$.

The equality $s_1 = s_1'$ follows from Eq. (5) together with $b = b'$, $a_1 = a_1'$, and $c = c'$. This shows the equalities in Eq. (8).

Altogether, $\mathcal{D}$ makes $|P|$ DL queries initiated by $\mathcal{B}$ (as in Eq. (6)) and $\nu - |P|$ additional DL queries (as in Eq. (7)) per initiated signing session. Thus, the total number of DL queries is exactly νq_s.

Neglecting the time needed to compute discrete logarithms and solve linear equation systems, the running time t' of $\mathcal{D}$ is twice the running time of $\mathcal{C}$, which itself is twice the running time of $\mathcal{B}$. The running time of $\mathcal{B}$ is the running time t of $\mathcal{A}$ plus the time needed to maintain tables T_{agg}, T_{non}, and T_{sig} (we assume each assignment takes unit time) and answer signing and hash queries. The sizes of T_{agg}, T_{non}, and T_{sig} are at most qN, q, and q respectively. Answering signing queries is dominated by the time needed to compute the aggregate key as well as the honest signer's effective nonce, which is at most Nt_{exp} and $(\nu - 1)t_{\text{exp}}$ respectively. Answering hash queries is dominated by the time to compute the aggregate nonce which is at most $(\nu - 1)t_{\text{exp}}$. Therefore, $t' = 4(t + q(N + 2\nu - 2))t_{\text{exp}} + O(qN)$.

Clearly, $\mathcal{D}$ is successful if $\text{Fork}^{\mathcal{C}}$ returns a non-$\perp$ answer and LinDep is not set to true. LinDep is set to true if, in the linear system corresponding to some $\text{SIGN}(k, \ldots)$ query, there are two identical values $b^{(\ell)} = b^{(\ell')}$ in two different execution components $\ell, \ell' \leq |P_k|$. By construction, $b^{(\ell)}$ and $b^{(\ell')}$ were assigned to two of the scalars $h_{\text{non},1}, h'_{\text{non},1}, h''_{\text{non},1}, h'''_{\text{non},1}, \ldots, h_{\text{non},q}, h'_{\text{non},q}, h''_{\text{non},q}, h'''_{\text{non},q}$. Since these $4q$ scalars are drawn from $\mathbb{Z}_p$ with $p \leq 2^{\lambda-1}$, we have $\Pr\left[\text{LinDep}\right] \leq (4q)^2/2^{\lambda-1} = 32q^2/2^\lambda$. Let $\varepsilon = \text{Adv}_{\mathcal{A}, \text{MuSig2}[\text{GrGen}, \nu]}^{\text{EUF-CMA}}(\lambda)$. By Lemmas 1 and 3, the success probability of $\text{Fork}^{\mathcal{C}}$ is at least

$$acc(\mathsf{Fork}^{\mathcal{C}}) \geq acc(\mathcal{C}) \left(\frac{acc(\mathcal{C})}{q} - \frac{1}{p} \right)$$

$$\geq \frac{(\varepsilon^2/q - 2(4q+1)/2^{\lambda})^2}{q} - \frac{\varepsilon^2/q - 2(4q+1)/2^{\lambda}}{2^{\lambda-1}}$$

$$\geq \frac{\varepsilon^4}{q^3} - \frac{(16+4/q)}{q \cdot 2^{\lambda}} - \frac{2}{q \cdot 2^{\lambda}} \geq \frac{\varepsilon^4}{q^3} - \frac{22}{2^{\lambda}}.$$

Altogether, the advantage of $\mathcal{D}$ is at least

$$\mathsf{Adv}_{\mathcal{D},\mathsf{GrGen}}^{\mathsf{AOMDL}}(\lambda) \geq acc(\mathsf{Fork}^{\mathcal{C}}) - \Pr\left[\mathsf{LinDep}\right] \geq \frac{\varepsilon^4}{q^3} - \frac{32q^2+22}{2^{\lambda}}$$

$\square$

References

1. Alper, H.K., Burdges, J.: Two-round trip schnorr multi-signatures via delinearized witnesses. In: CRYPTO 2021, 2021. https://eprint.iacr.org/2020/1245
2. Bagherzandi, A., Cheon, J.H., Jarecki, S.: Multisignatures secure under the discrete logarithm assumption and a generalized forking lemma. In: Ning, P., Syverson, P.F., Jha, S. (eds.) ACM CCS 2008, pp. 449–458. ACM Press, October 2008. https://doi.org/10.1145/1455770.1455827
3. Bellare, M., Namprempre, C., Pointcheval, D., Semanko, M.: The one-more-RSA-inversion problems and the security of Chaum's blind signature scheme. J. Cryptol. **16**(3), 185–215 (2003). https://doi.org/10.1007/s00145-002-0120-1
4. Bellare, M., Neven, G.: Multi-signatures in the plain public-key model and a general forking lemma. In: Juels, A., Wright, R.N., De Capitani di Vimercati, S. (eds.) ACM CCS 2006, pp. 390–399. ACM Press, October/November 2006. https://doi.org/10.1145/1180405.1180453
5. Bellare, M., Palacio, A.: GQ and schnorr identification schemes: proofs of security against impersonation under active and concurrent attacks. In: Yung, M. (ed.) CRYPTO 2002. LNCS, vol. 2442, pp. 162–177. Springer, Heidelberg (2002). https://doi.org/10.1007/3-540-45708-9_11
6. Bellare, M., Shoup, S.: Two-tier signatures, strongly unforgeable signatures, and Fiat-Shamir without Random Oracles. In: Okamoto, T., Wang, X. (eds.) PKC 2007. LNCS, vol. 4450, pp. 201–216. Springer, Heidelberg (2007). https://doi.org/10.1007/978-3-540-71677-8_14
7. Benhamouda, F., Lepoint, T., Loss, J., Orrù, M., Raykova, M.: On the (in)security of ROS. In: Canteaut, A., Standaert, F.-X. (eds.) EUROCRYPT 2021. LNCS, vol. 12696, pp. 33–53. Springer, Cham (2021). https://doi.org/10.1007/978-3-030-77870-5_2
8. Boldyreva, A.: Threshold signatures, multisignatures and blind signatures based on the gap-Diffie-Hellman-group signature scheme. In: Desmedt, Y.G. (ed.) PKC 2003. LNCS, vol. 2567, pp. 31–46. Springer, Heidelberg (2003). https://doi.org/10.1007/3-540-36288-6_3
9. Boneh, D., Drijvers, M., Neven, G.: Compact multi-signatures for smaller blockchains. In: Peyrin, T., Galbraith, S. (eds.) ASIACRYPT 2018. LNCS, vol. 11273, pp. 435–464. Springer, Cham (2018). https://doi.org/10.1007/978-3-030-03329-3_15

10. Chaum, D., Pedersen, T.P.: Wallet databases with observers. In: Brickell, E.F. (ed.) CRYPTO 1992. LNCS, vol. 740, pp. 89–105. Springer, Heidelberg (1993). https://doi.org/10.1007/3-540-48071-4_7
11. Drijvers, M., et al.: On the security of two-round multi-signatures. In: 2019 IEEE Symposium on Security and Privacy, pp. 1084–1101. IEEE Computer Society Press, May 2019. https://doi.org/10.1109/SP.2019.00050
12. Fuchsbauer, G., Kiltz, E., Loss, J.: The algebraic group model and its applications. In: Shacham, H., Boldyreva, A. (eds.) CRYPTO 2018. LNCS, vol. 10992, pp. 33–62. Springer, Cham (2018). https://doi.org/10.1007/978-3-319-96881-0_2
13. Fuchsbauer, G., Plouviez, A., Seurin, Y.: Blind schnorr signatures and signed ElGamal encryption in the algebraic group model. In: Canteaut, A., Ishai, Y. (eds.) EUROCRYPT 2020. LNCS, vol. 12106, pp. 63–95. Springer, Cham (2020). https://doi.org/10.1007/978-3-030-45724-2_3
14. Gentry, C., Wichs, D.: Separating succinct non-interactive arguments from all falsifiable assumptions. In: Fortnow, L., Vadhan, S.P. (eds.) 43rd ACM STOC, pp. 99–108. ACM Press, June 2011. https://doi.org/10.1145/1993636.1993651
15. Goldwasser, S., Kalai, Y.T.: Cryptographic assumptions: A position paper. Cryptology ePrint Archive, Report 2015/907 (2015). https://eprint.iacr.org/2015/907
16. Horster, P., Michels, M., Petersen, H.: Meta-multisignature schemes based on the discrete logarithm problem. In: IFIP/Sec '95, IFIP Advances in Information and Communication Technology, pp. 128–142. Springer (1995)
17. Itakura, K., Nakamura, K.: A public-key cryptosystem suitable for digital multisignatures. NEC Res. Dev. **71**, 1–8 (1983)
18. Komlo, C., Goldberg, I.: FROST: flexible round-optimized schnorr threshold signatures. In: SAC 2020, 2020. To be published. https://eprint.iacr.org/2020/852
19. Langford, S.K.: Weaknesses in some threshold cryptosystems. In: Koblitz, N. (ed.) CRYPTO 1996. LNCS, vol. 1109, pp. 74–82. Springer, Heidelberg (1996). https://doi.org/10.1007/3-540-68697-5_6
20. Ma, C., Weng, J., Li, Y., Deng, R.H.: Efficient discrete logarithm based multi-signature scheme in the plain public key model. Des. Codes Cryptogr. **54**(2), 121–133 (2010). https://doi.org/10.1007/s10623-009-9313-z
21. Maxwell, G., Poelstra, A., Seurin, Y., Wuille, P.: Simple Schnorr multi-signatures with applications to Bitcoin. IACR Cryptology ePrint Archive, 2018/068, Version 20180118:124757, 2018. Preliminary obsolete version of [22]. https://eprint.iacr.org/2018/068/20180118:124757
22. Maxwell, G., Poelstra, A., Seurin, Y., Wuille, P.: Simple Schnorr multi-signatures with applications to Bitcoin. Des. Codes Cryptogr. **87**(9), 2139–2164 (2019). https://eprint.iacr.org/2018/068.pdf
23. Micali, S., Ohta, K., Reyzin, L.: Accountable-subgroup multisignatures: extended abstract. In: Reiter, M.K., Samarati, P., (eds.) ACM CCS 2001, pp. 245–254. ACM Press, November 2001. https://doi.org/10.1145/501983.502017
24. Michels, M., Horster, P.: On the risk of disruption in several multiparty signature schemes. In: Kim, K., Matsumoto, T. (eds.) ASIACRYPT 1996. LNCS, vol. 1163, pp. 334–345. Springer, Heidelberg (1996). https://doi.org/10.1007/BFb0034859
25. Naor, M.: On cryptographic assumptions and challenges. In: Boneh, D. (ed.) CRYPTO 2003. LNCS, vol. 2729, pp. 96–109. Springer, Heidelberg (2003). https://doi.org/10.1007/978-3-540-45146-4_6
26. Nick, J.: Insecure shortcuts in MuSig (2019). https://medium.com/blockstream/insecure-shortcuts-in-musig-2ad0d38a97da

27. Nick, J., Ruffing, T., Seurin, Y.: MuSig2: simple two-round schnorr multi-signatures. Cryptology ePrint Archive, Report 2020/1261 (2020). https://eprint.iacr.org/2020/1261

28. Nick, J., Ruffing, T., Seurin, Y., Wuille, P.: MuSig-DN: schnorr multi-signatures with verifiably deterministic nonces. In: Ligatti, J., Ou, X., Katz, J., Vigna, G., (eds.) ACM CCS 20, pp. 1717–1731. ACM Press, November 2020. https://doi.org/10.1145/3372297.3417236

29. Nicolosi, A., Krohn, M.N., Dodis, Y., Mazières, D.: Proactive two-party signatures for user authentication. In: NDSS 2003. The Internet Society, February 2003. https://www.ndss-symposium.org/ndss2003/proactive-two-party-signatures-user-authentication/

30. Pointcheval, D., Stern, J.: Security arguments for digital signatures and blind signatures. J. Cryptol. **13**(3), 361–396 (2000). https://doi.org/10.1007/s001450010003

31. Ristenpart, T., Yilek, S.: The power of proofs-of-possession: securing multiparty signatures against rogue-key attacks. In: Naor, M. (ed.) EUROCRYPT 2007. LNCS, vol. 4515, pp. 228–245. Springer, Heidelberg (2007). https://doi.org/10.1007/978-3-540-72540-4_13

32. Schnorr, C.-P.: Efficient signature generation by smart cards. J. Cryptol. **4**(3), 161–174 (1991). https://doi.org/10.1007/BF00196725

33. Schnorr, C.P.: Security of blind discrete log signatures against interactive attacks. In: Qing, S., Okamoto, T., Zhou, J. (eds.) ICICS 2001. LNCS, vol. 2229, pp. 1–12. Springer, Heidelberg (2001). https://doi.org/10.1007/3-540-45600-7_1

34. Shoup, V.: Lower bounds for discrete logarithms and related problems. In: Fumy, W. (ed.) EUROCRYPT 1997. LNCS, vol. 1233, pp. 256–266. Springer, Heidelberg (1997). https://doi.org/10.1007/3-540-69053-0_18

35. Stinson, D.R., Strobl, R.: Provably secure distributed schnorr signatures and a (t, n) threshold scheme for implicit certificates. In: Varadharajan, V., Mu, Y. (eds.) ACISP 2001. LNCS, vol. 2119, pp. 417–434. Springer, Heidelberg (2001). https://doi.org/10.1007/3-540-47719-5_33

36. Syta, E., et al.: Keeping authorities "honest or bust" with decentralized witness cosigning. In: 2016 IEEE Symposium on Security and Privacy, pages 526–545. IEEE Computer Society Press, May 2016. https://doi.org/10.1109/SP.2016.38

37. Wagner, D.: A generalized birthday problem. In: Yung, M. (ed.) CRYPTO 2002. LNCS, vol. 2442, pp. 288–304. Springer, Heidelberg (2002). https://doi.org/10.1007/3-540-45708-9_19

38. Wuille, P., Nick, J., Ruffing, T.: Schnorr signatures for secp256k1. Bitcoin Improvement Proposal 340 (2020). https://github.com/bitcoin/bips/blob/master/bip-0340.mediawiki

Tighter Security for Schnorr Identification and Signatures: A High-Moment Forking Lemma for Σ-Protocols

Lior Rotem[(✉)] and Gil Segev

School of Computer Science and Engineering, Hebrew University of Jerusalem,
91904 Jerusalem, Israel
{lior.rotem,segev}@cs.huji.ac.il

Abstract. The Schnorr identification and signature schemes have been amongst the most influential cryptographic protocols of the past three decades. Unfortunately, although the best-known attacks on these two schemes are via discrete-logarithm computation, the known approaches for basing their security on the hardness of the discrete logarithm problem encounter the "square-root barrier". In particular, in any group of order p where Shoup's generic hardness result for the discrete logarithm problem is believed to hold (and is thus used for setting concrete security parameters), the best-known t-time attacks on the Schnorr identification and signature schemes have success probability t^2/p, whereas existing proofs of security only rule out attacks with success probabilities $(t^2/p)^{1/2}$ and $(q_{\mathsf{H}} \cdot t^2/p)^{1/2}$, respectively, where q_{H} denotes the number of random-oracle queries issued by the attacker.

We establish tighter security guarantees for identification and signature schemes which result from Σ-protocols with special soundness based on the hardness of their underlying relation, and in particular for Schnorr's schemes based on the hardness of the discrete logarithm problem. We circumvent the square-root barrier by introducing a high-moment generalization of the classic forking lemma, relying on the assumption that the underlying relation is "d-moment hard": The success probability of any algorithm in the task of producing a witness for a random instance is dominated by the d-th moment of the algorithm's running time.

In the concrete context of the discrete logarithm problem, already Shoup's original proof shows that the discrete logarithm problem is 2-moment hard in the generic-group model, and thus our assumption can be viewed as a highly-plausible strengthening of the discrete logarithm assumption in any group where no better-than-generic algorithms are currently known. Applying our high-moment forking lemma in this context shows that, assuming the 2-moment hardness of the discrete logarithm problem, any t-time attacker breaks the security of the Schnorr

L. Rotem and G. Segev—Supported by the European Union's Horizon 2020 Framework Program (H2020) via an ERC Grant (Grant No. 714253).

L. Rotem—Supported by the Adams Fellowship Program of the Israel Academy of Sciences and Humanities.

T. Malkin and C. Peikert (Eds.): CRYPTO 2021, LNCS 12825, pp. 222–250, 2021.
https://doi.org/10.1007/978-3-030-84242-0_9

identification and signature schemes with probabilities at most $(t^2/p)^{2/3}$ and $(q_\mathsf{H} \cdot t^2/p)^{2/3}$, respectively.

1 Introduction

The Schnorr identification and signature schemes [Sch89,Sch91] have been amongst the most influential cryptographic protocols of the past three decades, due to their conceptual simplicity and practical efficiency. Accordingly, the analysis of their security guarantees has attracted much attention over the years. Though from the onset, it was observed that their asymptotic security can be tied to that of the discrete logarithm problem, characterizing their concrete security has remained an elusive feat. On the one hand, to this day there are no known attacks on these schemes that improve upon the existing algorithms for computing discrete logarithms. On the other hand, essentially all known security reductions to the discrete logarithm problem are non-tight, which may lead to significant blowups when setting concrete security parameters (i.e., the group size), and hence to degraded efficiency.[1] Concretely, the known approaches for basing the security of the Schnorr identification and signature schemes on the hardness of the discrete logarithm problem encounter the "square-root barrier".

The Square-Root Barrier. In order to base the security of the Schnorr identification scheme and signature scheme on the hardness of the discrete logarithm problem, one has to transform any malicious impersonator and any malicious forger, respectively, into a discrete-logarithm algorithm. The existing approaches are based on the classic "forking lemma" of Pointcheval and Stern [PS00] (see also [AAB+02,BN06,BCC+16,KMP16] and the references therein). The difference between the various approaches is reflected by the different trade-offs between the success probability and the running time of their discrete-logarithm algorithms.

For the Schnorr identification scheme, any malicious impersonator that runs in time t and breaks the security of the scheme with probability ϵ, can be transformed for example into a discrete-logarithm algorithm that has success probability roughly ϵ^2 and runs in time roughly t. Similarly, for the Schnorr signature scheme, any malicious forger that runs in time t, issues q_H random-oracle queries and breaks the security of the scheme with probability ϵ, can be transformed into a discrete-logarithm algorithm that has success probability roughly ϵ^2/q_H and runs in time roughly t.

Thus, in any group of order p where Shoup's generic hardness result for computing discrete logarithms is believed to hold [Sho97], this leads to the bound $\epsilon \leq (t^2/p)^{1/2}$ on the security of the Schnorr identification scheme, and to the bound $\epsilon \leq (q_\mathsf{H} \cdot t^2/p)^{1/2}$ on the security of the Schnorr signature scheme (we refer the reader to Sect. 3 for a variety of other trade-offs that were established over the years, all of which lead to the same square-root bounds, as recently observed by Bellare and Dai [BD20] and by Jaeger and Tessaro [JT20]).

---

[1] These exclude reductions in the generic-group model [Sho97] and algebraic-group model [FKL18], as discussed below.

However, the best-known attack on the security the Schnorr identification and signature schemes is via discrete-logarithm computation, which has success probability t^2/p in such groups. For example, for a 256-bit prime p, the success probability of the best-known 2^{80}-time attack on the Schnorr identification scheme is roughly 2^{-96}, whereas the square-root bound only rules out attacks with success probability greater than 2^{-48} (for the Schnorr signature scheme this gap only increases due to the additional dependency on q_H).

A Wider Perspective: Identification and Signatures from Σ-Protocols. The square-root barrier is encountered not only when proving the security of the Schnorr identification and signatures schemes, but also when proving the security of additional ones, such as the Okamoto identification and signature schemes [Oka92] (see [AAB+02, KMP16] for various other examples). The Schnorr and Okamoto schemes are prime examples of the more general approach of constructing identification schemes based on Σ-protocols with special soundness, and of constructing signature schemes based on such identification schemes via the Fiat-Shamir paradigm [FS86, AAB+02]. In such schemes, the square-root barrier arises due to the rewinding-based methodology underlying their security proofs, as we further discuss in Sect. 3.

It should be noted that additional approaches were suggested as alternatives to basing the security of the Schnorr identification and signature schemes on the hardness of the discrete logarithm problem. Shoup [Sho97] and Fuchsbauer, Plouviez and Seurin [FPS20] provided tight security proofs in the generic-group model and in the algebraic-group model, respectively, and Bellare and Dai [BD20] provided tight security proofs based on the hardness of their multi-base discrete logarithm problem. These approaches do not encounter the square-root barrier, at the cost of considering either idealized models that considerably restrict attackers, or a newly-introduced interactive problem instead of the long-studied discrete logarithm problem.

1.1   Our Contributions

We establish tighter security guarantees for identification and signature schemes by circumventing the square-root barrier. Our approach applies to schemes that result from Σ-protocols with special soundness based on the hardness of their underlying relation $\mathcal{R} \subseteq \mathcal{X} \times \mathcal{W}$, and in particular to the Schnorr and Okamoto identification and signature schemes based on the hardness of the discrete logarithm problem.

We prove our results by introducing a high-moment generalization of the classic forking lemma, relying on the assumption that the success probability of any algorithm in the task of producing a witness $w \in \mathcal{W}$ given a random instance $x \in \mathcal{X}$ is dominated by the d-th moment of the algorithm's running time. In what follows we provide a high-level description of our assumption, and then state our bounds on the security of identification and signature schemes.

Our Assumption: d-Moment Hardness. Given a relation $\mathcal{R} \subseteq \mathcal{X} \times \mathcal{W}$ underlying a Σ-protocol, and a distribution $\mathcal{D}$ over pairs $(x, w) \in \mathcal{R}$, we put forward the d-moment assumption that considers the task of producing a witness w given an instance x that is sampled via $\mathcal{D}$. Informally, in its most simplistic form, our assumption asks that the success probability of any algorithm A in this task is at most $\mathbb{E}\left[(\mathsf{T}_{A,\mathcal{D}})^d\right]/|\mathcal{W}|$, where $\mathsf{T}_{A,\mathcal{D}}$ denotes the random variable corresponding to A's running time.[2] We refer the reader to Sect. 3 for a formal statement.

In the specific context of the discrete logarithm problem, instances are of the form $x = (\mathbb{G}, p, g, h)$ where $\mathbb{G}$ is a cyclic group of order p that is generated by g, and h is a group element. The relation $\mathcal{R}$ consists of all pairs $((\mathbb{G}, p, g, h), w)$ for which $h = g^w$, and the distribution $\mathcal{D}$ consists of a group-generation algorithm that produces the description $(\mathbb{G}, p, g)$ of the group, together with a uniformly-distributed group element h.

As recently observed by Jaeger and Tessaro [JT20], already Shoup's original proof shows that the discrete logarithm problem is 2-moment hard in the generic-group model [Sho97].[3] Thus, our assumption can be viewed a highly-plausible strengthening of the discrete logarithm assumption in any group where no better-than-generic algorithms are currently known for the discrete logarithm problem. In such groups, the generic hardness of the problem is used for setting concrete security parameters, and thus the assumption that the discrete logarithm problem is 2-moment hard can be viewed as identifying some of the core essence of the problem's generic hardness in the form of a standard-model assumption.

Tighter Security for Identification Schemes. Given an identification scheme resulting from a Σ-protocol for a relation $\mathcal{R}$, we follow the approach underlying the classic "forking lemma" of Pointcheval and Stern [PS00], and show that any attacker can be transformed into an algorithm A that takes as input an instance $x \in \mathcal{X}$ and produces (with a certain probability) a witness $w \in \mathcal{W}$ such that $(x, w) \in \mathcal{R}$. However, unlike existing variants of the forking lemma (see, for example, [AAB+02, BN06, KMP16, BCC+16, JT20]), we design our algorithm A with the goal of optimizing the trade-off between its success probability and the dth moment of its running time. Assuming the d-moment hardness of the relation $\mathcal{R}$, this trade-off leads to the following tighter bound on the success probability of the attacker when considering the standard notion of security against passive impersonation attacks (in Sect. 3 we demonstrate that the existing variants of the forking lemma do not circumvent the square-root barrier when relying on our assumption):

Theorem 1.1 (informal). *Let $\mathcal{ID}$ be an identification scheme with special soundness for a relation $\mathcal{R} \subseteq \mathcal{X} \times \mathcal{W}$. If $\mathcal{R}$ is d-moment hard, then any*

---

[2] More generally, our assumption asks that the latter probability is at most $\Delta \cdot \mathbb{E}\left[(\mathsf{T}_{A,\mathcal{D}})^d\right]/|\mathcal{W}|^\omega$ for functions Δ and ω of the security parameter. Looking ahead, the Schnorr identification and signature schemes will correspond to $\Delta = \omega = 1$, whereas the Okamoto identification and signature scheme will correspond to $\Delta = 1$ and $\omega = 1/2$.

[3] In fact, Shoup proved the following stronger statement: For any $t \geq 0$, the success probability of any algorithm in computing the discrete logarithm of a uniformly-distributed group element, conditioned on running in time at most t, is at most t^2/p. This implies, in particular, 2-moment hardness (with $\Delta = \omega = 1$).

attacker that runs in time t breaks the security of $\mathcal{ID}$ *with probability at most* $(t^d/|\mathcal{W}|)^{d/(2d-1)}$.

In particular, our theorem yields the following corollary for the Schnorr and Okamoto identification schemes (Table 1 exemplifies our concrete improvement over the square-root bound for a few typical choices of parameters):

Corollary 1.2 (informal). *Assuming that the discrete logarithm problem is 2-moment hard, then any attacker that runs in time t breaks the security of the Schnorr and Okamoto identification schemes with probability at most* $(t^2/p)^{2/3}$, *where p is the order of the underlying group.*

Tighter Security for Signature Schemes. We show that our approach extends to establishing tighter security guarantees for signature schemes that are obtained from identification schemes via the Fiat-Shamir paradigm [FS86]. The generic analysis of the Fiat-Shamir transform in this context [AAB+02], when combined with Theorem 1.1, yields the bound $\epsilon \leq q_{\mathsf{H}} \cdot (t^d/|\mathcal{W}|)^{d/(2d-1)}$ on the success probability of any malicious forger that runs in time t and issues q_{H} random-oracle queries assuming the d-moment hardness of the underlying relation. Although this bound may already be useful on its own, we nevertheless show that it can be further improved by applying our proof technique directly for reducing the dependence on q_{H}:

Theorem 1.3 (informal). *Let* $\mathcal{ID}$ *be an identification protocol with special soundness for a relation* $\mathcal{R} \subseteq \mathcal{X} \times \mathcal{W}$, *and let* $\mathcal{SIG}_{\mathcal{ID},\mathsf{H}}$ *be its corresponding signature schemes obtained via the Fiat-Shamir transform using the hash function* H. *If* $\mathcal{R}$ *is d-moment hard and* H *is modeled as a random oracle, then any attacker that runs in time t and issues* q_{H} *random-oracle queries breaks the security of* $\mathcal{SIG}_{\mathcal{ID},\mathsf{H}}$ *with probability at most* $(q_{\mathsf{H}} \cdot t^d/|\mathcal{W}|)^{d/(2d-1)}$.

As above, our theorem yields the following corollary for the Schnorr and Okamoto signature schemes (Table 2 exemplifies our concrete improvement over the square-root bound for a few typical choices of parameters):

Corollary 1.4 (informal). *Assuming that the discrete logarithm problem is 2-moment hard, then any attacker that runs in time t and issues* q_{H} *random-oracle queries breaks the security of the Schnorr and Okamoto signature schemes with probability at most* $(q_{\mathsf{H}} \cdot t^2/p)^{2/3}$, *where p is the order of the underlying group.*

1.2   Paper Organization

The remainder of this paper is organized as follows. First, in Sect. 2 we present the basic notation and standard cryptographic primitives that are used throughout the paper. In Sect. 3 we formally define our d-moment assumption, and demonstrate that the existing variants of the forking lemma do not circumvent the square-root barrier when relying on our assumption. In Sects. 4 and 5 we present and prove our bounds on the security of identification and signature schemes, respectively, from which in Sect. 6 we derive concrete security bounds for the Schnorr and Okamoto identification and signature schemes.

Table 1. A comparison of the security guarantees for the Schnorr and Okamoto identification schemes provided by the square-root bound and by our bound.

Attacker's running time t	Security parameter λ	Square-root bound $(t^2/p)^{1/2}$	Our bound $(t^2/p)^{2/3}$
2^{64}	256	2^{-64}	$2^{-85.34}$
2^{80}	256	2^{-48}	2^{-64}
2^{100}	512	2^{-156}	2^{-208}

Table 2. A comparison of the security guarantees for the Schnorr Okamoto signature schemes provided by the square-root bound and by our bound.

Attacker's running time t	Attacker's oracle queries q_H	Security parameter λ	Square-root bound $(q_H \cdot t^2/p)^{1/2}$	Our bound $(q_H \cdot t^2/p)^{2/3}$
2^{64}	2^{50}	256	2^{-39}	2^{-52}
2^{80}	2^{60}	256	2^{-18}	2^{-24}
2^{80}	2^{60}	512	2^{-146}	$2^{-194.67}$
2^{100}	2^{80}	512	2^{-116}	$2^{-142.67}$

2 Preliminaries

In this section we present the basic notions and standard cryptographic primitives that are used in this work. For an integer $n \in \mathbb{N}$ we denote by $[n]$ the set $\{1, \ldots, n\}$. For a distribution X we denote by $x \leftarrow X$ the process of sampling a value x from the distribution X. Similarly, for a set $\mathcal{X}$ we denote by $x \leftarrow \mathcal{X}$ the process of sampling a value x from the uniform distribution over $\mathcal{X}$.

Σ-Protocols. Let $\mathcal{R} = \{\mathcal{R}_\lambda\}_{\lambda \in \mathbb{N}}$ be a relation, where $\mathcal{R}_\lambda \subseteq \mathcal{X}_\lambda \times \mathcal{W}_\lambda$ for any $\lambda \in \mathbb{N}$, for sets $\mathcal{X} = \{\mathcal{X}_\lambda\}_{\lambda \in \mathbb{N}}$ and $\mathcal{W} = \{\mathcal{W}_\lambda\}_{\lambda \in \mathbb{N}}$. A Σ-protocol Π for the relation $\mathcal{R}$ is a 4-tuple $(\mathsf{P}_1, \mathsf{P}_2, \mathsf{V}, \mathcal{C})$, where P_1 is a probabilistic polynomial-time algorithm, P_2 and V are deterministic polynomial-time algorithms, and $\mathcal{C} = \{\mathcal{C}_x\}_{x \in \mathcal{X}}$ is an ensemble of efficiently sampleable sets. The protocol π is defined as follows:

1. The algorithm P_1 on input (x, w), where $x \in \mathcal{X}_\lambda$ and $w \in \mathcal{W}_\lambda$, produces a message α and a state st.
2. A challenge β is sampled uniformly at random from the challenge set $\mathcal{C}_x$.
3. The algorithm P_2 on input (st, β) produces a message γ.
4. The algorithm V on input $(x, \alpha, \beta, \gamma)$ determines the output of the protocol by outputting either 0 or 1.

In terms of completeness, we ask that for every $\lambda \in \mathbb{N}$ and for every $(x, w) \in \mathcal{R}_\lambda$, it holds that $\mathsf{V}(x, \alpha, \beta, \mathsf{P}_2(\mathsf{st}, \beta)) = 1$ with an overwhelming probability over the choice of $(\alpha, \mathsf{st}) \leftarrow \mathsf{P}_1(x, w)$ and $\beta \leftarrow \mathcal{C}_x$. In terms of soundness, we consider the following standard special soundness property for Σ-protocols. Roughly, the property requires that given an instance $x \in \mathcal{X}$ and two accepting transcripts for x which share the same first message α but differ on their second message β, one can efficiently compute a witness $w \in \mathcal{W}$ such that $(x, w) \in \mathcal{R}$.

Definition 2.1. *Let $\Pi = (P_1, P_2, V, \mathcal{C})$ be a Σ-protocol for a relation $\mathcal{R} \subseteq \mathcal{X} \times \mathcal{W}$, and let $t = t(\lambda)$ be a function of the security parameter $\lambda \in \mathbb{N}$. Then, Π has t-time special soundness if there exists a deterministic t-time algorithm WitnessExt for which to following holds: For every $\lambda \in \mathbb{N}$, for every instance $x \in \mathcal{X}_\lambda$, and for every $(\alpha, (\beta, \gamma), (\beta', \gamma'))$ such that $V(x, \alpha, \beta, \gamma) = V(x, \alpha, \beta', \gamma') = 1$ and $\beta \neq \beta'$ it holds that $(x, \text{WitnessExt}(x, \alpha, (\beta, \gamma), (\beta', \gamma')) \in \mathcal{R}$.*

Identification Schemes. An identification scheme consists of a Σ-protocol for a relation $\mathcal{R} \subseteq \mathcal{X} \times \mathcal{W}$ and of an algorithm Gen that produces a distribution over instances $x \in \mathcal{X}$ together with a corresponding witness $w \in \mathcal{W}$ such that $(x, w) \in \mathcal{R}$. We say that an identification protocol has t-time special soundness if its underlying Σ-protocol has t-time special soundness.

Additionally, we consider the standard notion of security against passive impersonation attacks, asking that a malicious prover on input an instance x produced by Gen should not be able to convince the verifier to accept even when given access to an oracle that produces honestly-generated transcripts for the instance x. In what follows, given an identification protocol, we let $\text{Trans}_{x,w}$ denote an oracle that (when queried without any input) runs an honest execution of the protocol on input (x, w) and returns the resulting transcript (α, β, γ).

Definition 2.2. *Let $t = t(\lambda)$ and $\epsilon = \epsilon(\lambda)$ be function of the security parameter $\lambda \in \mathbb{N}$. An identification scheme $\mathcal{ID} = (\text{Gen}, P_1, P_2, V, \mathcal{C})$ is (t, ϵ)-secure against passive impersonation attacks if for any t-time probabilistic prover $\bar{P} = (\bar{P}_1, \bar{P}_2)$ it holds that*

$$\mathbf{Adv}^{\text{PA-IMP}}_{\mathcal{ID}, \bar{P}}(\lambda) \overset{\text{def}}{=} \Pr\left[\text{PA-IMP}_{\mathcal{ID}, \bar{P}}(\lambda) = 1\right] \leq \epsilon(\lambda)$$

for all sufficiently large $\lambda \in \mathbb{N}$, where the experiment $\text{PA-IMP}_{\mathcal{ID}, \bar{P}}(\lambda)$ is defined as follows:

1. *$(x, w) \leftarrow \text{Gen}(1^\lambda)$.*
2. *$(\alpha, \text{st}) \leftarrow \bar{P}_1^{\text{Trans}_{x,w}}(1^\lambda, x)$.*
3. *$\gamma \leftarrow \bar{P}_2^{\text{Trans}_{x,w}}(\text{st}, \beta)$ for $\beta \leftarrow \mathcal{C}_x$.*
4. *If $V(x, \alpha, \beta, \gamma) = 1$ then output 1 and otherwise output 0.*

In this work we consider identification schemes that are *simulatable*: There exists an efficient algorithm that on input $x \in \mathcal{X}$, for $(x, w) \leftarrow \text{Gen}(1^\lambda)$, samples a transcript (α, β, γ) from the distribution of honest executions of the protocol on input (x, w).

Definition 2.3. *Let $t = t(\lambda)$ be function of the security parameter $\lambda \in \mathbb{N}$. An identification scheme $\mathcal{ID} = (\text{Gen}, P_1, P_2, V, \mathcal{C})$ is t-time simulatable if there exists a t-time algorithm Sim such that the distributions $\{(x, (\alpha, \beta, \gamma))\}_{\lambda \in \mathbb{N}}$ and $\{(x, \text{Sim}(1^\lambda, x))\}_{\lambda \in \mathbb{N}}$ are identical, where $(x, w) \leftarrow \text{Gen}(1^\lambda)$, $(\alpha, \text{st}) \leftarrow P_1(x, w)$, $\beta \leftarrow \mathcal{C}_x$ and $\gamma \leftarrow P_2(\text{st}, \beta)$.*

Note that for any simulatable identification scheme $\mathcal{ID}$ we can thus assume that malicious provers do not query the transcript-generation oracle $\mathsf{Trans}_{x,w}$ as such queries can be internally simulated given the instance x. Specifically, if $\mathcal{ID}$ is t_{Sim}-time simulatable then any malicious prover $\bar{\mathsf{P}}$ that runs in time $t_{\bar{\mathsf{P}}}$ and issues $q_{\bar{\mathsf{P}}}$ queries to the transcript-generation oracle can be simulated by a malicious prover that runs in time $t_{\bar{\mathsf{P}}} + q_{\bar{\mathsf{P}}} \cdot t_{\mathsf{Sim}}$ and does not issue any queries. Such a malicious prover is in fact attacking the Σ-protocol underlying $\mathcal{ID}$ with respect to the distribution over instances that is determined by Gen.

Finally, for considering the standard transformation of identification schemes to signature schemes via the Fiat-Shamir paradigm, we rely on the following notion of first-message unpredictability (originally referred to as "min-entropy of commitments" by Abdalla et al. [AAB+02]):

Definition 2.4. *Let $\delta = \delta(\lambda)$ be function of the security parameter $\lambda \in \mathbb{N}$. An identification scheme $\mathcal{ID} = (\mathsf{Gen}, \mathsf{P}_1, \mathsf{P}_2, \mathsf{V}, \mathcal{C})$ is δ-first-message unpredictable if for any $\lambda \in \mathbb{N}$, for any (x, w) produced by $\mathsf{Gen}(1^{\lambda})$ and for any α^* it holds that $\Pr\left[\alpha = \alpha^*\right] \leq \delta(\lambda)$, where $(\alpha, \mathsf{st}) \leftarrow \mathsf{P}_1(x, w)$.*

Signature Schemes. A signature scheme is a tuple $\mathcal{SIG} = (\mathsf{KG}, \mathsf{Sign}, \mathsf{Verify})$ of algorithms defined as follows:

- The algorithm KG is a probabilistic algorithm that receives as input the security parameter $\lambda \in \mathbb{N}$ and outputs a pair $(\mathsf{sk}, \mathsf{vk})$ of a signing key and a verification key.
- The algorithm Sign is a (possibly) probabilistic algorithm that receives as input a signing key sk and a message m and outputs a signature σ.
- The algorithm Verify is a deterministic algorithm that receives as input a verification key vk, a message m and a signature σ, and outputs a bit $b \in \{0, 1\}$.

In terms of correctness, the standard requirement for signature schemes asks that

$$\Pr\left[\mathsf{Verify}_{\mathsf{vk}}(m, \mathsf{Sign}_{\mathsf{sk}}(m)) = 1\right] = 1$$

for every $\lambda \in \mathbb{N}$ and for every message m, where the probability is taken over the choice of $(\mathsf{sk}, \mathsf{vk}) \leftarrow \mathsf{KG}(1^{\lambda})$ and over the internal randomness of Sign and Verify. In terms of security, we rely on the following standard notion of existential unforgeability under adaptive chosen-message attack (see, for example, [Gol04]) which naturally generalizes to the random-oracle model by providing all algorithm access to the oracle.

Definition 2.5. *Let $t = t(\lambda)$ and $\epsilon = \epsilon(\lambda)$ be function of the security parameter $\lambda \in \mathbb{N}$. A signature scheme $\mathcal{SIG} = (\mathsf{KG}, \mathsf{Sign}, \mathsf{Verify})$ is (t, ϵ)-existentially unforgeable under adaptive chosen-message attacks if for t-time probabilistic algorithm F it holds that*

$$\mathbf{Adv}_{\mathcal{SIG}, F}^{\mathsf{Forge}}(\lambda) \stackrel{\mathsf{def}}{=} \Pr\left[\mathsf{Forge}_{\mathcal{SIG}, F}(\lambda) = 1\right] \leq \epsilon(\lambda)$$

for all sufficiently large $\lambda \in \mathbb{N}$, where the experiment $\mathsf{Forge}_{\mathcal{SIG}, F}(\lambda)$ is defined as follows:

1. $(\mathsf{sk}, \mathsf{vk}) \leftarrow \mathsf{KG}(1^\lambda)$.
2. $(m^*, \sigma^*) \leftarrow F^{\mathsf{Sign}_{\mathsf{sk}}(\cdot)}(1^\lambda, \mathsf{vk})$. Let $\mathcal{Q}$ denote the set of all messages with which F queried its oracle.
3. If $\mathsf{Verify}_{\mathsf{vk}}(m^*, \sigma^*) = 1$ and $m^* \notin \mathcal{Q}$ then output 1, and otherwise output 0.

3   Our Assumption: d-Moment Hardness

In this section we first formally define the computational assumption on which our approach is based. Then, we demonstrate that the existing approaches for proving the security of identification schemes and signature schemes that are based on Σ-protocols with special soundness do not yield improved results when relying on our assumption.

The Assumption. In what follows, we consider relations $\mathcal{R} = \{\mathcal{R}_\lambda\}_{\lambda \in \mathbb{N}}$, where $\mathcal{R}_\lambda \subseteq \mathcal{X}_\lambda \times \mathcal{W}_\lambda$ for any $\lambda \in \mathbb{N}$, and distributions $\mathcal{D} = \{\mathcal{D}_\lambda\}_{\lambda \in \mathbb{N}}$ where each $\mathcal{D}_\lambda$ produces pairs $(x, w) \in \mathcal{R}_\lambda$. For any such distribution $\mathcal{D}$ and for any probabilistic algorithm A, we denote by $\mathsf{T}_{A, \mathcal{D}_\lambda}$ the random variable corresponding to the running time of A on input x where $(x, w) \leftarrow \mathcal{D}_\lambda$.

Definition 3.1. *Let* $d = d(\lambda)$, $\Delta = \Delta(\lambda)$ *and* $\omega = \omega(\lambda)$ *be functions of the security parameter* $\lambda \in \mathbb{N}$, *and let* $\mathcal{R} = \{\mathcal{R}_\lambda\}_{\lambda \in \mathbb{N}}$ *be a relation, where* $\mathcal{R}_\lambda \subseteq \mathcal{X}_\lambda \times \mathcal{W}_\lambda$ *for any* $\lambda \in \mathbb{N}$. *We say that* $\mathcal{R}$ *is* d-*moment* (Δ, ω)-*hard with respect to a distribution* $\mathcal{D} = \{\mathcal{D}_\lambda\}_{\lambda \in \mathbb{N}}$ *if for every algorithm* A *it holds that*

$$\Pr\left[(x, A(x)) \in \mathcal{R}_\lambda\right] \leq \frac{\Delta \cdot \mathbb{E}\left[(\mathsf{T}_{A, \mathcal{D}_\lambda})^d\right]}{|\mathcal{W}_\lambda|^\omega},$$

for all sufficiently large $\lambda \in \mathbb{N}$, *where the probability is taken over the choice of* $(x, w) \leftarrow \mathcal{D}_\lambda$ *and over the internal randomness of* A.

When $\Delta(\lambda) = 1$ and $\omega(\lambda) = 1$ for all $\lambda \in \mathbb{N}$, we will simply say that the relation $\mathcal{R}$ is d-moment hard. As discussed in Sect. 1.1, in the specific context of the discrete logarithm problem the relation $\mathcal{R}$ consists of all pairs $((\mathbb{G}, p, g, h), w)$ for which $h = g^w$, and the distribution $\mathcal{D}$ consists of a group-generation algorithm that produces the description $(\mathbb{G}, p, g)$ of the group, together with a uniformly-distributed group element h. Given that the discrete logarithm problem is 2-moment hard in the generic-group model [Sho97, JT20], the assumption that the discrete logarithm problem is 2-moment hard (in the standard model) can be viewed as identifying the core essence of the problem's generic hardness in the form of a standard-model assumption.

Existing Approaches. Extensive research has been devoted over the years for analyzing the security of identification schemes and signature schemes that are based on Σ-protocols with special soundness. For concreteness, we focus in this discussion on identification schemes as they already capture the main difficulties (the reader is referred to Sect. 5 for a discussion on transforming such schemes into signature schemes via the Fiat-Shamir paradigm [FS86]).

Given an identification scheme that is based on a Σ-protocol for a relation $\mathcal{R}$, the security of the scheme is proved by showing that any malicious prover $\bar{\mathsf{P}}$

can be transformed into an algorithm A that takes as input an instance $x \in \mathcal{X}$ and produces two accepting transcripts (α, β, γ) and $(\alpha, \beta', \gamma')$ with $\beta' \neq \beta$. The special soundness of the Σ-protocol guarantees that these two transcripts can then be used to retrieve a witness $w \in \mathcal{W}$ such that $(x, w) \in \mathcal{R}$. To the best of our knowledge, all known approaches for the construction of such an algorithm A are based on the following fundamental idea: The algorithm A uses the malicious prover $\bar{\mathsf{P}}$ to obtain an accepting transcript (α, β, γ), and then rewinds it to the same first message α and feeds it with fresh challenges β' with the hope of obtaining an additional accepting transcript $(\alpha, \beta', \gamma')$ with $\beta' \neq \beta$.

This fundamental idea traces back to the classic "forking lemma" of Pointcheval and Stern [PS00], later generalized and refined by Bellare and Neven [BN06], and by Kiltz, Masny and Pan [KMP16]. The difference between the existing approaches is reflected by the different trade-offs between the success probability of the algorithm A and its running time.

Given a malicious prover $\bar{\mathsf{P}}$ that runs in time t and breaks the security of the identification scheme with probability ϵ, then on one end of the spectrum $\bar{\mathsf{P}}$ is invoked roughly $1/\epsilon$ times, leading to an algorithm A with constant success probability and running time t/ϵ [KMP16]. On the other end of the spectrum, $\bar{\mathsf{P}}$ is invoked only twice, leading to an algorithm A with success probability roughly ϵ^2 and running time $2t$ [BN06]. When the relation $\mathcal{R}$ corresponds to the discrete logarithm problem in a group of order p where Shoup's generic hardness result is believed to hold, in both cases one obtains the bound $\epsilon \leq (t^2/p)^{1/2}$ (which is inferior to our bound $\epsilon \leq (t^2/p)^{2/3}$). More generally, if the discrete logarithm problem is d-moment (Δ, ω)-hard for some $d \geq 2$, $\Delta \geq 1$ and $\omega \leq 1$, one obtains the bound $\epsilon \leq (\Delta \cdot t^d/p^\omega)^{1/d}$ in the first case and the bound $\epsilon \leq (\Delta \cdot t^d/p^\omega)^{1/2}$ in the second case (both of which are inferior to our bound $\epsilon \leq (\Delta \cdot t^d/p^\omega)^{d/(2d-1)}$).

An approach that is closer to ours is to optimize the trade-off between the success probability of the algorithm A and its expected running time [PS00, BCC+16, JT20]. In their recent work, Jaeger and Tessaro [JT20] showed that in the generic-group model any algorithm A with an expected running time $\mathbb{E}[\mathsf{T}]$ computes the discrete logarithm of a random group element with probability at most $(\mathbb{E}[\mathsf{T}]^2/p)^{1/2}$ (omitting small constants for simplicity), and this can be used for establishing concrete bounds for algorithms that do not have a strict running time.[4]

In this setting, given a malicious prover $\bar{\mathsf{P}}$ that runs in time t and breaks the security of the identification scheme with probability ϵ, Bootle et al. [BCC+16] suggested the following algorithm A: It invokes $\bar{\mathsf{P}}$ once, and only if successful then it repeatedly rewinds A to the same first message and feeds it with a fresh

---

[4] More generally, if the discrete logarithm problem is d-moment hard for some $d \geq 2$, their approach shows that any algorithm A with an expected running time $\mathbb{E}[\mathsf{T}]$ computes the discrete logarithm of a random group element with probability at most $(\mathbb{E}[\mathsf{T}]^d/p)^{1/d}$.

challenge until it succeeds again.[5] A simple argument shows that A's success probability is roughly ϵ, and its expected running time is t. A similar algorithm A suggested by Pointcheval and Stern [PS00] has constant success probability and expected running time t/ϵ. In both cases, using the work of Jaeger and Tessaro one again obtains the bound $\epsilon \leq (t^2/p)^{1/2}$ as above (which is inferior to our bound $\epsilon \leq (t^2/p)^{2/3}$).[6]

4   Tighter Security for Σ-Protocols and Identification Schemes

In this section we introduce our high-moment forking lemma for establishing tighter security guarantee for Σ-protocols and identification schemes. We first focus on our result for Σ-protocols, and then extend it to identification schemes.

Given a Σ-protocol for a relation $\mathcal{R}$, we follow the approach underlying the forking lemma [PS00], and show that any malicious prover $\bar{P}$ can be transformed into an algorithm A that takes as input an instance $x \in \mathcal{X}$ and produces (with a certain probability) two accepting transcripts (α, β, γ) and $(\alpha, \beta', \gamma')$ for x such that $\beta' \neq \beta$. Assuming that Π has special soundness, these two transcripts can then be used to retrieve a witness $w \in \mathcal{W}$ such that $(x, w) \in \mathcal{R}$.

However, unlike existing variants of the forking lemma, we design our algorithm A with the goal of optimizing the trade-off between its success probability and the dth moment of its running time. Assuming that $\mathcal{R}$ is a d-moment (Δ, ω)-hard relation (recall Definition 3.1), this trade-off leads to an upper bound on the success probability of the malicious prover $\bar{P}$.

At a high level, given a malicious prover that runs in time t and convinces the verifier with probability ϵ, the description of our algorithm A is quite intuitive. First, it invokes the malicious prover to obtain a transcript (α, β, γ) of the protocol. Then, if this transcript is accepted by the verifier, it rewinds the malicious prover $B \approx 1/\epsilon^{1/d}$ times, providing it with randomly sampled challenges $\beta_1, \ldots, \beta_B$ and obtaining respective responses $\gamma_1, \ldots, \gamma_B$. If any one of these additional transcripts $(\alpha, \beta_i, \gamma_i)$ is accepted by the verifier and $\beta_i \neq \beta'$, then the algorithm A successfully retrieves a witness.

Ignoring various approximations and other technical challenges, we prove that the algorithm A has success probability roughly $B \cdot \epsilon^2 \approx \epsilon^{2-1/d}$, and the d-th moment of its running time is at most $\epsilon \cdot t^d/B^d \approx T^d$. Thus, assuming that $\mathcal{R}$ is a d-moment (Δ, ω)-hard relation leads to the bound $\epsilon \leq (\Delta \cdot t^d/|\mathcal{W}|^\omega)^{d/(2d-1)}$ on the probability of a t-time malicious prover to convince the verifier. This

---

[5] The rewinding technique of Bootle et al. is actually a more general one that is motivated by recent protocols with a generalized special soundness property (for which the classic forking lemma is insufficient).

[6] More generally, if the discrete logarithm problem is d-moment (Δ, ω)-hard, then using the expected-time rewinding techniques of Bootle et al. and of Pointcheval and Stern one obtains the bound $\epsilon \leq (\Delta \cdot t^d/p^\omega)^{1/d}$ (which is inferior to our bound $\epsilon \leq (\Delta \cdot t^d/p^\omega)^{d/(2d-1)}$).

should be compared with the approaches discussed in Sect. 3, leading roughly either to success probability ϵ^2 and dth moment t^d, or to success probability ϵ and dth moment at least t^d/ϵ^{d-1}, or to constant success probability and dth moment at least t^d/ϵ^d – all of which lead to inferior bounds. Formally, we prove the following theorem:

Theorem 4.1. *Let $d = d(\lambda)$, $\Delta = \Delta(\lambda)$, $\omega = \omega(\lambda)$, $t_W = t_W(\lambda)$ and $t_{\bar{P}} = t_{\bar{P}}(\lambda)$ be functions of the security parameter $\lambda \in \mathbb{N}$, and let $\Pi = (P_1, P_2, V, C)$ be a Σ-protocol with t_W-time special soundness for a relation $\mathcal{R} \subseteq \mathcal{X} \times \mathcal{W}$. If $\mathcal{R}$ is d-moment (Δ, ω)-hard with respect to a distribution $\mathcal{D}$ then for any malicious prover $\bar{P}$ that runs in time $t_{\bar{P}}$ it holds that*

$$\Pr\left[V(x, \alpha, \beta, \gamma) = 1\right] \leq \left(\frac{\Delta \cdot (16(t_{\bar{P}} + t_V + t_W))^d}{|\mathcal{W}_\lambda|^\omega}\right)^{\frac{d}{2d-1}} + \frac{2}{|\mathcal{C}_\lambda|},$$

for all sufficiently large $\lambda \in \mathbb{N}$, where the probability is taken over $(x, w) \leftarrow \mathcal{D}_\lambda$, $(\alpha, \mathsf{st}) \leftarrow \bar{P}_1(x)$, $\beta \leftarrow \mathcal{C}_x$ and $\gamma \leftarrow \bar{P}_2(\mathsf{st}, \beta)$, and where $t_V = t_V(\lambda)$ denotes the running time of the algorithm V, $|\mathcal{C}_\lambda|$ denotes the size of the challenge set $\mathcal{C}_x$ for any $x \in \mathcal{X}_\lambda$.

Recall that the notion of security against passive impersonations attacks for an identification scheme $\mathcal{ID} = (\mathsf{Gen}, P_1, P_2, V, C)$ is obtained from the experiment considered in Theorem 4.1 for its underlying Σ-protocol, by additionally providing the malicious prover with access to a transcript-generation oracle (recall Definition 2.2). As discussed in Sect. 2, if $\mathcal{ID}$ is t_{Sim}-time simulatable (recall Definition 2.3), then any malicious prover $\bar{P}$ that runs in time $t_{\bar{P}}$ and issues $q_{\bar{P}}$ queries to the transcript-generation oracle can be simulated by a malicious prover that runs in time $t_{\bar{P}} + q_{\bar{P}} \cdot t_{\mathsf{Sim}}$ and does not issue any queries. Thus, Theorem 4.1 immediately yields the following corollary:

Corollary 4.2. *Let $d = d(\lambda)$, $\Delta = \Delta(\lambda)$, $\omega = \omega(\lambda)$, $t_{\mathsf{Sim}} = t_{\mathsf{Sim}}(\lambda)$, $t_W = t_W(\lambda)$, $t_{\bar{P}} = t_{\bar{P}}(\lambda)$ and $q_{\bar{P}} = q_{\bar{P}}(\lambda)$ be functions of the security parameter $\lambda \in \mathbb{N}$, and let $\mathcal{ID} = (\mathsf{Gen}, P_1, P_2, V, C)$ be a t_{Sim}-time simulatable identification protocol with t_W-time special soundness for a relation $\mathcal{R} \subseteq \mathcal{X} \times \mathcal{W}$. If $\mathcal{R}$ is d-moment (Δ, ω)-hard with respect to Gen, then for any malicious prover $\bar{P}$ that runs in time $t_{\bar{P}}$ and issues $q_{\bar{P}}$ transcript-generation queries it holds that*

$$\mathbf{Adv}^{\mathsf{PA\text{-}IMP}}_{\mathcal{ID}, \bar{P}}(\lambda) \leq \left(\frac{\Delta \cdot (16(t_{\bar{P}} + q_{\bar{P}} \cdot t_{\mathsf{Sim}} + t_V + t_W))^d}{|\mathcal{W}_\lambda|^\omega}\right)^{\frac{d}{2d-1}} + \frac{2}{|\mathcal{C}_\lambda|},$$

for all sufficiently large $\lambda \in \mathbb{N}$, where $t_V = t_V(\lambda)$ denotes the running time of the algorithm V, and $|\mathcal{C}_\lambda|$ denotes the size of the challenge set $\mathcal{C}_x$ for any $x \in \mathcal{X}_\lambda$.

In the remainder of this section we prove Theorem 4.1.

Proof of Theorem 4.1. Let $\bar{P} = (\bar{P}_1, \bar{P}_2)$, and for any $\lambda \in \mathbb{N}$ let $\epsilon = \epsilon(\lambda) = \Pr[V(x, \alpha, \beta, \gamma) = 1]$, where $(x, w) \leftarrow \mathcal{D}_\lambda$, $(\alpha, \mathsf{st}) \leftarrow \bar{P}_1(x)$, $\beta \leftarrow \mathcal{C}_x$ and $\gamma = \bar{P}_2(\mathsf{st}, \beta)$ (without loss of generality we assume that $\bar{P}_2$ is deterministic given st). Let $B = \lceil 1/\epsilon^{1/d} - 1 \rceil$, and consider the following algorithm A:

The algorithm A

Input: An instance $x \in \mathcal{X}_\lambda$.

1. Sample $(\alpha, \mathsf{st}) \leftarrow \bar{\mathsf{P}}_1(x)$, $\beta_0 \leftarrow \mathcal{C}_x$ and compute $\gamma_0 = \bar{\mathsf{P}}_2(\mathsf{st}, \beta_0)$. If $\mathsf{V}(x, \alpha, \beta_0, \gamma_0) = 0$ then output $\bot$ and terminate.
2. For every $j \in [B]$ sample $\beta_j \leftarrow \mathcal{C}_x$ and compute $\gamma_j = \bar{\mathsf{P}}_2(\mathsf{st}, \beta_j)$. If for every $j \in [B]$ it holds that either $\mathsf{V}(x, \alpha, \beta_j, \gamma_j) = 0$ or $\beta_j = \beta_0$, then output $\bot$ and terminate.
3. Output $w = \mathsf{WitnessExt}(\alpha, (\beta_0, \gamma_0), (\beta_{j^*}, \gamma_{j^*}))$, where j^* is the minimal index for which $\mathsf{V}(x, \alpha, \beta_{j^*}, \gamma_{j^*}) = 1$ and $\beta_{j^*} \neq \beta_0$.

The following lemma establishes a lower bound on the success probability of the algorithm A:

Lemma 4.3. *For any $\lambda \in \mathbb{N}$ it holds that either $\Pr\left[(x, A(x)) \in \mathcal{R}\right] \geq B \cdot \epsilon^2/8$ or $\epsilon < 2/|\mathcal{C}_\lambda|$.*

Proof of Lemma 4.3. Whenever the algorithm A reaches Step 3 the witness extraction algorithm $\mathsf{WitnessExt}$ guarantees that $(x, A(x)) \in \mathcal{R}$. Therefore,

$$\Pr\left[(x, A(x)) \in \mathcal{R}\right]$$

$$= \Pr\left[\mathsf{V}(x, \alpha, \beta_0, \gamma_0) = 1 \ \wedge \ \left(\bigvee_{j=1}^{B} \left\{ \begin{matrix} \mathsf{V}(x, \alpha, \beta_j, \gamma_j) = 1 \\ \wedge \ \beta_j \neq \beta_0 \end{matrix} \right\}\right)\right]$$

$$= \sum_{\mathsf{st}} \left(\Pr\left[\mathsf{st}\right] \cdot \Pr\left[\mathsf{V}(x, \alpha, \beta_0, \gamma_0) = 1 \ \wedge \ \left(\bigvee_{j=1}^{B} \left\{ \begin{matrix} \mathsf{V}(x, \alpha, \beta_j, \gamma_j) = 1 \\ \wedge \ \beta_j \neq \beta_0 \end{matrix} \right\}\right)\right]\right)$$

where $(x, w) \leftarrow \mathcal{D}_\lambda$, $(\alpha, \mathsf{st}) \leftarrow \bar{\mathsf{P}}_1(x)$, $\beta_0, \dots, \beta_B \leftarrow \mathcal{C}_x$ and $\gamma_j = \bar{\mathsf{P}}_2(\mathsf{st}, \beta_j)$ for every $j \in \{0, \dots, B\}$; and we assume without loss of generality that for any $\lambda \in \mathbb{N}$, $x \in \mathcal{X}_\lambda$ and for any (α, st) produced by $\mathsf{P}_1^*(x)$ it holds that the state st consists of λ, x and α (in addition to any other information determined by P_1^*). In what follows, for every state st, let β_{st}^* denote the lexicographically first $\beta \in \mathcal{C}_x$ for which $\mathsf{V}(x, \alpha, \beta, \bar{\mathsf{P}}_2(\mathsf{st}, \beta)) = 1$. If no such β exists, let $\beta_{\mathsf{st}}^* = \bot$. It thus holds that

$$\Pr\left[(x, A(x)) \in \mathcal{R}\right]$$

$$= \sum_{\mathsf{st}} \left(\Pr\left[\mathsf{st}\right] \cdot \Pr\left[\mathsf{V}(x, \alpha, \beta_0, \gamma_0) = 1 \ \wedge \ \left(\bigvee_{j=1}^{B} \left\{ \begin{matrix} \mathsf{V}(x, \alpha, \beta_j, \gamma_j) = 1 \\ \wedge \ \beta_j \neq \beta_{\mathsf{st}}^* \end{matrix} \right\}\right)\right]\right)$$

where for every state st, the probability is taken only over the choice of $\beta_0, \dots, \beta_B \leftarrow \mathcal{C}_x$. Then, for every fixed state st, the events $\mathsf{V}(x, \alpha, \beta_0, \gamma_0) = 1$ and $\{\mathsf{V}(x, \alpha, \beta_j, \gamma_j) = 1 \wedge \beta_j \neq \beta_{\mathsf{st}}^*\}_j$ are independent, and therefore

$$\Pr\left[\bigvee_{j=1}^{B} \left\{ \begin{matrix} \mathsf{V}(x, \alpha, \beta_j, \gamma_j) = 1 \\ \wedge \ \beta_j \neq \beta_{\mathsf{st}}^* \end{matrix} \right\}\right]$$

$$= 1 - \Pr\left[\bigwedge_{j=1}^{B}\left\{\begin{matrix} \mathsf{V}(x,\alpha,\beta_j,\gamma_j) = 0 \\ \vee\ \beta_j = \beta_{\mathsf{st}}^* \end{matrix}\right\}\right]$$

$$= 1 - \prod_{j=1}^{B}\Pr\left[\begin{matrix} \mathsf{V}(x,\alpha,\beta_j,\gamma_j) = 0 \\ \vee\ \beta_j = \beta_{\mathsf{st}}^* \end{matrix}\right]$$

$$\geq 1 - \prod_{j=1}^{B}\min\left\{1,\Pr\left[\mathsf{V}(x,\alpha,\beta_j,\gamma_j) = 0\right] + \Pr\left[\beta_j = \beta_{\mathsf{st}}^*\right]\right\}$$

$$\geq 1 - \left(1 - \max\left\{0,\epsilon(\mathsf{st}) - \frac{1}{|\mathcal{C}_\lambda|}\right\}\right)^B,$$

where $\epsilon(\mathsf{st}) = \Pr_\beta\left[\mathsf{V}(x,\alpha,\beta,\bar{\mathsf{P}}_2(\mathsf{st},\beta)) = 1\right]$ for each st. Denoting

$$\widetilde{\epsilon}(\mathsf{st}) = \max\left\{0,\epsilon(\mathsf{st}) - 1/|\mathcal{C}_\lambda|\right\}$$

for every st, we obtain

$$\Pr\left[(x,A(x)) \in \mathcal{R}\right] \geq \sum_{\mathsf{st}}\left(\Pr[\mathsf{st}] \cdot \epsilon(\mathsf{st}) \cdot \left(1 - (1 - \widetilde{\epsilon}(\mathsf{st}))^B\right)\right)$$

$$= \mathbb{E}_{\mathsf{st}}\left[\widetilde{\epsilon}(\mathsf{st}) \cdot \left(1 - (1 - \widetilde{\epsilon}(\mathsf{st}))^B\right)\right].$$

The following claim (which is proved in the full version of the paper) provides a lower bound on the above term $\mathbb{E}_{\mathsf{st}}\left[\widetilde{\epsilon}(\mathsf{st}) \cdot \left(1 - (1 - \widetilde{\epsilon}(\mathsf{st}))^B\right)\right]$. Note that this term is the expectation of a non-convex function of $\widetilde{\epsilon}(\mathsf{st})$ over the interval $[0, 1]$, and therefore such a lower bound is not directly implied by Jensen's inequality.

Claim 4.4. *It holds that* $\mathbb{E}_{\mathsf{st}}\left[\widetilde{\epsilon}(\mathsf{st}) \cdot \left(1 - (1 - \widetilde{\epsilon}(\mathsf{st}))^B\right)\right] \geq \frac{1}{2} \cdot B \cdot \left(\epsilon - \frac{1}{|\mathcal{C}_\lambda|}\right)^2.$

Given Claim 4.4, it holds that either $\epsilon < 2/|\mathcal{C}_\lambda|$ or $\Pr\left[(x,A(x)) \in \mathcal{R}\right] \geq \frac{1}{2} \cdot B \cdot (\epsilon/2)^2$, and this concludes the proof of Lemma 4.3. ∎

The following lemma establishes an upper bound on the dth moment of the running time of the algorithm A (recall that $\mathsf{T}_{A,\mathcal{D}_\lambda}$ denotes the random variable corresponding to the running time of A on input x where $(x,w) \leftarrow \mathcal{D}_\lambda$):

Lemma 4.5. *For any* $\lambda \in \mathbb{N}$ *it holds that*

$$\mathbb{E}\left[(\mathsf{T}_{A,\mathcal{D}_\lambda})^d\right] \leq 2(1+B)^d \cdot (t_{\bar{\mathsf{P}}} + t_{\mathsf{V}} + t_{\mathsf{W}})^d \cdot \epsilon.$$

Proof of Lemma 4.5. The description of A yields that with probability $1 - \epsilon$ it runs in time at most $t_{\bar{\mathsf{P}}} + t_{\mathsf{V}}$, and with probability ϵ it runs in time at most $(1 + B) \cdot (t_{\bar{\mathsf{P}}} + t_{\mathsf{V}}) + t_{\mathsf{W}}$ (for simplicity we assume that the time required for sampling a uniform $\beta \in \mathcal{C}_x$ is subsumed by $t_{\bar{\mathsf{P}}} + t_{\mathsf{V}}$). Therefore,

$$\mathbb{E}\left[(\mathsf{T}_{A,\mathcal{D}_\lambda})^d\right] \leq (t_{\bar{\mathsf{P}}} + t_{\mathsf{V}})^d \cdot (1 - \epsilon) + ((1+B) \cdot (t_{\bar{\mathsf{P}}} + t_{\mathsf{V}} + t_{\mathsf{W}}))^d \cdot \epsilon$$

$$\leq (t_{\bar{P}} + t_V)^d + ((1 + B) \cdot (t_{\bar{P}} + t_V + t_W))^d \cdot \epsilon$$
$$\leq 2(1 + B)^d \cdot (t_{\bar{P}} + t_V + t_W)^d \cdot \epsilon. \tag{1}$$

where Eq. (1) follows from the fact that $B \geq 1/\epsilon^{1/d} - 1$ (and thus $1 \leq (1+B)^d \cdot \epsilon$). $\blacksquare$

Equipped with Lemmas 4.3 and 4.5, the assumption that $\mathcal{R}$ is a d-moment (Δ, ω)-hard relation with respect to the distribution $\mathcal{D}$ implies that either $\epsilon < 2/|\mathcal{C}_\lambda|$ or

$$\frac{B \cdot \epsilon^2}{8} \leq \Pr\left[(x, A(x)) \in \mathcal{R}\right]$$
$$\leq \frac{\Delta \cdot \mathbb{E}\left[(T_{A, \mathcal{D}_\lambda})^d\right]}{|\mathcal{W}_\lambda|^\omega}$$
$$\leq \frac{\Delta \cdot 2(1 + B)^d \cdot (t_{\bar{P}} + t_V + t_W)^d \cdot \epsilon}{|\mathcal{W}_\lambda|^\omega}$$
$$\leq \frac{\Delta \cdot 2^{d+1} B^d \cdot (t_{\bar{P}} + t_V + t_W)^d \cdot \epsilon}{|\mathcal{W}_\lambda|^\omega}$$
$$\leq \frac{\Delta \cdot B^d \cdot (2(t_{\bar{P}} + t_V + t_W))^d \cdot \epsilon}{|\mathcal{W}_\lambda|^\omega}$$

Our choice of $B = \lceil 1/\epsilon^{1/d} - 1 \rceil$ guarantees that $B^{d-1} \leq \epsilon^{1-1/d}$, and therefore

$$\epsilon^{2-\frac{1}{d}} \leq \frac{\epsilon}{B^{d-1}} \leq \frac{\Delta \cdot 8 \cdot (2(t_{\bar{P}} + t_V + t_W))^d}{|\mathcal{W}_\lambda|^\omega}$$

leading to

$$\epsilon \leq \left(\frac{\Delta \cdot 8 \cdot (2(t_{\bar{P}} + t_V + t_W))^d}{|\mathcal{W}_\lambda|^\omega}\right)^{\frac{d}{2d-1}}.$$

Therefore, overall we obtain

$$\epsilon \leq \max\left\{\left(\frac{\Delta \cdot 8 \cdot (2(t_{\bar{P}} + t_V + t_W))^d}{|\mathcal{W}_\lambda|^\omega}\right)^{\frac{d}{2d-1}}, \frac{2}{|\mathcal{C}_\lambda|}\right\}$$
$$\leq \left(\frac{\Delta \cdot (16(t_{\bar{P}} + t_V + t_W))^d}{|\mathcal{W}_\lambda|^\omega}\right)^{\frac{d}{2d-1}} + \frac{2}{|\mathcal{C}_\lambda|}.$$

$\blacksquare$

5   Tighter Security for Signature Schemes

In this section we show that our approach extends to establishing tighter security guarantees for signature schemes that are obtained from identification schemes via the Fiat-Shamir paradigm [FS86]. The generic analysis of the Fiat-Shamir transform in this context [AAB+02] shows that if any malicious prover that runs in time t breaks the security of the identification scheme with probability at most ϵ, then any malicious forger that runs in time roughly t and issues q_H random-oracle queries breaks the security of the signature scheme with probability at most roughly $q_H \cdot \epsilon$. Therefore, given our result from Sect. 4, if the relation $\mathcal{R} \subseteq \mathcal{X} \times \mathcal{W}$ underlying the identification scheme is a d-moment (Δ, ω)-hard relation, then any such forger breaks the security of the signature scheme with probability at most roughly $q_H \cdot (\Delta \cdot t^d / |\mathcal{W}|^\omega)^{d/(2d-1)}$.

Here, we show that the latter bound can be further improved by applying our proof technique directly, showing that any forger as above breaks the security of the signature scheme with probability at most roughly $(q_H \cdot \Delta \cdot t^d / |\mathcal{W}|^\omega)^{d/(2d-1)}$. Note that some dependency on q_H seems to be unavoidable, at least for a very large class of reductions which includes in particular all reductions based on the underlying paradigm of the forking lemma [PV05, GBL08, Seu12, FJS14]. In what follows, we first recall the standard transformation from identification schemes to signature schemes via the Fiat-Shamir paradigm [FS86, AAB+02], and then state and prove our result.

Let $\mathcal{ID} = (\mathsf{Gen}, \mathsf{P}_1, \mathsf{P}_2, \mathsf{V}, \mathcal{C})$ be an identification scheme for a relation $\mathcal{R} \subseteq \mathcal{X} \times \mathcal{W}$, and let H be a hash function mapping triplets of the form (x, m, α) to challenges in $\mathcal{C}_x$. The Fiat-Shamir paradigm then defines the following signature scheme $\mathcal{SIG}_{\mathcal{ID}, \mathsf{H}} = (\mathsf{KG}, \mathsf{Sign}, \mathsf{Verify})$:

- $\mathsf{KG}(1^\lambda)$ samples $(x, w) \leftarrow \mathsf{Gen}(1^\lambda)$ and outputs $\mathsf{sk} = (x, w)$ and $\mathsf{vk} = x$.
- $\mathsf{Sign}(\mathsf{sk}, m)$ parses $\mathsf{sk} = (x, w)$ and outputs $\sigma = (\alpha, \beta, \gamma)$, where $(\alpha, \mathsf{st}) \leftarrow \mathsf{P}_1(x, w)$, $\beta = \mathsf{H}(\mathsf{vk}, m, \alpha)$ and $\gamma \leftarrow \mathsf{P}_2(\mathsf{st}, \beta)$.
- $\mathsf{Verify}(\mathsf{vk}, m, \sigma)$ parses $\sigma = (\alpha, \beta, \gamma)$, and outputs 1 if and only $\mathsf{V}(\mathsf{vk}, \alpha, \beta, \gamma) = 1$ and $\beta = \mathsf{H}(\mathsf{vk}, m, \alpha)$.

Note that the value β in fact does not have to be included in the signature $\sigma = (\alpha, \beta, \gamma)$ as it can be computed given vk, m and α. Alternatively, in some identification protocols, for any x, β and γ there is a unique and efficiently computable α for which $\mathsf{V}(x, \alpha, \beta, \gamma) = 1$, and in such cases the value α does not have to be included in the signature $\sigma = (\alpha, \beta, \gamma)$.

We prove the following theorem (the reader is referred to Sect. 2 for the standard notions of t_Sim-time simulatability, t_W-time special soundness, and δ-first-message unpredictability for identification protocols):

Theorem 5.1. *Let $d = d(\lambda)$, $\Delta = \Delta(\lambda)$, $\omega = \omega(\lambda)$, $t_\mathsf{Sim} = t_\mathsf{Sim}(\lambda)$, $t_\mathsf{W} = t_\mathsf{W}(\lambda)$, $\delta = \delta(\lambda)$, $t_F = t_F(\lambda)$, $q_\mathsf{H} = q_\mathsf{H}(\lambda)$ and $q_\mathsf{Sign} = q_\mathsf{Sign}(\lambda)$ be functions of the security parameter $\lambda \in \mathbb{N}$, and let $\mathcal{ID} = (\mathsf{Gen}, \mathsf{P}_1, \mathsf{P}_2, \mathsf{V}, \mathcal{C})$ be a t_Sim-time simulatable identification protocol with t_W-time special soundness and δ-first-message unpredictability for a relation $\mathcal{R} \subseteq \mathcal{X} \times \mathcal{W}$. If $\mathcal{R}$ is d-moment (Δ, ω)-hard with respect to Gen, and the hash function H is modeled as a random oracle, then for every t_F-time algorithm F that issues q_H oracle queries and q_Sign signing queries it holds that*

$$\mathbf{Adv}_{\mathcal{SIG}_{ID},\mathsf{H},F}^{\mathsf{Forge}}(\lambda) \leq \left(\frac{q_{\mathsf{H}} \cdot \Delta \cdot (16(t_F + q_{\mathsf{Sign}} \cdot t_{\mathsf{Sim}} + t_{\mathsf{V}} + t_{\mathsf{W}}))^d}{|\mathcal{W}_\lambda|^\omega}\right)^{\frac{d}{2d-1}}$$

$$+ 2 \cdot \left(\frac{q_{\mathsf{H}}^2 + 1}{|\mathcal{C}_\lambda|} + q_{\mathsf{Sign}} \cdot q_{\mathsf{H}}^2 \cdot \delta\right)$$

for all sufficiently large $\lambda \in \mathbb{N}$, where $t_{\mathsf{V}} = t_{\mathsf{V}}(\lambda)$ denotes the running time of the algorithm V and $|\mathcal{C}_\lambda|$ denotes the size of the challenge set $\mathcal{C}_x$ for any $x \in \mathcal{X}_\lambda$.

At a high level, the proof of Theorem 5.1 follows a similar outline to that Theorem 4.1, while carefully handling additional technical challenges that arise when considering the unforgeability of signatures schemes in the random oracle model, as to minimize the increase in the adversary's success probability. Concretely, let F be a forger that runs in time t, issues at most q_{H} random-oracle queries and produces a successful forgery with probability ϵ. Our algorithm A invokes the forger to obtain a message-signature pair $(m, \sigma = (\alpha, \beta, \gamma))$, while simulating the random oracle and the signing oracle using the simulatability of the underlying Σ-protocol. Then, it checks that this pair is a valid one and that the forger queried the random oracle for the hash value of (x, m, α). If so, it rewinds the forger $B \approx 1/\epsilon^{1/d}$ times to the point just before (x, m, α) was queried, simulating a fresh random oracle from that point on each time, and obtaining respective message-signature pairs $(m_1, \sigma_1 = (\alpha_1, \beta_1, \gamma_1)), \ldots, (m_B, \sigma_B = (\alpha_B, \beta_B, \gamma_B))$. If any one of these additional pairs (m_i, σ_i) is a valid one, and in addition $\alpha_i = \alpha$ and $\beta_i \neq \beta$, then the algorithm A successfully retrieves a witness.

Technical challenges and approximations omitted, we prove that the algorithm A has success probability roughly $B \cdot \epsilon^2/q_{\mathsf{H}} \approx \epsilon^{2-1/d}/q_{\mathsf{H}}$, and the d-th moment of its running time is at most $\epsilon \cdot t^d/B^d \approx T^d$. Thus, assuming that $\mathcal{R}$ is a d-moment (Δ, ω)-hard relation leads to the bound $\epsilon \leq (q_{\mathsf{H}} \cdot \Delta \cdot t^d/|\mathcal{W}|^\omega)^{d/(2d-1)}$ on the advantage of a t-time forger which issues q_{H} random oracle queries in breaking the existential unforgeability of the signature schemes via an adaptive-chosen message attack.

Proof of Theorem 5.1. For any $\lambda \in \mathbb{N}$ let $\epsilon = \epsilon(\lambda) = \mathbf{Adv}_{\mathcal{SIG}_{ID},\mathsf{H},F}^{\mathsf{Forge}}(\lambda)$, and $B = \lceil 1/\epsilon^{1/d} - 1 \rceil$. We make the following assumptions about the forger F without loss of generality:

- F does not issue the same query twice to H, as F can always store the answers received from the oracle.
- After querying the signing oracle $\mathsf{Sign}(\mathsf{sk}, \cdot)$ on a message m and receiving a signature $\sigma = (\alpha, \beta, \gamma)$, F does not query H on (vk, m, α). This is without loss of generality, since in the real experiment $\mathsf{Forge}_{\mathcal{SIG}_{ID},\mathsf{H},F}(\lambda)$, it is always the case $\mathsf{H}(\mathsf{vk}, m, \alpha) = \beta$, and hence F can just store this value.
- If $F^{\mathsf{H},\mathsf{Sign}(\mathsf{sk},\cdot)}(\mathsf{vk})$ outputs a pair $(m, \sigma = (\alpha, \beta, \gamma))$ and F queried H for $y = \mathsf{H}(\mathsf{vk}, m, \alpha)$, then $\beta = y$. If this is not the case, then it necessarily holds that $\mathsf{Verify}(\mathsf{vk}, m, \sigma) = 0$ and thus $\mathsf{Forge}_{\mathcal{SIG}_{ID},\mathsf{H},F}(\lambda) = 0$.
- F never outputs a message m on which it has queried $\mathsf{Sign}(\mathsf{sk}, \cdot)$.

Consider the following algorithm A (which uses the algorithms Sim and WitnessExt provided by the simulatability and special soundness of $\mathcal{ID}$, respectively):

The Algorithm A

Input: An instance $x \in \mathcal{X}_\lambda$.

1. Set $\mathsf{vk} = x$, sample randomness $r \leftarrow \{0,1\}^*$ for F, sample q_{H} hash values $\boldsymbol{y_0} = (y_{0,1}, \ldots, y_{0,q_{\mathsf{H}}}) \leftarrow \mathcal{C}_x^q$, and sample q_{Sign} transcripts $(\alpha_0', \beta_0', \gamma_0'), \ldots, (\alpha_{q_{\mathsf{Sign}}}', \beta_{q_{\mathsf{Sign}}}', \gamma_{q_{\mathsf{Sign}}}') \leftarrow \mathsf{Sim}(x)$.
2. Invoke $(m_0, \alpha_0, \beta_0, \gamma_0) \leftarrow F^{\mathsf{H}, \mathsf{Sign}(\mathsf{sk}, \cdot)}(\mathsf{vk}; r)$ while simulating the oracles to F as follows:
   - H-queries: For each $i \in [q_{\mathsf{H}}]$ respond to the ith query with $y_{0,i}$.
   - Sign-queries: For each $i \in [q_{\mathsf{Sign}}]$ let m denote the ith query and responds as follows. If $\mathsf{H}(\mathsf{vk}, m, \alpha_i')$ was already queried and the response was different than β_i', then output $\perp$ and terminate. Otherwise, respond with the signature $\sigma = (\alpha_i', \beta_i', \gamma_i')$.
3. If $\mathsf{V}(x, m_0, \alpha_0, \beta_0, \gamma_0) = 0$ or if F did not query for $\mathsf{H}(\mathsf{vk}, m_0, \alpha_0)$ then output $\perp$ and terminate. Otherwise, let $i^* \in [q_{\mathsf{H}}]$ denote the index of query in which F queried for $\mathsf{H}(\mathsf{vk}, m_0, \alpha_0)$.
4. For every $j \in [B]$:
   (a) Sample $y_{j,i^*}, \ldots, y_{j,q} \leftarrow \mathcal{C}_x$. If $y_{j,i^*} = y_{0,i^*}$ then skip to the next iteration.
   (b) Invoke $(m_j, \alpha_j, \beta_j, \gamma_j) \leftarrow F^{\mathsf{H}, \mathsf{Sign}(\mathsf{sk}, \cdot)}(\mathsf{vk}; r)$ while simulating the oracles as in Step 2 with the following modification: For each $\ell \in \{i^*, \ldots, q\}$ respond to F's ℓth H-query with $y_{j,\ell}$.
   (c) If $m_j = m_0$, $\alpha_j = \alpha_0$, $\beta_j = y_{j,i^*}$ and $\mathsf{V}(x, \alpha_j, \beta_j, \gamma_j) = 1$ then output $w = \mathsf{WitnessExt}(\alpha_0, (\beta_0, \gamma_0), (\beta_j, \gamma_j))$ and terminate.
5. Output $\perp$.

The following lemma establishes a lower bound on the success probability of the algorithm A:

Lemma 5.2. *For any $\lambda \in \mathbb{N}$ it holds that either*

$$\Pr\left[(x, A(x)) \in \mathcal{R}\right] \geq \frac{B \cdot \epsilon^2}{8 \cdot q_{\mathsf{H}}}$$

or

$$\epsilon < 2 \cdot \left(\frac{q_{\mathsf{H}}^2 + 1}{|\mathcal{C}_\lambda|} + q_{\mathsf{Sign}} \cdot q_{\mathsf{H}}^2 \cdot \delta\right).$$

Proof of Lemma 5.2. Denote by I_0 the random variable corresponding to the index of the H-query in which F queries H with $(\mathsf{vk}, m_0, \alpha_0)$ in its invocation in Step 2. If in this invocation F does not query H with $(\mathsf{vk}, m_0, \alpha_0)$ or if $\beta_0 \neq y_{0, I_0}$, then we set $I_0 = 0$. Similarly, for each $j \in [B]$ denote by I_j the random variable corresponding to the index of the H-query in which F queries H with $(\mathsf{vk}, m_j, \alpha_j)$

in its invocation in the jth iteration of Step 4. If in this invocation F does not query $(\mathsf{vk}, m_j, \alpha_j)$ or if $\beta_j \neq y_{j,I_j}$, then we set $I_j = 0$.

For every $i \in [q_{\mathsf{Sign}}]$ let $\mathsf{Bad}_{0,i}$ denote the event in which A aborts in the ith Sign-query of F in its invocation in Step 2. That is, if we denote by m the ith Sign-query of F in its invocation in Step 2, then $\mathsf{Bad}_{0,i}$ is the event in which F already queried H with $(\mathsf{vk}, m, \alpha'_i)$ in an earlier stage of this invocation, and the response was different than β'_i. For every $j \in [B]$ and $i \in [q_{\mathsf{Sign}}]$, let $\mathsf{Bad}_{j,i}$ be defined analogously with respect to the jth invocation of F in Step 4, and let $\mathsf{Bad}_\ell = \bigvee_{i \in [q_{\mathsf{Sign}}]} \mathsf{Bad}_{\ell,i}$ for every $\ell \in \{0, \dots, B\}$. Since transcripts sampled using Sim are distributed identically as honestly-generated transcripts, then by the δ-first-message unpredictability of the identification scheme $\mathcal{ID}$, it holds that

$$
\Pr[\mathsf{Bad}_\ell] \leq \sum_{i=1}^{q_{\mathsf{Sign}}} \mathsf{Bad}_{\ell,i}
$$

$$
\leq \sum_{i=1}^{q_{\mathsf{Sign}}} q_{\mathsf{H}} \cdot \delta
$$

$$
\leq q_{\mathsf{Sign}} \cdot q_{\mathsf{H}} \cdot \delta.
$$

Whenever A reaches Step 4c, it is guaranteed that it invokes the witness extraction algorithm on two accepting transcripts with distinct challenges. Therefore,

$$
\Pr[(x, A(x)) \in \mathcal{R}]
$$

$$
= \Pr\left[\left(\begin{matrix} \mathsf{V}(x, m_0, \alpha_0, \beta_0, \gamma_0) = 1 \\ \wedge\ I_0 > 0 \wedge \overline{\mathsf{Bad}_0} \end{matrix} \right) \wedge \left(\bigvee_{j=1}^{B} \left\{ \begin{matrix} \mathsf{V}(x, m_j, \alpha_j, \beta_j, \gamma_j) = 1 \\ \wedge\ I_0 = I_j \wedge\ y_{j,I_j} \neq y_{0,I_0} \\ \wedge\ \overline{\mathsf{Bad}_j} \end{matrix} \right\} \right) \right]
$$

$$
= \sum_{i=1}^{q_{\mathsf{H}}} \Pr\left[\left(\begin{matrix} \mathsf{V}(x, m_0, \alpha_0, \beta_0, \gamma_0) = 1 \\ \wedge\ I_0 = i \wedge \overline{\mathsf{Bad}_0} \end{matrix} \right) \wedge \left(\bigvee_{j=1}^{B} \left\{ \begin{matrix} \mathsf{V}(x, m_j, \alpha_j, \beta_j, \gamma_j) = 1 \\ \wedge\ I_j = i \wedge\ y_{j,i} \neq y_{0,i} \\ \wedge\ \overline{\mathsf{Bad}_j} \end{matrix} \right\} \right) \right]
$$

$$
= \sum_{i=1}^{q_{\mathsf{H}}} \sum_{\substack{x, r, \{(\alpha'_\ell, \beta'_\ell, \gamma'_\ell)\}_{\ell \in [q_{\mathsf{Sign}}]} \\ y_{0,1}, \dots, y_{0,i-1}}} \left(\Pr\left[\begin{matrix} x \wedge\ r \wedge\ \{(\alpha'_\ell, \beta'_\ell, \gamma'_\ell)\}_{\ell \in [q_{\mathsf{Sign}}]} \\ \wedge\ y_{0,1}, \dots, y_{0,i-1} \end{matrix} \right] \right.
$$

$$
\left. \times \Pr\left[\begin{matrix} \mathsf{V}(x, m_0, \alpha_0, \beta_0, \gamma_0) = 1 \\ \wedge\ I_0 = i \wedge \overline{\mathsf{Bad}_0} \\ \wedge\ \left(\bigvee_{j=1}^{B} \left\{ \begin{matrix} \mathsf{V}(x, m_j, \alpha_j, \beta_j, \gamma_j) = 1 \\ \wedge\ I_j = i \wedge\ y_{j,i} \neq y_{0,i} \\ \wedge\ \overline{\mathsf{Bad}_j} \end{matrix} \right\} \right) \end{matrix} \right] \right).
$$

It thus holds that

$$
\Pr[(x, A(x)) \in \mathcal{R}]
$$

$$
\geq \sum_{i=1}^{q_{\mathsf{H}}} \sum_{\substack{x, r, \{(\alpha'_\ell, \beta'_\ell, \gamma'_\ell)\}_{\ell \in [q_{\mathsf{Sign}}]} \\ y_{0,1}, \dots, y_{0,i-1}}} \left(\Pr\left[\begin{matrix} x \wedge\ r \wedge\ \{(\alpha'_\ell, \beta'_\ell, \gamma'_\ell)\}_{\ell \in [q_{\mathsf{Sign}}]} \\ \wedge\ y_{0,1}, \dots, y_{0,i-1} \end{matrix} \right] \right.
$$

$$\times \Pr\left[\left(\begin{array}{c} V(x,m_0,\alpha_0,\beta_0,\gamma_0) = 1 \\ \wedge\ I_0 = i\ \wedge \overline{\mathsf{Bad}_0} \\ \wedge\ \left(\bigvee_{j=1}^{B}\left\{\begin{array}{c} V(x,m_j,\alpha_j,\beta_j,\gamma_j) = 1 \\ \wedge\ I_j = i\ \wedge \overline{\mathsf{Bad}_j} \\ \wedge\ \forall \ell \in \{i,\dots,q_{\mathsf{H}}\}\ :\ y_{j,\ell} \neq y_{0,\ell} \end{array}\right\}\right) \end{array}\right)\right]$$

where $(x,w) \leftarrow \mathsf{Gen}(1^\lambda)$, and the values $r, \{\{y_{j,\ell}\}_{\ell\in[q_{\mathsf{H}}]}, m_j, \alpha_j, \beta_j, \gamma_j\}_{j\in\{0,\dots,B\}}$ and $\{(\alpha'_\ell, \beta'_\ell, \gamma'_\ell)\}_{\ell\in[q_{\mathsf{Sign}}]}$ are distributed as in the description of A.

For every $y_{0,1}, \dots, y_{0,i-1}$ let us denote $\boldsymbol{y}[i-1] = (y_{0,1}, \dots, y_{0,i-1})$ and $\boldsymbol{\tau} = \{(\alpha'_\ell, \beta'_\ell, \gamma'_\ell)\}_{\ell\in[q_{\mathsf{Sign}}]}$. For every $i, x, r, \boldsymbol{\tau}$ and $\boldsymbol{y}[i-1]$, denote by $(y_i^*(i,x,r,\boldsymbol{\tau},\boldsymbol{y}[i-1]), \dots, y_{q_{\mathsf{H}}}^*(i,x,r,\boldsymbol{\tau},\boldsymbol{y}[i-1]))$ the lexicographically first tuple of $q_{\mathsf{H}} - i + 1$ values in C_x for which the following holds: In the simulation $F^{\mathsf{H},\mathsf{Sign}(\mathsf{sk},\cdot)}(x;r)$ (where the oracles are simulated to F as in the description of A using the values $\boldsymbol{\tau}$ and $\boldsymbol{y}[i-1], y_i^*(i,x,r,\boldsymbol{\tau},\boldsymbol{y}[i-1]), \dots, y_{q_{\mathsf{H}}}^*(i,x,r,\boldsymbol{\tau},\boldsymbol{y}[i-1]))$, F outputs (m,α,β,γ) such that:

- $V(x,m,\alpha,\beta,\gamma) = 1$;
- F's ith query to H is (x,m,α);
- For every $\ell \in [q_{\mathsf{Sign}}]$: If m_ℓ is the ℓth query of F to $\mathsf{Sign}(\mathsf{sk},\cdot)$, then F does not query H on (x,m_ℓ,α'_ℓ) before its ℓth query to $\mathsf{Sign}(\mathsf{sk},\cdot)$.

Then, it holds that

$$\Pr\left[(x,A(x)) \in \mathcal{R}\right]$$

$$\geq \sum_{i=1}^{q_{\mathsf{H}}} \sum_{\substack{x,r,\{(\alpha'_\ell,\beta'_\ell,\gamma'_\ell)\}_{\ell\in[q_{\mathsf{Sign}}]} \\ y_{0,1},\dots,y_{0,i-1}}} \left(\Pr\left[\begin{array}{c} x\ \wedge\ r\ \wedge\ \{(\alpha'_\ell,\beta'_\ell,\gamma'_\ell)\}_{\ell\in[q_{\mathsf{Sign}}]} \\ \wedge\ y_{0,1},\dots,y_{0,i-1} \end{array}\right]\right.$$

$$\left.\times \Pr\left[\left(\begin{array}{c} V(x,m_0,\alpha_0,\beta_0,\gamma_0) = 1 \\ \wedge\ I_0 = i\ \wedge \overline{\mathsf{Bad}_0} \\ \wedge\ \left(\bigvee_{j=1}^{B}\left\{\begin{array}{c} V(x,m_j,\alpha_j,\beta_j,\gamma_j) = 1 \\ \wedge\ I_j = i\ \wedge \overline{\mathsf{Bad}_j} \\ \wedge\ \forall \ell \in \{i,\dots,q\}\ :\ y_{j,\ell} \neq y_\ell^*(i,x,r,\boldsymbol{\tau},\boldsymbol{y}[i-1]) \end{array}\right\}\right) \end{array}\right)\right]\right)$$

For every fixing of i, x, r, $\{(\alpha'_\ell,\beta'_\ell,\gamma'_\ell)\}_{\ell\in[q_{\mathsf{Sign}}]}$ and $y_{0,1},\dots,y_{0,i-1}$, the event $V(x,m_0,\alpha_0,\beta_0,\gamma_0)) = 1\ \wedge\ I_0 = i\ \wedge\ \overline{\mathsf{Bad}_0}$ and the events

$$\left\{\begin{array}{c} V(x,m_j,\alpha_j,\beta_j,\gamma_j) = 1 \wedge\ I_j = i\ \wedge\ \overline{\mathsf{Bad}_j} \\ \wedge\ \forall \ell \in \{i,\dots,q\}\ :\ y_{j,i} \neq y_i^*(i,x,r,\boldsymbol{\tau},\boldsymbol{y}[i-1]) \end{array}\right\}_{j\in[B]}$$

are independent. Therefore,

$$\Pr\left[(x,A(x)) \in \mathcal{R}\right]$$

$$\geq \sum_{i=1}^{q_{\mathsf{H}}} \sum_{\substack{x,r,\{(\alpha'_\ell,\beta'_\ell,\gamma'_\ell)\}_{\ell\in[q_{\mathsf{Sign}}]} \\ y_{0,1},\dots,y_{0,i-1}}} \left(\Pr\left[\begin{array}{c} x\ \wedge\ r\ \wedge\ \{(\alpha'_\ell,\beta'_\ell,\gamma'_\ell)\}_{\ell\in[q_{\mathsf{Sign}}]} \\ \wedge\ y_{0,1},\dots,y_{0,i-1} \end{array}\right]\right.$$

$$\times \Pr\left[\begin{array}{c} \mathsf{V}(x, m_0, \alpha_0, \beta_0, \gamma_0) = 1 \\ \wedge\ I_0 = i\ \wedge\ \overline{\mathsf{Bad}_0} \end{array}\right]$$

$$\times \left(1 - \prod_{j=1}^{B} \Pr\left[\begin{array}{c} \mathsf{V}(x, m_j, \alpha_j, \beta_j, \gamma_j) = 0\ \vee\ I_j \neq i\ \vee\ \mathsf{Bad}_j \\ \vee\ \exists \ell \in \{i, \ldots, q\}\ :\ y_{j,i} = y_i^*(i, x, r, \boldsymbol{\tau}, \boldsymbol{y}[i-1]) \end{array}\right]\right)\right),$$

and for every $j \in [B]$ the union bound implies that

$$\Pr\left[\begin{array}{c} \mathsf{V}(x, m_j, \alpha_j, \beta_j, \gamma_j) = 0\ \vee\ I_j \neq i\ \vee\ \mathsf{Bad}_j \\ \vee\ \exists \ell \in \{i, \ldots, q\}\ :\ y_{j,i} = y_i^*(i, x, r, \boldsymbol{\tau}, \boldsymbol{y}[i-1]) \end{array}\right]$$

$$\leq \min\bigg\{1,\ \Pr\left[\mathsf{V}(x, m_j, \alpha_j, \beta_j, \gamma_j) = 0\ \vee\ I_j \neq i\right]$$

$$+ \Pr\left[\exists \ell \in \{i, \ldots, q\}\ :\ y_{j,i} = y_i^*(i, x, r, \boldsymbol{\tau}, \boldsymbol{y}[i-1])\right] + \Pr\left[\mathsf{Bad}_j\right]\bigg\}$$

$$\leq \min\bigg\{1,\ 1 - \Pr\left[\mathsf{V}(x, m_j, \alpha_j, \beta_j, \gamma_j) = 1\ \wedge\ I_j = i\right]$$

$$+ \frac{q_{\mathsf{H}}}{|\mathcal{C}_\lambda|} + q_{\mathsf{Sign}} \cdot q_{\mathsf{H}} \cdot \delta\bigg\}.$$

For every i, x, r, $\{(\alpha_\ell', \beta_\ell', \gamma_\ell')\}_{\ell \in [q_{\mathsf{Sign}}]}$ and $y_{0,1}, \ldots, y_{0,i-1}$ denote

$$\widetilde{\epsilon}_i(x, r, \boldsymbol{\tau}, \boldsymbol{y}[i-1])$$

$$= \max\bigg\{0,\ \Pr\left[\mathsf{V}(\mathsf{vk}, m_0, \alpha_0, \beta_0, \gamma_0) = 1\ \wedge\ I_0 = i\right] - \frac{q_{\mathsf{H}}}{|\mathcal{C}_\lambda|} - q_{\mathsf{Sign}} \cdot q_{\mathsf{H}} \cdot \delta\bigg\}.$$

Then, we obtain that

$$\Pr\left[(x, A(x)) \in \mathcal{R}\right]$$

$$\geq \sum_{i=1}^{q_{\mathsf{H}}} \sum_{\substack{x, r, \{(\alpha_\ell', \beta_\ell', \gamma_\ell')\}_{\ell \in [q_{\mathsf{Sign}}]} \\ y_{0,1}, \ldots, y_{0,i-1}}} \left(\Pr\left[\begin{array}{c} x\ \wedge\ r\ \wedge\ \{(\alpha_\ell', \beta_\ell', \gamma_\ell')\}_{\ell \in [q_{\mathsf{Sign}}]} \\ \wedge\ y_{0,1}, \ldots, y_{0,i-1} \end{array}\right]\right.$$

$$\left. \times \widetilde{\epsilon}_i(x, r, \boldsymbol{\tau}, \boldsymbol{y}[i-1]) \cdot \left(1 - (1 - \widetilde{\epsilon}_i(x, r, \boldsymbol{\tau}, \boldsymbol{y}[i-1]))^B\right)\right)$$

$$= \sum_{i=1}^{q_{\mathsf{H}}} \mathbb{E}\left[\widetilde{\epsilon}_i(x, r, \boldsymbol{\tau}, \boldsymbol{y}[i-1]) \cdot \left(1 - (1 - \widetilde{\epsilon}_i(x, r, \boldsymbol{\tau}, \boldsymbol{y}[i-1]))^B\right)\right],$$

where the expectation is taken over the choice of $x, r, y_{0,1}, \ldots, y_{0,i-1}$ and of $\{(\alpha_\ell', \beta_\ell', \gamma_\ell')\}_{\ell \in [q_{\mathsf{Sign}}]}$.

For each $i \in [q_{\mathsf{H}}]$, denote $\epsilon_i = \Pr\left[\mathsf{V}(x, m_0, \alpha_0, \beta_0, \gamma_0) = 1 \ \wedge\ I_0 = i\right]$ and $\widetilde{\epsilon}_i = \mathbb{E}\left[\widetilde{\epsilon}_i(x, r, \boldsymbol{\tau}, \boldsymbol{y}[i-1])\right]$. The following claim (which is proved in the full version of the paper) provides a lower bound on each of the terms in the above sum (note that each term is the expectation of a non-convex function, and therefore such a lower bound is not directly implied by Jensen's inequality)

Claim 5.3 *For every $i \in [q_{\mathsf{H}}]$ it holds that*

$$\mathbb{E}\left[\widetilde{\epsilon}_i(x, r, \boldsymbol{\tau}, \boldsymbol{y}[i-1]) \cdot \left(1 - (1 - \widetilde{\epsilon}_i(x, r, \boldsymbol{\tau}, \boldsymbol{y}[i-1]))^B\right)\right] \geq \frac{1}{2} \cdot B \cdot \widetilde{\epsilon}_i^2.$$

Claim 5.3 together with Jensen's inequality imply that

$$\Pr\left[(x, A(x)) \in \mathcal{R}\right]$$

$$\geq \frac{1}{2} \cdot B \cdot \sum_{i=1}^{q_{\mathsf{H}}} \widetilde{\epsilon}_i^2.$$

$$\geq \frac{1}{2 \cdot q_{\mathsf{H}}} \cdot B \cdot \left(\sum_{i=1}^{q_{\mathsf{H}}} \widetilde{\epsilon}_i\right)^2$$

$$\geq \frac{1}{2 \cdot q_{\mathsf{H}}} \cdot B \cdot \left(\sum_{i=1}^{q_{\mathsf{H}}} \left(\epsilon_i - \frac{q_{\mathsf{H}}}{|\mathcal{C}_\lambda|} - q_{\mathsf{Sign}} \cdot q_{\mathsf{H}} \cdot \delta\right)\right)^2$$

$$= \frac{B}{2 \cdot q_{\mathsf{H}}} \cdot \left(\Pr\left[\mathsf{V}(x, m_0, \alpha_0, \beta_0, \gamma_0) = 1 \ \wedge\ I_0 > 0\right] - \frac{q_{\mathsf{H}}^2}{|\mathcal{C}_\lambda|} - q_{\mathsf{Sign}} \cdot q_{\mathsf{H}}^2 \cdot \delta\right)^2.$$

Observe that when F outputs a pair $(m, \sigma = (\alpha, \beta, \gamma))$ without querying H on (vk, m, α), the view of F at termination is independent of the value $\mathsf{H}(\mathsf{vk}, m, \alpha)$. Hence, the probability that it outputs a value β such that $\mathsf{H}(\mathsf{vk}, m, \alpha) = \beta$ (which is a necessary condition for F to win the experiment) is at most $1/|\mathcal{C}_\lambda|$. Therefore,

$$\Pr\left[\mathsf{V}(x, m_0, \alpha_0, \beta_0, \gamma_0) = 1 \ \wedge\ I_0 > 0\right] \geq \epsilon - \frac{1}{|\mathcal{C}_\lambda|},$$

which implies that

$$\Pr\left[(x, A(x)) \in \mathcal{R}\right] \geq \frac{1}{2 \cdot q_{\mathsf{H}}} \cdot B \cdot \left(\epsilon - \frac{q_{\mathsf{H}}^2 + 1}{|\mathcal{C}_\lambda|} - q_{\mathsf{Sign}} \cdot q_{\mathsf{H}}^2 \cdot \delta\right)^2.$$

Then, either $\epsilon < 2 \cdot \left(\frac{q_{\mathsf{H}}^2 + 1}{|\mathcal{C}_\lambda|} + q_{\mathsf{Sign}} \cdot q_{\mathsf{H}}^2 \cdot \delta\right)$, or

$$\Pr\left[(x, A(x)) \in \mathcal{R}\right] \geq \frac{1}{8 \cdot q_{\mathsf{H}}} \cdot B \cdot \epsilon^2.$$

∎

The following lemma establishes an upper bound on the dth moment of the running time of the algorithm A (recall that $\mathsf{T}_{A, \mathsf{KG}(1^\lambda)}$ denotes the random variable corresponding to the running time of A on input x where $(x, w) \leftarrow \mathsf{KG}(1^\lambda)$):

Lemma 5.4. *For any $\lambda \in \mathbb{N}$ it holds that*

$$\mathbb{E}\left[(T_{A,KG(1^\lambda)})^d\right] \leq 2(1+B)^d \cdot (q_{Sign} \cdot t_{Sim} + t_F + t_V + t_W)^d \cdot \epsilon.$$

Proof of Lemma 5.4. The description of A yields that with probability $1 - \epsilon$ it runs in time at most $q_{Sign} \cdot t_{Sim} + t_F + t_V$, and with probability ϵ it runs in time at most $q_{Sign} \cdot t_{Sim} + (1 + B) \cdot (t_F + t_V) + t_W$ (for simplicity we assume that the time required for sampling a uniform $\beta \in C_x$ is subsumed by $t_F + t_V$). Therefore,

$$
\begin{aligned}
\mathbb{E}\left[(T_{A,KG(1^\lambda)})^d\right] &\leq (q_{Sign} \cdot t_{Sim} + t_F + t_V)^d \cdot (1 - \epsilon) \\
&\quad + (q_{Sign} \cdot t_{Sim} + (1+B) \cdot (t_F + t_V) + t_W)^d \cdot \epsilon \\
&\leq (q_{Sign} \cdot t_{Sim} + t_F + t_V)^d \\
&\quad + ((1+B) \cdot (q_{Sign} \cdot t_{Sim} + t_F + t_V + t_W))^d \cdot \epsilon \\
&\leq 2(1+B)^d \cdot (q_{Sign} \cdot t_{Sim} + t_F + t_V + t_W)^d \cdot \epsilon. \quad (2)
\end{aligned}
$$

where Eq. (2) follows from the fact that $B \geq 1/\epsilon^{1/d} - 1$ (and thus $1 \leq (1+B)^d \cdot \epsilon$). ∎

Lemma 5.2 and Lemma 5.4, together with the assumption that $\mathcal{R}$ is a d-moment (Δ, ω)-hard relation imply that either $\epsilon < 2 \cdot ((q_H^2 + 1)/|\mathcal{C}_\lambda| + q_{Sign} \cdot q_H^2 \cdot \delta)$ or

$$
\begin{aligned}
\frac{B \cdot \epsilon^2}{8 \cdot q_H} &\leq \Pr\left[(x, A(x)) \in \mathcal{R}\right] \\
&\leq \frac{\Delta \cdot \mathbb{E}\left[(T_{A,KG(1^\lambda)})^d\right]}{|\mathcal{W}_\lambda|^\omega} \\
&\leq \frac{\Delta \cdot 2(1+B)^d \cdot (q_{Sign} \cdot t_{Sim} + t_F + t_V + t_W)^d \cdot \epsilon}{|\mathcal{W}_\lambda|^\omega} \\
&\leq \frac{\Delta \cdot 2^{d+1} B^d \cdot (q_{Sign} \cdot t_{Sim} + t_F + t_V + t_W)^d \cdot \epsilon}{|\mathcal{W}_\lambda|^\omega} \\
&\leq \frac{\Delta \cdot B^d \cdot (2(q_{Sign} \cdot t_{Sim} + t_F + t_V + t_W))^d \cdot \epsilon}{|\mathcal{W}_\lambda|^\omega}
\end{aligned}
$$

Our choice of $B = \lceil 1/\epsilon^{1/d} - 1 \rceil$ guarantees that $B^{d-1} \leq \epsilon^{1-1/d}$, and therefore

$$
\epsilon^{2 - \frac{1}{d}} \leq \frac{\epsilon}{B^{d-1}} \leq \frac{8 \cdot q_H \cdot \Delta \cdot (2(q_{Sign} \cdot t_{Sim} + t_F + t_V + t_W))^d}{|\mathcal{W}_\lambda|^\omega}
$$

which yields

$$\epsilon \leq \left(\frac{8 \cdot q_{\mathsf{H}} \cdot \Delta \cdot (2(q_{\mathsf{Sign}} \cdot t_{\mathsf{Sim}} + t_F + t_{\mathsf{V}} + t_{\mathsf{W}}))^d}{|\mathcal{W}_\lambda|^\omega} \right)^{\frac{d}{2d-1}}.$$

Therefore, overall we obtain

$$\epsilon \leq \max \left\{ \begin{array}{c} \left(\frac{8 \cdot q_{\mathsf{H}} \cdot \Delta \cdot (2(q_{\mathsf{Sign}} \cdot t_{\mathsf{Sim}} + t_F + t_{\mathsf{V}} + t_{\mathsf{W}}))^d}{|\mathcal{W}_\lambda|^\omega} \right)^{\frac{d}{2d-1}}, \\ 2 \cdot \left(\frac{q_{\mathsf{H}}^2 + 1}{|\mathcal{C}_\lambda|} + q_{\mathsf{Sign}} \cdot q_{\mathsf{H}}^2 \cdot \delta \right) \end{array} \right\}$$

$$\leq \left(\frac{q_{\mathsf{H}} \cdot \Delta \cdot (16(q_{\mathsf{Sign}} \cdot t_{\mathsf{Sim}} + t_F + t_{\mathsf{V}} + t_{\mathsf{W}}))^d}{|\mathcal{W}_\lambda|^\omega} \right)^{\frac{d}{2d-1}}$$

$$+ 2 \cdot \left(\frac{q_{\mathsf{H}}^2 + 1}{|\mathcal{C}_\lambda|} + q_{\mathsf{Sign}} \cdot q_{\mathsf{H}}^2 \cdot \delta \right).$$

∎

6 Implications to the Schnorr and Okamoto Schemes

In this section we derive concrete security bounds for the Schnorr identification and signature schemes and for the Okamoto identification and signature schemes based on Corollary 4.2 and Theorem 5.1, assuming the 2-moment hardness of the discrete logarithm problem. In the description of the schemes, we rely on the existence of a group generation algorithm GroupGen, which takes as input the security parameter 1^λ and outputs a description $(\mathbb{G}, p, g)$ of a cyclic group $\mathbb{G}$ of prime order p, where g is a generator of the group. We focus on the typical case where the security parameter $\lambda \in \mathbb{N}$ determines a lower bound on the size of the group and thus $p \geq 2^\lambda$, and we denote by $t_{\mathsf{exp}} = t_{\mathsf{exp}}(\lambda)$ the time required for a single exponentiation in the group $\mathbb{G}$, where $(\mathbb{G}, p, g) \leftarrow \mathsf{GroupGen}(1^\lambda)$. Moreover, we assume for simplicity that the time required for multiplication in $\mathbb{G}$, for sampling elements in $\mathbb{Z}_p$, and for arithmetic computations in $\mathbb{Z}_p$ is subsumed by t_{exp}.

6.1 The Schnorr Identification and Signature Schemes

We start by recalling the definition of the Schnorr identification scheme $\mathcal{ID}_{\mathsf{Schnorr}} = (\mathsf{Gen}, \mathsf{P}_1, \mathsf{P}_2, \mathsf{V}, \mathcal{C})$ which is defined as follows:

Gen(1^λ):	$P_1(x, w)$:
1. $(\mathbb{G}, p, g) \leftarrow \mathsf{GroupGen}(1^\lambda)$	1. Parse x as $((\mathbb{G}, p, g), h)$
2. $w \leftarrow \mathbb{Z}_p$	2. $r \leftarrow \mathbb{Z}_p$
3. $x = ((\mathbb{G}, p, g), g^w)$	3. $\alpha = g^r$
4. Output (x, w)	4. $\mathsf{st} = (w, r)$
	5. Output (α, st)
$V(x, \alpha, \beta, \gamma)$:	
	$P_2(\mathsf{st}, \beta)$:
1. Parse x as $((\mathbb{G}, p, g), h)$	
2. If $\alpha = g^\gamma \cdot h^{-\beta}$ then output 1	1. Parse st as (w, r)
and otherwise output 0	2. Output $\gamma = w \cdot \beta + r \mod p$

Note that the scheme's challenge space $\mathcal{C} = \mathcal{C}_x$ is $\mathbb{Z}_p$ for any $x = ((\mathbb{G}, p, g), g^w)$ produced by Gen, and that $\mathcal{ID}_{\mathsf{Schnorr}}$ has a challenge space of size $|\mathcal{C}_\lambda| \geq 2^\lambda$ and δ-first message unpredictability for $\delta = \delta(\lambda) = 2^{-\lambda}$. Additionally, the verifier V preforms two exponentiations in the group $\mathbb{G}$ which yields a total running time of $t_V = t_V(\lambda) = 2t_{\mathsf{exp}}(\lambda)$. The following well-known claim establishes the special soundness and simulatability of $\mathcal{ID}_{\mathsf{Schnorr}}$.

Claim 6.1. *$\mathcal{ID}_{\mathsf{Schnorr}}$ is simulatable and has special soundness.*

For completeness, in the full version of the paper we present the simulator Sim establishing the simulatability of the scheme, and the extractor WitnessExt which establishes its special soundness. The simulator Sim runs in time $t_{\mathsf{Sim}} = 2t_{\mathsf{exp}}$, and the extractor WitnessExt performs only arithmetic operations in the ring $\mathbb{Z}_p$, and hence for our purposes its running time is dominated by that of the other algorithms under consideration. Given Claim 6.1 and the above observations, we obtain the following theorem, establishing concrete security bounds for the Schnorr identification scheme, as an immediate implication of Corollary 4.2.

Theorem 6.2. *Let $t_{\bar{\mathsf{P}}} = t_{\bar{\mathsf{P}}}(\lambda)$ and $q_{\bar{\mathsf{P}}} = q_{\bar{\mathsf{P}}}(\lambda)$ be functions of the security parameter $\lambda \in \mathbb{N}$. If the discrete logarithm problem is 2-moment hard with respect to Gen, then for any malicious prover $\bar{\mathsf{P}}$ that runs in time $t_{\bar{\mathsf{P}}}$ and issues $q_{\bar{\mathsf{P}}}$ transcript-generation queries it holds that*

$$\mathbf{Adv}_{\mathcal{ID}_{\mathsf{Schnorr}}, \bar{\mathsf{P}}}^{\mathsf{PA\text{-}IMP}}(\lambda) \leq \left(\frac{(16(t_{\bar{\mathsf{P}}} + 2(q_{\bar{\mathsf{P}}} + 1) \cdot t_{\mathsf{exp}})^2}{2^\lambda} \right)^{\frac{2}{3}} + \frac{2}{2^\lambda},$$

for all sufficiently large $\lambda \in \mathbb{N}$.

Recall that Schnorr signatures are obtained from $\mathcal{ID}_{\mathsf{Schnorr}}$ via the Fiat-Shamir transform relative to hash function H, as described in Sect. 5. Hence, we obtain the following theorem, establishing concrete security bounds for the Schnorr signature scheme, as a corollary of Theorem 5.1.

Theorem 6.3. *Let $t_F = t_F(\lambda)$, $q_{\mathsf{H}} = q_{\mathsf{H}}(\lambda)$ and $q_{\mathsf{Sign}} = q_{\mathsf{Sign}}(\lambda)$ be functions of the security parameter $\lambda \in \mathbb{N}$. If the discrete logarithm problem is 2-moment* *hard with respect to* Gen, *and the hash function* H *is modeled as a random oracle, then for every* t_F*-time algorithm* F *that issues* q_H *oracle queries and* q_{Sign} *signing queries it holds that*

$$\mathbf{Adv}^{\text{Forge}}_{\mathcal{SIG}_{\mathcal{ID}_{\text{Schnorr}}},H,F}(\lambda) \leq \left(\frac{q_H \cdot (16(t_F + 2(q_{\text{Sign}} + 1) \cdot t_{\text{exp}}))^2}{2^\lambda} \right)^{\frac{2}{3}}$$
$$+ 2 \cdot \left(\frac{(q_{\text{Sign}} + 1) \cdot q_H^2 + 1}{2^\lambda} \right)$$

for all sufficiently large $\lambda \in \mathbb{N}$.

6.2   The Okamoto Identification and Signature Schemes

The Okamoto identification scheme $\mathcal{ID}_{\text{Okamoto}}$ is defined as follows:

Gen(1^λ): 1. $(\mathbb{G}, p, g) \leftarrow \text{GroupGen}(1^\lambda)$ 2. $g_2 \leftarrow \mathbb{G}$ 3. $w_1, w_2 \leftarrow \mathbb{Z}_p$ 4. $w = (w_1, w_2)$ 5. $x = ((\mathbb{G}, p, g), g_2, g^{w_1} \cdot g_2^{w_2})$ 6. Output (x, w)	$\mathsf{P}_1(x, w)$: 1. Parse x as $((\mathbb{G}, p, g), g_2, h)$ 2. $r_1, r_2 \leftarrow \mathbb{Z}_p$ 3. $\alpha = g^r \cdot g_2^{r_2}$ 4. $\mathsf{st} = (w, r_1, r_2)$ 5. Output (α, st)
$\mathsf{V}(x, \alpha, \beta, \gamma)$: 1. Parse x as $((\mathbb{G}, p, g), g_2, h)$ and γ as (γ_1, γ_2) 2. If $\alpha = g^{\gamma_1} \cdot g_2^{\gamma_2} \cdot h^{-\beta}$ then output 1 and otherwise output 0	$\mathsf{P}_2(\mathsf{st}, \beta)$: 1. Parse st as (w_1, w_2, r_1, r_2) 2. $\gamma_i = w_i \cdot \beta + r_i \mod p$ for $i \in \{1, 2\}$ 3. Output $\gamma = (\gamma_1, \gamma_2)$

Observe that the scheme's challenge space $\mathcal{C} = \mathcal{C}_x$ is $\mathbb{Z}_p$ for any $x = ((\mathbb{G}, p, g), g^w)$ produced by Gen, and that $\mathcal{ID}_{\text{Okamoto}}$ has a challenge space of size $|\mathcal{C}_\lambda| \geq 2^\lambda$ and δ-first message unpredictability for $\delta = \delta(\lambda) = 2^{-\lambda}$. Moreover, the verifier V preforms three exponentiations in the group $\mathbb{G}$ which yields a total running time of $t_V = t_V(\lambda) = 3t_{\text{exp}}(\lambda)$.

Note that the instance-witness relation induced by Gen consists of all pairs of the form $((\mathbb{G}, p, g_1, g_2, h), (w_1, w_2))$ for which $h = g_1^{w_1} \cdot g_2^{w_2}$. We denote this relation by $\mathcal{R}_{2\text{DLog}}$. The following claim establishes the special soundness (with respect to the relation $\mathcal{R}_{2\text{Dlog}}$) and simulatability of $\mathcal{ID}_{\text{Okamoto}}$.

Claim 6.4. $\mathcal{ID}_{\text{Okamoto}}$ *is simulatable and has special soundness.*

For completeness, in the full version of the paper we present the simulator Sim establishing the simulatability of the scheme, and the extractor WitnessExt which establishes its special soundness. The simulator Sim runs in time $t_{\text{Sim}} = 3t_{\text{exp}}$, and the extractor WitnessExt performs only arithmetic operations in the ring $\mathbb{Z}_p$, and hence for our purposes its running time is dominated by that of the other algorithms under consideration.

Let $\mathcal{D} = \{\mathcal{D}_\lambda\}_{\lambda \in \mathbb{N}}$ be the distribution which outputs pairs of the form $((\mathbb{G}, p, g, h), w)$ where $(\mathbb{G}, p, g) \leftarrow \mathsf{GroupGen}(1^\lambda)$, $w \leftarrow \mathbb{Z}_p$ and $h = g^w$. It is well-known that the hardness of the relation $\mathcal{R}_{2\mathsf{DLog}}$ with respect to Gen is tightly implied by the hardness of the discrete logarithm relation with respect to $\mathcal{D}$. That is, for any algorithm A there exists an algorithm B such that $\mathsf{T}_{A,\mathsf{Gen}}$ and $\mathsf{T}_{B,\mathcal{D}}$ are identically distributed[7] and

$$
\Pr\left[g^w = h \,\middle|\, \begin{array}{c} (\mathbb{G}, p, g) \leftarrow \mathsf{GroupGen}(1^\lambda) \\ h \leftarrow \mathbb{G} \\ w \leftarrow A(\mathbb{G}, p, g, h) \end{array} \right]
$$
$$
= \Pr\left[g^{w_1} \cdot g_2^{w_2} = h \,\middle|\, \begin{array}{c} (\mathbb{G}, p, g) \leftarrow \mathsf{GroupGen}(1^\lambda) \\ g_2, h \leftarrow \mathbb{G} \\ (w_1, w_2) \leftarrow B(\mathbb{G}, p, g, g_2, h) \end{array} \right].
$$

It immediately follows that if the discrete logarithm relation is 2-moment hard, then the $\mathcal{R}_{2\mathsf{DLog}}$ relation is 2-moment ($\Delta = 1, \omega = 1/2$)-hard, where the parameter $\omega = 1/2$ comes from the fact that the witness space $\mathcal{W}_\lambda$ of $\mathcal{R}_{2\mathsf{DLog}}$ is of size p^2 where p is the order of the group. Hence, the following theorem which establishes concrete security bounds for the Okamoto identification scheme follows immediately from Corollary 4.2.

Theorem 6.5. *Let $t_{\bar{\mathsf{P}}} = t_{\bar{\mathsf{P}}}(\lambda)$ and $q_{\bar{\mathsf{P}}} = q_{\bar{\mathsf{P}}}(\lambda)$ be functions of the security parameter $\lambda \in \mathbb{N}$. If the discrete logarithm problem is 2-moment hard with respect to Gen, then for any malicious prover $\bar{\mathsf{P}}$ that runs in time $t_{\bar{\mathsf{P}}}$ and issues $q_{\bar{\mathsf{P}}}$ transcript-generation queries it holds that*

$$
\mathbf{Adv}_{\mathcal{ID}_{\mathsf{Okamoto}}, \bar{\mathsf{P}}}^{\mathsf{PA\text{-}IMP}}(\lambda) \leq \left(\frac{(16(t_{\bar{\mathsf{P}}} + 3(q_{\bar{\mathsf{P}}} + 1) \cdot t_{\mathsf{exp}})^2}{2^\lambda} \right)^{\frac{2}{3}} + \frac{2}{2^\lambda},
$$

for all sufficiently large $\lambda \in \mathbb{N}$.

The Okamoto signature scheme is obtained from $\mathcal{ID}_{\mathsf{Okamoto}}$ via the Fiat-Shamir transform relative to hash function H, as described in Sect. 5. Therefore, the following theorem which establishes concrete security bounds for the Okamoto signature scheme, is an immediate corollary of Theorem 5.1.

Theorem 6.6. *Let $t_F = t_F(\lambda)$, $q_{\mathsf{H}} = q_{\mathsf{H}}(\lambda)$ and $q_{\mathsf{Sign}} = q_{\mathsf{Sign}}(\lambda)$ be functions of the security parameter $\lambda \in \mathbb{N}$. If the discrete logarithm problem is 2-moment hard with respect to Gen, and the hash function H is modeled as a random oracle, then for every t_F-time algorithm F that issues q_{H} oracle queries and q_{Sign} signing queries it holds that*

---

[7] To be precise, the running time $\mathsf{T}_{B,\mathcal{D}}$ of B is distributed as $\mathsf{T}_{A,\mathsf{Gen}} + 2t_{\mathsf{exp}}$, since B performs two exponentiations and invokes A once. For simplicity of presentation, we assume that the term $2t_{\mathsf{exp}}$ is subsumed by $\mathsf{T}_{A,\mathsf{Gen}}$.

$$\mathbf{Adv}^{\mathsf{Forge}}_{\mathcal{SIG}_{\mathcal{ID}_{\mathsf{Okamoto}}},\mathsf{H},F}(\lambda) \leq \left(\frac{q_{\mathsf{H}} \cdot (16(t_F + 3(q_{\mathsf{Sign}} + 1) \cdot t_{\mathsf{exp}}))^2}{2^{\lambda}} \right)^{\frac{2}{3}}$$

$$+2 \cdot \left(\frac{(q_{\mathsf{Sign}} + 1) \cdot q_{\mathsf{H}}^2 + 1}{2^{\lambda}} \right)$$

for all sufficiently large $\lambda \in \mathbb{N}$.

References

[AAB+02] Abdalla, M., An, J.H., Bellare, M., Namprempre, C.: From identification to signatures via the Fiat-Shamir transform: minimizing assumptions for security and forward-security. In: Knudsen, L.R. (ed.) EUROCRYPT 2002. LNCS, vol. 2332, pp. 418–433. Springer, Heidelberg (2002). https://doi.org/10.1007/3-540-46035-7_28

[BCC+16] Bootle, J., Cerulli, A., Chaidos, P., Groth, J., Petit, C.: Efficient zero-knowledge arguments for arithmetic circuits in the discrete log setting. In: Fischlin, M., Coron, J.-S. (eds.) EUROCRYPT 2016. LNCS, vol. 9666, pp. 327–357. Springer, Heidelberg (2016). https://doi.org/10.1007/978-3-662-49896-5_12

[BD20] Bellare, M., Dai, W.: The multi-base discrete logarithm problem: tight reductions and non-rewinding proofs for schnorr identification and signatures. In: Bhargavan, K., Oswald, E., Prabhakaran, M. (eds.) INDOCRYPT 2020. LNCS, vol. 12578, pp. 529–552. Springer, Cham (2020). https://doi.org/10.1007/978-3-030-65277-7_24

[BN06] Bellare, M., Neven, G.: Multi-signatures in the plain public-key model and a general forking lemma. In: Proceedings of the ACM Conference on Computer and Communications Security, pp. 390–399 (2006)

[FJS14] Fleischhacker, N., Jager, T., Schröder, D.: On tight security proofs for schnorr signatures. In: Sarkar, P., Iwata, T. (eds.) ASIACRYPT 2014. LNCS, vol. 8873, pp. 512–531. Springer, Heidelberg (2014). https://doi.org/10.1007/978-3-662-45611-8_27

[FKL18] Fuchsbauer, G., Kiltz, E., Loss, J.: The algebraic group model and its applications. In: Shacham, H., Boldyreva, A. (eds.) CRYPTO 2018. LNCS, vol. 10992, pp. 33–62. Springer, Cham (2018). https://doi.org/10.1007/978-3-319-96881-0_2

[FPS20] Fuchsbauer, G., Plouviez, A., Seurin, Y.: Blind schnorr signatures and signed ElGamal encryption in the algebraic group model. In: Canteaut, A., Ishai, Y. (eds.) EUROCRYPT 2020. LNCS, vol. 12106, pp. 63–95. Springer, Cham (2020). https://doi.org/10.1007/978-3-030-45724-2_3

[FS86] Fiat, A., Shamir, A.: How to prove yourself: practical solutions to identification and signature problems. In: Odlyzko, A.M. (ed.) CRYPTO 1986. LNCS, vol. 263, pp. 186–194. Springer, Heidelberg (1987). https://doi.org/10.1007/3-540-47721-7_12

[GBL08] Garg, S., Bhaskar, R., Lokam, S.V.: Improved bounds on security reductions for discrete log based signatures. In: Wagner, D. (ed.) CRYPTO 2008. LNCS, vol. 5157, pp. 93–107. Springer, Heidelberg (2008). https://doi.org/10.1007/978-3-540-85174-5_6

[Gol04] Goldreich, O.: Foundations of Cryptography - Volume 2: Basic Applications. Cambridge University Press, Cambridge (2004)

[JT20]   Jaeger, J., Tessaro, S.: Expected-time cryptography: generic techniques and applications to concrete soundness. In: Proceedings of the 18th Theory of Cryptography Conference, pp. 414–443 (2020)

[KMP16] Kiltz, E., Masny, D., Pan, J.: Optimal security proofs for signatures from identification schemes. In: Robshaw, M., Katz, J. (eds.) CRYPTO 2016. LNCS, vol. 9815, pp. 33–61. Springer, Heidelberg (2016). https://doi.org/10.1007/978-3-662-53008-5_2

[Oka92] Okamoto, T.: Provably secure and practical identification schemes and corresponding signature schemes. In: Brickell, E.F. (ed.) CRYPTO 1992. LNCS, vol. 740, pp. 31–53. Springer, Heidelberg (1993). https://doi.org/10.1007/3-540-48071-4_3

[PS00]   Pointcheval, D., Stern, J.: Security arguments for digital signatures and blind signatures. J. Cryptol. **13**, 361–396 (2000)

[PV05]   Paillier, P., Vergnaud, D.: Discrete-log-based signatures may not be equivalent to discrete log. In: Roy, B. (ed.) ASIACRYPT 2005. LNCS, vol. 3788, pp. 1–20. Springer, Heidelberg (2005). https://doi.org/10.1007/11593447_1

[Sch89] Schnorr, C.P.: Efficient identification and signatures for smart cards. In: Brassard, G. (ed.) CRYPTO 1989. LNCS, vol. 435, pp. 239–252. Springer, New York (1990). https://doi.org/10.1007/0-387-34805-0_22

[Sch91] Schnorr, C.: Efficient signature generation by smart cards. J. Cryptol. **4**(3), 161–174 (1991)

[Seu12] Seurin, Y.: On the exact security of Schnorr-type signatures in the random Oracle model. In: Pointcheval, D., Johansson, T. (eds.) EUROCRYPT 2012. LNCS, vol. 7237, pp. 554–571. Springer, Heidelberg (2012). https://doi.org/10.1007/978-3-642-29011-4_33

[Sho97] Shoup, V.: Lower bounds for discrete logarithms and related problems. In: Fumy, W. (ed.) EUROCRYPT 1997. LNCS, vol. 1233, pp. 256–266. Springer, Heidelberg (1997). https://doi.org/10.1007/3-540-69053-0_18

DualRing: Generic Construction of Ring Signatures with Efficient Instantiations

Tsz Hon Yuen[1]([✉]) [iD], Muhammed F. Esgin[2,3], Joseph K. Liu[2], Man Ho Au[1] [iD], and Zhimin Ding[4]

[1] The University of Hong Kong, Pok Fu Lam, Hong Kong
{thyuen,allenau}@cs.hku.hk
[2] Department of Software Systems and Cybersecurity, Faculty of Information Technology, Monash University, Melbourne, Australia
{muhammed.esgin,joseph.liu}@monash.edu
[3] CSIRO's Data61, Melbourne, Australia
[4] Rice University, Houston, USA
zd21@rice.edu

Abstract. We introduce a novel generic ring signature construction, called *DualRing*, which can be built from several canonical identification schemes (such as Schnorr identification). *DualRing* differs from the classical ring signatures by its formation of *two* rings: a ring of commitments and a ring of challenges. It has a structural difference from the common ring signature approaches based on accumulators or zero-knowledge proofs of the signer index. Comparatively, *DualRing* has a number of unique advantages.

Considering the DL-based setting by using Schnorr identification scheme, our *DualRing* structure allows the signature size to be compressed into logarithmic size via an argument of knowledge system such as Bulletproofs. We further improve on the Bulletproofs argument system to eliminate about half of the computation while maintaining the same proof size. We call this *Sum Argument* and it can be of independent interest. This DL-based construction, named DualRing-EC, using Schnorr identification with *Sum Argument* has the shortest ring signature size in the literature without using trusted setup.

Considering the lattice-based setting, we instantiate *DualRing* by a canonical identification based on M-LWE and M-SIS. In practice, we achieve the shortest lattice-based ring signature, named DualRing-LB, when the ring size is between 4 and 2000. DualRing-LB is also $5\times$ faster in signing and verification than the fastest lattice-based scheme by Esgin et al. (CRYPTO'19).

Keywords: Ring signature · Generic construction · Sum argument · M-LWE/SIS

1 Introduction

Ring signatures [35] allow a signer to dynamically choose a set of public keys (including his/her own) and to sign messages on behalf of the set, without reveal-

© International Association for Cryptologic Research 2021
T. Malkin and C. Peikert (Eds.): CRYPTO 2021, LNCS 12825, pp. 251–281, 2021.
https://doi.org/10.1007/978-3-030-84242-0_10

ing who the real signer is. In addition, it is impossible to check if two signatures are issued by the same signer. Ring signatures provide anonymity and they are widely used in privacy-preserving protocols such as e-voting, whistleblowing and privacy-preserving cryptocurrencies.

Classical Ring Structure. The classical ring signatures [35] for a set of n public keys **pk** are constructed by computing $n - 1$ "pseudo-signatures" (the outputs computed from the verification function) sequentially in a *ring structure* first and then using one signer secret key to create a real signature. These n signatures together form a ring signature on behalf of **pk**.

Abe *et al.* [2] generalized this idea in a generic construction (AOS ring signature), which can be built from two types of standard signatures: Type-H (Hash-and-one-way type, e.g., RSA signature) and Type-T (Three-move type, e.g., Schnorr signature). Borromean ring signatures [33] used the ring structure in [2] to compress multiple ring signatures. Its variant is used in privacy-preserving cryptocurrency Monero.

From Accumulator to Zero-Knowledge Proof. The major drawback of the above ring structure approach is the signature size of $O(n)$. Therefore, researchers used other cryptographic primitives to build ring signatures.

An accumulator allows the signer to "compress" n public keys into a constant size *value* and there is a *witness* showing that the signer's public key is in the set of public keys. The advantage of the accumulator-based ring signature [17] is the constant signature size. However, most of the existing accumulators require a trusted setup, which is often not desirable.

Another main approach to constructing an efficient ring signature is to use a zero-knowledge proof to prove knowledge of the secret key with respect to one of the public keys in the ring. The state-of-the-art proof size is $O(\log n)$ by the use of one-out-of-many proof [22].

1.1 DualRing: New Generic Construction of Ring Signature

In this paper, we revisit the classical ring structure approach and design a novel *dual ring* structure to build a new generic construction of ring signatures. Let us first recall how a Type-T signature works and how the AOS ring signature [2] is built on top of it.

A Type-T signature involves the following three functions in its signing (we use Schnorr signature as a running example, indicated inside [ ], with a secret key sk, a public key $\text{pk} = g^{\text{sk}}$ and a message M): a commit function A, which outputs a commitment R $[A : g^r \rightarrow R]$; a hash function H, which outputs a challenge c $[H(M, R) \rightarrow c]$; and a response function Z, which outputs a response z $[Z : r - c \cdot \text{sk} \rightarrow z]$. A Type-T signature is then $\sigma = (c, z)$. For the verification algorithm, one runs a function V to reconstruct R from σ $[V : g^z \cdot \text{pk}^c \rightarrow R']$, and then runs H to check if c is correct $[H(M, R') \stackrel{?}{=} c]$.

Now, in a Type-T AOS *ring* signature for public keys $\text{pk} = \{\text{pk}_1, \ldots, \text{pk}_n\}$, the signer (with index j) follows the structure in Fig. 1, where the signer is

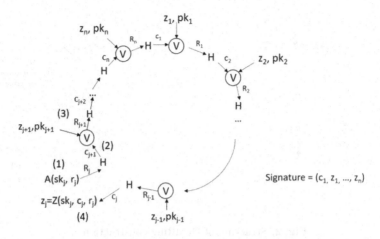

Fig. 1. Structure of the AOS ring signature from a Type-T Signature in [2].

assumed to have sk_j corresponding to pk_j. In particular, (1) the signer picks a randomness r_j to generate R_j via the commit function A. (2) The signer uses the commitment R_j to compute the $(j+1)$-th challenge c_{j+1} by the hash function H. (3) For $i = j+1, \ldots, n, 1, \ldots, j-1$ by picking a random $(i+1)$-th response z_i and the public key of the (i)-th user pk_i, the signer can reconstruct the (i)-th commitment R_i using the function V as in verification and generate the $(i+1)$-th challenge c_{i+1} by the hash function H. A *ring* is then formed sequentially. (4) The last step is to compute z_j from sk_j, c_j, r_j using the response function Z. The final ring signature is composed of a single challenge c_1 and n responses $(z_1, \ldots, z_n)$.

Overview of DualRing. We now describe our novel generic construction of ring signatures called *DualRing*. Let $\odot$ and $\otimes$ be two commutative group operations (e.g., modular multiplication and modular addition). We first modify the definition of a Type-T signature as follows:

- the verification function $V(pk, z, c)$ within the verification algorithm can be divided into two functions $V_1(z)$ and $V_2(pk, c)$ (pk is the public key, c is the challenge and z is the response) such that

$$V(pk, z, c) = V_1(z) \odot V_2(pk, c) \qquad [\text{Schnorr: } V_1 : g^z, V_2 : pk^c].$$

Using this property, we construct a ring signature with a dual-ring structure as in Fig. 2. Particularly, for a set of public keys $\mathbf{pk} = (pk_1, \ldots, pk_n)$ and a secret key sk_j, (1) the signer first picks some randomness r_j. (2) He further picks random challenges $c_1, \ldots, c_{j-1}, c_{j+1}, \ldots, c_n$, and (3) forms an R-ring using the group operation $\odot$ with the functions A and V_2. (4) Then he computes R as:

$$R = A(sk_j; r_j) \odot$$
$$V_2(pk_{j+1}, c_{j+1}) \odot \cdots \odot V_2(pk_n, c_n) \odot V_2(pk_1, c_1) \odot \cdots \odot V_2(pk_{j-1}, c_{j-1}).$$

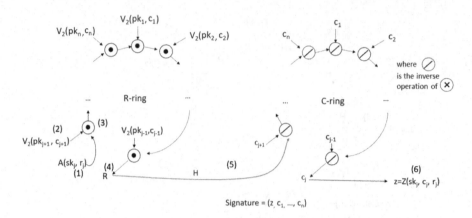

Fig. 2. Structure of DualRing construction

After that, the signer forms a C-ring using the group operation $\otimes$, where the "missing" challenge (5) c_j is computed as:

$$c_j = H(M, \mathbf{pk}, R) \oslash c_{j+1} \oslash \cdots \oslash c_n \oslash c_1 \oslash \cdots c_{j-1} (\text{where } \oslash \text{ is the inverse of } \otimes).$$

As a result, the following equation is satisfied

$$c_1 \otimes \cdots \otimes c_n = H(M, \mathbf{pk}, R) \tag{1}$$

to form the link connecting the two rings for the input message M and the list of public key $\mathbf{pk}$. (6) Lastly, the response z is computed by running $Z(\mathrm{sk}_j, c_j, r_j)$. The final ring signature is composed of a *single response* z and n challenges $(c_1, \ldots, c_n)$, in contrast of the AOS signature which is composed of a *single challenge* c_1 and n responses $(z_1, \ldots z_n)$.

Advantages of DualRing over the AOS Ring Signature. The advantage of DualRing is threefold. Firstly, the AOS ring signature is composed of a *single* challenge and n responses, while DualRing is composed of n challenges and a *single* response. When instantiated with cryptosystems having a small challenge size and a large response size (e.g., lattice-based cryptosystem), it leads to a significant saving in terms of signature size.

Secondly, we observe that the AOS ring signature includes the hash function H in the ring structure (Fig. 1), and this makes it difficult to further shorten the signature. On the other hand, DualRing uses two separate rings with simple group operations, which allows the use of an argument of knowledge to *efficiently* prove the relation in Eq. (1). We instantiate this in the discrete logarithm (DL) setting with communication complexity $O(\log n)$.

Thirdly, our DualRing, when instantiated with the Schnorr identification, has a simpler security reduction when compared to the alternative construction of the AOS ring signature in the Appendix A of [2]. They described that *"the reduction is quite costly because we may have to have at most n successful* *rewinding simulations*" and hence they did not give a full proof. On the other hand, our instantiation does not incur such security loss.

Technical Challenges. One of technical challenges we solve in this paper is to give a security proof for DualRing, as well as the Type-T AOS ring signature which has not been formally proven. Note that it has been an open problem to prove the security of the generic construction of the Type-T AOS ring signature [2] (only a security proof for the instantiation using the Schnorr signature was previously given). We solve this open problem by using *canonical identification* [1] (which is a three-move identification scheme that can be transformed to a Type-T *signature* by the Fiat-Shamir heuristic) in the construction and the security proofs. While the Type-T signature restricts the input to the hash function to include the *signer's public key*, the hash function H of the AOS ring signature takes the set of public keys **pk** as an input. This difference hinders the use of a forgery of the AOS ring signature to break the unforegability of the Type-T signature. On the other hand, the canonical identification does not have such a restriction on the generation of the challenge. The security proof of the Type-T AOS ring signature is given in the full version of the paper.

In order to prove the security of DualRing, we further define a variant called Type-T* *canonical identification*, with the following properties:

1. the verification $V(\mathsf{pk}, z, c)$ can be divided into two algorithms $V_1(z)$ and $V_2(\mathsf{pk}, c)$ such that $V(\mathsf{pk}, z, c) = V_1(z) \odot V_2(\mathsf{pk}, c)$;
2. V_1 is additively/multiplicatively homomorphic;
3. given the secret key sk corresponding to pk and a challenge c, there exists a function $\mathcal{T}$ which outputs $\hat{z} = \mathcal{T}(\mathsf{sk}, c)$ such that $V_1(\hat{z}) = V_2(\mathsf{pk}, c)$;
4. the challenge space Δ_c is a group.

Property 1 of Type-T* canonical identification allows us to build the R-ring as in Fig. 2. Looking ahead, Property 3 is needed in the proof of DualRing's unforgeability to calculate $\hat{z}_i$ such that $V_1(\hat{z}_i) = V_2(\mathsf{pk}_i, c_i)$ for $i \neq j$, and then we use Property 2 to combine z with all $\hat{z}_i$'s to break the Type-T* canonical identification. Property 4 is needed in the proof of DualRing's anonymity to make sure that the challenge c_j constructed in a specific way is indistinguishable from the others. We further define a new security model for canonical identification called *special impersonation*, which is a combination of the security models of impersonation and special soundness. Some standard identification schemes such as Schnorr identification and GQ identification [23] are examples of Type-T* canonical identification secure against special impersonation.

1.2   Efficient Instantiations of DualRing

DualRing-EC: Logarithmic DL-based Ring Signature by Sum Argument. Having established a secure generic construction, DualRing, we try to compress the n challenges $(c_1, \ldots c_n)$ via an argument of knowledge by exploiting the following simple algebraic structure:

$$c_1 \otimes \cdots \otimes c_n = H(M, \mathbf{pk}, R).$$

Table 1. $O(\log n)$-size DL-based ring signature schemes for n public keys, where p is a 256-bit prime.

Ring Signatures	# elements in signature		Signature Size (Bytes)				
	$\mathbb{G}$	$\mathbb{Z}_p$	$n = 2$	$n = 8$	$n = 64$	$n = 2048$	$n = 4096$
[29]	$4 \log n + 2$	$5 \log n + 4$	480	1070	1946	3114	3406
[22]	$4 \log n$	$3 \log n + 1$	260	716	1400	2540	2768
[11]	$\log n + 12$	$\frac{3}{2} \log n + 6$	669	831	1074	1479	1560
[36]	$2 \log n + 7$	7	521	653	851	1181	1247
[27]	$2 \log(n + 2) + 4$	5	424	523	721	1051	1117
DualRing-EC	$2 \log n + 1$	3	195	327	525	855	921

This is theoretically a new approach to construct efficient ring signatures by combining the classical ring structure approach with the argument of knowledge[1].

In the DL setting, the group operation $\otimes$ is the modular addition. We improve the Bulletproof's inner product argument [14] into a new proof system called *Sum Argument*, which allows a prover to convince a verifier that he/she has the knowledge of a vector of scalars $(c_1, \ldots, c_n)$ such that their summation is a public value (i.e., $H(M, \mathbf{pk}, R)$). Our *Sum Argument* only requires about half of the computation of Bulletproof while keeping the same proof size. We show how to obtain it by removing one of the two vectors of the inner product argument required in Bulletproof and to achieve a proof of size $O(\log n)$.

Based on DualRing, Schnorr identification and the sum argument above, we design DualRing-EC, the shortest ring signature scheme in the literature without using trusted setup, as shown in Table 1. The signature size is $O(\log(n))$. When implemented on an elliptic curve with a 256-bit modulus, DualRing-EC is at least 54% (resp., 27%, 18%) shorter than [27] for a ring size of 2 (resp. 64, 4096). Our scheme is at least 46% (resp., 64%, 67%) shorter than [29] for a ring size of 2 (resp. 64, 4096) at the same security level of 128-bit. Therefore, DualRing-EC is highly efficient and is useful for real world applications.

DualRing-LB: Shortest Lattice-based Ring Signature for Ring Size between 4 and 2000. We instantiate DualRing in the M-LWE/SIS setting and obtain DualRing-LB, the shortest lattice-based ring signature for a ring size between 4 and 2000. As mentioned above, DualRing-LB consists of a *single* response and n challenges. The size of a challenge (around 256 bits) in lattice-based identification is often much smaller than the size of a response (around a few KB). As a result, we obtain a compact lattice-based ring signature even without requiring a lattice-based sum argument. We compare with the shortest linear-size ring signature in [30] and shortest logarithmic-size ring signatures in [10,21] in Table 2. DualRing-LB is shorter than [10,21] for ring size less than about 2000 (note that our ring size can be arbitrary number). [30] is longer for all the ring sizes larger than 4, and it is based on a stronger NTRU assumption.

---

[1] Here, we do not require the zero-knowledge property since the anonymity of DualRing is provided by the ring structure.

Table 2. Lattice-based ring signatures for n public keys.

Ring Signatures	Signature Size (Bytes)						Assumption
	$n = 2$	$n = 8$	$n = 64$	$n = 1024$	$n = 2048$	$n = 4096$	
Raptor [30]	2532	10128	81024	1296384	2592768	6564888576	NTRU
Falafl (for 2) [10]	49000	50000	52000	54000	54500	55000	M-LWE+M-SIS
MatRiCT [21]	18000	19000	31000	48000	53000	59000	M-LWE+M-SIS
DualRing-LB (Algo. 3 + 6)	4480	4630	6020	31160	55500	106570	M-LWE+M-SIS

The isogeny-based construction in [10] is at a much lower security level (60 bits of quantum security), is extremely slow (in the order of minutes), and has longer signatures than ours in the range around 5–300.

It is estimated in [19] that the running time of [19] is faster than Raptor for medium/large-sized rings ($n \geq 1024$) and also the estimated runtimes of [19] are significantly faster than those in [10]. The construction in [21] is an optimized version of that in [19] to reduce the signature length at the cost of computational efficiency. Therefore, the scheme by Esgin et al. [19] is the fastest scalable ring signature from lattices. We implement DualRing-LB together with the scheme in [19] and find that our scheme is at least 5 times faster in terms of sign and verify. We, therefore, expect an optimized implementation of our scheme to run faster than Raptor [30] and Falafl [10] as well for most ring sizes.

1.3 Our Contributions

Our contributions can be summarized as follows.

- The main contribution of our paper is the introduction of the novel dual ring structure *DualRing* to design generic construction of ring signatures, which differs significantly from the mainstream zero-knowledge-based or accumulator-based approaches.
- DualRing consists of n challenges and a single response, while the AOS ring signature consists of a single challenge and n responses. This significant difference allows us to produce much shorter signatures in both DL-based and lattice-based setting.
- In the DL-based setting, the DualRing structure allows the signature size to be compressed into $O(\log n)$ size, where n is the number of users in the ring, by using argument of knowledge system such as Bulletproofs [14]. We further enhance the Bulletproofs by eliminating almost half of the computation while maintaining the same proof size and thus achieve much better efficiency. We call this new argument of knowledge *Sum Argument* which can be of independent interest. Our resulting DualRing-EC deploying Schnorr identification scheme with *Sum Argument* is the shortest ring signature in the literature without using trusted setup.
- In the lattice-based setting, we instantiate DualRing by constructing a canonical identification based on M-LWE and M-SIS assumptions. DualRing-LB is the shortest lattice-based ring signature for the most practical ring sizes of 4

up to 2000.[2] We also implement DualRing-LB and show that it is at least 5 times faster in signing and verification than the state-of-the-art fastest construction (in terms of running times of signing and verification) in [19].

2 Related Work

Accumulator-Based Approach. Ring signatures can be constructed by accumulators [17]. The advantage of the accumulator approach is the constant signature size. However, the existing RSA-based and pairing-based accumulators both require a trusted setup for generating system parameters, which is not desirable for systems without a mutually trusted party. There exists a lattice-based accumulator [28] with no trusted setup, but it is not practical (the signature size is in the order of several MBs). Merkle-tree based accumulator does not require trusted setup. However, the membership proof of Merkle-tree based accumulator involves expensive zero-knowledge proof on hash function input.

Zero-Knowledge Proof Based Approach. The mainstream approach to construct a ring signature is to use a zero-knowledge proof on a signer index with the corresponding secret key. Most efficient schemes in the literature is to design a specific zero-knowledge proof for the designated cryptosystem (e.g., DL-based, RSA-based or lattice-based). In particular, a one-out-of-many proof [22] shows that the prover knows an opening of one out of n commitments. The index of such commitment can be expressed as a binary string $(b_1, \ldots b_{\log n})$. The zero-knowledge proof demonstrates the correctness of such an index, and hence the proof size is $O(\log n)$. Since a public key can be viewed as a commitment to zero[3], there are multiple ring signature schemes proposed using one-out-of-many proofs, including the DL-based setting [11,22] and lattice-based setting [19–21]. These ring signatures have size of $O(\log n)$.

Logarithmic-Size Generic Construction. The logarithmic-size generic construction of ring signature in [3] is secure in the standard model by using a public key encryption, a standard signature, a somewhere perfectly binding hash function with private local opening, and a non-interactive witness-indistinguishable (NIWI) proof systems. Their DL-based construction has a signature size of $2(\log n)^2 + 4$ elements in $\mathbb{G}$ and $2 \log n$ elements in $\mathbb{Z}_p$ with an additional NIWI proof (not instantiated in [3]), and hence it is not as efficient as the schemes in Table 1. The lattice-based construction in [3] is also not efficient.

---

[2] A ring signature of n users has some inherent limitations such that it requires at least n operations in signing and verification and storage of n public keys. These two limitations restrict the ring size to go up a lot for many practical applications. On the other hand, for very small ring sizes of, say, 2–5, the anonymity guarantee is very weak. For example, there has been attacks against Monero (cf. [26,34]) that exploit the earlier use of very small rings of size < 6. Hence, one may argue that the most relevant range in practice falls inside 10–2000.

[3] E.g., a DL-based public key g^x is a Pedersen commitment to zero.

3 Preliminaries

Notations. In this paper, we use λ as the security parameter. For the notion $a \leftarrow_s S$, it means that we randomly pick an element a from a set S. We use bold letters such as $\mathbf{a}$ to represent a vector (or matrix for lattice-based construction).

Argument of Knowledge. An argument consists of three PPT algorithms $(\mathsf{S}, \mathcal{P}, \mathcal{V})$, which are CRS (Common Reference String) generator S, the prover $\mathcal{P}$ and the verifier $\mathcal{V}$. A CRS $\hat{\sigma}$ is produced by S on input λ and a transcript tr is produced by $\mathcal{P}$ and $\mathcal{V}$ on inputs s and t, which is denoted by $tr \leftarrow \langle \mathcal{P}(s), \mathcal{V}(t) \rangle$. We write $\langle \mathcal{P}(s), \mathcal{V}(t) \rangle = b$ to denote that the verifier $\mathcal{V}$ accepts $b = 1$ or rejects $b = 0$. We define the language:

$$\mathcal{L} = \{x \mid \exists w : (\hat{\sigma}, x, w) \in \mathcal{R}\},$$

where w is a witness and x is a set of statements u in the relation $\mathcal{R}$.

An argument of knowledge $(\mathsf{S}, \mathcal{P}, \mathcal{V})$ should satisfy *perfect completeness* and *statistical witness-extended emulation* [12]. Informally, completeness means that a prover with a witness w for $x \in \mathcal{L}$ can convince the verifier of this fact. Statistical witness-extended emulation means that given an adversary that produces an acceptable argument with probability ϵ, there exists an emulator that produces a similar argument with probability ϵ together with a witness w.

Definition 1 (Perfect completeness). *For any non-uniform polynomial time adversary $\mathcal{A}$, $(\mathsf{S}, \mathcal{P}, \mathcal{V})$ has perfect completeness if*

$$\Pr\left[(\hat{\sigma}, u, w) \notin \mathcal{R} \text{ or } \langle \mathcal{P}(\hat{\sigma}, u, w), \mathcal{V}(\sigma, u) \rangle = 1 \,\middle|\, \hat{\sigma} \leftarrow \mathsf{S}(\lambda), (u, w) \leftarrow \mathcal{A}(\hat{\sigma})\right] = 1.$$

Definition 2 (Statistical Witness-Extended Emulation). *For any deterministic polynomial time prover $\mathcal{P}^*$, $(\mathsf{S}, \mathcal{P}, \mathcal{V})$ has witness-extended emulation if there is a polynomial time emulator $\mathcal{E}$ such that for any pair of interactive adversaries $\mathcal{A}_1$ and $\mathcal{A}_2$ such that*

$$\Pr\left[\mathcal{A}_1(tr) = 1 \,\middle|\, \begin{array}{l} \hat{\sigma} \leftarrow \mathsf{S}(\lambda), \\ (u, s) \leftarrow \mathcal{A}_2(\hat{\sigma}), \\ tr \leftarrow \langle \mathcal{P}^*(\hat{\sigma}, u, s), \\ \mathcal{V}(\hat{\sigma}, u) \rangle \end{array} \right] \approx \Pr\left[\begin{array}{l} \mathcal{A}_1(tr) = 1 \wedge \\ (tr \text{ is accepting} \\ \Rightarrow (\hat{\sigma}, u, w) \in \mathcal{R}) \end{array} \,\middle|\, \begin{array}{l} \hat{\sigma} \leftarrow \mathsf{S}(\lambda), \\ (u, s) \leftarrow \mathcal{A}_2(\hat{\sigma}), \\ (tr, w) \leftarrow \mathcal{E}^{\mathcal{O}}(\hat{\sigma}, u) \end{array} \right],$$

where the oracle $\mathcal{O} = \langle \mathcal{P}^*(\hat{\sigma}, u, s), \mathcal{V}(\hat{\sigma}, u) \rangle$ can rewind to some point and resume with new randomness for the verifier $\mathcal{V}$ from this point onward.

Such an emulation above is used to define knowledge-soundness [12]. We consider s (which is the output of the adversary $\mathcal{A}_2$ in the above equation) as the internal state of $\mathcal{P}^*$ with randomness, which follows that $\mathcal{E}$ can extract a witness whenever $\mathcal{P}^*$ generates a convincing argument in s.

4   Security Model

We review the security model of a ring signature in [8]. A ring signature consists of four PPT algorithms as follows:

$$
\mathrm{RS} \begin{cases}
\mathsf{Setup}(\lambda) & \to \mathsf{param} \\
\mathsf{KeyGen}(\mathsf{param}) & \to (\mathsf{pk}, \mathsf{sk}) \\
\mathsf{Sign}(\mathsf{param}, M, \mathbf{pk}, \mathsf{sk}) & \to \sigma \\
\mathsf{Verify}(\mathsf{param}, M, \mathbf{pk}, \sigma) & \to 1/0
\end{cases}
$$

We use $\mathbf{pk}$ to represent a vector of public keys $(\mathsf{pk}_1, \ldots, \mathsf{pk}_n)$. For simplicity, we omit the input of system parameters param to algorithms other than Setup in the rest of this paper.

Unforgeability w.r.t. insider corruption. Unforgeability w.r.t. insider corruption [8] means that the adversary $\mathcal{A}$ cannot generate a valid signature without a secret key, even if he can adaptively corrupt some honest participants and obtain their secret keys.

Definition 3 (Unforgeability w.r.t. Insider Corruption). *For any polynomial time adversary $\mathcal{A}$, a ring signature is unforgeable if for some integer q_k polynomial in λ:*

$$
\Pr \left[
\begin{array}{l}
1 \leftarrow \mathsf{Verify}(M^*, \mathbf{pk}^*, \sigma^*), \\
\mathbf{pk}^* \subseteq S \setminus C, (M^*, \mathbf{pk}^*, \cdot) \\
\textit{was not the input of } \mathcal{SO}
\end{array}
\middle|
\begin{array}{l}
\mathsf{param} \leftarrow \mathsf{Setup}(\lambda), \; \textit{for } i \in [1, q_k]: \\
(\hat{\mathsf{pk}}_i, \hat{\mathsf{sk}}_i) \leftarrow \mathsf{KeyGen}(), S := \{\hat{\mathsf{pk}}_i\}_{i=1}^{q_k}, \\
(M^*, \mathbf{pk}^*, \sigma^*) \leftarrow \mathcal{A}^{\mathcal{CO}, \mathcal{SO}}(\mathsf{param}, S)
\end{array}
\right] \leq \mathsf{negl}(\lambda),
$$

where the oracles given to $\mathcal{A}$ is defined as:

- *$\mathcal{CO}(i)$ outputs $\hat{\mathsf{sk}}_i$. We denote C as the set of corrupted users queried in $\mathcal{CO}$.*
- *$\mathcal{SO}(M, \mathbf{pk}, j)$: On input a message M, a vector of public keys $\mathbf{pk}$ and the signer index j, the Signing Oracle outputs $\perp$ if $\hat{\mathsf{pk}}_j \notin \mathbf{pk}$. Otherwise, it outputs a signature $\sigma \leftarrow \mathsf{Sign}(M, \mathbf{pk}, \hat{\mathsf{sk}}_j)$.*

Anonymity against full key exposure. We use the strong anonymity model in [8] that the adversary $\mathcal{A}$ is given all randomness to generate the secret keys.

Definition 4 (Anonymity against Full Key Exposure). *For any polynomial time adversary $(\mathcal{A}_1, \mathcal{A}_2)$, a ring signature is anonymous if for some integer q_k polynomial in λ:*

$$
\left|
\Pr \left[
\begin{array}{l}
b = b', \\
\hat{\mathsf{pk}}_{i_0}, \hat{\mathsf{pk}}_{i_1} \\
\in S \cap \mathbf{pk}^*.
\end{array}
\middle|
\begin{array}{l}
\mathsf{param} \leftarrow \mathsf{Setup}(\lambda), \; \textit{for } i \in [1, q_k]: \\
(\hat{\mathsf{pk}}_i, \hat{\mathsf{sk}}_i) \leftarrow \mathsf{KeyGen}(\mathsf{param}; \omega_i), \\
S := \{\hat{\mathsf{pk}}_i\}_{i=1}^{q_k}, \\
(M^*, \mathbf{pk}^*, i_0, i_1, St) \leftarrow \mathcal{A}_1^{\mathcal{SO}}(\mathsf{param}, S), \\
b \leftarrow_s \{0, 1\}, \sigma \leftarrow \mathsf{Sign}(M^*, \mathbf{pk}^*, \hat{\mathsf{sk}}_{i_b}), \\
b' \leftarrow \mathcal{A}_2(\sigma, \{\omega_i\}_{i=1}^{q_k}, St)
\end{array}
\right] - \frac{1}{2}
\right| \leq \mathsf{negl}(\lambda).
$$

Note that the set of public keys $\mathbf{pk}^*$ chosen by $\mathcal{A}_1$ can include adversarially generated public keys.

Algorithm 1: Type-T Signature

---

1 **Procedure** SETUP(λ):	10 **Procedure** KEYGEN():
2 define $H : \{0,1\}^* \to \Delta_c$;	11 return (pk, sk);
3 return param; // including H	12 **Procedure** VERIFY(M, pk, σ):
4 **Procedure** SIGN(M, sk):	13 parse $\sigma = (z, c)$;
5 $r \leftarrow \Delta_r$;	14 $R' = V(\text{pk}, z, c)$;
6 $R = A(\text{sk}; r)$;	15 if $c \neq H(M, R')$ then
7 $c = H(M, R)$;	16 return 0;
8 $z = Z(\text{sk}, r, c)$;	17 return 1;
9 return $\sigma = (z, c)$;	

---

5 DualRing: Generic Ring Signature Construction

In this section, we show how to construct a generic ring signature scheme, Dual-Ring, from a special kind of canonical identification scheme.

5.1 AOS Ring Signature

The AOS ring signature [2] can be constructed from a standard signature of Type-H or Type-T. We review the definition of Type-T in Algorithm 1.

- The SIGN algorithm uses the algorithm A to generate a commitment R using a randomness r (chosen from a randomness domain Δ_r). Then, the message and R are hashed by H to obtain the hash value c (within the range of hash function Δ_c). Finally, the algorithm uses the function Z to generate the signature using the secret key sk, r and c.
- The VERIFY algorithm allows the reconstruction of R' from the public key pk, z and c using the function V. The signature is validated by using H on the message and R'.

Schnorr signature, Guillou-Quisquater signature [23], Katz-Wang signature [24] and EdDSA [9] are examples of Type-T signatures. Using Type-T signatures, a Type-T AOS ring signature can be constructed as shown in Fig. 1. However, as mentioned before, there is no security proof for this generic construction in [2], but only the instantiation with Schnorr signature is proven secure in [2]. We formally prove its security in the full version of the paper.

5.2 Canonical Identification

Canonical identification [1] is a three-move public-key authentication protocol of a specific form. We first give canonical identification in Algorithm 2, based on the definition of Type-T signature in [2]. We add the additional checking in line 17 of Algorithm 2, which is useful for lattice-based construction. It is known that after applying the Fiat-Shamir transformation to canonical identification, we obtain a Type-T signature.

Algorithm 2: Canonical Identification

---

1 **Procedure** SETUP(λ):
2   return param;

3 **Procedure** KEYGEN():
4   return (pk, sk);

5 **Procedure** PROOF1(sk):
6     $r \leftarrow_s \Delta_r$;
7     $R = A(\text{sk}; r)$;
8   return (R, r);

9 **Procedure** CH(R):
10   return c;

11 **Procedure** PROOF2(sk, r, c):
12   return $z = Z(\text{sk}, r, c)$;

13 **Procedure** VERIFY(pk, z, c):
14     $R' = V(\text{pk}, c, z)$;
15   if $c \neq \text{CH}(R')$ then
16   return 0;
17   auxiliary checking with R', c, z;
18   return 1;

We define a new security notion of *special impersonation under key only attack* for canonical identification. It can be viewed as a combination of the special soundness and the impersonation attack: the adversary wins by outputting two valid transcripts with the same commitment.

Definition 5. *A canonical identification is secure against special impersonation under key only attack for any polynomial time adversary $\mathcal{A}$:*

$$\Pr\left[\begin{array}{c} \text{VERIFY}(\text{pk}, z, c) \\ = \text{VERIFY}(\text{pk}, z', c') = 1 \\ \wedge\, c \neq c' \wedge c, c' \in \Delta_c \end{array} \middle| \begin{array}{c} \text{param} \leftarrow \text{SETUP}(\lambda), \\ (\text{pk}, \text{sk}) \leftarrow \text{KEYGEN}(), \\ (z, c, z', c') \leftarrow \mathcal{A}(\text{param}, \text{pk}) \end{array} \right] \leq \text{negl}(\lambda).$$

We use this new definition instead of *special soundness* together with *key recovery under key only attack* in this paper, because the standard special soundness definition [25] is not satisfied by the efficient lattice-based identification scheme used in Section 7. This stems from the so-called 'knowledge gap' in efficient lattice-based zero-knowledge proofs. In particular, the knowledge extractor in such schemes is *not* guaranteed to recover a secret key of a given public key, but rather recovers an 'approximate' witness of a *relaxed* relation closely related to the relation satisfied by a public-secret key pair. Therefore, to keep the generality of our results, we use the *special impersonation under key only attack*. We refer the reader to earlier works such as [19,20,31,32] for further discussion about this knowledge/soundness gap issue.

We also note that for the settings where the knowledge/soundness gap issue do not arise (i.e., standard special soundness is satisfied) such as the DL-setting, 'special impersonation under key only attack' implies the standard 'key recovery under key only attack' [25] since the knowledge extractor in that case recovers a secret key sk^* with $(\text{sk}^*, \text{pk}) \in \text{KEYGEN}()$ given a public key pk and two accepting transcripts.

Type-T* Canonical Identification. Next, we define Type-T* canonical identification, which is a canonical identification with the following properties.

1. The function V in the verify algorithm consists of two functions V_1 and V_2 during the reconstruction of R', such that line 14 in Algorithm 2 becomes:

$$R' = V_1(z) \odot V_2(\mathsf{pk}, c),$$

where $\odot$ is a commutative group operation for the domain of R'.
2. The function V_1 is additively/multiplicatively homomorphic, i.e., $V_1(z_1) \odot V_1(z_2) = V_1(z_1 \oplus z_2)$, where $\oplus$ is the additive/multiplicative operation. The homomorphic operation should be efficiently computable.
3. Given the secret key sk corresponding to pk and c, there exists a function $\mathcal{T}$ that outputs $\hat{z} = \mathcal{T}(\mathsf{sk}, c)$ such that $V_1(\hat{z}) = V_2(\mathsf{pk}, c)$.
4. The challenge space Δ_c is a group with operation "$\otimes$". We denote the inverse operation of $\otimes$ as $\oslash$. (For example, if $\otimes$ is defined as "$+$", $\oslash$ will be "$-$".) If c_1 and c_2 are uniformly distributed in Δ_c, then $c_1 \otimes c_2$ is also uniformly distributed in Δ_c.

It is easy to see that Schnorr identification and Guillou-Quisquater identification [23] are examples of Type-T* canonical identification. There are in fact many more examples from the literature. For many identification schemes reviewed in [6], the verification function V can be split into $V_1(z)$ and $V_2(pk, c)$, such as the FFS family, FF family, and Hs family. Apart from the above schemes, the identification scheme from Katz-Wong signature [24], Chaum-Pedersen identification [15] and the Okamoto-Schnorr identification are some examples of Type-T* canonical identification. Type-T* canonical identification can also be applied to the lattice-based setting, in particular, effectively to all "Fiat-Shamir with Aborts" [31,32]-based identification schemes (as shown in Sect. 7).

Schnorr identification. The SETUP algorithm outputs a cyclic group $\mathbb{G}$ of prime order p, with a generator g. For each KEYGEN execution, the algorithm picks a random $\mathsf{sk} \in \mathbb{Z}_p$ and computes $\mathsf{pk} = g^{\mathsf{sk}}$. The functions A, Z, V_1, V_2 are defined as:

$$R = A(\mathsf{sk}; r) := g^r,$$
$$z = Z(\mathsf{sk}, r, c) := r - c \cdot \mathsf{sk} \mod p,$$
$$R' = V_1(z) \odot V_2(\mathsf{pk}, c) := g^z \cdot \mathsf{pk}^c.$$

Note that V_1 is additively homomorphic: $V_1(z_1) \odot V_1(z_2) = g^{z_1} \cdot g^{z_2} = g^{z_1 + z_2} = V_1(z_1 + z_2)$. Given the secret key sk corresponding to pk and c, it is easy to compute $\hat{z} = \mathcal{T}(\mathsf{sk}, c) := \mathsf{sk} \cdot c \mod p$ such that $V_1(\hat{z}) = g^{\mathsf{sk} \cdot c} = \mathsf{pk}^c = V_2(\mathsf{pk}, c)$. The challenge space $\mathbb{Z}_p$ is a group under addition modulo p. Therefore, Schnorr identification is a Type-T* canonical identification.

Theorem 1. *Schnorr identification is secure against special impersonation under key only attack if the DL assumption holds.*

Proof. Suppose that $\mathcal{A}$ is an adversary breaking the special impersonation under key only attack. The algorithm $\mathcal{B}$ is given a DL problem (g, y) for a cyclic group $\mathbb{G}$ of prime order p. $\mathcal{B}$ gives $\mathsf{param} = (\mathbb{G}, p, g)$ and $\mathsf{pk} = y$ to $\mathcal{A}$.

$\mathcal{A}$ returns (c, z, c', z') where $c \neq c'$. Then we have:

$$g^z \cdot \mathsf{pk}^c = g^{z'} \cdot \mathsf{pk}^{c'}.$$

Therefore $\mathcal{B}$ can extract the secret key $\mathsf{sk} = \frac{z-z'}{(c'-c)}$ as the solution to the DL problem. □

Guillou-Quisquater (GQ) identification [23]. The SETUP algorithm outputs a pair (N, e), where $N = pq$, p and q are large prime numbers, e is a prime number less than $N/4$ and $\gcd(e, \phi(N)) = 1$. For each KEYGEN execution, the algorithm picks a random $\mathsf{sk} \in \mathbb{Z}_N$ and calculates $\mathsf{pk} = \mathsf{sk}^e$. The functions A, Z, V_1, V_2 are defined as:

$$R = A(\mathsf{sk}; r) := r^e,$$
$$z = Z(\mathsf{sk}, r, c) := \mathsf{sk}^c \cdot r \mod N,$$
$$R' = V_1(z) \odot V_2(\mathsf{pk}, c) := z^e \cdot \mathsf{pk}^{-c} \mod N.$$

Note that V_1 is multiplicatively homomorphic: $V_1(z_1) \odot V_1(z_2) = z_1^e \cdot z_2^e = (z_1 z_2)^e = V_1(z_1 \cdot z_2)$. Given the secret key sk corresponding to pk and c, it is easy to compute $\hat{z} = T(\mathsf{sk}, c) := \mathsf{sk}^{-c} \mod N$ such that $V_1(\hat{z}) = \hat{z}^e = \mathsf{sk}^{-ce} = \mathsf{pk}^{-c} = V_2(\mathsf{pk}, c)$. The challenge space of GQ identification is $\mathbb{Z}_e$ and it is a group under addition. Therefore, GQ identification is a Type-T* canonical identification.

Theorem 2. *GQ identification is secure against special impersonation under key only attack if the RSA assumption holds.*

Proof. Suppose that $\mathcal{A}$ is an adversary breaking the special impersonation under key only attack. The algorithm $\mathcal{B}$ is given a RSA problem (N, e, y). $\mathcal{B}$ gives $\mathsf{param} = (N, e)$ and $\mathsf{pk} = y$ to $\mathcal{A}$.

$\mathcal{A}$ returns (c, z, c', z'), where $c \neq c'$, we have $z^e \cdot \mathsf{pk}^{-c} = z'^e \cdot \mathsf{pk}^{-c'}$. Then:

$$(z/z')^e = \mathsf{pk}^{(c-c')}$$

Since e is a prime and $c, c' \in \mathbb{Z}_e$, $\mathcal{B}$ can compute integers A and B such that:

$$A \cdot e + B \cdot (c - c') = \gcd(e, (c - c')) = 1,$$

by the Euclidean algorithm. Hence we have:

$$(z/z')^{Be} = \mathsf{pk}^{1-Ae}$$

Therefore we can extract the secret key $\mathsf{sk} = (z/z')^B \mathsf{pk}^A$ as the solution to the RSA problem. □

Algorithm 3: DualRing

---

1 **Procedure** SETUP(λ):	11 **Procedure** KEYGEN(param):
2 $\quad$ define $H : \{0,1\}^* \to \Delta_c$;	12 $\quad$ return (pk, sk) $\leftarrow$
3 $\quad$ return param $\leftarrow$ T*.SETUP(λ);	$\quad\quad$ T*.KEYGEN(param);
4 **Procedure** SIGN(param, m, **pk** =	13 **Procedure** VERIFY(param, m, **pk** =
$\quad$ {pk$_1$, ..., pk$_n$}, sk$_j$):	$\quad$ {pk$_1$, ..., pk$_n$}, σ):
5 $\quad r \leftarrow_s \Delta_r, c_i \leftarrow_s \Delta_c$ for all $i \neq j$;	14 $\quad$ parse $\sigma = (c_1, ..., c_n, z)$;
6 $\quad R = A(\mathsf{sk}_j; r) \odot \bigodot_{i \neq j} V_2(\mathsf{pk}_i, c_i)$;	15 $\quad R = V_1(z) \odot \bigodot_{i=1}^n V_2(\mathsf{pk}_i, c_i)$;
7 $\quad c = H(m, \mathbf{pk}, R)$;	16 $\quad c = \bigotimes_{i=1}^n c_i$;
8 $\quad c_j = c \oslash \bigotimes_{i \neq j} c_i$;	17 $\quad$ if $c \neq H(m, \mathbf{pk}, R)$ then
9 $\quad z = Z(\mathsf{sk}_j, r, c_j)$;	18 $\quad\quad$ return 0;
10 $\quad$ return $\sigma = (c_1, ..., c_n, z)$;	19 $\quad$ auxiliary checking with (R, c, z);
	20 $\quad$ return 1;

5.3 Our Construction: DualRing

We denote a Type-T* canonical identification scheme by T*. We use the symbol $\odot$ and $\bigotimes$ to represent consecutive $\odot$ and $\otimes$ operations, respectively:

$$\bigodot_{i=1}^n a_i := a_1 \odot a_2 \odot \ldots \odot a_{n-1} \odot a_n, \quad \bigotimes_{i=1}^n b_i := b_1 \otimes b_2 \otimes \ldots \otimes b_{n-1} \otimes b_n.$$

DualRing is shown in Algorithm 3. The high level idea is that we use V_2 to add the decoy public keys pk$_i$ and their corresponding challenge values c_i to the commitment R first. After getting the real challenge value c, the signer with index j computes $c_j = c \oslash \bigotimes_{i \neq j} c_i \in \Delta_c$. The signer computes z according to the canonical identification scheme. To verify, the commitment R is reconstructed from all public keys and their corresponding challenge values. The value $\bigotimes_{\forall i} c_i$ should be equal to the real challenge value c.

Theorem 3. *DualRing is unforgeable w.r.t. insider corruption in the random oracle model if T^* is secure against special impersonation under key only attack and $|\Delta_c| > q_s(q_h + q_s - 1)$, where q_s and q_h are the number of queries to the signing oracle and the H oracle respectively.*

Proof. Denote $\mathcal{A}$ as a PPT adversary breaking the unforgeability w.r.t. insider corruption of DualRing. We build an algorithm $\mathcal{B}$ to break the special impersonation under key only attack of T*. Suppose the algorithm $\mathcal{B}$ is given a system parameters param and a public key pk* from its challenger $\mathcal{C}$.

Setup. $\mathcal{B}$ picks a random index $i^* \in [1, q_k]$. $\mathcal{B}$ runs $(\hat{\mathsf{pk}}_i, \hat{\mathsf{sk}}_i) \leftarrow$ KeyGen() for $i \in [1, q_k], i \neq i^*$. $\mathcal{B}$ sets $\hat{\mathsf{pk}}_{i^*} = \mathsf{pk}^*$. $\mathcal{B}$ gives param and $S := \{\hat{\mathsf{pk}}_i\}_{i=1}^{q_k}$ to $\mathcal{A}$.

Oracle Simulation. $\mathcal{B}$ answers the oracle queries as follows.

- H: $\mathcal{B}$ simulates H as a random oracle.

- $\mathcal{CO}$: On input i, $\mathcal{B}$ returns $\hat{\mathsf{sk}}_i$ (If $i = i^*$, $\mathcal{B}$ declares failure and exits.).
- $\mathcal{SO}$: On input a message M, a set of public key $\mathbf{pk} = (\mathsf{pk}_1, \ldots, \mathsf{pk}_n)$ and the signer index j, it outputs $\perp$ if $\hat{\mathsf{pk}}_j \notin \mathbf{pk}$. If $j \neq i^*$, then $\mathcal{B}$ returns $\sigma \leftarrow$ SIGN$(\mathrm{param}, M, \mathbf{pk}, \hat{\mathsf{sk}}_j)$.
Otherwise, $\mathcal{B}$ picks random $c_1, \ldots, c_n \in \Delta_c$ and z from the domain of response Δ_z according to the distribution of the output of $Z(\cdot)$. $\mathcal{B}$ computes $R = V_1(z) \odot \bigodot_{i=1}^{n} V_2(\mathsf{pk}_i, c_i)$. $\mathcal{B}$ sets $H(M, \mathbf{pk}, R) = \bigotimes_{i=1}^{n} c_i$ in the random oracle. If such value has been set in the random oracle, $\mathcal{B}$ declares failure and exits. $\mathcal{B}$ returns $\sigma = (c_1, \ldots, c_n, z)$.

Challenge. $\mathcal{A}$ returns a forgery $(M^*, \{\hat{\mathsf{pk}}_{i_j}\}_{j=1}^{n}, \sigma^* = (c_1^*, \ldots, c_{n^*}^*, z^*))$. If $\mathsf{pk}^* \neq \hat{\mathsf{pk}}_{i_j}$ for all $j \in [1, n]$, $\mathcal{B}$ declares failure and exits. Otherwise, we denote j^* as the index such that $\mathsf{pk}^* = \hat{\mathsf{pk}}_{i_{j^*}}$. Denote $\mathbf{pk}^* = \{\hat{\mathsf{pk}}_{i_j}\}_{j=1}^{n}$ and compute R^* as in the VERIFY algorithm. $\mathcal{B}$ rewinds to the point that $(M^*, \mathbf{pk}^*, R^*)$ is queried to H and returns a different c' instead. $\mathcal{A}$ returns another signature $\sigma' = (c_1', \ldots, c_n', z')$. Since both σ^* and σ' are valid signatures, We have:

$$R^* = V_1(z^*) \odot \bigodot_{j=1}^{n} V_2(\hat{\mathsf{pk}}_{i_j}, c_j^*) = V_1(z') \odot \bigodot_{j=1}^{n} V_2(\hat{\mathsf{pk}}_{i_j}, c_j').$$

Note that it is impossible to have $c_j^* = c_j'$ for all $j \in [1, n]$ (since $\bigotimes_{j=1}^{n} c_j^* \neq \bigotimes_{j=1}^{n} c_j'$). If $c_{j^*}^* = c_{j^*}'$, $\mathcal{B}$ declares failure and exits. With probability at least $1/n$, we have $c_{j^*}^* \neq c_{j^*}'$. Observe that:

$$V_1(z^*) \odot \bigodot_{j=1}^{n} V_2(\hat{\mathsf{pk}}_{i_j}, c_j^*)$$
$$= V_1(z^* \oplus \hat{z}_1^* \oplus \ldots \oplus \hat{z}_{j^*-1}^* \oplus \hat{z}_{j^*+1}^* \oplus \ldots \oplus \hat{z}_n^*) \odot V_2(\mathsf{pk}^*, c_{j^*}^*)$$
$$= V_1(\tilde{z}^*) \odot V_2(\mathsf{pk}^*, c_{j^*}^*),$$

where $\hat{z}_i^* = T(\hat{\mathsf{sk}}_i, c_i^*)$ for $i \in [1, n] \setminus j^*$ and $\tilde{z}^* = z^* \oplus \hat{z}_1^* \oplus \ldots \oplus \hat{z}_{j^*-1}^* \oplus \hat{z}_{j^*+1}^* \oplus \ldots \oplus \hat{z}_n^*$. Similarly we have $V_1(z') \odot \bigodot_{j=1}^{n} V_2(\hat{\mathsf{pk}}_{i_j}, c_j') = V_1(\tilde{z}') \odot V_2(\mathsf{pk}^*, c_{j^*}')$ for some $\tilde{z}'$. Then $\mathcal{B}$ can return $(c_{j^*}^*, \tilde{z}^*, c_{j^*}', \tilde{z}')$ to its challenger $\mathcal{C}$.

Probability Analysis. We analyse the probability of success (i.e., not aborting) in the above simulation. For q_c queries to the $\mathcal{CO}$, the probability of success in the first query is $(1 - \frac{1}{q_k})$. The probability of success in the second query is at least $(1 - \frac{1}{q_k-1})$. The probability of success after q_c queries is at least $(1 - \frac{1}{q_k})(1 - \frac{1}{q_k-1}) \cdots (1 - \frac{1}{q_k-q_c+1}) = \frac{q_k-q_c}{q_k} = 1 - \frac{q_c}{q_k}$. (It is implied by the security model that $q_k > q_c + n$.)

For q_s queries to the $\mathcal{SO}$, the probability of success in the first query is at least $(1 - \frac{q_h}{|\Delta_c|})$, where q_h is the number queries to the H oracle. The probability of success after q_s queries to $\mathcal{SO}$ is at least

$$(1 - \frac{q_h}{|\Delta_c|})(1 - \frac{q_h+1}{|\Delta_c|}) \cdots (1 - \frac{q_h+q_s-1}{|\Delta_c|}) \geq 1 - \frac{q_s(q_h+q_s-1)}{|\Delta_c|}.$$

Here we assume that $|\Delta_c| > q_s(q_h + q_s - 1)$.

The probability of $\mathsf{pk}^* \neq \hat{\mathsf{pk}}_{i_j}$ in the challenge phase is $(1 - \frac{1}{q_k - q_c})(1 - \frac{1}{q_k - q_c - 1}) \cdots (1 - \frac{1}{q_k - q_c - n + 1}) = \frac{q_k - q_c - n}{q_k - q_c}$. If the probability of forgery by $\mathcal{A}$ is ϵ, then the probability of $\mathcal{B}$ does not return failure before rewinding is

$$\epsilon_b := \epsilon(1 - \frac{q_c}{q_k})(1 - \frac{q_s(q_h + q_s - 1)}{|\Delta_c|})(1 - \frac{q_k - q_c - n}{q_k - q_c})$$

$$= \epsilon(1 - \frac{q_s(q_h + q_s - 1)}{|\Delta_c|})(\frac{n}{q_k}).$$

By the generalized forking lemma [4], the probability of a successful rewinding is at least $\frac{\epsilon_b}{8}$ if $|\Delta_c| > 8q_h/\epsilon_b$ (it runs in time $\tau \cdot 8q_n/\epsilon_b \cdot \ln(8n/\epsilon_b)$ if $\mathcal{A}$ runs in time τ). Finally we have $c_{j^*}^* \neq c_{j^*}'$ with probability at least $1/n$. As a result, the probability ϵ' of $\mathcal{B}$ breaking the special impersonation is:

$$\epsilon' \geq (\frac{\epsilon n}{8q_k})(1 - \frac{q_s(q_h + q_s - 1)}{|\Delta_c|}).$$

if $|\Delta_c| > q_s(q_h + q_s - 1)$ and $|\Delta_c| > 8q_h/\epsilon_b$[4]. We can further simplify the probability ϵ' if we take $|\Delta_c| \geq 2q_s(q_h + q_s - 1)$. Then if $|\Delta_c| > \frac{16q_h q_k}{\epsilon n}$, we have $\epsilon' \geq \frac{\epsilon n}{16q_k}$. □

Theorem 4. *DualRing is anonymous in the random oracle model, if $|\Delta_c| > q_s(q_h + q_s - 1)$, where q_s and q_h are the number of queries to the signing oracle and the H oracle respectively.*

Proof. We show how to build an algorithm $\mathcal{B}$ providing perfect anonymity in the random oracle model.

Setup. $\mathcal{B}$ runs param $\leftarrow$ SETUP(λ). $\mathcal{B}$ runs $(\mathsf{pk}_i, \mathsf{sk}_i) \leftarrow$ KeyGen(param; ω_i) for $i \in [1, q_k]$ with randomness ω_i. $\mathcal{B}$ gives param and $S := \{\mathsf{pk}_i\}_{i=1}^{q_k}$ to $\mathcal{A}_1$.

Oracle Simulation. $\mathcal{B}$ answers the oracle queries as follows.

- $\mathcal{SO}$: On input a message m, a set of public key **pk** with the signer index j, $\mathcal{B}$ returns $\sigma \leftarrow$ SIGN(param, m, **pk**, sk_j).
- H: $\mathcal{B}$ simulates H as a random oracle.

Challenge. $\mathcal{A}_1$ gives $\mathcal{B}$ a message m and a vector of public keys **pk** and two indices i_0, i_1. $\mathcal{B}$ picks random $c_1, \ldots, c_n \in \Delta_c$ and picks z from the domain of response Δ_z according to the distribution of the output of $Z(\cdot)$. $\mathcal{B}$ computes $R = V_1(z) \odot \bigodot_{i=1}^{n} V_2(\mathsf{pk}_i, c_i)$. $\mathcal{B}$ sets $H(m, \mathbf{pk}, R) = \bigotimes_{i=1}^{n} c_i$ in the random oracle. By Property 4, the distribution is correct. If the hash value is already set by the H oracle, $\mathcal{B}$ declares failure and exits. $\mathcal{B}$ returns $\sigma = (c_1, \ldots, c_n, z)$ and $\{\omega_i\}_{i=1}^{q_k}$ to $\mathcal{A}_2$. $\mathcal{B}$ picks a random bit b.

---

[4] The condition $|\Delta_c| > 8q_h/\epsilon_b$ is not needed if we use the forking lemma in [7] with a looser security bound.

Output. Finally, $\mathcal{A}_2$ outputs a bit b'. Observe that b is not used in the generation of σ. Therefore, $\mathcal{A}_2$ can only win with probability $1/2$.

Probability Analysis. We analyse the probability of success (i.e., not aborting) in the above simulation. For q_h queries to the H oracle and q_s queries to the $\mathcal{SO}$, the probability of success in the first query is at least $(1 - \frac{q_h}{|\Delta_c|})$. The probability of success after q_s queries to $\mathcal{SO}$ is at least

$$(1 - \frac{q_h}{|\Delta_c|})(1 - \frac{q_h + 1}{|\Delta_c|}) \cdots (1 - \frac{q_h + q_s - 1}{|\Delta_c|}) \geq 1 - \frac{q_s(q_h + q_s - 1)}{|\Delta_c|}.$$

Here we assume that $|\Delta_c| > q_s(q_h + q_s - 1)$. If $\mathcal{B}$ does not abort, then no PPT adversary can win with non-negligible probability over half. $\qquad\square$

Difference with AOS Ring Signature. Our ring signature is a bit different from the AOS ring signature. The AOS ring signature allows a mixture of different types of public keys, such as keys from the Schnorr signature and the RSA signature. The security proof for the generic construction of the AOS ring signature was not formally given in [2]. On the other hand, our scheme allows different types of public keys from different Type-T* canonical identification schemes, with the restriction that these canonical identification schemes should use the same V_1 function[5] (Otherwise, we do not know which V_1 function to use in the VERIFY algorithm). The security proof for our generic construction holds for different Type-T* canonical identification schemes satisfying the requirement above.

The AOS ring signature is generated sequentially by forming a "ring" of c_i in a loop and calculating z_i for n times. On the other hand, our signature is generated by forming a "R-ring" in one-shot during the commit phase, forming a "C-ring" in one-shot after getting the challenge c and calculating z for one time only. Therefore, our scheme is more efficient than the AOS ring signature.

Finally, our dual ring technique cannot be applied to the Type-H signature in [2]. Recall that for our Type-T* DualRing, we require the use of $V_2(\mathsf{pk}_i, c_i)$ (for all non-signer indices) to generate R. For Type-H, pk_i is tied with z by the one-way function $F(z, \mathsf{pk}_i)$. Hence, we cannot separate z and pk_i into V_1 and V_2 to form the R-ring similarly.

Difference with CDS OR-proofs. The C-Ring in DualRing is similar to the use of secret sharing in CDS 1-out-of-n OR proof [16]. Our construction of R-Ring leads to a single R and hence a single z in the signature. On the contrary, [16] does not have the formation of R-Ring and still has n commitments R_i's. It results in n responses z_i's. So, the ring signature constructed by [16] consists of (c_i, z_i) for $i \in [n]$. There is no trivial way to combine all z_i's, because each z_i is only related to R_i and c_i, and not to other z_j's. Hence, [16] does not (easily) achieve an $O(\log n)$ size ring signature in the DL-based setting.

---

[5] Which implicitly implies all users should use the same set of security parameters including the same group and generator for their sk and pk.

6   DualRing-EC: Our Succinct DL-based Ring Signature

We give a new *sum argument of knowledge* which is useful to reduce the signature size of DualRing from linear to logarithmic in the DL-based setting. The group operation $\otimes$ of the challenge space is modular addition. This is the first combination of the classical ring structure with the argument of knowledge.

Notations and Assumptions. For a security parameter λ, we use $\mathbb{G}$ to represent a cyclic group of prime order p. We use $[n]$ to denote the numbers $1, 2, ..., n$.

We use the following notations for vectors for our DL-based construction: $\mathbf{a}_{[:l]}$ and $\mathbf{a}_{[l:]}$ represent $(a_1, ..., a_l)$ and $(a_{l+1}, ..., a_n)$. $\mathbf{a} \circ \mathbf{b}$ is the Hadamard product $(a_1 b_1, a_2 b_2, ..., a_n b_n)$. $\langle \mathbf{a}, \mathbf{b} \rangle$ is the inner product $\sum_{i=1}^{n} a_i b_i$. $\mathbf{a}^b$, $\mathbf{a} + b$ and $\mathbf{a}^\mathbf{b}$ represent $(a_1^b, a_2^b, ..., a_n^b)$, $(a_1 + b, a_2 + b, ..., a_n + b)$ and $\prod_{i=1}^{n} a_i^{b_i}$ respectively. $\sum \mathbf{a}$ and $\prod \mathbf{a}$ denotes $\sum_{i=1}^{n} a_i$ and $\prod_{i=1}^{n} a_i$.

Definition 6 (Discrete Logarithm Assumption). *For all PPT adversaries $\mathcal{A}$ such that*

$$\Pr\left[y = g^a \mid g, y \leftarrow_s \mathbb{G}, a \leftarrow \mathcal{A}(\mathbb{G}, g, y)\right] \leq \mathsf{negl}(\lambda).$$

6.1   Sum Arguments of Knowledge

The sum argument of knowledge is a variant of inner product argument in [14]. The inner product argument is an efficient proof system for the following relation:

$$\left\{ (\mathbf{g}, \mathbf{h} \in \mathbb{G}^n, P \in \mathbb{G}, c \in \mathbb{Z}_p; \mathbf{a}, \mathbf{b} \in \mathbb{Z}_p^n) : P = \mathbf{g}^\mathbf{a} \mathbf{h}^\mathbf{b} \wedge c = \langle \mathbf{a}, \mathbf{b} \rangle \right\}$$

in which a prover $\mathcal{P}$ convinces a verifier $\mathcal{V}$ that c is the inner product of two committed vectors $\mathbf{a}, \mathbf{b}$. Bootle *et al.* [12] presented an efficient zero-knowledge proof for inner product argument, with communication complexity of $6 \log_2(n)$ (n is the dimension of vectors). Based on their works, Bünz *et al.* proposed Bulletproofs [14] to reduce the communication complexity to $2 \log_2(n)$. They achieve $O(\log n)$ complexity by running a recursive PF algorithm, such that in each round two vectors $\mathbf{a}, \mathbf{b}$ of size n are committed into two commitments (L, R), and two vector of proofs $\mathbf{a}', \mathbf{b}'$ of size $n/2$ are computed for challenge x, where $L^{x^2} P R^{x^{-2}}$ is equal to the commitment of $\mathbf{a}', \mathbf{b}'$ and $\langle \mathbf{a}', \mathbf{b}' \rangle$. In the next round, run the PF algorithm with input vectors $\mathbf{a}', \mathbf{b}'$ and the recursion ends when $n = 1$.

From Inner Product Argument to Sum Argument. To construct our logarithmic size ring signature, we propose a new argument of knowledge named Sum Argument. First we give the relation:

$$\left\{ (\mathbf{g} \in \mathbb{G}^n, P \in \mathbb{G}, c \in \mathbb{Z}_p; \mathbf{a} \in \mathbb{Z}_p^n) : P = \mathbf{g}^\mathbf{a} \wedge c = \sum \mathbf{a} \right\} \tag{2}$$

In a sum argument, a prover convinces a verifier that he/she has the knowledge of a vector of scalars $\mathbf{a}$, such that $P = \mathbf{g}^\mathbf{a}$ and $c = \sum \mathbf{a}$. Our sum argument looks like an inner product argument, where a vector of generators and a computation of multi-exponentiation is used. Although an inner product argument can be converted into a sum argument by setting the vector $\mathbf{b}$ to $\mathbf{1}^n$, this yields a less efficient protocol than ours.

Assume that the system parameter param includes a generator $u \in \mathbb{G}$ in group $\mathbb{G}$ with order p and two hash functions $H_Z, H_Z' : \{0,1\}^* \rightarrow \mathbb{Z}_p$. A Non-interactive Sum Argument (NISA) consists of a PROOF algorithm which takes $(\text{param}, \mathbf{g}, P, c, \mathbf{a})$ and outputs a proof π; and a VERIFY algorithm which takes $(\text{param}, \mathbf{g}, P, c, \pi)$ and outputs a bit 1/0. Our NISA is given in Algorithm 4. Observe that for the k-th recursion in PF, the value of $\mathbf{b}$ is $\prod_{i=1}^k (x_i + x_i^{-1})\mathbf{1}^{\frac{n}{2^k}}$, where x_i is the i-th output of H_Z. This $\mathbf{b}$ is known to the verifier and hence we do not need a vector of generators $\mathbf{h}$ to commit $\mathbf{b}$ in L, R as in [12]. As a result, we can set $\mathbf{h}$ as $\mathbf{1}^n$ and can save almost half of the exponentiation during the recursion. In addition, the computation of P is also not needed by the prover.

Theorem 5. *Our sum argument has statistical witness-extended emulation for non-trivial discrete logarithm relation among $\mathbf{g}, u$ or a valid witness $\mathbf{a}$.*

We defer its security proof to the full version of the paper.

Compared with [14], our protocol is simpler. In each iteration, we compute $(4n' + 2)$ exponentiations to generate a proof, then compute a multi-exponentiation of size $(1 + n + 2\log_2(n))$ to verify. For an inner product argument [14], the corresponding computations are $(8n' + 8)$ exponentiations and a multi-exponentiation of size $(1 + 2n + 2\log_2(n))$, respectively. The proof sizes are similar; however we omit almost half of exponentiations.

6.2 Logarithmic Size DL-based Ring Signature

We give the full construction of compact DL-based ring signature, by combining DualRing with the sum argument of knowledge and Schnorr identification. Then, we compare the efficiency with the existing ring signature schemes.

Matching Sum Argument with Ring Signature. Notice that the sum argument proves the relation for some $a_i \in \mathbb{Z}_p$, given $g_i, P \in \mathbb{G}$ and $c \in \mathbb{Z}_p$:

$$P = \prod_{i=1}^n g_i^{a_i} \quad \wedge \quad c = \sum_{i=1}^n a_i.$$

On the other hand, the verification of our generic ring signature includes:

$$R \odot (V_1(z))^{-1} = \bigodot_{i=1}^n V_2(\mathsf{pk}_i, c_i) \quad \wedge \quad H(m, \mathsf{pk}, R) = \bigotimes_{i=1}^n c_i.$$

Interestingly, the two examples (DL- and RSA-based) of the Type-T* canonical identification have $V_2(\mathsf{pk}_i, c_i) = \mathsf{pk}_i^{c_i}$. Therefore, we can use the sum argument for the relation:

$$R \cdot (V_1(z))^{-1} = \prod_{i=1}^n \mathsf{pk}_i^{c_i} \quad \wedge \quad H(m, \mathsf{pk}, R) = \sum_{i=1}^n c_i.$$

Algorithm 4: NISA

---

1 **Procedure** NISA.PROOF($\{$param$, \mathbf{g}, P, c\}, \mathbf{a}$):

2 $\quad\lfloor$ Run protocol PF on input $(\mathbf{g}, u^{H'_Z(P,u,c)}, \mathbf{a}, \mathbf{1}^n)$;

3 **Procedure** PF$(\mathbf{g}, \hat{u}, \mathbf{a}, \mathbf{b})$:

$\quad$ // **L**, **R** are initially empty, but maintain its memory throughout
$\quad\quad$ the recurrsion. n is the length of vector **a** and **b**.

4 $\quad$ **if** $n = 1$ **then**

5 $\quad\quad\lfloor$ Output $\pi = (\mathbf{L}, \mathbf{R}, a, b)$.

6 $\quad$ **else**

7 $\quad\quad$ Compute $n' = \frac{n}{2}$, $c_L = \langle \mathbf{a}_{[:n']}, \mathbf{b}_{[n':]} \rangle \in \mathbb{Z}_p$, $c_R = \langle \mathbf{a}_{[n':]}, \mathbf{b}_{[:n']} \rangle \in \mathbb{Z}_p$;

8 $\quad\quad$ $L = \mathbf{g}_{[n':]}^{\mathbf{a}_{[:n']}} \hat{u}^{c_L} \in \mathbb{G}$ and $R = \mathbf{g}_{[:n']}^{\mathbf{a}_{[n':]}} \hat{u}^{c_R} \in \mathbb{G}$;

9 $\quad\quad$ Add L to **L** and R to **R** and compute $x = H_Z(L, R)$;

10 $\quad\quad$ Compute $\mathbf{g}' = \mathbf{g}_{[:n']}^{x^{-1}} \circ \mathbf{g}_{[n':]}^{x} \in \mathbb{G}^{n'}$, $\mathbf{a}' = x \cdot \mathbf{a}_{[:n']} + x^{-1} \cdot \mathbf{a}_{[n':]} \in \mathbb{Z}_p^{n'}$ and
$\quad\quad$ $\mathbf{b}' = x^{-1} \cdot \mathbf{b}_{[:n']} + x \cdot \mathbf{b}_{[n':]} \in \mathbb{Z}_p^{n'}$;

11 $\quad\quad$ Run protocol PF on input $(\mathbf{g}', \hat{u}, \mathbf{a}', \mathbf{b}')$;

12 **Procedure** NISA.VERIFY(param$, \mathbf{g}, P, c, \pi = (\mathbf{L}, \mathbf{R}, a, b)$):

13 $\quad$ $P' = P \cdot u^{c \cdot H'_Z(P,u,c)}$;

14 $\quad$ Compute for all $j = 1, ..., \log_2 n$: $x_j = H_Z(L_j, R_j)$;

15 $\quad$ Compute for all $i = 1, ..., n$:

$$ y_i = \prod_{j \in [\log_2 n]} x_j^{f(i,j)}, f(i,j) = \begin{cases} 1 & \text{if } (i-1)\text{'s } j\text{-th bit is } 1 \\ -1 & \text{otherwise} \end{cases}; $$

16 $\quad$ Set $\mathbf{y} = (y_1, ..., y_n)$, $\mathbf{x} = (x_1, ..., x_{\log_2 n})$;

17 $\quad$ **if** $\mathbf{L}^{\mathbf{x}^2} P' \mathbf{R}^{\mathbf{x}^{-2}} = \mathbf{g}^{a \cdot \mathbf{y}} u^{ab \cdot H'_Z(P,u,c)}$ **then**

18 $\quad\quad\lfloor$ Output 1

19 $\quad$ Output 0

As a result, we can give a logarithmic size ring signature from Type-T* canonical identification scheme with matching non-interactive sum argument.

DualRing-EC Construction. Our DL-based construction DualRing-EC is shown in Algorithm 5, by using DUALRING and NISA for Relation 2.

Theorem 6. *DualRing-EC is unforgeable w.r.t. insider corruption if DUAL-RING is unforgeable w.r.t. insider corruption and the NISA has statistical witness-extended emulation.*

Proof. Suppose that $\mathcal{A}$ is an adversary breaking the unforgeability w.r.t. insider corruption of DualRing-EC. Then, we can construct an algorithm $\mathcal{B}$ breaking the unforgeability of DUALRING. $\mathcal{B}$ is given the system parameter param′ and a set of public keys S from the challenger of DUALRING. $\mathcal{B}$ picks a random generator $u \in \mathbb{G}$ and returns param $= ($param′$, u)$ to $\mathcal{A}$.

When $\mathcal{A}$ asks for a signing oracle query, $\mathcal{B}$ asks the signing oracle of DUALRING and obtains $\sigma' = (c_1, ..., c_n, z)$. $\mathcal{B}$ computes R by running DUAL-

---

Algorithm 5: DualRing-EC

---

1 **Procedure** SETUP(λ):
2   param$'$ $\leftarrow$ DUALRING.SETUP(λ);
3   pick a generator $u \leftarrow_s \mathbb{G}$;
4   return param $= ($param$', u)$;

5 **Procedure** SIGN(param, m, **pk**, sk_j):
6   $(c_1, \ldots, c_n, z) \leftarrow$ DUALRING.SIGN
  (param, m, **pk**, sk_j);
  // (c, R) is computed in DUALRING.SIGN
7   $\mathbf{a} \leftarrow (c_1, \ldots, c_n)$;
8   $P = R \odot (V_1(z))^{-1}$;
9   $\pi \leftarrow$ NISA.PROOF($\{$param, **pk**, $u, P, c\}, \mathbf{a}$);
10 return $\sigma = (z, R, \pi)$;

11 **Procedure** KEYGEN(param):
12 return (pk, sk) $\leftarrow$
  DUALRING.KEYGEN(param$'$);

13 **Procedure** VERIFY(param, m, **pk**, σ):
14 parse $\sigma = (z, R, \pi)$;
15 $c = H_Z(m, \textbf{pk}, R)$;
16 $P = R \odot (V_1(z))^{-1}$;
17 **if** $0 \leftarrow$ NISA.VERIFY(param, **pk**, u, P, c)
  then
18   return 0;
19 return 1;

RING.VERIFY on σ'. $\mathcal{B}$ computes $c = c_1 + \cdots + c_n$ and $P = R \odot (V_1(z))^{-1}$. $\mathcal{B}$ runs the NISA.PROOF and obtains π. $\mathcal{B}$ returns (c, z, R, π).

In the challenge phase, $\mathcal{A}$ returns a signature $\sigma^* = (c^*, z^*, R^*, \pi^*)$ with respect to a message M^* and $\{\textbf{pk}_i^*\}_{i=1}^n$. By the statistical witness-extended emulation of NISA, $\mathcal{B}$ can run an extractor $\mathcal{E}$ to obtain $(c_1^*, \ldots, c_n^*)$, where $P^* = R^* \odot (V_1(z^*))^{-1} = \bigodot_{i=1}^n V_2(\textbf{pk}_i^*, c_i^*)$. Then $\mathcal{B}$ returns the signature $\sigma' = (c_1^*, \ldots, c_n^*, z^*)$, the message M^* and $\{\textbf{pk}_i^*\}_{i=1}^n$ to the challenger of DUAL-RING. $\qquad\square$

Theorem 7. *DualRing-EC is anonymous if* DUALRING *is anonymous.*

Proof. Suppose that $\mathcal{A}$ is an adversary breaking the anonymity of DualRing-EC. Then, we can construct an algorithm $\mathcal{B}$ breaking the anonymity of DUALRING. $\mathcal{B}$ is given param$'$ and the set S from its challenger. $\mathcal{B}$ picks a random generator $u \in \mathbb{G}$ and gives param $= ($param$', u)$ to $\mathcal{A}$.

When $\mathcal{A}$ asks for a signing oracle query, $\mathcal{B}$ simulates it as in the proof of unforgeability. In the challenge phase, $\mathcal{A}$ gives M^*, **pk**, i_0, i_1 to $\mathcal{B}$ and $\mathcal{B}$ forwards it to its challenger. $\mathcal{B}$ receives $((c_1^*, \ldots, c_n^*, z^*), \{\omega_i\}_{i=1}^{q_k})$. $\mathcal{B}$ computes σ^* by line 7–9 of the SIGN algorithm and returns $(\sigma^*, \{\omega_i\}_{i=1}^{q_k})$ to $\mathcal{A}$.

Finally $\mathcal{A}$ returns a bit b' and $\mathcal{B}$ sends b' to its challenger to break the anonymity of DUALRING. $\qquad\square$

6.3 Efficiency Analysis

Signature Size. We compare our DL-based instantiation for n public keys with other $O(\log n)$-size DL-based ring signatures without trusted setup in Table 1. Most accumulator-based $O(1)$-size ring signatures require trusted setup. The lattice-based logarithmic ring signatures [19,20,28] are still at least 100 times longer than DL-based construction. Our ring signature is 789/921 bytes for the ring size $= 1024/4096$ with $\lambda = 128$. We can see that DualRing-EC (Algorithm 5 with Schnorr Identification) is the shortest ring signature without trusted setup. Figure 3 shows the concrete signature size when an element in $\mathbb{Z}_p$ is represented by 32 bytes and an element in $\mathbb{G}$ is represented by 33 bytes. Note that the

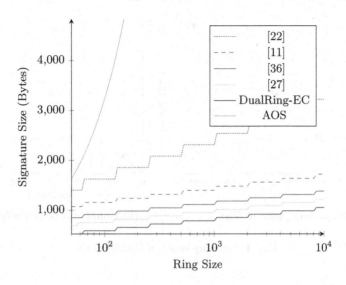

Fig. 3. The signature size of ring signature schemes for n public keys, when implemented on elliptic curve with $\lambda = 128$.

signature size for a ring with size $[\log(n-1) + 1, \log n]$ is the same. Therefore, the signature size increases for ring size 1025, 2049, 4097, etc.

Computational Efficiency. We implement our DualRing-EC in Python, using the P256 curve in the fastecdsa library. It is tested on a computer with Intel Core i5 2.3 GHz, 8 GB RAM with MacOS 10. The running time is shown in Fig. 4.

We compare the asymptotic running time of our scheme with [11,22][6]. The running time of the signer for both [22] and [11] are both dominated by $O(n \log n)$ exponentiations. On the other hand, the signer's running time for DualRing-EC is $O(n)$ exponentiations only. Comparing with [27,36], the major difference for the signer's running time is the use of the inner product argument in [27,36] and the use of NISA in our scheme. As discussed in the section of NISA, we only use half of the exponentiation used in the inner product argument. Verification time for out scheme is dominated by Line 17 of Algorithm 4, which contains $n + 2\log n + 1$ exponentiations for a ring size of n. [27,36] used Bulletproof which contains $2n + 2\log n + 1$ exponentiations in verification. To conclude, our DualRing-EC outperforms [11,22,27,36] in terms of signature size and the running time of the signer and the verifier.

7   DualRing-LB: Our Lattice-Based Ring Signature

In this section, we give a concrete ring signature construction based on standard (module) lattice assumptions using DualRing.

---

[6] For simplicity, we compare the schemes by assuming that a multi-exponentiation of size ℓ is the same as ℓ exponentiation in $\mathbb{G}$.

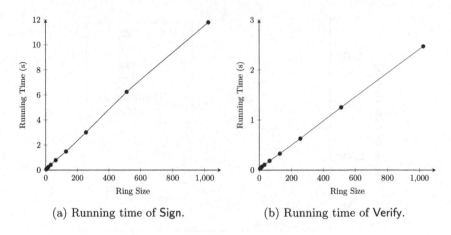

(a) Running time of Sign.   (b) Running time of Verify.

Fig. 4. Running times of DualRing-EC

Notations and Assumptions. We define q as an odd modulus and R_q as a ring $\mathbb{Z}_q[X]/(X^d+1)$ of dimension d. Define $\boldsymbol{I}_n$ as the identity matrix with size n, $\mathfrak{U}_k$ as a set of polynomials in $\mathbb{Z}[X]/(X^d+1)$ with infinity norm at most $k \in \mathbb{Z}^+$, and $\mathcal{U}$ as the uniform distribution. The Euclidean $\|\cdot\|$ and infinity $\|\cdot\|_\infty$ norms of a polynomial (or a vector of polynomials) are defined in the standard fashion w.r.t. the coefficient vector of the polynomial. Define the following challenge space:

$$\mathcal{C} = \{\, c \in \mathbb{Z}[X]/(X^d+1) \;:\; \|c\|_\infty = 1 \,\}. \tag{3}$$

Observe that $|\mathcal{C}| = 3^d$. That is, for $d = 128$, we have $|\mathcal{C}| = 3^{128} > 2^{202}$.

We review the hardness of Module-SIS (M-SIS) (defined in "Hermite normal form" as in [5]) and Module-LWE (M-LWE) problems [19].

Definition 7 (M-SIS$_{n,m,q,\beta_{SIS}}$ Assumption). *For all PPT adversaries* $\mathcal{A}$,

$$\Pr\begin{bmatrix} \boldsymbol{A}' \leftarrow_s \mathcal{U}(R_q^{n\times(m-n)}), & \boldsymbol{Az} = \boldsymbol{0} \in R_q^n, \\ \boldsymbol{A} = [\boldsymbol{I}_n\|\boldsymbol{A}'], \boldsymbol{z} \leftarrow \mathcal{A}(\boldsymbol{A}) & 0 < \|\boldsymbol{z}\| \le \beta_{SIS} \end{bmatrix} \le \mathsf{negl}(\lambda).$$

Definition 8 (M-LWE$_{n,m,q,\chi}$ Assumption). *Let* χ *be a distribution over* R_q *and* $\boldsymbol{s} \leftarrow_s \chi^n$ *be a secret key. Define* $LWE_{q,s}$ *as the distribution obtained by sampling* $\boldsymbol{a} \leftarrow_s R_q^n, e \leftarrow_s \chi$ *and outputting* $(\boldsymbol{a}, \langle \boldsymbol{a}, \boldsymbol{s}\rangle + e)$. *For all PPT adversaries* $\mathcal{A}$, *the probability of distinguishing between* m *samples from* $LWE_{q,s}$ *and* $\mathcal{U}(R_q^n, R_q)$ *is* $\mathsf{negl}(\lambda)$.

7.1   Lattice-Based Canonical Identification

We give a Type-T* canonical identification from M-LWE/SIS in Algorithm 6. We use the rejection sampling technique from [31] to make sure that no information about the signer's secret key is revealed in the response.

Algorithm 6: Lattice-based Type-T* Canonical Identification

---

1 **Procedure** $\text{SETUP}(\lambda)$:
2   set M-LWE parameters k, m, d, q;
3   define a hash function $\mathcal{H} : \{0,1\}^* \to \mathcal{C}$;
4   pick $\boldsymbol{G}' \leftarrow R_q^{k \times (m-k)}$;
5      $\boldsymbol{G} = [\,\boldsymbol{I}_k \,\|\, \boldsymbol{G}'\,]$;
6   return param $= (k, m, d, q, \boldsymbol{G}, \mathcal{H})$;

7 **Procedure** $\text{KEYGEN}()$:
8   pick $\boldsymbol{x} \leftarrow \mathfrak{U}_1^m$;
9   compute $c = \boldsymbol{G} \cdot \boldsymbol{x}$;
10   return $(\text{pk}, \text{sk}) = (c, \boldsymbol{x})$;

11 **Procedure** $\text{PROOF1}(\text{sk})$:
12   pick $\boldsymbol{r} \leftarrow \mathfrak{U}_{md^2}^m$;
13      $R = A(\text{sk}; \boldsymbol{r}) := \boldsymbol{G} \cdot \boldsymbol{r}$;
14   return $(R, \boldsymbol{r})$;

15 **Procedure** $\text{CH}(R)$:
16   pick $c \leftarrow \mathcal{C}$;
17   return c;

18 **Procedure** $\text{PROOF2}(\text{sk}, \boldsymbol{r}, c)$:
19      $z = Z(\text{sk}, \boldsymbol{r}, c) := c \cdot \text{sk} - \boldsymbol{r}$;
20   if $\|z\|_\infty > md^2 - d$ then
21   restart PROOF1;
22   return z;

23 **Procedure** $\text{VERIFY}(\text{pk}, z, c)$:
24      $R' = V_1(z) + V_2(\text{pk}, c) := -\boldsymbol{G} \cdot z + c \cdot \text{pk}$;
25   if $c \neq \text{CH}(R')$ then
26   return 0;
27   if $\|z\|_\infty > md^2 - d$ then
28   return 0;
29   return 1;

We can observe the following

1. The function V_1 is additively homomorphic:

$$V_1(\boldsymbol{z}_1) + V_1(\boldsymbol{z}_2) = -\boldsymbol{G} \cdot \boldsymbol{z}_1 - \boldsymbol{G} \cdot \boldsymbol{z}_2 = -\boldsymbol{G} \cdot (\boldsymbol{z}_1 + \boldsymbol{z}_2) = V_1(\boldsymbol{z}_1 + \boldsymbol{z}_2).$$

2. Given sk, pk and c, we can compute $\tilde{\boldsymbol{z}} = -c \cdot \text{sk}$ such that $V_1(\tilde{\boldsymbol{z}}) = \boldsymbol{G} \cdot (c \cdot \text{sk}) = V_2(\text{pk}, c)$.
3. The challenge space $\mathcal{C}$ is a group under addition mod 3.

Theorem 8. *Algorithm 6 is secure against special impersonation under key only attack if M-$\text{SIS}_{k,m+1,q,\beta_{\text{SIS}}}$ (in HNF) for $\beta_{\text{SIS}} \approx 2d^2 \sqrt{m} \cdot \left(1 + m\sqrt{d}\right)$ and M-$\text{LWE}_{m-k,k,q,\mathfrak{U}_1}$ are hard.*

Proof. Suppose that $\mathcal{A}$ is an adversary breaking the special impersonation under key only attack. Suppose that $\mathcal{B}$ is given $\hat{\boldsymbol{G}} = [\,\boldsymbol{I}_k \,\|\, \boldsymbol{G}' \,\|\, \boldsymbol{g}\,] \in R_q^{k \times (m+1)}$ as the M-SIS matrix where $\boldsymbol{G}'$ and $\boldsymbol{g}$ are sampled uniformly at random. Denote $\boldsymbol{G} = [\,\boldsymbol{I}_k \,\|\, \boldsymbol{G}'\,]$, which is used as the commitment key in the oracle simulations by $\mathcal{B}$. The number of public keys generated by the challenger is q_k. $\mathcal{B}$ sets

$$\text{pk} = \boldsymbol{G} \cdot \boldsymbol{r} + \boldsymbol{g} \tag{4}$$

for $\boldsymbol{r} \leftarrow \mathfrak{U}_1^m$. Observe that $\|\boldsymbol{r}'\| \leq \sqrt{md+1}$ for $\boldsymbol{r}' = \begin{pmatrix} \boldsymbol{r} \\ 1 \end{pmatrix}$. Also, note that we can write $\boldsymbol{G} \cdot \boldsymbol{r} = \boldsymbol{r}_0 + \boldsymbol{G}' \cdot \boldsymbol{r}_1$ for $\boldsymbol{r}_0 \in \mathfrak{U}_1^k$ and $\boldsymbol{r}_1 \in \mathfrak{U}_1^{m-k}$. Therefore, by M-$\text{LWE}_{m-k,k,q,\mathfrak{U}_1}$ assumption, $\boldsymbol{G} \cdot \boldsymbol{r}$ is computationally indistinguishable from a random element in R_q^k and so is $\text{pk} = \boldsymbol{G} \cdot \boldsymbol{r} + \boldsymbol{g}$. $\mathcal{B}$ gives param $= (k, m, d, q, \boldsymbol{G}, \mathcal{H})$ and pk to $\mathcal{A}$.

$\mathcal{A}$ returns $(c, \boldsymbol{z}, c', \boldsymbol{z}')$, where $c \neq c'$, we have:

$$-\boldsymbol{G} \cdot \boldsymbol{z} + c \cdot \text{pk} = -\boldsymbol{G} \cdot \boldsymbol{z}' + c' \cdot \text{pk}$$

$$(c - c') \cdot \mathsf{pk} = \boldsymbol{G} \cdot (\boldsymbol{z} - \boldsymbol{z}') = \hat{\boldsymbol{G}} \cdot \begin{pmatrix} \boldsymbol{z} - \boldsymbol{z}' \\ 0 \end{pmatrix}$$

Further, multiplying Eq. (4) by $(c - c')$, we have

$$(c - c') \cdot \mathsf{pk} = \boldsymbol{G} \cdot (c - c') \cdot \boldsymbol{r} + (c - c') \cdot \boldsymbol{g} = \hat{\boldsymbol{G}} \cdot (c - c') \cdot \begin{pmatrix} \boldsymbol{r} \\ 1 \end{pmatrix}.$$

Therefore, we get:

$$\hat{\boldsymbol{G}} \cdot (c - c') \cdot \begin{pmatrix} \boldsymbol{r} \\ 1 \end{pmatrix} = \hat{\boldsymbol{G}} \cdot \begin{pmatrix} \boldsymbol{z} - \boldsymbol{z}' \\ 0 \end{pmatrix}.$$

That is, $\hat{\boldsymbol{G}} \cdot \boldsymbol{s} = 0$ over R_q for $\boldsymbol{s} = (c - c') \cdot \begin{pmatrix} \boldsymbol{r} \\ 1 \end{pmatrix} - \begin{pmatrix} \boldsymbol{z} - \boldsymbol{z}' \\ 0 \end{pmatrix}$. Observe that $\boldsymbol{s}$ cannot be the zero vector as $c \neq c'$ and the last coordinate of $\boldsymbol{s}$ is $(c - c')$. Since $\|\boldsymbol{z}\|_\infty, \|\boldsymbol{z}'\|_\infty \leq md^2 - d$, we also have

$$\|\boldsymbol{s}\| \leq 2d\sqrt{d}\sqrt{md + 1} + 2 \cdot (md^2\sqrt{md}) \approx 2d^2\sqrt{m} \cdot \left(1 + m\sqrt{d}\right).$$

Hence, $\boldsymbol{s}$ is a solution to M-SIS$_{k,m+1,q,\beta_{\mathrm{SIS}}}$ for $\beta_{\mathrm{SIS}} \approx 2d^2\sqrt{m}\left(1 + m\sqrt{d}\right)$.   □

Remark. It is not known how to build an efficient lattice-based ZK proof for sum argument. There is a theoretical work on constructing a lattice analog of Bulletproofs in [13]. However, in practice, the construction is inefficient. As the lattice analog of the Sum Argument cannot be constructed efficiently, the signature size of our lattice-based construction remains at $O(n)$, while [10,19] achieve $O(\log n)$ signature size. Hence, after some point (around 1100), our construction eventually produces longer signatures.

7.2   Efficiency Analysis of DualRing-LB

Signature Size. The practical security estimations of M-SIS and M-LWE against known attacks are done by following the methodology detailed in [18, Section 3.2.4]. In particular, we aim for a "root Hermite factor" of around 1.0045. The root Hermite factor is a common metric used in lattice-based cryptography to measure practical hardness. We refer to [18] for further discussion. We refer to Table 3 for the concrete parameter setting. In general, for $d = 128$, the signature length can be approximated by the following formula:

$$|\sigma| = |\boldsymbol{z}| + n \cdot |c_i| \approx 4536 + 26n \text{ bytes.} \tag{5}$$

The above formula stems from the fact that $|c_i| = d \log 3/8$ bytes and $|\boldsymbol{z}| = md \log(2md^2)/8$ bytes since $\boldsymbol{z} \in R^m$ with $\|\boldsymbol{z}\|_\infty \leq md^2$. Plugging in $(d, m) = (128, 15)$ yields (5).

Although Theorems 3 and 8 imply that DualRing-LB is secure, they do not provide all the information required in the concrete parameter setting. Unlike

Table 3. The parameter setting of DualRing-LB. The root Hermite factor for both M-SIS and M-LWE are ≤ 1.0045. $d = 128$ always. The sizes are in KB.

n	k	m	$\log q$	Signature Size	PK Size	SK Size	Size of $(c_1, \ldots, c_n)$	Size of z
2	7	15	26	4.48	2.84	0.23	0.05	4.43
4	7	15	26	4.53	2.84	0.23	0.10	4.43
8	7	15	26	4.63	2.84	0.23	0.20	4.43
16	7	15	26	4.83	2.84	0.23	0.40	4.43
32	7	15	26	5.22	2.84	0.23	0.79	4.43
64	7	15	26	6.02	2.84	0.23	1.59	4.43
128	7	15	26	7.60	2.84	0.23	3.17	4.43
256	7	15	26	10.78	2.84	0.23	6.34	4.43
512	8	16	26	17.44	3.25	0.25	12.69	4.75
1024	8	16	26	30.13	3.25	0.25	25.38	4.75
2048	8	16	26	55.50	3.25	0.25	50.75	4.75
4096	8	17	27	106.57	3.38	0.27	101.50	5.07

the classical DL- or factoring-based constructions, in the lattice setting, it is important for the concrete parameter setting to know the precise (Euclidean) norm bound β_{SIS} of M-SIS solution that arises in the security reduction. This is because the practical security estimations depend on the β_{SIS} parameter of the M-SIS problem. Therefore, we also need to investigate in more detail the M-SIS solution length β_{SIS} for the *ring signature* (not the underlying Type-T* canonical identification as in Theorem 8) and see how it depends on the parameters. We do this in the full version of the paper and show concretely what the length of the M-SIS solution is for the ring signature, which gives $\beta_{SIS} \approx 2d\sqrt{md} \cdot (md + n)$. The proof follows the same blueprint in the generic unforgeability proof of DualRing (Theorem 3), but we keep track of the norms as the proof proceeds.

Computational Efficiency. First, the modulus q is always less than 32 bits in length for the parameters in Table 3. Therefore the values in our construction fit into 32-bit registers, boosting the computational efficiency. Another advantage of our construction is that no (discrete) Gaussian sampling is required, making the implementation easier to protect against side-channel attacks.

We show the running times of DualRing-LB in Fig. 5. The code is written in Python, using the polynomial arithmetic and NTT transform in the sympy library. It is tested on a computer with Intel Core i5 2.3GHz, 8GB RAM with MacOS 10. For our scheme, the expected number of iterations due to rejection sampling in SIGN is about 2.72 and our experiment matches this prediction. The running time for a single run of sign and verify algorithms are about the same. However, the expected number of iterations for sign is 2.72. Therefore, we have the running time for sign as in Fig. 5.

The construction in [19] is at least 5 times slower than DualRing-LB for both sign and verify. Some of the possible reasons include: (1) their expected number of iterations due to rejection sampling in SIGN is about 4.757, (2) they use a polynomial of degree $d = 256$. Their scheme does not exhibit a linear increase in running time since [19] changes the system parameters (e.g., matrix dimension, degree of polynomial) for different ring size to optimize their signature size.

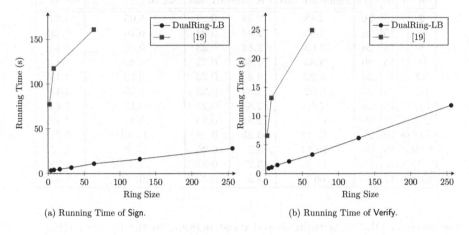

(a) Running Time of Sign.   (b) Running Time of Verify.

Fig. 5. Lattice-based ring signatures

8   Conclusion

In this paper, we propose a generic construction of ring signature scheme using a dual ring structure. When we instantiate in the DL-setting, it is the shortest ring signature scheme without using trusted setup. When instantiated in M-LWE/SIS, we have the shortest ring signature for ring size between 4 and 2000.

References

1. Abdalla, M., An, J.H., Bellare, M., Namprempre, C.: From identification to signatures via the fiat-shamir transform: necessary and sufficient conditions for security and forward-security. IEEE Trans. Inf. Theor. **54**(8), 3631–3646 (2008)
2. Abe, M., Ohkubo, M., Suzuki, K.: 1-out-of-n signatures from a variety of keys. In: Zheng, Y. (ed.) ASIACRYPT 2002. LNCS, vol. 2501, pp. 415–432. Springer, Heidelberg (2002). https://doi.org/10.1007/3-540-36178-2_26
3. Backes, M., Döttling, N., Hanzlik, L., Kluczniak, K., Schneider, J.: Ring signatures: logarithmic-size, no setup—from standard assumptions. In: Ishai, Y., Rijmen, V. (eds.) EUROCRYPT 2019. LNCS, vol. 11478, pp. 281–311. Springer, Cham (2019). https://doi.org/10.1007/978-3-030-17659-4_10
4. Bagherzandi, A., Cheon, J.H., Jarecki, S.: Multisignatures secure under the discrete logarithm assumption and a generalized forking lemma. In: CCS 2008, pp. 449–458. ACM (2008)
5. Baum, C., Damgård, I., Lyubashevsky, V., Oechsner, S., Peikert, C.: More efficient commitments from structured lattice assumptions. In: Catalano, D., De Prisco, R. (eds.) SCN 2018. LNCS, vol. 11035, pp. 368–385. Springer, Cham (2018). https://doi.org/10.1007/978-3-319-98113-0_20

6. Bellare, M., Namprempre, C., Neven, G.: Security proofs for identity-based identification and signature schemes. In: Cachin, C., Camenisch, J.L. (eds.) EUROCRYPT 2004. LNCS, vol. 3027, pp. 268–286. Springer, Heidelberg (2004). https://doi.org/10.1007/978-3-540-24676-3_17

7. Bellare, M., Neven, G.: Multi-signatures in the plain public-key model and a general forking lemma. In: CCS 2006, pp. 390–399. ACM (2006)

8. Bender, A., Katz, J., Morselli, R.: Ring signatures: stronger definitions, and constructions without random oracles. J. Cryptology $22(1)$, 114–138 (2009)

9. Bernstein, D.J., Duif, N., Lange, T., Schwabe, P., Yang, B.-Y.: High-speed high-security signatures. In: Preneel, B., Takagi, T. (eds.) CHES 2011. LNCS, vol. 6917, pp. 124–142. Springer, Heidelberg (2011). https://doi.org/10.1007/978-3-642-23951-9_9

10. Beullens, W., Katsumata, S., Pintore, F.: Calamari and Falafl: logarithmic (Linkable) ring signatures from isogenies and lattices. In: Moriai, S., Wang, H. (eds.) ASIACRYPT 2020. LNCS, vol. 12492, pp. 464–492. Springer, Cham (2020). https://doi.org/10.1007/978-3-030-64834-3_16

11. Bootle, J., Cerulli, A., Chaidos, P., Ghadafi, E., Groth, J., Petit, C.: Short accountable ring signatures based on DDH. In: Pernul, G., Ryan, P.Y.A., Weippl, E. (eds.) ESORICS 2015. LNCS, vol. 9326, pp. 243–265. Springer, Cham (2015). https://doi.org/10.1007/978-3-319-24174-6_13

12. Bootle, J., Cerulli, A., Chaidos, P., Groth, J., Petit, C.: Efficient Zero-Knowledge Arguments for Arithmetic Circuits in the Discrete Log Setting. In: Fischlin, M., Coron, J.-S. (eds.) EUROCRYPT 2016. LNCS, vol. 9666, pp. 327–357. Springer, Heidelberg (2016). https://doi.org/10.1007/978-3-662-49896-5_12

13. Bootle, J., Lyubashevsky, V., Nguyen, N.K., Seiler, G.: A Non-PCP approach to succinct quantum-safe zero-knowledge. In: Micciancio, D., Ristenpart, T. (eds.) CRYPTO 2020. LNCS, vol. 12171, pp. 441–469. Springer, Cham (2020). https://doi.org/10.1007/978-3-030-56880-1_16

14. Bünz, B., Bootle, J., Boneh, D., Poelstra, A., Wuille, P., Maxwell, G.: Bulletproofs: short proofs for confidential transactions and more. In: 2018 IEEE Symposium on Security and Privacy (SP), pp. 315–334 (2018)

15. Chaum, D., Pedersen, T.P.: Wallet databases with observers. In: Brickell, E.F. (ed.) CRYPTO 1992. LNCS, vol. 740, pp. 89–105. Springer, Heidelberg (1993). https://doi.org/10.1007/3-540-48071-4_7

16. Cramer, R., Damgård, I., Schoenmakers, B.: Proofs of partial knowledge and simplified design of witness hiding protocols. In: Desmedt, Y.G. (ed.) CRYPTO 1994. LNCS, vol. 839, pp. 174–187. Springer, Heidelberg (1994). https://doi.org/10.1007/3-540-48658-5_19

17. Dodis, Y., Kiayias, A., Nicolosi, A., Shoup, V.: Anonymous identification in *Ad Hoc* groups. In: Cachin, C., Camenisch, J.L. (eds.) EUROCRYPT 2004. LNCS, vol. 3027, pp. 609–626. Springer, Heidelberg (2004). https://doi.org/10.1007/978-3-540-24676-3_36

18. Esgin, M.F.: Practice-Oriented Techniques in Lattice-Based Cryptography. Ph.D. thesis, Monash University (5 2020). https://doi.org/10.26180/5eb8f525b3562

19. Esgin, M.F., Steinfeld, R., Liu, J.K., Liu, D.: Lattice-based zero-knowledge proofs: new techniques for shorter and faster constructions and applications. In: Boldyreva, A., Micciancio, D. (eds.) CRYPTO 2019. LNCS, vol. 11692, pp. 115–146. Springer, Cham (2019). https://doi.org/10.1007/978-3-030-26948-7_5

20. Esgin, M.F., Steinfeld, R., Sakzad, A., Liu, J.K., Liu, D.: Short lattice-based one-out-of-many proofs and applications to ring signatures. In: Deng, R.H., Gauthier-Umaña, V., Ochoa, M., Yung, M. (eds.) ACNS 2019. LNCS, vol. 11464, pp. 67–88. Springer, Cham (2019). https://doi.org/10.1007/978-3-030-21568-2_4

21. Esgin, M.F., Zhao, R.K., Steinfeld, R., Liu, J.K., Liu, D.: MatRiCT: efficient, scalable and post-quantum blockchain confidential transactions protocol. In: ACM CCS, pp. 567–584. ACM (2019), (Full version at ia.cr/2019/1287)

22. Groth, J., Kohlweiss, M.: One-out-of-many proofs: or how to leak a secret and spend a coin. In: Oswald, E., Fischlin, M. (eds.) EUROCRYPT 2015. LNCS, vol. 9057, pp. 253–280. Springer, Heidelberg (2015). https://doi.org/10.1007/978-3-662-46803-6_9

23. Guillou, L.C., Quisquater, J.-J.: A paradoxical indentity-based signature scheme resulting from zero-knowledge. In: Goldwasser, S. (ed.) CRYPTO 1988. LNCS, vol. 403, pp. 216–231. Springer, New York (1990). https://doi.org/10.1007/0-387-34799-2_16

24. Katz, J., Wang, N.: Efficiency improvements for signature schemes with tight security reductions. In: CCS 2003, pp. 155–164. ACM (2003)

25. Kiltz, E., Masny, D., Pan, J.: Optimal security proofs for signatures from identification schemes. In: Robshaw, M., Katz, J. (eds.) CRYPTO 2016. LNCS, vol. 9815, pp. 33–61. Springer, Heidelberg (2016). https://doi.org/10.1007/978-3-662-53008-5_2

26. Kumar, A., Fischer, C., Tople, S., Saxena, P.: A traceability analysis of Monero's blockchain. In: Foley, S.N., Gollmann, D., Snekkenes, E. (eds.) ESORICS 2017. LNCS, vol. 10493, pp. 153–173. Springer, Cham (2017). https://doi.org/10.1007/978-3-319-66399-9_9

27. Lai, R.W.F., Ronge, V., Ruffing, T., Schröder, D., Thyagarajan, S.A.K., Wang, J.: Omniring: scaling private payments without trusted setup. In: CCS 2019, pp. 31–48. ACM (2019)

28. Libert, B., Ling, S., Nguyen, K., Wang, H.: Zero-knowledge arguments for lattice-based accumulators: logarithmic-size ring signatures and group signatures without trapdoors. In: Fischlin, M., Coron, J.-S. (eds.) EUROCRYPT 2016. LNCS, vol. 9666, pp. 1–31. Springer, Heidelberg (2016). https://doi.org/10.1007/978-3-662-49896-5_1

29. Libert, B., Peters, T., Qian, C.: Logarithmic-size ring signatures with tight security from the DDH assumption. In: Lopez, J., Zhou, J., Soriano, M. (eds.) ESORICS 2018. LNCS, vol. 11099, pp. 288–308. Springer, Cham (2018). https://doi.org/10.1007/978-3-319-98989-1_15

30. Lu, X., Au, M.H., Zhang, Z.: Raptor: a practical lattice-based (Linkable) ring signature. In: Deng, R.H., Gauthier-Umaña, V., Ochoa, M., Yung, M. (eds.) ACNS 2019. LNCS, vol. 11464, pp. 110–130. Springer, Cham (2019). https://doi.org/10.1007/978-3-030-21568-2_6

31. Lyubashevsky, V.: Fiat-Shamir with aborts: applications to lattice and factoring-based signatures. In: Matsui, M. (ed.) ASIACRYPT 2009. LNCS, vol. 5912, pp. 598–616. Springer, Heidelberg (2009). https://doi.org/10.1007/978-3-642-10366-7_35

32. Lyubashevsky, V.: Lattice signatures without trapdoors. In: Pointcheval, D., Johansson, T. (eds.) EUROCRYPT 2012. LNCS, vol. 7237, pp. 738–755. Springer, Heidelberg (2012). https://doi.org/10.1007/978-3-642-29011-4_43

33. Maxwell, G., Poelstra, A.: Borromean ring signatures (2015). https://pdfs.semanticscholar.org/4160/470c7f6cf05ffc81a98e8fd67fb0c84836ea.pdf

34. Möser, M., et al.: An empirical analysis of traceability in the monero blockchain. PoPETs **2018**(3), 143–163 (2018)
35. Rivest, R.L., Shamir, A., Tauman, Y.: How to Leak a Secret. In: Boyd, C. (ed.) ASIACRYPT 2001. LNCS, vol. 2248, pp. 552–565. Springer, Heidelberg (2001). https://doi.org/10.1007/3-540-45682-1_32
36. Yuen, T.H., et al.: RingCT 3.0 for blockchain confidential transaction: shorter size and stronger security. In: Bonneau, J., Heninger, N. (eds.) FC 2020. LNCS, vol. 12059, pp. 464–483. Springer, Cham (2020). https://doi.org/10.1007/978-3-030-51280-4_25

Compact Ring Signatures from Learning with Errors

Rohit Chatterjee[1]([✉]), Sanjam Garg[2,3], Mohammad Hajiabadi[4],
Dakshita Khurana[5], Xiao Liang[1], Giulio Malavolta[6], Omkant Pandey[1],
and Sina Shiehian[1,2]

[1] Stony Brook University, Stony Brook, USA
rochatterjee@cs.stonybrook.edu
[2] University of California, Berkeley, USA
[3] NTT Research, Tokyo, Japan
[4] University of Waterloo, Waterloo, Canada
[5] University of Illinois Urbana-Champaign, Champaign, USA
[6] Max Planck Institute for Security and Privacy, Bochum, Germany

Abstract. Ring signatures allow a user to sign a message on behalf of a "ring" of signers, while hiding the true identity of the signer. As the degree of anonymity guaranteed by a ring signature is directly proportional to the size of the ring, an important goal in cryptography is to study constructions that minimize the size of the signature as a function of the number of ring members.

In this work, we present the first compact ring signature scheme (i.e., where the size of the signature grows logarithmically with the size of the ring) from the (plain) learning with errors (LWE) problem. The construction is in the standard model and it does not rely on a common random string or on the random oracle heuristic. In contrast with the prior work of Backes *et al.* [EUROCRYPT'2019], our scheme does not rely on bilinear pairings, which allows us to show that the scheme is post-quantum secure assuming the quantum hardness of LWE.

At the heart of our scheme is a new construction of compact and statistically witness indistinguishable ZAP arguments for NP ∩ coNP, that we show to be sound based on the plain LWE assumption. Prior to our work, statistical ZAPs (for all of NP) were known to exist only assuming *sub-exponential* LWE. We believe that this scheme might find further applications in the future.

1 Introduction

In a *ring signature* scheme, (introduced in [44]) a user can sign a message with respect to a *ring* of public keys. The ring can be arbitrarily chosen by the signer and the verification keys that populate the ring can be sampled locally by each user, i.e., no central coordination is required. No user or entity should be able to tell which user in the ring actually produced a given signature—a property referred to as *anonymity*. This is complemented with the standard notion of

© International Association for Cryptologic Research 2021
T. Malkin and C. Peikert (Eds.): CRYPTO 2021, LNCS 12825, pp. 282–312, 2021.
https://doi.org/10.1007/978-3-030-84242-0_11

unforgeability for signatures, which in this case requires that no user outside a specified ring should be able to produce valid signatures on behalf of this ring. A salient feature is the *online* or *setup-free* generation of ring signatures, which requires that signatures can be generated without any prior interaction between members of the ring. Ring signatures and their variants have found natural applications related to whistleblowing, authenticating leaked information, and more recently to cryptocurrencies [37,47].

There is a sizeable body of work [2,5,29,39] that construct ring signatures under various definitions and hardness assumptions. As the degree of anonymity guaranteed by the ring signature is directly proportional to the size of the ring, an important property of ring signatures becomes *compactness*, which requires that signatures only have a logarithmic (or lower) dependence on the size of the ring. Recently, the work of [2] provided a compact ring signature construction in the plain model (i.e., not needing a common random string or a setup). Their construction assumes the existence of the following: noninteractive witness indistinguishable proofs or NIWIs (which are known only from bilinear pairing based assumptions or indistinguishability obfuscation), somewhere perfectly binding (SPB) hashes, public key encryption with oblivious public key generation and pseudorandom ciphertexts, and a standard signature scheme. While most of these primitives are known under a variety of cryptographic assumptions including LWE, unfortunately, we currently do not know any constructions of NIWI proofs from LWE (please see the technical overview for related discussion).

This leads to the natural question of whether NIWIs are necessary to construct compact ring signatures in the plain model. The looming threat of quantum computers makes this question particularly pressing, since we would lose our only candidate construction to quantum attacks (due to the reliance on bilinear maps). We therefore ask the following open question:

Can we obtain compact (logarithmic size) ring signatures from the hardness of standard learning with errors (LWE) problem?

1.1   Our Results

Our main contribution resolves the open problem stated above. In other words, we obtain a ring signature construction from *plain* or *standard* LWE, i.e., only assuming polynomial hardness of the LWE problem with polynomial modulus-to-noise ratio. Our result is obtained as follows:

ZAPs for NP ∩ coNP. The first key step to our construction of ring signatures is realization of a new argument system that we call *relaxed ZAPs for extended* NP ∩ coNP. These are akin to ZAPs but with a few additional restrictions, and can also be viewed as a generalization of (non-adaptive) ZAPs for languages in NP ∩ coNP. We show how to construct these ZAPs from the plain (polynomially-hard) LWE. This is in contrast with the known constructions of ZAPs for NP [4,25,31] that assume *subexponential* hardness of LWE. Our ZAP construction also enjoys several other attractive properties such as statistical witness indistinguishability and proof compactness; which we expect will make them useful in other application contexts. We defer further exposition to our technical overview.

Compact Ring Signatures from LWE. Next, we show that our notion of relaxed ZAPs, along with SPB hash schemes and a special public key encryption scheme, is sufficient to construct compact ring signatures. All these components have constructions from plain LWE. Thus, we obtain the *first* construction of compact ring signatures in the plain model from purely post-quantum assumptions in the literature. In addition, we investigate security in the *fully quantum* setting, where the adversary can query the signing oracle on a superposition of messages. Towards this goal, we give a construction that retains unforgeability and anonymity in this setting.

1.2 Background

Fiat-Shamir Transformation, Trapdoor Σ-Protocols, and Correlation Intractability. A trapdoor Σ-protocol [14] for a language L is a 3-move (honest verifier) zero-knowledge protocol between a prover and a verifier, where the prover tries to convince the verifier about the veracity of a statement x. The protocol is instantiated with an *extractable* commitment scheme where there is an extraction trapdoor td which allows extracting the plaintexts in the commitments. In the first move of the protocol, the prover commits to a string a and sends this commitment $\mathsf{Com}(a)$ to the verifier. Next, in the second move, the verifier sends a challenge b to the prover. In the final round, based on the challenge b, the prover computes the final message and sends it to the verifier. The distinctive property of trapdoor sigma protocols is that for a false statement x, there is at most one *bad challenge* b^* which lets a malicious prover to successfully complete its proof, and this bad challenge is efficiently computable given a. Consequently, given the extraction trapdoor td, the bad challenge can be efficiently computed from $\mathsf{Com}(a)$.

The Fiat-Shamir transformation [20] can convert a trapdoor Σ-protocol (indeed any Σ-protocol) to a noninteractive protocol in the random oracle model. The way it works is that the prover evaluates a hash function on its first message to compute the challenge b, and then proceeds to send the full proof generated using this challenge to the verifier. To argue soundness, notice that since the bad challenge is unique and the hash function is modeled as a random oracle, a malicious prover has a negligible chance of finding a first message such that the hash of it equals the bad challenge b^*.

A line of work [14, 42] builds a special type of hash functions called *correlation intractable* (CI) hash functions, to securely instantiate the Fiat-Shamir heuristic in the plain model for trapdoor Σ-protocols, thus turning them into noninteractive protocols in the CRS model. In particular, the LWE-based CI hash functions in [42] allow building noninteractive zero knowledege protocols for all of NP from the LWE assumption. Informally, a hash function is CI for a class of circuits if for any circuit C in the class, given a random hash key k, it is hard to find an input z whose image under the hash function equals $C(z)$. We can securely replace CI hash functions with random oracles when we apply the Fiat-Shamir transformation to trapdoor Σ-protocols. To see this, notice that since in trapdoor Σ-protocols the bad challenge is efficiently computable given the prover's first message, a malicious prover that can find a first message which gets mapped to the bad challenge is breaking the correlation intractability of the hash function.

Somewhere Perfectly Binding Hash. A somewhere perfectly binding (SPB) hash is similar to a Merkle tree [34]: it can compress a large database of N records into a small digest. In a SPB hash with private local openings, binding holds perfectly for a single hidden index $i \in [N]$. In more detail, the SPB hash key generation algorithm takes as input a binding index $i \in [N]$ and outputs a pair of keys (hk, shk). The hash key hk can be used to generate a digest. The secret key shk, can be used to generate a short opening for the ith record in the database. Perfect binding says that a valid opening for the ith location of the database uniquely determines the value of that location. Also, the hash key hk is index hiding, i.e., it computationally hides the binding index i.

Compact Ring Signatures of [2]. The construction of [2] is based on four ingredients: a noninteractive witness indistinguishable argument system NIWI, a public key encryption scheme PKE, a standard signature scheme Sig, and a somewhere perfectly binding hash scheme SPB. In this scheme, each verification key consists of two components: a uniformly chosen public key pk (not generated through the key generation algorithm of PKE) and a standard signature verification key vk. The signing key consists of sk, the corresponding signing key for vk. To sign a message m using signing key sk_i corresponding to verification key $\mathsf{VK_i} = (vk_i, pk_i)$, and on behalf of ring $\mathsf{R} = (\mathsf{VK_1}, \cdots, \mathsf{VK_\ell})$, the signer

- first generates a standard signature σ for message m as $\sigma \leftarrow \mathsf{Sig.Sign}(sk_i, m)$,
- encrypts σ under pk_i with random coins r to get ciphertext $c \leftarrow \mathsf{PKE.Enc}(pk_i, \sigma; r)$,
- generates a binding SPB key pair for index i, $(hk, shk) \leftarrow \mathsf{SPB.Gen}(i)$,
- hashes the ring R with hk to get a short digest $h := \mathsf{SPB.Hash}(hk, \mathsf{R})$,
- creates an opening for the ith location $\tau \leftarrow \mathsf{SPB.Open}(hk, shk, \mathsf{R}, i)$,
- generates a NIWI proof π which using the short opening τ proves existence of a verification key $\mathsf{VK_i} = (vk_i, pk_i)$ in the ring R such that under pk_i, c encrypts a valid signature under verifiable with vk_i,
- finally, it publishes (π, c, hk) as the signature for message m.

To prove unforgeability, we switch to a hybrid where we generate each pk_i with a corresponding secret key sk_i. Consequently, perfect binding of SPB and soundness of NIWI imply that given a forgery (π, c, hk) for ring R, there exists a sk_i such that $\mathsf{PKE.Dec}(sk_i, c)$ is valid forgery against Sig. Proving anonymity involves techniques similar to [36].

1.3 Technical Overview

ZAP Instead of NIWI. As already mentioned, the issue that prevents [2] from basing their construction solely on LWE is their reliance on NIWIs. Our starting point is the observation of [6] which proposes using two-message public coin argument systems, known in the literature as ZAPs [18], instead of NIWIs. Namely, we can add a ZAP first message ρ to each verification key. The signer now picks the lexicographically smallest verification key $\mathsf{VK}_1 = (vk_1, pk_1, \rho_1) \in \mathsf{R}$ in the ring and uses ρ_1 to generate a proof. Using LWE-based ZAPs constructed in [4,25,31], this approach gives us LWE based compact ring signatures. However, there is a major caveat: none of the LWE-based ZAPs mentioned above are based on polynomial hardness assumptions. They all need super-polynomial hardness of LWE (in fact subexponential hardness if the goal is to achieve conventional λ bits of security). Therefore, using lattice based ZAPs generically seems to be unsatisfactory as the resulting construction would rely on qualitatively stronger assumptions.

ZAPs for NP ∩ coNP. Our next insight is that we may not need ZAPs for all of NP. Assume that in the forgery $\varSigma^* = (\pi^*, c^*, hk^*)$, the ciphertext c^* is guaranteed to be encrypted under one of the public keys pk_i. In the unforgeability game we can generate pk_is with corresponding secrets sk_i. In this case, given sk_i, checking that $\varSigma^*$ is a forgery can be done efficiently, i.e., sk_i is a witness for the fact that $\varSigma^*$ is not a valid signature. Therefore, ZAPs for NP ∩ coNP might suffice for our application.

It turns out that for NP ∩ coNP we can build ZAPs based on the polynomial hardness of LWE. We will now describe a ZAP protocol for any arbitrary language $L \in$ NP ∩ coNP. The ZAP that we describe here is constructed by following the general framework of converting a $\varSigma$-protocol to a noninteractive protocol using a CI hash function [14,42]. More specifically, we describe a two round commitment scheme and use it to instantiate [14,42]. Our commitment scheme is defined with respect to the complement language $\overline{L}$. To commit to a bit b and generate the second commitment message, the sender specifies a statement x. The receiver can recover the committed bit, if, when generating the first message it specified a (non-)witness $\overline{w}$ for the fact that $x \in \overline{L}$. If $x \notin \overline{L}$, the committed bit is hidden. The commitment scheme works as follows:

- The receiver sends an arbitrary bitstring $\overline{w}$ via the first message of a statistically sender private (1 out of 2) OT, $\mathsf{OT1}(\overline{w})$.
- The sender garbles the following circuit: on input $\overline{w}$, if $\overline{w}$ is a witness for $x \in \overline{L}$, output b, otherwise, output 0. The sender sends the garbled circuit along with a OT second message containing the labels $\mathsf{OT2}(\{\mathsf{lbl}_{i,0}, \mathsf{lbl}_{i,1}\})$.

We instantiate [14,42] for language L with our two round *witness extractable commitment* for $\overline{L}$, to get a ZAP for NP ∩ coNP: the verifier sends the commitment first message along with a key for a CI hash function, the prover uses the hash key and the commitment scheme to proceed as in [14]. Recall that to apply the transformation of [14,42], we have to make sure that when $x \notin L$, the commitments used in the underlying Σ-protocol are extractable given the extraction trapdoor. If $x \notin L$, the verifier can (undetectably) switch to generating the first commitment message using a non-witness $\overline{w_x}$ for $x \in \overline{L}$ and this will let the soundness proof go through.

Unfortunately, when trying to use our NP ∩ coNP ZAPs to build ring signatures we encounter two issues:

1. The ZAPs that we need for our ring signatures need to be adaptively sound. However, the ZAPs that we just constructed are only selectively sound. This is because, in the soundness reduction we have to switch to a commitment first message that depends on a non-witness $\overline{w}$ for the statement x (depends on a $\overline{w}$ such that $(x, \overline{w}) \in \overline{R}$).
2. We assumed the ciphertext c^* in the forgery is a valid encryption under one of the public keys of the ring. This may not be true. In particular, $\overline{L}$ might not be in NP.

The first issue seems relatively easy to resolve. Our ZAP construction already achieves a weak notion of adaptivity that is sufficient for our purpose: as long as the non-witness $\overline{w}$ is fixed in advance, the cheating prover cannot come up with a valid proof for a statement x where $(x, \overline{w}) \in \overline{R}$. In our case, the non-witnesses which are the secret keys corresponding to pk_is are clearly fixed in advance.

Extending the Complement language. For the second issue, our solution is to *extend* $\overline{L}$ to a language $\widetilde{L} \in$ NP and use a witness extractable commitment for this extended language $\widetilde{L}$. In more detail, given a forgery Σ^* for a ring R* of size ℓ, we define statement $x = (\Sigma^*, R^*)$. For a witness $\widetilde{w} = (sk_1, \cdots, sk_\ell)$ we say that $(x, \widetilde{w}) \in \widetilde{L}$, if each sk_i is a valid secret key for pk_i, and decrypting c^* with any sk_j does not yield a valid standard signature corresponding to vk_j. Accordingly, in the unforgeability game, we can generate each public key pk_i with a corresponding secret sk_i, and put these secret keys inside the witness extractable commitment first message. With this approach we encounter a new problem: the size of the commitment first message, and consequently the verifier's first message in the ZAP scheme, needs to scale at least linearly with the maximum number of members in a ring. However, the number of members in a ring can be arbitrarily large.

One Secret Key, Multiple Public Keys. To overcome this problem we use a public key cryptosystem which can generate multiple public keys having a single secret key. Using such a public key scheme, the first commitment message now only needs to hold one short secret key. Luckily, public key cryptosystems with this property already exist in the literature. In particular, Regev's cryptosystem [43] already has the ability to generate multiple pseudorandom public keys having a single uniformly chosen secret key. This cryptosystem also has another appealing feature: it has sparse valid public keys. In other words, a randomly chosen public key does not have a corresponding secret key (except with negligible probability). In the ring signature context, this sparseness property will be helpful in proving the anonymity of the scheme. Specifically, given a signature Σ for a ring R, if at least one verification key in R is generated honestly, or in particular if at least one public key $pk_i \in$ R is chosen uniformly at random, then $(\Sigma, R) \notin \tilde{L}$, and therefore, the commitment scheme is hiding.

Compactness Through Malicious Circuit Private FHE. The ZAP that we have constructed so far seems to satisfy the soundness and witness indistinguishibility properties that we need in the application to our ring signature scheme. However, upon a closer look, it seems that our resulting ZAP scheme suffers from a major flaw. Namely, the size of our ring signatures is linear in the size of the ring. This is because in the witness extractable commitment scheme, each commitment contains a garbling of a circuit that computes on each verification key in the ring separately. Specifically, while the size of the circuit for checking membership in L is independent of the size of the ring (thanks to the properties of SPB hashing), circuits for checking membership in $\tilde{L}$, and even the relevant statements, have size that depend on the ring. It seems that to overcome this, we need some form of a *compact* witness extractable commitment. Our final idea is to use a fully homomorphic encryption scheme [21] to build such a compact witness extractable commitment. The construction is as follows:

- The receiver generates a FHE key pair (FHE.pk, FHE.sk) and sends a ciphertext
  $ct \leftarrow$ FHE.Enc(FHE.$pk, \tilde{w}$) encrypting an arbitrary string $\tilde{w}$.
- The sender homomorphically evaluates the following circuit on ct: on input $\tilde{w}$, if $\tilde{w}$ is a witness for $x \in \tilde{L}$, output b, otherwise, output 0. The sender sends the evalauted ciphertext ct_{eval}.

Observe now that the compactness of the commitment scheme follows from the compactness of the FHE scheme. Clearly, if the receiver encrypts a non-witness for x, it can recover the committed bit b using the secret key FHE.sk. For this commitment scheme to be hiding, it is sufficient that in the FHE scheme, the evaluated ciphertext hides the circuit that has been evaluated on it, even if the initial FHE ciphertext and public key are maliciously generated. Fortunately, FHE schemes satisfying the aforementioned *malicious circuit privacy* have already been constructed from LWE [11,38].

1.4   Related Existing Work

The initial construction of ring signatures by Rivest, Shamir and Kalai [44] is in the random oracle model. Several subsequent constructions [1,9,27] were also given in the ROM. Constructions in the standard model were first obtained concurrently by Chow, Liu, Wei and Yuen [16] and Bender, Katz and Morselli [6]. Several works also construct schemes in the CRS model [10,45,46]. Brakerski and Kalai [12] gave a construction based on the SIS problem in the standard model, and there are subsequent lattice-based constructions [5,47] that give more practical constructions (these works actually construct *linkable* ring signatures). Park and Sealfon [39] give certain constructions based on SIS and others based on verifiable random functions that satisfy new and interesting definitions of repudiability and claimability that they develop. All of these constructions give ring signatures linear in the ring size.

Dodis et al. [17] gave the first sublinear size ring signatures in the ROM. Since then, constructing logarithmic size ring signatures in the ROM been the focus of many works [7,19,26,28,29,32]. In the CRS model, [15,23,24,30] build sublinear ring signatures under various assumptions. In the plain model, Backes et al. [3] construct sublinear ring signatures using a primitive called signatures with *flexible* public key, and Malavolta and Schroder [33] construct constant size ring signatures under a knowledge of exponent assumption, which is unfalsifiable. Finally, as mentioned, Backes et al. [2] construct the first logarithmic size ring signatures in the plain model under standard and falsifiable assumptions, namely DDH or LWE along with NIWI proofs.

2   Preliminaries

We denote the security parameter by λ. For any $\ell \in \mathbb{N}$, we denote the set of the first ℓ positive integers by $[\ell]$. For a set S, $x \leftarrow S$ denotes sampling a uniformly random element x from S.

2.1   Learning with Errors

We recall the Learning With Errors (LWE) problem, and its hardness based on worst-case lattice problems.

For a positive integer dimension n and modulus q, and an error distribution χ over $\mathbb{Z}$, the LWE distribution and decision problem are defined as follows. For an $\mathbf{s} \in \mathbb{Z}^n$, the LWE distribution $A_{\mathbf{s},\chi}$ is sampled by choosing a uniformly random $\mathbf{a} \leftarrow \mathbb{Z}_q^n$ and an error term $e \leftarrow \chi$, and outputting $(\mathbf{a}, b = \langle \mathbf{s}, \mathbf{a} \rangle + e) \in \mathbb{Z}_q^{n+1}$.

Definition 1. *The decision-LWE$_{n,q,\chi}$ problem is to distinguish, with non-negligible advantage, between any desired (but polynomially bounded) number of independent samples drawn from $A_{\mathbf{s},\chi}$ for a single $\mathbf{s} \leftarrow \mathbb{Z}_q^n$, and the same number of uniformly random and independent samples over $\mathbb{Z}_q^{n+1}$.*

A standard instantiation of LWE is to let χ be a *discrete Gaussian* distribution over $\mathbb{Z}$ with parameter $r = 2\sqrt{n}$. A sample drawn from this distribution has magnitude bounded by, say, $r\sqrt{n} = \Theta(n)$ except with probability at most 2^{-n}, and hence this tail of the distribution can be entirely removed. For this parameterization, it is known that LWE is at least as hard as *quantumly* approximating certain "short vector" problems on n-dimensional lattices, in the worst case, to within $\tilde{O}(q\sqrt{n})$ factors [41,43]. Classical reductions are also known for different parameterizations [13,40].

Fix a dimension $n = \text{poly}(\lambda)$. For the rest of this paper, when we refer to hardness of LWE, we mean hardness of LWE with polynomial modulus-to-noise ratio against polynomial sized adversaries, i.e., polynomial hardness of LWE$_{n,q,\chi}$ where, q is a polynomial in n, and χ is the error distribution described in the previous paragraph.

2.2 Correlation Intractable Hash Functions

We borrow the following the definition of CI hash functions from [42] verbatim.

Definition 2. *Let $C = \{C_\lambda\}$ be a family of circuits, i.e., a set of circuits for each λ. A hash function family* Hash $=$ (Gen, Eval) *is* correlation intractable (CI) *for C if for every non-uniform polynomial-size adversary $\mathcal{A} = \{\mathcal{A}_\lambda\}$ there exists a negligible function $\nu(\lambda)$ such that for every $C \in C_\lambda$,*

$$\Pr_{\substack{k \leftarrow \mathsf{Hash.Gen}(1^\lambda) \\ x \leftarrow \mathcal{A}_\lambda(k)}} [\mathsf{Hash.Eval}(k, x) = C(x)] \leq \nu(\lambda) . \tag{1}$$

We will also use CI hash construction of [42].

Theorem 1 ([42]). *Assuming hardness of LWE, there exists a polynomial $m = m(\lambda)$ such that, for every family of polynomial sized circuits C with output size at least m bits, there exists a hash function family which is CI for C. Furthermore, the key generation algorithm in this hash function family simply outputs a uniformly random key from its key space.*

2.3 Public Key Encryption

Similar to [2], we need a public key encryption scheme which has pseudorandom ciphertexts and public keys. For our application, we also require additional properties.

Definition 3. *A public key encryption scheme is a tuple of PPT algorithms* PKE $=$ (GenWithKey, Enc, Dec, Valid), *with the following interfaces, where for each security parameter $\lambda \in \mathbb{N}$, PK_λ, SK_λ and CT_λ are three sets where the uniform distribution is efficiently sampleable,*

- GenWithKey(sk), *on input a secret key $sk \in \mathsf{SK}_\lambda$ outputs a public key $pk \in \mathsf{PK}_\lambda$.*
- Enc(pk, b), *on input a public key pk, and a message $b \in \{0, 1\}$, outputs a ciphertext $ct \in \mathsf{CT}_\lambda$.*
- Dec(sk, ct), *on input a secret key sk and a ciphertext ct, outputs a bit b.*
- Valid(pk, sk), *on input a public pk and a secret key sk, either accepts or rejects.*

We consider the following properties:

1. Completeness: *for any $\lambda \in \mathbb{N}$, any key pair (pk, sk) such that* Valid(pk, sk) *accepts, and any message b,*

$$\Pr[\mathsf{Dec}(sk, ct) = b] = 1,$$

where $ct \leftarrow \mathsf{Enc}(pk, m)$. Furthermore, for any $\lambda \in \mathbb{N}$,

$$\Pr_{\substack{sk \leftarrow \mathsf{SK}_\lambda \\ pk \leftarrow \mathsf{GenWithKey}(sk)}} [\mathsf{Valid}(pk, sk) \ accepts] = 1.$$

2. Sparseness of valid public keys: *for any* $\lambda \in \mathbb{N}$,

$$\Pr_{pk \leftarrow \mathsf{PK}_\lambda} [\exists sk : \mathsf{Valid}(pk, sk) \ accepts] = \mathrm{negl}(\lambda).$$

3. Injectivity of key generation: *for any* sk,

$$\Pr_{pk \leftarrow \mathsf{GenWithKey}(sk)} [\exists sk' \neq sk : \mathsf{Valid}(pk, sk') \ accepts] = \mathrm{negl}(\lambda).$$

4. Pseudorandomness of public keys: *for every* $Q = \mathrm{poly}(\lambda)$, *the following two distributions*
   - *first, samples a uniformly random secret key* $sk \leftarrow \mathsf{SK}_\lambda$, *then outputs* $\{pk_i \leftarrow \mathsf{GenWithKey}(sk)\}_{i \in [Q]}$
   - *outputs* L *uniformly random public keys* $\{pk_i \leftarrow \mathsf{PK}_\lambda\}_{i \in [Q]}$,
   are computationally indistinguishable.
5. Closeness of ciphertexts to uniform: *for every message* b, *the output of the following two distributions*
   - *first, samples a uniformly random public key* $pk \leftarrow \mathsf{PK}_\lambda$, *then, outputs* $(pk, \mathsf{Enc}(pk, b))$,
   - *first, samples a uniformly random public key* $pk \leftarrow \mathsf{PK}_\lambda$, *then, chooses a uniformly random ciphertext* $ct \leftarrow \mathsf{CT}_\lambda$ *and outputs* (pk, ct),
   are statistically indistinguishable.

Consider Regev's public key cryptosystem [43]. For some appropriate parameters $n = \mathrm{poly}(\lambda), q = \mathrm{poly}(n), m \geq 2n \log q$, $B \ll q/4$, a secret key in this scheme is a vector $\mathbf{s} \in \mathbb{Z}_q^n$ and valid public keys for secret $\mathbf{s}$ are generated as

$$pk := \mathbf{A} = \begin{bmatrix} \bar{\mathbf{A}} \\ \mathbf{s}^t \bar{\mathbf{A}} + \mathbf{e}^t \end{bmatrix} \in \mathbb{Z}_q^{(n+1) \times m},$$

where, $\bar{\mathbf{A}} \leftarrow \mathbb{Z}_q^{n \times m}$ and $\mathbf{e}$ is chosen from some B-bounded distribution. For this cryptosystem we define the following validity check algorithm

- $\mathsf{Valid}(pk = \mathbf{A}, sk = \mathbf{s})$: Accept iff $|(\mathbf{s}^t, -1) \cdot \mathbf{A}|_\infty \leq B$.

Theorem 2. *Assuming hardness of LWE, there exists a public key encryption scheme satisfying all the properties in Definition 3.*

Proof. We briefly argue that equipped with algorithm Valid, Regev's cryptosystem satisfies all the properties in Definition 3. When q is a prime number, injectivity of key generation is an implication of Lemma 5.3 in [22]. The rest of the properties are already established in [35, 43].

2.4 Blum's Raw Protocol

Here, we formally define and state the properties of the raw version of Blum's sigma protocol [8]. In this abstraction, the prover does not use any commitment or encryption scheme to hide its first message and therefore, the protocol does not satisfy a conventional zero knowledge property. Using a commitment scheme, this protocol can be converted into an honest verifier zero knowledge protocol.

Definition 4. *Let* $L \in$ NP *be a language with a corresponding relation R. Blum's raw protocol for L, is a tuple of PPT algorithms $\Pi = ($P1, P2, V, BadChallenge, Sim$)$ with the following interfaces*

- P1(x, w), *on input a statement witness pair* $(x, w) \in L$, *it outputs a first message a, two substrings* (a_0, a_1) *of a corresponding to two subsets of indices S_0, S_1, and an internal state ζ. We implicitly assume (a_0, a_1) uniquely determine the subsets S_0, S_1.*
- P2(a, b, ζ), *on input first message a, a challenge bit $b \in \{0,1\}$, and internal state ζ, it outputs a second message c.*
- V(x, b, a_b, c), *on input an instance x, a challenge bit $b \in \{0,1\}$, an opening a_b, and a response c, it either accepts or rejects.*
- BadChallenge(a), *on input a first message a, it outputs a badchallenge bit $b \in \{0,1\}$.*
- Sim(b, x), *takes as input a challenge bit b, and an instance x, and outputs two strings a_b and c.*

These algorithms satisfy the following properties:

1. Completeness: *for any* $(x, w) \in L$, *any* $\ell \in \mathbb{N}$, *and any* $b \in \{0,1\}$,

$$\Pr[V(x, b, a_b, c) \text{ accepts }] = 1,$$

where, $(a, (a_0, a_1), \zeta) \leftarrow$ P1(x, w), *and* $c \leftarrow$ P2(a, b, ζ).
2. Soundness: *if* $x \notin L$, *then, for any two subsets of indices S_0, S_1, bit $b \neq$ BadChallenge(a), and any c,*

$$\Pr[V(x, b, a_b, c) \text{ rejects }] = 1,$$

where, a_b *denotes a subset of a specified by indices in S_b.*
3. Zero knowledge: *for any* $b \in \{0,1\}$ *and any* $(x, w) \in R$ *the following two distributions,*
    - *outputs* (b, a_b, c), *where* $(a, (a_0, a_1), \zeta) \leftarrow$ P1(x, w), *and* $c \leftarrow$ P2(a, b, ζ)
    - *outputs* $(b, \text{Sim}(b, x))$
    are identical.

Blum's raw protocol exists unconditionally for any language $L \in$ NP [8].

2.5 Maliciously Circuit Private FHE

We review the definition of maliciously circuit private FHE.

Definition 5 ([38]). *A maliciously circuit private leveled FHE scheme is a tuple of algorithms.*
FHE $= ($Gen, Enc, Eval, Dec, Sim$)$, *where, except for* Sim *the rest of the algorithms are PPT, having the following interfaces*

- Gen$(1^\lambda, 1^d)$, *given a security parameter $\lambda \in \mathbb{N}$ and a depth parameter $d \in \mathbb{N}$, outputs a public and private key pair* (pk, sk).

- Enc(pk, b), *given a public key pk and a message* $b \in \{0,1\}$, *outputs a ciphertext* $ct \in \{0,1\}^{\ell_{ct}(\lambda, d)}$.
- Eval$((ct_1, \cdots, ct_k), C; r)$, *given* k *ciphertexts* $ct_1, \cdots, ct_k$, *a boolean circuit* $C : \{0,1\}^k \to \{0,1\}$, *and random coins* r, *outputs an evaluated ciphertext* $ct_{eval} \in \{0,1\}^{\ell_{eval}}$.
- Dec(sk, ct), *given a secret key sk and a ciphertext ct, outputs a bit* $b \in \{0,1\}$.
- Sim$(pk^*, (ct_1^*, \cdots, ct_k^*), b)$, *on input a (not necessarily honestly generated) public-key* pk^* *and* k *(not necessarily honestly generated) ciphertexts* $ct_1^* \in \{0,1\}^{\ell_{ct}(\lambda,d)}, ..., ct_k^* \in \{0,1\}^{\ell_{ct}(\lambda,d)}$, *and a bit* b, *outputs a simulated ciphertext* ct_{sim}.

We consider FHE schemes that satisfy the following properties:

1. Completeness: *for every* $\lambda, d \in \mathbb{N}$, *every circuit* $C : \{0,1\}^k \to \{0,1\}$ *of depth at most* d *and every input* $m \in \{0,1\}^k$,

$$\Pr[\mathsf{Dec}(sk, ct_{eval}) = C(m)] = 1,$$

   where, $(pk, sk) \leftarrow \mathsf{Gen}(1^\lambda, 1^d)$, $ct_i \leftarrow \mathsf{Enc}(pk, m_i)$ *for every* $i \in [\ell]$, *and* $ct_{eval} \leftarrow \mathsf{Eval}((ct_1, \cdots, ct_\ell), C)$.
2. Compactness: *there exists fixed polynomials* $\ell_{eval} = \ell_{eval}(\lambda, d)$ *and* $\ell_{rand} = \ell_{rand}(\lambda, d)$, *such that evaluated ciphertexts have size* $\ell_{eval}(\lambda, d)$ *and the size of the randomness used in* Eval *algorithm is* $\ell_{rand}(\lambda, d)$, *i.e., the size of evaluated ciphertexts and the size of randomness in the evaluation algorithm only depend on the depth of the circuit being evaluated.*
3. Pseudorandomness of public keys: *the public key pk output by the* Gen *algorithm is pseudorandom.*
4. Pseudorandomness of ciphertexts: *for every non-uniform polynomial-size adversary* $\mathcal{A}$, *every* $d \in \mathbb{N}$ *and every* $b \in \{0,1\}$, *the probabilities*

$$\Pr[\mathcal{A}(pk, ct) = 1], \tag{2}$$

   in the following two experiments differ by only negl(λ):
   - *in experiment 1,* $(pk, sk) \leftarrow \mathsf{Gen}(1^\lambda, 1^d)$, $ct \leftarrow \mathsf{Enc}(pk, b)$
   - *in experiment 2,* $(pk, sk) \leftarrow \mathsf{Gen}(1^\lambda, 1^d)$, $ct \leftarrow \{0,1\}^{\ell_{ct}(\lambda,d)}$
5. Malicious circuit privacy: *for every (not necessarily honestly generated) public-key* pk^*, *every* $k \in \mathbb{N}$, *and every* k *(not necessarily honestly generated) ciphertexts* $ct_1^* \in \{0,1\}^{\ell_{ct}(\lambda,d)}, ..., ct_k^* \in \{0,1\}^{\ell_{ct}(\lambda,d)}$, *there exists a* $m^* \in \{0,1\}^k$ *such that, for every circuit* $C : \{0,1\}^k \to \{0,1\}$ *of depth at most* d,

$$\mathsf{Eval}((ct_1^*, \cdots, ct_k^*), C) \overset{s}{\approx} \mathsf{Sim}(pk^*, (ct_1^*, \cdots, ct_k^*), C(m^*)).$$

Theorem 3 ([11,38]). *Assuming hardness of LWE, there exists a maliciously circuit private leveled FHE, where the size of evaluated ciphertexts and secret keys only depend on the security parameter* λ.

2.6 Somewhere Perfectly Binding Hash

We next define the notion of somewhere perfectly binding hash or SPB schemes, which are very similar to somewhere statistically binding hash schemes (as can be surmised, the only change from the latter is that here we expect the somewhere binding property to hold with probability 1). As in the scheme of [2], we will only define and employ a slightly weaker primitive denoted as *somewhere perfectly binding hash with private local openings*, which is what we will need for our signature scheme as well. We direct the reader to [2] for further details. The definition is essentially identical to that in [2], and is as follows.

Definition 6 (SPB Hash). *A somewhere perfectly binding hash scheme with private local openings, denoted by* SPB, *consists of a tuple of probabilistic polynomial time algorithms* (Gen, Hash, Open, Verify), *with the following syntax:*

- Gen$(1^\lambda, n, \mathsf{ind})$, *given a security parameter* λ, *a database size* n, *and index* ind *as input, outputs a hash and secret key pair* (hk, shk).
- Hash(hk, db), *given a hash key* hk *and database* db *as input, outputs a hash value* h.
- Open$(hk, shk, \mathsf{db}, \mathsf{ind})$, *given a hash key* hk, *secret key* shk, *database* db *and index* ind *as input, outputs a witness* τ.
- Verify$(hk, h, \mathsf{ind}, x, \tau)$, *given as input a hash key* hk, *a hash value* h, *an index* ind, *a value* x *and a witness* τ, *either accepts or rejects.*

To maintain clarity, we will not explicitly specify the block size of databases as input to Gen, *but assume that this is clear from the specific usage and hardwired into the algorithm. We ask that the* SPB *scheme satisfies the following properties:*

1. Correctness: *for all* $\lambda \in \mathbb{N}$, $n = \mathrm{poly}(\lambda)$, *all databases* db *of size* n, *and all indices* ind $\in [n]$, *we have,*

$$\Pr[\mathsf{Verify}(hk, h, \mathsf{ind}, \mathsf{db_{ind}}, \tau) \ accepts\,] = 1,$$

where, $(hk, shk) \leftarrow$ Gen$(1^\lambda, n, \mathsf{ind})$, $h \leftarrow$ Hash(hk, db) *and* $\tau \leftarrow$ Open$(hk, shk, \mathsf{db}, \mathsf{ind})$.

2. Efficiency: *any hash keys* hk *and witnesses* τ *corresponding to size* n *databases, are of size* $\log(n) \cdot \mathrm{poly}(\lambda)$. *Further, for size* n *databases,* Verify *can be computed by a circuit of size* $\log(n) \cdot \mathrm{poly}(\lambda)$.

3. Somewhere perfectly binding: *for all* $\lambda, n \in \mathbb{N}$, *all databases* db *of size* n, *all indices* ind $\in [n]$, *all purported hashing keys* hk, *all purported witnesses* τ, *all* h *in the support of* Hash(hk, db), *if* Verify$(hk, h, \mathsf{ind}, x, \tau)$ *accepts, then* $x = \mathsf{db_{ind}}$.

4. Index hiding, *for any* $n \in \mathbb{N}$ *and any* $\mathsf{ind_0}, \mathsf{ind_1} \in [n]$,

$$\{hk : (hk, shk) \leftarrow \mathsf{Gen}(1^\lambda, n, \mathsf{ind_0})\} \stackrel{c}{\approx} \{hk : (hk, shk) \leftarrow \mathsf{Gen}(1^\lambda, n, \mathsf{ind_1})\}$$

Theorem 4 ([2]). *Assuming hardness of LWE, there exists a SPB hash.*

2.7 Ring Signatures

We review the definition of compact ring signatures as presented in [2].

Definition 7 (Compact Ring Signature [2]). *A compact ring signature scheme* RS *is described by a triple of PPT algorithms* (Gen, Sign, Verify) *that have the following interface:*

- Gen($1^\lambda, N$), *given a security parameter λ and the maximum number of members in a ring N, outputs a verification and signing key pair* (VK, SK).
- Sign(SK, m, R), *given a secret key* SK, *a message $m \in \mathcal{M}_\lambda$. and a list of verification keys (interpreted as a ring)* R = (VK$_1, \cdots,$ VK$_\ell$) *as input, outputs a ring signature Σ.*
- Verify(R, m, Σ), *given a ring* R = (VK$_1, \ldots,$ VK$_\ell$), *message $m \in \mathcal{M}_\lambda$ and ring signature Σ as input, either accepts or rejects.*

Further, we require that the ring signature satisfies the following properties:

1. Completeness: *for all $\lambda \in \mathbb{N}$, $N \in \mathbb{N}$, $\ell \leq N$, $i \in [\ell]$ and $m \in \mathcal{M}_\lambda$, we have:*

$$\Pr[\text{RS.Verify}(R, m, \Sigma) \ accepts] = 1,$$

where, (VK$_i$, SK$_i$) $\leftarrow$ Gen($1^\lambda, N$), $\Sigma \leftarrow$ Sign(SK$_i, m$, R) *(where* R = (VK$_1, \ldots, VK_\ell$))*.*

2. Unforgeability: *for any $N \in \mathbb{N}$, and any $Q = \text{poly}(\lambda)$, any PPT adversary $\mathcal{A}$ has negligible advantage in the following game:*

Experiment RS$-$Forge$^Q(\mathcal{A})$: *This experiment is run by a challenger that proceeds as follows:*

- *For each $i \in [Q]$, the challenger generates key pairs* (VK$_i$, SK$_i$) $\leftarrow$ Gen($1^\lambda, N; r_i$), *and stores these key pairs along with their corresponding randomness. It then sets $\mathcal{VK} = \{$VK$_1, \ldots,$ VK$_Q\}$ and initializes $\mathcal{C} = \emptyset$.*
- *The challenger sends $\mathcal{VK}$ to $\mathcal{A}$.*
- *$\mathcal{A}$ can now make the following two kinds of queries: signing queries* sign *to get signatures signed by a particular entity on a particular message with respect to a ring of its choice, and corruption queries* corrupt *to corrupt a particular entity. The challenger responds as follows:*
  - *Signing query* (sign, i, m, R): *The challenger first checks if* VK$_i \in$ R. *If so, it computes $\Sigma \leftarrow$ Sign(SK$_i, m$, R) and sends this to $\mathcal{A}$. It also keeps a list of all such queries made by $\mathcal{A}$.*
  - *Corruption query* (corrupt, i): *The challenger adds* VK$_i$ *to the set $\mathcal{C}$ and returns the randomness r_i to $\mathcal{A}$.*
- *Finally, $\mathcal{A}$ outputs a forgery attempt, namely a purported ring signature Σ^* with respect to a ring R* and message m^*. The challenger checks if:*
  - R$^* \subseteq \mathcal{VK} \setminus \mathcal{C}$,
  - *$\mathcal{A}$ never made a signing query with respect to m^* and R* (together, i.e. of the form* (sign, $\cdot, m^*$, R*)), *and*
  - Verify(R$^*, m^*, \Sigma^*$) *accepts.*
  If so, the challenger outputs 1, otherwise, it outputs 0.

The advantage *of the adversary* $\mathcal{A}$ *is defined to be* $\mathbf{Adv}_{\mathsf{RS-Forge}^Q}(\mathcal{A}) = \Pr[\mathsf{RS-Forge}^Q(\mathcal{A}) = 1]$.

3. Anonymity: *for all* $Q = \mathrm{poly}(\lambda)$, *any PPT adversary* $\mathcal{A}$ *has negligible advantage in the following game:*

Experiment $\mathsf{RS-Anon}^Q(\mathcal{A})$: *This experiment is run by a challenger that proceeds as follows:*

- *For each* $i \in [Q]$, *the challenger generates key pairs* $(\mathsf{VK}_i, \mathsf{SK}_i) \leftarrow \mathsf{Gen}(1^\lambda; r_i)$. *It sends these key pairs along with their corresponding randomness to* $\mathcal{A}$.
- *Eventually* $\mathcal{A}$ *sends a challenge to the challenger of the form* $(\mathsf{R}, m, i_0, i_1)$. *We stress that* R *might have keys that are not generated by the challenger in the previous step. In particular, it might contain maliciously generated keys. The challenger checks if* $\mathsf{VK}_{i_0}, \mathsf{VK}_{i_1} \in \mathsf{R}$. *If so, it first samples a uniform bit* $b \leftarrow \{0, 1\}$, *then computes* $\Sigma \leftarrow \mathsf{Sign}(\mathsf{SK}_{i_b}, m, \mathsf{R})$, *and sends this to* $\mathcal{A}$.
- $\mathcal{A}$ *sends back its guess bit* b'. *The challenger outputs 1 if* $b' = b$, *otherwise it outputs 0.*

The advantage *of the adversary* $\mathcal{A}$ *in this game is defined as*

$$\mathbf{Adv}_{\mathsf{RS-Anon}^Q}(\mathcal{A}) = |\Pr[\mathsf{RS-Anon}^Q(\mathcal{A}) = 1] - \frac{1}{2}|.$$

4. Compactness: *the size of a signature is upper-bounded by a polynomial in* λ *and* $\log N$.

We mention that the unforgeability and anonymity properties defined in Definition 7 correspond respectively to the notions of *unforgeability with insider corruption* and *anonymity with respect to full key exposure* presented in [6].

3   Compact Witness Extractable Commitments

In this section we define witness extractable commitments. A witness extractable commitment for a language $L \in \mathsf{NP}$ with corresponding NP relation R is a two round commitment protocol. The receiver's message is generated using a witness w, and the sender's commitment to a bit b is generated using a statement x. Informally speaking, the bit b can be efficiently extracted when $(x, w) \in R$, however, when $x \notin L$, b is statistically hidden.

For our application in this paper, we are interested in witness extractable commitments that are compact. This means that the size of a commitment second message does not depend on the size of the NP verifier circuit (except for maybe its depth).

3.1   Definition

Definition 8. *Fix a language* $L \in \mathsf{NP}$. *By* R *and* $\{C_{n,\ell} : \{0, 1\}^n \times \{0, 1\}^\ell \to \{0, 1\}\}_{n,\ell \in N}$ *denote the* NP *relation and the* NP *verification circuit corresponding* *to L respectively. Also, let $d = d(n, \ell)$ be the depth of $C_{n,\ell}$. When it is clear from the context, we use d instead of $d(n, \ell)$. A* witness extractable commitment scheme *for L, is a tuple of PPT algorithms* (Com1, Com2, Verify, Extract) *having the following interfaces:*

- Com1$(1^\lambda, 1^D, w)$, *given a security parameter* λ, *circuit depth upper bound* D, *and a witness* $w \in \{0,1\}^\ell$, *outputs the commitment first message* com1 $\in \{0,1\}^{\ell_{com1} = \ell_{com1}(\lambda, D, \ell)}$ *and a string* st $\in \{0,1\}^{\ell_{st}}$ *representing the internal state.*
- Com2(com1, $x, b; r$), *given a commitment first message* com1, *a statement* x, *a bit* b *to commit, and randomness* $r \in \{0,1\}^{\ell_r}$, *outputs a commitment* com2 $\in \{0,1\}^{\ell_{com2}}$.
- Verify(com1, com2, x, b, r), *given a commitment transcript* com1, com2, *a statement* x, *a bit* b, *and random coins* r, *it either accepts or rejects.*
- Extract(com2, st), *given a commitment* com2 *and internal state* st, *outputs a bit* b.

We consider the following properties:

1. Completeness: *for every* $\lambda \in \mathbb{N}$, *bit* b, *every statement* x, *every witness* w, *every* $D \geq d$,

$$\Pr[\text{Verify}(\text{com1}, \text{com2}, x, b, r) \text{ accepts}] = 1,$$

   where, com1 $\leftarrow$ Com1$(1^\lambda, 1^D, w)$, $r \leftarrow \{0,1\}^{\ell_r}$, *and* com2 $\leftarrow$ Com2(com1, $x, b; r$).
2. Statistical hiding: *if* $x \notin L$, *then, for any* $\ell \in \mathbb{N}$, *any* $D \geq d(|x|, \ell)$, *and any sequence of strings* $\{\text{com1}_\lambda \in \{0,1\}^{\ell_{com1}(\lambda, D, \ell)}\}_{\lambda \in \mathbb{N}}$,

$$\text{com1}_\lambda, \text{Com2}(\text{com1}_\lambda, x, 0) \overset{s}{\approx} \text{com1}_\lambda, \text{Com2}(\text{com1}_\lambda, x, 1) \tag{3}$$

3. Pseudorandomness of first message: *for any* w *and any* D,

$$\text{Com1}(1^\lambda, 1^D, w) \overset{c}{\approx} U_{\ell_{com1}} \tag{4}$$

4. Extractability: *if* $(x, w) \in R$, *then, for any bit* b, *any* $D \geq d$, *any* com1, st *in the support of* Com1$(1^\lambda, 1^D, w)$, *any randomness* r, *and any* com2 *such that* Verify(com1, com2, x, b, r) *accepts,*

$$\Pr[\text{Extract}(\text{com2}, \text{st}) = b] = 1. \tag{5}$$

5. Compactness: *the parameters* ℓ_{com2}, ℓ_r *and* ℓ_{st} *are upper-bounded by some language-independent fixed polynomials in* λ *and* D. *In particular, they are independent of the size of the* NP *verifier circuit* $C_{n,\ell}$ *and the size of the statement* x.

3.2 Construction

We will use the maliciously circuit private FHE scheme FHE = (FHE.Gen, FHE. Enc, FHE.Eval) of [38].

Construction 1. Here we use the same notation as in Definition 8.

- Com1($1^\lambda, 1^D, w$): run (FHE.pk, FHE.sk) $\leftarrow$ FHE.Gen($1^\lambda, 1^{D+1}$). Output com1 $\leftarrow$ FHE.Enc(FHE.pk, w). Keep st := FHE.sk as internal state. Notice that for any circuit C of depth D, the circuit constructed in Fig. 1 has depth $D + 1$.
- Com2(com1, x, b): on input first message com1 and bit b, output

$$\text{com2} \leftarrow \text{FHE.Eval}(\text{com1}, G_{x,b}; r),$$

where, $G_{x,b}$ is the circuit defined below and r represents the random coins used in the FHE evaluation algorithm.

- Extract(com2, st = FHE.sk): output FHE.Dec(FHE.sk, com2).
- Verify(com1, com2, x, b, r): accept iff com2 is equal to FHE.Eval(com1, $G_{x,b}; r$).

procedure $G_{x,b}(w)$
   if $C(x, w) = 1$ **then**
      Output b
   else
      Output 0

Fig. 1. Description of $G_{x,b}$

Extractability and completeness of Construction 1 follow immediately from completeness of FHE. Compactness also follows from compactness of FHE. In fact, using the FHE in [38], both ℓ_{st} and ℓ_{com2} only depend on λ. Finally, pseudorandomness of FHE ciphertext and public keys imply pseudorandomness of the first message in Construction 1.

Theorem 5. *If* FHE *is maliciously circuit private, then, the commitment scheme in Construction 1 is statistically hiding.*

4   Compact Relaxed ZAPs for Extended NP ∩ coNP

In this section, we define and construct a 2-round public-coin argument system. Our argument system can be viewed as a generalization of ZAPs for NP ∩ coNP. To describe this generalization, first we introduce the notion of *super-complement* of a language. A super-complement of a language is an extension of the complement of that language. Notably, the complement of a language is a super-complement of it.

Definition 9 (Super-Complement). *Let L, $\widetilde{L}$ be two languages where the elements of $\widetilde{L}$ are represented as pairs of bit strings. We say $\widetilde{L}$ is a super-complement of L, if*

$$\widetilde{L} \subseteq (\{0,1\}^* \setminus L) \times \{0,1\}^*,$$

i.e., $\widetilde{L}$ is a super complement of L if for any $x = (x_1, x_2)$,

$$x \in \widetilde{L} \Rightarrow x_1 \notin L.$$

Our argument system is defined for two NP languages $L, \widetilde{L}$, where, $\widetilde{L}$ is a super-complement of L. Notice that, while the complement of L might not be in NP, however we require that $\widetilde{L} \in$ NP. The language $\widetilde{L}$ is used to define the soundness property. Namely, producing a proof for a statement $x = (x_1, x_2) \in \widetilde{L}$, should be hard. We also use the fact that $\widetilde{L} \in$ NP to mildly strengthen the soundness property. In more detail, instead of having selective soundness where the statement $x \in \widetilde{L}$ is fixed in advance, now, we fix a non-witness $\widetilde{w}$ and let the statement x be adaptively chosen by the malicious prover from all statements which have $\widetilde{w}$ as a witness to their membership in $\widetilde{L}$.

For our application to compact ring signatures, we further require the size of the proofs to be compact with respect to $\widetilde{L}$. Roughly speaking, this means that size of a proof for a statement $x = (x_1, x_2)$ only depends on the size of x_1.

4.1   Definition

Definition 10. *Let $L, \widetilde{L} \in$ NP be two languages such that $\widetilde{L}$ is a super complement of L. By R and $\widetilde{R}$ denote the NP relations corresponding to L and $\widetilde{L}$ respectively. Let $\{C_{n,\ell}\}_{n,\ell \in N}$ and $\{\widetilde{C}_{n,\ell}\}_{n,\ell \in N}$ be the NP verification circuits for L and $\widetilde{L}$ respectively. Let $\widetilde{d} = \widetilde{d}(n,\ell)$ be the depth of $\widetilde{C}_{n,\ell}$. A compact relaxed ZAP for $L, \widetilde{L}$ is a tuple of PPT algorithms $(\mathsf{V}, \mathsf{P}, \mathsf{Verify})$ having the following interfaces (where $1^n, 1^\lambda$ are implicit inputs to $\mathsf{P}, \mathsf{Verify}$):*

- $\mathsf{V}(1^\lambda, 1^n, 1^{\widetilde{\ell}}, 1^{\widetilde{D}})$, *given a security parameter λ, statement length n for L, witness length $\widetilde{\ell}$ for $\widetilde{L}$, and NP verifier circuit depth upper-bound $\widetilde{D}$ for $\widetilde{L}$, outputs a first message ρ.*
- $\mathsf{P}(\rho, x = (x_1, x_2), w)$, *given a string ρ, a statement $(x_1 \in \{0,1\}^n, x_2)$, and a witness w such that $(x_1, w) \in R$, outputs a proof π.*
- $\mathsf{Verify}(\rho, x = (x_1, x_2), \pi)$, *given a string ρ, a statement x, and a proof π, either accepts or rejects.*

We consider the following properties:

1. *Completeness: for every $(x_1, w) \in L$, every $x_2 \in \{0,1\}^*$, every $\widetilde{\ell} \in \mathbb{N}$, every $\widetilde{D} \geq \widetilde{d}(|x_1| + |x_2|, \widetilde{\ell})$, and every $\lambda \in \mathbb{N}$,*

$$\Pr[\mathsf{Verify}(\rho, x = (x_1, x_2), \pi) \text{ accepts }] = 1,$$

where, $\rho \leftarrow \mathsf{V}(1^\lambda, 1^{|x_1|}, 1^{\widetilde{\ell}}, 1^{\widetilde{D}})$ and $\pi \leftarrow \mathsf{P}(\rho, x, w)$.

2. *Public coin:* $V(1^\lambda, 1^n, 1^{\tilde{\ell}}, 1^{\tilde{D}})$ *simply outputs a uniformly random string.*
3. *Selective non-witness and adaptive statement soundness: for every non-uniform polynomial-size "cheating" prover* $P^* = \{P_\lambda^*\}$ *there exists a negligible function* $\nu(\lambda)$ *such that for any* $n, \tilde{D} \in \mathbb{N}$ *and any non-witness* $\tilde{w} \in \{0,1\}^*$,

$$\Pr_{\substack{\rho \leftarrow V(1^\lambda, 1^n, 1^{|\tilde{w}|}, 1^{\tilde{D}}) \\ (x=(x_1, x_2), \pi^*) \leftarrow P_\lambda^*(\rho)}} [\text{Verify}(\rho, x, \pi^*) \text{ accepts} \wedge \tilde{D} \geq \tilde{d}(|x|, |\tilde{w}|) \wedge (x, \tilde{w}) \in \tilde{R}] \leq \nu(\lambda). \quad (6)$$

4. *Statistical witness indistinguishability: for every (possibly unbounded) "cheating" verifier* $V^* = (V_1^*, V_2^*)$, *and every* $n, \tilde{\ell}, \tilde{D} \in \mathbb{N}$ *the probabilities*

$$\Pr[V_2^*(\rho, x, \pi, \zeta) = 1 \wedge (x, w) \in \mathcal{R} \wedge (x, w') \in \mathcal{R}]$$

in the following two experiments differ only by $\text{negl}(\lambda)$:
   - *in experiment 1,* $(\rho, x, w, w', \zeta) \leftarrow V_1^*(1^\lambda, 1^n, 1^{\tilde{\ell}}, 1^{\tilde{D}}), \pi \leftarrow P(\rho, x, w)$
   - *in experiment 2,* $(\rho, x, w, w', \zeta) \leftarrow V_1^*(1^\lambda, 1^n, 1^{\tilde{\ell}}, 1^{\tilde{D}}), \pi \leftarrow P(\rho, x, w')$
5. *Compactness: bit-size of proof* π *is a fixed polynomial in* $n, \tilde{\ell}, \tilde{D}, |C|$ *and* λ. *In particular, it is independent of the size of* $\tilde{C}$ *and* x_2.

4.2 Construction

For languages $L, \tilde{L}$, we give the tuple of algorithms (V, P, Verify) that make up our relaxed ZAP scheme. In the construction we will use the following ingredients:

- A witness extractable commitment $\text{Com} = (\text{Com1}, \text{Com2}, \text{Verify}, \text{Extract})$ for $\tilde{L}$. We denote the sizes of the first commitment message, second commitment message, the internal state output by Com1, and the randomness for Com2, by $\ell_{com1}, \ell_{com2}, \ell_{st}$ and ℓ_r respectively.
- Blum's raw protocol $\Pi = (\text{P1}, \text{P2}, V, \text{BadChallenge}, \text{Sim})$ for L. We denote the size of the first and second prover messages by ℓ_{p1} and ℓ_{p2} respectively. For any $\ell \in N$, Π^ℓ means repeating the protocol Π, ℓ times in parallel and interpreting the inputs to the algorithms accordingly. When it is clear from the context, we drop the superscript ℓ.
- A hash family $\text{Hash}^{n, \ell_{rep}} = (\text{Gen}, \text{Eval})$ that for any $n \in \mathbb{N}$, and any polynomial $\ell_{rep} = \ell_{rep}(\lambda)$ that is larger than the polynomial $m(\lambda)$ in Theorem 1, is CI for a circuit family $\mathcal{C}^{n, \ell_{rep}}$ which we will define next. The circuit family is defined as

$$\mathcal{C}^{n, \ell_{rep}} = \{\mathcal{C}_\lambda^{n, \ell_{rep}}\}_{\lambda \in \mathbb{N}},$$

where for each $\lambda \in \mathbb{N}$,

$$\mathcal{C}_\lambda^{n, \ell_{rep}} = \{f_{st} : \{0,1\}^{\ell_{rep} \cdot \ell_{p1} \cdot \ell_{com2}} \to \{0,1\}^{\ell_{rep}}\}_{st \in \{0,1\}^{\ell_{st}(\lambda)}},$$

where, f_{st} is defined as

$$f_{st}(x) = \Pi^{\ell_{rep}}.\text{BadChallenge}(\text{Com.Extract}(x, st)),$$

i.e., f_{st} extracts a message from the input commitment and outputs the *bad challenge* corresponding to that message. We will drop the indices n, ℓ_{rep} when they are clear from the context.

Construction 2. Let $\ell_{rep} = \ell_{rep}(\lambda)$ be a polynomial that is larger than the polynomial $m(\lambda)$ in Theorem 1.

- $\mathsf{V}(1^\lambda, 1^n, 1^{\tilde{\ell}}, 1^{\tilde{D}})$: first, pick a uniformly random commitment first message $\mathsf{com1} \leftarrow \{0,1\}^{\ell_{com1}(\lambda, \tilde{D}, \tilde{\ell})}$, then, generate CI-hash key $k \leftarrow \mathsf{Hash}^{n, \ell_{rep}}.\mathsf{Gen}(1^\lambda)$. Output $\rho := (\mathsf{com1}, k)$.
- $\mathsf{P}(\rho = (\mathsf{com1}, k), x = (x_1, x_2), w)$: first, compute

$$(\mathbf{a}, \{a_{i,b}\}_{i \in [\ell_{rep}], b \in \{0,1\}}, \zeta) \leftarrow \Pi^{\ell_{rep}}.\mathsf{P1}(x_1, w),$$

and then send

$$\pi = (\mathsf{com2} = \mathsf{Com}.\mathsf{Com2}(\mathsf{com1}, x, \mathbf{a}; \mathbf{r}), I = \mathsf{Hash}.\mathsf{Eval}(k, \mathsf{com2}), \mathbf{c} = \Pi.\mathsf{P2}(\mathbf{a}, I, \zeta), \mathbf{r}_I, \mathbf{a}_I)$$

to the verifier, where, $\mathbf{a}_I = \{a_{i,I_i}\}_{i \in [\ell_{rep}]}$ and $\mathbf{r}_I$ denotes the subset of randomness used to commit to $\mathbf{a}_I$. Also, $\mathsf{com2}_I$ denotes the chunks of $\mathsf{com2}$ which commit to $\mathbf{a}_I$.
- $\mathsf{Verify}(\rho, x = (x_1, x_2), \pi)$: parse $\pi = (\mathsf{com2}, I, \mathbf{c}, \mathbf{r}_I, \mathbf{a}_I)$. Accept iff both $\Pi.\mathsf{V}(x, I, \mathbf{a}_I, \mathbf{c})$ and $\mathsf{Com}.\mathsf{Verify}(\mathsf{com1}, \mathsf{com2}_I, x, \mathbf{a}_I, \mathbf{r}_I)$ accept.

Completeness of Construction 2 follows directly from the completeness of Π and Com. It is also public coin because the CI hash keys are uniform. Compactness also follows from the compactness of Com, namely, it follows from the fact that ℓ_{com2}, ℓ_{st} and ℓ_r may only polynomially depend on the depth $\tilde{D}$ of $\tilde{C}$ and not its size.

Theorem 6. *The protocol described in Construction 2 satisfies selective non-witness adaptive statement soundness.*

Theorem 7. *The protocol described in Construction 2 is statistically witness indsitinguishable.*

5   Compact LWE-Based Ring Signature Scheme

In this section, we present our compact ring signature scheme. First, we briefly list the ingredients in our construction:

- A standard signature scheme $\mathsf{Sig} = (\mathsf{Gen}, \mathsf{Sign}, \mathsf{Verify})$ with EUF–CMA security.
- A public key encryption scheme $\mathsf{PKE} = (\mathsf{GenWithKey}, \mathsf{Enc}, \mathsf{Dec}, \mathsf{Valid})$ as defined in Definition 3.
- A somewhere perfectly binding hash function $\mathsf{SPB} = (\mathsf{Gen}, \mathsf{Hash}, \mathsf{Open}, \mathsf{Verify})$ with private local openings.
- A compact relaxed ZAP scheme $\mathsf{ZAP} = (\mathsf{V}, \mathsf{P}, \mathsf{Verify})$ as described in Sect. 4.

Next, we define the languages L and $\widetilde{L}$ that we will instantiate our relaxed ZAP construction for. The language L is identical to the language $\mathcal{L}$ used in the ring signature construction of [2]. For a statement $y_1 = (m, c, hk, h)$ and witness $w = (\mathsf{VK} = (vk, pk, \rho), i, \tau, \sigma, r_c)$, define relations R_1, R_2 and R_3 as follows:

$$(y_1, w) \in R_1 \Leftrightarrow \mathsf{SPB.Verify}(hk, h, i, \mathsf{VK}, \tau) \text{ accepts}$$
$$(y_1, w) \in R_2 \Leftrightarrow \mathsf{PKE.Enc}(pk, (\sigma, vk); r_c) = c$$
$$(y_1, w) \in R_3 \Leftrightarrow \mathsf{Sig.Verify}(vk, m, \sigma) \text{ accepts}$$

Next, define the relation R' as

$$R' := R_1 \cap R_2 \cap R_3.$$

Let L' be the language corresponding to R'. For statements of the form $(m, c_1, c_2, hk_1, hk_2, h_1, h_2)$, define the language L as

$$L = \{(m, c_1, c_2, hk_1, hk_2, h_1, h_2) | (m, c_1, hk_1, h_1) \in L' \vee (m, c_2, hk_2, h_2) \in L'\}.$$

Now, we define the language $\widetilde{L}$ and prove that it is a super-complement of L. Let $x_2 = \mathsf{R} = (\mathsf{VK}_1, \ldots, \mathsf{VK}_\ell)$, $y = (y_1, x_2)$, and $\widetilde{w} = s$. Define the following relations:

$$(y, \widetilde{w}) \in R_4 \Leftrightarrow \forall j \in [\ell] : \mathsf{PKE.Valid}(pk_j, s) \text{ accepts} \wedge h = \mathsf{SPB.Hash}(hk, \mathsf{R})$$
$$(y, \widetilde{w}) \in R_5 \Leftrightarrow \mathsf{PKE.Dec}(s, c) = (\sigma, vk) \wedge \mathsf{Sig.Verify}(vk, m, \sigma) \text{ accepts}$$
$$\wedge \, \exists \mathsf{VK} \in \mathsf{R} : \mathsf{VK} = (vk, pk, \rho) \text{ for some } pk \text{ and } \rho$$

where, for each $j \in [\ell]$, pk_j is the public key in VK_j. Let L_4, L_5 be the languages corresponding to R_4, R_5 respectively.

Define further the relation $\widehat{R}$ according to

$$\widehat{R} := R_4 \setminus R_5,$$

and let $\widehat{L}$ be the corresponding language. Finally, for statements of the form $x = (x_1 = (m, c_1, c_2, hk_1, hk_2, h_1, h_2), x_2 = \mathsf{R})$, let $\widetilde{L}$ be the language given by

$$\widetilde{L} = \{(m, c_1, c_2, hk_1, hk_2, h_1, h_2, \mathsf{R}) | (m, c_1, hk_1, h_1, \mathsf{R}) \in \widehat{L} \wedge (m, c_2, hk_2, h_2, \mathsf{R}) \in \widehat{L}\}.$$

Given the properties of the SPB and PKE we can quickly prove the following lemma.

Lemma 1. *If* SPB *is somewhere perfectly binding and* PKE *is complete,* $\widetilde{L}$ *is a super-complement of* L.

We will employ the relaxed ZAP scheme for the languages L and $\widetilde{L}$.

5.1 Construction

Construction 3. Let $\widetilde{D} = \widetilde{D}(\lambda, N)$ be the maximum depth of the NP verifier circuit for language $\widetilde{L}$ restricted to statements where the ring has at most N members, and the security parameter corresponding to SPB hash keys and values and PKE ciphertext is λ. By $n = n(\lambda, \log N)$ denote the maximum size of the statements of language L where the ring has at most N members and the security parameter is λ. Recall that for security parameter λ, secret keys in PKE have size $\widetilde{\ell} = \ell_{sk}(\lambda)$. We now describe our ring signature construction:

- $\mathsf{Gen}(1^\lambda, N)$:
  - sample signing and verification keys $(vk, sk) \leftarrow \mathsf{Sig.Gen}(1^\lambda)$,
  - sample pk uniformly from the keyspace of PKE,
  - compute the first message $\rho \leftarrow \mathsf{ZAP.V}(1^\lambda, 1^n, 1^{\widetilde{\ell}}, 1^{\widetilde{D}})$ for the relaxed ZAP scheme,
  - output the verification key $\mathsf{VK} = (vk, pk, \rho)$ and signing key $\mathsf{SK} = (sk, vk, pk, \rho)$.
- $\mathsf{Sign}(\mathsf{SK}, m, R = (\mathsf{VK}_1, \ldots, \mathsf{VK}_l))$:
  - parse $\mathsf{SK} = (sk, vk, pk, \rho)$,
  - compute $\sigma \leftarrow \mathsf{Sig.Sign}(sk, m)$,
  - let $\mathsf{VK} = \mathsf{VK}_i \in R$ be the verification key corresponding to SK,
  - sample hash keys $(hk_1, shk_1) \leftarrow \mathsf{SPB.Gen}(1^\lambda, |R|, i)$, and compute the hash $h_1 \leftarrow \mathsf{SPB.Hash}(hk_1, R)$,
  - compute the opening $\tau_1 \leftarrow \mathsf{SPB.Open}(hk_1, shk_1, R, i)$ to position i,
  - compute $c_1 \leftarrow \mathsf{PKE.Enc}(pk, (\sigma, vk); r_{c_1})$
  - sample hash keys $(hk_2, shk_2) \leftarrow \mathsf{SPB.Gen}(1^\lambda, |R|, i)$ and compute the hash $h_2 \leftarrow \mathsf{SPB.Hash}(hk_2, R)$,
  - sample c_2 randomly from the ciphertext space of PKE,
  - let $\mathsf{VK}_1 = (vk_1, pk_1, \rho_1)$ denote the lexicographically smallest member of R (as a string; note that this is necessarily unique).,
  - fix statement $x_1 = (m, c_1, c_2, hk_1, hk_2, h_1, h_2)$, witness $w = (vk, pk, i, \tau_1, \sigma, r_{c_1})$, and statement $x_2 = R$,
  - Compute $\pi \leftarrow \mathsf{ZAP.P}(\rho_1, x = (x_1, x_2), w)$,
  - output $\Sigma = (c_1, hk_1, c_2, hk_2, \pi)$.
- $\mathsf{Verify}(\Sigma, m, R)$:
  - identify the lexicographically smallest verification key VK_1 in R,
  - compute $h_1' = \mathsf{SPB.Hash}(hk_1, R)$,
  - compute $h_2' = \mathsf{SPB.Hash}(hk_2, R)$,
  - fix $x_1 = (m, c_1, c_2, hk_1, hk_2, h_1', h_2')$, and $x_2 = R$,
  - determine ρ_1 in VK_1,
  - compute and output $\mathsf{ZAP.Verify}(\rho_1, x, \pi)$.

Completeness of Construction 3 follows by the completeness of SPB and ZAP. For compactness, notice that $\widetilde{D}$ is upper-bounded by a polynomial in λ and $\log N$, and therefore, since Construction 2 is compact, Construction 3 is also compact.

5.2   Unforgeability

Here, we prove that our ring signature scheme possesses the unforgeability property as defined in Definition 7. The proof strategy is as follows: we leverage the selective non-witness adaptive statement soundness of ZAP to conclude that there must be a valid signature σ in the forgery attempt, and essentially try to obtain this signature with significantly high probability so that we can devise a reduction to the existential unforgeability of Sig.

Theorem 8. *Construction 3 is unforgeable, assuming* Sig *is* EUF−CMA *secure,* PKE *has injective key generation and pseudorandom public keys,* SPB *is somewhere perfectly binding, and* ZAP *satisfies selective non-witness adaptive statement soundness.*

Proof. We start by considering a PPT adversary $\mathcal{A}$ that participates in the unforgeability game. Let $Q = \text{poly}(\lambda)$ be an upper bound on the number of key queries made by $\mathcal{A}$.

We proceed with a hybrid argument to set up our reduction to the unforgeability of Sig. Consider the following hybrids:

Hybrid H_0: This is just the standard unforgeability game. In particular, for all $i \in [Q]$, the challenger in the game generates pk_i by sampling an element uniformly from the keyspace of PKE.

Hybrid H_1: In this experiment, the only difference is that, the challenger first picks a uniformly random secret key sk_{PKE} for PKE, and then generates the corresponding public keys for the adversary using this, namely $pk_i \leftarrow$ PKE.GenWithKey(sk_{PKE}), for all $i \in [Q]$. The challenger now stores sk_{PKE}.

Lemma 2. *Assuming* PKE *has pseudorandom public keys,* $H_0 \overset{c}{\approx} H_1$.

Proof. Let $\mathcal{A}$ be a PPT adversary attempting to distinguish H_0 and H_1. We use $\mathcal{A}$ to build an adversary $\mathcal{A}'$ having the same advantage against the pseudorandomness of public keys of PKE. Here, $\mathcal{A}'$ is either given $\{pk_i \leftarrow$ GenWithKey(sk)$\}_{i \in [Q]}$ for a sk chosen uniformly at random or $\{pk_i \leftarrow \mathsf{PK}_\lambda\}_{i \in [Q]}$. We define $\mathcal{A}'$ to proceed exactly as in H_0 but using the public keys that is given to it as input. Clearly, if pk_is are chosen with a single uniformly chosen secret key, then, the view of $\mathcal{A}$ is identical to H_1, whereas, if pk_is are chosen uniformly at random, the view of $\mathcal{A}$ is identical to H_0.

Now, we will proceed to show that unforgeability holds in H_1. Consider the adversary's forgery attempt $(\Sigma^* = (c_1^*, hk_1^*, c_2^*, hk_2^*, \pi^*), m^*, \mathsf{R}^*)$. Define x_1^* as the statement corresponding to Σ^* as $x_1^* = (m^*, c_1^*, c_2^*, hk_1^*, hk_2^*, h_1^*, h_2^*)$, where $h_1^* = \mathsf{SPB.Hash}(hk_1^*, \mathsf{R}^*)$ and $h_2^* = \mathsf{SPB.Hash}(hk_2^*, \mathsf{R}^*)$. Let $\mathsf{VK}_1^* = (vk_1^*, pk_1^*, \rho_1^*)$ be the lexicographically smallest verification key in R^*.

Our next step is to show that if π^* is a valid proof for $x^* = (x_1^*, x_2^* = \mathsf{R}^*)$ under ρ_1^*, then, with overwhelming probability, $x^* \notin \tilde{L}$.

Lemma 3. *In H_1, assuming ZAP satisfies selective non-witness adaptive statement soundness, and PKE has injective key generation,*

$$\Pr[x^* \in \widetilde{L} \wedge \mathsf{ZAP.Verify}(\rho_1^*, x^*, \pi^*) \text{ accepts}] = \mathrm{negl}(\lambda).$$

Proof. It is enough to show that for each $j \in [Q]$,

$$\Pr[x^* \in \widetilde{L} \wedge \mathsf{ZAP.Verify}(\rho_j, x^*, \pi^*) \text{ accepts}] = \mathrm{negl}(\lambda),$$

where ρ_j denotes the ZAP first message corresponding to the jth verification key VK_j generated in the game.

Let $\mathcal{A}$ be an adversary attempting to output a forgery such that $x^* \in \widetilde{L} \wedge$ $\mathsf{ZAP.Verify}(\rho_j, x^*, \pi^*)$ accepts. We build an adversary $\mathcal{A}'$ against the selective non-witness adaptive statement soundness of ZAP for languages L and $\widetilde{L}$ with fixed non-witness $\widetilde{w} = sk_{\mathsf{PKE}}$. The algorithm $\mathcal{A}'$ proceeds as follows:

- on input ZAP first message $\widehat{\rho}$, it sets $\rho_j = \widehat{\rho}$ and then proceeds exactly as H_1.
- upon recieving the forgery attempt Σ^* from $\mathcal{A}$, it constructs the corresponding x^* and π^*, and outputs (x^*, π^*).

To finish the proof of this lemma, we observe that if $x^* \in \widetilde{L}$, then, except with negligible probability, $(x^*, sk_{\mathsf{PKE}}) \in \widetilde{R}$. This is because, if $x^* \in \widetilde{L}$, then, by definition of $\widetilde{L}$, there exists a non-witness $\widetilde{w}^*$ such that,

$$\forall (vk_i^*, pk_i^*, \rho_i^*) \in R^* : \mathsf{PKE.Valid}(pk_i^*, \widetilde{w}^*) \text{ accepts},$$

and since PKE has injective key generation, it follows that except with negligible probability, $\widetilde{w}^* = sk_{\mathsf{PKE}}$.

In the next lemma we show that if $x^* \notin \widetilde{L}$, then, by decrypting c_1^* or c_2^*, we can find a forgery for Sig.

Lemma 4. *In H_1, assuming Sig is EUF$-$CMA secure, PKE has injective key generation, and SPB is somewhere perfectly binding,*

$$\Pr[x^* \notin \widetilde{L}] = \mathrm{negl}(\lambda).$$

Proof. Let $\mathcal{A}$ be an adversary attempting to output a forgery such that $x^* \notin \widetilde{L}$. We build an algorithm $\mathcal{A}'$ against the EUF$-$CMA security of Sig. The algorithm $\mathcal{A}'$ proceeds as follows,

- on input $\widehat{vk}$, first picks an index $j \leftarrow [Q]$ uniformly at random, and then sets $vk_j = \widehat{vk}$. It then proceeds as in H_1,
- when $\mathcal{A}$ sends a signing query, if it is using keys from a party other than the jth party, it proceeds as in H_1, otherwise, it uses the EUF$-$CMA game's signing oracle to obtain a signature for the jth party and then continues exactly as in H_1.
- if $\mathcal{A}$ tries to corrupt the jth party, $\mathcal{A}'$ aborts.

- upon recieving the forgery attempt Σ^* from $\mathcal{A}$, it decrypts c_1^* using sk_{PKE} to recover σ_1^*.
  If $\mathsf{Sig.Verify}(vk_j, m^*, \sigma_1^*)$ accepts, it sets $\widehat{\sigma} := \sigma_1^*$. Otherwise, it decrypts c_2^* with sk_{PKE} to recover σ_2^*, and sets $\widehat{\sigma} = \sigma_2^*$. It outputs $(m^*, \widehat{\sigma})$.

To finish the proof, we show that with probability at least

$$\frac{1}{Q}(\Pr[x^* \notin \widetilde{L}] - \mathrm{negl}(\lambda)),$$

$(m^*, \widehat{\sigma})$ is a valid forgery for key vk_j. Without loss of generality assume that

$$(m^*, c_1^*, hk_1^*, h_1^*, \mathsf{R}^*) \notin \widehat{L}.$$

Observe that due to the way H_1 generates the public keys and also by definition of h_1^*,

$$(m^*, c_1^*, hk_1^*, h_1^*, \mathsf{R}^*) \in L_4.$$

Therefore, by definition of $\widehat{L}$, there exists a string $\widetilde{w}$ such that,

$$((m^*, c_1^*, hk_1^*, h_1^*, \mathsf{R}^*), \widetilde{w}) \in R_5.$$

By an argument similar to the one presented in Lemma 3, it follows that except with negligible probability $\widetilde{w} = sk_{\mathsf{PKE}}$. Consequently, (i) $\mathsf{PKE.Dec}(sk_{PKE}, c_1^*) = (\sigma^*, vk^*)$, (ii) due to the somewhere perfectly binding property of SPB, there exists $\mathsf{VK}^* = (vk^*, pk^*, \rho^*)$ such that $\mathsf{VK}^* \in \mathsf{R}^*$, and finally (iii) $\mathsf{Sig.Verify}(vk^*, m^*, \sigma^*)$ accepts. We conclude that the adversary uses a verification key $\mathsf{VK}^* \in \mathsf{R}^*$ and that c_1^* encrypts (among other things) a signature σ^* that is valid for the forgery message m^* w.r.t. key vk^*. Since index j is chosen uniformly at random, $vk_j = vk^*$ with probability $1/Q$.

Lemma 3 and Lemma 4 show that any efficient adversary has negligible chance of winning the RS−FORGE game in hybrid H_1. We observe that winning the RS−FORGE game is an event that can be efficiently tested, therefore, by Lemma 2 no efficient adversary can win the RS−FORGE game in hybrid H_0, i.e., Construction 3 is unforgeable.

5.3   Anonymity

We now prove that our construction satisfies anonymity. Recall that this corresponds to an experiment where the adversary recieves the secret keys and randomness of all the existing parties, and then recieves a challenge signature created using the keys of one of two possible parties (of course, the challenge ring may also include parties that were created by the adversary). Our task is to show that the adversary cannot distinguish between a signature created by party i_0 and one created by party i_1 (for any distinct i_0, i_1). We will do this using a sequence of hybrids. Our strategy will be roughly as follows: we start with a signature produced using the signing key of party i_0. First, we switch

c_2 to valid encryptions of a signature under vk_{i_1} (along with vk_{i_1}) and hk_2 to a valid SPB hash key to the index for VK_{i_1} in the ring respectively. Next, we switch the witness used in π to use these values (instead of c_1 and hk_1). Then, we change c_1 to valid encryption of a signature under vk_{i_1} and a valid SPB hash key to the index for VK_{i_1} in the ring respectively. Finally, we change c_2 to a junk ciphertext, as in the honest signing algorithm. The final hybrid just outputs a signature using the keys for party i_1, and thus we only have to show that the adversary cannot detect any of the individual changes outlined above.

Theorem 9. *Assume* PKE *has close to uniform ciphertexts and sparse valid public keys as described in Definition 3,* SPB *is index hiding, and* ZAP *is statistically witness indistinguishable. Then the ring signature scheme in Construction 3 satisfies the anonymity property described in Definition 7.*

Proof. Let $\mathcal{A}$ be a PPT adversary participating in the anonymity game. Let $Q = \text{poly}(\lambda)$ be an upper bound on the number of key queries made by $\mathcal{A}$. Suppose that the adversary's eventual challenge is $(\mathsf{R}, m, i_0, i_1)$. Let t_0, t_1 be the indices of VK_{i_0}, VK_{i_1} in R respectively. Denote by ρ the ZAP first message corresponding to the lexicographically smallest VK in R. As pointed out, it suffices to show that a signature prepared using SK_{i_0} is indistinguishable from one prepared using SK_{i_1}, even when $\mathcal{A}$ has all the keys $\mathsf{VK}_1, \cdots, \mathsf{VK}_Q$ and the randomness used in creating them. We do so using the following hybrids:

Hybrid H_0: This hybrid simply runs the anonymity game honestly as the challenger, and sends an honest signature generated using SK_{i_0}, namely $\Sigma = (c_1, hk_1, c_2, hk_2, \pi)$, as the challenge to the adversary.

Hybrid H_1: The only change in this hybrid is that it samples hk_2 in the signature with index t_1, i.e. $(hk_2, shk_2) \leftarrow \mathsf{SPB.Gen}(1^\lambda, |\mathsf{R}|, t_1)$.

Hybrid H_2: The only difference between this hybrid and H_1 is that here, instead of sampling c_2 uniformly from the PKE ciphertext space, it generates c_2 as $c_2 \leftarrow \mathsf{PKE.Enc}(pk_{i_1}, (\sigma', vk_{i_1}); r_{c_2})$, where, $\sigma' \leftarrow \mathsf{Sig.Sign}(sk_{i_1}, m)$.

Hybrid H_3: This hybrid works exactly like the previous one, except that it uses a witness corresponding to (c_2, hk_2) to generate the proof π. Namely, it computes witness $w' = (vk_{i_2}, pk_{i_2}, t_1, \tau'_2, \sigma', r_{c_2})$, where, $\tau'_2 = \mathsf{SPB.Open}(hk_2, shk_2, \mathsf{R}, t_1)$, and proof π is generated as $\pi \leftarrow \mathsf{ZAP.P}(\rho, x, w')$.

Hybrid H_4: This hybrid is similar to H_3, except that it now computes c_1 by sampling it uniformly from the ciphertext space of PKE.

Hybrid H_5: This hybrid works exactly like the previous, with the only difference being that it generates hk_1 with respect to index t_1, i.e., $(hk_1, shk_1) \leftarrow \mathsf{SPB.Gen}(1^\lambda, |\mathsf{R}|, t_1)$.

Hybrid H_6: It is identical to H_5, except that here, $c_1 \leftarrow \mathsf{PKE.Enc}(pk_{i_1}, (\sigma', vk_{i_1}); r_{c_1})$ where $\sigma' \leftarrow \mathsf{Sig.Sign}(sk_{i_1}, m)$.

Hybrid H_7: The only change in this hybrid is that, it uses a witness corresponding to (c_1, hk_1) to generate the ZAP proof. Namely, it computes $w'' = (vk, pk, t_1, \tau_1', \sigma, r_{c_1},)$, where $\tau_1' = \mathsf{SPB.Open}(hk_1, shk_1, \mathsf{R}, t_1)$, and $\pi = \mathsf{ZAP.P}(\rho, x, w'')$, and uses this in Σ.

Hybrid H_8: This hybrids works exactly like the previous, except that it now computes c_2 by sampling it uniformly from the ciphertext space of Enc. Notice that this hybrid corresponds to generating the signature using SK_{i_1}.

Lemma 5. *Assuming* SPB *is index hiding,* $H_0 \overset{c}{\approx} H_1$.

Proof. Let $\mathcal{A}$ be an adversary attempting to distinguish H_0 and H_1. We use $\mathcal{A}$ to build an adversary $\mathcal{A}'$ having the same advantage against the index hiding property of SPB. $\mathcal{A}'$ runs $\mathcal{A}$ and interacts with it exactly like H_0, till the point where $\mathcal{A}$ sends its challenge $(\mathsf{R}, m, i_0, i_1)$. At this point, $\mathcal{A}'$ sends $(t_0, t_1, |\mathsf{R}|)$ to its index hiding challenger. $\mathcal{A}'$ then receives a SPB hash key hk^*, which is either $\mathsf{SPB.Gen}(1^\lambda, |\mathsf{R}|, t_0)$ or $\mathsf{SPB.Gen}(1^\lambda, |\mathsf{R}|, t_1)$. It uses hk^* as the key hk_2 for generating the challenge signature Σ for $\mathcal{A}$. If hk^* is generated for index t_0 then $\mathcal{A}$'s view is identical to its view in H_0. Otherwise, if hk^* corresponds to t_1, $\mathcal{A}$'s view is identical to its view in H_1.

Lemma 6. *If* PKE *has close to uniform ciphertexts,* $H_1 \overset{s}{\approx} H_2$.

Proof. This follows directly from the definition of close to uniform ciphertexts property described in Definition 3.

Lemma 7. *If* ZAP *is statistically witness indistinguishable, and* PKE *has sparse valid public keys,* $H_2 \overset{s}{\approx} H_3$.

Proof. At least two of the public-keys in R, pk_{i_0} and pk_{i_1} are generated uniformly at random. Consequently, since PKE has sparse valid public keys, except with negligible probability,

$$\nexists sk : (\forall (vk, pk, \rho) \in \mathsf{R} : \mathsf{PKE.Valid}(pk, sk) \text{ accepts }).$$

Thus, $x_1 \notin \widetilde{L}$, and consequently, the lemma follows from the definition of witness indistinguishability described in Definition 3.

Lemma 8. *If* PKE *has close to uniform ciphertexts,* $H_3 \overset{s}{\approx} H_4$.

Proof. This follows directly from the definition of close to uniform ciphertexts property described in Definition 3.

Lemma 9. *Assuming* SPB *is index hiding,* $H_4 \overset{c}{\approx} H_5$.

Proof. The proof of the lemma is almost identical to Lemma 5.

Lemma 10. *If* PKE *has close to uniform ciphertexts,* $H_5 \overset{s}{\approx} H_6$.

Proof. This follows directly from the definition of close to uniform ciphertexts property described in Definition 3.

Lemma 11. *If* ZAP *is statistically witness indistinguishable, and* PKE *has sparse valid public keys,* $H_6 \overset{s}{\approx} H_7$.

Proof. The proof for this lemma is very similar to Lemma 5.3 and we won't repeat it.

Lemma 12. *If* PKE *has close to uniform ciphertexts,* $H_7 \overset{s}{\approx} H_8$.

Proof. This follows directly from the definition of close to uniform ciphertexts property described in Definition 3.

This completes the proof of Definition 9.

Acknowledgments. We thank anonymous reviewers for pointing out issues in Definition 4 and Definition 8 in an earlier version of this work.

Omkant Pandey is supported in part by DARPA SIEVE Award HR00112020026, NSF grants 1907908 and 2028920, and a Cisco Research Award.

Sanjam Garg is supported in part by DARPA under Agreement No. HR00112020026, AFOSR Award FA9550-19-1-0200, NSF CNS Award 1936826, and research grants by the Sloan Foundation and Visa Inc.

Any opinions, findings and conclusions or recommendations expressed in this material are those of the author(s) and do not necessarily reflect the views of the United States Government, DARPA, AFOSR, NSF, Cisco, Sloan Foundation, or Visa Inc.

Dakshita Khurana is supported in part by DARPA SIEVE Award HR00112020024.

References

1. Abe, M., Ohkubo, M., Suzuki, K.: 1-out-of-n signatures from a variety of keys. In: Zheng, Y. (ed.) ASIACRYPT 2002. LNCS, vol. 2501, pp. 415–432. Springer, Heidelberg (2002). https://doi.org/10.1007/3-540-36178-2_26
2. Backes, M., Döttling, N., Hanzlik, L., Kluczniak, K., Schneider, J.: Ring signatures: logarithmic-size, no setup—from standard assumptions. In: Ishai, Y., Rijmen, V. (eds.) EUROCRYPT 2019. LNCS, vol. 11478, pp. 281–311. Springer, Cham (2019). https://doi.org/10.1007/978-3-030-17659-4_10
3. Backes, M., Hanzlik, L., Kluczniak, K., Schneider, J.: Signatures with flexible public key: introducing equivalence classes for public keys. In: Peyrin, T., Galbraith, S. (eds.) ASIACRYPT 2018. LNCS, vol. 11273, pp. 405–434. Springer, Cham (2018). https://doi.org/10.1007/978-3-030-03329-3_14
4. Badrinarayanan, S., Fernando, R., Jain, A., Khurana, D., Sahai, A.: Statistical ZAP arguments. In: Canteaut, A., Ishai, Y. (eds.) EUROCRYPT 2020. LNCS, vol. 12107, pp. 642–667. Springer, Cham (2020). https://doi.org/10.1007/978-3-030-45727-3_22
5. Baum, C., Lin, H., Oechsner, S.: Towards practical lattice-based one-time linkable ring signatures. In: ICICS, pp. 303–322 (2018)

6. Bender, A., Katz, J., Morselli, R.: Ring signatures: stronger definitions, and constructions without random Oracles. In: TCC, pp. 60–79 (2006)
7. Beullens, W., Katsumata, S., Pintore, F.: Calamari and Falafl: logarithmic (linkable) ring signatures from isogenies and lattices. In: Moriai, S., Wang, H. (eds.) ASIACRYPT 2020. LNCS, vol. 12492, pp. 464–492. Springer, Cham (2020). https://doi.org/10.1007/978-3-030-64834-3_16
8. Blum, M.: How to prove a theorem so no one else can claim it. In: Proceedings of the International Congress of Mathematicians, pp. 1444–1451 (1987)
9. Boneh, D., Gentry, C., Lynn, B., Shacham, H.: Aggregate and verifiably encrypted signatures from bilinear maps. In: Biham, E. (ed.) EUROCRYPT 2003. LNCS, vol. 2656, pp. 416–432. Springer, Heidelberg (2003). https://doi.org/10.1007/3-540-39200-9_26
10. Boyen, X., Haines, T.: Forward-secure linkable ring signatures. In: ACISP, pp. 245–264 (2018)
11. Brakerski, Z., Döttling, N.: Two-message statistically sender-private OT from LWE. In: TCC, pp. 370–390 (2018)
12. Brakerski, Z., Kalai, Y.T.: A framework for efficient signatures, ring signatures and identity based encryption in the standard model. Cryptology ePrint Archive, Report 2010/086 (2010). https://eprint.iacr.org/2010/086
13. Brakerski, Z., Langlois, A., Peikert, C., Regev, O., Stehlé, D.: Classical hardness of learning with errors. In: STOC, pp. 575–584 (2013)
14. Canetti, R., et al.: Fiat-Shamir: from practice to theory. In: STOC (2019, to appear)
15. Chandran, N., Groth, J., Sahai, A.: Ring signatures of sub-linear size without random Oracles. In: ICALP, pp. 423–434 (2007)
16. Chow, S.S.M., Wei, V.K., Liu, J.K., Yuen, T.H.: Ring signatures without random Oracles. In: ASIACCS, pp. 297–302 (2006)
17. Dodis, Y., Kiayias, A., Nicolosi, A., Shoup, V.: Anonymous identification in Ad Hoc groups. In: Cachin, C., Camenisch, J.L. (eds.) EUROCRYPT 2004. LNCS, vol. 3027, pp. 609–626. Springer, Heidelberg (2004). https://doi.org/10.1007/978-3-540-24676-3_36
18. Dwork, C., Naor, M.: Zaps and their applications. SIAM J. Comput. 36(6), 1513–1543 (2007)
19. Esgin, M.F., Zhao, R.K., Steinfeld, R., Liu, J.K., Liu, D.: Matrict: efficient, scalable and post-quantum blockchain confidential transactions protocol. In: CCS, pp. 567–584 (2019)
20. Fiat, A., Shamir, A.: How to prove yourself: practical solutions to identification and signature problems. In: Odlyzko, A.M. (ed.) CRYPTO 1986. LNCS, vol. 263, pp. 186–194. Springer, Heidelberg (1987). https://doi.org/10.1007/3-540-47721-7_12
21. Gentry, C.: A fully homomorphic encryption scheme. Ph.D. thesis, Stanford University (2009). http://crypto.stanford.edu/craig
22. Gentry, C., Peikert, C., Vaikuntanathan, V.: Trapdoors for hard lattices and new cryptographic constructions. In: STOC, pp. 197–206 (2008)
23. Ghadafi, E.: Sub-linear blind ring signatures without random Oracles. In: IMACC, pp. 304–323 (2013)
24. González, A.: A ring signature of size $\Theta(\sqrt[3]{n})$ without random oracles (2017). https://eprint.iacr.org/2017/905
25. Goyal, V., Jain, A., Jin, Z., Malavolta, G.: Statistical zaps and new oblivious transfer protocols. In: Canteaut, A., Ishai, Y. (eds.) EUROCRYPT 2020. LNCS, vol. 12107, pp. 668–699. Springer, Cham (2020). https://doi.org/10.1007/978-3-030-45727-3_23

26. Groth, J., Kohlweiss, M.: One-out-of-many proofs: or how to leak a secret and spend a coin. In: Oswald, E., Fischlin, M. (eds.) EUROCRYPT 2015. LNCS, vol. 9057, pp. 253–280. Springer, Heidelberg (2015). https://doi.org/10.1007/978-3-662-46803-6_9

27. Herranz, J., Sáez, G.: Forking lemmas for ring signature schemes. In: Johansson, T., Maitra, S. (eds.) INDOCRYPT 2003. LNCS, vol. 2904, pp. 266–279. Springer, Heidelberg (2003). https://doi.org/10.1007/978-3-540-24582-7_20

28. Libert, B., Ling, S., Nguyen, K., Wang, H.: Zero-knowledge arguments for lattice-based accumulators: logarithmic-size ring signatures and group signatures without trapdoors. In: Fischlin, M., Coron, J.-S. (eds.) EUROCRYPT 2016. LNCS, vol. 9666, pp. 1–31. Springer, Heidelberg (2016). https://doi.org/10.1007/978-3-662-49896-5_1

29. Libert, B., Peters, T., Qian, C.: Logarithmic-size ring signatures with tight security from the DDH assumption. In: ESORICS, pp. 288–308 (2018)

30. Libert, B., Nguyen, K., Peters, T., Yung, M.: One-shot fiat-shamir-based nizk arguments of composite residuosity in the standard model. Cryptology ePrint Archive, Report 2020/1334 (2020). https://eprint.iacr.org/2020/1334

31. Lombardi, A., Vaikuntanathan, V., Wichs, D.: 2-message publicly verifiable WI from (subexponential) LWE. Cryptology ePrint Archive, Report 2019/808, p. 808 (2019). https://eprint.iacr.org/2019/808

32. Lyubashevsky, V., Nguyen, N.K., Seiler, G.: SMILE: set membership from ideal lattices with applications to ring signatures and confidential transactions. In: CRYPTO (2021, to appear)

33. Malavolta, G., Schröder, D.: Efficient ring signatures in the standard model. In: Takagi, T., Peyrin, T. (eds.) ASIACRYPT 2017. LNCS, vol. 10625, pp. 128–157. Springer, Cham (2017). https://doi.org/10.1007/978-3-319-70697-9_5

34. Merkle, R.C.: A digital signature based on a conventional encryption function. In: Pomerance, C. (ed.) CRYPTO 1987. LNCS, vol. 293, pp. 369–378. Springer, Heidelberg (1988). https://doi.org/10.1007/3-540-48184-2_32

35. Micciancio, D.: Duality in lattice cryptography. In: Public Key Cryptography (2010). Invited talk

36. Naor, M., Yung, M.: Public-key cryptosystems provably secure against chosen ciphertext attacks. In: STOC, pp. 427–437 (1990)

37. Noether, S.: Ring signature confidential transactions for monero (2015). https://eprint.iacr.org/2015/1098

38. Ostrovsky, R., Paskin-Cherniavsky, A., Paskin-Cherniavsky, B.: Maliciously circuit-private FHE. In: Garay, J.A., Gennaro, R. (eds.) CRYPTO 2014. LNCS, vol. 8616, pp. 536–553. Springer, Heidelberg (2014). https://doi.org/10.1007/978-3-662-44371-2_30

39. Park, S., Sealfon, A.: It wasn't me! - repudiability and claimability of ring signatures. In: Boldyreva, A., Micciancio, D. (eds.) CRYPTO 2019. LNCS, vol. 11694, pp. 159–190. Springer, Cham (2019). https://doi.org/10.1007/978-3-030-26954-8_6

40. Peikert, C.: Public-key cryptosystems from the worst-case shortest vector problem. In: STOC, pp. 333–342 (2009)

41. Peikert, C., Regev, O., Stephens-Davidowitz, N.: Pseudorandomness of Ring-LWE for any ring and modulus. In: STOC, pp. 461–473 (2017)

42. Peikert, C., Shiehian, S.: Noninteractive zero knowledge for NP from (plain) learning with errors. In: Boldyreva, A., Micciancio, D. (eds.) CRYPTO 2019. LNCS, vol. 11692, pp. 89–114. Springer, Cham (2019). https://doi.org/10.1007/978-3-030-26948-7_4

43. Regev, O.: On lattices, learning with errors, random linear codes, and cryptography. J. ACM **56**(6), 1–40 (2009). Preliminary version in STOC 2005
44. Rivest, R.L., Shamir, A., Tauman, Y.: How to leak a secret. In: Boyd, C. (ed.) ASIACRYPT 2001. LNCS, vol. 2248, pp. 552–565. Springer, Heidelberg (2001). https://doi.org/10.1007/3-540-45682-1_32
45. Schäge, S., Schwenk, J.: A CDH-based ring signature scheme with short signatures and public keys. In: Financial Cryptography and Data Security, pp. 129–142 (2010)
46. Shacham, H., Waters, B.: Efficient ring signatures without random oracles. In: PKC, pp. 166–180 (2007)
47. Alberto Torres, W.A., et al.: Post-quantum one-time linkable ring signature and application to ring confidential transactions in blockchain (Lattice RingCT v1.0). In: Susilo, W., Yang, G. (eds.) ACISP 2018. LNCS, vol. 10946, pp. 558–576. Springer, Cham (2018). https://doi.org/10.1007/978-3-319-93638-3_32

Quantum Cryptography

A Black-Box Approach to Post-Quantum Zero-Knowledge in Constant Rounds

Nai-Hui Chia[1,2(✉)], Kai-Min Chung[3], and Takashi Yamakawa[4]

[1] QuICS, University of Maryland, College Park, USA
naichia@iu.edu
[2] Luddy School of Informatics, Computing, and Engineering, Indiana University,
Bloomington, USA
[3] Institute of Information Science, Academia Sinica, Taiwan, China
kmchung@iis.sinica.edu.tw
[4] NTT Secure Platform Laboratories, Tokyo, Japan
takashi.yamakawa.ga@hco.ntt.co.jp

Abstract. In a recent seminal work, Bitansky and Shmueli (STOC '20) gave the first construction of a constant round zero-knowledge argument for **NP** secure against quantum attacks. However, their construction has several drawbacks compared to the classical counterparts. Specifically, their construction only achieves computational soundness, requires strong assumptions of quantum hardness of learning with errors (QLWE assumption) and the existence of quantum fully homomorphic encryption (QFHE), and relies on non-black-box simulation.

In this paper, we resolve these issues at the cost of weakening the notion of zero-knowledge to what is called ε-zero-knowledge. Concretely, we construct the following protocols:

– We construct a constant round interactive proof for **NP** that satisfies *statistical* soundness and *black-box* ε-zero-knowledge against quantum attacks assuming the existence of *collapsing hash functions*, which is a quantum counterpart of collision-resistant hash functions. Interestingly, this construction is just an adapted version of the classical protocol by Goldreich and Kahan (JoC '96) though the proof of ε-zero-knowledge property against quantum adversaries requires novel ideas.

– We construct a constant round interactive argument for **NP** that satisfies computational soundness and *black-box* ε-zero-knowledge against quantum attacks only assuming the existence of post-quantum one-way functions.

At the heart of our results is a new quantum rewinding technique that enables a simulator to extract a committed message of a malicious verifier while simulating verifier's internal state in an appropriate sense.

1 Introduction

Zero-Knowledge Proof. Zero-knowledge (ZK) proof [GMR89] is a fundamental cryptographic primitive, which enables a prover to convince a verifier of a

T. Malkin and C. Peikert (Eds.): CRYPTO 2021, LNCS 12825, pp. 315–345, 2021.
https://doi.org/10.1007/978-3-030-84242-0_12

statement without giving any additional "knowledge" beyond that the statement is true. In the classical setting, there have been many feasibility results on ZK proofs for specific languages including quadratic residuosity [GMR89], graph isomorphism [GMW91], statistical difference problem [SV03] etc., and for all **NP** languages assuming the existence of one-way functions (OWFs) [GMW91,Blu86]. On the other hand, van de Graaf [Gra97] pointed out that there is a technical difficulty to prove security of these protocols against quantum attacks. Roughly, the difficulty comes from the fact that security proofs of these results are based on a technique called *rewinding*, which cannot be done when an adversary is quantum due to the no-cloning theorem. Watrous [Wat09] considered *post-quantum ZK proof*, which means a classical interactive proof that satisfies (computational) zero-knowledge property against quantum malicious verifiers, and showed that some of the classical constructions above are also post-quantum ZK. Especially, he introduced a new *quantum rewinding technique* which is also applicable to quantum adversaries and proved that 3-coloring protocol of Goldreich, Micali, and Wigderson [GMW91] is secure against quantum attacks assuming that the underlying OWF is post-quantum secure, i.e., uninvertible in quantum polynomial-time (QPT).[1] Since the 3-coloring problem is **NP**-complete, this means that there exists a post-quantum ZK proof for all **NP** languages assuming the existence of post-quantum OWFs.

Round Complexity. An important complexity measure of ZK proofs is *round complexity*, which is the number of interactions between a prover and verifier. In this aspect, the 3-coloring protocol [GMW91] (and its quantumly secure version [Wat09]) is not satisfactory since that requires super-constant number of rounds.[2] Goldreich and Kahan [GK96] gave the first construction of a constant round ZK proof for **NP** assuming the existence of collision-resistant hash function in the classical setting. However, Watrous' rewinding technique does not seem to work for this construction (as explained in Sect. 1.2), and it has been unknown if their protocol is secure against quantum attacks.

Recently, Bitansky and Shmueli [BS20] gave the first construction of post-quantum ZK *argument* [BC90] for **NP**, which is a weakened version of post-quantum ZK proof where soundness holds only against computationally bounded adversaries. In addition to weakening soundness to computational one, there are several drawbacks compared to classical counterparts. First, they assume strong assumptions of quantum hardness of learning with erros (QLWE assumption) [Reg09] and the existence of quantum fully homomorphic encryption (QFHE)

---

[1] Strictly speaking, Watrous' assumption is a statistically binding and post-quantum computationally hiding commitment scheme, and he did not claim that this can be constructed under the existence of post-quantum OWFs. However, we can see that such a commitment scheme can be obtained by instantiating the construction of [Nao91,HILL99] with a post-quantum OWF.

[2] 3-round suffices for achieving a constant soundness error, but super-constant times sequential repetitions are needed for achieving negligible soundness error (i.e., a cheating prover can let a verifier accept on a false statement only with a negligible probability). Negligible soundness error is a default requirement in this paper.

[Mah18a, Bra18]. Though the QLWE assumption is considered fairly standard due to reductions to worst-case lattice problems [Reg09, Pei09, BLP13], a construction of QFHE requires circular security of an QLWE-based encryption scheme, which has no theoretical evidence. In contrast, a constant round *classical* ZK argument for **NP** is known to exist under the minimal assumption of the existence of OWFs [FS90, PW09]. Second, their security proof of quantum ZK property relies on a novel *non-black-box* simulation technique, which makes use of the actual description of malicious verifier instead of using it as a black-box. In contrast, classical counterparts can be obtained by black-box simulation [FS90, GK96, PW09]. Therefore, it is of theoretical interest to ask if we can achieve constant round quantum ZK by black-box simulation. Third, somewhat related to the second issue, their construction also uses building blocks in a non-black-box manner, which makes the actual efficiency of the protocol far from practical. Again, classical counterparts are known based on black-box constructions [GK96, PW09].

Given the state of affairs, it is natural to ask the following questions:

1. Are there constant round post-quantum ZK proofs for **NP** instead of arguments?
2. Are there constant round post-quantum ZK proofs/arguments for **NP** from weaker assumptions than those in [BS20]?
3. Are there constant round post-quantum ZK proofs/arguments for **NP** based on black-box simulation and/or black-box construction?
4. Are known constructions of constant round classical ZK proofs/arguments for **NP** (e.g., [FS90, GK96, PW09]) secure against quantum attacks if we instantiate them with post-quantum building blocks?

1.1 Our Results

In this work, we partially answer the above questions affirmatively at the cost of weakening the quantum ZK property to *quantum ϵ-ZK*, which is the quantum version of ϵ-ZK introduced in [DNS04].[3]

Quantum ϵ-Zero-Knowledge. The standard quantum ZK property roughly requires that for any QPT V^*, there exists a QPT simulator $\mathcal{S}$ that simulates the interaction between V^* and an honest prover so that the simulation is indistinguishable from the real execution against any QPT distinguishers. On the other hand, in quantum ϵ-ZK, a simulator is allowed to depend on a "accuracy parameter" ϵ. That is, it requires that for any QPT malicious verifier V^* and a noticeable accuracy parameter ϵ, there exists a QPT simulator $\mathcal{S}$ *whose running time polynomially depends on* ϵ^{-1} that simulates the interaction between V^* and an honest prover so that no QPT distinguisher can distinguish it from real execution with advantage larger than ϵ. Though this is a significant relaxation of quantum ZK, this still captures meaningful security. For example, we can see

---

[3] ϵ-ZK was originally called ϵ-knowledge, but some later works [BKP18, FGJ18] call it ϵ-ZK. We use ϵ-ZK to clarify that this is a variant of ZK.

that quantum ϵ-ZK implies both quantum versions of witness indistinguishability and witness hiding similarly to the analogous claims in the classical setting [BKP19].[4] Moreover, by extending the observation in [DNS04] to the quantum setting, we can see the following: Suppose that a QPT malicious verifier solves some puzzle whose solution is efficiently checkable (e.g., finding a witness of an NP statement) after an interaction between an honest prover. Then, quantum ϵ-ZK implies that if the verifier succeeds in solving the puzzle with noticeable probability p after the interaction, then there is a QPT algorithm (whose running time polynomially depends on p^{-1}) that solves the same puzzle with noticeable probability (say, $p/2$) *without interacting with the honest prover*. This captures the naive intuition of the ZK property that "anything that can be done after the execution can be done without execution" in some sense, and this would be sufficient in many cryptographic applications. Thus we believe that quantum ϵ-ZK is conceptually a similar notion to the standard quantum ZK. More discussion on (quantum) ϵ-ZK and other related notions of ZK can be found in Sect. 1.3.

Our Constructions. We give two constructions of constant round quantum ϵ-ZK protocols.

– We construct a constant round quantum ϵ-ZK *proof* for NP assuming the existence of *collapsing hash functions* [Unr16b, Unr16a], which is considered as a counterpart of collision-resistant hash functions in the quantum setting. Especially, we can instantiate the construction based on the QLWE assumption. Our construction is fully black-box in the sense that both simulation and construction rely on black-box usage of building blocks and a malicious verifier. Interestingly, this construction is just an adapted version of the classical protocol of [GK96] though the proof of quantum ϵ-zero-knowledge property requires novel ideas.
– We construct a constant round quantum ϵ-ZK argument for NP assuming the minimal assumption of the existence of *post-quantum OWFs*. This construction relies on black-box simulation, but the construction itself is non-black-box.

At the heart of our results is a new quantum rewinding technique that enables a simulator to extract a committed message of a malicious verifier while simulating verifier's internal state in some sense. We formalize this technique as an *extraction lemma*, which we believe is of independent interest.

1.2 Technical Overview

Though we prove a general lemma which we call extraction lemma (Lemma 3.1) and then prove quantum ϵ-ZK of our constructions based on that in the main body, we directly explain the proof of quantum ϵ-ZK without going through such an abstraction in this overview.

---

[4] Actually, [BKP19] shows that even weaker notion called *weak ZK* suffices for witness indistinguishability and witness hiding. See also Sect. 1.3.

Known Classical Technique and Difficulty in Quantum Setting. First, we review a classical constant round ZK proof by Goldreich and Kahan [GK96] (referred to as GK protocol in the following), and explain why it is difficult to prove quantum ZK for this protocol by known techniques. GK protocol is based on a special type of 3-round proof system called Σ-protocol.[5] In a Σ-protocol, a prover sends the first message a, a verifier sends the second message e referred to as a *challenge*, which is just a public randomness, and the prover sends the third message z. A Σ-protocol satisfies a special type of honest-verifier ZK, which ensures that if a challenge e is fixed, then one can simulate the transcript (a, e, z) without using a witness. Though this may sound like almost the standard ZK property, a difficulty when proving ZK is that a malicious verifier may *adaptively* choose e depending on a, and thus we cannot fix e at the beginning. To resolve this issue, the idea of GK protocol is to let the verifier commit to a challenge e at the beginning of the protocol. That is, GK protocol roughly proceeds as follows:[6]

1. A verifier sends a commitment com to a challenge e of a Σ-protocol.
2. The prover sends the first message a of the Σ-protocol.
3. The verifier opens com to open a challenge e and its opening information r (i.e., the randomness used for the commitment).
4. The prover aborts if the verifier's opening is invalid. Otherwise it sends the third message z of the Σ-protocol.

When proving the ZK property of GK protocol, they rely on a *rewinding* argument. That is, a simulator first runs the protocol with a malicious verifier until Step 3 to extract a committed message e inside com, and then rewind the verifier's state back to just after Step 1, and then simulates the transcript by using the extracted knowledge of e.

On the other hand, this strategy does not work if we consider a quantum malicious verifier since a quantum malicious verifier may perform measurements in Step 3, which is in general not reversible. In other words, since we cannot copy the verifier's internal state after Step 1 due to the no-cloning theorem, we cannot recover that state after running the protocol until Step 3.

Watrous [Wat09] proved that we can apply a rewinding argument for quantum verifiers under a certain condition. Roughly speaking, the condition is that there is a simulator that succeeds in simulation for quantum verifiers with a fixed (verifier-independent) and noticeable probability. For example, if the challenge space is polynomial size, then a simulator that simply guesses a challenge e suffices. However, for achieving negligible soundness error, the challenge space should be super-polynomial size, in which case it seems difficult to construct such a simulator. Also, relaxing quantum ZK to quantum ϵ-ZK does not seem to resolve the issue in any obvious way.

---

[5] In this paper, we use Σ-protocol to mean a parallel repetition version where soundness error is reduced to negligible.

[6] We note that this construction is based on an earlier work of [BCY91].

Quantum Analysis of GK Protocol. In spite of the above mentioned difficulty, we succeed in proving quantum ϵ-ZK for a slight variant of GK protocol. In the following, we explain the idea for our results.

Simplified Goal: Simulation of Non-Aborting Case. First, we apply a general trick introduced in [BS20], which simplifies the task of proving quantum ZK. In GK protocol, we say that a verifier aborts if it fails to provide a valid opening to com in Step 3. Then, for proving quantum ZK of the protocol, it suffices to construct two simulators $\mathsf{Sim_a}$ and $\mathsf{Sim_{na}}$ that work only when the verifier aborts and does not abort and they do not change the probability that the verifier aborts too much, respectively. The reason is that if we randomly choose either of these two simulators and just run the chosen one, then the simulation succeeds with probability $1/2$ since the guess of if the verifier aborts is correct with probability $1/2$. Then, we can apply Watrous' rewinding technique to convert it to a full-fledged simulator. Essentially the same trick also works for quantum ϵ-ZK.

Moreover, it is easy to construct $\mathsf{Sim_a}$ because the first message of a Σ-protocol can be simulated without witness, and one need not provide the third message to the verifier when it aborts. Therefore, the problem boils down to constructing a simulator $\mathsf{Sim_{na}}$ that works only when the verifier does not abort.

Initial Observations. For explaining how to construct $\mathsf{Sim_{na}}$, we start by considering the simplest case where a verifier never aborts. Moreover, suppose that the commitment scheme used for committing to a challenge e satisfies the strict-binding property [Unr12], i.e., for any commitment com, there is at most one valid message and randomness. Then, a rewinding strategy similar to the classical case works since, in this case, the verifier's message in Step 3 is information-theoretically determined, and such a deterministic computation does not collapse a quantum state in general.[7] However, for ensuring statistical soundness, we have to use a statistically hiding commitment, which cannot be strict-binding. Fortunately, this problem can be resolved by using *collapse-binding* commitments [Unr16b], which roughly behave similarly to strict-binding commitments for any *computationally bounded* adversaries.[8] Since this is rather a standard technique, in the rest of this overview, we treat the commitment as if it satisfies the strict-binding property.

Next, we consider another toy example where a verifier sometimes aborts. Suppose that a malicious verifier V^* is given an initial state $\frac{1}{\sqrt{2}}(|\psi_a\rangle + |\psi_{na}\rangle)$ in its internal register $\mathbf{V}$ where $|\psi_a\rangle$ and $|\psi_{na}\rangle$ are orthogonal, and runs as follows:

1. V^* randomly picks e, honestly generates a commitment com to e, and sends it to the prover (just ignoring the initial state).

---

[7] This is also observed in [BS20].

[8] Strictly speaking, we need to use a slightly stronger variant of collapse-binding commitments which we call *strong collapse-binding* commitments. Such commitments can be constructed under the QLWE assumption or the existence of collapsing hash functions in more general. See Sect. 2.2 for more details.

2. After receiving a, V^* performs a projective measurement $\{|\psi_{\mathsf{a}}\rangle \langle\psi_{\mathsf{a}}| , I - |\psi_{\mathsf{a}}\rangle \langle\psi_{\mathsf{a}}|\}$ on $\mathbf{V}$, and immediately aborts if $|\psi_{\mathsf{a}}\rangle \langle\psi_{\mathsf{a}}|$ is applied, and otherwise honestly opens (e, r).

3. After completing the protocol, V^* outputs its internal state in $\mathbf{V}$.

It is trivial to construct a simulator for this particular V^* since it just ignores prover's messages. But for explaining our main idea, we examine what happens if we apply the same rewinding strategy as the classical case to the above verifier. After getting a commitment com from V^*, a simulator sends a random a to V^* to extract e. Since we are interested in constructing a simulator that works in the non-aborting case, suppose that V^* does not abort, i.e., sends back a valid opening (e, r). At this point, V^*'s internal state collapses to $|\psi_{\mathsf{na}}\rangle$. Then the simulator cannot "rewind" this state to the original verifier's state $\frac{1}{\sqrt{2}}(|\psi_{\mathsf{a}}\rangle + |\psi_{\mathsf{na}}\rangle)$ in general, and thus the simulation seems to get stuck. However, our key observation is that, conditioned on that V^* does not abort, V^*'s state always collapses to $|\psi_{\mathsf{na}}\rangle$ even in the real execution. Since our goal is to construct $\mathsf{Sim}_{\mathsf{na}}$ that is only required to work for the non-aborting case, it does not matter if V^*'s state collapses to $|\psi_{\mathsf{na}}\rangle$ when the simulator runs extraction. More generally, extraction procedure may collapse verifier's internal state if a similar collapsing happens even in the real execution conditioned on that the verifier does not abort.

Our Idea: Decompose Verifier's Space. To generalize the above idea, we want to decompose verifier's internal state after Step 1 into *aborting part* and *non-aborting part*. However, the definition of such a decomposition is non-trivial since a verifier may determine if it aborts depending on the prover's message a in addition to its internal state. Therefore, instead of decomposing it into always-aborting part and always-non-aborting part as in the example of the previous paragraph, we set a noticeable threshold t and decompose it into "not-abort-with-probability $< t$ part" and "not-abort-with-probability $\geq t$ part" over the randomness of a.

For implementing this idea, we rely on Jordan's lemma (e.g., see a lecture note by Regev [AR06]) in a similar way to the work by Nagaj, Wocjan, and Zhang [NWZ09] on the amplification theorem for $\mathbf{QMA}$. Let Π be a projection that corresponds to "Step 2 + Step 3 + Check if the verifier does not abort" in GK protocol. A little bit more formally, let $\mathbf{V}$ be a register for verifier's internal state and $\mathbf{Aux}$ be an auxiliary register. Then Π is a projection over $\mathbf{V} \otimes \mathbf{Aux}$ that works as follows:

1. Apply a unitary U_{aux} over $\mathbf{Aux}$ that maps $|0\rangle_{\mathbf{Aux}}$ to $\frac{1}{\sqrt{|\mathcal{R}|}} \sum_{\mathsf{rand}\in\mathcal{R}}$ $|\mathsf{rand}, a_{\mathsf{rand}}\rangle_{\mathbf{Aux}}$ where $\mathcal{R}$ is the randomness space to generate the first message of the Σ-protocol and a_{rand} is the first message derived from the randomness rand.[9]

---

[9] $\mathbf{Aux}$ stores multiple qubits, but we denote by $|0\rangle_{\mathbf{Aux}}$ to mean $|0^{\ell}\rangle_{\mathbf{Aux}}$ for the appropriate length ℓ for notational simplicity.

2. Apply a unitary U_V that corresponds to Step 3 for prover's message a_{rand} in **Aux** except for measurement,
3. Apply a projection to the subspace spanned by states that contain valid opening (e, r) for com in designated output registers,
4. Apply $(U_V U_{\mathsf{aux}})^\dagger$.

One can see that the probability that the verifier does not abort (i.e., sends a valid opening) is $\| \Pi \, |\psi\rangle_{\mathbf{V}} \, |0\rangle_{\mathbf{Aux}} \|^2$ where $|\psi\rangle_{\mathbf{V}}$ is verifier's internal state after Step 1. Then Jordan's lemma gives an orthogonal decomposition of the Hilbert space of $\mathbf{V} \otimes \mathbf{Aux}$ into many one- or two-dimensional subspaces $S_1, ..., S_N$ that are invariant under Π and $|0\rangle_{\mathbf{Aux}} \langle 0|_{\mathbf{Aux}}$ such that we have the following:

1. For any $j \in [N]$ and $|\psi_j\rangle_{\mathbf{V}} \, |0\rangle_{\mathbf{Aux}} \in S_j$, the projection Π succeeds with probability p_j, i.e., $\| \Pi \, |\psi_j\rangle_{\mathbf{V}} \, |0\rangle_{\mathbf{Aux}} \|^2 = p_j$.
2. A success probability of projection Π is "amplifiable" in each subspace. That is, there is an "amplification procedure" Amp that maps any $|\psi_j\rangle_{\mathbf{V}} \, |0\rangle_{\mathbf{Aux}} \in S_j$ to $\Pi \, |\psi_j\rangle_{\mathbf{V}} \, |0\rangle_{\mathbf{Aux}}$ with overwhelming probability within $\mathrm{poly}(\lambda, p_j^{-1})$ times iteration of the same procedure (that does not depend on j) for any $j \in [N]$. Moreover, this procedure does not cause any interference between different subspaces.

Then we define two subspaces

$$S_{<t} := \bigoplus_{j:p_j<t} S_j, \quad S_{\geq t} := \bigoplus_{j:p_j \geq t} S_j.$$

Then for any $|\psi\rangle_{\mathbf{V}}$, we can decompose it as

$$|\psi\rangle_{\mathbf{V}} = |\psi_{<t}\rangle_{\mathbf{V}} + |\psi_{\geq t}\rangle_{\mathbf{V}}$$

by using (sub-normalized) states $|\psi_{<t}\rangle_{\mathbf{V}}$ and $|\psi_{\geq t}\rangle_{\mathbf{V}}$ such that $|\psi_{<t}\rangle_{\mathbf{V}} \, |0\rangle_{\mathbf{Aux}} \in S_{<t}$ and $|\psi_{\geq t}\rangle_{\mathbf{V}} \, |0\rangle_{\mathbf{Aux}} \in S_{\geq t}$. In this way, we can formally define a decomposition of verifier's internal state into "not-abort-with-probability $< t$ part" and "not-abort-with-probability $\geq t$ part".

Extraction and Simulation. Then we explain how we can use the above decomposition to implement extraction of e for simulation of non-aborting case. First, we consider an easier case where the verifier's state after Step 1 only has $S_{\geq t}$ component $|\psi_{\geq t}\rangle_{\mathbf{V}}$. In this case, we can use Amp to map $|\psi_{\geq t}\rangle_{\mathbf{V}} \, |0\rangle_{\mathbf{Aux}}$ onto the span of Π within $\mathrm{poly}(\lambda, t^{-1})$ times iteration. After mapped to Π, we can extract (e, r) without collapsing the state by the definition of Π and our assumption that the commitment is strict-binding. This means that given $|\psi_{\geq t}\rangle_{\mathbf{V}}$, we can extract (e, r), which is information theoretically determined by com, with overwhelming probability. In general, such a deterministic computation can be implemented in a reversible manner, and thus we can extract (e, r) from $|\psi_{\geq t}\rangle_{\mathbf{V}}$ almost without damaging the state.

On the other hand, the same procedure does not work for $|\psi_{<t}\rangle_{\mathbf{V}}$ since $\mathrm{poly}(\lambda, t^{-1})$ times iteration is not sufficient for amplifying the success probability of Π to overwhelming in this subspace. Our idea is to let a simulator run

the above extraction procedure in superposition even though $S_{<t}$ component may be damaged.

Specifically, our extraction procedure Ext works as follows:

1. Given a verifier's internal state $|\psi\rangle_\mathbf{V}$ after Step 1, initialize $\mathbf{Aux}$ to $|0\rangle_\mathbf{Aux}$ and runs Amp for $\mathsf{poly}(\lambda, t^{-1})$ times iteration. Abort if a mapping onto Π does not succeed. Otherwise, proceed to the next step.
2. Apply $U_V U_{\mathsf{aux}}$, measure designated output registers to obtain $(e_{\mathsf{Ext}}, r_{\mathsf{Ext}})$, and apply $(U_V U_{\mathsf{aux}})^\dagger$. We note that $(e_{\mathsf{Ext}}, r_{\mathsf{Ext}})$ is always a valid opening of com since Ext runs this step only if it succeeds in mapping the state onto Π in the previous step. We also note that this step does not collapse the state at all by the strict-binding property of the commitment.
3. Uncompute Step 1 and measure $\mathbf{Aux}$. Abort if the measurement outcome is not 0. Otherwise, proceed to the next step.
4. Output the extracted opening $(e_{\mathsf{Ext}}, r_{\mathsf{Ext}})$ along with a "post-extraction state" $|\psi'\rangle_\mathbf{V}$ in register $\mathbf{V}$. For convenience, we express $|\psi'\rangle_\mathbf{V}$ as a sub-normalized state whose norm is the probability that Ext does not abort and the post-extraction state conditioned on that the extraction succeeds is $\frac{|\psi'\rangle_\mathbf{V}}{\||\psi'\rangle_\mathbf{V}\|}$.

In the following, we analyze Ext. We consider the decomposition of $|\psi\rangle_\mathbf{V}$ as defined in the previous paragraph:

$$|\psi\rangle_\mathbf{V} = |\psi_{<t}\rangle_\mathbf{V} + |\psi_{\geq t}\rangle_\mathbf{V} \, .$$

Suppose that Ext does not abort, i.e., it outputs a valid opening $(e_{\mathsf{Ext}}, r_{\mathsf{Ext}})$ along with a post-extraction state $|\psi'\rangle_\mathbf{V}$. Then, $|\psi'\rangle_\mathbf{V}$ can be expressed as

$$|\psi'\rangle_\mathbf{V} = |\psi'_{<t}\rangle_\mathbf{V} + |\psi'_{\geq t}\rangle_\mathbf{V}$$

for some $|\psi'_{<t}\rangle_\mathbf{V}$ and $|\psi'_{\geq t}\rangle_\mathbf{V}$ such that $|\psi'_{<t}\rangle_\mathbf{V}|0\rangle_\mathbf{Aux} \in S_{<t}$, $|\psi'_{\geq t}\rangle_\mathbf{V}|0\rangle_\mathbf{Aux} \in S_{\geq t}$, and $|\psi_{\geq t}\rangle_\mathbf{V} \approx |\psi'_{\geq t}\rangle_\mathbf{V}$ since there is no interference between $S_{<t}$ and $S_{\geq t}$ when running Amp and $S_{\geq t}$ component hardly changes as observed above. This is not even a close state to the original state $|\psi\rangle_\mathbf{V}$ in general since the $S_{<t}$ component may be completely different. However, our key observation is that, conditioned on that the verifier does not abort, at most "t-fraction" of $S_{<t}$ component survives even in the real execution by the definition of the subspace $S_{<t}$. That is, in the verifier's final output state conditioned on that it does not abort, the average squared norm of a portion that comes from $S_{<t}$ component is at most t. Thus, even if a simulator fails to simulate this portion, this only impacts the accuracy of the simulation by a certain function of t, which is shown to be $O(t^{1/3})$ in the main body.

With this observation in mind, the non-aborting case simulator $\mathsf{Sim}_{\mathsf{na}}$ works as follows.

1. Run Step 1 of the verifier to obtain com and let $|\psi\rangle_\mathbf{V}$ be verifier's internal state at this point.

2. Run Ext on input $|\psi\rangle_\mathbf{V}$. Abort if Ext aborts. Otherwise, obtain an extracted opening $(e_{\mathsf{Ext}}, r_{\mathsf{Ext}})$ and a post-extraction state $|\psi'\rangle_\mathbf{V}$, and proceed to the next step.
3. Simulate a transcript (a, e_{Ext}, z) by the honest-verifier ZK property of the Σ-protocol.
4. Send a to the verifier whose internal state is replaced with $|\psi'\rangle_\mathbf{V}$. Let (e, r) be the verifier's response. Abort if (e, r) is not a valid opening to com. Otherwise send z to the verifier.
5. Output the verifier's final output.

By the above analysis, we can see that $\mathsf{Sim}_{\mathsf{na}}$'s output distribution is close to the real verifier's output distribution with an approximation error $O(t^{1/3})$ conditioned on that the verifier does not abort. Furthermore, the probability that the verifier does not abort can only be changed by at most $O(t^{1/3})$. If we could set t to be a negligible function, then we would be able to achieve quantum ZK rather than quantum ϵ-ZK. However, since we have to ensure that Amp's running time $\mathrm{poly}(\lambda, t^{-1})$ is polynomial in λ, we can only set t to be noticeable. Since we can set t to be an arbitrarily small noticeable function, we can make the approximation error $O(t^{1/3})$ be an arbitrarily small noticeable function. This means that the protocol satisfies quantum ϵ-ZK.

Black-Box Simulation. So far, we did not pay attention to the black-box property of simulation. We briefly explain the definition of black-box quantum ZK and that our simulator satisfies it. First, we define black-box quantum ZK by borrowing the definition of quantum oracle machine by Unruh [Unr12]. Roughly, we say that a simulator is black-box if it only accesses unitary part of a verifier and its inverse in a black-box manner, and does not directly act on the verifier's internal registers. With this definition, one part where it is unclear if our simulator is black-box is the amplification procedure Amp. However, by a close inspection, we can see that Amp actually just performs sequential measurements $\{\Pi, I_{\mathbf{V},\mathbf{Aux}} - \Pi\}$ and $\{|0\rangle_{\mathbf{Aux}}\langle 0|_{\mathbf{Aux}}, I_{\mathbf{V},\mathbf{Aux}} - |0\rangle_{\mathbf{Aux}}\langle 0|_{\mathbf{Aux}}\}$, which can be done by black-box access to the verifier as seen from the definition of Π. Therefore, we can see that our simulator is black-box.

A Remark on Underlying Σ-Protocol. In the original GK protocol, any Σ-Protocol can be used as a building block. However, in our technique, we need to use *delayed-witness* Σ-protocol where the first message a can be generated without knowledge of a witness due to a technical reason. An example of delayed-witness Σ-protocol is Blum's Graph Hamiltonicity protocol [Blu86]. Roughly, the reason to require this additional property is for ensuring that a simulator can perfectly simulate the first message a of the Σ-protocol when running the extraction procedure. In the classical setting, a computationally indistinguishable simulation of a works, but we could not prove an analogous claim in our setting.

OWF-Based Construction. Next, we briefly explain our OWF-based quantum ϵ-ZK argument. The reason why we need a stronger assumption in our first construction is that we need to implement the commitment for the challenge by a constant round statistically hiding commitment, which is not known to exist from OWF. Then, a natural idea is to relax it to computationally hiding one if we only need computational soundness. We can show that the extraction technique as explained above also works for statistically binding commitments with a small tweak. However, we cannot prove soundness of the protocol without any modification due to a malleability issue. For explaining this, we recall that the first message a of a Σ-protocol itself is also implemented as a commitment. Then, the computational hiding of commitment does not prevent a computationally bounded prover, which is given a commitment com to e, from generating a "commitment" a whose committed message depends on e. Such a dependence leads to an attack against soundness. To prevent this, an extractable commitment scheme is used to generate a in the classical setting [PW09]. However, since it is unclear if the extractable commitment scheme used in [PW09] is secure against quantum adversaries, we take an alternative approach that we let a prover prove that it knows a committed message inside a by using a proof of knowledge before a verifier opens a challenge as is done in [Gol01, Sec.4.9], [Gol04, App.C.3]. A naive approach to implement this idea would be to use ZK proof of knowledge, but this does not work since a constant round ZK argument is what we are trying to construct. Fortunately, we can instead use witness indistinguishable proof of knowledge (WIPoK) with a simple OR proof trick. Specifically, we let a prover prove that "I know committed message in a" OR "I know witness w for x" where x is the statement being proven in the protocol. In the proof of soundness, since we assume x is a false statement, a witness for the latter statement does not exist. Then we can extract a committed message inside a to break the hiding property of the commitment scheme used by the verifier if the committed message depends on e. On the other hand, in the proof of ϵ-ZK property, we can use the real witness w in an intermediate hybrid to simulate WIPoK without using knowledge of a committed message. In such a hybrid, we can rely on honest-verifier ZK of the Σ-protocol to change a to a simulated one for an extracted challenge e.

Finally, we remark that though we are not aware of any work that explicitly claims the existence of a constant round WIPoK that works for quantum provers from OWFs, we observe that a combination of known works easily yields such a construction. (See the full version for more details.) As a result, we obtain constant round quantum ϵ-ZK argument from OWFs.

1.3 Related Work

ϵ-Zero-Knowledge and Related Notions. Though we are the first to consider ϵ-ZK in the quantum setting, there are several works that consider ϵ-ZK in the classical setting. We briefly review them. We note that all of these results are in the classical setting, and it is unknown if similar results hold in the quantum setting. The notion of ϵ-ZK (originally called ϵ-knowledge) was introduced by Dwork,

Naor, and Sahai [DNS04] in the context of concurrent ZK proofs. Bitansky, Kalai, and Paneth [BKP18] gave a construction of 4-round ϵ-ZK proof for **NP** assuming the existence of key-less multi-collision resistant hash function.[10] Barak and Lindell [BL02] showed the impossibility of constant round black-box ZK proof with strict-polynomial time simulation, and observed that strict-polynomial time simulation is possible if we relax ZK to ϵ-ZK. This can be understood as a theoretical separation between ZK and ϵ-ZK. On the other hand, Fleischhacker, Goyal, and Jain [FGJ18] showed that there does not exist 3-round ϵ-ZK proof for **NP** even with non-black-box simulation under some computational assumptions, which is the same lower bound as that for ZK proofs if we allow non-black-box simulation.

Another relaxation of ZK is *super-polynomial simulation (SPS)-ZK* [Pas03], where a simulator is allowed to run in super-polynomial time. One may find a similarity between ϵ-ZK and SPS-ZK in the sense that the latter can be seen as a variant of ϵ-ZK where we set the accuracy parameter ϵ to be negligible. On the other hand, it has been considered that ϵ-ZK is much more difficult to achieve than SPS-ZK. For example, the work of Bitansky, Khurana, and Paneth [BKP19] gave a construction of a 2-round argument for **NP** that achieves a weaker notion of ZK than ϵ-ZK, and the result is considered a significant breakthrough in the area even though there is a simple construction of 2-round SPS-ZK argument for **NP** [Pas03].

Several works considered other weakened notions of ZK [DNRS03,BP12, CLP15,JKKR17,BKP19]. Some of them are weaker than ϵ-ZK, and others are incomparable. For example, "weak ZK" in [BP12,CLP15] is incomparable to ϵ-ZK whereas "weak ZK" in [BKP19] is weaker than ϵ-ZK.

Post-Quantum Zero-Knowledge with Classical Computational Soundness. Ananth and La Placa [AL20] gave a construction of post-quantum ZK argument for **NP** with *classical* computational soundness assuming the QLWE assumption. Though such a protocol would be easy to obtain if we assume average-case classical hardness of certain problems in **BQP** (e.g., factoring) in addition to the QLWE assumption, what is interesting in [AL20] is that they only assume the QLWE assumption.

Post-Quantum Zero-Knowledge with Trusted Setup. Several works studied (non-interactive) post-quantum ZK proofs for **NP** in the common random/reference string model [Kob03,DFS04,PS19]. Among them, Peikert and Shiehian [PS19] proved that there exists non-interactive post-quantum ZK proof for **NP** in the common reference string model assuming the QLWE assumption.[11]

---

[10] The protocol achieves full-fledged ZK if we allow the simulator to take non-uniform advice or assume a super-polynomial assumption.

[11] In [PS19], they do not explicitly claim ZK against quantum adversaries. However, since their security proof does not rely on rewinding, it immediately extends to post-quantum security if we assume the underlying assumption against quantum adversaries.

Zero-Knowledge for **QMA**. The complexity class **QMA** is a quantum analogue of **NP**. Broadbent, Ji, Song, and Watrous [BJSW20] gave a construction of a ZK proof for **QMA**. Recently, Broadbent and Grilo [BG20] gave an alternative simpler construction of a ZK proof for **QMA**. Bitansky and Shmueli [BS20] gave a constant round ZK argument for **QMA** by combining the construction of [BG20] and their post-quantum ZK argument for **NP**. We believe that our technique can be used to construct a constant round ϵ-ZK proof for **QMA** by replacing the delayed-witness Σ-protocol for **NP** with the delayed-witness quantum Σ-protocol for **QMA** recently proposed by Brakerski and Yuen [BY20].[12] This is beyond the scope of this paper, and we leave a formal proof as a future work.

Several works studied non-interactive ZK proofs/arguments for **QMA** in preprocessing models [CVZ20, BG20, Shm20, ACGH20].

Collapsing Hash Functions. The notion of collapsing hash functions was introduced by Unruh [Unr16b] for a replacement of collision-resistant hash functions in post-quantum setting. Unruh [Unr16a] gave a construction of a collapsing hash function under the QLWE assumption. Actually, the construction is generic based on any lossy function with sufficiently large "lossy rate".[13] Currently, we are not aware of any other construction of collapsing hash function based on standard assumptions, but any new construction of collapsing hash function yields a new instantiation of our first construction.

Zhandry [Zha19] proved that any collision-resistant hash function that is not collapsing yields a stronger variant of public-key quantum money (with infinitely often security). Given the difficulty of constructing public key quantum money, he suggested that most natural post-quantum collision-resistant hash functions are likely already collapsing.

Relation to [CCY20]. Our idea of decomposing a verifier's internal space into "aborting space" and "non-aborting space" is inspired by a recent work of Chia, Chung, and Yamakawa [CCY20]. In [CCY20], the authors consider a decomposition of a prover's internal space into "know-answer space" and "not-know-answer space" to prove soundness of parallel repetition version of Mahadev's classical verification of quantum computation protocol [Mah18b]. Though the conceptual idea and some technical tools are similar, the ways of applying them to actual problems are quite different. For example, in our case, we need a careful analysis to make sure that a post-extraction state is close to the original one in some sense while such an argument does not appear in their work since their goal is proving soundness rather than ZK. On the other hand, their technical core is a approximated projection to each subspace, which is not needed in this paper.

Subsequent work. Subsequently to this work, Chia, Chung, Liu, and Yamakawa [CCLY21] proved that there does not exist a constant round post-quantum ZK

---

[12] Actually, their protocol is delayed-input, i.e., the first message generation does not use the statement either.

[13] A lossy function is defined similarly to a lossy trapdoor function [PW08] except that we do not require the existence of trapdoor.

argument for **NP** unless **NP** ∈ **BQP**, which is highly unlikely. This justifies the relaxation to ε-ZK in our constructions.

2 Preliminaries

Basic Notations. We use λ to denote the security parameter throughout the paper. For a positive integer $n \in \mathbb{N}$, $[n]$ denotes a set $\{1, 2, ..., n\}$. For a finite set $\mathcal{X}$, $x \xleftarrow{\$} \mathcal{X}$ means that x is uniformly chosen from $\mathcal{X}$. A function $f : \mathbb{N} \to [0, 1]$ is said to be negligible if for all polynomial p and sufficiently large $\lambda \in \mathbb{N}$, we have $f(\lambda) < 1/p(\lambda)$, said to be overwhelming if $1 - f$ is negligible, and said to be noticeable if there is a polynomial p such that we have $f(\lambda) \geq 1/p(\lambda)$ for sufficiently large $\lambda \in \mathbb{N}$. We denote by poly an unspecified polynomial and by negl an unspecified negligible function. We use PPT and QPT to mean (classical) probabilistic polynomial time and quantum polynomial time, respectively. For a classical probabilistic or quantum algorithm $\mathcal{A}$, $y \xleftarrow{\$} \mathcal{A}(x)$ means that $\mathcal{A}$ is run on input x and outputs y. When $\mathcal{A}$ is classical probabilistic algorithm, we denote by $\mathcal{A}(x; r)$ to mean the execution of $\mathcal{A}$ on input x and a randomness r. When $\mathcal{A}$ is a quantum algorithm that takes a quantum advice, we denote by $\mathcal{A}(x; \rho)$ to mean the execution of $\mathcal{A}$ on input x and an advice ρ. For a quantum algorithm $\mathcal{A}$, a unitary part of $\mathcal{A}$ means the unitary obtained by deferring all measurements by $\mathcal{A}$ and omitting these measurements. We use the bold font (like **X**) to denote quantum registers, and $\mathcal{H}_{\mathbf{X}}$ to mean the Hilbert space corresponding to the register **X**. For a quantum state ρ, $M_{\mathbf{X}} \circ \rho$ means a measurement in the computational basis on the register **X** of ρ. For quantum states ρ and ρ', $\mathsf{TD}(\rho, \rho')$ denotes trace distance between them. When we consider a sequence $\{X_\lambda\}_{\lambda \in \mathbb{N}}$ of some objects (e.g., bit strings, quantum states, sets, Hilbert spaces etc.) indexed by the security parameter λ, we often simply write X to mean X_λ or $\{X_\lambda\}_{\lambda \in \mathbb{N}}$, which will be clear from the context. Similarly, for a function f in the security parameter λ, we often simply write f to mean $f(\lambda)$.

Standard Computational Models

- A PPT algorithm is a probabilistic polynomial time (classical) Turing machine. A PPT algorithm is also often seen as a sequence of uniform polynomial-size circuits.
- A QPT algorithm is a polynomial time quantum Turing machine. A QPT algorithm is also often seen as a sequence of uniform polynomial-size quantum circuits.
- An adversary (or malicious party) is modeled as a non-uniform QPT algorithm $\mathcal{A}$ (with quantum advice) that is specified by sequences of polynomial-size quantum circuits $\{\mathcal{A}_\lambda\}_{\lambda \in \mathbb{N}}$ and polynomial-size quantum advice $\{\rho_\lambda\}_{\lambda \in \mathbb{N}}$. When $\mathcal{A}$ takes an input of λ-bit, $\mathcal{A}$ runs $\mathcal{A}_\lambda$ taking ρ_λ as an advice.

Interactive Quantum Machine and Oracle-Aided Quantum Machine. We rely on the definition of an interactive quantum machine and oracle-aided quantum

machine that is given oracle access to an interactive quantum machine following
[Unr12]. Roughly, an interactive quantum machine $\mathcal{A}$ is formalized by a unitary
over registers $\mathbf{M}$ for receiving and sending messages and $\mathbf{A}$ for maintaining
$\mathcal{A}$'s internal state. For two interactive quantum machines $\mathcal{A}$ and $\mathcal{B}$ that share
the same message register $\mathbf{M}$, an interaction between $\mathcal{A}$ and $\mathcal{B}$ proceeds by
alternating invocations of $\mathcal{A}$ and $\mathcal{B}$ while exchanging messages over $\mathbf{M}$.

An oracle-aided quantum machine $\mathcal{S}$ given oracle access to an interactive
quantum machine $\mathcal{A}$ with an initial internal state ρ (denoted by $\mathcal{S}^{\mathcal{A}(\rho)}$) is allowed
to apply unitary part of $\mathcal{A}$ and its inverse in a black-box manner where $\mathcal{S}$ can
act on $\mathcal{A}$'s internal register $\mathbf{A}$ only through oracle access. We refer to [Unr12] for
more formal definitions of interactive quantum machines and black-box access
to them.

Indistinguishability of Quantum States. We define computational and statistical
indistinguishability of quantum states similarly to [BS20].

We may consider random variables over bit strings or over quantum states.
This will be clear from the context. For ensembles of random variables $\mathcal{X} = \{X_i\}_{\lambda \in \mathbb{N}, i \in I_\lambda}$ and $\mathcal{Y} = \{Y_i\}_{\lambda \in \mathbb{N}, i \in I_\lambda}$ over the same set of indices $I = \bigcup_{\lambda \in \mathbb{N}} I_\lambda$
and a function δ, we write $\mathcal{X} \stackrel{comp}{\approx}_\delta \mathcal{Y}$ to mean that for any non-uniform QPT
algorithm $\mathcal{A} = \{\mathcal{A}_\lambda, \rho_\lambda\}$, there exists a negligible function negl such that for all
$\lambda \in \mathbb{N}$, $i \in I_\lambda$, we have

$$|\Pr[\mathcal{A}_\lambda(X_i; \rho_\lambda)] - \Pr[\mathcal{A}_\lambda(Y_i; \rho_\lambda)]| \leq \delta(\lambda) + \mathsf{negl}(\lambda).$$

Especially, when we have the above for $\delta = 0$, we say that $\mathcal{X}$ and $\mathcal{Y}$ are computationally indistinguishable, and simply write $\mathcal{X} \stackrel{comp}{\approx} \mathcal{Y}$.

Similarly, we write $\mathcal{X} \stackrel{stat}{\approx}_\delta \mathcal{Y}$ to mean that for any unbounded time algorithm
$\mathcal{A}$, there exists a negligible function negl such that for all $\lambda \in \mathbb{N}$, $i \in I_\lambda$, we have

$$|\Pr[\mathcal{A}(X_i)] - \Pr[\mathcal{A}(Y_i)]| \leq \delta(\lambda) + \mathsf{negl}(\lambda).$$

Especially, when we have the above for $\delta = 0$, we say that $\mathcal{X}$ and $\mathcal{Y}$ are statis-
tically indistinguishable, and simply write $\mathcal{X} \stackrel{stat}{\approx} \mathcal{Y}$. Moreover, we write $\mathcal{X} \equiv \mathcal{Y}$
to mean that X_i and Y_i are distributed identically for all $i \in I$[14].

2.1 Post-Quantum One-Way Functions and Collapsing Hash Functions

A post-quantum one-way function (OWF) is a classically computable function
that is hard to invert in QPT. A collapsing hash function is a quantum counterpart of collision-resistant hash function introduced by Unruh [Unr16b]. Unruh
[Unr16a] gave a construction of collapsing hash functions based on the QLWE

[14] In other words, $\mathcal{X} \stackrel{stat}{\approx}_\delta \mathcal{Y}$ means that there exists a negligible function negl such
that the trace distance between ρ_{X_i} and ρ_{Y_i} is at most $\delta(\lambda) + \mathsf{negl}(\lambda)$ for all $\lambda \in \mathbb{N}$
and $i \in I_\lambda$ where ρ_{X_i} and ρ_{Y_i} denote density matrices corresponding to X_i and Y_i.

assumption. We give formal definitions in the full version since they are only used for constructing other cryptographic primitives and not directly used in our constructions.

2.2 Commitment

We use commitments in our constructions. Though they are mostly standard, we need one new security notion which we call *strong collapse-binding*, which is a stronger variant of collapse-biding introduced by Unruh [Unr16b]. Roughly speaking, this security requires that for any superposition of messages and randomness corresponding the same commitment generated by an adversary, the adversary cannot distinguish if the message and randomness registers are measured or not. The difference from the original collapse-binding property is that both message and randomness registers are measured rather than only the message register. We observe that the collapse-binding commitment based on collapsing hash functions in [Unr16b] also satisfies the strong collapse-binding property. Especially, there exists a strong collapse-binding commitment under the QLWE assumption. See the full version for details of the definition and construction of strong collapse-binding commitments.

2.3 Interactive Proof and Argument

We define interactive proofs and arguments similarly to [BS20].

Notations. For an **NP** language L and $x \in L$, $R_L(x)$ is the set that consists of all (classical) witnesses w such that the verification machine for L accepts (x, w).

A (classical) interactive protocol is modeled as an interaction between interactive quantum machines P referred to as a prover and V referred to as a verifier that can be implemented by PPT algorithms. We denote by $\langle P(x_P), V(x_V) \rangle(x)$ an execution of the protocol where x is a common input, x_P is P's private input, and x_V is V's private input. We denote by $\mathsf{OUT}_V \langle P(x_P), V(x_V) \rangle(x)$ the final output of V in the execution. An honest verifier's output is $\top$ indicating acceptance or $\bot$ indicating rejection, and a quantum malicious verifier's output may be an arbitrary quantum state.

Definition 2.1 (Interactive Proof and Argument for NP). *An interactive proof or argument for an* **NP** *language L is an interactive protocol between a PPT prover P and a PPT verifier V that satisfies the following:*

Perfect Completeness. For any $x \in L$, and $w \in R_L(x)$, we have

$$\Pr[\mathsf{OUT}_V \langle P(w), V \rangle(x) = \top] = 1$$

Statistical/Computational Soundness. We say that an interactive protocol is statistically (resp. computationally) sound if for any unbounded-time (resp. non-uniform QPT) cheating prover P^*, there exists a negligible function negl such that for any $\lambda \in \mathbb{N}$ and any $x \in \{0,1\}^\lambda \setminus L$, we have

$$\Pr[\mathsf{OUT}_V \langle P^*, V \rangle(x) = \top] \leq \mathsf{negl}(\lambda).$$

We call an interactive protocol with statistical (resp. computational) soundness an interactive proof (resp. argument).

Delayed-Witness Σ-Protocol. We introduce a special type of Σ-protocol which we call *delayed-witness Σ-protocol* where the first message can be generated without witness.

Definition 2.2 (Delayed-Witness Σ-Protocol). *A (post-quantum) delayed-witness Σ-protocol for an **NP** language L is a 3-round interactive proof for **NP** with the following syntax.*

Common Input: An instance $x \in L \cap \{0,1\}^\lambda$ for security parameter $\lambda \in \mathbb{N}$.
P's **Private Input:** A classical witness $w \in R_L(x)$ for x.

1. P generates a "commitment" a and a state st. For this part, P only uses the statement x and does not use any witness w. We denote this procedure by $(a, \mathsf{st}) \xleftarrow{\$} \Sigma.P_1(x)$. Then it sends a to the verifier, and keeps st as its internal state.
2. V chooses a "challenge" $e \xleftarrow{\$} \{0,1\}^\lambda$ and sends e to P.
3. P generates a "response" z from st, witness w, and e. We denote this procedure by $z \xleftarrow{\$} \Sigma.P_3(\mathsf{st}, w, e)$. Then it sends z to V.
4. V verifies the transcript (a, e, z) and outputs $\top$ indicating acceptance or $\bot$ indicating rejection. We denote this procedure by $\top/\bot \xleftarrow{\$} \Sigma.V(x, a, e, z)$.

We require a delayed-witness Σ-protocol to satisfy the following property in addition to perfect completeness and statistical soundness.[15]

Special Honest-Verifier Zero-Knowledge. There exists a PPT simulator Sim_Σ such that we have

$$\{(a, z) : (a, \mathsf{st}) \xleftarrow{\$} \Sigma.P_1(x), z \xleftarrow{\$} \Sigma.P_3(\mathsf{st}, w, e)\}_{\lambda, x, w, e} \overset{comp}{\approx} \{(a, z) : (a, z) \xleftarrow{\$} \mathsf{Sim}_\Sigma(x, e)\}_{\lambda, x, w, e}$$

where $x \in L \cap \{0,1\}^\lambda$, $w \in R_L(x)$, and $e \in \{0,1\}^\lambda$.

---

[15] We do not require *special soundness*, which is often a default requirement of Σ-protocol.

Instantiations. An example of a delayed-witness Σ-protocol is a parallel repetition version of Blum's Graph Hamiltonicity protocol [Blu86]. In the protocol, we need a computationally hiding and perfectly binding non-interactive commitment scheme, which exists under the QLWE assumption as noted in Sect. 2.2. In summary, a delayed-input Σ-protocol for all **NP** languages exists under the QLWE assumption.

Quantum ϵ-Zero-Knowledge Proof and Argument. Here, we define quantum black-box ϵ-zero-knowledge proofs and arguments. The difference from the definition of quantum zero-knowledge in [BS20] are:

1. (ϵ-**Zero-Knowledge**) We allow the simulator to depend on a noticeable "accuracy parameter" ϵ, and allows its running time to polynomially depend on ϵ^{-1}, and
2. (**Black-Box Simulation**) the simulator is only given black-box access to a malicious verifier.

Definition 2.3 (Post-Quantum Black-Box ϵ-Zero-Knowledge Proof and Argument). *A post-quantum black-box ϵ-zero-knowledge proof (resp. argument) for an **NP** language L is an interactive proof (resp. argument) for L that satisfies the following property in addition to perfect completeness and statistical (resp. computational) soundness:*

Quantum Black-Box ϵ-Zero-Knowledge. There exists an oracle-aided QPT simulator Sim *such that for any non-uniform QPT malicious verifier* $V^* = \{V_\lambda^*, \rho_\lambda\}_{\lambda \in \mathbb{N}}$ *and any noticeable function* $\epsilon(\lambda)$*, we have*

$$\{\mathsf{OUT}_{V_\lambda^*}\langle P(w), V_\lambda^*(\rho_\lambda)\rangle(x)\}_{\lambda,x,w} \stackrel{comp}{\approx}_\epsilon \{\mathsf{OUT}_{V_\lambda^*}(\mathsf{Sim}^{V_\lambda^*(\rho_\lambda)}(x, 1^{\epsilon^{-1}}))\}_{\lambda,x,w}$$

where $\lambda \in \mathbb{N}$*,* $x \in L \cap \{0,1\}^\lambda$*,* $w \in R_L(\lambda)$*, and* $\mathsf{OUT}_{V_\lambda^*}(\mathsf{Sim}^{V_\lambda^*(\rho_\lambda)}(x))$ *is the state in the output register of* V_λ^* *after the simulated execution of* V_λ^* *by* Sim*.*

Remark 2.1. In the above definition of quantum black-box ϵ-zero-knowledge, we do not consider an entanglement between auxiliary input of a malicious verifier and distinguisher unlike the original definition of quantum zero-knowledge by Watrous [Wat09]. However, in the full version we show that the above definition implies indistinguishability against a distinguisher that may get an entangled state to verifier's auxiliary input by taking advantage of black-box simulation.

Witness Indistinguishable Proof of Knowledge. The definition of witness indistinguishable proof of knowledge is given in the full version.

2.4   Quantum Rewinding Lemma

Watrous [Wat09] proved a lemma that enables us to amplify the success probability of a quantum algorithm under certain conditions. The following form of the lemma is based on that in [BS20, Lemma 2.1].

Lemma 2.1 ([Wat09, BS20]). *There is an oracle-aided quantum algorithm* R *that gets as input the following:*

- *A quantum circuit* Q *that takes n-input qubits in register* Inp *and outputs a classical bit b (in a register outside* Inp*) and an m output qubits.*
- *An n-qubit state ρ in register* Inp*.*
- *A number $T \in \mathbb{N}$ in unary.*

$R(1^T, Q, \rho)$ *executes in time $T \cdot |Q|$ and outputs a distribution over m-qubit states $D_\rho := R(1^T, Q, \rho)$ with the following guarantees.*

For an n-qubit state ρ, denote by Q_ρ the conditional distribution of the output distribution $Q(\rho)$, conditioned on $b = 0$, and denote by $p(\rho)$ the probability that $b = 0$. If there exist $p_0, q \in (0, 1)$, $\gamma \in (0, \frac{1}{2})$ such that:

- *Amplification executes for enough time: $T \geq \frac{\log(1/\gamma)}{4p_0(1-p_0)}$,*
- *There is some minimal probability that $b = 0$: For every n-qubit state ρ, $p_0 \leq p(\rho)$,*
- *$p(\rho)$ is input-independent, up to γ distance: For every n-qubit state ρ, $|p(\rho) - q| < \gamma$, and*
- *q is closer to $\frac{1}{2}$: $p_0(1 - p_0) \leq q(1 - q)$,*

then for every n-qubit state ρ,

$$\mathsf{TD}(Q_\rho, D_\rho) \leq 4\sqrt{\gamma}\frac{\log(1/\gamma)}{p_0(1 - p_0)}.$$

Moreover, $R(1^T, Q, \rho)$ works in the following manner: It uses Q for only implementing oracles that perform the unitary part of Q and its inverse, acts on Inp *only through these oracles, and the output of* R *is the state in the output register of Q after the simulated execution. We note that* R *may directly act on Q's internal registers other than* Inp*.*

Remark 2.2. The final claim of the lemma ("Moreover...") is not explicitly stated in previous works. In the description of R in [Wat09], the first qubit of Inp is designated to output b, and thus the above requirement is not satisfied. However, this can be easily avoided by just letting Q output b in a register outside Inp as required above. Then one can see that R acts on the input register only through Q as seen from the description of R in [Wat09] (with the above modification in mind). Looking ahead, this is needed to show our ϵ-zero-knowledge simulators are black-box.

3   Extraction Lemma

In this section, we prove our main technical lemma, which we call the *extraction lemma*. Before giving a formal statement, we give an intuitive explanation. Suppose that we have a two-stage quantum algorithm $\mathcal{A} = (\mathcal{A}_{\mathsf{com}}, \mathcal{A}_{\mathsf{open}})$ that works as follows. $\mathcal{A}_{\mathsf{com}}$ is given pp of a commitment scheme and generates a commitment com, and passes a quantum state ρ_{st} in its internal register to $\mathcal{A}_{open}$. $\mathcal{A}_{open}$ is given the internal state ρ_{st}, and outputs a message-randomness pair (m, r) (which is not necessarily a valid opening to com) along with a classical output out, and let ρ'_{st} be its internal state after the execution. We call a successive execution of $\mathcal{A}_{com}$ and $\mathcal{A}_{open}$ a real experiment. On the other hand, we consider an *extraction experiment* where an "extractor" Ext runs on input ρ_{st} in between $\mathcal{A}_{com}$ and $\mathcal{A}_{open}$ to "extract" a committed message m_{Ext} while generating a simulated $\mathcal{A}$'s internal state ρ_{Ext}. Then we run $\mathcal{A}_{open}$ with the internal state ρ_{Ext} instead of ρ_{st} to complete the extraction experiment. Roughly, the extraction lemma claims that if the commitment scheme is strong collapse-binding (resp. statistically binding), then there exists an extractor Ext such that we have $m = m_{Ext}$ with high probability and distributions of (m, r, out, ρ'_{st}) in real and extraction experiments are computationally (resp. statistically) indistinguishable *conditioned on that* (m, r) *is a valid opening to* com.

The formal statement is given below.

Definition 3.1 (Extraction Experiments). *Let* Com = (Setup, Commit) *be a commitment scheme with message space* $\mathcal{M}$, *randomness space* $\mathcal{R}$, *commitment space* $\mathcal{COM}$, *and a public parameter space* $\mathcal{PP}$. *Let* $\mathcal{A} = \{\mathcal{A}_{com,\lambda}, \mathcal{A}_{open,\lambda}, \rho_\lambda\}_{\lambda \in \mathbb{N}}$ *be a sequence of two-stage non-uniform QPT algorithms with the following syntax:*

$\mathcal{A}_{com,\lambda}(pp; \rho_\lambda) \to (com, \rho_{st})$: *It takes as input* pp $\in \mathcal{PP}$ *and an advice* ρ_λ, *and outputs* com $\in \mathcal{COM}$ *and a quantum state* ρ_{st} *in register* **ST**.

$\mathcal{A}_{open,\lambda}(\rho_{st}) \to (m, r, out, \rho'_{st})$: *It takes as input a quantum state* ρ_{st} *in register* **ST**, *and outputs* $m \in \mathcal{M}$, $r \in \mathcal{R}$, *a classical string* out, *and a quantum state* ρ'_{st} *in register* **ST**.

Let Ext *be a QPT algorithm and* δ *be a function in* λ. *Then we define following experiments:*

$\mathsf{Exp}_{real}[\mathsf{Com}, \mathcal{A}](\lambda)$	$\mathsf{Exp}_{ext}[\mathsf{Com}, \mathcal{A}, \mathsf{Ext}](\lambda, \delta)$
pp $\xleftarrow{\$}$ Setup(1^λ),	pp $\xleftarrow{\$}$ Setup(1^λ),
$(com, \rho_{st}) \xleftarrow{\$} \mathcal{A}_{com,\lambda}(pp; \rho_\lambda)$,	$(com, \rho_{st}) \xleftarrow{\$} \mathcal{A}_{com,\lambda}(pp; \rho_\lambda)$,
	$(m_{Ext}, \rho_{Ext}) \xleftarrow{\$} \mathsf{Ext}(1^\lambda, 1^{\delta^{-1}}, pp, com, \mathcal{A}_{open,\lambda}, \rho_{st})$,
$(m, r, out, \rho'_{st}) \xleftarrow{\$} \mathcal{A}_{open,\lambda}(\rho_{st})$,	$(m, r, out, \rho'_{st}) \xleftarrow{\$} \mathcal{A}_{open,\lambda}(\rho_{Ext})$,
If Commit$(pp, m; r) \neq com$,	If Commit$(pp, m; r) \neq com \vee m \neq m_{Ext}$,
Output $\perp$	Output $\perp$
Else Output $(pp, com, m, r, out, \rho'_{st})$.	Else Output $(pp, com, m, r, out, \rho'_{st})$.

Lemma 3.1 (Extraction Lemma). *For any strong collapse-binding commitment scheme* Com = (Setup, Commit), *there exists a QPT algorithm* Ext *such that for any noticeable function* $\delta(\lambda)$ *and* $\mathcal{A} = \{\mathcal{A}_{com,\lambda}, \mathcal{A}_{open,\lambda}, \rho_\lambda\}_{\lambda \in \mathbb{N}}$ *as in Definition 3.1, we have*

$$\{\mathsf{Exp}_{real}[\mathsf{Com}, \mathcal{A}](\lambda)\}_{\lambda \in \mathbb{N}} \overset{comp}{\approx}_\delta \{\mathsf{Exp}_{ext}[\mathsf{Com}, \mathcal{A}, \mathsf{Ext}](\lambda, \delta)\}_{\lambda \in \mathbb{N}}.$$

If Com *is statistically binding instead of strong collapse-binding, we have*

$$\{\mathsf{Exp}_{\mathsf{real}}[\mathsf{Com},\mathcal{A}](\lambda)\}_{\lambda\in\mathbb{N}} \overset{stat}{\approx}_{\delta} \{\mathsf{Exp}_{\mathsf{ext}}[\mathsf{Com},\mathcal{A},\mathsf{Ext}](\lambda,\delta)\}_{\lambda\in\mathbb{N}}.$$

Moreover, $\mathsf{Ext}(1^{\lambda}, 1^{\delta^{-1}}, \mathsf{pp}, \mathsf{com}, \mathcal{A}_{\mathsf{open},\lambda}, \rho_{\mathsf{st}})$ *works in the following manner: It uses* $\mathcal{A}_{\mathsf{open},\lambda}$ *for only implementing oracles that perform unitary part of* $\mathcal{A}_{\mathsf{open},\lambda}$ *and its inverse, and acts on* **ST** *only through black-box access to the oracles. The second output* ρ_{Ext} *of* Ext *is the state in* **ST** *after the execution. We note that* Ext *may directly act on internal registers of* $\mathcal{A}_{\mathsf{open},\lambda}$ *other than* **ST**.

The above lemma abstracts our technical core, which is extraction of the verifier's committed challenge without collapsing verifier's internal state too much. (One can think of $\mathcal{A}$ in the above lemma as the verifier and ρ_{st} and ρ'_{st} as verifier's internal states before and after opening the commitment, respectively, in our constant round ϵ-zero-knowledge proofs/arguments.) Since the intuition of the proof is already explained in Sect. 1.2, we defer the proof to the full version.

4   Post-quantum ϵ-Zero-Knowledge Proof and Argument

In this section, we prove the following theorems.

Theorem 4.1. *If the QLWE assumption holds, then there exists a 5-round post-quantum black-box ϵ-zero-knowledge proof for all* **NP** *languages.*

Theorem 4.2. *If a collapsing hash function exists, then there exists a 5-round post-quantum black-box ϵ-zero-knowledge proof for all* **NP** *languages.*

Theorem 4.3. *If post-quantunm OWF exists, then there exists a 9-round post-quantum black-box ϵ-zero-knowledge argument for all* **NP** *languages.*

In the rest of this section, we prove Theorem 4.1 and 4.2. The proof of Theorem 4.3 is given in the full version.

4.1   Construction

Our construction is the same as the Golderich-Kahan protocol [GK96] except that we instantiate the verifier's commitment with a strong collapse-binding commitment and we rely on a post-quantum delayed-witness Σ-protocol. Specifically, our construction is built on the following ingredients:

- A commitment scheme (CBCom.Setup, CBCom.Commit) that is statistical hiding and strong collapse-binding with message space $\{0,1\}^{\lambda}$ and randomness space $\mathcal{R}$. As noted in Sect. 2.2, such a commitment scheme exists under the QLWE assumption.
- A delayed-witness Σ-protocol $(\Sigma.P_1, \Sigma.P_3, \Sigma.V)$ for an **NP** language L as defined in Definition 2.2. As noted in Sect. 2.3, such a protocol exists under the QLWE assumption.

Protocol 1

Common Input: An instance $x \in L \cap \{0,1\}^{\lambda}$ for security parameter $\lambda \in \mathbb{N}$.
P's Private Input: A classical witness $w \in R_L(x)$ for x.

1. **V's Commitment to Challenge:**
   (a) P computes $pp \xleftarrow{\$} \mathsf{CBCom.Setup}(1^{\lambda})$ and sends pp to V.
   (b) V chooses $e \xleftarrow{\$} \{0,1\}^{\lambda}$ and $r \xleftarrow{\$} \mathcal{R}$, computes $com \xleftarrow{\$} \mathsf{CBCom.Commit}(pp, e; r)$, and sends com to P.
2. **Σ-Protocol Execution:**
   (a) P generates $(a, st) \xleftarrow{\$} \Sigma.P_1(x)$ and sends a to V.
   (b) V sends (e, r) to P.
   (c) P aborts if $\mathsf{CBCom.Commit}(pp, e; r) \neq com$.
       Otherwise, it generates $z \xleftarrow{\$} \Sigma.P_3(st, w, e)$ and sends z to V.
   (d) V outputs $\Sigma.V(x, a, e, z)$.

Fig. 1. Constant-round post-quantum ϵ-zero-knowledge proof for $L \in \mathbf{NP}$

Then our construction of post-quantum black-box ϵ-zero-knowledge proof is given in Fig. 1.

The completeness of the protocol clearly follows from that of the underlying Σ-protocol. In Sect. 4.2 and 4.3, we prove that this protocol satisfies statistical soundness and quantum black-box ϵ-zero-knowledge. Then we obtain Theorem 4.1.

4.2 Statistical Soundness

This is essentially the same as the proof in [GK96], but we give a proof for completeness.

For $x \notin L$ an unbounded-time cheating prover P^*, we consider the following sequence of hybrids. We denote by win_i the event that P^* wins in Hyb_i.

Hyb_1: This is the original game. That is,
   1. P^* sends pp to V.
   2. V chooses $e \xleftarrow{\$} \{0,1\}^{\lambda}$ and $r \xleftarrow{\$} \mathcal{R}$, computes $com \xleftarrow{\$} \mathsf{CBCom.Commit}(pp, e; r)$, and sends com to P^*.
   3. P^* sends a to V.
   4. V sends (e, r) to P^*
   5. P^* sends z to V.
   We say that P^* wins if we have $\Sigma.V(x, a, e, z) = \top$.
Hyb_2: This hybrid is identical to the previous one except that in Step 4, V uniformly chooses r' such that $com = \mathsf{CBCom.Commit}(pp, e; r')$ and sends (e, r') to P^* instead of (e, r). We note that this procedure may be inefficient. This is just a conceptual change and thus we have $\Pr[win_1] = \Pr[win_2]$.

$\mathsf{Hyb_3}$: This hybrid is identical to the previous one except that in Step 2, V sends com $\xleftarrow{\$}$ CBCom.Commit(pp, 0^ℓ; r) and the generation of e is delayed to Step 4. Since no information of r is given to P^* due to the modification made in $\mathsf{Hyb_2}$, by the statistical hiding property of CBCom, we have $|\Pr[\mathsf{win_3}] - \Pr[\mathsf{win_2}]| = \mathsf{negl}(\lambda)$.

Now, it is easy to prove $\Pr[\mathsf{win_3}] = \mathsf{negl}(\lambda)$ by reducing it to the statistical soundness of the Σ-protocol. Namely, we consider a cheating prover $\Sigma.P^*$ against the Σ-protocol that works as follows.

1. $\Sigma.P^*$ runs P^* to get the first message pp.
2. $\Sigma.P^*$ computes com $\xleftarrow{\$}$ CBCom.Commit(pp, 0^ℓ; r), sends com to P^*, and gets the third message a. Then $\Sigma.P^*$ sends a to its own external challenger as the first message of the Σ-protocol.
3. Upon receiving a challenge e from the external challenger, $\Sigma.P^*$ uniformly chooses r' such that com = CBCom.Commit(pp, e; r'), sends (e, r') to P^*, and gets the P^*'s final message z. Then $\Sigma.P^*$ sends z to the external challenger.

It is easy to see that $\Sigma.P^*$ perfectly simulates the environment in $\mathsf{Hyb_3}$ for P^*. Therefore, $\Sigma.P^*$'s winning probability is equal to $\Pr[\mathsf{win_3}]$. On the other hand, by soundness of the Σ-protocol, $\Sigma.P^*$'s winning probability is $\mathsf{negl}(\lambda)$. Therefore we have $\Pr[\mathsf{win_3}] = \mathsf{negl}(\lambda)$.

Combining the above, we have $\Pr[\mathsf{win_1}] = \mathsf{negl}(\lambda)$, which means that the protocol satisfies the statistical soundness.

4.3   Quantum Black-Box ϵ-Zero-Knowledge

Structure of the Proof. A high-level structure of our proof is similar to that of [BS20]. Specifically, we first construct simulators $\mathsf{Sim_a}$ and $\mathsf{Sim_{na}}$ that simulate the "aborting case" and "non-aborting case", respectively. More precisely, $\mathsf{Sim_a}$ correctly simulates the verifier's view if the verifier aborts and otherwise returns a failure symbol Fail and $\mathsf{Sim_{na}}$ correctly simulates the verifier's view if the verifier does not abort and otherwise returns a failure symbol Fail. Then we consider a combined simulator $\mathsf{Sim_{comb}}$ that runs either of $\mathsf{Sim_a}$ or $\mathsf{Sim_{na}}$ with equal probability. Then $\mathsf{Sim_{comb}}$ correctly simulates the verifier's view conditioned on that the output is not Fail, and it returns Fail with probability almost $1/2$. By applying the Watrous' quantum rewinding lemma (Lemma 2.1) to $\mathsf{Sim_{comb}}$, we can convert it to a full-fledged simulator.

Though the above high-level structure is similar to [BS20], the analyses of simulators $\mathsf{Sim_a}$ and $\mathsf{Sim_{na}}$ are completely different from [BS20] since we consider different protocols. While the analysis of $\mathsf{Sim_a}$ is easy, the analysis of $\mathsf{Sim_{na}}$ is a little more complicated as it requires the extraction lemma (Lemma 3.1), which was developed in Sect. 3.

Proof of Quantum Black-Box ϵ-Zero-Knowledge. For clarity of exposition, we first show the quantum ϵ-zero-knowledge property ignoring that the simulator should be black-box. That is, we give the full description of the malicious verifier and its quantum advice as part of the simulator's input instead of only the oracle access to the verifier. At the end of the proof, we explain that the simulator is indeed black-box.

In quantum ϵ-zero-knowledge, we need to show a simulator Sim that takes an accuracy parameter $1^{\epsilon^{-1}}$ as part of its input. We assume $\epsilon(\lambda) = o(1)$ without loss of generality since the other case trivially follows from this case. Without loss of generality, we can assume that a malicious verifier V^* does not terminate the protocol before the prover aborts since it does not gain anything by declaring the termination. We say that V^* aborts if it fails to provide a valid opening (e, r) to com in Step 2b (i.e., the prover aborts in Step 2c).

First, we construct a simulator $\mathsf{Sim}_{\mathsf{comb}}$, which returns a special symbol Fail with probability roughly $1/2$ but almost correctly simulates the output of V_λ^* conditioned on that it does not return Fail. The simulator $\mathsf{Sim}_{\mathsf{comb}}$ uses simulators $\mathsf{Sim}_{\mathsf{a}}$ and $\mathsf{Sim}_{\mathsf{na}}$ as sub-protocols:

$\mathsf{Sim}_{\mathsf{comb}}(x, 1^{\epsilon^{-1}}, V_\lambda^*, \rho_\lambda)$:
1. Choose mode $\xleftarrow{\$} \{\mathsf{a}, \mathsf{na}\}$.
2. Run $\mathsf{Sim}_{\mathsf{mode}}(x, 1^{\epsilon^{-1}}, V_\lambda^*, \rho_\lambda)$.
3. Output what $\mathsf{Sim}_{\mathsf{mode}}$ outputs.

$\mathsf{Sim}_{\mathsf{a}}(x, 1^{\epsilon^{-1}}, V_\lambda^*, \rho_\lambda)$:[16]
1. Set V_λ^*'s internal state to ρ_λ.
2. Compute pp $\xleftarrow{\$}$ CBCom.Setup(1^λ) and send pp to V_λ^*.
3. V_λ^* returns com.
4. Compute $(a, \mathsf{st}) \xleftarrow{\$} \Sigma.P_1(x)$ and send a to V_λ^*.
5. V_λ^* returns (e, r).
6. Return Fail and abort if CBCom.Commit$(\mathsf{pp}, e; r) = \mathsf{com}$.
   Otherwise, let V_λ^* output the final output notifying that the prover aborts.
7. The final output of V_λ^* is treated as the output $\mathsf{Sim}_{\mathsf{a}}$.

$\mathsf{Sim}_{\mathsf{na}}(x, 1^{\epsilon^{-1}}, V_\lambda^*, \rho_\lambda)$:
1. Set V_λ^*'s internal state to ρ_λ.
2. Compute pp $\xleftarrow{\$}$ CBCom.Setup(1^λ) and send pp to V_λ^*.
3. V_λ^* returns com. Let ρ_{st} be the internal state of V_λ^* at this point.
4. Compute $(e_{\mathsf{Ext}}, \rho_{\mathsf{Ext}}) \xleftarrow{\$} \mathsf{Ext}(1^\lambda, 1^{\delta^{-1}}, \mathsf{pp}, \mathsf{com}, \mathcal{A}_{\mathsf{open},\lambda}, \rho_{\mathsf{st}})$ where Ext is as in Lemma 3.1 for the commitment scheme CBCom, $\delta := \frac{\epsilon^2}{3600 \log^4(\lambda)}$, and $\mathcal{A} = (\mathcal{A}_{\mathsf{com},\lambda}, \mathcal{A}_{\mathsf{open},\lambda})$ as defined below:
   $\mathcal{A}_{\mathsf{com},\lambda}(\mathsf{pp}; \rho_\lambda)$: It sets V_λ^*'s internal state to ρ_λ and sends pp to V_λ^*. Let com be the response by V_λ^* and ρ_{st} be the internal state of V_λ^* at this point. It outputs $(\mathsf{com}, \rho_{\mathsf{st}})$.
   $\mathcal{A}_{\mathsf{open},\lambda}(\rho_{\mathsf{st}})$: It generates $(a, \mathsf{st}) \xleftarrow{\$} \Sigma.P_1(x)$,[17] sets V_λ^*'s internal state to ρ_{st}, and sends a to V_λ^*. Let (e, r) be the response by V_λ^* and let

---

[16] Though $\mathsf{Sim}_{\mathsf{a}}$ does not depend on ϵ, we include $1^{\epsilon^{-1}}$ in the input for notational uniformity.

[17] We note that we consider x to be hardwired into $\mathcal{A}_{\mathsf{open},\lambda}$. We also note that though $\mathcal{A}_{\mathsf{open},\lambda}$ does not take explicit randomness, it can generate randomness by say, applying Hadamard on its working register and then measuring it.

ρ'_{st} be the internal state of V^*_λ at this point. It outputs $(e, r, \text{out} := (a, \text{st}), \rho'_{st})$.

Here, we remark that V^*_λ's internal register corresponds to **ST** and e corresponds to m in the notation of Lemma 3.1.

5. Set the verifier's internal state to ρ_{Ext}.
6. Compute $(a, z) \xleftarrow{\$} \text{Sim}_\Sigma(x, e_{Ext})$ and send a to V^*_λ.
7. V^*_λ returns (e, r).
8. Return Fail and abort if $e \neq e_{Ext}$ or $\text{CBCom.Commit}(pp, e; r) \neq \text{com}$. Otherwise, send z to V^*_λ.
9. The final output of V^*_λ is treated as the output Sim_{na}.

Intuitively, Sim_a (resp. Sim_{na}) is a simulator that simulates the verifier's view in the case that verifier aborts (resp. does not abort).

More formally, we prove the following lemmas.

Lemma 4.1 (Sim_a simulates the aborting case). *For any non-uniform QPT malicious verifier $V^* = \{V^*_\lambda, \rho_\lambda\}_{\lambda \in \mathbb{N}}$, let $\text{OUT}_{V^*_a}\langle P(w), V^*_\lambda(\rho_\lambda)\rangle(x)$ be the V^*_λ's final output that is replaced with Fail if V^*_λ does not abort. Then we have*

$$\{\text{OUT}_{V^*_a}\langle P(w), V^*_\lambda(\rho_\lambda)\rangle(x)\}_{\lambda,x,w} \equiv \{\text{Sim}_a(x, 1^{\epsilon^{-1}}, V^*_\lambda, \rho_\lambda)\}_{\lambda,x,w}.$$

where $\lambda \in \mathbb{N}$, $x \in L \cap \{0,1\}^\lambda$, and $w \in R_L(x)$.

Proof. Since Sim_a perfectly simulates the real execution for V^*_λ when it aborts, Lemma 4.1 immediately follows.

Lemma 4.2 (Sim_{na} simulates the non-aborting case). *For any non-uniform QPT malicious verifier $V^* = \{V^*_\lambda, \rho_\lambda\}_{\lambda \in \mathbb{N}}$, let $\text{OUT}_{V^*_{na}}\langle P(w), V^*_\lambda(\rho_\lambda)\rangle(x)$ be the V^*_λ's final output that is replaced with Fail if V^*_λ aborts. Then we have*

$$\{\text{OUT}_{V^*_{na}}\langle P(w), V^*_\lambda(\rho_\lambda)\rangle(x)\}_{\lambda,x,w} \stackrel{comp}{\approx}_\delta \{\text{Sim}_{na}(x, 1^{\epsilon^{-1}}, V^*_\lambda, \rho_\lambda)\}_{\lambda,x,w}$$

where $\lambda \in \mathbb{N}$, $x \in L \cap \{0,1\}^\lambda$, and $w \in R_L(x)$.

Proof. Here, we analyze $\text{Sim}_{na}(x, 1^{\epsilon^{-1}}, V^*_\lambda, \rho_\lambda)$. In the following, we consider hybrid simulators $\text{Sim}_{na,i}(x, w, 1^{\epsilon^{-1}}, V^*_\lambda, \rho_\lambda)$ for $i = 1, 2, 3$. We remark that they also take the witness w as input unlike Sim_{na}.

$\text{Sim}_{na,1}(x, w, 1^{\epsilon^{-1}}, V^*_\lambda, \rho_\lambda)$: This simulator works similarly to $\text{Sim}_{na}(x, 1^{\epsilon^{-1}}, V^*_\lambda, \rho_\lambda)$ except that it generates $(a, \text{st}) \xleftarrow{\$} \Sigma.P_1(x)$ and $z \xleftarrow{\$} \Sigma.P_3(\text{st}, w, e_{Ext})$ instead of $(a, z) \xleftarrow{\$} \text{Sim}_\Sigma(x, e_{Ext})$ in Step 6.
By the special honest-verifier zero-knowledge property of the Σ-protocol, we have

$$\{\text{Sim}_{na}(x, 1^{\epsilon^{-1}}, V^*_\lambda, \rho_\lambda)\}_{\lambda,x,w} \stackrel{comp}{\approx} \{\{\text{Sim}_{na,1}(x, w, 1^{\epsilon^{-1}}, V^*_\lambda, \rho_\lambda)\}_{\lambda,x,w}\}_{\lambda,x,w}$$

where $\lambda \in \mathbb{N}$, $x \in L \cap \{0,1\}^\lambda$, and $w \in R_L(x)$.

$\mathsf{Sim}_{\mathsf{na},2}(x, w, 1^{\epsilon^{-1}}, V_\lambda^*, \rho_\lambda)$: This simulator works similarly to $\mathsf{Sim}_{\mathsf{na},1}(x, w, 1^{\epsilon^{-1}}, V_\lambda^*, \rho_\lambda)$ except that the generation of z is delayed until Step 8 and it is generated as $z \xleftarrow{\$} \Sigma.P_3(\mathsf{st}, w, e)$ instead of $z \xleftarrow{\$} \Sigma.P_3(\mathsf{st}, w, e_{\mathsf{Ext}})$.

The modification does not affect the output distribution since it outputs Fail if $e \neq e_{\mathsf{Ext}}$ and if $e = e_{\mathsf{Ext}}$, then this simulator works in exactly the same way as the previous one. Therefore we have

$$\{\mathsf{Sim}_{\mathsf{na},1}(x, w, 1^{\epsilon^{-1}}, V_\lambda^*, \rho_\lambda)\}_{\lambda,x,w} \equiv \{\mathsf{Sim}_{\mathsf{na},2}(x, w, 1^{\epsilon^{-1}}, V_\lambda^*, \rho_\lambda)\}_{\lambda,x,w}$$

where $\lambda \in \mathbb{N}$, $x \in L \cap \{0,1\}^\lambda$, and $w \in R_L(x)$.

$\mathsf{Sim}_{\mathsf{na},3}(x, w, 1^{\epsilon^{-1}}, V_\lambda^*, \rho_\lambda)$: This simulator works similarly to $\mathsf{Sim}_{\mathsf{na},2}(x, w, 1^{\epsilon^{-1}}, V_\lambda^*, \rho_\lambda)$ except that Step 4 and 5 are deleted and the check of $e \neq e_{\mathsf{Ext}}$ in Step 8 is omitted. That is, it outputs Fail in Step 8 if and only if we have $\mathsf{CBCom.Commit}(\mathsf{pp}, e; r) \neq \mathsf{com}$.

We note that e_{Ext} and ρ_{Ext} are no longer used at all and thus need not be generated.

We can see that Step 3 is exactly the same as executing $(\mathsf{com}, \rho_{\mathsf{st}}) \xleftarrow{\$} \mathcal{A}_{\mathsf{com},\lambda}(\mathsf{pp}; \rho_\lambda)$ and Step 6 and 7 of previous and this experiments are exactly the same as executing $(e, r, \mathsf{out} = (a, \mathsf{st}), \rho'_{\mathsf{st}}) \xleftarrow{\$} \mathcal{A}_{\mathsf{open},\lambda}(\rho_{\mathsf{Ext}})$ and $(e, r, \mathsf{out} = (a, \mathsf{st}), \rho'_{\mathsf{st}}) \xleftarrow{\$} \mathcal{A}_{\mathsf{open},\lambda}(\rho_{\mathsf{st}})$, respectively where we define ρ'_{st} in simulated experiments as V_λ^*'s internal state after Step 7. Moreover, the rest of execution of the simulators can be done given $(\mathsf{pp}, \mathsf{com}, e, r, \mathsf{out} = (a, \mathsf{st}), \rho'_{\mathsf{st}})$. Therefore, by a straightforward reduction to Lemma 3.1, we have

$$\{\mathsf{Sim}_{\mathsf{na},2}(x, w, 1^{\epsilon^{-1}}, V_\lambda^*, \rho_\lambda)\}_{\lambda,x,w} \overset{comp}{\approx}_\delta \{\mathsf{Sim}_{\mathsf{na},3}(x, w, 1^{\epsilon^{-1}}, V_\lambda^*, \rho_\lambda)\}_{\lambda,x,w}$$

where $\lambda \in \mathbb{N}$, $x \in L \cap \{0,1\}^\lambda$, and $w \in R_L(x)$.

We can see that $\mathsf{Sim}_{\mathsf{na},3}(x, w, 1^{\epsilon^{-1}}, V_\lambda^*, \rho_\lambda)$ perfectly simulates the real execution for V_λ^* and outputs V_λ^*'s output conditioned on that V_λ^* does not abort, and just outputs Fail otherwise. Therefore, we have

$$\{\mathsf{Sim}_{\mathsf{na},3}(x, w, 1^{\epsilon^{-1}}, V_\lambda^*, \rho_\lambda)\}_{\lambda,x,w} \equiv \{\mathsf{OUT}_{V_{\mathsf{na}}^*}\langle P(w), V_\lambda^*(\rho_\lambda)\rangle(x)\}_{\lambda,x,w}$$

where $\lambda \in \mathbb{N}$, $x \in L \cap \{0,1\}^\lambda$, and $w \in R_L(x)$. Combining the above, Lemma 4.2 is proven.

By combining Lemmas 4.1 and 4.2, we can prove the following lemma.

Lemma 4.3 ($\mathsf{Sim}_{\mathsf{comb}}$ simulates V_λ^*'s output with probability almost 1/2). *For any non-uniform QPT malicious verifier $V^* = \{V_\lambda^*, \rho_\lambda\}_{\lambda \in \mathbb{N}}$, let $p_{\mathsf{comb}}^{\mathsf{suc}}(x, 1^{\epsilon^{-1}}, V_\lambda^*, \rho_\lambda)$ be the probability that $\mathsf{Sim}_{\mathsf{comb}}(x, 1^{\epsilon^{-1}}, V_\lambda^*, \rho_\lambda)$ does not return Fail and $D_{\mathsf{sim,comb}}(x, 1^{\epsilon^{-1}}, V_\lambda^*, \rho_\lambda)$ be a conditional distribution of $\mathsf{Sim}_{\mathsf{comb}}(x, 1^{\epsilon^{-1}}, V_\lambda^*, \rho_\lambda)$, conditioned on that it does not return Fail. There exists a negligible function negl such that for any $x = \{x_\lambda \in L \cap \{0,1\}^\lambda\}_{\lambda \in \mathbb{N}}$, we have*

$$\left| p_{\mathsf{comb}}^{\mathsf{suc}}(x, 1^{\epsilon^{-1}}, V_\lambda^*, \rho_\lambda) - 1/2 \right| \leq \delta/2 + \mathsf{negl}(\lambda). \tag{1}$$

Moreover, we have

$$\{\mathsf{OUT}_{V^*}\langle P(w), V_\lambda^*(\rho_\lambda)\rangle(x)\}_{\lambda,x,w} \overset{comp}{\approx}_{4\delta} \{D_{\mathsf{sim},\mathsf{comb}}(x, 1^{\epsilon^{-1}}, V_\lambda^*, \rho_\lambda)\}_{\lambda,x,w} \quad (2)$$

where $\lambda \in \mathbb{N}$, $x \in L \cap \{0,1\}^\lambda$, and $w \in R_L(x)$.

Proof. (sketch.) Intuition of the proof is very easy: By Lemma 4.1 and 4.2, Sim_a and Sim_{na} almost simulate the real output distribution of V_λ^* conditioned on that V_λ^* aborts and does not abort, respectively. Therefore, if we randomly guess if V_λ^* aborts and runs either of Sim_a and Sim_{na} that successfully works for the guessed case, the output distribution is close to the real output distribution of V_λ^* conditioned on that the guess is correct, which happens with probability almost $1/2$.

Indeed, the actual proof is based on the above idea, but for obtaining concrete bounds as in Eq. 1 and 2, we need some tedious calculations. We give a full proof in the full version since the proof is easy and very similar to that in [BS20] (once we obtain Lemma 4.1 and 4.2).

Then, we convert $\mathsf{Sim}_{\mathsf{comb}}$ to a full-fledged simulator that does not return Fail by using the quantum rewinding lemma (Lemma 2.1). Namely, we let Q be a quantum algorithm that takes ρ_λ as input and outputs $\mathsf{Sim}_{\mathsf{comb}}(x, 1^{\epsilon^{-1}}, V_\lambda^*, \rho_\lambda)$ where $b := 0$ if and only if it does not return Fail, $p_0 := \frac{1}{4}$, $q := \frac{1}{2}$, $\gamma := \delta$, and $T := 2\log(1/\delta)$. Then it is easy to check that the conditions for Lemma 2.1 is satisfied by Eq. 1 in Lemma 4.3 (for sufficiently large λ). Then by using Lemma 2.1, we can see that $\mathsf{R}(1^T, \mathsf{Q}, \rho_\lambda)$ runs in time $T \cdot |\mathsf{Q}| = \mathsf{poly}(\lambda)$ and its output (seen as a mixed state) has a trace distance bounded by $4\sqrt{\gamma}\frac{\log(1/\gamma)}{p_0(1-p_0)}$ from $D_{\mathsf{sim},\mathsf{comb}}(x, 1^{\epsilon^{-1}}, V_\lambda^*, \rho_\lambda)$. Since we have $\gamma = \delta = \frac{\epsilon^2}{3600\log^4(\lambda)} = 1/\mathsf{poly}(\lambda)$, we have $4\sqrt{\gamma}\frac{\log(1/\gamma)}{p_0(1-p_0)} < 30\sqrt{\gamma}\log^2(\lambda) = \frac{\epsilon}{2}$ for sufficiently large λ where we used $\log(1/\gamma) = \log(\mathsf{poly}(\lambda)) = o(\log^2(\lambda))$. Thus, by combining the above and Eq. 2 in Lemma 4.3, if we define $\mathsf{Sim}(x, 1^{\epsilon^{-1}}, V_\lambda^*, \rho_\lambda) := \mathsf{R}(1^T, \mathsf{Q}, \rho_\lambda)$, then we have

$$\mathsf{OUT}_{V^*}\langle P(w), V_\lambda^*(\rho_\lambda)\rangle(x) \overset{comp}{\approx}_{\frac{\epsilon}{2}+4\delta} \mathsf{Sim}(x, 1^{\epsilon^{-1}}, V_\lambda^*, \rho_\lambda).$$

We can conclude the proof of quantum ϵ-zero-knowledge by noting that we have $\frac{\epsilon}{2} + 4\delta < \epsilon$ since we have $\delta = \frac{\epsilon^2}{3600\log^4(\lambda)} < \frac{\epsilon}{8}$.

Black-Box Simulation. Here, we explain that the simulator Sim constructed as above only needs black-box access to the verifier. What we need to show are that Sim applies the unitary part $U_{V_\lambda^*}$ of V_λ^* and its inverse $U_{V_\lambda^*}^\dagger$ only as oracles and Sim does not directly act on V_λ^*'s internal register. There are two parts of the construction of Sim that are not obviously black-box. The first is Step 4 and 5 of Sim_{na} where it runs the extraction algorithm Ext of Lemma 3.1, and the second is the conversion from $\mathsf{Sim}_{\mathsf{comb}}$ to Sim using R in Lemma 2.1. In the following, we explain that both steps can be implemented by black-box access to the verifier.

1. By Lemma 3.1, Ext uses the unitary part of $\mathcal{A}_{\text{open},\lambda}$ and its inverse only in a black-box manner, and they can be implemented by black-box access to $U_{V_\lambda^*}$ and $U_{V_\lambda^*}^\dagger$. Moreover, since register **ST** in the notation of Lemma 3.1 corresponds to the internal register of V_λ^* in our context, the lemma ensures that Ext does not directly act on it. Also, Sim_{na} need not explicitly set V_λ^*'s internal register to ρ_{Ext} in Step 5 if we do the above black-box simulation since a state in the register automatically becomes ρ_{Ext} after the execution as stated in Lemma 3.1. Therefore, this step can be implemented by black-box access to V_λ^*.

2. Given the above observation, we now know that both Sim_{a} and Sim_{na} only need black-box access to V_λ^*. This means that Q only needs black-box access to V_λ^*. Since R only uses Q as oracles that perform the unitary part of Q and its inverse as stated in Lemma 2.1 and they can be implemented by black-box access to V_λ^*, R uses $U_{V_\lambda^*}$ and $U_{V_\lambda^*}^\dagger$ only as oracles. Moreover, since the register Inp in Lemma 2.1 corresponds to the internal register of V_λ^* in our context, R does not directly act on it.

By the above observations, we can see that the simulator Sim only needs black-box access to V_λ^*.

4.4 Instantiation from Collapsing Hash Function

Our construction in Fig. 1 is based on two building blocks: a statistically hiding and strong collapse-binding commitment scheme and a delayed-witness Σ-protocol. Though the former can be instantiated by a collapsing hash function, we do not know how to instantiate the latter by a collapsing hash function since it needs non-interactive commitment that is not known to be implied by collapsing hash functions. However, we can just use a 4-round version of a delayed-witness Σ-protocol where the first message "commitment" in the Σ-protocol is instantiated based on Naor's commitments [Nao91] instead of a non-interactive one. Since Naor's commitments can be instantiated under any OWF and collapsing hash function is trivially also one-way, we can instantiate the 4-round version of a delayed-witness Σ-protocol based on a collapsing hash function. We can prove security of the construction based on 4-round version of a delayed-witness Σ-protocol in essentially the same manner as the security proofs in Sect. 4.2 and 4.3. We also note that this does not increase the number of rounds of our construction. Based on these observations, we obtain Theorem 4.2.

Acknowledgement. NHC's research is support by the U.S. Department of Defense and NIST through the Hartree Postdoctoral Fellowship at QuICS and by NSF through IUCRC Planning Grant Indiana University: Center for Quantum Technologies (CQT) under award number 2052730. KMC's research is partially supported by MOST, Taiwan, under Grant no. MOST 109-2223-E-001-001-MY3 and Executive Yuan Data Safety and Talent Cultivation Project (ASKPQ-109-DSTCP).

References

[ACGH20] Alagic, G., Childs, A.M., Grilo, A.B., Hung, S.-H.: Non-interactive classical verification of quantum computation. In: Pass, R., Pietrzak, K. (eds.) TCC 2020, Part III. LNCS, vol. 12552, pp. 153–180. Springer, Cham (2020). https://doi.org/10.1007/978-3-030-64381-2_6

[AL20] Ananth, P., La Placa, R.L.: Secure quantum extraction protocols. In: Pass, R., Pietrzak, K. (eds.) TCC 2020, Part III. LNCS, vol. 12552, pp. 123–152. Springer, Cham (2020). https://doi.org/10.1007/978-3-030-64381-2_5

[AR06] Aharon, N., Regev, O.: Witness-preserving Amplification of QMA (lecture note) (2006). https://cims.nyu.edu/regev/teaching/quantum_fall_2005/ln/qma.pdf

[BC90] Brassard, G., Crepeau, C.: Sorting out zero-knowledge. In: Quisquater, J.-J., Vandewalle, J. (eds.) EUROCRYPT 1989. LNCS, vol. 434, pp. 181–191. Springer, Heidelberg (1990). https://doi.org/10.1007/3-540-46885-4_20

[BCY91] Brassard, G., Crépeau, C., Yung, M.: Constant-round perfect zero-knowledge computationally convincing protocols. Theor. Comput. Sci. 84(1), 23–52 (1991)

[BG20] Broadbent, A., Grilo, A.B.: QMA-hardness of consistency of local density matrices with applications to quantum zero-knowledge. In: 61st FOCS, pp. 196–205 (2020)

[BJSW20] Broadbent, A., Ji, Z., Song, F., Watrous, J.: Zero-knowledge proof systems for QMA. SIAM J. Comput. 49(2), 245–283 (2020)

[BKP18] Bitansky, N., Kalai, Y.T., Paneth, O.: Multi-collision resistance: a paradigm for keyless hash functions. In: 50th ACM STOC, pp. 671–684 (2018)

[BKP19] Bitansky, N., Khurana, D., Paneth, O.: Weak zero-knowledge beyond the black-box barrier. In: 51st ACM STOC, pp. 1091–1102 (2019)

[BL02] Barak, B., Lindell, Y.: Strict polynomial-time in simulation and extraction. In: 34th ACM STOC, pp. 484–493 (2002)

[BLP13] Brakerski, Z., Langlois, A., Peikert, C., Regev, O., Stehlé, D.: Classical hardness of learning with errors. In: 45th ACM STOC, pp. 575–584 (2013)

[Blu86] Blum, M.: How to prove a theorem so no one else can claim it. In: Proceedings of the International Congress of Mathematicians, pp. 1444–1451 (1986)

[BP12] Bitansky, N., Paneth, O.: Point obfuscation and 3-round zero-knowledge. In: Cramer, R. (ed.) TCC 2012. LNCS, vol. 7194, pp. 190–208. Springer, Heidelberg (2012). https://doi.org/10.1007/978-3-642-28914-9_11

[Bra18] Brakerski, Z.: Quantum FHE (almost) as secure as classical. In: Shacham, H., Boldyreva, A. (eds.) CRYPTO 2018, Part III. LNCS, vol. 10993, pp. 67–95. Springer, Cham (2018). https://doi.org/10.1007/978-3-319-96878-0_3

[BS20] Bitansky, N., Shmueli, O.: Post-quantum zero knowledge in constant rounds. In: 52nd ACM STOC, pp. 269–279 (2020)

[BY20] Brakerski, Z., Yuen, H.: Quantum Garbled Circuits. arXiv:2006.01085 (2020)

[CCLY21] Chia, N.-H., Chung, K.-M., Liu, Q., Yamakawa, T.: On the Impossibility of Post-Quantum Black-Box Zero-Knowledge in Constant Rounds. arXiv:2103.11244 (2021)

[CCY20] Chia, N.-H., Chung, K.-M., Yamakawa, T.: Classical verification of quantum computations with efficient verifier. In: Pass, R., Pietrzak, K. (eds.) TCC 2020, Part III. LNCS, vol. 12552, pp. 181–206. Springer, Cham (2020). https://doi.org/10.1007/978-3-030-64381-2_7

[CLP15] Chung, K.-M., Lui, E., Pass, R.: From weak to strong zero-knowledge and applications. In: Dodis, Y., Nielsen, J.B. (eds.) TCC 2015, Part I. LNCS, vol. 9014, pp. 66–92. Springer, Heidelberg (2015). https://doi.org/10.1007/978-3-662-46494-6_4

[CVZ20] Coladangelo, A., Vidick, T., Zhang, T.: Non-interactive zero-knowledge arguments for QMA, with preprocessing. In: Micciancio, D., Ristenpart, T. (eds.) CRYPTO 2020, Part III. LNCS, vol. 12172, pp. 799–828. Springer, Cham (2020). https://doi.org/10.1007/978-3-030-56877-1_28

[DFS04] Damgård, I., Fehr, S., Salvail, L.: Zero-knowledge proofs and string commitments withstanding quantum attacks. In: Franklin, M. (ed.) CRYPTO 2004. LNCS, vol. 3152, pp. 254–272. Springer, Heidelberg (2004). https://doi.org/10.1007/978-3-540-28628-8_16

[DNRS03] Dwork, C., Naor, M., Reingold, O., Stockmeyer, L.J.: Magic functions. J. ACM 50(6), 852–921 (2003)

[DNS04] Dwork, C., Naor, M., Sahai, A.: Concurrent zero-knowledge. J. ACM 51(6), 851–898 (2004)

[FGJ18] Fleischhacker, N., Goyal, V., Jain, A.: On the existence of three round zero-knowledge proofs. In: Nielsen, J.B., Rijmen, V. (eds.) EUROCRYPT 2018, Part III. LNCS, vol. 10822, pp. 3–33. Springer, Cham (2018). https://doi.org/10.1007/978-3-319-78372-7_1

[FS90] Feige, U., Shamir, A.: Zero knowledge proofs of knowledge in two rounds. In: Brassard, G. (ed.) CRYPTO 1989. LNCS, vol. 435, pp. 526–544. Springer, New York (1990). https://doi.org/10.1007/0-387-34805-0_46

[GK96] Goldreich, O., Kahan, A.: How to construct constant-round zero-knowledge proof systems for NP. J. Cryptol. 9(3), 167–190 (1996)

[GMR89] Goldwasser, S., Micali, S., Rackoff, C.: The knowledge complexity of interactive proof systems. SIAM J. Comput. 18(1), 186–208 (1989)

[GMW91] Goldreich, O., Micali, S., Wigderson, A.: Proofs that yield nothing but their validity for all languages in NP have zero-knowledge proof systems. J. ACM 38(3), 691–729 (1991)

[Gol01] Goldreich, O.: The Foundations of Cryptography - Volume 1: Basic Techniques. Cambridge University Press, Cambridge (2001)

[Gol04] Goldreich, O.: The Foundations of Cryptography - Volume 2: Basic Applications. Cambridge University Press, Cambridge (2004)

[Gra97] Graaf, J.V.D.: Towards a formal definition of security for quantum protocols. PhD thesis, University of Montreal, Montreal, Canada (1997)

[HILL99] Håstad, J., Impagliazzo, R., Levin, L.A., Luby, M.: A pseudorandom generator from any one-way function. SIAM J. Comput. 28(4), 1364–1396 (1999)

[JKKR17] Jain, A., Kalai, Y.T., Khurana, D., Rothblum, R.: Distinguisher-dependent simulation in two rounds and its applications. In: Katz, J., Shacham, H. (eds.) CRYPTO 2017, Part II. LNCS, vol. 10402, pp. 158–189. Springer, Cham (2017). https://doi.org/10.1007/978-3-319-63715-0_6

[Kob03] Kobayashi, H.: Non-interactive quantum perfect and statistical zero-knowledge. In: Ibaraki, T., Katoh, N., Ono, H. (eds.) ISAAC 2003. LNCS, vol. 2906, pp. 178–188. Springer, Heidelberg (2003). https://doi.org/10.1007/978-3-540-24587-2_20

[Mah18a] Mahadev, U.: Classical homomorphic encryption for quantum circuits. In: 59th FOCS, pp. 332–338 (2018)

[Mah18b] Mahadev, U.: Classical verification of quantum computations. In: 59th FOCS, pp. 259–267 (2018)

[Nao91] Naor, M.: Bit commitment using pseudorandomness. J. Cryptol. **4**(2), 151–158 (1991)

[NWZ09] Nagaj, D., Wocjan, P., Zhang, Y.: Fast Amplification of QMA. arXiv:0904.1549 (2009)

[Pas03] Pass, R.: Simulation in quasi-polynomial time, and its application to protocol composition. In: Biham, E. (ed.) EUROCRYPT 2003. LNCS, vol. 2656, pp. 160–176. Springer, Heidelberg (2003). https://doi.org/10.1007/3-540-39200-9_10

[Pei09] Peikert, C.: Public-key cryptosystems from the worst-case shortest vector problem: extended abstract. In: 41st ACM STOC, pp. 333–342 (2009)

[PS19] Peikert, C., Shiehian, S.: Noninteractive zero knowledge for NP from (plain) learning with errors. In: Boldyreva, A., Micciancio, D. (eds.) CRYPTO 2019, Part I. LNCS, vol. 11692, pp. 89–114. Springer, Cham (2019). https://doi.org/10.1007/978-3-030-26948-7_4

[PW08] Peikert, C., Waters, B.: Lossy trapdoor functions and their applications. In: 40th ACM STOC, pp. 187–196 (2008)

[PW09] Pass, R., Wee, H.: Black-box constructions of two-party protocols from one-way functions. In: Reingold, O. (ed.) TCC 2009. LNCS, vol. 5444, pp. 403–418. Springer, Heidelberg (2009). https://doi.org/10.1007/978-3-642-00457-5_24

[Reg09] Regev, O.: On lattices, learning with errors, random linear codes, and cryptography. J. ACM **56**(6), 34:1-34:40 (2009)

[Shm20] Shmueli, O.: Multi-theorem (Malicious) Designated-Verifier NIZK for QMA. arXiv:2007.12923 (2020)

[SV03] Sahai, A., Vadhan, S.P.: A complete problem for statistical zero knowledge. J. ACM **50**(2), 196–249 (2003)

[Unr12] Unruh, D.: Quantum proofs of knowledge. In: Pointcheval, D., Johansson, T. (eds.) EUROCRYPT 2012. LNCS, vol. 7237, pp. 135–152. Springer, Heidelberg (2012). https://doi.org/10.1007/978-3-642-29011-4_10

[Unr16a] Unruh, D.: Collapse-binding quantum commitments without random oracles. In: Cheon, J.H., Takagi, T. (eds.) ASIACRYPT 2016, Part II. LNCS, vol. 10032, pp. 166–195. Springer, Heidelberg (2016). https://doi.org/10.1007/978-3-662-53890-6_6

[Unr16b] Unruh, D.: Computationally binding quantum commitments. In: Fischlin, M., Coron, J.-S. (eds.) EUROCRYPT 2016, Part II. LNCS, vol. 9666, pp. 497–527. Springer, Heidelberg (2016). https://doi.org/10.1007/978-3-662-49896-5_18

[Wat09] Watrous, J.: Zero-knowledge against quantum attacks. SIAM J. Comput. **39**(1), 25–58 (2009)

[Zha19] Zhandry, M.: Quantum lightning never strikes the same state twice. In: Ishai, Y., Rijmen, V. (eds.) EUROCRYPT 2019, Part III. LNCS, vol. 11478, pp. 408–438. Springer, Cham (2019). https://doi.org/10.1007/978-3-030-17659-4_14

On the Concurrent Composition
of Quantum Zero-Knowledge

Prabhanjan Ananth[1]([✉]), Kai-Min Chung[2], and Rolando L. La Placa[3]

[1] UCSB, Santa Barbara, USA
prabhanjan@cs.ucsb.edu
[2] Academia Sinica, Taipei City, Taiwan
kmchung@iis.sinica.edu.tw
[3] MIT, Cambridge, USA
rlaplaca@mit.edu

Abstract. We study the notion of zero-knowledge secure against quantum polynomial-time verifiers (referred to as quantum zero-knowledge) in the concurrent composition setting. Despite being extensively studied in the classical setting, concurrent composition in the quantum setting has hardly been studied.

We initiate a formal study of concurrent quantum zero-knowledge. Our results are as follows:

- **Bounded Concurrent QZK for NP and QMA**: Assuming post-quantum one-way functions, there exists a quantum zero-knowledge proof system for NP in the bounded concurrent setting. In this setting, we fix a priori the number of verifiers that can simultaneously interact with the prover. Under the same assumption, we also show that there exists a quantum zero-knowledge proof system for QMA in the bounded concurrency setting.
- **Quantum Proofs of Knowledge**: Assuming quantum hardness of learning with errors (QLWE), there exists a bounded concurrent zero-knowledge proof system for NP satisfying quantum proof of knowledge property.

  Our extraction mechanism simultaneously allows for extraction probability to be negligibly close to acceptance probability (*extractability*) and also ensures that the prover's state after extraction is statistically close to the prover's state after interacting with the verifier (*simulatability*).

  Even in the standalone setting, the seminal work of [Unruh EUROCRYPT'12], and all its followups, satisfied a weaker version of extractability property and moreover, did not achieve simulatability. Our result yields a proof of *quantum knowledge* system for QMA with better parameters than prior works.

1 Introduction

Zero-knowledge [GMR85] is one of the foundational concepts in cryptography. A zero-knowledge system for NP is an interactive protocol between a prover P, who

© International Association for Cryptologic Research 2021
T. Malkin and C. Peikert (Eds.): CRYPTO 2021, LNCS 12825, pp. 346–374, 2021.
https://doi.org/10.1007/978-3-030-84242-0_13

receives as input an instance x and a witness w, and a verifier V who receives as input an instance x. The (classical) zero-knowledge property roughly states that the view of the malicious probabilistic polynomial-time verifier V^* generated after interacting with the prover P can be simulated by a PPT simulator, who doesn't know the witness w.

Protocol Composition in the Quantum Setting. Typical zero-knowledge proof systems only focus on the case when the malicious verifier is classical. The potential threat of quantum computers forces us to revisit this definition. There are already many works [ARU14, BJSW16, BG19, BS20, ALP20, VZ20, ABG+20], starting with the work of Watrous [Wat09], that consider the definition of zero-knowledge against verifiers modeled as quantum polynomial-time (QPT) algorithms; henceforth this definition will be referred to as quantum zero-knowledge. However, most of these works study quantum zero-knowledge only in the standalone setting. These constructions work under the assumption that the designed protocols work in isolation. That is, a standalone protocol is one that only guarantees security if the parties participating in an execution of this protocol do not partake in any other protocol execution. This is an unrealistic assumption. Indeed, the standalone setting has been questioned in the classical cryptography literature by a large number of works [DS98, DCO99, Can01, CLOS02, CF01, RK99, BS05, DNS04, PRS02, Lin03, Pas04, PV08, PTV14, GJO+13, CLP15, FKP19] that have focussed on designing cryptographic protocols that still guarantee security even when composed with the other protocols.

A natural question to ask is whether there exist *quantum* zero-knowledge protocols (without any setup) that still guarantee security under composition. Barring a few works [Unr10, JKMR06, ABG+20], this direction has largely been unaddressed. The couple of works [JKMR06, ABG+20] that do address composition only focus on parallel composition; in this setting, all the verifiers interacting with the prover should send the ith round messages before the $(i+1)^{th}$ round begins. The setting of parallel composition is quite restrictive; it disallows the adversarial verifiers from arbitrarily interleaving their messages with the prover. A more reasonable scenario, also referred to as *concurrent composition*, would be to allow the adversarial verifiers to choose the scheduling of their messages in any order they desire. So far, there has been no work that addresses concurrent composition in the quantum setting.

Concurrent Quantum Zero-Knowledge. In the concurrent setting, quantum zero-knowledge is defined as follows: there is a single prover, who on input instance-witness pair (x, w), can simultaneously interact with multiple verifiers, where all these verifiers are controlled by a single malicious quantum polynomial-time adversary. All the verifiers can potentially share an entangled state. Moreover, they can arbitrarily interleave their messages when they interact with the prover. For example, suppose the prover sends a message to the first verifier, instead of responding, it could let the second verifier send a message, after which the third verifier interacts with the prover and so on.

We say that zero-knowledge in this setting holds if there exists a quantum polynomial-time simulator (with access to the initial quantum state of all the verifiers) that can simultaneously simulate the interaction between the prover and all the verifiers.

We ask the following question in this work:

Do there exist quantum zero-knowledge proof systems that are secure under concurrent composition?

1.1   Our Contributions

Bounded Concurrent QZK for NP. We initiate a formal study of concurrent composition in the quantum setting. We work in the bounded concurrent setting: where the prover interacts only with a bounded number of verifiers where this bound is fixed at the time of protocol specification. This setting has been well studied in the classical concurrency literature [Lin03, PR03, Pas04, PTW09]. Moreover, we note that the only other existing work that constructs quantum zero-knowledge against multiple verifiers albeit in the parallel composition setting, namely [ABG+20][1], also works in the bounded setting. We prove the following.

Theorem 1 (Informal). *Assuming the existence of post-quantum one-way functions[2], there exists a bounded concurrent quantum zero-knowledge proof system for NP. Additionally, our protocol is a public coin proof system.*

Our construction satisfies quantum black-box zero-knowledge[3]. We note that achieving public-coin *unbounded* concurrrent ZK is impossible [PTW09] even in the classical setting.

Quantum Proofs of Knowledge. Our construction, described above, only satisfies the standard soundness guarantee. A more desirable property is quantum proof of knowledge. Roughly speaking, proof of knowledge states the following: suppose a malicious (computationally unbounded) prover can convince a verifier to accept an instance x with probability ε. Let the state of the prover at the end of interaction with the verifier be $|\Psi\rangle$[4]. Then there exists an efficient extractor,

---

[1] They achieve bounded parallel ZK under the assumption of quantum learning with errors and circular security assumption in constant rounds. While the notion they consider is sufficient for achieving MPC, the parallel QZK constructed by [ABG+20] has the drawback that the simulator aborts even if one of the verifiers abort. Whereas the notion of bounded concurrent QZK we consider allows for the simulation to proceed even if one of the sessions abort. On the downside, our protocol runs in polynomially many rounds.

[2] That is, one-way functions secure against (non-uniform) quantum polynomial-time algorithms.

[3] The simulator has oracle access to the unitary V and $V^\dagger$, where V is the verifier.

[4] We work in the purified picture and thus we can assume that the output of the prover is a pure state.

with black-box access to the prover, that can output a witness w for x with probability δ. Additionally, it also outputs a quantum state $|\Phi\rangle$. Ideally, we require the following two conditions to hold: (i) $|\varepsilon - \delta|$ is negligible and, (ii) the states $|\Psi\rangle$ and $|\Phi\rangle$ are close in trace distance; this property is also referred to as simulatability property. Unruh [Unr12] presented a construction of quantum proofs of knowledge; their construction satisfies (i) but not (ii). Indeed, the prover's state, after it interacts with the extractor, could be completely destroyed. Condition (ii) is especially important if we were to use quantum proofs of knowledge protocols as a sub-routine inside larger protocols, for instance in secure multiparty computation protocols.

Since Unruh's work, there have been other works that present constructions that satisfy both the above conditions but they demonstrate extraction only against *computationally bounded* adversaries [HSS11, BS20, ALP20]. Thus, it has been an important open problem to design quantum proofs of knowledge satisfying both of the above conditions.

We show the following.

Theorem 2 (Informal). *Assuming that learning with errors is hard against QPT algorithms (QLWE), there exists a bounded concurrent quantum zero-knowledge proof system for NP satisfying quantum proofs of knowledge property.*

Unlike all of the previous quantum proof of knowledge protocols which make use of Unruh's rewinding technique, we make black-box use of Watrous rewinding lemma in conjunction with novel cryptographic tools to prove the above theorem. On the downside, our protocol runs in polynomially many rounds, while Unruh's technique works for the existing 3-message Σ protocols.

Bounded Concurrent QZK for QMA. We also show how to extend our result to achieve bounded concurrrent zero-knowledge proof system for QMA [KSVV02] (a quantum-analogue of MA).

We show the following.

Theorem 3 (Informal). *Assuming post-quantum one-way functions, there exists a bounded concurrent quantum zero-knowledge proof system for QMA.*

This improves upon the existing QZK protocols for QMA [BJSW16, BG19, CVZ20, BS20] which only guarantee security in the standalone setting.

Our construction considers a simplified version of the framework of [BJSW16][5] and instantiates the underlying primitives in their protocol with bounded concurrent secure constructions.

We could combine the recent work of Coladangelo et al. [CVZ20] with our quantum proof of knowledge system for NP to obtain a proof of *quantum* knowledge system for QMA. This result yields better parameters than the one guaranteed in prior works [CVZ20, BG19]. Specifically, if the malicious prover convinces

---

[5] For the reader familiar with [BJSW16], we consider a coin-flipping protocol secure against explainable adversaries as against malicious adversaries as considered in [BJSW16].

the verifier with probability negligibly close to 1 then the extractor (in our result) can extract a state that is negligibly close to the witness state whereas the previous works did not have this guarantee.

1.2 Guide to the Reader

We present the overview of our results in the technical sections, just before presenting a formal description of the results.

- In Sect. 2, we present the definitions of concurrent QZK proof systems for NP and QMA. In the same section, we present definitions of quantum proof of knowledge.
- **Bounded Concurrent QZK**: In Sect. 3, we present the construction of bounded concurrent QZK for NP. We first begin with an overview of the construction and then present the formal construction in the same section. The proofs are presented in the Appendix (see the relevant references at the end of Sect. 3).
- **QZK Proof of Knowledge**: In Sect. 4.1, we present the construction of bounded concurrent QZK proof of knowledge for NP. We first begin with an overview of the construction and then present the formal construction in the same section. This construction involves the tool of oblivious transfer; we present the definition and the construction of oblivious transfer in the Appendix.
- **Bounded Concurrent QZK for QMA**: Finally, we present a construction of bounded concurrent QZK for QMA in Sect. 5.

2   Concurrent Quantum ZK Proof Systems: Definitions

We denote the security parameter by λ.

We denote the (classical) computational indistiguishability of the two distributions $\mathcal{D}_0$ and $\mathcal{D}_1$ by $\mathcal{D}_0 \approx_{c,\varepsilon} \mathcal{D}_1$, where ε is the distinguishing advantage. In the case when ε is negligible, we drop ε from this notation.

We define two distributions $\mathcal{D}_0$ and $\mathcal{D}_1$ to be quantum computationally indistinguishable if they cannot be distinguished by QPT distinguishers; we define this formally in the full version. We denote this by $\mathcal{D}_0 \approx_{\mathcal{Q},\varepsilon} \mathcal{D}_1$, where ε is the distinguishing advantage. We denote the process of an algorithm A being executed on input a sample from a distribution $\mathcal{D}$ by the notation $A(\mathcal{D})$.

Languages and Relations. A language $\mathcal{L}$ is a subset of $\{0,1\}^*$. A (classical) relation $\mathcal{R}$ is a subset of $\{0,1\}^* \times \{0,1\}^*$. We use the following notation:

- Suppose $\mathcal{R}$ is a relation. We define $\mathcal{R}$ to be *efficiently decidable* if there exists an algorithm A and fixed polynomial p such that $(x,w) \in \mathcal{R}$ if and only if $A(x,w) = 1$ and the running time of A is upper bounded by $p(|x|, |w|)$.

– Suppose $\mathcal{R}$ is an efficiently decidable relation. We say that $\mathcal{R}$ is a NP relation if $\mathcal{L}(\mathcal{R})$ is a NP language, where $\mathcal{L}(\mathcal{R})$ is defined as follows: $x \in \mathcal{L}(R)$ if and only if there exists w such that $(x, w) \in \mathcal{R}$ and $|w| \leq p(|x|)$ for some fixed polynomial p.

In Sect. 2.1, we define the notion of bounded concurrent QZK for NP. In Sect. 2.2, we define the notion of bounded concurrent ZK for QMA. We present the definition of quantum proof of knowledge in Sect. 2.3.

2.1 Bounded Concurrent QZK for NP

We start by recalling the definitions of the completeness and soundness properties of a classical interactive proof system.

Definition 1 (Proof System). *Let Π be an interactive protocol between a classical PPT prover P and a classical PPT verifier V. Let $\mathcal{R}(\mathcal{L})$ be the NP relation associated with Π.*

Π is said to satisfy **completeness** *if the following holds:*

– **Completeness***: For every $(x, w) \in \mathcal{R}(\mathcal{L})$,*

$$\Pr[\mathsf{Accept} \leftarrow \langle P(x, w), V(x) \rangle] \geq 1 - \mathsf{negl}(\lambda),$$

for some negligible function negl.

Π is said to satisfy **(unconditional) soundness** *if the following holds:*

– **Soundness***: For every prover P^* (possibly computationally unbounded), every $x \notin \mathcal{R}(\mathcal{L})$,*

$$\Pr[\mathsf{Accept} \leftarrow \langle P^*(x), V(x) \rangle] \leq \mathsf{negl}(\lambda),$$

for some negligible function negl.

Remark 1. We will later define a stronger property called proof of knowledge property that subsumes the soundness property.

To define (bounded) concurrent QZK, we first define Q-session adversarial verifiers. Roughly speaking, a Q-session adversarial verifier is one that invokes Q instantiations of the protocol and in each instantiation, the adversarial verifier interacts with the honest prover. In particular, the adversarial verifier can interleave its messages from different instantiations.

Definition 2 (Q-session Quantum Adversary). *Let $Q \in \mathbb{N}$. Let Π be an interactive protocol between a (classical) PPT prover and a (classical) PPT verifier V for the relation $\mathcal{R}(\mathcal{L})$. Let $(x, w) \in \mathcal{R}(\mathcal{L})$. We say that an adversarial non-uniform QPT verifier V^* is a Q-session adversary if it invokes Q sessions with the prover $P(x, w)$.*

Moreover, we assume that the interaction of V^* with P is defined as follows: denote by V_i^* to be the verifier algorithm used by V^* in the ith session and denote by P_i to be the ith invocation of $P(x, w)$ interacting with V_i^*. Every message sent by V^* is of the form $\big((1, \mathsf{msg}_1), \ldots, (Q, \mathsf{msg}_Q)\big)$, where msg_i is defined as:

$$\mathsf{msg}_i = \begin{cases} \mathsf{N/A}, & \text{if } V_i^* \text{ doesn't send a message,} \\ (t, z), & \text{if } V_i^* \text{ sends } z \text{ in the round } t \end{cases}$$

P_i responds to msg_i. If $\mathsf{msg}_i = \mathsf{N/A}$ then it sets $\mathsf{msg}_i' = \mathsf{N/A}$. If V_i^* has sent the messages in the correct order[6], then P_i applies the next message function on its own private state and msg_i to obtain z' and sets $\mathsf{msg}_i' = (t + 1, z')$. Otherwise, it sets $\mathsf{msg}_i' = (\bot, \bot)$. Finally, V^* receives $\big((1, \mathsf{msg}_1'), \ldots, (Q, \mathsf{msg}_Q')\big)$. In total, V^* exchanges $\ell_{\mathsf{prot}} \cdot Q$ number of messages, ℓ_{prot} is the number of the messages in the protocol.

While the above formulation of the adversary is not typically how concurrent adversaries are defined in the concurrency literature, we note that this formulation is without loss of generality and does capture all concurrent adversaries.

We define quantum ZK for NP in the concurrent setting below.

Definition 3 (Concurrent Quantum ZK for NP). *An interactive protocol Π between a (classical) PPT prover P and a (classical) PPT verifier V for a language $\mathcal{L} \in$ NP is said to be a **concurrent quantum zero-knowledge (QZK) proof system** if it satisfies completeness, unconditional soundness and the following property:*

– Concurrent Quantum Zero-Knowledge: *For every sufficiently large $\lambda \in \mathbb{N}$, every polynomial $Q = Q(\lambda)$, every Q-session QPT adversary V^* there exists a QPT simulator Sim such that for every $(x, w) \in \mathcal{R}(\mathcal{L})$, poly$(\lambda)$-qubit bipartite advice state, ρ_{AB}, on registers A and B, the following holds:*

$$\mathsf{View}_{V^*} \langle P(x, w), V^*(x, \rho_{AB}) \rangle \approx_Q \mathsf{Sim}(x, \rho_{AB})$$

where V^* and Sim only have access to register A. In other words, only the identity is performed on register B.

In this work, we consider a weaker setting, called bounded concurrency. The number of sessions, denoted by Q, in which the adversarial verifier interacts with the prover is fixed ahead of time and in particular, the different complexity measures of a protocol can depend on Q.

Definition 4 (Bounded Concurrent Quantum ZK for NP). *Let $Q \in \mathbb{N}$. An interactive protocol between a (classical) probabilistic polynomial time (in Q) prover P and a (classical) probabilistic polynomial time (in Q) verifier V for a language $\mathcal{L} \in$ NP is said to be a **bounded concurrent quantum zero-knowledge (QZK) proof system** if it satisfies completeness, unconditional soundness and the following property:*

---

[6] That is, it has sent $(1, z_1)$ first, then $(2, z_2)$ and so on.

– Bounded Concurrent Quantum Zero-Knowledge: *For every sufficiently large* $\lambda \in \mathbb{N}$, *every Q-session concurrent QPT adversary* V^*, *there exists a QPT simulator* Sim *such that for every* $(x, w) \in \mathcal{R}(\mathcal{L})$, poly($\lambda$)*-qubit bipartite advice state,* ρ_{AB}, *on registers A and B, the following holds:*

$$\text{View}_{V^*}\langle P(x, w), V^*(x, \rho_{AB})\rangle \approx_Q \text{Sim}(x, \rho_{AB})$$

where V^* *and* Sim *only have access to register A. In other words, only the identity is performed on register B.*

2.2 Bounded Concurrent QZK for QMA

We start by recalling the definitions of completeness and soundness properties of a quantum interactive proof system for promise problems.

Definition 5 (Interactive Quantum Proof System for QMA). Π *is an interactive proof system between a QPT prover P and a QPT verifier V, associated with a promise problem* $A = A_{yes} \cup A_{no} \in$ QMA, *if the following two conditions are satisfied.*

– **Completeness**: *For all* $x \in A_{yes}$, *there exists a* poly($|x|$)*-qubit state* $|\psi\rangle$ *such that the following holds:*

$$\Pr[\text{Accept} \leftarrow \langle P(x, |\Psi\rangle), V(x)\rangle] \geq 1 - \text{negl}(|x|),$$

for some negligible function negl.

Π *is said to satisfy* (**unconditional**) **soundness** *if the following holds:*

– **Soundness**: *For every prover* P^* *(possibly computationally unbounded), every* $x \in A_{no}$, *the following holds:*

$$\Pr[\text{Accept} \leftarrow \langle P^*(x), V(x)\rangle] \leq \text{negl}(|x|),$$

for some negligible function negl.

To define bounded concurrent QZK for QMA, we first define the notion of Q-session adversaries.

Definition 6 (Q-session adversary for QMA). *Let* $Q \in \mathbb{N}_{\geq 1}$. *Let* Π *be a quantum interactive protocol between a QPT prover and a QPT verifier V for a* QMA *promise problem* $A = A_{yes} \cup A_{no}$. *We say that an adversarial non-uniform QPT verifier* V^* *is a Q-session adversary if it invokes Q sessions with the prover* $P(x, |\psi\rangle)$.

As in the case of concurrent verifiers for NP, we assume that the interaction of V^* *with P is defined as follows: denote by* V_i^* *to be the verifier algorithm used by* V^* *in the* i^{th} *session and denote by* P_i *to be the* i^{th} *invocation of* $P(x, w)$ *interacting with* V_i^*. *Every message sent by* V^* *is of the form* $((1, \text{msg}_1), \ldots, (Q, \text{msg}_Q))$, *where* msg_i *is defined as:*

$$\text{msg}_i = \begin{cases} \text{N/A}, & \text{if } V_i^* \text{ doesn't send a message,} \\ (t, \rho), & \text{if } V_i^* \text{ sends the state } \rho \text{ in the round } t \end{cases}$$

P_i responds to msg_i. If $\mathsf{msg}_i = \mathsf{N/A}$ then it sets $\mathsf{msg}_i' = \mathsf{N/A}$. If V_i^* has sent the messages in the correct order, P_i applies the next message function (modeled as a quantum circuit) on msg_i and its private quantum state to obtain ρ' and sets $\mathsf{msg}_i' = (t+1, \rho')$. Otherwise, it sets $\mathsf{msg}_i' = (\perp, \perp)$. Finally, V^* receives $((1, \mathsf{msg}_1'), \ldots, (Q, \mathsf{msg}_Q'))$. In total, V^* exchanges $\ell_{\mathsf{prot}} \cdot Q$ number of messages, where ℓ_{prot} is the number of the messages in the protocol.

Remark 2. To invoke Q different sessions, we assume that the prover has Q copies of the witness state.

Remark 3. We assume, without loss of generality, the prover will measure the appropriate registers to figure out the round number for each verifier. This is because the malicious verifier can always send the superposition of the ordering of messages.

We define quantum ZK for QMA in the bounded concurrent setting below.

Definition 7 (Bounded Concurrent QZK for QMA). *Let $Q \in \mathbb{N}$. An interactive protocol Π between a QPT prover P (running in time polynomial in Q) and a QPT verifier V (running in time polynomial in Q) for a QMA promise problem $\mathcal{A} = \mathcal{A}_{yes} \cup \mathcal{A}_{no}$ if it satisfies completeness, unconditional soundness and the following property:*

- **Bounded Concurrent Quantum Zero-Knowledge:** *For every sufficiently large $\lambda \in \mathbb{N}$, for every Q-session QPT adversary V^*, there exists a QPT simulator Sim such that for every $x \in \mathcal{A}_{yes}$ and any witness $|\psi\rangle$, $\mathrm{poly}(\lambda)$-qubit bipartite advice state, ρ_{AB}, on registers A and B, the following holds:*

$$\mathsf{View}_{V^*} \langle P(x, |\psi\rangle), V^*(x, \rho_{AB}) \rangle \approx_Q \mathsf{Sim}(x, \rho_{AB})$$

where V^* and Sim only have access to register A. In other words, only the identity is performed on register B.

2.3 Quantum Proofs of Knowledge

We present the definition of quantum proof of knowledge; this is the traditional notion of proof of knowledge, except that the unbounded prover could be a quantum algorithm and specifically, its intermediate states could be quantum states.

Definition 8 (Quantum Proof of Knowledge). *We say that an interactive proof system (P, V) for a NP relation $\mathcal{R}$ satisfies (ε, δ)-proof of knowledge property if the following holds: suppose there exists a malicious (possibly computationally unbounded prover) P^* such that for every x, and quantum state ρ it holds that:*

$$\Pr\left[(\widetilde{\rho}, \mathsf{decision}) \leftarrow \langle P^*(x, \rho), V(x)\rangle \bigwedge \mathsf{decision} = \mathsf{accept} \right] = \varepsilon$$

Then there exists a quantum polynomial-time extractor Ext, *such that:*

$$\Pr\left[(\tilde{\rho}', \text{decision}, w) \leftarrow \text{Ext}(x, \rho) \bigwedge \text{decision} = \text{accept}\right] = \delta$$

Moreover, we require $T(\tilde{\rho}, \tilde{\rho}') = \text{negl}(|x|)$, *where* $T(\cdot, \cdot)$ *denotes the trace distance and* negl *is a negligible function.*

We drop (ε, δ) *from the notation if* $|\delta - \varepsilon| \leq \text{negl}(|x|)$, *for a negligible function* negl.

Remark 4 (Comparison with Unruh's Proof of Knowledge [Unr12]). Our definition is a special case of Unruh's quantum proof of knowledge definition. Any proof system satisfying our definition is a quantum proof of knowledge system (according to Unruh's definition) with knowledge error κ, for any κ. Moreover, in Unruh's definition, the extraction probability is allowed to be polynomially related to the acceptance probability whereas in our case, the extraction probability needs to be negligibly close to the acceptance probability.

Definition 9 (Concurrent Quantum ZK PoK). *We say that a concurrent (resp., bounded) quantum ZK is a concurrent (resp., bounded) QZKPoK if it satisfies proof of knowledge property.*

2.4 Intermediate Tool: Quantum Witness-Indistinguishable Proofs for NP

For our construction, we use a proof system that satisfies a property called quantum witness indistinguishability. We recall this notion below.

Definition 10 (Quantum Witness-Indistinguishability). *An interactive protocol between a (classical) PPT prover P and a (classical) PPT verifier V for a language* $L \in$ NP *is said to be a **quantum witness-indistinguishable proof system** if in addition to completeness, unconditional soundness, the following holds:*

– **Quantum Witness-Indistinguishability***: For every* $x \in \mathcal{L}$ *and* w_1, w_2 *such that* $(x, w_1) \in \mathcal{R}(\mathcal{L})$ *and* $(x, w_2) \in \mathcal{R}(\mathcal{L})$, *for every QPT verifier* V^* *with* $\text{poly}(\lambda)$-*qubit advice* ρ, *the following holds:*

$$\{\text{View}_{V^*}(\langle P(x, w_1), V^*(x, \rho)\rangle)\} \approx_{\mathcal{Q}} \{\text{View}_{V^*}(\langle P(x, w_2), V^*(x, \rho)\rangle)\}$$

Instantiation. By suitably instantiating the constant round WI argument system of Blum [Blu86] with statistically binding commitments (which in turn can be based on post-quantum one-way functions [Nao91]), we achieve a 4 round quantum WI proof system for NP. Moreover, this proof system is a public-coin proof system; that is, the verifier's messages are sampled uniformly at random.

3 Bounded Concurrent QZK for NP

We first give an overview of bounded concurrent QZK for NP.

3.1 Bounded Concurrent QZK for NP

Black Box QZK via Watrous Rewinding. The traditional rewinding technique that has been used to prove powerful results on classical zero-knowledge cannot be easily ported to the quantum setting. The fundamental reason behind this difficulty is the fact that to carry out rewinding, it is necessary to clone the state of the verifier. While cloning comes for free in the classical setting, the no-cloning theorem of quantum mechanics prevents us from being able to clone arbitrary states. Nonetheless, the seminal work of Watrous [Wat09] demonstrates that there are rewinding techniques that are amenable to the quantum setting. Watrous used this technique to present the first construction of quantum zero-knowledge for NP. This technique is so powerful that all quantum zero-knowledge protocols known so far (including the ones with non-black box simulation [BS20, ABG+20]!) either implicitly or explicitly use this technique.

We can abstractly think of Watrous technique as follows: to prove that a classical protocol is quantum zero-knowledge, first come up with a (classical) PPT simulator that simulates a (classical) malicious PPT verifier. The classical simulator needs to satisfy the following two conditions:

- **Oblivious Rewinding**: There is a distribution induced on the decision bits of the simulator to rewind in any given round i. This distribution could potentially depend on the randomness of the simulator and also the state of the verifier.

  The oblivious rewinding condition requires that this distribution should be independent of the state of the verifier. That is, this distribution should remain the same irrespective of the state of the verifier[7].

- **No-recording**: Before rewinding any round, the simulator could record (or remember) the transcript generated so far. This recorded transcript along with the rewound transcript will be used for simulation. For instance, in Goldreich and Kahan [GK96], the simulator first commits to garbage values and then waits for the verifier to decommit its challenges. The simulator then records the decommitments before rewinding and then changing its own commitments based on the decommitted values.

  The no-recording condition requires the following to hold: in order for the simulator to rewind from point i to point j $(i > j)$, the simulator needs to forget the transcript generated from j^{th} round to the ith round. Note that the simulator of [GK96] does not satisfy the no-recording condition.

Once such a classical simulator is identified, we can then simulate quantum verifiers as follows: run the classical simulator and the quantum verifier[8] in superposition and then at the end of each round, measure the appropriate register to figure out whether to rewind or not. The fact that the distribution associated with the decision bits are independent of the verifier's state is used to argue

---

[7] A slightly weaker property where the distribution is *"approximately"* independent of the state of the verifier also suffices.

[8] Without loss of generality, we can consider verifiers whose next message functions are implemented as unitaries and they perform all the measurements in the end.

that the state, after measuring the decision register, is essentially not disturbed. Using this fact, we can then reverse the computation and go back to an earlier round. Once the computation is reversed (or rewound to an earlier round), the simulator forgets all the messages exchanged from the point – to which its being rewound to – until the current round.

Incompatibility of Existing Concurrent ZK Techniques. To realize our goal of building bounded concurrent QZK, a natural direction to pursue is to look for classical concurrent ZK protocols with the guarantee that the classical simulator satisfies both the oblivious rewinding and no-recording conditions. However, most known classical concurrent ZK techniques are such that they satisfy one of these two conditions but not both. For example, the seminal work of [PRS02] proposes a concurrent ZK protocol and the simulator they describe satisfies the oblivious rewinding condition but not the no-recording condition. More relevant to our work is the work of Pass et al. [PTW09], who construct a bounded concurrent ZK protocol whose simulator satisfies the no-recording condition but not the oblivious rewinding condition.

In more detail, at every round, the simulator (as described in [PTW09]) makes a decision to rewind based on which session verifier sends a message in that round. This means that the probability of whether the simulator rewinds any given round depends on the scheduling of the messages of the verifiers. Unfortunately, the scheduling itself could be a function of the state of the verifier. The malicious verifier could look at the first bit of its auxiliary state. If it is 0, it will ask the first session verifier to send a message and if it is 1, it will ask the second session verifier to send a message and so on. This means that a simulator's decision to rewind could depend on the state of the verifier.

Bounded Concurrent QZK. We now discuss our construction of bounded concurrent QZK and how we overcome the aforementioned difficulties. Our construction is identical to the bounded concurrent (classical) ZK construction of Pass et al. [PTW09], modulo the setting of parameters. We recall their construction below.

The protocol is divided into two phases. In the first phase, a sub-protocol, referred to as *slot*, is executed many times. We will fix the number of executions later when we do the analysis. In the second phase, the prover and the verifier execute a witness-indistinguishable proof system.

In more detail, one execution of a slot is defined as follows:

- Prover sends a commitment of a random bit b to the verifier. This commitment is generated using a statistically binding commitment scheme that guarantees hiding property against quantum polynomial-time adversaries (also referred to as quantum concealing).
- The verifier then sends a uniformly random bit b' to the prover.

We say that a slot is *matched* if $b = b'$.

In the second phase, the prover convinces the verifier that either the instance is in the language or there is a large fraction, denoted by τ, of matched slots. This is done using a proof system satisfying witness-indistinguishability property against efficient quantum verifiers. Of course, τ needs to be carefully set such that the simulator will be able to satisfy this constraint while a malicious prover cannot. Before we discuss the precise parameters, we first outline the simulator's strategy to prove zero-knowledge. As remarked earlier, the classical simulation strategy described in Pass et al. [PTW09] is incompatible with Watrous rewinding. We first discuss a new classical simulation strategy, that we call *block rewinding*, for this protocol and then we discuss how to combine this strategy along with Watrous rewinding to prove quantum zero-knowledge property of the above protocol.

Block Rewinding. Suppose Q be the number of sessions the malicious verifier initiates with the simulator. Since this is a bounded concurrent setting, Q is known even before the protocol is designed. Let ℓ_{prot} be the number of messages in the protocol. Note that the total number of messages exchanged in all the sessions is at most $\ell_{\text{prot}} \cdot Q$. We assume for a moment that the malicious verifier never aborts. Thus, the number of messages exchanged between the prover and the verifier is exactly $\ell_{\text{prot}} \cdot Q$.

The simulator partitions the $\ell_{\text{prot}} \cdot Q$ messages into many blocks with each block being of a fixed size (we discuss the parameters later). The simulator then runs the verifier till the end of first block. At this point, it checks if this block contains a slot. Note that the verifier can stagger the messages of a particular session across the different blocks such that the first message of a slot is in one block but the second message of this slot could be in a different block. The simulator only considers those slots such that both the messages of these slots are contained inside the first block. Let the set of all the slots in the first block be denoted by $\mu(B_1)$, where B_1 denotes the first block. Now, the simulator picks a random slot from the set $\mu(B_1)$. It then checks if this slot is matched or not. That is, it checks if the bit committed in the slot equals the bit sent by the verifier. If indeed they are equal, it continues to the next block, else it rewinds to the beginning of the first block and then executes the first block again. Before rewinding, it forgets the transcript collected in the first block. It repeats this process until the slot it picked is matched. The simulator then moves on to the second block and repeats the entire process. When the simulator needs to compute a witness-indistinguishable proof for a session, it first checks if the fraction of matched slots for that particular session is at least τ. If so, it uses this information to complete the proof. Otherwise, it aborts.

It is easy to see why the no-recording condition is satisfied: the simulator never stores the messages sent in a block. Let us now analyze why the oblivious rewinding condition is satisfied. Suppose we are guaranteed that in every block there is at least one slot. Then, we claim that the probability that the simulator rewinds is $\frac{1}{2} \pm \mathsf{negl}(\lambda)$, where negl is a negligible function and λ is the security parameter. This is because the simulator rewinds only if the slot is not matched and the probability that a slot is not matched is precisely $\frac{1}{2} \pm \mathsf{negl}(\lambda)$, from the hiding property of the commitment scheme. If we can show that every block contains a slot, then the oblivious rewinding condition would also be satisfied.

ABSENCE OF SLOTS AND ABORTING ISSUES: We glossed over a couple of issues in the above description. Firstly, the malicious verifier could abort all the sessions in some block. Moreover, it can also stagger the messages across blocks such that there are blocks that contain no slots. In either of the above two cases, the simulator will not rewind these blocks and this violates the oblivious rewinding condition: the decision to rewind would be based on whether the verifier aborted or whether there were any slots within a block. In turn, these two conditions could depend on the state of the verifier.

To overcome these two issues, we fix the simulator as follows: at the end of every block, it checks if there are any slots inside this block. If there are slots available, then the simulator continues as detailed above. Otherwise, it performs a dummy rewind: it picks a bit uniformly at random and rewinds only if the bit is 0. If the bit is 1, it continues its execution. This ensures that the simulator will rewind with probability $\frac{1}{2} \pm \mathsf{negl}(\lambda)$ irrespective of whether there are any slots inside a block. Thus, with this fix, the oblivious rewinding condition is satisfied as well.

PARAMETERS AND ANALYSIS: We now discuss the parameters associated with the system. We set the number of slots in the system to be $120Q^7\lambda$. We set τ to be $\lfloor \frac{60Q^7\lambda + Q^4\lambda}{120Q^7\lambda} \rfloor$. We set the number of blocks to be $24Q^6\lambda$. Thus, the size of each block is $\lfloor \frac{120Q^7\lambda}{24Q^6\lambda} \rfloor$. Recall that the reason why we need to set these parameters carefully is to ensure that the malicious prover cannot match more than τ slots with better than negligible probability whereas the simulator can beat this threshold with overwhelming probability.

We now argue that the classical simulator can successfully simulate all the Q sessions. To simulate any given session, say the ith session, the number of matched slots needs to be at least $60Q^7\lambda + Q^4\lambda$. Note that the number of blocks is $24Q^6\lambda$; the best case scenario is that each of these blocks contain at least one slot of the ith session and the simulator picks this slot every time. Even in this best case scenario, the simulator can match at most $24Q^6\lambda$ slots and thus, there still would remain $60Q^7\lambda + Q^4\lambda - 24Q^6\lambda$ number of slots to be matched. Moreover, even the likelihood of this best case scenario is quite low.

Instead, we argue the following:

- The simulator only needs to match $3Q^4\lambda$ number of slots for the ith session. We argue that with overwhelming probability, there are $3Q^4\lambda$ blocks such that (i) there is at least one slot from the ith session and, (ii) the simulator happens to choose a slot belonging to this session in each of these blocks.
- Roughly, $\frac{120Q^7\lambda - 3Q^4\lambda}{2} \gg 60Q^7\lambda - 2Q^4\lambda$ number of slots are matched by luck, even without the simulator picking these slots and trying to match. This follows from the fact that with probability $\frac{1}{2}$, a slot is matched and the number of remaining slots that need to be matched are $120Q^7\lambda - 3Q^4\lambda$.

From the above two bullet points, it follows that with overwhelming probability, the total number of slots matched is at least $60Q^7\lambda + Q^4\lambda$.

We note that although the simulation strategy of Pass et al. [PTW09] is quite different, their analysis follows the same template as above.

SIMULATION OF QUANTUM VERIFIERS: So far we have demonstrated a simulator that can simulate classical verifiers. We describe, at a high level, how to simulate quantum verifiers. The quantum simulator runs the classical simulator in superposition. At the end of every block, it measures a single-qubit register, denoted by **Dec**, which indicates whether the simulator needs to rewind this block or not. If this register has 0, the simulator does not rewind, otherwise it rewinds. We can show that, no matter what the auxiliary state of the malicious verifier is, at the end of a block, the quantum state is of the following form:

$$\sqrt{p}|0\rangle_{\mathsf{Dec}}|\Psi_{\mathsf{Good}}\rangle + \sqrt{1-p}|1\rangle_{\mathsf{Dec}}|\Psi_{\mathsf{Bad}}\rangle,$$

where $|\Psi_{\mathsf{Good}}\rangle$ is a superposition of all the transcripts where the chosen slot is matched and on the other hand, $|\Psi_{\mathsf{Bad}}\rangle$ is a superposition of all the transcripts where the chosen slot is not matched. Moreover, using the hiding property of the commitment scheme, we can argue that $|p - \frac{1}{2}| \leq \mathsf{negl}(\lambda)$. Then we can apply the Watrous rewinding lemma, to obtain a state that is close to $|\Psi_{\mathsf{Good}}\rangle$. This process is repeated for every block. At the end of the protocol, the simulator measures the registers containing the transcript of the protocol and outputs this along with the private state of the verifier.

3.2 Construction

We present the construction of quantum zero-knowledge proof system for NP in the bounded concurrent setting in Fig. 1. As remarked earlier, the construction is the same as the classical bounded concurrent ZK by Pass et al. [PTW09], whereas our proof strategy is significantly different from that of Pass et al.

The relation associated with the bounded concurrent system will be denoted by $\mathcal{R}(\mathcal{L})$, with $\mathcal{L}$ being the associated NP language. Let Q be an upper bound on the number of sessions. We use the following tools in our construction.

- Statistically-binding and quantum-concealing commitment protocol, denoted by $(\mathsf{Comm}, \mathsf{R})$.
- Four round quantum witness-indistinguishable proof system Π_{WI} (Definition 10). The relation associated with Π_{WI}, denoted by $\mathcal{R}_{\mathsf{WI}}$, is defined as follows:

$$\mathcal{R}_{\mathsf{WI}} = \left\{ \left(\left(x, \mathbf{r}_1, \mathbf{c}_1, b_1', \ldots, \mathbf{r}_{120Q^7\lambda}, \mathbf{c}_{120Q^7\lambda}, b_{120Q^7\lambda}' \right) ; \left(w, r_1, \ldots, r_{120Q^7\lambda} \right) \right) : (x, w) \in \mathcal{R}(\mathcal{L}) \bigvee \right.$$
$$\left. \left(\exists j_1, \ldots, j_{60Q^7\lambda+Q^4\lambda} \in [120Q^7\lambda] \text{ s.t. } \bigwedge_{i=1}^{60Q^7\lambda+Q^4\lambda} \mathsf{Comm}(1^\lambda, \mathbf{r}_{j_i}, b_{j_i}'; r_{j_i}) = \mathbf{c}_{j_i} \right) \right\}$$

We present the proofs of completeness, soundness and quantum zero-knowledge in the full version.

Input of P: Instance $x \in \mathcal{L}$ along with witness w.
Input of V: Instance $x \in \mathcal{L}$.

Stage 1: For $j = 1$ to $120Q^7\lambda$,

- $P \leftrightarrow V$: Sample $b_j \xleftarrow{\$} \{0,1\}$ uniformly at random. P commits to b_j using the statistical-binding commitment scheme. Let the verifier's message (verifier plays the role of the receiver) be $\mathbf{r}_j$ and let the prover's message be $\mathbf{c}_j$.
- $V \rightarrow P$: Sample $b'_j \xleftarrow{\$} \{0,1\}$ uniformly at random. Respond with b'_j.

// *We refer to one execution as a slot. So, P and V execute $120Q^7\lambda$ number of slots.*

Stage 2: P and V engage in Π_{WI} with the common input being the following:

$$(x, \mathbf{r}_1, \mathbf{c}_1, b'_1, \ldots, \mathbf{r}_{120Q^7\lambda}, \mathbf{c}_{120Q^7\lambda}, b'_{120Q^7\lambda})$$

Additionally, P uses the witness $(w, \bot, \ldots, \bot)$.

Fig. 1. Construction of classical bounded concurrent ZK for NP.

4 Quantum Proofs of Knowledge

We first present a construction of standalone quantum proof of knowledge for NP. We extend this construction to the bounded concurrent setting in Sect. 3.1.

4.1 Standalone Quantum Proofs of Knowledge

Towards building a bounded-concurrent QZK system satisfying quantum proof of knowledge property, we first focus on the standalone QZK setting. The quantum proof of knowledge property roughly says the following: for every unbounded prover convincing a verifier to accept an instance x with probability p, there exists an extractor that outputs a witness w with probability negligibly close to p and it also outputs a state $|\Phi\rangle$ that is close (in trace distance) to the output state of the real prover.

Our approach is to design a novel extraction mechanism that uses oblivious transfer to extract a bit from a quantum adversary.

Main Tool: Statistical Receiver-Private Oblivious Transfer. Our starting point is an oblivious transfer (OT) protocol [Rab05]. This protocol is defined between two entities: a sender and a receiver. The sender has two bits (m_0, m_1) and the receiver has a single bit b. At the end of the protocol, the receiver receives the bit m_b.

The security against malicious senders (receiver privacy) states that the sender should not be able to distinguish (with non-negligible probability) whether the receiver's bit is 0 or 1. The security against malicious receivers (also called sender privacy) states that there is a bit b' such that the receiver cannot distinguish (with non-negligible probability) the case when the sender's input is (m_0, m_1) versus the setting when the sender's input is $(m_{b'}, m_{b'})$.

We require receiver privacy to hold against unbounded senders while we require sender privacy to hold against quantum polynomial-time receivers. The reason we require receiver privacy against unbounded senders is because our goal is to design extraction mechanism against computationally unbounded provers.

We postpone discussing the construction of statistical receiver-private oblivious transfer to the Appendix. We will now see how to use this to achieve extraction.

One-bit Extraction with $\left(\frac{1}{2} \pm \mathsf{negl}\right)$-error. We begin with a naive attempt to design the extraction mechanism for extracting a single secret bit, say s[9]. The prover and the verifier execute the OT protocol; prover takes on the role of the OT sender and the verifier takes on the receiver's role. The prover picks bits b and α uniformly at random and then sets the OT sender's input to be (s, α) if $b = 0$, otherwise if $b = 1$, it sets the OT sender's input to be (α, s). The verifier sets the receiver's bit to be 0. After the OT protocol ends, the prover sends the bit b. Note that if the bit b picked by the prover was 0 then the verifier can successfully recover s, else it recovers α.

We first discuss the classical extraction process. The quantum extractor runs the classical extractor in superposition as we did in the case of quantum zero-knowledge. The extraction process proceeds as follows: the extractor picks a bit $\tilde{b}$ uniformly at random and sets $\tilde{b}$ to be the receiver's bit in the OT protocol. By the statistical receiver privacy property of OT, it follows that the probability that the extractor succeeds in recovering s is negligibly close to $\frac{1}{2}$. Moreover, the success probability is independent of the initial state of the prover. This means that we can apply the Watrous rewinding lemma and amplify the success probability.

MALICIOUS PROVERS: However, we missed a subtle issue: the malicious prover could misbehave. For instance, the prover can set the OT sender's input to be (r, r) and thus, not use the secret bit s at all.

---

[9] For instance, s could be the first bit of the witness.

We resolve this issue by additionally requiring the prover to prove to the verifier that one of its inputs in the OT protocol is the secret bit[10] s. This is realized by using a quantum zero-knowledge protocol, denoted by Π.

Error amplification. A malicious verifier can successfully recover the secret s with probability $\frac{1}{2}$. To reduce the verifier's success probability, we execute the above process (i.e., first executing the OT protocol and then executing the ZK protocol) λ number of times, where λ is the security parameter. First, the prover will additively secret share the bit s into secret shares $sh_1, \ldots, sh_\lambda$. It also samples the bits $b_1, \ldots, b_\lambda$ uniformly at random. In the ith execution, it sets the OT sender's input to be (sh_i, α_i) if $b_i = 0$, otherwise it sets the OT sender's input to be (α_i, sh_i), where α_i is sampled uniformly at random. After all the OT protocols are executed, the prover is going to prove using a QZK protocol Π, as considered above, that the messages in the OT protocols were correctly computed.

We first argue that even in this protocol, the extraction still succeeds with overwhelming probability. In each OT execution, the extractor applies Watrous rewinding, as before, to extract all the shares $sh_1, \ldots, sh_\lambda$. From this, it can recover s. All is left is to argue that this template satisfies quantum zero-knowledge property. It turns out that arguing this is challenging[11].

Challenges in Proving QZK and Distinguisher-Dependent Hybrids. We first define the simulator as follows:

- The simulator uses (α_i, α_i) as the sender's input in the ith OT execution, where α_i is sampled uniformly at random.
- It then simulates the protocol Π.

To prove that the output distribution of the simulated world is computationally indistinguishable from the real world, we adopt a hybrid argument. The first hybrid, Hyb_1, corresponds to the real world. In the second hybrid, Hyb_2, simulate the protocol Π. The indistinguishability of Hyb_1 and Hyb_2 follows from the QZK property of Π. Next, we define the third hybrid, Hyb_3, that executes the simulator. To prove the indistinguishability of Hyb_2 and Hyb_3, we consider a sequence of intermediate hybrids, denoted by $\{\mathsf{Hyb}_{2.j}\}_{j\in[\lambda]}$. Using this sequence of hybrids, we change the inputs in all the λ OT executions one at a time. Finally, we define the third hybrid, Hyb_3, that corresponds to the ideal world. Proving

---

[10] For now, assume that there exists a predicate that can check if s is a valid secret bit.

[11] We would like to point out that we are designing the standalone PoK protocol as a stepping stone towards the bounded concurrent PoK protocol. If one were to be interested in just the standalone setting, then it might be possible to avoid the subtleties described above by making use of a simulation-secure OT rather than an indistinguishable-secure OT. The reason why we use an indistinguishable-secure OT in the concurrent PoK setting instead of a simulation-secure OT is because we want to avoid using more than one simulator in the analysis; otherwise, we would have multiple simulators trying to rewind the verifier, making the analysis significantly complicated.

the indistinguishability of the consecutive hybrids, $\mathsf{Hyb}_{2.j}$ and $\mathsf{Hyb}_{2.j+1}$, in this sequence turns out to be challenging.

The main issue is the following: suppose we are in the jth intermediate hybrid $\mathsf{Hyb}_{2.j}$, for $j \leq \lambda$. At this point, we have changed the inputs to the first j OT executions and we are about to change the input to the $(j+1)^{th}$ OT. But what exactly are the inputs we are using for the first j OT executions? It is unclear whether we use the input (sh_i, sh_i) or the input (α_i, α_i), for $i \leq j$, in the ith OT execution. Note that the OT security states that we can either switch the real sender's inputs to either (sh_i, sh_i) or (α_i, α_i), based on the sender's and the distinguisher's randomness. And hence, we define an *inefficient* intermediate hybrid, which is a function (not necessarily computable), that determines for every i, where $i \leq j$, whether to use (sh_i, sh_i) or (α_i, α_i). Moreover, *this hybrid depends on the distinguisher*, that distinguishes the two intermediate hybrids.

The indistinguishability of the consecutive pair of inefficient hybrids, say $\mathsf{Hyb}_{2.j}$ and $\mathsf{Hyb}_{2.j+1}$, is proven by a non-uniform reduction that receives as input the advice corresponding to the first j executions of OT, where the sender's inputs are correctly switched to either (sh_i, sh_i) or (α_i, α_i), for $i \leq j$. This in turn depends on the distinguisher distinguishing these two hybrids. Then, the reduction uses the $(j+1)^{th}$ OT execution in the protocol to break the sender privacy property of OT. If the two hybrids can be distinguished with non-negligible probability then the reduction can succeed with the same probability.

In the hybrid $\mathsf{Hyb}_{2.\lambda-1}$, we additionally include an abort condition: if the inputs in the first $\lambda - 1$ OT executions are all switched to (sh_i, sh_i) then we abort. We show that the probability that $\mathsf{Hyb}_{2.\lambda-1}$ aborts is negligible. This is necessary to argue that the verifier does not receive all the shares of the secret.

Note that only the intermediate hybrids, namely $\{\mathsf{Hyb}_{2.j}\}_{j\in[\lambda]}$, are inefficient, and in particular, the final hybrid Hyb_3 is still efficient.

Extraction of Multiple Bits. To design a quantum proof of knowledge protocol, we need to be able to extract not just one bit, but multiple bits. To achieve this, we design the prover as follows: on input a witness w, it sequentially executes the above extraction template for each bit of the witness. That is, for every $i \in [\ell_w]$, where ℓ_w is the length of w, it additively secret shares w_i into the shares $(sh_{i,1}, \ldots, sh_{i,\lambda})$. It then invokes $\ell_w \cdot \lambda$ number of OT executions, where in the $(i,j)^{th}$ execution, it chooses the input $(sh_{i,j}, \alpha_{i,j})$ if $b_{i,j} = 0$, or the input $(\alpha_{i,j}, sh_{i,j})$ if $b_{i,j} = 1$, where $\alpha_{i,j}, b_{i,j}$ are sampled uniformly at random. Finally, it uses a QZK protocol to prove that it behaved honestly in the earlier OT executions.

The proofs of quantum proof of knowledge and the QZK properties follow along the same lines as the single-bit extraction case.

4.2   Construction of (Standalone) QZKPoK

We construct a (standalone) QZKPoK (P, V) for an NP relation $\mathcal{R}(\mathcal{L})$. The following tools are used in our construction:

- A post-quantum statistical receiver-private oblivious transfer protocol, $\Pi_{\mathsf{OT}} = (\mathsf{S}, \mathsf{R})$ satisfying perfect correctness property.
  We say that a transcript τ is valid with respect to sender's randomness r and its input bits (m_0, m_1) if τ can be generated with a sender that uses r as randomness for the protocol and uses (m_0, m_1) as inputs.
- A (standalone) QZK proof system Π_{zk} for $\mathcal{R}(\mathcal{L}_{\mathsf{zk}})$. We describe the relation $\mathcal{R}(\mathcal{L}_{\mathsf{zk}})$, parameterized by security parameter λ, below.

$$\mathcal{R}\left(\mathcal{L}_{\mathsf{zk}}\right) = \left\{ \left(\left(x, \{\tau_{\mathsf{OT}}^{(i,j)}, b_{i,j}\}_{i \in [\ell_w], j \in [\lambda]} \right) ; \left(w, \{r_{\mathsf{OT}}^{(i,j)}, sh_{i,j}, \alpha_{i,j}\}_{i \in [\ell_w], j \in [\lambda]} \right) \right) : \right.$$
$$\left. \left(\begin{array}{c} \forall i \in [\ell_w], j \in [\lambda], \\ \tau_{\mathsf{OT}}^{(i,j)} \text{ is valid w.r.t} \\ r_{\mathsf{OT}}^{(i,j)} \text{ and } (((1-b_{i,j})sh_{i,j}+b_{i,j}\cdot\alpha_{i,j}), (b_{i,j}sh_{i,j}+(1-b_{i,j})\cdot\alpha_{i,j})) \end{array} \right) \wedge \left(\begin{array}{c} \forall i \in [\ell_w], \\ \oplus_{j=1}^{\lambda} sh_{i,j} = w_i \end{array} \right) \wedge (x, w) \in \mathcal{R}(\mathcal{L}) \right\}$$

In other words, the relation checks if the shares $\{sh_{i,j}\}$ used in all the OT executions so far are defined to be such that the XOR of the shares $sh_{i,1}, \ldots, sh_{i,\lambda}$ yields the bit w_i. Moreover, the relation also checks if $w_1 \cdots w_{\ell_w}$ is the witness to the instance x.

We describe the construction in Fig. 2.

We present the proofs of completeness, quantum proof of knowledge and quantum zero-knowledge in the full version.

4.2.1 Quantum PoK in the Bounded Concurrent Setting

Our construction of bounded concurrent quantum proof of knowledge is the same as the one described in Sect. 4.1, except that we instantiate Π using the bounded concurrent QZK protocol that we constructed in Sect. 3[12].

However, proving the bounded concurrent QZK protocol turns out to be even more challenging than the standalone setting. To grasp the underlying difficulties, let us revisit the proof of QZK in Sect. 4.1. To prove the indistinguishability of the real and the ideal world, we first simulated the protocol Π. Since we are in the bounded concurrent setting, the simulator of Π is now simultaneously simulating multiple sessions of the verifier. Then using a sequence of intermediate hybrids, we changed the inputs used in the OT executions of all the sessions one at a time. However, in the bounded concurrent setting, the OT messages can be interleaved with QZK messages. This means that the simulator of QZK could be rewinding the OT messages along with the QZK messages. This makes it difficult to invoke the security of OT.

To reduce the indistinguishability of hybrids to breaking OT, we will carefully design the security reduction such that it does not rewind the blocks (the definition of a block is the same as the one described in Sect. 3.1) containing the messages of the OT protocol. This ensures that we can embed the messages exchanged with the external challenger (in the OT game) without the fear of being rewound. Of course, we need to be cautious: the decision to not

---

[12] We emphasize that we use the specific bounded concurrent QZK protocol that we constructed earlier and we do not know how to provide a generic transformation.

Input of P: Instance $x \in \mathcal{L}$ along with witness w. The length of w is denoted to be ℓ_w.

Input of V: Instance $x \in \mathcal{L}$.

- For every $i \in [\ell_w]$, P samples the shares $sh_{i,1}, \ldots, sh_{i,\lambda}$ uniformly at random conditioned on $\oplus_{j=1}^{\lambda} sh_{i,j} = w_i$, where w_i is the ith bit of w.

- For every $i \in [\ell_w]$, P samples the bits $\alpha_{i,1}, \ldots, \alpha_{i,\lambda}$ uniformly at random.

- For $i \in [\ell_w], j \in [\lambda]$, do the following:
  - $P \leftrightarrow V$: P and V execute Π_{OT} with V playing the role of the receiver in Π_{OT} and P playing the role of the sender in Π_{OT}. The input of the receiver in this protocol is 0, while the input of the sender is set to be $(sh_{i,j}, \alpha_{i,j})$ if $b_{i,j} = 0$, otherwise it is set to be $(\alpha_{i,j}, sh_{i,j})$ if $b_{i,j} = 1$, where the bit $b_{i,j}$ is sampled uniformly at random.
  Call the resulting transcript of the protocol to be $\tau_{\mathsf{OT}}^{(i,j)}$ and let $r_{\mathsf{OT}}^{(i,j)}$ be the randomness used by the sender in OT.

  - $P \to V$: P sends $b_{i,j}$ to V.

- $P \leftrightarrow V$: P and V execute Π_{zk} with P playing the role of the prover of Π_{zk} and V playing the role of the verifier of Π_{zk}. The instance is $\left(x, \left\{ \tau_{\mathsf{OT}}^{(i,j)}, b_{i,j} \right\}_{i \in [\ell_w], j \in [\lambda]} \right)$ and the witness is $\left(w, \left\{ r_{\mathsf{OT}}^{(i,j)}, sh_{i,j}, \alpha_{i,j} \right\}_{i \in [\ell_w], j \in [\lambda]} \right)$. If the verifier in Π_{zk} rejects, then V rejects.

Fig. 2. Construction of (standalone) QZKPoK for NP.

rewind a specific block could leak information about the private state of the verifier and this could affect the zero-knowledge property of the underlying QZK protocol. To overcome this issue, for a block containing the OT messages, we perform a dummy rewind where the transcript of conversation in this block does not change. Thus, we can still interact with the external challenger using the messages in this block. Another issue that arises is that we might end up not rewinding as many blocks as the round complexity of the underlying OT protocol, which is polynomially many rounds. We show that the simulator of the bounded concurrent QZK we constructed in Sect. 3.1 can be modified in such a way that it can successfully simulate all the sessions even if polynomially many blocks are ignored.

We present the formal details in Sect. 3.1.

5   Bounded Concurrent QZK for QMA

We show a construction of bounded concurrent QZK for QMA. Our starting point is the QZK protocol for QMA from [BJSW16], which constructs QZK for QMA from QZK for NP, a commitment scheme and a coin-flipping protocol. We first simplify the protocol of [BJSW16] as follows: their protocol requires security of the coin-flipping protocol to hold against malicious adversaries whereas we only require the security to hold against adversaries who don't deviate from the protocol specification. Once we simplify this step, the resulting protocol will satisfy the property that the QZK simulator only rewinds during the execution of the underlying simulator simulating the QZK protocol for NP. This modification makes it easier for us to extend this protocol to the bounded concurrent setting. We simply instantiate the underlying QZK for NP protocol with its bounded concurrent version.

5.1   Bounded Concurrent QZK for QMA

We first recall the QZK for QMA construction from [BJSW16]. Their protocol is specifically designed for the QMA promise problem called k-local Clifford Hamiltonian, which they showed to be QMA-complete for $k = 5$. We restate it here for completeness.

Definition 11 (k-local Clifford Hamiltonian Problem [BJSW16]). *For all $i \in [m]$, let $H_i = C_i |0^{\otimes k}\rangle\langle 0^{\otimes k}| C_i^\dagger$ be a Hamiltonian term on k-qubits where C_i is a Clifford circuit.*

- *Input: $H_1, H_2, \ldots, H_m$ and strings 1^p, 1^q where p and q are positive integers satisfying $2^p > q$.*
- *Yes instances (A_{yes}): There exists an n-qubit state such that $\mathsf{Tr}[\rho \sum_i H_i] \leq 2^{-p}$*
- *No instances (A_{no}): For every n-qubit state ρ, the following holds: $\mathsf{Tr}[\rho \sum_i H_i] \geq \frac{1}{q}$*

BJSW Encoding. A key idea behind the construction from [BJSW16] is for the prover to encode its witness, $|\psi\rangle$, using a secret-key quantum authentication code (that also serves as an encryption) that satisfies the following key properties needed in the protocol. For any state $|\psi\rangle$, denote the encoding of $|\psi\rangle$ under the secret-key s by $\mathsf{E}_s(|\psi\rangle)$.

1. *Homomorphic evaluation of Cliffords.* Given $\mathsf{E}_s(|\psi\rangle)$, and given any Clifford circuit C, it is possible to compute $\mathsf{E}_{s'}(C|\psi\rangle)$ efficiently. Moreover, s' can be determined efficiently by knowing C and s.
2. *Homomorphic measurements of arbitrary Clifford basis.* For any Clifford circuit C and any state $|\psi\rangle$, a computational basis measurement on $C|\psi\rangle$ can be recovered from a computational basis measurement on $\mathsf{E}_{s'}(C|\psi\rangle)$ along with C and s. Formally, there is a classically efficiently computable function

g such that if y is sampled from the distribution induced by measuring the state $\mathsf{E}_{s'}(C|\psi\rangle)$ in the computational basis, then $g(s, C, y)$ is sampled from the distribution induced by measuring the state $C|\psi\rangle$ in the computational basis.

3. *Authentication of measurement outcomes.* For any s and any clifford C, there is a set $\mathcal{S}_{s,C}$ such that for any state $|\psi\rangle$, and any computational basis measurement outcome y performed on $\mathsf{E}_{s'}(C|\psi\rangle)$, it holds that $y \in \mathcal{S}_{s,C}$. Furthermore, for any y, given s and C, it can be efficiently checked whether $y \in \mathcal{S}_{s,C}$.

4. *Simulatability of authenticated states*: there exists an efficient QPT algorithm B such that for any adversary $\mathcal{A}$, every $x \in A_{\mathsf{yes}}$ along with witness $|\psi\rangle$, poly(λ)-qubit advice ρ, the following holds: the probability that $\mathcal{P}(s, C_{r*}^\dagger, \mathcal{A}(\mathsf{E}_s(|\psi\rangle)))$ outputs 1 is negligibly close to the probability that $\mathcal{P}(s, C_{r*}^\dagger, \mathcal{A}(B(x, s, r^*))))$ outputs 1, where $\mathcal{P}$ is defined below.

$$\mathcal{P}(s, C^\dagger, y) = \begin{cases} 1 \text{ if } g(s, C^\dagger, y) \neq 0 \\ 0 \text{ otherwise} \end{cases}$$

In both the events, s and r^* are chosen uniformly at random.

The QMA verifier of the k-local Clifford Hamiltonian problem measures terms of the form $C|0^{\otimes k}\rangle\langle 0^{\otimes k}|C^\dagger$ where C is a Clifford circuit on a witness $|\psi\rangle$. Specifically, a verifier will first apply $C^\dagger$ and then measure in the computational basis. If the outcome of the measurement is the 0 string, it rejects. Otherwise, it accepts. In the zero-knowledge case, the witness will be encoded, $\mathsf{E}_s(|\psi\rangle)$, but the verifier can still compute $\mathsf{E}_s(C^\dagger|\psi\rangle)$ and measure to obtain some string y. Then, the prover can prove to the verifier (in NP) that y corresponds to a non-zero outcome on a measurement of $C^\dagger|\psi\rangle$ instead using the predicate $\mathcal{P}$.

We follow the approach of BJSW [BJSW16], except that we instantiate the coin-flipping protocol in a specific way in order to get concurrency when instantiating the underlying QZK for NP with our bounded concurrent construction.

Construction. We use the following ingredients in our construction:

- Statistical-binding and quantum-concealing commitment scheme, $(\mathsf{Comm}, \mathsf{R})$.
- Bounded concurrent QZK proof system, denoted by Π_{NP}, for the following language (Sect. 3.2).

$$\mathcal{L} = \left\{ ((\mathbf{r}, \mathbf{c}, \mathbf{r}', \mathbf{c}', r^*, y, b) ; (s, \ell, a, \ell')) : \begin{array}{c} \mathcal{P}(s, C_{r*}^\dagger, y)=1 \\ \wedge \\ \mathsf{Comm}(1^\lambda, \mathbf{r}, s; \ell)=\mathbf{c} \\ \wedge \\ \mathsf{Comm}(1^\lambda, \mathbf{r}', a; \ell')=\mathbf{c}' \\ \wedge \\ a \oplus b = r^* \end{array} \right\}$$

Let Q be the maximum number of sessions associated with the protocol.

We describe the construction of bounded concurrent QZK for QMA (with bound Q) in Fig. 3. We prove the following.

Instance: A k-local Clifford Hamiltonian, $H = \sum_{r=1}^{M} C_r |0^{\otimes k}\rangle\langle 0^{\otimes k}| C_r^\dagger$.

Witness: $|\psi\rangle$

- $P \leftrightarrow V$: Prover P samples a secret-key $s \xleftarrow{\$} \{0,1\}^{\text{poly}(k,M)}$, and commits to s using the commitment protocol (Comm, R). Let $\mathbf{r}$ be the first message of the receiver (sent by V) and $\mathbf{c}$ be the commitment.
  // We call this commitment, the secret-key commitment.

- $P \rightarrow V$: P sends $\mathsf{E}_s(|\psi\rangle)$.

- $P \leftrightarrow V$: Prover samples a random string $a \xleftarrow{\$} \{0,1\}^{\log(M)}$, and commits to a using the commitment protocol (Comm, R). Let $\mathbf{r}'$ be the first message of the receiver and $\mathbf{c}'$ be the commitment.
  // We call this commitment, the coin-flipping commitment.

- $V \rightarrow P$: Verifier samples a random string $b \xleftarrow{\$} \{0,1\}^{\log(M)}$. Verifier sends b to the prover.

- $P \rightarrow V$: Prover sends $r^* := a \oplus b$ to the verifier.

- Verifier computes $\mathsf{Eval}\left(C_{r^*}^\dagger, \mathsf{E}_s(|\Psi\rangle)\right) \rightarrow \mathsf{E}_s(C_{r^*}^\dagger |\psi\rangle)$ and measures in the computational basis. Let y denote the measurement outcome. Verifier sends y to the prover.

- Prover checks that $y \in \mathcal{S}_{s,C_{r^*}^\dagger}$ and that $\mathcal{P}(s, C_{r^*}^\dagger, y) = 1$. If not, it aborts.

- Prover and verifier engage in a QZK protocol for NP, Π_{NP}, for the statement $(\mathbf{r}, \mathbf{c}, \mathbf{r}', \mathbf{c}', r^*, y, b)$ and the witness (s, ℓ, a, ℓ').

Fig. 3. Bounded-concurrent QZK for QMA

Theorem 4. *Assuming that Π_{NP} satisfies the definition of bounded concurrent QZK for NP, the protocol given in Fig. 3 is a bounded concurrent QZK protocol for QMA with soundness $\frac{1}{\text{poly}}$.*

Remark 5. The soundness of the above protocol can be amplified by sequential repetition. In this case, the prover needs as many copies of the witness as the number of repetitions.

Proof (Proof Sketch).
Completeness follows from [BJSW16].

Soundness. Once we argue that r^* produced in the protocol is uniformly distributed, even when the verifier is interacting with the malicious prover, we can then invoke the soundness of [BJSW16] to prove the soundness of our protocol.

Suppose the verifier accepts the Π_{NP} proof produced during the execution of the above protocol. From the soundness of Π_{NP}, we have that $r^* = a \oplus b$ where a is the string that the prover initially committed to in $\mathbf{c}'$. By the statistical binding security of the commitment, and the fact that b is chosen at random after a has been committed to, we have that r^* is sampled uniformly from $[M]$.

Bounded-Concurrent Quantum Zero-Knowledge. Suppose $x \in A_{\mathsf{yes}}$. Suppose V^* is a non-uniform malicious QPT Q-session verifier. Then we construct a QPT simulator Sim as follows.

Description of Sim: it starts with the registers $\mathbf{X}_{zk}, \mathbf{X}_{anc}, \mathbf{M}, \mathbf{Aux}$. The register $\mathbf{X}_{zk}$ is used by the simulator of the bounded concurrent QZK protocol, $\mathbf{X}_{anc}$ is an ancillary register, $\mathbf{M}$ is used to store the messages exchanged between the simulator and the verifier and finally, the register $\mathbf{Aux}$ is used for storing the private state of the verifier. Initialize the registers $\mathbf{X}_{zk}, \mathbf{M}$ with all zeroes. Initialize the register $\mathbf{X}_{anc}$ with $(\bigotimes_{j=1}^{Q} |s_j\rangle\langle s_j|) \otimes (\bigotimes_{j=1}^{Q} |r_j^*\rangle\langle r_j^*|) \otimes (\bigotimes_{j=1}^{Q} \rho_j) \otimes |0^{\otimes \mathrm{poly}}\rangle\langle 0^{\otimes \mathrm{poly}}|$, where s_i, r_i^* are generated uniformly at random and $\rho_j \leftarrow B(x, s_j, r_j^*)$ is defined in bullet 4 under BJSW encoding.

Sim applies the following unitary for Q times on the above registers. This unitary is defined as follows: it parses the message $((1, \mathsf{msg}_1), \ldots, (Q, \mathsf{msg}_Q))$ in the register $\mathbf{M}$. For every round of conversation, it does the following: if it is V^*'s turn to talk, it applies V^* on $\mathbf{Aux}$ and $\mathbf{M}$. Otherwise,

- Let S_1 be the set of indices such that for every $i \in S_1$, msg_i is a message in the protocol Π_{NP}. Finally, let $S_2 = [Q] \backslash S_1$.
- It copies $((1, \mathsf{msg}_1), \ldots, (Q, \mathsf{msg}_Q))$ into $\mathbf{X}_{zk}$ (using many CNOT operations) and for every $i \notin S_1$, replaces msg_i with N/A. We note that msg_i is a quantum state (for instance, it could be a superposition over different messages).
- For every $i \in S_2$, if msg_i is the first prover's message of the ith session, then set msg_i' to be $|\mathbf{c}_i\rangle\langle \mathbf{c}_i| \otimes \rho_i$, where $\mathbf{c}_i$ is the secret-key commitment of 0. If msg_i corresponds to the coin-flipping commitment, then set msg_i' to be $|\mathbf{c}_i'\rangle\langle \mathbf{c}_i'|$ where $\mathbf{c}_i'$ is a commitment to 0.
- It applies the simulator of Π_{NP} on $\mathbf{X}_{zk}$ to obtain $((1, \mathsf{msg}_{1, zk}'), \ldots (Q, \mathsf{msg}_{Q, zk}'))$. The ith session simulator of Π_{NP} takes as input $(\mathbf{r}_i, \mathbf{c}_i, \mathbf{r}_i', \mathbf{c}_i', r_i^*, y_i, b_i)$, where r_i^* was generated in the beginning and $\mathbf{r}_i, \mathbf{c}_i, \mathbf{r}_i', \mathbf{c}_i', y_i, b_i$ are generated as specified in the protocol.
- Determine $((1, \mathsf{msg}_1'), \ldots, (Q, \mathsf{msg}_Q'))$ as follows. Set $\mathsf{msg}_i' = \mathsf{msg}_{i, zk}$, if $i \in S_1$. Output of this round is $((1, \mathsf{msg}_1'), \ldots, (Q, \mathsf{msg}_Q'))$.

We claim that the output distribution of Sim (ideal world) is computationally indistinguishable from the output distribution of V^* when interacting with the prover (real world).

$\underline{\mathsf{Hyb}_1}$: This corresponds to the real world.

$\underline{\mathsf{Hyb}_2}$: This is the same as Hyb_1 except that the verifier V^* is run in superposition and the transcript is measured at the end.

The output distributions of Hyb_1 and Hyb_2 are identical.

$\underline{\mathsf{Hyb}_3}$: Simulate the zero-knowledge protocol Π_{NP} simultaneously for all the sessions. Other than this, the rest of the hybrid is the same as before.

The output distributions of Hyb_2 and Hyb_3 are computationally indistinguishable from the bounded concurrent QZK property of Π_{NP}.

$\underline{\mathsf{Hyb}_{4.i}}$ for $i \in [Q]$: For every $j \leq i$, the coin-flipping commitment in the jth session is a commitment to 0 instead of a_i. For all $j > i$, the commitment is computed as in the previous hybrid.

The output distributions of $\mathsf{Hyb}_{4.i-1}$ (or Hyb_3 if $i = 1$) and $\mathsf{Hyb}_{4.i}$ are computationally indistinguishable from the quantum concealing property of $(\mathsf{Comm}, \mathsf{R})$.

$\underline{\mathsf{Hyb}_{5.i}}$ for $i \in [Q]$: For every $j \leq i$, the secret-key commitment in the jth session is a commitment to 0. For all $j > i$, the commitment is computed as in the previous hybrid.

The output distributions of $\mathsf{Hyb}_{5.i-1}$ (or $\mathsf{Hyb}_{4.Q}$ if $i = 1$) and $\mathsf{Hyb}_{5.i}$ are computationally indistinguishable from the quantum concealing property of $(\mathsf{Comm}, \mathsf{R})$.

$\underline{\mathsf{Hyb}_{6.i}}$ for $i \in [Q]$: For every $j \leq i$, the encoding of the state is computed instead using $B(x, s_i, r_i^*)$, where s_i, r_i^* is generated uniformly at random.

The output distributions of $\mathsf{Hyb}_{6.i-1}$ and $\mathsf{Hyb}_{6.i}$ are statistically indistinguishable from simulatability of authenticated states property of BJSW encoding (bullet 4). This follows from the following fact: conditioned on the prover not aborting, the output distributions of the two worlds are identical. Moreover, the property of simulatability of authenticated states shows that the probability of the prover aborting in the previous hybrid is negligibly close to the probability of the prover aborting in this hybrid.

$\underline{\mathsf{Hyb}_7}$: This corresponds to the ideal world.

The output distributions of $\mathsf{Hyb}_{6.Q}$ and Hyb_7 are identical.

Proof of Quantum Knowledge with better witness quality. We can define an anologous notion of proof of knowledge in the context of interactive protocols for QMA. This notion is called proof of *quantum* knowledge. See [CVZ20] for a definition of this notion. Coladangelo, Vidick and Zhang [CVZ20] show how to achieve quantum proof of quantum knowledge generically using quantum proof of classical knowledge. Their protocol builds upon [BJSW16] to achieve their goal. We can adopt their idea to achieve proof of quantum knowledge property for a bounded concurrent QZK for QMA system. In Fig. 3, include a quantum proof of classical knowledge system for NP (for instance, the one we constructed in

Sect. 4.2) just after the prover sends encoding of the witness state $|\Psi\rangle$, encoded using the key s. Using the quantum proof of classical knowledge system, the prover convinces the verifier of its knowledge of the s. The rest of the protocol is the same as Fig. 3. To see why this satisfies proof of quantum knowledge, note that an extractor can extract s with probability negligibly close to the acceptance probability and using s, can recover the witness $|\Psi\rangle$.

For the first time, we get proof of quantum knowledge (even in the standalone setting) with $(1 - \mathsf{negl})$-quality if the acceptance probability is negligibly close to 1, where the quality denotes the closeness to the witness state. Previous proof of quantum knowledge [BG19, CVZ20] achieved only $1 - \frac{1}{\mathsf{poly}}$ quality; this is because these works use Unruh's quantum proof of classical knowledge technique [Unr12] and the extraction probability in Unruh is not negligibly close to the acceptance probability.

Acknowledgements. We thank Abhishek Jain for many enlightening discussions, Zhengzhong Jin for patiently answering questions regarding [GJJM20], Dakshita Khurana for suggestions on constructing oblivious transfer, Ran Canetti for giving an overview of existing classical concurrent ZK techniques, Aram Harrow and Takashi Yamakawa for discussions on the assumption of cloning security (included in a previous version of this paper) and Andrea Coladangelo for clarifications regarding [CVZ20]. RL was funded by NSF grant CCF-1729369. MIT-CTP/5289.

References

[ABG+20] Agarwal, A., Bartusek, J., Goyal, V., Khurana, D., Malavolta, G.: Post-quantum multi-party computation in constant rounds. arXiv preprint arXiv:2005.12904 (2020)

[ALP20] Ananth, P., La Placa, R.L.: Secure quantum extraction protocols. In: Pass, R., Pietrzak, K. (eds.) TCC 2020, Part III. LNCS, vol. 12552, pp. 123–152. Springer, Cham (2020). https://doi.org/10.1007/978-3-030-64381-2_5

[ARU14] Ambainis, A., Rosmanis, A., Unruh, D.: Quantum attacks on classical proof systems: the hardness of quantum rewinding. In: 2014 IEEE 55th Annual Symposium on Foundations of Computer Science, pp. 474–483. IEEE (2014)

[BG19] Broadbent, A., Grilo, A.B.: Zero-knowledge for QMA from locally simulatable proofs. arXiv preprint arXiv:1911.07782 (2019)

[BJSW16] Broadbent, A., Ji, Z., Song, F., Watrous, J.: Zero-knowledge proof systems for QMA. In: 2016 IEEE 57th Annual Symposium on Foundations of Computer Science (FOCS), pp. 31–40. IEEE (2016)

[Blu86] Blum, M.: How to prove a theorem so no one else can claim it. In: Proceedings of the International Congress of Mathematicians, vol. 1, p. 2. Citeseer (1986)

[BS05] Barak, B., Sahai, A.: How to play almost any mental game over the net-concurrent composition via super-polynomial simulation. In: 46th Annual IEEE Symposium on Foundations of Computer Science (FOCS 2005), pp. 543–552. IEEE (2005)

[BS20] Bitansky, N., Shmueli, O.: Post-quantum zero knowledge in constant rounds. In: STOC (2020)

[Can01]   Canetti, R.: Universally composable security: a new paradigm for crypto-graphic protocols. In: Proceedings 42nd IEEE Symposium on Foundations of Computer Science, pp. 136–145. IEEE (2001)

[CF01]   Canetti, R., Fischlin, M.: Universally composable commitments. In: Kilian, J. (ed.) CRYPTO 2001. LNCS, vol. 2139, pp. 19–40. Springer, Heidelberg (2001). https://doi.org/10.1007/3-540-44647-8_2

[CLOS02] Canetti, R., Lindell, Y., Ostrovsky, R., Sahai, A.: Universally compos-able two-party and multi-party secure computation. In: Proceedings of the Thirty-Fourth Annual ACM Symposium on Theory of Computing, pp. 494–503 (2002)

[CLP15]   Chung, K.-M., Lin, H., Pass, R.: Constant-round concurrent zero-knowledge from indistinguishability obfuscation. In: Gennaro, R., Robshaw, M. (eds.) CRYPTO 2015, Part I. LNCS, vol. 9215, pp. 287–307. Springer, Heidelberg (2015). https://doi.org/10.1007/978-3-662-47989-6_14

[CVZ20]   Coladangelo, A., Vidick, T., Zhang, T.: Non-interactive zero-knowledge arguments for QMA, with preprocessing. In: Micciancio, D., Ristenpart, T. (eds.) CRYPTO 2020, Part III. LNCS, vol. 12172, pp. 799–828. Springer, Cham (2020). https://doi.org/10.1007/978-3-030-56877-1_28

[DCO99]   Di Crescenzo, G., Ostrovsky, R.: On concurrent zero-knowledge with pre-processing. In: Wiener, M. (ed.) CRYPTO 1999. LNCS, vol. 1666, pp. 485–502. Springer, Heidelberg (1999). https://doi.org/10.1007/3-540-48405-1_31

[DNS04]   Dwork, C., Naor, M., Sahai, A.: Concurrent zero-knowledge. J. ACM (JACM) 51(6), 851–898 (2004)

[DS98]   Dwork, C., Sahai, A.: Concurrent zero-knowledge: reducing the need for timing constraints. In: Krawczyk, H. (ed.) CRYPTO 1998. LNCS, vol. 1462, pp. 442–457. Springer, Heidelberg (1998). https://doi.org/10.1007/BFb0055746

[FKP19]   Freitag, C., Komargodski, I., Pass, R.: Non-uniformly sound certificates with applications to concurrent zero-knowledge. In: Boldyreva, A., Mic-ciancio, D. (eds.) CRYPTO 2019, Part III. LNCS, vol. 11694, pp. 98–127. Springer, Cham (2019). https://doi.org/10.1007/978-3-030-26954-8_4

[GJJM20] Goyal, V., Jain, A., Jin, Z., Malavolta, G.: Statistical zaps and new obliv-ious transfer protocols. In: Canteaut, A., Ishai, Y. (eds.) EUROCRYPT 2020, Part III. LNCS, vol. 12107, pp. 668–699. Springer, Cham (2020). https://doi.org/10.1007/978-3-030-45727-3_23

[GJO+13] Goyal, V., Jain, A., Ostrovsky, R., Richelson, S., Visconti, I.: Concurrent zero knowledge in the bounded player model. In: Sahai, A. (ed.) TCC 2013. LNCS, vol. 7785, pp. 60–79. Springer, Heidelberg (2013). https://doi.org/10.1007/978-3-642-36594-2_4

[GK96]   Goldreich, O., Kahan, A.: How to construct constant-round zero-knowledge proof systems for NP. J. Cryptol. 9(3), 167–190 (1996)

[GMR85]   Goldwasser, S., Micali, S., Rackoff, C.: The knowledge complexity of inter-active proof-systems. In: STOC, pp. 291–304 (1985)

[HSS11]   Hallgren, S., Smith, A., Song, F.: Classical cryptographic protocols in a quantum world. In: Rogaway, P. (ed.) CRYPTO 2011. LNCS, vol. 6841, pp. 411–428. Springer, Heidelberg (2011). https://doi.org/10.1007/978-3-642-22792-9_23

[JKMR06] Jain, R., Kolla, A., Midrijanis, G., Reichardt, B,W.: On parallel compo-sition of zero-knowledge proofs with black-box quantum simulators. arXiv preprint quant-ph/0607211 (2006)

[KSVV02] Kitaev, A.Y., Shen, A., Vyalyi, M.N., Vyalyi, M.N.: Classical and Quantum Computation, vol. 47. American Mathematical Society, Providence (2002)

[Lin03] Lindell, Y.: Bounded-concurrent secure two-party computation without setup assumptions. In: Proceedings of the Thirty-Fifth Annual ACM Symposium on Theory of Computing, pp. 683–692 (2003)

[Nao91] Naor, M.: Bit commitment using pseudorandomness. J. Cryptol. **4**(2), 151–158 (1991)

[Pas04] Pass, R.: Bounded-concurrent secure multi-party computation with a dishonest majority. In: STOC, pp. 232–241 (2004)

[PR03] Pass, R., Rosen, A.: Bounded-concurrent secure two-party computation in a constant number of rounds. In: 44th Annual IEEE Symposium on Foundations of Computer Science, 2003. Proceedings, pp. 404–413. IEEE (2003)

[PRS02] Prabhakaran, M., Rosen, A., Sahai, A.: Concurrent zero knowledge with logarithmic round-complexity. In: FOCS, pp. 366–375. IEEE (2002)

[PTV14] Pass, R., Tseng, W.-L.D., Venkitasubramaniam, M.: Concurrent zero knowledge, revisited. J. Cryptol. **27**(1), 45–66 (2014)

[PTW09] Pass, R., Tseng, W.-L.D., Wikström, D.: On the composition of public-coin zero-knowledge protocols. In: Halevi, S. (ed.) CRYPTO 2009. LNCS, vol. 5677, pp. 160–176. Springer, Heidelberg (2009). https://doi.org/10.1007/978-3-642-03356-8_10

[PV08] Pass, R., Venkitasubramaniam, M.: On constant-round concurrent zero-knowledge. In: Canetti, R. (ed.) TCC 2008. LNCS, vol. 4948, pp. 553–570. Springer, Heidelberg (2008). https://doi.org/10.1007/978-3-540-78524-8_30

[Rab05] Rabin, M.O.: How to exchange secrets with oblivious transfer. IACR Cryptol. ePrint Arch., 2005(187) (2005)

[RK99] Richardson, R., Kilian, J.: On the concurrent composition of zero-knowledge proofs. In: Stern, J. (ed.) EUROCRYPT 1999. LNCS, vol. 1592, pp. 415–431. Springer, Heidelberg (1999). https://doi.org/10.1007/3-540-48910-X_29

[Unr10] Unruh, D.: Universally composable quantum multi-party computation. In: Gilbert, H. (ed.) EUROCRYPT 2010. LNCS, vol. 6110, pp. 486–505. Springer, Heidelberg (2010). https://doi.org/10.1007/978-3-642-13190-5_25

[Unr12] Unruh, D.: Quantum proofs of knowledge. In: Pointcheval, D., Johansson, T. (eds.) EUROCRYPT 2012. LNCS, vol. 7237, pp. 135–152. Springer, Heidelberg (2012). https://doi.org/10.1007/978-3-642-29011-4_10

[VZ20] Vidick, T., Zhang, T.: Classical zero-knowledge arguments for quantum computations. Quantum **4**, 266 (2020)

[Wat09] Watrous, J.: Zero-knowledge against quantum attacks. SIAM J. Comput. **39**(1), 25–58 (2009)

Multi-theorem Designated-Verifier NIZK for QMA

Omri Shmueli[✉]

Tel Aviv University, Tel Aviv, Israel
omrishmueli@mail.tau.ac.il

Abstract. We present a designated-verifier non-interactive zero-knowledge argument system for QMA with multi-theorem security under the Learning with Errors Assumption. All previous such protocols for QMA are only single-theorem secure. We also relax the setup assumption required in previous works. We prove security in the malicious designated-verifier (MDV-NIZK) model (Quach, Rothblum, and Wichs, EUROCRYPT 2019), where the setup consists of a mutually trusted random string and an untrusted verifier public key.

Our main technical contribution is a general compiler that given a NIZK for NP and a quantum sigma protocol for QMA generates an MDV-NIZK protocol for QMA.

1 Introduction

Zero-knowledge protocols allow to prove statements without revealing anything but the mere fact that they are true. Since their introduction by Goldwasser, Micali, and Rackoff [GMR89] they have had a profound impact on modern cryptography and theoretical computer science at large. While standard zero-knowledge protocols are interactive, Blum, Feldman, and Micali [BFM19] introduced the concept of a non-interactive zero-knowledge (NIZK) protocol, which consists of a single message sent by the prover to the verifier. NIZK protocols cannot exist in the plain model (i.e. a language with such a NIZK protocol can be decided by an efficient algorithm) but can be realized with a pre-computed setup. The point of the setup is that it can be computed instance-independently and usually, the setup is executed by a trusted third party that generates and publishes a string of bits and sometimes trapdoors are handed to the prover or verifier (or both).

Although existing zero-knowledge protocols for NP cover an array of diverse tasks and in particular, under standard computational assumptions it is known how to construct NIZK protocols for NP [CCH+19,PS19,BKM20], far less is

---

O. Shmueli—Supported by ISF grants 18/484 and 19/2137, by Len Blavatnik and the Blavatnik Family Foundation, and by the European Union Horizon 2020 Research and Innovation Program via ERC Project REACT (Grant 756482).

T. Malkin and C. Peikert (Eds.): CRYPTO 2021, LNCS 12825, pp. 375–405, 2021.
https://doi.org/10.1007/978-3-030-84242-0_14

known about the class QMA, the quantum generalization of NP. This knowledge gap between NP and QMA, which is present in both interactive and non-interactive zero-knowledge protocols, stems from the fact that many of the techniques that work for constructing protocols for NP, implicitly rely on the assumption that information in the system is classical. Accordingly, these techniques fail when this assumption no longer holds.

The first gap between classical and quantum NIZK protocols is that of setup requirements, that is, how much trust and resources the setup needs. The standard setup in NIZK is called the common reference string (CRS) model, where the trusted party samples a classical string from some specified distribution and publishes it. If the reference string is simply uniformly random then the setup is in the common *random* string model, which is considered to require minimal trust in the NIZK setting. While NIZK arguments for NP are known to exist in the common random string model under LWE [CCH+19, PS19], in current QMA constructions the setup is comprised at least of a common reference string sampled by the trusted party, and an additional public and secret verification keys (pvk, svk) where pvk is published along with the CRS and svk is kept by the verifier, such that either:

– pvk is a quantum state that needs to stay coherent while waiting for the proof by the prover, or
– The pair (pvk, svk) can be sampled only by the trusted party and not the verifier.

Aside from the above, a more elementary missing part in current NIZK protocols for QMA is multi-theorem security, which provides the main efficiency advantage to a NIZK protocol over an interactive protocol. Multi-theorem security considers the *reusability of the setup*, that is, once the setup is computed, any prover can send a proof by a single message repeatedly for many different statements and there is no need to re-compute the setup for every new proof sent, and in relation to the above QMA setups: once the CRS and public verification key are published, they are reusable.

Given the gap of knowledge in NIZK techniques between NP and QMA, improving the power of NIZKs for QMA and specifically constructing a reusable non-interactive zero-knowledge protocol for QMA seem as a natural cryptographic goal which we explore in this work.

1.1   Results

Under the Learning with Errors (LWE) assumption [Reg09] we resolve the above question. Specifically, we construct a multi-theorem-secure NIZK argument for QMA in the malicious designated-verifier model, which is the following:

1. The trusted party samples only a common random string crs.
2. Given crs, any verifier can sample a pair of classical public and secret verification keys (pvk, svk), in particular it is possible that the published pvk is maliciously-generated.

Given crs and pvk, any prover can repeatedly give a non-interactive zero-knowledge proof by a single quantum message $|\pi\rangle$. The MDV-NIZK model is introduced by Quach, Rothblum, and Wichs in [QRW19] and has the same minimal trust requirements as the common random string model (but is privately verifiable).

Theorem 1 (informal). *Assuming that LWE is hard for polynomial-time quantum algorithms, there exists a reusable, non-interactive computational zero-knowledge argument system for QMA in the malicious designated-verifier model.*

Main Technical Contribution: General Sigma Protocol MDV-NIZK Compilation. Technically, we deviate from previous NIZK constructions for QMA and aim for a simple and classical technique which is post-quantum (i.e. preserves security also for quantum protocols). Specifically, our main contribution is showing how given a NIZK for NP it is possible to compile a quantum sigma protocol into a reusable MDV-NIZK protocol. Further details are given in the technical overview below.

1.2 Technical Overview

We next describe our construction of a multi-theorem-secure MDV-NIZK protocol for QMA. For a discussion about the possibility of constructing a NIZK protocol for QMA in the CRS model see Subsect. 1.3, and for an overview of NIZK models and previous work on NIZK for QMA see Subsect. 1.3.

As we are aiming for a classical (quantum-secure) technique we currently restrict our attention to a purely-classical question: Given any sigma protocol $(\Sigma.\mathsf{P}, \Sigma.\mathsf{V})$, generically compile it into a multi-theorem-secure MDV-NIZK while assuming minimal properties of the protocol[1]. We will start with considering classical sigma protocols and later see what changes should take place in order for the technique to work for quantum protocols.

From a Sigma Protocol to a Single-Theorem-Secure MDV-NIZK. A sigma protocol is a 3-message public-coin proof system (with some mild zero knowledge properties), where the 3 messages are denoted by α, β and γ (i.e. β is a random string and is called "the challenge string"). Our first step is to construct a MDV-NIZK protocol with only single-theorem security out of a sigma protocol and is very simple.

In a sigma protocol, since the verifier's message β is a random string it is independent of any other information, additionally, our second need from it is that it stays hidden (until after the prover sends its first message α). The verifier can compute its public verification key, which is computed instance-independently, as a function of β: The public verification key pvk is an FHE-encrypted random challenge β and the secret verification key svk is the FHE decryption key and the challenge string,

$$\mathsf{pvk} = \mathsf{FHE}.\mathsf{Enc}_{\mathsf{fhek}}(\beta), \quad \mathsf{svk} = (\beta, \mathsf{fhek}) \ .$$

---

[1] In particular, we do not assume that the message α is classical.

Given the public verification key pvk, the 1-message proof procedure for $x \in \mathcal{L}$ goes as follows:

- P computes the first sigma protocol message $\alpha \leftarrow \Sigma.\mathsf{P}(x, w)$, where $w \in \mathcal{R}_\mathcal{L}(x)$.
- P computes γ the last protocol message under the encryption, that is, P performs the homomorphic evaluation $\hat{\mathsf{ct}}_\mathsf{P} \leftarrow \mathsf{FHE.Eval}(\Sigma.\mathsf{P}_3, \mathsf{FHE.Enc}_{\mathsf{fhek}}(\beta))$.
- As the proof, P sends α out in the open and γ under the encryption, that is, the proof is $\pi = (\alpha, \hat{\mathsf{ct}}_\mathsf{P})$.

In order for the proof to stay zero-knowledge, the homomorphic evaluation needs to be circuit-private. The verification algorithm is straightforward: Given svk, an instance x and a proof $\pi = (\alpha, \hat{\mathsf{ct}}_\mathsf{P})$, the verifier decrypts $\hat{\mathsf{ct}}_\mathsf{P}$ to get γ, and accepts iff the sigma protocol verifier accepts $\Sigma.\mathsf{V}(x, \alpha, \beta, \gamma) = 1$.

Is the Above Protocol Multi-theorem-Secure? While it is intuitively clear that the described construction is secure for a single use of the setup (that is, the above should, with some modifications, yield a single-theorem-secure MDV-NIZK) it is provably not multi-theorem-secure. Sigma protocols are usually parallel repetitions of 3-message zero-knowledge protocols, for example, consider the sigma protocol which is the parallel repetition of the zero-knowledge protocol for Graph Hamiltonicity [Blu86], which is as follows: Given a Hamiltonian cycle C in a graph $G = (V, E)$, the prover samples a random permutation $\varphi : V \to V$ of the vertices and commits to the permuted graph $\varphi(G)^2$. The verifier then sends a random bit b, and the prover answers accordingly:

- If $b = 0$ it is considered as a validity check, and the prover opens all commitments and sends φ. The verifier accepts if indeed the committed graph is $\varphi(G)$.
- If $b = 1$ it is considered as the cycle check, and the prover opens commitments only for the subgraph $\varphi(C)$. The verifier accepts if the opening shows a Hamiltonian cycle.

If the sigma protocol used in the above MDV-NIZK construction is the parallel repetition of the zero-knowledge protocol for Hamiltonicity[3], then there is a polynomial-time malicious prover P* that given multiple access to the verifier's verdict function $\mathsf{V}(\mathsf{svk}, \cdot)$ using the same public/secret verification key pair, can decode the encrypted challenge string β (which is polynomially-many random bits, each bit is for the i-th parallel repetition of the zero-knowledge protocol) and consequently break the soundness.

P* takes a Hamiltonian graph G and a Hamiltonian cycle C in it, and will decode the entire $\beta = (b_1, b_2, \cdots, b_k)$ bit-by-bit: To decode b_i, P* will honestly

---

[2] That is, the prover commits to all of the cells in the adjacency matrix that represents the graph $\varphi(G)$.

[3] We take the Hamiltonicity protocol only as a concrete easy example and in fact any other sigma protocol can take the role of this protocol in our context of attacking the soundness.

execute the zero-knowledge protocol prover's algorithm for all indices but index i (that is, for all $j \neq i$, it will honestly compute $\mathsf{Com}(\varphi_j(G))$ and under the encryption, the opening of either the entire graph and the permutation of just the cycle $\varphi_j(C)$), for which it is going to operate as follows. P^* will guess that $b_i = 0$ and send a commitment to a permutation of the graph out in the open and under the encryption act as if $b_i = 0$ regardless of the actual value of b_i. By the verifier's acceptance or rejection it will know whether the bit was 0 or 1. After decoding β the prover can now use this information to "prove" that any graph G is Hamiltonian.

From Single-Theorem to Multi-theorem Security. In the above attack the prover heavily relied on a specific operation: It uses a yes-instance (in the above case, a Hamiltonian graph G), in order to decode the random challenge β and then goes on to use the knowledge of β to give a false proof for a no-instance (again, in the above, a non Hamiltonian graph G^*).

Crucially, P^* does not know how to decode β when the graph is not Hamiltonian. More specifically, in the above we decode β bit-by-bit rather than all at once, and this ability comes from the fact that G is Hamiltonian and the zero-knowledge protocol is complete, thus P^* can be sure that if it honestly executes the zero-knowledge protocol for all indices but i, the only index that can make the proof get rejected is i. In this isolation, checking whether the challenge bit b_i is 0 or 1 becomes easy. However, if the graph is not Hamiltonian then the prover cannot know which index made the proof get rejected because all k indices are prone to rejection. Formally, by the soundness of the sigma protocol, we know that the answer from the verdict function of the verifier in this case will always be a rejection for any polynomial (or even sub-exponential) number of queries, with overwhelming probability. This means in particular that the prover cannot decode anything through the oracle access to the verdict function.

Our fix to the first protocol is based on the above observation: If we could make the random challenge β change with the instance at hand it seems that the decoding attack is neutralized, because even if the prover decodes β_G the challenge for a Hamiltonian graph G, it doesn't have information about β_{G^*} the challenge of some non Hamiltonian G^*. Since the instance x *is in particular a classical string* we can make the challenge change with the instance: The public verification key will not be an encrypted challenge β but instead will be a secret key prfk of a pseudorandom function PRF. The prover will compute α out in the open as before but the homomorphic evaluation changes: under the encryption, P will compute the challenge string as the PRF's output on the instance $\beta_x = \mathsf{PRF.F}_{\mathsf{prfk}}(x)$, and then compute γ for the challenge β_x.

Extraction by Non-interactive Zero Knowledge for NP. Up to this point we only came close to constructing a provably-secure MDV-NIZK. Indeed, we didn't even use any NIZK tools yet for NP, and in order to prove the security of our construction we need knowledge extraction from both the prover and verifier.

To prove soundness, our thought process is roughly the following: We know that the prover computes γ obliviously under the FHE, more precisely, it homomorphically evaluates the circuit $C_{x,r}$ that computes $\beta_x = \mathsf{PRF.F}_{\mathsf{prfk}}(x)$ and then given β_x computes γ. The part of the circuit $C_{x,r}$ that computes γ from β_x is the "non-trivial" part of the circuit and is determined by a secret string r (which is the information that the honest sigma protocol prover uses in order to compute γ, this information is the randomness of the prover and possibly the witness). If we could extract r from a prover (e.g. by the prover giving a proof of knowledge on the non-trivial part of the circuit $C_{x,r}$) that successfully cheats in the NIZK protocol then we could get a successfully cheating prover for the sigma protocol and thus prove security. To see this, note that by the hiding of the FHE and by the pseudorandomness of the PRF, even if as the public verification key we send an encryption of 0 instead of an encryption of the PRF secret key, the string r still needs to yield a circuit $C_{x,r}$ that does well in generating a satisfying γ for a now-truly-random challenge β.

On the zero knowledge side we also need extraction; we recall a basic property of a sigma protocol: if the sigma protocol simulator knows the challenge string β before sending the first message α then it can simulate a view that is indistinguishable from the real interaction with the honest prover. This means that the information we want to extract from the malicious verifier is the secret PRF key prfk that in particular holds the information for obtaining β_x.

We solve both extraction tasks by a combination of a two-sided NP NIZK and a public-key encryption scheme with pseudorandom public keys. Given the existence of a PKE scheme (PKE.Gen, PKE.Enc, PKE.Dec) with pseudorandom public keys of length ℓ we take the common random string of our protocol to be (1) the common random string of an NP NIZK (NIZK.Setup, NIZK.P, NIZK.V) protocol which we denote with crs, concatenated with (2) a random string of length ℓ which we denote with ek (for extraction key).

We will let each of the parties encrypt, using $\text{PKE.Enc}_{ek}(\cdot)$, the secrets that we want to extract and then use the NIZK to prove consistency between the content of the PKE encryption and the protocol computations. More precisely, as part of its 1-message proof, the prover will give a proof π_P that the string r encrypted using the PKE yields the (canonical) circuit $C_{x,r}$ that it used for the (circuit-private) homomorphic evaluation that generated γ, and the verifier, as part of its public verification key, will give a proof π_V that the PRF key prfk that is encrypted using the PKE is the same key encrypted with the FHE. Note that the information that the parties encrypt using a random string instead of a real PKE key stays secure due to the fact that a real key is indistinguishable from a random string, and thus an adversary that manages to break the PKE when it uses a random string as the public key can break the pseudorandomness property of the public keys.

When wanting to extract information (either in the soundness reduction or in the zero-knowledge simulation), we will sample ek using the PKE key-generation algorithm $(ek, sk) \leftarrow \text{PKE.Gen}$, and since the public keys are pseudorandom the change in key distribution won't be felt by either of the parties. At that point the parties encrypt their secrets and prove they do so using the NIZK, and the extractor can just use the PKE decryption $\text{PKE.Dec}_{sk}(\cdot)$ to obtain the secrets.

Compiling Quantum Protocols. Our technique so far is entirely classical and compiles classical sigma protocols. We now ask whether it works to compile quantum sigma protocols. This can be answered in turn by answering the following question: what properties of the sigma protocol *exactly* did we use in order for the MDV-NIZK protocol to work?

It can be verified that even if we don't assume nothing on the sigma protocol that we compile, every action in the MDV-NIZK protocol except the homomorphic evaluation of the circuit $C_{x,r}$ can stay exactly the same. Regarding the homomorphic evaluation, the issue that we have is the following: In order to still be able to extract the information r of the circuit $C_{x,r}$ from the prover, the computation that takes β_x and outputs γ needs to be a classical circuit. This is not necessarily the case in a quantum protocol. For example, in the quantum zero-knowledge protocol for QMA of [BJSW16] (which is also the basis for the quantum NIZK protocol of [CVZ19]), in order to generate γ given α, β, first a quantum Clifford operation that is chosen with respect to β needs to be executed on α, followed by a measurement. Then, the prover proves in ZK that the classical string obtained by the measurement satisfies some properties[4]. With this goal in mind, we identify a different quantum protocol that in fact does satisfy the property that γ can be computed by an entirely classical circuit.

We consider the Consistency of Local Density Matrices (CLDM) problem [Liu06], which is a QMA problem with some special properties. In [BG19] Broadbent and Grilo show that CLDM is QMA-complete and how to construct a very simple quantum zero-knowledge protocol for it. The [BG19] zero-knowledge protocol for CLDM is as follows: Given a quantum witness $|w\rangle$, the protocol starts with the prover sending a quantum one-time pad encryption of $|w\rangle$ as the message α. More precisely, for a length-l witness it samples classical random pads $a, b \leftarrow \{0, 1\}^l$, applies

$$\bigotimes_{i \in [l]} \left(X^{a_i} \cdot Z^{b_i} \right) \cdot |w\rangle \ ,$$

and then sends as α the transformed quantum state and classical commitments to the QOTP keys a, b. For a random challenge β, the prover response γ is an opening to part of the state. We find the CLDM problem and specifically the zero-knowledge protocol for it especially attractive for our purposes as γ *is only a function of the randomness of the prover and the challenge* β, which in particular means that the circuit $C_{x,r}$ can stay classical in our setting.

Finally, by using the sigma protocol yielded by the parallel repetition of the zero-knowledge protocol from [BG19] we obtain a clean and simple noninteractive computational zero-knowledge argument system for the class QMA in the malicious designated-verifier model:

---

[4] in that protocol it is also needed that the verifier itself makes the Clifford operation and measurement, which makes the protocol more challenging to use for a NIZK protocol.

1. **Common Random String:** (crs, ek).
2. **Public and Secret Verification Keys:** $prfk \leftarrow$ PRF.Gen(1^λ), fhek $\leftarrow$ FHE.Gen(1^λ),

$$pvk = \big(FHE.Enc_{fhek}(prfk), PKE.Enc_{ek}(prfk), \pi_V\big), \quad svk = (prfk, fhek) \ .$$

For any prover that wishes to give a proof for an instance $x \in \mathcal{L}_{yes}$, it executes the following:

- **Proof:** If π_V is valid, P computes $\alpha \leftarrow \Xi.P(|w\rangle; r)$ and sends

$$|\pi\rangle = \big(\alpha, FHE.Eval(C_{x,r}, FHE.Enc(prfk)), PKE.Enc_{ek}(r), \pi_P\big) \ .$$

1.3 Related Work

In this section we discuss the main challenges in the construction of non-interactive zero-knowledge protocols for QMA (specifically in the CRS model) and the previous works on QMA NIZKs.

Can We Build a NIZK Protocol for QMA in the CRS Model? In short, the answer to the above question is that we don't know, and this section does not aim to answer it. This section is intended to give some evidence to why constructing a NIZK for QMA in the CRS model seem to require a different set of techniques from what we currently have for NP. In what follows we will start with briefly recalling how NIZKs for NP are constructed and then understand why current approaches fail in the setting of quantum proofs.

NP, Fiat-Shamir and Correlation Intractability. In order to construct a non-interactive zero-knowledge protocol for NP under standard assumptions, the construction starts with a sigma protocol $(\Sigma.P, \Sigma.V)$. To make the protocol non-interactive, the Fiat-Shamir transform is applied: By assuming public oracle access to a random function F, the prover applies it to α and treat its (random-string) output $F(\alpha)$ as the challenge string β. It then computes γ and sends all of this information to the verifier, who makes sure that β was rightfully generated $\beta = F(\alpha)$, and that the sigma protocol verifier $\Sigma.V(\alpha, \beta, \gamma)$ accepts. Since we don't know how to construct a cryptographic primitive that acts as a publicly-computable random function, the above protocol is secure only in the random oracle model, that is, only if we directly assume public access to such random function F.

In order to prove the security of the NIZK protocol in the standard model (with access to a common reference string rather than a random oracle), the final part of the construction involves swapping the random function F with a new, special hash function H - this general technique of swapping F with a special hash function H is usually called the Correlation Intractability (CI) paradigm [CGH04]. The properties of the hash function H or the meaning of correlation intractability are less relevant to this overview, but it is suffices to say that under the LWE assumption it is known how to construct a hash function H that can be swapped with F in the FS transform and where the protocol can be proven secure [CCH+19, PS19].

Can we use Known Classical NIZK Techniques for Quantum Protocols? There are two known routes for getting a quantum-secure NIZK for NP in the CRS model, the first is through the FS transform and CI (which also uses only standard assumptions, described above) and the second is through the hidden bits model and indistinguishability obfuscation. It is natural to ask whether we can use these techniques for QMA (the question of whether the FS transform can be used for quantum protocols was asked as one of the open questions in Sect. 1.4 of [BG19]).

We first review the ability to use the FS transform (and in particular correlation intractability) for QMA and explain why there is an issue with the no-cloning theorem. In the quantum setting, sigma protocols ($\varXi.P, \varXi.V$) [BG19, BJSW16] are quite the same but with the main difference that the first message α is quantum (and of course, the prover takes as input a quantum witness $|w\rangle$ rather than classical). Recall that when we use the FS transform on a sigma protocol in order to generate a NIZK, for the protocol to be complete, when the parties act honestly then the verifier needs to verify that the random function F yields the challenge, that is $F(\alpha) = \beta$. This means that now F needs to be a quantum transformation such that for $x \in \mathcal{L}_{yes}$ and an honestly generated $\alpha \leftarrow \varXi.P(|w\rangle)$, $F(\alpha)$ is always the same classical string (with overwhelming probability). Also, for the protocol to be sound we need that the *entire* output of F will be the challenge β and it cannot be the case for example that the output $F(\alpha)$ will contain one register with the classical string β and another register with some quantum state $|\psi\rangle$. Now, denote by s the classical string s.t. $F(\alpha) = s$, and we have a generating circuit for the quantum witness: $|w\rangle = \varXi.P^{\dagger}(\cdot) \cdot F^{\dagger} \cdot |s\rangle$, where the inverse versions of F and $\varXi.P$ are purified. This seems to violate the no-cloning theorem in the following manner: the prover gets a copy of the witness and can generate a generating circuit for the witness state, this circuit can be used to generate arbitrarily many copies of the state. Finally, because we can always consider a trivial language with a dummy witness, and take the quantum witness to be some unclonable state (for example, a pseudorandom quantum state) we get a contradiction to the no-cloning theorem.

Even if we aim to construct a NIZK using the FS transform for QCMA, the subclass of QMA where the verification algorithm is still quantum but the witness is classical, the problem is not seemed to be solved. The reason, is that we don't know how to construct sigma protocols for QCMA where the first message α is classical, and the same contradiction to the no-cloning theorem holds.

The second known route of obtaining a quantum-secure NIZK protocol for NP in the CRS model is through the hidden bits model [FLS99] which is implementable by sub-exponentially-secure indistinguishability obfuscation [BP15]. In the hidden bits model, intuitively (and roughly), the trusted party samples as the common reference string a commitment to a string sampled from some distribution (where by using a trapdoor permutation, the prover can open the commitments efficiently), and the prover proves that the instance at hand $x \in \mathcal{L}_{yes}$

satisfies some property related to the string underlying the commitments. Even if we are willing to assume the very strong cryptographic assumptions which are needed for the realization of this protocol (i.e. sub-exponentially-secure post-quantum indistinguishability obfuscation), it is currently unknown how to use the hidden bits model to instantiate non-interactive zero-knowledge quantum protocols.

Relaxations of the CRS Model and Previous Work. The constructions of NIZKs for NP discussed in Subsect. 1.3 are implicitly in the CRS model, where the setup consists of a string that is sampled and published by the trusted party, in particular, nor the prover or verifier hold any trapdoors over the setup. Sometimes when it is unknown how to build a NIZK in the CRS model (or unknown how to minimize the assumptions for building one) we turn to relaxations of the CRS model. For example, in the designated-verifier model (DV-NIZK) [PV+06] the trusted party samples, along with the CRS, a pair of public and secret verification keys (pvk, svk), publishes pvk along with the CRS and hands svk only to the verifier. Another example is the designated prover model (DP-NIZK) [KW19], which is analogous to the DV-NIZK model, only that the prover is the one who gets a secret, now-*proof* key.

It is a well known fact in the design of NIZKs that when the verifier holds a secret verification key (e.g. in the DV-NIZK model) then multi-theorem zero knowledge can be achieved generically by the compiler of [FLS99], but multi-theorem soundness becomes non-trivial. For example, it is possible (and is sometimes provably the case) that the prover can decode the verifier's secret key by having access multiple times to the verifier's verdict function, consequently breaking the soundness of the protocol. Indeed, one example is that until the works of [QRW19, LQR+19], based on [PV+06] it was only known how to get single-theorem-secure DV-NIZK for NP, and another example is that this is the current situation with QMA constructions of NIZK protocols.

The QMA NIZK protocol of Broadbent and Grilo [BG19] is in the secret parameters model (i.e. the protocol is both designated-prover and designated-verifier and both parties get secret keys from the trusted party) but is a proof system and has *statistical* soundness rather than the computational soundness we achieve. The protocol of Coladangelo, Vidick and Zhang [CVZ19] is in a model that is somewhat between the common reference string model and the DV-NIZK model, where the trusted party samples a common reference string and the verifier itself samples a pair (pvk, svk) where pvk is a quantum state. Morimae [Mor20] shows a classical-designated-verifier NIZK proof system for QMA with a quantum trusted setup. Outside of the standard model, an additional construction by Alagic, Childs, Grilo and Hung [ACGH19] yields a QMA NIZK argument in the quantum random oracle model (with additional setup in the secret parameters model) which is classical-verifier. All of the abovementioned protocols are not reusable.

There are two main issues with letting the trusted party sample secret keys for any of the parties: First, the trust requirements of the setup now increase as the party receiving the secret key should assume that the trusted party handles its secret information securely. The second issue is that of centralization of computational resources: for example, in the DV-NIZK model, the trusted party is now responsible for sampling a fresh pair (pvk, svk) for every new verifier that wishes to use the protocol, which is very different from the CRS setting where it samples a string and from that point on can terminate.

The *malicious* designated-verifier (MDV-NIZK) model [QRW19, LQR+19] seeks to solve the above two problems, which is also the model of our protocol. In the MDV-NIZK model the trusted party only samples a common random string, and then, any verifier wishing to use the protocol can sample *by itself* a pair of classical keys (pvk, svk) and publish pvk. The protocol then stays secure even if the public key pvk is maliciously-generated.

1.4 Subsequent Work

Subsequently to this work, several related constructions for NIZK protocols for QMA are shown. Morimae and Yamakawa construct a classically verifiable dual-mode NIZK for QMA, with quantum preprocessing [MY21]. The result is essentially in the same model of the protocol of Coladangelo, Vidick and Zhang [CVZ19], that is, the CRS is published, and then the verifier sends an instance-independent quantum message to the prover, keeping a classical trapdoor. Given the instance, witness and the verifier's quantum message, the prover can perform an efficient quantum procedure and send a classical message to the verifier which acts as a proof. The improvement of [MY21] over [CVZ19] is that the protocol is dual-mode and has two modes: (1) a proof (with statistical soundness) and computational ZK guarantee and (2) an argument (with computational soundness guarantee) and statistical ZK, rather than only an argument mode, that [CVZ19] enables.

Bartusek, Coladangelo, Khurana and Ma also construct an MDV-NIZK protocol for QMA [BCKM20], and improve our result in two aspects. First, in order to get adaptive soundness (over standard soundness) we need to assume the subexponential (quantum) hardness of LWE, while [BCKM20] only requires assuming the polynomial (quantum) hardness of LWE. Second, our protocol requires polynomially-many copies of the quantum witness for the QMA instance x, while the protocol of [BCKM20] is a single-witness protocol.

2 Preliminaries

We rely on standard notions of classical Turing machines and Boolean circuits:

- A PPT algorithm is a probabilistic polynomial-time Turing machine.
- Let M be a PPT and let x denote the random variable which is the output of M. Whenever the entropy of the output of M is non-zero, we denote the random experiment of sampling x with $x \leftarrow M(\cdot)$. If the entropy of the output of M is zero (i.e. M is deterministic), we denote $x = M(\cdot)$.

- We sometimes think about PPT algorithms as polynomial-size uniform families of circuits, these are equivalent models. A polynomial-size circuit family $\mathcal{C}$ is a sequence of circuits $\mathcal{C} = \{C_\lambda\}_{\lambda \in \mathbb{N}}$, such that each circuit C_λ is of polynomial size $\lambda^{O(1)}$. We say that the family is uniform if there exists a deterministic polynomial-time algorithm M that on input 1^λ outputs C_λ.
- For a PPT algorithm M, we denote by $M(x; r)$ the output of M on input x and random coins r. For such an algorithm and any input x, we write $m \in M(x)$ to denote the fact that m is in the support of $M(x; \cdot)$.

We follow standard notions from quantum computation.

- A QPT algorithm is a quantum polynomial-time Turing machine.
- We sometimes think about QPT algorithms as polynomial-size uniform families of quantum circuits, these are equivalent models. A polynomial-size quantum circuit family $\mathcal{C}$ is a sequence of quantum circuits $\mathcal{C} = \{C_\lambda\}_{\lambda \in \mathbb{N}}$, such that each circuit C_λ is of polynomial size $\lambda^{O(1)}$. We say that the family is uniform if there exists a deterministic polynomial-time algorithm M that on input 1^λ outputs C_λ.
- An interactive algorithm M, in a two-party setting, has input divided into two registers and output divided into two registers. For the input, one register I_m is for an input message from the other party, and a second register I_a is an auxiliary input that acts as an inner state of the party. For the output, one register O_m is for a message to be sent to the other party, and another register O_a is again for auxiliary output that acts again as an inner state. For a quantum interactive algorithm M, both input and output registers are quantum.

The Adversarial Model. Throughout, efficient adversaries are modeled as quantum circuits with non-uniform quantum advice (i.e. quantum auxiliary input). Formally, *a polynomial-size adversary* $\mathsf{A}^* = \{\mathsf{A}_\lambda^*, \rho_\lambda\}_{\lambda \in \mathbb{N}}$, consists of a polynomial-size non-uniform sequence of quantum circuits $\{\mathsf{A}_\lambda^*\}_{\lambda \in \mathbb{N}}$, and a sequence of polynomial-size mixed quantum states $\{\rho_\lambda\}_{\lambda \in \mathbb{N}}$.

For an interactive quantum adversary in a classical protocol, it can be assumed without loss of generality that its output message register is always measured in the computational basis at the end of computation. This assumption is indeed without the loss of generality, because whenever a quantum state is sent through a classical channel then qubits decohere and are effectively measured in the computational basis.

Indistinguishability in the Quantum Setting

- Let $f : \mathbb{N} \to [0, 1]$ be a function.
    - f is negligible if for every constant $c \in \mathbb{N}$ there exists $N \in \mathbb{N}$ such that for all $n > N$, $f(n) < n^{-c}$.
    - f is noticeable if there exists $c \in \mathbb{N}, N \in \mathbb{N}$ such that for every $n \geq N$, $f(n) \geq n^{-c}$.
    - f is overwhelming if it is of the form $1 - \mu(n)$, for a negligible function μ.

- We may consider random variables over bit strings or over quantum states. This will be clear from the context.
- For two random variables X and Y supported on quantum states, quantum distinguisher circuit D with, quantum auxiliary input ρ, and $\mu \in [0, 1]$, we write $X \approx_{\mathsf{D}, \rho, \mu} Y$ if

$$|\Pr[\mathsf{D}(X; \rho) = 1] - \Pr[\mathsf{D}(Y; \rho) = 1]| \leq \mu.$$

- Two ensembles of random variables $\mathcal{X} = \{X_i\}_{\lambda \in \mathbb{N}, i \in I_\lambda}$, $\mathcal{Y} = \{Y_i\}_{\lambda \in \mathbb{N}, i \in I_\lambda}$ over the same set of indices $I = \cup_{\lambda \in \mathbb{N}} I_\lambda$ are said to be *computationally indistinguishable*, denoted by $\mathcal{X} \approx_c \mathcal{Y}$, if for every polynomial-size quantum distinguisher $\mathsf{D} = \{\mathsf{D}_\lambda, \rho_\lambda\}_{\lambda \in \mathbb{N}}$ there exists a negligible function $\mu(\cdot)$ such that for all $\lambda \in \mathbb{N}, i \in I_\lambda$,

$$X_i \approx_{\mathsf{D}_\lambda, \rho_\lambda, \mu(\lambda)} Y_i .$$

- The trace distance between two distributions X, Y supported over quantum states, denoted $\mathrm{TD}(X, Y)$, is a generalization of statistical distance to the quantum setting and represents the maximal distinguishing advantage between two distributions supported over quantum states, by unbounded quantum algorithms. We thus say that ensembles $\mathcal{X} = \{X_i\}_{\lambda \in \mathbb{N}, i \in I_\lambda}$, $\mathcal{Y} = \{Y_i\}_{\lambda \in \mathbb{N}, i \in I_\lambda}$, supported over quantum states, are statistically indistinguishable (and write $\mathcal{X} \approx_s \mathcal{Y}$), if there exists a negligible function $\mu(\cdot)$ such that for all $\lambda \in \mathbb{N}, i \in I_\lambda$,

$$\mathrm{TD}(X_i, Y_i) \leq \mu(\lambda) .$$

In what follows, we introduce the cryptographic tools used in this work. By default, all algorithms are classical and efficient, and security holds against polynomial-size non-uniform quantum adversaries with quantum advice.

2.1 Cryptographic Tools

Interactive Proofs and Sigma Protocols. We define interactive proof systems and then proceed to describe sigma protocols, which are a special case of interactive proof systems. In what follows, we denote by (P, V) a protocol between two parties P and V. For common input x, we denote by $\mathsf{OUT}_{\mathsf{V}}\langle \mathsf{P}, \mathsf{V}\rangle(x)$ the output of V in the protocol. For honest verifiers, this output will be a single bit indicating acceptance or rejection of the proof. Malicious quantum verifiers may have arbitrary quantum output.

Definition 1 (Quantum Proof Systems for QMA). *Let (P, V) be a quantum protocol with an honest QPT prover P and an honest QPT verifier V for a problem $\mathcal{L} \in \mathbf{QMA}$, satisfying:*

1. **Statistical Completeness:** *There is a polynomial $k(\cdot)$ and a negligible function $\mu(\cdot)$ s.t. for any $\lambda \in \mathbb{N}$, $x \in \mathcal{L} \cap \{0,1\}^{\lambda}$, $|w\rangle \in \mathcal{R}_{\mathcal{L}}(x)^5$,*

$$\Pr[\mathsf{OUT}_{\mathsf{V}}\langle\mathsf{P}(|w\rangle^{\otimes k(\lambda)}), \mathsf{V}\rangle(x) = 1] \geq 1 - \mu(\lambda) \ .$$

2. **Statistical Soundness:** *There exists a negligible function $\mu(\cdot)$, such that for any (unbounded) prover P^*, any security parameter $\lambda \in \mathbb{N}$, and any $x \in \{0,1\}^{\lambda} \setminus \mathcal{L}$,*

$$\Pr\left[\mathsf{OUT}_{\mathsf{V}}\langle\mathsf{P}^*, \mathsf{V}\rangle(x) = 1\right] \leq \mu(\lambda) \ .$$

We use the abstraction of *Sigma Protocols*, which are public-coin three-message proof systems with a weak zero-knowledge guarantee. We define quantum Sigma Protocols for gap problems in QMA.

Definition 2 (Quantum Sigma Protocol for QMA). *A quantum sigma protocol for $\mathcal{L} \in \mathbf{QMA}$ is a quantum proof system $(\varXi.\mathsf{P}, \varXi.\mathsf{V})$ (as in Definition 1) with 3 messages and the following syntax.*

- $\alpha = \varXi.\mathsf{P}(|w\rangle^{\otimes k(\lambda)}; r)$: *Given $k(\lambda)$ copies of the quantum witness $w \in \mathcal{R}_{\mathcal{L}}(x)$ and classical randomness r, the first prover message consists of a quantum message α generated by a quantum unitary computation $\varXi.\mathsf{P}$.*
- $\beta \leftarrow \varXi.\mathsf{V}(x)$: *The verifier simply outputs a string of $\mathrm{poly}(|x|)$ random bits.*
- $\gamma = \varXi.\mathsf{P}_3(\beta, r)$: *Given the verifier's β and the randomness r, the prover outputs a response γ by a classical computation $\varXi.\mathsf{P}_3$.*

The protocol satisfies the following.

Special Zero-Knowledge: *There exists a QPT simulator $\varXi.\mathsf{Sim}$ such that,*

$$\left\{(\alpha,\gamma) \mid r \leftarrow U_{\ell(\lambda)}, \alpha = \varXi.\mathsf{P}(|w\rangle^{\otimes k(\lambda)}; r), \gamma = \varXi.\mathsf{P}_3(\beta, r)\right\}_{\lambda, x, |w\rangle, \beta}$$

$$\approx_c \{(\alpha,\gamma) \mid (\alpha,\gamma) \leftarrow \varXi.\mathsf{Sim}(x, \beta)\}_{\lambda, x, |w\rangle, \beta} \ ,$$

where $\lambda \in \mathbb{N}$, $x \in \mathcal{L} \cap \{0,1\}^{\lambda}$, $|w\rangle \in \mathcal{R}_{\mathcal{L}}(x)$, $\beta \in \{0,1\}^{\mathrm{poly}(\lambda)}$ and $\ell(\lambda)$ is the amount of randomness needed for the first prover message.

Instantiations. Quantum sigma protocols follow from the parallel repetition of the 3-message quantum zero-knowledge protocols of [BG19] for QMA.

Leveled Fully-Homomorphic Encryption with Circuit Privacy. We define a leveled fully-homomorphic encryption scheme with circuit privacy, that is, for an encryption $\mathsf{ct} = \mathsf{FHE.Enc}(x)$ and a circuit C, a C-homomorphically-evaluated ciphertext $\hat{\mathsf{ct}} = \mathsf{FHE.Eval}(C, \mathsf{ct})$ reveals nothing on C but $C(x)$.

---

[5] For a problem $\mathcal{L} = (\mathcal{L}_{yes}, \mathcal{L}_{no})$ in QMA, for an instance $x \in \mathcal{L}_{yes}$, the set $\mathcal{R}_{\mathcal{L}}(x)$ is the (possibly infinite) set of quantum witnesses that make the BQP verification machine accept with some overwhelming probability $1 - \mathrm{negl}(\lambda)$.

Definition 3 (Circuit-Private Fully-Homomorphic Encryption). *A circuit-private, leveled fully-homomoprhic encryption scheme* (FHE.Gen, FHE.Enc, FHE.Eval, FHE.Dec) *has the following syntax:*

- sk $\leftarrow$ FHE.Gen($1^\lambda, 1^{s(\lambda)}$) : *a probabilistic algorithm that takes a security parameter 1^λ and a circuit size bound $s(\lambda)$ and outputs a secret key* sk.
- ct $\leftarrow$ FHE.Enc$_{\text{sk}}(x)$: *a probabilistic algorithm that given the secret key, takes a string $x \in \{0,1\}^*$ and outputs a ciphertext* ct.
- ĉt $\leftarrow$ FHE.Eval(C, ct) : *a probabilistic algorithm that takes a (classical) circuit C and a ciphertext* ct *and outputs an evaluated ciphertext* ĉt.
- $\hat{x}$ = FHE.Dec$_{\text{sk}}$(ĉt) : *a deterministic algorithm that takes a ciphertext* ĉt *and outputs a string $\hat{x}$.*

The scheme satisfies the following.

- **Perfect Correctness:** *For any polynomial $s(\cdot)$, for any $\lambda \in \mathbb{N}$, size-$s(\lambda)$ classical circuit C and input x for C,*

$$
\Pr\left[\text{FHE.Dec}_{\text{sk}}(\hat{\text{ct}}) = C(x) \;\middle|\; \begin{array}{l} \text{sk} \leftarrow \text{FHE.Gen}(1^\lambda, 1^{s(\lambda)}), \\ \text{ct} \leftarrow \text{FHE.Enc}_{\text{sk}}(x), \\ \hat{\text{ct}} \leftarrow \text{FHE.Eval}(C, \text{ct}) \end{array}\right] = 1 \ .
$$

- **Input Privacy:** *For every polynomial $\ell(\cdot)$ (and any polynomial $s(\lambda)$),*

$$
\left\{\text{ct} \;\middle|\; \begin{array}{l} \text{sk} \leftarrow \text{FHE.Gen}(1^\lambda, 1^{s(\lambda)}), \\ \text{ct} \leftarrow \text{FHE.Enc}_{\text{sk}}(x_0) \end{array}\right\}_{\lambda, x_0, x_1} \approx_c \left\{\text{ct} \;\middle|\; \begin{array}{l} \text{sk} \leftarrow \text{FHE.Gen}(1^\lambda, 1^{s(\lambda)}), \\ \text{ct} \leftarrow \text{FHE.Enc}_{\text{sk}}(x_1) \end{array}\right\}_{\lambda, x_0, x_1} ,
$$

where $\lambda \in \mathbb{N}$ and $x_0, x_1 \in \{0,1\}^{\ell(\lambda)}$.

- **Statistical Circuit Privacy:** *There exist unbounded algorithms, probabilistic* Sim *and deterministic* Ext *such that:*
  - *For every $x \in \{0,1\}^*$, ct $\in$ FHE.Enc(x), the extractor outputs* Ext(ct) = x.
  - *For any polynomial $s(\cdot)$,*

$$
\{\text{FHE.Eval}(C, \text{ct}^*)\}_{\lambda, C, \text{ct}^*} \approx_s \{\text{Sim}(\ 1^\lambda, C(\text{Ext}(1^\lambda, \text{ct}^*))\ )\}_{\lambda, C, \text{ct}^*} ,
$$

where $\lambda \in \mathbb{N}$, C is a $s(\lambda)$-size circuit, and ct* $\in \{0,1\}^*$.

The next claim follows directly from the circuit privacy property, and will be used throughout the analysis.

Claim (Evaluations of Agreeing Circuits are Statistically Close). For any polynomial $s(\cdot)$,

$$
\{\text{FHE.Eval}(C_0, \text{ct}^*)\}_{\lambda, C_0, C_1, \text{ct}} \approx_s \{\text{FHE.Eval}(C_1, \text{ct}^*)\}_{\lambda, C_0, C_1, \text{ct}} ,
$$

where $\lambda \in \mathbb{N}$, C_0, C_1 are two $s(\lambda)$-size functionally-equivalent circuits, and ct* $\in \{0,1\}^*$.

Instantiations. Circuit-private leveled FHE schemes are known based on LWE [OPCPC14, BD18].

Pseudorandom-Key Public-Key Encryption. We define a public-key encryption scheme with pseudorandom public keys.

Definition 4 (Pseudorandom-key   Public-key   Encryption). *A pseudorandom-key public-key encryption scheme* (PKE.Gen, PKE.Enc, PKE.Dec) *has the following syntax:*

- (pk, sk) $\leftarrow$ PKE.Gen(1^λ) : *a probabilistic algorithm that takes a security parameter* 1^λ *and outputs a pair of public and secret keys* (pk, sk).
- ct $\leftarrow$ PKE.Enc$_{pk}(x)$: *a probabilistic algorithm that given the public key, takes a string* $x \in \{0,1\}^*$ *and outputs a ciphertext* ct.
- $x =$ PKE.Dec$_{sk}$(ct) : *a deterministic algorithm that given the secret key, takes a ciphertext* ct *and outputs a string* x.

The scheme satisfies the following.

- **Statistical Correctness Against Malicious Encryptors:** *There is a negligible function* negl($\cdot$) *such that for any* $\lambda \in \mathbb{N}$ *and input* $x \in \{0,1\}^*$, *the following perfect correctness holds with probability at least* $1 -$ negl(λ) *over sampling* (pk, sk) $\leftarrow$ PKE.Gen(1^λ):

$$\Pr\left[\text{PKE.Dec}_{sk}(\text{ct}) = x \mid \text{ct} \leftarrow \text{PKE.Enc}_{pk}(x)\right] = 1 \ .$$

- **Public-key Pseudorandomness:** *For* $\lambda \in \mathbb{N}$ *let* $\ell(\lambda)$ *be the length of the public key generated by* PKE.Gen(1^λ), *then,*

$$\left\{\text{pk} \mid (\text{pk}, \text{sk}) \leftarrow \text{PKE.Gen}(1^\lambda)\right\}_{\lambda \in \mathbb{N}} \approx_c \left\{U_{\ell(\lambda)}\right\}_{\lambda \in \mathbb{N}} \ .$$

- **Encryption Security:** *For every polynomial* $l(\cdot)$,

$$\left\{(\text{pk}, \text{ct}) \,\middle|\, \begin{array}{l} (\text{pk}, \text{sk}) \leftarrow \text{PKE.Gen}(1^\lambda), \\ \text{ct} \leftarrow \text{PKE.Enc}_{pk}(x_0) \end{array} \right\}_{\lambda, x_0, x_1} \approx_c \left\{(\text{pk}, \text{ct}) \,\middle|\, \begin{array}{l} (\text{pk}, \text{sk}) \leftarrow \text{PKE.Gen}(1^\lambda), \\ \text{ct} \leftarrow \text{PKE.Enc}_{pk}(x_1) \end{array} \right\}_{\lambda, x_0, x_1} ,$$

where $\lambda \in \mathbb{N}$ *and* $x_0, x_1 \in \{0,1\}^{l(\lambda)}$.

Instantiations. Pseudorandom-key public-key encryption schemes are known based on LWE [Reg09].

Pseudorandom Function

Definition 5 (Pseudorandom Function (PRF)). *A pseudorandom function scheme* (PRF.Gen, PRF.F) *has the following syntax:*

- sk $\leftarrow$ PRF.Gen($1^\lambda, 1^{\ell(\lambda)}$) : *a probabilistic algorithm that takes a security parameter* 1^λ *and an output size* $\ell(\lambda)$ *and outputs a secret key* sk.
- $y =$ PRF.F$_{sk}(x)$: *a deterministic algorithm that given the secret key, takes a string* $x \in \{0,1\}^*$ *and outputs a string* $y \in \{0,1\}^{\ell(\lambda)}$.

The scheme satisfies the following property.

- **Pseudorandomness:** *For every quantum polynomial-size distinguisher* $D = \{D_\lambda, \rho_\lambda\}_{\lambda \in \mathbb{N}}$ *and polynomial* $\ell(\cdot)$ *there is a negligible function* $\mu(\cdot)$ *such that for all* $\lambda \in \mathbb{N}$,

$$\left| \Pr_{sk \leftarrow \text{PRF.Gen}(1^\lambda, 1^{\ell(\lambda)})}[D_\lambda(\rho_\lambda)^{\text{PRF.F}_{sk}(\cdot)} = 1] - \Pr_{f \leftarrow (\{0,1\}^{\ell(\lambda)})^{(\{0,1\}^*)}}[D_\lambda(\rho_\lambda)^{f(\cdot)} = 1] \right| \leq \mu(\lambda) \ .$$

NIZK Argument for NP in the Common Random String Model. We define non-interactive computational zero-knowledge arguments for NP in the common random string model, with adaptive multi-theorem security.

Definition 6 (NICZK Argument for NP). *A non-interactive computational zero-knowledge argument system in the common random string model for a language $\mathcal{L} \in NP$ consists of 3 algorithms* (NIZK.Setup, NIZK.P, NIZK.V) *with the following syntax:*

- crs $\leftarrow$ NIZK.Setup(1^λ) : *A classical algorithm that on input security parameter λ simply samples a common uniformly random string* crs.
- π $\leftarrow$ NIZK.P(crs, x, w) : *A probabilistic algorithm that on input* crs, *an instance $x \in \mathcal{L}$ and a witness $w \in \mathcal{R}_\mathcal{L}(x)$, outputs a proof π.*
- NIZK.V(crs, x, π) $\in \{0, 1\}$: *A deterministic algorithm that on input* crs, *an instance $x \in \mathcal{L}$ and a proof π, outputs a bit.*

The protocol satisfies the following properties.

- **Perfect Completeness:** *For any $\lambda \in \mathbb{N}$, $x \in \mathcal{L} \cap \{0, 1\}^\lambda$, $w \in \mathcal{R}_\mathcal{L}(x)$,*

$$\Pr_{\substack{\text{crs} \leftarrow \text{NIZK.Setup}(1^\lambda), \\ \pi \leftarrow \text{NIZK.P}(\text{crs}, x, w)}} \left[\text{NIZK.V}(\text{crs}, x, \pi) = 1 \right] = 1 \ .$$

- **Adaptive Computational Soundness:** *For every quantum polynomial-size prover* NIZK.P$^* = \{$NIZK.P$^*_\lambda, \rho_\lambda\}_{\lambda \in \mathbb{N}}$ *there is a negligible function $\mu(\cdot)$ such that for every security parameter $\lambda \in \mathbb{N}$,*

$$\Pr_{\substack{\text{crs} \leftarrow \text{NIZK.Setup}(1^\lambda), \\ (x, \pi^*) \leftarrow \text{NIZK.P}^*_\lambda(\rho_\lambda, \text{crs})}} \left[(x \notin \mathcal{L}) \wedge \left(1 = \text{NIZK.V}(\text{crs}, x, \pi^*) \right) \right] \leq \mu(\lambda) \ .$$

- **Multi-Theorem Adaptive Computational Zero Knowledge:** *There exists a polynomial-time simulator* NIZK.Sim *such that for every quantum polynomial-size distinguisher* D$^* = \{$D$^*_\lambda, \rho_\lambda\}_{\lambda \in \mathbb{N}}$ *there is a negligible function $\mu(\cdot)$ such that for every security parameter $\lambda \in \mathbb{N}$,*

$$|P_{\lambda, \text{Real}} - P_{\lambda, \text{Simulated}}| \leq \mu(\lambda) \ ,$$

where,

$$P_{\lambda, \text{Real}} := \Pr_{\text{crs} \leftarrow \text{NIZK.Setup}(1^\lambda)} \left[\text{D}^*_\lambda(\rho_\lambda, \text{crs})^{\text{NIZK.P}(\text{crs}, \cdot, \cdot)} = 1 \right] \ ,$$

$$P_{\lambda, \text{Simulated}} := \Pr_{(\tilde{\text{crs}}, \text{td}) \leftarrow \text{NIZK.Sim}(1^\lambda)} \left[\text{D}^*_\lambda(\rho_\lambda, \tilde{\text{crs}})^{\text{NIZK.Sim}(\text{td}, \cdot)} = 1 \right] \ ,$$

where,
  - *In every query that* D* *makes to the oracle, it sends a pair (x, w) where $x \in \mathcal{L} \cap \{0, 1\}^\lambda$ and $w \in \mathcal{R}_\mathcal{L}(x)$.*
  - NIZK.P(crs, $\cdot$, $\cdot$) *is the prover algorithm and* NIZK.Sim($\cdot$, $\cdot$) *acts only on its sampled trapdoor* td *and on x.*

Instantiations. Non-interactive computational zero-knowledge arguments for NP in the common random string model with both adaptive soundness and zero knowledge are known based on LWE [CCH+19,PS19].

Malicious Designated-Verifier Non-interactive Zero-Knowledge for QMA. We define non-interactive zero-knowledge protocols in the malicious designated-verifier model (MDV-NIZK) for QMA, with adaptive (and non-adaptive) multi-theorem security.

Definition 7 (MDV-NICZK Argument for QMA). *A non-interactive computational zero-knowledge argument system for in the malicious designated-verifier model for a gap problem* $(\mathcal{L}_{yes}, \mathcal{L}_{no}) = \mathcal{L} \in \textbf{QMA}$ *consists of 4 algorithms* (Setup , VSetup , P , V) *with the following syntax:*

- crs $\leftarrow$ Setup(1^λ) : *A classical algorithm that on input security parameter* λ *simply samples a common uniformly random string* crs.
- (pvk, svk) $\leftarrow$ VSetup(crs) : *A classical algorithm that on input* crs *samples a pair of public and secret verification keys.*
- $|\pi\rangle$ $\leftarrow$ P(crs, pvk, x, $|w\rangle^{\otimes k(\lambda)}$) : *A quantum algorithm that on input* crs, *the public verification key* pvk, *an instance* $x \in \mathcal{L}_{yes}$ *and polynomially-many identical copies of a witness* $|w\rangle \in \mathcal{R}_\mathcal{L}(x)$ *(*$k(\cdot)$ *is some polynomial), outputs a quantum state* $|\pi\rangle$.
- V(crs, svk, x, $|\pi\rangle$) $\in \{0, 1\}$: *A quantum algorithm that on input* crs, *secret verification key* svk, *an instance* $x \in \mathcal{L}$ *and a quantum proof* $|\pi\rangle$, *outputs a bit.*

The protocol satisfies the following properties.

- **Statistical Completeness:** *There is a polynomial* $k(\cdot)$ *and a negligible function* $\mu(\cdot)$ *s.t. for any* $\lambda \in \mathbb{N}$, $x \in \mathcal{L}_{yes} \cap \{0, 1\}^\lambda$, $|w\rangle \in \mathcal{R}_\mathcal{L}(x)$, crs $\in$ Setup(1^λ), (pvk, svk) $\in$ VSetup(crs),

$$\Pr_{|\pi\rangle \leftarrow P(crs, pvk, x, |w\rangle^{\otimes k(\lambda)})} \left[V(crs, svk, x, |\pi\rangle) = 1 \right] \geq 1 - \mu(\lambda) \ .$$

- **Multi-Theorem Adaptive Computational Soundness:** *For every quantum polynomial-size prover* P$^* = \{P_\lambda^*, \rho_\lambda\}_{\lambda \in \mathbb{N}}$ *there is a negligible function* $\mu(\cdot)$ *such that for every security parameter* $\lambda \in \mathbb{N}$,

$$\Pr_{\substack{crs \leftarrow Setup(1^\lambda), \\ (pvk, svk) \leftarrow VSetup(crs), \\ (x, |\pi^*\rangle) \leftarrow P_\lambda^*(\rho_\lambda, crs, pvk)^{V(crs, svk, \cdot, \cdot)}}} \left[(x \in \mathcal{L}_{no}) \wedge \left(1 = V(crs, svk, x, |\pi^*\rangle) \right) \right] \leq \mu(\lambda) \ .$$

- **Multi-Theorem Adaptive Computational Zero Knowledge:** *There exists a quantum polynomial-time simulator* Sim *such that for every quantum polynomial-size distinguisher* D$^* = \{D_\lambda^*, \rho_\lambda\}_{\lambda \in \mathbb{N}}$ *there is a negligible function* $\mu(\cdot)$ *such that for every security parameter* $\lambda \in \mathbb{N}$,

$$\left| \Pr_{crs \leftarrow Setup(1^\lambda)} \left[D_\lambda^*(\rho_\lambda, crs)^{P(crs, \cdot, \cdot, \cdot)} = 1 \right] - \Pr_{(\tilde{crs}, td) \leftarrow Sim(1^\lambda)} \left[D_\lambda^*(\rho_\lambda, \tilde{crs})^{Sim(td, \cdot, \cdot)} = 1 \right] \right| \leq \mu(\lambda) \ ,$$

where,

- *In every query that D^* makes to the oracle, it sends a triplet $(\mathsf{pvk}^*, x, |w\rangle^{\otimes k(\lambda)})$ where pvk^* can be arbitrary, $x \in \mathcal{L}_{yes} \cap \{0,1\}^\lambda$ and $|w\rangle \in \mathcal{R}_\mathcal{L}(x)$.*
- $\mathsf{P}(\mathsf{crs}, \cdot, \cdot, \cdot)$ *is the prover algorithm and* $\mathsf{Sim}(\cdot, \cdot)$ *acts only on its sampled trapdoor* td *and on* pvk^*, x.

We note that the standard (non-adaptive) soundness guarantees the following:

Definition 8 (MDV-NICZK Argument for QMA with Standard Soundness). *A non-interactive computational zero-knowledge argument system in the malicious designated-verifier model for a gap problem* $(\mathcal{L}_{yes}, \mathcal{L}_{no}) = \mathcal{L} \in \mathbf{QMA}$ *has standard non-adaptive soundness if it satisfies the same properties described in Definition 7, with the only change that instead of satisfying multi-theorem adaptive soundness, it satisfies the following guarantee:*

- **Multi-Theorem Computational Soundness:** *For every quantum polynomial-size prover* $\mathsf{P}^* = \{\mathsf{P}^*_\lambda, \rho_\lambda\}_{\lambda \in \mathbb{N}}$ *and* $\{x_\lambda\}_{\lambda \in \mathbb{N}}$ *where* $\forall \lambda \in \mathbb{N} : x_\lambda \in \mathcal{L}_{no}$, *there is a negligible function* $\mu(\cdot)$ *such that for every security parameter* $\lambda \in \mathbb{N}$,

$$\Pr_{\substack{\mathsf{crs} \leftarrow \mathsf{Setup}(1^\lambda), \\ (\mathsf{pvk}, \mathsf{svk}) \leftarrow \mathsf{VSetup}(\mathsf{crs}), \\ |\pi^*\rangle \leftarrow \mathsf{P}^*_\lambda(\rho_\lambda, \mathsf{crs}, \mathsf{pvk})^{\mathsf{V}(\mathsf{crs}, \mathsf{svk}, \cdot, \cdot)}}} \left[1 = \mathsf{V}(\mathsf{crs}, \mathsf{svk}, x, |\pi^*\rangle) \right] \leq \mu(\lambda) \ .$$

3   Non-interactive Zero-Knowledge Protocol

In this section we describe a non-interactive computational zero-knowledge argument system in the malicious designated-verifier model for an arbitrary $\mathcal{L} \in \mathbf{QMA}$, according to Definition 7.

Ingredients and notation

- A non-interactive zero-knowledge argument for NP (NIZK.Setup, NIZK.P, NIZK.V) in the common random string model.
- A pseudorandom function (PRF.Gen, PRF.F).
- A leveled fully-homomorphic encryption scheme (FHE.Gen, FHE.Enc, FHE.Eval, FHE.Dec) with circuit privacy.
- A public-key encryption scheme (PKE.Gen, PKE.Enc, PKE.Dec) with pseudorandom public keys.
- A 3-message quantum sigma protocol $(\varXi.\mathsf{P}, \varXi.\mathsf{V})$ for QMA.

We describe the protocol in Fig. 1.

The (statistical) completeness of the protocol follows readily from the perfect completeness of the NIZK scheme, the perfect correctness of FHE and the statistical completeness of the quantum sigma protocol $(\varXi.\mathsf{P}, \varXi.\mathsf{V})$. We next prove the soundness and zero knowledge of the protocol.

3.1 Soundness

We prove that the protocol has multi-theorem computational soundness (as in Definition 8). By standard generic compilation and sub-exponential hardness of LWE we extend our soundness to be adaptive (as in Definition 7).

Protocol 1

Common Input: An instance $x \in \mathcal{L}_{yes} \cap \{0,1\}^{\lambda}$, for security parameter $\lambda \in \mathbb{N}$.
P's private input: Polynomially many identical copies of a witness for x: $|w\rangle^{\otimes k(\lambda)}$ s.t. $|w\rangle \in \mathcal{R}_{\mathcal{L}}(x)$.

1. **Common Random String:** Setup samples the common random string of the NP NIZK argument, crs $\leftarrow$ NIZK.Setup(1^{λ}) and an additional random string ek $\leftarrow U_{\ell(\lambda)}$ where $\ell(\lambda)$ is the size of a public key generated by PKE.Gen(1^{λ}). Setup publishes (crs, ek) as the common random string.
2. **Public and Secret Verification Keys:** VSetup samples public and secret verification keys:
   - Samples prfk $\leftarrow$ PRF.Gen(1^{λ}), fhek $\leftarrow$ FHE.Gen(1^{λ}) and encrypts the PRF key using the FHE encryption, $\mathsf{ct_V} \leftarrow$ FHE.Enc$_{\mathsf{fhek}}$(prfk).
   - Let r_{V} be the randomness used for PRF.Gen, FHE.Gen, FHE.Enc. VSetup encrypts $\mathsf{ct}_{r_{\mathsf{V}}} \leftarrow$ PKE.Enc$_{\mathsf{ek}}(r_{\mathsf{V}})$ and computes a NIZK proof $\pi_{\mathsf{V}} \leftarrow$ NIZK.P(crs, ($\mathsf{ct_V}, \mathsf{ct}_{r_{\mathsf{V}}}$, ek)), for the NP statement declaring that the tuple ($\mathsf{ct_V}, \mathsf{ct}_{r_{\mathsf{V}}}$, ek) is consistent.[a]

   The key values are: pvk = ($\mathsf{ct_V}, \mathsf{ct}_{r_{\mathsf{V}}}, \pi_{\mathsf{V}}$), svk = (prfk, fhek).
3. **Non-interactive Zero-knowledge Proof:** Given (crs, ek) and pvk, P first checks that $1 = $ NIZK.V(crs, ($\mathsf{ct_V}, \mathsf{ct}_{r_{\mathsf{V}}}$, ek), π_{V}) and aborts otherwise.
   - P computes the sigma protocol message $\alpha = \Xi.\mathsf{P}(|w\rangle^{\otimes k(\lambda)}; r_{\Xi})$, for randomness r_{Ξ}.
   - P computes $\hat{\mathsf{ct}}_{\mathsf{P}} \leftarrow$ FHE.Eval($C_{x,r_{\Xi}}, \mathsf{ct_V}$), where $C_{x,r_{\Xi}}$ is the following circuit: Given input prfk a PRF secret key, $C_{x,r_{\Xi}}$ computes $\beta_x = $ PRF.F$_{\mathsf{prfk}}(x)$, and then outputs $\gamma = \Xi.\mathsf{P}_3(\beta_x, r_{\Xi})$.
   - P encrypts $\mathsf{ct}_{r_{\Xi}} \leftarrow$ PKE.Enc$_{\mathsf{ek}}(r_{\Xi})$ and computes a NIZK proof $\pi_{\mathsf{P}} \leftarrow$ NIZK.P(crs, ($\hat{\mathsf{ct}}_{\mathsf{P}}, \mathsf{ct}_{r_{\Xi}}$, ek)), for the NP statement declaring that the tuple ($\hat{\mathsf{ct}}_{\mathsf{P}}, \mathsf{ct}_{r_{\Xi}}$, ek) is consistent.[b]

   P sends $|\pi\rangle = (\alpha, \hat{\mathsf{ct}}_{\mathsf{P}}, \mathsf{ct}_{r_{\Xi}}, \pi_{\mathsf{P}})$ to V.
4. **Verification:** Given (crs, ek), svk and $|\pi\rangle$, V accepts iff all of the following holds:
   - $1 = $ NIZK.V(crs, ($\hat{\mathsf{ct}}_{\mathsf{P}}, \mathsf{ct}_{r_{\Xi}}$, ek), π_{P}).
   - Let $\beta_x = $ PRF.F$_{\mathsf{prfk}}(x)$, $\gamma = $ FHE.Dec$_{\mathsf{fhek}}(\hat{\mathsf{ct}}_{\mathsf{P}})$, then $1 = \Xi.\mathsf{V}(x, \alpha, \beta_x, \gamma)$.

---

[a]Formally, there exist r_1, r_2 s.t. $\mathsf{ct_V}$ is generated by using PRF.Gen, FHE.Gen, FHE.Enc with randomness r_1, and $\mathsf{ct}_{r_{\mathsf{V}}} = $ PKE.Enc$_{\mathsf{ek}}(r_1; r_2)$.
[b]Formally, there exist r_{Ξ}, r_1, r_2 s.t. $\hat{\mathsf{ct}}_{\mathsf{P}} = $ FHE.Eval($C_{x,r_{\Xi}}, \mathsf{ct_V}; r_1$), $\mathsf{ct}_{r_{\Xi}} = $ PKE.Enc$_{\mathsf{ek}}(r_{\Xi}; r_2)$.

Fig. 1. A non-interactive computational zero-knowledge argument system for $\mathcal{L} \in$ **QMA** in the malicious designated-verifier model.

Proposition 1 (The Protocol has Multi-theorem Computational Soundness). *For every quantum polynomial-size prover* $\mathsf{P}^* = \{\mathsf{P}^*_\lambda, \rho_\lambda\}_{\lambda \in \mathbb{N}}$ *there is a negligible function* $\mu(\cdot)$ *such that for every security parameter* $\lambda \in \mathbb{N}$ *and* $x \in \mathcal{L}_{no} \cap \{0,1\}^\lambda$,

$$\Pr_{\substack{(\mathsf{crs},\mathsf{ek}) \leftarrow \mathsf{Setup}(1^\lambda), \\ ((\mathsf{ct}_V, \mathsf{ct}_{r_V}, \pi_V), (\mathsf{prfk}, \mathsf{fhek})) \leftarrow \mathsf{VSetup}(\mathsf{crs},\mathsf{ek}), \\ |\pi^*\rangle \leftarrow \mathsf{P}^*_\lambda(\rho_\lambda, (\mathsf{crs},\mathsf{ek}), (\mathsf{ct}_V, \mathsf{ct}_{r_V}, \pi_V))^{V((\mathsf{crs},\mathsf{ek}),(\mathsf{prfk},\mathsf{fhek}),\cdot,\cdot)}}} \left[1 = \mathsf{V}((\mathsf{crs},\mathsf{ek}), (\mathsf{prfk}, \mathsf{fhek}), x, |\pi^*\rangle) \right] \leq \mu(\lambda) \ .$$

Proof. Let $\mathsf{P}^* = \{\mathsf{P}^*_\lambda, \rho_\lambda\}_{\lambda \in \mathbb{N}}$ a polynomial-size quantum prover and let $\{x_\lambda\}_{\lambda \in \mathbb{N}}$ s.t. $\forall \lambda \in \mathbb{N} : x_\lambda \in \mathcal{L}_{no} \cap \{0,1\}^\lambda$. We prove soundness by a hybrid argument, that is, we consider a series of computationally-indistinguishable hybrid processes with output over $\{0,1\}$, starting from the output of the verifier (for the prover's false proof) in the real interaction, until we get to a distribution where the output of the verifier can be 1 with at most negligible probability. We define the following processes.

- Hyb_0 : The output distribution of the verifier in the real interaction, that is, for

$$(\mathsf{crs}, \mathsf{ek}) \leftarrow \mathsf{Setup}(1^\lambda) \ , \left((\mathsf{ct}_V, \mathsf{ct}_{r_V}, \pi_V), (\mathsf{prfk}, \mathsf{fhek}) \right) \leftarrow \mathsf{VSetup}(\mathsf{crs}, \mathsf{ek}) \ ,$$

$$|\pi^*\rangle \leftarrow \mathsf{P}^*_\lambda \left(\rho_\lambda, (\mathsf{crs}, \mathsf{ek}), (\mathsf{ct}_V, \mathsf{ct}_{r_V}, \pi_V) \right)^{V((\mathsf{crs},\mathsf{ek}),(\mathsf{prfk},\mathsf{fhek}),\cdot,\cdot)} \ ,$$

  the output bit $\mathsf{V}((\mathsf{crs}, \mathsf{ek}), (\mathsf{prfk}, \mathsf{fhek}), x, |\pi^*\rangle)$.
- Hyb_1 : This hybrid process is identical to Hyb_0, with the exception that ek is sampled as a public key for the PKE scheme $(\mathsf{ek}, \mathsf{sk}) \leftarrow \mathsf{PKE.Gen}(1^\lambda)$, rather than as a random string of the same length. To move to this hybrid we will use the fact that the public keys of the PKE scheme are pseudorandom.
- Hyb_2 : This hybrid process is identical to Hyb_1, with the exception that the verification algorithm (described in step 4 of the protocol) changes. The new verifier $\check{\mathsf{V}}$ still makes sure that π_P is a valid proof for $(\hat{\mathsf{ct}}_P, \mathsf{ct}_{r_\Xi}, \mathsf{ek})$, but the second check changes to the following: Let $r_\Xi = \mathsf{PKE.Dec}_{\mathsf{sk}}(\mathsf{ct}_{r_\Xi})$, and let $\gamma = \Xi.\mathsf{P}_3(\beta_x, r_\Xi)$. Then $\check{\mathsf{V}}$ accepts if $1 = \Xi.\mathsf{V}(x, \alpha, \beta_x, \gamma)$. To move to this hybrid we will use the (adaptive) soundness property of the NP NIZK proof that P^* provides.
- Hyb_3 : This hybrid process is identical to Hyb_2, with the exception that when generating the CRS $(\mathsf{crs}, \mathsf{ek})$ and the public verification key $\mathsf{pvk} = (\mathsf{ct}_V, \mathsf{ct}_{r_V}, \pi_V)$, (1) the CRS for the NP NIZK is simulated $(\mathsf{crs}, \mathsf{td}) \leftarrow \mathsf{NIZK.Sim}(1^\lambda)$, (2) the proof π_V is simulated $\pi_V \leftarrow \mathsf{NIZK.Sim}(\mathsf{td}, (\mathsf{ct}_V, \mathsf{ct}_{r_V}, \mathsf{ek}))$ rather than generated by the NP NIZK prover. To move to this hybrid we use the zero-knowledge property of the NP NIZK proof that V provides.
- Hyb_4 : This hybrid process is identical to Hyb_3, with the exception that when generating $\mathsf{pvk} = (\mathsf{ct}_V, \mathsf{ct}_{r_V}, \pi_V)$, ct_{r_V} is just an encryption of a string of zeros (of the same length) rather than the randomness r_V. To move to this hybrid we use the security of the PKE scheme.

- Hyb_5 : This hybrid process is identical to Hyb_4, with the exception that when generating $\mathsf{pvk} = (\mathsf{ct}_\mathsf{V}, \mathsf{ct}_{r_\mathsf{V}}, \pi_\mathsf{V})$, ct_V is just an encryption of a string of zeros (of the same length) rather than the FHE encryption of the secret PRF key prfk. To move to this hybrid we use the security of the FHE scheme.
- Hyb_6 : This hybrid process is identical to Hyb_5, with the exception that the modified verification algorithm $\tilde{\mathsf{V}}$ from Hyb_2 is now going to be a new *stateful* algorithm $\tilde{\mathsf{V}}_s$. The new verifier $\tilde{\mathsf{V}}_s$ still makes sure that π_P is a valid proof for $(\hat{\mathsf{ct}}_\mathsf{P}, \mathsf{ct}_{r_\Xi}, \mathsf{ek})$, but the second check changes to the following: It is identical to that of $\tilde{\mathsf{V}}$, except that β_x is now lazily sampled as a truly random string, that is, every time P^* sends a query for some x', instead of computing $\beta_{x'} = \mathsf{PRF.F}_{\mathsf{prfk}}(x')$, $\tilde{\mathsf{V}}_s$ samples $\beta_{x'}$ a truly random string of the same length and remembers it for future queries by the prover (for the same x'). To move to this hybrid we use the pseudorandomnes guarantee of the PRF.
- Hyb_7 : This hybrid process is identical to Hyb_6, with the exception that the behaviour of the verification algorithm $\tilde{\mathsf{V}}_s$ changes in the following way: Consider t the *first* time step in the execution of P^* (in Hyb_6) such that with a noticeable probability, P^* sends a pair $(x', |\pi^*\rangle)$ such that (1) $x' \in \mathcal{L}_{no}$ and (2) the modified verification algorithm $\tilde{\mathsf{V}}_s$ accepts - this proof can be sent either as a query to the verification oracle, or as the final output of P^* (in that case, t is the last time step of P^* and $x' = x$).

  Now we define Hyb_7: the verification algorithm works as in Hyb_6 with the one change that if P^* sends a query to the verification oracle before its time step t and this query is for a no-instance $x' \in \mathcal{L}_{no}$, then we simply return 0 to P^* as the verifier's answer, without computing anything. Note that checking whether $x' \in \mathcal{L}_{no}$ takes $2^{O(|x'|)}$ time[6], and thus the execution of this hybrid is inefficient. If such time step t does not exist (i.e. in each of the prover's time steps, the probability for it to generate a false proof is only negligible), this process is identical to Hyb_6.

We now explain why the outputs of each two consecutive hybrids are computationally indistinguishable[7]. We will then use the last hybrid process to show that soundness of the protocol follows from the soundness of the quantum sigma protocol $(\Xi.\mathsf{P}, \Xi.\mathsf{V})$.

- $\mathsf{Hyb}_0 \approx_c \mathsf{Hyb}_1$: Follows readily from the pseudorandomness property of the public keys generated by $\mathsf{PKE.Gen}(1^\lambda)$.
- $\mathsf{Hyb}_1 \approx_c \mathsf{Hyb}_2$: Follows from the adaptive soundness of the NIZK protocol for NP, the statistical correctness of the PKE scheme and the perfect correctness of the FHE scheme. We explain in more detail: Assume the output bits of

---

[6] We assume that our gap problem $\mathcal{L} \in \mathbf{QMA}$ has exponential-time algorithms that solve it, that is, for $x \in \mathcal{L}$ we can decide whether $x \in \mathcal{L}_{yes}$ or $x \in \mathcal{L}_{no}$ in $2^{O(|x|)}$ time. It is also enough for our proof to assume that $\mathcal{L}$ is solvable in general exponential time i.e. $O(2^{|x|^c})$ time for some constant $c \in \mathbb{N}$.

[7] the output bits of the hybrids are in fact *statistically* indistinguishable, because any two distributions over a bit are statistically indistinguishable if they are computationally indistinguishable, but we won't care about this in our analysis.

Hyb_1 and Hyb_2 are distinguishable with some noticeable advantage, then by the perfect correctness of the FHE evaluation, it follows that with a noticeable probability, either (1) there was an error in the decryption process of the PKE scheme at least once, or (2) P^* generated a false proof for the NP NIZK scheme at least once. We prove that both happen with at most negligible probability, and thus the statistical distance between the output bits of Hyb_1 and Hyb_2 is at most negligible.

The correctness guarantee of the PKE scheme is that when the public key is sampled honestly, which is true in our case, then with overwhelming probability over the randomness of $\mathsf{PKE.Gen}(1^\lambda)$, the decryption is perfectly correct, regardless of the randomness used for the encryption (which in our case is possibly malicious, as it is chosen by P^*). This implies that with at most negligible probability there is an error in the decryption process $\mathsf{PKE.Dec_{sk}}(\cdot)$.

If P^* manages to give a false proof π_P^* for some tuple $(\hat{\mathsf{ct}}_\mathsf{P}, \mathsf{ct}_{r_\Xi}, \mathsf{ek})$ with a noticeable probability ε then we can use it to break the adaptive soundness of the NP NIZK scheme: We guess the index of the query (to the verification oracle $\tilde{\mathsf{V}}((\mathsf{crs}, \mathsf{ek}), (\mathsf{prfk}, \mathsf{fhek}), \cdot, \cdot))$ where P^* gives such false proof, and with probability at least $\varepsilon \cdot \frac{1}{t}$, where t is the (polynomial) running time of P^*, we find such false proof. This implies that ε has to be at most negligible i.e. P^* cannot produce a false proof for the NP NIZK with a noticeable probability.

– $\mathsf{Hyb}_2 \approx_c \mathsf{Hyb}_3$: Assume toward contradiction that the output bits of Hyb_2 and Hyb_3 are distinguishable with some noticeable advantage, we use the prover P^* in order to construct a distinguisher D that breaks the zero-knowledge property of the NP NIZK scheme (it seems that we don't have to use the fact that the zero knowledge property of the NP NIZK is adaptive, but we will use it for the convenience of the proof and because it does not cause an extra cost in computational assumptions).

D will sample $(\mathsf{ek}, \mathsf{sk}) \leftarrow \mathsf{PKE.Gen}(1^\lambda)$, honestly sample $(\mathsf{ct_V}, \mathsf{ct}_{r_V})$ with randomness r, and then get a common random string crs from the NIZK zero knowledge challenger. D then hands $(\mathsf{ct_V}, \mathsf{ct}_{r_V}, \mathsf{ek})$ along with the NP witness r and gets back either a real proof or a simulated proof. it then proceeds to run the malicious prover P^* and at the end, by the verdict of the (modified) verification algorithm $\tilde{\mathsf{V}}$ for the prover's proof and instance, distinguishes between whether it got a simulated proof or a real proof. This follows from the fact that whenever D gets a real proof (and CRS) then the view of P^* is exactly its view in Hyb_2 and whenever D gets a simulated proof (and CRS) then the view of P^* is exactly its view in Hyb_3.

– $\mathsf{Hyb}_3 \approx_c \mathsf{Hyb}_4$: Follows readily from the security of the PKE scheme.
– $\mathsf{Hyb}_4 \approx_c \mathsf{Hyb}_5$: Follows readily from the security of the FHE scheme.
– $\mathsf{Hyb}_5 \approx_c \mathsf{Hyb}_6$: Follows readily from the security of the PRF scheme.
– $\mathsf{Hyb}_6 \approx_c \mathsf{Hyb}_7$: Note that by how we defined the time step t it follows that the change of returning 0 on queries for no-instances before time step t (rather than actually evaluating the verification algorithm $\tilde{\mathsf{V}}_s$) is unnoticeable to the prover P^*.

Now, assume toward contradiction that P^* succeeds in breaking the soundness with a noticeable probability in the original execution of the protocol (i.e.

in the process Hyb_0), and by the fact $\mathsf{Hyb}_0 \approx_c \mathsf{Hyb}_7$ it follows that the verifier accepts the prover's false proof with some noticeable probability in the hybrid experiment Hyb_7. By the fact that with some noticeable probability P^* succeeds in cheating in Hyb_7, it follows that a time step t exists where P^* sends a pair $(x', |\pi^*\rangle)$ such that $x' \in \mathcal{L}_{no}$ and $\tilde{\mathsf{V}}_s$ accepts the proof (this follows because in the last step of P^*'s execution it sends noticeably often a successful false proof for $x \in \mathcal{L}_{no}$).

Now we consider the execution process of Hyb_7 and fix by an averaging argument the snapshot $|\psi\rangle$ of the execution in the exact moment where P^* sends a pair $(x', |\pi^*\rangle)$ in its time step t, such that the snapshot maximizes the probability that $x' \in \mathcal{L}_{no}$ and $\tilde{\mathsf{V}}_s$ accepts the proof $|\pi^*\rangle$ (as a side note, this snapshot includes (1) all of the randomness (including setup information) in the process Hyb_7 until P^*'s step t, (2) the inner quantum state of P^* in step t, and of course a pair $(x', |\pi^*\rangle)$ such that $x' \in \mathcal{L}_{no}$.). It follows that the part α and the extracted γ (both obtained from $|\pi^*\rangle$, recall γ is obtained by the extracted randomness r_Ξ and the random string $\beta_{x'}$) make a quantum sigma protocol verifier $\Xi.\mathsf{V}$ accept the proof for a random challenge β with a noticeable probability.

We now describe a malicious prover $\Xi.\mathsf{P}^*$ that breaks the soundness of the quantum sigma protocol $(\Xi.\mathsf{P}, \Xi.\mathsf{V})$, by using P^* and the quantum advice $|\psi\rangle$ in order to convince $\Xi.\mathsf{V}$ to accept the no-instance $x' \in \mathcal{L}_{no}$. $\Xi.\mathsf{P}^*$ uses the snapshot $|\psi\rangle$ and takes α from $|\pi^*\rangle$ and sends it as the first sigma protocol message to $\Xi.\mathsf{V}$. $\Xi.\mathsf{V}$ returns a random challenge β, and $\Xi.\mathsf{P}^*$ treats this random challenge as the random $\beta_{x'}$ for the verification procedure $\tilde{\mathsf{V}}_s$. $\Xi.\mathsf{P}^*$ then derives γ from $|\pi^*\rangle$ (as usual in $\tilde{\mathsf{V}}_s$) and sends it to $\Xi.\mathsf{V}$. Recall that we know $\Xi.\mathsf{V}$ accepts the proof with a noticeable probability, and thus $\Xi.\mathsf{P}^*$ breaks the soundness of the quantum sigma protocol with noticeable probability, in contradiction.

We next use standard complexity leveraging to make the soundness adaptive, that is, by assuming that the security of our cryptographic primitives is sub-exponential we prove that the prover cannot choose the no-instance $x \in \mathcal{L}_{no}$ adaptively. As mentioned in the preliminaries, the security of all of our primitives can be based on the hardness of LWE, and thus based on the sub-exponential hardness of LWE we can get adaptive soundness.

Proposition 2 (The Protocol has Multi-theorem Adaptive Computational Soundness). *Assume there is a constant $\varepsilon \in (0,1)$ such that the cryptographic ingredients we use are secure against $O(2^{\lambda^\varepsilon})$-time quantum algorithms for security parameter λ. Then, by executing the protocol with security parameter $\lambda := |x|^{\frac{2}{\varepsilon}}$ rather than $\lambda = |x|$, for every quantum polynomial-size prover $\mathsf{P}^* = \{\mathsf{P}^*_\lambda, \rho_\lambda\}_{\lambda \in \mathbb{N}}$ there is a negligible function $\mu(\cdot)$ such that for every security parameter $\lambda \in \mathbb{N}$,*

$$\Pr\left[(x \in \mathcal{L}_{no}) \wedge \left(1 = \mathsf{V}((\mathsf{crs}, \mathsf{ek}), (\mathsf{prfk}, \mathsf{fhek}), x, |\pi^*\rangle))\right)\right] \leq \mu(\lambda) \ ,$$

where the probability is above the following experiment:

$$(\mathsf{crs}, \mathsf{ek}) \leftarrow \mathsf{Setup}(1^\lambda), \quad ((\mathsf{ct}_\mathsf{V}, \mathsf{ct}_{r_\mathsf{V}}, \pi_\mathsf{V}), (\mathsf{prfk}, \mathsf{fhek})) \leftarrow \mathsf{VSetup}(\mathsf{crs}, \mathsf{ek}),$$

$$(x, |\pi^*\rangle) \leftarrow \mathsf{P}_\lambda^*\big(\rho_\lambda, (\mathsf{crs}, \mathsf{ek}), (\mathsf{ct}_\mathsf{V}, \mathsf{ct}_{r_\mathsf{V}}, \pi_\mathsf{V})\big)^{\mathsf{V}((\mathsf{crs},\mathsf{ek}),(\mathsf{prfk},\mathsf{fhek}),\cdot,\cdot)} .$$

Proof. The proof is almost identical to the proof of Proposition 1, with minor technical changes. Let $\mathsf{P}^* = \{\mathsf{P}_\lambda^*, \rho_\lambda\}_{\lambda \in \mathbb{N}}$ a polynomial-size quantum prover in Protocol 1 and as before, we prove soundness by a hybrid argument by considering almost the same series of hybrids processes, and the reductions that show the outputs of each consecutive pair of hybrids are indistinguishable, are also going to be slightly different.

More precisely, consider the exact same hybrids $\mathsf{Hyb}_0, \cdots, \mathsf{Hyb}_7$ from the proof of Proposition 1, with only the following differences:

- With accordance to the fact that we consider adaptive provers, in each hybrid process, the output of the malicious prover at the end of the execution is a pair $(x, |\pi^*\rangle)$ rather than only a proof $|\pi^*\rangle$.
- The output of each hybrid process is still a bit, but going to be the logical AND of (1) the verifier accepting the prover's proof and instance x, and (2) the instance x is indeed a no-instance $x \in \mathcal{L}_{no}$ (note that in the proof for Proposition 1 the output bit of the hybrids only considers the verdict of the verifier, as the no-instance $x \in \mathcal{L}_{no}$ is already fixed).

We will next claim that the outputs of each pair of consecutive hybrids are computationally indistinguishable. For this, we will use the fact that given $x \in \mathcal{L} = \mathcal{L}_{yes} \cup \mathcal{L}_{no}$, we can decide whether $x \in \mathcal{L}_{no}$ or not in $2^{O(|x|)}$ time.[8] We also use the fact that our primitives are assumed to be secure against sub-exponential time algorithms and we run the protocol with increased security parameter, more specifically, we assume that our primitives are secure against $O(2^{\lambda^\varepsilon})$-time algorithms and we use security parameter $\lambda = |x|^{\frac{2}{\varepsilon}}$, thus it follows that no $O(2^{\lambda^\varepsilon}) = O(2^{|x|^2})$-time algorithm can break the security of the primitives.

In continuance to the above, by the exact same reductions from the proof of Proposition 1 with a single change, we have

$$\mathsf{Hyb}_0 \approx_c \mathsf{Hyb}_1 \approx_c \mathsf{Hyb}_2 \approx_c \mathsf{Hyb}_3 \approx_c \mathsf{Hyb}_4 \approx_c \mathsf{Hyb}_5 \approx_c \mathsf{Hyb}_6 \approx_c \mathsf{Hyb}_7 .$$

The single change that we refer to is the check that the reduction makes when getting the final output of the prover. In the proof of Proposition 1, the final output of P^* is a false proof $|\pi^*\rangle$ for a specific and pre-chosen x, while in our case (the adaptive case) it is a pair $(x, |\pi^*\rangle)$ for an adaptively-chosen x. Instead of checking only the verdict of V, which can be done in polynomial time, the reduction in our case will also check that $x \in \mathcal{L}_{no}$, which can be done in time $2^{O(|x|)}$. This implies that our security reductions take $2^{O(|x|)}$ time to execute, but they break primitives with security against $O(2^{|x|^2})$-time algorithms, which constitutes the needed contradiction. Finally, the algorithm $\varXi.\mathsf{P}^*$ that uses P^* in the process Hyb_7 in order to break the soundness of the quantum sigma protocol is exactly the same as before, and our proof is finished.

---

[8] As noted before, the proof is not sensitive to the fact that the time complexity is $2^{O(|x|)}$ and not $O(2^{|x|^c})$ time for some constant $c \in \mathbb{N}$.

As mentioned before, by the fact that the security of the cryptographic ingredients in our protocol can be based on the hardness of LWE and the security reductions for the primitives are polynomial-time, we get the following corollary.

Corollary 1. *Assume there is a constant $\varepsilon \in (0,1)$ such that LWE is hard for $O(2^{n^\varepsilon})$-time quantum algorithms (for LWE secret of n bits). Then, for every quantum polynomial-size prover $\mathsf{P}^* = \{\mathsf{P}^*_\lambda, \rho_\lambda\}_{\lambda \in \mathbb{N}}$ there is a negligible function $\mu(\cdot)$ such that for every security parameter $\lambda \in \mathbb{N}$,*

$$\Pr\left[(x \in \mathcal{L}_{no}) \wedge \left(1 = \mathsf{V}((\mathsf{crs}, \mathsf{ek}), (\mathsf{prfk}, \mathsf{fhek}), x, |\pi^*\rangle))\right)\right] \leq \mu(\lambda) \ ,$$

where the probability is above the following experiment:

$$(\mathsf{crs}, \mathsf{ek}) \leftarrow \mathsf{Setup}(1^\lambda), \ \ ((\mathsf{ct}_\mathsf{V}, \mathsf{ct}_{r_\mathsf{V}}, \pi_\mathsf{V}), (\mathsf{prfk}, \mathsf{fhek})) \leftarrow \mathsf{VSetup}(\mathsf{crs}, \mathsf{ek}),$$

$$(x, |\pi^*\rangle) \leftarrow \mathsf{P}^*_\lambda\left(\rho_\lambda, (\mathsf{crs}, \mathsf{ek}), (\mathsf{ct}_\mathsf{V}, \mathsf{ct}_{r_\mathsf{V}}, \pi_\mathsf{V})\right)^{\mathsf{V}((\mathsf{crs}, \mathsf{ek}), (\mathsf{prfk}, \mathsf{fhek}), \cdot, \cdot)} \ .$$

3.2   Zero Knowledge

We show that the protocol is multi-theorem adaptive computational zero-knowledge[9], which holds even when the trusted setup samples only a common uniformly random string, and an adversarial polynomial-time (quantum) verifier samples its public verification key maliciously.

We next describe the simulator and then prove that the view that it generates is indistinguishable from the real one, against adaptive distinguishers that choose the statement to be proven only after seeing the common random string. $\mathsf{Sim}(1^\lambda)$:

1. **CRS Simulation:** Given a security parameter λ, the first simulator output is the simulation of the CRS for the NP NIZK protocol and swapping ek with a public key for the PKE scheme, that is, Sim samples:

$$(\mathsf{crs}, \mathsf{td}) \leftarrow \mathsf{NIZK.Sim}(1^\lambda) \ , (\mathsf{ek}, \mathsf{sk}) \leftarrow \mathsf{PKE.Gen}(1^\lambda) \ ,$$

   outputs $(\mathsf{crs}, \mathsf{ek})$ as the simulated CRS and $(\mathsf{td}, \mathsf{sk})$ as the simulator trapdoor.
2. **Proof Simulation:** Given the trapdoor $(\mathsf{td}, \mathsf{sk})$, a (possibly malicious) public verification key $\mathsf{pvk} = (\mathsf{ct}_\mathsf{V}, \mathsf{ct}_{r_\mathsf{V}}, \pi_\mathsf{V})$ and a yes-instance $x \in \mathcal{L}_{yes}$, the simulator does the following:
   (a) Sim checks that π_V is a valid proof for the tuple $(\mathsf{ct}_\mathsf{V}, \mathsf{ct}_{r_\mathsf{V}}, \mathsf{ek})$ and also actually verifies some of the statement itself: It decrypts $r_\mathsf{V} = \mathsf{PKE.Dec}_\mathsf{sk}(\mathsf{ct}_{r_\mathsf{V}})$ and checks that ct_V is obtained by running $\mathsf{PRF.Gen}, \mathsf{fhek} \leftarrow \mathsf{FHE.Gen}, \mathsf{FHE.Enc}_\mathsf{fhek}$ with randomness r_V. If the check is not accepted, Sim returns $\bot$.

---

[9] It would have been enough to show that the protocol is *single-theorem* adaptive computational zero-knowledge, and then by the single-to-multi-theorem compiler for NIZKs of [FLS99] get a MDV-NICZK argument with adaptive *multi-theorem* security, but for the sake of completeness, because our construction can be shown to be multi-theorem zero-knowledge without the FLS compilation and because it does not change the main ideas in the proof, we prove the multi-theorem case directly.

(b) Sim derives prfk from r_V, computes $\beta_x = \mathsf{PRF.F}_{\mathsf{prfk}}(x)$ and then executes $(\alpha, \gamma) \leftarrow \varXi.\mathsf{Sim}(x, \beta_x)$.

(c) Sim performs a circuit-private homomorphic evaluation $\hat{\mathsf{ct}}_\mathsf{P} \leftarrow \mathsf{FHE.Eval}(C_\gamma, \mathsf{ct}_V)$, where C_γ is the circuit that always outputs γ.

(d) Sim encrypts $\mathsf{ct}_{r_\varXi} \leftarrow \mathsf{PKE.Enc}_{\mathsf{ek}}(0^\ell)$, where ℓ is the length of the randomness for the prover in the quantum sigma protocol.

(e) Finally, Sim simulates the non-interactive zero-knowledge proof π_P, by executing $\pi_\mathsf{P} \leftarrow \mathsf{NIZK.Sim}(\mathsf{td}, (\hat{\mathsf{ct}}_\mathsf{P}, \mathsf{ct}_{r_\varXi}, \mathsf{ek}))$.

Sim outputs $(\alpha, \hat{\mathsf{ct}}_\mathsf{P}, \mathsf{ct}_{r_\varXi}, \pi_\mathsf{P})$.

We now prove that the simulated proofs that the simulator generates are computationally indistinguishable from the real proofs that the prover generates.

Proposition 3 (The Protocol is Multi-theorem Adaptive Computational Zero-knowledge). *For every quantum polynomial-size distinguisher* $\mathsf{D}^* = \{\mathsf{D}_\lambda^*, \rho_\lambda\}_{\lambda \in \mathbb{N}}$ *there is a negligible function* $\mu(\cdot)$ *such that for every security parameter* $\lambda \in \mathbb{N}$,

$$\left| P_{\lambda,\mathsf{Real}} - P_{\lambda,\mathsf{Simulated}} \right| \le \mu(\lambda) \ ,$$

where,

$$P_{\lambda,\mathsf{Real}} := \Pr_{(\mathsf{crs},\mathsf{ek}) \leftarrow \mathsf{Setup}(1^\lambda)} \left[\mathsf{D}_\lambda^*(\rho_\lambda, (\mathsf{crs}, \mathsf{ek}))^{\mathsf{P}((\mathsf{crs},\mathsf{ek}),\cdot,\cdot,\cdot)} = 1 \right] \ ,$$

$$P_{\lambda,\mathsf{Simulated}} := \Pr_{((\mathsf{crs},\mathsf{ek}),(\mathsf{td},\mathsf{sk})) \leftarrow \mathsf{Sim}(1^\lambda)} \left[\mathsf{D}_\lambda^*(\rho_\lambda, (\mathsf{crs}, \mathsf{ek}))^{\mathsf{Sim}((\mathsf{td},\mathsf{sk}),\cdot,\cdot)} = 1 \right] \ ,$$

where in every query that D^* *makes to the oracle, it sends a triplet* $(\mathsf{pvk}^*, x, |w\rangle^{\otimes k(\lambda)})$ *such that* pvk^* *can be arbitrary,* $x \in \mathcal{L}_{yes} \cap \{0,1\}^\lambda$ *and* $|w\rangle \in \mathcal{R}_\mathcal{L}(x)$.

Proof. Let $\mathsf{D}^* = \{\mathsf{D}_\lambda^*, \rho_\lambda\}_{\lambda \in \mathbb{N}}$ a polynomial-size quantum distinguisher. We prove zero knowledge by a hybrid argument, that is, we consider a series of computationally-indistinguishable hybrid processes with 1-bit outputs, starting from the output of D^* when getting real proofs, until we get to the output of D^* when getting simulated proofs. We define the following processes.

- Hyb_0 : The output of D^* when getting honestly-generated proofs, that is, it gets the CRS from $(\mathsf{crs}, \mathsf{ek}) \leftarrow \mathsf{Setup}(1^\lambda)$ and the proofs from $\mathsf{P}^*((\mathsf{crs}, \mathsf{ek}), \cdot, \cdot, \cdot)$, as described in the experiment of P_{Real}.

- Hyb_1 : This hybrid process is identical to Hyb_0, with the exception that ek is sampled as a public key for the PKE scheme $(\mathsf{ek}, \mathsf{sk}) \leftarrow \mathsf{PKE.Gen}(1^\lambda)$, rather than as a random string of the same length. To move to this hybrid we will use the fact that the public keys of the PKE scheme are pseudorandom.

- Hyb_2 : This hybrid process is identical to Hyb_1, with the exception that the prover adds another validity check, over the one checking the validity of the proof π_V: It decrypts $r_V = \mathsf{PKE.Dec}_{\mathsf{sk}}(\mathsf{ct}_{r_V})$ and checks that ct_V is obtained by running $\mathsf{PRF.Gen}, \mathsf{fhek} \leftarrow \mathsf{FHE.Gen}, \mathsf{FHE.Enc}_{\mathsf{fhek}}$ with randomness r_V. To move to this hybrid we will use the adaptive soundness of the NP NIZK.

- Hyb_3 : This hybrid process is identical to Hyb_2, with the exception that we simulate the NP NIZK proofs, that is, (1) when sampling the NP NIZK common random string crs from the total CRS (crs, ek), we sample a simulated CRS (crs, td) $\leftarrow$ NIZK.Sim(1^λ) instead of crs $\leftarrow$ NIZK.Setup(1^λ), and (2) every time we compute an NP NIZK proof π_P as part of the QMA NIZK proof $|\pi\rangle$, we use the NP NIZK simulator $\pi_\mathsf{P} \leftarrow$ NIZK.Sim(td, ($\hat{\mathsf{ct}}_\mathsf{P}, \mathsf{ct}_{r_\Xi}, \mathsf{ek}$)) rather than $\pi_\mathsf{P} \leftarrow$ NIZK.P(crs, ($\hat{\mathsf{ct}}_\mathsf{P}, \mathsf{ct}_{r_\Xi}, \mathsf{ek}$)) (where we execute NIZK.P along with a witness for the statement). To move to this hybrid we will use the adaptive zero knowledge property of the NP NIZK.
- Hyb_4 : This hybrid process is identical to Hyb_3, with the exception that ct_{r_Ξ} is an encryption of zeros rather than the randomness for the circuit C_{x,r_Ξ}, which is homomorphically evaluated. To move to this hybrid we will use the security of the PKE scheme.
- Hyb_5 : This hybrid process is identical to Hyb_4, with the exception that when computing the evaluated ciphertext $\hat{\mathsf{ct}}_\mathsf{P}$, instead of homomorphically evaluating the circuit C_{x,r_Ξ}, we compute C_{x,r_Ξ} in the clear and inject the result by circuit-private evaluation. More precisely, the prover does the following: First, it regularly computes $\alpha = \Xi.\mathsf{P}(|w\rangle^{\otimes k(\lambda)}; r_\Xi)$, for randomness r_Ξ. It derives prfk from the decrypted randomness r_V, computes $\beta_x = \mathsf{PRF.F}_\mathsf{prfk}(x)$, $\gamma = \Xi.\mathsf{P}_3(\beta_x, r_\Xi)$, and then $\hat{\mathsf{ct}}_\mathsf{P} \leftarrow \mathsf{FHE.Eval}(C_\gamma, \mathsf{ct}_\mathsf{V})$, where C_γ is the circuit that always outputs γ. To move to this hybrid we will use the circuit-privacy property of the FHE's evaluation algorithm.
- Hyb_6 : This hybrid process is identical to Hyb_5, with the exception that when computing (α, γ) we use the quantum sigma protocol (special zero-knowledge) simulator, that is, the prover first computes β_x (from prfk which is derived from r_V) and then computes $(\alpha, \gamma) \leftarrow \Xi.\mathsf{Sim}(x, \beta_x)$ and as before, α is sent in the clear and γ is sent through homomorphically evaluating the circuit C_γ on ct_V. To move to this hybrid we will use the special zero knowledge property of the quantum sigma protocol. Note that the actions of the prover in this hybrid process are exactly the ones of the QMA NIZK simulator Sim and thus Hyb_6 is exactly the process described in the experiment of $P_\mathsf{Simulated}$.

We now claim that the outputs of each two consecutive hybrids are computationally indistinguishable, which will finish our proof.

- $\mathsf{Hyb}_0 \approx_s \mathsf{Hyb}_1$: Follows readily from the pseudorandomness property of the public keys generated by PKE.Gen(1^λ).
- $\mathsf{Hyb}_1 \approx_s \mathsf{Hyb}_2$: Follows from the adaptive soundness of the NIZK protocol for NP and the statistical correctness of the PKE scheme. We explain in more detail: First, note that whenever the NP statement that D^* proves in π_V is correct and the decryption of the PKE is correct, then the output distribution of the proof oracle is identical between the two hybrid processes, as the additional check that is made in Hyb_2 passes successfully. Also note that whenever the proof π_V is invalid, then both processes output $\perp$ and are identical. It follows that the only times that the output distributions of the proof oracles are not identical is whenever there is an error in the decryption

of the PKE, or the proof π_V checks successfully but the statement is false i.e. whenever D^* breaks the adaptive soundness of the NP NIZK protocol. Since both of the above happen with at most negligible probability, it follows that only with negligible probability the outputs of Hyb_1 and Hyb_2 can be distinguished, and the statistical closeness between them follows.

– $\mathsf{Hyb}_2 \approx_c \mathsf{Hyb}_3$: Follows readily from the adaptive zero-knowledge property of the NP NIZK protocol.

– $\mathsf{Hyb}_3 \approx_c \mathsf{Hyb}_4$: Follows from the security of the PKE scheme. Specifically, the encrypted randomness r_Ξ for every query is simply a random string (independent of all other operations in the process) and thus all of these random strings can be chosen at the beginning of the execution of the process, and thus we fix by an averaging argument the strings $r_\Xi^1, \cdots, r_\Xi^q$ that maximize the distinguishability of D^*, where the q is the (polynomial) number of queries that D^* makes to the proof oracle. It then follows that if D^* distinguishes between Hyb_3 and Hyb_4 then it distinguishes between encryptions of $r_\Xi^1, \cdots, r_\Xi^q$ and encryptions of zeros, and since the single-message security of public-key encryption schemes implies many-message security the indistinguishability $\mathsf{Hyb}_3 \approx_c \mathsf{Hyb}_4$ follow.

– $\mathsf{Hyb}_4 \approx_s \mathsf{Hyb}_5$: Follows by a hybrid argument, by the circuit-privacy property of the FHE scheme and from the fact that the prover makes the additional check on the public verification key, which checks that ct_V is obtained by running $\mathsf{PRF.Gen}, \mathsf{fhek} \leftarrow \mathsf{FHE.Gen}, \mathsf{FHE.Enc}_{\mathsf{fhek}}$ with the extracted randomness r_V. More precisely, let q be the number of queries that D^* makes to the proof oracle, and for $i \in \{0, 1, \cdots, q\}$ we define Hyb_4^i as the process that performs the homomorphic evaluation of C_{x, r_Ξ} (rather than computing it in the clear and then injecting the result, as done in Hyb_5) starting from query number $i + 1$ that D^* makes, thus $\mathsf{Hyb}_4^0 = \mathsf{Hyb}_4$, $\mathsf{Hyb}_4^q = \mathsf{Hyb}_5$.
If Hyb_4 and Hyb_5 are distinguishable then for some $i \in \{0, 1, \cdots, q-1\}$, Hyb_4^i and Hyb_4^{i+1} are distinguishable. We fix by an averaging argument a snapshot of the execution until after the point that D^* sends the $(i + 1)$-th query to the proof oracle. If the check that the prover makes in the beginning, which includes both checking the validity of the NP proof π_V and also checking the validity of creating ct_V from the extracted randomness r_V, fails, then the hybrid processes are the same as the answer of the proof oracle will be $\perp$. In case the check is successful, it follows that the outputs of the circuits C_{x, r_Ξ} and C_γ on the input prfk (which is encrypted inside ct_V) are the same, and thus it follows that the distinguisher between the hybrids Hyb_4^i and Hyb_4^{i+1} can be used to break the (even statistical) circuit privacy of the FHE evaluation.

– $\mathsf{Hyb}_5 \approx_c \mathsf{Hyb}_6$: The proof is very similar to the proof for the indistinguishability $\mathsf{Hyb}_4 \approx_c \mathsf{Hyb}_5$, as the indistinguishability follows by a hybrid argument and from the special zero knowledge property of the quantum sigma protocol. More precisely, for $i \in \{0, 1, \cdots, q\}$ we define Hyb_5^i as the process that uses $\Xi.\mathsf{P}$ (and the polynomially-many copies of the quantum witness) in order to generate (α, γ) (rather than computing it using the simulator) starting from query number $i + 1$ that D^* makes, thus $\mathsf{Hyb}_5^0 = \mathsf{Hyb}_5$, $\mathsf{Hyb}_5^q = \mathsf{Hyb}_6$.

If Hyb_5 and Hyb_6 are distinguishable then for some $i \in \{0, 1, \cdots, q-1\}$, Hyb_5^i and Hyb_5^{i+1} are distinguishable. We fix by an averaging argument a snapshot of the execution until after the point that D^* sends the $(i+1)$-th query to the proof oracle, this in particular fixes the yes instance $x \in \mathcal{L}_{yes}$, the quantum witness $|w\rangle$ and the pseudorandomness β_x. It follows that the distinguisher between the hybrids Hyb_5^i and Hyb_5^{i+1} can be used to tell the difference between a tuple (α, γ) that was generated by $\varXi.\mathsf{P}$ and a tuple that was generated by $\varXi.\mathsf{Sim}$, in contradiction the special zero knowledge property of the protocol $(\varXi.\mathsf{P}, \varXi.\mathsf{V})$.

Acknowledgments. We thank Nir Bitansky and Zvika Brakerski for helpful discussions during the preparation of this work.

References

[ACGH19] Alagic, G., Childs, A.M., Grilo, A.B., Hung, S.H.: Non-interactive classical verification of quantum computation. arXiv, pages arXiv-1911 2019)

[BCKM20] Bartusek, J., Coladangelo, A., Khurana, D., Ma, F.: On the round complexity of two-party quantum computation. arXiv preprint arXiv:2011.11212 (2020)

[BD18] Brakerski, Z., Döttling, N.: Two-message statistically sender-private OT from LWE. In: Beimel, A., Dziembowski, S. (eds.) TCC 2018. LNCS, vol. 11240, pp. 370–390. Springer, Cham (2018). https://doi.org/10.1007/978-3-030-03810-6_14

[BFM19] Blum, M., Feldman, P., Micali, S.: Non-interactive zero-knowledge and its applications. In: Providing Sound Foundations for Cryptography: On the Work of Shafi Goldwasser and Silvio Micali, pP. 329–349 (2019)

[BG19] Broadbent, A., Grilo, A.B.: Zero-knowledge for qma from locally simulatable proofs. arXiv preprint arXiv:1911.07782 (2019)

[BJSW16] Broadbent, A., Ji, Z., Song, F., Watrous, J.: Zero-knowledge proof systems for qma. In: 2016 IEEE 57th Annual Symposium on Foundations of Computer Science (FOCS), pp. 31–40. IEEE (2016)

[BKM20] Brakerski, Z., Koppula, V., Mour, T.: Nizk from lpn and trapdoor hash via correlation intractability for approximable relations. IACR Cryptol. ePrint Arch. **2020**, 258 (2020)

[Blu86] Blum, M.: How to prove a theorem so no one else can claim it. In: Proceedings of the International Congress of Mathematicians, vol. 1, p. 2. Citeseer (1986)

[BP15] Bitansky, N., Paneth, O.: ZAPs and non-interactive witness indistinguishability from indistinguishability obfuscation. In: Dodis, Y., Nielsen, J.B. (eds.) TCC 2015. LNCS, vol. 9015, pp. 401–427. Springer, Heidelberg (2015). https://doi.org/10.1007/978-3-662-46497-7_16

[CCH+19] Canetti, R., et al.: Fiat-shamir: from practice to theory. In: Proceedings of the 51st Annual ACM SIGACT Symposium on Theory of Computing, pp. 1082–1090 (2019)

[CGH04] Canetti, R., Goldreich, O., Halevi, S.: The random oracle methodology, revisited. J. ACM (JACM) **51**(4), 557–594 (2004)

[CVZ19]   Coladangelo, A., Vidick, A., Zhang, T.: Non-interactive zero-knowledge arguments for qma, with preprocessing. arXiv preprint arXiv:1911.07546 (2019)

[FLS99]   Feige, U., Lapidot, D., Shamir, A.: Multiple noninteractive zero knowledge proofs under general assumptions. SIAM J. Comput. **29**(1), 1–28 (1999)

[GMR89]   Goldwasser, S., Micali, S., Rackoff, C.: The knowledge complexity of interactive proof systems. SIAM J. Comput. **18**(1), 186–208 (1989)

[KW19]   Kim, S., Wu, D.J.: Multi-theorem preprocessing nizks from lattices. J. Cryptol., pp. 1–84 (2019)

[Liu06]   Liu, Y.-K.: Consistency of local density matrices is QMA-complete. In: Díaz, J., Jansen, K., Rolim, J.D.P., Zwick, U. (eds.) APPROX/RANDOM -2006. LNCS, vol. 4110, pp. 438–449. Springer, Heidelberg (2006). https:// doi.org/10.1007/11830924_40

[LQR+19]   Lombardi, A., Quach, W., Rothblum, R.D., Wichs, D., Wu, D.J.: New constructions of reusable designated-verifier NIZKs. In: Boldyreva, A., Micciancio, D. (eds.) CRYPTO 2019. LNCS, vol. 11694, pp. 670–700. Springer, Cham (2019). https://doi.org/10.1007/978-3-030-26954-8_22

[Mor20]   Morimae, T.: Information-theoretically-sound non-interactive classical verification of quantum computing with trusted center. arXiv preprint arXiv:2003.10712 (2020)

[MY21]   Morimae, T., Yamakawa, T.: Classically verifiable (dual-mode) nizk for qma with preprocessing. arXiv preprint arXiv:2102.09149, 2021

[OPCPC14]   Ostrovsky, R., Paskin-Cherniavsky, A., Paskin-Cherniavsky, B.: Maliciously circuit-private FHE. In: Garay, J.A., Gennaro, R. (eds.) CRYPTO 2014. LNCS, vol. 8616, pp. 536–553. Springer, Heidelberg (2014). https:// doi.org/10.1007/978-3-662-44371-2_30

[PS19]   Peikert, C., Shiehian, S.: Noninteractive zero knowledge for NP from (plain) learning with errors. In: Boldyreva, A., Micciancio, D. (eds.) CRYPTO 2019. LNCS, vol. 11692, pp. 89–114. Springer, Cham (2019). https://doi.org/10.1007/978-3-030-26948-7_4

[PV+06]   Pass, R., Vaikuntanathan, V., et al.: Construction of a non-malleable encryption scheme from any semantically secure one. In: Dwork, C. (ed.) CRYPTO 2006. LNCS, vol. 4117, pp. 271–289. Springer, Heidelberg (2006). https://doi.org/10.1007/11818175_16

[QRW19]   Quach, W., Rothblum, R.D., Wichs, D.: Reusable designated-verifier NIZKs for all NP from CDH. In: Ishai, Y., Rijmen, V. (eds.) EUROCRYPT 2019. LNCS, vol. 11477, pp. 593–621. Springer, Cham (2019). https://doi.org/10.1007/978-3-030-17656-3_21

[Reg09]   Regev, O.: On lattices, learning with errors, random linear codes, and cryptography. J. ACM **56**(6), 34:1–34:40 (2009)

On the Round Complexity of Secure Quantum Computation

James Bartusek[1](✉), Andrea Coladangelo[1], Dakshita Khurana[2],
and Fermi Ma[3,4]

[1] UC Berkeley, Berkeley, USA
[2] UIUC, Champaign, USA
dakshita@illinois.edu
[3] Princeton University, Princeton, USA
fermima@alum.mit.edu
[4] NTT Research, Palo Alto, USA

Abstract. We construct the first *constant-round* protocols for secure quantum computation in the two-party (2PQC) and multi-party (MPQC) settings with security against *malicious* adversaries. Our protocols are in the common random string (CRS) model.

- Assuming two-message oblivious transfer (OT), we obtain (*i*) three-message 2PQC, and (*ii*) five-round MPQC with only three rounds of *online* (input-dependent) communication; such OT is known from quantum-hard Learning with Errors (QLWE).
- Assuming sub-exponential hardness of QLWE, we obtain (*i*) three-round 2PQC with two online rounds and (*ii*) four-round MPQC with two online rounds.
- When only one (out of two) parties receives output, we achieve *minimal interaction* (two messages) from two-message OT; classically, such protocols are known as non-interactive secure computation (NISC), and our result constitutes the first maliciously-secure quantum NISC.

Additionally assuming reusable malicious designated-verifier NIZK arguments for NP (MDV-NIZKs), we give the first MDV-NIZK for QMA that only requires one copy of the quantum witness.

Finally, we perform a preliminary investigation into *two-round* secure quantum computation where each party must obtain output. On the negative side, we identify a broad class of simulation strategies that suffice for *classical* two-round secure computation that are *unlikely* to work in the quantum setting. Next, as a proof-of-concept, we show that two-round secure quantum computation exists with respect to a quantum oracle.

1 Introduction

Secure computation allows mutually distrusting parties to compute arbitrary functions on their private inputs, revealing only the outputs of the computation while hiding all other private information [12,18,27,40]. With the emergence of quantum

© International Association for Cryptologic Research 2021
T. Malkin and C. Peikert (Eds.): CRYPTO 2021, LNCS 12825, pp. 406–435, 2021.
https://doi.org/10.1007/978-3-030-84242-0_15

computers, it becomes important to understand the landscape of secure *quantum* computation over distributed, private quantum (or classical) states. In the most general setting, n parties hold (possibly entangled) quantum inputs $x_1, \ldots, x_n$, and would like to evaluate a quantum circuit $Q(x_1, \ldots, x_n)$. The output is of the form $(y_1, \ldots, y_n)$, so at the end of the protocol party i holds state y_i.

Secure computation with classical inputs and circuits forms a centerpiece of classical cryptography. Solutions to this problem in the classical setting were first obtained nearly 35 years ago, when [40] built garbled circuits to enable secure two-party computation, and [12,18,27] obtained the first secure multi-party computation protocols. Since then, there has been an extensive body of work in this area, of which a large chunk focuses on understanding the amount of back-and-forth interaction required to implement these protocols. Notably, the work of Beaver, Micali and Rogaway [9] obtained the first constant-round classical multi-party computation protocols in the dishonest majority setting. There have been several subsequent works including but not limited to [5,7,14, 19,25,31] that have nearly completely characterized the *exact* round complexity of classical secure computation.

The problem of secure *quantum* computation on distributed quantum states is not nearly as well-understood as its classical counterpart. The quantum setting was first studied by [11,20], who obtained unconditional maliciously-secure multi-party quantum computation with honest majority. Just like the classical setting, when half (or more) of the players are malicious, secure quantum computation also requires computational assumptions due to the impossibility of unconditionally secure quantum bit commitment [21,32,35].

In the dishonest majority setting, [23] gave a two-party quantum computation (2PQC) protocol secure against the quantum analogue of semi-honest adversaries (specious adversaries); this was later extended to the malicious setting by [24]. A work of [22] constructed maliciously-secure *multi-party* quantum computation (MPQC) with dishonest majority from any maliciously-secure post-quantum classical MPC, where the round complexity grows with the size of the circuit *and* the number of participants. Very recently, [4] constructed MPQC with identifiable abort, and with round complexity that does not grow with the circuit size but grows with the number of participants.

However, the feasibility of maliciously-secure MPQC with *constant* rounds has remained open until this work. In addition to settling this question, we also make several headways in understanding the *exact* round complexity of secure quantum computation with up to all-but-one malicious corruptions.

1.1   Our Results

We assume that parties have access to a common random string (CRS), and obtain answers to a range of fundamental questions, as we discuss next[1].

---

[1] We point out that the post-quantum MPC protocol of [1] can be used to generate a CRS in constant rounds. This, combined with our results, yields the first constant round multi-party quantum computation protocols without trusted setup in the standard model.

Quantum Non-interactive Secure Computation. Our first result pertains to the most basic setting for secure (quantum) computation: a sender holds input $\mathbf{y}$, a receiver holds input $\mathbf{x}$, and the goal is for the receiver to obtain $Q(\mathbf{x}, \mathbf{y})$ for some quantum circuit Q. We construct a protocol achieving *minimal interaction*—commonly known as non-interactive secure computation (NISC) [30]—where the receiver publishes an encryption of $\mathbf{x}$, the sender replies with an encryption of $\mathbf{y}$, and the receiver subsequently obtains $Q(\mathbf{x}, \mathbf{y})$. Our result constitutes the first maliciously-secure NISC for quantum computation (Q-NISC).

Theorem 1. *(Informal) Maliciously-secure NISC for quantum computation exists assuming post-quantum maliciously-secure two-message oblivious transfer (OT) with straight-line simulation.*

Such OT protocols are known from the post-quantum hardness of Learning with Errors (LWE) [36]. We remark that our Q-NISC result also extends to the *reusable* setting where the receiver has a classical input that they would like to reuse across multiple quantum computations on different sender inputs.

Application: Malicious Designated-Verifier NIZK Arguments for QMA. As an application of our maliciously-secure Q-NISC, we construct (reusable) *malicious designated-verifier non-interactive zero-knowledge arguments* (MDV-NIZKs) for QMA in the common random string model. Specifically, our MDV-NIZK enables the following interaction for any QMA language: a verifier can publish a classical public key pk that enables a prover to send an instance x and quantum message $\mathbf{m}$, such that the verifier holding the corresponding secret key sk can determine if x is a valid instance.

Theorem 2. *(Informal) There exists a reusable MDV-NIZK for* QMA *with a classical CRS and classical proving key assuming the existence of post-quantum maliciously-secure two-message oblivious transfer with straight-line simulation in the CRS model, and post-quantum (adaptively sound) reusable MDV-NIZK for NP. All of the underlying primitives exist assuming the quantum hardness of learning with errors.*

We briefly elaborate on the security guarantees of our reusable MDV-NIZK. Reusability means that soundness holds for multiple proofs (of potentially different statements) computed with respect to the same setup (i.e., the common random string and the public key), even if the prover learns whether or not the verifier accepted each proof; we remark that reusable security is sometimes referred to as multi-theorem security. Malicious security means that the zero-knowledge property holds even against verifiers that generate the public key maliciously. Previously, such a reusable MDV-NIZK for QMA required the prover to have access to multiple copies of the quantum witness [37], while our MDV-NIZK only requires the prover to have a single copy.

Constant-Round 2PQC and MPQC. Our next set of results concerns the general setting for 2PQC and MPQC *where all parties obtain output*. We focus on minimizing total round complexity as well as *online* round complexity, where the latter refers to the number of *input-dependent* rounds; if a protocol has round complexity d and online round complexity k, then the parties can perform the first $d - k$ rounds *before* they receive their inputs.[2]

We obtain various results, some from the generic assumption of quantum polynomially-secure two-message oblivious transfer, and others from the specific assumption of sub-exponential QLWE. Our results in this section are summarized in Table 1.[3]

Table 1. Maliciously-secure quantum computation in the CRS model

	From OT	From sub-exp QLWE
Two-party	3 rounds (3 online)	3 rounds (2 online)
Multi-party	5 rounds (3 online)	4 rounds (2 online)

In order to prove the security of these protocols, we develop a delayed simulation technique, which we call "simulation via teleportation", which may be of independent interest.

Is Two-Round Secure Quantum Computation Possible? A natural next question is whether it is possible to construct two-round secure quantum computation *without* pre-processing. This appears to be a challenging question to resolve, either positively or negatively. We provide some preliminary results on both fronts: we give a negative result indicating that common simulation strategies from the classical setting will not suffice in the quantum setting, but we also provide a proof-of-concept positive result, with a new simulation strategy, assuming virtual-black-box obfuscation of quantum circuits. We stress that the latter result is primarily to give intuition, as virtual-black-box obfuscation is known to be impossible even for classical circuits [8]. We limit the scope of this preliminary investigation to the *two-party* setting.

First, we give some intuition for why it seems hard to design a two-round two-party protocol by showing that, under a plausible quantum information-theoretic conjecture, a large class of common simulation techniques would *not* suffice. We consider any simulator that learns which player (between Alice and Bob) is corrupted only *after* it has generated the simulated CRS. We call such a simulator an *oblivious simulator*. To the best of our knowledge, all existing

---

[2] We remark that a k-online round protocol can also be viewed as a k-round protocol in a quantum pre-processing model, i.e. a model where parties receive some quantum correlations as setup.

[3] The results below are in the setting of security with abort, as opposed to security with *unanimous* abort (which is only a distinction in the multi-party setting). If one wants security with unanimous abort, the overall round complexity will not change, but one more round of online communication will be required.

classical and quantum two-party computation protocols in the CRS model either (1) already admit oblivious simulation, or (2) can generically be transformed to admit oblivious simulation via post-quantum NIZK proofs of knowledge for NP.

In the quantum setting, we show, roughly, that any two-round 2PQC protocol for general quantum functionalities *with an oblivious simulator* would yield an *instantaneous nonlocal quantum computation* protocol [10,28,38,39] for general quantum functionalities, with polynomial-size pre-processing.

Instantaneous nonlocal quantum computation is well-studied in the quantum information literature [10,28,38,39], and the best known protocols for general functionalities require exponential-size pre-processing [10]. Thus, a two-round 2PQC for general functionalities with oblivious simulation would immediately yield an exponential improvement in the size of the pre-processing for this task.

Theorem 3. *(Informal) Under the conjecture that there exists a quantum functionality that does not admit an instantaneous nonlocal quantum computation protocol with polynomial-size pre-processing, there exists a quantum functionality that cannot be securely computed in two rounds in the classical CRS model with an oblivious simulator.*

Towards getting around this potential barrier, we give a proof-of-concept construction of a protocol with non-oblivious simulation. Specifically, we assume a (strong) form of VBB obfuscation for quantum circuits that contain unitary and measurement gates, where the former may be classically controlled on the outcome of measurement gates. We point out, however, that VBB-obfuscation of circuits with measurement gates is potentially even more powerful than the VBB obfuscation for unitaries that was formalized in [3] (further discussion on this is available in the full version). Under this assumption, we obtain a two-round two-party secure quantum computation protocol in the CRS model.

Theorem 4. *(Informal) Two-round two-party secure quantum computation in the common reference string model exists assuming a strong form of VBB or ideal obfuscation for quantum circuits as discussed above.*

We remark that while there exist (contrived) examples of functionalities that cannot be VBB obfuscated [2,3,6], it is still plausible that many quantum functionalities can be obfuscated. However, without any candidate constructions of obfuscation for quantum circuits, we stress that our result should only be taken as a proof-of-concept.

1.2   Paper Organization

In Sect. 2, we provide technical intuition for all of our results. In Sect. 3, we give a full technical specification of our three-message 2PQC protocol. We prove that security holds against a malicious Alice, and we defer a security proof for malicious Bob to the full version (as will become clear in Sect. 2, handling malicious Alice is the more challenging case). We defer the remainder of our results to the full version, which includes the two-round 2PQC with preprocessing, the

MPQC results, the technical formalization of [15] C+M garbling, MDV-NIZKs for QMA, our oblivious simulation barrier, and our VBB-based proof-of-concept construction.

2 Technical Overview

2.1 Quantum Background

We briefly recap some relevant concepts from quantum computation.

Notation. We use bold letters to write the density matrix of a quantum state $\mathbf{x}$. We use the shorthand $U(\mathbf{x})$ to mean $U\mathbf{x}U^\dagger$, the result of applying unitary U to $\mathbf{x}$. The notation $(\mathbf{x}, \mathbf{y})$ denotes a state on two registers, where $\mathbf{x}$ and $\mathbf{y}$ are potentially entangled. The k-fold tensor product of a state $\mathbf{x} \otimes \mathbf{x} \otimes \cdots \otimes \mathbf{x}$ will be written as $\mathbf{x}^k$.

The Pauli Group. The Pauli group on a single qubit, denoted by $\mathscr{P}_1$, is generated by the unitary operations X (bit flip) and Z (phase flip), defined as $X = \begin{bmatrix} 0 & 1 \\ 1 & 0 \end{bmatrix}, Z = \begin{bmatrix} 1 & 0 \\ 0 & -1 \end{bmatrix}$. The Pauli group on n qubits, denoted by $\mathscr{P}_n$, is the n-fold tensor product of the single qubit Pauli group. Any unitary in the Pauli group $\mathscr{P}_n$ can be written (up to global phase) as $\bigotimes_{i \in [n]} X^{r_i} Z^{s_i}$ for $r, s \in \{0, 1\}^n$.

The Clifford Group. The Clifford group on n qubits, denoted by $\mathscr{C}_n$, is the group of unitaries that normalize $\mathscr{P}_n$, i.e. $C \in \mathscr{C}_n$ if and only if for all $U \in \mathscr{P}_n$, we have $CUC^\dagger \in \mathscr{P}_n$. Alternatively, we can think of a Clifford unitary C as an operation where for any choice of $r, s \in \{0, 1\}^n$, there exists a choice of $r', s' \in \{0, 1\}^n$ such that

$$C \left(\bigotimes_{i \in [n]} X^{r_i} Z^{s_i} \right) = \left(\bigotimes_{i \in [n]} X^{r'_i} Z^{s'_i} \right) C.$$

Intuitively, this means that with a suitable update of the Pauli operation, one can swap the order in which a Clifford and a Pauli are applied.

Clifford Authentication Codes. We will make extensive use of Clifford authentication codes. Clifford authentication codes are an information-theoretic encoding scheme for quantum states that provides both secrecy and authentication. An n-qubit quantum state $\mathbf{x}$ can be encoded in a Clifford authentication code as follows: prepare a λ-qubit all 0's state which we denote as $\mathbf{0}^\lambda$ (where λ is a security parameter), sample a random Clifford unitary $C \leftarrow \mathscr{C}_{n+\lambda}$, and output $C(\mathbf{x}, \mathbf{0}^\lambda)$. The Clifford C serves as a secret key, while the $\mathbf{0}^\lambda$ qubits enable authentication, and are called "trap" qubits. A party without knowledge of C cannot modify the encoding without modifying the trap qubits (except with negligible probability). Therefore, decoding works by applying $C^\dagger$ and then measuring the λ trap qubits in the computational basis. If these measurements are all 0, this ensures that with all but negligible probability, the n remaining registers hold the originally encoded state $\mathbf{x}$.

Clifford + Measurement Circuits. We will rely heavily on the "Clifford + Measurement" representation of quantum circuits (henceforth "C+M circuits") due to [16]. In this representation, a quantum circuit can be decomposed into layers. Each layer consists of a Clifford unitary whose output wires are partitioned into wires that will be fed as inputs into the next layer, and wires that will be measured. The latter group of wires are measured in the computational basis, resulting in a classical bitstring that is used to select the Clifford unitary to be applied in the subsequent layer. The first layer takes in all of the inputs to the quantum circuit, ancilla **0** states, and "magic" **T** states defined as $\mathbf{T} := (|0\rangle + e^{i\pi/4}|1\rangle)/\sqrt{2}$. The final layer only produces output wires (i.e. its output registers have no wires to be measured), which are interpreted as the output of the circuit. [16] demonstrate that, with constant multiplicative factor overhead in size, any quantum circuit can be written as a "C + M circuit" or equivalently, in a magic state representation.

Therefore, for the purposes of this technical overview, we will assume that any quantum circuit F is written as a C+M circuit F_{CM}, and its evaluation on an input $\mathbf{x}$ is computed as $F(\mathbf{x}) = F_{\mathrm{CM}}(\mathbf{x}, \mathbf{T}^k, \mathbf{0}^k)$. For simplicity, we use the same k to denote the number of **T** states and the number of ancilla **0** states.

Magic State Distillation. In settings where malicious parties are tasked with providing the **T** states, we will use cryptographic techniques such as "cut-and-choose" to ensure that F_{CM} is evaluated on an input of the form $(\mathbf{x}, \widehat{\mathbf{T}^k}, \mathbf{0}^k)$ where $\widehat{\mathbf{T}^k}$ is a state guaranteed to be "somewhat" close to $\mathbf{T}^k$. However, correctness of F_{CM} will require states that are negligibly close to real magic states. To that end, we will make use of a magic state distillation C+M circuit D due to [22] which takes in somewhat-close magic states $\widehat{\mathbf{T}^k}$ and outputs states negligibly close to $\mathbf{T}^{k'}$, for $k' < k$. Therefore, the representation of any functionality F will in fact be a C+M circuit $F_{\mathrm{CM},D}$ that first applies D to $\widehat{\mathbf{T}^k}$, and then runs F_{CM}.

2.2   Why Is Malicious Security Hard to Achieve?

We begin this technical overview by describing our results in the two-party setting. Before this, we briefly explain why malicious security does not follow readily from existing techniques. Indeed, a candidate two-message 2PQC (where one party receives output) with *specious* security (the quantum analogue of classical semi-honest security [23]) was recently proposed in [15]. Alternatively, any construction of quantum fully-homomorphic encryption (QFHE) naturally yields a two-message 2PQC protocol: (1) Alice QFHE-encodes her input and sends it to Bob, (2) Bob evaluates the functionality on his input and Alice's encoded input, and (3) Bob sends Alice the encryption of her output.

One might hope to compile this QFHE-based protocol or the [15] protocol into a maliciously secure protocol by having the parties include proofs that their messages are well-formed. Unfortunately, it is unclear how to implement this in the quantum setting. In both of these approaches, the parties would have to prove (in zero-knowledge) statements of the form "**y** is the result of evaluating quantum circuit C on **x**." Crucially, the *statement* the parties need to prove explicitly makes reference to a quantum state. This is beyond the reach of what one can prove with, say, NIZKs for QMA, in which witnesses are quantum but the statements are entirely classical.

Therefore, we design our malicious 2PQC so that parties do not have to prove general statements about quantum states. A core ingredient in our protocol is a quantum garbled circuit construction sketched in [15, §2.5], where the circuit garbling procedure is entirely classical.[4] Combining this with a post-quantum maliciously-secure *classical* 2PC, we will ensure valid circuit garbling against malicious quantum adversaries.

2.3 A Garbling Scheme for **C** + **M** Circuits

Our first step is to formalize the proposal sketched in [15, §2.5] for garbling C + M circuits. The starting point for the [15, §2.5] construction is a simple technique for garbling any quantum circuit that consists of a single Clifford unitary F.[5] The idea is to sample a random Clifford E and give out $FE^\dagger$ as the garbled circuit; note that the description of $FE^\dagger$ will be entirely classical. Since the Clifford unitaries form a group, $FE^\dagger$ is a uniformly random Clifford unitary independent of F. To garble the input quantum state **x**, simply compute $E(\mathbf{x})$. The construction in [15, §2.5] extends this simple construction to any circuit.

To build intuition, we will consider a two-layer C + M circuit $Q = (F_1, f)$, where F_1 is the first layer Clifford unitary, and f is a classical circuit that takes as input a single bit measurement result m, and outputs a classical description of F_2, the second layer Clifford unitary. On input **x**, the circuit operates as follows:

1. Apply F_1 to **x**.
2. Measure the last output wire in the computational basis to obtain $m \in \{0,1\}$, and feed the remaining wires to the next layer. Compute the second layer Clifford unitary $F_2 = f(m)$.
3. Apply F_2 to the non-measured output wires from the first layer. Return the result.

One could try to extend the simple idea for one-layer garbling to this circuit. We still sample a random input-garbling Clifford E_0 and compute $F_1 E_0^\dagger$. To hide the second layer Clifford, a natural idea is to sample yet another random Clifford E_1 to be applied to the non-measured output wires of F_1. That is, we replace $F_1 E_0^\dagger$ with $(E_1 \otimes \mathbb{I}) F_1 E_0^\dagger$, and release the description of a function g such that $g(m) = f(m) E_1^\dagger$.

---

[4] We remark that the 2PQC proposed in [15] is based on their "main" quantum garbled circuit construction, which crucially does *not* have a classical circuit garbling procedure. The advantage of their main construction is that garbling can be done in low depth, whereas the alternative construction requires an expensive but classical garbling procedure.

[5] [15] call this *group-randomizing quantum randomized encoding*.

However, this may in general be insecure. Let $F_2^{(0)}$ be the Clifford output by function f when $m = 0$, and $F_2^{(1)}$ the Clifford output by function f when $m = 1$. Suppose $F_2^{(0)} - F_2^{(1)} = A$ for some invertible matrix A. Then, an attacker with access to g could obtain $F_2^{(0)} E_1^\dagger - F_2^{(1)} E_1^\dagger$, and multiplying the result by A^{-1} yields $A^{-1}(F_2^{(0)} E_1^\dagger - F_2^{(1)} E_1^\dagger) = A^{-1} A E_1^\dagger = E_1^\dagger$.

Therefore, instead of giving out g, the construction of [15, §2.5] gives out a classical garbling of g. To accommodate this, the output wire from the first layer that is measured to produce $m \in \{0, 1\}$ must be replaced by a collection of wires that produces the corresponding label lab_m for the garbled circuit. This can be easily achieved by applying a suitable "label unitary" to the m wire (and ancilla wires) within the garbled gate for the first layer.

There is one last issue with this approach: an attacker that chooses not to measure the wires containing lab_m can obtain a superposition over two valid labels. Recall that the standard definition of security for classical garbled circuits only guarantees simulation of one label, not a quantum superposition of both labels. To ensure the attacker cannot get away with skipping the computational basis measurement, the [15, §2.5] construction applies a Z-twirl to m before the "label unitary" is applied. Recall that a Z-twirl is simply a random application of a Pauli Z gate, i.e. Z^b for a uniformly random bit b; applying Z^b to a wire is equivalent to performing a computational basis measurement (without recording the result).

To recap, a garbled 2-layer $\mathsf{C} + \mathsf{M}$ circuit Q consists of three components: an "input garbling" Clifford E_0, an initial Clifford unitary to be applied to the garbled input $D_0 := (E_1 \otimes \mathbb{I}) F_1 E_0^\dagger$, and a classical garbled circuit $\tilde{g}$. Extrapolating, we see that in general a garbled $\mathsf{C} + \mathsf{M}$ circuit takes the form

$$(E_0, D_0, \tilde{g}_1, \ldots, \tilde{g}_d) := (E_0, \tilde{Q}),$$

where the $\tilde{g}_i$'s are garblings of classical circuits. Crucially, all of these components can be generated by an entirely classical circuit. The only quantum operation involved in the garbling process is the application of E_0 to the input $\mathbf{x}$ to garble the input. Next, we show how we can take advantage of this mostly classical garbling procedure to obtain maliciously-secure 2PQC.

2.4 A Three-Message Protocol with Malicious Security

In this section, we describe a three-message 2PQC protocol where both parties obtain output. This implies the two-message 2PQC result with one-sided output described in the first part of our results section, and fills in the upper left corner of Table 1.

We begin with a plausible but *insecure* construction of a three-message 2PQC based on the above quantum garbled circuit construction. We will then highlight the ways a malicious attacker might break this construction, and arrive at our final construction by implementing suitable modifications.

Our protocol relies only on a *classical* two-message 2PC with one-sided output that is (post-quantum) secure against malicious adversaries; this can be realized by combining (post-quantum) classical garbled circuits [40] with (post-quantum) two-message oblivious transfer [36] following e.g. [30].

We will consider two parties: Alice with input $\mathbf{x}_A$ and Bob with input $\mathbf{x}_B$. They wish to jointly compute a quantum circuit Q on their inputs whose output is delivered to both players. Q is represented as a Clifford+Measurement circuit that takes input $(\mathbf{x}_A, \mathbf{x}_B, \mathbf{T}^k, \mathbf{0}^k)$. We denote by $(\mathbf{y}_A, \mathbf{y}_B)$ the joint outputs of Alice and Bob. At a high level, the parties will use the first two messages (Bob $\rightarrow$ Alice, Alice $\rightarrow$ Bob) to jointly encode their quantum inputs, while in parallel computing a two-message classical 2PC that outputs the classical description of a quantum garbled circuit to Bob. By evaluating the garbled circuit, Bob can learn his own output, as well as Alice's encoded output, which he sends to Alice in the 3rd message.

In more detail, the classical functionality $\mathcal{F}[Q]$ to be computed by the classical 2PC is defined as follows. It takes as input (the classical description of) a Clifford unitary $C_{B,\text{in}}$ from Bob and Clifford unitaries $(C_{A,\text{in}}, C_{A,\text{out}})$ from Alice. Let Q_B be a modification of Q that outputs $(C_{A,\text{out}}(\mathbf{y}_A, \mathbf{0}^\lambda), \mathbf{y}_B)$ in place of $(\mathbf{y}_A, \mathbf{y}_B)$; looking ahead, this will enable Bob to evaluate (a garbling of) Q_B on (a garbling of) their joint inputs without learning Alice's output. The functionality computes a garbling $(E_0, \widetilde{Q_B})$ of Q_B. Finally, it computes $W := E_0 \cdot (\mathbb{I} \otimes C_{B,\text{in}}^{-1} \otimes \mathbb{I}) \cdot C_{A,\text{in}}^{-1}$ (where the registers implied by the tensor product will become clear below), and outputs $(W, \widetilde{Q_B})$ to Bob.

The (insecure) protocol template is as follows:

- **First Message (Bob $\rightarrow$ Alice).** Bob picks a random Clifford $C_{B,\text{in}}$ and uses it to encrypt and authenticate his input $\mathbf{x}_B$ as $\mathbf{m}_1 := C_{B,\text{in}}(\mathbf{x}_B, \mathbf{0}^\lambda)$. He also computes the first round message m_1 of the classical 2PC, using $C_{B,\text{in}}$ as his input. He sends $(\mathbf{m}_1, m_1)$ to Alice.
- **Second Message (Alice $\rightarrow$ Bob).** After receiving $(\mathbf{m}_1, m_1)$, Alice picks a random Clifford $C_{A,\text{in}}$ and uses it to encrypt her input $\mathbf{x}_A$ along with Bob's encoding $\mathbf{m}_1$, k copies of a $\mathbf{T}$ state, and $k + \lambda$ copies of a $\mathbf{0}$ state. The result of this is $\mathbf{m}_2 := C_{A,\text{in}}(\mathbf{x}_A, \mathbf{m}_1, \mathbf{T}^k, \mathbf{0}^{k+\lambda})$. Alice also samples another random Clifford $C_{A,\text{out}}$ that will serve to encrypt and authenticate her output, and computes the second round message m_2 of the classical 2PC using input $(C_{A,\text{in}}, C_{A,\text{out}})$. She sends $(\mathbf{m}_2, m_2)$ to Bob.
- **Third Message (Bob $\rightarrow$ Alice).** After receiving $(\mathbf{m}_2, m_2)$, Bob can compute his output of the classical 2PC, which is $(W, \widetilde{Q_B})$. He computes

$$W(\mathbf{m}_2) = E_0 \cdot (\mathbb{I} \otimes C_{B,\text{in}}^{-1} \otimes \mathbb{I}) \cdot C_{A,\text{in}}^{-1} \left(C_{A,\text{in}}(\mathbf{x}_A, \mathbf{m}_1, \mathbf{T}^k, \mathbf{0}^{k+\lambda}) \right) = E_0(\mathbf{x}_A, \mathbf{x}_B, \mathbf{T}^k, \mathbf{0}^{k+\lambda}).$$

Recall that $E_0(\mathbf{x}_A, \mathbf{x}_B, \mathbf{T}^k, \mathbf{0}^{k+\lambda})$ corresponds to a garbled input for $\widetilde{Q_B}$. He evaluates $\widetilde{Q_B}$ on this garbled input and obtains $(C_{A,\text{out}}(\mathbf{y}_A, \mathbf{0}^\lambda), \mathbf{y}_B)$.
At this point, Bob has his output $\mathbf{y}_B$ in the clear. Next he sets $\mathbf{m}_3 = C_{A,\text{out}}(\mathbf{y}_A, \mathbf{0}^\lambda)$, and sends $\mathbf{m}_3$ to Alice. Upon receiving $\mathbf{m}_3$, Alice can recover her output by computing $C_{A,\text{out}}^{-1}(\mathbf{m}_3)$.

The above protocol can already be shown to be secure against malicious Bob by relying on security of the classical two-party computation protocol against malicious adversaries. But malicious Alice can break security by generating ill-formed auxiliary states. We now describe this issue in some more detail and then present modifications to address the problem.

Malicious Generation of Auxiliary States. In the second message of the protocol, Alice is instructed to send a quantum state $C_{A,\text{in}}(\mathbf{x}_A, \mathbf{m}_1, \mathbf{T}^k, \mathbf{0}^{k+\lambda})$. A malicious Alice can deviate from honest behavior by submitting arbitrary states in place of the magic $\mathbf{T}$ states and the auxiliary $\mathbf{0}$ states, either of which may compromise security.

We therefore modify the classical 2PC to include randomized checks that will enable Bob to detect if Alice has deviated from honest behavior.

We check validity of $\mathbf{0}$ states using the "random linear map" technique of [22]. The classical 2PC will sample a uniformly random matrix $M \in \mathbb{F}_2^{k \times k}$, and apply a unitary U_M that maps the quantum state $\mathbf{v} = |v\rangle \langle v|$ for any $v \in \mathbb{F}_2^k$ to the state $\mathbf{Mv} = |Mv\rangle \langle Mv|$. For any $M \in \mathbb{F}_2^{k \times k}$, there exists an efficient Clifford unitary U_M implementing this map. This check takes advantage of the fact that $U_M(\mathbf{0}^k) = \mathbf{0}^k$ for any M, but on any other pure state $\mathbf{v} = |v\rangle \langle v|$ for non-zero $v \in \mathbb{F}_2^k$, we have $U_M(\mathbf{v}) \neq \mathbf{0}^k$ with overwhelming probability in k.

More precisely, our protocol will now ask Alice to prepare twice $(2k)$ the required number of $\mathbf{0}$ states. The classical 2PC will generate a Clifford unitary U_M implementing a random linear map $M \in \mathbb{F}_2^{2k \times 2k}$, and incorporate U_M into its output Clifford W, which is now $W = (E_0 \otimes \mathbb{I}) \cdot (\mathbb{I} \otimes C_{B,\text{in}}^{-1} \otimes \mathbb{I}) \cdot (\mathbb{I} \otimes U_M) \cdot C_{A,\text{in}}^{-1}$. Now when Bob applies W to Alice's message $C_{A,\text{in}}(\mathbf{x}_A, C_{B,\text{in}}(\mathbf{x}_B, \mathbf{0}^\lambda), \mathbf{T}^k, \mathbf{0}^{2k})$, it has the effect of stripping off $C_{A,\text{in}}$ by applying $C_{A,\text{in}}^{-1}$, and then applying U_M to the last $2k$ registers. The rest of the application of W has the same effect as before the modification, so it undoes the application of $C_{B,\text{in}}$, and then re-encodes *all but the last k registers* under the input garbling Clifford E_0 to produce a garbled input. Crucially, the last k registers are designated "$\mathbf{0}$-state check registers", which Bob can simply measure in the computational basis to detect if Alice prepared the $\mathbf{0}$ states properly.

Unfortunately, this technique does not extend to checking validity of $\mathbf{T}$ states. To do so, we would have to map $\mathbf{T}$ states to $\mathbf{0}$ states, but there is no Clifford unitary that realizes this transformation.[6] The problem with using a non-Clifford unitary is that security of W relies on the fact that it is the product of a random Clifford $C_{A,\text{in}}$ and some other Clifford W'. Since the Clifford unitaries form a group, multiplication by a random $C_{A,\text{in}}$ perfectly masks the details of W', but only when W' is Clifford.

We will therefore employ the "cut-and-choose" technique from [22]. The protocol will now have Alice prepare $\lambda(k+1)$-many $\mathbf{T}$ states instead of just k. The classical 2PC will generate a random permutation π on $[\lambda(k+1)]$, which will move a random selection of λ of the $\mathbf{T}$ states into "$\mathbf{T}$-state check registers." The application of π will be implemented by a unitary U_π incorporated into W.

---

[6] The existence of such a Clifford would imply that Clifford + Measurement circuits *without* magic states are universal for quantum computing, contradicting the Gottesman-Knill theorem (assuming BPP $\neq$ BQP).

After applying W, Bob will apply a projective measurement onto $\mathbf{T}$ to each of the $\mathbf{T}$-state check registers, and will abort if any of the λ measurements fails.

If all of the λ measurements pass, this means the remaining λk un-tested $\mathbf{T}$ states are "somewhat close" to being real $\mathbf{T}$ states. However, being "somewhat close" will not be sufficient; for instance, an attacker who prepares exactly one completely invalid $\mathbf{T}$ state will only be caught with $1/(k+1)$ probability.

We will therefore need to apply magic-state distillation to transform these into states which are negligibly close to real $\mathbf{T}$ states. For this, we use a magic-state distillation circuit of [22, §2.5] (which builds on [16]). This circuit consists solely of Clifford gates and computational basis measurements. To apply this circuit we modify our underlying functionality, so that we now give out a garbling of a circuit that first implements magic-state distillation and only then applies Q_B.

This completes an overview of our protocol, and a formal construction and analysis can be found in Sect. 3.

2.5   Application: Reusable MDV-NIZK for QMA

Now we briefly describe how the above techniques readily give a reusable malicious designated-verifier NIZK for QMA in the CRS model. Note that NIZK for QMA is a special case of two-party quantum computation, where the functionality being computed is the verification circuit $\mathcal{V}$ for some QMA language, the prover (previously Alice) has the quantum witness $\mathbf{w}$ as input, and the verifier (previously Bob) has no input and receives a binary output indicating whether $\mathcal{V}(x, \mathbf{w})$ accepts or rejects, where x is the (classical) description of the instance they are considering.

Since the prover does not receive output, there is no need for the third message in the protocol of Sect. 2.4. Furthermore, since the verifier has no input, there is no need for any quantum message from him in the first message. The verifier only needs to send a first-round classical 2PC message which then functions as a proving key. The (classical) left-over state is the verifier's secret verification key. After this, the prover just sends one quantum message (the Second Message in the above protocol), proving that $\mathcal{V}(x, \mathbf{w}) = 1$.

In order to make the above template reusable, we can first instantiate the underlying classical 2PC with a reusable 2PC. Once this is in place, the verifier's first-round message is necessarily independent. Then, to ensure that a cheating prover cannot break soundness by observing whether the verifier accepts its proofs or not, we modify the classical functionality to take as input a PRF key from the verifier, and generate all required randomness (used for the $\mathbf{0}$ and $\mathbf{T}$ checks, and the quantum garbling procedure) by applying this PRF to the (classical) description of the instance x. By security of the reusable 2PC and the PRF, a verifier will never accept a maliciously sampled proof for any instance x not in the language.

2.6   Challenges in Achieving a Two-Round Protocol in the Quantum Setting

The previous sections show that we can achieve 2PQC in two messages if only one party receives output, which is optimal in terms of round complexity. Now we ask whether both parties can obtain output with just two rounds of simultaneous exchange. Indeed, in the classical setting, there is a natural approach to obtaining a two-round protocol, given a two-message protocol where one party receives output. The parties simply run two parallel executions of the two-message protocol on the same inputs - one in which Alice speaks first and the functionality only computes her part of the output, and another in which Bob speaks first and the functionality only computes his part of the output. Unfortunately, this natural approach completely fails in the quantum setting, for at least two reasons.

- Running two parallel executions of the same protocol on the same set of inputs seems to require *cloning* those inputs, which is in general impossible if the inputs may be arbitrary quantum states.
- Running two parallel executions of a randomized functionality requires the parties to fix the same random coins to be used in each execution, as otherwise their outputs may not be properly jointly distributed. This is not possible in the quantum setting, since randomness can come from measurement, and measurement results cannot be fixed and agreed upon beforehand.

These issues motivate the rest of our work. Since running two protocols in parallel on the same inputs is problematic, we take as our guiding principle that one party must be performing the actual computation at some point in the protocol, and then distributing the outputs.

Interestingly, while the first issue mentioned above is unique to the setting of quantum inputs, the second issue applies even if the parties wish to compute a quantum circuit over just *classical* inputs, which we regard as a very natural setting. Thus, while this paper focuses on the most general case of secure quantum computation over potentially quantum inputs, we stress that all the results we achieve are the best known even for the classical input setting. Furthermore, note that both issues also exist in the specious setting, so it doesn't appear to be straightforward to achieve two-round 2PQC even in this setting. While the focus of this paper is on the setting of malicious security, exploring these questions in the specious setting is also an interesting direction.

2.7   A Two-Round Protocol with Pre-processing

Our next result is a three-round protocol for 2PQC which requires only two *online* rounds of communication, filling in the upper right corner of Table 1.

In fact, we construct a protocol in which the pre-input phase only consists of a *single* message from Bob to Alice (computed with respect to a CRS). We take our three sequential message protocol as a starting point, and introduce several modifications. The first modification will immediately achieve the goal of removing input-dependence from Bob's first message, and all the subsequent modifications will be necessary to restore correctness and security.

Modification 1: Removing Input-Dependence via Teleportation. Before sending his first message, Bob samples n EPR pairs, where n is the number of qubits of the input $\mathbf{x}_B$. We denote these EPR pairs by $(\mathbf{epr}_1, \mathbf{epr}_2)$, where $\mathbf{epr}_1$ denotes the left n qubits, and $\mathbf{epr}_2$ denotes the right n qubits. In place of sending $C_{B,\text{in}}(\mathbf{x}_B, \mathbf{0}^\lambda)$, Bob sends $\mathbf{m}_{B,1} := C_{B,\text{in}}(\mathbf{epr}_1, \mathbf{0}^\lambda)$. Note that the classical 2PC only requires input $C_{B,\text{in}}$, which is a random Clifford that Bob samples for himself, so Bob's entire first round message $(\mathbf{m}_{B,1}, m_{B,1})$ can now be sent *before* Bob receives his input. The idea is that later on, when Bob learns his input $\mathbf{x}_B$, he will perform Bell measurements on $(\mathbf{x}_B, \mathbf{epr}_2)$ to teleport $\mathbf{x}_B$ into $\mathbf{epr}_1$.

Issue: Incorporating Bob's Teleportation Errors. Teleporting $\mathbf{x}_B$ into $\mathbf{epr}_1$ will require Bob to somehow correct $\mathbf{epr}_1$ later in the protocol using the results of his Bell measurements on $(\mathbf{x}_B, \mathbf{epr}_2)$. But enabling Bob to do this in a way that does not compromise security will be tricky, as we now explain.

After receiving the second round message from Alice in our original malicious 2PQC protocol, Bob learns the output of the classical 2PC, which includes (1) a (classical description of a) quantum garbled circuit $\widetilde{Q}$, and (2) a Clifford unitary W. Bob applies W to Alice's quantum message $\mathbf{m}_{A,2}$, performs the appropriate $\mathbf{0}$ and $\mathbf{T}$ state checks, and conditioned on the checks passing, is left with a state of the form $E_0(\mathbf{x}_A, \mathbf{x}_B, \widehat{\mathbf{T}}, \mathbf{0})$, where $\widehat{\mathbf{T}}$ is a state "somewhat close" to $\mathbf{T}^k$. But at this point in our newly modified protocol, Bob is holding the state $E_0(\mathbf{x}_A, \mathbf{epr}_1, \widehat{\mathbf{T}}, \mathbf{0})$. To restore correctness, we somehow need to modify the protocol so that Bob can apply $X^{x_{\text{inp}}} Z^{z_{\text{inp}}}$ to $\mathbf{epr}_1$ "inside" the E_0 mask, where $x_{\text{inp}}, z_{\text{inp}}$ are the result of Bell basis measurements on $(\mathbf{x}_B, \mathbf{epr}_2)$.

Recall that the structure of W is $W = E_0 \cdot U_{\text{dec-check}}^\dagger$, where E_0 is the input garbling Clifford for the quantum garbled circuit, and $U_{\text{dec-check}}$ is the matrix that undoes $C_{A,\text{in}}$, undoes $C_{B,\text{in}}$, and then applies a permutation π and a random linear map M, and rearranges all the to-be-checked registers to the last few (rightmost) register slots. The multiplication by E_0 is applied only to the non-checked registers.

Thus, it seems like correctness would have to be restored by inserting the unitary $(\mathbb{I} \otimes X^{x_{\text{inp}}} Z^{z_{\text{inp}}} \otimes \mathbb{I})$ in between E_0 and $U_{\text{dec-check}}^\dagger$. But if Bob can learn $E_0(\mathbb{I} \otimes X^{x_{\text{inp}}} Z^{z_{\text{inp}}} \otimes \mathbb{I}) U_{\text{dec-check}}^\dagger$ for even two different values of x_{inp} and z_{inp}, security of the input garbling Clifford E_0 may be lost entirely.

Modification 2: Classical Garbling + Quantum Multi-Key Fully Homomorphic Encryption. In order to resolve this issue, we will split up the matrix $E_0(\mathbb{I} \otimes X^{x_{\text{inp}}} Z^{z_{\text{inp}}} \otimes \mathbb{I}) U_{\text{dec-check}}^\dagger$ into two matrices

$$U_{x_{\text{inp}}, z_{\text{inp}}} := E_0(\mathbb{I} \otimes X^{x_{\text{inp}}} Z^{z_{\text{inp}}} \otimes \mathbb{I}) U_{\text{rand}}^\dagger$$
$$U_{\text{check}} := U_{\text{rand}} U_{\text{dec-check}}^\dagger$$

where U_{rand} is a "re-randomizing" Clifford.

The matrix U_{check} is independent of Bob's teleportation errors, and will now be output to Bob by the classical 2PC. But to preserve security, we will have Bob obtain $U_{x_{\mathrm{inp}}, z_{\mathrm{inp}}}$ by evaluating a *classical* garbled circuit $\widetilde{f}_{\mathrm{inp}}$ where $f_{\mathrm{inp}}(x_{\mathrm{inp}}, z_{\mathrm{inp}}) := U_{x_{\mathrm{inp}}, z_{\mathrm{inp}}}$; the garbled circuit $\widetilde{f}_{\mathrm{inp}}$ is included in the output of the classical 2PC.

But now we are faced with a new problem: how does Bob obtain the (classical) labels for $\widetilde{f}_{\mathrm{inp}}$? Since we only have one round of interaction remaining, Bob won't be able to run an OT to learn the correct labels (Bob could learn the labels by the end of the two online rounds, but then we would still need another round for Bob to send Alice her encrypted output).

We resolve this problem with *quantum multi-key fully-homomorphic encryption* (QMFHE), which we will use in tandem with our classical garbled circuit $\widetilde{f}_{\mathrm{inp}}$ to enable Bob to compute (a homomorphic encryption of) $U_{x_{\mathrm{inp}}, z_{\mathrm{inp}}}$ without leaking anything else. Before we continue, we give a brief, intuition-level recap of QMFHE (we refer the reader to the full version for a formal description). Recall that a standard fully-homomorphic encryption (FHE) allows one to apply arbitrary efficient computation to encrypted data (without needing to first decrypt). *Multi-key* FHE (MFHE) extends FHE to enable computation over multiple ciphertexts encrypted under different keys; the output of such a homomorphic computation is a "multi-key" ciphertext which can only be decrypted given all the secret keys for all of the ciphertexts involved in the computation [33]. Finally, QMFHE extends MFHE a step further to allow arbitrary efficient *quantum* computation over encrypted (classical or quantum) data [1,13,29,34].

We will encrypt each of the garbled circuit labels for $\widetilde{f}_{\mathrm{inp}}$ under an independent QMFHE key. All of these encrypted labels along with the corresponding QMFHE public keys (to enable quantum computations over these ciphertexts) will also be output to Bob as part of the classical 2PC. We remark that this requires a QMFHE scheme where encryptions of classical plaintexts are themselves classical; such schemes are known assuming the quantum hardness of the learning with errors (QLWE) assumption [1].[7]

To recap, Bob obtains from the classical 2PC a collection of QMFHE ciphertexts, one for each of the garbled circuit labels for $\widetilde{f}_{\mathrm{inp}}$. Bob picks out the ciphertexts corresponding to $x_{\mathrm{inp}}, z_{\mathrm{inp}}$ and performs quantum multi-key evaluation of $\widetilde{f}_{\mathrm{inp}}$ over these ciphertexts, obtaining a QMFHE encryption of the output of $\widetilde{f}_{\mathrm{inp}}$, i.e. $\mathsf{QMFHE.Enc}(\mathsf{pk}_{x_{\mathrm{inp}}, z_{\mathrm{inp}}}, U_{x_{\mathrm{inp}}, z_{\mathrm{inp}}})$ where $\mathsf{pk}_{x_{\mathrm{inp}}, z_{\mathrm{inp}}}$ denotes the collection of QMFHE public keys corresponding to $x_{\mathrm{inp}}, z_{\mathrm{inp}}$. The classical 2PC output also includes U_{check} in the clear, which Bob can apply to $\mathbf{m}_{A,2}$ to obtain $U_{\mathrm{rand}}(\mathbf{x}_A, \mathbf{epr}_1, \widehat{\mathbf{T}}, \mathbf{0})$ (after performing appropriate measurement checks). Then Bob can homomorphically compute the ciphertext $\mathsf{QMFHE.Enc}(\mathsf{pk}_{x_{\mathrm{inp}}, z_{\mathrm{inp}}}, E_0(\mathbf{x}_A, \mathbf{x}_B, \widehat{\mathbf{T}}, \mathbf{0}))$, and proceed to homomorphically evaluate his quantum garbled circuit to obtain $\mathsf{QMFHE.Enc}(\mathsf{pk}_{x_{\mathrm{inp}}, z_{\mathrm{inp}}}, (C_{A,\mathrm{out}}(\mathbf{y}_A, \mathbf{0}^\lambda), \mathbf{y}_B))$.

In order for Bob to obtain his final output in the clear, we will have Bob send Alice $x_{\mathrm{inp}}, z_{\mathrm{inp}}$ in the first online round. In response, in the second online round Alice will reply with $\mathsf{sk}_{x_{\mathrm{inp}}, z_{\mathrm{inp}}}$; security of the QMFHE will

---

[7] We only require *leveled* QMFHE, which can be based solely on the QLWE assumption. Unleveled QMFHE requires an additional circularity security assumption.

guarantee that Bob cannot decrypt ciphertexts corresponding to any other choice of the teleportation errors. In the second online round, Bob will send Alice $\mathsf{QMFHE.Enc}(\mathsf{pk}_{x_{\mathrm{inp}},z_{\mathrm{inp}}},(C_{A,\mathrm{out}}(\mathbf{y}_A,\mathbf{0}^\lambda)))$, which she can decrypt to obtain $\mathbf{y}_A$. Finally, Bob produces his output by performing QMFHE decryption with $\mathsf{sk}_{x_{\mathrm{inp}},z_{\mathrm{inp}}}$.

Issue: Simulating a Quantum Garbled Circuit with Unknown Output. At this point, we have a correct protocol whose first round is completely input-independent. However, we will run into issues when attempting to prove malicious security.

The problem arises in the security proof for a malicious Bob. In the original three-round maliciously secure protocol, the simulator is able to extract $\mathbf{x}_B$ from Bob's first round message to Alice; this is done by first extracting $C_{B,\mathrm{in}}$ from Bob's first round classical message for the classical 2PC, and then applying $C_{B,\mathrm{in}}^{-1}$ to Bob's first round quantum message. Extracting $\mathbf{x}_B$ from Bob's first round message to Alice is crucial for proving security, since it enables the simulator to query the ideal functionality on $\mathbf{x}_B$, learn the output $\mathbf{y}_B$, and finally simulate the quantum garbled circuit using Bob's output $\mathbf{y}_B$ before computing Alice's simulated second round message to be sent to Bob. This second round message reveals to Bob the quantum garbled circuit, so it is crucial that the quantum garbled circuit simulator has been executed at this point.

Not surprisingly, this simulation strategy runs into a major problem in our newly modified protocol. Bob's first message is independent of $\mathbf{x}_B$, so the simulator cannot query the ideal functionality, and therefore seemingly cannot simulate the quantum garbled circuit before computing Alice's message, which in particular reveals the quantum garbled circuit to Bob. In summary, the simulator must provide Bob with the quantum garbled circuit (part of Alice's first online round message), *before* it has enough information to extract Bob's input. This appears quite problematic since simulating a garbled circuit certainly requires knowing the output. However, since Bob can only obtain an *encryption* of the output of the garbled circuit after receiving Alice's first message, it is still reasonable to expect that the protocol is secure.

Modification 3: Simulation via Teleportation. We fix this problem through a new technique we call *simulation via teleportation*. The idea is as follows. Instead of running the quantum garbled circuit simulator on the output of the circuit (which the simulator does not yet know), the simulator will first prepare fresh EPR pairs $\mathbf{epr}_1',\mathbf{epr}_2'$ and then run the quantum garbled circuit simulator on $(C_{A,\mathrm{out}}(\mathbf{0},\mathbf{0}^\lambda),\mathbf{epr}_1')$ (where $\mathbf{0}$ takes the place of Alice's input $\mathbf{x}_A$ and $\mathbf{epr}_1'$ takes the place of Bob's output $\mathbf{y}_B$). In the following round, after Bob has teleported over his input state $\mathbf{x}_B$, the simulator will query the ideal functionality, learn $\mathbf{y}_B$, and then *teleport* $\mathbf{y}_B$ *into* $\mathbf{epr}_1'$.

Implementing the final teleportation step requires some care. When the simulator learns $\mathbf{y}_B$, it performs Bell measurements on $(\mathbf{y}_B,\mathbf{epr}_2')$, obtaining measurement outcomes $x_{\mathrm{out}},z_{\mathrm{out}}$. It must then find some way to apply $x_{\mathrm{out}},z_{\mathrm{out}}$ to the state $\mathbf{epr}_1'$ so that Bob can obtain his correct output.

So we further modify the protocol so that the garbled circuit Bob receives from the classical 2PC is modified to output $(C_{A,\text{out}}(\mathbf{y}_A, \mathbf{0}^\lambda), X^{x_{\text{out}}} Z^{z_{\text{out}}} \mathbf{y}_B)$ instead of $(C_{A,\text{out}}(\mathbf{y}_A, \mathbf{0}^\lambda), \mathbf{y}_B)$, as before. That is, in the real protocol, an honest Alice will sample random $x_{\text{out}}, z_{\text{out}}$, and then the 2PC will output the circuit implementing this functionality. Alice will send $x_{\text{out}}, z_{\text{out}}$ to Bob in the second online round, and Bob will first apply Pauli corrections $X^{x_{\text{out}}} Z^{z_{\text{out}}}$ to his output to obtain $\mathbf{y}_B$. In the simulated protocol, however, $x_{\text{out}}, z_{\text{out}}$ are not sampled by the simulator. Instead, they are the result of the simulator's Bell measurements on $(\mathbf{y}_B, \mathbf{epr}_2')$. The simulator thus simulates a garbled circuit that outputs $(C_{A,\text{out}}(\mathbf{0}, \mathbf{0}^\lambda), \mathbf{epr}_1')$, and then sends $x_{\text{out}}, z_{\text{out}}$ in the second online round. Note that this teleportation step occurs *exclusively within the simulation*.

Modification 4: Alice (Equivocally) Commits to Pauli Corrections. To arrive at a fully secure protocol, we need to address one last issue. As currently described, there is nothing that prevents a malicious Alice from misreporting her choice of $x_{\text{out}}, z_{\text{out}}$. This can introduce arbitrary Pauli errors into Bob's output that he has no way of detecting. However, this can easily be fixed using equivocal commitments. That is, Alice inputs $x_{\text{out}}, z_{\text{out}}$ to the classical 2PC, along with commitment randomness s. Bob obtains the commitment as part of the output of the classical 2PC, and later when Alice sends $x_{\text{out}}, z_{\text{out}}$ in the second online round, she must also send along s. The equivocality property enables the simulation strategy to work as before, as the simulator will have the power to send Bob a commitment to an arbitrary value, and after learning $x_{\text{out}}, z_{\text{out}}$ from its Bell measurements, use equivocation to produce a valid opening.

2.8   The Multi-party Setting

In this section, we describe our results in the multi-party setting, filling in the bottom row of Table 1.

We begin by describing our approach to obtaining a five-round protocol from quantum-secure OT. Our approach follows the same high-level idea as the three-message 2PQC protocol described in Sect. 2.4, where one party (the "designated party", or P_1) will evaluate a quantum garbled circuit on encodings of each party's input, and then distribute the encoded outputs to each party. However, implementing this template in the multi-party setting requires resolving a host of new challenges.

Input Encoding. Recall that in our two-party protocol, Alice received an encoding of Bob's input, concatenated their own input, re-randomized the entire set of registers with a random Clifford C, and then sent the re-randomized state to Bob. This re-randomization ensures that the only meaningful computation Bob can perform is to apply the quantum garbled circuit, whose classical description is re-randomized with $C^\dagger$. A natural extension of this idea to the multi-party setting goes as follows. First, each party sends their encoded input to P_1. Then P_1 concatenates all inputs together and re-randomizes the resulting set of registers with their own random Clifford C_1. Then, these registers are passed around in a circle, each party P_i applying their own re-randomizing Clifford C_i. Finally, P_1

receives the fully re-randomized state, along with some classical description of a quantum garbled circuit obtained via classical MPC, and re-randomized with $C_1^\dagger \ldots C_n^\dagger$. The fact that each party applies their own re-randomizing Clifford is necessary, since we are in the dishonest majority setting. Indeed, if only one party P_i is honest, their security will crucially rely on the fact that the adversary does not know their re-randomizing Clifford C_i. This approach of encrypting and sending a state around the circle of parties for re-randomization is similar to [22]'s "input encoding" protocol, in which each individual party's input is sent around the circle of parties for re-randomization.

Unfortunately, the round complexity of this encoding step will grow linearly with the number of parties. To obtain a constant-round protocol, our idea is to round-collapse this input-encoding via the use of quantum teleportation. In the first round, parties will send EPR pairs to each other following the topology of the computation described above. That is, each party sets up EPR pairs with P_1 that will be used to teleport their encoded inputs to P_1, and each consecutive pair of parties will set up EPR pairs that will be used to teleport the encoded state around the circle. After this setup, the parties can *simultaneously* apply re-randomization Cliffords and teleport the encoded state around the circle. This will introduce teleportation errors, but since the re-randomization operations are Clifford, these can be later corrected. Indeed, this correction will be facilitated by a classical MPC protocol that takes as input each party's Clifford and set of teleportation errors.

0 and T State Checks. The next challenge is how to enforce 0 and T state checks in the multi-party setting. Recall that in the two-party setting, we had the non-evaluator party (Alice) prepare the 0 and T states, which were then checked by the garbled circuit evaluator (Bob). This approach works because we know that if Alice is malicious and tried to cheat during preparation of these states, then Bob must be honest and will then refuse to evaluate the garbled circuit. However, this does not carry over to the multi-party setting. If we try to fix some party P_i to prepare the 0 and T states and then have the evaluator P_1 check them, it may be the case that *both* P_i and P_1 are malicious, which would be problematic.

Thus, we take a different approach, instructing P_1 to prepare the 0 and T states, and designing a *distributed* checking protocol, similar to that of [22]. We now briefly describe the T state check, leaving a description of the 0 state check to the body. P_1 will be instructed to concatenate all parties' inputs with their own T states, and then send the resulting state around the circle for re-randomization. Later, they receive the re-randomized state, along with a unitary from the classical MPC that i) undoes the re-randomization, ii) samples a different subset of T states for each party, iii) Clifford-encodes each subset, and iv) garbles the inputs together with the remaining T states. Thus, P_1 obtains n encoded subsets of T states, and is supposed to send one to each party. Each party will then receive their encoded subset, decode (using information obtained from the classical MPC), and measure in the T-basis. Each party will then abort the protocol if their check failed. Only if *no* parties abort will the classical MPC send information to each party allowing them to decrypt their output from the quantum garbled circuit. It is crucial that *no* party receives output until all honest parties indicate that their T state check passed, because using malformed T states in the quantum garbled circuit could result in outputs that leak information about honest party inputs.

The Five-Round Protocol. We give a high-level overview of the five rounds of the protocol.

- Round 1: Each party P_i generates EPR pairs and sends half of each pair to its neighbor P_{i+1}. Additionally, party P_1 generates enough EPR pairs so that it can send EPR pair halves to every other party P_i for $i \neq 1$.
- Round 2: Teleport inputs to P_1 and teleport the resulting state around the circle (with re-randomization Cliffords C_i applied along the way). Input teleportation errors and $\{C_i\}_{i \in [n]}$ to the classical MPC.
- Round 3: Classical MPC delivers unitary to P_1 that samples subsets of T states and garbles inputs, along with classical description of the quantum garbled circuit.
- Round 4: P_1 evaluates the unitary and garbled circuit, then delivers encoded subsets of T states and encrypted outputs to each party.
- Round 5: If no parties abort after their T state check, the classical MPC delivers key to each party allowing them to decrypt their output.

Note that the distributed T state check is the reason that the protocol requires five rounds. The first round is used for setting up EPR pairs. At this point the parties can perform quantum teleportation and obtain their Pauli errors. Now, these must be corrected by the classical MPC, which takes a minimum of two rounds. Thus, P_1 can only obtain output from the MPC, and thus from the quantum garbled circuit, after Round 3. Then, Round 4 must be used to distribute subsets of T states, and Round 5 must be used to deliver decryption keys conditioned on all parties being happy with their T states. As we describe in the body, the actual computation of the garbled circuit can be delayed one round (at the cost of settling for security with abort rather than unanimous abort), giving a five-round protocol with three online rounds.

Now we discuss how to instantiate the classical MPC. We are going to need an MPC that supports *reactive* functionalities, where inputs may depend on previous outputs obtained from the MPC. Moreover, we need the MPC to be *round-optimal*, in the sense that outputs delivered in round i may depend on inputs from round $i - 1$. We observe that the round-collapsing compiler of [26] gives exactly this—an $\ell + 1$ round MPC for a reactive functionality with ℓ rounds of output. Thus, we can rely solely on quantum-secure two-message OT to construct the above five-round quantum MPC.

The Four-Round Protocol. Finally, we observe that there is some slack in the aforementioned protocol. Indeed, P_1 does not obtain any output from the classical MPC until after round 3, when in principle the classical MPC can be used to compute some output in only two rounds. The reason we waited three rounds is that we wanted to include the parties' teleportation errors in the computation performed by the MPC, and these are not known until the beginning of the second round.

However, we can use ideas similar to those in Sect. 2.7 in order to allow the MPC to compute something meaningful during the first two rounds without yet knowing the teleportation errors. In particular, we make use of classical garbled circuits and quantum multi-key FHE to provide a mechanism by which the classical MPC can output information allowing P_1 to (homomorphically) compute a function of the teleportation errors after Round 2. This allows us to collapse the total number of required rounds to 4. Moreover, a similar idea allows the parties to delay teleportation of their inputs another round, giving a four-round protocol with (optimal) *two* rounds of online interaction. Equivalently, our protocol can be seen as two-round MPQC in a quantum pre-processing model.

2.9   Two Round 2PQC Without Pre-processing: Challenges and Possibilities

In this section, we explore the possibility of achieving a two-round 2PQC protocol in the CRS model *without pre-processing*. We stress that this model *does not permit pre-shared entanglement* between the two parties, as we consider sharing of entanglement to be a pre-processing step.

The Challenge of Oblivious Simulation. In the classical setting, all known two-round two-party computation protocols (in the CRS model) can be modified so that security is proven via (what we call) an *oblivious simulator*.[8] That is, the simulator (1) only makes black-box queries to the adversary, (2) is straight-line (meaning it only runs the adversary a single time without rewinding), and (3) it generates the simulated CRS *independently of the choice of corrupted party* (between Alice and Bob).

By focusing on protocols with oblivious simulation, we can highlight an apparent difficulty of building secure two-round protocols for quantum functionalities in the CRS model. Assume without loss of generality that Alice is adversarial (the identical argument applies to Bob). Observe that if the first message that Alice sends is not computationally binding to her input $\mathbf{x}_A$, she can potentially cheat by *equivocating*, i.e. acting as if she had received a different input, and subsequently learn multiple outputs of the functionality. If the simulation is oblivious, then this reasoning applies simultaneously to Alice and Bob—that is, both parties must, in the first round, send computationally-binding commitments to their respective inputs. This is immediately problematic for quantum inputs, since no-cloning implies that their leftover states will have no (computationally) useful information about their original inputs. Thus, it is unclear how a general computation can be performed on their *joint* inputs before

---

[8] Each party will use a NIZK proof of knowledge to prove that their first message is well-formed, using their input and randomness as witness. Then, a simulator programming the CRS may extract either party's input.

the start of the second round, as the parties have effectively swapped their initial states. And somehow, after just one more round of messaging, they must hold their correctly computed output states.

Our negative result formalizes this intuitive difficulty. If the simulator is oblivious, then by roughly following the above reasoning, at the end of the first round:

- Alice holds a computationally binding commitment to Bob's input x_B,
- Bob holds a computationally binding commitment to Alice's input x_A, and
- Neither party has information about their original inputs.

Moreover, the correctness of oblivious simulation implies that for a computationally indistinguishable CRS, there exists a "trapdoor" that would enable Alice to extract x_B and would enable Bob to extract x_A. But now their states can be viewed as the states of two parties at the *beginning of a one-round protocol with polynomial-size pre-processing* in which the parties' inputs are *swapped*; the pre-processing step is necessary to give both parties the trapdoor information of the simulator. The resulting one-round protocol no longer satisfies any meaningful security guarantees, but crucially, it still satisfies correctness. Moreover, the one-round protocol falls into a model of "instantaneous non-local computation" that has been previously studied in the quantum information literature [10]. It is currently open whether this model enables general quantum computation with only polynomial-size preprocessing, and a positive result for two-round 2PQC with oblivious simulation would affirmatively answer this question.

A Proof-of-Concept Construction from Quantum VBB Obfuscation. Given the above barrier, one could attempt to construct a two-round protocol whose security relies crucially on a *non-oblivious* simulation strategy. In this work, we take an initial step in this direction by providing a proof-of-concept construction from a strong form of quantum VBB obfuscation that handles obfuscation of quantum circuits that include both unitary gates and measurement gates (further discussion is available in the full version).

In our construction, Alice will send an encryption of her input to Bob in round 1, who will then homomorphically compute the functionality over their joint inputs and respond with Alice's encrypted output in round 2. Alice will also send a message in round 2 that allows Bob to decrypt his output. However, the key is that this interaction will actually be indistinguishable from an interaction in which the *opposite* flow of computation is occuring. In particular, if the CRS if sampled differently (but in an indistinguishable way), it will be the case that Bob is actually sending his encrypted input to Alice in the first round, and then Alice homomorphically computes the functionality and sends Bob's encrypted output back in the second round.

To instantiate this template, we provide a number of quantum obfuscations in the CRS, three per party. First, there are the "input" obfuscations $\mathcal{O}_{A,\mathsf{inp}}$ and $\mathcal{O}_{B,\mathsf{inp}}$. $\mathcal{O}_{A,\mathsf{inp}}$ will take as input Alice's input x_A along with a "dummy" input d_A, and output Clifford encodings of each. Alice is instructed to send the first output of this obfuscation as her first message, and keep the second output as her state. In the real protocol, the obfuscated functionality will be such that the first output will be the Clifford encoding of the first input (Alice's real input $\mathbf{x}_A$), and the second output will be the Clifford encoding of the second input (Alice's dummy input $\mathbf{d}_A$). On the other hand, $\mathcal{O}_{B,\text{inp}}$ will obfuscate the functionality that does the exact opposite, setting its first output to be a Clifford encoding of its second input, and its second output to be a Clifford encodings of its first input. Thus, in round 1, Alice sends a Clifford encoding of her real input and keeps a Clifford encoding of her dummy input in her state, while Bob sends a Clifford encoding of his dummy input and keeps a Clifford encoding of his real input in his state.

The next obfuscations $\mathcal{O}_{A,\text{cmp}}$ and $\mathcal{O}_{B,\text{cmp}}$ share secret randomness with the input obfuscations (in the form of PRF keys) and can thus decrypt Clifford encodings output by the input obfuscations. They each are defined to decrypt and check the authenticity of their inputs, apply the functionality Q that the parties wish to compute, and then encode the outputs with freshly sampled Cliffords. Each party will run their respective obfuscation on their state and the other party's first round message. Note that then Alice is just using $\mathcal{O}_{A,\text{cmp}}$ to compute Q over dummy inputs, while Bob is using $\mathcal{O}_{B,\text{cmp}}$ to compute Q over their real inputs. Alice will send an encrypted dummy output to Bob in round 2, while Bob will send an encrypted real output to Alice.

Finally, each party applies their respective output obfuscation $\mathcal{O}_{A,\text{out}}$ and $\mathcal{O}_{B,\text{out}}$ to their final state and other party's second round message. $\mathcal{O}_{A,\text{out}}$ will ignore Alice's state (which contains Alice's dummy output) and decrypt and output Bob's second round message (which contains Alice's real output). On the other hand, $\mathcal{O}_{B,\text{out}}$ will ignore Alice's second round message and decrypt and output Bob's state.

Now, it is possible to argue (under the assumption that the obfuscations in the CRS are in fact VBB obfuscations) that, because all intermediate states and messages are Clifford-encoded, "switching the direction" of the input and output obfuscations cannot be noticed by the parties. Note that if each of $\mathcal{O}_{A,\text{inp}}$ and $\mathcal{O}_{B,\text{inp}}$ are re-defined to permute the order of their outputs, then the flow of computation will be completely reversed. In particular, Alice will be computing the functionality over real inputs with $\mathcal{O}_{A,\text{cmp}}$, and Bob will be computing the functionality over dummy inputs with $\mathcal{O}_{B,\text{cmp}}$. Thus, depending on how the simulator programs the CRS, it can either extract directly from Alice's first round message OR it can extract directly from Bob's first round message, but it could never extract from both simultaneously.

Thus, this template represents a potential method for securely computing a quantum functionality in two rounds, where one of the two parties actually performs the computation between rounds 1 and 2 and then distributes the output in round 2. In other words, it is an instantiation of our guiding principle mentioned in Sect. 2.6 in a model without pre-processing.

3 Quantum Non-interactive Secure Computation

3.1 Useful Lemmas

Lemma 1 (Magic State Distillation [16,22]). *Let $p(\cdot)$ be a polynomial. Then there exists a* $\mathrm{poly}(\lambda)$ *size* $\mathsf{C} + \mathsf{M}$ *circuit Q from $\lambda p(\lambda)$ input qubits to $p(\lambda)$ output qubits such that the following holds. Take any state $\mathbf{x}$ on $\lambda p(\lambda) + \lambda$ qubits. Apply a uniformly random permutation to the registers of $\mathbf{x}$ and then measure the final λ qubits in the T-basis to obtain a bitstring s. Let $\widetilde{\mathbf{x}}$ be the remaining $\lambda p(\lambda)$ registers. Then there exist negligible functions μ, ν such that*

$$\Pr\left[(s = 0) \wedge \left(\left\|Q(\widetilde{\mathbf{x}}) - \mathbf{T}^{p(\lambda)}\right\|_1 > \mu(\lambda)\right)\right] \le \nu(\lambda).$$

Proof. This follows from applying [22, Lemma I.1] with parameters $n = \lambda p(\lambda)$, $k = \lambda$, $\delta = 1/2$ followed by [22, Lemma 2.7] with parameters $m = \lambda p(\lambda)$, $\ell = m/2, t = p(\lambda)$.

Lemma 2 ([22]). *For any $n \in \mathbb{N}$ and projector Π on $2n$ qubits, define the quantum channel $\mathcal{L}^{\Pi}$ by*

$$\mathcal{L}^{\Pi}(\mathbf{x}) := \Pi \mathbf{x} \Pi + |\bot\rangle \langle \bot| \mathrm{Tr}[(\mathbb{I}^{2n} - \Pi)\mathbf{x}],$$

where $|\bot\rangle$ is a distinguished state on $2n$ qubits with $\Pi|\bot\rangle = 0$. For any $t \in \{0,1\}^n$, let $\Pi_{t,\mathsf{Full}} := |0^{2n}\rangle \langle 0^{2n}|$ if $t = 0^n$ and $\Pi_{t,\mathsf{Full}} := 0$ otherwise. Let $\Pi_{t,\mathsf{Half}} := \mathbb{I}^n \otimes |t\rangle \langle t|$. Then for any QRV $\mathbf{x}$ on $2n$ registers and $t \in \{0,1\}^n$,

$$\left\| \mathcal{L}^{\Pi_{t,\mathsf{Full}}}(\mathbf{x}) - \mathop{\mathbb{E}}_{U \leftarrow \mathsf{GL}(2n, \mathbb{F}_2)} \left[\mathcal{L}^{\Pi_{t,\mathsf{Half}}}(U(\mathbf{x}))\right] \right\|_1 = \mathrm{negl}(n).$$

3.2 The Protocol

In what follows, we describe our protocol for two-party quantum computation in the setting of sequential messages. This protocol requires three messages of interaction when both players desire output, and two messages in a setting where only one party obtains an output, which can be seen as a Q-NISC (Quantum Non-interactive Secure Computation) protocol.

Ingredients. Our protocol will make use of the following cryptographic primitives: (1) Quantum-secure two-message two-party classical computation in the CRS model ($2\mathsf{PC.Gen}, 2\mathsf{PC}_1, 2\mathsf{PC}_2, 2\mathsf{PC}_{\mathsf{out}}$) with a straight-line black-box simulator (see Sect. 3.4 of the full version), and (2) a garbling scheme for $\mathsf{C} + \mathsf{M}$ circuits ($\mathsf{QGarble}, \mathsf{QGEval}, \mathsf{QGSim}$). (see Sect. 4 of the full version).

Notation. The protocol below computes a two-party quantum functionality represented by a $\mathsf{C}+\mathsf{M}$ circuit Q that takes n_A+n_B input qubits, produces m_A+m_B output qubits, and requires n_Z auxiliary **0** states and n_T auxiliary **T** states. Let λ be the security parameter. The total number of quantum registers used will be $s = n_A + (n_B + \lambda) + (2n_Z + \lambda) + (n_T + 1)\lambda$, and we'll give a name to different groups of these registers.

Given a $\mathsf{C}+\mathsf{M}$ circuit Q and a Clifford $C_{\mathsf{out}} \in \mathscr{C}_{m_A+\lambda}$, we define another $\mathsf{C}+\mathsf{M}$ circuit $Q_{\mathsf{dist}}[C_{\mathsf{out}}]$. This circuit takes as input $n_A + n_B + n_Z + \lambda + n_T\lambda$ qubits $(\mathbf{x}_A, \mathbf{x}_B, \mathbf{z}_{\mathsf{inp}}, \mathsf{trap}_A, \mathbf{t}_{\mathsf{inp}})$ on registers $(\mathsf{A}, \mathsf{B}, \mathsf{Z}_{\mathsf{inp}}, \mathsf{Trap}_A, \mathsf{T}_{\mathsf{inp}})$. It will first apply the magic state distillation circuit from Lemma 1 with parameters $(n_T\lambda, \lambda)$ to $\mathbf{t}_{\mathsf{inp}}$ to produce QRV $\mathbf{t}$ of size n_T. It will then run Q on $(\mathbf{x}_A, \mathbf{x}_B, \mathbf{z}_{\mathsf{inp}}, \mathbf{t})$ to produce $(\mathbf{y}_A, \mathbf{y}_B)$. Finally, it will output $(C_{\mathsf{out}}(\mathbf{y}_A, \mathsf{trap}_A), \mathbf{y}_B)$ (Fig. 1).

Protocol 1: Classical Functionality $\mathcal{F}[Q]$

Common Information: Security parameter λ, and $\mathsf{C}+\mathsf{M}$ circuit Q to be computed with $n_A + n_B$ input qubits, $m_A + m_B$ output qubits, n_Z auxiliary **0** states, and n_T auxiliary **T** states. Let $s = n_A + (n_B + \lambda) + (2n_Z + \lambda) + (n_T + 1)\lambda$.

Party A Input: Classical descriptions of $C_A \in \mathscr{C}_s$ and $C_{\mathsf{out}} \in \mathscr{C}_{m_A+\lambda}$.
Party B Input: Classical description of $C_B \in \mathscr{C}_{n_B+\lambda}$.

The Functionality:

1. Sample the unitary $U_{\mathsf{dec-check}}$ as follows:
   - Sample a random permutation π on $(n_T + 1)\lambda$ elements.
   - Sample a random element $M \leftarrow \mathsf{GL}(2n_T, \mathbb{F}_2)$.
   - Compute a description of the Clifford U_{check} that operates as follows on registers $(\mathsf{A}, \mathsf{B}, \mathsf{Trap}_B, \mathsf{Z}_A, \mathsf{Trap}_A, \mathsf{T}_A)$.
     (a) Rearrange the registers of T_A according to the permutation π and then partition the registers into $(\mathsf{T}_{\mathsf{inp}}, \mathsf{T}_{\mathsf{check}})$.
     (b) Apply the linear map M to the registers Z_A and then partition the registers into $(\mathsf{Z}_{\mathsf{inp}}, \mathsf{Z}_{\mathsf{check}})$.
     (c) Re-arrange the registers to $(\mathsf{A}, \mathsf{B}, \mathsf{Z}_{\mathsf{inp}}, \mathsf{Trap}_A, \mathsf{T}_{\mathsf{inp}}, \mathsf{Z}_{\mathsf{check}}, \mathsf{Trap}_B, \mathsf{T}_{\mathsf{check}})$.
   - Define $U_{\mathsf{dec-check}}$ as:

   $$U_{\mathsf{dec-check}} := U_{\mathsf{check}} \left(\mathbb{I}^{n_A} \otimes C_B^\dagger \otimes \mathbb{I}^{(2n_Z+\lambda)+(n_T+1)\lambda} \right) C_A^\dagger.$$

2. Sample $(E_0, D_0, \widetilde{g}_1, \ldots, \widetilde{g}_d) \leftarrow \mathsf{QGarble}(1^\lambda, Q_{\mathsf{dist}}[C_{\mathsf{out}}])$.
3. Compute a description of $U_{\mathsf{dec-check-enc}} := \left(E_0 \otimes \mathbb{I}^{(n_Z+\lambda)+\lambda} \right) U_{\mathsf{dec-check}}^\dagger$.

Party B Output: (1) A unitary $U_{\mathsf{dec-check-enc}}$ on s qubits (to be applied on registers $(\mathsf{A}, \mathsf{B}, \mathsf{Trap}_B, \mathsf{Z}_A, \mathsf{Trap}_A, \mathsf{T}_A)$), and (2) A QGC $(D_0, \widetilde{g}_1, \ldots, \widetilde{g}_d)$ (to be applied to registers $(\mathsf{A}, \mathsf{B}, \mathsf{Z}_{\mathsf{inp}}, \mathsf{Trap}_A, \mathsf{T}_{\mathsf{inp}})$).

Fig. 1. Classical functionality to be used in Protocol 2.

Protocol 2: Three-message two-party quantum computation

Common Information: (1) Security parameter λ, and (2) a $\mathsf{C} + \mathsf{M}$ circuit Q over $n_A + n_B$ input qubits, $m_A + m_B$ output qubits, n_Z auxiliary $\mathbf{0}$ states, and n_T auxiliary $\mathbf{T}$ states. Let $s = n_A + (n_B + \lambda) + (2n_Z + \lambda) + (n_T + 1)\lambda$.

Party A Input: $\mathbf{x}_A$
Party B Input: $\mathbf{x}_B$

The Protocol:
Setup. Run classical 2PC setup: $\mathsf{crs} \leftarrow 2\mathsf{PC.Gen}(1^\lambda)$.

Round 1. *Party B:*

1. Sample $C_B \leftarrow \mathscr{C}_{n_B + \lambda}$ and compute $\mathbf{m}_{B,1} := C_B(\mathbf{x}_B, \mathbf{0}^\lambda)$.
2. Compute $(m_{B,1}, \mathsf{st}) \leftarrow 2\mathsf{PC}_1(1^\lambda, \mathcal{F}[Q], \mathsf{crs}, C_B)$.
3. Send to Party A: $(m_{B,1}, \mathbf{m}_{B,1})$.

Round 2. *Party A:*

1. Sample $C_A \leftarrow \mathscr{C}_s$ and $C_{\mathsf{out}} \leftarrow \mathscr{C}_{m_A + \lambda}$.
2. Compute $\mathbf{m}_{A,2} := C_A(\mathbf{x}_A, \mathbf{m}_{B,1}, \mathbf{0}^{2n_Z}, \mathbf{0}^\lambda, \mathbf{T}^{(n_T+1)\lambda})$.
3. Compute $m_{A,2} \leftarrow 2\mathsf{PC}_2(1^\lambda, \mathcal{F}[Q], \mathsf{crs}, m_{B,1}, (C_A, C_{\mathsf{out}}))$.
4. Send to Party B: $(m_{A,2}, \mathbf{m}_{A,2})$.

Round 3. *Party B:*

1. Compute $(U_{\mathsf{dec-check-enc}}, D_0, \tilde{g}_1, \dots, \tilde{g}_d) \leftarrow 2\mathsf{PC}_{\mathsf{out}}(1^\lambda, \mathsf{st}, m_{A,2})$.
2. Compute $(\mathbf{m}_{\mathsf{inp}}, \mathbf{z}_{\mathsf{check}}, \mathbf{trap}_B, \mathbf{t}_{\mathsf{check}}) := U_{\mathsf{dec-check-enc}}(\mathbf{m}_2)$, where
   - $\mathbf{m}_{\mathsf{inp}}$ is on registers $(\mathsf{A}, \mathsf{B}, \mathsf{Z}_{\mathsf{inp}}, \mathsf{Trap}_A, \mathsf{T}_{\mathsf{inp}})$,
   - $(\mathbf{z}_{\mathsf{check}}, \mathbf{trap}_B, \mathbf{t}_{\mathsf{check}})$ is on registers $(\mathsf{Z}_{\mathsf{check}}, \mathsf{Trap}_B, \mathsf{T}_{\mathsf{check}})$.
3. Measure each qubit of $(\mathbf{z}_{\mathsf{check}}, \mathbf{trap}_B)$ in the standard basis and abort if any measurement is not zero.
4. Measure each qubit of $\mathbf{t}_{\mathsf{check}}$ in the T-basis and abort if any measurement is not zero.
5. Compute $(\widehat{\mathbf{y}}_A, \mathbf{y}_B) \leftarrow \mathsf{QGEval}((D_0, \tilde{g}_1, \dots, \tilde{g}_d), \mathbf{m}_{\mathsf{inp}})$, where $\widehat{\mathbf{y}}_A$ consists of $m_A + \lambda$ qubits and $\mathbf{y}_B$ consists of m_B qubits.
6. Send to Party A: $\widehat{\mathbf{y}}_A$.

Output Reconstruction.

- *Party A:* Compute $(\mathbf{y}_A, \mathbf{trap}_A) := C_{\mathsf{out}}^\dagger(\widehat{\mathbf{y}}_A)$, where $\mathbf{y}_A$ consists of m_A qubits and $\mathbf{trap}_A$ consists of λ qubits. Measure each qubit of $\mathbf{trap}_A$ in the standard basis and abort if any measurement is not zero. Otherwise, output $\mathbf{y}_A$.
- *Party B:* Output $\mathbf{y}_B$.

Fig. 2. Three-message two-party quantum computation.

3.3 Security

Theorem 5. *Assuming post-quantum maliciously-secure two-message oblivious transfer, there exists maliciously-secure NISC for quantum computation and maliciously-secure three-message two-party quantum computation.*

Proof. Let Π be the protocol described in Protocol 2 computing some quantum circuit Q. Here, we only show security against a malicious party A and defer the remainder of the proof to the full version.

The simulator. Consider any QPT adversary $\mathsf{Adv} = \{\mathsf{Adv}_\lambda\}_{\lambda \in \mathbb{N}}$ corrupting party A. The simulator Sim is defined as follows. Whenever we say that the simulator aborts, we mean that it sends $\perp$ to the ideal functionality and to the adversary. $\mathsf{Sim}^{\mathcal{I}[\mathbf{x}_B](\cdot)}(\mathbf{x}_A, \mathbf{aux}_{\mathsf{Adv}})$:

- Compute $(crs, \tau, m_{B,1}) \leftarrow 2\mathsf{PC}.\mathsf{Sim}_A^{(1)}(1^\lambda)$, sample $C_B \leftarrow \mathscr{C}_{n_B + \lambda}$, compute $m_{B,1} := C_B(0^{n_B}, 0^\lambda)$, and send $(crs, m_{B,1}, \mathbf{m}_{B,1})$ to $\mathsf{Adv}_\lambda(\mathbf{x}_A, \mathbf{aux}_{\mathsf{Adv}})$.
- Receive $(m_{A,2}, \mathbf{m}_{A,2})$ from Adv_λ and compute out $\leftarrow 2\mathsf{PC}.\mathsf{Sim}_A^{(1)}(1^\lambda, \tau, m_{A,2})$. If out $= \perp$ then abort. Otherwise, parse out as (C_A, C_{out}).
- Using (C_A, C_B), sample $U_{\mathsf{dec-check}}$ as in the description of $\mathcal{F}[Q]$. Compute

$$(\mathbf{x}_A', \mathbf{x}_B', \mathbf{z}_{\mathsf{inp}}, \mathsf{trap}_A, \mathsf{t}_{\mathsf{inp}}, \mathbf{z}_{\mathsf{check}}, \mathsf{trap}_B, \mathsf{t}_{\mathsf{check}}) := U_{\mathsf{dec-check}}(\mathbf{m}_{A,2}).$$

Measure each qubit of $\mathbf{z}_{\mathsf{check}}$ and trap_B in the standard basis and each qubit of $\mathsf{t}_{\mathsf{check}}$ in the T-basis. If any measurement is non-zero, then abort.
- Forward $\mathbf{x}_A'$ to $\mathcal{I}[\mathbf{x}_B](\cdot)$ and receive back $\mathbf{y}_A$. Compute $\widehat{\mathbf{y}}_A := C_{\mathsf{out}}(\mathbf{y}_A, \mathsf{trap}_A)$, send $\widehat{\mathbf{y}}_A$ to Adv_λ, send ok to $\mathcal{I}[\mathbf{x}_B]$, and output the output of Adv_λ.

We consider a sequence of hybrid distributions, where the first hybrid $\mathcal{H}_0$ is $\mathsf{REAL}_{\Pi,\mathsf{Q}}(\mathsf{Adv}_\lambda, \mathbf{x}_A, \mathbf{x}_B, \mathbf{aux}_{\mathsf{Adv}})$, i.e. the real interaction between the adversary $\mathsf{Adv}_\lambda(\mathbf{x}_A, \mathbf{aux}_{\mathsf{Adv}})$ and an honest party $B(1^\lambda, \mathbf{x}_B)$. In each hybrid, we describe the differences from the previous hybrid.

- $\mathcal{H}_1$: Simulate 2PC as described in Sim, using $2\mathsf{PC}.\mathsf{Sim}_A^{(1)}$ to compute $m_{B,1}$ and $2\mathsf{PC}.\mathsf{Sim}_A^{(2)}$ to extract an input (C_A, C_{out}) (or abort). Use (C_A, C_{out}) to sample an output $(U_{\mathsf{dec-check-enc}}, D_0, \widetilde{g}_1, \ldots, \widetilde{g}_d)$ of the classical functionality. Use this output to run party B's honest Message 3 algorithm.
- $\mathcal{H}_2$: In this hybrid, we change how B's third round message $\widehat{\mathbf{y}}_A$ is sampled. In particular, rather than evaluating the quantum garbled circuit on $\mathbf{m}_{\mathsf{inp}}$, we will directly evaluate $Q_{\mathsf{dist}}[C_{\mathsf{out}}]$ on the input. In more detail, given $\mathbf{m}_{A,2}$ returned by Adv_λ, (C_A, C_{out}) extracted from Adv_λ, and C_B sampled in Message 1, $\widehat{\mathbf{y}}_A$ is sampled as follows. Sample $U_{\mathsf{dec-check}}$ as in Step 1 of $\mathcal{F}[Q]$. Compute

$$(\mathbf{x}_A', \mathbf{x}_B', \mathbf{z}_{\mathsf{inp}}, \mathsf{trap}_A, \mathsf{t}_{\mathsf{inp}}, \mathbf{z}_{\mathsf{check}}, \mathsf{trap}_B, \mathsf{t}_{\mathsf{check}}) := U_{\mathsf{dec-check}}(\mathbf{m}_{A,2})$$

and carry out the checks on $\mathbf{z}_{\mathsf{check}}, \mathsf{trap}_B, \mathsf{t}_{\mathsf{check}}$ as described in Steps 3.(c) and 3.(d) of Protocol 2, aborting if needed. Then, compute

$$(\widehat{\mathbf{y}}_A, \mathbf{y}_B) \leftarrow Q_{\mathsf{dist}}[C_{\mathsf{out}}](\mathbf{x}_A', \mathbf{x}_B', \mathbf{z}_{\mathsf{inp}}, \mathsf{trap}_A, \mathsf{t}_{\mathsf{inp}})$$

and return $\widehat{\mathbf{y}}_A$ to Adv_λ.
- $\mathcal{H}_3$: Compute $m_{B,1}$ as $C_B(0^{n_B}, 0^\lambda)$, and substitute $\mathbf{x}_B$ for $\mathbf{x}_B'$ before applying $Q_{\mathsf{dist}}[C_{\mathsf{out}}]$ to the registers described above in $\mathcal{H}_2$.

- $\mathcal{H}_4$: Rather than directly computing $Q_{\text{dist}}[C_{\text{out}}]$, query the ideal functionality with $\mathbf{x}'_A$, receive $\mathbf{y}_A$, and send $\widehat{\mathbf{y}}_A := C_{\text{out}}(\mathbf{y}_A, \text{trap}_A)$ to Adv_λ. This hybrid is $\text{IDEAL}_{\Pi, Q, A}(\text{Sim}, \boldsymbol{\rho}_\lambda, \mathbf{x}_A, \mathbf{x}_B, \text{aux})$.

We show indistinguishability between each pair of hybrids.

- $\mathcal{H}_0 \approx_c \mathcal{H}_1$: This follows from the security against corrupted A of 2PC.
- $\mathcal{H}_1 \approx_s \mathcal{H}_2$: This follows from the statistical correctness of QGC.
- $\mathcal{H}_2 \approx_s \mathcal{H}_3$: First, by the security of the Clifford authentication code, conditioned on all measurements of qubits in trap_B returning 0, we have that $\mathbf{x}'_B \approx_s \mathbf{x}_B$. Next, switching $\mathbf{x}_B$ to $\mathbf{0}^{n_B}$ in B's first message is perfectly indistinguishable due to the perfect hiding of the Clifford authentication code.
- $\mathcal{H}_3 \approx_s \mathcal{H}_4$: First, by Lemma 2, conditioned on all measurements of qubits in $\mathbf{z}_{\text{check}}$ returning 0, we have that $\mathbf{z}_{\text{inp}} \approx_s \mathbf{0}^{n_Z}$.
  Next, the above observation, along with Lemma 1, implies that, conditioned on all T-basis measurements of qubits in $\mathbf{t}_{\text{check}}$ returning 0, it holds that the output of $Q_{\text{dist}}[C_{\text{out}}](\mathbf{x}'_A, \mathbf{x}_B, \mathbf{z}_{\text{inp}}, \text{trap}_A, \mathbf{t}_{\text{inp}})$ is statistically close to the result of computing $(\mathbf{y}_A, \mathbf{y}_B) \leftarrow Q(\mathbf{x}'_A, \mathbf{x}_B, \mathbf{0}^{n_Z}, \mathbf{T}^{n_T})$ and returning $(C_{\text{out}}(\mathbf{y}_A, \text{trap}_A), \mathbf{y}_B)$. This is precisely what is being computed in $\mathcal{H}_4$.

On Reusable Security against Malicious A. We remark that the two-message special case of the above protocol, that is, our Quantum NISC protocol, can be lightly modified to also achieve *reusable* security. A reusable classical NISC protocol (see, e.g. [17]) retains security against malicious A in a setting where A and B execute many instances of secure computation that *reuse* the first message of B. A natural quantum analogue of this protocol enables computation of quantum circuits while guaranteeing security against malicious A, in a setting where A and B execute many instances of secure computation that *reuse* the first message of B. Here we assume that B's input is classical, and so functionality will hold over repeated executions. We note that our protocol can be lightly modified to achieve reusable security against malicious A, by replacing the underlying classical 2PC with a reusable classical 2PC. The proof of security remains identical, except that the indistinguishability between hybrids 0 and 1 relies on the reusable security of the underlying classical two-party computation protocol. In the full version, we discuss how to achieve reusable MDV-NIZKs for NP, which can be viewed as a special case of reusable Q-NISC.

References

1. Agarwal, A., Bartusek, J., Goyal, V., Khurana, D., Malavolta, G.: Post-quantum multi-party computation. In: Canteaut, A., Standaert, F.-X. (eds.) EUROCRYPT 2021. LNCS, vol. 12696, pp. 435–464. Springer, Cham (2021). https://doi.org/10.1007/978-3-030-77870-5_16
2. Alagic, G., Brakerski, Z., Dulek, Y., Schaffner, C.: Impossibility of quantum virtual black-box obfuscation of classical circuits. arXiv preprint arXiv:2005.06432 (2020)
3. Alagic, G., Fefferman, B.: On quantum obfuscation. ArXiv abs/1602.01771 (2016)

4. Alon, B., Chung, H., Chung, K.M., Huang, M.Y., Lee, Y., Shen, Y.C.: Round efficient secure multiparty quantum computation with identifiable abort. Cryptology ePrint Archive, Report 2020/1464 (2020). https://eprint.iacr.org/2020/1464
5. Ananth, P., Choudhuri, A.R., Jain, A.: A new approach to round-optimal secure multiparty computation. In: Katz, J., Shacham, H. (eds.) CRYPTO 2017, Part I. LNCS, vol. 10401, pp. 468–499. Springer, Cham (2017). https://doi.org/10.1007/978-3-319-63688-7_16
6. Ananth, P., La Placa, R.L.: Secure software leasing. arXiv preprint arXiv:2005.05289 (2020)
7. Badrinarayanan, S., Goyal, V., Jain, A., Kalai, Y.T., Khurana, D., Sahai, A.: Promise zero knowledge and its applications to round optimal MPC. In: Shacham, H., Boldyreva, A. (eds.) CRYPTO 2018, Part II. LNCS, vol. 10992, pp. 459–487. Springer, Cham (2018). https://doi.org/10.1007/978-3-319-96881-0_16
8. Barak, B., et al.: On the (Im)possibility of Obfuscating Programs. In: Kilian, J. (ed.) CRYPTO 2001. LNCS, vol. 2139, pp. 1–18. Springer, Heidelberg (2001). https://doi.org/10.1007/3-540-44647-8_1
9. Beaver, D., Micali, S., Rogaway, P.: The round complexity of secure protocols (extended abstract). In: 22nd ACM STOC, pp. 503–513. ACM Press, May 1990
10. Beigi, S., Koenig, R.: Simplified instantaneous non-local quantum computation with applications to position-based cryptography. J. Phys. **13**(9), 093036 (2011)
11. Ben-Or, M., Crépeau, C., Gottesman, D., Hassidim, A., Smith, A.: Secure multiparty quantum computation with (only) a strict honest majority. In: 47th FOCS, pp. 249–260. IEEE Computer Society Press, October 2006
12. Ben-Or, M., Goldwasser, S., Wigderson, A.: Completeness theorems for non-cryptographic fault-tolerant distributed computation (extended abstract). In: 20th ACM STOC, pp. 1–10. ACM Press, May 1988
13. Brakerski, Z.: Quantum FHE (Almost) as secure as classical. In: Shacham, H., Boldyreva, A. (eds.) CRYPTO 2018, Part III. LNCS, vol. 10993, pp. 67–95. Springer, Cham (2018). https://doi.org/10.1007/978-3-319-96878-0_3
14. Brakerski, Z., Halevi, S., Polychroniadou, A.: Four round secure computation without setup. In: Kalai, Y., Reyzin, L. (eds.) TCC 2017, Part I. LNCS, vol. 10677, pp. 645–677. Springer, Cham (2017). https://doi.org/10.1007/978-3-319-70500-2_22
15. Brakerski, Z., Yuen, H.: Quantum garbled circuits. arXiv preprint arXiv:2006.01085 (2020)
16. Bravyi, S., Kitaev, A.: Universal quantum computation with ideal clifford gates and noisy ancillas. Phys. Rev. A **71**(2), 022316 (2005)
17. Chase, M., et al.: Reusable non-interactive secure computation. In: Boldyreva, A., Micciancio, D. (eds.) CRYPTO 2019, Part III. LNCS, vol. 11694, pp. 462–488. Springer, Cham (2019). https://doi.org/10.1007/978-3-030-26954-8_15
18. Chaum, D., Crépeau, C., Damgård, I.: Multiparty unconditionally secure protocols (abstract) (informal contribution). In: Pomerance, C. (ed.) CRYPTO 1987. LNCS, vol. 293, p. 462. Springer, Heidelberg (1988). https://doi.org/10.1007/3-540-48184-2_43
19. Choudhuri, A.R., Ciampi, M., Goyal, V., Jain, A., Ostrovsky, R.: Round optimal secure multiparty computation from minimal assumptions. In: Theory of Cryptography - 18th International Conference, TCC 2020, Durham, NC, USA, 16–19 November 2020, Proceedings, Part II, pp. 291–319 (2020)
20. Crépeau, C., Gottesman, D., Smith, A.: Secure multi-party quantum computation. In: 34th ACM STOC, pp. 643–652. ACM Press, May 2002
21. D'Ariano, G.M., Schlingemann, D., Werner, R., Kretschmann, D.: Quantum bit commitment revisited: the possible and the impossible. Tech. rep. (2006)

22. Dulek, Y., Grilo, A.B., Jeffery, S., Majenz, C., Schaffner, C.: Secure multi-party quantum computation with a dishonest majority. In: Canteaut, A., Ishai, Y. (eds.) EUROCRYPT 2020, Part III. LNCS, vol. 12107, pp. 729–758. Springer, Cham (2020). https://doi.org/10.1007/978-3-030-45727-3_25

23. Dupuis, F., Nielsen, J.B., Salvail, L.: Secure two-party quantum evaluation of unitaries against specious adversaries. In: Rabin, T. (ed.) CRYPTO 2010. LNCS, vol. 6223, pp. 685–706. Springer, Heidelberg (2010). https://doi.org/10.1007/978-3-642-14623-7_37

24. Dupuis, F., Nielsen, J.B., Salvail, L.: Actively secure two-party evaluation of any quantum operation. In: Safavi-Naini, R., Canetti, R. (eds.) CRYPTO 2012. LNCS, vol. 7417, pp. 794–811. Springer, Heidelberg (2012). https://doi.org/10.1007/978-3-642-32009-5_46

25. Garg, S., Mukherjee, P., Pandey, O., Polychroniadou, A.: The exact round complexity of secure computation. In: Fischlin, M., Coron, J.-S. (eds.) EUROCRYPT 2016, Part II. LNCS, vol. 9666, pp. 448–476. Springer, Heidelberg (2016). https://doi.org/10.1007/978-3-662-49896-5_16

26. Garg, S., Srinivasan, A.: Two-round multiparty secure computation from minimal assumptions. In: Nielsen, J.B., Rijmen, V. (eds.) EUROCRYPT 2018, Part II. LNCS, vol. 10821, pp. 468–499. Springer, Cham (2018). https://doi.org/10.1007/978-3-319-78375-8_16

27. Goldreich, O., Micali, S., Wigderson, A.: How to play any mental game or A completeness theorem for protocols with honest majority. In: Aho, A. (ed.) 19th ACM STOC, pp. 218–229. ACM Press, May 1987

28. Gonzales, A., Chitambar, E.: Bounds on instantaneous nonlocal quantum computation. IEEE Trans. Inf. Theory **66**(5), 2951–2963 (2020)

29. Goyal, R.: Quantum multi-key homomorphic encryption for polynomial-sized circuits. Cryptology ePrint Archive, Report 2018/443 (2018). https://eprint.iacr.org/2018/443

30. Ishai, Y., Kushilevitz, E., Ostrovsky, R., Prabhakaran, M., Sahai, A.: Efficient non-interactive secure computation. In: Paterson, K.G. (ed.) EUROCRYPT 2011. LNCS, vol. 6632, pp. 406–425. Springer, Heidelberg (2011). https://doi.org/10.1007/978-3-642-20465-4_23

31. Ciampi, M., Ostrovsky, R., Siniscalchi, L., Visconti, I.: Round-optimal secure two-party computation from trapdoor permutations. In: Kalai, Y., Reyzin, L. (eds.) TCC 2017. LNCS, vol. 10677, pp. 678–710. Springer, Cham (2017). https://doi.org/10.1007/978-3-319-70500-2_23

32. Lo, H.K., Chau, H.F.: Why quantum bit commitment and ideal quantum coin tossing are impossible. Physica D Nonlinear Phenom. **120**(1–2), 177–187 (1998)

33. López-Alt, A., Tromer, E., Vaikuntanathan, V.: On-the-fly multiparty computation on the cloud via multikey fully homomorphic encryption. In: Karloff, H.J., Pitassi, T. (eds.) 44th ACM STOC, pp. 1219–1234. ACM Press, May 2012

34. Mahadev, U.: Classical homomorphic encryption for quantum circuits. In: Thorup, M. (ed.) 59th FOCS, pp. 332–338. IEEE Computer Society Press, October 2018

35. Mayers, D.: Unconditionally secure quantum bit commitment is impossible. Phys. Rev. Lett. **78**(17), 3414 (1997)

36. Peikert, C., Vaikuntanathan, V., Waters, B.: A framework for efficient and composable oblivious transfer. In: Wagner, D. (ed.) CRYPTO 2008. LNCS, vol. 5157, pp. 554–571. Springer, Heidelberg (2008). https://doi.org/10.1007/978-3-540-85174-5_31

37. Shmueli, O.: Multi-theorem (malicious) designated-verifier NIZK for QMA (2020)

38. Speelman, F.: Instantaneous non-local computation of low t-depth quantum circuits. In: Broadbent, A. (ed.) 11th Conference on the Theory of Quantum Computation, Communication and Cryptography, TQC 2016, 27–29 September 2016, Berlin, Germany. LIPIcs, vol. 61, pp. 9:1–9:24. Schloss Dagstuhl - Leibniz-Zentrum für Informatik (2016)
39. Vaidman, L.: Instantaneous measurement of nonlocal variables. Phys. Rev. Lett. **90**, 010402 (2003)
40. Yao, A.C.C.: How to generate and exchange secrets (extended abstract). In: 27th FOCS, pp. 162–167. IEEE Computer Society Press, October 1986

Round Efficient Secure Multiparty Quantum Computation with Identifiable Abort

Bar Alon[1], Hao Chung[2], Kai-Min Chung[3]([⊠]), Mi-Ying Huang[3,4], Yi Lee[3], and Yu-Ching Shen[3]

[1] Department of Computer Science, Ariel University, Ariel, Israel
[2] Department of Electrical and Computer Engineering, Carnegie Mellon University, Pittsburgh, USA
haochung@andrew.cmu.edu
[3] Institute of Information Science, Academia Sinica, Taipei City, Taiwan
{kmchung,yuching}@iis.sinica.edu.tw, ylee1228@umd.edu
[4] Department of Computer Science and Information Engineering, National Taiwan University, Taipei City, Taiwan
mining.huang@usc.edu

Abstract. A recent result by Dulek et al. (EUROCRYPT 2020) showed a secure protocol for computing any quantum circuit even without the presence of an honest majority. Their protocol, however, is susceptible to a "denial of service" attack and allows even a single corrupted party to force an abort. We propose the first quantum protocol that admits *security-with-identifiable-abort*, which allows the honest parties to agree on the identity of a corrupted party in case of an abort. Additionally, our protocol is the first to have the property that the number of rounds where quantum communication is required is *independent of the circuit complexity*. Furthermore, if there exists a post-quantum secure classical protocol whose round complexity is independent of the circuit complexity, then our protocol has this property as well. Our protocol is secure under the assumption that classical quantum-resistant fully homomorphic encryption schemes with decryption circuit of logarithmic depth exist. Interestingly, our construction also admits a reduction from quantum fair secure computation to classical fair secure computation.

B. Alon—This work was supported by ISF grant 152/17 and by the Ariel Cyber Innovation Center in conjunction with the Israel National Cyber directorate in the Prime Minister's Office. Part of the work was done while visiting Academia Sinica.

H. Chung and Y.-C. Shen—This research is partially supported by the Young Scholar Fellowship (Einstein Program) of the Ministry of Science and Technology (MOST) in Taiwan, under grant number MOST 108-2636-E-002-014 and Executive Yuan Data Safety and Talent Cultivation Project (ASKPQ-109-DSTCP).

K.-M. Chung—This research is partially supported by the Air Force Office of Scientific Research under award number FA2386-20-1-4066, and MOST, Taiwan, under Grant no. MOST 109-2223-E-001-001-MY3.

M.-Y. Huang—This work is supported by the Young Scholar Fellowship (Einstein Program) of the Ministry of Science and Technology (MOST) in Taiwan, under grant number MOST 109-2636-E-002-025.

Y. Lee—This work was done in part while the author was affiliated to National Taiwan University.

T. Malkin and C. Peikert (Eds.): CRYPTO 2021, LNCS 12825, pp. 436–466, 2021.
https://doi.org/10.1007/978-3-030-84242-0_16

1 Introduction

In the setting of secure multiparty computation (MPC), the goal is to allow a set of mutually distrustful parties to compute some function of their private inputs in a way that preserves some security properties, even in the face of adversarial behavior by some of the parties. Some of the desired properties of a secure protocol include correctness (cheating parties can only affect the output by choosing their inputs), privacy (nothing but the specified output is learned), fairness (all parties receive an output or none do), and even guaranteed output delivery (meaning that all honestly behaving parties always learn an output). Informally speaking, a protocol π computes a functionality f with full-security if it provides all of the above security properties.

It is well-known that, assuming an honest majority and a broadcast channel, any functionality can be computed with full-security [RBO89]. However, achieving fairness, and hence full-security, is impossible in general assuming no honest majority [Cle86]. Instead, one usually settles on a weaker notion called *security-with-abort*, which completely disregards fairness. Roughly, security-with-abort guarantees that either the protocol terminates successfully, in which case the honest parties receive their outputs, or the protocol aborts, in which case all honest parties learn that there was an attack. Note that since fairness is not guaranteed, it might be the case where the adversary learns the output of the corrupted parties. In many setting, however, security-with-abort is not enough, as an adversary can cause a *denial-of-service* attack by repeatedly aborting the protocol. Thus, it is highly desirable to consider the stronger security notion called *security-with-identifiable-abort* (SWIA) [IOZ14]. Here, if the protocol is aborted, then all honest parties additionally agree on an identity of a corrupted party. It is well-known that there are protocols admitting SWIA for any number of corrupted parties, e.g., the GMW protocol [GMW87].

In this work we consider the quantum version of MPC. In the *fully quantum* setting, the functionality – including the inputs and outputs – is quantum. As such, the parties, as well as the adversary attacking the protocol, are quantum. Secure multiparty quantum computation (MPQC) in the fully quantum setting, was first studied by [CGS02], who constructed a fully secure n-party protocol tolerating strictly less than $n/6$. The threshold $n/6$ was subsequently improved the more general honest majority setting [BOCG+06], assuming the availability of a classical broadcast channel. Similarly to the classical setting, if there is no honest majority, then full-security is impossible to achieve in general [ABDR04, Kit].[1] Moreover, [DNS12] presented a secure-with-abort protocol in the two-party case, and recently [DGJ+20] extended it to the multiparty case, tolerating any number of corrupted parties.

---

[1] The impossibility proof is in the information theoretic setting, where the adversary is unbounded. However, even though Cleve's impossibility result is stated for classical protocols, the proof can still be applied for quantum protocols.

The protocol of [DGJ+20], however, does not admit *identifiable abort*. This follows from the fact that it is impossible to broadcast a quantum state. Therefore a corrupted party can accuse an honest party of not sending it a message, thus, not only is the quantum state lost, but the other parties cannot identify the corrupted party. When compared to the classical setting, this raises the following natural question.

Can any multiparty quantum circuit be computed with security-with-identifiable-abort, tolerating any number of corrupted parties?

1.1 Our Results

In this paper, we answer the above question affirmatively. Additionally, our protocol is the first to have the property that the number of rounds where quantum communication is required is independent of the circuit complexity. Furthermore, if there exists a post-quantum secure classical protocol whose round complexity is independent of the circuit complexity, then our protocol has this property as well.

Similarly to [DGJ+20, DNS12], we present the results and the protocol, assuming the availability of a reactive trusted party, called cMPC, that is able to compute any *classical* multiparty functionality. We refer to this as the cMPC-*hybrid model*. Furthermore, we assume that the parties are able to broadcast classical messages. The implementation of cMPC can be done by first removing the reactive assumption using standard techniques, and then implement each call using a post-quantum secure-with-identifiable-abort protocol. We refer the reader to Sect. 3.2 for more details. We prove the following.

Theorem 1 (Informal). *Assume the existence of a classical quantum-resistant fully homomorphic encryption scheme with decryption circuit of logarithmic depth. Then any multiparty quantum circuit can be computed with security-with-identifiable-abort tolerating any number of corrupted parties in the cMPC-hybrid model. Moreover, the round complexity of the quantum communication of the protocol is independent of the circuit complexity.*

The formal statement of the theorem appears in Sect. 4. A few notes are in place. First, Brakerski and Vaikuntanathan [BV11] showed that the existence of a fully-homomorphic encryption satisfying the conditions stated in Theorem 1 can be reduced to the *learning with errors* assumption.

Second, we note that the protocol can be split into an online phase and an offline phase, where the parties have yet to receive their inputs. In the offline phase, the parties prepare auxiliary magic states in order to compute quantum gates later in the online phase. In fact, it suffices that the parties know only an upper bound on the number of gates in the circuit before interacting in the offline phase.

Third, although the number of rounds requiring quantum information to be sent is independent of the circuit complexity (i.e., independent of the number of gates), it still depends on the number of parties, the number of input-qubits and output-qubits of the circuit, and the security parameter. Specifically, the offline phase consists of $O(n^4 \cdot \kappa)$ rounds, and the online phase consists of $O(n^3 \cdot (\ell_{\mathsf{in}} + \ell_{\mathsf{out}}))$ rounds, where n is the number of parties, κ is the security parameter, and ℓ_{in} and ℓ_{out} upper-bound the number of input-qubits and output-qubits of the circuit, respectively.

Fourth, although our protocol admits security-with-identifiable-abort, any single corrupted party can cause it to abort. It is arguably more desirable and an interesting open problem to have a protocol that requires the adversary to corrupt more parties to cause an abort.

Finally, an interesting consequence of our construction is that quantum fair secure computation can be implemented assuming the hybrid functionality cMPC is fair.[2]

In the following sections, we present the ideas behind the construction.

1.2 Our Techniques

In this section, we present the main ideas behind the construction of our protocol.

A Warm-Up: Reliable Transmission of Quantum States

Before presenting the general construction, let us consider the following simple task. Suppose that there are n parties $P_1, \ldots, P_n$, where P_1 – called the sender – holds a quantum state ρ. The goal of the parties is to send ρ to P_n – called the receiver – such that if either the sender or the receiver is corrupted and deviate from the protocol, then the other parties can identify which of them is corrupted. Moreover, this should hold even the corrupted party collude with some of the other parties in $\{P_2, \ldots, P_{n-1}\}$.

As stated before, simply having P_1 send ρ to P_n, and have P_n broadcast a complaint in case it did not receive a message, does not work. Indeed, it could be the case where the receiver is corrupted, and falsely accuse the sender of not sending ρ. Since broadcasting a quantum state is impossible, to the other parties, this scenario is identical to the case where a corrupted sender did not send ρ. Thus, the desired security property is not met. Moreover, due to the no-cloning theorem, the state ρ is now permanently lost, making it unclear as to how to proceed the protocol.

Dealing with False Accusations. As such "packet loss" seems unavoidable, our first idea is to not send ρ directly, but rather to encode ρ using a *quantum error-correcting code* (QECC), that can tolerate d deletions, where d will be determined below. This generates an q-qubit codeword $(\sigma_k)_{k=1}^q$, for some q, which will then be transmitted qubit-by-qubit as explained below.[3] By doing so, P_n can still recover ρ as long as it receives enough qubits of the codeword.

We next explain how the parties can transmit the codeword's qubits in such a way that will allow them to identify the corrupted party, if such exists. For

---

[2] Intuitively, fair computation means that either all parties receive their respective outputs, or none of them do.

[3] Here we abuse the notation that we denote the kth qubit of the codeword σ_k, while these q qubits may be entangled.

simplicity of the current discussion, let us assume that the adversary can perform one of the following two attacks. Either it does not send a message, or it can falsely accuse a party of not sending a message. Below we will explain how to remove this assumption and how to resist general malicious attackers. Under these simplifying assumptions, we can make the following observation. If P_n accused P_1 of not sending a message, then all parties know that at least one of them is corrupted. Therefore, they can agree to remove the channel between them, and have P_1 send the next qubit of the codeword via a different path. The parties continue in this fashion until either enough σ_k's where successfully transmitted to the receiver, or until there is no path from the sender to the receiver. Formally, the parties keep track of a simple and undirected graph G, which represents *trust* between parties, i.e., an edge between two vertices exists if and only if there was no accusation between the two parties that the vertices represent. Observe that in the above protocol, all honest parties form a clique in G. Thus, if G becomes disconnected, the honest parties can agree on a corrupted party *not* connected to them. Therefore, using a QECC that can tolerate $d = \Theta(n^2)$ deletions results in a secure protocol.

Dealing with General Malicious Behavior. Next, we show to remove the simplifying assumption of the behavior of the adversary, and allow it to tamper with the messages arbitrarily. Here, we utilize *quantum authentication codes* [BCG+02], that allow a party to verify if a quantum state was tampered with. However, in our protocol the parties must know where on the path the message had been tampered with (if any tampered occurred), in order to later remove the corresponding edge. To achieve this, we define a new primitive, which we call *sequential authentication* (SA), that allows the sender to transmit a qubit to the receiver along some path, so that if the qubit was tampered with, all parties know where on the path the tampering occurred. We then combine SA with the previous protocol that dealt with false accusations, to construct a secure-with-identifiable-abort protocol for the transmission of a quantum state. One subtlety in the final construction, is that any path from P_1 to P_n must go through all parties, so as to ensure that at least one honest party can verify the integrity of the message.

We now describe the construction of a protocol for sequential authentication. The construction is inspired by the swaddling notion from [DNS12] and the public authentication test from [DGJ+20], which are both based on *Clifford authentication codes*. Let us first recall Clifford codes [ABOE10]. Given a m-qubit state ρ and a security parameter κ, the Clifford encryption[4] appends an auxiliary register $|0^\kappa\rangle\langle 0^\kappa|$, called *traps*. Then, a random Clifford operator E is sampled from the Clifford group acting on $m + \kappa$ qubits. Finally, the encryption outputs the ciphertext $E(\rho \otimes |0^\kappa\rangle\langle 0^\kappa|)E^\dagger$, where E serves as the secret key. The decryption of a Clifford ciphertext σ, simply applies $E^\dagger$ to σ and measures the

---

[4] It is more common to use the term Clifford encoding. However, in the quantum setting authentication implies encryption. Thus, we refer to these as encryptions to remove confusion with the QECC encoding.

last κ trap qubits. If the measurement outcome is all-zero, then the decoding algorithm outputs the resulting state of the first m qubits. Otherwise, it rejects. The security of Clifford codes stems from the fact that any operation that is applied to the ciphertext, will flip each qubit in the trap with noticeable probability upon measurement. Moreover, the secret key of the Clifford code can be sampled efficiently by a classical algorithm [DLT02].

Constructing a Sequential Authentication Protocol. We utilize these property to build a protocol for SA. Suppose that a message ρ is going to be transmitted through ℓ parties. Let us first present a naïve solution. The first party on the path will append $\ell\kappa$ qubits of $|0\rangle$ to ρ. Then, using the classical MPC functionality cMPC, the parties will securely sample for P_1 a Clifford key E_1 to encrypt its state. It then sends the encrypted message to P_2. To verify the authenticity of the state, the parties will again use cMPC for sampling a Clifford $V_2 = E_2 E_1^\dagger$, where E_2 acts only on the first $(\ell-1)\kappa$ qubits. We then let P_2 receive V_2 and apply it to the encrypted message it received from P_1. This allows P_2 to measure the last κ qubits and compare them to zero. For each party P_i on the transmitting path, P_i measures κ qubits of traps. The parties can then continue in this fashion. Notice, however, that a corrupt P_1 might only append the last κ qubits honestly, which will not be immediately detected by P_2. This could later result in an honest party accusing another honest party. To overcome this issue, we use a similar trick to the public authentication test [DGJ+20], and have the Clifford V_2 that cMPC sampled include a random invertible linear transformation over $\mathbb{F}_2$ acting on all traps. Specifically, we let $V_2 = E_2 G_2 E_1^\dagger$, where we abuse notations and let $G_2|x\rangle = |G_2(x)\rangle$. Observe that if P_1 did not prepare the traps correctly, then upon measurement with high probability P_2 will not obtain all-zero.

Security With Packet Drops

With the above technique, it is natural to incorporate it into the construction of [DGJ+20]. This naïve solution, however, does not work. Towards explaining the issue, let us first briefly describe the protocol of [DGJ+20]. Roughly, their protocol starts with an input encoding phase, such that at the end of the phase each party's input is encrypted under a Clifford code with cMPC holding the secret Clifford key. This is done similarly to the sequential authentication protocol described earlier. The parties then proceed to perform computation over the encrypted inputs. Computation over single-qubit Clifford gates can be done by simply letting cMPC update its key, while CNOT gates require communication since the inputs to CNOT gates are encrypted separately under different Clifford keys.

While the input encoding phase can be modified to admit security-with-identifiable-abort, it is unclear how to modify the computation phase of the protocol. This follows from the fact that the parties are required to use QECC over their inputs in the input encoding phase, thus at the end of this phase, each party will hold a Clifford encoding of each qubit of its input's codeword. As a result, the parties have to either perform the computation over QECC codewords in some way, or decode the Clifford encrypted codewords and perform computation similarly to [DGJ+20]. We next give an intuitive explanation as to why both solutions fail.

Let us first argue why the second solution fails. That is, suppose the parties decode all QECC encodings before starting to perform any computation. The issue here is that once the parties decode the QECC they lose its protection, hence the protocol cannot tolerate losing quantum states after this step. Since the protocol of [DGJ+20] requires communicating quantum messages to compute CNOT gates, this causes inevitable packet drops *during computation*, causing the honest parties to output incorrect values.

The former solution fails due to the fact that a corrupted party might not encode its qubit correctly using the QECC. Observe that our sequential authentication protocol will not be able to detect such error, since it is able to detect an attack only after a Clifford had been applied. Furthermore, this error might propagate into the evaluation. Indeed, consider the following example.

Suppose that the parties use repetition code as an implementation of the QECC.[5] In repetition code, a logical zero $|\bar{0}\rangle$ is encoded as $|000\rangle$ and a logical one $|\bar{1}\rangle$ is encoded as $|111\rangle$. The decoding is done by taking the majority, e.g., $|000\rangle$, $|001\rangle$, $|010\rangle$ and $|100\rangle$ are all decoded to $|\bar{0}\rangle$. Suppose three parties wish to compute the following circuit, where the CNOTs are applied transversally, and where the inputs $|\psi_i\rangle$ are repetition codes of logical $|\bar{0}\rangle$.

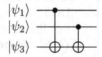

Clearly, in an honest execution the value of $|\psi_3\rangle$ becomes $|000\rangle$ which decodes to $|0\rangle$. Now, suppose the two parties holding $|\psi_1\rangle$ and $|\psi_2\rangle$ are corrupted and prepares $|\psi_1\rangle = |001\rangle$ and $|\psi_2\rangle = |010\rangle$. Then the value of $|\psi_3\rangle$ under such an attack becomes $|011\rangle$. Consequently, even if all codewords are of logical 0 at the beginning, the decoding would result in a logical 1.

A possible way to try and fix this issue, would be to try to *correct* the QECC codewords. However, this in particular would require the parties to compute a multi-qubit gate (e.g., CNOT), which as stated before, cannot be done without losing the quantum states due to a potential attack.

With this state of affairs, we aim to construct a protocol that has the property that no adversary can cause qubits to be "dropped" during the computation of the circuit. Thus, we first propose an abstraction of a security notion that allows the adversary to "drop" some of the input-states and output-states. We call this security notion secure-with-identifiable-abort-and-packet-drop (IDPD-security). We then show how to reduce the problem of constructing a secure-with-identifiable-abort protocol to the problem of constructing an IDPD-secure protocol.

---

[5] Repetition codes only resist bit-flip error (i.e., Pauli X attack). However, it is sufficient for the purposes of demonstration here.

Defining IDPD-Security. Let us now define IDPD-security. Similarly to other notions of security in multiparty computation, here we follow the standard ideal vs. real paradigm. Roughly, the ideal-world follows similar instructions to that of the security-with-identifiable-abort ideal-world, with the following two additions. First, when the parties send their inputs to the trusted party, the adversary additionally sends it a bounded-sized set, representing which input-qubits are to be replaced with $|0\rangle$ (modelling "packet drop"). Note that it might be the case where a single party holds several qubits as inputs, and the adversary changes only a subset of them to the 0 state. The second change we make is done after the adversary receives its output from the trusted party. Here, the adversary either instructs the trusted party to abort while revealing the identity of a corrupted party, or it instructs the trusted party to continue and drop some qubits from the output.[6] In case the adversary instructed to continue, the trusted party then sends to all other parties their respective outputs that remained. Additionally, the trusted party reveals which input-qubits and which output-qubits were dropped. The formal definition of IDPD-security can be found in Sect. 3.1.

Reducing SWIA to IDPD-security. We now show a simple reduction from SWIA to IDPD-security. The reduction makes use of a QECC. Let C be the circuit that the parties wish to compute. First, each party encodes its input using the QECC. The parties then use an IDPD-secure protocol in order to compute the circuit C' that first decodes its inputs using the QECC, then applies C, and finally re-encodes each output using the QECC. Upon receiving their encoded outputs, each party locally decodes it to obtain their output. To see why this reduction works, observe that the adversary can only drop some of the qubits in the input to C' and some of the qubits in the output. Therefore, by the properties of the QECC and IDPD-security, either the original state can be reconstructed, or the adversary has revealed the identity of a corrupted party.

Securely Computing A General Circuit
We next explain how to achieve a secure protocol for computing a general circuit. With the above reduction, it suffices to construct an IDPD-secure protocol. Unfortunately, previous approaches, such as that of [DGJ+20], for constructing secure protocols fail to achieve IDPD-security. Indeed, as stated before, the protocol of [DGJ+20] requires communicating quantum messages to compute CNOT gates, which causes inevitable packet drops during computation and thus fails to achieve IDPD-security.

Our Approach. To circumvent the aforementioned issue, the parties need a way to perform computation *without* quantum communication. To do so, our main idea is to delegate the computation to some designated party, say P_1, and let it perform computation under *verifiable quantum fully homomorphic encryption*

---

[6] Formally, the ideal-world is parametrized by two polynomial in the security parameter that bound the number input-qubits and number of output-qubits that can be dropped.

(VQFHE) [ADSS17]. More precisely, the first step of our protocol will encrypt all parties' input using the VQFHE scheme of [ADSS17], called TrapTP, send their encrypted inputs to P_1, and store the VQFHE classical secret key sk in cMPC. We refer to this step as the *pre-computation* step. This allows us to let P_1 perform the computation homomorphically to obtain encrypted output without any quantum communication. Furthermore, the verification of the evaluation can be done using the help of cMPC holding sk. If the verification passes, P_1 delivers the output to each party. Note that an additional advantage of our approach is that the round complexity of our protocol is independent of the circuit complexity.

VQFHE scheme TrapTP. We first review some useful facts about the TrapTP scheme. In TrapTP, the encryption of a 1-qubit state $|\psi\rangle$ consists of a quantum part and a classical part. The quantum part is a *trap code* encryption of $|\psi\rangle$

$$\Pi X^x Z^z (\text{QECC.Enc}(|\psi\rangle) \otimes |0\rangle^{\otimes\kappa} \otimes |+\rangle^{\otimes\kappa}),$$

where Π is a random permutation over 3κ qubits (which is part of the secret key sk) and $x, z \leftarrow \{0,1\}^{3\kappa}$ are sampled independent and uniformly at random. The classical part is a classical FHE encryption of the Pauli key x, z. Homomorphic evaluation requires a quantum evaluation key ρ_{evk}, which consists of multiple TrapTP encryptions of magic states, including ancilla zero states, phase (P) states $|P\rangle := P|+\rangle$, Hadamard (H) states $|H\rangle := (H \otimes I)\text{CNOT}(|+\rangle \otimes |0\rangle)$, T states $|T\rangle := T|+\rangle$, and a special gadget state $|\gamma\rangle$ (see Sect. 7.3 in the full version [ACC+20] for a more detailed definition of $|\gamma\rangle$). These (encrypted) states are used to perform computation homomorphically over the underlying trap codes.

The Pre-Computation Step. Recall that the goal is to send TrapTP encrypted inputs to P_1, with the secret key stored in cMPC. The first step is to let each party send their input to P_1 using the technique we developed in Sect. 1.2. Namely, we let each party to send Clifford encryptions of their input qubits using sequential authentication protocol through paths determined by a trust graph G. We formalize this as an *authenticated routing* (AR) protocol that achieves the following functionality with IDPD-security.

> **Authenticated Routing (AR):** As input, each sender P_i holds multiple quantum messages $\rho_1, \ldots, \rho_\ell$ (the "packets") to send to P_1. As output, the receiver P_1 receives Clifford ciphertexts $\sigma_j = E_j(\rho_j \otimes |0^t\rangle\langle 0^t|)E_j^\dagger$ with trap size t and cMPC receives the Clifford keys E_j for $j \in [\ell]$ with at most n^2 packet drop.

We note that in AR, a packet ρ_j can consist of multiple qubits and the trap size can be set arbitrarily; these properties will be useful later. Here, we let each P_i send their input qubit-by-qubit to P_1 using AR with trap size $3\kappa - 1$. After that, P_1 holds Clifford encodings of all parties' input (with certain packet drops). Note that AR allows to drop at most n^2 input states, while it is acceptable in IDPD-security.

However, in TrapTP, the quantum messages are encrypted under trap code instead of Clifford code. We next use the following simple *re-encrypt* protocol to turn Clifford codes into trap codes: Let $\sigma = E(\rho \otimes |0^{3\kappa-1}\rangle\langle 0^{3\kappa-1}|)E^\dagger$ be a Clifford encoding of ρ held by P_1 with the corresponding Clifford key E held by cMPC. We simply let cMPC send to P_1 the Clifford operator

$$V = X^x Z^z \Pi (U_{\mathsf{Enc}} \otimes I^{\otimes\kappa} \otimes H^{\otimes\kappa})E^\dagger,$$

where U_{Enc} is an unitary operator maps $\rho \otimes |0^{\kappa-1}\rangle\langle 0^{\kappa-1}|$ into an QECC codeword. Observe that if P_1 applies V to σ, the result would be a trap-code encryption of ρ, which is also the quantum part of the TrapTP encryption of ρ. Also note that since the Clifford key E is uniformly random to P_1, it serves as a one-time pad, hence P_1 learns nothing about the trap code secret Π, x, z from V. After that, we can let cMPC generate and send the classical part of the TrapTP encryption of ρ to P_1 so that it obtains a complete TrapTP encryption of ρ.

It is worth mentioning that a natural alternative is to use trap code to construct SA in AR to avoid using two different codes with re-encryption. However, this does not provide a secure protocol since, unlike Clifford codes, in trap codes each qubit is encrypted individually. If only one qubit has been tampered with, then there is no guarantee that the adversary would be immediately caught.

To conclude the pre-computation step, it is left to prepare the evaluation key ρ_{evk} for P_1, which consists of multiple TrapTP encryptions of auxiliary magic states and a special gadget state. Preparing such states turns out to be involved, which we discuss next.

Magic State Preparation (except T). We first note that it suffices to generate Clifford encryption of these states, and we can apply the above re-encryption protocol to turn them into TrapTP encryption.

Let us start with the simplest case of ancilla zero state $|0\rangle$. For this, we can use the AR protocol to send the empty state, denoted ε, with trap size 3κ to prepare it. Indeed, the Clifford encoding outputs

$$E(\varepsilon \otimes |0^{3\kappa}\rangle\langle 0^{3\kappa}|)E^\dagger = E(|0\rangle\langle 0| \otimes |0^{3\kappa-1}\rangle\langle 0^{3\kappa-1}|)E^\dagger,$$

as required. Note that AR protocol takes as input a list of "packets," where n^2 packets may be dropped. Since magic state preparation is independent to parties' private states, the parties actually call AR protocol with $n^2 + 1$ packets to make sure that at least one packet can be delivered. Then, the server and cMPC keep the lexicographically first remaining packet. For simplicity, we omit the number of initial packets.

Next, consider preparing a $|P\rangle$ magic state. Since a P gate is a Clifford, we can generate it by preparing encoding of $|0\rangle$ and update the Clifford key held by cMPC. Specifically, if cMPC updates its Clifford E to $E(PH)^\dagger$ (where PH is applied only to the first qubit of the codeword), then decrypting the ciphertext with the updated key would result in

$$(E(PH)^\dagger)^\dagger E(|0\rangle \otimes |0^{3\kappa-1}\rangle) = PH(|0\rangle \otimes |0^{3\kappa-1}\rangle) = |P\rangle \otimes |0^{3\kappa-1}\rangle.$$

The $|H\rangle$ magic state, is also generated by a Clifford, but consists of two qubits. To generate this, we first use AR to send the empty state with trap size 6κ and view it as

$$E(|0\rangle^{M_1} \otimes |0\rangle^{M_2} \otimes |0^{3\kappa-1}\rangle^{T_1} \otimes |0^{3\kappa-1}\rangle^{T_2}),$$

where the gray superscript denote the registers the qubits are stored in. Then, we let cMPC send to P_1 the Clifford operator

$$V = (E_1^{M_1 T_1} \otimes E_2^{M_2 T_2})(H \otimes I)\mathsf{CNOT}(H \otimes I)^{M_1 M_2} E^\dagger,$$

where E_1 and E_2 are two Clifford sampled uniformly at random and independently, and where the gray superscript denote the registers on which each operator acts. Observe that upon applying V to its codeword, P_1 will obtain an encrypted H state. Additionally, as V is distributed like a uniform random Clifford operator, it follows that a corrupted P_1 will gain no new information.

More generally, the above examples suggest that we can prepare any ℓ-qubit state in the Clifford group by first preparing Clifford encoding of $3\ell\kappa$ qubits $E|0^{3\ell\kappa}\rangle$ using AR, and letting cMPC send Clifford operator V to instruct P_1 to prepare the Clifford state and split it into ℓ Clifford encodings of each qubit. We note that the special gadget state $|\gamma\rangle$ is of this type and therefore can be prepared in this way.

T Magic State Preparation. Among all magic states, the preparation of $T := T|+\rangle$ magic state is the most difficult, since T is not a Clifford operator. We follow a similar approach to that of [DGJ+20], but with modifications to achieve security-with-identifiable-abort. Here, we give a brief overview of their construction and discuss the required modifications.

At a high-level, the protocol asks a party, say P_1, to prepare a large number N of (supposedly) $|T\rangle$ states under Clifford encoding with Clifford keys stored in cMPC. This can be done by, e.g., letting P_1 send these states using AR in our context. Then, the parties randomly distribute these encoded states among themselves, and have $P_2, \ldots, P_n$ verify that they are indeed $|T\rangle$ states. This is done by sending the Clifford keys to P_i, and having P_i measure the decoded states in the $\{|T\rangle, |T^\perp\rangle\}$-basis. If any $|T^\perp\rangle$ outcome is detected, the protocol aborts. If not, then we know that the states held in P_1 contains only a small number of errors with high probability. The protocol then apply a T state distillation circuit (over the encoded states) to distill the desired T magic states.

To achieve security-with-identifiable-abort, we cannot let the protocol be aborted when an error is detected, since the parties cannot distinguish the case where the error was due to a malicious P_1 preparing incorrect states, or a malicious party P_i falsely reporting the error. Thus, to identify the malicious party, we let each party P_i report its *error rate* ϵ_i, i.e., the fraction of $|T^\perp\rangle$ outcomes it obtained, to cMPC with ϵ_1 set to 0. cMPC then sort these numbers, and check if there are two consecutive numbers with difference greater than a certain threshold δ that is larger than expected sampling errors. If so, cMPC finds the smallest such pairs, say, they are $\epsilon_i < \epsilon_j$ reported by P_i and P_j, respectively, and publish the result. The parties then abort, with an honest party P_k identifying P_i

(resp., P_j) as the malicious party if $\epsilon_k \geq \epsilon_j$ (resp., $\epsilon_k \leq \epsilon_i$). Intuitively, this works since all honest parties should obtain roughly the same error rate up to a small sampling error, and hence they will belong to the same side and accuse the same party being the malicious party. Also, if the protocol does not abort, it means that all reported error rates are small, since $\epsilon_1 = 0$ and we still have the guarantee that the error rate of the states held in P_1 is small.

The second issue is that we need to be able to apply the T state distillation circuit to the (Clifford encrypted) states held by P_1, which is a classically-controlled Clifford circuit (A circuit consists of Clifford gates and measurements, and which Clifford gates should be applied depends on all previous measurement outcomes.). If these states are encrypted separately, then we do not know how to compute the distillation circuit without quantum communication, as this is the problem we want to solve to begin with. Fortunately, as discussed above, if these states are encrypted as a single Clifford ciphertext of a multi-qubit message, then we can perform Clifford operation on the underlying message and split it into multiple Clifford ciphertexts of smaller messages by letting cMPC sending proper Clifford instruction to P_1. We can further extend it to evaluate classically-controlled Clifford circuit. Based on this observation, we let P_1 to prepare the N copies of $|T\rangle$ states and send it as a N-qubit quantum message $\rho = |T\rangle^{\otimes N}$ in AR (with a sufficiently large trap size). This allows us to distribute the states to all parties (by splitting the ciphertexts) and apply the T state distillation circuit to the states held by P_1 later.

Final Issue: Re-encryption to Clifford Codes. The computation step is rather straightforward, so we do not discuss the details here but just state that as a result, P_1 holds trap code encoding of the output. All that is left is to show how it can distribute each output to its corresponding party. The idea is to reverse the operations done until now. That is, to first re-encrypt the trap codes back to Clifford codes, and then use AR to distribute the outputs. The final issue is that re-encrypting trap code to Clifford cannot be done in the same way as it was done in the other direction. This is because before, we use the randomness of the Clifford key as one-time pad to protect the trap code key, but now the randomness in the trap code key is not enough to protect the Clifford key.

To resolve the issue, we again use AR. Let us say σ is a trap code that P_1 needs to send to a party P_i. We let P_1 send ρ as a 3κ-qubit message to itself using AR. As a result, P_1 will receive a Clifford encoding $\sigma = E(\rho \otimes |0^t\rangle\langle 0^t|)E^\dagger$ (with a sufficiently large trap size t) for which we can let P_1 perform Clifford operation on the underlying message ρ. Note that if P_1 is malicious, the underlying message ρ of σ may not be a valid trap code. Thus, we let P_1 and cMPC verify and decode the supposedly trap code ρ. Specifically, cMPC will check the classical parts of the computation. If the verification rejects, we abort and identify P_1 as the malicious party. If it passes, then we obtain a Clifford encoding of the qubit underlying the trap code as desired. Finally, we remind the reader that some of the trap codes in ρ may be dropped by AR, but this is allowed since IDPD-security allows to drop part of the output qubits.

1.3   Roadmap

In Sect. 2 we provide the required preliminaries. In Sect. 3 we explain in detail the model of our computation. Then, in Sect. 4 we state our main theorem and show the reduction to IDPD-security. In Sect. 5 we give the construction of sequential authentication, and in Sect. 6 we use it to construct authenticated routing. These constructions admits information theoretic security. Following that, in Sect. 7 we show how to prepare all required magic states. In Sect. 8 we show how to securely compute the pre-computation protocol, Sect. 9 is dedicated to performing the computation of the circuit, and finally, in Sect. 10 we show how the parties can distribute the output securely. We note that only the computation protocol from Sect. 9 has computational security.

2   Preliminaries

For space considerations, most standard definitions and notations are deferred to the full version [ACC+20]. We next provide the definitions that we find more essential for the readability of the bulk of the paper.

For $n \in \mathbb{N}$, let $[n] = \{1, 2 \ldots n\}$. We also let Sym_n to denote the symmetric group over n symbols. Given a binary string x, we write $|x|$ to denote the length of x, and $w(x)$ to denote the *relative Hamming weight* of x which equals to Hamming weight of x divided by $|x|$. For a string x and a subset $S \subseteq [|x|]$, we use x_S to denote the substring of x indicated by S.

Given a set S, we write $s \leftarrow S$ to indicate that s is selected uniformly at random from S. Similarly, given a random variable (or a distribution) X, we write $x \leftarrow X$ to indicate that x is selected according to X. A function $\mu \colon \mathbb{N} \rightarrow [0, 1]$ is called negligible, if for every positive polynomial $p(\cdot)$ and all sufficiently large n, it holds that $\mu(n) < 1/p(n)$. We use $\mathrm{neg}(\cdot)$ to denote an unspecified negligible function.

For $n \in \mathbb{N}$, we use $\mathcal{H}^n$ to denote the Hilbert space of n qubits. We write $D(\mathcal{H})$ to denote the set of density matrices over the Hilbert space $\mathcal{H}$, and let $\mathcal{D}^n := D(\mathcal{H}^n)$. We define $\mathcal{D}^* := \bigcup_{n=0}^{\infty} D(\mathcal{H}^n)$ to denote the set of the density matrices acting on the Hilbert space of arbitrary number of qubits. We use lowercase Greek alphabets, e.g., ρ, σ, τ, to denote quantum state. We use capital Latin alphabets, e.g., A, B, M, T, to denote quantum registers. For a quantum register A, we write $|A|$ to denote the number of qubits in it. We denote the Hilbert space of a quantum register A by $\mathcal{H}_A$. The Hilbert space $\mathcal{H}_{AB}$ of a joint quantum register AB is the tensor product of the Hilbert spaces of each subsystems, that is, $\mathcal{H}_{AB} = \mathcal{H}_A \otimes \mathcal{H}_B$. It will be convenient to denote by $\varepsilon \in \mathcal{D}^0$ the empty state.

The trace distance between two quantum states ρ and σ, denoted as $\Delta(\rho, \sigma)$, is define by $\Delta(\rho, \sigma) = \frac{1}{2}\|\rho - \sigma\|_1$, where $\|M\|_1 = \mathrm{tr}\left(\sqrt{M^\dagger M}\right)$ is the trace norm of a matrix. Let $|+\rangle = \frac{1}{\sqrt{2}}(|0\rangle + |1\rangle)$ and $|-\rangle = \frac{1}{\sqrt{2}}(|0\rangle - |1\rangle)$. An EPR pair is the two-qubit state $|\Phi^+\rangle = \frac{1}{\sqrt{2}}(|00\rangle + |11\rangle)$.

A *state ensemble* $\rho = \{\rho_{a,\kappa}\}_{a\in\mathcal{D}_\kappa,\kappa\in\mathbb{N}}$ is an infinite sequence of quantum states indexed by $a \in \mathcal{D}_\kappa$ and $\kappa \in \mathbb{N}$, where $\mathcal{D}_\kappa$ is a domain that might depend on κ. When the domains of a and κ are clear from context, we remove them for brevity. We write $\rho \approx_{\mathrm{neg}(\kappa)} \sigma$ if there exists a negligible function μ, such that for all $\kappa \in \mathbb{N}$ and $a \in \mathcal{D}_\kappa$, it holds that $\Delta(\rho_{a,\kappa}, \sigma_{a,\kappa}) \leq \mu(\kappa)$. We sometimes abuse notations and write $\rho_{a,\kappa} \approx_{\mathrm{neg}(\kappa)} \sigma_{a,\kappa}$.

Let QPT stand for quantum polynomial time. Computational indistinguishability is defined as follows.

Definition 1. *Let* $\rho = \{\rho_{a,\kappa}\}_{a\in\mathcal{D}_\kappa,\kappa\in\mathbb{N}}$ *and* $\sigma = \{\sigma_{a,\kappa}\}_{a\in\mathcal{D}_\kappa,\kappa\in\mathbb{N}}$ *be two ensembles. We say that* ρ *and* σ *are computationally indistinguishable, denoted* $\rho \stackrel{c}{\equiv} \sigma$, *if for every non-uniform* QPT *distinguisher* D, *there exists a negligible function* $\mu(\cdot)$, *such that for all* $\kappa \in \mathbb{N}$ *and* $a \in \mathcal{D}_\kappa$, *it holds that*

$$|\mathrm{Pr}\,[\mathsf{D}(\rho_{a,\kappa}) = 1] - \mathrm{Pr}\,[\mathsf{D}(\sigma_{a,\kappa}) = 1]| \leq \mu(\kappa).$$

For a quantum operator U, we write U^A to specify that the quantum operator U acts on register A. Similarly, we write ρ^A to specify that the quantum state ρ lies in register A. Here, the register written in gray on the superscript is only for reminder, and whether it is written does not change the meaning of the operator or the state. That is, $U^A = U$ and $\rho^A = \rho$. We write χ^A to denote the maximally mixed state $I^A/|A|$ of register A. For $n \in \mathbb{N}$ we let $\mathcal{C}_n$ denote the set of Clifford operators acting on n qubits.

In this paper we make use of quantum error-correcting codes (QECC) and quantum authentication scheme (QAS) [ABOE10]. A QAS is a way to ensure that quantum state was not tampered with. We refer the reader to Sect. 2 of the full version [ACC+20] for a formal definition of a QAS. To remove confusion with the encoding and decoding of QECC, we view QAS as an encryption scheme.

We make use of Clifford codes [ABOE10]. Roughly, they are defined as follows. The encryption procedure, denoted $\mathsf{CAuth.Enc}_E$, encrypt a quantum message ρ using a Clifford E as its key (sampled uniformly at random). The procedure first append to ρ a *trap* $|0^t\rangle\langle 0^t|$, where t is considered the security parameter, and then applies the Clifford E to $\rho \otimes |0^t\rangle\langle 0^t|$. The decoding procedure, denoted $\mathsf{CAuth.Dec}_E$, accepts if and only if after applying $E^\dagger$ to its input and measure the traps, the value of the trap is $|0^t\rangle\langle 0^t|$. We refer the reader to Sect. 2 of the full version [ACC+20] for a formal definition alongside the security properties of Clifford encodings.

We also use trapcodes [BGS13]. A trapcode encrypts a single qubit ρ^M held in register M as follows. First, apply QECC.Enc on register M, and append t-qubits from register T_X in the state $(|0\rangle\langle 0|)^{\otimes t}$, and append t-qubits from register T_Z in the states $(|+\rangle\langle +|)^{\otimes t}$. Then permute the qubits of $\tilde{M}T_XT_Z$ according to Π, where $\tilde{M}$ is the register holding the encoding of the qubit ρ. Finally, apply X^xZ^z on register $\tilde{M}T_XT_Z$. That is,

$$\mathsf{TAuth.Enc}_{\Pi,x,z}(\rho) := X^x Z^z \Pi \left(\mathsf{QECC.Enc}(\rho) \otimes (|0\rangle\langle 0|)^{\otimes t} \otimes (|+\rangle\langle +|)^{\otimes t}\right) (X^x Z^z \Pi)^\dagger.$$

The decryption applies $(X^x Z^z \Pi)^\dagger$ onto register $\tilde{M}T_XT_Z$, and measure the register T_X in computational basis, and measure the register T_Z in Hadamard

$\{|+\rangle, |-\rangle\}$-basis. If the outcome of T_X is all zeros and the outcome of T_Z is all $+$, then apply QECC.Dec on register $\tilde{M}$ and set $|\mathsf{Acc}\rangle\langle\mathsf{Acc}|$ in F. Otherwise, replace the state in M with $|\bot\rangle\langle\bot|$ and set $|\mathsf{Rej}\rangle\langle\mathsf{Rej}|$ in F. Since $X^x Z^z$ is a Pauli operator up to a phase ± 1 or $\pm i$, we sometimes write $\mathsf{TAuth.Enc}_{\Pi,P}$ and $\mathsf{TAuth.Dec}_{\Pi,P}$, where P is a Pauli operator. We refer the reader to Sect. 2 of the full version [ACC+20] for a formal definition alongside the security and homomorphic properties of trapcodes.

We define the trap code *partial decryption* operation $\mathsf{TAuth.PDec}$, as the unitary part of $\mathsf{TAuth.Dec}$. That is, it decodes the permutation and quantum one time pad, perform the (unitary part of) QECC decoding on the first t qubits, and then apply Hadamards on the last t qubits to map $|+\rangle$ to $|0\rangle$. Formally, we define it as follows.

Definition 2. *Let $x, z \in \{0,1\}^m$ and let $\Pi \in \mathrm{Sym}_m$. Then,*

$$\mathsf{TAuth.PDec}_{\Pi,x,z} := (U_{\mathsf{Dec}} \otimes I^{\otimes 2t})(I^{\otimes 2t} \otimes H^{\otimes t})(X^x Z^z \Pi)^\dagger,$$

where U_{Dec} is the unitary operator corresponding to the QECC.Dec circuit.

Notice that when applied to a $\mathsf{TAuth.Enc}$ encoding of ρ using the same keys, the result is $\rho \otimes |0^{2t}\rangle\langle 0^{2t}|$. Similarly, we define the trap code *partial encryption* operation $\mathsf{TAuth.PEnc}$ as the unitary part of $\mathsf{TAuth.Enc}$.

Definition 3. *Let $x, z \in \{0,1\}^m$ and let $\Pi \in \mathrm{Sym}_m$. Then,*

$$\mathsf{TAuth.PEnc}_{\Pi,x,z} := X^x Z^z \Pi (U_{\mathsf{Enc}} \otimes I^{\otimes t} \otimes H^{\otimes t}),$$

where U_{Enc} is the unitary operator corresponding to the QECC.Enc circuit.

3   The Model of Computation

The security of multiparty computation protocols is defined using the real vs. ideal paradigm. In this paradigm, we consider the real-world model, in which protocols are executed. Here, an n-party quantum protocol π for computing a quantum circuit family $C = \{C_\kappa\}_{\kappa\in\mathbb{N}}$ is defined by a set of n interactive uniform QPT circuits $\mathcal{P} = \{\mathsf{P}_1, \ldots, \mathsf{P}_n\}$. To alleviate notation, we simply write C for the circuit. We then formulate an ideal model for executing the task. This ideal model involves a trusted party whose functionality captures the security requirements of the task. Finally, we show that the real-world protocol "emulates" the ideal-world protocol, i.e., for any real-world adversary $\mathcal{A}$ there exists an ideal-world adversary Sim (called the simulator) such that the global output of an execution of the protocol with $\mathcal{A}$ in the real-world is distributed similarly to the global output of running Sim in the ideal model.

In this work we are mainly interested in the security notion called *security-with-identifiable-abort*. Due to space considerations, the formal definition is deferred to Sect. 3 of the full version [ACC+20].

3.1 Security with Packet Drops

We now introduce a relaxed security notion of security-with-identifiable-abort that allows the adversary to drop some of the input-qubits and some of the output-qubits. We call this security notion *IDPD-security*. This security notion is parameterized with two polynomials $d_{\mathsf{in}} = d_{\mathsf{in}}(\kappa)$ and $d_{\mathsf{out}} = d_{\mathsf{out}}(\kappa)$ representing an upper bound on the number of input-qubits and output-qubits, respectively, the adversary is allowed to drop from the computation. The definition follows the standard ideal vs. real paradigm.

Informally, in the ideal world, in addition to sending inputs, the adversary also instructs the trusted party which single qubits are to be replaced with 0. Then, upon receiving the output, the adversary can decide to either abort the protocol while revealing the identity of a corrupted party, or to instruct the trusted party to discard some of the qubits in the output and distribute it.

We now formally describe the $(d_{\mathsf{in}}, d_{\mathsf{out}})$-IDPD ideal model, which specifies the requirements for an IDPD-secure computation of a circuit C with security parameter κ. Unlike the informal discussion from Sect. 1.2, it will be more convenient to have the adversary send to the trusted party the set of *remaining* qubits. Let $\mathcal{A}$ be an adversary in the ideal-world, which is given an auxiliary quantum state ρ_{aux} and corrupts a subset $\mathcal{I}$ of the parties.

Security with identifiable abort and packet drops

Inputs: Each honest party P_i holds the security parameter 1^κ where $\kappa \in \mathbb{N}$ and an input $\rho_i = (\rho_{ij})_{j=1}^{\ell_{\mathsf{in}}}$ where each $\rho_{ij} \in \mathcal{D}^1$ is single-qubit. The adversary is given 1^κ, input ρ_i of every corrupted party $P_i \in \mathcal{I}$, and an auxiliary input ρ_{aux}. Finally, the trusted party T is given the security parameter 1^κ.

Parties send inputs: Each honest P_i sends ρ_i to T. For every corrupted party P_i, the adversary sends a state ρ_i^* to T as the input of P_i.

The adversary instructs T to drop some input-qubits: The adversary sends to T a set $\mathcal{R}_{\mathsf{in}} \subseteq \{(i,j) \in \mathbb{N}^2 \mid i \in [n], j \in [\ell_{\mathsf{in}}]\}$ of size $|\mathcal{R}_{\mathsf{in}}| \geq n\ell_{\mathsf{in}} - d_{\mathsf{in}}$ (note that it could be the case that $n\ell_{\mathsf{in}} < d_{\mathsf{in}}$, in which case no restriction are imposed on $\mathcal{R}_{\mathsf{in}}$). Denote

$$\rho'_{ij} = \begin{cases} |0\rangle\langle 0| & \text{if } (i,j) \notin \mathcal{R}_{\mathsf{in}} \\ \rho_{ij} & \text{if } (i,j) \in \mathcal{R}_{\mathsf{in}} \text{ and } i \notin \mathcal{I} \\ \rho_{ij}^* & \text{if } (i,j) \in \mathcal{R}_{\mathsf{in}} \text{ and } i \in \mathcal{I} \end{cases}$$

and let $\rho' = (\hat{\rho}_{ij})_{i \in [n], j \in [\ell_{\mathsf{in}}]}$.

The trusted party performs the computation: The trusted party T prepares ancilla zero states ρ_0 and computes $C(\rho', \rho_0)$. Let $(\sigma_1, \ldots, \sigma_n, \sigma_{\mathsf{discard}})$ be the resulting output-states, where σ_i is the output associated with party P_i. The trusted party sends $\sigma_{\mathcal{I}}$ to $\mathcal{A}$.

Adversary instructs T to drop some output-qubits or halt: For every $i \in [n]$ write $\sigma_i = (\sigma_{ij})_{j=1}^{\ell_{\mathsf{out}}}$, where each $\sigma_{ij} \in \mathcal{D}^1$ is single-qubit. The adversary $\mathcal{A}$ sends to T either $(\texttt{continue}, \mathcal{R}_{\mathsf{out}})$ where

$\mathcal{R}_{\text{out}} \subseteq \{(i,j) \in \mathbb{N}^2 \mid i \in [n], j \in [\ell_{\text{out}}]\}$ is of size $|\mathcal{R}_{\text{out}}| \geq \ell_{\text{out}} - d_{\text{out}}$, or (abort, P_i) for some $P_i \in \mathcal{I}$. If the adversary sent $(\text{continue}, \mathcal{R}_{\text{out}})$, then for every honest party $P_i \notin \mathcal{I}$, the trusted party sends it $(\mathcal{R}_{\text{in}}, \mathcal{R}_{\text{out}}, \sigma'_i)$, where $\sigma'_i = (\sigma'_{ij})_{j=1}^{\ell_{\text{out}}}$ are defined as

$$\sigma'_{ij} = \begin{cases} \sigma_{ij} & \text{if } (i,j) \in \mathcal{R}_{\text{out}} \\ \bot & \text{if } (i,j) \notin \mathcal{R}_{\text{out}} \end{cases}$$

Otherwise, if $\mathcal{A}$ sent (abort, P_i), then T sends (abort, P_i) to all honest parties.

Outputs: Each honest party outputs whatever it received from the trusted party, the parties in $\mathcal{I}$ output nothing, and the adversary outputs some function of its view.

Observe that if $d_{\text{in}} = d_{\text{out}} = 0$ then the above process is identical to the security-with-identifiable-abort process. We denote by $\text{IDEAL}^{(d_{\text{in}}, d_{\text{out}})\text{-IDPD}}_{C, \mathcal{A}(\rho_{\text{aux}})}$ $(\kappa, (\rho_i)_{i=1}^n)$ the joint output of the adversary $\mathcal{A}$ and the honest parties in an execution of the above ideal-world computation of C, on security parameter κ, inputs $(\rho_i)_{i=1}^n$, auxiliary input ρ_{aux}, and packet-drop bounds d_{in} and d_{out}. When d_{in} and d_{out} are clear from context, we remove them from the notations.

We next give the definition of IDPD-security.

Definition 4 (IDPD-security). *Let π be a protocol for computing a circuit C, and let $d_{\text{in}} = d_{\text{in}}(\cdot)$ and $d_{\text{out}} = d_{\text{out}}(\cdot)$ be two polynomials. We say that π computes C with computational $(d_{\text{in}}, d_{\text{out}})$-IDPD-security, if the following holds. For every non-uniform QPT adversary $\mathcal{A}$, controlling a set $\mathcal{I} \subset \mathcal{P}$ in the real-world, there exists a non-uniform QPT adversary $\mathsf{Sim}_{\mathcal{A}}$, controlling $\mathcal{I}$ in the IDPD ideal-world, such that*

$$\left\{ \text{IDEAL}^{(d_{\text{in}}, d_{\text{out}})\text{-IDPD}}_{C, \mathsf{Sim}_{\mathcal{A}}(\rho_{\text{aux}})} \left(\kappa, (\rho_i)_{i=1}^n \right) \right\}_{\kappa \in \mathbb{N}, \rho_1, \ldots, \rho_n, \rho_{\text{aux}} \in \mathcal{D}^*}$$
$$\overset{C}{\equiv} \left\{ \text{REAL}_{\pi, \mathcal{A}(\rho_{\text{aux}})} \left(\kappa, (\rho_i)_{i=1}^n \right) \right\}_{\kappa \in \mathbb{N}, \rho_1, \ldots, \rho_n, \rho_{\text{aux}} \in \mathcal{D}^*} \quad (1)$$

Statistical and perfect security are defined similarly by replacing $\overset{C}{\equiv}$ with $\approx_{\text{neg}(\kappa)}$ and $=$, respectively, and assuming unbounded adversaries and simulators.

In Sect. 4, we reduce the problem of constructing a secure-with-identifiable-abort protocol, to the problem of constructing an IDPD-secure protocol.

3.2 The Hybrid Model

The *hybrid model* is a model that extends the real model with a trusted party that provides ideal computation for specific circuits. The parties communicate with this trusted party as specified by the ideal model.

Let C be a quantum circuit. Then, an execution of a protocol π computing a circuit C' in the C-hybrid model involves the parties sending normal messages to each other (as in the real model) and in addition, having access to a trusted party computing C. It is essential that the invocations of C are done sequentially, meaning that before an invocation of C begins, the preceding invocation must finish. In particular, there is at most a single call to C per round, and no other messages are sent during any round in which C is called.

Let type be an ideal world. Let $\mathcal{A}$ be a non-uniform QPT machine with auxiliary input ρ_{aux} controlling a subset $\mathcal{I} \subset \mathcal{P}$ of the parties. We denote by $\mathrm{HYBRID}_{\pi,\mathcal{A}(\rho_{\mathsf{aux}})}^{C,\mathsf{type}}(\kappa, \rho_1, \ldots, \rho_n)$ the joint output of the adversary and of the honest parties, following an execution of π with ideal calls to a trusted party computing C according to the ideal model "type," on inputs $\rho_1, \ldots, \rho_n$, auxiliary input ρ_{aux} given to $\mathcal{A}$, and security parameter κ. We call this the (C, type)-hybrid model. When type is clear from context we remove it for brevity.

The Classical MPC Hybrid Model

Following [DNS12, DGJ+20], throughout the paper, we assume the availability of a *trusted party*, denoted cMPC, that is able to compute any efficiently computable *classical* multiparty functionality. Furthermore, we assume cMPC is a *reactive* functionality, i.e., it is allowed to have an internal state that may be taken into account the next time it is invoked. One particular classical functionality we employ is the broadcast functionality. Thus, we implicitly assume that each party can broadcast a classical message at any given round of the protocol.

Similarly to [DGJ+20], we can implement cMPC using a post-quantum secure protocol. Specifically, we first remove the assumption that cMPC is reactive via standard techniques. To maintain security-with-identifiable-abort, this is done as follows. At the end of each call to cMPC, its state s will be shared in an additive n-out-of-n secret sharing scheme. Let s_i denote the ith share. The functionality then uses a post-quantum secure signature scheme to sign each share. Let σ_i denote the signature of s_i. The output of P_i will now additionally include s_i, σ_i, and the verification key of the signature scheme (which is the same for all parties). Note that the parties do not keep the signing key. In the next call to cMPC, the parties will additionally send their signed shares and keys to cMPC. If the keys are not all equal, then cMPC sends to party P_i the output (abort, P), where P is the lexicographically smallest party whose key differs from the key of P_i. Otherwise, if all the keys are the same, cMPC verifies all shares, sending the identity of a party whose verification failed if such a party exists, and reconstruct the state s and continue with the computation otherwise. Note that since the honest parties forward the output they received from the previous call, in case of abort they all agree on the identity of a corrupted party.

Finally, we can implement each call to cMPC assuming a correlated randomness setup, using the information theoretic UC-secure protocol of [IOZ14] and apply [Unr10]'s lifting theorem, to obtain post-quantum security. Furthermore, pre-computing the randomness in an off-line phase yields a protocol in the pre-processing model [DPSZ12]. Such protocols have an off-line phase which admits computational security, however, assuming no attack was successful during this phase, their online-phase admit information theoretic security.

Furthermore, for the sake of presentation, we sometimes abuse the existence of cMPC, and construct some of the ideal worlds with the ability to interact with it. Although this cannot happen in the standalone model, such an assumption can be removed using the techniques described above, i.e., each party will hold a signed share of cMPC's input and receive a signed share of its output.

We denote by $\mathrm{HYBRID}_{\pi,\mathcal{A}(\rho_{\mathsf{aux}})}^{\mathsf{cMPC}}\left(\kappa, (\rho_i)_{i=1}^n\right)$ the joint output of the adversary $\mathcal{A}$, cMPC, and of the honest parties in a random execution of π in the cMPC-hybrid model on security parameter $\kappa \in \mathbb{N}$, inputs $\rho_1, \ldots, \rho_n$, and an auxiliary input ρ_{aux}.

4   Statement of Our Main Result

In this section we present the main theorem of the paper, namely that any multiparty quantum functionality can be computed with security-with-identifiable-abort against any number of corrupted parties.

Theorem 2. *Assume the existence of a classical quantum-resistant fully homomorphic encryption scheme with decryption circuit of logarithmic depth. Let C be an n-ary quantum circuit. Then C can be computed with computational security-with-identifiable-abort in the cMPC-hybrid model. Moreover, the round complexity of the protocol is independent of the circuit depth.*

Toward proving Theorem 2 we first show how to reduce the problem to the problem of constructing an IDPD-secure protocol for a related circuit. The following lemma states the existence of such an IDPD-secure protocol.

Lemma 1. *Assume the existence of a classical quantum-resistant fully homomorphic encryption scheme with decryption circuit of logarithmic depth. Let C be an n-ary quantum circuit. Then C can be computed with computational $(n^2, 2n^2)$-IDPD security in the cMPC-hybrid model. Moreover, the round complexity of the protocol is independent of the circuit depth.*

The proof of Lemma 1 is given in Sect. 10. Toward proving it, in the following sections we construct several building blocks used in the construction of the final protocol. We now use it to prove Theorem 2. It suffices to prove the following claim, asserting that security-with-identifiable-abort can be reduced to IDPD-security.

Claim 3. *Let C be an n-ary quantum circuit and let $d_{\mathsf{in}} = d_{\mathsf{in}}(\kappa)$ and $d_{\mathsf{out}} = d_{\mathsf{out}}(\kappa)$ be two polynomials. Additionally, let QECC denote a quantum error-correcting code that can tolerate $\max\{d_{\mathsf{in}}, d_{\mathsf{out}}\}$ errors. Then C can be computed with perfect security-with-identifiable-abort in the $(C', (d_{\mathsf{in}}, d_{\mathsf{out}})\text{-IDPD})$-hybrid model, where*

$$C' = \mathsf{QECC.Enc}^{\otimes n\ell_{\mathsf{out}}} \circ C \circ \mathsf{QECC.Dec}^{\otimes n\ell_{\mathsf{in}}}.$$

That is, C' transversely decodes each of its inputs using the QECC, computes C, and then re-encode each output.

Due to space considerations, the formal proof is deferred to Sect. 4 of the full version [ACC+20].

5 Sequential Authentication

In this section, we present a protocol, called *sequential authentication* (SA), that allows a party – called the sender – to send an encryption of its input along a predetermined path known to everyone, to a designated party called the receiver (not necessarily different from the sender). The security achieved by this protocol roughly guarantees that in case the protocol is aborted, the parties will identify two parties, one of which is guaranteed to be corrupted. Later, in Sect. 6, using sequential calls to SA we show how to use it in order to augment the security to obtain an IDPD-secure protocol.

Let us first formally define the ideal world of SA. To simplify the presentation, we assume that cMPC is an additional party that will receive an output. Additionally, the parties have two common inputs, in addition to the security parameter. These are a path PATH and number of traps t. The domain of PATH is the set of all (non-simple) paths that goes through all parties, whose length is exactly[7] $\ell := n^2$. To remove confusion with the parties themselves, we call the parties along the path *relays* and denote by Q_i the ith party along the path (note that a single party may be multiple relays on the path). Furthermore, we call Q_1 the sender, and call Q_ℓ the receiver.

Ideal world of sequential authentication

Inputs: Each party P_i and cMPC holds the security parameter 1^κ, a path description $PATH = (Q_1, \cdots, Q_\ell)$ that goes through every party at least once, and the number of traps $t = t(\kappa)$ required for the output ciphertext. The sender Q_1 holds an m-qubit input state ρ. The adversary $\mathcal{A}$ is given an auxiliary quantum state ρ_{aux}.

The sender sends input: If $Q_1 \notin \mathcal{I}$, then it sends ρ as its input to T. Otherwise, the adversary chooses an input ρ^* to be given to T. Let ρ' be the input received by the trusted party.

The trusted party encodes the state and sends $\mathcal{A}$ its output: T samples a Clifford $E \leftarrow \mathcal{C}_{m+t}$ and encode ρ' to obtain $\sigma \leftarrow$ CAuth.Enc$_E(\rho')$. If $Q_\ell \in \mathcal{I}$, then T sends σ to $\mathcal{A}$.

The adversary instructs trusted party to continue or to abort: The adversary $\mathcal{A}$ sends to T either continue or (abort, Q_i, Q_{i+1}) where $1 \leq i < \ell$ and where either Q_i or Q_{i+1} is corrupted. If $\mathcal{A}$ sent continue, then T sends E to cMPC. Additionally, if the receiver $Q_\ell \notin \mathcal{I}$ is honest, then T sends it σ. Otherwise, if $\mathcal{A}$ sends (abort, Q_i, Q_{i+1}), then T forwards it to the cMPC and all honest parties.

Outputs: The honest parties output whatever they received from T, the corrupted parties in $\mathcal{I}$ output nothing, and the adversary outputs some function of its view.

---

[7] The reason for the fixed length is due to a technicality that follows from the way SA is used.

We denote by $\mathsf{SA}_{\mathcal{A}(\rho_{\mathsf{aux}})}(\kappa, \mathsf{PATH}, t, \rho)$ the joint output of $\mathcal{A}$, the honest parties, and cMPC, in an execution of the above ideal world, on security parameter κ, input ρ, auxiliary input ρ_{aux}, path PATH, and the number of traps t.

As mentioned in Sect. 1.2, our construction is similar to swaddling from [DNS12] and the public authentication test from [DGJ+20], both of which are based on Clifford code. Due to space limitations the construction alongside its proof of security is deferred to Sect. 5 of the full version [ACC+20].

We also make use of a variant of SA, where the input – instead of an arbitrary state – is encrypted under Clifford encryption, with the key being held by cMPC. We call this variant *input-ciphertext* SA (CTSA). The protocol follows the same lines as the protocol for computing SA and is presented in Sect. 5.2 of the full version [ACC+20]. We stress that unlike the protocol for SA, this protocol is *not* secure and will only be used as a subroutine in other protocols.

6   Authenticated Routing

In this section, we present a protocol, called *authenticated routing* (AR), that allows the parties to securely send an encryption of their inputs to a designated party. The security achieved by this protocol is *IDPD-security* (i.e., security-with-identifiable-abort-and-packet-drops), as was defined in Sect. 3.1. We extensively use AR as a building block in order to construct a secure-with-identifiable-abort protocol for a general circuit.

We next define the AR functionality. For a polynomial $t = t(\kappa) \geq \kappa$, representing *trap-size*, denote by $\mathsf{AR} = \mathsf{AR}_t$ the following mapping. Each party P_i holds ℓ_{in} packets $\rho_i = (\rho_{ij})_{j=1}^{\ell_{\mathsf{in}}}$, where each $\rho_{ij} \in \mathcal{D}^m$. An output is given only to P_1 – called the receiver – and to cMPC. Specifically, cMPC receives a collection of Cliffords $(E_{ij})_{i \in [n], j \in [\ell_{\mathsf{in}}]}$, where $E_{ij} \leftarrow \mathcal{C}_{m+t}$ are sampled independently and uniformly at random, and the receiver P_1 receives the Clifford encoding of each packet ρ_{ij} under E_{ij}; that is, P_1 receives $(\mathsf{CAuth.Enc}_{E_{ij}}(\rho_{ij}))_{i \in [n], j \in [\ell_{\mathsf{in}}]}$. In the following section we present a protocol that computes AR with $(n^2, 0)$-IDPD-security in the cMPC-hybrid model, i.e., at most n^2 input-packets can be dropped by the adversary while no output-packets can be dropped.

6.1   The Authenticated Routing Protocol

In this section, we present our protocol for authenticated routing. Roughly, the idea is as follows. Throughout the entire interaction, we let cMPC maintain a graph G that represents *trustfulness*. In more details, each vertex in G corresponds to party and the graph is initialized as the complete graph. Then, whenever a party accuses another party, the corresponding edge will be removed from G.[8] Following the initialization, each party P_i tries to send its packets

---

[8] We note that this technique, of using the graph to allow honest parties to unanimously agree on the identity of a corrupted party, was independently used in another recent paper by [BMMMQ20].

(ρ_{ij}), one by one, to P_1 along a path that goes through all parties. Such a path can be computed, and thus agreed upon, by having cMPC repeatedly applying BFS/DFS to find a path from P_i to P_2, then to P_3 until it reaches the last party P_n, from which it finds a path to P_1. The parties will send the packets along the path using the SA functionality.[9] If SA aborted, then the parties now hold two identities P_a and P_b given to them by SA, one of which is guaranteed to be corrupted. cMPC will then remove the edge ab from the graph G. Now, party P_i will try to send the rest of its packets using a *different* route that does not pass through the edge ab. The parties continue in this fashion until either most qubits were sent successfully, or until G becomes disconnected, in which case all honest parties are in the same connected component. Therefore, they can agree to identify a party *not* connected to them as malicious.

Let us now consider the case where a call SA ended in abort. Here, a single packet had been dropped, and so by the ideal-world definition of IDPD-security, the parties must agree to replace this packet with the 0 state. To do this, the parties will call SA again with the *empty state* $\varepsilon \in \mathcal{D}^0$ and $m + \kappa$ traps. To see why this work, notice that the Clifford encoding of the empty state with $m + \kappa$ traps, is equivalent to a Clifford encoding of $|0^m\rangle$ with κ traps. Moreover, by the security of Clifford encoding, if the adversary changes the traps from 0 then SA will abort again, which will remove another edge from the graph. Thus, this can be done repeatedly until either G becomes disconnected or the parties successfully encode the 0 state.

The IDPD-security of the protocol described so far can still be breached by a malicious adversary, due to the following difficulty one would encounter while constructing a simulator. Suppose that the adversary corrupted the receiver P_1, and consider a call to SA, for a packet $(1, j)$ for some $j \in [\ell_{\text{in}}]$, i.e., the receiver sends to itself an encoding of the packet. To generate the corresponding transcript, the simulator in the ideal-world must query the adversary for its input ρ to the SA functionality and must send to $\mathcal{A}$ an output in return. Observe that $\mathcal{A}$ expects to receive $\sigma = \text{CAuth.Enc}_E(\rho)$ where the key E is held by the cMPC. Since the simulator does not know the key E, it cannot generate a-priori a value σ that is consistent with the output of cMPC. On the other hand, the simulator may not be ready to send inputs to the trusted party either, as it must hold *all* input packets from the adversary. Since rewinding the adversary can help the environment to distinguish between the real world and ideal world, it seems to be the case where there are no good ways to generate this output of SA. One possible solution is to modify the AR ideal functionality so it will immediately encode and output each received packet before receiving the next packet. Unfortunately, the resulting ideal functionality would be too weak for our purposes later.

It is possible to overcome this challenge by tweaking the protocol. A simple solution to this issue would be to have the receiver, after it has received all of the packets, to send them to itself again using CTSA (that is, the ciphertext-input

---

[9] Recall that SA requires the path to be of length n^2. Note that the way cMPC computes the path always generates a path of length at most n^2. If the path is shorter, then cMPC can just add the last party repeatedly.

version of SA). With this modification, the simulator can send authentication of 0s to the receiver as the outputs of SA. To see why this works, recall that Clifford authentication ciphertexts are identical to maximally mixed states due to Clifford twirling. Thus, the simulator can then collect all input packets and interact with the trusted party to receive the correct outputs. When the receiver sends the dummy ciphertexts to itself, the simulator collects and verifies them, before replacing them with the correct outputs.

Although this approach works, as CTSA is not secure as a standalone protocol, it hard to formally argue the security of the above protocol. Instead, we slightly modify the protocol and also construct a slightly different simulator. The idea is to have the simulator send halves of EPR pairs as the output of SA, instead of authentications of 0s. Since halves of EPR pairs are indistinguishable from Clifford authentication ciphertexts, the adversary will reply with the same messages in both the real and the ideal world. After the simulator collects all packets and interact with the trusted party, it then replaces these halves of EPR pairs with the correct output via quantum teleportation. To complete the teleportation, the simulator must send a Pauli operator for the adversary to apply. Thus, we correspondingly add a key-update step at the end of the protocol to provide an opportunity for this.

Protocol 1 Authenticated Routing protocol π_{AR}

Inputs: Each party P_i holds private input $\rho_i = (\rho_{ij})_{j=1}^{\ell_{\mathsf{in}}}$ where $\rho_{ij} \in \mathcal{D}^m$.
Common input: The security parameter 1^κ and the packet-size m.

1. cMPC initializes G as the complete graph with n vertices where each vertex represents a party, and initializes a set $\mathcal{R}_{\mathsf{in}} = \emptyset$, which will keep track of all packets that were sent successfully.
2. For each packet $(i,j) \in [n] \times [\ell_{\mathsf{in}}]$:
   (a) cMPC computes a path PATH_{ij} in G from P_i to P_1 that goes through all parties of size exactly n^2, and send it to all parties.
   (b) The parties call SA with P_i's input being ρ_{ij}, with κ as the common trap-size, and PATH as the common path.
      – If SA outputs $(\mathbf{abort}, P_a, P_b)$ for some $a, b \in [n]$, then cMPC removes the edge ab from the graph G. If G becomes disconnected, then cMPC sends ab to all parties. Each party then outputs $(\mathbf{abort}, P)$, where $P \in \{P_a, P_b\}$ is the party on the edge *not* connected to it on the graph, and halts.
      – Otherwise SA terminates successfully, sending a uniform random Clifford $F_{ij} \leftarrow \mathcal{C}_{m+\kappa}$ to cMPC, sending σ_{ij} to P_1, where $\sigma_{ij} = \mathsf{CAuth.Enc}_{F_{ij}}(\rho_{ij})$, and sending $\mathbf{continue}$ to all other parties. In this case, cMPC adds (i,j) to $\mathcal{R}_{\mathsf{in}}$.
3. For each dropped packet $(i,j) \in ([n] \times [\ell_{\mathsf{in}}]) \setminus \mathcal{R}_{\mathsf{in}}$:
   (a) cMPC finds a path PATH'_{ij} in G from P_1 to itself that passes through every party and send it to all parties.
   (b) The parties call SA, trap-size $m + \kappa$, no private inputs, and PATH'_{ij} as the common input.

- If SA outputs $(\texttt{abort}, P_a, P_b)$ for some $a, b \in [n]$, then, similarly to Step 2b, cMPC removes the edge ab from the graph G. If G becomes disconnected, then cMPC sends ab to all parties. Each party P then outputs $(\texttt{abort}, P')$, where $P' \in \{P_a, P_b\}$ is the party on the edge *not* connected to P, and halt. Otherwise, if the graph is still connected, then the parties go back to Step 3a.
- Otherwise SA terminates successfully, sending a uniform random Clifford $F_{ij} \leftarrow \mathcal{C}_{m+\kappa}$ to cMPC, sending σ_{ij} to P_1, where $\sigma_{ij} \leftarrow \texttt{CAuth.Enc}_{F_{ij}}(\varepsilon)$, and sending $\texttt{continue}$ to all other parties.

4. For all packets $(i, j) \in [n] \times [\ell_{\text{in}}]$:
   (a) cMPC samples a Pauli independently and uniformly at random $P_{ij} \leftarrow \mathcal{P}_{m+\kappa}$ and sends it to P_1.
   (b) P_1 applies P_{ij} to σ_{ij}, obtaining τ_{ij}.
   (c) cMPC updates its Clifford key to be $E_{ij} = P_{ij} F_{ij}$.
5. cMPC sends $\mathcal{R}_{\text{in}}$ to all parties.
6. Each party outputs $(\texttt{continue}, \mathcal{R}_{\text{in}})$, cMPC additionally outputs the Cliffords $\{E_{ij}\}_{ij \in S_{\text{input}}}$, and P_1 additionally outputs $\{\tau_{ij}\}_{ij \in S_{\text{input}}}$.

We next state the security of the protocol.

Lemma 2. *Protocol π_{AR} computes the functionality* AR *with perfect $(n^2, 0)$-IDPD-security in the $\{\text{cMPC}, \text{SA}\}$-hybrid model.*

The proof of security is deferred to Sect. 6 of the full version [ACC+20]. We also make use of the *input-ciphertext* variant of AR, denoted CTAR. Similarly to CTSA, this is also insecure in general, so we only describe the protocol. Here, unlike in AR, there is only a single sender, denoted P_1, and multiple receivers. The goal of this variant is to send each *plaintext* from the P_1 to its designated receiver, encrypted under a *new* key. The protocol follows similar ideas to π_{AR} and is given in Sect. 6.2 of the full version [ACC+20]. We let π_{CTAR} be the protocol for computing the input-ciphertext variant of the AR functionality.

7 Magic State Preparation

Recall that we aim to have a single designated party to homomorphically evaluate a universal circuit over encrypted values. Towards achieving this, the parties require five kinds of magic states. These include ancilla zero states, P magic states, T magic states, H magic state and gadgets γ. In all magic state preparation protocols, an output will be given to only two parties: the server P_1 and cMPC. Furthermore, since the preparation is independent of the parties' inputs, these can be prepared in advance in an offline phase (in fact, the parties only require to know an upper bound on the number of gates in the circuit).

For space considerations, we will only present a rough overview of the construction of the protocol for preparing T magic states. The rest of the magic states can be prepared by using simpler protocols. These protocols can be found in the full version [ACC+20]. To simplify the presentation, the protocol and the functionality will prepare a single magic state. This, however, can be easily generalized to create more magic T states using the same number of rounds (see the full version for more details).

We next define the functionality MSP_T for preparing a single T magic state, $|T\rangle := T|+\rangle$. The other functionalities are denoted $\mathsf{MSP}_{\mathsf{ms}}$, where $\mathsf{ms} \in \{Z, P, H, \gamma\}$, are defined similarly (here ms represents either the ancilla zero state, $|P\rangle := P|+\rangle$ state, $|H\rangle := (H \otimes I)|\Phi^+\rangle$ state, or a gadget state $|\gamma\rangle$ defined in Sect. 7.3 of the full version [ACC+20], respectively). MSP_T is a no-input functionality whose output is defined as follows. Let $E \leftarrow \mathcal{C}_{3\kappa}$ be a uniform random Clifford. Then the mapping outputs to P_1 a Clifford encryption of the T magic state $\mathsf{CAuth.Enc}_E(|T\rangle\langle T|)$ and outputs to cMPC the corresponding key E.

7.1 T Magic State Preparation Protocol

Our protocol is a modification of the protocol of [DGJ+20] for preparing T magic states, which achieves only security-with-abort. Let us first give an overview of the protocol of [DGJ+20]. First, recall the result of magic state distillation [BK05] (or see the discussion in Sect. 2.4 of the full version [ACC+20]), that given $\mathrm{poly}(\log(1/\delta_0))$ copies of noisy T magic states with a constant fraction error, using the T distillation circuit we can obtain δ_0-close $|T\rangle$ state. Now, in [DGJ+20], the server P_1 prepares κn copies of $|T\rangle$. Then, the parties execute the *secure-with-abort* input-encoding protocol of [DGJ+20], which generates a Clifford encoding of each $|T\rangle$ state, i.e., $(\mathsf{CAuth.Enc}_{E_j}(|T\rangle\langle T|))_{j=1}^{\kappa n}$, and outputs to cMPC the corresponding Clifford keys. Following this, cMPC samples disjoint sets $S_1, \cdots, S_n \subseteq [\kappa n]$, each of size κ, uniformly at random, and sends them to all parties. For each subset S_i, the server P_1 sends $\{\mathsf{CAuth.Enc}_{E_j}(|T\rangle\langle T|)\}_{j \in S_i}$ to P_i and cMPC sends $\{E_j\}_{j \in S_i}$ to P_i. Then, party P_i decrypts and measures the received states in the $\{|T\rangle, |T^\perp\rangle\}$-basis, and broadcast an abort if it gets $|T^\perp\rangle$ in any of the measurements. We refer to this step as the *random sampling test*. Upon receiving an abort from a party, all parties abort and halt. Otherwise, [DGJ+20] showed that the remaining copies the server holds differ by a constant fraction from $\{\mathsf{CAuth.Enc}_{E_j}(|T\rangle\langle T|)\}_{j \in S_1}$ with respect to the trace distance. The server can then get a state of negligible trace distance from $\mathsf{CAuth.Enc}_E(|T\rangle\langle T|)$ with respect to a new key E, by running the T distillation circuit (guaranteed to exist by Theorem 2.8 in the full version [ACC+20]).

Clearly, the above protocol does not admits security-with-identifiable-abort. Indeed, not only is the input-encoding protocol of [DGJ+20] does not admit security-with-identifiable-abort, it further holds that a corrupted party may accuse an honest server by lying about the states that it measured. To overcome this two issues, we perform the following modifications to the protocol of [DGJ+20].

First, we make the following observations. Regardless of what the server prepares, assuming all states were successfully sent during the random sampling test, with overwhelming probability all honest parties will have roughly the same number of $|T^\perp\rangle$ states upon measurement. Therefore, instead of broadcasting abort, we consider each party's *error rate*, defined to be number of $|T^\perp\rangle$ it holds divided by κ. These will be sent to cMPC, who compares them. If there are two parties whose error rates are significantly far apart, then cMPC can publish them, and the honest parties can agree on which is corrupted.

Second, note that the previous observation holds only if the states were faithfully distributed by during the random sampling test. Indeed, the corrupted parties can bias the error rates by dropping the packets. Consider the following example. Suppose that P_1 is corrupted and $P_2, \ldots, P_n$ are honest. The server P_1 prepares each state to be $|T\rangle$ with probability $1/2$ and $|T^\perp\rangle$ with probability $1/2$. Then, after cMPC sends to P_1 the set S_2, the adversary drops the all $|T\rangle$ states that belong to S_2. As for the states that belong to S_3, the adversary will drop the $|T^\perp\rangle$ states. Consequently, the error rate ϵ_2 will be much higher than $1/2$ while ϵ_3 will be much lower than $1/2$. To solve this issue, we would like that for any state that was dropped, the error rate will not include it. We achieve this as follows. The server first prepares $N_0 := 3n^2 + 1$ copies of $|T\rangle\langle T|^{\otimes \kappa n}$. Then, for each copy of $|T\rangle\langle T|^{\otimes \kappa n}$ a random sampling test is applied, where each party receives κ of the qubits among $|T\rangle\langle T|^{\otimes \kappa n}$. Moreover, the qubits will be transmitted to their destination using the AR functionality, to ensure that the adversary cannot drop too many qubits. If there is a state that was lost during the transmission, all parties start the random sampling test for another copy of $|T\rangle\langle T|^{\otimes \kappa n}$.

Third, the parties need to be able to sample a subset of the qubits held by P_1, even if $|T\rangle\langle T|^{\otimes \kappa n}$ are encrypted under a Clifford code. The idea is to have cMPC update the encryption keys so that they will randomly permute the qubits and re-encrypt using a new key of the form $(E_1 \otimes \cdots \otimes E_n)$, where each $E_i \leftarrow \mathcal{C}_{\kappa+t}$, where t is the number of traps. Additionally, the permutation must ensure that each κ of the T states have t trap states $|0\rangle$ appended to. Observe that decrypting using such key would result in n pieces of T states, each of size κ and encrypted under a different key with t traps. The parties can then use input-ciphertext authenticated routing (formally defined as Protocol 5 in the full version [ACC+20]) to distribute the states.

Finally, we encounter the following difficulty when constructing the simulator. The T distillation circuit is not deterministic in the sense that which gates should be applied depend on previous measurement outcomes. To simplify the security proof, after performing the T distillation, the parties execute π_{CTAR} to have the server P_1 route all ciphertexts generated by the T distillation circuit *to itself*. Now, similarly to π_{AR}, we let cMPC updating its key using a random Pauli. Then, similarly to the simulation for AR, the simulator can send halves of EPR pairs as the output during the execution of π_{CTAR}. Among the remaining packets after π_{CTAR}, the simulator can teleport the output it got from the trusted party to P_1.

The formal description of the protocol alongside its proof of security are deferred to Sect. 7.4 of the full version [ACC+20].

8   Secure Delegation of the Computation – Preparation

In this section, we present a protocol, which we call *pre-computation*, that allows the parties to securely delegate the computation to a designated party, called the server. More concretely, at the end of the protocol, the server will hold an encryption of each of the parties' inputs, while cMPC will hold the keys used for the encryption. Later, in Sect. 9, we show how the server and cMPC can homomorphically evaluate a quantum circuit over the encrypted inputs. Thus, we require that the encryption used by the parties to be the TrapTP VQFHE scheme of [ADSS17]. Recall that a VQFHE is four-tuple of QPT algorithms (KeyGen, Enc, Eval, Dec), that generate keys, encrypt plaintext, evaluate a circuit of an encrypted message, and decrypt a ciphertext while verifying the evaluation was performed honestly. Our pre-computation protocol can thus be viewed as a way to implement TrapTP.KeyGen and TrapTP.Enc – the key generation and encryption algorithms of TrapTP, respectively – in a distributed manner. We next present a formal definition of the functionality we wish to compute.

Let $L = L(\kappa)$ be a polynomial (this will later represent an upper-bound on the size of a circuit to be evaluated and the number of ancilla 0 states it requires). Denote by $\mathsf{PreComp} = \mathsf{PreComp}_L$ the following mapping. Party P_i holds an ℓ_{in}-qubit input $\rho_i = (\rho_{ij})_{j=1}^{\ell_{in}}$, where $\ell_{in} = \ell_{in}(\kappa) \in \mathbb{N}$ is some polynomial. Only the server P_1 and cMPC are given outputs, defined as follows. Let $(\mathsf{sk}, \rho_{evk}) \leftarrow \mathsf{TrapTP.KeyGen}(1^\kappa, 1^L)$ (recall that $\mathsf{sk} \in \{0,1\}^*$ is a classical string and ρ_{evk} is a quantum state). Then cMPC receives sk and P_1 receives the encryptions of each input-qubit, encryptions of 0 states, and the evaluation key ρ_{evk}, i.e., it receives $(\hat{\rho}, \hat{\rho}_0, \rho_{evk})$ where $\hat{\rho} = (\mathsf{TrapTP.Enc}_{\mathsf{sk}}(\rho_{ij}))_{(i,j) \in [n] \times [\ell_{in}]}$, and $\hat{\rho}_0 = (\mathsf{TrapTP.Enc}_{\mathsf{sk}}(|0\rangle\langle 0|))_{i=1}^{L}$.

We now present a rough overview of our protocol for computing $\mathsf{PreComp}$ with $(n^2, 0)$-IDPD-security that outputs ciphertexts of size 3κ. The formal description of the protocol alongside its proof of security are deferred to Sect. 8 of the full version [ACC+20]. Conceptually, the protocol consists of three main steps. First, the private inputs of each party are routed to P_1 by a call to AR. This results in P_1 holding the Clifford ciphertexts of all private inputs, and cMPC holding the keys. Second, the parties call the magic state preparation functionalities. This include MSP_Z that prepares ancilla 0 states, MSP_P that prepares magic P states, MSP_H that prepares magic H states, MSP_T that prepares magic T states, and MSP_γ that prepares gadget states. At the end of the call, the server P_1 holds the Clifford ciphertexts of all these magic states, while cMPC holds the Clifford keys. Finally, as we use the TrapTP scheme, the homomorphic evaluation can only be applied to trap-code ciphertexts. Thus, we show how the server and cMPC can *re-encrypt* all Clifford ciphertexts to trap-code ciphertext.

9   Secure Delegation of the Computation – Computation

In the previous section we introduced the PreComp protocol for generating a key of TrapTP and outputs to the server P_1 encryptions of all inputs. In this section, we present a protocol that securely implements evaluation and verified decryption. This in turn, allows P_1 to perform the circuit evaluation, while ensuring to the other parties that the evaluation was done correctly. Looking ahead, as the server would need to distribute the outputs, unlike in PreComp, the resulting encrypted value held by the server would be under Clifford code. In Sect. 10 below, we will show how to securely distribute these Clifford ciphertexts.

Formally, let C be an n-ary circuit. Define the functionality Comp as follows. Let ℓ_{in} and ℓ_{out} be the number of input-qubits and output-qubits, respectively, of each party P_i. Denote the input of P_i as ρ_i. An output is given only to the server P_1 and cMPC, as follows. cMPC receives a uniform random Clifford for each output-qubit, namely it receives $(E_{ij})_{(i,j)\in[n]\times[\ell_{out}]}$ where $E_{ij} \leftarrow \mathcal{C}_{1+n^2\kappa}$ are sampled independently and uniformly at random. The server P_1 receives the Clifford encryptions of each of the output-qubits encrypted with the Cliffords given to cMPC. That is, P_1 receives $\mathsf{CAuth.Enc}_{E_{ij}}(\sigma_{ij})$, where for all $i \in [n]$ and $j \in [\ell_{out}]$ it holds that $\sigma_{ij} \in \mathcal{D}^1$ is a single qubit, and these are defined as $(\sigma_{ij})_{(i,j)\in[n]\times[\ell_{out}]} = C(\rho_1,\ldots,\rho_n)$.

Roughly, our protocol works as follows. First, the parties prepare the values required to run TrapTP.Eval. That is, they generate keys and ciphertexts of their inputs under TrapTP using PreComp. The server P_1 can now run TrapTP.Eval on the ciphertexts to homomorphically evaluate the circuit, obtaining the outcome $\hat{\sigma}_{ij}$ for every party i and qubit j (possibly after some qubits where dropped). As $\hat{\sigma}_{ij}$ is encrypted using TrapTP, the parties now need to re-encrypt it to a Clifford ciphertext. To do this, the parties call AR, to have the server route the encrypted results *to itself*. This results in a Clifford ciphertext τ_{ij} of a trap code ciphertext of the outputs.

We now explain how cMPC can verify the computation. Let us first recall two important properties of TrapTP.Eval and TrapTP.VerDec. Recall that TrapTP.Eval, in addition to performing a computation over trap codes, if further produces a log of the computation, that includes all the classical messages including randomness, computation steps, and all intermediate results during evaluation. Next recall, that although TrapTP.VerDec is a quantum procedure, it includes a classical subroutine that verifies these logs. We denote this subroutine by CheckLogs. It is given a secret key sk (generated from TrapTP.KeyGen used in PreComp) and a log to be checked, and outputs updated Pauli keys and a flag to indicate whether the computation was performed faithfully. We refer the reader to [ADSS17] for a detailed construction of the classical algorithm.

Now, P_1 sends log to cMPC who applies CheckLogs to check validity. Then, the server split the trap registers into Z_1 and Z_2 for each ciphertext τ_{ij}, and cMPC sends it the Clifford

$$V_{ij} = (E_{ij}^{MZ_2} \otimes R_{ij}^{S} \otimes \mathsf{TAuth.PEnc}_{\Pi_{ij},Q_{ij}}^{TZ_1})\mathsf{TAuth.PDec}_{\Pi_0,P_{ij}}^{MST} F_{ij}^{\dagger}.$$

Here, the first term $F_{ij}^{\dagger}$ would remove the Clifford encryption added by AR, resulting in a trap code ciphertext. Then the partial decryption of the trap code TAuth.PDec is applied (see Definition 2), using the global permutation Π_0, and the Pauli P_{ij} it got from checking the logs using CheckLogs. This converts the trap code ciphertext into a plaintext in register M, traps to be verified in register T, and the syndrome in register S (recall that trap codes use QECC in their construction). The term E_{ij} is a new Clifford that re-encrypts the plaintexts under a Clifford code, the term R_{ij} is a random Pauli that overwrites the syndromes to prevent leak of information, and TAuth.PEnc$_{\Pi_{ij}, Q_{ij}}$ perform partial encryption of the trap code (see Definition 3), to re-encrypt the traps in register T under trap code with a newly sampled key. The server is then asked to homomorphically measure these traps and send the measurement results to cMPC to verify, who aborts if the verification failed. Specifically, the verification compares the measured traps to 0's. If the protocol does not abort, the server outputs the computation results that is now under a Clifford code, and cMPC outputs the corresponding keys.

The proof of security is done by reducing it to the security of the TrapTP scheme. The formal description of the protocol alongside its proof of security are deferred to Sect. 9 of the full version [ACC+20].

10   Secure Computation of a Quantum Circuit with Packet Drops

In this section, we are finally ready to present our protocol for computing an arbitrary quantum circuit C with IDPD-security. That is, we prove Lemma 1. We do so by constructing a protocol in the {cMPC, Comp}-hybrid model. Given the functionality Comp from the previous section, the protocol is rather simple. The parties first call Comp, which ensures that P_1 will hold a Clifford encoding of the output of each party, and cMPC will hold the keys. The parties then execute π_{CTAR} to route each output held by P_1 to the correct party. Finally, if the protocol did not yet abort, then cMPC will send the keys to each output to the corresponding party.

The formal description of the protocol and its proof of security are deferred to Sect. 10 of the full version [ACC+20].

Remark 1. Interestingly, assuming that cMPC sends all Clifford keys to the parties *simultaneously*, it follows that identifiable fair[10] classical MPC is sufficient for identifiable fair quantum MPC (see Appendix A of the full version [ACC+20] for a formal definition). Indeed, observe that until cMPC sends the Clifford keys, all quantum states held by each party is encrypted. Therefore, an adversary that causes the protocol to abort gains no information on the output. Thus, if the last call to cMPC is fair, then all parties will receive the keys to their respective encrypted output simultaneously. This results in a fair MPQC protocol in the cMPC-hybrid model.

---

[10] In addition to fairness, identifiable fair computation have the added property that in case the protocol aborts, the honest parties agree on the identity of at least one corrupted party.

Acknowledgements. The authors would like to thank the anonymous reviewers for their useful comments and suggestions, and in particular for pointing out the existence of NC^1 decryption of classical fully homomorphic encryption schemes [BV11]. We would also like to thank Eran Omri for many useful conversations.

References

[ABDR04] Ambainis, A., Buhrman, H., Dodis, Y., Rohrig, H.: Multiparty quantum coin flipping. In: Proceedings of the 19th IEEE Annual Conference on Computational Complexity 2004, pp. 250–259. IEEE (2004)

[ABOE10] Aharonov, D., Ben-Or, M., Eban, E.: Interactive proofs for quantum computations. In: Chi-Chih Yao, A. (ed.) Innovations in Computer Science - ICS 2010, Tsinghua University, 5–7 January 2010, Beijing, China. Proceedings, pp. 453–469. Tsinghua University Press (2010)

[ACC+20] Alon, B., Chung, H., Chung, K.-M., Huang, M.-Y., Lee, Y., Shen, Y.-C.: Round efficient secure multiparty quantum computation with identifiable abort. Cryptology ePrint Archive, Report 2020/1464, 2020. https://eprint.iacr.org/2020/1464

[ADSS17] Alagic, G., Dulek, Y., Schaffner, C., Speelman, F.: Quantum fully homomorphic encryption with verification (2017)

[BCG+02] Barnum, H., Crepeau, C., Gottesman, D., Smith, A., Tapp, A.: Authentication of quantum messages. In: The 43rd Annual IEEE Symposium on Foundations of Computer Science 2002 Proceedings. IEEE Comput. Soc (2002) Authentication of quantum messages. In *The 43rd Annual IEEE Symposium on Foundations of Computer Science, 2002. Proceedings*. IEEE Comput. Soc, 2002

[BGS13] Broadbent, A., Gutoski, G., Stebila, D.: Quantum one-time programs. In: Canetti, R., Garay, J.A. (eds.) CRYPTO 2013. LNCS, vol. 8043, pp. 344–360. Springer, Heidelberg (2013). https://doi.org/10.1007/978-3-642-40084-1_20

[BK05] Bravyi, S., Kitaev, A.: Universal quantum computation with ideal Clifford gates and noisy ancillas. Physical Review A (2005)

[BMMMQ20] Brandt, N.-P., Maier, S., Müller, T., Müller-Quade, J.: Constructing secure multi-party computation with identifiable abort. IACR Cryptol. ePrint Arch. 2020, vol. 153 (2020)

[BOCG+06] Ben-Or, M., Crepeau, C., Gottesman, D., Hassidim, A., Smith, A.: Secure multiparty quantum computation with (only) a strict honest majority. In: 2006 47th Annual IEEE Symposium on Foundations of Computer Science (FOCS 2006). IEEE (2006)

[BV11] Brakerski, Z., Vaikuntanathan, V.: Efficient fully homomorphic encryption from (standard) LWE. In: Ostrovsky, R. (ed.) IEEE 52nd Annual Symposium on Foundations of Computer Science, FOCS 2011, 22–25 October 2011, Palm Springs, CA, USA, pp. 97–106. IEEE Computer Society (2011)

[CGS02] Crépeau, C., Gottesman, D., Smith, A.: Secure multi-party quantum computation. In: Proceedings of the Thiry-Fourth Annual ACM Symposium on Theory of Computing - STOC 2002. ACM Press (2002)

[Cle86] Cleve, R.: Limits on the security of coin flips when half the processors are faulty. In: Proceedings of the Eighteenth Annual ACM Symposium on Theory of Computing, pp. 364–369 (1986)

[DGJ+20] Dulek, Y., Grilo, A.B., Jeffery, S., Majenz, C., Schaffner, C.: Secure multi-party quantum computation with a dishonest majority. Advances in Cryptology - EUROCRYPT 2020 (2020)

[DLT02] DiVincenzo, D.P., Leung, D.W., Terhal, B.M.: Quantum data hiding. IEEE Trans. Inf. Theory **48**(3), 580–598 (2002)

[DNS12] Dupuis, F., Nielsen, J.B., Salvail, L.: Actively secure two-party evaluation of any quantum operation. In: Safavi-Naini, R., Canetti, R. (eds.) CRYPTO 2012. LNCS, vol. 7417, pp. 794–811. Springer, Heidelberg (2012). https://doi.org/10.1007/978-3-642-32009-5_46

[DPSZ12] Damgård, I., Pastro, V., Smart, N., Zakarias, S.: Multiparty computation from somewhat homomorphic encryption. In: Safavi-Naini, R., Canetti, R. (eds.) CRYPTO 2012. LNCS, vol. 7417, pp. 643–662. Springer, Heidelberg (2012). https://doi.org/10.1007/978-3-642-32009-5_38

[GMW87] Goldreich, O., Micali, S., Wigderson, A.: How to play ANY mental game. In: Proceedings of the Nineteenth Annual ACM Conference on Theory of Computing - STOC 1987. ACM Press (1987)

[IOZ14] Ishai, Y., Ostrovsky, R., Zikas, V.: Secure multi-party computation with identifiable abort. In: Garay, J.A., Gennaro, R. (eds.) CRYPTO 2014. LNCS, vol. 8617, pp. 369–386. Springer, Heidelberg (2014). https://doi.org/10.1007/978-3-662-44381-1_21

[Kit] Kitaev, A.: Quantum coin-flipping. Talk at QIP 2003 (slides and video at MSRI), December 2002

[RBO89] Rabin, T., Ben-Or, M.: Verifiable secret sharing and multiparty protocols with honest majority. In: Proceedings of the Twenty-First Annual ACM Symposium on Theory of Computing, pp. 73–85 (1989)

[Unr10] Unruh, D.: Universally composable quantum multi-party computation. In: Gilbert, H. (ed.) EUROCRYPT 2010. LNCS, vol. 6110, pp. 486–505. Springer, Heidelberg (2010). https://doi.org/10.1007/978-3-642-13190-5_25

One-Way Functions Imply Secure Computation in a Quantum World

James Bartusek[1(✉)], Andrea Coladangelo[1], Dakshita Khurana[2],
and Fermi Ma[3]

[1] UC Berkeley, Berkeley, USA
[2] UIUC, Champaign, USA
dakshita@illinois.edu
[3] Princeton University and NTT Research, Princeton, USA
fermima@alum.mit.edu

Abstract. We prove that quantum-hard one-way functions imply *simulation-secure* quantum oblivious transfer (QOT), which is known to suffice for secure computation of arbitrary quantum functionalities. Furthermore, our construction only makes *black-box* use of the quantum-hard one-way function.

Our primary technical contribution is a construction of *extractable and equivocal* quantum bit commitments based on the black-box use of quantum-hard one-way functions in the standard model. Instantiating the Crépeau-Kilian (FOCS 1988) framework with these commitments yields simulation-secure QOT.

1 Introduction

The complexity of cryptographic primitives is central to the study of cryptography. Much of the work in the field focuses on establishing *reductions* between different primitives, typically building more sophisticated primitives from simpler ones. Reductions imply relative measures of complexity among different functionalities, and over the years have resulted in an expansive hierarchy of assumptions and primitives, as well as separations between them.

One-way functions (OWFs) lie at the center of cryptographic complexity: their existence is the minimal assumption necessary for nearly all classical cryptography [22,23,28]. One-way functions are equivalent to so-called "minicrypt" primitives like pseudorandom generators, pseudorandom functions and symmetric encryption; but provably cannot imply key exchange when used in a black-box way [3,24]. Thus, the existence of key exchange is believed to be a stronger assumption than the existence of one-way functions. Oblivious transfer (OT) is believed to be *even stronger*: it implies key exchange, but cannot be obtained from black-box use of a key exchange protocol [29].

The importance of OT stems from the fact that it can be used to achieve secure computation, which is a central cryptographic primitive with widespread applications. In a nutshell, secure computation allows mutually distrusting participants to compute any public function over their joint private inputs while revealing no private information beyond the output of the computation.

The Quantum Landscape. The landscape of cryptographic possibilities changes significantly when participants have quantum computation and communication capabilities. For one, *unconditionally* secure key distribution—commonly known as *quantum key distribution* (QKD)—becomes possible [5]. Moreover, *quantum* oblivious transfer (QOT) is known to be achievable from special types of commitments, as we discuss next.

Crépeau and Kilian [11] first proposed a protocol for QOT using quantum bit commitments. The central idea in these QKD and QOT protocols is the use of (what are now known as) "BB84 states". These are single qubit states encoding either 0 or 1 in either the computational or Hadamard basis. Crucially, measuring (or essentially attempting to copy the encoded bit) in the wrong basis completely destroys information about the encoded bit. Then [6] presented a transmission-error resistant version of the [11] protocol. These protocols did not come with a proof of security, but subsequently Mayers and Salvail [31] proved that the [11] protocol is secure against a restricted class of attackers that only perform single-qubit measurements. This was later improved by Yao [37], who extended the [31] result to handle general quantum adversaries.

By an unfortunate historical accident, the aforementioned security proofs claimed the [11] QOT could be *information-theoretically secure*, since at the time it was believed that information-theoretic quantum bit commitment was possible [9]. Several years later, Mayers [30] and Lo and Chau [27] independently proved the impossibility of information-theoretic quantum bit commitment, and as a consequence, the precise security of [11] QOT was once again unclear. This state of affairs remained largely unchanged until 2009, when Damgard, Fehr, Lunemann, Salvail, and Schaffner [13] proved that bit commitment schemes satisfying certain additional properties, namely *extraction and equivocation*, suffice to instantiate [11] QOT. [13] called their commitments *dual-mode* commitments, and provided a construction based on the quantum hardness of the learning with errors (QLWE) assumption. We remark that assumptions about the hardness of specific problems like QLWE are qualitatively even worse than general assumptions like QOWFs and QOT. Thus, the following basic question remains

Do quantum-hard one-way functions suffice for quantum oblivious transfer?

Quantum OT: The Basis of Secure Quantum Computation. There is a natural extension of secure computation to the quantum world, where Alice and Bob wish to compute a *quantum* circuit on (possibly entangled) *quantum* input states. This setting, usually referred to as secure *quantum* computation, has been previously studied and in fact has a strong tradition in the quantum cryptography literature.

[4,10] constructed unconditional maliciously-secure *multi-party* quantum computation with honest majority. The setting where half (or more) of the players are malicious requires computational assumptions due to the impossibility of unconditionally secure quantum bit commitment [27,30].

In this computational setting, [16,17] showed the feasibility of two-party quantum computation (2PQC) assuming post-quantum OT. More recently, [15] constructed maliciously-secure general multi-party quantum computation (MPQC) secure against a *dishonest* majority from any maliciously-secure post-quantum multi-party computation (MPC) protocol for classical functionalities, which can itself be obtained from post-quantum OT [2].

Nevertheless, the following natural question has remained unanswered:

Can secure (quantum) computation be obtained from quantum-hard one-way functions?

1.1   Our Results

Our main result is the following:

Quantum oblivious transfer can be based on the assumption that quantum-hard one-way functions exist.

In fact, we prove a stronger result: we show that quantum oblivious transfer can be based on the *black-box use of any statistically binding, quantum computationally hiding commitment*. Such commitments can be based on the black-box use of quantum-hard one-way functions. This in turn implies secure two-party computation of classical functionalities, in the presence of quantum computation and communication capabilities, from (black-box use of) quantum-hard one-way functions [26]. The latter can then be used to obtain secure two-party *quantum* computation, by relying on the work of [17]. Quantum OT can also be used to obtain *multi-party* secure computation of all classical functionalities, in the presence of quantum computation and communication capabilities, and additionally assuming the existence of authenticated channels. This follows from the techniques in [12,14,25,26] which obtain classical MPC based on black-box use of any OT protocol. By relying on [15], this also implies multi-party secure *quantum* computation.

In summary, our main result implies that: (1) 2PQC can be obtained from (black-box use of) quantum-hard OWFs and (2) assuming the existence of authenticated channels, MPQC can be obtained from (black-box use of) quantum-hard OWFs.

This gives a potential separation between the complexity of cryptographic primitives in the classical and quantum worlds. In the former, (two-party) secure computation provably cannot be based on black-box use of quantum-hard one-way functions. It is only known from special types of enhanced public-key encryption schemes or from the hardness of specific problems, both of which are believed to be much stronger assumptions than one-way functions. But in the quantum world, prior to our work, (two-party) secure computation was only known from the special commitments required in the protocol of [13], which can be based on QLWE following [13], or post-quantum OT (implicit in [2,7,20])—but were not known to be achievable from quantum-hard one-way functions.

On the Significance of the Black-Box use of Cryptography in the Quantum Setting. Making black-box use of a cryptographic primitive refers to only having oracle access to its input/output behavior, without having the ability to examine the actual code (i.e., representation as a sequence of symbols) of the primitive. For instance, proving in zero-knowledge that a committed value satisfies some given predicate often requires explicit knowledge of the commitment algorithm; classifying the resulting proof as making "non-black-box" use of the one-way function. In the literature, constructions that make black-box use of cryptographic primitives are often preferred over those that make non-black-box use of cryptography. Besides their conceptual simplicity and elegance, black-box constructions are also of practical interest since they avoid expensive NP reductions involving circuits of primitives. Perhaps most importantly, in the case of black-box constructions, one can instantiate the underlying primitive with an arbitrary implementation, including physical implementations via secure hardware or those involving quantum communication.

In many quantum protocols, which involve quantum states being transferred between two or more players, black-box constructions are not only significantly preferable but often become *a necessity*. Let us illustrate this with an example. The GMW protocol [18] first showed that secure multi-party computation can be based on any oblivious transfer protocol; however the protocol involved zero-knowledge proofs involving the description of the (classical) oblivious transfer protocol. Due to the GMW [18] protocol being non-black-box in the underlying OT, our OT protocols cannot be used with GMW to obtain multi-party computation of classical functionalities. We instead need to rely on compilers like [12,14,25,26] that only make *black-box use* of the underlying OT protocol. As discussed above, the black-box nature of these compilers makes them applicable irrespective of whether they are instantiated with classical or QOT.

In a similar vein, we believe that our *black-box* use of any statistically binding, quantum computationally hiding commitment in our QOT protocol is of particular significance. For instance, one can substitute our statistically binding, quantum computationally hiding commitment with an unconditionally secure one in the quantum random oracle model [34], resulting in *unconditional quantum OT in the quantum random oracle model*. Moreover if in the future, new constructions of statistically binding, quantum computationally hiding commitments involving quantum communication are discovered based on assumptions weaker than quantum-hard one-way functions, it would be possible to plug those into our protocol compilers to obtain QOT. These applications would not have been possible had we required non-black-box use of the underlying commitment.

Primary Tool: Stand-alone Extractable and Equivocal Commitments. As discussed earlier, [13] show that simulation-secure QOT can be obtained from commitments satisfying certain properties, namely *extraction* and *equivocation*.

- At a high level, extraction requires that there exist an efficient quantum "extractor" that is able to extract a committed message from any quantum committer.
- Equivocality requires that there exist an efficient quantum "equivocator" capable of simulating an interaction with any quantum receiver such that it can later open the commitment to any message of its choice.

These two properties are crucial for proving simulation security of the [11] OT protocol: extraction implies receiver security and equivocality implies sender security[1]. Our key technical contribution is the following:

Extractable and equivocal commitments can be based on the black-box use of quantum-hard one-way functions.

We obtain this result via the following transformations, each of which only makes *black-box* use of the underlying primitives.

- *Step 1: Quantum Equivocal Commitments from Quantum-Hard One-Way Functions.* We describe a generic unconditional compiler to turn any commitment into an equivocal commitment in the plain model. By applying our compiler to Naor's statistically binding commitment [32]—which can be based on quantum-hard one-way functions—we obtain a statistically binding, equivocal commitment.
- *Step 2: Quantum Extractable Commitments from Quantum Equivocal Commitments.* We show that the [8,11,13] framework can be used to obtain an extractable commitment that leverages quantum communication, and can be based on the existence of any quantum equivocal commitment. This combined with the previous step implies the existence of quantum extractable commitments based on the existence of quantum-hard one-way functions.
  This is in contrast to existing approaches (e.g., [20]) that require classical communication but rely on qualitatively stronger assumptions like classical OT with post-quantum security.
- *Step 3: From Extractable Commitments to Extractable and Equivocal Commitments.* We apply the black-box equivocality compiler from the first step to the quantum extractable commitment obtained above, to produce an extractable and equivocal commitment.
  We point out that it is generally straightforward to make a classical commitment equivocal using zero-knowledge proofs, but this approach does not apply to quantum commitment protocols. We therefore devise our own equivocality compiler capable of handling quantum commitments and use it in both Step 1 and Step 3.

Plugging our quantum extractable and equivocal commitments into the [11] framework yields a final QOT protocol with an interaction pattern that readers familiar with [5,11] may find interesting: the sender sends the receiver several BB84 states, after which the receiver proves to the sender that it has honestly measured the sender's BB84 states by *generating more BB84 states of their own and asking the sender to prove that they have measured the receiver's BB84 states.* An intriguing open question is whether obtaining QOT from one-way

---

[1] It is important to note that extraction and equivocation are only made possible in an ideal world where a simulator has access to the adversary's state. Participants in the real protocol cannot access each others' state, which prevents them from extracting or equivocating.

functions *requires* this type of two-way quantum communication or, alternatively, quantum memory.[2]

1.2 Related Work

For some readers, it may appear that the central claim of this work—that quantum-hard one-way functions suffice for oblivious transfer—has already been established [8,13]. Indeed, prior work [8,13] showed that statistically binding and computational hiding commitments (which are weaker than extractable and equivocal commitments), known to exist from one-way functions, can be plugged into the [11] template to achieve an oblivious transfer protocol satisfying *indistinguishability-based* security.

However, the indistinguishability-based security definition for oblivious transfer is *not* standard in the cryptographic literature. When cryptographers refer to "oblivious transfer", they almost always mean the standard *simulation-based* security notion. Indeed, the fundamental importance of oblivious transfer in modern cryptography is due to the fact that it is necessary and sufficient for secure computation, but this is only true for the simulation-based notion.

1.3 Concurrent and Independent Work

In a concurrent and independent work, Grilo, Lin, Song, and Vaikuntanathan [19] also construct simulation-secure quantum oblivious transfer from quantum-hard one way functions via the intermediate primitive of extractable and equivocal commitments. However, the two works take entirely different approaches to constructing these commitments. We briefly summarize these strategies below.

This work:

1. Construct equivocal commitments from statistically binding commitments via a new "equivocality compiler" based on Watrous [35] rewinding.
2. Construct extractable commitments from equivocal commitments via a new "extractability compiler" based on the [11] template.
3. Construct extractable and equivocal commitments from extractable commitments via the same compiler from Step 1.

[19]:

1. Construct selective opening secure commitments with inefficient simulation against malicious committers from statistically binding commitments and zero-knowledge proofs.
2. Construct QOT with inefficient simulation against malicious receivers from selective opening secure commitments with inefficient simulation against malicious committers, following the [11] QOT template.[3]

---

[2] Naive approaches to removing one direction of quantum communication appear to require the honest parties to be entangled and subsequently perform quantum teleportation.

[3] [19] point out that the conclusions of Steps 1 and 2 together had also been established in prior works of [8,13,33].

3. Construct parallel QOT with inefficient simulation against malicious receivers from (stand-alone) QOT with inefficient simulation against malicious receivers via a new lemma for parallel repetition of protocols.
4. Construct verifiable conditional disclosure of secrets, a new primitive introduced in [19], from parallel QOT with inefficient simulation against malicious receivers, statistically binding commitments, Yao's garbled circuits, and zero-knowledge proofs.
5. Construct extractable commitments from verifiable conditional disclosure of secrets, statistically binding commitments, and zero-knowledge proofs.
6. Construct extractable and equivocal commitments from extractable commitments and zero-knowledge proofs.

We believe that our result is easier to understand and conceptually simpler, as we do not need to define additional primitives beyond extractable and/or equivocal commitments. Aside from differences in approach, there are several other places where the results differ:

- **This Work: Black-Box Use of One-Way Functions.** A significant advantage of our work over [19] is that we construct quantum OT from *black-box use* of statistically binding commitments or one-way functions. The OT in [19] makes non-black-box use of the underlying one-way function. As discussed above, making black-box use of underlying cryptographic primitives is particularly useful in the quantum setting. Due to the extensive use of zero-knowledge proofs and garbled circuits in [19], it appears difficult to modify their approach to be black-box in the underlying one-way function.
- **This Work: One-Sided Statistical Security.** Additionally, our oblivious transfer protocol offers *one-sided statistical security*. As written, our quantum OT protocol satisfies statistical security against malicious senders (and computational security against malicious receivers). Moreover, this OT can be reversed following the techniques in e.g., [36] to obtain a quantum OT protocol that satisfies statistical security against malicious receivers (and computational security against malicious senders). On the other hand, the quantum OT protocol in [19] appears to achieve computational security against both malicious senders and malicious receivers.
- [19]: **Verifiable Conditional Disclosure of Secrets.** Towards achieving their main result, [19] introduce and construct verifiable conditional disclosure of secrets (vCDS). This primitive may be of independent interest.
- [19]: **Constant Rounds in the CRS Model.** While both works construct poly(λ)-round protocols in the plain model, [19] additionally construct a constant round OT protocol in the CRS model based on (non-black-box use of) quantum-hard one-way functions.
  In an earlier version of this work, we did not consider the CRS model. After both works were posted to the Cryptology ePrint Archive, we realized that our techniques could be straightforwardly adapted to achieve constant round complexity in the CRS model, while still making black-box use of one-way functions. However, unlike [19], our CRS is non-reusable. For the interested reader, we sketch how this can be achieved in the full version.

2   Technical Overview

This work establishes that (1) black-box use of post-quantum one-way functions suffices for post-quantum *extractable and equivocal* commitment schemes and moreover, that (2) [11] quantum oblivious transfer instantiated with such commitments is a standard *simulation-secure* oblivious transfer. Crucially, the standard notion of simulation-secure (quantum) oblivious transfer that we achieve is sequentially composable and suffices to achieve general-purpose secure quantum computation. Before explaining our technical approach, we provide a complete review of the original [11] protocol.

2.1   Recap: Quantum Oblivious Transfer from Commitments

In quantum oblivious transfer (QOT), a quantum sender holding two classical messages m_0, m_1 engages in an interactive protocol over a quantum channel with a quantum receiver holding a classical choice bit b. Correctness requires the receiver to learn m_b by the end of the protocol. Informally, security demands that a malicious receiver only learn information about one of m_0, m_1, and that a malicious sender learn nothing about b. Somewhat more formally, as discussed earlier, our focus is on the standard simulation-based notion of security. This stipulates the existence of an efficient quantum simulator that generates the view of an adversary (sender/receiver) when given access to an ideal OT functionality. In particular, when simulating the view of a malicious sender, this simulator must extract the sender's inputs (m_0, m_1) without knowledge of the receiver's input b. And when simulating the view of a malicious receiver, the simulator must extract the receiver's input b, and then simulate the receiver's view given just m_b.

We recall the construction of quantum oblivious transfer due to [11] (henceforth CK88), which combines the information theoretic quantum key distribution protocol of [5] (henceforth BB84) with cryptographic bit commitments.

CK88 First Message. The first message of the CK88 protocol exactly follows the beginning of the BB84 protocol. For classical bits y, z, let $|y\rangle_z$ denote $|y\rangle$ if $z = 0$, and $(|0\rangle + (-1)^y|1\rangle)/\sqrt{2}$ if $z = 1$, i.e. the choice of z specifies whether to interpret y as a computational or Hadamard basis vector. Let λ denote the security parameter. The sender samples two random 2λ-bit strings x and θ, and constructs "BB84 states" $|x_i\rangle_{\theta_i}$ for $i \in [2\lambda]$. The sender forwards these 2λ BB84 states $(|x_i\rangle_{\theta_i})_{i\in[2\lambda]}$ to the receiver. Next, the receiver samples a 2λ-bit string $\hat{\theta}$, measures each $|x_i\rangle_{\theta_i}$ in the basis specified by $\hat{\theta}_i$, and obtains a 2λ-bit measurement result string $\hat{x}$.

CK88 Measurement-Check Subprotocol. At this point, the CK88 and BB84 protocols diverge. Since the BB84 protocol is an interaction between two *honest* parties, it assumes the parties comply with the protocol instructions. However, in the CK88 protocol, a malicious receiver who does not measure these BB84 states will be able to compromise sender privacy later in the protocol. Therefore, the next phase of CK88 is a measurement-check subprotocol designed to catch a malicious receiver who skips the specified measurements. This subprotocol requires the use of a quantum-secure classical commitment scheme; for the purposes of this recap, one should imagine a commitment with idealized hiding and binding properties. The subprotocol proceeds as follows:

- For each $i \in [2\lambda]$, the receiver commits to $(\hat{\theta}_i, \hat{x}_i)$.
- Next, the sender picks a random set T of λ indices from $[2\lambda]$, and challenges the receiver to open the corresponding commitments.
- The receiver sends $(\hat{\theta}_i, \hat{x}_i)$ along with the corresponding opening for each $i \in T$.
- The sender verifies each commitment opening, and furthermore checks that $\hat{x}_i = x_i$ for each $i \in T$ where $\hat{\theta}_i = \theta_i$. If any of these checks fail, the sender aborts.

The rough intuition for the subprotocol is simple: from the receiver's point of view, the BB84 states are maximally mixed and therefore completely hide x_i and θ_i. For any index i that the receiver does not measure, it must guess $\hat{x}_i$. From the receiver's perspective, the sender checks $\hat{x}_i$ against x_i if two $1/2$-probability events occur: (1) i is included in T, and (2) $\hat{\theta}_i = \theta_i$. This means a malicious receiver who skips a significant number of measurements will be caught with overwhelming probability.

CK88 Privacy Amplification. If all the subprotocol checks pass, the sender continues to the final stage of the CK88 protocol. For convenience, relabel the λ indices in $[2\lambda] \setminus T$ from 1 to λ; all indices corresponding to opened commitments are discarded for the remainder of the protocol.

For each $i \in [\lambda]$, the sender reveals the correct measurement basis θ_i. The receiver then constructs the index set I_b—where b is its choice bit for the oblivious transfer—as the set of all $i \in [\lambda]$ where $\theta_i = \hat{\theta}_i$. It sets I_{1-b} to be the remaining indices, and sends (I_0, I_1) to the sender. Note that by the hiding property of the commitments, the sender should not be able to deduce b from (I_0, I_1); furthermore, I_0 and I_1 will both be close to size $\lambda/2$, since for each $i \in [\lambda]$, the receiver committed to $\hat{\theta}_i$ before obtaining θ_i.

On receiving I_0, I_1, the sender sets $x_0 := (x_i)_{i \in I_0}$ and $x_1 := (x_i)_{i \in I_1}$. The intuition is that if a receiver honestly constructs (I_0, I_1), it will only have information about x_b corresponding to its choice bit b. However, it turns out that even if the receiver maliciously constructs (I_0, I_1), at least one of x_0 and x_1 will have high min-entropy from its point of view. Thus, by standard privacy amplification techniques, the sender can complete the oblivious transfer as follows. It samples two universal hash functions h_0 and h_1, both with ℓ-bit outputs, and uses $h_0(x_0)$ to mask the ℓ-bit message m_0, and uses $h_1(x_1)$ to mask m_1. That is, the sender sends $(h_0, h_1, h_0(x_0) \oplus m_0, h_1(x_1) \oplus m_1)$ to the receiver, who can then use x_b to recover m_b. Since x_{1-b} will have high entropy, the leftover hash lemma implies that $h_{1-b}(x_{1-b})$ is statistically close to uniform, which hides m_{1-b} from the receiver.

Simulation-Based Security. Turning this intuition into a proof of simulation-based security of the resulting QOT requires some additional insights [13], and requires the commitments used in the measurement-check subprotocol to satisfy two additional properties: extractability and equivocality. In what follows, we briefly summarize why these properties help achieve simulation-based security.

To argue that the resulting QOT protocol satisfies security against a malicious sender, one must demonstrate the existence of a simulator that simulates the sender's view by generating messages on behalf of an honest receiver, and extracts both QOT inputs of the sender[4]. Now, the measurement-check subprotocol described above is designed to ensure that at least one of the sender's inputs is hidden from a receiver. To nevertheless enable the simulator to extract both sender inputs, the idea in [13] is to modify the commitments used in the measurement-check subprotocol with *equivocal commitments* that allow the simulator to later open these commitments to any value of its choice. This enables the simulator to defer any measurements until after it obtains the set T from the sender, and then selectively measure *only* the states that correspond to indices in T. All other states are left untouched until the sender reveals its measurement bases in the final stage of the CK88 protocol. Upon obtaining the sender's "correct" measurement bases, the simulator measures all the remaining states in the correct bases, allowing it to learn both the inputs of the sender.

To demonstrate that the resulting QOT protocol satisfies security against a malicious receiver, one must demonstrate the existence of a simulator that simulates the receiver's view by generating messages on behalf of an honest sender, and extracts the receiver's choice bit. Again by design, the measurement-check subprotocol ensures that the receiver's choice bit hidden is hidden from the sender. To nevertheless enable the simulator to extract this choice bit, [13] modify the commitments in the measurement-check subprotocol so that the simulator is able to extract all of the $\{(\widehat{\theta}_i, \widehat{x}_i)\}_{i \in [2\lambda]}$ from the receiver's commitments. This enables the simulator to compute which one of the sets I_0, I_1 contain more indices i for which $\theta_i = \widehat{\theta}_i$; clearly the set with more indices corresponds to the receiver's choice bit. In summary, the key tool that enables simulation against a malicious receiver is an *extractable* commitment, that forces the receiver to use commitments for which the simulator can extract the committed value, without ever running the opening phase.

To conclude, following [13] the CK88 protocol can be shown to satisfy simulation-based security as long as the commitments used in the measurement-check subprotocol satisfy both the *extractability* and *equivocality* properties that were informally described above.

With this in mind, we now describe our primary technical contribution: a construction of the required extractable and equivocal commitments based on black-box use of quantum-hard one-way functions.

---

[4] We refer the reader to Sect. 6.1 for a formal definition of simulation-based QOT.

2.2 Our Construction: A High-Level Overview

The rest of this technical overview describes our *black-box* construction of simultaneously *extractable and equivocal* quantum bit commitments from any quantum-hard one-way function.

The ingredients for our construction are the following:

- A general-purpose "equivocality compiler" that turns any bit commitment scheme—classical or quantum—into an *equivocal* quantum commitment scheme. Moreover, if the original commitment scheme is *extractable*, this compiler outputs an *extractable and equivocal* commitment scheme.
- A general-purpose "extractability compiler" that turns any *equivocal* bit commitment scheme—classical or quantum—into an *extractable but not equivocal* commitment scheme.

Both of these compilers require no additional computational assumptions beyond those of the original commitment schemes. Given these compilers, we build extractable and equivocal commitments via the following steps:

- **Instantiation:** Begin with Naor's statistically-binding, computationally hiding commitments [32]. Naor's construction makes black-box use of one-way functions and achieves post-quantum computational hiding assuming post-quantum security of the one-way function.[5]
- **Step 1:** Plug Naor's commitments into our equivocality compiler to obtain an *equivocal* quantum bit commitment scheme.
- **Step 2:** Feed the resulting equivocal quantum bit commitments into our extractability compiler to obtain an *extractable but not equivocal* quantum bit commitment.
- **Step 3:** Run the equivocality compiler *a second time*, but now starting with the extractable commitments produced by the previous step. This gives the desired *extractable and equivocal* quantum bit commitments.

2.3 Making Any Quantum (or Classical) Commitment Equivocal

Recall that a quantum commitment protocol is *equivocal* if an efficient quantum algorithm called the *equivocator*, with access to the receiver, can generate commitments that can be opened to any value. More precisely, for any receiver

---

[5] In slightly more detail, Naor's commitment scheme makes black-box use of any pseudo-random generator (PRG). It is straightforward to verify that if the PRG is post-quantum secure, the commitment satisfies computational hiding against quantum attackers. A black-box construction of pseudo-random generators from one-way functions is due to [21]; Aaronson [1] and Zhandry [38] observed that [21] applies to non-uniform quantum attackers with *classical* advice. This can be extended to handle non-uniform quantum advice by giving the one-way function attacker constructed in the [21] reduction many copies of the PRG attacker's non-uniform quantum advice (which only requires some polynomial upper bound on the number of times the reduction invokes the PRG attacker).

(modeled as an efficient malicious quantum algorithm), there must exist an equivocator who can generate a computationally indistinguishable commitment that the equivocator can later open arbitrarily.

In this subsection, we describe a *black-box* compiler for a fairly general task (which may be of independent interest): making any *classical or quantum* commitment equivocal. Recall from Sect. 2.2 that we will need to invoke our equivocality compiler *twice*, once on a classical bit commitment scheme, and once on an extractable quantum bit commitment scheme; in the latter case, our compiler will need to preserve the extractability of the original commitment. Since classical commitments are a subclass of quantum commitments, our exposition will focus on challenges unique to the quantum setting.

Our Equivocality Compiler. In our construction, to commit to a bit b, the committer and receiver will perform λ sequential repetitions of the following subprotocol:

- The (honest) committer samples 2 uniformly random bits u_0, u_1, and commits to each one *twice* using the base commitment scheme. Let the resulting commitments be $\mathbf{c}_0^{(0)}, \mathbf{c}_0^{(1)}, \mathbf{c}_1^{(0)}, \mathbf{c}_1^{(1)}$, where the first two are to u_0 and the second two are to u_1. Note that since the base commitment scheme can be an arbitrary quantum interactive commitment, each commitment $\mathbf{c}_{b_1}^{(b_2)}$ corresponds to the receiver's quantum state after the commitment phase of the base commitment.
- The receiver sends the committer a random challenge bit β.
- The committer opens the two base commitments $\mathbf{c}_\beta^{(0)}, \mathbf{c}_\beta^{(1)}$. If the openings are invalid or the revealed messages are different, the receiver aborts the entire protocol.

If these λ executions pass, the receiver is convinced that a majority of the committer's remaining 2λ unopened commitments are honestly generated, i.e. most pairs of commitments are to the same bit.

Rewriting the (honest) committer's unopened bits as $u_1, \ldots, u_\lambda$, the final step of the commitment phase is for the committer to send $h_i := u_i \oplus b$ for each $i \in [\lambda]$ (recall that b is the committed bit).

To decommit, the committer reveals each u_i by picking one of the two corresponding base commitments at random, and opening it. The receiver accepts if each one of the base commitment openings is valid, and the opened u_i satisfies $h_i \oplus u_i = b$ for every i.

The (statistical) binding property of the resulting commitment can be seen to follow from the (statistical) binding of the underlying commitment. For any commitment, define the unique committed value as the majority of $(h_i \oplus u_i)$ values in the unopened commitments, setting u_i to $\perp$ if both committed bits in the ith session differ. Due to the randomized checks by the receiver, any committer that tries to open to a value that differs from the unique committed value will already have been caught in the commit phase, and the commitment will have been rejected with overwhelming probability. A similar argument also allows us to establish that this transformation preserves extractability of the underlying commitment. We now discuss why the resulting commitment is *equivocal*.

Quantum Equivocation. The natural equivocation strategy should have the equivocator (somehow) end up with λ pairs of base commitments where for each $i \in [\lambda]$, the pair of commitments is to u_i and $1 - u_i$ for some random bit u_i. This way, it can send an appropriately distributed string $h_1, \cdots, h_\lambda$, and later open to any b by opening the commitment to $b \oplus h_i$ for each i.

We construct our equivocator using Watrous's quantum rewinding lemma [35] (readers familiar with Watrous's technique may have already noticed our construction is tailored to enable its use).

We give a brief, intuition-level recap of the rewinding technique as it pertains to our equivocator. Without loss of generality, the malicious quantum receiver derives its challenge bit β by performing some binary outcome measurement on the four quantum commitments it has just received (and on any auxiliary states). Our equivocator succeeds (in one iteration) if it can prepare four quantum commitments $\mathbf{c}_0^{(0)}, \mathbf{c}_0^{(1)}, \mathbf{c}_1^{(0)}, \mathbf{c}_1^{(1)}$ where:

1. $\mathbf{c}_\alpha^{(0)}, \mathbf{c}_\alpha^{(0)}$ are commitments to the same random bit,
2. $\mathbf{c}_{1-\alpha}^{(0)}, \mathbf{c}_{1-\alpha}^{(0)}$ are commitments to a random bit and its complement,
3. on input $\mathbf{c}_0^{(0)}, \mathbf{c}_0^{(1)}, \mathbf{c}_1^{(0)}, \mathbf{c}_1^{(1)}$, the receiver produces challenge bit $\beta = \alpha$.

That is, the equivocator is successful if the receiver's challenge bit β corresponds to the bit α that it can open honestly. Watrous's [35] rewinding lemma applies if the distribution of β is *independent* of the receiver's choice of α, which is guaranteed here by the hiding of the base commitments. Thus, the rewinding lemma yields a procedure for obtaining an honest-looking interaction where all three properties above are met. Given the output of the rewinding process, the equivocator has successfully "fooled" the committer on this interaction and proceeds to perform this for all λ iterations. As described above, fooling the committer on all λ iterations enables the equivocator to later open the commitment arbitrarily.

2.4   An Extractability Compiler for Equivocal Commitments

In this subsection, we compile any classical or quantum *equivocal* bit commitment into a quantum *extractable* bit commitment. We stress that even though this compiler is applied to equivocal bit commitments, the resulting commitment is *not* guaranteed to be simultaneously *extractable and equivocal*; we refer the reader to Sect. 2.2 for details on how this compiler fits into our final construction. Recall that a commitment scheme is *extractable* if for any adversarial quantum committer that successfully completes the commitment phase, there exists an efficient quantum algorithm (called the extractor) which outputs the committed bit.

Construction. The committer, who intends to commit to a classical bit b, begins by sampling 2λ-bit strings x and θ. It generates the corresponding 2λ BB84 states $|x_i\rangle_{\theta_i}$ and sends this to the receiver. The receiver picks 2λ random measurement bases $\hat{\theta}_i$, and measures each $|x_i\rangle_{\theta_i}$ in the corresponding basis, obtaining outcomes $\hat{x}_i$.

Next, the receiver and committer engage in a CK88-style measurement-check subprotocol. That is, they temporarily switch roles (for the duration of the subprotocol), and perform the following steps:

1. The receiver (acting as a committer in the subprotocol), commits to each $\hat{\theta}_i$ and $\hat{x}_i$ (for each $i \in [2\lambda]$) with an *equivocal* commitment.
2. The committer (acting as a receiver in the subprotocol), asks the receiver to open the equivocal commitments for all $i \in T$, where $T \subset [2\lambda]$ is a random set of size λ.
3. The receiver (acting as a committer in the subprotocol) opens the λ commitments specified by T.

Provided the receiver passes the measurement-check subprotocol, the committer generates the final message of the commitment phase as follows:

- Discard the indices in T and relabel the remaining λ indices from 1 to λ.
- Partition $\{x_1, \ldots, x_\lambda\}$ into $\sqrt{\lambda}$ strings $\boldsymbol{x}_1, \ldots, \boldsymbol{x}_{\sqrt{\lambda}}$ each of length $\sqrt{\lambda}$.
- Sample $\sqrt{\lambda}$ universal hash functions $h_1, \ldots, h_{\sqrt{\lambda}}$ each with 1-bit output.
- Finally, send $(\theta_i)_{i \in [\lambda]}, (h_j, h_j(\boldsymbol{x}_j) \oplus b)_{j \in [\sqrt{\lambda}]}$.

This concludes the commitment phase.

To decommit, the committer reveals b and $(\boldsymbol{x}_1, \ldots, \boldsymbol{x}_{\sqrt{\lambda}})$. The receiver accepts if (1) for each j, the bit b and the value $\boldsymbol{x}_j$ are consistent with the claimed value of $h_j(\boldsymbol{x}_j) \oplus b$ from the commit phase, and (2) for each index $i \in [\lambda]$ where $\theta_i = \hat{\theta}_i$, the x_i from the opening is consistent with $\hat{x}_i$.

Extraction. The use of equivocal commitments in the measurement-check subprotocol makes extraction simple. Given any malicious committer, we construct an extractor as follows.

The extractor plays the role of the receiver and begins an interaction with the malicious committer. But once the committer sends its 2λ BB84 states, the extractor skips the specified measurements, instead leaving these states unmeasured. Next, instead of performing honest commitments to each $\hat{\theta}_i, \hat{x}_i$, the extractor invokes (for each commitment) the equivocator algorithm of the underlying equivocal commitment scheme. Since the equivocator is guaranteed to produce an indistinguishable commitment from the point of view of any malicious receiver for the equivocal commitment, this dishonest behavior by the extractor will go undetected.

When the malicious committer responds with a challenge set $T \subset [2\lambda]$, the extractor samples uniformly random bases $\hat{\theta}_i$ for each $i \in T$, measures the corresponding BB84 states to obtain $\hat{x}_i$ values, and sends $(\hat{\theta}_i, \hat{x}_i)_{i \in T}$. Moreover, the equivocator (for each commitment) will enable the extractor to generate valid-looking openings for all of these claimed values.

Thus, the malicious committer proceeds with the commitment protocol, and sends

$$(\theta_i)_{i \in [\lambda]}, (h_j, h_j(\boldsymbol{x}_j) \oplus b)_{j \in [\sqrt{\lambda}]}$$

to the extractor. These correspond to the λ BB84 states that the extractor has not yet measured, so it can simply read off the bases θ_i, perform the specified measurements, and extract the committer's choice of b.

Statistical Hiding. Intuitively, statistical hiding of the above commitment protocol follows because the measurement-check subprotocol forces the receiver to measure states in arbitrary bases, which destroys information about the corresponding x_i values whenever $\widehat{\theta}_i \neq \theta_i$. The formal argument is a straightforward application of a quantum sampling lemma of [8], devised in part to simplify analysis of [11]-style protocols, and we defer further details to the full version.

2.5 Putting It Together: From Commitments to Secure Computation

Plugging the compilers of Sects. 2.3 and 2.4 into the steps described in Sect. 2.2 yields a black-box construction of simultaneously extractable and equivocal quantum bit commitments from quantum-hard one-way functions. Following [13], these commitments can be plugged into CK88 to obtain maliciously simulation-secure QOT (see Sect. 6 for further details). Finally, going from QOT to arbitrary secure computation (in a black-box way) follows from prior works of [15,17,25,26]; a more thorough discussion is available in the full version.

3 Preliminaries

Notation. We will write density matrices/quantum random variables (henceforth, QRVs) in lowercase bold font, e.g. $\mathbf{x}$. A quantum register X will be written in uppercase (grey) serif font. A collection of (possibly entangled) QRVs will be written as $(\mathbf{x}, \mathbf{y}, \mathbf{z})$.

Throughout this paper, λ will denote a cryptographic security parameter. We say that a function $\mu(\lambda)$ is *negligible* if $\mu(\lambda) = 1/\lambda^{\omega(1)}$.

The trace distance between two QRVs $\mathbf{x}$ and $\mathbf{y}$ will be written as $\|\mathbf{x} - \mathbf{y}\|_1$. Recall that the trace distance captures the maximum probability that two QRVs can be distinguished by any (potentially inefficient) procedure. We therefore say that two infinite collections of QRVs $\{\mathbf{x}_\lambda\}_{\lambda \in \mathbb{N}}$ and $\{\mathbf{y}_\lambda\}_{\lambda \in \mathbb{N}}$ are *statistically indistinguishable* if there exists a negligible function $\mu(\lambda)$ such that $\|\mathbf{x}_\lambda - \mathbf{y}_\lambda\|_1 \leq \mu(\lambda)$, and we will frequently denote this with the shorthand $\{\mathbf{x}_\lambda\}_{\lambda \in \mathbb{N}} \approx_s \{\mathbf{y}_\lambda\}_{\lambda \in \mathbb{N}}$.

Non-uniform Quantum Advice. We will consider non-uniform quantum polynomial-time (QPT) algorithms *with quantum advice*, denoted by $\mathcal{A} = \{\mathcal{A}_\lambda, \boldsymbol{\rho}_\lambda\}_{\lambda \in \mathbb{N}}$, where each $\mathcal{A}_\lambda$ is the classical description of a poly(λ)-size quantum circuit, and each $\boldsymbol{\rho}_\lambda$ is some (not necessarily efficiently computable) non-uniform poly(λ)-qubit quantum advice. We remark that "non-uniform quantum polynomial-time algorithms" often means non-uniform *classical advice*, but the cryptographic applications in this work will require us to explicitly consider quantum advice.

Definitions for Cryptographic Commitments. Full definitions of cryptographic commitments can be found in the full version.

4   A Quantum Equivocality Compiler

In this section, we show a generic black-box compiler that takes any quantum-secure bit commitment scheme and produces a quantum-secure *equivocal* bit commitment scheme.

The compiler is described in Protocol 1, where (Commit, Decommit) denotes some statistically binding and computationally hiding bit commitment scheme. We describe how to equivocally commit to a single bit, and note that commitment to an arbitrary length string follows by sequential repetition.

Furthermore, we show that if the underlying commitment (Commit, Decommit) is *extractable*, then the resulting commitment is both extractable and equivocal.

These results are captured in the following theorems.

Theorem 1. *For $\mathcal{X} \in \{quantum\ extractability, statistical\ binding\}$ and $\mathcal{Y} \in \{computationally, statistically\}$, if Commit is a $\mathcal{Y}$-hiding quantum bit commitment satisfying $\mathcal{X}$, then Protocol 1 is a $\mathcal{Y}$-equivocal bit commitment satisfying $\mathcal{X}$.*

These theorems follow from establishing statistical binding, equivocality, and extractability of the commitment in Protocol 1, as we do next. First, we note that if Commit is statistically binding, then Protocol 1 is statistically binding. For any adversarial committer strategy, consider the λ unopened pairs of commitments after the commit phase. Since Commit is statistically binding, we can assume that each of the 2λ commitments is binding to a particular bit, except with negligible probability. Now, if any single pair contains binding commitments to the same bit d_i, then the committer will only be able to open its Protocol 1 commitment to the bit $d_i \oplus e_i$. Thus, to violate binding, the adversarial committer will have to have committed to different bits in each of the λ unopened pairs. However, in this case, the committer will be caught and the receiver will abort except with probability $1/2^\lambda$.

4.1   Equivocality

The equivocal simulator ($\mathcal{Q}_{\mathcal{R}^*,\mathrm{com}}, \mathcal{Q}_{\mathcal{R}^*,\mathrm{open}}$) is obtained via the use of Watrous's quantum rewinding lemma [35]; a full statement of the lemma is available in

---

Protocol 1

Committer C Input: Bit $b \in \{0,1\}$.
The Protocol: Commit Phase

1. C samples uniformly random bits $d_{i,j}$ for $i \in [\lambda]$ and $j \in \{0,1\}$.
2. For every $i \in [\lambda]$, C and R sequentially perform the following steps.
   (a) C and R execute four sessions sequentially, namely:
     – $\mathbf{x}_{0,0}, \mathbf{y}_{0,0} \leftarrow \mathsf{Commit}\langle C(d_{i,0}), R\rangle$,
     – $\mathbf{x}_{0,1}, \mathbf{y}_{0,1} \leftarrow \mathsf{Commit}\langle C(d_{i,0}), R\rangle$,
     – $\mathbf{x}_{1,0}, \mathbf{y}_{1,0} \leftarrow \mathsf{Commit}\langle C(d_{i,1}), R\rangle$ and
     – $\mathbf{x}_{1,1}, \mathbf{y}_{1,1} \leftarrow \mathsf{Commit}\langle C(d_{i,1}), R\rangle$.
   (b) R sends a choice bit $c_i \leftarrow \{0,1\}$.
   (c) C and R execute two decommitments, obtaining the opened bits:
     – $u \leftarrow \mathsf{Decommit}\langle C(\mathbf{x}_{c_i,0}), R(\mathbf{y}_{c_i,0})\rangle$ and
     – $v \leftarrow \mathsf{Decommit}\langle C(\mathbf{x}_{c_i,1}), R(\mathbf{y}_{c_i,1})\rangle$.
     If $u \neq v$, R aborts. Otherwise, C and R continue.
3. For $i \in [\lambda]$, C sets $e_i = b \oplus d_{i,1-c_i}$ and sends $\{e_i\}_{i\in[\lambda]}$ to R.

The Protocol: Decommit Phase

1. C sends b to R. In addition,
   – For $i \in [\lambda]$, C picks $\alpha_i \leftarrow \{0,1\}$ and sends it to R.
   – C and R execute $\widehat{d_i} \leftarrow \mathsf{Decommit}\langle C(\mathbf{x}_{1-c_i,\alpha_i}), R(\mathbf{y}_{1-c_i,\alpha_i})\rangle$.
2. R accepts the decommitment and outputs b if for every $i \in [\lambda]$, $\widehat{d_i} = b \oplus e_i$.

Fig. 1. Equivocal bit commitment.

the full version. For the purposes of defining the simulation strategy, it will be sufficient (w.l.o.g.) to consider a restricted receiver R^* as follows, for the ith sequential step of the protocol. In our simulation, the state of R^* will be initialized to the final state at the end of simulating the $(i-1)^{th}$ step.

1. R^* takes a quantum register W, representing its auxiliary quantum input. R^* will use two additional quantum registers that function as work space: V, which is an arbitrary (polynomial-size) register, and A, which is a single qubit register. The registers V and A are initialized to their all-zero states before the protocol begins.
2. Let M denote the polynomial-size register used by C to send messages to R^*. After carrying out step 2(a) by running on registers (W, V, A, M), R^* measures the register A to obtain a bit c_i, for Step 2(b), which it sends back to C.
3. Next, R^* computes the decommitment phases (with messages from C placed in register M) according to Step 2(c). R^* outputs registers (W, V, A, M).

Any polynomial-time quantum receiver can be modeled as a receiver of this restricted form followed by some polynomial-time post-processing of the

484   J. Bartusek et al.

restricted receiver's output. The same post-processing can be applied to the output of the simulator that will be constructed for the given restricted receiver.

Following [35], we define a simulator that uses two additional registers, C and Z. C is a one qubit register, while Z is an auxiliary register used to implement the computation that will be described next. Consider a quantum procedure $\mathcal{Q}_{\text{partial}}$ that implements the strategy described in Protocol 2 using these registers.

Protocol 2

Circuit $\mathcal{Q}_{\text{partial}}$.

1. Sample a uniformly random classical bit $\widehat{c}$, and store it in register C.
2. Sample uniformly random bits (z, d).
3. If $\widehat{c} = 0$, initialize committer input as follows, corresponding to four sequential sessions:
   - For the first two sessions, set committer input to z.
   - For the third and fourth sessions, set committer input to d and $1 - d$ respectively.
4. If $\widehat{c} = 1$, initialize committer input as follows, corresponding to four sequential sessions:
   - For the first and second sessions, set committer input to d and $1 - d$ respectively.
   - For the last two sessions, set committer input to z.
5. Run the commitment phase interaction between the honest committer and $\mathcal{R}^*$'s sequence of unitaries on registers initialized as above.
6. Measure the qubit register A to obtain a bit c. If $c = \widehat{c}$, output 0, otherwise output 1.

Fig. 2. Equivocal simulator.

Next, we would like to apply Watrous's quantum rewinding lemma to the $\mathcal{Q}_{\text{partial}}$ circuit. In order to do this, we will argue that the probability $p(\psi)$ that this circuit outputs 0 is such that $|p(\psi) - \frac{1}{2}| = \mathsf{negl}(\lambda)$, regardless of the auxiliary input $|\psi\rangle$ to $\mathcal{R}^*$. This follows from the fact that the commitments are (statistically/computationally) hiding. In more detail, by definition, Step 5 produces a distribution on the $\mathcal{R}^*$'s side that is identical to the distribution generated by $\mathcal{R}^*$ in its interaction with the committer. If $|p(\psi) - \frac{1}{2}|$ were non-negligible, then the sequence of unitaries applied by $\mathcal{R}^*$ could be used to distinguish commitments generated according to the case $\widehat{c} = 0$ from commitments generated according to the case $\widehat{c} = 1$, leading to a contradiction.

Now consider the state of the residual qubits of $\mathcal{Q}_{\text{partial}}$ conditioned on a measurement of its output qubit being 0. The output state of the general quantum circuit $\widehat{\mathcal{Q}}$ resulting from applying Watrous's quantum rewinding lemma will have negligible trace distance from this state. This state is over all of the registers discussed above, so the simulator $\mathcal{Q}_{\text{com},\mathcal{R}^*}$ must further process this state as:

- Measure the register C, obtaining challenge c.
- Compute decommitment information corresponding to challenge c, as in Step 2(c) of the protocol (recall that this information is stored in the message register M).
- Output registers (W, V, A, M). All remaining registers are traced out.

The simulator $\mathcal{Q}_{\mathcal{R}^*,\mathsf{com}}$ executes all i sequential interactions in this manner, and then samples $e_1, \ldots, e_\lambda \leftarrow \{0,1\}^\lambda$, as the committer messages for Step 3 of Protocol 1. It runs the receiver's unitary on the resulting protocol, and outputs the resulting registers (W, V, A, M). It additionally outputs private state $\mathsf{st} = (c_1, d_1, \ldots, c_\lambda, d_\lambda)$ where c_i, d_i were sampled during the ith execution of Protocol 2.

The simulator $\mathcal{Q}_{\mathcal{R}^*,\mathsf{open}}(b, \mathsf{st}, \mathbf{w}, \mathbf{v}, \mathbf{a}, \mathbf{m})$ parses st as $(c_1, d_1, \ldots, c_\lambda, d_\lambda)$. For every $i \in [\lambda]$ it does the following:

- Let $\widehat{d}_i = b \oplus e_i$.
- If $c_i = 0$, it executes the decommitment phase for the $((\widehat{d}_i \oplus d_i) + 2)^{th}$ session.
- If $c_i = 1$, it executes the decommitment phase for the $(\widehat{d}_i \oplus d_i)^{th}$ session.

$\mathcal{Q}_{\mathcal{R}^*,\mathsf{open}}$ then executes the receiver's algorithm on these decommitments and outputs the resulting state. Note that each decommitment will be to the bit $\widehat{d}_i = b \oplus e_i$.

To complete the proof of equivocality, we must establish that the view of the receiver interacting with an honest committer the view of the receiver interacting with the equivocator are indistinguishable. This follows from the (statistical/computational) hiding of the commitment scheme, via an identical argument to the one used above. In particular, if the equivocal simulator produces a distribution that is distinguishable from the real distribution, then there exists a session $i \in [\lambda]$ such that the distribution in the real and ideal experiments upto the $i - 1^{th}$ session are indistinguishable, but upto the ith session are distinguishable. This contradicts the above guarantee given by the quantum rewinding lemma, since for any i, the post-processed residual qubits of $\mathcal{Q}_{\mathsf{partial}}$ are indistinguishable from the state of $\mathcal{R}^*$ after the ith sequential session in the real protocol (due to the hiding of the commitment scheme).

4.2 Extractability

Next, we prove that Protocol 1 satisfies extractability as long as the underlying commitment (Commit, Decommit) is extractable; in other words, this compiler preserves extractability. Consider the following extractor $\mathcal{E}_{\mathcal{C}^*}$.

- For $i \in [\lambda]$:
    • Execute four sequential commitment sessions with $\mathcal{C}^*$, where the extractor of Commit is run on all sessions. Obtain outputs $(\rho_{\mathcal{C}^*}, \mathsf{st}_{\mathcal{R},i,0}, d'_{i,0}, \mathsf{st}_{\mathcal{R},i,1}, d'_{i,1})$, where $\rho_{\mathcal{C}^*}$ is the final state of the committer after engaging in all four sequential sessions, and $\mathsf{st}_{\mathcal{R},i,0}$, $\mathsf{st}_{\mathcal{R},i,1}$ are receiver states output by the extractor corresponding to the first and third sessions.

- Corresponding to Step 2(b), compute and send $c_i \leftarrow \{0,1\}$.
- Execute Step 2(c) identically to Protocol 1.
- Executes Step 3 of Protocol 1, receiving bits $\{e_i\}_{i \in [\lambda]}$. Fix b^* to be the most frequently occurring bit in $\{e_i \oplus d'_{i,1-c_i}\}_{i \in [\lambda]}$, and output the final state of $\mathcal{C}^*$, the receiver states $\{\mathsf{st}_{\mathcal{R},i,0}, \mathsf{st}_{\mathcal{R},i,1}\}_{i \in [\lambda]}$, and the extracted bit b^*.

Indistinguishability between the distributions Real and Ideal defined by the above extractor follows by a hybrid argument, and is based on the definition of extractability of the underlying commitment (Commit, Decommit). In more detail, recall that Real denotes the distribution $(\rho_{\mathcal{C}^*,\mathsf{final}}, b)$ where $\rho_{\mathcal{C}^*,\mathsf{final}}$ denotes the final state of $\mathcal{C}^*$ and b the output of the receiver, and Ideal denotes the final committer state and opened bit after the opening phase of the scheme is run on the output of the extractor.

Note that there are a total of 4λ commitment sessions. For each $i \in [\lambda], j \in [0,3]$, define $\mathsf{Hyb}_{i,j}$ to be the distribution of the committer's state and receiver output when extracting from all commitments in sessions $1, \ldots, i-1$ and extracting from the first j commitments in the ith session, but computing the receiver's output as in the honest protocol.

Claim. There exists a negligible function $\mu(\cdot)$ such that for every $i \in [\lambda], j \in [0,2]$, and every QPT distinguisher $\mathcal{D}$,

$$|\Pr[\mathcal{D}(\mathsf{Hybrid}_{i,j}) = 1] - \Pr[\mathcal{D}(\mathsf{Hybrid}_{i,j+1}) = 1]| = \mu(\lambda),$$

and for every $i \in [\lambda]$ and every QPT distinguisher $\mathcal{D}$,

$$|\Pr[\mathcal{D}(\mathsf{Hybrid}_{i,3}) = 1] - \Pr[\mathcal{D}(\mathsf{Hybrid}_{i+1,0}) = 1]| = \mu(\lambda).$$

Proof. Suppose this is not the case, then there exists an adversarial committer $\mathcal{C}^*$, a distinguisher $\mathcal{D}$, a polynomial $p(\cdot)$, and an initial committer state ψ that corresponds to a state just before the beginning of the $(i, j+1)^{th}$ commitment, and where

$$\Pr[\mathcal{D}(\mathsf{Hybrid}_{i,j}) = 1] - \Pr[\mathcal{D}(\mathsf{Hybrid}_{i,j+1}) = 1]| \geq \frac{1}{p(\lambda)}.$$

Consider a reduction/adversarial committer $\widetilde{\mathcal{C}}$ that obtains initial state ψ, then internally runs $\mathcal{C}^*$, forwarding all messages between an external receiver and $\mathcal{C}^*$ for the $(i, j+1)^{th}$ commitment. It then begins the opening phase, running $\mathcal{C}^*$ internally and forwarding the opening of the $(i, j+1)^{th}$ commitment (if it is executed) to an external receiver. Finally, it outputs the final state of the committer, and b is output by the external receiver. The claim being false directly implies that $\widetilde{\mathcal{C}}$ contradicts extractability of the bit commitment. $\square$

Now for every commitment strategy, every $i \in [\lambda]$, the probability that $d'_{i,1-c_i}$ is not equal to the other bit committed in its pair, and yet the receiver does not abort in Step 2(c) in the ith sequential repetition, is $\leq \frac{1}{2} + \mathsf{negl}(\lambda)$. Then with probability $1 - \mathsf{negl}(\lambda)$, the same also holds for the extracted bits. Thus, by the correctness of the extractor, this implies that the probability that an adversarial committer opens to $1 - b^*$ is at most $1/2^{\lambda/2} + \mathsf{negl}(\lambda) = \mathsf{negl}(\lambda)$. This implies that $\mathsf{Hybrid}_{\lambda,2}$ is indistinguishable from the Ideal distribution defined by the extractor defined above, since the only difference lies in the computation of the receiver's output b^*. Since Real is indistinguishable from $\mathsf{Hybrid}_{1,0}$, this completes the proof.

5   Quantum Extractable Commitments

We construct extractable commitments by making use of the following building blocks.

- We let (EqCommit, EqDecommit) denote any statistically binding, equivocal quantum commitment scheme. Such a commitment can be obtained by applying the compiler from last section to Naor's commitment scheme [32].
- For a suitable polynomial $k(\cdot)$, let $h : \{0,1\}^{k(\lambda)} \times \{0,1\}^{\lambda^2} \rightarrow \{0,1\}$ be a universal hash function that is evaluated on a random seed $s \in \{0,1\}^{k(\lambda)}$ and input $x \in \{0,1\}^{\lambda^2}$.

Our extractable commitment scheme is described formally in Fig. 3. We show how to commit to a single bit, though commitment to any arbitrary length string follows by sequential repetition. Correctness of the protocol follows by inspection. In the remainder of this section, we prove the following theorem.

Theorem 2. *Protocol 3 describes a quantum statistically hiding and extractable bit commitment whenever* (EqCommit, EqDecommit) *is instantiated with any quantum statistically binding and equivocal bit commitment scheme.*

Throughout, we will consider non-uniform adversaries, but for ease of exposition we drop the indexing by λ.

5.1   Extractability

Consider any adversarial committer $\mathcal{C}^*$ with advice ρ. The extractor $\mathcal{E}_{\mathcal{C}^*}(\rho)$ is constructed as follows.

1. Run the first message algorithm of $\mathcal{C}^*$ on input ρ, obtaining message ψ.
2. For $i \in [2\lambda^3]$, sequentially execute equivocal commitment sessions with the equivocal simulator $\mathcal{Q}_{R^*,\mathsf{com}}$, where R^* is the part of $\mathcal{C}^*$ that participates as receiver in the ith session. Session i results in output $(\mathbf{z}_i, \mathbf{y}_{\mathsf{com},i})$, where $\mathbf{z}_i$ is stored by the extractor, and $\mathbf{y}_{\mathsf{com},i}$ is the current state of $\mathcal{C}^*$, which is fed as input into the next session.

Protocol 3

Committer $\mathcal{C}$ Input: Bit $b \in \{0, 1\}$.

The Protocol: Commit Phase.

1. $\mathcal{C}$ chooses $x \leftarrow \{0, 1\}^{2\lambda^3}$, $\theta \leftarrow \{+, \times\}^{2\lambda^3}$ and sends $|x\rangle_\theta$ to $\mathcal{R}$.
2. $\mathcal{R}$ chooses $\widehat{\theta} \leftarrow \{+, \times\}^{2\lambda^3}$ and obtains $\widehat{x} \in \{0, 1\}^{2\lambda^3}$ by measuring $|x\rangle_\theta$ in basis $\widehat{\theta}$.
   $\mathcal{R}$ commits to $\widehat{\theta}$ and $\widehat{x}$ position-wise: $\mathcal{R}$ and $\mathcal{C}$ execute sequentially $2\lambda^3$ equiv-ocal commitment sessions with $\mathcal{R}$ as committer and $\mathcal{C}$ as receiver. That is, for each $i \in [2\lambda^3]$, they compute $(\mathsf{x}_{\mathsf{com},i}, \mathsf{y}_{\mathsf{com},i}) \leftarrow \mathsf{EqCommit}\langle \mathcal{R}(\widehat{\theta}_i, \widehat{x}_i), \mathcal{C} \rangle$.
3. $\mathcal{C}$ sends a random test subset $T \subset [2\lambda^3]$ of size λ^3 to $\mathcal{R}$.
4. For every $i \in T$, $\mathcal{R}$ and $\mathcal{C}$ engage in $(\widehat{\theta}_i, \widehat{x}_i) \leftarrow \mathsf{EqDecommit}\langle \mathcal{R}(\mathsf{x}_{\mathsf{com},i}), \mathcal{C}(\mathsf{y}_{\mathsf{com},i}) \rangle$, and $\mathcal{C}$ aborts if any commitment fails to open.
5. $\mathcal{C}$ checks that $x_i = \widehat{x}_i$ whenever $\theta_i = \widehat{\theta}_i$. If all tests pass, $\mathcal{C}$ proceeds with the protocol, otherwise, $\mathcal{C}$ aborts.
6. The tested positions are discarded by both parties: $\mathcal{C}$ and $\mathcal{R}$ restrict x and θ, respectively $\widehat{x}$ and $\widehat{\theta}$, to the λ^3 indices $i \in \overline{T}$. $\mathcal{C}$ sends θ to $\mathcal{R}$.
7. $\mathcal{C}$ partitions the remaining λ^3 bits of x into λ different λ^2-bit strings $x^{(1)}, \ldots, x^{(\lambda)}$. For each $\ell \in [\lambda]$, sample a seed $s_\ell \leftarrow \{0, 1\}^{k(\lambda)}$ and compute $d_\ell := h(s_\ell, x^{(\ell)})$. Then output $(s_\ell, b \oplus d_\ell)_{\ell \in [\lambda]}$.

The Protocol: Decommit Phase.

1. $\mathcal{C}$ sends b and $(x^{(1)}, \ldots, x^{(\lambda)})$ to $\mathcal{R}$.
2. If either of the following fails, $\mathcal{R}$ rejects and outputs $\perp$. Otherwise, $\mathcal{R}$ accepts and outputs b.
   - Let $\{s_\ell, v_\ell\}_{\ell \in [\lambda]}$ be the message received by $\mathcal{R}$ in step 7. Check that for all $\ell \in [\lambda]$, $v_\ell = b \oplus h(s_\ell, x^{(\ell)})$.
   - For each $j \in [\lambda^3]$ such that $\widehat{\theta}_j = \theta_j$, check that $\widehat{x}_j = x_j$.

Fig. 3. Extractable commitment.

3. Obtain T from $\mathcal{C}^*$, and sample $\widehat{\theta} \leftarrow \{+, \times\}^{2\lambda^3}$. Let ψ_i denote the ith qubit of ψ, and measure the qubits ψ_i for $i \in T$, each in basis $\widehat{\theta}_i$. Let $\{\widehat{x}_i\}_{i \in [T]}$ be the results of the measurements.
4. Let $\mathsf{x}_{\mathsf{com}}$ be the current state of $\mathcal{C}^*$. For each $i \in [T]$, execute $\mathcal{Q}_{R^*,\mathsf{open}}((\widehat{\theta}_i, \widehat{x}_i), \mathsf{z}_i, \mathsf{x}_{\mathsf{com}})$, where R^* is the part of $\mathcal{C}^*$ that participates in the ith opening, and $\mathsf{x}_{\mathsf{com}}$ is updated to be the current state of $\mathcal{C}^*$ after each sequential session.
5. If $\mathcal{C}^*$ aborts at any point, abort and output $\perp$, otherwise continue.
6. Discard tested positions and restrict $\widehat{\theta}$ to the indices in $\overline{T}$. Obtain $\theta \in \{+, \times\}^{\lambda^3}$ from $\mathcal{C}^*$. Measure the qubits ψ_i in basis θ_i to obtain $\widehat{x}_i$ for $i \in \overline{T}$, and then partition $\widehat{x}$ into λ different λ^2-bit strings $\widehat{y}_1, \ldots, \widehat{y}_\lambda$.

7. Obtain $\{s_\ell, v_\ell\}_{\ell \in [\lambda]}$ from $\mathcal{C}^*$. Let b^* be the most frequently occurring bit in $\{h(s_\ell, \widehat{x}^{(\ell)}) \oplus v_\ell\}_{\ell \in [\lambda]}$. Output $(\mathbf{x}_{\text{com}}, \mathbf{y}_{\text{com}}, b^*)$, where $\mathbf{x}_{\text{com}}$ is the resulting state of $\mathcal{C}^*$ and $\mathbf{y}_{\text{com}} = (\theta, \widehat{\theta}, \widehat{x})$.

We now prove that $\mathcal{E}_{\mathcal{C}^*}$ is a secure extractor; for space reasons, a full definition of extractability in the quantum setting is in the full version.

Hyb_1. Define distribution Hyb_1 identically to Real (the honest interaction), except that in Step 2, for $i \in [2\lambda^3]$, sequentially execute equivocal commitment sessions using the equivocal simulator $\mathcal{Q}_{R^*,\text{com}}$, as described in the extractor. In Step 4, for every $i \in T$, open the i'th commitment to $(\widehat{\theta}_i, \widehat{x}_i)$ using $\mathcal{Q}_{R^*,\text{open}}$, as described in the extractor.

By the equivocal property of Commit, for any QPT distinguisher $(\mathcal{D}^*, \sigma)$, there exists a negligible function $\nu(\cdot)$ such that

$$\left| \Pr[\mathcal{D}^*(\sigma, \mathsf{Hyb}_1) = 1] - \Pr[\mathcal{D}^*(\sigma, \mathsf{Hyb}_0) = 1] \right| = \nu(\lambda).$$

Hyb_2. This is identical to Hyb_1, except that the verifier measures qubits of $|x\rangle_\theta$ *only after* obtaining a description of the set T, and *only measures* the qubits $i \in [T]$. The output of this experiment is identical to Hyb_1, therefore for any QPT distinguisher $(\mathcal{D}^*, \sigma)$,

$$\Pr[\mathcal{D}^*(\sigma, \mathsf{Hyb}_3) = 1] = \Pr[\mathcal{D}^*(\sigma, \mathsf{Hyb}_2) = 1].$$

Moreover, the only difference between Hyb_2 and Ideal is that Ideal outputs FAIL when the message b opened by $\mathcal{C}^*$ is not $\bot$ and differs from the one extracted by $\mathcal{E}_{\mathcal{C}^*}$. Therefore, to derive a contradiction it will suffice to prove that there exists a negligible function $\nu(\cdot)$ such that

$$\Pr[\mathsf{FAIL}|\mathsf{Ideal}] = \nu(\lambda).$$

Consider any sender $\mathcal{C}^*$ that produces a committer state $\mathbf{x}_{\text{com}}$ and then decommits to message b' using strings $(y_1, \ldots, y_\lambda)$ during the decommit phase. Let $T' \subseteq [\lambda]$ denote the set of all indices $\ell \in [\lambda]$ such that the corresponding $x^{(\ell)} \neq v_\ell$, where $\widehat{x}^{(\ell)}$ denotes the values obtained by the extractor in Step 6. Then we have the following claim.

Claim. There exists a negligible function $\nu(\cdot)$ such that

$$\Pr[|T'| > \lambda/2] = \nu(\lambda)$$

where the probability is over the randomness of the extractor.

Proof. For every $\ell \in [\lambda]$, we have that (over the randomness of the extractor):

$$\Pr\left[\mathcal{R}_{\text{open}}(\mathbf{y}_{\text{com}}) \text{ outputs } \bot \text{ in } \langle \mathcal{C}^*_{\text{open}}(\mathbf{x}_{\text{com}}), \mathcal{R}_{\text{open}}(\mathbf{y}_{\text{com}})\rangle \,\Big|\, x^{(\ell)} \neq \widehat{x}^{(\ell)} \right] \geq \frac{1}{2}.$$

Indeed, the receiver will reject if for some position i for which $x^{(\ell)} \neq \widehat{x}^{(\ell)}$, it holds that $\theta_i = \widehat{\theta}_i$. Since $\widehat{\theta}$ was sampled uniformly at random, this will occur for a single i with independent probability $1/2$. This implies that $\Pr[|T'| > \lambda/2] \leq \frac{1}{2^{\lambda/2}}$, and the claim follows. $\square$

By construction of $\mathcal{E}_{C^*}$, $\Pr[\mathsf{FAIL}|\mathsf{Ideal}] < \Pr[\|T'\| > \lambda/2]$, and therefore it follows that there exists a negligble function $\nu(\cdot)$ such that

$$\Pr[\mathsf{FAIL}|\mathsf{Ideal}] = \nu(\lambda).$$

The proof of that the extractable commitment scheme described in Fig. 3 is statistically hiding follows readily from quantum sampling techniques developed by [8], and is deferred to the full version.

6   Quantum Oblivious Transfer from Extractable and Equivocal Commitments

6.1   Definitions for Oblivious Transfer with Quantum Communication

An oblivious transfer with quantum communication is a protocol between a quantum interactive sender $\mathcal{S}$ and a quantum interactive receiver $\mathcal{R}$, where the sender $\mathcal{S}$ has input $m_0, m_1 \in \{0,1\}^\lambda$ and the receiver $\mathcal{R}$ has input $b \in \{0,1\}$. After interaction the sender outputs (m_0, m_1) and the receiver outputs (b, m_b).

Let $\mathcal{F}(\cdot, \cdot)$ be the following functionality. $\mathcal{F}(b, \cdot)$ takes as input either (m_0, m_1) or abort from the sender, returns end to the sender, and outputs m_b to the receiver in the non-abort case and $\perp$ in the abort case. $\mathcal{F}(\cdot, (m_0, m_1))$ takes as input either b or abort from the receiver, returns m_b to the receiver, and returns end to the sender in the non-abort case, and returns $\perp$ to the sender in the abort case.

Definition 1. *We let $\langle S(m_0, m_1), R(b) \rangle$ denote an execution of the OT protocol with sender input (m_0, m_1) and receiver input bit b. We denote by $\rho_{\mathsf{out},S^*}\langle S^*(\rho), R(b) \rangle$ and $\mathsf{OUT}_R\langle S^*(\rho), R(b) \rangle$ the final state of a non-uniform malicious sender $S^*(\rho)$ and the output of the receiver $R(b)$ at the end of an interaction (leaving the indexing by λ implicit). We denote by $\rho_{\mathsf{out},R^*}\langle S(m_0, m_1), R^*(\rho) \rangle$ and $\mathsf{OUT}_S\langle S(m_0, m_1), R^*(\rho) \rangle$ the final state of a non-uniform malicious receiver $R^*(\rho)$ and the output of the sender $S(m_0, m_1)$ at the end of an interaction. We require OT to satisfy the following security properties:*

- **Receiver Security.** *For every QPT non-uniform malicious sender S^*, there exists a simulator Sim_{S^*} such that the following holds. For any non-uniform advice ρ, σ where ρ and σ may be entangled, bit $b \in \{0,1\}$, and QPT non-uniform distinguisher D^*, $\mathsf{Sim}_{S^*}(\rho)$ sends inputs (m_0, m_1) or abort to the ideal functionality $\mathcal{F}_{\mathsf{OT}}(b, \cdot)$, and outputs a final state $\rho_{\mathsf{Sim},\mathsf{out},S^*}$. The output of the ideal functionality to the receiver in this experiment is denoted by OUT_R. It must hold that*

$$\left| \Pr\left[D^* \left(\sigma, \left(\rho_{\mathsf{Sim},\mathsf{out},S^*}, \mathsf{OUT}_R \right) \right) = 1 \right] \right.$$

$$\left. - \Pr\left[D^* \left(\sigma, \left(\rho_{\mathsf{out},S^*}\langle S^*(\rho), R(b) \rangle, \mathsf{OUT}_R\langle S^*(\rho), R(b) \rangle \right) \right) = 1 \right] \right| = \mathsf{negl}(\lambda).$$

- **Sender Security.** *For every QPT non-uniform malicious receiver R^*, there exists a simulator Sim_{R^*} such that the following holds. For any non-uniform advice ρ, σ where ρ and σ may be entangled, pair of sender inputs (m_0, m_1), and QPT non-uniform distinguisher D^*, $\mathsf{Sim}_{R^*}(\rho)$ sends bit b or abort to the ideal functionality $\mathcal{F}_{\mathsf{OT}}(m_0, m_1, \cdot)$, and outputs a final state $\rho_{\mathsf{Sim,out},R^*}$. The output of the ideal functionality to the sender in this experiment is denoted by OUT_S. It must hold that*

$$\Big| \Pr\left[D^* \left(\sigma, (\rho_{\mathsf{Sim,out},R^*}, \mathsf{OUT}_S) \right) = 1 \right]$$

$$- \Pr\left[D^* \left(\sigma, (\rho_{\mathsf{out},R^*} \langle S(m_0, m_1), R^*(\rho) \rangle, \mathsf{OUT}_S \langle S(m_0, m_1), R^*(\rho) \rangle) \right) = 1 \right] \Big| = \mathsf{negl}(\lambda).$$

6.2 Our Construction

We construct simulation-secure quantum oblivious transfer by making use of the following building blocks.

- Let $(\mathsf{EECommit}, \mathsf{EEDecommit})$ denote any quantum bit commitment scheme satisfying extractability and equivocality. Such a commitment scheme may be obtained by applying the compiler from Sect. 4 to the extractable commitment constructed in Sect. 5.
- Let $h : \{0,1\}^{k(\lambda)} \times \mathcal{X} \to \{0,1\}^{\lambda}$ be a universal hash with seed length $k(\lambda) = \mathsf{poly}(\lambda)$ and domain $\mathcal{X}$ the set of all binary strings of length *at most* 8λ.

Our QOT protocol is described in Protocol 4, which is essentially the [11] protocol instantiated with our extractable and equivocal commitment scheme.

Theorem 3. *The protocol in Fig. 4 is a simulation-secure QOT protocol whenever $(\mathsf{EECommit}, \mathsf{EEDecommit})$ is instantiated with a quantum bit commitment satisfying extractability and equivocality.*

We prove that the resulting QOT protocol satisfies standard simulation-based notions of receiver and sender security.

The proof of sender security follows readily from quantum sampling techniques developed by [8], and is deferred to the full version.

6.3 Receiver Security

Consider any adversarial sender S^* with advice ρ. The simulator $\mathsf{Sim}_{S^*}(\rho)$ is constructed as follows.

1. Run the first message algorithm of S^* on input ρ to obtain message ψ.
2. Execute 16λ sequential sessions of $\mathsf{EECommit}$. In each session, run the equivocator $\mathcal{Q}_{\mathcal{R}^*,\mathsf{com}}$, where $\mathcal{R}^*$ denotes the portion of S^* that participates as receiver in the ith sequential $\mathsf{EECommit}$ session.
3. Obtain test subset T of size 8λ from S^*.

Protocol 4

Sender S Input: Messages $m_0, m_1 \in \{0,1\}^\lambda \times \{0,1\}^\lambda$
Receiver R Input: Bit $b \in \{0,1\}$

The Protocol:

1. S chooses $x \leftarrow \{0,1\}^{16\lambda}$ and $\theta \leftarrow \{+,\times\}^{16\lambda}$ and sends $|x\rangle_\theta$ to R.
2. R chooses $\widehat{\theta} \leftarrow \{+,\times\}^{16\lambda}$ and obtains $\widehat{x} \in \{0,1\}^{16\lambda}$ by measuring $|x\rangle_\theta$ in basis $\widehat{\theta}$. Then, S and R execute 16λ sessions of EECommit sequentially with R acting as committer and S as receiver. In session i, R commits to the bits $\widehat{\theta}_i, \widehat{x}_i$.
3. S sends a random test subset $T \subset [16\lambda]$ of size 8λ to R.
4. For each $i \in T$, R and S sequentially execute the i'th EEDecommit, after which S receives the opened bits $\widehat{\theta}_i, \widehat{x}_i$.
5. S checks that $x_i = \widehat{x}_i$ whenever $\theta_i = \widehat{\theta}_i$. If all tests pass, S accepts, otherwise, S rejects and aborts.
6. The tested positions are discarded by both parties: S and R restrict x and θ, respectively $\widehat{x}$ and $\widehat{\theta}$, to the 8λ indices $i \in \overline{T}$. S sends θ to R.
7. R partitions the positions of $\overline{T}$ into two parts: the "good" subset $I_b = \{i : \theta_i = \widehat{\theta}_i\}$ and the "bad" subset $I_{1-b} = \{i : \theta_i \neq \widehat{\theta}_i\}$. R sends (I_0, I_1) to S.
8. S samples seeds $s_0, s_1 \leftarrow \{0,1\}^{k(\lambda)}$ and sends $(s_0, h(s_0, x_0) \oplus m_0, s_1, h(s_1, x_1) \oplus m_1)$, where x_0 is x restricted to the set of indices I_0 and x_1 is x restricted to the set of indices I_1.
9. R decrypts s_b using $\widehat{x}_b$, the string $\widehat{x}$ restricted to the set of indices I_b.

Fig. 4. Quantum oblivious transfer.

4. For each $i \in T$, sample $\widehat{\theta}_i \leftarrow \{+,\times\}$. Obtain $\widehat{x}_i$ by measuring the ith qubit of ψ in basis $\widehat{\theta}_i$. For each $i \in T$, sequentially execute the equivocal simulator $\mathcal{Q}_{\mathcal{R}^*,\mathsf{open}}$ on input $(\widehat{\theta}_i, \widehat{x}_i)$ and the state obtained from $\mathcal{Q}_{\mathcal{R}^*,\mathsf{com}}$.
5. If S^* continues, discard positions indexed by T. Obtain θ_i for $i \in \overline{T}$ from S^*, and compute x_i for $i \in \overline{T}$ by measuring the ith qubit of ψ in basis θ_i.
6. For every $i \in \overline{T}$, sample bit $d_i \leftarrow \{0,1\}$. Partition the set $\overline{T}$ into two subsets (I_0, I_1), where for every $i \in \overline{T}$, place $i \in I_0$ if $d = 0$ and otherwise place $i \in I_1$. Send (I_0, I_1) to S.
7. Obtain (y_0, y_1) from S. Set x_0 to be x restricted to the set of indices I_0 and x_1 to be x restricted to the set of indices I_1. For $b \in \{0,1\}$, parse $y_b = (s_b, t_b)$ and compute $m_b = t_b \oplus h(s_b, x_b)$.
8. If S^* aborts anywhere in the process, send abort to the ideal functionality. Otherwise, send (m_0, m_1) to the ideal functionality. Output the final state of S^*.

Next, we establish receiver security according to Definition 1. Towards a contradiction, suppose there exists a bit $b \in \{0,1\}$, a non-uniform QPT sender

(S^*, ρ), a non-uniform QPT distinguisher (D^*, σ), and polynomial $\mathsf{poly}(\cdot)$ s.t.

$$\left| \Pr\left[D^* \left(\sigma, (\rho_{\mathsf{Sim,out},S^*}, \mathsf{OUT}_R) \right) = 1 \right] \right.$$
$$\left. - \Pr\left[D^* \left(\sigma, (\rho_{\mathsf{out},S^*} \langle S^*(\rho), R(b) \rangle, \mathsf{OUT}_R \langle S^*(\rho), R(b) \rangle) \right) = 1 \right] \right| \geq \frac{1}{\mathsf{poly}(\lambda)}.$$

Fix any such b, sender (S^*, ρ) and distinguisher (D^*, σ). We derive a contradiction via an intermediate hybrid experiment, defined as follows with respect to bit b and sender (S^*, ρ).

Hyb. In this hybrid, we generate the QOT receiver commitments via the equivocal simulator $\mathcal{Q}_{\mathcal{R}^*}$ (where $\mathcal{R}^*$ is derived from the malicious QOT sender S^*), and otherwise follow the honest QOT receiver's algorithm.

1. Run the first message algorithm of S^* on input ρ to obtain message ψ.
2. Choose $\widehat{\theta} \leftarrow \{+, \times\}^{16\lambda}$ and obtain $\widehat{x} \in \{0,1\}^{16\lambda}$ by measuring ψ in basis $\widehat{\theta}$. Execute 16λ sequential sessions of EECommit. In each session, run the equivocator $\mathcal{Q}_{\mathcal{R}^*,\mathsf{com}}$, where $\mathcal{R}^*$ denotes the portion of S^* that participates as receiver in the ith sequential EECommit session.
3. Obtain test subset T of size 8λ from S^*.
4. For each $i \in T$, sequentially execute the equivocal simulator $\mathcal{Q}_{\mathcal{R}^*,\mathsf{open}}$ on input $\widehat{\theta}_i, \widehat{x}_i$ and the state obtained from $\mathcal{Q}_{\mathcal{R}^*,\mathsf{com}}$.
5. If S^* continues, discard positions indexed by T. Obtain θ_i for $i \in \overline{T}$ from S^*.
6. Partition the set $\overline{T}$ into two subsets: the "good" subset $I_b = \{i : \theta_i = \widehat{\theta}_i\}$ and the "bad" subset $I_{1-b} = \{i : \theta_i \neq \widehat{\theta}_i\}$. Send (I_0, I_1) to S.
7. Obtain (y_0, y_1) from S. Set x_b to be $\widehat{x}$ restricted to the set of indices I_b, and compute and set $m_b = t_b \oplus h(s_b, x_b)$. If S^* aborts anywhere in the process, let $\perp$ be the output of the receiver, otherwise let m_b be the output of the receiver.

The output of Hyb is the joint distribution of the final state of S^* and the output of the receiver. Receiver security then follows from the following two claims.

Claim. $\Pr\left[D^* \left(\sigma, (\rho_{\mathsf{Sim,out},S^*}, \mathsf{OUT}_R) \right) = 1 \right] \equiv \Pr\left[D^*(\sigma, \mathsf{Hyb}) = 1 \right].$

Proof. The only differences in the simulated distribution are (1) that measurements of S^*'s initial message ψ are delayed (which cannot be noticed by S^*), and (2) a syntactic difference in that the ideal functionality is queried to produce the receiver's output. □

Claim. There exists a negligible function $\nu(\cdot)$ such that

$$\left| \Pr[D^*(\sigma, \mathsf{Hyb}) = 1] - \Pr\left[D^* \left(\sigma, (\rho_{\mathsf{out},S^*} \langle S^*(\rho), R(b) \rangle, \mathsf{OUT}_R \langle S^*(\rho), R(b) \rangle) \right) = 1 \right] \right| = \nu(\lambda).$$

Proof. The only difference between the two distributions is that in the first, the receiver generates commitments according to the honest commit algorithms of EECommit while in the second, commitments in step 2 are generated via the equivocal simulator $\mathcal{Q}_{\mathcal{R}^*}$ of EECommit. Therefore, this claim follows by the equivocality of (EECommit, EEDecommit). □

Finally, Theorems 1, Theorem 2, and Theorem 3 give the following.

Corollary 1. *Quantum oblivious transfer (QOT) satisfying Definition 1 can be based on black-box use of statistically binding bit commitments, or on black-box use of quantum-hard one-way functions.*

Acknowledgments. The authors are grateful to the Simons Institute programs on *Lattices: Algorithms, Complexity and Cryptography*, and *The Quantum Wave in Computing* for fostering this collaboration. Thanks also to Alex Grilo, Huijia Lin, Fang Song, and Vinod Vaikuntanathan for discussions about similarities and differences with [19]. A.C. is supported by DoE under grant DOD ONR Federal. This material is based on work supported in part by DARPA under Contract No. HR001120C0024 (for DK). Any opinions, findings and conclusions or recommendations expressed in this material are those of the author(s) and do not necessarily reflect the views of the United States Government or DARPA.

References

1. Aaronson, S.: Quantum copy-protection and quantum money. In: 2009 24th Annual IEEE Conference on Computational Complexity, pp. 229–242. IEEE (2009)
2. Agarwal, A., Bartusek, J., Goyal, V., Khurana, D., Malavolta, G.: Post-quantum multi-party computation. Cryptology ePrint Archive, Report 2020/1395 (2020). https://eprint.iacr.org/2020/1395
3. Barak, B., Mahmoody-Ghidary, M.: Merkle puzzles are optimal — an $O(n^2)$-query attack on any key exchange from a random oracle. In: Halevi, S. (ed.) CRYPTO 2009. LNCS, vol. 5677, pp. 374–390. Springer, Heidelberg (2009). https://doi.org/10.1007/978-3-642-03356-8_22
4. Ben-Or, M., Crépeau, C., Gottesman, D., Hassidim, A., Smith, A.: Secure multi-party quantum computation with (only) a strict honest majority. In: 47th FOCS, pp. 249–260. IEEE Computer Society Press, October 2006
5. Bennett, C.H., Brassard, G.: Quantum cryptography: public key distribution and coin tossing. In: Proceedings of the IEEE International Conference on Computers, Systems, and Signal Processing, pp. 175–179 (1984)
6. Bennett, C.H., Brassard, G., Crépeau, C., Skubiszewska, M.-H.: Practical quantum oblivious transfer. In: Feigenbaum, J. (ed.) CRYPTO 1991. LNCS, vol. 576, pp. 351–366. Springer, Heidelberg (1992). https://doi.org/10.1007/3-540-46766-1_29
7. Bitansky, N., Shmueli, O.: Post-quantum zero knowledge in constant rounds. In: Makarychev, K., Makarychev, Y., Tulsiani, M., Kamath, G., Chuzhoy, J. (eds.) Proccedings of the 52nd Annual ACM SIGACT Symposium on Theory of Computing, STOC 2020, Chicago, IL, USA, 22–26 June, 2020, pp. 269–279. ACM (2020)
8. Bouman, N.J., Fehr, S.: Sampling in a quantum population, and applications. In: Rabin, T. (ed.) CRYPTO 2010. LNCS, vol. 6223, pp. 724–741. Springer, Heidelberg (2010). https://doi.org/10.1007/978-3-642-14623-7_39
9. Brassard, G., Crépeau, C., Jozsa, R., Langlois, D.: A quantum bit commitment scheme provably unbreakable by both parties. In: 34th FOCS, pp. 362–371. IEEE Computer Society Press, November 1993
10. Crépeau, C., Gottesman, D., Smith, A.: Secure multi-party quantum computation. In: 34th ACM STOC, pp. 643–652. ACM Press, May 2002

11. Crépeau, C., Kilian, J.: Achieving oblivious transfer using weakened security assumptions (extended abstract). In: 29th FOCS, pp. 42–52. IEEE Computer Society Press, October 1988
12. Crépeau, C., van de Graaf, J., Tapp, A.: Committed oblivious transfer and private multi-party computation. In: Coppersmith, D. (ed.) CRYPTO 1995. LNCS, vol. 963, pp. 110–123. Springer, Heidelberg (1995). https://doi.org/10.1007/3-540-44750-4_9
13. Damgård, I., Fehr, S., Lunemann, C., Salvail, L., Schaffner, C.: Improving the security of quantum protocols via commit-and-open. In: Halevi, S. (ed.) CRYPTO 2009. LNCS, vol. 5677, pp. 408–427. Springer, Heidelberg (2009). https://doi.org/10.1007/978-3-642-03356-8_24
14. Damgård, I., Ishai, Y.: Constant-round multiparty computation using a black-box pseudorandom generator. In: Shoup, V. (ed.) CRYPTO 2005. LNCS, vol. 3621, pp. 378–394. Springer, Heidelberg (2005). https://doi.org/10.1007/11535218_23
15. Dulek, Y., Grilo, A.B., Jeffery, S., Majenz, C., Schaffner, C.: Secure multi-party quantum computation with a dishonest majority. In: Canteaut, A., Ishai, Y. (eds.) EUROCRYPT 2020, Part III. LNCS, vol. 12107, pp. 729–758. Springer, Cham (2020). https://doi.org/10.1007/978-3-030-45727-3_25
16. Dupuis, F., Nielsen, J.B., Salvail, L.: Secure two-party quantum evaluation of unitaries against specious adversaries. In: Rabin, T. (ed.) CRYPTO 2010. LNCS, vol. 6223, pp. 685–706. Springer, Heidelberg (2010). https://doi.org/10.1007/978-3-642-14623-7_37
17. Dupuis, F., Nielsen, J.B., Salvail, L.: Actively secure two-party evaluation of any quantum operation. In: Safavi-Naini, R., Canetti, R. (eds.) CRYPTO 2012. LNCS, vol. 7417, pp. 794–811. Springer, Heidelberg (2012). https://doi.org/10.1007/978-3-642-32009-5_46
18. Goldreich, O., Micali, S., Wigderson, A.: How to prove all NP statements in zero-knowledge and a methodology of cryptographic protocol design (extended abstract). In: Odlyzko, A.M. (ed.) CRYPTO 1986. LNCS, vol. 263, pp. 171–185. Springer, Heidelberg (1987). https://doi.org/10.1007/3-540-47721-7_11
19. Grilo, A.B., Lin, H., Song, F., Vaikuntanathan, V.: Oblivious transfer is in miniqcrypt. CoRR abs/2011.14980 (2020)
20. Hallgren, S., Smith, A., Song, F.: Classical cryptographic protocols in a quantum world. In: Rogaway, P. (ed.) CRYPTO 2011. LNCS, vol. 6841, pp. 411–428. Springer, Heidelberg (2011). https://doi.org/10.1007/978-3-642-22792-9_23
21. Håstad, J., Impagliazzo, R., Levin, L.A., Luby, M.: A pseudorandom generator from any one-way function. SIAM J. Comput. 28(4), 1364–1396 (1999)
22. Impagliazzo, R., Levin, L.A., Luby, M.: Pseudo-random generation from one-way functions (extended abstracts). In: 21st ACM STOC, pp. 12–24. ACM Press, May 1989
23. Impagliazzo, R., Luby, M.: One-way functions are essential for complexity based cryptography (extended abstract). In: 30th FOCS, pp. 230–235. IEEE Computer Society Press, October/November 1989
24. Impagliazzo, R., Rudich, S.: Limits on the provable consequences of one-way permutations. In: Goldwasser, S. (ed.) CRYPTO 1988. LNCS, vol. 403, pp. 8–26. Springer, New York (1990). https://doi.org/10.1007/0-387-34799-2_2
25. Ishai, Y., Prabhakaran, M., Sahai, A.: Founding cryptography on oblivious transfer – efficiently. In: Wagner, D. (ed.) CRYPTO 2008. LNCS, vol. 5157, pp. 572–591. Springer, Heidelberg (2008). https://doi.org/10.1007/978-3-540-85174-5_32
26. Kilian, J.: Founding cryptography on oblivious transfer. In: 20th ACM STOC, pp. 20–31. ACM Press, May 1988

27. Lo, H.K., Chau, H.F.: Is quantum bit commitment really possible? Phys. Rev. Lett. **78**(17), 3410 (1997)
28. Luby, M., Rackoff, C.: Pseudo-random permutation generators and cryptographic composition. In: 18th ACM STOC, pp. 356–363. ACM Press, May 1986
29. Mahmoody, M., Maji, H.K., Prabhakaran, M.: On the power of public-key encryption in secure computation. In: Lindell, Y. (ed.) TCC 2014. LNCS, vol. 8349, pp. 240–264. Springer, Heidelberg (2014). https://doi.org/10.1007/978-3-642-54242-8_11
30. Mayers, D.: Unconditionally secure quantum bit commitment is impossible. Phys. Rev. lett. **78**(17), 3414 (1997)
31. Mayers, D., Salvail, L.: Quantum oblivious transfer is secure against all individual measurements. In: Proceedings Workshop on Physics and Computation. PhysComp 1994, pp. 69–77. IEEE (1994)
32. Naor, M.: Bit commitment using pseudorandomness. J. Cryptology **4**(2), 151–158 (1991)
33. Unruh, D.: Random Oracles and auxiliary input. In: Menezes, A. (ed.) CRYPTO 2007. LNCS, vol. 4622, pp. 205–223. Springer, Heidelberg (2007). https://doi.org/10.1007/978-3-540-74143-5_12
34. Unruh, D.: Quantum position verification in the random Oracle model. In: Garay, J.A., Gennaro, R. (eds.) CRYPTO 2014, Part II. LNCS, vol. 8617, pp. 1–18. Springer, Heidelberg (2014). https://doi.org/10.1007/978-3-662-44381-1_1
35. Watrous, J.: Zero-knowledge against quantum attacks. In: Kleinberg, J.M. (ed.) 38th ACM STOC, pp. 296–305. ACM Press, May 2006
36. Wolf, S., Wullschleger, J.: Oblivious transfer is symmetric. In: Vaudenay, S. (ed.) EUROCRYPT 2006. LNCS, vol. 4004, pp. 222–232. Springer, Heidelberg (2006). https://doi.org/10.1007/11761679_14
37. Yao, A.C.C.: Security of quantum protocols against coherent measurements. In: 27th ACM STOC, pp. 67–75. ACM Press, May/Jun 1995
38. Zhandry, M.: How to construct quantum random functions. In: 53rd FOCS, pp. 679–687. IEEE Computer Society Press, October 2012

Impossibility of Quantum Virtual Black-Box Obfuscation of Classical Circuits

Gorjan Alagic[1,2], Zvika Brakerski[3], Yfke Dulek[4,6(✉)], and Christian Schaffner[5,6]

[1] Joint Center for Quantum Information and Computer Science,
University of Maryland, College Park, MD, USA
galagic@umd.edu
[2] National Institute of Standards and Technology, Gaithersburg, MD, USA
[3] Weizmann Institute of Science, Rehovot, Israel
zvika.brakerski@weizmann.ac.il
[4] Centrum Wiskunde & Informatica, Amsterdam, The Netherlands
dulek@cwi.nl
[5] University of Amsterdam, Amsterdam, The Netherlands
c.schaffner@uva.nl
[6] QuSoft, Amsterdam, The Netherlands

Abstract. Virtual black-box obfuscation is a strong cryptographic primitive: it encrypts a circuit while maintaining its full input/output functionality. A remarkable result by Barak et al. (Crypto 2001) shows that a general obfuscator that obfuscates classical circuits into classical circuits cannot exist. A promising direction that circumvents this impossibility result is to obfuscate classical circuits into quantum states, which would potentially be better capable of hiding information about the obfuscated circuit. We show that, under the assumption that Learning With Errors (LWE) is hard for quantum computers, this quantum variant of virtual black-box obfuscation of classical circuits is generally impossible. On the way, we show that under the presence of dependent classical auxiliary input, even the small class of classical point functions cannot be quantum virtual black-box obfuscated.

1 Introduction

The obfuscation of a circuit is an object, typically another circuit, that allows a user to evaluate the functionality of the original circuit without learning any additional information about the structure of the circuit. Obfuscation is useful for publishing software without revealing the code, but it also has more fundamental applications in cryptography. For example, the strongest notion called *virtual black-box* obfuscation can transform any private-key encryption scheme into a public-key scheme, and transform public-key schemes into fully-homomorphic schemes. Unfortunately, this notion turns out to be impossible for general circuits [BGI+01] – at least, if we require the obfuscation of a circuit to be a circuit itself.

© International Association for Cryptologic Research 2021
T. Malkin and C. Peikert (Eds.): CRYPTO 2021, LNCS 12825, pp. 497–525, 2021.
https://doi.org/10.1007/978-3-030-84242-0_18

The impossibility result from [BGI+01] leaves open an intriguing possibility: what if the obfuscation of a (classical) circuit is allowed to be a *quantum state*? Could a quantum state contain all the information about a functionality, allowing a user to produce correct outputs, without revealing all that information? This possibility seems hopeful, due to the unrevealing nature of quantum states, but the extent to which no-cloning affects cryptography is not fully understood. The question whether quantum obfuscation of classical circuits is possible appeared in Aaronson's list of semi-grand challenges in quantum computing [Aar05]. At least one candidate construction was proposed [Chr14], but subsequently broken. An attempt to prove impossibility [AF16] also encountered several obstacles (discussed below). As a result, the question remained far from settled.

In this work, we answer the question by showing that virtual-black-box obfuscating classical circuits into quantum states is not possible. We adopt ideas from the classical proof [BGI+01], but while using a similar proof outline is natural, the actual execution is non-trivial: our work requires tools such as quantum fully homomorphic encryption [Mah18] and compute-and-compare obfuscation [WZ17,GKW17] that were only developed in recent years.

1.1   Related Work

Barak et al. defined the obfuscating property of virtual black-box (vbb) obfuscators as follows: any information that an adversary can learn about a circuit from its obfuscation can also be learned by a simulator that does not have access to the obfuscation, but only to an oracle for the circuit's functionality [BGI+01]. In this definition, the crucial difference between the adversary and the simulator is that the adversary has access to a short representation of the circuit (namely, the obfuscation), whereas the simulator only has access to an input/output interface that implements the functionality. Some circuit classes allow the adversary to exploit this difference by using the obfuscation as an input value to the circuit itself. Those circuit classes are unobfuscatable in the vbb sense, rendering vbb obfuscation impossible for the general class of circuits in **P** [BGI+01].

In more detail, the impossibility proof in [BGI+01] relies on point functions, which output zero everywhere except at a single input value α, where they output a string β. The circuits in the unobfuscatable class can, depending on the input, do all of the following: (1) apply that point function, (2) return an encryption of α, (3) homomorphically evaluate a gate, or (4) check whether a ciphertext decrypts to β. An adversary holding the obfuscation is able to divide it into single gates, and can use those to homomorphically evaluate option (1), thereby converting a ciphertext for α into a ciphertext for β. That way, the adversary can tell whether he is holding an obfuscation with a point function from α to β, or one with the all-zero function. (In the second case, the homomorphic evaluation would yield a ciphertext for zero, rather than one for β.) A simulator, only having access to the input/output behavior, cannot perform the homomorphic evaluation, because it cannot divide the functionality into single gates.

The above construction rules out the existence of an obfuscator that maps classical circuits to classical circuits. It leaves open the possibility of an obfuscator that maps classical circuits to *quantum states*: such a quantum state, together with a fixed public 'interpreter map', could be used to evaluate the obfuscated circuit. The possibility of quantum obfuscation was the object of study for Alagic and Fefferman [AF16], who attempted to port the impossibility proof from [BGI+01] to the quantum setting. In doing so, they encountered two issues:

Homomorphic Evaluation. The interpreter map, that runs the obfuscation state on a chosen input, is a quantum map. It will likely have quantum states as intermediate states of the computation, so in order to homomorphically run the point function, one needs the ability to evaluate quantum gates on quantum ciphertexts. The unobfuscatable circuit class will thus need to contain quantum circuits to perform homomorphic evaluation steps.

Reusability. In the construction from [BGI+01], the obfuscated circuit needs to be used multiple times: for example, each homomorphic gate evaluation requires a separate call to the obfuscated circuit. If the obfuscation is a (classical or quantum) circuit, this poses no problem, but if it is a quantum *state*, multiple uses are not guaranteed.

These two issues limit the extent of the impossibility results in [AF16]: they show that it is impossible to vbb obfuscate *quantum* circuits into *reusable* obfuscated states (e.g., quantum circuits).

After it became clear [BGI+01] that obfuscating all classical circuits is impossible, efforts were made to construct obfuscators for smaller, but still nontrivial, classes of circuits. Successful constructions have been found for several classes of evasive functions, such as point functions [Wee05, CD08] and compute-and-compare functions [WZ17, GKW17]. Currently, no quantum obfuscators are known for circuit classes that cannot be classically obfuscated.

1.2   Our Contributions

We strengthen the impossibility of virtual-black-box obfuscation of classical circuits by showing that classical circuits cannot be obfuscated into quantum states. We assume the existence of classical-client quantum fully homomorphic encryption and classical obfuscation of compute-and-compare functions. Both of these can be constructed from the learning-with-errors (LWE) assumption [Mah18, Bra18, WZ17, GKW17]. The compute-and-compare construction requires the strongest assumption in terms of the LWE parameters.

Theorem (informal). *If LWE is hard for quantum algorithms, then it is impossible to quantum vbb obfuscate the class of polynomial-size classical circuits (even with non-negligible correctness and security error, and even if the obfuscation procedure is inefficient).*

Our result uses the same proof strategy as in [BGI+01] and [AF16], overcoming the two main issues described above as follows:

Homomorphic Evaluation. The constructions in [BGI+01] and [AF16] rely on the obfuscator to implement the homomorphic evaluations, by obfuscating the functionality "decrypt, then apply a gate, then re-encrypt". However, by now, we know how to build quantum fully-homomorphic encryption schemes directly [Mah18, Bra18], based on the learning-with-errors (LWE) assumption. Thus, in our construction, we can remove the homomorphic gate evaluation from the obfuscated circuits: the adversary can do the homomorphic evaluation of the point function herself, using a quantum fully-homomorphic encryption scheme. With the homomorphic evaluation removed from it, the class of circuits that we prove impossible to obfuscate can remain classical.

This solution introduces a slight complication: part of the functionality of the circuit we construct is now to return the public evaluation key. However, unless one is willing to make an assumption on the circular security of the homomorphic encryption, the size of this key (and therefore the size of the circuit) scales with the size of the circuit that needs to be homomorphically evaluated. To get rid of this inconvenient dependence, our unobfuscatable circuit returns the public key in small, individual blocks that can be independently computed. We argue that any classical-key quantum fully-homomorphic encryption scheme has public keys that can be decomposed in this way.

Reusability. The circuits that we consider are classical and deterministic. Therefore, if the interpreter map is run on an obfuscation state ρ for a circuit C, plus a classical input x, then by correctness, the result is (close to) a computational-basis state $|C(x)\rangle$. This output can be copied out to a separate wire without disturbing the state, and the interpreter map can be reversed, recovering the obfuscation ρ to be used again. If the interpreter map is not unitary, then it can be run coherently (i.e., keeping purification registers around instead of measuring wires), and this coherent version can be reversed as long as the purification registers are not measured.

At one point in our proof, we will need to run the interpreter map homomorphically on (an encryption of) ρ and x. This may result in a superposition of different ciphertexts for $C(x)$, which cannot cleanly be copied out to a separate wire without entangling that wire with the output. Thus, recovering ρ is not necessarily possible after the homomorphic-evaluation step.

We circumvent this problem by making sure that the homomorphic evaluation occurs last, so that ρ is not needed anymore afterwards. This reordering is achieved by classically obfuscating the part of the circuit that checks whether a ciphertext decrypts to the value β. That way, this functionality becomes a constant output value that a user can request and store before performing the homomorphic evaluation, and use afterwards. To obfuscate the decryption check, we use a classical vbb obfuscator for compute-and-compare functions, which relies on a variant of the LWE assumption [WZ17, GKW17]. These vbb obfuscators have previously been successfully applied in a similar way, in the context of quantum extraction [AL20a, BS20].

Our impossibility result compares to the classical impossibility result from Barak et al. [BGI+01] as follows. First, as mentioned, we extend the realm of impossible obfuscators to include obfuscators that produce a quantum state, rather than a classical circuit. Second, the impossibility result from [BGI+01] is unconditional, whereas we require the (standard) assumption that learning-with-errors is hard for quantum adversaries. It may be possible to relax this assumption if ρ can be recovered after the homomorphic evaluation, see Sect. 1.3 below. Third, the class of classical circuits that cannot be obfuscated is slightly different: in our work, it does not have the homomorphic-evaluation functionality built into it, and is therefore arguably simpler, strengthening the impossibility result. However, we stress that in both works, the unobfuscatable circuit class itself is somewhat contrived: the main implication is that its superclass $\mathbf{P}$ is unobfuscatable.

As an intermediate result, we show that it is impossible to vbb obfuscate even just the class of classical multi-bit-output point functions into a quantum state, if the adversary and simulator have access to auxiliary classical information that contains an encryption of the non-zero input value α and a vbb obfuscation of a function depending on the secret key for that encryption.

Theorem (informal). *If LWE is hard for quantum algorithms, then it is impossible to quantum vbb obfuscate multi-bit-output point functions and the all-zero function under the presence of classical dependent auxiliary information (even with non-negligible soundness and security error).*

At first glance, that may seem to contradict constructions in [WZ17, GKW17], where vbb obfuscation for point functions is constructed, even in the presence of dependent auxiliary information. The crucial difference is that the constructions in [WZ17, GKW17] only allow a limited dependency of the auxiliary information, whereas in our impossibility proof, the dependence is slightly stronger. This subtle difference seems to indicate that the gap between possibility and impossibility of vbb obfuscation is closing.

Comparison with Concurrent Work. Independently of this work, Ananth and La Placa [AL20b] have concurrently shown the general impossibility of quantum copy-protection, thereby also ruling out quantum obfuscation of classical circuits. Their techniques are very similar to ours, but their adversary allows to completely de-obfuscate the program given non-black-box access (a property that we did not attempt to achieve). They also present some positive results in their work in the context of software protection. Their result requires an additional assumption compared to ours. Specifically, in addition to LWE being quantum-secure, they also require that the underlying homomorphic-encryption scheme is circularly secure. We avoid circularity by introducing a notion of decomposable public keys for homomorphic encryption. Our technique could be used to remove the circularity assumption from the copy-protection impossibility result [AL20b] as well.

1.3 Open Questions

The strongest assumption in our work is the existence of the classical vbb obfuscator for compute-and-compare functions, which relies on a variant of LWE. It is necessary because the QFHE evaluation may destroy the obfuscation state when the superposition of output ciphertexts is measured. However, it is not clear if this measurement actually destroys any information on the *plaintext* level, since the plaintext value is deterministic. Thus, it may be possible to recover the (plaintext) obfuscation state after the QFHE evaluation. In that case, it is not necessary to classically obfuscate the compute-and-compare function: it can simply be part of the quantum-obfuscated functionality.

Other open questions are about possibilities rather than impossibilities. What circuit classes *can* be vbb obfuscated into quantum states? Is quantum vbb obfuscation stronger than classical vbb obfuscation, in the sense that it can obfuscate circuit classes that classical vbb cannot? Also, the weaker notion of indistinguishability obfuscation (iO) (also introduced in [BGI+01]) is not affected by our impossibility result: it may still be possible to classically or quantumly iO obfuscate classical functionalities. Could such a construction be lifted into the quantum realm, so that we can (quantum) iO obfuscate [BK20] quantum functionalities?

1.4   Structure of This Work

In Sect. 2, we give preliminary definitions of the relevant concepts for this work: (classical and quantum) obfuscation, quantum fully homomorphic encryption, and compute-and-compare functions. We also describe how the input of an (almost) deterministic quantum circuit can be recovered. In Sect. 4, we prove impossibility of quantum obfuscation of point functions under dependent auxiliary input. Building on the concepts in that section, Sect. 5 proves our main result, impossibility of quantum obfuscation of classical circuits without any auxiliary input.

2   Preliminaries

2.1   Notation

PPT stands for probabilistic polynomial-time algorithm, and QPT stands for quantum polynomial-time algorithm. If a classical or quantum algorithm A has oracle access to a classical function f, we write A^f. If A has access to multiple oracles with separate input/output interfaces, we write, e.g., $A^{f,g}$. Since our oracles will model or emulate evaluation of a known circuit, our quantum algorithms will always have superposition access to a classical oracle f. This amounts to oracle access to the unitary map $|x\rangle |y\rangle \mapsto |x\rangle |y \oplus f(x)\rangle$ where $\oplus$ is the bit-wise XOR operation.

Let $\mathsf{poly}(x)$ denote an unspecified polynomial $p(x)$. Similarly, let $\mathsf{negl}(x)$ denote an unspecified negligible function $\mu(x)$, i.e., for all constants $c \in \mathbb{N}$ there exists an $x_0 \in \mathbb{R}$ such that for all $x > x_0$, $|\mu(x)| < x^{-c}$. Let $\mathbf{Z}_n : \{0,1\}^n \to \{0^n\}$ denote the all-zero function on n input bits: $\mathbf{Z}_n(x) = 0^n$ for all x.

If D is a distribution, we write $x \leftarrow D$ to signify that x is sampled according to D. For a finite set S, we write $x \leftarrow_R S$ to signify that x is sampled uniformly at random from the set S. Two distribution ensembles $\{D_\lambda\}_{\lambda \in \mathbb{N}}$ and $\{D'_\lambda\}_{\lambda \in \mathbb{N}}$ are computationally indistinguishable, written $D_\lambda \overset{c}{\approx} D'_\lambda$, if no poly-time algorithm can distinguish between a sample from one distribution or the other, i.e., for all PPT A,

$$\left| \Pr_{x \leftarrow D_\lambda} [A(x) = 1] - \Pr_{y \leftarrow D'_\lambda} [A(y) = 1] \right| \leq \mathsf{negl}\,(\lambda) .$$

We sometimes write $x \overset{c}{\approx} y$ if it is clear from which distributions x and y are sampled. If not even a QPT algorithm can distinguish them, the distributions are quantum-computationally indistinguishable.

A pure quantum state is written $|\psi\rangle$ or $|\varphi\rangle$, and a mixed quantum state is usually denoted by ρ or σ. As a special case, a computational-basis state is written $|x\rangle$ for some classical string $x \in \{0,1\}^*$. We sometimes abuse notation and give a classical input x to a quantum algorithm A, writing $A(x)$: in that case, the algorithm A is actually given $|x\rangle$ as input.

X and Z denote the bit-flip gate and phase-flip gate, respectively. If we write X^a for some $a \in \{0,1\}$, we mean that the gate X is applied if $a = 1$; otherwise, identity is applied.

Finally, for a mixed state ρ, let $\| \rho \|_{\mathrm{tr}} := \mathrm{Tr}\left(\sqrt{\rho^\dagger \rho} \right)$ denote the trace norm. The trace distance $\frac{1}{2} \| \rho - \sigma \|_{\mathrm{tr}}$ is a measure for how different two mixed states ρ and σ are.

2.2   Classical and Quantum Virtual-Black-Box Obfuscation

In this work we consider so-called *circuit* obfuscators: the functionalities to be hidden are represented by circuits. A virtual-black-box circuit obfuscator hides the functionality in such a way that the obfuscation looks like a "black box": the only way to get information about its functionality is to evaluate it on an input and observe the output.

Definition 2.1 ([BGI+01, **Definition 2.2**]). *A classical virtual black-box obfuscator for the circuit class $\mathfrak{F}$ is a probabilistic algorithm $\mathcal{O}$ such that*

1. *(polynomial slowdown) For every circuit $C \in \mathfrak{F}$, $|\mathcal{O}(C)| = \mathrm{poly}\,(|C|)$;*
2. *(functional equivalence) For every circuit $C \in \mathfrak{F}$, the string $\mathcal{O}(C)$ describes a circuit that computes the same function as C;*
3. *(virtual black-box) For any PPT adversary A, there exists a PPT simulator S such that for all circuits $C \in \mathfrak{F}$,*

$$\left| \Pr\left[A(\mathcal{O}(C)) = 1 \right] - \Pr\left[A(S^C(1^{|C|})) = 1 \right] \right| \leq \mathsf{negl}\,(|C|) .$$

As a variation on the third requirement, one may assume that some auxiliary information (which may depend on the circuit C) is present alongside the obfuscation $\mathcal{O}(C)$. In that case, a simulator with access to that auxiliary information should still be able to simulate the adversary's output distribution:

Definition 2.2 ([GK05, **Definition 3**]). *A classical virtual black-box obfuscator w.r.t. dependent auxiliary input for a circuit class $\mathfrak{F}$ is a probabilistic algorithm $\mathcal{O}$ that satisfies Definition 2.1, with the "virtual black-box" property redefined as follows:*

3. *(virtual black-box) For any PPT adversary A, there exists a PPT simulator S such that for all circuits $C \in \mathfrak{F}$ and all strings $\mathsf{aux} \in \{0,1\}^{\mathsf{poly}(|C|)}$ (which may depend on C),*

$$\left| \Pr\left[A(\mathcal{O}(C), \mathsf{aux}) = 1\right] - \Pr\left[A(S^C(1^{|C|}, \mathsf{aux})) = 1\right] \right| \leq \mathsf{negl}\,(|C|).$$

In the quantum setting, we consider quantum obfuscators for classical circuit classes: that is, the obfuscation $\mathcal{O}(C)$ may be a quantum state. We adapt Definition 5 from [AF16], which defines quantum obfuscators for quantum circuits.

Definition 2.3. *A quantum virtual black-box obfuscator for the classical circuit class $\mathfrak{F}$ is a quantum algorithm $\mathcal{O}$ and a QPT $\mathcal{J}$ such that*

1. *(polynomial expansion) For every circuit $C \in F$, $\mathcal{O}(C)$ is an m-qubit quantum state with $m = \mathsf{poly}\,(n)$;*
2. *(functional equivalence) For every circuit $C \in F$ and every input x,*

$$\frac{1}{2} \left\| \mathcal{J}(\mathcal{O}(C) \otimes |x\rangle\langle x|) - |C(x)\rangle\langle C(x)| \right\|_{\mathrm{tr}} \leq \mathsf{negl}\,(|C|);$$

3. *(virtual black-box) For every QPT adversary $\mathcal{A}$, there exists a QPT simulator S (with superposition access to its oracle) such that for all circuits $C \in \mathfrak{F}$,*

$$\left| \Pr[\mathcal{A}(\mathcal{O}(C)) = 1] - \Pr[S^C(1^{|C|}) = 1] \right| \leq \mathsf{negl}\,(|C|).$$

There are a few differences with the classical definition. First, the obfuscation is a quantum state, and not a (classical or quantum) circuit. Second, due to the probabilistic nature of quantum computation, we allow a negligible error in the functional equivalence. Third, the simulator is slightly more powerful because of its superposition access to the functionality of C: a query performs the unitary operation specified by $|x\rangle\,|z\rangle \mapsto |x\rangle\,|z \oplus C(x)\rangle$. Note that a quantum adversary can always use a (classical or quantum) obfuscation to compute the obfuscated functionality on a superposition of inputs, obtaining a superposition of outputs. For this reason, the simulator gets superposition access to its oracle in the quantum setting. Throughout this work, all oracles supplied to quantum algorithms allow for superposition access.

We can again strengthen the virtual black-box property to include (classical or quantum) dependent auxiliary information: this auxiliary string or state would be provided to both the adversary and the simulator, in the same way as in Definition 2.2.

2.3 Quantum Fully Homomorphic Encryption

A fully homomorphic encryption (FHE) of a message m provides privacy by hiding the message, but allows ciphertexts to be transformed in a meaningful way. Given a ciphertext for m, some party that only knows the public key can produce a ciphertext for $f(m)$ for any efficiently computable function f. Any information that is necessary for this transformation is contained in the public key (in particular, we do not make a distinction between the public key and the evaluation key).

A *quantum* fully homomorphic encryption (QFHE) scheme allows quantum computations on encrypted quantum data. From the Learning with Errors assumption, it is possible to construct secure QFHE schemes where all client-side operations (key generation, encryption, and decryption) are classical [Mah18, Bra18].

Definition 2.4. *A quantum fully homomorphic encryption scheme* QFHE *consists of four algorithms, as follows:*

- **Key Generation:** $(pk, sk) \leftarrow$ QFHE.KeyGen(1^λ) *produces a public key pk and a secret key sk, given a security parameter λ. This is a classical PPT algorithm.*
- **Encryption:** $c \leftarrow$ QFHE.Enc$_{pk}(m)$ *encrypts a single-bit message $m \in \{0,1\}$. For multi-bit messages $m \in \{0,1\}^\ell$, we write* QFHE.Enc$_{pk}(m)$ *to denote the bit-by-bit encryption*

$$(\text{QFHE.Enc}_{pk}(m_1), \text{QFHE.Enc}_{pk}(m_2), \ldots, \text{QFHE.Enc}_{pk}(m_\ell)).$$

This algorithm is in general QPT but it only uses a classical random tape, and furthermore whenever m is classical, so is the encryption algorithm.
- **Decryption:** $m' =$ QFHE.Dec$_{sk}(c)$ *decrypts a ciphertext c into a single-bit message m', using the secret key sk. If c is a ciphertext for a multi-bit message, we write* QFHE.Dec$_{sk}(c)$ *for the bit-by-bit decryption. Again this is QPT in general, but can be classical if c is classical.*
- **Homomorphic evaluation:** $c' \leftarrow$ QFHE.Eval$_{pk}(C, c)$ *takes as input the public key, a classical description of a BQP circuit C with ℓ input wires and ℓ' output wires, and a bit-by-bit encrypted ciphertext c encrypting ℓ bits. It produces a c', a sequence of ℓ' output ciphertexts. This is a QPT algorithm.*

We say that a (Q)FHE scheme is (perfectly) correct if the homomorphic evaluation of any BQP circuit C on a ciphertext has the effect of applying C to the plaintext, i.e.,

$$\text{QFHE.Dec}_{sk}\left(\text{QFHE.Eval}_{pk}\left(C, \text{QFHE.Enc}_{pk}(m)\right)\right) = C(m)$$

for all m, C, and $(pk, sk) \leftarrow$ QFHE.KeyGen(1^λ). A (Q)FHE scheme is secure if its encryption function is secure. We usually require quantum indistinguishability under chosen plaintext attacks (q-IND-CPA) [BJ15].

The QFHE schemes from [Mah18, Bra18] encrypt a message m using a quantum one-time-pad with random keys $a, b \in \{0, 1\}$, attaching classical FHE ciphertexts of the one-time pad keys:

$$\mathsf{QFHE.Enc}_{pk}(m) = \mathsf{X}^a \mathsf{Z}^b \ket{m} \otimes \ket{\mathsf{FHE.Enc}_{pk}(a), \mathsf{FHE.Enc}_{pk}(b)}.$$

Note that this ciphertext can be classically represented as the tuple

$$(m \oplus a, \mathsf{FHE.Enc}_{pk}(a), \mathsf{FHE.Enc}_{pk}(b)),$$

so that encryption may be seen as a classical procedure. Conversely, a classical homomorphic encryption $\tilde{m} \leftarrow \mathsf{FHE.Enc}_{pk}(m)$ can easily be turned into a valid quantum homomorphic encryption by preparing the state $\ket{0} \otimes \ket{\tilde{m}, \mathsf{FHE.Enc}_{pk}(0)}$, which decrypts to m. Thus, it is possible to freely switch back and forth between quantum ciphertexts and classical ciphertexts, as long as the message is known to be classical.

The quantum one-time pad encryption also straightforwardly extends to encrypting general quantum states $\ket{\psi}$, rather than only computational-basis states $\ket{m}$: the quantum one-time pad is simply applied to the state $\ket{\psi}$, and the one-time-pad keys encrypted into a computational-basis state as above. Of course, encryption becomes a quantum procedure in this setting. We will use encryption of quantum states in our work, where we supply the encryption of a quantum-state obfuscation as the input to a homomorphic evaluation.

Leveled FHE and Bootstrappable FHE. In many cases in the literature, we wish to consider FHE schemes which require an a priori upper bound (polynomial in the security parameter) on the depth of circuits to be homomorphically evaluated. In the current state of the art, such schemes (referred to as *leveled* FHE) can be constructed under milder assumptions than unleveled schemes: in particular, they do not require circular-security-type assumptions. There are a few variants of leveled FHE defined in the literature, but for the purpose of this work we use the following.

Definition 2.5 (Leveled FHE). *A leveled (Q)FHE scheme is a scheme where the key generation takes an additional parameter* $\mathsf{KeyGen}(1^\lambda, 1^d)$ *and outputs* (sk, pk) *for a (Q)FHE scheme. Correctness holds only for evaluating circuits of total depth at most* d. *Furthermore, the length of sk and the complexity of decryption are independent of* d.

We assume w.l.o.g. that the random tape used by KeyGen is always of length λ and does not depend on d (this is w.l.o.g. since it is always possible to use a PRG to stretch the random tape into the desired length).

One way to construct leveled FHE is via the bootstrapping technique as suggested by Gentry [Gen09]. Gentry showed that given a base scheme with homomorphic capacity greater than its decryption depth, it is possible to create a leveled scheme with the following properties.

Definition 2.6 (Leveled Bootstrapped FHE). *A leveled bootstrapped (Q)FHE is a scheme where there exists a base-scheme with a key-generation algorithm* SubKeyGen(1^λ) *and encryption, decryption and evaluation algorithms, such that the key generation algorithm* KeyGen$(1^\lambda, 1^d)$ *takes the following form.*

1. *Run* SubKeyGen(1^λ) *with fresh randomness* $(d+1)$ *times to generate sub-keys* (sk_i, pk_i) *for* $i = 0, \ldots, d$.
2. *Encrypt* $c_i^* = \mathsf{Enc}_{pk_i}(sk_{i-1})$ *for all* $i = 1, \ldots, d$.
3. *Output* $pk = (pk_0, (pk_1, c_1^*), \ldots, (pk_d, c_d^*))$ *and* $sk = sk_d$.

For our purposes, we will assume that the random tape that is being used for the SubKeyGen *executions is generated using a pseudorandom function. That is, the random tape of* KeyGen *is used as a seed for a PRF, and for the ith execution of* SubKeyGen *we use a random tape that is derived by applying a PRF on* i.

For the sake of completeness we note that the decryption algorithm of the bootstrapped scheme is the same as that of the base scheme, and that for the sake of encryption only pk_0 is needed.

2.4 Point Functions and Compute-and-Compare Functions

The class of compute-and-compare functions, as well as its subclass of point functions, plays an important role in this work. In this section we define these function classes.

Definition 2.7 (Point function). *Let* $y \in \{0,1\}^n$. *The point function* $\mathbf{P}_y$ *is defined by*

$$\mathbf{P}_y(x) := \begin{cases} 1 & \text{if } x = y \\ 0 & \text{otherwise.} \end{cases} \tag{1}$$

The value y is called the *target value*. Point functions are a special type of compute-and-compare function, where the function f is the identity:

Definition 2.8 (Compute-and-compare function). *Let* $f : \{0,1\}^m \to \{0,1\}^n$ *and* $y \in \{0,1\}^n$. *The compute-and-compare function* $\mathbf{CC}_{f,y}$ *is defined by*

$$\mathbf{CC}_{f,y}(x) := \begin{cases} 1 & \text{if } f(x) = y \\ 0 & \text{otherwise.} \end{cases} \tag{2}$$

One can also consider point functions or compute-and-compare functions with *multi-bit output*: in that case, the function outputs either some string z (instead of 1), or the all-zero string (instead of 0). We denote such functions with $\mathbf{P}_{y,z}$ and $\mathbf{CC}_{f,y,z}$.

2.5   Recovering the Input of a Quantum Circuit

We will consider (efficient) quantum operations as (polynomial-size) circuits, consisting of the following set of basic operations: unitary gates from some fixed constant-size gate set, measurements in the computational basis, and initialization of auxiliary wires in the $|0\rangle$ state.

While unitary gates are always reversible by applying their transpose ($U^\dagger U = I$ for any unitary U), measurement gates may not be, as they can possibly collapse a state. However, we can effectively delay all measurements in a circuit C until the very end, as follows. Define U_C as the unitary that computes C *coherently*: that is, for every computational-basis measurement in C on some wire w, U_C performs a CNOT operation from w onto a fresh auxiliary target wire initialized in the state $|0\rangle$. The circuit C is now equivalent to the following operation: initialize all auxiliary target wires in the $|0\rangle$ state[1], apply the unitary U_C, and measure all auxiliary target wires in the computational basis.

In this work, we will encounter circuits C which, for specific inputs, yield a specific state in the computational basis with very high probability. In the proof of the following lemma, we specify how to use coherent computation in order to learn the output value while preserving the input quantum state.

Lemma 2.9. *Let C be a quantum circuit. There exists an input-recovering circuit C_{rec} such that for all inputs ρ_{in}, the following holds: if $\frac{1}{2} \| C(\rho_{\text{in}}) - |x\rangle\langle x| \|_{\text{tr}} \leq \varepsilon$ for some classical string x and some $\varepsilon > 0$, then*

$$\frac{1}{2} \| C_{\text{rec}}(\rho_{\text{in}}) - (\rho_{\text{in}} \otimes |x\rangle\langle x|) \|_{\text{tr}} \leq 2\sqrt{\varepsilon}.$$

The specification of C_{rec} is independent of the specific input state ρ_{in}. However, C_{rec} cannot necessarily recover *all* possible inputs ρ_{in}, only those that lead to an almost-classical output.

The input-recovering circuit consists of running C coherently, copying out the output register, and reverting the coherent computation of C. We formally prove Lemma 2.9 in Appendix A.

3   FHE with Decomposable Public Keys

For the purpose of our result in Sect. 5, we will need to obfuscate a class of circuits that allow to (quantumly) homomorphically evaluate operations of arbitrary polynomial depth. We nevertheless wish to rely only on leveled FHE for the sake of minimizing our assumptions. We therefore would like to define a class of circuits that are a priori polynomially bounded in size, but which are capable of

---

[1] If, apart from the targets of the aforementioned CNOTs, the circuit C contains any other wires that are initialized in the $|0\rangle$ state inside the circuit, those wires are also considered part of the input of the unitary U_C. They should be initialized to $|0\rangle$ here as well.

encapsulating public-key generation of a leveled scheme for some depth d that is not fixed a priori. Note that in a leveled scheme even the length of pk depends on d.

To this end, we define the notion of a scheme with *decomposable* public key, which is defined below. Intuitively, in such a scheme, the public key can be generated by first generating a sequence of blocks, each of some size independent of d. These blocks can then be combined into the actual pk of the scheme. Crucially, the generation of the blocks can be done in parallel, and the complexity of generating each block (given the security parameter and the random tape) is independent of d. In other words, a decomposable public key can be generated on the fly, involving small "chunks" of computation that are independent of d. Formally, we recall Definition 2.5 and define decomposability as follows.

Definition 3.1 (Decomposable public key). *A leveled (Q)FHE scheme has a decomposable public key if there exists a polynomial $K = K(\lambda, d)$ and a polynomial-time deterministic function* $\mathsf{BlockGen}(1^\lambda, i, r, r')$ *(where $r, r' \in \{0,1\}^\lambda$) that generates classical strings ("blocks") c_i such that the following holds:*

1. **Correctness:** *there exists a QPT* $\mathsf{Assemble}$ *such that for all $\lambda, d, r,$ and r', letting $K = K(\lambda, d)$, it holds that*

$$\mathsf{Assemble}(c_0, c_1, c_2, \ldots, c_K) = pk,$$

   where $(pk, sk) = \mathsf{KeyGen}(1^\lambda, 1^d; r)$, and $c_i = \mathsf{BlockGen}(1^\lambda, i, r, r')$ for all i.
2. **Simulatability:** *there exists a QPT simulator S such that for all d and r,*

$$\mathcal{S}(1^\lambda, pk) \stackrel{c}{\approx} (c_0, c_1, c_2, \ldots, c_K),$$

   where $(pk, sk) = \mathsf{KeyGen}(1^\lambda, d, r)$, and the distribution on $(c_1, c_2, \ldots, c_K)$ on the right-hand side is generated by selecting a uniformly random r', and then for all i, setting $c_i = \mathsf{BlockGen}(1^\lambda, i, r, r')$.

We emphasize that in Definition 3.1, the randomness strings r and r' are the same for every run of $\mathsf{BlockGen}$. The reason for this choice is twofold. First, with our final goal in mind of obfuscating the $\mathsf{BlockGen}$ functionality, we want to avoid having to specify K independent randomness strings (as that would considerably increase the size of the circuit to obfuscate). Second, most schemes require some form of correlation to exist between the different blocks. Thinking of r and r' as short random seeds for a PRF, this correlation can be realized by running the PRF on the same inputs (see, for example Sect. 3.1).

3.1   Instantiation from Bootstrapped Schemes

For bootstrapped schemes (see Definition 2.6), decomposability follows immediately by definition. In this case, we do not even need the extra randomness r' and can simply set $\mathsf{BlockGen}(1^\lambda, i, r, r')$ to be the process that evaluates $PRF_r(i-1)$

and $PRF_r(i)$ to generate random tapes for SubKeyGen, uses this randomness to generate (sk_{i-1}, pk_{i-1}) and (sk_i, pk_i), generates c_i^* based on these values, and outputs (pk_i, c_i^*). In addition, for $i = 0$, it simply computes $PRF_r(0)$, and uses the resulting randomness to generate pk_0.

Existing QFHE schemes are based on bootstrapping [Mah18, Bra18]. Without affecting security, we can assume that their randomness is sampled using a PRF as just described.

Lemma 3.2. *Bootstrapping-based leveled QFHE schemes with keys generated from a PRF have decomposable public keys.*

Proof. Define $K(\lambda, d) := d$, and $c_0 := pk_0$. For $i > 0$, define the blocks c_i, which are generated by BlockGen$(1^\lambda, i, r, r')$, as follows:

$$c_i := (pk_i, c_i^* = \mathsf{Enc}_{pk_i}(sk_{i-1})), \text{ where } (pk_i, sk_i) \leftarrow \mathsf{SubKeyGen}(1^\lambda; PRF_r(i)),$$
$$(pk_{i-1}, sk_{i-1}) \leftarrow \mathsf{SubKeyGen}(1^\lambda; PRF_r(i-1)). \tag{3}$$

Note that for public keys of this form, BlockGen does not make use of the additional randomness r'.

The assembly function Assemble$(c_0, c_1, \ldots, c_d)$ is a straightforward concatenation of all the blocks: Assemble$(c_0, c_1, \ldots, c_d) := (c_0, c_1, \ldots, c_d)$.

Simulatability as in Definition 3.1 is also easily satisfied: a simulator $\mathcal{S}$, for a public key pk and index i, reads out the pair (pk_i, c_i^*). It can thereby exactly produce the list $(c_1, \ldots, c_d)$.

3.2 Instantiation from Any Leveled (Q)FHE

We now observe that we can instantiate the a (Q)FHE with decomposable public keys from any leveled scheme, even ones that are not bootstrapped. Decomposing the public key of a general QFHE scheme is done via garbled circuits [Yao86, App17], as we will briefly outline here. A block c_i corresponds to a single garbled gate of the circuit for KeyGen. That is, BlockGen$(1^\lambda, i, r, r')$ returns a garbling of the ith gate[2] of KeyGen$(1^\lambda, d, r)$, using r' as a PRF seed to generate sufficient randomness for the garbling. A separate block (e.g., c_0) contains the required encoding/decoding information to use the garbled circuit. To assemble the public key, a user concatenates all garbled gates, and evaluates the garbled circuit to obtain the output pk. Conversely, by the privacy property of garbled circuits [BHR12], a simulator given only the security parameter λ and the output pk of the garbled circuit, can reproduce a garbled circuit that is indistinguishable from the actual garbled circuit. It can then return the gates of that simulated garbled circuit as the blocks c_i.

Any result relying on the decomposability of the public key of a non-/bootstrapping based QFHE scheme of course also relies on any computational assumptions required for the security of the garbled-circuit construction.

---

[2] The total number of blocks, $K(\lambda, d)$, will be the number of gates in KeyGen$(1^\lambda, 1^d, r)$. Since the number of gates is polynomial in λ, it suffices for the length of the PRF seed r' to be linear in λ.

4 Impossibility with Respect to Dependent Auxiliary Information

In this section, we show impossibility of virtual-black-box quantum obfuscation of classical point functions under dependent auxiliary information. It sets the stage for our main result, Theorem 5.1, where we incorporate the auxiliary information into the circuit, constructing a circuit class which is unobfuscatable even without the presence of any auxiliary information. Although the result in the current section is perhaps less surprising, the proof contains the most important technical details of our work.

The impossibility result requires two cryptographic primitives, both of which can be built from the hardness of LWE [Mah18, WZ17, GKW17]: (1) quantum fully homomorphic encryption with classical client-side operations (see Sect. 2.3), and (2) classical vbb obfuscation of compute-and-compare functions. Our result therefore holds under the assumption that LWE is hard. The least favorable LWE parameters are required for the obfuscation of compute-and-compare functionalities, and are discussed in Sect. 4.1.

In Sect. 4.1, we describe the classical obfuscator for compute-and-compare functions that we use. We will apply the construction from [WZ17, GKW17] to a specific class of compute-and-compare functions with a specific type of auxiliary information. In Sect. 4.2, we use this specific application to define a class of circuits and auxiliary-information strings that is unobfuscatable in the quantum vbb sense. The impossibility proof follows in Sect. 4.3.

4.1 Classical Obfuscation of Compute-and-Compare Functions

The works of [WZ17, GKW17] showed that under the assumption that LWE (with polynomial dimension and exponential modulus in the security parameter λ) is hard, it is possible to classically obfuscate compute-and-compare functions [WZ17, GKW17]. We will write "LWE*" to denote their specific variant of the LWE assumption. We note that LWE is known to be at least as hard as worst-case lattice problems [Reg05, PRS17]. In particular, the aforementioned parameter regime LWE* translates to the worst-case hardness of the Gap Shortest Vector Problem (GapSVP) with sub-exponential approximation factor (in the dimension of the lattice). There is currently no known super-polynomial quantum speedup for GapSVP, and the best known quantum (and classical) algorithms require sub-exponential running time.

The works of [WZ17, GKW17] achieve so-called distributional virtual-black-box obfuscation of functions $\mathbf{CC}_{f,y}$, assuming that the target value y has sufficient pseudo-entropy given a description of the function f. The obfuscation is even secure in the presence of (dependent) auxiliary information, so long as the pseudo-entropy of the target value remains high, even conditioned on this auxiliary information.

In our construction, we provide a classically-obfuscated compute-and-compare function as auxiliary information to a quantum obfuscation. We will require that the target value of the compute-and-compare function is sufficiently random, even given the rest of the auxiliary information (including the quantum obfuscation).

More specifically, for any IND-secure public-key encryption scheme (KeyGen, Enc, Dec), fixed bit string α, and a classical obfuscation procedure $\mathcal{O}(\cdot)$, define a distribution ensemble $\{D_\lambda^{\alpha,d}\}_{\lambda \in \mathbb{N}}$ that samples

$$(pk, \tilde{\alpha}, o_{sk,\beta}) \leftarrow D_\lambda^{\alpha,d} \quad \text{as} \quad (pk, sk) \leftarrow \mathsf{KeyGen}(1^\lambda, 1^d),$$
$$\tilde{\alpha} \leftarrow \mathsf{Enc}_{pk}(\alpha),$$
$$\beta \leftarrow_R \{0,1\}^\lambda,$$
$$o_{sk,\beta} \leftarrow \mathcal{O}\left(\mathbf{CC}_{\mathsf{Dec}_{sk},\beta}\right), \tag{4}$$

where $\mathbf{CC}_{\mathsf{Dec}_{sk},\beta}$ is a compute-and-compare function as in Definition 2.8. For each α and λ, the target value β is chosen independently from all other information: its pseudo-entropy is λ, even conditioned on pk, $\tilde{\alpha}$ and Dec_{sk}. Therefore, there exists an obfuscation procedure for this class of compute-and-compare programs that has distributional indistinguishability in the following sense:

Lemma 4.1 (Application of [WZ17, Theorem 5.2]). *Under the LWE** *assumption, there exists a classical obfuscation procedure $O_{\mathbf{CC}}(\cdot)$ and a (non-uniform) simulator S such that for all α and d,*

$$(pk, \tilde{\alpha}, o_{sk,\beta}) \overset{c}{\approx} (pk, \tilde{\alpha}, S(1^\lambda, \mathsf{params})), \tag{5}$$

where $(pk, \tilde{\alpha}, o_{sk,\beta}) \leftarrow D_\lambda^{\alpha,d}$ using $O_{\mathbf{CC}}(\cdot)$ as the obfuscation procedure $\mathcal{O}(\cdot)$, and params is some information that is independent of sk and β (e.g., it may contain the size of the circuit and/or λ).

In the rest of this work, $O_{\mathbf{CC}}(\cdot)$ will implicitly be the obfuscation procedure used in the distributions $D_\lambda^{\alpha,d}$.

We note that the proofs in [WZ17,GKW17] showed a classical reduction from the hardness of distinguishing the aforementioned distributions to the hardness of solving LWE. We note that proofs by (either Karp or Turing) classical polynomial-time reduction from A to B implies that any solver for A can be translated into a solver for B with comparable complexity, in particular if the solver for A runs in quantum polynomial time then so will the resulting solver for B.

As a consequence of Lemma 4.1, we show that it is hard to guess the value of α, given only a ciphertext $\tilde{\alpha}$ for α, and an obfuscation of the compute-and-compare function. Intuitively, since the information α is completely independent of the target value β, the obfuscation effectively hides the secret key sk that would be necessary to learn α.

Lemma 4.2. *Under the LWE* assumption, there exists a negligible function* negl $(\cdot)$ *such that for any QPT algorithm A and any d,*

$$\Pr[A(pk, \tilde{\alpha}, o_{sk,\beta}) = \alpha] \leq \mathsf{negl}(\lambda). \tag{6}$$

Here, the probability is over $\alpha \leftarrow_R \{0,1\}^\lambda$, $(pk, \widetilde{\alpha}, o_{sk,\beta}) \leftarrow D_\lambda^{\alpha,d}$, and the execution of A.

Proof. The result follows almost directly from Lemma 4.1, except that we want to bound the probability that A outputs the multi-bit string α, whereas Lemma 4.1 only deals with algorithms with a single-bit output.

To bridge the gap, define an algorithm A'_α that runs A on its input, and compares the output of A to α: if they are equal, A'_α outputs 1; otherwise, it outputs 0.

For any *fixed* value of α, we have

$$\Pr[A(pk, \widetilde{\alpha}, o_{sk,\beta}) = \alpha] = \Pr[A'_\alpha(pk, \widetilde{\alpha}, o_{sk,\beta}) = 1] \tag{7}$$

$$\overset{(*)}{\approx} \Pr[A'_\alpha(pk, \widetilde{\alpha}, \mathcal{S}(1^\lambda, \mathsf{params})) = 1] \tag{8}$$

$$= \Pr[A(pk, \widetilde{\alpha}, \mathcal{S}(1^\lambda, \mathsf{params})) = \alpha]. \tag{9}$$

The approximation $(*)$ follows from Lemma 4.1, and holds up to a difference of $\mathsf{negl}\,(\lambda)$.

To complete the proof, note that $\mathcal{S}(1^\lambda, \mathsf{params})$ depends neither on α nor on sk. Thus, randomizing over α again, and invoking privacy of the encryption, we get

$$\Pr[A(pk, \widetilde{\alpha}, o_{sk,\beta}) = \alpha] \approx \Pr[A(pk, \widetilde{\alpha}, \mathcal{S}(1^\lambda, \mathsf{params})) = \alpha] \le \mathsf{negl}\,(|\alpha|) = \mathsf{negl}\,(\lambda). \tag{10}$$

We have thus established that, even in the presence of an obfuscated compute-and-compare function that depends on the secret key, encryptions remain secure (in the one-way sense). For this security to hold, it is important that the target value β is sufficiently independent of the plaintext α.

4.2   An Unobfuscatable Circuit Class

In this subsection, we define the class of circuits and auxiliary-information strings that we will prove unobfuscatable. Like in [BGI+01], we will exploit the idea that access to an object (circuit or quantum state) that allows the evaluation of a function is more powerful than mere black-box access to the functionality: in particular, it allows to evaluate the function homomorphically. For this argument to work, it is important that the function is not easily learnable through black-box access. We will use point functions, as in [BGI+01]: with black-box access only, it is hard to tell the difference between a point function and the all-zero function $\mathbf{Z}_\lambda$, that accepts inputs of length λ, and always returns 0^λ.

Consider the class $\mathcal{C}_{\lambda,d}^{\mathsf{point}} \cup \mathcal{C}_{\lambda,d}^{\mathsf{zero}}$ of circuits plus auxiliary information, where

$$\mathcal{C}_{\lambda,d}^{\mathsf{point}} := \{(\mathbf{P}_{\alpha,\beta}, (pk, \widetilde{\alpha}, o_{sk,\beta})) \mid \alpha \in \{0,1\}^\lambda, (pk, \widetilde{\alpha}, o_{sk,\beta}) \in \mathrm{supp}(D_\lambda^{\alpha,d})\}, \tag{11}$$

$$\mathcal{C}_{\lambda,d}^{\mathsf{zero}} := \{(\mathbf{Z}_\lambda, (pk, \widetilde{\alpha}, o_{sk,\beta})) \mid \alpha \in \{0,1\}^\lambda, (pk, \widetilde{\alpha}, o_{sk,\beta}) \in \mathrm{supp}(D_\lambda^{\alpha,d})\}. \tag{12}$$

The class $\mathcal{C}_{\lambda,d}^{\mathsf{point}}$ contains all λ-bit point functions, together with an encryption of the point input α, a public key that enables evaluation of circuits up to depth d, and a function that checks whether a ciphertext decrypts to the target value β. $\mathcal{C}_{\lambda,d}^{\mathsf{zero}}$ contains the all-zero function $\mathbf{Z}_\lambda$ (which is itself a point function), but still with auxiliary information for the possible values of α and β.

Suppose that some quantum obfuscation $(O_Q(\cdot)), \mathcal{J})$ exists. We define a QPT algorithm A, which expects an obfuscation $\rho = O_Q(\mathbf{P}_{\alpha,\beta})$ (or $O_Q(\mathbf{Z}_\lambda)$), together with the classical auxiliary information $\mathsf{aux} = (pk, \widetilde{\alpha}, o_{sk,\beta})$. On general inputs ρ and $\mathsf{aux} = (\mathsf{key}, \mathsf{ctxt}, \mathsf{obf})$ of this form, let A do as follows:

1. Run $\mathsf{QFHE.Eval}_{\mathsf{key}}(\mathcal{J}, \mathsf{Enc}_{\mathsf{key}}(\rho) \otimes |\mathsf{ctxt}\rangle\langle\mathsf{ctxt}|)$ to homomorphically evaluate the interpreter algorithm $\mathcal{J}$. If $\rho = O_Q(\mathbf{P}_{\alpha,\beta})$, $\mathsf{key} = pk$, and $\mathsf{ctxt} = \widetilde{\alpha}$, then this step results in an encryption of β with high probability. If $\rho = O_Q(\mathbf{Z}_\lambda)$, $\mathsf{key} = pk$, $\mathsf{ctxt} = \widetilde{\alpha}$, and d is at least the depth of $\mathcal{J}$, then it results in an encryption of 0^λ. Note that we use classical and quantum ciphertexts for the QFHE scheme interchangeably here: see Sect. 2.3 for a justification.
2. Run obf on the output of the previous step. If $\mathsf{obf} = o_{sk,\beta}$, this will indicate whether the previous step resulted in a ciphertext for β or not.

The above algorithm A will almost certainly output 1 when given an element from $\mathcal{C}_{\lambda,d}^{\mathsf{point}}$ for a sufficiently high value of d, because of the functional equivalence of the two obfuscations and the correctness of the homomorphic evaluation. Similarly, when given an element from $\mathcal{C}_{\lambda,d}^{\mathsf{zero}} - \mathcal{C}_{\lambda,d}^{\mathsf{point}}$, it will almost certainly output 0. Formally, for all $\alpha, \beta \in \{0,1\}^\lambda - \{0^\lambda\}$, and d at least the depth of $\mathcal{J}$,

$$\Pr\left[A(O_Q(\mathbf{P}_{\alpha,\beta}), pk, \widetilde{\alpha}, o_{sk,\beta}) = 1\right] \geq 1 - \mathsf{negl}\,(\lambda)\,, \tag{13}$$

$$\Pr\left[A(O_Q(\mathbf{Z}_\lambda), pk, \widetilde{\alpha}, o_{sk,\beta}) = 1\right] \leq \mathsf{negl}\,(\lambda)\,. \tag{14}$$

The vastly different output distribution of A when given an obfuscation of a point function versus the zero function are due the fact that A has an actual representation, ρ, of the function to feed into the interpreter $\mathcal{J}$. In the proof in the next subsection, we will see that a simulator, with only black-box access to these functionality, will not be able to make that distinction.

4.3   Impossibility Proof

We are now ready to state and prove the impossibility theorem for quantum obfuscation of classical circuits with dependent auxiliary input. We reiterate that the two assumptions (quantum FHE and compute-and-compare obfuscation) can be realized under the LWE* assumption.

Define $\mathcal{C}_\lambda^{\mathsf{point}} := \bigcup_{d \in [2^\lambda]} \mathcal{C}_{\lambda,d}^{\mathsf{point}}$, and similarly $\mathcal{C}_\lambda^{\mathsf{zero}} := \bigcup_{d \in [2^\lambda]} \mathcal{C}_{\lambda,d}^{\mathsf{zero}}$.

Theorem 4.3 (Impossibility of quantum obfuscation w.r.t. auxiliary input). *Suppose that a classical-client quantum fully homomorphic encryption scheme QFHE exists that satisfies Definition 2.4, and a classical obfuscation procedure $O_{\mathbf{CC}}(\cdot)$ for compute-and-compare functionalities exists that satisfies*

Lemma 4.1. Then any (not necessarily efficient) quantum obfuscator $(O_Q(\cdot), \mathcal{J})$ for the class $\mathcal{C}_\lambda^{\mathsf{point}} \cup \mathcal{C}_\lambda^{\mathsf{zero}}$ satisfying conditions 1 (polynomial expansion) and 2 (functional equivalence) from Definition 2.3 cannot be virtual black-box under the presence of classical dependent auxiliary input, i.e., cannot satisfy condition 3 from Definition 2.3 where both $\mathcal{A}$ and $\mathcal{S}$ get access to a classical string aux (which may depend on C).

It may seem that the class $\mathcal{C}_\lambda^{\mathsf{point}} \cup \mathcal{C}_\lambda^{\mathsf{zero}}$, consisting of point functions, is classically obfuscatable using $O_{\mathbf{CC}}(\cdot)$ from [WZ17,GKW17]. That obfuscation is secure if α (wich is the target value if we view $\mathbf{P}_{\alpha,\beta}$ as the multi-bit output compute-and-compare function $\mathbf{CC}_{\mathsf{id},\alpha,\beta}$) is unpredictable given the auxiliary information aux $= (pk, \widetilde{\alpha}, o_{sk,\beta})$. On the surface, that seems to be the case: only an encryption of α is available in the auxiliary information. However, the secret key sk is present as part of the compute-and-compare function $\mathbf{CC}_{\mathsf{Dec}_{sk},\beta}$. That function is obfuscated, but the obfuscation is not secure in the presence of (an obfuscation of) $\mathbf{P}_{\alpha,\beta}$. Thus, the obfuscation result from [WZ17,GKW17] *almost* applies to the class $\mathcal{C}_\lambda^{\mathsf{point}} \cup \mathcal{C}_\lambda^{\mathsf{zero}}$, but not quite. Hence we are able to prove impossibility of obfuscating it, which we do below.

Proof. The proof structure is similar to [BGI+01], and is by contradiction: assume that a quantum obfuscation $(O_Q(\cdot), \mathcal{J})$ for the class $\mathcal{C}_\lambda^{\mathsf{point}} \cup \mathcal{C}_\lambda^{\mathsf{zero}}$ does exist that satisfies all three conditions. We will show that the output distribution of the algorithm A defined in Sect. 4.2 is approximately the same for every element of the class, contradicting Eqs. (13) and (14).

By the assumption of the existence of a secure quantum obfuscation $(O_Q(\cdot), \mathcal{J})$, there exists a simulator $\mathcal{S}$ such that

$$\left| \Pr[A(O_Q(\mathbf{P}_{\alpha,\beta}), \mathsf{aux}) = 1] - \Pr[\mathcal{S}^{\mathbf{P}_{\alpha,\beta}}(1^\lambda, \mathsf{aux}) = 1] \right| \le \mathsf{negl}\,(\lambda), \text{ and} \quad (15)$$

$$\left| \Pr[A(O_Q(\mathbf{Z}_\lambda), \mathsf{aux}) = 1] - \Pr[\mathcal{S}^{\mathbf{Z}_\lambda}(1^\lambda, \mathsf{aux}) = 1] \right| \le \mathsf{negl}\,(\lambda). \quad (16)$$

The probability is taken over $\alpha \leftarrow_R \{0,1\}^\lambda$ and aux $= (pk, \widetilde{\alpha}, O_{\mathbf{CC}}(\mathbf{CC}_{\mathsf{Dec}_{sk},\beta}))$ $\leftarrow D_\lambda^{\alpha,q}$ for q the depth of the interpreter circuit $\mathcal{J}$. Note that $\mathcal{S}$ does not depend on α, β, sk, or pk.

In the remainder of this proof we show that for any $\mathcal{S}$ (independent of α, β, sk, pk),

$$\left| \Pr[\mathcal{S}^{\mathbf{P}_{\alpha,\beta}}(1^\lambda, \mathsf{aux}) = 1] - \Pr[\mathcal{S}^{\mathbf{Z}_\lambda}(1^\lambda, \mathsf{aux}) = 1] \right| \le \mathsf{negl}\,(\lambda), \quad (17)$$

from which it can be concluded that

$$\left| \Pr[A(O_Q(\mathbf{P}_{\alpha,\beta}), \mathsf{aux}) = 1] - \Pr[A(O_Q(\mathbf{Z}_\lambda), \mathsf{aux}) = 1] \right| \le \mathsf{negl}\,(\lambda). \quad (18)$$

Since Eqs. 13 and 14 imply that this difference must be at least $1 - \mathsf{negl}\,(\lambda)$, Eq. 18 yields a contradiction.

To show that Eq. (17) holds, i.e., to bound the difference in output probabilities of $\mathcal{S}$ when given an oracle for $\mathbf{P}_{\alpha,\beta}$ versus an oracle for $\mathbf{Z}_\lambda$, we employ the one-way to hiding theorem as it is stated in [AHU19, Theorem 3]. It says that there exists a QPT algorithm B such that

$$\left|\Pr[\mathcal{S}^{\mathbf{P}_{\alpha,\beta}}(1^\lambda, \mathsf{aux}) = 1] - \Pr[\mathcal{S}^{\mathbf{Z}_\lambda}(1^\lambda, \mathsf{aux}) = 1]\right| \leq 2d' \cdot \sqrt{\Pr[B^{\mathbf{Z}_\lambda}(1^\lambda, \mathsf{aux}) = \alpha]},$$
(19)

where $d' = \mathsf{poly}\,(\lambda)$ is the query depth of $\mathcal{S}$. However, by Lemma 4.2, the probability that B outputs α when given the auxiliary information $\mathsf{aux} = (pk, \widetilde{\alpha}, o_{sk,\beta})$ is negligible in λ. Granting B access to the zero-oracle and the additional input 1^λ does not increase this probability, since the value of λ can already be deduced from aux.

We can thus conclude that the difference in Eq. (19) is negligible, and Eq. (17) holds, as desired.

We end this section with a few remarks: we describe some variants and generalizations of Theorem 4.3 which almost immediately follow from the presented proof.

Remark 4.4. The proof for Theorem 4.3 also works if we replace $O_{\mathsf{CC}}(\mathbf{CC}_{\mathsf{Dec}_{sk},\beta})$ inside the distributions $D_\lambda^{\alpha,d}$ with $O_Q(\mathbf{CC}_{\mathsf{Dec}_{sk},\beta})$, the quantum obfuscation we get from the assumption. This adaptation renders a quantum obfuscator for point functions impossible with respect to dependent auxiliary *quantum* input: a slightly weaker statement, but it does not require the existence of a classical obfuscator for compute-and-compare programs. In particular, the required LWE parameters are better, because we only need the assumption of quantum fully homomorphic encryption.

Remark 4.5. Even a quantum obfuscator $(O_Q(\cdot), \mathcal{J})$ for $\mathcal{C}_\lambda^{\mathsf{point}} \cup \mathcal{C}_\lambda^{\mathsf{zero}}$ with non-negligible errors in the functional equivalence and/or the virtual-black-box property would lead to a contradiction in the proof of Theorem 4.3. Concretely, let ε_f denote the error for functional equivalence, and ε_s denote the error for security in the virtual-black-box sense (they are both $\mathsf{negl}\,(|C|) = \mathsf{negl}\,(\lambda)$ in Definition 2.3). The impossibility proof works for any values of $\varepsilon_f, \varepsilon_s$ such that $\varepsilon_f + \varepsilon_s \leq \frac{1}{2} - \frac{1}{\mathsf{poly}(\lambda)}$. So in particular, even a quantum obfuscator with small constant (instead of negligible) errors in both conditions cannot exist.

5   Impossibility Without Auxiliary Information

In this section, we will show that quantum virtual-black-box obfuscation of classical circuits is impossible even when no auxiliary information is present. We will rely heavily on the class constructed in Sect. 4, essentially showing how the auxiliary information can be absorbed into the obfuscated circuit. As a result, the unobfuscatable circuit class itself becomes perhaps less natural, but still consists of classical polynomial-size circuits. Thus, our theorem implies impossibility of quantum vbb obfuscation of the class of all efficient classical circuits.

We would like to consider circuits of the following form:

$$C_{\alpha,\beta,\text{aux}}(b,x) := \begin{cases} \text{aux} = (pk, \widetilde{\alpha}, o_{sk,\beta}) & \text{if } b = 0 \\ \mathbf{P}_{\alpha,\beta}(x) & \text{if } b = 1, \end{cases} \tag{20}$$

where $(pk, \widetilde{\alpha}, o_{sk,\beta})$ is generated from $D_\lambda^{\alpha,d}$, as in Sect. 4. The input bit b is a choice bit: if it is set to 1, the function $\mathbf{P}_{\alpha,\beta}$ (or $\mathbf{Z}_\lambda$) is evaluated on the actual input x, whereas if it is set to 0, the auxiliary information is retrieved.

The idea would then be to retrieve the auxiliary information, followed by a homomorphic evaluation of the branch for $b = 1$. There is a problem with this approach, however: since the auxiliary information aux contains the public evaluation key pk, the circuit C grows with d, which affects the length of pk. But as the circuit grows, a (non-circularly-secure) QFHE scheme may require a larger pk to perform all evaluation steps.

To get around this issue, the unobfuscatable circuit will generate the public key step-by-step, in a construction inspired by [CLTV15]. We will assume that the public key of the leveled QFHE scheme is decomposable in the sense of Definition 3.1.

Given a scheme with a decomposable public key, we redefine the unobfuscatable circuit class as follows. Instead of returning the entire public key at once, the circuit allows the user to request individual blocks c_i, up to some depth d. An honest user can run the circuit $K + 1 = K(d, \lambda) + 1$ times to obtain $pk = \text{Assemble}(c_0, c_1, \ldots, c_K)$. The depth d will not be fixed a priori, although it will be (exponentially) upper bounded: the circuit will only be able to handle inputs i where $|i| \leq \lambda$. Thus, only up to 2^λ blocks c_i can be retrieved.

The circuit class we consider in this section consists of circuits of the following form:

$$\hat{C}_{\alpha,\beta,d,r,r',\widetilde{\alpha},o_{sk,\beta}}(b,x) := \begin{cases} (\widetilde{\alpha}, o_{sk,\beta}) & \text{if } b = 0, \\ \text{BlockGen}(1^\lambda, x, r, r') & \text{if } b = 1 \text{ and } x \leq K(d, \lambda), \\ \bot & \text{if } b = 1 \text{ and } x > K(d, \lambda), \\ \mathbf{P}_{\alpha,\beta}(x) & \text{if } b = 2. \end{cases} \tag{21}$$

or

$$\hat{C}'_{\alpha,\beta,d,r,r',\widetilde{\alpha},o_{sk,\beta}}(b,x) := \begin{cases} (\widetilde{\alpha}, o_{sk,\beta}) & \text{if } b = 0, \\ \text{BlockGen}(1^\lambda, x, r, r') & \text{if } b = 1 \text{ and } x \leq K(d, \lambda), \\ \bot & \text{if } b = 1 \text{ and } x > K(d, \lambda), \\ \mathbf{Z}_\lambda(x) & \text{if } b = 2. \end{cases} \tag{22}$$

The first input b is now a choice trit: depending on its value, a different branch of the circuit is executed.

We alter the distribution $D_\lambda^{\alpha,d}$ from Eq. 4, so that it does not explicitly generate the public key anymore. That information is now generated on-the-fly by setting $b = 1$. The public and secret key are deterministically computed using r to generate the auxiliary information $(\widetilde{\alpha}, o_{sk,\beta})$ for $b = 0$. Consider the distribution ensemble $\{D_\lambda^{\alpha,d,r}\}_{\lambda \in \mathbb{N}}$, where

$$(\widetilde{\alpha}, o_{sk,\beta}) \leftarrow D_\lambda^{\alpha,d,r} \quad \text{as} \quad (pk, sk) = \mathsf{KeyGen}(1^\lambda, 1^d, r),$$
$$\widetilde{\alpha} \leftarrow \mathsf{Enc}_{pk}(\alpha),$$
$$\beta \leftarrow_R \{0,1\}^\lambda$$
$$o_{sk,\beta} \leftarrow \mathbf{CC}_{\mathsf{Dec}_{sk},\beta}. \tag{23}$$

Note that the value of d does not influence the size of $\widetilde{\alpha}$ or $o_{sk,\beta}$ (and thereby the circuit size of $\hat{C}$ and $\hat{C}'$).

We can then define the following parametrized circuit classes:

$$\hat{\mathcal{C}}_{\lambda,d}^{\mathsf{point}} := \{\hat{C}_{\alpha,\beta,d,r,r',\widetilde{\alpha},o_{sk,\beta}} \mid \alpha \in \{0,1\}^\lambda, r, r' \in \{0,1\}^\lambda, (\widetilde{\alpha}, o_{sk,\beta}) \in \mathrm{supp}(D_\lambda^{\alpha,d,r})\}, \tag{24}$$

$$\hat{\mathcal{C}}_{\lambda,d}^{\mathsf{zero}} := \{\hat{C}'_{\alpha,\beta,d,r,r',\widetilde{\alpha},o_{sk,\beta}} \mid \alpha \in \{0,1\}^\lambda, r, r' \in \{0,1\}^\lambda, (\widetilde{\alpha}, o_{sk,\beta}) \in \mathrm{supp}(D_\lambda^{\alpha,d,r})\}. \tag{25}$$

Define the circuit class $\hat{\mathcal{C}}_\lambda^{\mathsf{point}} \cup \hat{\mathcal{C}}_\lambda^{\mathsf{zero}}$, where $\hat{\mathcal{C}}_\lambda^{\mathsf{point}} := \bigcup_{d \in [2^\lambda]} \hat{\mathcal{C}}_{\lambda,d}^{\mathsf{point}}$ and similarly $\hat{\mathcal{C}}_\lambda^{\mathsf{zero}} := \bigcup_{d \in [2^\lambda]} \hat{\mathcal{C}}_{\lambda,d}^{\mathsf{zero}}$. Note that in all circuits in this class, the "auxiliary information" $(\widetilde{\alpha}, o_{sk,\beta})$ is fixed. Hence, when the obfuscation of the compute-and-compare function is requested by setting $b = 0$, the circuit always returns the same obfuscation that depends on the same secret key sk.

Similarly to the setting with auxiliary input, there exists a QPT algorithm A' that has significantly different output distributions when given a circuit from $\hat{\mathcal{C}}_{\lambda,d}^{\mathsf{point}}$ versus a circuit from $\hat{\mathcal{C}}_{\lambda,d}^{\mathsf{zero}}$. Here, we define the algorithm A' that is able to distinguish *only* if it receives a circuit for $d = q$, where q is the depth of the interpreter circuit. If $d < q$, then A' will not be able to retrieve a long enough evaluation key, and will always output zero. However, for our impossibility result, a single value of d on which A' succeeds in distinguishing is sufficient. Note that we cannot define our circuit class to contain only circuits with $d = q$, since q depends on the specific obfuscator/interpreter pair.

On an input state ρ, we define A' as follows:

1. Run $\mathcal{J}_{\mathsf{rec}}(\rho, |b = 0\rangle\langle b = 0| \otimes |0^\lambda\rangle\langle 0^\lambda|)$, where $\mathcal{J}_{\mathsf{rec}}$ is the input-recovering version of the interpreter circuit (see Lemma 2.9). If ρ is an obfuscation of a circuit in $\hat{\mathcal{C}}^{\mathsf{point}} \cup \hat{\mathcal{C}}^{\mathsf{zero}}$, this will result in a state (negligibly close to) $\rho \otimes |\widetilde{\alpha}\rangle\langle\widetilde{\alpha}| \otimes |o_{sk,\beta}\rangle\langle o_{sk,\beta}|$. Measure the second and third registers to obtain $\widetilde{\alpha}$ and $o_{sk,\beta}$.
2. Let q be the depth of the interpreter $\mathcal{J}$. Because the interpreter is efficient, $q = \mathrm{poly}(\lambda)$. Sequentially run $\mathcal{J}_{\mathsf{rec}}(\rho, |b = 1\rangle\langle b = 1| \otimes |i\rangle\langle i|)$ for all $0 \le i \le K = K(q, \lambda)$ to obtain $(c_0, c_1, \ldots, c_K)$, and compute the public evaluation

key $pk = \mathsf{Assemble}(c_0, c_1, \ldots, c_K)$, suitable for homomorphic evaluations of up to depth q. Note that the key pk is only revealed in its entirety if the given circuit has parameter $d = q$. If $d < q$, A' will notice that $\bot$ is returned for some queries, and outputs 0 at this point.

3. Run $\mathsf{QFHE.Eval}_{pk}(\mathcal{J}, \mathsf{Enc}_{pk}(\rho) \otimes |\mathsf{Enc}_{pk}(b = 2)\rangle\langle\mathsf{Enc}_{pk}(b = 2)| \otimes |\tilde{\alpha}\rangle\langle\tilde{\alpha}|)$. Similarly to Sect. 4.2, this will result in a ciphertext for β (if ρ was an obfuscation of a circuit in $\hat{\mathcal{C}}_\lambda^{\mathsf{point}}$) or a ciphertext for 0^λ (if ρ was an obfuscation of a circuit in $\hat{\mathcal{C}}_\lambda^{\mathsf{zero}}$), provided that $d = q$.

4. Run $o_{sk,\beta}$ on the output of the previous step. Doing so will indicate whether the previous step resulted in a ciphertext for β or not. If yes, output 1; otherwise output 0.

Let $(O_Q(\cdot), \mathcal{J})$ be an obfuscator. The algorithm A', when given a random obfuscated circuit from $\hat{\mathcal{C}}_{\lambda,q}^{\mathsf{point}}$, will almost certainly output 1, where q is the depth of $\mathcal{J}$. At the same time, an element from $\hat{\mathcal{C}}_{\lambda,q}^{\mathsf{zero}} - \hat{\mathcal{C}}_{\lambda,q}^{\mathsf{point}}$ will almost certainly result in the output 0. More formally, for all $\alpha, r \in \{0,1\}^\lambda$ and $d = q$,

$$\Pr\left[A'(O_Q(\hat{C}_{\alpha,\beta,d,r,r',\tilde{\alpha},o_{sk,\beta}})) = 1\right] \geq 1 - \mathsf{negl}(\lambda), \tag{26}$$

$$\Pr\left[A'(O_Q(\hat{C}'_{\alpha,\beta,d,r,r',\tilde{\alpha},o_{sk,\beta}})) = 1\right] \leq \mathsf{negl}(\lambda). \tag{27}$$

The probability is taken over $D_\lambda^{\alpha,d,r}$, r', and the internal randomness of A'. Compare these inequalities to Eqs. 13 and 14.

We are now ready to state our main theorem.

Theorem 5.1 (Impossibility of quantum obfuscation). *Suppose that a classical/client quantum fully homomorphic encryption scheme* QFHE *exists that satisfies Definition 2.4 and 3.1, and a classical obfuscation procedure* $O_{\mathsf{CC}}(\cdot)$ *for compute-and-compare functionalities exists that satisfies Lemma 4.1. Then any (not necessarily efficient) quantum obfuscator* $(O_Q(\cdot), \mathcal{J})$ *for the class* $\hat{\mathcal{C}}_\lambda^{\mathsf{point}} \cup \hat{\mathcal{C}}_\lambda^{\mathsf{zero}}$ *satisfying conditions 1 (polynomial expansion) and 2 (functional equivalence) from Definition 2.3 cannot be virtual black-box, i.e., cannot satisfy condition 3 from Definition 2.3.*

Corollary 5.2. *If the LWE* assumption holds, the class of classical polynomial-size circuits cannot be quantum virtual-black-box obfuscated in the sense of Definition 2.3.*

Proof (Proof of Theorem 5.1). We again prove the statement by contradiction, assuming that there does exist an obfuscator $(O_Q(\cdot), \mathcal{J})$ that securely obfuscates $\hat{\mathcal{C}}_\lambda^{\mathsf{point}} \cup \hat{\mathcal{C}}_\lambda^{\mathsf{zero}}$. Let q be the depth of $\mathcal{J}$, so that $K(q, \lambda)$ is the number of blocks c_i of the evaluation key required by A' to successfully distinguish between an element of $\hat{\mathcal{C}}_\lambda^{\mathsf{point}}$ and of $\hat{\mathcal{C}}_\lambda^{\mathsf{zero}}$.

By the assumption that $(O_Q(\cdot), \mathcal{J})$ is secure, there must exist a simulator $\mathcal{S}_0$ such that for all $\alpha, r \in \{0,1\}^\lambda$ (and setting $d = q$),

$$\left| \Pr[A'(O_Q(\hat{C}_{\alpha,\beta,q,r,r',\tilde{\alpha},o_{sk,\beta}})) = 1] - \Pr[\mathcal{S}_0^{\hat{C}_{\alpha,\beta,q,r,r',\tilde{\alpha},o_{sk,\beta}}}(1^\lambda) = 1] \right| \leq \mathsf{negl}(\lambda),$$

$$(28)$$

$$\left| \Pr[A'(O_Q(\hat{C}'_{\alpha,\beta,q,r,r',\tilde{\alpha},o_{sk,\beta}})) = 1] - \Pr[\mathcal{S}_0^{\hat{C}'_{\alpha,\beta,q,r,r',\tilde{\alpha},o_{sk,\beta}}}(1^\lambda) = 1] \right| \leq \mathsf{negl}(\lambda).$$

$$(29)$$

The probabilities are taken over $(\tilde{\alpha}, o_{sk,\beta}) \leftarrow D_\lambda^{\alpha,d,r}$ and $r' \leftarrow_R \{0,1\}^\lambda$, and the internal randomness of A' and $\mathcal{S}_0$.

The output distribution of $\mathcal{S}_0$ can be exactly simulated by another simulator, $\mathcal{S}_1$, that has access only to an oracle for $\mathbf{P}_{\alpha,\beta}$ or $\mathbf{Z}_\lambda$, and gets the auxiliary information pk, $\tilde{\alpha}$, and $o_{sk,\beta}$ as input. $\mathcal{S}_1$ can simply run $\mathcal{S}_0$, simulating each oracle query using its own oracle, auxiliary input, or a combination thereof. If (part of) the query of $\mathcal{S}_0$ is for some block c_i, $\mathcal{S}_1$ can use the decomposability of pk to compute the individual blocks. We formally show the existence of such an $\mathcal{S}_1$ in Corollary B.2.

We can thus conclude that for all $\alpha, r \in \{0,1\}^\lambda$,

$$\left| \Pr[A'(O_Q(\hat{C}_{\alpha,\beta,q,r,r',\tilde{\alpha},o_{sk,\beta}})) = 1] - \Pr[\mathcal{S}_1^{\mathbf{P}_{\alpha,\beta}}(1^\lambda, \tilde{\alpha}, o_{sk,\beta}, pk) = 1] \right| \leq \mathsf{negl}(\lambda),$$

$$(30)$$

$$\left| \Pr[A'(O_Q(\hat{C}'_{\alpha,\beta,q,r,r',\tilde{\alpha},o_{sk,\beta}})) = 1] - \Pr[\mathcal{S}_1^{\mathbf{Z}_\lambda}(1^\lambda, \tilde{\alpha}, o_{sk,\beta}, pk) = 1] \right| \leq \mathsf{negl}(\lambda).$$

$$(31)$$

Again, the probabilities are over $D_\lambda^{\alpha,d,r}$ and r', A', and $\mathcal{S}_1$.

However, by Eq. (17) in the proof of Theorem 4.3, the output distribution of $\mathcal{S}_1$ can only differ negligibly between the two different oracles. Thus, we have

$$\left| \Pr[A'(O_Q(\hat{C}_{\alpha,\beta,q,r,r',\tilde{\alpha},o_{sk,\beta}})) = 1] - \Pr[A'(O_Q(\hat{C}'_{\alpha,\beta,q,r,r',\tilde{\alpha},o_{sk,\beta}})) = 1] \right| \leq \mathsf{negl}(\lambda).$$

$$(32)$$

This contradicts our observation in Eqs. 26 and 27 that on input $\hat{C}_{\alpha,\beta,q,r,r',\tilde{\alpha},o_{sk,\beta}}$, A' will almost always output 1, whereas on input $\hat{C}'_{\alpha,\beta,q,r,r',\tilde{\alpha},o_{sk,\beta}}$, it will almost always output 0.

Acknowledgements. We thank Andrea Coladangelo, Urmila Mahadev and Alexander Poremba for useful discussions, and Serge Fehr for pointing out an error in the proof of Lemma 2.9. GA acknowledges support from the NSF under grant CCF-1763736, from the U.S. Army Research Office under Grant Number W911NF-20-1-0015, and from the U.S. Department of Energy under Award Number DE-SC0020312. ZB is supported by the Binational Science Foundation (Grant No. 2016726), and by the European Union Horizon 2020 Research and Innovation Program via ERC Project REACT

(Grant 756482) and via Project PROMETHEUS (Grant 780701). YD is supported by the Dutch Research Council (NWO/OCW), as part of the Quantum Software Consortium programme (project number 024.003.037). CS is supported by a NWO VIDI grant (Project No. 639.022.519). Part of this work was done while the authors were attending https://simons.berkeley.edu/programs/quantum2020. The Quantum Wave in Computing at the Simons Institute for the Theory of Computing.

A   Proof of Lemma 2.9

Proof. The input-recovering circuit C_{rec} will consist of running C coherently, copying out the output register, and reverting the coherent computation of C. Suppose the circuit C contains k measurement gates, ℓ initializations of wires in the $|0\rangle$ state, and outputs of length n. Define C_{rec} as:

1. Run U_C on input $\rho_{\text{in}}^{A_1} \otimes |0^\ell\rangle\langle 0^\ell|^{A_2} \otimes |0^k\rangle\langle 0^k|^{M}$, where U_C is the unitary that coherently executes C, $A = (A_1, A_2)$ is a register that contains the actual input and the auxiliary input $|0\rangle$ states for C, and M is the register that contains the auxiliary wires for the coherent measurements.
2. Copy the wires that are supposed to contain the output $C(\rho_{\text{in}})$ into a register Y, initialized to $|0^n\rangle\langle 0^n|$, using CNOTs. The source of the CNOTs is a register O, the subregister of A containing those output wires. Write $\overline{O}$ for the registers in A that are not in O (these wires are normally discarded after the execution of C).
3. Run $U_C^\dagger$ to recover the original input, and discard the registers A_2 and M.

The behavior of C_{rec} can be summarized as

$$C_{\text{rec}}(\rho_{\text{in}}) = \text{Tr}_{A_2 M}\left[U_C^\dagger \text{CNOT}_{O,Y}^{\otimes n} \left(U_C \left(\rho_{\text{in}}^{A_1} \otimes |0^{\ell+k}\rangle\langle 0^{\ell+k}|^{A_2 M} \right) U_C^\dagger \otimes |0\rangle\langle 0|^{Y} \right) \right.$$
$$\left. (\text{CNOT}_{O,Y}^{\otimes n})^\dagger U_C \right]. \tag{33}$$

To see that C_{rec} acts as promised, let ρ_{in}, x, and ε be s.t. $\| C(\rho_{\text{in}}) - |x\rangle\langle x| \|_{\text{tr}} \leq \varepsilon$. If ε is small, the CNOT in Step 2. does not create a lot of entanglement, since the control wires are (close to) the computational-basis state $|x\rangle\langle x|$. The output is therefore (almost) perfectly copied out.

More formally, note that $C(\rho_{\text{in}}) = \text{Tr}_{\overline{O}M}\left[U_C(\rho_{\text{in}} \otimes |0^{\ell+k}\rangle\langle 0^{\ell+k}|)U_C^\dagger \right]$. By Lemma A.1 in [ABC+19], the closeness of $C(\rho_{\text{in}})$ and $|x\rangle\langle x|$ implies that there exists a density matrix $\chi^{\overline{O}M}$ such that

$$\frac{1}{2}\left\| U_C(\rho_{\text{in}} \otimes |0^{\ell+k}\rangle\langle 0^{\ell+k}|)U_C^\dagger - |x\rangle\langle x| \otimes \chi^{\overline{O}M} \right\|_{\text{tr}} \leq \sqrt{\varepsilon}. \tag{34}$$

Next, we use the fact that a quantum map cannot increase the trace distance between two states to derive two inequalities from Eq. 34.

For the first inequality, we append $|x\rangle\langle x|$ on both sides (into a separate Y register):

$$\frac{1}{2}\left\| U_C(\rho_{\text{in}} \otimes |0^{\ell+k}\rangle\langle 0^{\ell+k}|)U_C^\dagger \otimes |x\rangle\langle x|^Y - |x\rangle\langle x| \otimes \chi^{\overline{OM}} \otimes |x\rangle\langle x|^Y \right\|_{\text{tr}} \leq \sqrt{\varepsilon}. \tag{35}$$

For the second inequality, we instead append $|0\rangle\langle 0|$ into the Y register, followed by CNOTs from O onto Y. Note that on the second term inside the trace norm, the effect is the same as before:

$$\frac{1}{2}\left\| \text{CNOT}_{O,Y}^{\otimes n} \left(U_C(\rho_{\text{in}} \otimes |0^{\ell+k}\rangle\langle 0^{\ell+k}|)U_C^\dagger \otimes |0\rangle\langle 0|^Y \right) (\text{CNOT}_{O,Y}^{\otimes n})^\dagger \right.$$
$$\left. - |x\rangle\langle x| \otimes \chi^{\overline{OM}} \otimes |x\rangle\langle x|^Y \right\|_{\text{tr}} \leq \sqrt{\varepsilon}. \tag{36}$$

Thus, by the triangle inequality, the left-hand terms inside the trace norms in Eqs. 35 and 36 are $2\sqrt{\varepsilon}$-close. Applying the map $\text{Tr}_{A_2 M}\left[U_C^\dagger(\cdot)U_C \right]$ to both terms, which again does not increase the trace difference, we arrive at the desired statement:

$$\frac{1}{2}\left\| (\rho_{\text{in}} \otimes |x\rangle\langle x|) - C_{\text{rec}}(\rho_{\text{in}}) \right\|_{\text{tr}} \leq 2\sqrt{\varepsilon}. \tag{37}$$

B   Auxiliary Lemmas for Theorem 5.1

Lemma B.1. *Let $g : \{0,1\}^m \to \{0,1\}^n$ for $m, n \in \mathbb{N}$, and let $c \in \{0,1\}^n$. Let $f : \{0,1\} \times \{0,1\}^m \to \{0,1\}^n$ be defined by*

$$f(b,x) := \begin{cases} c & \text{if } b = 0 \\ g(x) & \text{if } b = 1. \end{cases} \tag{38}$$

Then for every QPT A, there exists a simulator S such that for all f, g of the form described above, and all input states ρ:

$$\Pr[A^f(\rho) = 1] = \Pr[S^g(\rho, c) = 1]. \tag{39}$$

Proof. Recall that since A and S are quantum algorithms, they access their oracles in superposition: that is, A has access to the map defined by $|x\rangle|z\rangle \mapsto |x\rangle|z \oplus f(x)\rangle$, and S has access to the map defined by $|x\rangle|z\rangle \mapsto |x\rangle|z \oplus g(x)\rangle$. The simulator S runs A on input ρ, and simulates any oracle calls to f (on inputs registers BX and output register Z) using two oracle calls to g. It only needs to prepare an auxiliary register in the state $|0^n\rangle$, and run the following circuit:

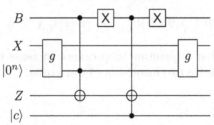

To see that this circuit exactly simulates a query to f on BXZ, consider an arbitrary query state

$$\sum_i \alpha_i \, |b_i, x_i\rangle_{BX} \, |z_i\rangle_Z \, |\varphi_i\rangle_R \, , \qquad (40)$$

where R is some purifying register. The state on $BXZR$ (plus the two auxiliary registers containing $|0^n\rangle$ and $|c\rangle$) after the above circuit is executed, is equal to

$$\sum_i \alpha_i \, |b_i, x_i\rangle_{XB} \, |0^n\rangle \, |z_i \oplus b \cdot g(x_i) \oplus (1-b) \cdot c\rangle_Z \, |c\rangle \, |\varphi_i\rangle_R \qquad (41)$$

$$= \sum_i \alpha_i \, |b_i, x_i\rangle_{XB} \, |0^n\rangle \, |z_i \oplus f(x_i)\rangle_Z \, |c\rangle \, |\varphi_i\rangle_R \, , \qquad (42)$$

which is exactly the state that would result from a direct query to f.

Corollary B.2. *Let $\hat{\mathcal{C}}_\lambda^{\mathsf{point}}$ and q be as in Sect. 5. Then for any QPT $\mathcal{S}_0$, there exists a QPT simulator $\mathcal{S}_1$ such that for all $\alpha, r \in \{0,1\}^\lambda$,*

$$\left| \Pr[\mathcal{S}_0^{\hat{C}_{\alpha,\beta,q,r,r',\tilde{\alpha},o_{sk,\beta}}}(1^\lambda) = 1] - \Pr[\mathcal{S}_1^{\mathbf{P}_{\alpha,\beta}}(1^\lambda, \tilde{\alpha}, o_{sk,\beta}, pk) = 1] \right| \le \mathsf{negl}\,(\lambda) \, .$$
$$(43)$$

A similar statement holds for circuits from $\hat{\mathcal{C}}_\lambda^{\mathsf{zero}}$.

Proof. The statement is proven via an intermediate simulator $\mathcal{S}_2$. This simulator is constructed by repeated application of Lemma B.1, so that for all α, r,

$$\left| \Pr[\mathcal{S}_0^{\hat{C}_{\alpha,\beta,q,r,r',\tilde{\alpha},o_{sk,\beta}}}(1^\lambda) = 1] - \Pr[\mathcal{S}_2^{\mathbf{P}_{\alpha,\beta}}(1^\lambda, \tilde{\alpha}, o_{sk,\beta}, c_0, c_1, c_2, \ldots, c_K, \perp) = 1] \right|$$
$$(44)$$

is at most $\mathsf{negl}\,(\lambda)$, where $K = K(q, \lambda)$ as in Definition 3.1. On the right-hand side, the probability is additionally over a random choice of r' (resulting in the sequence $(c_0, c_1, c_2, \ldots, c_K)$).

Next, we apply the simulatability property of Definition 3.1. It states that there exists a simulator $\mathcal{S}_3$ that, given a public key, can generate the distribution over $(c_0, c_1, c_2, \ldots, c_K)$ itself. Define

$$\mathcal{S}_1^{\mathbf{P}_{\alpha,\beta}}(1^\lambda, \tilde{\alpha}, o_{sk,\beta}, pk) := \mathcal{S}_2^{\mathbf{P}_{\alpha,\beta}}(1^\lambda, \tilde{\alpha}, o_{sk,\beta}, \mathcal{S}_3(pk), \perp), \qquad (45)$$

and the corollary follows.

References

[Aar05] Aaronson, S.: Ten semi-grand challenges for quantum computing theory. Blog post (2005). https://www.scottaaronson.com/writings/qchallenge. html

[ABC+19] Aharonov, D., Brakerski, Z., Chung, K.-M., Green, A., Lai, C.-Y., Sattath, O.: On quantum advantage in information theoretic single-server PIR. In: Ishai, Y., Rijmen, V. (eds.) EUROCRYPT 2019. LNCS, vol. 11478, pp. 219–246. Springer, Cham (2019). https://doi.org/10.1007/978-3-030-17659-4_8

[AF16] Alagic, G., Fefferman, B.: On quantum obfuscation. arxiv preprint arXiv: 1602.01771 (2016)

[AHU19] Ambainis, A., Hamburg, M., Unruh, D.: Quantum security proofs using semi-classical oracles. In: Boldyreva, A., Micciancio, D. (eds.) CRYPTO 2019. LNCS, vol. 11693, pp. 269–295. Springer, Cham (2019). https://doi.org/10.1007/978-3-030-26951-7_10

[AL20a] Ananth, P., La Placa, R.L.: Secure quantum extraction protocols. In: Pass, R., Pietrzak, K. (eds.) TCC 2020. LNCS, vol. 12552, pp. 123–152. Springer, Cham (2020). https://doi.org/10.1007/978-3-030-64381-2_5

[AL20b] Ananth, P., La Placa, R.L.: Secure software leasing. arXiv arXiv: 2005.05289 (2020)

[App17] Applebaum, B.: Garbled circuits as randomized encodings of functions: a primer. In: Tutorials on the Foundations of Cryptography. ISC, pp. 1–44. Springer, Cham (2017). https://doi.org/10.1007/978-3-319-57048-8_1

[BGI+01] Barak, B., et al.: On the (Im)possibility of obfuscating programs. In: Kilian, J. (ed.) CRYPTO 2001. LNCS, vol. 2139, pp. 1–18. Springer, Heidelberg (2001). https://doi.org/10.1007/3-540-44647-8_1

[BHR12] Bellare, M., Hoang, V.T., Rogaway, P.: Foundations of garbled circuits. In: Proceedings of the 19th ACM SIGSAC Conference on Computer and Communications Security (CCS), pp. 784–796. ACM (2012). https://doi.org/10.1145/2382196.2382279

[BJ15] Broadbent, A., Jeffery, S.: Quantum homomorphic encryption for circuits of low T-gate complexity. In: Gennaro, R., Robshaw, M. (eds.) CRYPTO 2015. LNCS, vol. 9216, pp. 609–629. Springer, Heidelberg (2015). https://doi.org/10.1007/978-3-662-48000-7_30

[BK20] Broadbent, A., Kazmi, R.A.: Indistinguishability obfuscation for quantum circuits of low t-count. arXiv: 2005.14699 (2020)

[Bra18] Brakerski, Z.: Quantum FHE (Almost) as secure as classical. In: Shacham, H., Boldyreva, A. (eds.) CRYPTO 2018. LNCS, vol. 10993, pp. 67–95. Springer, Cham (2018). https://doi.org/10.1007/978-3-319-96878-0_3

[BS20] Bitansky, N., Shmueli, O.: Post-quantum zero knowledge in constant rounds. In: Proceedings of the 52nd Annual ACM SIGACT Symposium on Theory of Computing, pp. 269–279 (2020)

[CD08] Canetti, R., Dakdouk, R.R.: Obfuscating point functions with multibit output. In: Smart, N. (ed.) EUROCRYPT 2008. LNCS, vol. 4965, pp. 489–508. Springer, Heidelberg (2008). https://doi.org/10.1007/978-3-540-78967-3_28

[Chr14] Christiano, P.: Quantum obfuscation of classical circuits. Seminar talk in the Quantum Games and Protocols program, Simons Insitute for the Theory of Computing (2014). Online: https://simons.berkeley.edu/talks/paul-christiano-2014-02-25

[CLTV15] Canetti, R., Lin, H., Tessaro, S., Vaikuntanathan, V.: Obfuscation of probabilistic circuits and applications. In: Dodis, Y., Nielsen, J.B. (eds.) TCC 2015. LNCS, vol. 9015, pp. 468–497. Springer, Heidelberg (2015). https://doi.org/10.1007/978-3-662-46497-7_19

[Gen09] Gentry, C.: Fully homomorphic encryption using ideal lattices. In: Proceedings of the 41st Annual ACM Symposium on Theory of Computing (STOC), pp. 169–178. ACM (2009). https://doi.org/10.1145/1536414.1536440

[GK05]   Goldwasser, S., Kalai, Y.T.: On the impossibility of obfuscation with auxiliary input. In: Proceedings of the 46th Annual Symposium on Foundations of Computer Science (FOCS), pp. 553–562. IEEE (2005). https://doi.org/10.1109/SFCS.2005.60

[GKW17] Goyal, R., Koppula, V., Waters, B.: Lockable obfuscation. In: Proceedings of the 58th Annual Symposium on Foundations of Computer Science (FOCS), pp. 612–621. IEEE (2017). https://doi.org/10.1109/FOCS.2017.62

[Mah18] Mahadev, U.: Classical homomorphic encryption for quantum circuits. In: Proceedings of the 59th Annual Symposium on Foundations of Computer Science (FOCS), pp. 332–338. IEEE (2018). https://doi.org/10.1109/FOCS.2018.00039

[PRS17] Peikert, C., Regev, O., Stephens-Davidowitz, N.: Pseudorandomness of ring-LWE for any ring and modulus. In: Proceedings of the 49th Annual ACM Symposium on Theory of Computing (STOC), pp. 461–473. ACM (2017). https://doi.org/10.1145/3055399.3055489

[Reg05] Regev, O.: On lattices, learning with errors, random linear codes, and cryptography. In: Proceedings of the 37th Annual ACM Symposium on Theory of Computing (STOC), pp. 84–93. ACM (2005). https://doi.org/10.1145/1060590.1060603

[Wee05] Wee, H.: On obfuscating point functions. In: Proceedings of the 37th Annual ACM Symposium on Theory of Computing (STOC), pp. 523–532. ACM (2005). https://doi.org/10.1145/1060590.1060669

[WZ17]   Wichs, D., Zirdelis, G.: Obfuscating compute-and-compare programs under LWE. In: Proceedings of the 58th Annual Symposium on Foundations of Computer Science (FOCS), pp. 600–611. IEEE (2017). https://doi.org/10.1109/FOCS.2017.61

[Yao86] Yao, A.C.: How to generate and exchange secrets. In: Proceedings of the 27th Annual Symposium on Foundations of Computer Science (FOCS), pp. 162–167. IEEE (1986). https://doi.org/10.1109/SFCS.1986.25

New Approaches for Quantum Copy-Protection

Scott Aaronson[1]([⊠]), Jiahui Liu[1], Qipeng Liu[2], Mark Zhandry[3], and Ruizhe Zhang[1]

[1] The University of Texas at Austin, Austin, USA
{aaronson,jiahui,rzzhang}@cs.utexas.edu
[2] Princeton University, Princeton, USA
qipengl@cs.princeton.edu
[3] Princeton University and NTT Research, Princeton, USA
mzhandry@princeton.edu

Abstract. Quantum copy-protection uses the unclonability of quantum states to construct quantum software that provably cannot be pirated. copy-protection would be immensely useful, but unfortunately, little is known about achieving it in general. In this work, we make progress on this goal, by giving the following results:

- We show how to copy-protect any program that cannot be learned from its input-output behavior relative to a *classical* oracle. This construction improves on Aaronson (CCC 2009), which achieves the same relative to a quantum oracle. By instantiating the oracle with post-quantum candidate obfuscation schemes, we obtain a heuristic construction of copy-protection.
- We show, roughly, that any program which can be watermarked can be copy *detected*, a weaker version of copy-protection that does not prevent copying, but guarantees that any copying can be detected. Our scheme relies on the security of the assumed watermarking, plus the assumed existence of public-key quantum money. Our construction is publicly detectable and applicable to many recent watermarking schemes.

1 Introduction

Quantum copy-protection, proposed by Aaronson [Aar09], aims to use the unclonability of quantum states to achieve programs that cannot be copied. That is, the program f is given as a quantum state $|\psi_f\rangle$. $|\psi_f\rangle$ allows for computing f on arbitrary inputs; meanwhile, it is infeasible to copy the state $|\psi_f\rangle$, or even convert $|\psi_f\rangle$ into two arbitrary states that both allow for computing f. The quantum no-cloning theorem shows that quantum states, in general, cannot be copied. Copy protection takes this much further, augmenting the unclonable state with the ability to evaluate programs. Copy-protection would have numerous applications to intellectual property management and to cryptography generally.

© International Association for Cryptologic Research 2021
T. Malkin and C. Peikert (Eds.): CRYPTO 2021, LNCS 12825, pp. 526–555, 2021.
https://doi.org/10.1007/978-3-030-84242-0_19

Progress on quantum copy-protection has unfortunately been slow. On the negative side, copy-protection for general programs is impossible. As explained by Aaronson [Aar09], any *learnable* program—that is, a program whose description can be learned from just its input/output behavior—cannot be copy-protected. Indeed, given the (copy-protected) code for the program, an attacker can just query the code on several inputs and learn the original program from the results. The attacker can then copy the original program indefinitely. A more recent result of Ananth and La Placa [AP20] shows, under certain computational assumptions, that certain contrived unlearnable programs cannot be copy-protected.

On the positive side, Aaronson demonstrates a quantum oracle[1] relative to which copy-protection exists for any unlearnable program. Due to the negative result above, this scheme cannot be instantiated in general. Worse, even for programs that are not subject to the impossibility result, it remains unclear how even heuristically to instantiate the scheme. Very recently, Ananth and La Placa [AP20] build a version of copy-protection, which they call software leasing, which guarantees a sort of copy *detection* mechanism. Unfortunately, their work explicitly allows copying the functionality and only ensures that such copying can be detected. Also, their construction only works for a certain class of "evasive" functions, which accept a hidden sparse set of inputs. The work of Ben-David and Sattath [BDS16] and more recently Amos et al. [AGKZ20] can be seen as copy-protecting specific cryptographic functionalities.

1.1 This Work

In this work, we give new general results for copy-protection. Our two main results are:

- Any unlearnable functionality can be copy-protected, relative to a *classical* oracle.
- Any functionality that can be *watermarked* in a certain sense, can be copy-detected assuming just the existence of public-key quantum money.

Both of our results are very general, applying to a wide variety of learning and watermarking settings, including settings where functionality preservation is not required. Along the way to obtaining our results, we give new definitions for security of copy-protection (as well as copy-detection and watermarking), which provide stronger guarantees.

Our first result improves Aaronson [Aar09] to use a classical oracle, which can then heuristically be instantiated using candidate post-quantum obfuscation (e.g. [BGMZ18,BDGM20]), resulting in a concrete candidate copy-protection scheme. Of course, the impossibility of Ananth and La Placa [AP20] means the resulting scheme cannot be secure in the standard model for arbitrary programs. Still, it can be conjectured to be secure for programs not subject to the impossibility.

---

[1] That is, an oracle that implements a quantum operation.

Our second result complements Ananth and La Placa [AP20]'s positive result for copy-detecting certain evasive functions by copy-detecting arbitrary watermarkable functions. For our purposes, watermarkable functions are those that can have a publicly observable "mark" embedded into the program, such that it is infeasible to remove the mark without destroying the functionality. We note that the results (and techniques) are incomparable to [AP20]. First, watermarkable functions are never evasive, so the class of functions considered are disjoint. Second, our security guarantee is much stronger than theirs, which we discuss in Sect. 1.2.

Taken together, we believe our results strongly suggest that watermarkable functions may be copy-protectable. Concretely, the impossibility result of Ananth and La Placa also applies to copy detection, and our second result shows that watermarkable functions, therefore, circumvent the impossibility. Based on this, we conjecture that our first result, when instantiated with candidate obfuscators, is a secure copy-protection scheme for watermarkable functions. We leave proving or disproving our conjecture as an interesting direction for future work.

1.2 Technical Overview

Definitional Work. We first investigate the definition of quantum copy-protection. We find that existing definitions and other straightforward attempts have several limitations. We therefore carefully develop a strong and general definition of copy-protection to resolve these limitations. In particular, our definition captures attacks where (1) the program is meaningfully copied even if the functionality is technically different, and (2) the program is copied only with a small but detectable probability.

Consider the following attempt of defining quantum copy-protection: we say an adversary successfully pirates a quantum program for computing a function f if it outputs two quantum programs σ_1, σ_2, each of them able to compute f correctly on a large fraction of inputs. Now consider applying this definition to the case where f is a signing algorithm with a particular signing key hard-coded, and suppose there are many valid signatures for each message. Consider a hypothetical adversary who "splits" the program into two pieces, each computing valid signatures; but neither computing the same signature that f produces. Such programs are "good enough" for forging signatures, and the ability to copy a signature-producing program in this way would naturally be considered an attack. However, the usual notions of security for copy-protection do not apply to such programs.

Another example is the copy-protection of public-key encryption. Let f be a decrypting algorithm with a particular decryption key hard-coded. Suppose the split two program pieces only work correctly on a sparse set: they can only decrypt correctly on ciphertexts of m_0, m_1; for ciphertexts of other messages, the output is arbitrary. This splitting attack does not violate the security notion either since both functions produced by the adversary differ from the original program on most inputs. But again, such programs are "good enough" for breaking the semantic security of the encryption scheme, and therefore would reasonably count as an attack.

Similar definitional issues are discussed in the context of watermarking [GKM+19] but have not been explored in the setting of copy-protection. Inspired by the watermarking case, our solution is to define "compute f correctly" by a general relation. The relation takes some random coins r, the function f (with some additional information about f hard-coded in the circuit); it samples an input and runs the (quantum) program on that classical input; finally, it checks the output of the quantum program, testing (in superposition) if the output z together with f, r is in the relation. As an example, if f is a signing circuit (with the signing key hard-coded), the relation is defined as: use random coins r to generate a random message m, run the quantum program on m and test in superposition if it is a valid signature, by applying the verification algorithm $\mathsf{Ver}(\mathsf{vk}, m, \cdot\, ; r)$.

Therefore, we propose a general definition that can capture a broader class of attacks, especially in the context of cryptographic functionalities.

Unfortunately, another uniquely quantum issue arises when trying to formulate a definition. We intuitively want to consider a program to be a valid copy if it computes f correctly on a non-trivial fraction of the domain. Unfortunately, there is no physical way to actually test if a program represented as a quantum state satisfies the property when an algorithm only receives a single copy of the program, especially in game-based security definitions.

Generally, any attempt at assigning a non-trivial property to quantum states (e.g., "valid program" vs. "invalid program") will be physically meaningless. Indeed, given any valid program P_1 and any invalid program P_2 (regardless of the meaning of "valid"), what is the uniform superposition $|P_1\rangle + |P_2\rangle$ of the two programs? Is it valid or invalid? Regardless of which, because the three programs are not orthogonal quantum states, no measurement can determine all three states' validity.

At a more operational level, the classical way to test for correctly computing f is to evaluate the function on all points and report the fraction of inputs where the program computed correctly. Alternatively, one can efficiently *estimate* the fraction of inputs that are computed correctly by simply testing a polynomial number of random points. Regardless, testing involves running the program on multiple points.

In the setting of quantum programs, however, the uncertainty principle implies that the moment one tests the first input, the quantum program state is irreversibly altered, potentially affecting the subsequent evaluations of the program. Thus, the fraction of inputs computed correctly is ever-changing, and simply evaluating the program on several points will not give a meaningful indication of the program's validity at any single point in time.

To illustrate further issues, consider the adversary which takes its quantum program P and simply produces $\frac{1}{\sqrt{2}}(|P\rangle\,|D\rangle\,|0\rangle + |D\rangle\,|P\rangle\,|1\rangle)$ where D is a dummy program that outputs junk. The two halves of this bipartite system each have probability $1/2$ of outputting the right answer on a random input. And yet, this "attack" is rather useless and should not be considered a break.

On the other hand, consider a hypothetical attacker which produces $\frac{1}{\sqrt{2}}|P\rangle|P\rangle + \frac{1}{\sqrt{2}}|D\rangle|D\rangle$. The two halves of this bipartite system each separately has probability $1/2$ of outputting the right answer on a random input. However, if we measure both halves, there is a $1/2$ chance of obtaining two copies of P, which each answers correctly with probability 1. Therefore, this attack should likely be considered a break.

Thus, we see that any characterization of program validity which just tests the program on a random input cannot distinguish cases that should be considered breaks from those that are not. On the other hand, if we test multiple random inputs, we run into the problem that testing each input causes the program state to change, meaning we may not get meaningful results.

Our solution will be to use recent ideas from Zhandry [Zha20], who considered similar issues in the context of traitor tracing. At a high level, the issue above is that we are trying to assign a property to a quantum state (whether the state is a good program), but this property is non-physical and does not make sense for mixed or entangled states. Instead, we want "a program is good" to be a measurement that can be applied to the state. We would naturally also want the measurement to be projective, so that if a program is once tested to be "good", it will always be "good".

Let $\mathcal{M} = (M_0, M_1)$ be binary positive operator-valued measures (POVMs) that represents choosing random coins and testing if the quantum program computes correctly with respect to the random coins. For a mixed quantum program state σ, the probability the program evaluates correctly relative to this test is given as $\mathrm{Tr}[M_0\sigma]$. Let $\mathcal{M}'$ be the (inefficient) projective measurement $\{P_p\}_{p \in [0,1]}$, projecting onto the eigenspaces of M_0, where p ranges over the corresponding eigenvalues of M_0[2] Zhandry showed that the measurement below results in an equivalent POVM as $\mathcal{M}$:

– Apply the projective measurement $\mathcal{M}'$, and obtain p;
– Output 0 with probability p, and output 1 with probability $1 - p$.

Intuitively, $\mathcal{M}'$ will project a state to an eigenvector with eigenvalue p. The leftover state computes correctly on p-fraction of all inputs.

Therefore, we say a quantum program σ is tested to be γ-good, if the measurement $\mathcal{M}'$ has outcome $p \geq \gamma$. We say an adversary successfully pirates a quantum program for computing f if the two programs are both tested to be γ-good with non-negligible probability. We will show an efficient algorithm that approximates the measurement. Thus, our new definition provides an operational game-based security definition that resolves all the issues we mentioned above. Besides, although the definition may be laborious, this definition implies the previous definitions in [Aar09, CMP20] and etc., and we find proving secu-

---

[2] Since $M_0 + M_1$ is the identity, M_1 shares the same eigenvectors, with eigenvalue $1 - p$.

rity with this definition is considerably easier. Using similar ideas, we also define quantum unlearnability of programs and quantum copy-detection.

Our Copy-Protection Scheme. We give a quantum copy-protection construction for all unlearnable functions based on (1) classical oracles, and (2) subspace states, or more abstractly, any tokenized signature scheme [BDS16].

Note the difference between classical and quantum oracles: a classical oracle is a classical functionality that can be (superposition) queried in a black-box way, while a quantum oracle is a quantum unitary operation used as a black-box. It is more feasible to implement classical oracles heuristically considering existing candidates of (post-quantum) obfuscations for classical circuits [BDGM20]. Therefore our construction is a significant improvement from the result in [Aar09].

A tokenized signature generates a signature token $|\text{sig}\rangle$ which we call a signing token. A signer who gets one copy of the signing token can sign a single bit b of her choice. $\text{Sign}(b, |\text{sig}\rangle)$ outputs a classical signature whose correctness guarantee is the same as classical signatures: namely, verification will accept the result as a signature on b. Importantly, the signing procedure is a unitary and will produce a superposition of all valid signatures of b; to obtain a classical signature, a measurement to the state is necessary, leading to a collapse of the token state. Thus, a signature token $|\text{sig}\rangle$ can only be used to produce one classical signature of a single bit, and any attempt to produce a classical signature of the other bit would fail. [BDS16] formalizes this idea and constructs a tokenized signature scheme relative to a classical oracle (a subspace membership oracle).

The high-level idea of our copy-protection scheme is that it requires an authorized user to query an oracle twice on signatures of bits 0 and 1. Let f be the function we want to copy-protect. Define the following classical circuits:

$$\mathcal{O}_1(x, \text{sig}) = \begin{cases} H(x) & \text{if } \text{Ver}(vk, 0, \text{sig}) = 1 \\ \perp & \text{otherwise} \end{cases},$$

$$\mathcal{O}_2(x, \text{sig}) = \begin{cases} f(x) \oplus H(x) & \text{if } \text{Ver}(vk, 1, \text{sig}) = 1 \\ \perp & \text{otherwise} \end{cases}.$$

Here H is a random function. The copy-protected program of f is a signature token $|\text{sig}\rangle$ and obfuscations of $\mathcal{O}_1, \mathcal{O}_2$, which we will heuristically treat as oracles to $\mathcal{O}_1, \mathcal{O}_2$. We denote this program as $(|\text{sig}\rangle, \mathcal{O}_1, \mathcal{O}_2)$.

To obtain $f(x)$, a user has to query on signatures of both bits and get $H(x)$ and $H(x) \oplus f(x)$. Note that even if one can only produce one of the classical signatures with token $|\text{sig}\rangle$, a user can still query both oracles $\mathcal{O}_1, \mathcal{O}_2$ multiple times. To obtain $H(x)$, a user can compute the superposition of all valid signatures of 0 by applying a unitary and feed the quantum state together with x to $\mathcal{O}_1$. It then measures the output register. The user never actually measures the signature. Because the output register contains a unique output $H(x)$, by Gentle Measurement Lemma [Aar04], it can rewind the quantum state back to $|\text{sig}\rangle$. Thus, our copy-protection scheme allows a copy-protected program to be evaluated on multiple inputs multiple times.

We next show how to prove anti-piracy security. Let σ_1, σ_2 be two (potentially entangled) program states pirated by an adversary, which makes oracle access to both $\mathcal{O}_1, \mathcal{O}_2$ and breaks the anti-piracy security. Let $\mathcal{O}_\perp$ be an oracle that always outputs $\perp$. If σ_1 never queries the oracle $\mathcal{O}_2$, we know the two programs $(\sigma_1, \mathcal{O}_1, \mathcal{O}_2)$ and $(\sigma_1, \mathcal{O}_1, \mathcal{O}_\perp)$ will have identical output distributions. Moreover, $(\sigma_1, \mathcal{O}_1, \mathcal{O}_\perp)$ can be simulated even without querying f because $\mathcal{O}_1$ is simply a random oracle (on valid inputs). Therefore, the program can be used to break the unlearnability of f. Similarly, if σ_2 never queries the oracle $\mathcal{O}_1$, the program $(\sigma_2, \mathcal{O}_\perp, \mathcal{O}_2)$ can be used to break the unlearnability of f.

Since f is unlearnable, the above two cases can not happen. We show that under this case, we can extract signatures of both 0 and 1. Intuitively, since $(\sigma_1, \mathcal{O}_1, \mathcal{O}_2)$ makes queries to $\mathcal{O}_2$, we can run the program on random inputs and measure a random query to $\mathcal{O}_2$, thereby extracting a signature of 1. Similarly, it holds for $(\sigma_2, \mathcal{O}_1, \mathcal{O}_2)$ and one could extract a signature of 0. Unfortunately, this intuition does not quite work since σ_1 and σ_2 are potentially entangled. It means there can be correlations between the outcomes of the measurements producing the two signatures: perhaps, if the measurement on $(\sigma_1, \mathcal{O}_1, \mathcal{O}_2)$ produces a valid signature on 1, then the measurement on $(\sigma_2, \mathcal{O}_1, \mathcal{O}_2)$ is guaranteed to fail to produce a signature. We show by a delicate argument that, in fact, adversaries cannot cheat using such correlations. Intuitively, although σ_1, σ_2 are entangled, we show there exists an efficient measurement: by applying this measurement to (σ_1, σ_2), with non-negligible probability, the resulting programs (σ_1', σ_2') have the following properties:

- They are both "good" programs. Thus, we can extract a signature of 1 in σ_1'.
- The resulting program σ_2'' after applying any measurement on σ_1' is still "good". Similarly, we can extract a signature of 0 in σ_2''.

Note that the above argument does not directly work for the original programs (σ_1, σ_2).

Our Copy-Detection Scheme. Inspired by [AP20], we propose a weaker definition called copy-detection, which has an additional checking procedure. A user can publicly verify a program's validity by running this checking procedure. The security guarantees that, given one copy of the program, no adversary can produce two programs such that both programs pass the checking procedure and both are 'functionally correct' (as in the copy-protection definition)—in other words, *honest* users can always identify the pirate. Looking ahead, we note that copy-detection is similar to secure software leasing (SSL, [AP20]), with the major differences are (1) the checking procedure is public, (2) 'functionally correct' in the security of copy-detection is average-case while that in the security of SSL is worst-case.

We construct a copy-detection scheme for any function family that can be watermarked. A watermarking scheme roughly consists of the following procedure: Mark takes a circuit and a message, and outputs a circuit embedded with that mark; Extract takes a marked circuit and produces the embedded mark. A watermarking scheme requires: (1) the watermarked circuit

$\tilde{f} = \mathsf{Mark}(f, m)$ should preserve its intended functionality as f; (2) any efficient adversary given a marked $\tilde{f}$, can not generate a new marked circuit with a different mark (or remove the mark) while preserving its functionality. Watermarking primitives have been studied in previous works, including [CHN+18, KW17, QWZ18, KW19, GKM+19].

Our construction also requires a public key quantum money scheme. It consists two procedures: a generation procedure and a verification procedure. The generation procedure outputs a quantum banknote $|\$\rangle$. Verification is public, takes a quantum money banknote, and outputs either a (classical) serial number of that banknote or $\perp$ indicating it is an invalid banknote. The security requires no efficient adversary could use a quantum banknote $|\$\rangle$ to prepare two quantum banknotes $|\$_1\rangle |\$_2\rangle$ such that both banknotes pass the verification and their serial numbers are equal to that of $|\$\rangle$. We note that this version of quantum money corresponds to a "mini-scheme" as defined by [AC12].

The copy-detection scheme takes a function f, samples a banknote $|\$\rangle$ with serial number s, lets $\tilde{f} \leftarrow \mathsf{Mark}(f, s)$ and outputs a copy-detection program as $(\tilde{f}, |\$\rangle)$. To evaluate the function, it simply runs the classical program $\tilde{f}$. To check a program is valid, it extracts the serial number from the money state and compares it with the mark of the program.

The security requires that no efficient adversary could produce $\tilde{f}_1, |\$_1\rangle$ and $\tilde{f}_2, |\$_2\rangle$ such that two programs pass the check and both classical circuits preserve the functionality. Let s be the serial number of $|\$\rangle$, s_b be the serial number of $|\$_b\rangle$ for $b = 1, 2$. To pass the check, there are two possible cases:

- $s_1 = s_2 = s$. In this case, $|\$_1\rangle |\$_2\rangle$ breaks the security of the quantum money scheme because one successfully duplicates a banknote with the same serial number.
- At least one of $s_b \neq s$. Because the mark of $\tilde{f}_b$ is also equal to s_b, one of $\tilde{f}_b$ breaks the security of the watermarking scheme, as it preserves the functionality, while having a different mark from s.

We show that the above construction and proof apply to a wide range of watermarking primitives.

Copy-Protection in the Standard Model? The security of our copy-protection scheme requires treating the obfuscated programs as oracles. While we prove security for all unlearnable programs, we cannot expect such security to hold in the standard model: as shown in [AP20], there are unlearnable functions that can not be copy-protected or even copy-detected. On the other hand, watermarkable programs are a natural class of programs that are necessarily immune to the style of counter-example of Barak et al. [BGI+01], on which the copy-protection impossibility is based. Namely, the counter-example works by giving programs that are unlearnable, but such that having any (even approximate [BP15]) code for the program lets you recover the original program. Such programs *cannot* be watermarkable, as the adversary can always recover the original program from the (supposedly) watermarked program.

Thus, we broadly conjecture that all watermarkable functions can be copy-protected. Our copy-detection result gives some evidence that this may be feasible. Concretely, we conjecture that our copy-protection construction is secure for any watermarkable program when the oracles are instantiated with post-quantum obfuscation constructions. We leave justifying either the broad or concrete conjectures as fascinating open questions.

1.3   Other Related Works

Quantum Copy Protection. Quantum copy-protection was proposed by Aaronson in [Aar09]; this paper gave two candidate schemes for copy-protecting point functions without security proofs and showed that any functions that are not quantum learnable could be quantum copy-protected relative to a quantum oracle (an oracle which could perform an arbitrary unitary).

[AP20] gave a conditional impossibility of general copy-protection: they construct a quantum unlearnable circuit using the quantum FHE scheme and compute-and-compare obfuscation [WZ17, GKW17], which is not copy-protectable once a QPT adversary has non-black-box access to the program. [AP20] also gave a new definition that is weaker than the standard copy-protection security, called Secure Software Leasing (SSL) and an SSL construction for a subclass of evasive functions, namely, searchable compute-and-compare circuits.

[BL19] and [GZ20] introduced two new notions respectively, unclonable encryption/decryption schemes; [CMP20] gave a construction for copy-protecting point functions in the quantum random oracle model with techniques inspired by [BL19] and the construction can be extended to copy-protecting compute-and-compare circuits. [BJL+21] then constructed information-theoretic SSL for point functions.

1.4   Concurrent and Independent Work

Very recently, [KNY20] presents a secure software leasing for a subclass of evasive functions and PRFs, using watermarking and two-tier quantum-lightning, which can be built from the LWE assumption. Their main observation is that the full power of public-key quantum money is not needed in the verification of SSL, and they introduce a new primitive in between public-key and private-key quantum money, which they call two-tier quantum lightning. While their construction can be built from LWE alone, our construction aims at a more generalized definition in terms of successful piracy and functionality-preserving; our copy detection construction also works for a broader class of cryptographic functionalities such as encryption and signature.

2   Preliminaries

We denote by λ the security parameter, and when inputted into an algorithm, λ will be represented in unary. We say a function $\epsilon(x)$ is *negligible* if for all inverse polynomials $1/p(x)$, $\epsilon(x) < 1/p(x)$ for all large enough x. We denote a negligible function by $\mathsf{negl}(x)$. We use QPT to denote quantum polynomial time.

2.1 Quantum Computation

Definition 1 (Trace distance). *Let $\rho, \sigma \in \mathbb{C}^{2^n \times 2^n}$ be the density matrices of two quantum states. The trace distance between ρ and σ is*

$$\|\rho - \sigma\|_{tr} := \frac{1}{2}\sqrt{Tr[(\rho - \sigma)^\dagger(\rho - \sigma)]},$$

Here, we only state a key lemma for our construction: the Gentle Measurement Lemma proposed by Aaronson [Aar04], which gives a way to perform measurements without destroying the state.

Lemma 1 (Gentle Measurement Lemma [Aar04]). *Suppose a measurement on a mixed state ρ yields a particular outcome with probability $1 - \epsilon$. Then after the measurement, one can recover a state $\tilde{\rho}$ such that $\|\tilde{\rho} - \rho\|_{\mathrm{tr}} \leq \sqrt{\epsilon}$. Here $\|\cdot\|_{\mathrm{tr}}$ is the trace distance (defined in Definition 1).*

We give other basic definitions of quantum computation and quantum information in the full version.

2.2 Quantum Oracle Algorithm

We consider the quantum query model in this work, which gives quantum circuits access to some oracles.

Definition 2 (Classical Oracle). *A classical oracle $\mathcal{O}$ on input query x is a unitary transformation of the form $U_f |x, y, z\rangle \rightarrow |x, y + f(x), z\rangle$ for classical function $f : \{0,1\}^n \rightarrow \{0,1\}^m$. Note that a classical oracle can be queried in quantum superposition.*

In the rest of the paper, we refer to the word "oracle" as "classical oracle". A quantum oracle algorithm with oracle access to $\mathcal{O}$ is a sequence of unitary U_i and oracle access to $\mathcal{O}$ (or U_f). Thus, the query complexity of a quantum oracle algorithm is defined as the number of $\mathcal{O}$ access.

In the analysis of the security of the copy-protection scheme in Sect. 5.2, we will use the following theorem from [BBBV97] to bound the change in adversary's state when we change the oracle's input-output behavior at places where the adversary hardly ever queries on.

Theorem 1 ([BBBV97]). *Let $|\phi_i\rangle$ be the superposition of quantum Turing machine $\mathcal{M}$ with oracle $\mathcal{O}$ on input x at time i. Define $W_y(|\phi_i\rangle)$ to be the sum of squared magnitudes in $|\phi_i\rangle$ of configurations of $\mathcal{M}$ which are querying the oracle on string y. For $\epsilon > 0$, let $F \subseteq [0, T-1] \times \Sigma^*$ be the set of time-string pairs such that $\sum_{(i,y) \in F} W_y(|\phi_i\rangle) \leq \epsilon^2/T$.*

Now suppose the answer to each query $(i, y) \in F$ is modified to some arbitrary fixed $a_{i,y}$ (these answers need not be consistent with an oracle). Let $|\phi_i'\rangle$ be the superposition of $\mathcal{M}$ on input x at time i with oracle $\mathcal{O}$ modified as stated above. Then $\||\phi_T\rangle - |\phi_T'\rangle\|_{\mathrm{tr}} \leq \epsilon$.

2.3   Direct-Product Problem and Quantum Signature Tokens

In this section, we will define direct-product problems, which are key components of the quantum signature token scheme by Ben-David and Sattath [BDS16] and also our quantum copy-protection scheme.

Definition 3 (Dual Subspace). *Given a subspace S of a vector space V, let $S^\perp$ be the orthogonal complement of S: the set of $y \in V$ such that $x \cdot y = 0$ for all $x \in S$. It is not hard to show: $S^\perp$ is also a subspace of V; $(S^\perp)^\perp = S$.*

Definition 4 (Subspace Membership Oracles). *A subspace membership oracle for a subspace $A \subseteq \mathbb{F}^n$, denoted as U_A, on input vector v, will output 1 if $v \in A$, $v \neq 0$ and output 0 otherwise.*

Definition 5 (Subspace State). *For a subspace $A \subseteq \mathbb{F}^n$, the state $|A\rangle$ is defined as $\frac{1}{\sqrt{|A|}} \sum_{v \in A} |v\rangle$, which is a uniform superposition of all vectors in A.*

Direct-Product Problem. Our construction relies on the following problem called the "Direct-Product Problem" in [AC12]: for any QPT adversary $\mathcal{A}$, given one copy of $|A\rangle$ and oracle access to $U_A, U_{A^\perp}$, the problem is to finds two *non-zero* vectors such that $u \in A$ and $v \in A^\perp$.

Ben-David and Sattath [BDS16] proved the hardness of the direct-product problem for the construction of quantum signature tokens. More precisely, a signature token is a subspace state $|A\rangle$ in their construction. All vectors in $A \setminus \{0\}$ are signatures for bit 0 and all vectors in $A^\perp \setminus \{0\}$ are signatures for bit 1. Therefore, to generate valid signatures for both 0 and 1, it is required to solve the "Direct-Product Problem". We believe that our copy-protection scheme works for general signature token schemes. To keep the statements and proofs simple, we focus on the construction in [BDS16].

Theorem 2 ([BDS16]). *Let $\epsilon > 0$ be such that $1/\epsilon = o(2^{n/2})$. Let A be a random subspace $\mathbb{F}^n$, and $\dim(A) = n/2$. Given one copy of $|A\rangle$ and access to both subspace membership oracles of U_A and $U_{A^\perp}$, an adversary needs $\Omega(\sqrt{\epsilon} 2^{n/4})$ queries to output a pair of non-zero vectors (u, v) such that $u \in A$ and $v \in A^\perp$ with probability at least ϵ.*

We will refer to the direct-product problem as a security game, which is defined as follows:

Definition 6 (Direct-Product Game). *A direct-product game consists of the following steps:*

Setup Phase: *the challenger takes in a security parameter λ, samples a random $\lambda/2$-dimensional subspace A from $\mathbb{F}^\lambda$; then prepares the membership oracle U_A for A, $U_{A^\perp}$ for the dual subspace $A^\perp$ and a quantum state $|A\rangle$.*

Query Phase: *the challenger sends $|A\rangle$ to the adversary; the adversary can query $U_A, U_{A^\perp}$ for polynomially many times.*

Output Phase: *the adversary outputs two vectors (u, v).*

The challenger checks if $u \in A \setminus \{0\}, v \in A^{\perp} \setminus \{0\}$. If this is satisfied, then the adversary wins the game.

Theorem 2 shows that for any QPT adversary, the winning probability of the direct-product game is negligible.

2.4 Testing Quantum Programs: Measurement Implementation

In classical cryptographic security games, the challenger typically gets some information from the adversary and checks if this information satisfies certain properties.

However, in the quantum world, when a challenger tries to decide if a quantum adversary has produced a state with certain properties, especially in the context of security games for properties related to unclonability, classical definitions of "testing properties" may result in various failures as discussed in [Zha20]. Such an issue has also been discussed in the introduction.

To deal with this issue, [Zha20] formalized a measurement procedure for testing an adversary's state. This is best understood with an example.

Consider a security game where the adversary needs to produce a state that can decrypt a challenge ciphertext. First, the challenger's behavior is abstracted into the following:

- Encrypt a random message bit m to get c using randomness rand, note that randomness rand is used to sample m and random coins for encryption;
- Run the adversary's state on the resulting ciphertext c;
- Output 1 or 0 depending on whether the adversary's state correctly decrypts or not.

Fixing the ciphertext c, the procedure of outputting 1 or 0 depending on whether the adversary's state correctly decrypts c can be described as a projective measurement $\mathcal{P}_{m,c} = (P_{m,c}, Q_{m,c})$ where $P_{m,c}$ corresponds to output 1, $Q_{m,c}$ corresponds to output 0 and $(P_{m,c}, Q_{m,c})$ can be efficiently implemented given subscript m, c. The challenger uses m, c as a control to decide which projective measurement to be applied to the state.

More generally, let $\mathcal{R}$ be the set of randomness, $\mathcal{I}$ be the control set (similar to the role of m, c in the above example). Let D be a function from $\mathcal{R}$ to $\mathcal{I}$. For a uniform randomness rand, $D(\text{rand})$ defines a distribution over $\mathcal{I}$. Therefore we will use the word "distribution" for D in the rest of the discussion. For every control (or index) $i \in \mathcal{I}$, we have a projective measurement $\mathcal{P}_i = (P_i, Q_i)$. Let $\mathcal{P} = \{\mathcal{P}_i = (P_i, Q_i)\}$ be a collection of binary projective measurements. We define a mixture of projective measurement $\mathcal{P}_D$ as follows.

Definition 7 (Mixture of Projective Measurement $\mathcal{P}_D$). *For $\mathcal{P} = \{P_i, Q_i\}_{i \in \mathcal{I}}$ and $D : \mathcal{R} \to \mathcal{I}$, a mixture of projective measurement $\mathcal{P}_D = (P_D, Q_D)$ is a POVM defined as the following:*

$$P_D = \sum_{i \in \mathcal{I}} \Pr[i \leftarrow D(R)] P_i, \qquad Q_D = \sum_{i \in \mathcal{I}} \Pr[i \leftarrow D(R)] Q_i,$$

where R is a uniform random variable in $\mathcal{R}$.

In other words, $\mathcal{P}_D$ is implemented in the following way: sample randomness rand $\leftarrow \mathcal{R}$, compute index/control $i \leftarrow D(\text{rand})$ and apply projective measurement $\mathcal{P}_i = (P_i, Q_i)$.

Thus, for any quantum state ρ, $\text{Tr}[\mathcal{P}_D \rho]$ is the probability that a random sampled projective measurement $\mathcal{P}_i = (P_i, Q_i)$ (according to the distribution D) applies on ρ and outputs 1.

Definition 8 (Projective Implementation). *Let $\mathcal{P} = (P, Q)$ be a binary outcome POVM. Let $\mathcal{D}$ be a finite set of distributions $(p, 1 - p)$ over outcomes $\{0, 1\}$. Let $\mathcal{E} = \{E_p\}_{(p,1-p)\in\mathcal{D}}$ be a projective measurement with index set $\mathcal{D}$. Consider the following measurement experiment:*

- *Measure under the projective measurement $\mathcal{E}$ and obtain a distribution $(p, 1 - p)$ over $\{0, 1\}$;*
- *Output a bit according to the distribution: output 1 with probability p and output 0 with probability $1 - p$.*

We say the measurement $\mathcal{E}$ is a projective implementation of $\mathcal{P}$ if the above experiment and $\mathcal{P}$ produce identical outcomes on any quantum states. We denote $\mathcal{E}$ by $\mathsf{ProjImp}(\mathcal{P})$.

Note that if the collapsed state is an eigenvector of P corresponding to eigenvalue p, then it is also an eigenvector of Q corresponding to eigenvalue $1 - p$.

Lemma 2 (A variation of Lemma 1 in [Zha20]). *Any binary outcome POVM $\mathcal{P} = (P, Q)$ has a unique projective measurement $\mathsf{ProjImp}(\mathcal{P})$.*

In this work, we propose the following new definition corresponding to ProjImp.

Definition 9 (Threshold Implementation). *A threshold implementation with parameter γ of a binary POVM $\mathcal{P} = (P, Q)$ is a variant of projective implementation $\mathsf{ProjImp}(\mathcal{P})$, denoted as $(\mathsf{TI}_\gamma(\mathcal{P}), \mathbf{I} - \mathsf{TI}_\gamma(\mathcal{P}))$:*

- *Measure under the projective measurement $\mathcal{E}$ ($\mathsf{ProjImp}(\mathcal{P})$) and obtain a distribution $(p, 1 - p)$ over $\{0, 1\}$;*
- *Output a bit according to the distribution $(p, 1 - p)$: output 1 if $p \geq \gamma$, or 0 otherwise.*

Remark 1. For any quantum state ρ, the threshold implementation outputs 1 with probability $\text{Tr}[\mathsf{TI}_\gamma(\mathcal{P})\rho]$, and 0 with probability $1 - \text{Tr}[\mathsf{TI}_\gamma(\mathcal{P})\rho]$.

Remark 2. For a binary outcome measurement $\mathcal{P} = (P, Q)$, we usually say "perform measurement P on ρ" if $\mathcal{P}$ was performed on ρ. For example, if we say a threshold implementation $\mathsf{TI}(\mathcal{P}_D)$ on a quantum state ρ outputs 1, we refer to apply $(\mathsf{TI}_\gamma(\mathcal{P}_D), \mathbf{I} - \mathsf{TI}_\gamma \mathcal{P}_D)$ on ρ and the outcome is 1.

Approximating Projective Implementation. Before describing the theorem of the approximation algorithm, we give two definitions that characterize how good an approximation projective implementation is, which were first introduced in [Zha20].

Definition 10 (Shift Distance). *For two distributions D_0, D_1, the shift distance with parameter ϵ is defined as $\Delta_{\mathsf{Shift}}^{\epsilon}(D_0, D_1)$, which is the smallest quantity δ such that for all $x \in \mathbb{R}$:*

$$\Pr[D_0 \leq x] \leq \Pr[D_1 \leq x + \epsilon] + \delta,$$
$$\Pr[D_1 \leq x] \leq \Pr[D_0 \leq x + \epsilon] + \delta.$$

For two real-valued measurements $\mathcal{M}$ and $\mathcal{N}$ over the same quantum system, the shift distance between $\mathcal{M}$ and $\mathcal{N}$ with parameter ϵ is defined as,

$$\Delta_{\mathsf{Shift}}^{\epsilon}(\mathcal{M}, \mathcal{N}) := \sup_{|\psi\rangle} \Delta_{\mathsf{Shift}}^{\epsilon}\left(\mathcal{M}(|\psi\rangle), \mathcal{N}(|\psi\rangle)\right).$$

Definition 11 ((ϵ, δ)-Almost Projective). *A real-valued quantum measurement $\mathcal{M}$ is said to be (ϵ, δ)-almost projective if for all quantum state $|\psi\rangle$, apply $\mathcal{M}$ twice in a row to $|\psi\rangle$, obtaining outcomes X and Y. Then we have $\Pr[|X - Y| \leq \epsilon] \geq 1 - \delta$.*

The following theorem gives a way to approximate any projective implementation:

Theorem 3 (Theorem 2 in [Zha20]). *Let D be any probability distribution over some control set $\mathcal{I}$ and $\mathcal{P}$ be a collection of projective measurements. For any $0 < \epsilon, \delta < 1$, there exists an algorithm of measurement $\mathsf{API}_{\mathcal{P},D}^{\epsilon,\delta}$ that satisfies the followings:*

- *$\Delta_{\mathsf{Shift}}^{\epsilon}(\mathsf{API}_{\mathcal{P},D}^{\epsilon,\delta}, \mathsf{ProjImp}(\mathcal{P}_D)) \leq \delta$.*
- *$\mathsf{API}_{\mathcal{P},D}^{\epsilon,\delta}$ is (ϵ, δ)-almost projective.*
- *The expected running time of $\mathsf{API}_{\mathcal{P},D}^{\epsilon,\delta}$ is $T_{\mathcal{P},D} \cdot \mathsf{poly}(1/\epsilon, \log(1/\delta))$ where $T_{\mathcal{P},D}$ is the combined running time of D, the procedure mapping i to (P_i, Q_i) and the run-time of measurement (P_i, Q_i).*

3   Learning Game Definitions

In this section, we define unlearnability, copy-protection, copy-detection, and watermarking with respect to a function family and a testing distribution.

We assume a function f is sampled uniformly at random from a function family $\mathcal{F}_\lambda$. To test the correctness of a quantum program (for computing f), it samples an input x from a testing distribution D_λ, runs the quantum program on x, and checks if the output is $f(x)$.

We will give the generalized definitions (for unlearnability, copy-protection, copy-detection, and watermarking) in the full version, which allow for more general sampling procedures and functionality testing. Since our constructions naturally extend to these settings, we leave all the discussions about definitions and proofs in the full version of the paper.

Definition 12 (Quantum Program with Classical Inputs and Outputs).
A quantum program with classical inputs is a pair of quantum state ρ and unitaries $\{U_x\}_{x\in[N]}$ (where $[N]$ is the domain), such that the state of the program evaluated on input x is equal to $U_x\rho U_x^\dagger$. To obtain an output, it measures the first register of $U_x\rho U_x^\dagger$. Moreover, $\{U_x\}_{x\in[N]}$ has a compact classical description which means "applying U_x" can be efficiently computed given x.

Notation-wise, the input and output space N, M are functions of λ.

3.1   Unlearnability

First, we define γ-goodness testing with respect to a fixed function f and a testing distribution D (over inputs).

Definition 13 (γ-Goodness Test with respect to f, D). *Let $(\rho, \{U_x\}_{x\in[N]})$ be a quantum program for computing a classical function $f : [N] \to [M]$. Let D be a testing distribution over the input space $[N]$.*

- *Define $\mathcal{P}_x = (P_x, Q_x)$ be the following projective measurement:*

  • *On input x, it runs U_x on the quantum state ρ;*
  • *It measures whether the output register is equal to $f(x)$; output 1 if yes, and 0 otherwise.*

  Let $\mathcal{P} = \{\mathcal{P}_x\}$ be a collection of projective measurements.

- *D is the distribution that samples an input: given randomness* rand, *output $x = D(\mathsf{rand})$.*
- *Let $\mathcal{P}_D = (P_D, Q_D)$ be the mixture of projective measurement defined in Definition 7.*
- *We say a quantum program is tested γ-**good** with respect to f, D, if the threshold implementation $\mathsf{TI}_\gamma(\mathcal{P}_D)$ outputs 1.*

We then define a learning game for a function family $\mathcal{F}$ and a set of testing distribution $\mathcal{D}$. Note that we assume for a fixed security parameter λ, f is drawn *uniformly at random* from $\mathcal{F}_\lambda$ and the testing distribution D_f is efficiently sampleable given the description f.

Definition 14 (Learning Game for $\mathcal{F}, \mathcal{D}$). *A learning game for a function family $\mathcal{F} = \{\mathcal{F}_\lambda : [N] \to [M]\}$, a distribution family $\mathcal{D} = \{D_f\}$, a threshold $\gamma \in (0, 1)$, and an adversary $\mathcal{A}$ is denoted as* LearningGame$_{\mathcal{F},\mathcal{D},\gamma}^{\mathcal{A}}(1^\lambda)$, *which consists of the following steps:*

1. *Sampling Phase: At the beginning of the game, the challenger takes a security parameter λ and samples a function $f \leftarrow \mathcal{F}_\lambda$ uniformly at random;*
2. *Query Phase: $\mathcal{A}$ then gets oracle access to f;*
3. *Output Phase: Finally, $\mathcal{A}$ outputs a quantum program $(\rho, \{U_x\}_{x\in[N]})$.*

The game outputs 1 if and only if the program is tested γ-good with respect to f, D_f.

Definition 15 (Quantum Unlearnability of $\mathcal{F}$ with Testing Distribution $\mathcal{D}$). *A family of functions $\mathcal{F}$ with respect to $\mathcal{D}$ is called γ quantum unlearnable if for any QPT adversary $\mathcal{A}$, there exists a negligible function $\mathsf{negl}(\cdot)$ such that the following holds for all λ:*

$$\Pr\left[b = 1,\ b \leftarrow \mathsf{LearningGame}_{\mathcal{F},\mathcal{D},\gamma}^{\mathcal{A}}(1^\lambda)\right] \leq \mathsf{negl}(\lambda)$$

3.2 Copy-Protection

Definition 16 (Quantum Copy-Protection). *A quantum copy-protection scheme for $\mathcal{F}, \mathcal{D}$ consists of the following procedures:*

$\mathsf{Setup}(1^\lambda) \to \mathsf{sk}$: *the setup algorithm takes in a security parameter λ in unary and generates a secret key sk.*

$\mathsf{Generate}(\mathsf{sk}, f) \to (\rho_f, \{U_{f,x}\}_{x \in [N]})$: *on input $f \in \mathcal{F}_\lambda$ and secret key sk, the vendor generates a quantum program $(\rho_f, \{U_{f,x}\}_{x \in [N]})$.*

$\mathsf{Compute}(\rho_f, \{U_{f,x}\}_{x \in [N]}, x) \to y$: *given a quantum program, a user can compute the function $f(x)$ on input x by applying $U_{f,x}$ on ρ_f and measuring the first register of the state.*

Efficiency: Setup, Compute and Generate should run in $\mathsf{poly}(\lambda)$ time.

Correctness: There exists a negligible function $\mathsf{negl}(\cdot)$ such that: all $\lambda \in \mathbb{N}$, every $f \in \mathcal{F}_\lambda$, all $\mathsf{sk} \leftarrow \mathsf{Setup}(1^\lambda)$, all $(\rho_f, \{U_{f,x}\}_{x \in [N]}) \leftarrow \mathsf{Generate}(\mathsf{sk}, f)$, for all $x \in [N]$, apply $U_{f,x}$ on ρ_f and measure the first register, with probability at least $1 - \mathsf{negl}(\lambda)$, the output is a fixed value $z_{f,x}$; moreover, $z_{f,x} = f(x)$.

Security: The γ-anti-piracy security defined below.

Note that correctness ensures that the copy-protected program can be evaluated polynomially many times.

Definition 17 (γ-Anti-Piracy Security Game). *An anti-piracy security game for $\mathcal{F}, \mathcal{D}$ and adversary $\mathcal{A}$ is denoted as $\mathsf{CopyProtectionGame}_{\mathcal{F},\mathcal{D},\gamma}^{\mathcal{A}}(1^\lambda)$, which consists of the following steps:*

1. **Setup Phase:** *At the beginning of the game, the challenger takes a security parameter λ and obtains a secret key $\mathsf{sk} \leftarrow \mathsf{Setup}(1^\lambda)$.*
2. **Sampling Phase:** *A function f is sampled uniformly at random, $f \leftarrow \mathcal{F}_\lambda$.*
3. **Query Phase:** *$\mathcal{A}$ makes a single query to the challenger and obtains a copy-protection program for f: $(\rho_f, \{U_{f,x}\}_{x \in [N]}) \leftarrow \mathsf{Generate}(\mathsf{sk}, f)$.*
4. **Output Phase:** *Finally, $\mathcal{A}$ outputs a (possibly mixed and entangled) state σ over two registers R_1, R_2 and two sets of unitaries $(\{U_{R_1,x}\}_x, \{U_{R_2,x}\}_x)$ They can be viewed as programs $P_1 = (\sigma[R_1], \{U_{R_1,x}\}_{x \in [N]})$ and $P_2 = (\sigma[R_2], \{U_{R_2,x}\}_{x \in [N]})$.*

The game outputs 1 if and only if both programs P_1, P_2 are tested to be γ-good with respect to $f, \mathcal{D}_f$.

Definition 18 (γ-Anti-Piracy-Security). *A copy-protection scheme for $\mathcal{F}$ and $\mathcal{D}$ has γ-anti-piracy security, if for any QPT adversary $\mathcal{A}$, there exists a negligible function negl($\cdot$) such that the following holds for all $\lambda \in \mathbb{N}$:*

$$\Pr\left[b = 1, b \leftarrow \mathsf{CopyProtectionGame}_{\mathcal{F},\mathcal{D},\gamma}^{\mathcal{A}}(1^\lambda)\right] \leq \mathsf{negl}(\lambda) \tag{1}$$

In the full version, we will show our new anti-piracy security implies previous security, defined in [Aar09].

3.3 Copy-Detection

A copy-detection scheme is very similar to the copy-protection scheme, except it has an additional procedure Check which applies a projective measurement and checks if the quantum state is valid.

Definition 19 (Quantum Copy-Detection). *A quantum copy-detection scheme for $\mathcal{F}, \mathcal{D}$ consists of the following procedures:*

Setup(1^λ), *Generate*(sk, f) *and* Compute($\rho_f, \{U_{f,x}\}_{x\in[N]}, x$) *are the same as those in Definition 16, except* Setup *additionally samples a public key for* Check.

Check(pk, $\rho_f, \{U_{f,x}\}_{x\in[N]}$) $\rightarrow b, \rho'$: *on input a quantum program, it applies a binary projective measurement (P_0, P_1) on ρ_f that depends on $\{U_{f,x}\}_{x\in[N]}$; it outputs the outcome b and the leftover state ρ'.*

Correctness (Generate): The same as the security of Definition 16.

Correctness (Check): For every efficient $\mathcal{A}$, there exists a negligible function negl($\cdot$) such that, all $\lambda \in \mathbb{N}$, (pk, sk) $\leftarrow$ Setup(1^λ), every $f \in \mathcal{F}_\lambda$, all $(\rho_f, \{U_{f,x}\}_{x\in[N]}) \leftarrow$ Generate(sk, f), Check(pk, $\rho_f, \{U_{f,x}\}_{x\in[N]}$) outputs 1 with probability at least $1 - \mathsf{negl}(\lambda)$.

Security: The γ-copy-detection security defined below.

Definition 20 (γ-Copy-Detection Security Game). *A copy-detection security game for $\mathcal{F}, \mathcal{D}$ and adversary $\mathcal{A}$ is denoted as* CopyDetectionGame$_{\mathcal{F},\mathcal{D},\gamma}^{\mathcal{A}}(1^\lambda)$, *which consists of the following steps:*

1. **Setup Phase:** *At the beginning of the game, the challenger takes a security parameter λ and obtains keys* (pk, sk) $\leftarrow$ Setup(1^λ).
2. **Sampling Phase:** *A function f is sampled uniformly at random, $f \leftarrow \mathcal{F}_\lambda$.*
3. **Query Phase:** *$\mathcal{A}$ makes a single query to the challenger and obtains a quantum program for f:* $(\rho_f, \{U_{f,x}\}_{x\in[N]}) \leftarrow$ Generate(sk, f).
4. **Output Phase:** *Finally, $\mathcal{A}$ outputs a (possibly mixed and entangled) state σ over two registers R_1, R_2 and two sets of unitaries $(\{U_{R_1,x}\}_x, \{U_{R_2,x}\}_x)$ They can be viewed as programs $P_1 = (\sigma[R_1], \{U_{R_1,x}\}_{x\in[N]})$ and $P_2 = (\sigma[R_2], \{U_{R_2,x}\}_{x\in[N]})$.*

The game outputs 1 if and only if

- *Apply* Check *on* P_i *respectively and both outcomes are 1. Let* P'_i *be the collapsed program conditioned on outcomes are 1.*
- *Both programs* P'_1, P'_2 *are tested* γ-*good with respect to* f, D_f.

Definition 21 (γ-Copy-Detection-Security). *A copy-detection scheme for* $\mathcal{F}, \mathcal{D}$ *has* γ-*copy-detection security, if for any QPT adversary* $\mathcal{A}$, *there exists a negligible function* negl$(\cdot)$ *such that the following holds for all* $\lambda \in \mathbb{N}$:

$$\Pr\left[b = 1, b \leftarrow \mathsf{CopyDetectionGame}^{\mathcal{A}}_{\mathcal{F}, \mathcal{D}, \gamma}(1^\lambda)\right] \leq negl(\lambda) \tag{2}$$

3.4 Watermarking Primitives with Public Extraction

In this section, we formalize watermarking. We will give the generalized notations in the full version.

Definition 22 (Watermarking Primitives for $\mathcal{F}, \mathcal{D}$). *A watermarking scheme for* $\mathcal{F}, \mathcal{D}$ *consists of the following classical algorithms:*

Setup(1^λ): *it takes as input a security parameter* 1^λ *and outputs keys* (xk, mk). xk *is the extracting key and* mk *is the marking key. We only consider the publicly extractable watermarking schemes. Thus,* xk *is always public.*

Mark(mk, f, τ): *it takes a circuit* f *and a message* $\tau \in \mathcal{M}_\lambda$, *outputs a marked circuit* $\tilde{f}$.

Extract(xk, f'): *it takes a circuit* f' *and outputs a message in* $\{\bot\} \cup \mathcal{M}_\lambda$.

It satisfies the following properties.

Definition 23 (Correctness of Mark (Functionality Preserving)). *For for every efficient algorithm* $\mathcal{A}$, *there exists a negligible function* negl, *for all* (xk, mk) $\leftarrow$ Setup(1^λ), *and every* $\tau \in \mathcal{M}_\lambda$, *all* λ,

$$\Pr\left[\tilde{f}(x) = f(x) : \begin{matrix} f \leftarrow \mathcal{F}_\lambda \\ \tilde{f} \leftarrow \mathsf{Mark}(\mathsf{mk}, f, \tau) \\ x \leftarrow D_f \end{matrix}\right] \geq 1 - negl(\lambda).$$

Definition 24 (Correctness of Extract). *For every efficient algorithm* $\mathcal{A}$, *there exists a negligible function* negl$(\cdot)$, *for all* (xk, mk) $\leftarrow$ Setup(1^λ), *and every* $\tau \in \mathcal{M}_\lambda$, *all* λ,

$$\Pr\left[\tau \neq \mathsf{Extract}(\mathsf{xk}, \tilde{f}) : \begin{matrix} f \leftarrow \mathcal{F}_\lambda \\ \tilde{f} \leftarrow \mathsf{Mark}(\mathsf{mk}, f, \tau) \end{matrix}\right] \leq negl(\lambda).$$

Definition 25. (γ-Unremovability with respect to $\mathcal{F}, \mathcal{D}$). *Consider the following game, denoted as* WaterMarkingGame$^{\mathcal{A}}_{\mathcal{F}, \mathcal{D}, \gamma}$:

1. **Setup:** *The challenger samples* (xk, mk) $\leftarrow$ Setup(1^λ). $\mathcal{A}$ *then gets* xk.
2. **Sampling Phase:** *A function* f *is sampled uniformly at random in* $\mathcal{F}_\lambda$.
3. **Query Phase:** $\mathcal{A}$ *has classical access to* Mark(mk, $f, \cdot$) *at any time. Define* Q *be the set of messages that* $\mathcal{A}$ *has queried on.*
4. **Output Phase:** *Finally, the algorithm outputs a circuit* f^*.

The adversary wins the game if and only if

$$\mathsf{Extract}(\mathsf{xk}, f^*) \notin Q \ \wedge \ \Pr_{x \leftarrow D_f}[f^*(x) = f(x)] \geq \gamma$$

We say a watermarking scheme has γ-unremovability with respect to $\mathcal{F}, \mathcal{D}$, if for all QPT $\mathcal{A}$, it wins the above game with negligible probability in λ.

Remark 3. Here, we only consider a weaker security notion where a quantum adversary only has classical oracle access in the query phase. We claim it is practical and good enough in most of the settings since the watermarking key mk is only in the hands of the challenger: whenever adversary queries Mark(mk, $f, \cdot$), the challenger can always measure this query.

Remark 4. Watermarking primitives should also satisfy 'meaningfulness' property [GKM+19] but since we do not use this property in our construction, we omit it here.

4   Approximating Threshold Implementation

By applying $\mathsf{API}_{\mathcal{P},D}^{\epsilon,\delta}$ and checking if the outcome is greater than or smaller than γ, we get a approximated threshold implementation $\mathsf{ATI}_{\mathcal{P},D,\gamma}^{\epsilon,\delta}$. Here, we use $(\mathsf{ATI}_{\mathcal{P},D,\gamma}^{\epsilon,\delta}, \mathbf{I} - \mathsf{ATI}_{\mathcal{P},D,\gamma}^{\epsilon,\delta})$ to denote this binary POVM.

Theorem 3 gives the following theorem on approximating threshold implementation:

Theorem 4. *For any $\epsilon, \delta, \gamma, \mathcal{P}, D$, the algorithm of measurement $\mathsf{ATI}_{\mathcal{P},D,\gamma}^{\epsilon,\delta}$ that satisfies the followings:*

- *For all quantum state ρ, $Tr[\mathsf{ATI}_{\mathcal{P},D,\gamma-\epsilon}^{\epsilon,\delta} \cdot \rho] \geq Tr[\mathsf{TI}_\gamma(\mathcal{P}_D) \cdot \rho] - \delta$.*
- *By symmetry, for all quantum state ρ, $Tr[\mathsf{TI}_{\gamma-\epsilon}(\mathcal{P}_D) \cdot \rho] \geq Tr[\mathsf{ATI}_{\mathcal{P},D,\gamma}^{\epsilon,\delta} \cdot \rho] - \delta$.*
- *For all quantum state ρ, let ρ' be the collapsed state after applying $\mathsf{ATI}_{\mathcal{P},D,\gamma}^{\epsilon,\delta}$ on ρ (conditioned on outcome 1). Then, $Tr[\mathsf{TI}_{\gamma-2\epsilon}(\mathcal{P}_D) \cdot \rho'] \geq 1 - 2\delta$.*
- *The expected running time is the same as $\mathsf{API}_{\mathcal{P},D}^{\epsilon,\delta}$.*

Intuitively the theorem says that if a quantum state ρ has weight p on eigenvectors with eigenvalues at least γ, the measurement $\mathsf{ATI}_{\mathcal{P},D,\gamma-\epsilon}^{\epsilon,\delta}$ with probability at least $p - \delta$ will produce a collapsed state which has weight $1 - 2\delta$ on eigenvectors with eigenvalues at least $\gamma - 2\epsilon$. Also note that the running time is proportional to $\mathsf{poly}(1/\epsilon, 1/(\log \delta))$, which is a polynomial in λ as long as ϵ is any inverse polynomial and δ is any inverse sub-exponential function. The proof of the above theorem is in the full version.

We can also consider approximating the measurements on a bipartite (possibly entangled) quantum state. In this case, we will prove a similar statement as Theorem 4.

Lemma 3. *Let $\mathcal{P}_1$ and $\mathcal{P}_2$ be two collections of projective measurements and D_1 and D_2 be any probability distributions defined on the index set of $\mathcal{P}_1$ and $\mathcal{P}_2$ respectively. For any $0 < \epsilon, \delta, \gamma < 1$, the algorithms $\mathsf{ATI}_{\mathcal{P}_1, D_1, \gamma}^{\epsilon, \delta}$ and $\mathsf{ATI}_{\mathcal{P}_2, D_2, \gamma}^{\epsilon, \delta}$ satisfy the followings:*

- *For any bipartite (possibly entangled, mixed) quantum state $\rho \in \mathcal{H}_{\mathcal{L}} \otimes \mathcal{H}_{\mathcal{R}}$,*

$$Tr\left[(\mathsf{ATI}_{\mathcal{P}_1, D_1, \gamma-\epsilon}^{\epsilon, \delta} \otimes \mathsf{ATI}_{\mathcal{P}_2, D_2, \gamma-\epsilon}^{\epsilon, \delta})\rho\right] \geq Tr\left[(\mathsf{TI}_\gamma(\mathcal{P}_{D_1}) \otimes \mathsf{TI}_\gamma(\mathcal{P}_{D_2}))\rho\right] - 2\delta.$$

- *For any (possibly entangled, mixed) quantum state ρ, let ρ' be the collapsed state after applying $\mathsf{ATI}_{\mathcal{P}_1, D_1, \gamma}^{\epsilon, \delta} \otimes \mathsf{ATI}_{\mathcal{P}_2, D_2, \gamma}^{\epsilon, \delta}$ on ρ (and normalized). Then,*

$$Tr\left[(\mathsf{TI}_{\gamma-2\epsilon}(\mathcal{P}_{D_1}) \otimes \mathsf{TI}_{\gamma-2\epsilon}(\mathcal{P}_{D_2}))\rho'\right] \geq 1 - 4\delta.$$

We defer the proof of the above Lemma to the full version.

5   Quantum Copy-Protection Scheme

Let λ be the security parameter. Let $\mathcal{F} = \{\mathcal{F}_\lambda\}_{\lambda \in \mathbb{N}}$ be a class of circuits. We assume $\mathcal{F}$ is quantum unlearnable with respect to $\mathcal{D}$ (see Definition 15) and can be computed by polynomial-sized classical circuits. The construction for quantum copy-protection of function class $\mathcal{F}_\lambda$ is defined in Fig. 1.

Note that this construction works for general quantum unlearnable function families as well. By simply changing the notation in the proof to that in the general quantum unlearnability case, we prove it for general quantum unlearnable function families. More discussion will be given in the full version.

Oracle Heuristics. In practice we use a quantum-secure PRF [Zha12] to implement function g; and we use quantum-secure (classical) VBB obfuscation to implement each of $(\mathcal{O}_1, \mathcal{O}_2, U_A, U_{A^\perp})$. We can replace VBB obfuscation programs with oracles that only allow black-box access by the security of VBB obfuscation; afterwards, we can also replace PRF g with a real random function by the property of PRF. The heuristic analysis is straightforward and we omit them here.

5.1   Correctness and Efficiency

Correctness. For the quantum program $\left(\rho = |A\rangle \langle A|, \{U_x\}_{x \in [N]}\right)$ produced by the Generate algorithm, it performs the following computation:

1. Make an oracle query $\mathcal{O}_1$ on the state $|0\rangle |x\rangle |A\rangle$, the resulting state is statistically close to $|y_1\rangle |x\rangle |A\rangle$. Note that $|A\rangle$ with overwhelming probability $1 - 1/|A|$ contains a non-zero vector in A. It measures y_1, which is $y_1 = f(x) \oplus g(x)$.
2. It then prepares a state by applying QFT on the third register and the resulting state is is statistically close to $|0\rangle |x\rangle |A^\perp\rangle$. It makes an oracle query $\mathcal{O}_2$ on the state $|0\rangle |x\rangle |A^\perp\rangle$, the resulting state is statistically close to $|y_2\rangle |x\rangle |A^\perp\rangle$ where $y_2 = g(x)$.

Therefore, with overwhelming probability, the output is $y_1 \oplus y_2 = f(x)$.

Setup(1^λ) → sk: The setup algorithm takes in security parameter 1^λ.
  - Pick a uniformly random subspace $A \subseteq \mathbb{F}^\lambda$ of dimension $\lambda/2$.
  - Output sk $= A$, where A is described by a set of orthogonal basis vectors.

Generate(sk, $f \in \mathcal{F}_\lambda$): The Generate algorithm receives sk $= A$ and a function f from $\mathcal{F}_\lambda$.
  - Prepare a subspace state on n qubits corresponding to A, $|A\rangle = \frac{1}{\sqrt{|A|}} \sum_{v \in A} |v\rangle$.
  - Generate oracles $U_A, U_{A^\perp}$ which compute subspace membership functions for subspace A and its dual subspace $A^\perp$ respectively.
  - Generate oracles $\mathcal{O}_1, \mathcal{O}_2$ such that

$$\mathcal{O}_1(x,v) = \begin{cases} f(x) \oplus g(x) & \text{if } v \in A \text{ and } v \neq 0, \\ \perp & \text{otherwise.} \end{cases}$$

$$\mathcal{O}_2(x,v) = \begin{cases} g(x) & \text{if } v \in A^\perp \text{ and } v \neq 0, \\ \perp & \text{otherwise.} \end{cases}$$

where g is a uniformly random function, with the same input and output length as f.
  - Finally, the Generate algorithm outputs a quantum program $(\rho = |A\rangle \langle A|, \{U_x\}_{x \in [N]})$, which describes the following procedure:
    • On input x, prepare the state $|0\rangle \langle 0| \otimes |x\rangle \langle x| \otimes \rho$ and make an oracle query U_A and measure the first register (output register) to get y_1; the remaining state is $|x\rangle \langle x| \otimes \rho'$.
    • Apply QFT on the third register ρ' to get ρ''.
    • Prepare the state $|0\rangle \langle 0| \otimes |x\rangle \langle x| \otimes \rho''$ and make an oracle query $U_{A^\perp}$ and measure the first register to get y_2.
    • Output $y_1 \oplus y_2$.

The description of $\{U_x\}_{x \in [N]}$ requires the oracle of $U_A, U_{A^\perp}$ (or the VBB obfuscations).

Fig. 1. Quantum copy-protection scheme.

Efficiency. In Generate algorithm, as shown in [AC12], given the basis of A, the subspace state $|A\rangle$ can be prepared in polynomial time using QFT. For the oracles $\mathcal{O}_1, \mathcal{O}_2$, it only needs to check the membership of A and $A^\perp$ and compute functions f and g. f can be prepared in polynomial time by definition. As we discussed above, we can prepare the function g as a PRF. Therefore, the oracles $\mathcal{O}_1, \mathcal{O}_2$ can be generated in polynomial time. The Compute algorithm is clearly efficient.

5.2 Anti-Piracy Security

We show that for a *quantum unlearnable* families of functions $\mathcal{F}$ with respect to $\mathcal{D}$ defined in Definition 15, the quantum copy-protection scheme has anti-piracy security against any quantum polynomial-time adversaries. More formally:

Theorem 5 (Main Theorem). *Let $\mathcal{F}$ be a function families that is γ-quantum-unlearnable with respect to distribution $\mathcal{D}$ (γ is a non-negligible function of λ). The above copy-protection scheme for $\mathcal{F}, \mathcal{D}$ has $(\gamma(\lambda) - 1/\text{poly}(\lambda))$-anti-piracy security, for all polynomial poly.*

In order to describe the quantum query behavior of quantum programs made to oracles, we give the following definitions and notations.

We recall that in Definition 13, a QPT adversary $\mathcal{A}$ in the anti-piracy security game $\textsf{CopyProtectionGame}_{\mathcal{F},\mathcal{D},\gamma}^{\mathcal{A}}(1^\lambda)$, will produce a state σ over registers R_1, R_2 and unitaries $\{U_{R_1,x}\}_{x\in[N]}, \{U_{R_2,x}\}_{x\in[N]}$, the challenger will then perform γ-goodness test on σ using threshold implementations $\textsf{TI}_\gamma(P_{R_1,f})$ and $\textsf{TI}_\gamma(P_{R_2,f})$. For simplicity we will describe the unitary ensembles $\{U_{R_1,x}\}_{x\in[N]}, \{U_{R_2,x}\}_{x\in[N]}$ as U_{R_1}, U_{R_2} and describe threshold implementations $\textsf{TI}_\gamma(P_{R_1,f}), \textsf{TI}_\gamma(P_{R_2,f})$ as $\textsf{TI}_{R_1,\gamma}, \textsf{TI}_{R_2,\gamma}$. Similarly, let $\textsf{ATI}_{R_1,\gamma-\epsilon}$ and $\textsf{ATI}_{R_2,\gamma-\epsilon}$ denote the approximation threshold implementation $\textsf{ATI}_{R_1,\gamma-\epsilon}^{\epsilon,\delta}$ and $\textsf{ATI}_{R_2,\gamma-\epsilon}^{\epsilon,\delta}$ respectively, for some inverse polynomial ϵ and inverse subexponential function δ (in other words, $\log(1/\delta)$ is polynomial in λ).

In this particular construction, $\mathcal{A}$'s behavior can be described as follows: $\mathcal{A}$ "splits" the copy-protection state ρ into two potentially entangled states $\sigma[R_1], \sigma[R_2]$. $\mathcal{A}$ prepares $(\sigma[R_1], U_{R_1})$ with oracle access to $(\mathcal{O}_1, \mathcal{O}_2)$ as pirate program $\textsf{P}_1$; and prepares $(\sigma[R_2], U_{R_2})$ with oracle access $(\mathcal{O}_1, \mathcal{O}_2)$ as pirate program $\textsf{P}_2$. Therefore, $\textsf{TI}_{R_b,\gamma}$ and $\textsf{ATI}_{R_b,\gamma-\epsilon}$ both make oracle queries to $\mathcal{O}_1, \mathcal{O}_2$.

We can assume the joint state of R_1, R_2 has been purified and the overall state is a pure state over register R_1, R_2, R_3 where $\textsf{P}_1$ has only access to R_1 and $\textsf{P}_2$ has only access to R_2.

Quantum Query Weight. Let σ be any quantum state of R_1, R_2, R_3. We consider the program $\textsf{P}_1$. $\textsf{P}_1$ has access to register R_1 and oracle access to $\mathcal{O} = (\mathcal{O}_1, \mathcal{O}_2)$. We denote $|\phi_i\rangle$ to be the overall state of registers R_1, R_2, R_3 before $\textsf{P}_1$ makes i-th query to $\mathcal{O}_1$, *when it applies* $\textsf{ATI}_{R_1,\gamma-\epsilon}$ *on* $\sigma[R_1]$.

$$|\phi_i\rangle = \sum_{x,v,z} \alpha_{x,v,z} |x,v,z\rangle .$$

where (x, v) is the query to oracle $\mathcal{O}_1$ and z is working space of $\textsf{P}_1$, the registers of R_2, R_3. Note that when $\textsf{ATI}_{R_1,\gamma-\epsilon}$ is applied on $\sigma[R_1]$, it in fact applies some unitary and eventually makes a measurement, during which the unitary makes queries to oracles $\mathcal{O}_1, \mathcal{O}_2$. Therefore such a query weight is well-defined.

We denote by $W_{1,A,i}$ to be the sum of squared amplitudes in $|\phi_i\rangle$, which are querying $\mathcal{O}_1$ on input (x, v) such that $v \in A \setminus \{0\}$:

$$W_{1,A,i} = \sum_{x,v,z:v\in A\setminus\{0\}} |\alpha_{x,v,z}|^2$$

Then we sum up all the squared amplitudes $W_{1,A,i}$ in all the queries made by P_1 to $\mathcal{O}_1$, where $v \in A \setminus \{0\}$. We denote this sum as $W_{1,A} = \sum_{i \in [\ell_1]} W_{1,A,i}$, where $\ell_1 = \ell_1(\lambda)$ is the number of queries made by P_1 to $\mathcal{O}_1$.

Similarly, we write $W_{1,A^\perp} = \sum_{i \in [\ell_2]} W_{1,A^\perp,i} = \sum_{i \in [\ell_2]} \sum_{x,v,z : v \in A^\perp \setminus \{0\}} |\alpha_{x,v,z}|^2$ to be the sum of squared amplitudes in $|\phi_i\rangle$ where $v \in A^\perp \setminus \{0\}$, in the ℓ_2 queries made by P_1 to $\mathcal{O}_2$.

Accordingly, for the other program P_2 and threshold implementation $\mathsf{ATI}_{R_2,\gamma-\epsilon}$, we denote these sums of squared amplitudes as $W_{2,A} = \sum_{i \in [m_1]} W_{2,A,i}$ and $W_{2,A^\perp} = \sum_{i \in [m_2]} W_{2,A^\perp,i}$, where m_1, m_2 are the number of queries made by P_2 to oracles $\mathcal{O}_1, \mathcal{O}_2$ respectively.

Case One. Fixing a function f, let $(\sigma, U_{R_1}, U_{R_2})$ be the two programs output by the adversary which are both tested γ-good with respect to f, D_f with some non-negligible probability.

Let $\mathcal{O}_\perp$ be an oracle that always outputs $\perp$. We hope one of the following events will happen:

1. The program $(\sigma[R_1], U_{R_1})$ with oracle access to $\mathcal{O}_1, \mathcal{O}_\perp$ is tested $(\gamma - 2\epsilon)$-good with respect to f, D_f, with non-negligible probability.
2. The program $(\sigma[R_2], U_{R_2})$ with oracle access to $\mathcal{O}_\perp, \mathcal{O}_2$ is tested $(\gamma - 2\epsilon)$-good with respect to f, D_f, with non-negligible probability.

Let $\widetilde{\mathsf{ATI}}_{R_1,\gamma-\epsilon}$ be the same as $\mathsf{ATI}_{R_1,\gamma-\epsilon}$ except with oracle access to $\mathcal{O}_1, \mathcal{O}_\perp$ and $\widetilde{\mathsf{ATI}}_{R_2,\gamma-\epsilon}$ be the same as $\mathsf{ATI}_{R_2,\gamma-\epsilon}$ except with oracle access to $\mathcal{O}_\perp, \mathcal{O}_2$. Similarly, let $\widetilde{\mathsf{TI}}_{R_b,\gamma-2\epsilon}$ be the same threshold implementation as $\mathsf{TI}_{R_b,\gamma-2\epsilon}$ except with oracle access to $\mathcal{O}_1, \mathcal{O}_\perp$ and $\mathcal{O}_\perp, \mathcal{O}_2$ respectively.

Since $(\sigma[R_1], U_{R_1})$ and $(\sigma[R_2], U_{R_2})$ are both γ-good with respect to f, D_f with non-negligible probability, for some non-negligible function $\beta(\cdot)$,

$$\mathrm{Tr}[(\mathsf{TI}_{R_1,\gamma} \otimes \mathsf{TI}_{R_2,\gamma}) \cdot \sigma] \geq \beta(\lambda)$$

From the property of the approximated threshold implementation (Lemma 3),

$$\mathrm{Tr}[(\mathsf{ATI}_{R_1,\gamma-\epsilon} \otimes \mathsf{ATI}_{R_2,\gamma-\epsilon}) \cdot \sigma] \geq \beta(\lambda) - 2\delta$$

Thus, for any $b \in \{1,2\}$, we have $\mathrm{Tr}[\mathsf{ATI}_{R_b,\gamma-\epsilon} \cdot \sigma[R_b]] \geq \beta(\lambda) - 2\delta$. Since δ is negligible, both probabilities are still non-negligible.

We then define the following two events:

E_1: Let E_1 be the event denotes $\mathrm{Tr}[\widetilde{\mathsf{ATI}}_{R_1,\gamma-\epsilon} \cdot \sigma[R_1]]$ is non-negligible. If E_1 happens, by Theorem 4,

$$\mathrm{Tr}\left[\widetilde{\mathsf{TI}}_{R_1,\gamma-2\epsilon} \cdot \sigma[R_1]\right] \geq \mathrm{Tr}\left[\widetilde{\mathsf{ATI}}_{R_1,\gamma-\epsilon} \cdot \sigma[R_1]\right] - \delta$$

which is still non-negligible. In other words, $(\sigma[R_1], U_{R_1})$ with oracle access to $\mathcal{O}_1, \mathcal{O}_\perp$ is tested $(\gamma - 2\epsilon)$-good with respect to f, D_f with non-negligible probability.

E_2: Similarly, define E_2 as the program $(\sigma[R_2], U_{R_2})$ with oracle access to $\mathcal{O}_\perp, \mathcal{O}_2$ is $(\gamma - 2\epsilon)$-good with respect to f, D_f with non-negligible probability.

Case Two. Fixing a function f, let $(\sigma, U_{R_1}, U_{R_2})$ be the two programs output by the adversary which are both γ-good with respect to f, D_f, with non-negligible probability.

If $\mathsf{E}_1 \vee \mathsf{E}_2$ does not happen, we are in the case $\bar{\mathsf{E}}_1 \wedge \bar{\mathsf{E}}_2$. By definition, there exist negligible functions $\mathsf{negl}_1, \mathsf{negl}_2$ such that

$$\mathrm{Tr}\left[\widetilde{\mathsf{ATI}}|_{R_1,\gamma-\epsilon} \cdot \sigma[R_1]\right] \leq \mathsf{negl}_1(\lambda), \qquad \mathrm{Tr}\left[\widetilde{\mathsf{ATI}}|_{R_2,\gamma-\epsilon} \cdot \sigma[R_2]\right] \leq \mathsf{negl}_2(\lambda).$$

We look at the following thought experiments:

1. We apply $\mathsf{ATI}|_{R_1,\gamma-\epsilon} \otimes \mathsf{ATI}|_{R_2,\gamma-\epsilon}$ on σ, by Lemma 3, there exists a non-negligible function $\beta(\cdot)$ such that

$$\mathrm{Tr}\left[(\mathsf{ATI}|_{R_1,\gamma-\epsilon} \otimes \mathsf{ATI}|_{R_2,\gamma-\epsilon}) \cdot \sigma\right] \geq \beta(\lambda) - 2\delta.$$

2. We apply $\mathsf{ATI}|_{R_1,\gamma-\epsilon} \otimes \widetilde{\mathsf{ATI}}|_{R_2,\gamma-\epsilon}$ on σ. We have,

$$\mathrm{Tr}\left[(\mathsf{ATI}|_{R_1,\gamma-\epsilon} \otimes \widetilde{\mathsf{ATI}}|_{R_2,\gamma-\epsilon}) \cdot \sigma\right] \leq \mathrm{Tr}\left[(I \otimes \widetilde{\mathsf{ATI}}|_{R_2,\gamma-\epsilon}) \cdot \sigma\right] \leq \mathsf{negl}_2(\lambda).$$

3. Note that in 1 and 2, the only difference is the oracle access: in 1, it has oracle access to $\mathcal{O}_1, \mathcal{O}_2$; in 2, it has oracle access to $\mathcal{O}_\perp, \mathcal{O}_2$. Let σ' be the state which we apply $(\mathsf{ATI}|_{R_1,\gamma-\epsilon} \otimes I)$ on σ and obtain a outcome 1, which happens with non-negligible probability. Let $W_{2,A}$ be the query weight defined on the state σ'. We know that $W_{2,A}$ can not be negligible otherwise by Theorem 1 (BBBV), the probability difference in 1 and 2 can not be non-neglibile.
   Define M_{R_2} be the operator that measures a random query of $\mathsf{ATI}|_{R_2,\gamma-\epsilon}$ to $\mathcal{O}_1$ and the query (x, v) satisfies $v \in A \setminus \{0\}$. By the above discussion, there exists a non-negligible function $\beta_1(\cdot)$,

$$\mathrm{Tr}\left[(\mathsf{ATI}|_{R_1,\gamma-\epsilon} \otimes M_{R_2}) \cdot \sigma\right] \geq \beta_1(\lambda).$$

4. We apply $\widetilde{\mathsf{ATI}}|_{R_1,\gamma-\epsilon} \otimes M_{R_2}$ on σ. We have,

$$\mathrm{Tr}\left[(\widetilde{\mathsf{ATI}}|_{R_1,\gamma-\epsilon} \otimes M_{R_2}) \cdot \sigma\right] \leq \mathrm{Tr}\left[(\widetilde{\mathsf{ATI}}|_{R_1,\gamma-\epsilon} \otimes I) \cdot \sigma\right] \leq \mathsf{negl}_1(\lambda).$$

5. By a similar argument of 3, let M_{R_1} be the operator that measures a random query of $\mathsf{ATI}|_{R_1,\gamma-\epsilon}$ to $\mathcal{O}_2$ and the query (x, v) satisfies $v \in A^\perp \setminus \{0\}$. There exists a non-negligible function $\beta_2(\cdot)$,

$$\mathrm{Tr}\left[(M_{R_1} \otimes M_{R_2}) \cdot \sigma\right] \geq \beta_2(\lambda).$$

Thus, in the case, one can extract a pair of vectors $(u, v) \in (A \setminus \{0\}) \times (A^\perp \setminus \{0\})$ with non-negligible probability. To conclude it, we have the following lemma,

Lemma 4. *Fixing a function f, let $(\sigma, U_{R_1}, U_{R_2})$ be the two programs output by the adversary which are both γ-good with respect to f, D_f, with non-negligible probability. If $\mathsf{E}_1 \vee \mathsf{E}_2$ does not happen, by randomly picking and measuring a query of $\mathsf{ATI}|_{R_1,\gamma-\epsilon}$ to $\mathcal{O}_2$ and a query of $\mathsf{ATI}|_{R_2,\gamma-\epsilon}$ to $\mathcal{O}_1$, one can obtain a pair of vectors $(u, v) \in (A \setminus \{0\}) \times (A^\perp \setminus \{0\})$ with non-negligible probability.*

Then we show a reduction to violate unlearnability in case of E_1 or E_2 and a reduction to violate direct product hardness in case of $\bar{E}_1 \wedge \bar{E}_2$. We have the following lemmas:

Lemma 5. *Let* $\Pr[E_1]$ *be the probability of* E_1 *taken over all randomness of* $\mathsf{CopyProtectionGame}^{\mathcal{A}}_{\mathcal{F},\mathcal{D},\gamma}(1^\lambda)$. *If* $\Pr[E_1]$ *is non-negligible, there exists an adversary* $\mathcal{A}_1$ *that wins* $\mathsf{LearningGame}^{\mathcal{A}_1}_{\mathcal{F},\mathcal{D},\gamma-2\epsilon}(1^\lambda)$ *with non-negligible probability.*

Proof. The challenger in the copy-protection security game plays as the quantum unlearnability adversary $\mathcal{A}_1$ for function $f \leftarrow \mathcal{F}$, given only black-box access to f; we denote this black box as oracle $\mathcal{O}_f$, which on query $|x, z\rangle$, answers the query with $|x, f(x) + z\rangle$.

Next, we show that $\mathcal{A}_1$ can simulate the copy-protection security game for $\mathcal{A}$ using the information given and uses $\mathcal{A}$ to quantumly learn f. $\mathcal{A}_1$ samples random $\lambda/2$-dimensional subspace A over $\mathbb{F}$ and prepares the membership oracles (two unitaries) $U_A, U_A^\perp$ as well as state $|A\rangle$.

Using $U_A, U_A^\perp$ and given oracle access to f in the unlearnability game, $\mathcal{A}_1$ simulates the copy-protection oracles $\mathcal{O}_1, \mathcal{O}_2$ for $\mathcal{A}$ in the query phase of anti-piracy game.

There is one subtlety in the proof: $\mathcal{A}_1$ needs to simulate the oracles in the anti-piracy game slightly differently: $\mathcal{A}_1$ simulates the oracles with their functionalities partially swapped:

$$\mathcal{O}'_1(x, v) = \begin{cases} g(x) & \text{if } v \in A \text{ and } v \neq 0, \\ \perp & \text{otherwise.} \end{cases}$$

$$\mathcal{O}'_2(x, v) = \begin{cases} f(x) \oplus g(x) & \text{if } v \in A^\perp \text{ and } v \neq 0, \\ \perp & \text{otherwise.} \end{cases}$$

That is, a random function $g(x)$ is output when queried on $u \in A \setminus \{0\}$, and $f(x) \oplus g(x)$ is output when queried on $u \in A^\perp \setminus \{0\}$. The distributions of $\mathcal{O}_1, \mathcal{O}_2$ and $\mathcal{O}'_1, \mathcal{O}'_2$ are identical. Note that $g(x)$ can be simulated by a quantum secure PRF or a $2t$-wise independent hash function where t is the number of oracle queries made by $\mathcal{A}$ [Zha12].

In the output phase, $\mathcal{A}$ outputs $(\sigma, U_{R_1}, U_{R_2})$ and sends to $\mathcal{A}_1$. $\mathcal{A}_1$ simply outputs $(\sigma[R_1], U_{R_1})$ with oracle access to $\mathcal{O}'_1, \mathcal{O}_\perp$. The program does not need access to oracle f because $\mathcal{O}'_1$ is only about $g(\cdot)$ and $\mathcal{O}_\perp$ is a dummy oracle. If E_1 happens, the program is a $(\gamma - 2\epsilon)$-good with non-negligible probability, by the definition of E_1. Because $\Pr[E_1]$ is also non-negligible, $\mathcal{A}_1$ breaks $(\gamma - 2\epsilon)$-quantum-unlearnability of $\mathcal{F}, \mathcal{D}$. $\square$

Lemma 6. *Let* $\Pr[E_2]$ *be the probability of* E_2 *taken over all randomness of* $\mathsf{CopyProtectionGame}^{\mathcal{A}}_{\mathcal{F},\mathcal{D},\gamma}(1^\lambda)$. *If* $\Pr[E_2]$ *is non-negligible, there exists an adversary* $\mathcal{A}_2$ *that wins* $\mathsf{LearningGame}^{\mathcal{A}_2}_{\mathcal{F},\mathcal{D},\gamma-2\epsilon}(1^\lambda)$ *with non-negligible probability.*

Proof (Proof Sketch). The proof is almost identical to the proof for Lemma 6 except oracles $\mathcal{O}_1, \mathcal{O}_2$ are simulated in the same way as that in the construction.

$\mathcal{O}_1(x,v)$ outputs $f(x) \oplus g(x)$ if $v \in A \setminus \{0\}$, and otherwise outputs $\bot$. Similarly, $\mathcal{O}_2(x,v)$ outputs $g(x)$ if $v \in A^{\perp} \setminus \{0\}$, and otherwise outputs $\bot$ □

As discussed above, if $\Pr[\mathsf{E}_1 \vee \mathsf{E}_2]$ is non-negligible, we can break the quantum unlearnability. Otherwise, $\Pr[\bar{\mathsf{E}}_1 \wedge \bar{\mathsf{E}}_2]$ is overwhelming. We show that in the case, one can use the adversary $\mathcal{A}$ to break the direct-product problem Theorem 2.

Lemma 7. *Let* $\Pr[\bar{\mathsf{E}}_1 \wedge \bar{\mathsf{E}}_2]$ *be the probability taken over all randomness of the game* $\mathsf{CopyProtectionGame}^{\mathcal{A}}_{\mathcal{F},\mathcal{D},\gamma}(1^{\lambda})$. *If* $\Pr[\bar{\mathsf{E}}_1 \wedge \bar{\mathsf{E}}_2]$ *is non-negligible, there exists an adversary* $\mathcal{A}_3$ *that breaks the direct-product problem.*

Proof. The challenger in the copy-protection security game plays as the adversary in breaking direct-product problem, denoted as $\mathcal{A}_3$. In the reduction, $\mathcal{A}_3$ is given the access to membership oracles $U_A, U_A^{\perp}$ and one copy of $|A\rangle$.

Next, we show that $\mathcal{A}_3$ can simulate the anti-piracy security game for $\mathcal{A}$ using the information given and uses $\mathcal{A}$ to obtain the two vectors. $\mathcal{A}_3$ samples $f \leftarrow \mathcal{F}$, and simulates a γ-anti-piracy game, specifically simulating the copy-protection oracle $\mathcal{O}_1, \mathcal{O}_2$ for adversary $\mathcal{A}$. In the output phase, $\mathcal{A}$ outputs $(\sigma, U_{R_1}, U_{R_2})$.

$\mathcal{A}_1$ upon taking the output, it randomly picks and measures a query of $\mathsf{ATI}_{R_1,\gamma-\epsilon}$ to $\mathcal{O}_2$ and a query of $\mathsf{ATI}_{R_2,\gamma-\epsilon}$ to $\mathcal{O}_1$, and obtain a pair of vectors (u,v). If $\bar{\mathsf{E}}_1 \wedge \bar{\mathsf{E}}_2$ happens. By Lemma 4, (u,v) breaks the direct-product problem with non-negligible probability. Since $\Pr[\bar{\mathsf{E}}_1 \wedge \bar{\mathsf{E}}_2]$ is non-negligible, the overall probability is non-negligible.   □

Note that the proof does not naturally extend to q-collusion resistant anti-piracy. We leave this as an interesting open problem.

6   Quantum Copy-Detection

6.1   Construction

We construct a copy-detection scheme for a watermarkable function family $\mathcal{F}$ with respect to an input distribution $\mathcal{D}$. Let QM and WM be a public key quantum money scheme and a publicly extractable watermarking scheme for $\mathcal{F}, \mathcal{D}$, whose serial number space $\mathcal{S}_{\lambda}$ of QM is a subset of the message space $\mathcal{M}_{\lambda}$ of WM. We construct a copy-detection scheme in Fig. 2. The definition of quantum money schemes, our general scheme and full proofs are in the full version of this paper.

6.2   Efficiency and Correctness

First, for all $\lambda \in \mathbb{N}$, all efficient $\mathcal{A}$, every $f \in \mathcal{F}_{\lambda}$, the copy-detection program is $(\rho_f, \{U_{f,x}\}_{x\in[N]})$. We have $\mathsf{Compute}(\rho_f, \{U_{f,x}\}_{x\in[N]}, x) = \tilde{f}(x)$, where $\tilde{f} = \mathsf{WM.Mark}(\mathsf{mk}, f, s)$ for some serial number s. From the correctness of WM, it satisfies the correctness of copy-detection.

The correctness of Check comes from the correctness of WM.Extract and **unique serial number** property of QM. Check is a projection since QM.Ver is also a projection. Efficiency is straightforward.

Setup(1^λ): it runs WM.Setup(1^λ) to get xk, mk, let sk = mk and pk = xk.
Generate(sk, f):
  – it runs QM.Gen(1^λ) to get a money state $|\$\rangle$ and a serial number
    s (by applying QM.Ver to the banknote);
  – let $\tilde{f}$ = WM.Mark(mk, f, s) which is classical;
  – it outputs the quantum state $\rho_f = (\tilde{f}, |\$\rangle)$, and $\{U_{f,x}\}_{x\in[N]}$;
  – let $\{U_{f,x}\}_{x\in[N]}$ describe the following unitary: on input a quantum
    state ρ, treat the first register as a classical function g, compute
    $g(x)$ in superposition.
Check(pk, $(\rho_f, \{U_{f,x}\}_{x\in[N]})$):
  – it parses and measures the first register, which is $(f', |\$'\rangle)$;
  – it checks if QM.Ver($|\$'\rangle$) is valid and it gets the serial number s';
  – it then checks if s' = WM.Extract(pk = xk, f');
  – if all the checks pass, it outputs 1; otherwise, it outputs 0.

Fig. 2. Quantum copy-detection scheme.

6.3   Security

Theorem 6. *Assume* QM *is a quantum money scheme and* WM *is a watermarking scheme for* $\mathcal{F}, \mathcal{D}$ *with* γ*-unremovability, the above copy-detection scheme for* $\mathcal{F}, \mathcal{D}$ *has* γ*-copy-detection-security.*

Proof. Let $\mathcal{A}$ be a QPT algorithm that tries to break the security of the copy-detection scheme. Let $(\sigma, U_{R_1}, U_{R_2})$ be the programs output by $\mathcal{A}$ which wins the game CopyDetectionGame$^{\mathcal{A}}_{\mathcal{F}, \mathcal{D}, \gamma}$. To win the game, the program $(\sigma, U_{R_1}, U_{R_2})$ should pass the following two tests:

1. Apply the projective measurement (defined by Check(pk, $\cdot$)) on both $\sigma[R_1]$ and $\sigma[R_2]$, and both outcomes are 1.
2. Let σ' be the state that passes step 1. Then both programs $(\sigma'[R_1], U_{R_1})$, $(\sigma'[R_2], U_{R_2})$ are tested to be γ-good with non-negligible probability.

In our construction, Check first measures the program registers. The resulting state is $\tilde{f}_1, \tilde{f}_2, \sigma$, where $\tilde{f}_1, \tilde{f}_2$ are supposed to be classical (marked) circuits that computes f and σ are (possibly entangled) states that are supposed to be quantum money state for each of the program.

Next, Check applies QM.Ver on both registers of σ and computes serial numbers. Define S_b be the random variable of QM.Ver applying on $\sigma[R_b]$ representing the serial number of ρ_b, for $b = 1, 2$. Define S be the random variable of QM.Ver($|\$\rangle$) representing the serial number of the quantum money state in the Generate procedure.

Define E be the event that both WM.Extract(xk, $\tilde{f}_b$) = S_b and at least one of S_1, S_2 is not equal to S. Define E' be the event that both S_1, S_2 are equal to S and both WM.Extract(xk, $\tilde{f}_b$) = S_b. If $\tilde{f}_1, \tilde{f}_2, \sigma$ passes the step 1, exactly one of E and E' happens.

In step 2, it simply tests if $\tilde{f}_1$ and $\tilde{f}_2$ are γ-good with respect to f, D_f. Since $\tilde{f}_1, \tilde{f}_2$ are classical circuits, it is equivalent to check whether they work correctly on at least γ fraction of all inputs. If it passes step 2, we have for all $b \in \{1, 2\}$, $\Pr_{x \leftarrow D_\lambda}[\tilde{f}_b(x) = f(x)] \geq \gamma$.

Therefore, the probability of $\mathcal{A}$ breaks the security game is indeed,

$$\Pr_{(\tilde{f}_1, \tilde{f}_2, \sigma)}\left[(E \vee E') \wedge \forall b, \Pr_{x \leftarrow D_\lambda}[\tilde{f}_b(x) = f(x)] \geq \gamma\right]$$

$$\leq \Pr_{(\tilde{f}_1, \tilde{f}_2, \sigma)}\left[E \wedge \forall b, \Pr_{x \leftarrow D_\lambda}[\tilde{f}_b(x) = f(x)] \geq \gamma\right] + \Pr_{(\tilde{f}_1, \tilde{f}_2, \sigma)}[E']$$

Note that the probability is taken over the randomness of $\mathsf{CopyDetectionGame}^{\mathcal{A}}_{\mathcal{F}, D, \gamma}$. Next we are going to show both probabilities are negligible, otherwise we can break the quantum money scheme or watermarking scheme.

Claim 1. $\Pr_{(\tilde{f}_1, \tilde{f}_2, \sigma)}[E'] \leq \mathsf{negl}(\lambda)$.

Proof. It corresponds to the security game of the quantum money scheme. Assume $\Pr[E']$ is non-negligible, we can construct an adversary $\mathcal{B}$ for the quantum money scheme with non-negligible advantage. Given a quantum money state $|\$\rangle$, the algorithm $\mathcal{B}$ simulates the challenger for the copy-detection game and can successfully 'copy' a money state. □

Claim 2. $\Pr_{(\tilde{f}_1, \tilde{f}_2, \sigma)}\left[E \wedge \forall b, \Pr_{x \leftarrow D_\lambda}[\tilde{f}_b(x) = f(x)] \geq \gamma\right] \leq \mathsf{negl}(\lambda)$.

Proof. It corresponds to the security game of the underlying watermarking scheme. Since if E happens, at least one of the circuit has different mark than s and it satisfies the correctness requirement. □

Thus, the probability of $\mathcal{A}$ breaks the game is negligible. □

Acknowledgements. We thank Paul Christiano for suggesting the idea of quantum copy-protection based on [AC12] hidden subspace oracles.

J. L., Q. L., M. Z. and R. Z.'s research is supported by NSF Grant; S. A. is supported by Vannevar Bush Faculty Fellowship from the US Department of Defense, the Simons Foundation's It from Qubit Collaboration, and a Simons Investigator Award.

References

[Aar04] Aaronson, S.: Limitations of quantum advice and one-way communication. In: Proceedings. 19th IEEE Annual Conference on Computational Complexity, 2004, pp. 320–332. IEEE (2004)

[Aar09] Aaronson, S.: Quantum copy-protection and quantum money. In 2009 24th Annual IEEE Conference on Computational Complexity, pp. 229–242. IEEE (2009)

[AC12]   Aaronson, S., Christiano, P.: Quantum money from hidden subspaces. In: Proceedings of the Forty-Fourth Annual ACM Symposium on Theory of Computing, pp. 41–60. ACM (2012)

[AGKZ20] Amos, R., Georgiou, M., Kiayias, A., Zhandry, M.: One-shot signatures and applications to hybrid quantum/classical authentication. In: Proceedings of the 52nd Annual ACM SIGACT Symposium on Theory of Computing, STOC 2020, pp. 255–268. Association for Computing Machinery (2020)

[AP20]   Ananth, P., La Placa, R.L.: Secure software leasing (2020)

[BBBV97] Bennett, C.H., Bernstein, E., Brassard, G., Vazirani, U.: Strengths and weaknesses of quantum computing. SIAM J. Comput. 26(5), 1510–1523 (1997)

[BDGM20] Brakerski, Z., Döttling, N., Garg, S., Malavolta, G.: Factoring and pairings are not necessary for io: circular-secure lwe suffices. Cryptology ePrint Archive, Report 2020/1024 (2020). https://eprint.iacr.org/2020/1024

[BDS16]   Ben-David, S., Sattath, O.: Quantum tokens for digital signatures. arXiv preprint arXiv:1609.09047 (2016)

[BGI+01] Barak, B., et al.: On the (im)possibility of obfuscating programs. In: Kilian, J. (ed.) CRYPTO 2001. LNCS, vol. 2139, pp. 1–18. Springer, Heidelberg (2001). https://doi.org/10.1007/3-540-44647-8_1

[BGMZ18] Bartusek, J., Guan, J., Ma, F., Zhandry, M.: Preventing zeroizing attacks on ggh15. In: Proceedings of TCC 2018 (2018)

[BJL+21] Broadbent, A., Jeffery, S., Podder, S., Sundaram, A.: Secure software leasing without assumptions. Sébastien Lord (2021)

[BL19]   Broadbent, A., Lord, S.: Uncloneable quantum encryption via random oracles. IACR Cryptol. ePrint Arch. 2019, 257 (2019)

[BP15]   Bitansky, N., Paneth, O.: On non-black-box simulation and the impossibility of approximate obfuscation. SIAM J. Comput. 44(5), 1325–1383 (2015)

[CHN+18] Cohen, A., Holmgren, J., Nishimaki, R., Vaikuntanathan, V., Wichs, D.: Watermarking cryptographic capabilities. SIAM J. Comput. 47(6), 2157–2202 (2018)

[CMP20]   Coladangelo, A., Majenz, C., Poremba, A.: Quantum copy-protection of compute-and-compare programs in the quantum random oracle model (2020)

[GKM+19] Goyal, R., Kim, S., Manohar, N., Waters, B., Wu, D.J.: Watermarking public-key cryptographic primitives. In: Boldyreva, A., Micciancio, D. (eds.) CRYPTO 2019. LNCS, vol. 11694, pp. 367–398. Springer, Cham (2019). https://doi.org/10.1007/978-3-030-26954-8_12

[GKW17]   Goyal, R., Koppula, V., Waters, B.: Lockable obfuscation. In: 2017 IEEE 58th Annual Symposium on Foundations of Computer Science (FOCS), pp. 612–621. IEEE (2017)

[GZ20]   Georgiou, M., Zhandry, M.: Unclonable decryption keys. Cryptology ePrint Archive, Report 2020/877 (2020). https://eprint.iacr.org/2020/877

[KNY20]   Kitagawa, F., Nishimaki, R., Yamakawa, T.: Secure software leasing from standard assumptions (2020)

[KW17]   Kim, S., Wu, D.J.: Watermarking cryptographic functionalities from standard lattice assumptions. In: Katz, J., Shacham, H. (eds.) CRYPTO 2017. LNCS, vol. 10401, pp. 503–536. Springer, Cham (2017). https://doi.org/10.1007/978-3-319-63688-7_17

[KW19] Kim, S., Wu, D.J.: Watermarking PRFs from lattices: stronger security via extractable PRFs. In: Boldyreva, A., Micciancio, D. (eds.) CRYPTO 2019. LNCS, vol. 11694, pp. 335–366. Springer, Cham (2019). https://doi.org/10.1007/978-3-030-26954-8_11

[QWZ18] Quach, W., Wichs, D., Zirdelis, G.: Watermarking PRFs under standard assumptions: public marking and security with extraction queries. In: Beimel, A., Dziembowski, S. (eds.) TCC 2018. LNCS, vol. 11240, pp. 669–698. Springer, Cham (2018). https://doi.org/10.1007/978-3-030-03810-6_24

[WZ17] Wichs, D., Zirdelis, G.: Obfuscating compute-and-compare programs under lwe. In: 2017 IEEE 58th Annual Symposium on Foundations of Computer Science (FOCS), pp. 600–611. IEEE (2017)

[Zha12] Zhandry, M.: How to construct quantum random functions. In 2012 IEEE 53rd Annual Symposium on Foundations of Computer Science, pp. 679–687. IEEE (2012)

[Zha20] Zhandry, M.: Schrödinger's pirate: how to trace a quantum decoder. Cryptology ePrint Archive, Report 2020/1191 (2020). https://eprint.iacr.org/2020/1191

Hidden Cosets and Applications
to Unclonable Cryptography

Andrea Coladangelo[1]([✉]), Jiahui Liu[2], Qipeng Liu[3], and Mark Zhandry[4]

[1] University of California, Berkeley, USA
[2] The University of Texas at Austin, Austin, USA
jiahui@cs.utexas.edu
[3] Princeton University, Princeton, USA
qipengl@cs.princeton.edu
[4] Princeton University and NTT Research, Princeton, USA
mzhandry@princeton.edu

Abstract. In 2012, Aaronson and Christiano introduced the idea of *hidden subspace states* to build public-key quantum money [STOC '12]. Since then, this idea has been applied to realize several other cryptographic primitives which enjoy some form of unclonability.

In this work, we propose a generalization of hidden subspace states to hidden *coset* states. We study different unclonable properties of coset states and several applications:

- We show that, assuming indistinguishability obfuscation (iO), hidden coset states possess a certain *direct product hardness* property, which immediately implies a tokenized signature scheme in the plain model. Previously, a tokenized signature scheme was known only relative to an oracle, from a work of Ben-David and Sattath [QCrypt '17].
- Combining a tokenized signature scheme with extractable witness encryption, we give a construction of an unclonable decryption scheme in the plain model. The latter primitive was recently proposed by Georgiou and Zhandry [ePrint '20], who gave a construction relative to a classical oracle.
- We conjecture that coset states satisfy a certain natural (information-theoretic) monogamy-of-entanglement property. Assuming this conjecture is true, we remove the requirement for extractable witness encryption in our unclonable decryption construction, by relying instead on compute-and-compare obfuscation for the class of unpredictable distributions. As potential evidence in support of the monogamy conjecture, we prove a weaker version of this monogamy property, which we believe will still be of independent interest.
- Finally, we give the first construction of a copy-protection scheme for pseudorandom functions (PRFs) in the plain model. Our scheme is secure either assuming iO, OWF and extractable witness encryption, or assuming iO, OWF, compute-and-compare obfuscation for the class of unpredictable distributions, and the conjectured monogamy property mentioned above.

© International Association for Cryptologic Research 2021
T. Malkin and C. Peikert (Eds.): CRYPTO 2021, LNCS 12825, pp. 556–584, 2021.
https://doi.org/10.1007/978-3-030-84242-0_20

1   Introduction

The no-cloning principle of quantum mechanics asserts that quantum information cannot be generically copied. This principle has profound consequences in quantum cryptography, as it puts a fundamental restriction on the possible strategies that a malicious party can implement. One of these consequences is that quantum information enables cryptographic tasks that are provably impossible to realize classically, the most famous example being information-theoretically secure key distribution [BB84].

Beyond this, the no-cloning principle opens up an exciting avenue to realize cryptographic tasks which enjoy some form of *unclonability*, e.g. quantum money [Wie83, AC12, FGH+12, Zha19a, Kan18], quantum tokens for digital signatures [BS16], copy-protection of programs [Aar09, ALL+20, CMP20], and more recently unclonable encryption [Got02, BL19] and decryption [GZ20].

In this work, we revisit the *hidden subspace* idea proposed by Aaronson and Christiano, which has been employed towards several of the applications above. We propose a generalization of this idea, which involves hidden *cosets* (affine subspaces), and we show applications of this to signature tokens, unclonable decryption and copy-protection.

Given a subspace $A \subseteq \mathbb{F}_2^n$, the corresponding *subspace state* is defined as a uniform superposition over all strings in the subspace A, i.e.

$$|A\rangle := \frac{1}{\sqrt{|A|}} \sum_{x \in A} |x\rangle,$$

The first property that makes this state useful is that applying a Hadamard on all qubits creates a uniform superposition over all strings in $A^{\perp}$, the orthogonal complement of A, i.e. $H^{\otimes n}|A\rangle = |A^{\perp}\rangle$.

The second property, which is crucial for constructing unclonable primitives with some form of verification, is the following. Given one copy of $|A\rangle$, where $A \subseteq \mathbb{F}_2^n$ is uniformly random of dimension $n/2$, it is impossible to produce two copies of $|A\rangle$ except with negligible probability. As shown by [AC12], unclonability holds even when given quantum access to oracles for membership in A and $A^{\perp}$, as long as the number of queries is polynomially bounded. On the other hand, such membership oracles allow for verifying the state $|A\rangle$, leading to publicly-verifiable quantum money, where the verification procedure is the following:

- Given an alleged quantum money state $|\psi\rangle$, query the oracle for membership in A on input $|\psi\rangle$. Measure the outcome register, and verify that the outcome is 1.
- If so, apply $H^{\otimes n}$ to the query register, and query the oracle for membership in $A^{\perp}$. Measure the outcome register, and accept the money state if the outcome is 1.

It is not difficult to see that the unique state that passes this verification procedure is $|A\rangle$.

In order to obtain a quantum money scheme in the plain model (without oracles), Aaronson and Christiano suggest instantiating the oracles with some form of program obfuscation. This vision is realized subsequently in [Zha19a], where access to the oracles for subspace membership is replaced by a suitable obfuscation of the membership programs, which can be built from indistinguishability obfuscation (iO). More precisely, Zhandry shows that, letting P_A and $P_{A^\perp}$ be programs that check membership in A and $A^\perp$ respectively, any computationally bounded adversary who receives a uniformly random subspace state $|A\rangle$ together with $iO(P_A)$ and $iO(P_{A^\perp})$ cannot produce two copies of $|A\rangle$ except with negligible probability.

The subspace state idea was later employed to obtain *quantum tokens* for digital signatures [BS16]. What these are is best explained by the (award-winning) infographic in [BS16] (see the ancillary arXiv files there). Concisely, a quantum signature token allows Alice to provide Bob with the ability to sign *one and only one* message in her name, where such signature can be publicly verified using Alice's public key. The construction of quantum tokens for digital signatures from [BS16] is the following.

- Alice samples a uniformly random subspace $A \subseteq \mathbb{F}_2^n$, which constitutes her secret key. A signature token is the state $|A\rangle$.
- Anyone in possession of a token $|A\rangle$ can sign message 0 by outputting a string $v \in A$ (this can be obtained by measuring $|A\rangle$ in the computational basis), and can sign message 1 by outputting a string $w \in A^\perp$ (this can be done by measuring $|A\rangle$ in the Hadamard basis).
- Signatures can be publicly verified assuming access to an oracle for subspace membership in A and in $A^\perp$ (such access can be thought of as Alice's public key).

In order to guarantee security of the scheme, i.e. that Bob cannot produce a valid signature for more than one message, Ben-David and Sattath prove the following strengthening of the original property proven by Aaronson and Christiano. Namely, they show that any query-bounded adversary with quantum access to oracles for membership in A and $A^\perp$ cannot produce, except with negligible probability, a pair (v, w) where $v \in A \setminus \{0\}$ and $w \in A^\perp \setminus \{0\}$. We refer to this property as a *direct product hardness* property.

The natural step to obtain a signature token scheme in the plain model is to instantiate the subspace membership oracles using iO, analogously to the quantum money application. However, unlike for the case of quantum money, here one runs into a technical barrier, which we expand upon in Sect. 2.1. Thus, a signature token scheme is not known in the plain model, and this has remained an open question since [BS16].

In general, a similar difficulty in obtaining schemes that are secure in the plain model as opposed to an oracle model seems prevalent in works about other unclonable primitives. For example, in the case of copy-protection of programs, we know that copy-protection of a large class of evasive programs, namely compute-and-compare programs, is possible with provable non-trivial security against fully malicious adversaries in the quantum random oracle model

(QROM) [CMP20]. Other results achieving provable security in the plain model are secure only against a restricted class of adversaries [AP21,KNY20,BJL+21]. To make the contrast between plain model and oracle model even more stark, all unlearnable programs can be copy-protected assuming access to (highly structured) oracles [ALL+20], but we know, on the other hand, that a copy-protection scheme for all unlearnable programs in the plain model does not exist (assuming Learning With Errors is hard for quantum computers) [AP21].

Likewise, for the recently proposed task of unclonable decryption, the only currently known scheme is secure only in a model with access to subspace membership oracles [GZ20].

1.1   Our Results

We propose a generalization of subspace states, which we call *coset* states. For $A \subseteq \mathbb{F}_2^n$, and $s, s' \in \mathbb{F}_2^n$, the corresponding coset state is:

$$|A_{s,s'}\rangle := \sum_{x \in A} (-1)^{\langle x, s' \rangle} |x + s\rangle,$$

where here $\langle x, s' \rangle$ denotes the inner product of x and s'. In the computational basis, the quantum state is a superposition over all elements in the coset $A + s$, while, in the Hadamard basis, it is a superposition over all elements in $A^\perp + s'$. Let P_{A+s} and $P_{A^\perp+s'}$ be programs that check membership in the cosets $A + s$ and $A^\perp + s'$ respectively. To check if a state $|\psi\rangle$ is a coset state with respect to A, s, s', one can compute P_{A+s} in the computational basis, and check that the outcome is 1; then, apply $H^{\otimes n}$ followed by $P_{A^\perp+s'}$, and check that the outcome is 1.

Computational Direct Product Hardness. Our first technical result is establishing a *computational direct product hardness* property in the plain model, assuming post-quantum iO and one-way functions.

Theorem 1 (Informal). *Any quantum polynomial-time adversary who receives* $|A_{s,s'}\rangle$ *and programs* iO(P_{A+s}) *and* iO($P_{A^\perp+s'}$) *for uniformly random* $A \subseteq \mathbb{F}_2^n$, $s, s' \in \mathbb{F}_2^n$, *cannot produce a pair* $(v, w) \in (A + s) \times (A^\perp + s')$, *except with negligible probability in* n.

As we mentioned earlier, this is in contrast to regular subspace states, for which a similar direct product hardness is currently not known in the plain model, but only in a model with access to subspace membership oracles.

We then apply this property to obtain the following primitives.

Signature Tokens. Our direct product hardness immediately implies a *signature token* scheme in the plain model (from post-quantum iO and one-way functions), thus resolving the main question left open in [BS16].

Theorem 2 (Informal). *Assuming post-quantum* iO *and one-way functions, there exists a signature token scheme.*

In this signature token scheme, the public verification key is the pair of programs $(\mathrm{iO}(P_{A+s}), \mathrm{iO}(P_{A^\perp+s'}))$, and a signature token is the coset state $|A_{s,s'}\rangle$. Producing signatures for both messages 0 and 1 is equivalent to finding elements in both $A + s$ and $A^\perp + s'$, which violates our computational direct product hardness property.

Unclonable Decryption. Unclonable decryption, also known as *single-decryptor encryption*, was introduced in [GZ20]. Informally, a single-decryptor encryption scheme is a (public-key) encryption scheme in which the secret key is a *quantum state*. The scheme satisfies a standard notion of security (in our case, CPA security), as well as the following additional security guarantee: no efficient quantum algorithm with one decryption key is able to produce two working decryption keys. We build a single-decryptor encryption scheme using a signature tokens scheme and extractable witness encryption in a black-box way. By leveraging our previous result about the existence of a signature token scheme in the plain model, we are able to prove security without the need for the structured oracles used in the original construction of [GZ20].

Theorem 3 (Informal). *Assuming post-quantum* iO, *one-way functions, and extractable witness encryption, there exists a public-key single-decryptor encryption scheme.*

Copy-Protection of PRFs. The notion of a copy-protection scheme was introduced by Aaronson in [Aar09] and recently explored further in [AP21, CMP20, ALL+20, BJL+21].

In a copy-protection scheme, the vendor of a classical program wishes to provide a user the ability to run the program on any input, while ensuring that the functionality cannot be "pirated": informally, the adversary, given one copy of the program, cannot produce two programs that enable evaluating the program correctly.

Copy-protection is trivially impossible classically, since classical information can always be copied. This impossibility can be in principle circumvented if the classical program is encoded in a quantum state, due to the no-cloning principle. However, positive results have so far been limited. A copy-protection scheme [CMP20] is known for a class of evasive programs, known as compute-and-compare programs, with provable non-trivial security against fully malicious adversaries in the Quantum Random Oracle Model (QROM). Other schemes in the plain model are only secure against restricted classes of adversaries (which behave honestly in certain parts of the protocol) [AP21, KNY20, BJL+21]. Copy-protection schemes for more general functionalities are known [ALL+20], but these are only secure assuming very structured oracles (which depend on the functionality that is being copy-protected).

In this work, we present a copy-protection scheme for a family of pseudorandom functions (PRFs). In such a scheme, for any classical key K for the PRF, anyone in possession of a *quantum key* ρ_K is able to evaluate $PRF(K, x)$ on any input x.

The copy-protection property that our scheme satisfies is that given a quantum key ρ_K, no efficient algorithm can produce two (possibly entangled) keys such that these two keys allow for simultaneous correct evaluation on uniformly random inputs, with noticeable probability.

Similarly to the unclonable decryption scheme, our copy-protection scheme is secure assuming post-quantum iO, one-way functions, and extractable witness encryption.

Theorem 4 (Informal). *Assuming post-quantum iO, one-way functions, and extractable witness encryption, there exists a copy-protection scheme for a family of PRFs.*

We remark that our scheme requires a particular kind of PRFs, namely puncturing and extracting with small enough error. However, PRFs satisfying these properties can be built from just one-way functions.

The existence of extractable witness encryption is considered to be a very strong assumption. In particular, it was shown to be impossible in general (under a special-purpose obfuscation conjecture) [GGHW17]. However, we emphasize that no provably secure copy-protection schemes with standard malicious security in the plain model are known at all. Given the central role of PRFs in the construction of many other cryptographic primitives, we expect that our copy-protection scheme, and the techniques developed along the way, will play an important role as a building block to realize *unclonable* versions of other primitives.

To avoid the use of extractable witness encryption, we put forth a (information-theoretic) conjecture about a *monogamy of entanglement* property of coset states, which we discuss below. Assuming this conjecture is true, we show that both unclonable decryption and copy-protection of PRFs can be constructed *without* extractable witness encryption, by relying instead on compute-and-compare obfuscation [WZ17, GKW17] (more details on the latter can be found in Sect. 3.1).

Theorem 5 (Informal). *Assuming post-quantum iO, one-way functions, and obfuscation of compute-and-compare programs against unpredictable distributions, there exist: (i) a public-key single-decryptor encryption scheme, and (ii) a copy-protection scheme for a family of PRFs.*

As potential evidence in support of the monogamy-of-entanglement conjecture, we prove a weaker version of the monogamy of entanglement property, which we believe will still be of independent interest (more details on this are below).

Remark 1. While iO was recently constructed based on widely-believed computational assumptions [JLS20], the latter construction is not quantum resistant, and the situation is less clear quantumly. However, several works have proposed candidate post-quantum obfuscation schemes [BGMZ18, WW20, BDGM20], and based on these works iO seems plausible in the post-quantum setting as well.

Remark 2. Compute-and-compare obfuscation against unpredictable distributions is known to exist assuming LWE (or iO) and assuming the existence of

Extremely Lossy Functions (ELFs) [Zha19c] [WZ17,GKW17]. Unfortunately, the only known constructions of ELFs rely on hardness assumptions that are broken by quantum computers (exponential hardness of decisional Diffie-Hellman). To remedy this, we give a construction of computate-and-compare obfuscation against *sub-exponentially* unpredictable distributions, from plain LWE (see Theorem 6, and its proof in the full version). The latter weaker obfuscation is sufficient to prove security of our single-decryptor encryption scheme, and copy-protection scheme for PRFs, if one additionally assumes *sub-exponentially* secure iO and one-way functions.

Monogamy-of-Entanglement. As previously mentioned, we conjecture that coset states additionally satisfy a certain (information-theoretic) *monogamy of entanglement* property, similar to the one satisfied by BB84 states, which is studied extensively in [TFKW13]. Unlike the monogamy property of BB84 states, the monogamy property we put forth is well-suited for applications with public verification, in a sense made more precise below.

This monogamy property states that Alice, Bob and Charlie cannot cooperatively win the following game with a challenger, except with negligible probability. The challenger first prepares a uniformly random coset state $|A_{s,s'}\rangle$ and gives the state to Alice. Alice outputs two (possibly entangled) quantum states and sends them to Bob and Charlie respectively. Finally, Bob and Charlie both get the description of the subspace A. The game is won if Bob outputs a vector in $A + s$ and Charlie outputs a vector in $A^\perp + s'$.

Notice that if Alice were told A before she had to send the quantum states to Bob and Charlie, then she could recover s and s' (efficiently) given $|A_{s,s'}\rangle$. Crucially, A is only revealed to Bob and Charlie *after* Alice has sent them the quantum states (analogously to the usual monogamy-of-entanglement game based on BB84 states, where θ is only revealed to Bob and Charlie after they receive their states from Alice.).

We note that the hardness of this game is an *information-theoretic* conjecture. As such, there is hope that it can be proven unconditionally.

Under this conjecture, we show that the problem remains hard (computationally) even if Alice additionally receives the programs iO(P_{A+s}) and iO($P_{A^\perp+s'}$). Based on this result, we then obtain unclonable decryption and copy-protection of PRFs from post-quantum iO and one-way functions, and compute-and-compare obfuscation against unpredictable distributions. We thus remove the need for extractable witness encryption (more details on this are provided in the technical overview, Sect. 2.1).

As evidence in support of our conjecture, we prove a weaker information-theoretic monogamy property, namely that Alice, Bob and Charlie cannot win at a monogamy game that is identical to the one described above, except that at the last step, Bob and Charlie are each required to return a pair in $(A+s) \times (A^\perp+s')$, instead of a single element each. Since coset states have more algebraic structure than BB84 states, a more refined analysis is required to prove this (weaker) property compared to that of [TFKW13]. We again extend this monogamy result to the case where Alice receives programs iO(P_{A+s}) and iO($P_{A^\perp+s'}$).

We emphasize that our monogamy result for coset states differs from the similar monogamy result for BB84 states in one crucial way: the result still holds when Alice receives programs that allow her to verify the correctness of her state (namely $iO(P_{A+s})$ and $iO(P_{A^\perp+s'})$). This is not the case for the BB84 monogamy result. In fact, Lutomirski [Lut10] showed that an adversary who is given $|x^\theta\rangle$ and a public verification oracle that outputs 1 if the input state is correct and 0 otherwise, can efficiently copy the state $|x^\theta\rangle$. At the core of this difference is the fact that coset states are highly entangled, whereas strings of BB84 states have no entanglement at all.

For this reason, we believe that the monogamy property of coset states may be of independent interest, and may find application in contexts where public verification of states is important.

2   Technical Overview

2.1   Computational Direct Product Hardness for Coset States

Our first technical contribution is to establish a *computational* direct product hardness property for coset states. In this section, we aim to give some intuition for the barrier to proving such a property for regular subspace states, and why resorting to coset states helps.

We establish the following: a computationally bounded adversary who receives $|A_{s,s'}\rangle$ and programs $iO(P_{A+s})$ and $iO(P_{A^\perp+s'})$ for uniformly random A, s, s', cannot produce a pair (v, w), where $v \in A + s$ and $w \in A^\perp + s'$, except with negligible probability.

The first version of this direct product hardness property involved regular subspace states, and was *information-theoretic*. It was proven by Ben-David and Sattath [BS16], and it established the following: given a uniformly random subspace state $|A\rangle$, where $A \subseteq \mathbb{F}_2^n$ has dimension $n/2$, no adversary can produce a pair of vectors v, w such that $v \in A$ and $w \in A^\perp$ respectively, even with access to oracles for membership in A and in $A^\perp$.

The first successful instantiation of the membership oracles in the plain model is due to Zhandry, in the context of public-key quantum money [Zha19a]. Zhandry showed that replacing the membership oracles with indistinguishability obfuscations of the membership programs P_A and $P_{A^\perp}$ is sufficient to prevent an adversary from copying the subspace state, and thus is sufficient for public-key quantum money. In what follows, we provide some intuition as to how one proves this "computational no-cloning" property, and why the same proof idea does not extend naturally to the direct product hardness property for regular subspace states.

In [Zha19a], Zhandry shows that iO realizes what he refers to as a *subspace-hiding obfuscator*. A subspace hiding obfuscator shO has the property that any computationally bounded adversary who chooses a subspace A cannot distinguish between $shO(P_A)$ and $shO(P_B)$ for a uniformly random superspace B of A (of not too large dimension). In turn, a subspace hiding obfuscator can then be used to show that an adversary who receives $|A\rangle$, $shO(P_A)$ and $shO(P_{A^\perp})$, for a uniformly random A, cannot produce two copies of $|A\rangle$. This is done in the following way. For the rest of the section, we assume that $A \subseteq \mathbb{F}_2^n$ has dimension $n/2$.

- Replace $\mathsf{shO}(P_A)$ with $\mathsf{shO}(P_B)$ for a uniformly random superspace B of A, where $\dim(B) = \frac{3}{4}n$. Replace $\mathsf{shO}(P_{A^\perp})$ with $\mathsf{shO}(P_C)$ for a uniformly random superspace C of $A^\perp$, where $\dim(C) = \frac{3}{4}n$.
- Argue that the task of copying a subspace state $|A\rangle$, for a uniformly random subspace $C^\perp \subseteq A \subseteq B$ (even knowing B and C directly) is just as hard as the task of copying a uniformly random subspace state of dimension $|A'\rangle \subseteq \mathbb{F}_2^{n/2}$ where $\dim(A') = \frac{n}{4}$. The intuition for this is that knowing $C^\perp$ fixes $\frac{n}{4}$ dimensions out of the $\frac{n}{2}$ original dimensions of A. Then, you can think of the first copying task as equivalent to the second up to a change of basis. Such reduction completely removes the adversary's knowledge about the membership programs.
- The latter task is of course hard (it would even be hard with access to membership oracles for A' and $A'^\perp$).

One can try to apply the same idea to prove a *computational direct product hardness property* for subspace states, where the task is no longer to copy $|A\rangle$, but rather we wish to show that a bounded adversary receiving $|A\rangle$ and programs $\mathsf{iO}(P_A)$ and $\mathsf{iO}(P_{A^\perp})$, for uniformly random A, cannot produce a pair (v, w), where $v \in A$ and $w \in A^\perp$. Applying the same replacements as above using shO allows us to reduce this task to the task of finding a pair of vectors in $A \times A^\perp$ given $|A\rangle, B, C$, such that $C^\perp \subseteq A \subseteq B$. Unfortunately, unlike in the case of copying, this task is easy, because any pair of vectors in $C^\perp \times B^\perp$ also belongs to $A \times A^\perp$. This is the technical hurdle that ones runs into when trying to apply the proof idea from [Zha19a] to obtain a computational direct hardness property for subspace states.

Our first result is that we overcome this hurdle by using coset states. In the case of cosets, the natural analog of the argument above results in a replacement of the program that checks membership in $A + s$ with a program that checks membership in $B + s$. Similarly, we replace $A^\perp + s'$ with $C + s'$. The crucial observation is that, since $B + s = B + s + t$ for any $t \in B$, the programs P_{B+s} and P_{B+s+t} are functionally equivalent. So, an adversary who receives $\mathsf{iO}(P_{B+s})$ cannot distinguish this from $\mathsf{iO}(P_{B+s+t})$ for any t. We can thus argue that t functions as a randomizing mask that prevents the adversary from guessing s and finding a vector in $A + s$.

Signature Tokens. The computational direct product hardness immediately gives a signature token scheme in the plain model:

- Alice samples a key (A, s, s') uniformly at random. This constitutes her secret key. The verification key is $(\mathsf{iO}(P_{A+s}), \mathsf{iO}(P_{A^\perp + s'}))$. A signature token is $|A_{s,s'}\rangle$.
- Anyone in possession of a token can sign message 0 by outputting a string $v \in A + s$ (this can be obtained by measuring the token in the computational

basis), and can sign message 1 by outputting a string $w \in A^\perp + s'$ (this can be done by measuring the token in the Hadamard basis).

- Signatures can be publicly verified using Alice's public key.

If an algorithm produces both signatures for messages 0 and 1, it finds vectors $v \in A+s$ and $w \in A^\perp+s'$, which violates computational direct product hardness.

2.2 Unclonable Decryption

Our second result is an *unclonable decryption* scheme (also known as a *single-decryptor encryption* scheme [GZ20] - we will use the two terms interchangeably in the rest of the paper) from black-box use of a signature token scheme and extractable witness encryption. This construction removes the need for structured oracles, as used in the construction of [GZ20].

Additionally, we show that, assuming the conjectured monogamy property described in Sect. 1.1, we obtain an unclonable decryption scheme from just iO and post-quantum one-way functions, where iO is used to construct obfuscators for both subspace-membership programs and compute-and-compare programs [GKW17, WZ17].

In this overview, we focus on the construction from the monogamy property, as we think it is conceptually more interesting.

Recall that a single-decryptor encryption scheme is a public-key encryption scheme in which the secret key is a quantum state. On top of the usual encryption security notions, one can define "single-decryptor" security: this requires that it is not possible for an adversary who is given the secret key to produce two (possibly entangled) decryption keys, which both enable simultaneous successful decryption of ciphertexts. A simplified version of our single-decryptor encryption scheme is the following. Let $n \in \mathbb{N}$.

- The key generation procedure samples uniformly at random $A \subseteq \mathbb{F}_2^n$, with $\dim(A) = \frac{n}{2}$ and $s, s' \in \mathbb{F}_2^n$ uniformly at random. The public key is the pair $(\mathrm{iO}(P_{A+s}), \mathrm{iO}(P_{A^\perp+s'}))$. The (quantum) secret key is the coset state $|A_{s,s'}\rangle$.
- To encrypt a message m, sample uniformly $r \leftarrow \{0,1\}$, and set $R = \mathrm{iO}(P_{A+s})$ if $r = 0$ and $R = \mathrm{iO}(P_{A^\perp+s'})$ if $r = 1$. Then, let C be the following program: C: on input v, output the message m if $R(v) = 1$ and otherwise output $\perp$. The ciphertext is then $(r, \mathrm{iO}(C))$.
- To decrypt a ciphertext $(r, \mathrm{iO}(C))$ with the quantum key $|A_{s,s'}\rangle$, one simply runs the program $\mathrm{iO}(C)$ coherently on input $|A_{s,s'}\rangle$ if $r = 0$, and on $H^{\otimes n}|A_{s,s'}\rangle$ if $r = 1$.

In the full scheme, we actually amplify security by sampling $r \leftarrow \{0,1\}^\lambda$, and having λ coset states, but we choose to keep the presentation in this section as simple as possible.

The high level idea for single-decryptor security is the following. Assume for the moment that iO were an ideal obfuscator (we will argue after this that iO is good enough). Consider a pirate who receives a secret key, produces two copies of it, and gives one to Bob and the other to Charlie. Suppose both Bob and Charlie can decrypt ciphertexts $(r, \mathrm{iO}(C))$ correctly with probability close to 1, over the randomness in the choice of r (which is crucially chosen only after Bob and Charlie have received their copies). Then, there must be some efficient quantum algorithm, which uses Bob's (resp. Charlie's) auxiliary quantum information (whatever state he has received from the pirate), and is able to output a vector in $A + s$. This is because in the case of $r = 0$, the program C outputs the plaintext message m exclusively on inputs $v \in A+s$. Similarly, there must be an algorithm that outputs a vector in $A^{\perp} + s'$ starting from Bob's (resp. Charlie's) auxiliary quantum information. Notice that this doesn't imply that Bob can *simultaneously* output a pair in $(A+s) \times (A^{\perp}+s')$, because explicitly recovering a vector in one coset might destroy the auxiliary quantum information preventing recovery of a vector in the other (and this very fact is of course crucial to the direct product hardness). Hence, in order to argue that it is not possible for both Bob and Charlie to be decrypting with probability close to 1, we have to use the fact that Bob and Charlie have separate auxiliary quantum information, and that each of them can recover vectors in $A + s$ or $A^{\perp} + s'$, which means that this can be done simultaneously, now violating the direct product hardness property.

The crux of the security proof is establishing that iO is a good enough obfuscator to enable this argument to go through.

To this end, we first notice that there is an alternative way of computing membership in $A + s$, which is functionally equivalent to the program C defined above.

Let $\mathsf{Can}_A(s)$ be a function that computes the lexicographically smallest vector in $A + s$ (think of this as a representative of the coset). It is not hard to see that a vector t is in $A + s$ if and only if $\mathsf{Can}_A(t) = \mathsf{Can}_A(s)$. Also Can_A is efficiently computable given A. Therefore, a functionally equivalent program to C, in the case that $r = 0$, is:

$\widetilde{C}$: on input v, output m if $\mathsf{Can}_A(v) = \mathsf{Can}_A(s)$, otherwise output $\perp$.

By the security of iO, an adversary can't distinguish $\mathrm{iO}(C)$ from $\mathrm{iO}(\widetilde{C})$.

The key insight is that now the program $\widetilde{C}$ is a *compute-and-compare* program [GKW17, WZ17]. The latter is a program described by three parameters: an efficiently computable function f, a target y and an output z. The program outputs z on input x if $f(x) = y$, and otherwise outputs $\perp$. In our case, $f = \mathsf{Can}_A$, $y = \mathsf{Can}_A(s)$, and $z = m$. Goyal et al. [GKW17] and Wichs et al. [WZ17] show that, assuming LWE or assuming iO and certain PRGs, a compute-and-compare program can be obfuscated provided y is (computationally) unpredictable given the function f and the auxiliary information. More precisely, the obfuscation guarantee is that the obfuscated compute-and-compare program is indistinguishable from the obfuscation of a (simulated) program that outputs zero on every input (notice, as a sanity check, that if y is unpredictable given f, then the compute-and-compare program must output zero almost everywhere as well).

We will provide more discussion on compute-and-compare obfuscation for unpredictable distributions in the presence of quantum auxiliary input in Sect. 3.1 and the full version.

- By the security of iO, we can replace the ciphertext $(0, iO(C))$, with the ciphertext $(0, iO(CC.Obf(\widetilde{C})))$ where CC.Obf is an obfuscator for compute-and-compare programs (this is because C has the same functionality as $CC.Obf(\widetilde{C})$).
- By the security of CC.Obf, we can replace the latter with $(0, iO(CC.Obf(Z)))$, where Z is the zero program. It is clearly impossible to decrypt from the latter, since no information about the message is present.

Thus, assuming iO cannot be broken, a Bob that is able to decrypt implies an adversary breaking the compute-and-compare obfuscation. This implies that there must be an efficient algorithm that can predict $y = Can_A(s)$ with non-negligible probability given the function Can_A and the auxiliary information received by Bob. Similarly for Charlie.

Therefore, if Bob and Charlie, with their own quantum auxiliary information, can both independently decrypt respectively $(0, iO(C))$ and $(1, iO(C'))$ with high probability (where here C and C' only differ in that the former releases the encrypted message on input a vector in $A + s$, and C' on input a vector in $A^{\perp} + s'$), then there exist efficient quantum algorithms for Bob and Charlie that take as input the descriptions of $Can_A(\cdot)$ and $Can_{A^{\perp}}(\cdot)$ respectively (or of the subspace A), and their respective auxiliary information, and recover $Can_A(s)$ and $Can_{A^{\perp}}(s')$ respectively with non-negligible probability. Since $Can_A(s) \in A + s$ and $Can_{A^{\perp}}(s') \in A^{\perp} + s'$, this violates the strong monogamy property of coset states described in Sect. 1.1.

Recall that this states that Alice, Bob and Charlie cannot cooperatively win the following game with a challenger, except with negligible probability. The challenger first prepares a uniformly random coset state $|A_{s,s'}\rangle$ and gives the state to Alice. Alice outputs two (possibly entangled) quantum states and sends them to Bob and Charlie respectively. Finally, Bob and Charlie both get the description of the subspace A. The game is won if Bob outputs a vector in $A + s$ and Charlie outputs a vector in $A^{\perp} + s'$. Crucially, in this monogamy property, Bob and Charlie will both receive the description of the subspace A in the final stage, yet it is still not possible for both of them to be simultaneously successful.

What allows to deduce the existence of efficient extracting algorithms is the fact that the obfuscation of compute-and-compare programs from [GKW17, WZ17] holds provided y is computationally unpredictable given f (and the auxiliary information). Thus, an algorithm that breaks the obfuscation property implies an efficient algorithm that outputs y (with noticeable probability) given f (and the auxiliary information).

In our other construction from signature tokens and extractable witness encryption, one can directly reduce unclonable decryption security to direct product hardness. We do not discuss the details of this construction here, instead we refer the reader to the full version.

2.3   Copy-Protecting PRFs

Our last contribution is the construction of copy-protected PRFs assuming post-quantum iO, one-way functions and the monogamy property we discussed in the previous section. Alternatively just as for unclonable decryption, we can do away with the monogamy property by assuming extractable witness encryption.

A copy-protectable PRF is a regular PRF $F : \{0,1\}^k \times \{0,1\}^m \rightarrow \{0,1\}^{m'}$, except that it is augmented with a *quantum key* generation procedure, which we refer to as QKeyGen. This takes as input the classical PRF key K and outputs a quantum state ρ_K. The state ρ_K allows to efficiently compute $F(K, x)$ on any input x (where correctness holds with overwhelming probability). Beyond the standard PRF security, the copy-protected PRF satisfies the following additional security guarantee: any computationally bounded adversary that receives ρ_K cannot process ρ_K into two states, such that each state enables efficient evaluation of $F(K, \cdot)$ on uniformly random inputs.

A simplified version of our construction has the following structure. For the rest of the section, we take all subspaces to be of $\mathbb{F}_2^n$ with dimension $n/2$.

– The quantum key generation procedure QKeyGen takes as input a classical PRF key K and outputs a quantum key. The latter consists of a number of uniformly sampled coset states $|(A_i)_{s_i,s_i'}\rangle$, for $i \in [\lambda]$, together with a (classical) *obfuscation* of the classical program P that operates as follows. P takes an input of the form $(x, v_1, \ldots, v_\lambda)$; checks that each vector v_i belongs to the correct coset ($A_i + s_i$ if $x_i = 0$, and $A_i^\perp + s_i'$ if $x_i = 1$); if so, outputs the value $F(K, x)$, otherwise outputs $\perp$.
– A party in possession of the quantum key can evaluate the PRF on input x as follows: for each i such that $x_i = 1$, apply $H^{\otimes n}$ to $|(A_i)_{s_i,s_i'}\rangle$. Measure each resulting coset state in the standard basis to obtain vectors $v_1, \ldots, v_\lambda$. Run the obfuscated program on input $(x, v_1, \ldots, v_\lambda)$.

Notice that the program has the classical PRF key K hardcoded, as well as the values A_i, s_i, s_i', so giving the program in the clear to the adversary would be completely insecure: once the adversary knows the key K, he can trivially copy the functionality $F(K, \cdot)$; and even if the key K is hidden by the obfuscation, but the A_i, s_i, s_i' are known, a copy of the (classical) obfuscated program P, together with the A_i, s_i, s_i' is sufficient to evaluate $F(K, \cdot)$ on any input.

So, the hope is that an appropriate obfuscation will be sufficient to hide all of these parameters. If this is the case, then the intuition for why the scheme is secure is that in order for two parties to simultaneously evaluate correctly on uniformly random inputs, each party should be able to produce a vector in $A_i + s$ or in $A_i^\perp + s_i'$. If the two parties accomplish this separately, then this implies that it is possible to simultaneously extract a vector in $A_i + s_i$ and one in $A_i^\perp + s_i'$, which should not be possible.[1]

We will use iO to obfuscate the program P. In the next part of this overview, we will discuss how we are able to deal with the fact that the PRF key K and the cosets are hardcoded in the program P. First of all, we describe a bit more precisely the copy-protection security that we wish to achieve. The latter is captured by the following security game between a challenger and an adversary (A, B, C):

- The challenger samples a uniformly random PRF key K and runs QKeyGen to generate ρ_K. Sends ρ_K to A.
- A sends quantum registers to two spatially separated parties B and C.
- The challenger samples uniformly random inputs x, x' to $F(K, \cdot)$. Sends x to B and x' to C.
- B and C return y and y' respectively to the challenger.

(A, B, C) wins if $y = F(K, x)$ and $y' = F(K, x')$.

Since the obfuscation we are using is not VBB, but only iO, there are two potential issues with security. B and C could be returning correct answers not because they are able to produce vectors in the appropriate cosets, but because:

(i) iO(P) leaks information about the PRF key K.
(ii) iO(P) leaks information about the cosets.

We handle issue (i) via a delicate "puncturing" argument [SW14]. At a high level, a puncturable PRF F is a PRF augmented with a procedure that takes a key K and an input value x, and produces a "punctured" key $K \setminus \{x\}$, which enables evaluation of $F(K, \cdot)$ at any point other than x. The security guarantee is that a computationally bounded adversary possessing the punctured key $K\setminus\{x\}$ cannot distinguish between $F(K, x)$ and a uniformly random value (more generally, one can puncture the key at any polynomially sized set of points). Puncturable PRFs can be obtained from OWFs using the [GGM86] construction [BW13].

By puncturing K precisely at the challenge inputs x and x', one is able to hardcode a punctured PRF key $K \setminus \{x, x'\}$ in the program P, instead of K, and setting the output of program P at x to uniformly random z and z', instead of to $F(K, x)$ and $F(K, x')$ respectively. The full argument is technical, and relies on the "hidden trigger" technique introduced in [SW14], which allows the "puncturing" technique to work even when the program P is generated before x and x' are sampled.

Once we have replaced the outputs of the program P on the challenge inputs x, x' with uniformly random outputs z, z', we can handle issue (ii) in a similar way to the case of unclonable decryption in the previous section.

---

[1] Again, we point out that we could not draw this conclusion if only a single party were able to do the following two things, each with non-negligible probability: produce a vector in $A + s_i$ and produce a vector in $A^\perp + s_i'$. This is because in a quantum world, being able to perform two tasks with good probability, does not imply being able to perform both tasks simultaneously. So it is crucial that both parties are able to separately recover the vectors.

By the security of iO, we can replace the behaviour of program P at x by a suitable functionally equivalent compute-and-compare program that checks membership in the appropriate cosets. We then replace this by an obfuscation of the same compute-and-compare program, and finally by an obfuscation of the zero program. We can then perform a similar reduction as in the previous section from an adversary breaking copy-protection security (and thus the security of the compute-and-compare obfuscation) to an adversary breaking the monogamy of entanglement game described in the previous section.

As in the previous section, we can replace the reliance on the conjectured monogamy property by extractable witness encryption. In fact, formally, we directly reduce the security of our copy-protected PRFs to the security of our unclonable decryption scheme.

3   Preliminaries

In this paper, we use λ to denote security parameters. We denote a function belonging to the class of polynomial functions by $\mathsf{poly}(\cdot)$. We say a function $f(\cdot) : \mathbb{N} \to \mathbb{R}^+$ is negligible if for all constant $c > 0$, $f(n) < \frac{1}{n^c}$ for all large enough n. We use $\mathsf{negl}(\cdot)$ to denote a negligible function. We say a function $f(\cdot) : \mathbb{N} \to \mathbb{R}^+$ is sub-exponential if there exists a constant $0 < c \leq 1$, such that $f(n) \geq 2^{n^c}$ for all large enough n. We use $\mathsf{subexp}(\cdot)$ to denote a sub-exponential function. When we refer to a probabilistic algorithm $\mathcal{A}$, sometimes we need to specify the randomness r used by $\mathcal{A}$ when running on some input x. We write this as $\mathcal{A}(x; r)$. For a finite set S, we use $x \leftarrow S$ to denote uniform sampling of x from the set S. We denote $[n] = \{1, 2, \cdots, n\}$. A binary string $x \in \{0,1\}^\ell$ is represented as $x_1 x_2 \cdots x_\ell$. For two strings x, y, $x \| y$ is the concatenation of x and y. We refer to a probabilistic polynomial-time and quantum polynomial time algorithm as PPT and QPT respectively.

For the rest of this paper, we will assume that all the classical cryptographic primitives used are post-quantum secure, and we sometimes omit this description for simplicity, except in formal definitions and theorems.

We omit the definitions of extracting, puncturable PRFs, injective puncturable PRFs, indistinguishability obfuscation (iO), and subspace hiding obfuscation (shO). We refer the reader to the full version for these.

3.1   Compute-and-Compare Obfuscation

Definition 1 (Compute-and-Compare Program). *Given a function $f : \{0,1\}^{\ell_{in}} \to \{0,1\}^{\ell_{out}}$ along with a target value $y \in \{0,1\}^{\ell_{out}}$ and a message $z \in \{0,1\}^{\ell_{msg}}$, we define the compute-and-compare program:*

$$\mathsf{CC}[f, y, z](x) = \begin{cases} z & \text{if } f(x) = y \\ \bot & \text{otherwise} \end{cases}$$

We define the following class of *unpredictable distributions* over pairs of the form $(\mathsf{CC}[f, y, z], \mathsf{aux})$, where aux is auxiliary quantum information. These distributions are such that y is computationally unpredictable given f and aux.

Definition 2 (Unpredictable/Sub-exponentially Unpredictable Distributions). *We say that a family of distributions $D = \{D_\lambda\}$ where D_λ is a distribution over pairs of the form* $(\mathsf{CC}[f, y, z], \mathsf{aux})$ *where* aux *is a quantum state, belongs to the class of* unpredictable distributions *if the following holds. There exists a negligible function* negl, *for all QPT algorithms $\mathcal{A}$,*

$$\Pr_{(\mathsf{CC}[f,y,z],\mathsf{aux})\leftarrow D_\lambda} \left[A(1^\lambda, f, \mathsf{aux}) = y\right] \leq \mathsf{negl}(\lambda).$$

If there exists a sub-exponential function subexp *such that, for all QPT algorithms $\mathcal{A}$, the above probability is at most $1/\mathsf{subexp}(\lambda)$, we say it belongs to the class of sub-exponentially unpredictable distributions.*

Definition 3 (Compute-and-Compare Obfuscation). *A PPT algorithm* $\mathsf{CC.Obf}$ *is an obfuscator for the class of unpredictable distributions (or subexponentially unpredictable distributions) if for any family of distributions $D = \{D_\lambda\}$ belonging to the class, the following holds:*

- *Functionality Preserving: there exists a negligible function* negl *such that for all λ, every program P in the support of D_λ,*

$$\Pr[\forall x, \ \widetilde{P}(x) = P(x), \ \widetilde{P} \leftarrow \mathsf{CC.Obf}(1^\lambda, P)] \geq 1 - \mathsf{negl}(\lambda)$$

- *Distributional Indistinguishability: there exists an efficient simulator* Sim *such that:*

$$(\mathsf{CC.Obf}(1^\lambda, P), \mathsf{aux}) \approx_c (\mathsf{Sim}(1^\lambda, P.\mathsf{param}), \mathsf{aux})$$

where $(P, \mathsf{aux}) \leftarrow D_\lambda$ and $P.\mathsf{param}$ consists the parameters of the circuit, including input size, output size, circuit size and etc.

Combining the results of [WZ17, GKW17] with those of [Zha19c], one obtains the following theorem. We refer to the full version for proofs and discussions.

Theorem 6. *Assuming the existence of post-quantum* iO *and the quantum hardness of LWE, there exist obfuscators for sub-exponentially unpredictable distributions, as in Definition 3.*

4 Coset States

This section is organized as follows. In Sect. 4.1, we introduce coset states. In Sect. 4.2, we show that coset states satisfy both an information-theoretic and a computational *direct product hardness* property. The latter immediately yields a signature token scheme in the plain model assuming iO, (this is described in Sect. 5). In Sect. 4.3 we show that coset states satisfy both an information-theoretic *monogamy of entanglement* property (analogous to that satisfied by BB84 states [TFKW13]), and a computational monogamy of entanglement property. The latter is used to obtain an unclonable decryption scheme from iO and extractable witness encryption (which will be presented in the full version). In Sect. 4.4, we describe a *strong version* of the monogamy property, which we conjecture to be true. The latter is used in Sect. 6.2 to obtain an unclonable decryption scheme which does not assume extractable witness encryption.

4.1   Definitions

In this subsection, we provide the basic definitions and properties of coset states.

For any subspace A, its complement is $A^\perp = \{b \in \mathbb{F}^n \mid \langle a, b \rangle \bmod 2 = 0\,,\, \forall a \in A\}$. It satisfies $\dim(A) + \dim(A^\perp) = n$. We also let $|A| = 2^{\dim(A)}$ denote the size of the subspace A.

Definition 4 (Subspace States). *For any subspace $A \subseteq \mathbb{F}_2^n$, the subspace state $|A\rangle$ is defined as*

$$|A\rangle = \frac{1}{\sqrt{|A|}} \sum_{a \in A} |a\rangle.$$

Note that given A, the subspace state $|A\rangle$ can be constructed efficiently.

Definition 5 (Coset States). *For any subspace $A \subseteq \mathbb{F}_2^n$ and vectors $s, s' \in \mathbb{F}_2^n$, the coset state $|A_{s,s'}\rangle$ is defined as:*

$$|A_{s,s'}\rangle = \frac{1}{\sqrt{|A|}} \sum_{a \in A} (-1)^{\langle s', a \rangle} |a + s\rangle.$$

Note that by applying $H^{\otimes n}$, which is QFT for $\mathbb{F}_2^n$, to the state $|A_{s,s'}\rangle$, one obtains exactly $|A^\perp_{s',s}\rangle$.

Additionally, note that given $|A\rangle$ and s, s', one can efficiently construct $|A_{s,s'}\rangle$ as follows:

$$\sum_a |a\rangle \xrightarrow{\text{add } s} \sum_a |a + s\rangle \xrightarrow{H^{\otimes n}} \sum_{a' \in A^\perp} (-1)^{\langle a', s \rangle} |a'\rangle$$

$$\xrightarrow{\text{adding } s'} \sum_{a' \in A^\perp} (-1)^{\langle a', s \rangle} |a' + s'\rangle \xrightarrow{H^{\otimes n}} \sum_{a \in A} (-1)^{\langle a, s' \rangle} |a + s\rangle$$

For a subspace A and vectors s, s', we define $A + s = \{v + s : v \in A\}$, and $A^\perp + s' = \{v + s' : v \in A^\perp\}$.

When it is clear from the context, for ease of notation, we will write $A + s$ to mean the *program* that checks membership in $A + s$. For example, we will often write $\mathsf{iO}(A + s)$ to mean an iO obfuscation of the program that checks membership in $A + s$.

4.2   Direct Product Hardness

We describe the computational *direct product hardness* property satisfied by coset states. For more details, and a proof, we refer the reader to the full version.

Theorem 7. *Assume the existence of post-quantum* iO *and one-way function. Let $A \subseteq \mathbb{F}_2^n$ be a uniformly random subspace of dimension $n/2$, and s, s' be uniformly random in $\mathbb{F}_2^n$. Given one copy of $|A_{s,s'}\rangle$, $\mathsf{iO}(A+s)$ and $\mathsf{iO}(A^\perp + s')$, any polynomial time adversary outputs a pair (v, w) such that $v \in A + s$ and $w \in A^\perp + s'$ with negligible probability.*

The proof follows a similar outline to the proof of security of public-key quantum money in [Zha19a]. The main difference is that our proof handles (and leverages) coset states, instead of regular subspace states.

4.3 Monogamy-of-Entanglement Property

In this subsection, we argue that coset states satisfy an information-theoretic and a computational monogamy-of-entanglement property. We will not make use of these properties directly, instead we will have to rely on a stronger conjectured monogamy-of-entanglement property, which is presented in Subsect. 4.4. Thus, the properties that we prove in this subsection serve merely as "evidence" in support of the stronger conjecture. Due to lack of space, we only discuss the computational monogamy-of-entanglement property.

The game is between a challenger and an adversary $(\mathcal{A}_0, \mathcal{A}_1, \mathcal{A}_2)$.

- The challenger picks a uniformly random subspace $A \subseteq \mathbb{F}^n$ of dimension $\frac{n}{2}$, and two uniformly random elements $s, s' \in \mathbb{F}_2^n$. It sends $|A_{s,s'}\rangle$, $\mathsf{iO}(A+s)$, and $\mathsf{iO}(A^\perp + s')$ to $\mathcal{A}_0$.
- $\mathcal{A}_0$ creates a bipartite state on registers B and C. Then, $\mathcal{A}_0$ sends register B to $\mathcal{A}_1$, and C to $\mathcal{A}_2$.
- The description of A is then sent to both $\mathcal{A}_1, \mathcal{A}_2$.
- $\mathcal{A}_1$ and $\mathcal{A}_2$ return respectively (s_1, s_1') and (s_2, s_2').

$(\mathcal{A}_0, \mathcal{A}_1, \mathcal{A}_2)$ wins if, for $i \in \{1, 2\}$, $s_i \in A + s$ and $s_i' \in A^\perp + s'$.

Let $\mathsf{CompMonogamy}((\mathcal{A}_0, \mathcal{A}_1, \mathcal{A}_2), n)$ be a random variable which takes the value 1 if the game above is won, and takes the value 0 otherwise.

Theorem 8. *Assume the existence of post-quantum* iO *and one-way function, there exists a negligible function* $\mathsf{negl}(\cdot)$, *for any QPT adversary* $(\mathcal{A}_0, \mathcal{A}_1, \mathcal{A}_2)$,

$$\Pr[\mathsf{CompMonogamy}((\mathcal{A}_0, \mathcal{A}_1, \mathcal{A}_2), n) = 1] = \mathsf{negl}(n).$$

4.4 Conjectured Strong Monogamy Property

In this section, we describe a stronger version of the monogamy property, which we conjecture to hold. The monogamy property is a slight (but significant) variation of the one stated in the last section (which we proved to be true). Recall that there $\mathcal{A}_1$ and $\mathcal{A}_2$ are required to return pairs (s_1, s_1') and (s_2, s_2') respectively, such that both $s_1, s_2 \in A + s$ and $s_1', s_2' \in A^\perp + s'$. Now, we require that it is hard for $\mathcal{A}_1$ and $\mathcal{A}_2$ to even return a single string s_1 and s_2 respectively such that $s_1 \in A + s$ and $s_2 \in A^\perp + s'$.

Formally, consider the following game between a challenger and an adversary $(\mathcal{A}_0, \mathcal{A}_1, \mathcal{A}_2)$.

- The challenger picks a uniformly random subspace $A \subseteq \mathbb{F}_2^n$ of dimension $\frac{n}{2}$, and two uniformly random elements $s, s' \in \mathbb{F}_2^n$. It sends $|A_{s,s'}\rangle$ to $\mathcal{A}_0$.
- $\mathcal{A}_0$ creates a bipartite state on registers B and C. Then, $\mathcal{A}_0$ sends register B to $\mathcal{A}_1$, and C to $\mathcal{A}_2$.
- The description of A is then sent to both $\mathcal{A}_1, \mathcal{A}_2$.
- $\mathcal{A}_1$ and $\mathcal{A}_2$ return respectively s_1 and s_2.

Let $\mathsf{ITStrongMonogamy}((\mathcal{A}_0, \mathcal{A}_1, \mathcal{A}_2), n)$ be a random variable which takes the value 1 if the game above is won by adversary $(\mathcal{A}_0, \mathcal{A}_1, \mathcal{A}_2)$, and takes the value 0 otherwise. We conjecture the following:

Conjecture 1. There exists a sub-exponential function subexp such that, for any (unbounded) adversary $(\mathcal{A}_0, \mathcal{A}_1, \mathcal{A}_2)$,

$$\Pr[\mathsf{ITStrongMonogamy}((\mathcal{A}_0, \mathcal{A}_1, \mathcal{A}_2), n) = 1] \leq 1/\mathsf{subexp}(n).$$

Assuming the conjecture is true, and assuming post-quantum iO and one-way functions, we are able to prove the following computational strong monogamy statement. Consider a game between a challenger and an adversary $(\mathcal{A}_0, \mathcal{A}_1, \mathcal{A}_2)$, which is identical to the one described above except that all $\mathcal{A}_0$ additionally gets the membership checking programs $\mathsf{iO}(A + s)$ and $\mathsf{iO}(A^\perp + s')$.

- The challenger picks a uniformly random subspace $A \subseteq \mathbb{F}_2^n$ of dimension $\frac{n}{2}$, and two uniformly random elements $s, s' \in \mathbb{F}_2^n$. It sends $|A_{s,s'}\rangle$, $\mathsf{iO}(A + s)$, and $\mathsf{iO}(A^\perp + s')$ to $\mathcal{A}_0$.
- $\mathcal{A}_0$ creates a bipartite state on registers B and C. Then, $\mathcal{A}_0$ sends register B to $\mathcal{A}_1$, and C to $\mathcal{A}_2$.
- The description of A is then sent to both $\mathcal{A}_1, \mathcal{A}_2$.
- $\mathcal{A}_1$ and $\mathcal{A}_2$ return respectively s_1 and s_2.

$(\mathcal{A}_0, \mathcal{A}_1, \mathcal{A}_2)$ wins if, for $s_1 \in A + s$ and $s_2 \in A^\perp + s'$.

Let $\mathsf{CompStrongMonogamy}((\mathcal{A}_0, \mathcal{A}_1, \mathcal{A}_2), n)$ be a random variable which takes the value 1 if the game above is won, and takes the value 0 otherwise.

Theorem 9. *Assuming Conjecture 1 holds, and assuming the existence of post-quantum iO and one-way functions, then there exists a negligible function $\mathsf{negl}(\cdot)$, for any QPT adversary $(\mathcal{A}_0, \mathcal{A}_1, \mathcal{A}_2)$,*

$$\Pr[\mathsf{CompStrongMonogamy}((\mathcal{A}_0, \mathcal{A}_1, \mathcal{A}_2), n) = 1] = \mathsf{negl}(n).$$

We can further show a 'sub-exponential strong monogamy property' if we additionally assume sub-exponentially secure iO and one-way functions.

Theorem 10. *Assuming Conjecture 1 holds, and assuming the existence of sub-exponentially secure post-quantum iO and one-way functions, then for any QPT adversary $(\mathcal{A}_0, \mathcal{A}_1, \mathcal{A}_2)$,*

$$\Pr[\mathsf{CompStrongMonogamy}((\mathcal{A}_0, \mathcal{A}_1, \mathcal{A}_2), n) = 1] \leq 1/\mathsf{subexp}(n).$$

In the rest of the work, whenever we mention the 'strong monogamy property', we refer to the computational monogamy property of Theorem 9 above. Whenever we mention the 'sub-exponentially strong monogamy property', we refer to the computational monogamy property of Theorem 10.

5   Tokenized Signature Scheme from iO

In this section, we present tokenized signature scheme based on the computational direct product hardness property (Theorem 7).

5.1   Definitions

Definition 6 (Tokenized signature scheme). *A tokenized signature (TS) scheme consists of a tuple of QPT algorithms* (KeyGen, TokenGen, Sign, Verify) *with the following properties:*

- KeyGen(1^λ) $\to$ (sk, pk)*: Takes as input* 1^λ*, where* λ *is a security parameter, and outputs a secret key, public (verification) key pair* (sk, pk)*.*
- TokenGen(sk) $\to$ |tk⟩*: Takes as input a secret key* sk *and outputs a signing token* |tk⟩*.*
- Sign(m, |tk⟩) $\to$ (m, sig)/$\perp$*: Takes as input a message* $m \in \{0,1\}^*$ *and a token* |tk⟩*, and outputs either a message, signature pair* (m, sig) *or* $\perp$*.*
- Verify(pk, m, sig) $\to$ 0/1*: Takes as input an verification key, an alleged message, signature pair* (m, sig)*, and outputs 0 ("reject") or 1 ("accept").*

These algorithms satisfy the following. First is correctness. There exists a negligible function negl($\cdot$), for any $\lambda \in \mathbb{N}$, $m \in \{0,1\}^*$,

$$\Pr[\mathsf{Verify}(\mathsf{pk}, m, \mathsf{sig}) = 1 : (m, \mathsf{sig}) \leftarrow \mathsf{Sign}(m, |\mathsf{tk}\rangle), |\mathsf{tk}\rangle \leftarrow \mathsf{TokenGen}(\mathsf{sk}),$$
$$(\mathsf{sk}, \mathsf{pk}) \leftarrow \mathsf{KeyGen}(1^\lambda)] \geq 1 - \mathsf{negl}(\lambda).$$

Definition 7 (Length restricted TS scheme). *A TS scheme is* r*-restricted if it holds only for* $m \in \{0,1\}^r$*. We refer to a scheme that is* 1*-restricted as a one-bit TS scheme.*

For notational purposes, we introduce an additional algorithm Verify_ℓ. The latter takes as input a public key pk and ℓ pairs $(m_\ell, \mathsf{sig}_\ell), \ldots, (m_\ell, \mathsf{sig}_\ell)$. It checks that $m_i \neq m_j$ for all $i \neq j$, and $\mathsf{Verify}(m_i, \mathsf{sig}_i) = 1$ for all $i \in [\ell]$; it outputs 1 if and only if they all hold. Next we define unforgeability.

Definition 8 (1-Unforgeability). *A TS scheme is* 1*-unforgeable if for every QPT adversary* $\mathcal{A}$*, there exists a negligible function* negl($\cdot$)*, for every* λ*:*

$$\Pr\left[\begin{array}{l} (m_0, \mathsf{sig}_0, m_1, \mathsf{sig}_1) \leftarrow \mathcal{A}(\mathsf{pk}, |\mathsf{tk}\rangle) \\ \mathsf{Verify}_2(\mathsf{pk}, m_0, \mathsf{sig}_0, m_1, \mathsf{sig}_1) = 1 \end{array} : \begin{array}{l} (\mathsf{sk}, \mathsf{pk}) \leftarrow \mathsf{KeyGen}(1^\lambda) \\ |\mathsf{tk}\rangle \leftarrow \mathsf{TokenGen}(\mathsf{sk}) \end{array} \right] \leq \mathsf{negl}(\lambda).$$

Definition 9 (Unforgeability). *A TS scheme is unforgeable if for every QPT adversary* $\mathcal{A}$*, there exists a negligible function* negl($\cdot$)*, for every* λ*,* $l = \mathsf{poly}(\lambda)$*:*

$$\Pr\left[\begin{array}{l} \{m_i, \mathsf{sig}_i\}_{i \in [l+1]} \leftarrow \mathcal{A}(\mathsf{pk}, \{|\mathsf{tk}_i\rangle\}_{i \in [l]}) \\ \mathsf{Verify}_{l+1}(\mathsf{pk}, \{m_i, \mathsf{sig}_i\}_{i \in [l+1]}) = 1 \end{array} : \begin{array}{l} (\mathsf{sk}, \mathsf{pk}) \leftarrow \mathsf{KeyGen}(1^\lambda) \\ |\mathsf{tk}_1\rangle \leftarrow \mathsf{TokenGen}(\mathsf{sk}) \\ \vdots \\ |\mathsf{tk}_l\rangle \leftarrow \mathsf{TokenGen}(\mathsf{sk}) \end{array} \right] \leq \mathsf{negl}(\lambda).$$

A tokenized signature scheme should also satisfy a revocability property. The revocability property follows straightforwardly from unforgeability [BS16]. Thus to show a construction is secure, we only need to focus on proving unforgeability.

The following theorem says that 1-unforgeability is sufficient to achieve a full blown TS scheme.

Theorem 11 ([BS16]). *A one-bit 1-unforgeable TS scheme implies a (full blown) TS scheme, assuming the existence of a quantum-secure digital signature scheme.*

In the next section, we give our construction of a one-bit 1-unforgeable TS scheme from coset states.

5.2   Tokenized Signature Construction

Construction.

- KeyGen(1^λ): *Set* $n = \mathsf{poly}(\lambda)$. *Sample uniformly* $A \subseteq \mathbb{F}_2^n$. *Sample* $s, s' \leftarrow \mathbb{F}_2^n$. *Output* $\mathsf{sk} = (A, s, s')$ *(where by A we mean a description of the subspace A) and* $\mathsf{pk} = (\mathsf{iO}(A + s), \mathsf{iO}(A^\perp + s'))$.
- TokenGen(sk): *Takes as input* sk *of the form* (A, s, s'). *Outputs* $|\mathsf{tk}\rangle = |A_{s,s'}\rangle$.
- Sign($m, |\mathsf{tk}\rangle$): *Takes as input* $m \in \{0, 1\}$ *and a state* $|\mathsf{tk}\rangle$ *on n qubits. Compute* $H^{\otimes n}|\mathsf{tk}\rangle$ *if $m = 1$, otherwise do nothing to the quantum state. It then measures in the standard basis. Let* sig *be the outcome. Output* (m, sig).
- Verify(pk, (m, sig)): *Parse* pk *as* $\mathsf{pk} = (C_0, C_1)$ *where C_0 and C_1 are circuits. Output* $C_m(\mathsf{sig})$.

Theorem 12. *Assuming post-quantum iO and one-way function, the scheme of Construction 5.2 is a one-bit 1-unforgeable tokenized signature scheme.*

Proof. Security follows immediately from Theorem 7.   □

Corollary 1. *Assuming post-quantum iO, one-way function(which implies digital signature) and a quantum-secure digital signature scheme, there exists a (full blown) tokenized signature scheme.*

Proof. This is an immediate consequence of Theorems 11 and 12.   □

6   Single-Decryptor Encryption

In this section, we formally introduce unclonable decryption, i.e. single-decryptor encryption [GZ20]. Then we describe two constructions and prove their security.

Our first construction (Sect. 6.2) relies on the strong monogamy-of-entanglement property (Conjecture 1), the existence of post-quantum one-way function, indistinguishability obfuscation and compute-and-compare obfuscation for (sub-exponentially) unpredictable distributions (whose existence has been discussed in Theorem 3.1). Our second construction has a similar structure.

It does not rely on the strong monogamy-of-entanglement property for coset states, but on the (weaker) direct product hardness property (Theorem 7). However, the construction additionally relies on a much stronger cryptographic primitive – post-quantum extractable witness encryption (as well post-quantum one-way functions and indistinguishability obfuscation). Due to lack of space, we refer the reader to the full version for further the latter construction.

6.1 Definitions

Definition 10 (Single-Decryptor Encryption Scheme). *A single-decryptor encryption scheme consists of the following efficient algorithms:*

- Setup$(1^\lambda) \rightarrow (\mathsf{sk}, \mathsf{pk})$: *a (classical) probabilistic algorithm that takes as input a security parameter λ and outputs a classical secret key sk and public key pk.*
- QKeyGen$(\mathsf{sk}) \rightarrow \rho_{\mathsf{sk}}$: *a quantum algorithm that takes as input a secret key sk and outputs a quantum secret key ρ_{sk}.*
- Enc$(\mathsf{pk}, m) \rightarrow \mathsf{ct}$: *a (classical) probabilistic algorithm that takes as input a public key pk, a message m and outputs a classical ciphertext ct.*
- Dec$(\rho_{\mathsf{sk}}, \mathsf{ct}) \rightarrow m/\bot$: *a quantum algorithm that takes as input a quantum secret key ρ_{sk} and a ciphertext ct, and outputs a message m or a decryption failure symbol $\bot$.*

A secure single-decryptor encryption scheme should satisfy the following:

Correctness: There exists a negligible function $\mathsf{negl}(\cdot)$, for all $\lambda \in \mathbb{N}$, for all $m \in \mathcal{M}$,

$$\Pr\left[\mathsf{Dec}(\rho_{\mathsf{sk}}, \mathsf{ct}) = m \ \middle| \ \begin{array}{c} (\mathsf{sk}, \mathsf{pk}) \leftarrow \mathsf{Setup}(1^\lambda), \rho_{\mathsf{sk}} \leftarrow \mathsf{QKeyGen}(\mathsf{sk}) \\ \mathsf{ct} \leftarrow \mathsf{Enc}(\mathsf{pk}, m) \end{array}\right] \geq 1 - \mathsf{negl}(\lambda)$$

Note that correctness implies that a honestly generated quantum decryption key can be used to decrypt correctly polynomially many times, from the gentle measurement lemma [Aar05].

CPA Security: The scheme should satisfy (post-quantum) CPA security, i.e. indistinguishability under chosen-plaintext attacks: for every (stateful) QPT adversary $\mathcal{A}$, there exists a negligible function $\mathsf{negl}(\cdot)$ such that for all $\lambda \in \mathbb{N}$, the following holds:

$$\Pr\left[\mathcal{A}(\mathsf{ct}) = b : \begin{array}{c} (\mathsf{sk}, \mathsf{pk}) \leftarrow \mathsf{Setup}(1^\lambda) \\ ((m_0, m_1) \in \mathcal{M}^2) \leftarrow \mathcal{A}(1^\lambda, \mathsf{pk}) \\ b \leftarrow \{0, 1\}; \mathsf{ct} \leftarrow \mathsf{Enc}(\mathsf{pk}, m_b) \end{array}\right] \leq \frac{1}{2} + \mathsf{negl}(\lambda),$$

Anti-Piracy Security. Next, we define anti-piracy security via the anti-piracy game below. Recall that, intuitively, anti-piracy security says that it is infeasible for a pirate who receives a quantum secret key to produce two quantum keys, which both allow successful decryption. This can be formalized as:

(CPA-style Anti-piracy) We ask the pirate to provide a pair of messages (m_0, m_1) along with two quantum secret keys, and we test whether the two keys allow to (simultanoeusly) distinguish encryptions of m_0 and m_1.

In order to describe the security games, it is convenient to first introduce the concept of a *quantum decryptor*. The following definition is implicitly with respect to some single-decryptor encryption scheme (Setup, QKeyGen, Enc, Dec).

Definition 11 (Quantum decryptor). *A quantum decryptor for ciphertexts of length n, is a pair (ρ, U) where ρ is a state, and U is a general quantum circuit acting on $n + m$ qubits, where m is the number of qubits of ρ.*

For a ciphertext c of length n, we say that we run the quantum decryptor (ρ, U) on ciphertext c to mean that we execute the circuit U on inputs $|c\rangle$ and ρ.

We are now ready to describe the CPA-style anti-piracy game.

Definition 12 (Anti-Piracy Game, CPA-style). *Let $\lambda \in \mathbb{N}^+$. The CPA-style anti-piracy game is the following game between a challenger and an adversary $\mathcal{A}$.*

1. **Setup Phase:** *The challenger samples keys $(\mathsf{sk}, \mathsf{pk}) \leftarrow \mathsf{Setup}(1^\lambda)$.*
2. **Quantum Key Generation Phase:** *The challenger sends $\mathcal{A}$ the classical public key pk and one copy of quantum decryption key $\rho_{\mathsf{sk}} \leftarrow \mathsf{QKeyGen}(\mathsf{sk})$.*
3. **Output Phase:** *$\mathcal{A}$ outputs a pair of distinct messages (m_0, m_1). It also outputs a (possibly mixed and entangled) state σ over two registers R_1, R_2 and two general quantum circuits U_1 and U_2. We interpret $\mathcal{A}$'s output as two (possibly entangled) quantum decryptors $\mathsf{D}_1 = (\sigma[R_1], U_1)$ and $\mathsf{D}_2 = (\sigma[R_2], U_2)$.*
4. **Challenge Phase:** *The challenger samples b_1, b_2 and r_1, r_2 uniformly at random and generates ciphertexts $c_1 = \mathsf{Enc}(\mathsf{pk}, m_{b_1}; r_1)$ and $c_2 = \mathsf{Enc}(\mathsf{pk}, m_{b_2}; r_2)$. The challenger runs quantum decryptor D_1 on c_1 and D_2 on c_2, and checks that D_1 outputs m_{b_1} and D_2 outputs m_{b_2}. If so, the challenger outputs 1 (the game is won by the adversary), otherwise outputs 0.*

We denote by $\mathsf{AntiPiracyCPA}(1^\lambda, \mathcal{A})$ a random variable for the output of the game.

Note that an adversary can succeed in this game with probability at least $1/2$. It simply gives ρ_{sk} to the first quantum decryptor and the second decryptor randomly guesses the plaintext.

We remark that one could have equivalently formulated this definition by having the pirate send registers R_1 and R_2 to two separated parties Bob and Charlie, who then receive ciphertexts from the challenger sampled as in the Challenge Phase above. The two formulations are equivalent upon identifying the quantum circuits U_1 and U_2.

Definition 13 (Anti-Piracy Security, CPA-style). *Let $\gamma : \mathbb{N}^+ \to [0, 1]$. A single-decryptor encryption scheme satisfies γ-anti-piracy security, if for any QPT adversary $\mathcal{A}$, there exists a negligible function $\mathsf{negl}(\cdot)$ such that the following holds for all $\lambda \in \mathbb{N}$:*

$$\Pr\left[b = 1, b \leftarrow \mathsf{AntiPiracyCPA}(1^\lambda, \mathcal{A})\right] \leq \frac{1}{2} + \gamma(\lambda) + \mathsf{negl}(\lambda) \qquad (1)$$

It is not difficult to show that if γ-anti-piracy security holds for all inverse poly γ, then this directly implies CPA security (we refer the reader to the full version for the proof of this implication).

6.2   Construction from Strong Monogamy Property

In this section, we give our first construction of a single-decryptor encryption scheme, whose security relies on the strong monogamy-of-entanglement property from Sect. 4.4.

In the rest of the paper, to simplify notation, whenever it is clear from the context, we will denote a program that checks membership in a set S simply by S.

Construction 13.

- Setup(1^λ) → (sk, pk) :
    - *Sample κ random $(n/2)$-dimensional subspaces $A_i \subseteq \mathbb{F}_2^n$ for $i = 1, 2, \cdots, \kappa$, where $n = \lambda$ and $\kappa = \kappa(\lambda)$ is a polynomial in λ.*
    - *For each $i \in [\kappa]$, choose two uniformly random vectors $s_i, s_i' \in \mathbb{F}_2^n$.*
    - *Prepare the programs* iO($A_i + s_i$) *and* iO($A_i^\perp + s_i'$) *(where we assume that the programs $A_i + s_i$ and $A_i^\perp + s_i'$ are padded to some appropriate length).*
    - *Output* sk $= \{A_i, s_i, s_i'\}_{i \in [\kappa]}$, pk $= \{$iO($A_i + s_i$), iO($A_i^\perp + s_i'$)$\}_{i \in [\kappa]}$.
- QKeyGen(sk) → ρ_{sk} : *on input* sk $= \{A_i, s_i, s_i'\}_{i \in [\kappa]}$, *output the "quantum secret key"* $\rho_{sk} = \{|A_{i,s_i,s_i'}\rangle\}_{i \in [\kappa]}$. *Recall that each $|A_{i,s_i,s_i'}\rangle$ is*

$$|A_{i,s_i,s_i'}\rangle = \frac{1}{\sqrt{|A_i|}} \sum_{a \in A_i} (-1)^{\langle a, s_i'\rangle} |a + s_i\rangle.$$

- Enc(pk, m) → ct : *on input a public key* pk $= \{$iO($A_i + s_i$), iO($A_i^\perp + s_i'$)$\}_{i \in [\kappa]}$ *and message m:*
    - *Sample a uniformly random string $r \leftarrow \{0,1\}^\kappa$.*
    - *Let r_i be the i-th bit of r. Define $R_i^0 = $ iO($A_i + s_i$) and $R_i^1 = $ iO($A_i^\perp + s_i'$). Let $P_{m,r}$ be the following program:*

On input $u = u_1 \| u_2 \| \cdots \| u_\kappa$ (where each $u_i \in \mathbb{F}_2^n$):
 1. If for all $i \in [\kappa]$, $R_i^{r_i}(u_i) = 1$:
        Output m
 2. Else:
        Output $\perp$

Fig. 1. Program $P_{m,r}$

- *Let $\hat{P}_{m,r} = $ iO($P_{m,r}$). Output ciphertext* ct $= (\hat{P}_{m,r}, r)$.

- $\mathsf{Dec}(\rho_{\mathsf{sk}}, \mathsf{ct}) \to m/\bot$: *on input* $\rho_{\mathsf{sk}} = \{|A_{i,s_i,s_i'}\rangle\}_{i \in [\kappa]}$ *and* $\mathsf{ct} = (\hat{P}_{m,r}, r)$:
  - *For each* $i \in [\kappa]$, *if* $r_i = 1$, *apply* $H^{\otimes n}$ *to the i-th state* $|A_{i,s_i,s_i'}\rangle$; *if* $r_i = 0$, *leave the i-th state* $|A_{i,s_i,s_i'}\rangle$ *unchanged. Denote the resulting state by* ρ_{sk}^*.
  - *Evaluate the program* $\hat{P}_{m,r}$ *on input* ρ_{sk}^* *in superposition; measure the evaluation register and denote the outcome by* m'. *Output* m'.
  - *Rewind by applying the operations in the first step again.*

Correctness. Correctness and efficiency easily follow from the construction.

For security, we have the following theorem (proved in the full version) (Fig. 1):

Theorem 14 (Regular Anti-Piracy). *Assuming the existence of post-quantum iO, one-way functions, compute-and-compare obfuscation for the class of unpredictable distributions (as in Definition 3), and the strong monogamy-of-entanglement property (Conjecture 1), the single-decryptor encryption scheme of Construction 13 has regular γ-anti-piracy security for $\gamma = 0$.*

Similarly, assuming the existence of post-quantum sub-exponentially secure iO, one-way functions, the quantum hardness of LWE and assuming the strong monogamy-of-entanglement property (Conjecture 1), the single-decryptor encryption scheme of Construction 13 has regular γ-anti-piracy security for $\gamma = 0$.

In the above theorem, the quantum hardness of LWE is used to build compute-and-compare obfuscation for sub-exponentially unpredictable distributions.

7 Copy-Protection of Pseudorandom Functions

In this section, we formally define copy-protection of pseudorandom functions. Then, we describe a construction that essentially builds on the single-decryptor encryption scheme described in Sect. 6.2 (together with post-quantum sub-exponentially secure one-way functions and iO). We remark that all of the PRFs that we use can be constructed from post-quantum one-way functions. We refer the reader to [SW14] and the full version for further details.

7.1 Definitions

In what follows, the PRF $F : [K] \times [N] \to [M]$, implicitly depends on a security parameter λ. We denote by $\mathsf{Setup}(\cdot)$ the procedure that samples a PRF key.

Definition 14 (Copy-Protection of PRF). *A copy-protection scheme for a PRF $F : [K] \times [N] \to [M]$ consists of the following polynomial-time algorithms:*

$\mathsf{QKeyGen}(K)$: *takes a key K and outputs a quantum key ρ_K;*
$\mathsf{Eval}(\rho_K, x)$: *takes a quantum key ρ_K and an input $x \in [N]$. It outputs a classical string $y \in [M]$.*

A copy-protection scheme should satisfy the following properties:

Definition 15 (Correctness). *There exists a negligible function* $\mathsf{negl}(\cdot)$, *for all* λ, *all* $K \leftarrow \mathsf{Setup}(1^\lambda)$, *all inputs* x,

$$\Pr[\mathsf{Eval}(\rho_K, x) = F(K, x) : \rho_K \leftarrow \mathsf{QKeyGen}(K)] \geq 1 - \mathsf{negl}(\lambda).$$

Note that the correctness property implies that the evaluation procedure has an "almost unique" output. This means that the PRF can be evaluated (and rewound) polynomially many times, without disturbing the quantum key ρ_K, except negligibly.

Definition 16 (Anti-Piracy Security). *Let* $\lambda \in \mathbb{N}^+$. *Consider the following game between a challenger and an adversary* $\mathcal{A}$:

1. *The challenger samples* $K \leftarrow \mathsf{Setup}(1^\lambda)$ *and* $\rho_K \leftarrow \mathsf{QKeyGen}(K)$. *It gives* ρ_K *to* $\mathcal{A}$;
2. $\mathcal{A}$ *returns to the challenger a bipartite state* σ *on registers* R_1 *and* R_2, *as well as general quantum circuits* U_1 *and* U_2.
3. *The challenger samples uniformly random* $u, w \leftarrow [N]$. *Then runs* U_1 *on input* $(\sigma[R_1], u)$, *and runs* U_2 *on input* $(\sigma[R_2], w)$. *The outcome of the game is 1 if and only if the outputs are* $F(K, u)$ *and* $F(K, w)$ *respectively.*

Denote by $\mathsf{CopyProtectionGame}(1^\lambda, \mathcal{A})$ *a random variable for the output of the game.*

We say the scheme has anti-piracy security if for every polynomial-time quantum algorithm $\mathcal{A}$, *there exists a negligible function* $\mathsf{negl}(\cdot)$, *for all* $\lambda \in \mathbb{N}^+$,

$$\Pr\left[b = 1, b \leftarrow \mathsf{CopyProtectionGame}(1^\lambda, \mathcal{A})\right] = \mathsf{negl}(\lambda).$$

7.2 Construction

In this section, we describe a construction of a copy-protection scheme for a class of PRFs. We will eventually reduce security of this construction to security of the single-decryptor encryption scheme of Sect. 6.2, and we will therefore inherit the same assumptions.

Let λ be the security parameter. Our construction copy-protects a PRF $F_1 :$ $[K_\lambda] \times [N_\lambda] \rightarrow [M_\lambda]$ where $N = 2^{n(\lambda)}$ and $M = 2^{m(\lambda)}$, for some polynomials $n(\lambda)$ and $m(\lambda)$, satisfying $n(\lambda) \geq m(\lambda) + 2\lambda + 4$. For convenience, we will omit writing the dependence on λ, when it is clear from the context. Moreover, F_1 should be a puncturable extracting PRF with error $2^{-\lambda-1}$. Such PRFs exist assuming post-quantum one-way functions.

Our copy-protection construction for F_1, will make use of the following additional building blocks:

1. A puncturable extracting PRF $F_1(K_1, \cdot)$ that accepts inputs of length $n = \ell_0 + \ell_1 + \ell_2$ and outputs strings of length m. It is extracting when the input min-entropy is greater than $m + 2\lambda + 4$. By Theorem 3 in [SW14], assuming one-way functions exist, as long as $n \geq m + 2\lambda + 4$, F_1 is a puncturable extracting PRF with error less than $2^{-\lambda-1}$.

2. A puncturable statistically injective PRF $F_2(K_2, \cdot)$ that accepts inputs of length ℓ_2 and outputs strings of length ℓ_1. By Theorem 2 in [SW14], assuming one-way functions exist, as long as $\ell_1 \geq 2\ell_2 + \lambda$, F_2 is a puncturable statistically injective PRF with failure probability $2^{-\lambda}$.

3. A puncturable PRF $F_3(K_3, \cdot)$ that accepts inputs of length ℓ_1 and outputs strings of length ℓ_2. By Theorem 1 in [SW14], assuming one-way functions exist, F_3 is a puncturable PRF.

Note that PRF $F_1(K_1, \cdot)$ is the PRF functionality we will copy-protect. The PRFs $F_2(K_2, \cdot)$, $F_3(K_3, \cdot)$ are just building blocks in the construction.

In Figs. 2, 3, we describe a copy-protection construction for PRF F_1.

QKeyGen(K_1): Sample uniformly random subspaces A_i of dimension $\lambda/2$ and vectors s_i, s_i' for $i = 1, 2, \cdots, \ell_0$. Sample PRF keys K_2, K_3 for F_2, F_3. Prepare the programs $R_i^0 = \text{iO}(A_i + s_i)$ and $R_i^1 = \text{iO}(A_i^{\perp} + s_i')$ (with appropriately padded length), and let P be the program described in Figure 3. Output the quantum key $\rho_K = (\{|A_{i,s_i,s_i'}\rangle\}_{i \in [\ell_0]}, \text{iO}(P))$.

Eval(ρ_K, x): Let $\rho_K = (\{|A_{i,s_i,s_i'}\rangle\}_{i \in [\ell_0]}, \text{iO}(P))$. Let $x = x_0 \| x_1 \| x_2$ and x_0 is of length ℓ_0. For all $i \in [\ell_0]$, if $x_{0,i}$ is 1, apply $H^{\otimes n}$ to $|A_{i,s_i,s_i'}\rangle$. Otherwise, leave the state unchanged.

Let σ be the resulting state. Run $\text{iO}(P)$ coherently on input x and σ, and measure the final output register to obtain y.

Fig. 2. Quantum copy-protection scheme for PRFs.

The program P takes as input x and a list of ℓ_0 vectors $v_1, \cdots, v_{\ell_0}$ and has two modes. If x is not in the sparse hidden trigger set (not passing the 'if' check in the first line), the program is in the *normal mode*: it only outputs a PRF evaluation of x if every v_i is in the corresponding coset. Otherwise, the program is in the *hidden trigger mode*. It will compute a circuit Q' from the input x and output $Q'(v_1, \cdots, v_{\ell_0})$. On almost all inputs except those sparse hidden triggers, the program runs in its normal mode.

We obtain the following theorem (which we prove in the full version):

Theorem 15. *Assuming the existence of post-quantum iO, one-way functions, compute-and-compare obfuscation for the class of unpredictable distributions (as in Definition 3), and the strong monogamy-of-entanglement property (Conjecture 1), our construction satisfies anti-piracy security (as in Definition 16).*

Similarly, assuming the existence of post-quantum sub-exponentially secure iO, one-way functions, the quantum hardness of LWE and assuming the strong monogamy-of-entanglement property (Conjecture 1), our construction satisfies anti-piracy security.

Hardcoded: Keys $K_1, K_2, K_3, R_i^0, R_i^1$ for all $i \in [\ell_0]$.
On input $x = x_0 \| x_1 \| x_2$ and vectors $v_1, \cdots, v_{\ell_0}$:

1. If $F_3(K_3, x_1) \oplus x_2 = x_0' \| Q'$ and $x_0 = x_0'$ and $x_1 = F_2(K_2, x_0' \| Q')$:
   Hidden Trigger Mode: It treats Q' as a (classical) circuit and outputs $Q'(v_1, \cdots, v_{\ell_0})$.
2. Otherwise, it checks if the following holds: for all $i \in [\ell_0]$, $R^{x_0, i}(v_i) = 1$.
   Normal Mode: If all hold, it outputs $F_1(K_1, x)$. Otherwise, it outputs $\perp$.

Fig. 3. Program P

Acknowledgements. A.C. is supported by the Simons Institute for the Theory of Computing, through a Quantum Postdoctoral Fellowship. J. L., Q. L. and M. Z. are supported by the NSF. J. L. is also supported by Scott Aaronson's Simons Investigator award. The authors are grateful for the support of the Simons Institute, where this collaboration was initiated.

References

[Aar05]   Aaronson, S.: Limitations of quantum advice and one-way communication. In: Theory of Computing, vol. 1, no. 1, pp. 1–28 (2005). https://doi.org/10.4086/toc.2005.v001a001

[Aar09]   Aaronson, S.: Quantum copy-protection and quantum money. In: 2009 24th Annual IEEE Conference on Computational Complexity, pp. 229–242. IEEE (2009)

[AC12]   Aaronson, S., Christiano, P.: Quantum money from hidden subspaces. In: Proceedings of the Forty-Fourth Annual ACM Symposium on Theory of Computing, pp. 41–60. ACM (2012)

[ALL+20] Aaronson, S., Liu, J., Zhandry, M., Zhang, R., Liu, Q.: New approaches for quantum copy-protection (2020)

[AP21]   Ananth, P., La Placa, R.L.: Secure Software Leasing (2021)

[BB84]   Bennett, C.H., Brassard, G.: Proceedings of the IEEE International Conference on Computers, Systems and Signal Processing (1984)

[BDGM20] Brakerski, Z., Döttling, N., Garg, S., Malavolta, G.: Factoring and pairings are not necessary for iO: circular-secure LWE suffices. Cryptology ePrint Archive, Report 2020/1024 (2020). https://eprint.iacr.org/2020/1024

[BGMZ18] Bartusek, J., Guan, J., Ma, F., Zhandry, M.: Preventing zeroizing attacks on GGH15. In: Proceedings of TCC 2018 (2018)

[BJL+21] Broadbent, A., Jeffery, S., Lord, S., Podder, S., Sundaram, A.: Secure software leasing without assumptions (2021). arXiv: 2101.12739 [quant-ph]

[BL19]   Broadbent, A., Lord, S.: Uncloneable quantum encryption via random oracles. In: IACR Cryptology ePrint Archive 2019, p. 257 (2019)

[BS16]   Ben-David, S., Sattath, O.: Quantum tokens for digital signatures. arXiv preprint arXiv:1609.09047 (2016)

584   A. Coladangelo et al.

[BW13] Boneh, D., Waters, B.: Constrained pseudorandom functions and their applications. In: Sako, K., Sarkar, P. (eds.) ASIACRYPT 2013. LNCS, vol. 8270, pp. 280–300. Springer, Heidelberg (2013). https://doi.org/10.1007/978-3-642-42045-0_15

[CMP20] Coladangelo, A., Majenz, C., Poremba, A.: Quantum copy-protection of compute-and-compare programs in the quantum random oracle model (2020). arXiv: 2009.13865 [quant-ph]

[FGH+12] Farhi, E., Gosset, D., Hassidim, A., Lutomirski, A., Shor, P.: Quantum money from knots. In: Proceedings of the 3rd Innovations in Theoretical Computer Science Conference, pp. 276–289 (2012)

[GGHW17] Garg, S., Gentry, C., Halevi, S., Wichs, D.: On the implausibility of differing-inputs obfuscation and extractable witness encryption with auxiliary input. Algorithmica **79**(4), 1353–1373 (2017)

[GGM86] Goldreich, O., Goldwasser, S., Micali, S.: How to construct random functions. J. ACM **33**(4), 792–807 (1986). ISSN: 0004-5411, https://doi.org/10.1145/6490.6503

[GKW17] Goyal, R., Koppula, V., Waters, B.: Lockable obfuscation. In: 2017 IEEE 58th Annual Symposium on Foundations of Computer Science (FOCS), pp. 612–621. IEEE (2017)

[Got02] Gottesman, D.: Uncloneable encryption. arXiv preprint quant-ph/0210062 (2002)

[GZ20] Georgiou, M., Zhandry, M.: Unclonable Decryption Keys. Cryptology ePrint Archive, Report 2020/877 (2020). https://eprint.iacr.org/2020/877

[JLS20] Jain, A., Lin, H., Sahai, A.: Indistinguishability obfuscation from well-founded assumptions. Cryptology ePrint Archive, Report 2020/1003 (2020). https://eprint.iacr.org/2020/1003

[Kan18] Kane, D.: Quantum money from modular forms (2018). arXiv preprint arXiv:1809.05925

[KNY20] Kitagawa, F., Nishimaki, R., Yamakawa, T.: Secure Software Leasing from Standard Assumptions (2020). arXiv: 2010. 11186 [quant-ph] .

[Lut10] Lutomirski, A.: An online attack against Wiesner's quantum money (2010). In: arXiv preprint arXiv:1010.0256

[SW14] Sahai, A., Waters, B.: How to use indistinguishability obfuscation: deniable encryption, and more. In: Proceedings of the Forty-Sixth Annual ACM Symposium on Theory of Computing, pp. 475–484 (2014)

[TFKW13] Tomamichel, M., Fehr, S., Kaniewski, J., Wehner, S.: A monogamy-of-entanglement game with applications to device-independent quantum cryptography. New J. Phys. **15**(10), 103002 (2013)

[Wie83] Wiesner, S.: Conjugate coding. ACM Sigact News **15**(1), 78–88 (1983)

[WW20] Wee, H., Wichs, D.: Candidate obfuscation via oblivious LWE sampling. Cryptology ePrint Archive, Report 2020/1042 (2020). https://eprint.iacr.org/2020/1042

[WZ17] Wichs, D., Zirdelis, G.: Obfuscating compute-and compare programs under LWE. In: 2017 IEEE 58th Annual Symposium on Foundations of Computer Science (FOCS), pp. 600–611. IEEE (2017)

[Zha19a] Zhandry, M.: Quantum lightning never strikes the same state twice. In: Ishai, Y., Rijmen, V. (eds.) EUROCRYPT 2019. LNCS, vol. 11478, pp. 408–438. Springer, Cham (2019). https://doi.org/10.1007/978-3-030-17659-4_14

[Zha19c] Zhandry, M.: The magic of ELFs. J. Cryptol. **32**(3), 825–866 (2019)

On Tight Quantum Security of HMAC and NMAC in the Quantum Random Oracle Model

Akinori Hosoyamada[1,2](✉) and Tetsu Iwata[2]

[1] NTT Secure Platform Laboratories, Tokyo, Japan
akinori.hosoyamada.bh@hco.ntt.co.jp
[2] Nagoya University, Nagoya, Japan
{hosoyamada.akinori,tetsu.iwata}@nagoya-u.jp

Abstract. HMAC and NMAC are the most basic and important constructions to convert Merkle-Damgård hash functions into message authentication codes (MACs) or pseudorandom functions (PRFs). In the quantum setting, at CRYPTO 2017, Song and Yun showed that HMAC and NMAC are quantum pseudorandom functions (qPRFs) under the standard assumption that the underlying compression function is a qPRF. Their proof guarantees security up to $O(2^{n/5})$ or $O(2^{n/8})$ quantum queries when the output length of HMAC and NMAC is n bits. However, there is a gap between the provable security bound and a simple distinguishing attack that uses $O(2^{n/3})$ quantum queries. This paper settles the problem of closing the gap. We show that the tight bound of the number of quantum queries to distinguish HMAC or NMAC from a random function is $\Theta(2^{n/3})$ in the quantum random oracle model, where compression functions are modeled as quantum random oracles. To give the tight quantum bound, based on an alternative formalization of Zhandry's compressed oracle technique, we introduce a new proof technique focusing on the symmetry of quantum query records.

Keywords: Symmetric-key cryptography · Post-quantum cryptography · Provable security · Quantum security · Compressed oracle technique · HMAC · NMAC

1 Introduction

In recent years, post-quantum cryptography is one of the most active research areas in cryptography. NIST is holding the standardization process for post-quantum *public-key* schemes such as public-key encryption, key-establishment algorithms, and signatures [28], and it is anticipated that currently used public-key schemes (such as RSA-based schemes) will be replaced with post-quantum ones in a near future. In the post-quantum era, it is desirable that we have some mathematical evidence that *symmetric-key* schemes also have post-quantum security. Studying post-quantum security of typical symmetric-key schemes is

© International Association for Cryptologic Research 2021
T. Malkin and C. Peikert (Eds.): CRYPTO 2021, LNCS 12825, pp. 585–615, 2021.
https://doi.org/10.1007/978-3-030-84242-0_21

also an interesting problem from the view point of cryptographic theories, and there have been a significant number of recent papers that focus on this topic [14,18,21,32].

There exist two post-quantum security notions for cryptographic schemes: *standard security* and *quantum security* [33]. If a scheme S is proven to be secure in the setting where adversaries have quantum computers but they make only *classical* queries to keyed oracles, S is said to have *standard security*. If S is proven to be secure even if adversaries are allowed to make quantum superposed queries to keyed oracles, S is said to have *quantum security*. Quantum security is the ultimate security since, if S has quantum security, S satisfies arbitrary intermediate security notions between standard security and quantum security[1].

Message authentication codes (MACs) are the most important symmetric-key schemes to achieve data integrity. Some of them including block cipher based MACs such as CBC-MAC [5,7,22] and PMAC [8] do not have quantum security, since there exist polynomial time attacks on them [23]. However, they have standard security since their classical security proofs remain valid if adversaries are allowed to make only classical queries to keyed oracles and the underlying block ciphers are post-quantum secure.

On the other hand, classical security proofs are not necessarily applicable to the (post-quantum) standard security for hash based MACs where the proofs use idealized models such as the random oracle model (when underlying hash functions are built on the Merkle-Damgård construction, e.g., SHA-2 [26]) or the ideal permutation model (when underlying hash functions are built on the sponge construction, e.g., SHA-3 [27]). Since adversaries can implement compression functions and permutations used in the hash functions on their own quantum computers to make quantum queries, the security of hash based MACs should be proven in the corresponding idealized quantum models such as the quantum random oracle model (QROM) [9] or quantum ideal permutation model [2,21].

The main focus of this paper is to study the tight quantum pseudorandom function security (qPRF security) of HMAC and its variant NMAC [4], which are the most basic and important constructions to convert Merkle-Damgård hash functions into pseudorandom functions (PRFs) or MACs, in the QROM where compression functions are modeled as quantum random oracles (QROs).

HMAC and NMAC. For a compression function $h : \{0,1\}^{m+n} \rightarrow \{0,1\}^n$, the Merkle-Damgård construction MD^h is defined as follows[2]: Let $IV \in \{0,1\}^n$ be a fixed public initialization vector. For each input message $M \in \{0,1\}^*$, the construction pads M (with a fixed padding function) and splits it into m-bit message blocks $M[1], \ldots, M[\ell]$. The state is first set as $S_0 := IV$, and iteratively

---

[1] Please do not confuse the notions of standard/quantum security with the standard model or the quantum random oracle model. The two notions are independent of the models, and it is possible that a scheme has quantum security in the standard model or standard security in the quantum random oracle model.

[2] n is the length of chaining values, and m is the length of message blocks.

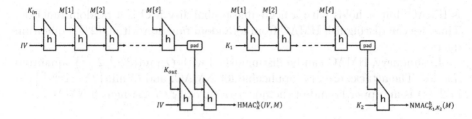

Fig. 1. HMAC and NMAC. Note that $\mathsf{pad}(M) = M[1]||\cdots||M[\ell]$.

updated as $S_{i+1} := h(M[i+1]||S_i)$, and S_ℓ becomes the final output. We assume $m \geq n$, which is the case for usual concrete hash functions such as SHA-2.

For a key length $k \leq m$, HMAC is defined to be the keyed function HMAC^h : $\{0,1\}^k \times \{0,1\}^n \times \{0,1\}^* \to \{0,1\}^n$ such that $\mathsf{HMAC}^h(K, IV, M) := \mathsf{MD}^h(IV, K_{out}||\mathsf{MD}^h(IV, K_{in}||M))$. Here, $K_{in} := (K||0^{m-k}) \oplus \mathsf{ipad}$, $K_{out} := (K||0^{m-k}) \oplus \mathsf{opad}$, and $\mathsf{ipad}, \mathsf{opad} \in \{0,1\}^m$ are fixed public constants such that $\mathsf{ipad} \neq \mathsf{opad}$. We sometimes write $\mathsf{HMAC}_K^h(IV, M)$ to denote $\mathsf{HMAC}^h(K, IV, M)$ for simplicity. See also Fig. 1.

NMAC is a two-key variant of HMAC. Mathematically, it is a keyed function $\mathsf{NMAC}^h : \{0,1\}^n \times \{0,1\}^n \times \{0,1\}^* \to \{0,1\}^n$ defined by $\mathsf{NMAC}^h(K_1, K_2, M) := \mathsf{MD}^h(K_2, \mathsf{MD}^h(K_1, M))$. Here, $K_1, K_2 \in \{0,1\}^n$ are chosen independently and uniformly at random.[3] We sometimes write $\mathsf{NMAC}_{K_1,K_2}^h(M)$ instead of NMAC^h (K_1, K_2, M) for simplicity. See also Fig. 1.

Quantum Security of HMAC and NMAC

Simple Quantum Distinguishing Attacks on HMAC and NMAC. There are two simple quantum attacks to distinguish HMAC from a random function. Suppose that we are given an oracle $\mathcal{O}$ that is either of HMAC or a random function, in addition to the quantum random oracle h.

The first attack is the one that tries to recover the secret key K. Once we succeed in recovering the correct key K (when $\mathcal{O}$ is HMAC) or realizing that there is no plausible candidate for K (when $\mathcal{O}$ a random function), we can distinguish HMAC from a random function. Since the exhaustive key search of k-bit keys can be done with $O(2^{k/2})$ queries by using Grover's algorithm [17], we can distinguish HMAC from a random function with $O(2^{k/2})$ quantum queries.

The second attack uses a collision for $\mathcal{O}$. Suppose that the padding function pad in the Merkle-Damgård construction satisfies the condition that there exists a function $\mathsf{p} : \mathbb{Z}_{\geq 0} \to \{0,1\}^*$ such that $\mathsf{pad}(M) = M||\mathsf{p}(|M|)$, which is the case for usual hash functions such as SHA-2. First, we try to find $M, M' \in \{0,1\}^m$ such that $\mathcal{O}(M) = \mathcal{O}(M')$, which can be done with $O(2^{n/3})$ quantum queries by using the BHT algorithm [11]. When we find such messages, we check whether $\mathcal{O}(M||0^m) = \mathcal{O}(M'||0^m)$ holds. This equality holds with a high probability if $\mathcal{O}$

---

[3] Note that there is no IV involved in NMAC and the key-length is always $n+n = 2n$.

is HMAC, but it holds with a negligible probability if $\mathcal{O}$ is a random function. Thus, we can distinguish HMAC from a random function with $O(2^{n/3})$ quantum queries.

In summary, HMAC can be distinguished with $O(\min\{2^{n/3}, 2^{k/2}\})$ quantum queries. The attacks are also applicable for NMAC, and $O(\min\{2^{n/3}, 2^{2n/2}\}) = O(2^{n/3})$ is an upper bound of the query complexity to distinguish NMAC.

Previous Results on Quantum Security of HMAC and NMAC. Song and Yun proved that HMAC and NMAC become secure quantum pseudorandom functions (qPRFs) against polynomial-time quantum adversaries in the *standard model* under the assumption that $h(\cdot\|K) : \{0,1\}^m \to \{0,1\}^n$ is a qPRF when $K \in \{0,1\}^n$ is randomly chosen [32]. They for the first time showed that HMAC and NMAC are secure even in the quantum setting, which has great importance in theory because it enables domain extension for qPRFs.

Roughly speaking, their proof guarantees security up to $O(2^{n/5})$ or $O(2^{n/8})$ quantum queries when the underlying function h_K is ideally random for each key K.[4] In other words, $\Omega(2^{n/5})$ or $\Omega(2^{n/8})$ is currently the best proven lower bound of quantum query complexity to distinguish HMAC or NMAC from a random function.

Results in standard models and those in (quantum) random oracles are not directly comparable, but there exists a large gap between the current best lower bound and the upper bound $O(2^{n/3})$ (when k is large enough) given in the above distinguishing attacks.

The gap between $\Omega(2^{n/5})$ (or $\Omega(2^{n/8})$) and $O(2^{n/3})$ may not be significant in an ideal world where adversaries are modeled as polynomial-time machines, but it is indeed significant in the real world applications, which we explain below.

Closing the Gap. In the real world, closing the gap between $\Omega(2^{n/5})$ (or $\Omega(2^{n/8})$) and $O(2^{n/3})$ is relevant for the following reasons.

Recall that there exist two security notions in the quantum setting: quantum security and standard security. The standard security of HMAC will have practical importance in a very near future because it is quite reasonable to assume that an adversary has a quantum computer on which h is implemented, but the attack target (HMAC) is implemented on a classical device.

Now, the problem is that exiting results guarantee the security of HMAC and NMAC only up to $O(2^{n/5})$ or $O(2^{n/8})$ queries, not only for the quantum security but also for the standard security (in the QROM). This is problematic since when HMAC is instantiated with SHA-256, where $n = 256$, the security is not guaranteed after about $2^{n/5} \approx 2^{52}$ (or $2^{n/8} \approx 2^{32}$) *classical* queries. It is completely unacceptable in practice, as the number is modest even with the current standard, and is too small to guarantee a longer term security.

---

[4] Actually, the previous work [32] did not give concrete security bound, but we can reasonably deduce that the security is guaranteed up to $O(2^{n/8})$ quantum queries. We have the bound $O(2^{n/5})$ instead of $O(2^{n/8})$ if we assume a conjecture. See Section A of this paper's full version [20] for details. .

In theory, the security up to $O(2^{n/3})$ queries can be guaranteed with the previous result if the security parameter is changed from n to $5n/3$ (or $8n/3$), by replacing the underlying hash function with the one with a longer output length. However, in the real world, it requires many years to change parameters or primitives of widely used symmetric-key cryptosystems such as HMAC, or sometimes it is simply infeasible, as we illusrtare below:

- Some small IoT devices (e.g., RFID tags) need MACs but do not have enough area for hardware implementation of primitives with large parameters.
- Some banking systems are still using Triple-DES although 20 years have already passed after the standardization of AES [3]. This is because even a small change (changing the block cipher) in financial systems is too costly.
- Artificial satellites require MACs to prevent accepting commands from malicious attackers. Changing primitives embedded as hardware is infeasible after satellites are launched into the outer space [31].

Hence, giving a precise security bound is relevant from a practical view point, and is one of the most important topics to study in symmetric-key cryptography, even if the improvement will be from $O(2^{n/5})$ (or $O(2^{n/8})$) to $O(2^{n/3})$.

We also note that there has been a long line of research to close the gap for HMAC and NMAC in the classical setting, and it was eventually addressed by Gazi et al. at CRYPTO 2014 [16] showing the upper bound and the matching lower bound. However, the analysis in the quantum setting does not reach this point, and closing the gap is important also from a theoretical view point.

1.1 Our Contributions

The main result of this paper is the following theorem, which shows that the tight bound of the number of quantum queries to distinguish HMAC or NMAC from a random function is in $\Theta(2^{n/3})$ (when k is large enough).

Theorem 1 (Lower bound, informal). *Assume $m \geq n$. Suppose that the maximum length of messages that we can query to HMAC, NMAC, or a random function* RF *(which is independent of h) is at most $m \cdot \ell$. Then, the following claims hold in the model where h is a quantum random oracle.*

1. *To distinguish HMAC from* RF *with a constant probability by making at most Q queries to HMAC or* RF *and at most q_h queries to h, $q_h \cdot \ell^{5/3} + Q \cdot \ell^{5/3} \geq \Omega(2^{n/3})$, or $q_h + Q \cdot \ell \geq \Omega(2^{k/2})$ have to be satisfied.*
2. *To distinguish NMAC from* RF *with a constant probability by making at most Q queries to NMAC or* RF *and at most q_h queries to h, $q_h \cdot \ell^{5/3} + Q \cdot \ell^{5/3} \geq \Omega(2^{n/3})$ has to be satisfied.*

Remark 1. Our tightness claim focuses on the number of quantum queries, neglecting the effect of the lengths of the queries (see also Fig. 2). Nevertheless, our result still has practical importance. For instance, when HMAC-SHA-256 is used to authenticate TCP/IP packets on Ethernet, $\ell < 32$ always holds since

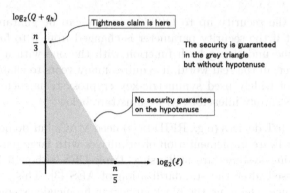

Fig. 2. The area that our result guarantees security (the grey triangle). We claim tightness of the bound for $\ell = O(1)$.

Maximum Segment Size (MSS) is about 1500-byte. In such a use-case our result guarantees about 85-bit security ($2^{n/3} \approx 2^{85}$ for $n = 256$), while previous works do only about 52-bit security or 32-bit security (in the QROM).

Remark 2. Some readers may think that results in the standard model are always superior to those in the (Q)ROM, but we emphasize that the standard model and (Q)ROM are theoretically incomparable.

To show the theorem, we use an alternative formalization [18,19] of Zhandry's *compressed oracle technique* [34]. One of the most difficult issues in proving security of cryptographic schemes against quantum adversaries is to record quantum queries to oracles. Zhandry [34] solved the issue by developing the compressed oracle technique, which can be used to record queries to QROs and efficiently simulate QROs. Intuitively, by using the technique, we can use the classical *lazy sampling* for quantum random oracles to some extent. The technique is so powerful that it is used to prove security of many cryptographic schemes [6,12,18,24,25,34]. However, efficient simulations of QROs are not necessary when we focus on the number of quantum queries made by adversaries and when their running time is irrelevant. Based on this observation, Hosoyamada and Iwata developed an alternative formalization of the compressed oracle technique that achieved a simpler formalization by ignoring efficient simulations of QROs and introducing notions of error terms, which is named *recording standard oracle with errors (* RstOE*)* [18,19]. Since our main focus is information theoretic adversaries of which computational resources are unlimited except for the number of quantum queries, we use RstOE instead of the original technique.

The technically hardest part to prove Theorem 1 is to show the indistinguishability of the function $F_1^h(u,v) := h(v, f(u))$ from a random function, where $u \in \{0,1\}^n, v \in \{0,1\}^m$, and $f : \{0,1\}^n \to \{0,1\}^n$ is a random function that is independent of h. (Adversaries have a direct oracle access to the quantum random oracle h, but only indirect access to f. That is, adversaries can query

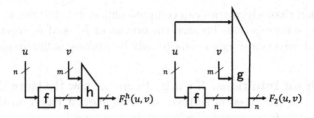

Fig. 3. F_1^h and F_2. h is a quantum random oracle that adversaries can directly access. f and g are random functions that are independent from h.

to f only through queries to F_1^h, and cannot observe the output values of f. See also Fig. 3.) Once we show the indistinguishability of F_1^h, the remaining proofs can be done with simpler proof techniques.

It turns out that previous techniques cannot be directly used to prove the indistinguishability of F_1^h. Thus we introduce a technique which we call *equivalent databases*. We explain the details in the next subsection.

1.2 Technical Overview

Let us denote the distinguishing advantage of an adversary $\mathcal{A}$ between (pair of) oracles $(\mathcal{O}_1^h, h)$ and $(\mathcal{O}_2, h)$ by $\mathbf{Adv}_{(\mathcal{O}_1^h,h),(\mathcal{O}_2,h)}^{\text{dist}}(\mathcal{A})$, where h is a quantum random oracle and $\mathcal{O}_1^h$ depends on h. Let RF be a random function that is independent of h. As mentioned above, the technically hardest part to show the tight security bound of HMAC and NMAC is to show the following proposition[5].

Proposition 1 (Technically hardest proposition to show, informal). *If $\mathcal{A}$ makes at most q queries to each oracle, $\mathbf{Adv}_{(F_1^h,h),(\mathsf{RF},h)}^{\text{dist}} \leq O(\sqrt{q^3/2^n})$ holds.*

Let F_2 be the function defined by $F_2(u,v) := g(u,v,f(u))$, where $g : \{0,1\}^n \times \{0,1\}^m \times \{0,1\}^n \to \{0,1\}^n$ is another random function (see also Fig. 3). Then, since g is a random function, $\mathbf{Adv}_{(F_1^h,h),(\mathsf{RF},h)}^{\text{dist}}(\mathcal{A}) = \mathbf{Adv}_{(F_1^h,h),(F_2,h)}^{\text{dist}}(\mathcal{A})$ holds. In what follows, we present an overview of how we show

$$\mathbf{Adv}_{(F_1^h,h),(F_2,h)}^{\text{dist}}(\mathcal{A}) \leq O(\sqrt{q^3/2^n}), \tag{1}$$

instead of directly showing Proposition 1. For bit strings x and y, we identify the concatenation $x\|y$ and the pair (x,y). [6]

Following usual terminology on provable security in symmetric-key cryptology, we call (direct) queries to h *offline queries* because h is an ideal model of a

---

[5] In [34] Zhandry showed that F_1^h is indifferentiable from a QRO when h and g are QROs. His result implies qPRF security of F_1^h up to $O(2^{n/4})$ quantum queries, while Proposition 1 guarantees security up to $O(2^{n/3})$ queries. .

[6] We consider F_2 instead of RF so that there exists a useful correspondence between "good" databases for F_1^h and those for F_2, which we will elaborate later.

public function that adversaries can compute offline. In addition, we call queries to F_1^h and F_2 *online queries* because the oracles of F_1^h and F_2 model the keyed functions that adversaries can compute only by making online queries.

Classical Proof Intuitions. If our goal were to show the indistinguishability of F_1^h and F_2 in the *classical* setting, we could show it based on the following idea by using the *lazy sampling* technique to f, g, and h:

> *If $\mathcal{A}$ cannot guess outputs of f, and outputs of f do not collide, then the outputs of F_1^h and F_2 seem completely random and indistinguishable.*

More precisely, a (classical) adversary $\mathcal{A}$ cannot distinguish F_1^h and F_2 as long as the following two bad events hit and coll do not happen.[7]

hit: $\mathcal{A}$ succeeds in guessing a previous output of f and queries it to h. That is, $\mathcal{A}$ has queried $u\|v'$ to the online keyed oracle (F_1^h or F_2) before, and now $\mathcal{A}$ queries $v\|f(u)$ to h (for some $v \in \{0,1\}^m$).

coll: A new output of f (which is sampled during an online query) happens to collide with either of (a) a previous output of f, or (b) the least significant n-bit ζ of a previous offline query $v\|\zeta$ to h.

Our proof for the *classical* indistinguishability would be as follows: First, we show that F_1^h and F_2 are completely indistinguishable as long as hit and coll do not happen. Second, we show that $\Pr[\mathsf{hit}]$ and $\Pr[\mathsf{coll}]$ are small. Let coll_i denote the event that coll happens at the i-th query. Then, by using the randomness of outputs of f, we can show $\Pr[\mathsf{coll}_i] \leq O(i/2^n)$ for each i, which implies that $\Pr[\mathsf{coll}] \leq \sum_{1 \leq i \leq q} \Pr[\mathsf{coll}_i] \leq \sum_{1 \leq i \leq q} O(i/2^n) = O(q^2/2^n)$. Similarly, $\Pr[\mathsf{hit}] \leq O(q^2/2^n)$ can be shown. (Actually there exists a qualitative difference between the proof for $\Pr[\mathsf{coll}] \leq O(q^2/2^n)$ and that for $\Pr[\mathsf{hit}] \leq O(q^2/2^n)$, which will be explained later). Hence we can show $\mathbf{Adv}_{(F_1^h,h),(F_2,h)}^{\mathrm{dist}}(\mathcal{A}) \leq \Pr[\mathsf{coll}] + \Pr[\mathsf{hit}] \leq O(q^2/2^n)$ in the classical setting.

How to Show Quantum Indistinguishability? When we show the *quantum* indistinguishability of F_1^h and F_2, it is natural to combine the above *classical* idea with some quantum proof techniques developed in previous works. Indeed, our first idea toward a quantum proof is to combine the above classical idea with a quantum technique introduced in [18,19].[8] However, actually it turns out that they cannot be simply combined. The issue is attributed to our situation where

---

[7] We use the symbols u and ζ to denote n-bit strings and v to denote an m-bit string.

[8] In Zhandry's paper that introduced the compressed oracle technique, quantum indifferentiability of the *fixed-input-length* Merkle-Damgård construction is proved [34]. Note that the *variable-input-length* Merkle-Damgård construction that is used in HMAC and NMAC is not indifferentiable in the random oracle model even in the classical setting [13]. In addition, the security bound of the indifferentiability is proved up to $O(2^{n/4})$ (but not $O(2^{n/3})$) quantum queries in [34]. Thus, we start from the proof technique used in [18,19] instead of [34].

we have to deal with the bad event hit that "$\mathcal{A}$'s *offline* query to h collides with a previous output of f in the *online* oracle".

Below, we explain (1) an overview of the previous quantum proof technique, (2) what kind of issue arises if we combine the above classical idea with the previous quantum technique, and that (3) we can solve the issue by introducing a new proof technique which we name *equivalent databases*.

Proof Technique in [18,19]. The previous work [18,19] showed quantum indistinguishability (Proposition 4 in [19]) of certain two oracles as follows:[9]

1. Suppose that random functions from which the oracles are built (in our case, f, g, and h) are implemented by using RstOE so that we can use intuitions of classical lazy sampling in quantum proofs to some extent (let D_f, D_g, and D_h denote *databases* associated with RstOE for f, g, and h, respectively, which correspond to transcripts of queries in the classical setting).
2. Based on classical proof ideas of using good and bad events, define the notion of *good* and *bad* for tuples of databases (in our case, (D_f, D_h) for F_1^h and (D_f, D_g, D_h) for F_2) in such a way that
   (a) There exists a one-to-one correspondence between good databases for one oracle (in our case, good databases (D_f, D_h) for F_1^h) and good databases for the other oracle (in our case, good databases (D_f, D_g, D_h) for F_2).
   (b) The behavior of one oracle (in our case, F_1^h) on a good database is the same as that of the other oracle (in our case, F_2) on the corresponding good database.
3. By using (a) and (b), show that the oracles (in our case, the pairs of the oracles (F_1^h, h) and (F_2, h)) are completely indistinguishable as long as databases are good.
4. Show that the probability (in some sense) that good databases change to bad databases is very small at each query.

Note that, unlike the setting, even if the record "x has been queried to f and responded with y" is stored in a database D_f for f, there is a possibility that the record will be overwritten as "x has not been queried to f before", or "x has been queried to f and responded with y'" for some y' such that $y \neq y'$ [10]. Hence it is not necessarily trivial how to define good and bad databases in such a way that we can formally prove both of (a) and (b) hold.

Next, we explain what kind of issue happens when we apply the above idea to our situation. In short, the issue lies in the last one of the above four steps.

---

[9] Some technical errors are contained in the Asiacrypt version of the previous work [18], which are corrected in the revised version [19]. Our technical overview in this section and formal proofs in later sections are based on the revised version. For completeness, we do not rely on any propositions in [18,19] that is related to the technical errors in [18]. The propositions from [18,19] that we use in this paper are the ones of which correctness can be confirmed just by straightforward algebraic calculation (Proposition 2 and Proposition 3).

[10] This may seem somewhat strange, but some differences between quantum oracles and classical oracles are explained by using this strange property.

An Issue with Our Situation. In the previous work [18,19], each adversary can access to only a single *keyed* oracle. Roughly speaking, a good database changes to bad only when a fresh value x is (indirectly) queried to a random function RF, and the newly sampled value $y := \mathsf{RF}(x)$ happens to collide with an existing record in a database (i.e., a bad event that correspond to coll in our situation).

On the other hand, in our situation, a good database also changes to bad when *an adversary succeeds to query* $v \| \zeta$ *to* h *such that* ζ *collides with a previous output of* f *(i.e.,* hit *occurs)*.

This difference causes an issue to prove that the "bad" probability is small. Unlike the lazy sampling that always chooses values uniformly at random, (quantum) adversaries can choose offline (quantum) queries to h arbitrarily and *adaptively*. Thus, an adversary may have strong ability to succeed to cause hit, even if the probability of coll is small.

Note that how to deal with adaptive queries to offline queries is not an easy issue even in the classical setting. To reduce the arguments on adaptive queries into those on non-adaptive arguments, sophisticated proof techniques such as the coefficients H technique [29] are usually used.

How to Solve the Issue. Our key intuition to solve the issue is, for arbitrary good database (D_f, D_h) for F_1^h that an adversary $\mathcal{A}$ is trying to change to be bad, there would be sufficiently many good databases (D_f', D_h') that $\mathcal{A}$ cannot distinguish from (D_f, D_h).

Suppose that (I) $\mathcal{A}$ is running relative to F_1^h and h, and has made $(i-1)$ queries in total, (II) both of the bad events coll and hit have not happened, and (III) now $\mathcal{A}$ chooses a bit string $\tilde{v} \| \tilde{\zeta}$ to query to h, trying to cause hit at the i-th query.

Let D_f and D_h be the current databases for f and h (before the i-th query). Then there exist $u_1, \ldots, u_s, \alpha_1, \ldots, \alpha_s \in \{0,1\}^n$ $(s \leq i-1)$ such that $D_f = ((u_1, \alpha_1), \ldots, (u_s, \alpha_s))$. Intuitively, α_j is equal to $f(u_j)$. Since bad events have not happened yet, D_f does not contain any collision (i.e., $\alpha_i \neq \alpha_j$ for $i \neq j$).

Let hit_i denote the event that hit occurs at the i-th query (to h). Then, hit_i occurs when $\mathcal{A}$ successfully chooses a value $\tilde{v} \| \tilde{\zeta}$ such that $\tilde{\zeta} = \alpha_j$ holds for some j. Our current goal is to prove that $\Pr[\mathsf{hit}_i]$ is very small.

To achieve this goal, we show that $\Pr\left[\mathsf{hit}_i \middle| \mathcal{A} \text{ chooses } \tilde{v} \| \tilde{\zeta}\right]$ is very small for arbitrary $\tilde{v} \| \tilde{\zeta}$, by focusing on the freedom of the choices of the values $f(u_1) = \alpha_1, \ldots, f(u_s) = \alpha_s$. Intuitively, even if the value $\alpha_j (= f(u_j))$ in the element $(u_j, \alpha_j) \in D_f$ is replaced with another value α_j', $\mathcal{A}$ does not notice since $\mathcal{A}$ does not observe output values of f. This means that the choices of the values $f(u_1) = \alpha_1, \ldots, f(u) = \alpha_s$ have some degree of freedom, even after $\mathcal{A}$ has chosen which value $\tilde{v} \| \tilde{\zeta}$ to query to h. We use this degree of freedom to bound the probability $\Pr\left[\mathsf{hit}_i \middle| \mathcal{A} \text{ chooses } \tilde{v} \| \tilde{\zeta}\right]$ (actually we will show a stronger result).

To provide a proof based on the above intuition, we introduce the notion of *equivalent databases* as follows.

Definition 1 (Equivalent database, informal). *A (good) database* (D'_f, D'_h) *is said to be equivalent to* (D_f, D_h) *if* $|D'_f| = |D_f|$, $|D'_h| = |D_h|$, *and* (D'_f, D'_h) *is equal to* (D_f, D_h) *except for the choices of the output values of* f.

We present an example to illustrate the intuition on equivalent databases. Let $D_f := ((u_1, \alpha_1), (u_2, \alpha_2))$ and $D_h := ((v_1 || \alpha_1, w_1), (v_2^{(1)} || \alpha_2, w_2^{(1)}), (v_2^{(2)} || \alpha_2, w_2^{(2)}), (v_3 || \zeta_3, w_3))$. This corresponds to the situation where $u_1 || v_1$, $u_2 || v_2^{(1)}$, $u_2 || v_2^{(2)}$ have been queried to F_1^h, and $v_3 || \zeta_3$ has been queried to h. See also Fig. 4. The adversary observes that $F_1^h(u_1 || v_1) = w_1$, $F_1^h(u_2 || v_2^{(1)}) = w_2^{(1)}$, $F_1^h(u_2 || v_2^{(2)}) = w_2^{(2)}$, and $h(v_3 || \zeta_3) = w_3$, but does not know the values $\alpha_1 = f(u_1)$ and $\alpha_2 = f(u_2)$. Suppose $\alpha_1, \alpha_2, \zeta_3$ are distinct, which implies that (D_f, D_h) is a good database. Then, another good database (D'_f, D'_h) is equivalent to (D_f, D_h) if and only if there exist α'_1 and α'_2 such that $\alpha'_1, \alpha'_2, \zeta_3$ are distinct, $D'_f = ((u_1, \alpha'_1), (u_2, \alpha'_2))$, and $D'_h = ((v_1 || \alpha'_1, w_1), (v_2^{(1)} || \alpha'_2, w_2^{(1)}), (v_2^{(2)} || \alpha'_2, w_2^{(2)}), (v_3 || \zeta_3, w_3))$.

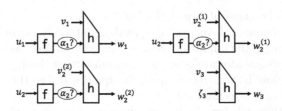

Fig. 4. The situation that corresponds to the good database (D_f, D_h). $\mathcal{A}$ has no information on α_1 and α_2 expect that $\alpha_1, \alpha_2, \zeta_3$ are distinct. We say that another good database (D'_f, D'_h) is equivalent to (D'_f, D'_h) if and only if (D_f, D_h) is equal to (D_f, D_h) except for the choice of the values for α_1 and α_2.

Let $\mathsf{Equiv}(D_f, D_h)$ be the set of good databases that are equivalent to (D_f, D_h). Then, intuitively, the following properties hold:

1. The probability that a database happens to become (D_f, D_h) (after $\mathcal{A}$ made $(i-1)$ queries) is equal to the probability that the database happens to become (D'_f, D'_h), for any $(D'_f, D'_h) \in \mathsf{Equiv}(D_f, D_h)$.
2. The ratio between (I) the number of $(D'_f, D'_h) \in \mathsf{Equiv}(D_f, D_h)$ that leads to the bad event hit_i (i.e., $\alpha_j = \zeta$ for some j) and (II) the size of the entire set $\mathsf{Equiv}(D_f, D_h)$ is at most about $\approx |D_f|/2^n \leq O(i/2^n)$.[11]

---

[11] This holds due to the following reasoning. For simplicity, assume that nothing has been *directly* queried to h before, and D_f has $(i-1)$ entries $(u_1, \alpha_1), \ldots, (u_{i-1}, \alpha_{i-1})$ (other cases can be shown similarly). Then $|\mathsf{Equiv}(D_f, D_h)|$ is equal to the number of choices of the tuple $(\alpha_1, \ldots, \alpha_{i-1})$ such that $\alpha_j \neq \alpha_k$ for $j \neq k$. Hence $|\mathsf{Equiv}(D_f, D_h)| = \binom{2^n}{i-1}$. In addition, the number of $(D'_f, D'_h) \in \mathsf{Equiv}(D_f, D_h)$ such that $\alpha_j = \zeta$ for some j is $(i-1) \cdot \binom{2^n}{i-2}$. Thus the ratio is $(i-1) \cdot \binom{2^n}{i-2} / \binom{2^n}{i-1} = \frac{(i-1)}{(2^n-i+2)} \leq O(i/2^n)$.

From the above two properties it follows that, for arbitrary $\tilde{v}||\tilde{\zeta}$ *and arbitrary* *good* (D_f, D_h), $\Pr\left[\text{hit}_i \middle| \mathcal{A} \text{ chooses } \tilde{v}||\tilde{\zeta} \wedge \text{ database is equivalent to } (D_f, D_h)\right] \leq O(i/2^n)$ holds. This implies that $\Pr\left[\text{hit}_i\right] \leq O(i/2^n)$.

The above explanations are in fact based on classical intuitions. To show they also work in the quantum setting, we carefully analyze quantum amplitude (complex coefficients) of state vectors.

Finishing the Proof. Now we have $\Pr\left[\text{hit}_i\right] \leq O(\frac{i}{2^n})$ in the quantum setting. We can also show $\Pr\left[\text{coll}_i\right] \leq O(\frac{i}{2^n})$ with the technique in the previous work [18].

In the classical setting, the distinguishing advantage is upper bounded by $\mathbf{Adv}^{\text{dist}}_{(F_1^h,h),(F_2,h)}(\mathcal{A}) \leq \Pr\left[\text{hit}\right] + \Pr\left[\text{coll}\right] \leq \sum_{1 \leq i \leq q} \Pr\left[\text{hit}_i\right] + \sum_{1 \leq i \leq q} \Pr\left[\text{coll}_i\right]$. On the other hand, roughly speaking, the quantum distinguishing advantage is upper bounded by $\mathbf{Adv}^{\text{dist}}_{(F_1^h,h),(F_2,h)}(\mathcal{A}) \leq \sum_{1 \leq i \leq q} \sqrt{\Pr\left[\text{hit}_i\right]} + \sum_{1 \leq i \leq q} \sqrt{\Pr\left[\text{coll}_i\right]}$. Therefore, we obtain the bound as $\mathbf{Adv}^{\text{dist}}_{(F_1^h,h),(F_2,h)}(\mathcal{A}) \leq \sum_{1 \leq i \leq q} O\left(\sqrt{i/2^n}\right) + \sum_{1 \leq i \leq q} O\left(\sqrt{i/2^n}\right) \leq O\left(\sqrt{q^3/2^n}\right)$ in the quantum setting, instead of the classical bound $O(q^2/2^n)$.

The intuition behind the notion of equivalent databases might seem simple or even trivial, though, the important point is that we can provide a rigorous proof that the intuition actually works in the quantum setting through RstOE. (Recall that it was unclear how to record quantum queries before the development of the compressed oracle technique.)

As we mentioned before, it is quite important to show the tight security bound in symmetric cryptology because even the improvement from $O(2^{n/5})$ (or $O(2^{n/8})$) to $O(2^{n/3})$ has significant importance in the real world. Bad events like hit that an adversary succeeds to guess an output of a random function often appear in classical provable security for symmetric-key cryptosystems. To deal with such bad events when showing quantum tight security bounds, proof techniques like our equivalent databases seem indispensable. We believe that our technique broadens the applicability of quantum provable security in symmetric-key cryptology.

1.3   Limitations and Future Directions

Our security bound is tight and any further improvement is impossible in terms of the number of queries. However, there is a room for improvement in terms of the length of messages. When an adversary makes a single classical query of very long length (e.g., a message of $m \cdot 2^{n/5}$ bits, or equivalently $\ell = 2^{n/5}$) to the keyed oracle of HMAC or NMAC, our result no longer guarantees any security. (Note that this does not invalidate the practical importance of our result. See Remark 1 for details.) However, we do not find any quantum attack that actually breaks the security of HMAC or NMAC by making only a few queries of which length is $O(m \cdot 2^{n/5})$, and we expect that there does not exist such an attack. Improving the security bound in terms of message lengths is an interesting future work.

1.4   Related Works

There are various notions on quantum MAC security such as EUF-qCMA security [10] and blind unforgeability [1]. There also exists another security notion for one-time MAC security [15]. MACs built from qPRFs satisfy all these security notions. Boneh and Zhandry showed that qPRFs become quantum secure MACs (in the sense of EUF-qCMA) and showed quantum security of the Carter-Wegman MACs [10]. Czajkowski et al. showed quantum security of random sponge, which can be seen as a variant of CBC-MAC [14].

1.5   Paper Organization

Section 2 describes notation, definitions, and some basic lemmas used in later sections. Section 3 gives an overview on the alternative formalization (RstOE) of Zhandry's compressed oracle technique. Section 4 gives the formal proof of the technically most hardest proposition (Proposition 1) and introduces the new proof technique. Section 5 shows quantum security bound of HMAC and NMAC.

2   Preliminaries

In this paper, all adversaries are quantum algorithms. I_n denotes the identity operator on n-qubit quantum states. We often write just I instead of I_n when it will cause no confusion. For a unitary operator U, we denote the operators $U \otimes I$ and $I \otimes U$ by the same symbol U, when it will cause no confusion. We identify the set of bit strings $\{0,1\}^n$ with the set of integers $\{0, 1, \ldots, 2^n - 1\}$ for any positive integer n. In addition, we identify the pair $(x, y) \in \{0,1\}^m \times \{0,1\}^n$ with the concatenation $x \| y \in \{0,1\}^{m+n}$. $\{0,1\}^*$ denotes the set $\coprod_{n=0}^{\infty} \{0,1\}^n$, where $\{0,1\}^0$ denotes the set that includes only the empty string. For a positive integer m, $(\{0,1\}^m)^+$ denotes the set $\coprod_{i=1}^{\infty} \{0,1\}^{im}$. $\mathsf{td}(\cdot, \cdot)$ denotes the trace distance function. For a vector $|\phi\rangle$ and a positive integer n, we also denote $|\phi\rangle \otimes |0^n\rangle$ and $|0^n\rangle \otimes |\phi\rangle$ by $|\phi\rangle$, when it will cause no confusion.

2.1   Quantum Algorithms and Quantum Oracles

When we consider the computational resources of adversaries, we focus on the number of queries made by adversaries, and we do not care about their running time and memory usage (i.e., we consider quantum information theoretic adversaries). Here we describe how we model (oracle-aided) quantum algorithms and quantum oracles in the case that each adversary is given an oracle access to a single quantum oracle.

Following previous works (e.g., [9]), we model an (oracle-aided) quantum algorithm $\mathcal{A}$ that makes at most q quantum queries to a single oracle as a sequence of unitary operators $(U_0, U_1, \ldots, U_q)$, where U_i corresponds to $\mathcal{A}$'s offline computation after the i-th oracle query for $i \geq 1$, and U_0 corresponds to $\mathcal{A}$'s initial computation. In addition, the quantum state space of $\mathcal{A}$ is a tensor product $\mathcal{H}_{\text{query}} \otimes \mathcal{H}_{\text{answer}} \otimes \mathcal{H}_{\text{work}}$, where $\mathcal{H}_{\text{query}}$, $\mathcal{H}_{\text{answer}}$, and $\mathcal{H}_{\text{work}}$ correspond to the register to make queries to the oracle, the register to receive answers from the oracle, and the register for $\mathcal{A}$'s offline computations, respectively. After the application of the final unitary operator U_q, $\mathcal{A}$'s entire state is measured, and (a part of) the measurement result (classical bit string) is returned as the output. When $\mathcal{A}$ does not take any initial input, we assume that $\mathcal{A}$'s initial state is set to be $|0^s\rangle$ for some positive integer s. When $\mathcal{A}$ takes a classical input $x \in \{0,1\}^m$, we assume that $\mathcal{A}$'s initial state is set to be $|x\rangle$ by convention. (This paper does not treat the situation that $\mathcal{A}$ takes quantum states as inputs.)

A quantum oracle $\mathcal{O}$ is modeled as a tuple of unitary operator O, quantum state space $\mathcal{H}_{\text{query}} \otimes \mathcal{H}_{\text{answer}} \otimes \mathcal{H}_{\text{state}}$, and a vector (initial state) $|\text{init}\rangle \in \mathcal{H}_{\text{state}}$. Here, the state space $\mathcal{H}_{\text{query}} \otimes \mathcal{H}_{\text{answer}}$ (i.e., the registers to send queries and receive answers) is shared with adversaries, and $\mathcal{H}_{\text{state}}$ is the oracle's private space that adversaries cannot access directly. O may be chosen randomly according to a distribution at the beginning of each game.

When the adversary $\mathcal{A}$ runs relative to the quantum oracle $\mathcal{O}$ on input x, the initial whole quantum state is $|x\rangle \otimes |\text{init}\rangle$. The whole quantum state just before the i-th query is $U_{i-1}OU_{i-2}O \cdots OU_0 |x\rangle \otimes |\text{init}\rangle$, and the whole quantum state just before the final measurement is $U_q O U_{q-1} O \cdots O U_0 |x\rangle \otimes |\text{init}\rangle$. Let $z \leftarrow \mathcal{A}^{\mathcal{O}}(x)$ denote the event that the quantum algorithm $\mathcal{A}$ returns z as the final output when $\mathcal{A}$ takes x as an input and runs relative to $\mathcal{O}$.

Example: Quantum oracle of a fixed function and a quantum random oracle. According to the above model, the quantum oracle $\mathcal{O}_f$ of a fixed function $f : \{0,1\}^m \rightarrow \{0,1\}^n$ is modeled as follows: the state space of $\mathcal{O}_f$ is empty. The unitary operator O_f that processes queries made to $\mathcal{O}_f$ is defined by $O_f : |x\rangle |y\rangle \mapsto |x\rangle |y \oplus f(x)\rangle$ for all $x \in \{0,1\}^m$ and $y \in \{0,1\}^n$.

In addition, a quantum random oracle (QRO) is defined to be the quantum oracle such that, $f : \{0,1\}^m \rightarrow \{0,1\}^n$ is chosen uniformly at random at the beginning of each game (for some m and n), and quantum oracle access to $\mathcal{O}_f$ is given to adversaries.

Even if a function f admits input messages M and M' of which lengths differ, we assume that the quantum oracle of O_f admits queries of superpositions of M and M'. In such a case, we assume that length $|M|$ of each message M is encoded with M. However, for ease of notation, we just write $|M\rangle$ instead of $|(|M|, M)\rangle$ for each message M.

2.2   How to Model Accesses to Multiple Quantum Oracles

Suppose that an adversary $\mathcal{A}$ is given oracle accesses to multiple quantum oracles $\mathcal{O}_1, \ldots, \mathcal{O}_s$, and $\mathcal{A}$ makes q queries to each oracle $\mathcal{O}_1, \ldots, \mathcal{O}_s$ in a sequential order. That is, for each $1 \leq j < s$, after $\mathcal{A}$ makes the i-th query to $\mathcal{O}_j$, $\mathcal{A}$ performs some offline computations, and then makes the i-th query to $\mathcal{O}_{j+1}$. Similarly, after $\mathcal{A}$ makes the i-th query to $\mathcal{O}_s$, $\mathcal{A}$ performs some offline computations, and then makes the $(i+1)$-th query to $\mathcal{O}_1$. Here we explain how to model the behavior of $\mathcal{A}$ and multiple quantum oracles $\mathcal{O}_1, \ldots, \mathcal{O}_s$ as sequential applications of unitary operators, in the case that $\mathcal{A}$ makes queries in a sequential order as above.

We assume that the oracles share a state space that is described as the tensor product $\mathcal{H}_{\text{query}} \otimes \mathcal{H}_{\text{answer}} \otimes \mathcal{H}_{\text{state}}$. Here, $\mathcal{H}_{\text{query}} \otimes \mathcal{H}_{\text{answer}}$ is the partial state space of $\mathcal{A}$ (thus the adversary and the oracles share the registers to send queries and receive answers). $\mathcal{H}_{\text{state}}$ is oracles' private space that adversaries cannot access directly.

For each quantum oracle $\mathcal{O}_i$, let O_i denote the unitary operator to process queries. We assume that the initial state of $\mathcal{A}$ is set to be $|x\rangle$ when $\mathcal{A}$ takes x as an input (when $\mathcal{A}$ does not take any initial input, by convention we assume that the initial state of $\mathcal{A}$ is $|0^\alpha\rangle$ for some α). Let $|\text{init}\rangle$ be the initial state of the oracles' private space $\mathcal{H}_{\text{state}}$. Then we model that the quantum state of $\mathcal{A}$ and the oracles before the final measurement becomes $\left(\prod_{j=1}^{q} U_{s,j} O_s \cdots U_{1,j} O_1 \right) U_0 |x\rangle \otimes |\text{init}\rangle$, where the adversary $\mathcal{A}$ is modeled as the sequence of unitary operators $(U_0, U_{1,1}, \ldots, U_{s,1}, U_{1,2}, \ldots, U_{s,q})$, and $U_{i,j}$ corresponds to the offline computation by $\mathcal{A}$ after the j-th query to $\mathcal{O}_i$. By $z \leftarrow \mathcal{A}^{\mathcal{O}_1, \ldots, \mathcal{O}_s}(x)$, we denote the event that $\mathcal{A}$ finally outputs the classical string z when $\mathcal{A}$ takes x as an input and runs relative to the oracles $\mathcal{O}_1, \ldots, \mathcal{O}_s$.

The Model of Adversaries of Which Queries Are Not in a Sequential Order. In the above model we considered the special case that the adversary queries to oracles $\mathcal{O}_1, \ldots, \mathcal{O}_s$ in a sequential order. However, even if an adversary $\mathcal{B}$ (given oracle accesses to $\mathcal{O}_1, \ldots, \mathcal{O}_s$) does not make queries in such a sequential order, the behavior of $\mathcal{B}$ can be captured with the above model: Suppose that $\mathcal{B}$ makes at most q_i quantum queries to $\mathcal{O}_i$ for each i, and s is a constant. Then, we can make another adversary $\mathcal{A}$ such that $\mathcal{A}$'s output distributions are the same as that of $\mathcal{B}$, and $\mathcal{A}$ makes $O(\max\{q_1, \ldots, q_s\})$ queries to each oracle in a sequential order as in the above model, by appropriately increasing the number of queries. Thus all reasonable adversaries are captured by the above model.

2.3 Security Advantages

Quantum Distinguishing Advantage. For quantum oracles $\mathcal{O}_1, \ldots, \mathcal{O}_s$ and $\mathcal{O}'_1, \ldots, \mathcal{O}'_s$, we define the quantum distinguishing advantage of an adversary $\mathcal{A}$ by $\mathbf{Adv}^{\text{dist}}_{(\mathcal{O}_1, \ldots, \mathcal{O}_s),(\mathcal{O}'_1, \ldots, \mathcal{O}'_s)}(\mathcal{A}) := \Big| \Pr\left[1 \leftarrow \mathcal{A}^{\mathcal{O}_1, \ldots, \mathcal{O}_s}()\right] - \Pr\left[1 \leftarrow \mathcal{A}^{\mathcal{O}'_1, \ldots, \mathcal{O}'_s}()\right] \Big|$.

qPRF Advantage in QROM. Let h be a QRO and F_K^h be a keyed function that may depend on h. By the same symbol F_K^h we denote the quantum oracle such that the key K is chosen at random, and the quantum oracle access to F_K^h is given to adversaries. In addition, let RF be the quantum oracle of a random function that is independent of h. Then, we define the

quantum pseudorandom function advantage (qPRF advantage) of $\mathcal{A}$ on F_K^h by
$$\mathbf{Adv}_{F_K^h}^{\mathrm{qPRF}}(\mathcal{A}) := \mathbf{Adv}_{(F_K^h,h),(\mathrm{RF},h)}^{\mathrm{dist}}(\mathcal{A}).$$

Here we introduce a basic proposition from a previous work [30] for later use.

Lemma 1 (Lemma 2.2 of [30]). *Let* $h : \{0,1\}^{m+n} \to \{0,1\}^n$ *be a quantum random oracle. For a random key* $K \in \{0,1\}^k$ *($k < m + n$), define* $F_K^h : \{0,1\}^{m+n-k} \to \{0,1\}^n$ *by* $F_K^h(x) = h(x||K)$. *Then, for each adversary* $\mathcal{A}$ *that makes at most* q_h *quantum queries to* h, $\mathbf{Adv}_{F_K^h}^{\mathrm{qPRF}}(\mathcal{A}) \leq O\left(q_h/2^{k/2}\right)$ *holds.*

qPRG Advantage. Let h be a quantum random oracle and $\rho^h : \{0,1\}^{k_1} \to \{0,1\}^{k_2}$ be a function that may depend on h. Then, we define the quantum PRG advantage $\mathbf{Adv}_{\rho^h}^{\mathrm{qPRG}}(\mathcal{A})$ of $\mathcal{A}$ on ρ^h by $\mathbf{Adv}_{\rho^h}^{\mathrm{qPRG}}(\mathcal{A}) := \left| \Pr\left[K_1 \xleftarrow{\$} \{0,1\}^{k_1} : 1 \leftarrow \mathcal{A}^h(\rho^h(K_1)) \right] - \Pr\left[K_2 \xleftarrow{\$} \{0,1\}^{k_2} : 1 \leftarrow \mathcal{A}^h(K_2) \right] \right|$. In addition, we introduce the following lemma for later use.

Lemma 2. *Let* $h : \{0,1\}^{m+n} \to \{0,1\}^n$ *be a quantum random oracle, and* $k \leq m$. *Let* $\Delta \in \{0,1\}^m$ *and* $IV \in \{0,1\}^n$ *be public constants such that* $\Delta \neq 0^m$. *Define* $\rho^h : \{0,1\}^k \to \{0,1\}^{2n}$ *by* $\rho^h(K) = h(K||0^{m-k}||IV)||h((K||0^{m-k} \oplus \Delta)||IV)$. *Then, for any quantum adversary* $\mathcal{A}$ *that makes at most* q_h *quantum queries to* h, $\mathbf{Adv}_{\rho^h}^{\mathrm{qPRG}}(\mathcal{A}) \leq O\left(q_h/2^{k/2}\right)$ *holds.*

Lemma 2 can easily be shown by slightly modifying the proof of Lemma 1 (Lemma 2.2 in [30]). See Section B of this paper's full version [20] for details.

3   An Overview on How to Record Quantum Queries

Here, we give an overview of the recording standard oracle with errors [18,19], which is an alternative formalization of Zhandry's compressed oracle technique [34].

The Primal Definition of QRO. Let us begin with recalling the primal definition of QRO (see Sect. 2 for details). A QRO is the quantum oracle such that

1. a function f is chosen from $\mathsf{Func}(\{0,1\}^m, \{0,1\}^n)$, the set of all functions from $\{0,1\}^m$ to $\{0,1\}^n$, uniformly at random, and
2. a quantum oracle access to f is given to adversaries.

Here, m and n are positive integers. Note that the quantum oracle of f is described as the unitary operator O_f that is defined by $O_f : |x\rangle |y\rangle \mapsto |x\rangle |y \oplus f(x)\rangle$ for all $x \in \{0,1\}^m$ and $y \in \{0,1\}^n$. In the QROM, an adversary $\mathcal{A}$ makes quantum queries to a QRO (and quantum queries to additional oracles that may depend on the QRO) and finally returns some outputs.

An Alternative View of QRO: The Standard Oracle. Here, let us define a quantum oracle named the *standard oracle*, which is an alternative view of QRO. First, suppose that each function $f : \{0,1\}^m \to \{0,1\}^n$ is encoded into the $2^m \cdot (n+1)$-bit string $(0||f(0))||\cdots||(0||f(2^m-1))$, and identify f with this bit string[12]. Second, let stO be the unitary operator defined by

$$\mathsf{stO} : |x\rangle\,|y\rangle \otimes |S\rangle \mapsto |x\rangle\,|y \oplus S_x\rangle \otimes |S\rangle, \tag{2}$$

where $x \in \{0,1\}^m$, $y \in \{0,1\}^n$, and $S = (b_0||S_0)||\cdots||(b_{2^m-1}||S_{2^m-1})$ ($b_i \in \{0,1\}$ and $S_i \in \{0,1\}^n$ for each i. Essentially, the operator stO does not act on the register for b_i for each i). Then we have $\mathsf{stO}\,|x\rangle\,|y\rangle \otimes |f\rangle = |x\rangle\,|y \oplus f(x)\rangle \otimes |f\rangle$ for each function f.

Definition 2 (Standard oracle). *The standard oracle is the quantum oracle such that the initial state of the oracle is $\sum_f \sqrt{1/2^{n2^m}}\,|f\rangle$ and each quantum query is processed with the unitary operator* stO.

By the same symbol stO we denote not only the unitary operator (2) but also the standard oracle if it will cause no confusion. The following lemma clearly holds.

Lemma 3. *For any quantum algorithm $\mathcal{A}$ and any possible output z (classical bit string), $\Pr\left[z \leftarrow \mathcal{A}^{\mathrm{QRO}}\right] = \Pr\left[z \leftarrow \mathcal{A}^{\mathsf{stO}}\right]$ holds.*

The Recording Standard Oracle with Errors. Let IH, U_{toggle}, and CH be the unitary operators that act on $2^m \cdot (n+1)$-qubit states defined by $\mathsf{IH} := (I \otimes H^{\otimes n})^{2^m}$, $U_{\mathrm{toggle}} := (I_1 \otimes |0^n\rangle\,\langle 0^n| + X \otimes (I_n - |0^n\rangle\,\langle 0^n|))^{2^m}$, and $\mathsf{CH} := (CH)^{2^m}$. Here, X is the 1-qubit bit-flip operation such that $X\,|b\rangle = |b \oplus 1\rangle$ and $CH := |0\rangle\,\langle 0| \otimes I_n + |1\rangle\,\langle 1| \otimes H^{\otimes n}$. Let $U_{\mathrm{enc}} := \mathsf{CH} \cdot U_{\mathrm{toggle}} \cdot \mathsf{IH}$ and $U_{\mathrm{dec}} := U_{\mathrm{enc}}^*$, and define the unitary operator RstOE that acts on $(m + n + (n+1) \cdot 2^m)$-qubit quantum states by

$$\mathsf{RstOE} := (I_{m+n} \otimes U_{\mathrm{enc}}) \cdot \mathsf{stO} \cdot (I_{m+n} \otimes U_{\mathrm{dec}}). \tag{3}$$

Then the recording standard oracle with errors RstOE is defined as follows.

Definition 3 (Recording standard oracle with errors). *The recording standard oracle with errors is the quantum oracle such that its initial state is $|0^{2^m(n+1)}\rangle$ and each quantum query is processed with the unitary operator* RstOE.

By the same symbol RstOE we denote not only the unitary operator (3) but also the recording standard oracle with errors if it will cause no confusion.

---

[12] Here, the bit "0" concatenated with each $f(i)$ is redundant, but it is necessary so that the notation for stO is compatible with that for the recording standard oracle with errors introduced later.

Intuition Behind the Definition of RstOE. RstOE is the composition of U_{dec}, stO, and U_{enc}. The first operator U_{dec} decodes superpositions of databases into the uniform superposition of all functions $\sum_f \sqrt{1/2^{n2^m}} |f\rangle$. The second stO responds to queries in the same way as the original standard oracle. Finally, U_{enc} encodes the uniform superposition of functions into a superposition of databases. Recall that $U_{\mathrm{enc}} = \mathsf{CH} \cdot U_{\mathrm{toggle}} \cdot \mathsf{IH}$. Intuitively, after the action of the first unitary operator IH, the register of the function f that corresponds to the value $f(x)$ changes to $|0^n\rangle$ if adversary has no information on $f(x)$, and changes to some non-zero value if adversary has some information on $f(x)$. If the value of the register is non-zero, database should record the value of $f(x)$. The second operator U_{toggle} checks if the register is non-zero, and set $b_x := 1$ to indicate that "the value of $f(x)$ should be recorded". Finally, the third operator CH constructs a (superposition of) database D in such a way that the value $f(x)$ is recorded in D if and only if $b_x = 1$.

Next, we give some notation used to describe the property of RstOE. Let $D := (b_0||y_0)|| \cdots ||(b_{2^m-1}||y_{2^m-1})$ be a $2^m \cdot (n+1)$-bit bit string, where $b_i \in \{0,1\}$ and $y_i \in \{0,1\}^n$ for $0 \le i \le 2^m - 1$. We call D a *valid database* if $\neg(b_i = 0 \wedge y_i \neq 0^n)$ holds for all i. If $b_i = 0 \wedge y_i \neq 0^n$ holds for some i, we call D an *invalid database*. Intuitively, a valid database D will be a quantum version of "transcript" for a random oracle: $b_x = 1 \wedge y_x = y$ implies that "the adversary queried x to the random oracle before, and the query was responded with y".

Let $D = (b_0||y_0)|| \cdots ||(b_{2^m-1}||y_{2^m-1})$ be a valid database, and $I_D \subset \{0,1\}^m$ be the set of indices such that $i \in I_D$ if and only if $b_i = 1$. Then, we can define a set $S_D \subset \{0,1\}^m \times \{0,1\}^n$ from D by $S_D := \{(i, y_i)\}_{i \in I_D}$. Similarly, if a subset $S \subset \{0,1\}^m \times \{0,1\}^n$ satisfies the condition

$$x \neq x' \text{ for distinct elements } (x, s_x), (x', s_{x'}) \in S, \tag{4}$$

we can define a valid database D_S from S by $D_S := (b_0||y_0)|| \cdots ||(b_{2^m-1}||y_{2^m-1})$, where $b_x = 1$ and $y_x = s_x$ if $(x, s_x) \in S$ and $b_x = 0$ and $y_x = 0^n$ otherwise. Each of the maps $D \mapsto S_D$ and $S \mapsto D_S$ is the inverse of the other, and we identify valid databases and the subsets that satisfy (4). Furthermore, we identify a set $S \subset \{0,1\}^m \times \{0,1\}^n$ that satisfies (4) with the partially defined function f_S such that $f_S(x) = y$ if and only if $(x, y) \in S$, and $f_S(x) = \bot$ if $(x, y) \notin S$ for any y. Particularly, we use the same symbol D to denote S_D and f_{S_D}.

Remark 3. Pay attention not to confuse the (valid) databases with the encoding of functions $f : \{0,1\}^m \to \{0,1\}^n$ that is used when we defined the standard oracle stO. The encoding of functions are used only in the definition of stO, but the notion of databases are used throughout the rest of the paper.

By definition of RstOE, the proposition below immediately follows (see arguments in Sect. 3 of [18,19] for details).

Proposition 2. *The recording standard oracle with errors* RstOE *is completely indistinguishable from the quantum random oracle. That is, for any quantum algorithm $\mathcal{A}$ and any possible output z, $\Pr\left[z \leftarrow \mathcal{A}^{\mathrm{QRO}}\right] = \Pr\left[z \leftarrow \mathcal{A}^{\mathrm{RstOE}}\right]$ holds.*

In addition, if we measure the database register of RstOE *just before* $\mathcal{A}$ *makes the i-th query, the database after the measurement contains at most* $(i-1)$ *entries.*

The following proposition shows the main properties of RstOE that are shown in the previous work [18,19].

Proposition 3 (Proposition 1 in [18,19]). *Let* $x \in \{0,1\}^m$ *and* $D = (b_0 \| y_0) \| \cdots \| (b_{2^m-1} \| y_{2^m-1})$ *be a valid database such that* $D(x) = \bot$ *(in particular,* $b_x = 0$ *and* $y_x = 0^n$ *hold). In addition, for* $z \neq 0^n$ *let* $D \cup (x,z)^{\mathsf{invalid}}$ *be the invalid database* $D \cup (x,z)^{\mathsf{invalid}} := (b_0' \| y_0') \| \cdots (b_{2^m-1}' \| y_{2^m-1}')$ *such that* $b_t' = b_t \wedge y_t = y_t'$ *if* $t \neq x$, *and* $b_x = 0 \wedge y_x = z$.

1. *For any* $y, \alpha \in \{0,1\}^n$, *there exists a vector* $|\epsilon_1\rangle$ *such that*

$$\mathsf{RstOE}\, |x,y\rangle \otimes |D \cup (x,\alpha)\rangle = |x, y \oplus \alpha\rangle \otimes |D \cup (x,\alpha)\rangle + |\epsilon_1\rangle \tag{5}$$

and $\||\epsilon_1\rangle\| \leq O(\sqrt{1/2^n})$ *hold. More precisely,*

$$|\epsilon_1\rangle = \frac{1}{\sqrt{2^n}} |x, y \oplus \alpha\rangle \left(|D\rangle - \left(\sum_{\beta \in \{0,1\}^n} \frac{1}{\sqrt{2^n}} |D \cup (x,\beta)\rangle \right) \right) \tag{6}$$

$$- \frac{1}{\sqrt{2^n}} \sum_{\beta \in \{0,1\}^n} \frac{1}{\sqrt{2^n}} |x, y \oplus \beta\rangle \left(|D \cup (x,\beta)\rangle - |D_\beta^{\mathsf{invalid}}\rangle \right) \tag{7}$$

$$+ \frac{1}{2^n} |x\rangle |\widehat{0^n}\rangle \left(2 \sum_{\beta \in \{0,1\}^n} \frac{1}{\sqrt{2^n}} |D \cup (x,\beta)\rangle - |D\rangle \right) \tag{8}$$

holds, where $|D_\beta^{\mathsf{invalid}}\rangle$ *is a superposition of invalid databases for each* β *defined by* $|D_\beta^{\mathsf{invalid}}\rangle = \sum_{\gamma \neq 0^n} \frac{(-1)^{\beta \cdot \gamma}}{\sqrt{2^n}} |D \cup (x,\gamma)^{\mathsf{invalid}}\rangle$ *and* $|\widehat{0^n}\rangle := H^{\otimes n} |0^n\rangle$.

2. *For any* y, *there exists a vector* $|\epsilon_2\rangle$ *such that*

$$\mathsf{RstOE}\, |x,y\rangle \otimes |D\rangle = \sum_{\alpha \in \{0,1\}^n} \frac{1}{\sqrt{2^n}} |x, y \oplus \alpha\rangle \otimes |D \cup (x,\alpha)\rangle + |\epsilon_2\rangle \tag{9}$$

and $\||\epsilon_2\rangle\| \leq O(\sqrt{1/2^n})$ *hold. More precisely,*

$$|\epsilon_2\rangle = \frac{1}{\sqrt{2^n}} |x\rangle |\widehat{0^n}\rangle \left(|D\rangle - \sum_{\beta \in \{0,1\}^n} \frac{1}{\sqrt{2^n}} |D \cup (x,\beta)\rangle \right) \tag{10}$$

holds, where $|\widehat{0^n}\rangle := H^{\otimes n} |0^n\rangle$.

The first and second properties (especially, (5) and (9)) in this proposition correspond to the classical intuition for lazy sampling such that, when x is queried to a
random function, (i) if x has been queried before and responded with α, respond
with α again, and (ii) if x has not been queried before, sample α uniformly at
random and respond with α, respectively. This intuition works well when the
initial state $|x, y\rangle \otimes |D \cup (x, \alpha)\rangle$ or $|x, y\rangle \otimes |D\rangle$ are not superposed. When the
initial states are superposed, the effect of the error terms $|\epsilon_1\rangle$ and $|\epsilon_2\rangle$ become
significant, and quantum-specific property such that "an entry $(x, \alpha) \in D$ is
deleted from D at a query" or "an entry $(x, \alpha) \in D$ is overwritten with another
data (x, α') at a query" emerge.

4   Technical Proposition

The goal of this section is to show the following proposition, which is the technically hardest part to show quantum security of HMAC and NMAC.[13] Once
we prove it, the remaining proofs for HMAC and NMAC can be shown by using
simpler techniques. See also Sect. 1.2 for proof intuition.

Proposition 4. *Let $h : \{0,1\}^{m+n} \to \{0,1\}^n$ be a quantum random oracle. Let
$f : \{0,1\}^{n+m'} \to \{0,1\}^n$ be a random function, and $F_1^h : \{0,1\}^{n+m'} \times \{0,1\}^m \to
\{0,1\}^n$ be the function defined by $F_1^h(u, v) := h(v, f(u))$. Let $\mathcal{A}$ be an algorithm
that runs relative to the quantum oracle of F_1^h and the quantum random oracle h,
or the quantum oracle of a random function RF and the quantum random oracle
h. Suppose that $\mathcal{A}$ makes at most q_h quantum queries to h and Q quantum queries
to F_1^h or RF. Let $q := \max\{Q, q_h\}$, and suppose that q is in $o(2^{n/3})$. Then*

$$\mathbf{Adv}_{F_1^h}^{\mathrm{qPRF}}(\mathcal{A}) \leq O\left(\sqrt{q^3/2^n}\right) \tag{11}$$

holds.

Let F_2 be the function defined by $F_2(u, v) := g(u, v, f(u))$, where $g : \{0,1\}^{n+m'} \times
\{0,1\}^m \times \{0,1\}^n \to \{0,1\}^n$ is another random function. Then, since g is a random
function, $\mathbf{Adv}_{F_1^h}^{\mathrm{qPRF}}(\mathcal{A}) = \mathbf{Adv}_{(F_1^h,h),(F_2,h)}^{\mathrm{dist}}(\mathcal{A})$ holds. To simplify proofs, instead
of directly showing (11), we show that $\mathbf{Adv}_{(F_1^h,h),(F_2,h)}^{\mathrm{dist}}(\mathcal{A}) \leq O\left(\sqrt{q^3/2^n}\right)$ holds.

4.1   Proof of Proposition 4

Here we give a proof for the case $m' = 0$. The claims for $m' > 0$ can be shown
in the same way. We assume that $\mathcal{A}$ makes queries to F_1^h and h (or, F_2 and
h) in a sequential order and model the adversary and oracles as in Sect. 2.2. In
particular, by convention we assume that $\mathcal{A}$'s $(2i - 1)$-th query is made to F_1^h
(or F_2) and $2i$-th query is made to h for $1 \leq i \leq q$. (For instance, $\mathcal{A}$ first queries

---

[13] The proposition is a formal restatement of Proposition 1 in Sect. 1.2 for the case
$u \in \{0,1\}^{n+m'}$.

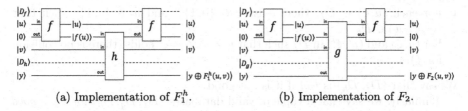

(a) Implementation of F_1^h.   (b) Implementation of F_2.

Fig. 5. Implementations of F_1^h and F_2. "in" and "out" denote the registers to send queries and receive answers, respectively. The dotted lines (and $|D_f\rangle, |D_h\rangle, |D_g\rangle$) appear only when f, h, g are implemented with RstOE, which correspond to the database registers.

to F_1^h (or F_2) and second queries to h.) We call queries to F_1^h and F_2 *online queries* and queries to h *offline queries* since, in practical settings, computations of h are done offline on adversaries' (quantum) computers.

We assume that the unitary operators to process queries to F_1^h and F_2 are implemented as follows:

Quantum Oracle of F_1^h.

1. Take $|u, v\rangle |y\rangle$ as an input, where $u, y \in \{0, 1\}^n$ and $v \in \{0, 1\}^m$.
2. Query u to f and obtain

$$|u, v\rangle |y\rangle \otimes |f(u)\rangle. \tag{12}$$

3. Query $(v, f(u))$ to h and add the answer into the y register to obtain

$$|u, v\rangle |y \oplus F_1^h(u, v)\rangle \otimes |f(u)\rangle. \tag{13}$$

4. Uncompute Step 2 to obtain $|u, v\rangle |y \oplus F_1^h(u, v)\rangle$.

We assume that the quantum oracle of F_2 is implemented in the same way as F_1^h, except that the query $(v, f(u))$ to h in Step 3 is replaced with the query $(u, v, f(u))$ to g. See also Fig. 5.

We show the hardness of distinguishing F_1^h and F_2 by using the recording standard oracle with errors (RstOE): We assume that the quantum oracles of f, g, and h are implemented by using RstOE (quantum queries are processed with RstOE). Let RstOE_f, RstOE_g, and RstOE_h be the recording standard oracle with errors for f, g, and h, respectively. We use the symbols D_f, D_g, and D_h to denote databases for f, g, and h, respectively. Then the unitary operator $O_{F_1^h}$ (resp., O_{F_2}) to process queries to F_1^h (resp., F_2) can be decomposed as $O_{F_1^h} = \mathsf{RstOE}_f^* \cdot \mathsf{RstOE}_h \cdot \mathsf{RstOE}_f$ (resp., $O_{F_2} = \mathsf{RstOE}_f^* \cdot \mathsf{RstOE}_g \cdot \mathsf{RstOE}_f$). See also Fig. 5 for the intuition about which registers the different RstOEs act.

Good and Bad Databases. Here we introduce the notion of good and bad databases for F_1^h and F_2. When we use the symbols u, ζ, v, w, we assume that $u, \zeta, w \in \{0, 1\}^n$ and $v \in \{0, 1\}^m$. We say that a pair of valid database (D_f, D_h) for F_1^h is *good* if and only if the following properties are satisfied.

1. For each $(u, \zeta) \in D_f$, there exist $v \in \{0,1\}^m$ and $w \in \{0,1\}^n$ such that $((v, \zeta), w) \in D_h$.
2. For (u, ζ) and (u', ζ') in D_f such that $u \neq u', \zeta \neq \zeta'$ holds (there is no collision for f).

We say that (D_f, D_h) is *bad* if it is not good.

Similarly, we say that a tuple of valid databases (D_f, D_g, D_h) for F_2 is *good* if and only if the following properties are satisfied.

1. For each $(u, \zeta) \in D_f$, there exist $v \in \{0,1\}^m$ and $w \in \{0,1\}^n$ such that $((u, v, \zeta), w) \in D_g$.
2. For each $((u, v, \zeta), w) \in D_g$, $(u, \zeta) \in D_f$.
3. For (u, ζ) and (u', ζ') in D_f such that $u \neq u', \zeta \neq \zeta'$ holds (i.e., there is no collision for f).
4. For each $((v, \zeta), w) \in D_h$ and $(u', \zeta') \in D_f$, $\zeta \neq \zeta'$ holds (i.e., the most significant n bits of inputs to h and the outputs of f do not collide).

We say that (D_f, D_g, D_h) is *bad* if it is not good.

Intuition Behind Good databases. Intuitively, a database (D_f, D_h) for F_1^h is defined to be good if and only if D_f does not contain collisions (the second condition on F_1^h). The first condition on F_1^h is included so that a weird situation such as "u has been queried to f, but $(v, f(u))$ has not been queried to h for any v" will not happen for good databases. Similarly, a database (D_f, D_g, D_h) for F_2 is defined to be good if and only if D_f does not contain collisions (the third condition condition on F_2) and the least significant n bits of inputs to h do not collide with outputs of f (the fourth condition on F_2). The first and second conditions on F_2 is included so that weird situations such as "u has been queried to f, but $(u, v, f(u))$ has not been queried to g for any v" or "(u, v, ζ) has been queried to g, but u has not been queried to f" will not happen for good databases.

One-to-one Correspondence for Good Databases. For a good database (D_f, D_g, D_h) for F_2, let $D_g \star D_h$ be the valid database for h such that $((v, \zeta), w) \in D_g \star D_h$ if and only if $((v, \zeta), w) \in D_h$ or $((u, v, \zeta), w) \in D_g$ for some u. Then $(D_f, D_g \star D_h)$ becomes a good database for F_1^h. Let us denote $(D_f, D_g \star D_h)$ by $[(D_f, D_g, D_h)]_1$. Then, it can easily be shown that the map $[\cdot]_1 : (D_f, D_g, D_h) \mapsto [(D_f, D_g, D_h)]_1 = (D_f, D_g \star D_h)$ is a bijection between the set of good databases for F_2 and that for F_1^h. Let $[\cdot]_2$ denote the inverse map of $[\cdot]_1$.

The bijections extend to (partially defined) isometries between the state spaces. Let $\mathcal{H}_{\mathcal{A}}$ be the state space of the adversary, and $\mathcal{H}_{D_f D_h}$ (resp., $\mathcal{H}_{D_f D_g D_h}$) be the state space of the databases for F_1^h (resp., F_2^h). In addition, let $V_{\text{good}}^{(1)} \subset \mathcal{H}_{D_f D_h}$ (resp., $V_{\text{good}}^{(2)} \subset \mathcal{H}_{D_f D_g D_h}$) be the subspace spanned by good databases. Then, the linear map from $\mathcal{H}_{\mathcal{A}} \otimes V_{\text{good}}^{(1)}$ to $\mathcal{H}_{\mathcal{A}} \otimes V_{\text{good}}^{(2)}$ that maps $|\eta\rangle \otimes |D_f, D_h\rangle$ to $|\eta\rangle \otimes |[D_f, D_h]_2\rangle$ for $|\eta\rangle \in \mathcal{H}_{\mathcal{A}}$ and a good database (D_f, D_h) becomes an isometry. We denote this isometry and its inverse also by $[\cdot]_2$ and $[\cdot]_1$, respectively.

Equivalent Good Databases. Next, we define the notion of *equivalent databases*. First, we define the notion for equivalent good databases for F_1^h. Let (D_f, D_h) be a good database for F_1^h, and let

$$S := \{\zeta \in \{0,1\}^n | \exists v, w \text{ s.t. } ((v, \zeta), w) \in D_h \text{ and } (u, \zeta) \notin D_f \text{ for all } u\}.$$

We say that another good database (D'_f, D'_h) is equivalent to (D_f, D_h) if and only if they are the same except for the output values of f, i.e., there exists a permutation π on $\{0,1\}^n$ such that

1. $\pi(\zeta) = \zeta$ for all $\zeta \in S$,
2. $(u, \zeta) \in D_f$ if and only if $(u, \pi(\zeta)) \in D'_f$, and
3. $((v, \zeta), w) \in D_h$ if and only if $((v, \pi(\zeta)), w) \in D'_h$ holds.

We define that a good database (D'_f, D'_g, D'_h) for F_2 is equivalent to another good database (D_f, D_g, D_h) in the same way, except that S is defined as $S := \{\zeta \in \{0,1\}^n | \exists v, w \text{ s.t. } ((v, \zeta), w) \in D_h\}$ and the following condition is additionally imposed.

3^+. $((u, v, \zeta), w) \in D_g$ if and only if $((u, v, \pi(\zeta)), w) \in D'_g$ hold.

As explained in Sect. 1.2, intuitively, two good databases are defined to be equivalent if and only if any adversary cannot distinguish them. By definition of equivalent databases, if a good database (D_f, D_g, D_h) for F_2 is equivalent to another good database (D'_f, D'_g, D'_h), then $D'_h = D_h$ holds.

Notations for State Vectors. Let $|\phi_{2i-1}\rangle$ be the whole quantum state just before $\mathcal{A}$'s i-th query to F_1^h when $\mathcal{A}$ runs relative to F_1^h and h. In addition, let $|\phi_{2i}\rangle$ be the whole quantum state just before $\mathcal{A}$'s i-th query to h when $\mathcal{A}$ runs relative to F_1^h and h. Define $|\psi_{2i-1}\rangle$ and $|\psi_{2i}\rangle$ similarly when $\mathcal{A}$ runs relative to F_2 and h. For ease of notation, let $|\phi_{2q+1}\rangle$ and $|\psi_{2q+1}\rangle$ be the quantum states just before the final measurement when $\mathcal{A}$ runs relative to (F_1^h, h) and (F_2, h), respectively.

We will show that Proposition 4 follows from the proposition below.

Proposition 5. *For each $j = 1, \ldots, 2q + 1$, there exist $|\phi_j^{\text{good}}\rangle$, $|\phi_j^{\text{bad}}\rangle$, $|\psi_j^{\text{good}}\rangle$, and $|\psi_j^{\text{bad}}\rangle$ that satisfy the following properties:*

1. $|\phi_j\rangle = |\phi_j^{\text{good}}\rangle + |\phi_j^{\text{bad}}\rangle$ and $|\psi_j\rangle = |\psi_j^{\text{good}}\rangle + |\psi_j^{\text{bad}}\rangle$.
2. $|\phi_j^{\text{good}}\rangle \in \mathcal{H}_{\mathcal{A}} \otimes V_{\text{good}}^{(1)}$ and $|\psi_j^{\text{good}}\rangle \in \mathcal{H}_{\mathcal{A}} \otimes V_{\text{good}}^{(2)}$.
3. $|\phi_j^{\text{good}}\rangle = \left[|\psi_j^{\text{good}}\rangle \right]_1$.
4. *There exists a complex number $a_{uvyzD_f D_g D_h}^{(j)}$ such that*

$$|\psi_j^{\text{good}}\rangle = \sum_{\substack{u,v,y,z,D_f,D_g,D_h; \\ (D_f, D_g, D_h):good}} a_{uvyzD_f D_g D_h}^{(j)} |u, v\rangle |y\rangle |z\rangle \otimes |D_f, D_g, D_h\rangle \quad (14)$$

and $a^{(j)}_{uvyzD_fD_gD_h} = a^{(j)}_{uvyzD'_fD'_gD'_h}$ if (D_f, D_g, D_h) and (D'_f, D'_g, D'_h) are equivalent, where (u, v), y, and z correspond to $\mathcal{A}$'s register to send queries, to receive answers from oracles, and for offline computations, respectively.[14]

5. For a good database (D_f, D_g, D_h) with non-zero coefficient in $|\psi^{\text{good}}_{2i-1}\rangle$ (resp., in $|\psi^{\text{good}}_{2i}\rangle$), $|D_g| \leq i - 1$, $|D_f| \leq 2(i - 1)$, and $|D_h| \leq i - 1$ hold (resp., $|D_g| \leq i$, $|D_f| \leq 2i$, and $|D_h| \leq i - 1$ hold).

6. $\| |\phi^{\text{bad}}_j\rangle \| \leq \| |\phi^{\text{bad}}_{j-1}\rangle \| + O\left(\sqrt{j/2^n}\right)$ and $\| |\psi^{\text{bad}}_j\rangle \| \leq \| |\psi^{\text{bad}}_{j-1}\rangle \| + O\left(\sqrt{j/2^n}\right)$ hold (we regard that $\| |\phi^{\text{bad}}_0\rangle \| = \| |\psi^{\text{bad}}_0\rangle \| = 0$).

Intuitive Interpretation of Proposition 5. The first and second properties show that $|\phi_j\rangle$ and $|\psi_j\rangle$ are divided into good and bad components. The third property shows that the good component of $|\phi_j\rangle$ matches to that of $|\psi_j\rangle$ through the isometry $[\cdot]_1$, which intuitively means that $\mathcal{A}$ cannot distinguish the two oracles as long as databases are good. The fourth property shows that the coefficients of equivalent databases are perfectly equal, which intuitively means that $\mathcal{A}$ cannot distinguish equivalent good databases. The fifth property shows the upper bound of the size of databases. The sixth property shows that the chance for good databases change to bad is very small at each query.

Overview of the Proof of Proposition 5. The proposition is shown by induction on j. The claim for $j = 1$ obviously holds by setting $|\phi^{\text{bad}}_1\rangle = |\psi^{\text{bad}}_1\rangle = 0$. Inductive steps are separated into two cases.

(Online queries): If the claim for $j = 2i - 1$ (i.e., before the i-th query to F_1^h or F_2) holds, then the claim for $j = 2i$ (i.e., after the query) holds.

(Offline queries): If the claim for $j = 2i$ (i.e., before the i-th query to h) holds, then the claim for $j = 2i + 1$ (i.e., after the query) holds.

Proof for Online Queries. Recall that $O_{F_1^h}$ (resp., O_{F_2}) are decomposed as $O_{F_1^h} = \text{RstOE}^*_f \cdot \text{RstOE}_h \cdot \text{RstOE}_f$ (resp., $O_{F_2} = \text{RstOE}^*_f \cdot \text{RstOE}_g \cdot \text{RstOE}_f$). We show that Properties 1–6 listed in Proposition 5 hold at each action of RstOE_f, RstOE_h (resp., RstOE_g), and RstOE^*_f. A state vector after an action of RstOE can be decomposed into three components.[15]

(i) The one that was (pre-)good before the action and still remains (pre-)good.

(ii) The one that was (pre-)good before the action but changed to bad.

(iii) The one that was already bad before the action.

---

[14] To be precise, we have to use the symbol (v, ζ) instead of (u, v) when $j = 2i$ since we always use the symbol $v\|\zeta$ to denote an input to h. However, here we use (u, v) to simplify notations. In the proof we use the symbol $a^{(2i)}_{v\zeta yzD_fD_gD_h}$ instead of $a^{(2i)}_{uvyzD_fD_gD_h}$.

[15] Pre-good databases are defined in the complete proof of Proposition 5 presented in Section C of this paper's full version [20].

Roughly speaking, we define (i) to be a new good vector, and the sum of (ii) and (iii) to be a new bad vector.[16] Then Properties 1 and 5 of Proposition 5 can easily be shown.

Intuitively, we defined good databases so that the behavior of the oracle of F_1^h on good databases will be the same for that of F_2 on the corresponding good databases. Thus we can show that Property 3 still holds for the new good vectors by keeping track of how the coefficients of basis vectors change, using Proposition 3.

The intuition for the proof of Property 4 is as follows. Let $\mathcal{DB}_0 := (D_f, D_g, D_h)$ and $\mathcal{DB}_1 := (D'_f, D'_f, D'_h)$ (resp., $\widehat{\mathcal{DB}}_0 := (\tilde{D}_f, \tilde{D}_g, \tilde{D}_h)$ and $\widehat{\mathcal{DB}}_1 := (\tilde{D}'_f, \tilde{D}'_f, \tilde{D}'_h)$) be equivalent good databases in $|\psi_{2i-1}^{\text{good}}\rangle$ (resp., $|\psi_{2i}^{\text{good}}\rangle$). In addition, by p_{ij} we ambiguously denote the "probability" that $\mathcal{DB}_i$ changes to $\widehat{\mathcal{DB}}_j$ for $i, j \in \{0, 1\}$ (p_{ij} has the information on the ratio of the coefficient of the vector corresponding to $\mathcal{DB}_i$ and that of $\widehat{\mathcal{DB}}_j$). Then we can show $p_{ij} = p_{i'j'}$ holds for all $(i, j), (i', j') \in \{0, 1\} \times \{0, 1\}$ by using symmetry of equivalent databases and Proposition 3. Since the coefficients corresponding to $\mathcal{DB}_0$ and $\mathcal{DB}_1$ are equal due to Property 4 on $|\psi_{2i-1}^{\text{good}}\rangle$, this implies that Property 4 also holds for $|\psi_{2i}^{\text{good}}\rangle$.

Property 6 is proven by showing the norm of the component (iii) is in $O(\sqrt{i/2^n})$. Intuitively, this corresponds to showing the probability that the event coll in Sect. 1.2 happens at the query is $O(i/2^n)$. We carefully prove it by using Proposition 3, taking into account that records in databases may be deleted or overwritten.

<u>Proof for Offline Queries.</u> The proof for offline queries are similar[17], except that showing $\|(\text{iii})\| \leq O(\sqrt{i/2^n})$ corresponds to showing $\Pr[\text{hit}_i] \leq O(i/2^n)$ in Sect. 1.2. See the explanations around page 596 for the intuition on $\Pr[\text{hit}_i] \leq O(i/2^n)$. To formally prove the bound, we use the inductive hypothesis that Property 4 holds for $j = 2i$.

See Section C of this paper's full version [20] for a complete proof.

Proof (of Proposition 4). Let tr_{D1} (resp., tr_{D2}) denote the partial trace operations over the quantum states of the databases for (F_1^h, h) (resp., (F_2, h)). Then

$$\mathbf{Adv}_{F_1^h, F_2}^{\text{dist}}(\mathcal{A}) \leq \text{td}\left(\text{tr}_{D1}(|\phi_{2q+1}\rangle\langle\phi_{2q+1}|), \text{tr}_{D2}(|\psi_{2q+1}\rangle\langle\psi_{2q+1}|)\right)$$

$$\leq \text{td}\left(\text{tr}_{D1}(|\phi_{2q+1}^{\text{good}}\rangle\langle\phi_{2q+1}^{\text{good}}|), \text{tr}_{D2}(|\psi_{2q+1}^{\text{good}}\rangle\langle\psi_{2q+1}^{\text{good}}|)\right) \tag{15}$$

$$+ \||\phi_{2q+1}^{\text{bad}}\rangle\| + \||\psi_{2q+1}^{\text{bad}}\rangle\| \tag{16}$$

---

[16] To be more precise, we sometimes include small "good" terms into the new bad vector so that the analysis will be easier.

[17] Actually the proof for offline queries are even simpler because the offline oracle is just a single random oracle h while the online oracles consist of two random functions.

holds. By Property 3 of Proposition 5, the term (15) is equal to zero. In addition,

$$(16) \leq \sum_{1 \leq j \leq 2q+1} O\left(\sqrt{j/2^n}\right) + \sum_{1 \leq j \leq 2q+1} O\left(\sqrt{j/2^n}\right) \leq O\left(\sqrt{q^3/2^n}\right) \text{ follows}$$

from Property 6 of Proposition 5. Hence Proposition 4 follows.   □

5 Quantum Security Proofs for HMAC and NMAC

The goal of this section is to show the following proposition.

Proposition 6. *Let* $h : \{0,1\}^{m+n} \to \{0,1\}^n$ *be a quantum random oracle. Assume* $m \geq n$. *Suppose that the padding function* pad *for the Merkle-Damgård construction is injective and there exists a function* $\mathsf{p} : \mathbb{Z}_{\geq 0} \to \{0,1\}^*$ *such that* $\mathsf{pad}(M) = M \| \mathsf{p}(|M|)$[18]. *Let* $\mathcal{A}$ *be a quantum adversary that runs relative to two quantum oracles* $\mathcal{O}^h$ *and* h[19] *such that (i)* $|\mathsf{pad}(M)| \leq m \cdot \ell$ *for arbitrary* M *that* $\mathcal{A}$ *queries to* $\mathcal{O}^h$ *when* $\mathcal{O}^h$ *is* HMAC_K^h *or* $\mathsf{NMAC}_{K_1,K_2}^h$, *and (ii)* $\mathcal{A}$ *makes at most* Q *queries to* $\mathcal{O}^h$ *and* q_h *queries to* h. *Then* $\mathbf{Adv}_{\mathsf{HMAC}_K^h}^{\mathrm{qPRF}}(\mathcal{A}) \leq$

$$O\left(\sqrt{\frac{(q_h+Q)^3\ell^5}{2^n}} + \frac{q_h+Q\ell}{2^{k/2}}\right) \text{ and } \mathbf{Adv}_{\mathsf{NMAC}_{K_1,K_2}^h}^{\mathrm{qPRF}}(\mathcal{A}) \leq O\left(\sqrt{\frac{(q_h+Q)^3\ell^5}{2^n}}\right) \text{ hold.}$$

Recall that HMAC_K^h (resp., $\mathsf{NMAC}_{K_1,K_2}^h$) is the composition of the functions $\mathsf{MD}^h(IV, K_{in}\|\cdot)$ and $\mathsf{MD}^h(IV, K_{out}\|\cdot)$ (resp., $\mathsf{MD}^h(K_1, \cdot)$ and $\mathsf{MD}^h(K_2, \cdot)$). Let us call the first (resp., second) function the *inner function* (resp., *outer function*). In addition, let $\mathsf{MD}'^h : \{0,1\}^n \times (\{0,1\}^m)^+ \to \{0,1\}^n$ be the function that is defined in the same way as MD^h but without padding. Then, to prove Proposition 6, it suffices to prove the claim in the case that the inner function of HMAC_K^h (resp., $\mathsf{NMAC}_{K_1,K_2}^h$) is replaced with $\mathsf{MD}'^h(IV, K_{in}\|\cdot)$ (resp., $\mathsf{MD}'^h(K_1, \cdot)$) and the lengths of messages queried by $\mathcal{A}$ is always a multiple of m and at most $\ell \cdot m$, since this change does not decrease adversaries' ability to distinguish.

Thus, in what follows, we prove Proposition 6 in the case where HMAC_K^h and $\mathsf{NMAC}_{K_1,K_2}^h$ are modified as above. We show it by introducing $(2\ell + 2)$ games $G_{0,H}, G_{0,N}, G_i$ $(1 \leq i \leq \ell)$, G_i' $(1 \leq i \leq \ell)$.

Game $G_{0,H}$. This is the game that the adversary is given oracle access to the quantum oracle of HMAC_K^h, in addition to h.

Game $G_{0,N}$. This is the game that the adversary is given oracle access to the quantum oracle of $\mathsf{NMAC}_{K_1,K_2}^h$, in addition to h.

---

[18] These conditions are satisfied for usual concrete hash functions such as SHA-2. Recall that $(\{0,1\}^m)^+$ is the set of bit strings of length positive multiple of m bits.
[19] $\mathcal{O}^h$ will be HMAC_K^h, $\mathsf{NMAC}_{K_1,K_2}^h$, or a random function.

Game G_i for $1 \le i \le \ell$. In the game G_i, the adversary is given quantum oracle access to the function H_i^h (in addition to h) that is defined as follows. Let $M := M[1]||\cdots||M[j]$ ($M[t] \in \{0,1\}^m$ for each t) be an input message for H_i^h.

1. If $j < i$, $H_i^h(M) := g_j(M)$ for a random function $g_j : \{0,1\}^{mj} \to \{0,1\}^n$.
2. If $j = i$, $H_i^h(M) := f_{out}(f_i(M))$ for a random function $f_i : \{0,1\}^{mi} \to \{0,1\}^n$ and $f_{out} : \{0,1\}^n \to \{0,1\}^n$.
3. If $j > i$, first $S_i := f_i(M[1]||\cdots||M[i])$ is computed, and then $S_t := h(M[t]|| S_{t-1})$ is iteratively computed for $i < t \le j$, and finally $H_i^h(M)$ is set as $H_i^h(M) := f_{out}(S_j)$.

See also Fig. 6.

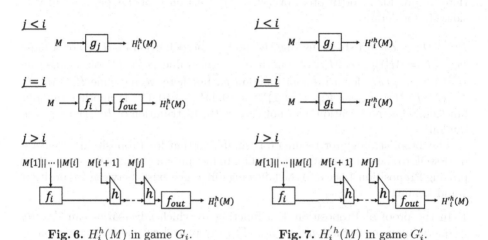

Fig. 6. $H_i^h(M)$ in game G_i.   **Fig. 7.** $H_i'^h(M)$ in game G_i'.

Game G_i' for $1 \le i \le \ell$. In the game G_i', the adversary is given quantum oracle access to the function $H_i'^h$ (in addition to h) that is defined as follows. Let $M := M[1]||\cdots||M[j]$ ($M[t] \in \{0,1\}^m$ for each t) be an input for $H_i'^h$.

1. If $j \le i$, $H_i'^h(M) := g_j(M)$ for a random function $g_j : \{0,1\}^{mj} \to \{0,1\}^n$.
2. If $j > i$, first $S_i := f_i(M[1]||\cdots||M[i])$ is computed, and then $S_t := h(M[t] ||S_{t-1})$ is iteratively computed for $i < t \le j$, and finally $H_i'^h(M)$ is set as $H_i'^h(M) := f_{out}(S_j)$. Here, $f_i : \{0,1\}^{mi} \to \{0,1\}^n$ and $f_{out} : \{0,1\}^n \to \{0,1\}^n$ are random functions.

See also Fig. 7. Since the lengths of messages queried by $\mathcal{A}$ is at most $m \cdot \ell$, G_ℓ' becomes the ideal game that $\mathcal{A}$ runs relative to a random function and h.

For the distinguishing advantage between $G_{0,N}$ and G_1 and the distinguishing advantage between $G_{0,H}$ and G_1, the following two lemmas hold.

Lemma 4 ($G_{0,N}$ and G_1). *It holds that* $\mathbf{Adv}_{(\mathrm{NMAC}_{K_1,K_2}^h,h),(H_1^h,h)}^{\mathrm{dist}}(\mathcal{A})$ *is in* $O(\sqrt{(q_h + Q\ell)^3/2^n})$.

Lemma 5 ($G_{0,H}$ and G_1). $\mathbf{Adv}^{\mathrm{dist}}_{(\mathrm{HMAC}^h_K,h),(H^h_1,h)}(\mathcal{A})$ *is in* $O(\sqrt{(q_h + Q\ell)^3/2^n}$ $+ (q_h + Q\ell)/2^{k/2})$.

It is straightforward to show that these lemmas follow from Lemma 1, Lemma 2, and Proposition 4. See Section D and Section E of this paper's full version [20] for complete proofs.

For the distinguishing advantage between G_i and G'_i for $1 \leq i \leq \ell$, the following lemma holds.

Lemma 6 (G_i and G'_i). $\mathbf{Adv}^{\mathrm{dist}}_{(H^h_i,h),(H'^h_i,h)}(\mathcal{A})$ *is in* $O(\sqrt{q^3\ell^3/2^n})$, *where* $q = \max\{Q, q_h\}$.

Here we provide a rough proof overview. See Section F of this paper's full version [20] for details.

Proof Overview. First, let us slightly modify the definition of H'^h_i. For a message $M = M[1]\|\cdots\|M[i]$ of length $m \cdot i$, the value $H'^h_i(M)$ was defined as $H'^h(M) := g_i(M)$ for a random function g_i, but here we re-define $H'^h_i(M) := f'_{out}(M, f_i(M))$, where $f'_{out} : \{0,1\}^{mi} \times \{0,1\}^n \to \{0,1\}^n$ is another random function. This modification does not change the distribution of H'^h_i since f'_{out} is random.

Our proof strategy for Lemma 6 is similar to that for Proposition 4, and we use RstOE to show the indistinguishability. In fact proving Lemma 6 is easier than proving Proposition 4 because the following difference exists between Proposition 4 and Lemma 6.

1. In the proof of Proposition 4, a function to which adversaries can *directly* query in one construction (i.e., h in F^h_1) is replaced with another function to which adversaries can query *only indirectly* in the other construction (i.e., g in F_2).
2. On the other hand, in Lemma 6, a function to which adversaries can query *only indirectly* in one construction (i.e., f_{out} in H^h_i of G_i) is replaced with another function to which adversaries can query *only indirectly* in the other construction (i.e., f'_{out} in H'^h_i of G'_i).

In the proof of Proposition 4, we had to assure that the probability that an adversary directly queries to h a value that is recorded in a database is very small (i.e., the probability of the bad event hit in Sect. 1.2 is very small). This is the reason that we introduced the notion of equivalent databases. On the other hand, in Lemma 6, adversaries can query to both of f_{out} and f'_{out} only indirectly (adversaries do not have full control on inputs to f_{out} and f'_{out}). In particular, we can define bad events in Lemma 6 in such a way that whether they happen or not do not depend on the values of $\mathcal{A}$'s queries, and their probability can be bounded by using the randomness of outputs of random functions (like coll in Sect. 1.2). Therefore we do not have to introduce the notion of equivalent databases in Lemma 6. Hence it easier to prove Lemma 6 than to prove Proposition 4.

For the distinguishing advantage between G'_i and G_{i+1} for $1 \leq i < \ell$, the following lemma holds.

Lemma 7 (G_i' and G_{i+1}). $\mathbf{Adv}^{\mathrm{dist}}_{(H_i'^h,h),(H_{i+1}^h,h)}(\mathcal{A})$ *is in* $O\left(\sqrt{(q_h+Q\ell)^3/2^n}\right)$.

Proof. Let $f_{i+1}'^h : \{0,1\}^{m(i+1)} \to \{0,1\}^n$ be the function defined by $f_{i+1}'^h(M[1]\|\cdots\|M[i+1]) := h(M[i+1]\|f_i(M[1]\|\cdots\|M[i]))$.

For an adversary $\mathcal{A}$ to distinguish $(H_i'^h,h)$ from (H_{i+1}^h,h) that makes at most Q quantum queries to $H_i'^h$ or H_{i+1}^h and at most q_h quantum queries to h, we construct another adversary $\mathcal{B}$ to distinguish $(f_{i+1}'^h,h)$ and (f_{i+1},h) by making $O(Q)$ queries to $f_{i+1}'^h$ or f_{i+1} and $O(q_h+Q\ell)$ queries to h, as follows.

$\mathcal{B}$ is given a quantum oracle access to $\mathcal{O}^h$, which is $f_{i+1}'^h$ or f_{i+1}, in addition to a quantum oracle access to h. First, $\mathcal{B}$ chooses functions $\tilde{g}_j : \{0,1\}^{jm} \to \{0,1\}^n$ for $j = 1,\ldots,i$ and $f_{out} : \{0,1\}^n \to \{0,1\}^n$ uniformly at random, and runs $\mathcal{A}$. When $\mathcal{A}$ makes a query to the second oracle (which is supposed to be h), $\mathcal{B}$ responds by querying to h. When $\mathcal{A}$ queries $M = M[1]\|\cdots\|M[j]$ to the first oracle (which is supposed to be $H_i'^h$ or H_{i+1}^h), $\mathcal{B}$ responds to $\mathcal{A}$ as follows:

1. If $j \leq i$, $\mathcal{B}$ computes $T = \tilde{g}_j(M)$ by itself, and responds to $\mathcal{A}$ with T.
2. If $j > i$, $\mathcal{B}$ computes $S_{i+1} := \mathcal{O}^h(M)$, $S_u := h(M[u]\|S_{u-1})$ for $u = i+2,\ldots,j$, and $T := f_{out}(S_j)$, by making queries to $\mathcal{O}^h$ and h. Then $\mathcal{B}$ responds to $\mathcal{A}$ with T.

Finally, $\mathcal{B}$ returns $\mathcal{A}$'s output as its own output.

Then $\mathcal{B}$ perfectly simulates $H_i'^h$ or H_{i+1}^h depending on whether $\mathcal{O}^h = f_{i+1}'^h$ or $\mathcal{O}^h = f_{i+1}$, which implies that $\mathbf{Adv}^{\mathrm{dist}}_{(H_i'^h,h),(H_{i+1}^h,h)}(\mathcal{A}) = \mathbf{Adv}^{\mathrm{dist}}_{(f_{i+1}'^h,h),(f_{i+1},h)}(\mathcal{B})$. In addition, $\mathcal{B}$ makes at most $O(Q)$ quantum queries to $f_{i+1}'^h$ or f_{i+1} and $O(q_h + Q\ell)$ quantum queries to h. Therefore

$$\mathbf{Adv}^{\mathrm{dist}}_{(H_i'^h,h),(H_{i+1}^h,h)}(\mathcal{A}) = \mathbf{Adv}^{\mathrm{dist}}_{(f_{i+1}'^h,h),(f_{i+1},h)}(\mathcal{B}) \leq O\left(\sqrt{\frac{(q_h+Q\ell)^3}{2^n}}\right) \quad (17)$$

follows from Proposition 4. □

Proof (of Proposition 6). The claim of the proposition immediately follows from Lemma 4, Lemma 5, Lemma 6, and Lemma 7. □

Acknowledgements. The second author was supported in part by JSPS KAKENHI Grant Number JP20K11675.

References

1. Alagic, G., Majenz, C., Russell, A., Song, F.: Quantum-access-secure message authentication via blind-unforgeability. In: Canteaut, A., Ishai, Y. (eds.) EURO-CRYPT 2020. LNCS, Part III, vol. 12107, pp. 788–817. Springer, Cham (2020). https://doi.org/10.1007/978-3-030-45727-3_27
2. Alagic, G., Russell, A.: Quantum-secure symmetric-key cryptography based on hidden shifts. In: Coron, J.-S., Nielsen, J.B. (eds.) EUROCRYPT 2017. LNCS, Part III, vol. 10212, pp. 65–93. Springer, Cham (2017). https://doi.org/10.1007/978-3-319-56617-7_3

3. ANSI: Retail Financial Services Symmetric Key Management Part 1: Using Symmetric Techniques. ANSI X9.24-1-2017 (2017)
4. Bellare, M., Canetti, R., Krawczyk, H.: Keying hash functions for message authentication. In: Koblitz, N. (ed.) CRYPTO 1996. LNCS, vol. 1109, pp. 1–15. Springer, Heidelberg (1996). https://doi.org/10.1007/3-540-68697-5_1
5. Bellare, M., Kilian, J., Rogaway, P.: The security of cipher block chaining message authentication code. In: Desmedt, Y.G. (ed.) CRYPTO 1994. LNCS, vol. 839, pp. 341–358. Springer, Heidelberg (1994). https://doi.org/10.1007/3-540-48658-5_32
6. Bindel, N., Hamburg, M., Hövelmanns, K., Hülsing, A., Persichetti, E.: Tighter proofs of CCA security in the quantum random oracle model. In: Hofheinz, D., Rosen, A. (eds.) TCC 2019. LNCS, Part II, vol. 11892, pp. 61–90. Springer, Cham (2019). https://doi.org/10.1007/978-3-030-36033-7_3
7. Black, J., Rogaway, P.: CBC MACs for arbitrary-length messages: the three-key constructions. In: Bellare, M. (ed.) CRYPTO 2000. LNCS, vol. 1880, pp. 197–215. Springer, Heidelberg (2000). https://doi.org/10.1007/3-540-44598-6_12
8. Black, J., Rogaway, P.: A block-cipher mode of operation for parallelizable message authentication. In: Knudsen, L.R. (ed.) EUROCRYPT 2002. LNCS, vol. 2332, pp. 384–397. Springer, Heidelberg (2002). https://doi.org/10.1007/3-540-46035-7_25
9. Boneh, D., Dagdelen, Ö., Fischlin, M., Lehmann, A., Schaffner, C., Zhandry, M.: Random oracles in a quantum world. In: Lee, D.H., Wang, X. (eds.) ASIACRYPT 2011. LNCS, vol. 7073, pp. 41–69. Springer, Heidelberg (2011). https://doi.org/10.1007/978-3-642-25385-0_3
10. Boneh, D., Zhandry, M.: Quantum-secure message authentication codes. In: Johansson, T., Nguyen, P.Q. (eds.) EUROCRYPT 2013. LNCS, vol. 7881, pp. 592–608. Springer, Heidelberg (2013). https://doi.org/10.1007/978-3-642-38348-9_35
11. Brassard, G., HØyer, P., Tapp, A.: Quantum cryptanalysis of hash and claw-free functions. In: Lucchesi, C.L., Moura, A.V. (eds.) LATIN 1998. LNCS, vol. 1380, pp. 163–169. Springer, Heidelberg (1998). https://doi.org/10.1007/BFb0054319
12. Chiesa, A., Manohar, P., Spooner, N.: Succinct arguments in the quantum random oracle model. In: Hofheinz, D., Rosen, A. (eds.) TCC 2019. LNCS, Part II, vol. 11892, pp. 1–29. Springer, Cham (2019). https://doi.org/10.1007/978-3-030-36033-7_1
13. Coron, J.-S., Dodis, Y., Malinaud, C., Puniya, P.: Merkle-Damgård revisited: how to construct a hash function. In: Shoup, V. (ed.) CRYPTO 2005. LNCS, vol. 3621, pp. 430–448. Springer, Heidelberg (2005). https://doi.org/10.1007/11535218_26
14. Czajkowski, J., Hülsing, A., Schaffner, C.: Quantum indistinguishability of random sponges. In: Boldyreva, A., Micciancio, D. (eds.) CRYPTO 2019. LNCS, Part II, vol. 11693, pp. 296–325. Springer, Cham (2019). https://doi.org/10.1007/978-3-030-26951-7_11
15. Garg, S., Yuen, H., Zhandry, M.: New security notions and feasibility results for authentication of quantum data. In: Katz, J., Shacham, H. (eds.) CRYPTO 2017. LNCS, Part II, vol. 10402, pp. 342–371. Springer, Cham (2017). https://doi.org/10.1007/978-3-319-63715-0_12
16. Gaži, P., Pietrzak, K., Rybár, M.: The exact PRF security of NMAC and HMAC. In: Garay, J.A., Gennaro, R. (eds.) CRYPTO 2014. LNCS, Part I, vol. 8616, pp. 113–130. Springer, Heidelberg (2014). https://doi.org/10.1007/978-3-662-44371-2_7
17. Grover, L.K.: A fast quantum mechanical algorithm for database search. In: ACM STOC 1996, Proceedings, pp. 212–219 (1996)

18. Hosoyamada, A., Iwata, T.: 4-round Luby-Rackoff construction is a qPRP. In: Galbraith, S.D., Moriai, S. (eds.) ASIACRYPT 2019. LNCS, Part I, vol. 11921, pp. 145–174. Springer, Cham (2019). https://doi.org/10.1007/978-3-030-34578-5_6

19. Hosoyamada, A., Iwata, T.: 4-round Luby-Rackoff construction is a qPRP: tight quantum security bound. IACR Cryptol. ePrint Arch. 2019/243, version 20200720:101411 (2020). (A revised version of [18].)

20. Hosoyamada, A., Iwata, T.: On tight quantum security of HMAC and NMAC in the quantum random oracle model (2021). to appear on IACR Cryptology ePrint Archive

21. Hosoyamada, A., Yasuda, K.: Building quantum-one-way functions from block ciphers: Davies-Meyer and Merkle-Damgård constructions. In: Peyrin, T., Galbraith, S. (eds.) ASIACRYPT 2018. LNCS, vol. 11272, pp. 275–304. Springer, Cham (2018). https://doi.org/10.1007/978-3-030-03326-2_10

22. Iwata, T., Kurosawa, K.: OMAC: one-key CBC MAC. In: FSE 2003, Proceedings, pp. 129–153 (2003)

23. Kaplan, M., Leurent, G., Leverrier, A., Naya-Plasencia, M.: Breaking symmetric cryptosystems using quantum period finding. In: Robshaw, M., Katz, J. (eds.) CRYPTO 2016. LNCS, Part II, vol. 9815, pp. 207–237. Springer, Heidelberg (2016). https://doi.org/10.1007/978-3-662-53008-5_8

24. Liu, Q., Zhandry, M.: On finding quantum multi-collisions. In: Ishai, Y., Rijmen, V. (eds.) EUROCRYPT 2019. LNCS, Part III, vol. 11478, pp. 189–218. Springer, Cham (2019). https://doi.org/10.1007/978-3-030-17659-4_7

25. Liu, Q., Zhandry, M.: Revisiting post-quantum Fiat-Shamir. In: Boldyreva, A., Micciancio, D. (eds.) CRYPTO 2019. LNCS, Part II, vol. 11693, pp. 326–355. Springer, Cham (2019). https://doi.org/10.1007/978-3-030-26951-7_12

26. NIST: Secure Hash Standard (SHS). NIST FIPS PUB 180-4 (2015)

27. NIST: SHA-3 Standard: Permutation-Based Hash and Extendable-Output Functions. NIST FIPS PUB 202 (2015)

28. NIST: Announcing request for nominations for public-key post-quantum cryptographic algorithms. National Institute of Standards and Technology (2016)

29. Patarin, J.: The "coefficients H" technique. In: Avanzi, R.M., Keliher, L., Sica, F. (eds.) SAC 2008. LNCS, vol. 5381, pp. 328–345. Springer, Heidelberg (2009). https://doi.org/10.1007/978-3-642-04159-4_21

30. Saito, T., Xagawa, K., Yamakawa, T.: Tightly-secure key-encapsulation mechanism in the quantum random oracle model. In: Nielsen, J.B., Rijmen, V. (eds.) EUROCRYPT 2018. LNCS, Part III, vol. 10822, pp. 520–551. Springer, Cham (2018). https://doi.org/10.1007/978-3-319-78372-7_17

31. Sanchez, I.A., Fischer, D.: Authenticated encryption in civilian space missions: context and requirements. DIAC - Directions in Authenticated Ciphers (2012)

32. Song, F., Yun, A.: Quantum security of NMAC and related constructions. In: Katz, J., Shacham, H. (eds.) CRYPTO 2017. LNCS, Part II, vol. 10402, pp. 283–309. Springer, Cham (2017). https://doi.org/10.1007/978-3-319-63715-0_10

33. Zhandry, M.: How to construct quantum random functions. In: FOCS 2012, Proceedings, pp. 679–687. IEEE (2012)

34. Zhandry, M.: How to record quantum queries, and applications to quantum indifferentiability. In: Boldyreva, A., Micciancio, D. (eds.) CRYPTO 2019. LNCS, Part II, vol. 11693, pp. 239–268. Springer, Cham (2019). https://doi.org/10.1007/978-3-030-26951-7_9

Quantum Collision Attacks on Reduced SHA-256 and SHA-512

Akinori Hosoyamada[1,2(✉)] and Yu Sasaki[1]

[1] NTT Secure Platform Laboratories, Tokyo, Japan
{akinori.hosoyamada.bh,yu.sasaki.sk}@hco.ntt.co.jp
[2] Nagoya University, Nagoya, Japan
hosoyamada.akinori@nagoya-u.jp

Abstract. In this paper, we study dedicated quantum collision attacks on SHA-256 and SHA-512 for the first time. The attacks reach 38 and 39 steps, respectively, which significantly improve the classical attacks for 31 and 27 steps. Both attacks adopt the framework of the previous work that converts many semi-free-start collisions into a 2-block collision, and are faster than the generic attack in the cost metric of time-space tradeoff. We observe that the number of required semi-free-start collisions can be reduced in the quantum setting, which allows us to convert the previous classical 38 and 39 step semi-free-start collisions into a collision. The idea behind our attacks is simple and will also be applicable to other cryptographic hash functions.

Keywords: Symmetric key cryptography · Hash function · SHA-256 · SHA-512 · Collision attack · Quantum attack · Conversion from semi-free-start collisions

1 Introduction

Cryptographic hash functions take an arbitrary length message as input and generate a fixed-length bit string. One of the most important security criteria is collision resistance. For a hash function $\mathcal{H} : \{0,1\}^* \to \{0,1\}^n$, the complexity to find two distinct values x_1 and x_2 such that $\mathcal{H}(x_1) = \mathcal{H}(x_2)$ should be $O(2^{n/2})$. The collision resistance is a practically relevant notion. For example, Stevens et al. [37], in their attack against SHA-1, forged two PDF documents with the same hash digest that display different arbitrarily-chosen visual contents.

The SHA-2 family is one of the most important hash functions at the present time, which is specified and standardized by NIST [32]. There are two core algorithms; SHA-256 and SHA-512, depending on the word size. Moreover four schemes are additionally specified depending on the output size. SHA-2 are used in wide range of communication protocols such as TLS/SSL, SSH, and IPsec. SHA-2 are also used by the digital currency such as Bitcoin. After the recent break of SHA-1 [22], industry accelerated the migration to SHA-2.

© International Association for Cryptologic Research 2021
T. Malkin and C. Peikert (Eds.): CRYPTO 2021, LNCS 12825, pp. 616–646, 2021.
https://doi.org/10.1007/978-3-030-84242-0_22

History of SHA-2 Cryptanalysis. SHA-2 received a massive amount of security analysis. Preimage attacks were studied in [1,13,18,20] and a conversion to pseudo-collisions was studied in [23]. Those would work relatively a large number of rounds, say 52 out of 64 steps of SHA-256 [20], while those only achieve a marginal amount of speed up. Those are interesting theoretical results but not strongly related to this research. As a non-random property, second-order differential collisions defined over four distinct inputs were studied [3].

More relevant works to this research are the attempts to apply previous collision finding techniques to SHA-2 or to find collisions on reduced-step SHA-2. The challenge to find a collision on reduced-step SHA-2 was initiated by [31], which found a collision on 19 out of 64 steps of SHA-224. This is a pioneering work to construct differential characteristic only having a single local collision. Then, this type of local collisions were manually optimized to find collisions of 21 steps of SHA-256 [33], and later improved to 22 steps [35], and to 24 steps and extended to SHA-512 [17,36]. However, it was indicated that the local collision by [33] could work only up to 24 rounds [17] and indeed this was the last work for improving the manually detected local collision.

The most recent technical innovation is the development of automated differential characteristic search tools, which was initiated by Mendel et al. [27] to find a collision on 27 steps of SHA-256. Because of the search space, the efficiency of the algorithm is crucial for the automated search tool. Mendel et al. improved the algorithm and presented a 31-step collision attack and a 38-step semi-free-start collision attack against SHA-256 [29].[1] This is the current best (semi-free-start) collision attacks for SHA-256. The algorithm was further improved to apply it to SHA-512 [10], SHA-512/224 and SHA-512-256 [7]. For SHA-512, 27-step collisions and 39-step semi-free-start collisions [7] are the current best results.

Techniques for Finding SHA-2 Collisions. For the attack on SHA-256, Mendel et al. [29] presented a framework to convert semi-free-start collision attacks having some special property into a 2-block collision. The framework is illustrated in Fig. 1. The attacker first analyzes the second block without fixing IV for the second block, IV_{second}. A semi-free-start collision attack that can work for 2^X choices, typically for any unfixed X bits, of IV_{second} is located in the second block. Then, the attacker tests 2^{n-X} messages for the first block to hit one of 2^X choices of IV_{second}, typically to hit the fixed $n-X$ bits of IV_{second}. Finally, the attacker determines the rest part of the second block to generate a 2-block collision.

The cost for the first block is 2^{256-X} for SHA-256. To be faster than the birthday paradox, X must satisfy $X > 128$. To achieve such a semi-free-start collision attack, the previous work [29] generated a differential characteristic such that the characteristic can be satisfied for any value of the first five message words. Hence, it achieves $X = 160$. (As explained later, those five message words can be adjusted to achieve a fixed 160-bit internal state value for any 160 bits of IV_{second}.)

---

[1] For readers who are not familiar with various types of collisions, we explain the difference among collisions, semi-free-stard collisions, and free-start collisions in Section A of this paper's full version [15].

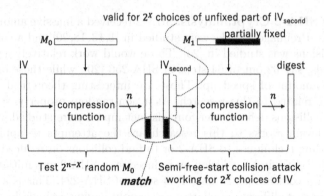

Fig. 1. Converting Semi-free-start Collisions into 2-block Collisions.

Dedicated Quantum Collision Attacks. Recently, it has been shown that collision attacks on hash functions with quantum machines can break more rounds than the attacks with classical machines [14]. Whether a hash function is attacked or not is judged by comparing the complexity of the generic attack (birthday paradox) and a dedicated attack. To find a collision, dedicated attacks mostly apply differential cryptanalysis. With quantum machines, the speed of finding a value satisfying a differential characteristic becomes a square root compared to classical machines, while the speed of the generic collision attack cannot be a square root of the birthday paradox, $O(2^{n/4})$. Indeed, the tight bound of the query complexity to find a collision was proven to be $O(2^{n/3})$ [38]. As a result, dedicated attacks can be stronger when quantum machines are available. In fact, such cases were observed for AES hashing modes [9,14] and Gimli [11].

In the quantum setting, the generic attack complexity of finding collisions depends on settings about the resource that an attacker can use. The previous work discussed three settings. In the first setting, a small (polynomial size) quantum computer and a large (exponential size) qRAM. In the second setting, a small (polynomial size) quantum computer and a large (exponential size) classical memory, In the third setting, efficiency of quantum algorithms are evaluated by their time-space tradeoff.

In this paper, we focus on the third setting, of which details are as follows. Note that we do not take error corrections into account and consider that the running time of a quantum circuit is proportional to the depth of the circuit.

Cost metric of time-space tradeoff. The efficiency of an attack is evaluated by the tradeoff between T and S, where T is the attack time complexity (or, the depth of the quantum circuit) and S is the hardware size required for the attack (i.e., S is the maximum size of quantum computers (or, width of quantum circuits) and classical computers). S can be exponentially large, and we do not make distinction between qubits for computation and qubits for memory. Bernstein [2] observed that, when a *classical* computer of size S is available, by using the parallel rho method [34] we can find a collision of a random function in time $T = O(2^{n/2}/S)$. There does not exist a quantum attack on a random function that achieves a better tradeoff than this classical attack.[2] Hence, a dedicated quantum collision attack on a concrete hash function that uses a quantum computer of size S is considered to be valid if its time complexity T is less than $2^{n/2}/S$.

The condition $T < 2^{n/2}/S$ is equivalent to $T \cdot S < 2^{n/2}$. Hence the efficiency of a quantum attack in the time-space tradeoff metric is evaluated by the multiplication of T and S, and the threshold for the attack to be valid is $2^{n/2}$.

Jaques and Schanck [19] showed that when error correction is necessary and quantum memory is actively corrected, it is realistic to model that the cost of a quantum attack is proportional to the multiplication of the depth and the width of the quantum circuit used in the attack. Therefore, although we do not care about error corrections in our complexity analysis, the cost metric of time-space tradeoff is in fact reasonable from the view point of cost estimation *including* quantum error correction (when quantum memory is actively corrected).

Research Challenge. The collision resistance of SHA-2 family in the quantum setting has not been studied before.[3] In fact, this is not a simple task. As mentioned before, the current differential characteristics for SHA-2 collision attacks consist of a single local collision. The previous work showed [14] that the cost to satisfy an uncontrolled part of the differential characteristic can be square root, while the differential characteristic for SHA-2 does not have such a form. Thus this issue deserves careful investigation.

Our Contributions. In this paper, we present quantum collision attacks on SHA-256 and on SHA-512 that break more rounds than the attacks in the classical setting. Our attacks are valid in the time-space tradeoff cost metric. The number of attacked steps is compared in Table 1.

To generate collisions, we follow the same approach as the previous work. Namely, we locate a semi-free-start collision in the second block and find a first-block message to hit one of IVs that is acceptable for the second block. In the previous work, it is principally inevitable that the semi-free-start collision attack must work for at least 2^X choices of IVs, where $X > 128$ for SHA-256. This is a strong requirement, which significantly restricts the search space to find a suitable differential characteristic. We observe that if quantum machines are available, we can construct an attack with an intuitive condition of $X > 0$ by ignoring the constant factor. In practice, the constant factor cannot be ignored and we will show a rigorous complexity analysis.

---

[2] There is no proof that the bound $O(2^{n/2}/S)$ is the best, but achieving a better bound is hard.

[3] From the view point of provable security, there is a previous work that suggests that the SHA-2 mode is reasonable in the quantum setting [16].

Table 1. Comparison of the attack results. The quantum attacks on SHA-256 and SHA-512 are faster than the generic attack as long as $S < 2^{12}$ and $S < 2^{6.6}$, respectively.

Target	Setting	Type	Steps	Complexity	Reference
SHA-256	Classic	Collision	28/64	Practical	[29]
	Classic	Collision	31/64	$2^{65.5}$	[29]
	Classic	Semi-free-start collision	38/64	Practical	[29]
	Quantum	Collision	38/64	$2^{122}/\sqrt{S}$	Sect. 5
SHA-512	Classic	Collision	24/80	Practical	[17,36]
	Classic	Collision	27/80	Practical	[7]
	Classic	Semi-free-start collision	38/80	Practical	[10]
	Classic	Semi-free-start collision	39/80	Practical	[7]
	Quantum	Collision	39/80	$2^{252.7}/\sqrt{S}$	Sect. 6

For SHA-256, the previous work [29] found a differential characteristic with $X > 128$ up to 31 steps, while unconditioned semi-free-start collisions could be generated for 38 steps. Hence we start from the 38-step semi-free-start collision example generated by [29] and slightly modify its message words so that semi-free-start collisions can be generated for multiple IVs. We achieve $X \approx 20$ for 38-step SHA-256. If we have a quantum computer of size S, the attack complexity is about $c \cdot \sqrt{2^{256-20}/S} = 2^{122}/\sqrt{S}$, where c is a small constant and rigorous analysis shows $c \approx 2^4$. Because the generic attack cost under the time-space metric is $2^{128}/S$, our attack is faster than the generic attack when $S < 2^{12}$.

For SHA-512, it seems difficult to build a differential characteristic with a lot of degrees of freedom such as $X > 256$. In fact, the previous work [7] could not apply the 2-block conversion, and the current strategy is limited to be a single-block attack. In this paper, we observe that the 39-step semi-free-start collision attack [7] can accept multiple choices of IV with some X that is much smaller than 256, and will convert it into 2-block collision in the quantum setting.

As we mentioned before, the previous work [14] discussed three settings depending on available computational resources. In fact our attacks are valid only in the setting of time-space tradeoff because the time complexity exceed the generic complexity in other settings. Nevertheless, we would like to remark that dedicated attacks that are valid in this setting (including our attacks) are always better than the generic attacks in other settings from the viewpoint of time-space tradeoff. This is because the generic attacks in other settings have time-space tradeoff $T^2 \cdot S = 2^n$, which is worse than the trade-off $T \cdot S = 2^n$ of the generic attack in our setting.[4]

---

[4] The generic attacks in other two settings are the BHT algorithm [5] and the CNS algorithm [6]. The BHT algorithm runs in time $T = O(2^{n/3})$ and uses $S = O(2^{n/3})$ qRAM. The CNS algorithm runs in time $T = O(2^{2n/5})$ and uses no qRAM, but requires $S = O(2^{n/5})$ classical memory.

Some readers may think that our attacks are invalid because the margin of our attacks (compared to the generic attack) are too small while we do not take the overhead for quantum computation, or their complexity does not significantly outperform the classical complexity. However, security of symmetric-key primitives is generally measured under the most vulnerable environment (they must resist any attacks in any nitpicked setting like $S = 1$). The principle of security under the most vulnerable environment makes it natural to ignore the overhead because the overhead for quantum computation may drastically be reduced by future technical developments. In addition, when reduced-step variants of symmetric-key primitives are analyzed, the most important factors is the number of attacked steps rather than the attack cost. Our quantum attacks break significantly more steps than the classical attacks.

Remark 1. For reference, we also provide discussions on comparison between our attacks and a generic collision attack based on the multi-target preimage search. See Section B of this paper's full version [15] for details.

Future Directions. Due to its simplicity, we believe that the idea of our 2-block quantum collision attacks is applicable to other cryptographic hash functions. It will also be interesting to study optimizations of differential characteristics for the classical semi-free-start collision attack with respect to the conversion to the quantum collision attack. Some observations and initial work will be provided in the last part of the paper.

Paper Organization. Section 2 is preliminaries. Section 3 explains the previous collision and semi-free-start collision attacks. Section 4 explains our observation that is used in our quantum attacks. Sections 5 and 6 show the attack algorithms and their evaluations. Section 7 provides discussion toward future applications of our attack idea. Finally, we conclude this paper in Sect. 8.

2 Preliminaries

For n-bit strings x and y, $\neg x$, $x \wedge y$, $x \vee y$ and $x \oplus y$ denote the bit-wise negation of x, the bit-wise AND on x and y, the bit-wise OR on x and y, and the bit-wise XOR on x and y, respectively. For an n-bit string x and a non-negative integer m such that $m \leq n$, $x \gg m$ (resp., $x \ggg m$) denotes the m-bit right shift operation on x (resp., the m-bit *circular* right shift operation on x). We identify the set of n-bit strings $\{0,1\}^n$ with the sets $\{0, \ldots, 2^n - 1\}$ and $\mathbb{Z}/2^n\mathbb{Z}$. $x + y$ denotes the modular addition of x and y for $x, y \in \mathbb{Z}/2^n\mathbb{Z}$, unless otherwise noted. Sometimes we use the symbol $\boxplus$ instead of $+$. We assume that readers are familiar with basics on quantum computation[5].

---

[5] Knowledge on quantum computations is required to fully understand our complexity analysis, though, essentially the quantum algorithms we use are only the (parallelized) Grover search, and we use them in an almost black-box manner.

2.1 Specification of SHA-256 and SHA-512

SHA-256 and SHA-512 adopt the Merkle-Damgård construction, and their compression functions adopt the Davies-Meyer construction. Let w be the word size, which is 32 for SHA-256 and 64 for SHA-512. The length of message blocks is $16w$ bits (512 bits for SHA-256 and 1024 bits for SHA-512), and the length of chaining values and final outputs is $8w$ bits (256 bits for SHA-256 and 512 bits for SHA-512).

Given a chaining value (or the initial value IV) $H = (H_0, \ldots, H_7) \in (\{0,1\}^w)^8$ and a message block $M = (M_0, \ldots, M_{15}) \in (\{0,1\}^w)^{16}$, the output value of the compression function $f(H, M)$ is computed by iteratively updating internal states as follows. The number of steps, which is denoted by r, is 64 for SHA-256 and 80 for SHA-512.

1. (Message expansion.) Compute W_i $(i = 0, \ldots, r - 1)$ by

$$W_i := \begin{cases} M_i & \text{for } i = 0, \ldots, 15, \\ \sigma_1(W_{i-2}) + W_{i-7} + \sigma_0(W_{i-15}) + W_{i-16} & \text{for } i = 16, \ldots, r - 1. \end{cases}$$

   The functions $\sigma_0, \sigma_1 : \{0,1\}^w \to \{0,1\}^w$ are defined later.
2. (Iterative state updates.) Set $st_{-1} := H$. For $i = 0, \ldots, r - 1$, update the $8w$-bit state $st_{i-1} = (A_{i-1}, A_{i-2}, A_{i-3}, A_{i-4}, E_{i-1}, E_{i-2}, E_{i-3}, E_{i-4})$ to $st_i = (A_i, A_{i-1}, A_{i-2}, A_{i-3}, E_i, E_{i-1}, E_{i-2}, E_{i-3})$, where

$$E_i := E_{i-4} + A_{i-4} + \Sigma_1(E_{i-1}) + \text{IF}(E_{i-1}, E_{i-2}, E_{i-3}) + K_i + W_i,$$
$$A_i := \Sigma_0(A_{i-1}) + \text{MAJ}(A_{i-1}, A_{i-2}, A_{i-3}) + E_i - A_{i-4}.$$

   The functions $\text{IF}, \text{MAJ} : (\{0,1\}^w)^3 \to \{0,1\}^w$ and $\Sigma_0, \Sigma_1 : \{0,1\}^w \to \{0,1\}^w$ are defined later. K_i is a step-dependent constant. Since the value of K_i does not affect our attacks, we omit the value of K_i. See also Fig. 2.
3. Compute the next chaining value $f(H, M)$ as $f(H, M) := st_{r-1} + H$. (Only here, the symbol "+" denotes the word-wise modular addition.)

The functions $\text{IF}, \text{MAJ} : (\{0,1\}^w)^3 \to \{0,1\}^w$ are defined as

$$\text{IF}(x, y, z) = (x \wedge y) \oplus ((\neg x) \wedge z), \quad \text{MAJ}(x, y, z) = (x \wedge y) \oplus (y \wedge z) \oplus (z \wedge x)$$

for both of SHA-256 and SHA-512. In addition, $\Sigma_0, \Sigma_1, \sigma_0, \sigma_1$ are defined by

$$\Sigma_0(x) = (x \ggg 2) \oplus (x \ggg 13) \oplus (x \ggg 22),$$
$$\sigma_0(x) = (x \ggg 7) \oplus (x \ggg 18) \oplus (x \gg 3),$$
$$\Sigma_1(x) = (x \ggg 6) \oplus (x \ggg 11) \oplus (x \ggg 25),$$
$$\sigma_1(x) = (x \ggg 17) \oplus (x \ggg 19) \oplus (x \gg 10)$$

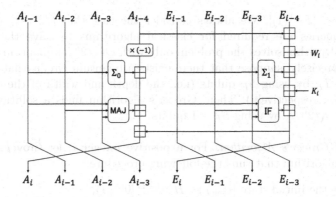

Fig. 2. This is an alternative representation of the state update function devised by the previous work [27]. The operation "$\times(-1)$" denotes the multiplication by (-1) in $\mathbb{Z}/2^w\mathbb{Z}$.

for SHA-256, and

$$\Sigma_0(x) = (x \ggg 28) \oplus (x \ggg 34) \oplus (x \ggg 39),$$
$$\sigma_0(x) = (x \ggg 1) \oplus (x \ggg 8) \oplus (x \gg 7),$$
$$\Sigma_1(x) = (x \ggg 14) \oplus (x \ggg 18) \oplus (x \ggg 41),$$
$$\sigma_1(x) = (x \ggg 19) \oplus (x \ggg 61) \oplus (x \gg 6)$$

for SHA-512.

Let $W_{i,j}$ denote bit j of W_i, where $W_{i,0}$ is the least significant bit and $W_{i,w-1}$ is the most significant bit. We also use the same notation to denote bit positions for other variables such as A_i and E_i.

2.2   Quantum Computation

We use the quantum circuit model as the model of quantum computation. Let H denote the Hadamard operator defined by $H\,|b\rangle = \sum_{c\in\{0,1\}}(-1)^{b\cdot c}\,|c\rangle$ for $b \in \{0,1\}$. The quantum oracle of a function $f : \{0,1\}^m \to \{0,1\}^n$ is the unitary operator O_f defined by $O_f\,|x\rangle\,|y\rangle = |x\rangle\,|y \oplus f(x)\rangle$ for $x \in \{0,1\}^m$ and $y \in \{0,1\}^n$.

Grover's Algorithm. Grover's algorithm [12] is the quantum algorithm to solve the following database search problem.

Problem 1. Let $F : \{0,1\}^n \to \{0,1\}$ be a function such that $|F^{-1}(1)| > 0$. Given a (quantum) oracle access to F, find x such that $F(x) = 1$.

Let $t := |F^{-1}(1)|$. We always consider the case that $t/2^n \ll 1$. Though $O(2^n/t)$ queries are required for classical algorithms to solve the problem, Grover's algorithm solves the problem only with $O(\sqrt{2^n/t})$ quantum queries.

More precisely, suppose that there exists a quantum circuit that computes F in time T_F by using S_F qubits (i.e., the depth and width of the circuit are T_F and S_F, respectively). Then, Grover's algorithm finds a solution in time $T_F \cdot (\pi/4) \cdot \sqrt{2^n/t}$, by using $S_F + 1$ qubits.

Details of Grover's Algorithm. For a positive integer i, let $\mathsf{Grov}(F, i)$ be the quantum algorithm that runs the following procedure:

1. Prepare the initial state $|\psi_{\mathsf{init}}\rangle := H^{\otimes(n+1)} |0^n\rangle |1\rangle$.
2. Let θ be the value that satisfies $\sin^2 \theta = t/2^n$ and $0 \le \theta \le \pi/2$. Apply the unitary operator $Q_F := -(H^{\otimes n} \otimes I)(O_0 \otimes I)(H^{\otimes n} \otimes I)O_F$ iteratively i times on $|\psi_{\mathsf{init}}\rangle$. Here, O_F is the quantum oracle of F, and O_0 is the operator such that $O_0 |x\rangle = (-1)^{\delta_{x,0^n}} |x\rangle$ ($\delta_{x,y}$ is Kronecker's delta such that $\delta_{x,y} = 1$ if $x = y$ and $\delta_{x,y} = 0$ if $x \ne y$).
3. Measure the resulting state $Q_F^i |\psi_{\mathsf{init}}\rangle$, and output the most significant n bits.

Boyer et al. showed that, when we set the number of iterations i to be $\lfloor \pi/4\theta \rfloor$, the algorithm $\mathsf{Grov}(F, \lfloor \pi/4\theta \rfloor)$ outputs x such that $F(x) = 1$ with a probability at least $1 - t/N$ [4]. Since $\pi/4\theta \le \pi/(4 \sin \theta) = (\pi/4)\sqrt{2^n/t}$ holds, the running time of $\mathsf{Grov}(F, \lfloor \pi/4\theta \rfloor)$ is at most $T_F \cdot (\pi/4)\sqrt{2^n/t}$.

Remark 2. In the above arguments, we implicitly assume that t is known in advance. If t is not known in advance, we have to perform a more sophisticated procedure, which increases the total number of queries to F by a constant factor [4].

Parallelization. When $P \ge 2$ quantum computers are available, by running P copies of $\mathsf{Grov}(F, \lfloor \pi/4\theta\sqrt{P} \rfloor)$ in parallel, we can find a solution in time $T_F \cdot \frac{\pi}{4}\sqrt{2^n/(t \cdot P)}$ with a probability at least $1 - 1/e$ (we always consider the case that $(t \cdot P)/2^n \ll 1$). For completeness, we provide detailed explanations on the success probability in Section C of this paper's full version [15]

Cost Evaluation. As mentioned in Sect. 1, we evaluate the complexity of the attacks in the setting of time-space tradeoff. We do not take costs of quantum error corrections into account, and we consider that the running time of a quantum circuit is proportional to the depth of the circuit.

In each attack, we assume that there exists an implementation of the attack target primitive (i.e., SHA-256 or SHA-512) on a quantum circuit $\mathcal{C}$, and we regard that the unit of depth (resp., width) of quantum circuits is the depth (resp., width) of $\mathcal{C}$, so that our cost estimation will be independent from implementation methods of primitives.

In addition, we do not take communication costs into account. That is, we assume that arbitrary two-qubit quantum gate can be applied to arbitrary pair of qubits. The communication costs will not be significant in our attacks because we use quantum circuits just for running the Grover search (or, its simple parallelization) that requires only several times as much qubits as implementations of SHA-2 use.

3   Previous Works

This section provides an overview on the collision attack on 31-step SHA-256 in [29], the semi-free-start collision attack on 38-step SHA-256 in [29], and the semi-free-start collision attack on 39-step SHA-512 in [7,8].

3.1   Collision Attack on 31-Step SHA-256

The collision attack on 31-step SHA-256 in [29] finds a 2-block collision with time complexity $2^{65.5}$. Intuitively, a 2-block collision $(\tilde{M}||M, \tilde{M}||M')$ (here, $\tilde{M}, M, M'$ are in $\{0,1\}^{512}$, and $M \neq M'$) is constructed by searching for a random message $\tilde{M}$ for the first block and a semi-free-start collision (M, M') for the second block such that the output of the first block is the IV of the second block.

Semi-free-start collisions in the second block are constructed based on a local collision that starts at step 5 and ends at step 18, which is found by using heuristic automated search tools. The tool finds both of differential characteristics and conditions for message pairs (M, M') at the same time. See Table 2 for the differential characteristic and conditions for (M, M') shown in [29]. The meanings of the notations in Table 2 are as follows:

1. "-" indicates that the bit associated with M at the position must be equal to the corresponding bit associated with M'.
2. "0" indicates that the bit at the position must be 0 for both of M and M'.
3. "1" indicates that the bit at the position must be 1 for both of M and M'.
4. "u" indicates that the bit at the position must be 1 for M and 0 for M'.
5. "n" indicates that the bit at the position must be 0 for M and 1 for M'.

See also Remark 3. For each i, by A_i, E_i, W_i we denote the words of internal states and expanded messages as described in Sect. 2.1.

The authors of [29] also show an example of a semi-free-start collision of 31-step SHA-256 that satisfies the differential characteristic. See Table 6 of this paper's full version [15] for details.

Attack Procedure. Next, we describe the attack procedure. The important features of the differential characteristic in Table 2 are summarized as follows:

1. Only seven message words $(W_5, \dots, W_9, W_{16}, W_{18})$ have differences. Since $W_0, \dots, W_4, W_{10}, \dots, W_{15}$ do not have differences, $W_{17}, W_{19}, W_{26}, \dots, W_{30}$ do not have differences, either. The differences at $W_{20}, \dots, W_{25}$ need to be canceled out (see Table 3).

626   A. Hosoyamada and Y. Sasaki

Table 2. The 31-step differential characteristic for SHA-256 shown in [29].

i	ΔA_i	ΔE_i	ΔW_i
-4	---- ---- ---- ---- ---- ---- ---- ----	---- ---- ---- ---- ---- ---- ---- ----	
-3	---- ---- ---- ---- ---- ---- ---- ----	---- ---- ---- ---- ---- ---- ---- ----	
-2	---- ---- ---- ---- ---- ---- ---- ----	---- ---- ---- ---- ---- ---- ---- ----	
-1	---- ---- ---- ---- ---- ---- ---- ----	---- ---- ---- ---- ---- ---- ---- ----	
0	---- ---- ---- ---- ---- ---- ---- ----	---- ---- ---- ---- ---- ---- ---- ----	---- ---- ---- ---- ---- ---- ---- ----
1	---- ---- ---- ---- ---- ---- ---- ----	---- ---- ---- ---- ---- ---- ---- ----	---- ---- ---- ---- ---- ---- ---- ----
2	---- ---- ---- ---- ---- ---- ---- ----	---- ---- ---- ---- ---- ---- ---- ----	---- ---- ---- ---- ---- ---- ---- ----
3	---- ---- ---- ---- ---- ---- --0-	-0-- ---- ---- ---- --0- ---- ---- ----	---- ---- ---- ---- ---- ---- ---- ----
4	---- ---- ---- ---- ---- ---- --00	-1-- ---- ---1 ---- -01- --1- 0--0 --10	---- ---- ---- ---- ---- ---- ---- ----
5	-nnn -n-n -11- ---n --nu -1-- ---- -0n-	0nnn n1uu -0-1 101n -1nu --0- 11-1 -0n1	u--- uunu ---- ---n ---n ---- ---- --n-
6	unnn n--- ---- ---- ---- ---- ---- --0-	n-n1 0111 n--u 11u0 0n10 u1n- nn1n -1uu	nn1- n--- nu-n n--1 u--0 -un0 --n0 -nn-
7	---- ---- ---- ---n ---- ---- ---- n-0u	101u 0nn1 0-11 011u -n11 1n11 0un1 -nnn	00nn 0n10 1-n1 nnn1 u0nn -n01 1u-1 n0--
8	---- ---- ---- ---- ---- ---- ---- ----	1-uu 1111 0--0 u101 10n- 1010 1010 -0n0	0001 u000 1-00 0nuu un1n 01nn -01n uuuu
9	---- ---- ---- ---- ---- ---- ---- ----	1011 00uu 1111 11nu 1110 01-- 0111 10nn	---- -1-- ---- ---u n--- 0--- -11 un--
10	---- ---- ---- ---- u--- ---- ---- -u--	1-00 u110 1001 101u n00- -000 1--u 1n00	---0 ---- ---- ---- ---- ---- ---- --1-
11	---- ---- ---- ---- ---- ---- ---- ----	0101 00u0 nu1u uuuu u100 1000 000n 1u10	---- ---- ---- ---- ---- ---- ---- ----
12	---- ---- ---- ---- ---- ---- ---- ----	111n uuuu uuuu uuuu u001 1111 0110 0n00	---- ---- ---- ---- ---- ---- ---- ----
13	---- ---- ---- ---- ---- ---- ---- ----	---1 01-1 1-1- ---- 1--- ---- ---0 -0--	---- ---- ---- ---- ---- ---- ---- ----
14	---- ---- ---- ---- ---- ---- ---- ----	---1 00-- -001 1111 u--- ---- 1--- -u--	---- ---- ---- ---- ---- ---- ---- ----
15	---- ---- ---- ---- ---- ---- ---- ----	---- ---- ---- ---- 0--- ---- ---- -0--	---- ---- ---- ---- ---- ---- ---- ----
16	---- ---- ---- ---- ---- ---- ---- ----	---- ---- ---- ---- 1--- ---- ---- -1--	---- ---- ---- -unn nunn nnnn nnnn nn--
17	---- ---- ---- ---- ---- ---- ---- ----	---- ---- ---- ---- ---- ---- ---- ----	---- ---- ---- ---- ---- ---- ---- ----
18	---- ---- ---- ---- ---- ---- ---- ----	---- ---- ---- ---- ---- ---- ---- ----	---- ---- ---- ---- ---- n--- ---- -n--
19	---- ---- ---- ---- ---- ---- ---- ----	---- ---- ---- ---- ---- ---- ---- ----	---- ---- ---- ---- ---- ---- ---- ----
20	---- ---- ---- ---- ---- ---- ---- ----	---- ---- ---- ---- ---- ---- ---- ----	---- ---- ---- ---- ---- ---- ---- ----
21	---- ---- ---- ---- ---- ---- ---- ----	---- ---- ---- ---- ---- ---- ---- ----	---- ---- ---- ---- ---- ---- ---- ----
22	---- ---- ---- ---- ---- ---- ---- ----	---- ---- ---- ---- ---- ---- ---- ----	---- ---- ---- ---- ---- ---- ---- ----
23	---- ---- ---- ---- ---- ---- ---- ----	---- ---- ---- ---- ---- ---- ---- ----	---- ---- ---- ---- ---- ---- ---- ----
24	---- ---- ---- ---- ---- ---- ---- ----	---- ---- ---- ---- ---- ---- ---- ----	---- ---- ---- ---- ---- ---- ---- ----
25	---- ---- ---- ---- ---- ---- ---- ----	---- ---- ---- ---- ---- ---- ---- ----	---- ---- ---- ---- ---- ---- ---- ----
26	---- ---- ---- ---- ---- ---- ---- ----	---- ---- ---- ---- ---- ---- ---- ----	---- ---- ---- ---- ---- ---- ---- ----
27	---- ---- ---- ---- ---- ---- ---- ----	---- ---- ---- ---- ---- ---- ---- ----	---- ---- ---- ---- ---- ---- ---- ----
28	---- ---- ---- ---- ---- ---- ---- ----	---- ---- ---- ---- ---- ---- ---- ----	---- ---- ---- ---- ---- ---- ---- ----
29	---- ---- ---- ---- ---- ---- ---- ----	---- ---- ---- ---- ---- ---- ---- ----	---- ---- ---- ---- ---- ---- ---- ----
30	---- ---- ---- ---- ---- ---- ---- ----	---- ---- ---- ---- ---- ---- ---- ----	---- ---- ---- ---- ---- ---- ---- ----

2. No condition is imposed on the first five message words $W_0, \ldots, W_4$, thus those can be chosen freely.

By using these properties, the authors of [29] first show an attack with complexity $2^{99.5}$, and then show how to reduce the complexity to $2^{65.5}$.

The First Attack with Complexity $2^{99.5}$. Let f denote the (31-step) compression function. The procedure of the collision attack with complexity $2^{99.5}$ is as follows.

I. Use the automatic search tool to determine the message words $W_5, \ldots, W_{12}$ and the internal states from the beginning of step 5 to the end of step 12 (in the second block). Though $W_0, \ldots, W_4$ have not been chosen yet at this step, the values of the variables $E_1, \ldots, E_4$ and $A_{-3}, \ldots, A_4$ are completely

Table 3. The position of the message words where non-zero differences appear. "○" indicates that the word has non-zero difference. "×" indicates that the word is computed from previous words with non-zero differences but the difference is canceled out. (W_i is computed from W_{i-2}, W_{i-7}, W_{i-15}, and W_{i-16} for $i \geq 16$.)

W_i	0	1	2	3	4	5	6	7	8	9	10	11	12	13	14	15
Difference						○	○	○	○	○						
W_i	16	17	18	19	20	21	22	23	24	25	26	27	28	29	30	
Difference	○		○		×	×	×	×	×	×						

determined by the internal state at the beginning of step 5 (see also Fig. 4 of this paper's full version [15] for details). Note that $A_{-1}||A_{-2}||A_{-3}$ correspond to the 96 most significant bits of the initial value of the second block.

II. Find a message $\tilde{M}$ for the first block such that the 96 most significant bits of $f(\text{IV}, \tilde{M})$ is equal to $A_{-1}||A_{-2}||A_{-3}$. Compute the (uniquely determined) values $W_0, \ldots, W_4$ that is compatible with the chaining value $f(\text{IV}, \tilde{M})$ and the state at the beginning of step 5.

III. Now, $W_0, \ldots, W_{12}$ have been chosen. Use degrees of freedom in W_{13}, W_{14}, W_{15} to fulfill the conditions on E_{13}, E_{14}, E_{15}, W_{16}, and W_{18} (in addition to the cancellation of differences at $W_{20}, \ldots, W_{25}$). If it fails, go back to Step II.

Step II requires time 2^{96}. According to the authors of [29], Step I of the attack takes only seconds, and Step III succeeds with a probability about $1/12$ due to the lack of degrees of freedom in W_{13}, W_{14}, W_{15}, which was verified experimentally. The total time complexity is estimated as $12 \cdot 2^{96} \approx 2^{99.5}$.

The Second Attack with Complexity $2^{65.5}$. The attack complexity is reduced from $2^{99.5}$ to $2^{65.5}$ by computing many solutions in Step I. The idea is as follows. Suppose that ℓ solutions can be found for Step I (they are stored in a list). Then, the complexity of Step II can be reduced from 2^{96} to $2^{96}/\ell$. If a single solution in Step I can be found in time T_I, then the overall complexity of the attack becomes $T_I \cdot \ell + 12 \cdot 2^{96}/\ell$.

The authors of [29] claim that $T_I \approx 2^{25.5}$, and their experiments indicate that they can expect $\ell \approx 2^{34}$. Based on these observations, they deduced that a collision can be found with complexity $2^{25.5} \cdot 2^{34} + 12 \cdot 2^{96}/2^{34} \approx 2^{65.5}$.

3.2 Semi-Free-Start Collision Attack on 38-Step SHA-256

As well as the semi-free-start collisions in the 31-step collision attack, the semi-free-start collision of 38-step SHA-256 in [29] is constructed based on a local collision that starts at step 7 and ends at step 24, which are also found by using the heuristic automated search tool.

See Table 4 for the differential characteristic and the conditions for confirming message pairs shown in [29]. (See also Remark 3.) The semi-free-start collision of 38-step SHA-256 given in [29] is shown in Table 7 of this paper's full version [15].

3.3 Semi-Free-Start Collision Attack on 39-Step SHA-512

The semi-free-start collision of 39-step SHA-512 in [7,8] is also constructed based on a local collision that starts at step 8 and ends at step 26, which is also found by using the heuristic automated search tool.

See Table 5 of this paper's full version [15] for the differential characteristic and the conditions for confirming message pairs shown in [8]. (See also Remark 3.) The semi-free-start collision of 39-step SHA-512 given in [7,8] is shown in Table 8 of this paper's full version [15].

Table 4. The 38-step differential characteristic for SHA-256 shown in [29].

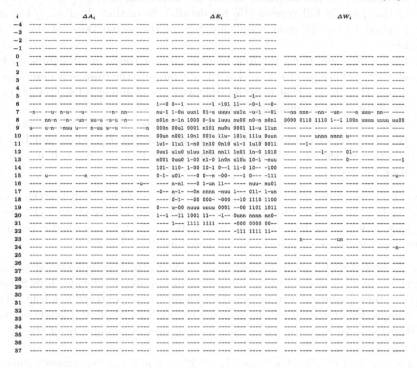

Remark 3. To be precise some bits in the differential characteristics in Tables 2, 4, and 5 of this paper's full version [15] have additional conditions. They are shown in the original papers [7,8,29] but we omit to show them because they are not significantly relevant to the basic idea of our attacks.

4   Observations and Ideas for Quantum Collision Attacks

For SHA-256, the previous 38-step semi-free-start collision is not converted into a collision while the 31-step semi-free-start collision is converted. For SHA-512, the previous 39-step semi-free-start collision is not converted.

In Sect. 4.1, we explain details on the reason that the semi-free-start collisions of 38-step SHA-256 and 39-step SHA-512 are not converted into collisions in the classical setting, based on the explanation in [7,8]. In Sect. 4.2, we explain our basic ideas on how to apply the conversion in the quantum setting.

4.1   Obstacles for Conversions in the Classical Setting

Summary of 31-Step SHA-256. Recall that the 31-step collision is obtained by matching the IV produced from the first block and semi-free-start collisions in the second block. Also recall that the attack consists of three steps.

In Step II of the attack, the degrees of freedom in the message words $W_0, \ldots, W_4$ are used to make the output of the first block and the local collision in the second block compatible. Let α denote the number of free bits in the message words that can be used to make those two values compatible. Since $W_0, \ldots, W_4$ can be chosen freely, $\alpha = 5 \cdot 32 = 160$ holds. For a randomly chosen $\tilde{M}$ and a single solution in Step I, the probability that they can be compatible is $2^\alpha/2^n$.

If we have ℓ solutions in Step I and if Step III succeeds with a probability p, a randomly chosen $\tilde{M}$ leads to a collision with probability $\ell \cdot (2^\alpha/2^n) \cdot p$. Thus the time complexity T is estimated as $T = \frac{1}{\ell \cdot (2^\alpha/2^n) \cdot p} = 2^n/(\ell \cdot 2^\alpha \cdot p)$ (by ignoring the complexity of Step I).

It is claimed in [29] that one can expect $\ell = 2^{34}$ and $p \approx 1/12 \approx 2^{-3.5}$, and the complexity $2^{65.5}$ is obtained as $T = 2^{256}/(2^{34} \cdot 2^{160} \cdot 2^{-3.5}) = 2^{65.5}$.

Remark 4. Let 2^X be the number of IVs of the second block that will be compatible with the local collisions in the second block. Then, the time complexity to find the first message block will be $T = 2^n/2^X$. The attack is valid as long as $X > n/2 = 128$.

Lack of Degrees of Freedom in 38-Step SHA-256. We observe that in the differential characteristic for the 38-step semi-free-start collision of SHA-256 (Table 4), almost all the bits of state variable E_i have conditions for $i = 7, \ldots, 20$, which implies that both of the values and the differences for $W_7, \ldots, W_{20}$ will be fixed. When 16 successive message words are fixed, all the message words are fixed (due to the message expansion). Thus, among the message words $W_0, \ldots, W_7$ that can be used to make the first block and the local collision in the second block compatible, only the two words W_5 and W_6 will have degrees of freedom, and the number of free bits is $\alpha = 2 \cdot 32 = 64$ in total.

Thus the time complexity will be $2^n/(\ell \cdot 2^\alpha \cdot p) = 2^{192}/(\ell \cdot p)$ when ℓ solutions are available. Considering that ℓ is about 2^{34} for 31-step collisions, the complexity will be larger than 2^{128} of the birthday paradox.

Remark 5. From another point of view, the 38-step semi-free-start collision cannot be converted into a collision because $X < 128$.

Lack of Degrees of Freedom in 39-Step SHA-512. The 39-step semi-free-start collision of SHA-512 in [8,29] cannot be converted into a collision for the same reason.

In the differential characteristic (Table 5 of this paper's full version [15]), almost all bits of the internal state variable E_i have some conditions for $i = 8, \ldots, 22$, which implies that both of the internal states and the message words in steps 8–22 will be fixed. Due to the constraint derived from the message expansion, only the single word W_7 will have degrees of freedom among the first 8 message words that can be used to make the first block and the local collision in the second block compatible (i.e., $\alpha = 64$). In addition, ℓ will not be large since the differential characteristic has dense conditions for $i = 8, \ldots, 22$. Thus the time complexity $2^n/(\ell \cdot 2^\alpha \cdot p)$ will be larger than 2^{256} of the birthday paradox.

4.2 Observations and Ideas on Conversion in the Quantum Setting

As mentioned in Remark 4, $X > n/2$ must be satisfied to be a valid attack. On the other hand, in the quantum setting of time-space tradeoff, it may be possible to mount valid 2-block collision attacks even if $X < n/2$. For example, assume that we can decrease the time complexity of 2-block collision attacks from $2^n/2^X$ to $\sqrt{2^n/2^X}$ by applying the Grover search and the Grover search requires negligible memory. It becomes a valid quantum collision attack in the setting of time-space tradeoff if $\sqrt{2^n/2^X} < 2^{n/2}$, which is equivalent to $X > 0$. Actually this idea is too naive and we cannot achieve a valid quantum attack in such a simple way. Nevertheless, this idea shows the possibility of valid 2-block quantum collision attacks with the Grover search.

With this in mind, we mount quantum collision attacks on 38-step SHA-256 and 39-step SHA-512 by converting the semi-free-start collisions into 2-block collisions with the Grover search. To achieve this goal, we have to take the following two points into account.

1. In the classical attack on 31-step SHA-256, by storing ℓ solutions in Step I, the complexity of Step II is decreased by the factor of ℓ. This strategy works well since memory is relatively cheap in the classical setting. On the other hand, memory is expensive in the quantum setting of time-space tradeoff, and memory-less algorithms are favorable.
2. In the classical attack on 31-step SHA-256, we can choose $W_0, \ldots, W_4$ freely because those values do not affect the steps with dense conditions in the differential characteristic (i.e., steps 5–12). On the other hand, in the attack on 38-step SHA-256 (resp., 39-step SHA-512), we have to choose the message words $W_0, \ldots, W_6$ (resp., $W_0, \ldots, W_7$) carefully because they affect on some of the message words in the steps with dense conditions, i.e., $W_7, \ldots, W_{20}$ (resp., $W_8, \ldots, W_{22}$), through the message expansion.

We will set $\ell = 1$ to minimize the required memory size. On the choice of the message words $W_0, \ldots, W_6$ for 38-step SHA-256, we observe the following.

We can modify W_6 to another value $\hat{W}_6$ without changing $W_7, \ldots, W_{21}$ by modifying W_j to $\hat{W}_j := W_j - (\sigma_0(\hat{W}_{j+1}) - \sigma_0(W_{j+1}))$ for $j = 5, 4, \ldots, 0$ step by step.

Indeed, if the value of W_6 is changed to another value $\hat{W}_6$, then W_{21} and W_{22} will be changed because $W_i = \sigma_1(W_{i-2}) + W_{i-7} + \sigma_0(W_{i-15}) + W_{i-16}$ holds for $i \geq 16$. However, the change of the value of W_{21} can be canceled out by modifying W_5 to $\hat{W}_5 := W_5 - (\sigma_0(\hat{W}_6) - \sigma_0(W_6))$. By modifying W_j to $\hat{W}_j := W_j - (\sigma_0(\hat{W}_{j+1}) - \sigma_0(W_{j+1}))$ similarly for $j = 4, \ldots, 0$, we can also keep $W_{20}, \ldots, W_{16}$ unchanged. Since $W_7, \ldots, W_{15}$ are not affected by the modification of $W_0, \ldots, W_6$, the words $W_7, \ldots, W_{15}$ are also kept unchanged.

We obtain a similar observation on the choice of the message words $W_0, \ldots, W_7$ for 39-step SHA-512. That is, we can modify W_7 to another value $\hat{W}_7$ without changing $W_8, \ldots, W_{22}$, by modifying W_j to $\hat{W}_j := W_j - (\sigma_0(\hat{W}_{j+1}) - \sigma_0(W_{j+1}))$ for $j = 6, \ldots, 0$ step by step.

We mount quantum 2-block collision attacks based on these observations.

Attack Idea. Here we explain basic ideas of our quantum attacks that are common between 38-step SHA-256 and 39-step SHA-512. We will explain details that are specific to each function in the next section.

Let i denote the number of the step where the local collision starts in the differential characteristic ($i = 7$ for 38-step SHA-256 and $i = 8$ for 39-step SHA-512). The attack procedure is as follows (see also Fig. 5 of this paper's full version [15]).

I.   Find a pair of messages (M, M') and an initial value for the second block that yield a semi-free-start collision. Let S_{start} be the internal state at the beginning of step i. For each j, let W_j and W'_j denote message word j expanded from M and M', respectively. Note that $W_0 = W'_0, \ldots, W_{i-1} = W'_{i-1}$ hold.

II. With the Grover search, find a message $\tilde{M}$ (for the first block) that satisfies the followings.

  (a) S_{start} and the input chaining value for the second block IV_{second} derived from $\tilde{M}$ can be compatible by modifying the message words $W_0, \ldots, W_{i-1}, W'_0, \ldots, W'_{i-1}$, while keeping the message words $W_i, \ldots, W_{i+14}, W'_i, \ldots, W'_{i+14}$ unchanged. Let $\hat{M}$ and $\hat{M}'$ be the messages for the second block after the modification, i.e., $\hat{M} := \hat{W}_0 || \cdots || \hat{W}_{i-1} || W_i || \cdots || W_{15}$ and $\hat{M}' := \hat{W}_0 || \cdots || \hat{W}_{i-1} || W'_i || \cdots || W'_{15}$.

  (b) S_{start} and the modified message pair $(\hat{M}, \hat{M}')$ yield a collision at the end of the second block.

III. By using $\tilde{M}$ found in Step II, perform the computations in Steps II-(a) and II-(b) again to obtain the pair $(\hat{M}, \hat{M}')$ that yield a collision at the end of the second block. (This step may seem redundant, but we separate this step from Step II so that we can apply the Grover search on $\tilde{M}$ in Step II.) Output $(\tilde{M} || \hat{M}, \tilde{M} || \hat{M}')$.

Step I of the above procedure corresponds to Step I of the classical collision attack on 31-step SHA-256. We store only a single solution in Step I of our attack so that the attack will be memory-less. Since only a single solution is required in this step, we just use the values shown in the previous works (i.e., the values M, M', h_0 in Table 7 and Table 8 of this paper's full version [15]).

Step II-(a) corresponds to Step II of the classical collision attack on 31-step SHA-256. Step II-(b) corresponds to Step III of the classical collision attack on 31-step SHA-256. We allow the remaining words $W_{i+15}, W_{i+16}, \ldots$ and $W'_{i+15}, W'_{i+16}, \ldots$ to be changed since the steps with dense conditions are up to $i+14$ and thus to probabilistically satisfy all the conditions from step $i+15$ by randomly changed $W_{i+15}, W_{i+16}, \ldots$ and $W'_{i+15}, W'_{i+16}, \ldots$ is not difficult.

Attack Complexity and Validity. Let F be the Boolean function to which Grover's algorithm is applied in Step II of our attack[6]. That is, F is defined by $F(\tilde{M}) := 1$ if and only if $\tilde{M}$ satisfies the two conditions II-(a) and II-(b). Let p be the probability that $F(\tilde{M}) = 1$ when we pick a message $\tilde{M}$ for the first block uniformly at

---

[6] More precisely, we run $\mathsf{Grov}(F, \lfloor \pi/4\theta \rfloor)$ in Step II, where $\theta = \arcsin(\sqrt{p})$.

random. In addition, suppose that F can be implemented on a quantum circuit of which width is S_F and depth is T_F.

The time complexity of Step I is negligible since we just use the values from previous works. The time complexity of Step III is also negligible compared to that of Step II. Thus the time complexity of our attacks is dominated by the time complexity of the Grover search on F, which is at most $T_F \cdot \frac{\pi}{4}\sqrt{1/p}$.

If a quantum computer of size $S(>S_F)$ is available, the Grover search can be parallelized[7] and sped up by the factor of $\sqrt{S/S_F}$, and the attack time complexity becomes

$$\left(T_F \cdot (\pi/4)\sqrt{1/p}\right) / \sqrt{S/S_F} = T_F \cdot (\pi/4) \cdot \sqrt{S_F/pS}. \tag{1}$$

Let n be the output length of the hash function. Since the time complexity of the generic attack is $2^{n/2}/S$ when a quantum computer of size S is available, our attack is valid as long as

$$T_F \cdot (\pi/4) \cdot \sqrt{S_F/pS} < 2^{n/2}/S \tag{2}$$

holds.

Remark 6. When we run the same procedure in the classical setting, the Grover search is replaced with the usual exhaustive search and the attack time complexity will be $(T_F \cdot S_F)/p$ (here we do not consider parallelizations for simplicity). Since the generic complexity is $2^{n/2}$, the attack becomes valid if and only if $(T_F \cdot S_F)/p < 2^{n/2}$, which is equal to

$$p > (T_F \cdot S_F)/2^{n/2}. \tag{3}$$

In particular, the classical attack is invalid if $p < 2^{-n/2}$. On the other hand, the condition (2) is equivalent to $p > S_F \cdot (\pi^2/16) \cdot T_F^2/2^n$ (when $S = 1$), and the quantum attack may be valid even if $p < 2^{-n/2}$.

5   Quantum Collision Attack on 38-Step SHA-256

This section shows a quantum collision attack on 38-step SHA-256 based on the attack idea in Sect. 4.2.

Let (M, M') and h_0 be the semi-free-start collision and the initial value shown in the previous work (i.e., (M, M') and h_0 in Table 7 of this paper's full version [15]). Let W_j and W_j' denote message word j associated with M and M', respectively. Recall that the local collision starts at step 7 in the differential characteristic in Table 4. Let S_{start} be the state at the beginning of step 7 that is computed from (M, M') and h_0.

Section 5.1 provides some observations on Step II of the quantum attack. Section 5.2 provides an implementation of F and analyzes the depth and width of the circuit of F. In Sect. 5.3 we analyze the total complexity when the quantum attack is mounted with the implementation of F in Sect. 5.2.

---

[7] See Sect. 2 for details on parallelization. We use the quantum computer of size S as S/S_F independent small quantum computers.

5.1   Observation on Step II

We provide two observations.

First Observation. The internal state variables $A_{-1}, \ldots, A_6$ and $E_3, \ldots, E_6$ are determined from $S_{\text{start}} = A_6 || \cdots || A_3 || E_6 || \cdots || E_3$. (These variables are common between M and M'. See also Fig. 4 of this paper's full version [15].) There exists a tuple $(\hat{W}_0, \ldots, \hat{W}_6)$ that is compatible with $\text{IV}_{\text{second}}$ and S_{start} if and only if A_{-1} matches the most significant 32 bits of $\text{IV}_{\text{second}}$. If A_{-1} matches, $A_{-2}, A_{-3}, A_{-4}, E_{-1}, \ldots, E_{-4}$ are determined by the equation $\text{IV}_{\text{second}} = A_{-1} || \cdots || A_{-4} || E_{-1} || \cdots || E_{-4}$, and the message words $\hat{W}_0, \ldots, \hat{W}_6$ are uniquely determined from $A_{-4}, \ldots, A_6$ and $E_{-4}, \ldots, E_{-1}, E_3, \ldots, E_6$.

Second Observation. By exhaustively checking all the possible values for $\hat{W}_6 \in \{0, 1\}^{32}$, we verified that there exist 1179647 ($> 2^{20}$) tuples $(\hat{W}_0, \ldots, \hat{W}_6)$ that satisfy the following conditions.[8]

(i) $\hat{W}_j = W_j - (\sigma_0(\hat{W}_{j+1}) - \sigma_0(W_{j+1}))$ holds for $j = 0, \ldots, 5$.
(ii) S_{start} and the messages $(\hat{M}, \hat{M}')$ for the second block, where $\hat{M} := \hat{W}_0 || \cdots || \hat{W}_6 || W_7 || \cdots || W_{15}$ and $\hat{M}' := \hat{W}_0 || \cdots || \hat{W}_6 || W_7' || \cdots || W_{15}'$, yield a collision at the end of the second block.

Remark 7. From another point of view, the second observation shows that we can make semi-free-start collisions for at least 2^{20} initial values.

5.2   Implementation and Analysis of F

Below we provide an implementation of F and its analysis. In particular, we show $T_F \leq 6.8$ and $S_F \leq 3.9$, where S_F denotes the width of the quantum circuit of F and T_F denotes the running time (depth) of the circuit.

Implementation of F: Basic Idea. Before describing a formal implementation of F with notations of quantum computation, we give a basic idea behind the implementation.

First, we compute the following values (from Table 7 of this paper's full version [15]) and store them into memory.

(a) The internal state S_{start} at the beginning of step 7.
(b) The message words $W_0 = W_0', \ldots, W_6 = W_6', W_7, \ldots, W_{21}, W_7', \ldots W_{21}'$.
(c) The internal state variable A_{-1} that is uniquely determined from S_{start}.

Note that these values are computed and stored before the start and kept unchanged throughout the attack.

Given an input $\tilde{M}$, the output value $F(\tilde{M})$ is computed as follows.

---

[8] We actually implemented to count the number of semi-free-start collisions for all 2^{32} choices of W_6 and accordingly modified $W_5 \ldots, W_0$.

1. Compute the output of the first block from $\tilde{M}$, and let $\text{IV}_{\text{second}}$ denote the output.
2. Check if the condition that the most significant 32 bits of $\text{IV}_{\text{second}}$ is equal to A_{-1} is satisfied. If it is satisfied, proceed to the next step. Otherwise output 0 and abort.
3. Compute the unique $(\hat{W}_0, \ldots, \hat{W}_6)$ that is compatible with $\text{IV}_{\text{second}}$ and S_{start}.
4. Check if the following conditions are satisfied.
   (i) $\hat{W}_j = W_j - (\sigma_0(\hat{W}_{j+1}) - \sigma_0(W_{j+1}))$ holds for $j = 0, \ldots, 5$.
   (ii) S_{start} and the messages $(\hat{M}, \hat{M}')$ yield a collision at the end of the second block, where $\hat{M} := \hat{W}_0 || \cdots || \hat{W}_6 || W_7 || \cdots || W_{15}$ and $\hat{M}' := \hat{W}_0 || \cdots || \hat{W}_6 || W_7' || \cdots || W_{15}'$.
   If both of (i) and (ii) are satisfied, output 1. Otherwise output 0.

Remark 8. When we implement a quantum circuit, each computational step has to be reversible, and the running time of the circuit has to be independent from inputs. We ignored such properties in the above explanations for simplicity but they are taken into account in the formal description below.

Implementation of F: Formal Description. Let L be the list to store the values explained in (a)–(c) above, and f be the 38-step compression function. Given an input $\tilde{M}$, the output value $F(\tilde{M})$ is computed as follows.

0. At the beginning, the quantum state is $|\tilde{M}\rangle |L\rangle |y\rangle$. ($|y\rangle$ is the single qubit register where the value $F(\tilde{M})$ will be added.)
1. Compute the output of the first block from $\tilde{M}$. Let $\text{IV}_{\text{second}}$ denote the output. Check if A_{-1} is equal to the most significant 32 bits of $\text{IV}_{\text{second}}$. If they are equal, set $b := 1$. If they are not equal, set $b := 0$. The current quantum state is $|\tilde{M}\rangle |L\rangle |y\rangle \otimes |\text{IV}_{\text{second}}\rangle |b\rangle$.
2. Let $\text{IV}'_{\text{second}}$ denote the concatenation of A_{-1} and the least significant 224 bits of $\text{IV}_{\text{second}}$ ($\text{IV}'_{\text{second}} = \text{IV}_{\text{second}}$ holds if $b = 1$). Compute the unique $(\hat{W}_0, \ldots, \hat{W}_6)$ that is compatible with the initial chaining value $\text{IV}'_{\text{second}}$ and S_{start}. The current quantum state is $|\tilde{M}\rangle |L\rangle |y\rangle \otimes |\text{IV}_{\text{second}}\rangle |b\rangle |\hat{W}_0, \ldots, \hat{W}_6\rangle$.
3. Let $\hat{M}$ denote $\hat{W}_0 || \cdots || \hat{W}_6 || W_7 || \cdots || W_{15}$ and $\hat{M}'$ denote $\hat{W}_0 || \cdots || \hat{W}_6 || W_7' || \cdots || W_{15}'$. Compute the values $f(\text{IV}'_{\text{second}}, \hat{M})$, $f(\text{IV}'_{\text{second}}, \hat{M}')$. The current quantum state is $|\tilde{M}\rangle |L\rangle |y\rangle \otimes |\text{IV}_{\text{second}}\rangle |b\rangle |\hat{W}_0, \ldots, \hat{W}_6\rangle |f(\text{IV}'_{\text{second}}, \hat{M})\rangle |f(\text{IV}'_{\text{second}}, \hat{M}')\rangle$.
4. Recall that $F(\tilde{M}) = 1$ if and only if $b = 1$ and the following (i) and (ii) hold.
   (i) $f(\text{IV}'_{\text{second}}, \hat{M}) = f(\text{IV}'_{\text{second}}, \hat{M}')$.
   (ii) $\hat{W}_j = W_j - (\sigma_0(\hat{W}_{j+1}) - \sigma_0(W_{j+1}))$ holds for $j = 0, \ldots, 5$.
   Compute $F(\tilde{M})$ by checking if $b = 1$, and (i) and (ii) hold, and add the value $F(\tilde{M})$ to the $|y\rangle$ register. The current quantum state is $|\tilde{M}\rangle |L\rangle |y \oplus F(\tilde{M})\rangle \otimes |\text{IV}_{\text{second}}\rangle |b\rangle |\hat{W}_0, \ldots, \hat{W}_6\rangle |f(\text{IV}'_{\text{second}}, \hat{M})\rangle |f(\text{IV}'_{\text{second}}, \hat{M}')\rangle$.
5. Uncompute Steps 1–3 to obtain $|\tilde{M}\rangle |L\rangle |y \oplus F(\tilde{M})\rangle$.

Analysis. We regard that the unit of depth (resp., width) of quantum circuits is the depth (resp., width) required to implement 38-step SHA-256 that takes 1-block inputs. In particular, we regard that the depth required to compute a single step of SHA-512 is equal to $1/38$. Since the input length of 1-block SHA-256 is 512 bits and the output length is 256 bits, at least $512 + 256 = 768$ qubits are required to implement the function on a quantum circuit.

Depth (T_F). Step 1 of the implementation computes the compression function once. The depth required to Step 2 is $7/38$ since the message words in the first 7 steps in the second block are computed in Step 2. Step 3 computes the compression function twice. The cost of Step 4 is dominated by the computation for (ii), of which cost is at most 6 steps of SHA-256. Thus the depth required for Step 4 is at most $6/38$. In summary, the depth required to implement Steps 1–4 is $1 + 7/38 + 2 + 6/38 \leq 3.4$. Since we have to perform uncomputations in Step 5, we have $T_F \leq 3.4 \times 2 = 6.8$.

Width (S_F). The length of $\tilde{M}$ is 16 words. L contains data of $8 + (7 + 15 + 15) + 1 = 46$ words in total. y is a single bit. Thus, $(16 + 46) \times 32 + 1 = 62 \times 32 + 1$ qubits are used in Step 0 of the implementation. Step 1 requires additional $8 \times 32 + 1$ qubits to store $\text{IV}_{\text{second}}$ and b. Step 2 requires additional 7×32 qubits to store $\hat{W}_0, \ldots, \hat{W}_6$. Step 3 requires additional $(8 + 8) \times 32 = 16 \times 32$ qubits to store $f(\text{IV}_{\text{second}}, \hat{M})$ and $f(\text{IV}_{\text{second}}, \hat{M}')$. Therefore, to store intermediate values shown in the above implementation, $(62 + 8 + 7 + 16) \times 32 + 2 = 2978$ qubits are used in total. Hence we have $S_F \leq 2978/768 \leq 3.9$.

Remark 9. On the estimation of the width S_F, more ancilla qubits may be required to compute the intermediate variables (such as $\text{IV}_{\text{second}}$) used in the implementation of F. However, we expect that they will be as much ancilla qubits as required to implement 1-block 38-step SHA-256. In particular, we expect that the ratio between the number of qubits to implement F and the number of qubits to implement 1-block 38-step SHA-256 will be about 3.9, even if we take the ancilla qubits to compute the intermediate variables into account.

Remark 10. Note that we could remove $|L\rangle$ from the computation since L is a list of classical data and computations that depend on L can be executed by classically controlling the gates. However, this has no consequence on the Time-memory tradeoff sine it is just converting qubits into classical bits.

5.3 Total Complexity

This section analyzes the total complexity when the quantum attack in Sect. 4.2 is mounted with the implementation of F in Sect. 5.2.

Let p denote the probability that $F(\tilde{M}) = 1$ holds when $\tilde{M}$ is randomly chosen. $F(\tilde{M}) = 1$ holds if and only if $\tilde{M}$ satisfies the conditions in the second and fourth steps of the implementation of F. A random $\tilde{M}$ satisfies the condition in the second step with probability 2^{-32}. From the observation on

Step II in Sect. 5.1, (i) and (ii) in the fourth step are satisfied with probability $\left(1179647/(2^{32})^7\right) > 2^{20}/2^{224}$. Therefore

$$p = 2^{-32} \cdot \left(1179647/(2^{32})^7\right) > 2^{-32} \cdot \left(2^{20}/2^{224}\right) = 2^{-236} \qquad (4)$$

holds.

The attack time complexity can be computed as in Eq. (1). We showed $T_F \leq 6.8$ and $S_F \leq 3.9$ in Sect. 5.2, and $p > 2^{-236}$ in (4). Therefore, when a quantum computer of size S is available, our attack finds a collision in time $6.8 \cdot (\pi/4)\sqrt{3.9/(2^{-236} \cdot S)} = \frac{6.8\pi\sqrt{3.9}}{4} \cdot 2^{118}/\sqrt{S} \leq 2^{122}/\sqrt{S}$. In addition, the attack time complexity $2^{122}/\sqrt{S}$ is lower than the generic complexity $2^{128}/S$ when $S < 2^{12}$. Therefore our attack is valid as long as $3.9 \leq S < 2^{12}$.

Remark 11. Some may consider that our complexity analysis is invalid since the first equality in (4) holds only if the output distribution of the first block is exactly equal to the uniform distribution over $\{0,1\}^{256}$, which will not be the case for 38-step SHA-256. However, still we can reasonably expect that the analysis is valid. See Section D of this paper's full version [15] for details.

6   Quantum Collision Attack on 39-Step SHA-512

This section shows a quantum collision attack on 39-step SHA-512 based on the attack idea in Sect. 4.2.

Let (M, M') and h_0 be the semi-free-start collision and the initial value shown in the previous work (i.e., (M, M') and h_0 in Table 8 of this paper's full version [15]). Let W_j and W'_j denote message word j associated with M and M', respectively.

The difference between the attack on 39-step SHA-512 from the one on 38-step SHA-256 is summarized as follows.

1. The local collision starts from step 8 but not step 7 (we denote the internal state at the beginning of step 8 by S_{start}).
2. The probability $p\ (= |F^{-1}(1)|/2^{512})$ satisfies $p > 2^{-498.4}$.
3. The implementation of F satisfies $T_F \leq 6.8$ and $S_F \leq 4.1$.

The attack finds a collision in time $2^{252.7}/\sqrt{S}$, which is valid when $4.1 < S < 2^{6.6}$.

Section 6.1 provides some observations on Step II of the quantum attack. Section 6.2 provides an implementation of F and analyzes the depth and width of the circuit of F. In Sect. 6.3 we analyze the total complexity when the quantum attack is mounted with the implementation of F in Sect. 6.2.

6.1   Observation on Step II

We provide two observations.

First Observation. Given a chaining initial input value $\text{IV}_{\text{second}}$, *there always exists a unique tuple* $(\hat{W}_0, \ldots, \hat{W}_7)$ that is compatible with $\text{IV}_{\text{second}}$ and S_{start}. This is because the local collision starts at step 8 in the differential characteristic for 39-step SHA-512 (see also Fig. 4 of this paper's full version [15] for details).

Second Observation. We experimentally verified that there exist 13184 ($>2^{13.6}$) tuples $(\hat{W}_0, \ldots, \hat{W}_7)$ that satisfies the following conditions.

 (i) $\hat{W}_j = W_j - (\sigma_0(\hat{W}_{j+1}) - \sigma_0(W_{j+1}))$ holds for $j = 0, \ldots, 6$.
 (ii) S_{start} and the messages $(\hat{M}, \hat{M}')$, where $\hat{M} := \hat{W}_0 \| \cdots \| \hat{W}_7 \| W_8 \| \cdots \| W_{15}$ and $\hat{M}' := \hat{W}_0 \| \cdots \| \hat{W}_7 \| W_8' \| \cdots \| W_{15}'$, yield a collision at the end of the second block.
 (iii) $\hat{W}_{23,j} = W_{23,j}$ for $j = 5, \ldots, 29$, where $\hat{W}_{23,j}$ and $W_{23,j}$ are bit j of message word 23 derived from $\hat{M}$ and M, respectively.

The condition (iii) is added to decrease the search space for $\hat{W}_7$. We chose bit 5, bit 6, $\ldots$, bit 29 because the differential characteristic (Table 5 of this paper's full version [15]) has strict conditions on these bit positions of E_{23}.

Remark 12. From another view of point, the second observation shows that we can make semi-free-start collisions for at least $2^{13.6}$ initial values.

6.2 Implementation and Analysis of F

In what follows we provide description and analysis of the implementation of F used in the attack on 39-step SHA-512 and show $T_F \leq 6.8$ and $S_F \leq 4.1$.

Implementation of F: Basic Idea. Since the basic idea of the implementation is similar to that for 38-step SHA-256 in Sect. 5.2, here we only provide the difference from Sect. 5.2.

In the attack on 39-step SHA-512, there always exists a unique tuple $(\hat{W}_0, \ldots, \hat{W}_7)$ that is compatible with $\text{IV}_{\text{second}}$ and S_{start} for arbitrary $\text{IV}_{\text{second}}$ due to the first observation in Sect. 6.1. Therefore we skip the step (in the implementation of F in Sect. 5.2) to check if A_{-1} is equal to the most significant 32 bits of $\text{IV}_{\text{second}}$.

Let $\tilde{M}$ be a message for the first block, and $\text{IV}_{\text{second}}$ be the initial vector for the second block that is computed from $\tilde{M}$. We define $F(\tilde{M}) := 1$ if and only if the conditions (i)–(iii) in the second observation in Sect. 6.1 are satisfied for the unique tuple $(\hat{W}_0, \ldots, \hat{W}_7)$ that is compatible with $\text{IV}_{\text{second}}$ and S_{start}.

Formal Implementation of F. First, we compute the following values (from Table 8 of this paper's full version [15]) and store them into a list L.

(a) The internal state S_{start} at the beginning of step 8.
(b) The message words $W_0 = W_0', \ldots, W_7 = W_7', W_8, \ldots, W_{22}, W_8', \ldots W_{22}', W_{23}$.

Given an input $\tilde{M}$, the output value $F(\tilde{M})$ is computed as follows.

0. At the beginning, the quantum state is $|\tilde{M}\rangle\,|L\rangle\,|y\rangle$. ($|y\rangle$ is the single qubit register where the value $F(\tilde{M})$ will be added.)
1. Compute the output of the first block from $\tilde{M}$. Let $\mathrm{IV}_{\mathrm{second}}$ denote the output. The current quantum state is $|\tilde{M}\rangle\,|L\rangle\,|y\rangle \otimes |\mathrm{IV}_{\mathrm{second}}\rangle$.
2. Compute the unique $(\hat{W}_0, \ldots, \hat{W}_7)$ that is compatible with $\mathrm{IV}_{\mathrm{second}}$ and S_{start}. The current quantum state is $|\tilde{M}\rangle\,|L\rangle\,|y\rangle \otimes |\mathrm{IV}_{\mathrm{second}}\rangle\,|\hat{W}_0, \ldots, \hat{W}_7\rangle$.
3. Let $\hat{M}$ denote $\hat{W}_0||\cdots||\hat{W}_7||W_8||\cdots||W_{15}$ and $\hat{M}'$ denote $\hat{W}_0||\cdots||\hat{W}_7$ $||W'_8||\cdots||W'_{15}$. Compute $f(\mathrm{IV}_{\mathrm{second}}, \hat{M})$, $f(\mathrm{IV}_{\mathrm{second}}, \hat{M}')$, and $\hat{W}_{23}$, where $\hat{W}_{23}$ is word 23 derived from $\hat{M}$. The current quantum state is $|\tilde{M}\rangle\,|L\rangle\,|y\rangle \otimes$ $|\mathrm{IV}_{\mathrm{second}}\rangle\,|\hat{W}_0, \ldots, \hat{W}_7\rangle\,|f(\mathrm{IV}_{\mathrm{second}}, \hat{M})\rangle\,|f(\mathrm{IV}_{\mathrm{second}}, \hat{M}')\rangle\,|\hat{W}_{23}\rangle$.
4. Recall that $F(\tilde{M}) := 1$ if and only if the following (i)–(iii) hold.
   (i) $f(\mathrm{IV}_{\mathrm{second}}, \hat{M}) = f(\mathrm{IV}_{\mathrm{second}}, \hat{M}')$.
   (ii) $\hat{W}_j = W_j - (\sigma_0(\hat{W}_{j+1}) - \sigma_0(W_{j+1}))$ holds for $j = 0, \ldots, 6$.
   (iii) $\hat{W}_{23,j} = W_{23,j}$ holds for $j = 5, \ldots, 29$
   Compute $F(\tilde{M})$ by checking if (i)–(iii) hold, and add the value $F(\tilde{M})$ to the $|y\rangle$ register. The current quantum state is $|\tilde{M}\rangle\,|L\rangle\,|y \oplus F(\tilde{M})\rangle \otimes$ $|\mathrm{IV}_{\mathrm{second}}\rangle\,|\hat{W}_0, \ldots, \hat{W}_7\rangle\,|f(\mathrm{IV}_{\mathrm{second}}, \hat{M})\rangle\,|f(\mathrm{IV}_{\mathrm{second}}, \hat{M}')\rangle\,|\hat{W}_{23}\rangle$.
5. Uncompute Steps 1–3 to obtain $|\tilde{M}\rangle\,|L\rangle\,|y \oplus F(\tilde{M})\rangle$.

Analysis. We regard that the unit of depth (resp., width) of quantum circuits is the depth (resp., width) required to implement 39-step SHA-512 that takes 1-block inputs. In particular, we regard that the depth required to compute a single step of SHA-512 is equal to $1/39$. Since the input length of 1-block SHA-512 is 1024 bits and the output length is 512 bits, at least $1024 + 512 = 1536$ qubits are required to implement the function on a quantum circuit.

Depth (T_F). Step 1 of the implementation computes the compression function once. Since the message words in the first 8 steps in the second block are computed in Step 2, the depth required for Step 2 is $8/39$. Step 3 computes the compression function twice. The cost of Step 4 is dominated by the computation for (ii), which is at most 7 steps of SHA-512. Thus the depth required for Step 4 is at most $7/39$. In summary, the depth required to implement Steps 1–4 is $1 + 8/39 + 2 + 7/39 \leq 3.4$. Since we have to perform uncomputations in Step 5, we have $T_F \leq 3.4 \times 2 = 6.8$.

Width (S_F). The length of $\tilde{M}$ is 16 words. L contains data of $8+(8+15+15+1) = 47$ words in total. y is a single bit. Thus, $(16+47) \times 64+1 = 63 \times 64+1$ qubits are used in Step 0 of the implementation. Step 1 requires additional 8×64 qubits to store $\mathrm{IV}_{\mathrm{second}}$. Step 2 requires additional 8×64 qubits to store $\hat{W}_0, \ldots, \hat{W}_7$. Step 3 requires additional $(8 + 8 + 1) \times 64 = 17 \times 64$ qubits to store $f(\mathrm{IV}_{\mathrm{second}}, \hat{M})$, $f(\mathrm{IV}_{\mathrm{second}}, \hat{M}')$, and $\hat{W}_{23}$. Therefore, to store intermediate values shown in the above implementation, $(63 + 8 + 8 + 17) \times 64 + 1 = 6145$ qubits are used in total. Hence we have $S_F \leq 6145/1536 \leq 4.1$.

Remark 13. On the estimation of the width S_F, more ancilla qubits may be required to compute the intermediate variables (such as $\mathrm{IV}_{\mathrm{second}}$) used in the implementation of F. However, we expect that they will be as much as ancilla qubits required to implement 2-block 39-step SHA-512. In particular, we expect that the ratio between the number of qubits to implement F and the number of qubits to implement 2-block 39-step SHA-512 will be as much as 4.1, even if we take the ancilla qubits to compute the intermediate variables into account.

6.3   Total Complexity

Let p denote the probability that $F(\tilde{M}) = 1$ holds when $\tilde{M}$ is randomly chosen. $F(\tilde{M}) = 1$ holds if and only if the conditions (i)–(iii) in the fourth step of the implementation of F are satisfied. From the second observation on Step II in Sect. 6.1, (i)–(iii) are satisfied with probability at least $2^{13.6}/(2^{64})^8$. Therefore $p > 2^{13.6}/(2^{64})^8 = 2^{-498.4}$ holds.

The attack time complexity can be computed as in Eq. (1). We showed $T_F \leq 6.8$ and $S_F \leq 4.1$ in Sect. 6.2, and $p > 2^{-498.4}$ above. Therefore, when a quantum computer of size S is available, our attack finds a collision in time $6.8 \cdot (\pi/4)\sqrt{4.1/(2^{-498.4} \cdot S)} = \frac{6.8\sqrt{4.1}\pi}{4} \cdot 2^{249.2}/\sqrt{S} \leq 2^{252.7}/\sqrt{S}$. In addition, the attack time complexity $2^{252.7}/\sqrt{S}$ is lower than the generic complexity $2^{256}/S$ when $S < 2^{6.6}$. Therefore our attack is valid as long as $4.1 \leq S < 2^{6.6}$.

7   Discussion

The previous sections exploited the existing semi-free-start collision attacks to mount quantum collision attacks for SHA-256 and SHA-512. This brings the following two questions. First, is it possible to optimize differential characteristics for the classical semi-free-start collision attack with respect to the conversion to the quantum collision attack? Second, is it possible to extend the conversion framework so that a wider class of the classical attack on other computation structure can be converted into a quantum collision attack? This section answers those questions. We hope those will provide future researchers with useful knowledge to find new quantum collision attacks.

7.1   Towards Searching for New Semi-Free-Start Collision Attacks

The attacks on SHA-256 and SHA-512 in Sects. 5 and 6 directly used the differential characteristics from the previous works, but it is possible to search for new differential characteristics from scratch in future works to be optimized in our conversion. More importantly, differential characteristics that cannot be exploited in the classical setting may still be exploited in the quantum setting.

Properties Required for Differential Characteristics. Our conversion is applied when the differential characteristic for the semi-free-collision attack satisfies the following properties.

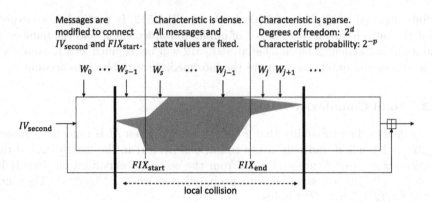

Fig. 3. Form of Semi-free-start Collision Attacks that can be Converted into Collisions.

- The characteristic is dense, i.e. requiring many conditions, only in a relatively small number of steps. Let FIX_{start} and FIX_{end} be the input and output state values of these steps, respectively.
- For multiple choices of IV_{second}, it is possible to modify message words W_0 to W_{s-1} so that IV_{second} and FIX_{start} are connected.
- The probability to satisfy the characteristic from FIX_{end} is high enough to be faster than the generic attack.

Given those, we can view that the characteristic is composed of three parts as shown in Fig. 3.[9]

Properties for the Sparse Part. In our attacks on SHA-256 and SHA-512, (almost) all the message words are fixed after modifying W_0 to W_{s-1}, thus degrees of freedom to satisfy the characteristic from FIX_{end} to the end is provided by generating the first message block many times, which requires significant computational cost. Besides, the probability from FIX_{end} is reasonably high, thus the attack procedure could be provided without special attention. Here we give a decent analysis with respect to the condition to be faster than the generic attack, which should be taken into account for finding new characteristic.

Suppose that the first k message words are independently chosen and the dense part of the characteristic is located between step s and $j - 1$, where $0 < s < j < k$. Then, after modifying W_0 to W_{s-1} to connect IV_{second} and FIX_{start}, the attacker can still have degrees of freedom in message words W_j to W_{k-1}. Let 2^d and 2^{-p} be the amount of degrees of freedom available to the attacker and the probability of the differential characteristic in the remaining steps. If $d \geq p$, degrees of freedom in W_j to W_{k-1} is sufficient, thus only the single choice of IV_{second} is sufficient to find a collision. This is advantageous because the cost of computing the first block directly impacts to the overall attack complexity. If

---

[9] In Sects. 5 and 6, we considered the special case where s is the number of the starting step of a local collision.

$d < p$, degrees of freedom in W_j to W_{k-1} is insufficient, thus the generation of IV_{second} in the first block must be repeated multiple times.

Whether the attack can be faster than the generic attack depends on the relationship between d and p. To evaluate the attack complexity, we first discuss the complexity in the classical setting. Let 2^f be the complexity to generate an IV_{second}.[10] In the classical setting, when $d \geq p$, the attacker needs to generate a single choice of IV_{second} and examine 2^p choices of message words for the last part of the characteristic. Hence, the attack complexity is $2^f + 2^p$. When $d < p$, the attacker needs to generate 2^{p-d} choices of IV_{second} and, for each of them, examine 2^d choices of message words for the last part of the characteristic. Hence, the attack complexity is $2^f \cdot 2^{p-d} + 2^{p-d} \cdot 2^d$, which is equal to $2^f \cdot 2^{p-d} + 2^p$. To be a valid attack, this complexity must be faster than the generic attack complexity, which is $2^{n/2}$ in the classical setting. Hence, $\max(f, p) < n/2$ when $d \geq p$ and $\max(p, f + p - d) \leq n/2$ when $d < p$. The closed formula for both cases is $\max(p, f + \max(p - d, 0)) < n/2$. Therefore, $p < n/2$ must be satisfied in the classical setting, namely, the probability of the differential characteristic for the last part cannot be smaller than $2^{-n/2}$.

The complexity evaluation in the quantum setting is as follows. When $d \geq p$, the cost for generating an IV_{second} and examining 2^p choices of message for the last part of the characteristic decreases to $\sqrt{2^f}$ and $\sqrt{2^p}$, respectively, by using the Grover search. Hence the attack complexity becomes $\sqrt{2^f} + \sqrt{2^p}$. When $d < p$, similarly we obtain quadratic speed up for each subroutine with the Grover search, and the attack complexity decreases to $\sqrt{2^f \cdot 2^{p-d}} + \sqrt{2^p}$. A quantum attack can be valid in the cost metric of time-space tradeoff if its complexity is below $2^{n/2}$, i.e., $\max(p, f + \max(p - d, 0)) < n$. In particular, a quantum attack can be valid even if $p \geq n/2$, i.e., the probability of the differential characteristic for the last part can be smaller than $2^{-n/2}$.

Note that $d \geq p$ may occur in practice. In fact, the 31-step (not 38-step) semi-free-start collision attack by Mendel et al. against SHA-256 is exactly the case with $d \geq p$. As introduced in Sect. 3.1, the authors of [29] explained that Step III succeeds with a probability about $1/12$ due to the lack of degrees of freedom in W_{13}, W_{14}, W_{15}. However, if it is analyzed carefully, $1/12$ is a part of probability that the generated IV_{second} is suitable, i.e. there are additional condition of 3.5 bits besides the match of the most significant 96 bits. The sparse characteristic in Fig. 3 corresponds to the characteristic from Step 13 to 31 in Table 2. There are 28 conditions on ΔE_{13} to ΔE_{16}, thus $p = 28$.[11] Degrees of freedom exist in all bits of W_{13} to W_{15}, thus $d = 96$. Hence, this is the case with $d \geq p$.

Remark 14. Roughly speaking, the attack of Sect. 5 (resp., Sect. 6) is the case with $s = 7$, $j = 22$, $d = 0$, $p > 20$, and $f = 32$ (resp., $s = 8$, $j = 23$, $d = 0$, $p > 13.6$, and $f = 0$).

---

[10] In other words, 2^f is the complexity to find a first block message M that can be connected to FIX_{start}.

[11] While Table 2 shows only 26 conditions on ΔE_{13} to ΔE_{16}, the original paper implies two additional conditions. Hence we deduce that $p = 28$. See also Remark 3.

Suitable Choice of s. The step index s is the border between the first and the second part of the characteristic in Fig. 3, where the state value is fully fixed after Step s. Suppose that the length of each message word is w-bit and the internal state size of hash functions is $t \cdot w$-bit. (In the case of SHA-256, $w = 32$ and $t = 8$.) Then the parameter f increases much and the attack may not work if s is too small or too large compared to t. The reason is as follows.

If s is too small compared to t (e.g., $s < t/2$), then degrees of freedom in $W_0, \ldots, W_{s-1}$ become too small and the probability that a randomly chosen IV_{second} can be connected to FIX_{start} becomes too small. Hence the parameter f becomes too large.

If s is too large (e.g., $s > 2t$), then the degrees of freedom in $W_0, \ldots, W_{s-1}$ will remain enough. However, this time it may be unclear which choice of $W_0, \ldots, W_{s-1}$ is compatible with IV_{second} and FIX_{start} for a random given IV_{second}, and the complexity to find a compatible choice becomes high. This implies that the parameter f also increases in this case.

Therefore we expect that an index s that is close to t (e.g., $t/2 < s < 2t$) will be suitable. (Indeed s is close to t in our attacks in Sects. 5 and 6.)

Remark on Memory. Memory is quite expensive in the quantum setting while cheap in the classical setting.[12] Thus differential characteristics that lead to memory-less attacks but seem non-optimal in the classical setting are worth investigating in the quantum setting.

7.2   Towards Application to Other Hash Functions

A natural question that arises after seeing our results is whether we can apply the same idea to other hash functions by using similar differential characteristics shown in previous works. In earlier sections we focused on semi-free-start collisions on SHA-256 and SHA-512, which are single-branch hash functions, but we do not have to restrict ourselves to semi-free-start collisions nor single-branch hash functions: Differential characteristics for free-start collisions or double-branch hash functions may also lead to quantum collision attacks if their structures are close to Fig. 3.[13]

Indeed, some previous works use such differential characteristics. Examples are the semi-free-start collision attack on reduced HAS-160 in [26], the free-start collision attacks on reduced SHA-2 family in [7] and reduced SM3 in [28], and the semi-free-start collision attacks on full RIPEMD-128 in [21] and reduced RIPEMD-160 in [24,25,30]. The differential characteristics used in these attacks look similar to Fig. 3 and they are found by using automated search tools in a similar way to the differential characteristics that we used in Sects. 5 and 6.

---

[12] The situation may change if we adopt the cost-metric that assumes the existence of quantum RAM instead of the cost-metric of time-memory tradeoff, but we expect that finding attacks that are valid in the latter is easier than finding ones valid in the former.

[13] Recall that a collision $((IV, M), (IV', M'))$ for a compression function h is called a semi-free-start collision if $IV = IV'$ and *free-start collision* if $IV \neq IV'$.

We investigated whether we could use those differential characteristics to mount quantum 2-block collision attacks. We elaborate observations that we obtained so far in Section G of this paper's full version [15]. Unfortunately, we have not succeeded yet, and with this respect, the analysis here is a failure report. Nevertheless, we believe that those are valuable to report because we observe that some of the applications are close to be valid collision attacks while others are very far. By sharing the experience of those analysis, it would be possible to search for new differential characteristics that satisfy properties in Sect. 7.1 in order to break more rounds than classical collision attack.

8   Concluding Remarks

In this paper, we showed collision attacks on 38 and 39 steps of SHA-256 and SHA-512, respectively, when the attacker can access to quantum machines under the time-space tradeoff metric. The complexity is $2^{122}/\sqrt{S}$ and $2^{252.7}/\sqrt{S}$ where $S < 2^{12}$ and $S < 2^{6.6}$ for SHA-256 and SHA-512, respectively.

Both attacks followed the same approach as the previous work, where a semi-free-start collision attack that works for 2^X choices of IVs ($X > \frac{n}{2}$) is converted into a 2-block collision. We observed that even a small X may lead to an attack faster than the generic one.

A possible future direction is to study applications to other cryptographic hash functions. Since the idea behind our quantum collision attacks is very simple, we believe that it has broad applications. It will also be interesting to study optimizations of differential characteristics for the classical semi-free-start collision attack with respect to the conversion to the quantum collision attack.

Acknowledgments. We thank anonymous reviewers for their insightful comments, especially for pointing out errors in previous versions of the paper.

References

1. Aoki, K., Guo, J., Matusiewicz, K., Sasaki, Y., Wang, L.: Preimages for step-reduced SHA-2. In: Matsui, M. (ed.) ASIACRYPT 2009. LNCS, vol. 5912, pp. 578–597. Springer, Heidelberg (2009). https://doi.org/10.1007/978-3-642-10366-7_34

2. Bernstein, D.J.: Cost analysis of hash collisions: will quantum computers make SHARCS obsolete? In: SHARCS (2009)

3. Biryukov, A., Lamberger, M., Mendel, F., Nikolić, I.: Second-order differential collisions for reduced SHA-256. In: Lee, D.H., Wang, X. (eds.) ASIACRYPT 2011. LNCS, vol. 7073, pp. 270–287. Springer, Heidelberg (2011). https://doi.org/10.1007/978-3-642-25385-0_15

4. Boyer, M., Brassard, G., Høyer, P., Tapp, A.: Tight bounds on quantum searching. Fortschritte der Physik: Prog. Phys. **46**(4–5), 493–505 (1998)

5. Brassard, G., Høyer, P., Tapp, A.: Quantum cryptanalysis of hash and claw-free functions. In: Lucchesi, C.L., Moura, A.V. (eds.) LATIN 1998. LNCS, vol. 1380, pp. 163–169. Springer, Heidelberg (1998). https://doi.org/10.1007/BFb0054319

6. Chailloux, A., Naya-Plasencia, M., Schrottenloher, A.: An efficient quantum collision search algorithm and implications on symmetric cryptography. In: Takagi, T., Peyrin, T. (eds.) ASIACRYPT 2017. LNCS, vol. 10625, pp. 211–240. Springer, Cham (2017). https://doi.org/10.1007/978-3-319-70697-9_8

7. Dobraunig, C., Eichlseder, M., Mendel, F.: Analysis of SHA-512/224 and SHA-512/256. In: Iwata, T., Cheon, J.H. (eds.) ASIACRYPT 2015. LNCS, vol. 9453, pp. 612–630. Springer, Heidelberg (2015). https://doi.org/10.1007/978-3-662-48800-3_25

8. Dobraunig, C., Eichlseder, M., Mendel, F.: Analysis of SHA-512/224 and SHA-512/256. IACR Cryptology ePrint Archive 2016/374 (2016). The full version of [7]

9. Dong, X., Sun, S., Shi, D., Gao, F., Wang, X., Hu, L.: Quantum collision attacks on AES-like hashing with low quantum random access memories. In: Moriai, S., Wang, H. (eds.) ASIACRYPT 2020. LNCS, vol. 12492, pp. 727–757. Springer, Cham (2020). https://doi.org/10.1007/978-3-030-64834-3_25

10. Eichlseder, M., Mendel, F., Schläffer, M.: Branching heuristics in differential collision search with applications to SHA-512. In: Cid, C., Rechberger, C. (eds.) FSE 2014. LNCS, vol. 8540, pp. 473–488. Springer, Heidelberg (2015). https://doi.org/10.1007/978-3-662-46706-0_24

11. Flórez Gutiérrez, A., Leurent, G., Naya-Plasencia, M., Perrin, L., Schrottenloher, A., Sibleyras, F.: New results on Gimli: full-permutation distinguishers and improved collisions. In: Moriai, S., Wang, H. (eds.) ASIACRYPT 2020. LNCS, vol. 12491, pp. 33–63. Springer, Cham (2020). https://doi.org/10.1007/978-3-030-64837-4_2

12. Grover, L.K.: A fast quantum mechanical algorithm for database search. In: ACM STOC 1996, pp. 212–219. ACM (1996)

13. Guo, J., Ling, S., Rechberger, C., Wang, H.: Advanced meet-in-the-middle preimage attacks: first results on full tiger, and improved results on MD4 and SHA-2. In: Abe, M. (ed.) ASIACRYPT 2010. LNCS, vol. 6477, pp. 56–75. Springer, Heidelberg (2010). https://doi.org/10.1007/978-3-642-17373-8_4

14. Hosoyamada, A., Sasaki, Y.: Finding hash collisions with quantum computers by using differential trails with smaller probability than birthday bound. In: Canteaut, A., Ishai, Y. (eds.) EUROCRYPT 2020. LNCS, vol. 12106, pp. 249–279. Springer, Cham (2020). https://doi.org/10.1007/978-3-030-45724-2_9

15. Hosoyamada, A., Sasaki, Y.: Quantum collision attacks on reduced SHA-256 and SHA-512. IACR Cryptology ePrint Archive 2021/292 (2021). The full version of this paper

16. Hosoyamada, A., Yasuda, K.: Building quantum-one-way functions from block ciphers: Davies-Meyer and Merkle-Damgård constructions. In: Peyrin, T., Galbraith, S. (eds.) ASIACRYPT 2018. LNCS, vol. 11272, pp. 275–304. Springer, Cham (2018). https://doi.org/10.1007/978-3-030-03326-2_10

17. Indesteege, S., Mendel, F., Preneel, B., Rechberger, C.: Collisions and other non-random properties for step-reduced SHA-256. In: Avanzi, R.M., Keliher, L., Sica, F. (eds.) SAC 2008. LNCS, vol. 5381, pp. 276–293. Springer, Heidelberg (2009). https://doi.org/10.1007/978-3-642-04159-4_18

18. Isobe, T., Shibutani, K.: Preimage attacks on reduced tiger and SHA-2. In: Dunkelman, O. (ed.) FSE 2009. LNCS, vol. 5665, pp. 139–155. Springer, Heidelberg (2009). https://doi.org/10.1007/978-3-642-03317-9_9

19. Jaques, S., Schanck, J.M.: Quantum cryptanalysis in the RAM model: claw-finding attacks on SIKE. In: Boldyreva, A., Micciancio, D. (eds.) CRYPTO 2019. LNCS, vol. 11692, pp. 32–61. Springer, Cham (2019). https://doi.org/10.1007/978-3-030-26948-7_2

20. Khovratovich, D., Rechberger, C., Savelieva, A.: Bicliques for preimages: attacks on Skein-512 and the SHA-2 family. In: Canteaut, A. (ed.) FSE 2012. LNCS, vol. 7549, pp. 244–263. Springer, Heidelberg (2012). https://doi.org/10.1007/978-3-642-34047-5_15

21. Landelle, F., Peyrin, T.: Cryptanalysis of full RIPEMD-128. In: Johansson, T., Nguyen, P.Q. (eds.) EUROCRYPT 2013. LNCS, vol. 7881, pp. 228–244. Springer, Heidelberg (2013). https://doi.org/10.1007/978-3-642-38348-9_14

22. Leurent, G., Peyrin, T.: SHA-1 is a shambles: first chosen-prefix collision on SHA-1 and application to the PGP web of trust. In: Capkun, S., Roesner, F. (eds.) USENIX Security 2020, pp. 1839–1856. USENIX Association (2020)

23. Li, J., Isobe, T., Shibutani, K.: Converting meet-in-the-middle preimage attack into pseudo collision attack: application to SHA-2. In: Canteaut, A. (ed.) FSE 2012. LNCS, vol. 7549, pp. 264–286. Springer, Heidelberg (2012). https://doi.org/10.1007/978-3-642-34047-5_16

24. Liu, F., Dobraunig, C., Mendel, F., Isobe, T., Wang, G., Cao, Z.: New semi-free-start collision attack framework for reduced RIPEMD-160. IACR Trans. Symmetric Cryptol. **2019**(3), 169–192 (2019)

25. Liu, F., Mendel, F., Wang, G.: Collisions and semi-free-start collisions for round-reduced RIPEMD-160. In: Takagi, T., Peyrin, T. (eds.) ASIACRYPT 2017. LNCS, vol. 10624, pp. 158–186. Springer, Cham (2017). https://doi.org/10.1007/978-3-319-70694-8_6

26. Mendel, F., Nad, T., Schläffer, M.: Cryptanalysis of round-reduced HAS-160. In: Kim, H. (ed.) ICISC 2011. LNCS, vol. 7259, pp. 33–47. Springer, Heidelberg (2012). https://doi.org/10.1007/978-3-642-31912-9_3

27. Mendel, F., Nad, T., Schläffer, M.: Finding SHA-2 characteristics: searching through a minefield of contradictions. In: Lee, D.H., Wang, X. (eds.) ASIACRYPT 2011. LNCS, vol. 7073, pp. 288–307. Springer, Heidelberg (2011). https://doi.org/10.1007/978-3-642-25385-0_16

28. Mendel, F., Nad, T., Schläffer, M.: Finding collisions for round-reduced SM3. In: Dawson, E. (ed.) CT-RSA 2013. LNCS, vol. 7779, pp. 174–188. Springer, Heidelberg (2013). https://doi.org/10.1007/978-3-642-36095-4_12

29. Mendel, F., Nad, T., Schläffer, M.: Improving local collisions: new attacks on reduced SHA-256. In: Johansson, T., Nguyen, P.Q. (eds.) EUROCRYPT 2013. LNCS, vol. 7881, pp. 262–278. Springer, Heidelberg (2013). https://doi.org/10.1007/978-3-642-38348-9_16

30. Mendel, F., Peyrin, T., Schläffer, M., Wang, L., Wu, S.: Improved cryptanalysis of reduced RIPEMD-160. In: Sako, K., Sarkar, P. (eds.) ASIACRYPT 2013. LNCS, vol. 8270, pp. 484–503. Springer, Heidelberg (2013). https://doi.org/10.1007/978-3-642-42045-0_25

31. Mendel, F., Pramstaller, N., Rechberger, C., Rijmen, V.: Analysis of step-reduced SHA-256. In: Robshaw, M. (ed.) FSE 2006. LNCS, vol. 4047, pp. 126–143. Springer, Heidelberg (2006). https://doi.org/10.1007/11799313_9

32. National Institute of Standards and Technology: Secure Hash Standard (SHS). FIPS PUB 180-4 (August 2015)

33. Nikolić, I., Biryukov, A.: Collisions for step-reduced SHA-256. In: Nyberg, K. (ed.) FSE 2008. LNCS, vol. 5086, pp. 1–15. Springer, Heidelberg (2008). https://doi.org/10.1007/978-3-540-71039-4_1

34. van Oorschot, P.C., Wiener, M.J.: Parallel collision search with application to hash functions and discrete logarithms. In: ACM CCS 1994, pp. 210–218. ACM (1994)
35. Sanadhya, S.K., Sarkar, P.: 22-step collisions for SHA-2. CoRR abs/0803.1220 (2008)
36. Sanadhya, S.K., Sarkar, P.: New collision attacks against up to 24-step SHA-2. In: Chowdhury, D.R., Rijmen, V., Das, A. (eds.) INDOCRYPT 2008. LNCS, vol. 5365, pp. 91–103. Springer, Heidelberg (2008). https://doi.org/10.1007/978-3-540-89754-5_8
37. Stevens, M., Bursztein, E., Karpman, P., Albertini, A., Markov, Y.: The first collision for full SHA-1. In: Katz, J., Shacham, H. (eds.) CRYPTO 2017. LNCS, vol. 10401, pp. 570–596. Springer, Cham (2017). https://doi.org/10.1007/978-3-319-63688-7_19
38. Zhandry, M.: A note on the quantum collision and set equality problems. Quantum Info. Comput. 15(7–8), 557–567 (2015)

Succinct Arguments

Halo Infinite: Proof-Carrying Data
from Additive Polynomial Commitments

Dan Boneh[1]([✉]), Justin Drake[2], Ben Fisch[1], and Ariel Gabizon[3]

[1] Stanford, Stanford, USA
dabo@stanford.edu
[2] Ethereum Foundation, Zug, Switzerland
[3] AZTEC Protocol, Bury Saint Edmunds, UK

Abstract. Polynomial commitment schemes (PCS) have recently been in the spotlight for their key role in building SNARKs. A PCS provides the ability to commit to a polynomial over a finite field and prove its evaluation at points. A *succinct* PCS has commitment and evaluation proof size sublinear in the degree of the polynomial. An *efficient* PCS has sublinear proof verification. Any efficient and succinct PCS can be used to construct a SNARK with similar security and efficiency characteristics (in the random oracle model).

Proof-carrying data (PCD) enables a set of parties to carry out an indefinitely long distributed computation where every step along the way is accompanied by a proof of correctness. It generalizes *incrementally verifiable computation* and can even be used to construct SNARKs. Until recently, however, the only known method for constructing PCD required expensive SNARK recursion. A system called *Halo* first demonstrated a new methodology for building PCD without SNARKs, exploiting an aggregation property of the *Bulletproofs* inner-product argument. The construction was *heuristic* because it makes non-black-box use of a concrete instantiation of the Fiat-Shamir transform. We expand upon this methodology to show that PCD can be (heuristically) built from any homomorphic polynomial commitment scheme (PCS), even if the PCS evaluation proofs are neither succinct nor efficient. In fact, the Halo methodology extends to any PCS that has an even more general property, namely the ability to aggregate linear combinations of commitments into a new succinct commitment that can later be opened to this linear combination. Our results thus imply new constructions of SNARKs and PCD that were not previously described in the literature and serve as a blueprint for future constructions as well.

1 Introduction

A polynomial commitment scheme (PCS) enables a prover to commit to a polynomial $f \in \mathbb{F}[X]$ of degree at most d. Later, given two public values $x, y \in \mathbb{F}$, the prover can convince a verifier that the committed polynomial f satisfies $y = f(x)$ and that f has degree at most d. This is done using a public coin evaluation protocol called Eval. The PCS is said to be *efficient* if the verifier

© International Association for Cryptologic Research 2021
T. Malkin and C. Peikert (Eds.): CRYPTO 2021, LNCS 12825, pp. 649–680, 2021.
https://doi.org/10.1007/978-3-030-84242-0_23

runs in time $o(d \log |\mathbb{F}|)$, and is said to be *succinct* if the commitment string and the communication complexity of Eval is $o(d \log |\mathbb{F}|)$.

This important concept was first introduced by Kate, Zaverucha, and Goldberg (KZG) [54], and has emerged as a key tool for building succinct and efficient non-interactive argument systems called SNARKs [14]. A succinct and efficient PCS can be used to compile an information theoretic interactive proof system known as a *Polynomial Interactive Oracle Proof* [23] (PIOP), or equivalently *Algebraic Holographic Proofs* [32]), into a SNARK. There are many examples of *efficient* PIOPs for NP languages, where the verifier complexity is logarithmic or even constant in the size of the statement being proven. This construction paradigm led to several recent SNARK systems with improved characteristics, including very efficient pre-processing SNARKs with a universal trusted setup [32,42,59] or no trusted setup [23,34,55,63].

The original PCS, called the KZG PCS [54], is both efficient and succinct. It is based on pairings and requires a linear size reference string generated by a trusted setup (a recent improvement shrinks the size of the reference string [24]). Another PCS, called the Bulletproofs PCS [19,22], does not require pairings or a trusted setup, and is succinct, but is not efficient. Some schemes are both efficient and succinct and do not require a trusted setup: DARK [23] is based on groups of unknown order, and very recently Dory [57] uses pairing-based commitments and generalized inner-product arguments [24]. A post-quantum efficient and succinct PCS without trusted setup can be built using FRI [13,55,65]. In practice, these schemes all have very different performance profiles and properties.

A proof-carrying data (PCD) system [15,35] is a powerful primitive that is more general than a SNARK. Consider a distributed computation that runs along a path of t ordered nodes. The computation is defined by a function $F : \mathbb{F}^{\ell_1} \times \mathbb{F}^{\ell_2} \to \mathbb{F}^{\ell_1}$ in which node i takes two inputs: the output $z_{i-1} \in \mathbb{F}^{\ell_1}$ of node $(i-1)$, and a local input $\mathsf{loc}_i \in \mathbb{F}^{\ell_2}$. The node outputs $z_i = F(z_{i-1}, \mathsf{loc}_i) \in \mathbb{F}^{\ell_1}$. A PCD system enables each node to provide a proof to the next node which attests not only to the correctness of its local computation, but also to the correctness of all prior computations along the path. The work to produce/verify each local proof is proportional to the size of the local computation and is independent of the length of the path. A PCD system can be more generally applied to any distributed computation over a directed acyclic graph of nodes. An important performance metric of a PCD system is its *recursion threshold*: the minimum size complexity of F for which recursion is possible. PCD is currently being used in practice to construct a "constant-size blockchain" system [18,56], where the latest proof attests to the validity of all state transitions (i.e., transactions) in the blockchain history.

PCD systems generalize *incrementally verifiable computation* (IVC), proposed by Valiant [64], where a machine outputs a proof after each step of computation that attests to the correct history of computation steps. This can be used to construct SNARKs for *succinct bounded RAM programs*, which captures many programs in practice that have a small memory footprint relative to their running time. It is also theoretically sufficient for constructing preprocessing SNARKs for arithmetic circuits [9].

1.1 Contributions

We define several abstract properties of a PCS and show that these abstract properties are sufficient to construct powerful proof systems, including PCD and IVC. These abstract constructions give a general and unified approach to understanding recent PCD constructions. We show that the PCS schemes mentioned above satisfy some or all of our abstract properties. In some cases, instantiating our abstract proof systems with these PCS schemes leads to new proof systems that were not previously known. In fact, we could instantiate the PCS in two different ways from *any* collision-resistant linear hash function $h : \mathbb{F}^d \to \mathbb{G}$, one that optimizes for the size of proofs passed along nodes of the PCD, and the other that optimizes for prover time (i.e., the size of the recursive statement).[1]

We begin by defining an **additive** PCS as a simple refinement of a PCS, where the space of commitment strings form a computational group $\mathbb{G}$ under some binary operation add. Group elements must have representation size $\mathsf{poly}(\lambda)$ in terms of the security parameter λ of the PCS and add must run in time $\mathsf{poly}(\lambda)$. This means that it is possible to efficiently compute integer linear combinations of commitments. Moreover, a second requirement is that the prover can efficiently derive a valid opening string to open the linear combination of commitments to the same linear combination of the underlying committed polynomials. Because $\mathbb{G}$ is finite, the size of the linearly combined commitments is bounded, independent of the number of summands or sizes of the integer coefficients. A trivial way to impose a group structure on the commitment space of any PCS is to define $\mathbb{G}$ as the group of formal linear combinations of commitment strings, however, this trivial group is not bounded and therefore does not qualify the PCS as additive.

A useful property of an additive PCS is the ability to *aggregate* PCS evaluations, akin to signature aggregation. We define two flavors of **PCS aggregation schemes**: private and public. First, consider a tuple $(C, x, y) \in \mathbb{G} \times \mathbb{F}^2$, where C is a commitment to some polynomial $f \in \mathbb{F}^{(<d)}[X]$. We say that the prover has a witness for this tuple, if when the prover runs the Eval protocol with the verifier on input (C, x, y), the verifier accepts with probability one. A **(private) aggregation scheme** is an interactive protocol between a prover and a verifier where the public input known to both is ℓ tuples $(C_1, x_1, y_1), \ldots, (C_\ell, x_\ell, y_\ell) \in \mathbb{G} \times \mathbb{F}^2$, and the public output is a single tuple $(C^*, x^*, y^*) \in \mathbb{G} \times \mathbb{F}^2$. At the end of the protocol, the verifier is convinced that if the prover has a witness for (C^*, x^*, y^*), then it must also have witnesses for (C_i, x_i, y_i) for all $i \in [\ell]$. A private aggregation scheme is non-trivial if it is more efficient than running the Eval protocol on the $\ell + 1$ tuples. It is *efficient* if the verifier complexity is sublinear in the degree of the committed polynomials.

---

[1] A homomorphism $h : \mathbb{Z}^d \to \mathbb{G}$ that is collision-resistant modulo p suffices, i.e. finding collisions where $\mathbf{x} \neq \mathbf{y} \bmod p$ is intractable.

A **public aggregation scheme** enables a prover who does not know the witnesses for the ℓ input tuples to aggregate the non-interactive proofs for these tuples. This is also a two-party protocol where, for each $i \in [\ell]$, both parties receive a tuple $(C_i, x_i, y_i) \in \mathbb{G} \times \mathbb{F}^2$ and a corresponding non-interactive proof π_i. The common output is a tuple $(C^*, x^*, y^*) \in \mathbb{G} \times \mathbb{F}^2$ for which the prover has a witness. The prover can subsequently produce a non-interactive proof for this output tuple. Informally, a valid proof for the output tuple demonstrates the validity of each input proof for the input tuples. As there is no information asymmetry between the two parties, the protocol is only interesting if the verifier does significantly less work than the prover.

A key theorem of this paper is that every additive PCS has an efficient private aggregation scheme. In fact, the theorem is more general. It is possible that a PCS is not additive, but there is still an efficient algorithm that takes as input a list of ℓ commitments along with ℓ integer coefficient weights, and outputs a new poly(λ)-size commitment in $\mathbb{G}$ to the linear combination of the underlying committed input polynomials, along with a proof of correctness. We call this a **linear combination scheme** (LCS). The LCS is *efficient* if the verifier is sublinear in the degree of the committed polynomials. Moreover, if the LCS verifier complexity is asymptotically faster than running the Eval verifier ℓ times, then we call the PCS *linearly amortizable* because it allows for opening linear combinations of commitments with amortized efficiency gains. If the PCS is additive it suffices to compute linear combinations of commitments over $\mathbb{G}$ and no additional proof is required, hence every additive PCS is linearly amortizable. We prove that:

Theorem 1.1 (informal). *Every PCS that has an efficient linear combination scheme has an efficient private aggregation scheme. Every succinct additive PCS has an efficient public aggregation scheme.*

The formal statement of this result is in Theorem 4.2 and Theorem 5.2. As a concrete implication, we can take any linear collision-resistant hash function $h : \mathbb{F}^d \to \mathbb{G}$ and build a trivial PCS where the evaluation proof outputs the entire polynomial. Although this is not succinct, it is still additive and thus, as the theorem states, it has an efficient private aggregation scheme. Additionally, combining this hash function with a succinct protocol for proving pre-images of h would give a succinct additive PCS, which has an efficient public aggregation scheme. In fact, there exists a generic succinct protocol for proving pre-images of h (Sect. 5).

The first part of the result (private aggregation, Theorem 4.2) is based on a novel batched evaluation protocol for opening commitments to distinct polynomials at distinct points. Previously, standard batched evaluation techniques for homomorphic polynomial commitments included: (1) opening distinct commitments at the same point, and (2) opening a single commitment at multiple points. The first is accomplished by opening a random linear combination of the original commitments. The second is accomplished by interpolating a degree-n polynomial t over the n opening points such that the committed polynomial f is equal to t over the domain H of these points, and proving that $f - t$ is divisible by the zero polynomial z_H over this domain. The prover computes a commitment C_q to the quotient polynomial $q := \frac{f-t}{z_H}$ and proves that $q \cdot Z_H = (f - t)$ by opening C_q and C_f at a random challenge point. Both of these standard batch evaluation protocols are single-round. We elegantly compose these two approaches to get a two-round protocol for batch opening *multiple* polynomials at *multiple* points. While the analysis of the standard batch evaluation protocol for a multiple commitments at a common point is based on the invertibility of a Vandermonde matrix, the analysis of our protocol relies on the invertibility of the Hadamard product of a random Vandermonde matrix with a square matrix of non-zero field elements (Lemma 4.7).

Our result for public aggregation (Theorem 5.2) leverages the generic private aggregation scheme from Theorem 4.2 combined with a generic succinct proof of knowledge of the classical homomorphism pre-image problem (Sect. 5), which has its roots in the Bulletproofs protocol. Public aggregation is a factor $O(\log d)$ more costly (in communication size) than private aggregation.

Aggregation schemes have a number of important applications to constructing PCS-based SNARKs. First, aggregation schemes can be used for batch evaluation of polynomial commitments in order to reduce the work of the verifier (Sect. 4). Second, in Sect. 6 we discuss a fascinating and powerful application of PCS aggregation to recursive proof systems. This application generalizes a construction by Bowe, Grigg, and Hopwood called Halo [21], which was also formalized and generalized by Bünz et al. [26].

PCD and IVC from PCS aggregation. Suppose $F : \mathbb{F}^\ell \to \mathbb{F}^\ell$ and we wish to prove the correctness of t iterations of F, i.e. that $F^{(t)}(z_0) = z_t$. It turns out that given any succinct PCS with an efficient aggregation scheme, it is possible to construct an efficient non-interactive proof system for this type of statement whose proof size and verification complexity is proportional to the size and verification complexity of the PCS on polynomials of degree $|F|$, completely independent of t. As our results have shown, this includes any additive PCS and even non-additive schemes that have an efficient linear combination scheme. Most significantly, the PCS itself does not need to have efficient verification.

In fact, a PCS with an efficient aggregation scheme can be used to construct a PCD system. Not only does this mean that PCD, IVC, and preprocessing SNARKs can be constructed from any PCS with an efficient linear combination scheme, but we also expect this should lead to practical improvements over the prior proof bootstrapping techniques [9,34] whenever the verification complexity of the private aggregation is smaller than the verification complexity of Eval. We leave concrete performance analysis for future work, although follow up work [25] has already shown that the instantiation of PCD based on our private aggregation scheme using a simple Pedersen hash function achieves an order-of-magnitude reduction in the size of the recursive statement (reducing the recursion threshold accordingly).

Theorem 1.2 (informal). *PCD with proofs linear in the predicate size can be constructed from any PCS that has an efficient linear combination scheme. PCD with sublinear proofs can be constructed from any PCS with an efficient public aggregation scheme.*

In summary, our results pave the way for novel constructions of PCD, IVC, and SNARKs with new efficiency and security characteristics by directing the research effort towards PCS constructions that have the simple abstract additivity properties formalized in this paper. The constructions of PCD/IVC following this methodology do require a *heuristic* security assumption because they involve instantiating random oracles (more specifically, the Fiat-Shamir transform) with concrete hash functions. All known constructions of PCD/IVC require heuristic security (i.e., knowledge assumptions or concrete instantiations of random oracles) and there is evidence that this is inherent [33].

1.2   Related Work

The construction of general purpose efficient SNARK systems is a hotly pursued topic. There are many examples of such proof systems that work for any NP relation [8,15,16,21,23,32,34,42,43,46,47,50,58–60,63]. In addition to the PCS constructions mentioned earlier, there is also a scheme by Bootle et al. [19] that achieves $\sqrt{n}$ commitment size and Eval complexity based on any additively homomorphic commitment, and a similar lattice-based construction by Baum et al. [4,5]. In Sect. 5 we describe a construction of a PCS from any collision-resistant homomorphism based on our succinct proof of homomorphism pre-images (HPI) that has constant size commitment, logarithmic size proofs and linear verification time.[2] Attema and Cramer [2] described a generalization of Bulletproofs to proving linear forms of Pedersen committed vectors, which is a special case of our HPI protocol.

Constructions of IVC/PCD use *recursive composition*, which enables the prover to prove knowledge of a proof that the verification algorithm would accept. Until recently, constructions following this paradigm placed a complete description of the proof verifier inside the recursive statement. Thus, PCD was limited to proof systems where the verifier description is sublinear in the statement being proven (i.e., SNARKs) [12,15,34,64]. The Halo protocol [21,26] was the first construction of PCD from an underlying inefficient proof system (combining the Sonic PIOP [59] and the Bulletproofs PCS). There were two key ideas. The first was, in our terminology, a public aggregation scheme for the Bulletproofs PCS. The second was that the recursive statement can omit the inefficient portion of the proof system's verifier, i.e. the Eval verifier. The Eval proof inputs to a PCD step are aggregated along with the output Eval proofs, and the recursive statement only checks that aggregation was done correctly. This aggregates all

---

[2] This can be combined with the technique of Bootle et al. [19] to get a PCS with $\sqrt{n}$ commitment size, $\sqrt{n}$ verification time, and logarithmic proof size based on any collision-resistant homomorphism. We do not include the details in this work.

Eval proofs into a single evaluation proof that is checked once at the end, amortizing the cost of Eval verification over the distributed computation length (i.e., recursion depth). Bünz et al. [26] generalize this proof technique further using a primitive they call SNARK *accumulation schemes.* They also define PCS accumulation schemes, which can be combined with PIOP-based SNARKs to get a SNARK accumulation scheme. Our notion of public aggregation coincides with PCS accumulation. A small tweak to the definition of PCS accumulation we call *private* accumulation coincides with private aggregation and can be used to construct PCD with larger proofs (linear in the predicate size). Our results are thus perfectly complementary.

2 Preliminaries

Basic notations. For an integer $n \geq 1$, we write $[n]$ to denote the set of integers $\{1, \ldots, n\}$. For any mathematical set $\mathcal{S}$ the notation $|\mathcal{S}|$ denotes the cardinality of $\mathcal{S}$. Unless specified otherwise, we use λ to denote the security parameter. We say a function $f(\lambda)$ is negligible in λ, denoted by $\mathsf{negl}(\lambda)$, if $f(\lambda) = o(1/\lambda^c)$ for all $c \in \mathbb{N}$. We say an algorithm is efficient if it runs in probabilistic polynomial time in the length of its input. We use $\mathsf{poly}(\lambda)$ to denote a quantity whose value is bounded by a fixed polynomial in λ. For a field $\mathbb{F}$, we use $\mathbb{F}^{(<d)}[X]$ for the set of polynomials in $\mathbb{F}[X]$ of degree at most d. We use $\{0,1\}^*$ to denote binary strings of arbitrary length and ε to denote the empty string. We may use the notations $\mathbb{F}_p$ and $\mathbb{Z}_p$ interchangeably to denote the unique prime field of characteristic p. For modular arithmetic, we use the notation $a \equiv b \pmod{n}$ to denote that integers $a, b \in \mathbb{Z}$ are equivalent modulo $n \in \mathbb{Z}$. The notation $a \bmod n$ denotes the unique integer $b \in [0, n)$ such that $a \equiv b \pmod{n}$.

For an abstract group, $\mathbb{G}$ denotes the set of elements in the group, and for any $g_1, g_2 \in \mathbb{G}$ the element $g_1 + g_2$ is the result of applying the binary operation to g_1 and g_2. The inverse of $g \in \mathbb{G}$ is denoted $-g$ and $g_1 - g_2 := g_1 + (-g_2)$. For any $n \in \mathbb{N}$ and $g \in \mathbb{G}$ the element $n \cdot g$ is defined as adding n copies of g. For $n \in \mathbb{Z}$, $n < 0$, then $n \cdot g$ is defined as $-(|n| \cdot g)$. The group $\mathbb{G}$ is called a *computational group* if there exist efficient algorithms for implementing the addition and inversion operations.

Proofs of knowledge. An NP relation $\mathcal{R}$ is a subset of strings $x, w \in \{0,1\}^*$ such that there is a decision algorithm to decide $(x, w) \in \mathcal{R}$ that runs in time polynomial in $|x|$ and $|w|$. The language of $\mathcal{R}$, denoted $\mathcal{L}_R$, is the set $\{x \in \{0,1\}^* : \exists w \in \{0,1\}^* \ s.t. \ (x, w) \in \mathcal{R}\}$. The string w is called the *witness* and x the *instance*. An **interactive proof of knowledge** for an NP relation $\mathcal{R}$ is a special kind of two-party interactive protocol between a prover denoted $\mathcal{P}$ and a verifier denoted $\mathcal{V}$, where $\mathcal{P}$ has a private input w and both parties have a common public input x such that $(x, w) \in \mathcal{R}$. Informally, the protocol is *complete* if $\mathcal{P}(w)$ always causes $\mathcal{V}(pp, x)$ to output 1 for any $(x, w) \in \mathcal{R}$. The protocol is *knowledge sound* if there exists an extraction algorithm $\mathcal{E}$ called the *extractor* such that for every x and adversarial prover $\mathcal{A}$ that causes $\mathcal{V}(pp, x)$ to output 1 with non-negligible probability, $\mathcal{E}$ outputs w such that $(x, w) \in \mathcal{R}$ with overwhelming probability given access[3] to $\mathcal{A}$.

Definition 2.1 (Interactive Proof with Efficient[4] Prover). *Let Setup(λ) denote a non-interactive setup algorithm that outputs public parameters pp given a security parameter λ. Let $\Pi\big(\mathcal{P}(w), \mathcal{V}(pp, x)\big)$ denote a two-party interactive protocol between $\mathcal{P}$ and $\mathcal{V}$, where $\mathcal{P}$ has private input w and $\mathcal{V}$ has the common public input (pp, x). Let $\langle \mathcal{P}(w), \mathcal{V}(pp, x) \rangle$ be a random variables that is the output of $\mathcal{V}$. All algorithms run in time poly($\lambda, |pp|, |x|, |w|$). The pair (Setup, Π) is called a* proof of knowledge *for relation $\mathcal{R}$ if for all non-uniform adversaries $\mathcal{A}$ the following properties hold:*

- *Perfect Completeness.*

$$\Pr\left[\begin{array}{c} (x, w) \notin \mathcal{R} \text{ or} \\ \langle \mathcal{P}(w), \mathcal{V}(pp, x) \rangle = 1 \end{array} : \begin{array}{c} pp \leftarrow \textsf{Setup}(\lambda) \\ (x, w) \leftarrow \mathcal{A}(pp) \end{array} \right] = 1$$

- *Knowledge soundness [6] There exists a probabilistic oracle machine $\mathcal{E}$ called the* extractor *such that for every adversarial interactive prover algorithm $\mathcal{A}$ that is only given the public inputs (pp, x) and every $x \in \mathcal{L}_R$ the following holds: if $\langle \mathcal{A}(\cdot), \mathcal{V}(pp, x) \rangle = 1$ with probability $\epsilon(x) > \textsf{negl}(\lambda)$ then $\mathcal{E}^{\mathcal{A}}(pp, x)$ with oracle access to $\mathcal{A}$ runs in time poly($|x|, \lambda$) and outputs w such that $(x, w) \in R$ with probability $1 - \textsf{negl}(\lambda)$.*

Forking lemmas. The following "forking lemma" is helpful for proving knowledge soundness of multi-round public coin interactive protocols over an exponentially large challenge space (i.e., where each verifier message is a uniform sample from a space $\mathcal{X}$ that has size at least 2^λ). It says that if the adversary succeeds with non-negligible probability $\epsilon = 1/\textsf{poly}(\lambda)$, then there is an $O(\textsf{poly}(\lambda))$-time algorithm for generating a tree of accepting transcripts defined as follows. For an r-round protocol, an $(n_1, ..., n_r)$-**tree of accepting transcripts** for $n_i \geq 0$ is a tree where (i) every node v of the tree corresponds to a partial transcript tr_v, (ii) every level-i node v has n_i children nodes that correspond to continuations of tr_v with distinct ith round challenges, and (iii) every leaf node corresponds to a full transcript in which the verifier accepts. More generally, the property that each pair of challenges on sibling nodes are distinct can be replaced with any property $\pi : \mathcal{X}^2 \rightarrow \{0, 1\}$ which outputs 1 on a random pair of challenges with overwhelming probability. This forking lemma generalizes a similar lemma by Bootle *et al.* [19]. We provide a proof in the full version.

---

[3] The extractor can run $\mathcal{A}$ for any specified number of steps, inspect the internal state of $\mathcal{A}$, and even rewind $\mathcal{A}$ to a previous state.

[4] A classical interactive proof does not require the prover to be efficient. However, our definition of an interactive proof with efficient prover should also not be confused with an interactive *argument*, which only requires soundness against efficient adversaries. In our definition, the prover is required to be efficient for correctness, but soundness must hold against adversaries with unbounded running time.

Lemma 2.2 (Forking Lemma). *Let $(\mathcal{P}, \mathcal{V})$ be an r-round public-coin interactive proof system and $\mathcal{A}$ an adversary that runs in expected time $t_{\mathcal{A}}$ such that $\langle \mathcal{A}(\cdot), \mathcal{V}(pp, x) \rangle = 1$ with probability ϵ on public input x and public parameters pp. Let $\{\pi_i\}_{i=1}^r$ be a set of properties $\pi_i : \mathcal{X}^2 \to \{0, 1\}$ such that $\forall_i \ Pr[\pi(x_1, x_2) = 1 : x_1, x_2 \xleftarrow{\$} \mathcal{X}] > 1 - negl(\lambda)$. If $r \in O(\log \lambda)$ then for any constants $n_1, ..., n_r \in \mathbb{N}$ there exists an algorithm $\mathcal{T}$ that runs in time $poly(\lambda) \cdot (t_{\mathcal{A}}/\epsilon)$ and with probability at least $1 - negl(\lambda)/\epsilon^2$ outputs an $(n_1, ..., n_r)$-tree of accepting transcripts such that for $i \in [1, r]$ all pairs of sibling-node challenges $x_1, x_2 \in \mathcal{X}$ at level i satisfy $\pi_i(x_1, x_2) = 1$.*

Fiat-Shamir tranform. The Fiat-Shamir transform preserves knowledge soundness for any constant-round public-coin interactive proof in the random oracle model, i.e. when the "hash function" is modeled as a random oracle [45, 62]. The interactive protocol must have a negligible soundness error. More generally, Fiat-Shamir preserves knowledge soundness for multi-round interactive proofs that satisfy a property called *state restoration soundness* [11], also equivalent to *round-by-round soundness* [27, 52]. There are also special classes of constant-round protocols for which the Fiat-Shamir transform can be instantiated using correlation-intractable hash functions [27, 28, 53], or even simpler non-cryptographic hash functions [29]. In general, the security of the Fiat-Shamir transform applied to a knowledge-sound interactive proof system using a concrete hash function is heuristic. There are known examples where the transform fails to preserve soundness.

Definition 2.3. *A knowledge-sound interactive proof system $(\mathcal{P}, \mathcal{V})$ is **FS compatible** if there exists a hash family $\mathcal{H}$ such that the non-interactive proof system $(\mathcal{P}_{FS}, \mathcal{V}_{FS})$ obtained from applying Fiat-Shamir using an explicit hash sampled from $\mathcal{H}$ is knowledge-sound.*

Zero Knowledge. An interactive proof satisfies **honest verifier zero-knowledge** (HVZK) if there exists a simulator that does not have access to the prover's private witness yet can produce convincing transcripts between the prover and an honest verifier that are statistically indistinguishable from real transcripts. The Fiat-Shamir transform compiles public-coin proofs that have HVZK into non-interactive proofs that have statistical zero-knowledge (for possibly malicious verifiers).

2.1 Polynomial Commitment Scheme (PCS)

A **polynomial commitment scheme**, or PCS, is a triple of PPT algorithms, Setup, Commit, and Verify along with an evaluation protocol Eval, where:

- Setup(λ, d) $\to pp$ a deterministic algorithm that outputs public parameters pp for committing to polynomials of degree d. The parameters pp include a specification of an abelian commitment group $\mathbb{G}$, as defined below.

- Commit$(pp, f) \to (C, \text{open})$ outputs a commitment $C \in \mathbb{G}$ to the polynomial $f \in \mathbb{F}^{(<d)}[X]$ and an opening "hint" open $\in \{0, 1\}^*$.

- Verify(pp, f, open, C) checks the validity of an opening hint open for a commitment $C \in \mathbb{G}$ to the polynomial $f \in \mathbb{F}^{(<d)}[X]$ and outputs 1 (accept) or 0 (reject).

- Eval$(\mathcal{P}(f, \text{open}), \mathcal{V}(pp, C, z, y)) \to (\bot, b)$ is a public-coin interactive protocol between a prover who has the private input (f, open) for $f \in \mathbb{F}^{(<d)}[X]$ and a verifier who has the common public input pp and $(C, z, y) \in \mathbb{G} \times \mathbb{F}^2$. The verifier outputs $b \in \{0, 1\}$ and the prover has no output. The purpose of the protocol is to convince the verifier that $f(z) = y$ and $\deg(f) < d$.

All the algorithms run in time polynomial in λ and d. Furthermore, a scheme is **correct** if for all polynomials $f \in \mathbb{F}^{(<d)}[X]$ and all points $z \in \mathbb{F}$, with probability 1 the verification Verify(pp, f, open, C) outputs 1 and likewise $\mathcal{V}$ outputs 1 in interaction with $\mathcal{P}$ in the Eval protocol on valid inputs.

Commitment group. A **commitment group** $\mathbb{G}$ is a computational group accompanied by two PPT algorithms: if open$_f$ and open$_g$ are opening hints for commitments C_f and C_g to polynomials $f, g \in \mathbb{F}^{(<d)}[X]$, then add$^*(\text{open}_f, \text{open}_g)$ outputs an opening for $C_f + C_g$ to the polynomial $f + g$ and invert$^*(\text{open}_f)$ outputs an opening for $-C_f$ to the polynomial $-f$. This is a non-standard part of the PCS definition and may appear overly restrictive. However, it does not reduce the generality of a PCS. The default way to define $\mathbb{G}$ is the space of formal linear combinations of commitments to elements of $\mathbb{F}^{(<d)}[X]$. The default add* would simply be concatenation.

Explicit specification of $\mathbb{G}$, add*, and invert* is convenient for defining the additivity properties of a PCS discussed in Sect. 3. This also serves to highlight how additivity is merely a refinement on $\mathbb{G}$. The existence of $\mathbb{G}$, add*, and invert* is not a distinguished property on its own.

Efficiency/Succinctness. If the Eval verifier runs in time $o(d)$, i.e. sublinear in the degree of the committed polynomial, then the PCS is called **efficient**. If both the size of commitments and communication complexity of the Eval protocol are $o(d)$ then the scheme is called **succinct**.

A PCS could be succinct and not efficient. One example is a PCS based on the Bulletproofs system [19, 22]. Some PCS applications may have stricter efficiency/succinctness requirements (e.g., polylog(d) length or run time). A non-succinct PCS is only interesting if it is hiding, and only distinguished from a regular hiding commitment scheme if it has a zero-knowledge evaluation protocol (defined below).

Non-interactive. Eval An interactive PCS Eval protocol may be compiled into a non-interactive Eval proof via the Fiat-Shamir transform. We use the notation $\pi \leftarrow \text{NI-Eval}(pp, f, \text{open}, C, x, y)$ and $b \leftarrow \mathcal{V}_{\text{Eval}}(pp, \pi, C, x, y)$. The PCS Eval may already be non-interactive (e.g., KZG [54]) in which case Fiat-Shamir is not needed.

Security properties. The scheme's algorithms (Setup, Commit, Verify) must be binding as a standard commitment scheme. Furthermore, the protocol Eval should be complete and a proof of knowledge. Informally, this means that any successful prover in the Eval protocol on common input (C, z, y) must *know* a polynomial $f(X) \in \mathbb{F}^{(<d)}[X]$ such that $f(z) = y$ and C is a commitment to $f(X)$. The two of these properties together also imply that the scheme is *evaluation binding*, which means that no efficient adversary can output pp and two pairs (C, z, y) and (C, z, y') where $y \neq y'$, and then succeed in Eval on both pairs (C, z, y) and (C, z, y'). The requirement that Eval is a proof of knowledge is stronger than evaluation binding alone, but is necessary for the application to SNARKs.

Definition 2.4 (Binding PCS). *A PCS is **binding** if for all PPT adversaries $\mathcal{A}$:*

$$\Pr\left[b_0 = b_1 = 1 \wedge f_0 \neq f_1 : \begin{array}{l} pp \leftarrow Setup(\lambda, d) \\ (f_0, \mathsf{open}_0, \mathsf{C}_0, f_1, \mathsf{open}_1, \mathsf{C}_1) \leftarrow \mathcal{A}(pp) \\ b_0 \leftarrow Verify(pp, f_0, \mathsf{open}_0, \mathsf{C}_0) \\ b_1 \leftarrow Verify(pp, f_1, \mathsf{open}_1, \mathsf{C}_1) \end{array} \right] \leq negl(\lambda)$$

Definition 2.5 (Knowledge soundness). *A PCS has **knowledge soundness** if for all pp output by $Setup(\lambda, d)$ and $d \in \mathbb{N}$, the interactive public-coin protocol Eval is a proof of knowledge for the NP relation $\mathcal{R}_{Eval}(pp, d)$ defined as follows:*

$$\mathcal{R}_{Eval}(pp, d) = \left\{ \langle (\mathsf{C}, z, y), (f, \mathsf{open}) \rangle : \begin{array}{l} f \in \mathbb{F}^{(<d)}[X] \wedge f(z) = y \\ Verify(pp, f, \mathsf{open}, \mathsf{C}) = 1 \end{array} \right\}$$

Hiding and Zero Knowledge. A PCS scheme **hiding** if it satisfies the standard definition of a hiding commitment, i.e. commitments to distinct polynomials are statistically indistinguishable. A PCS scheme is **zero-knowledge** if its Eval protocol is a public-coin HVZK interactive proof for the relation $\mathcal{R}_{Eval}(pp, d)$.

Bounded witness ZK. Eval The regular definition of a zero-knowledge PCS scheme requires that the Eval protocol is a zero-knowledge proof for the relation $\mathcal{R}_{Eval}(pp, d)$. This means that Eval cannot leak any information at all about the prover's witness (f, open) for the commitment open, other than the public statements $f(z) = y$, $f \in \mathbb{F}^{(<d)}[X]$, and open is valid. Some schemes, such as DARK [23], do not satisfy this strongest definition of zero-knowledge, but rather satisfy a weaker zero-knowledge PCS property that is generally sufficient in practice. Let $\mathbb{H}$ be a set containing all possible opening hints and let $\mathcal{N} : \mathbb{H} \to \mathbb{R}$ be any non-negative efficiently computable function. Let $\{\mathsf{Eval}(B) : B \in \mathbb{R}\}$ denote a family of evaluation protocols that take an extra parameter $B \in \mathbb{R}$. A PCS satisfies **bounded witness zero-knowledge** for $\mathcal{N}$ if $\mathsf{Eval}(B)$ is a public-coin HVZK interactive proof for the modified relation:

$$\mathcal{R}_{Eval}(pp, d, \mathcal{N}, B) = \left\{ \langle (\mathsf{C}, z, y), (f, \mathsf{open}) \rangle : \begin{array}{l} f \in \mathbb{F}^{(<d)}[X] \wedge f(z) = y \wedge \mathcal{N}(\mathsf{open}) \leq B \\ Verify(pp, f, \mathsf{open}, \mathsf{C}) = 1 \end{array} \right\}$$

"Relaxed" PCS openings. For any PCS scheme, the Verify function can be relaxed such that it will accept an opening of the commitment $t \cdot C_f$ to the polynomial $h = t \cdot f$ for a integer $t \in \mathbb{Z}$ as a valid opening of C_f to the polynomial f.

Lemma 2.6. *Let* $\mathcal{PCS} = (\mathsf{Setup}, \mathsf{Commit}, \mathsf{Verify}, \mathsf{Eval})$ *denote a PCS for polynomials over a field* $\mathbb{F}$ *of characteristic* p. *If the algorithm* Verify *is replaced with an algorithm* Verify^* *that accepts* $(f, (t, \mathsf{open}), \mathsf{C})$ *if and only if* $t \neq 0 \bmod p$ *and* Verify *accepts* $(h, \mathsf{open}, t \cdot \mathsf{C})$ *where* $h = t \cdot f$, *then the new PCS is still binding.*

Proof. Suppose an adversary outputs openings $(f_1, (t_1, \mathsf{open}_1))$ and $(f_2, (t_2, \mathsf{open}_2))$ to a commitment C such that Verify^* accepts both and $f_1 \neq f_2$. This implies that Verify accepts both $(h_1, \mathsf{open}_1, t_1 \cdot \mathsf{C})$ and $(h_2, \mathsf{open}_2, t_2 \cdot \mathsf{C})$ where $h_1 = t_1 \cdot f_1$ and $h_2 = t_2 \cdot f_2$. Using the add^* operation, it would be possible to compute valid openings of $t_1 t_2 \cdot \mathsf{C}$ to both $t_1 h_2 = t_1 t_2 \cdot f_2$ and $t_2 h_1 = t_1 t_2 \cdot f_1$. Since $f_1 \neq f_2$ it follows that $t_1 h_2 \neq t_2 h_1$. Thus, this would contradict the binding property of the original PCS. □

Lemma 2.7. *Given two vectors of commitments* $\mathbf{C}, \mathbf{C}^* \in \mathbb{G}^n$, *a system of equations* $\mathbf{AC} = \mathbf{C}^*$ *for an integer matrix* $\mathbf{A} \in \mathbb{Z}^{n \times n}$ *that is invertible over* $\mathbb{F}_p$, *and a vector of openings of* $\mathbf{C}^*$ *to a vector of polynomials* $\mathbf{f}^* = (f_1^*, ..., f_n^*) \in (\mathbb{F}^{(<d)}[X])^n$, *there is an efficient algorithm to derive polynomials* $\mathbf{f} = (f_1, ..., f_n) \in (\mathbb{F}^{(<d)}[X])^n$, *an integer* $t \in \mathbb{Z}$ *such that* $t \neq 0 \bmod p$, *and openings for each* $t \cdot \mathbf{C}_i$ *to the polynomial* $t \cdot f_i \bmod p$ *such that* $\mathbf{A} \cdot \mathbf{f} \equiv \mathbf{f}^* (\bmod\ p)$.

Proof. Since $det(\mathbf{A}) \neq 0$, the matrix $\mathbf{A}$ is invertible over $\mathbb{Q}$. Let $\mathbf{A}^{-1}$ denote the inverse of $\mathbf{A}$ over $\mathbb{Q}$ and let $\mathbf{I}$ denote the identity matrix over $\mathbb{Z}$. Set $\mathbf{L}$ to be the matrix obtained by clearing the denominators of $\mathbf{A}^{-1}$, i.e. $\mathbf{L} = t \cdot \mathbf{A}^{-1}$ where $t \neq 0$ is the least common multiple of all denominators of the rational entries of $\mathbf{A}^{-1}$. We have $t \cdot \mathbf{C} = \mathbf{L} \cdot \mathbf{A} \cdot \mathbf{C} = \mathbf{L} \cdot \mathbf{C}^*$. From each linear combination of $\mathbf{C}^*$, we use add^* to derive an opening of $t \cdot \mathbf{C}_i$ to a polynomial $g_i = \langle \mathbf{L}_i, \mathbf{f}^* \rangle \in \mathbb{F}[X]$. Let $\mathbf{g} = (g_1, ..., g_n)$. Finally, solve for the vector of polynomials $\mathbf{f}$ such that $\mathbf{A} \cdot \mathbf{f} = \mathbf{f}^*$ by computing $\mathbf{A}^{-1} \bmod p$. Note that $\mathbf{L} \cdot \mathbf{A} \cdot \mathbf{f} = t \cdot \mathbf{f} = \mathbf{L} \cdot \mathbf{f}^*$. Thus, $t f_i = g_i$, for which we have a valid opening of $t \cdot \mathbf{C}_i$. □

3   Additive Polynomial Commitments

This section defines an **additive** PCS as a simple refinement of a PCS, where the group of commitments is a computational group of bounded size. Recall that in our definition from Sect. 2.1, a PCS includes a specification of a family of commitment groups indexed by the parameters (λ, d). We remarked that this is without loss of generality.

Definition 3.1. *A PCS is* **additive** *if every abelian commitment group* $\mathbb{G}_{\lambda,d}$ *determined by the public parameters* $pp \xleftarrow{\$} \mathsf{Setup}(\lambda, d)$ *is a computational group of size at most* $2^{poly(\lambda)}$. *An additive PCS for polynomials in* $\mathbb{F}^{(<d)}[X]$ *is* **additively succinct** *if the size of* $\mathbb{G}_{\lambda,d}$ *is* $o(|\mathbb{F}|^d)$.

There may be a group $\mathbb{G}$ that satisfies the size constraints of Definition 3.1 but does not qualify as a commitment group but the add^* operation only works for a bounded number of operations. Examples include DARK and lattice-based schemes [4,23]. We call them *bounded additive*.

Definition 3.2. *A PCS over a field $\mathbb{F}$ is **homomorphic** if for any $\lambda, d \in \mathbb{N}$ the parameters $pp \leftarrow \mathsf{Setup}(\lambda, d)$ determine two computational groups $(\mathbb{G}, \mathbb{H})$ and two polynomial time computable homomorphisms $\phi : \mathbb{H} \rightarrow \mathbb{G}$ and $\chi : \mathbb{H} \rightarrow \mathbb{F}^{(<d)}[X]$ such that the algorithm $\mathsf{Verify}(pp, f, \mathsf{C}, \mathsf{open})$ returns 1 if and only if $\phi(\mathsf{open}) = \mathsf{C}$ and $\chi(\mathsf{open}) = f$.*

We call $\mathbb{H}$ the "hint" group. For a homomorphic PCS to be binding, the homomorphism $\phi : \mathbb{H} \rightarrow \mathbb{G}$ must be collision resistant over equivalence classes in $\mathbb{H}/ker(\chi)$ (i.e., finding $x_1, x_2 \in \mathbb{H}$ such that $\chi(x_1) \neq \chi(x_2)$ and $\phi(x_1) = \phi(x_2)$ must be hard).

An additive PCS gives a homomorphic PCS. Any additive PCS over a prime field $\mathbb{F} = \mathbb{F}_p$ and commitment group $\mathbb{G}$, can be efficiently transformed into a non-hiding homomorphic PCS with the same commitment group $\mathbb{G}$. The transformation maintains succinctness if the PCS is additively succinct. The new commitment algorithm will give a homomorphism $\phi : \mathbb{Z}^d \rightarrow \mathbb{G}$.

3.1 Linear Combination Schemes

It is possible that a PCS is not additive, yet there is still an efficient scheme to linearly combine polynomial commitments into a succinct aggregate commitment and later open this at points.

Definition 3.3 (Linear Combination Scheme). *A linear combination scheme for a PCS with commitment group $\mathbb{G}$ is a public-coin interactive protocol $\mathsf{LinCombine}$ defined as follows. Given any $\mathbf{f} \in \mathbb{F}^{(<d)}[X]^\ell$, $\boldsymbol{\alpha} \in \mathbb{F}^\ell$, $\mathbf{C} \in \mathbb{G}^\ell$, and a vector of openings $\mathsf{open} = (\mathsf{open}_1, ..., \mathsf{open}_\ell)$ such that $\mathsf{Verify}(pp, f_i, \mathsf{open}_i, \mathsf{C}_i) = 1$ for all $i \in [\ell]$, the protocol $\mathsf{LinCombine}$ does:*

$$\mathsf{LinCombine}\big(\mathcal{P}(\mathbf{f}, \mathbf{open}), \mathcal{V}(pp, \mathbf{C}, \boldsymbol{\alpha})\big) \rightarrow (\mathbf{open}^*, (C^*, b)).$$

The public output is $(C^*, b) \in \mathbb{G} \times \{0,1\}$ where $b \in \{0,1\}$ indicates success or failure. The private output is an opening open^* for C^* to the polynomial $\sum_{i=1}^\ell \alpha_i \cdot f_i$. As for the security, $\mathsf{LinCombine}$ composed with Eval on the output C^* is a proof of knowledge for the relation:

$$\mathcal{R}_{LinComb}(pp, d) = \left\{ \langle (\mathbf{C}, C^*, \boldsymbol{\alpha}), (f, \mathsf{open}, \mathsf{open}^*) \rangle : \begin{array}{l} (C^*, (f, \mathsf{open}^*)) \in \mathcal{R}_{Eval}(pp, d) \\ (\mathsf{C}, (f, \mathsf{open})) \in \mathcal{R}_{Eval}(pp, d) \\ \mathsf{C} = \sum_i \alpha_i \cdot \mathsf{C}_i \end{array} \right\}$$

The trivial linear combination scheme simply returns the linear combination of the input commitments over the commitment group. This clearly satisfies the security definition because $C^* = \mathsf{C}$ in this case. When a scheme is additively succinct then the trivial linear combination scheme is the most natural to use. The purpose of a non-trivial LinCombine is to return a C* that is more succinct than C. We call the scheme **size-optimal** if the aggregate commitment size is bounded by the worst case size of commitments to polynomials of degree d.

We remark that every PCS has a relatively uninteresting generic size-optimal linear combination protocol. The prover can simply compute a fresh commitment C* to $f = \sum_{i=1}^{\ell} \alpha_i \cdot f_i$ and run $\ell + 1$ instances of Eval on C* and each C_i at a common random point ρ selected by the verifier. The verifier can check the linear relation between the opening value of C* at ρ and opening values of the list of C_i at ρ. This satisfies the security definition simply because the LinCombine protocol itself is a proof of knowledge of an opening of C* to f and each C_i to f_i such that $f = \sum \alpha_i \cdot f_i$. A linear combination scheme is interesting when it is more efficient than this generic one.

We say that a linear combination scheme is **efficient** if the verifier complexity in the protocol LinCombine is sublinear in the maximum degree of the input polynomials.

3.2   PCS Examples and Their Additive Properties

The table below summarizes the properties of several schemes. All major PCS constructions have efficient linear combination schemes, which beat the generic one. The linear combination scheme (LCS) amortization ratio (column 3) indicates the ratio of the communication/verification complexity of using the LCS to prove the evaluation of a linear combination (i.e. run Eval on the output of the LCS) versus the generic protocol of running ℓ separate instances of Eval. This ratio is most relevant for the efficiency of batch evaluation (Sect. 4). The complexity ratio of the LCS verifier to the Eval verifier (column 5) is most relevant for the efficiency[5] of proof recursion (i.e., IVC/PCD) discussed in Sect. 6. The parameter ℓ is the number of polynomial commitments being linearly combined and d is their maximum degree.

	additive	LCS amortization	$|\mathcal{V}_{\text{LinCombine}}|$	$\frac{|\mathcal{V}_{\text{LinCombine}}|}{|\mathcal{V}_{\text{Eval}}|}$
Bulletproofs	yes	$1/\ell$	$O_\lambda(\ell)$	$\ell/\Omega(d)$
Dory	yes	$1/\ell$	$O_\lambda(\ell)$	$\ell/\Omega(\log d)$
KZG	yes	$1/\ell$	$O_\lambda(\ell)$	$\ell/\Omega(1)$
DARK	Bounded	$1/\ell$	$O_\lambda(\ell)$	$\ell/\Omega(\log d)$

FRI: a non-additive PCS. The Fast Reed-Solomon IOP of Proximity (FRI) [7] is a protocol for proving that a committed vector in $\mathbb{F}^n$ is δ-close (in relative

---

[5] The asymptotic ratio for KZG hides the fact that $\mathcal{V}_{\text{Eval}}$ involves a pairing operation while $\mathcal{V}_{\text{LinCombine}}$ has only $\ell \cdot \lambda$ curve additions and thus is cheaper for small ℓ.

Hamming distance) to a Reed-Solomon (RS) codeword. FRI can be used to construct a PCS that is post-quantum.

The FRI PCS is not additive by Definition 3.1, but it does have a protocol for opening a *random* linear combination that achieves amortized efficiency ratio of $\frac{1}{\ell} + \frac{1}{\Omega(\log d)}$ over ℓ commitments, which can also be extended to achieve amortized batch evaluation (e.g., Algorithm 8.2 of Aurora [10]).

4   Batch Evaluation and Private Aggregation

For the purpose of this section $\mathbb{F} := \mathbb{F}_p$, for some prime number p. It may be possible to generalize our results to work over extension fields, but that is beyond scope.

The batch evaluation problem. Let $f_1, \ldots, f_\ell \in \mathbb{F}^{(<d)}[X]$ and let C_i be a commitment to f_i for $i \in [\ell]$. The verifier has pp and $C_1, \ldots, C_\ell$. For each $i \in [\ell]$ the verifier also has $(z_{i,1}, y_{i,1}), \ldots, (z_{i,\ell_i}, y_{i,\ell_i}) \in \mathbb{F}^2$. The prover wants to convince the verifier that $f_i(z_{i,j}) = y_{i,j}$ for all $i \in [\ell]$ and $j \in [\ell_i]$.

An alternative formulation of the batch evaluation problem is as follows. For each $i \in [\ell]$:

- let $\Omega_i = \{z_{i,1}, \ldots, z_{i,\ell_i}\} \subseteq \mathbb{F}$, and
- let t_i be the unique degree-$(\ell_i - 1)$ polynomial that satisfies $t_i(z_{i,j}) = y_{i,j}$ for all $j \in [\ell_i]$.

The verifier has (C_i, Ω_i, t_i) for $i \in [\ell]$. The batch evaluation problem is for the prover to convince the verifier that $f_i(x) = t_i(x)$ for all $i \in [\ell]$ and $x \in \Omega_i$. We will use this formulation of the problem from now on.

When all the polynomials t_i in the batch evaluation problem are identically zero (i.e., $t_i \equiv 0$ for all $i \in [\ell]$) then the problem is called *batch zero testing*.

Aggregation scheme. We define PCS proof *aggregation*, akin to signature aggregation. The aggregation of tuples $(C_1, x_1, y_1), \ldots, (C_\ell, x_\ell, y_\ell)$ is a single tuple (C^*, x^*, y^*) such that running Eval to open $C^* \in \mathbb{G}$ at point $x^* \in \mathbb{F}$ to $y^* \in \mathbb{F}$ suffices to open each $C_i \in \mathbb{G}$ at $x_i \in \mathbb{F}$ to $y_i \in \mathbb{F}$. Aggregation enables batch evaluation, as shown in Fig. 1.

Definition 4.1 (Aggregation). *Let* $\mathcal{PCS}$ = (Setup, Commit, Verify, Eval) *denote a PCS with commitment group* $\mathbb{G}$. *An aggregation scheme for* $\mathcal{PCS}$ *is a public-coin interactive protocol* Aggregate *with public inputs* $\mathbf{C} = (C_1, \ldots, C_\ell) \in \mathbb{G}^\ell$, $\mathbf{x} \in \mathbb{F}^\ell$, $\mathbf{y} \in \mathbb{F}^\ell$, *and private inputs* $\mathbf{f} \in \mathbb{F}^{(<d)}[X]^\ell$ *and* open = $(\text{open}_1, \ldots, \text{open}_\ell)$ *such that* Verify$(pp, f_i, \text{open}_i, C_i) = 1$ *for all* $i \in [\ell]$:

$$\text{Aggregate}\big(\mathcal{P}(\mathbf{f}, \mathbf{open}), \mathcal{V}(\mathbf{C}, \mathbf{x}, \mathbf{y})\big) \to ((\text{open}^*, f^*), (C^*, x^*, y^*, b))$$

The public output is a tuple in $\mathbb{G} \times \mathbb{F}^2 \times \{0, 1\}$ *and* $|C^*| = \text{poly}(\lambda)$ *independent of* ℓ. *The security requirement is that the batch evaluation protocol shown in Fig. 1 is a proof of knowledge for the relation:*

$$\mathcal{R}_{BatchEval}(pp, d) = \big\{ \langle (\mathbf{C}, \mathbf{x}, \mathbf{y}), (\mathbf{f}, \mathbf{open}) \rangle : ((C_i, x_i, y_i), (f_i, \text{open}_i)) \in \mathcal{R}_{Eval}(pp, d) \big\}$$

As for correctness, if the inputs to $\mathcal{P}$ satisfy $\mathcal{R}_{\mathsf{BatchEval}}(pp, d)$ then $\mathcal{V}$ outputs $b = 1$ and the private output (open^*, f^*) satisfies $\mathsf{Verify}(pp, f^*, \mathsf{open}^*, C^*) = 1$.

$\mathcal{P}(\mathbf{C}, \mathbf{z}, \mathbf{y}, \mathbf{open}, \mathbf{f})$	$\mathcal{V}(\mathbf{C}, \mathbf{z}, \mathbf{y})$
$((\mathsf{open}^*, f^*), (C^*, z^*, y^*, b_1)) \leftarrow \mathsf{Aggregate}(\mathcal{P}(\mathbf{f}, \mathbf{open}), \mathcal{V}(\mathbf{C}, \mathbf{z}, \mathbf{y}))$	
	Reject if $b_1 = 0$
$(\bot, b_2) \leftarrow \mathsf{Eval}(\mathcal{P}(f^*, \mathsf{open}^*), \mathcal{V}(pp, C^*, z^*, y^*))$	
	Accept if $b_2 = 1$

Fig. 1. A batch evaluation protocol for multiple commitments at multiple points based on a PCS aggregation scheme.

Theorem 4.2. *Any PCS that has a linear combination scheme* LinCombine *(Definition 3.3) also has an aggregation scheme* Aggregate *(Definition 4.1) that on ℓ input commitments makes a single call to* LinCombine *on $\ell + 2$ commitments with λ-bit integer coefficients. Both the prover and verifier do an additional $O(\ell \log \ell)$ operations in $\mathbb{F}$, and the prover makes one call to* Commit *on a polynomial of degree $max_i\{deg(f_i)\}$. The additional communication is one $\mathbb{G}$ element and two $\mathbb{F}$ elements.*

Corollary 4.3. *Every additive PCS (Definition 3.1) has an aggregation scheme with prover complexity $O(\ell \log \ell)$ operations in $\mathbb{F}$ plus one* Commit *to a polynomial of degree $max_i\{deg(f_i)\}$, verifier complexity $O(\ell \log \ell)$ operations in $\mathbb{F}$ plus $O(\ell \cdot \lambda)$ operations in $\mathbb{G}$, and communication of one $\mathbb{G}$ element plus two $\mathbb{F}$ elements.*

We will say that an aggregation scheme is **efficient** if the verifier complexity of the protocol Aggregate is sublinear in the maximum degree of the input polynomials. By Corollary 4.3, every additive PCS, and more generally any PCS with an efficient linear combination scheme, has an efficient aggregation scheme.

Corollary 4.4. *If a PCS has an efficient linear combination scheme then it has an efficient aggregation scheme.*

4.1 A Protocol for Batch Zero Testing

We first construct a general protocol for batch zero testing. Batch evaluation is a simple generalization. The entire protocol is shown in Fig. 2. The communication is comprised of one extra commitment and one evaluation protocol, independent of the number of input polynomials k. In Theorem 4.5 we show that the protocol is knowledge-sound.

The protocol preserves zero-knowledge. The zero-knowledge simulator for this protocol samples $\tilde{\rho}, \tilde{r} \leftarrow \mathbb{F}$, computes an integer representative $\hat{z} \in [0, p)$ for

$z(\tilde{r})^{-1}$, sets $\tilde{C}_q := \sum_{i=1}^{k} \tilde{\rho}^{i-1} z_i(\tilde{r}) \cdot \hat{z} \cdot C_i$, and sets $\tilde{C}_g := \sum_{i=1}^{k} \tilde{\rho}^{i-1} z_i(\tilde{r}) \cdot C_i - z(\tilde{r}) \cdot \tilde{C}_q$. If there exists an opening for each C_i then there exists an opening of $C_i - z(\tilde{r}) \cdot (\hat{z} \cdot C_i)$ to the zero-polynomial, and thus there exists an opening of $\tilde{C}_g$ to the zero-polynomial. The simulator calls the Eval simulator on public input $(\tilde{C}_g, \tilde{r}, 0)$ to get a simulated transcript $\tilde{\pi}$. It output the final simulated transcript $(\tilde{\rho}, \tilde{C}_q, \tilde{r}, \tilde{\pi})$.

$\mathcal{P}((f_1, \mathsf{open}_1, \Omega_1), \ldots, (f_k, \mathsf{open}_k, \Omega_k))$ $\qquad\qquad$ $\mathcal{V}((C_1, \Omega_1), \ldots, (C_k, \Omega_k))$

$\Omega := \bigcup_{i=1}^{k} \Omega_i$ $\qquad\qquad\qquad\qquad\qquad\qquad\qquad\qquad$ $\Omega := \bigcup_{i=1}^{k} \Omega_i$

$z(X) := \prod_{\omega \in \Omega}(X - \omega)$ $\qquad\qquad\qquad\qquad\qquad\qquad$ $z(X) := \prod_{\omega \in \Omega}(X - \omega)$

$\forall_i \; \bar{\Omega}_i := \Omega \setminus \Omega_i$ $\qquad\qquad\qquad\qquad\qquad\qquad\qquad\quad$ $\forall_i \; \bar{\Omega}_i := \Omega \setminus \Omega_i$

$\forall_i \; z_i(X) := \prod_{\omega \in \bar{\Omega}_i}(X - \omega)$ $\qquad\qquad\qquad\qquad\qquad$ $\forall_i \; z_i(X) := \prod_{\omega \in \bar{\Omega}_i}(X - \omega)$

$\qquad\qquad\qquad\qquad\qquad\qquad\qquad \overset{\rho}{\longleftarrow} \qquad\qquad \rho \overset{\$}{\leftarrow} [0, p)$

$q(X) := \sum_{i=1}^{k} \rho^{i-1} z_i f_i / z$

$(C_q, \mathsf{open}_q) \leftarrow \mathsf{Commit}(pp, q) \qquad \overset{C_q}{\longrightarrow}$

$\qquad\qquad\qquad\qquad\qquad\qquad\qquad\qquad\qquad\qquad r \overset{\$}{\leftarrow} [0, p)$

$\qquad\qquad\qquad\qquad\qquad\qquad\qquad \overset{r}{\longleftarrow}$

$g(X) := \sum_{i=1}^{k} \rho^{i-1} z_i(r) f_i(X) - z(r) q(X) \qquad \forall_i \text{ compute } z_i(r) \in \mathbb{F}$

$\quad$ (if all is valid then $g(r) = 0$)

$\qquad\qquad\qquad\qquad\qquad\qquad\qquad\qquad\qquad C' := \sum_{i=1}^{k} \rho^{i-1} z_i(r) \cdot C_i$

$\qquad\qquad\qquad\qquad\qquad\qquad\qquad\qquad\qquad C_g := C' - z(r) \cdot C_q$

$\qquad\qquad\qquad \mathsf{Eval}(\mathcal{P}(g, \mathsf{open}_g), \mathcal{V}(C_g, r, 0))$
$\qquad\qquad\qquad \longleftrightarrow$

Fig. 2. A zero test for multiple polynomials on distinct sets: $(C_i, \mathsf{open}_i) \leftarrow \mathsf{Commit}(pp, f_i)$ and Ω_i is a non-empty subset of $\mathbb{F}$ for all $i \in [k]$. The prover computes open_g from $\rho, r, \mathsf{open}_1, \ldots, \mathsf{open}_k$ (not shown).

Theorem 4.5. *If Eval is knowledge sound, then the protocol in Fig. 2 is a proof of knowledge for the relation:*

$$\mathcal{R}_{ZTest}(pp, d) := \left\{ \langle (C, \Omega), (\mathbf{f}, \mathbf{open}) \rangle : \begin{array}{l} \mathbf{f} = (f_1, \ldots, f_k) \; s.t. f_i \in \mathbb{F}^{(<d)}[X] \\ \forall i \in [k] \forall_{\omega \in \Omega_i} f_i(\omega) = 0 \\ \forall i \in [k] \; Verify(pp, C_i, open_i, f_i) = 1 \end{array} \right\}$$

The proof is included in the full version of this paper.

4.2 Batch Evaluation Protocol

The protocol for batch evaluation is a small generalization of the zero-testing protocol in Fig. 2. Here, for $i \in [k]$, the verifier has (C_i, Ω_i, t_i) where $t_i \in \mathbb{F}^{(<d)}[X]$,

and needs to be convinced that $f_i(x) = t_i(x)$ for all $i \in [k]$ and all $x \in \Omega_i$. This is the same as proving that every polynomial $\hat{f}_i := f_i - t_i$ is zero on all of Ω_i. Thus, we can apply the protocol in Fig. 2 to $\hat{f}_1, \dots, \hat{f}_k$.

Naively, the verifier would need to compute a commitment to each $\hat{f}_i$, which it can do from C_i and t_i. However, we can optimize the verifier by observing that the verifier only uses $t_i(X)$ to compute $t_i(r)$ for some random $r \in \mathbb{F}$. Hence, we can replace the verifier's computation of C' in Fig. 2 by instead computing $C' := \sum_{i=1}^{k} \rho^{i-1} z_i(r) \cdot (C_i - t_i(r) \cdot C^{(1)})$ where $C^{(1)}$ is a commitment to the polynomial $f \equiv 1$. In doing so, we save the verifier the work to compute commitments to $\hat{f}_1, \dots, \hat{f}_k$.

Theorem 4.6. *If Eval is knowledge sound, then the batch evaluation protocol based on Fig. 2 is a proof of knowledge for the relation $\mathcal{R}_{BatchEval}(pp, d)$.*

The complete proof of Theorem 4.6 is included in the full version of this paper. The proof applies the forking lemma (Lemma 2.2) to show that it is possible to generate a depth-2 tree of $2k$ protocol transcripts where:

1. There are k distinct first-round challenges $\rho_1 \neq \cdots \neq \rho_k \neq 0 \bmod p$
2. For all $i \in [k]$, two transcripts share the first-round challenge ρ_i and have distinct second-round challenges r_i and r'_i such that $z(r_i) \neq z(r'_i) \neq 0$.
3. Letting $\mathbf{V} \in \mathbb{Z}^{k \times k}$ denote the Vandermonde matrix with jth row $(1, \rho_j, \dots, \rho_j^{k-1})$ and letting $\mathbf{R} \in \mathbb{Z}^{k \times k}$ be the matrix with (i,j)th coordinate $z_i(r_j)$, the Hadamard product of these matrices $\mathbf{A} := \mathbf{V} \circ \mathbf{R}$ is invertible over $\mathbb{F}_p$.

The first two conditions are easy to guarantee because collisions among first round challenges occur with negligible probability, and similarly $z(r) \neq z(r') \neq 0$ with overwhelming probability over $r, r' \xleftarrow{\$} \mathbb{F}$. The third condition is guaranteed by the fact (proven in Lemma 4.7) that if every entry of $\mathbf{R}$ is non-zero over $\mathbb{F}_p$, then for $\{\rho_j\}$ sampled uniformly and independently the matrix $\mathbf{A}$ is invertible with overwhelming probability. For $\{r_j\}$ sampled uniformly and independently, $z_i(r_j) \neq 0 \bmod p$ except with probability $\frac{k}{|\mathbb{F}|}$.

For each of these transcripts, the Eval extractor is invoked to extract an opening of each $C'_j = \sum_{i=1}^{k} \rho_j^{i-1} z_i(r_j) \cdot C_i$ to a polynomial f'_j. This gives a system of equations that can be solved to obtain openings of the input commitments $(C_1, \dots, C_k)$ to polynomials $(f_1, \dots, f_k) = \mathbf{A}^{-1} \cdot (f'_1, \dots, f'_k)$.

The protocol is still zero-knowledge if the PCS is hiding and Eval is zero-knowledge. The description of the simulator is nearly identical to the simulator for the protocol in Fig. 2 so we will not repeat the details.

Lemma 4.7. *Let $\mathbf{M}$ be an $n \times n$ matrix over $\mathbb{F}_p^\times$. Let $\mathbf{V}$ be a random Vandermonde matrix over $\mathbb{F}_p$, sampled uniformly and independent of $\mathbf{A}$. Their Hadamard product $\mathbf{V} \circ \mathbf{M}$ is invertible with probability at least $1 - \frac{n^2}{|\mathbb{F}|}$.*

Proof. Let $\mathbf{V}(\mathbf{X})$ denote the Vandermonde matrix over formal variables $X_1, \dots, X_n$. Using the Leibnitz formula, $det(\mathbf{V}(\mathbf{X}))$ is an n-variate polynomial, which is an alternating sum of $n!$ distinct monomials. The determinant of the Hadamard product, $det(\mathbf{V}(\mathbf{X}) \circ \mathbf{M})$ is also an alternating sum of $n!$ distinct monomials where the coefficient on each distinct monomial is a distinct summand of the Leibnitz formula for $det(\mathbf{M})$. All coefficients are non-zero since all entries of $\mathbf{A}$ are non-zero. Therefore, this n-variate polynomial is not identically zero. Let $p(X_1, ..., X_n)$ denote this polynomial, which has total degree less than n^2. A random Vandermonde matrix $\mathbf{V}$ is a random assignment $\mathbf{x} = (x_1, ..., x_n)$ to the n variables $X_1, ..., X_n$ and thus $det(\mathbf{V} \circ \mathbf{M}) = p(x_1, ..., x_n)$. By the Schwartz-Zippel lemma, the probability that $p(x_1, ..., x_n) = 0$ is at most $\frac{n^2}{|\mathbb{F}|}$. $\square$

4.3   Aggregation Scheme (proof of Theorem 4.2)

When the PCS has a linear combination scheme (Definition 3.3), then the protocol from Sect. 4.2 together with the linear aggregation protocol LinCombine results in an aggregation scheme for the PCS. Concretely, the protocol on public inputs $\mathbf{C} = (C_1, ..., C_k) \in \mathbb{G}^k$, $\mathbf{x} = (x_1, ..., x_k) \in \mathbb{F}^k$, and $\mathbf{y} = (y_1, ..., y_k) \in \mathbb{F}^k$ with prover private inputs $\mathbf{f} = (f_1, ..., f_k) \in \mathbb{F}^{(<d)}[X]^k$ and $\mathsf{open} = (\mathsf{open}_1, ..., \mathsf{open}_k)$ operates as follows:

$\mathsf{Aggregate}\big(\mathcal{P}(\mathbf{f}, \mathbf{open}), \mathcal{V}(\mathbf{C}, \mathbf{x}, \mathbf{y})\big) \to ((\mathsf{open}^*, f^*), (C^*, x^*, y^*, b))$

1. Let $\Omega_i = \{x_i\}$ for $i \in [1, k]$, and let $t_i := y_i$.
2. Run the protocol in Sect. 4.2 with public inputs $\{(C_i, \Omega_i, t_i)\}_{i \in [k]}$ and prover private inputs $\{(f_i, \mathsf{open}_i)\}_{i \in [k]}$ up until the point that $\mathcal{P}$ and $\mathcal{V}$ derive C_g, the prover $\mathcal{P}$ has privately derived $g(X)$, and the verifier $\mathcal{V}$ has sent the challenge $r \in \mathbb{F}$. Note that C_g is a linear combination of the input commitments $\mathbf{C}$, the C_q sent during the protocol, and $C^{(1)}$ (the commitment to 1).
3. The prover and verifier will run LinCombine to produce a succinct commitment C^* to the same polynomial as C_g:
   - Let $\mathbf{C}' := (C_1, ..., C_k, C^{(1)}, C_q)$
   - Let $\mathbf{f}' := (f_1, ..., f_k, 1, q)$ and let $\mathbf{open}' = (\mathsf{open}_1, ..., \mathsf{open}_k, \mathsf{open}^{(1)}, \mathsf{open}_q)$
   - For $i \in [k]$ let $\alpha_i := \rho^{i-1} \cdot z_i(r) \cdot f_i$, let $\alpha_{k+1} := -\sum_{i=1}^{k} \rho^{i-1} \cdot z_i(r) \cdot y_i$, and let $\alpha_{k+2} := -z(r)$. Let $\boldsymbol{\alpha} := (\alpha_1, ..., \alpha_{k+2})$.
   - Run the protocol $\mathsf{LinCombine}\big(\mathcal{P}(\mathbf{f}', \mathbf{open}'), \mathcal{V}(pp, \mathbf{C}', \boldsymbol{\alpha})\big) \to (\mathsf{open}^*, (C^*, b))$.
   - The prover's private output is (open^*, g) and the verifier's public output is $(C^*, r, 0, b)$.

In the case that $(C^*, \mathsf{open}^*) = (C_g, \mathsf{open}_g)$, i.e. the PCS is additive, then composing this protocol with an Eval on C_g is a special case of the batch evaluation protocol in Sect. 4.2, which by Theorem 4.6 is a proof of knowledge for relation $\mathcal{R}_{\mathsf{BatchEval}}(pp, d)$. More generally, by the security property of the linear combination scheme LinCombine, composing the protocol with an Eval on $(C^*, r, 0)$ is equivalent to running Eval on $(C_g, r, 0)$, i.e. it is a proof of knowledge of an opening for C_g at the pair $(r, 0)$. Thus, this provides the extractor from Theorem 4.6 with the same information it needs to extract an $\mathcal{R}_{\mathsf{BatchEval}}(pp, d)$ witness.

The prover complexity in the aggregation protocol is $O(k \log k)$ operations in $\mathbb{F}$ using FFTs plus the complexity of a single call to Commit on a polynomial of degree at most d. The verifier complexity is $O(k \log k)$ operations in $\mathbb{F}$ and $O(k \cdot \lambda)$ operations in $\mathbb{G}$.

5   Homomorphic PCS Public Aggregation

The aggregation scheme in Definition 4.1 requires the aggregator, who plays the role of a prover, to know openings of all the input commitments. In a *public aggregation scheme*, the aggregator isn't required to know the openings of the input commitments but performs more work than the verifier. We define public aggregation only for a PCS with a non-interactive evaluation protocol NI-Eval.

The verifier in the Aggregate protocol receives NI-Eval proofs π_i for each (C_i, x_i, y_i) input tuple. The prover's output is (open^*, f^*) and the verifier's output is (C^*, x^*, y^*, b). If the prover succeeds in the aggregation protocol (i.e., the verifier outputs $b = 1$) and the verifier separately verifies the membership of (C^*, x^*, y^*) in $\mathcal{R}_{\mathsf{Eval}}(pp, d)$ then it should be convinced that each input tuple is also in $\mathcal{R}_{\mathsf{Eval}}(pp, d)$ with overwhelming probability.

Definition 5.1 (Public Aggregation). *Let* $\mathcal{PCS} = ($Setup, Commit, Verify, NI-Eval$)$ *denote a PCS with commitment group* $\mathbb{G}$ *and a non-interactive evaluation protocol. A public aggregation scheme for* $\mathcal{PCS}$ *is a public-coin interactive protocol* Aggregate *that has public inputs* $\mathbf{C} = (C_1, ..., C_\ell) \in \mathbb{G}^\ell$, $\mathbf{x} \in \mathbb{F}^\ell$, $\mathbf{y} \in \mathbb{F}^\ell$, *and* $\boldsymbol{\pi} = (\pi_1, ..., \pi_\ell)$:

$$\mathsf{Aggregate}\big(\mathcal{P}, \mathcal{V}(pp, \boldsymbol{\pi}, \mathbf{C}, \mathbf{x}, \mathbf{y})\big) \rightarrow \big((\mathsf{open}^*, f^*), (C^*, x^*, y^*, b)\big)$$

In a correct scheme, if the inputs satisfy $\mathcal{V}_{\mathsf{Eval}}(\pi_i, C_i, x_i, y_i) = 1$ *for all* $i \in [\ell]$, *then the outputs satisfy* $b = 1$ *and* Verify$(pp, f^*, \mathsf{open}^*, C^*) = 1$. *The soundness requirement is that the following probability is negligible:*

$$\Pr\left[\begin{array}{l} b \wedge \mathcal{V}_{\mathsf{Eval}}(\pi^*, C^*, x^*, y^*) = 1 \\ \exists_i \mathcal{V}_{\mathsf{Eval}}(pp, \pi_i, C_i, x_i, y_i) \neq 1 \end{array} : \begin{array}{l} pp \leftarrow \mathsf{Setup}(\lambda, d) \\ (\mathbf{C}, \mathbf{x}, \mathbf{y}, \boldsymbol{\pi}) \leftarrow \mathcal{A}(pp) \\ ((\mathsf{open}^*, f^*), (C^*, x^*, y^*, b)) \leftarrow \mathsf{Aggregate}(\mathcal{P}, \mathcal{V}(pp, \boldsymbol{\pi}, \mathbf{C}, \mathbf{x}, \mathbf{y})) \\ \pi^* \leftarrow \mathsf{NI\text{-}Eval}(pp, f^*, \mathsf{open}^*, C^*, x^*, y^*) \end{array}\right]$$

A public aggregation scheme is **efficient** if the verifier complexity of the protocol Aggregate is sublinear in the maximum degree of the input polynomials.

Theorem 5.2. *There is a black-box compilation from any additive PCS over a prime field* $\mathbb{F} = \mathbb{F}_p$ *and commitment group* $\mathbb{G}$ *into a publicly aggregatable homomorphic PCS with the same commitment group* $\mathbb{G}$. *The overhead of the new* Eval *is:*

- *Communication:* $O(\log d)$ *additional elements of* $\mathbb{G} \times \mathbb{F}$
- *Prover:* $O((\log p + \lambda) \cdot n)$ *additional operations in* $\mathbb{G}$

– *Verifier: $O(\log d)$ additional operations in $\mathbb{G} \times \mathbb{F}$*

The public aggregation scheme complexity for ℓ commitments is:

– *Communication: One $\mathbb{G}$ element and two $\mathbb{F}$ elements.*
– *Prover: $O(\ell \log \ell)$ operations in $\mathbb{F}$, $O(\log p \cdot n)$ operations in $\mathbb{G}$, and $O(\ell \cdot n)$ multiplications of λ-bit integers*
– *Verifier: $O(\ell \log \ell)$ operations in $\mathbb{F}$ and $O(\ell \cdot \lambda)$ operations in $\mathbb{G}$.*

Theorem 5.2 is proven in two parts. First, there is a simple transformation from any additive PCS into a homomorphic PCS with the same commitment group and opening group $\mathbb{H} = \mathbb{Z}^n$. Second, we present a compiler from any homomorphic PCS with opening group $\mathbb{H} = \mathbb{Z}^n$ into a new homomorphic PCS together with a public aggregation scheme that meets the performance requirements of the theorem. A key ingredient is a protocol for *succinct proof of knowledge of homomorphism pre-image*, which we present next.

5.1   A Succinct PoK for Homomorphism Pre-image

Let $\phi : \mathbb{Z}^n \to \mathbb{G}$ be any homomorphism where $\mathbb{G}$ is an abelian computational group. We will present a succinct public-coin interactive proof of knowledge for the following relation:

$$\mathcal{R}^*_{\mathsf{HPI}}(\phi, \mathbb{G}, p) = \{((\mathbf{x} \in \mathbb{Z}^n, t \in \mathbb{Z}), y \in \mathbb{G}) : \phi(\mathbf{x}) = t \cdot y \wedge t \neq 0 \bmod p\}$$

In the special case that $p\mathbb{Z} \subseteq ker(\phi)$, e.g. when $\mathbb{G}$ has order p or is an $\mathbb{F}_p$-vector space, a proof of knowledge for this relation is equivalent to a proof of knowledge for the standard homomorphism pre-image relation. In this case, given a witness $(\mathbf{x}, t)$ for $\mathcal{R}^*_{\mathsf{HPI}}$ it is possible to efficiently compute an integer vector $\mathbf{x}'$ such that $\phi(\mathbf{x}') = y$ by computing $\hat{t} \in \mathbb{Z}$ such that $\hat{t} \equiv t^{-1} \bmod p$ and setting $\mathbf{x}' := \hat{t} \cdot x$.

Let $\{e_i\}_{i \in [n]}$ denote the standard basis of $\mathbb{Z}^n$ and define $g_i := \phi(e_i)$. The homomorphism ϕ may be rewritten as the $\mathbb{Z}$-linear map $\phi(\mathbf{x}) = \langle \mathbf{x}, \mathbf{g} \rangle = \sum_{i=1}^{n} x_i \cdot g_i$. We will use $[\![\mathbf{x}]\!]_{\mathbf{g}}$ as a shorthand notation for $\langle \mathbf{x}, \mathbf{g} \rangle$ give $\mathbf{x} \in \mathbb{Z}^n$ and $\mathbf{g} \in \mathbb{G}^n$. Note the following two properties of $[\![\cdot]\!]$:

1. **Decomposition** If $\mathbf{x} = (\mathbf{x}_L, \mathbf{x}_R)$ for $\mathbf{x}_L \in \mathbb{Z}^{n_1}$ and $\mathbf{x}_R \in \mathbb{Z}^{n_2}$ such that $n_1 + n_2 = n$ and $\mathbf{g} = (\mathbf{g}_L, \mathbf{g}_R)$ for $\mathbf{g}_L \in \mathbb{G}^{n_1}$ and $\mathbf{g}_R \in \mathbb{G}^{n_2}$, then $[\![\mathbf{x}]\!]_{\mathbf{g}} = [\![\mathbf{x}_L]\!]_{\mathbf{g}_L} + [\![x_R]\!]_{\mathbf{g}_R}$.

2. **Bilinearity** If $\alpha, \beta \in \mathbb{Z}$, $\mathbf{x} \in \mathbb{Z}^n$, and $\mathbf{g}, \mathbf{h} \in \mathbb{G}^n$ then $\alpha[\![\mathbf{x}]\!]_{\mathbf{g}} + \beta[\![\mathbf{x}]\!]_{\mathbf{h}} = [\![\alpha\mathbf{x}]\!]_{\mathbf{g}} + [\![\beta\mathbf{x}]\!]_{\mathbf{h}} = [\![\mathbf{x}]\!]_{\alpha\mathbf{g}+\beta\mathbf{h}}$

The public coin interactive proof is illustrated in Fig. 3. The verifier's public-coin challenges are sampled uniformly from the set $\mathcal{X} := [0, 2^\lambda)$.

Correctness. If the prover follows the protocol honestly, then $[\![\mathbf{x}]\!]_{\mathbf{g}} = [\![\mathbf{x}_L]\!]_{\mathbf{g}_L} + [\![\mathbf{x}_R]\!]_{\mathbf{g}_R}$, and:

$$y' = y_L + \alpha^2 y_R + \alpha y = [\![\mathbf{x}_L]\!]_{\mathbf{g}_R} + [\![\alpha^2 \mathbf{x}_R]\!]_{\mathbf{g}_L} + [\![\alpha\mathbf{x}_L]\!]_{\mathbf{g}_L} + [\![\alpha\mathbf{x}_R]\!]_{\mathbf{g}_R}$$
$$= [\![\mathbf{x}']\!]_{\mathbf{g}_R} + [\![\alpha\mathbf{x}']\!]_{\mathbf{g}_L} = [\![\mathbf{x}']\!]_{\mathbf{g}_R + \alpha\mathbf{g}_L}$$

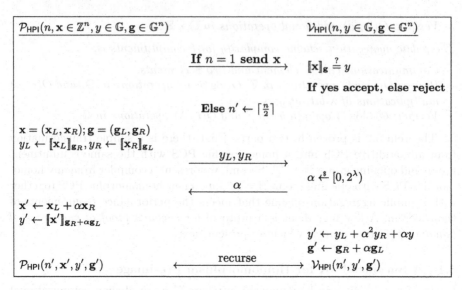

Fig. 3. *A succinct interactive protocol for HPI.* For simplicity n is a power of 2.

Thus, in each recursive round, if $\mathbf{x}$ is a valid witness for $(y, n, \mathbf{g})$ then $\mathbf{x}'$ is a valid witness for $(y', n', \mathbf{g}')$.

Theorem 5.3. *The protocol in Fig. 3 is a proof of knowledge for the relation* $\mathcal{R}^*_{HPI}(\phi, \mathbb{G}, p)$.

Proof. Our analysis will show the protocol is a proof of knowledge for the relation $\mathcal{R}^*_{HPI}(\llbracket \cdot \rrbracket, \mathbb{G}, p)$. For simplicity we assume n is a power of 2. We define a knowledge extractor $\mathcal{E}$ that runs with an adversary $\mathcal{A}$ who succeeds for public input $(\mathbf{x}, y, \mathbf{g})$ with probability $\epsilon = 1/\mathsf{poly}(\lambda)$. $\mathcal{E}$ begins by invoking the forking lemma to generate a tree of accepting transcripts with the following characteristics:

- The tree has depth $\log n$ and branching factor 3. We will index nodes by $v \in [0, n^{\log 3})$.
- The root is labeled with the verifier's input $(y, \mathbf{g})$.
- Each non-leaf node v distinct from the root is labeled with a challenge α_v and a prover message $(y_{v,0}, y_{v,1})$.
- Each non-leaf node v has three children each labeled with three distinct verifier challenges. $\alpha_{v,1} \neq \alpha_{v,2} \neq \alpha_{v,3}$.
- Each leaf node v is labeled with a prover message $x_v \in \mathbb{Z}$.

Since the probability of collision on a pair of challenges sampled uniformly from $\mathcal{X}$ is $1/2^\lambda$, by the forking lemma (Lemma 2.2) this tree-finding algorithm runs for time polynomial in λ and succeeds excepts with negligible probability in λ.

For any non-leaf node v with parent w and message pair $(y_{v,0}, y_{v,1})$ and challenge α_v define $y_v := y_{w,0} + \alpha_v^2 \cdot y_{w,1} + \alpha_v \cdot y_w$. For any leaf node v the value of y_v is already defined by the transcript. For the root node rt define $y_{\text{rt}} := y$, where y is the input. We also define a value $\mathbf{g}_v$ for every node v as follows: if v is the root then $\mathbf{g}_v := \mathbf{g}$, else if v has a parent w then $\mathbf{g}_v := \mathbf{g}_{w,0} + \alpha_v \cdot \mathbf{g}_{w,1}$ where $\mathbf{g}_w = (\mathbf{g}_{w,0}, \mathbf{g}_{w,1})$ is the concatenation of equal length vectors $\mathbf{g}_{w,0}, \mathbf{g}_{w,1}$. If v is a node on the ith level up from the leaves then $\mathbf{g}_v \in \mathbb{G}^{2^i}$. Every component of $\mathbf{g}_v$ is a linear combination of the elements in $\mathbf{g}$ derived from challenges along a path up the tree. Thus, for each $\mathbf{g}_v$ the extractor also knows a matrix $\mathbf{U}_v \in \mathbb{Z}^{2^i \times n}$ such $\mathbf{U}_v \cdot \mathbf{g} = \mathbf{g}_v$. By construction, for every root to leaf path of nodes $v_1, ..., v_{\log n}$ the sequence of values $(\alpha_{v_i}, y_{v_i,0}, y_{v_i,1})$ form an accepting transcript between the prover and verifier where $(\mathbf{g}_{v_i}, y_{v_i})$ are the verifier's local inputs in the ith round. Moreover, the leaf node labels satisfy $x_v \cdot \mathbf{g}_v = y_v$.

We will show that given this tree, the extractor can compute $(t_v, \mathbf{x}_v) \in \mathbb{Z} \times \mathbb{Z}^n$ for each node v such that $[\![\mathbf{x}_v]\!]_{\mathbf{g}} = t_v \cdot y_v$. In particular, this means that the extractor obtains a witness $(t_{\text{rt}}, \mathbf{x}_{\text{rt}}) \in \mathbb{Z} \times \mathbb{Z}^n$ for $y \in \mathbb{G}$ such that $[\![\mathbf{x}_{\text{rt}}]\!]_{\mathbf{g}} = t_{\text{rt}} \cdot y$. This is a valid pair for the relation $\mathcal{R}^*_{\text{HPI}}([\![\cdot]\!], \mathbb{Z}^n, \mathbb{G})$. The extractor begins at the leaves. Every leaf node is already labeled with $x_v \in \mathbb{Z}$ such that $x_v \cdot \mathbf{g}_v = x_v \cdot \mathbf{U}_v \cdot \mathbf{g} = y_v$ where $\mathbf{U}_v \in \mathbb{Z}^{1 \times n}$. The extractor sets $\mathbf{x}_v := x_v \cdot \mathbf{U}_v$. Next, suppose the extractor has already successfully computed an $(t_v, \mathbf{x}_v)$ pair for all children nodes of a node w. For ease of notation, temporarily let y_1, y_2, y_3 denote the y_v values for the three children and $\alpha_1, \alpha_3, \alpha_3$ denote their respective challenge labels. Similarly, let $(\mathbf{x}_i, t_i) \in \mathbb{Z}^n \times \mathbb{Z}$ for $i \in [3]$ denote the extracted labels for the children nodes. By construction, $y_i = y_w + \alpha_i^2 y_{w,0} + \alpha_i y_{w,1}$ for $i \in [3]$. Defining $\mathbf{A} \in \mathbb{Z}^{3 \times 3}$ to be the matrix with rows $(1, \alpha_i^2, \alpha_i)$, $\mathbf{T}$ the diagonal matrix with diagonal entries $t_1, t_2, t_3 \neq 0 \bmod p$, and $\mathbf{X} \in \mathbb{Z}^{3 \times n}$ the integer matrix with rows $\mathbf{x}_1, \mathbf{x}_2, \mathbf{x}_3$, we can summarize the relations:

$$\mathbf{A} \cdot \begin{bmatrix} y_w \\ y_{w,0} \\ y_{w,1} \end{bmatrix} = \begin{bmatrix} y_1 \\ y_2 \\ y_3 \end{bmatrix} \qquad \mathbf{T} \cdot \begin{bmatrix} y_1 \\ y_2 \\ y_3 \end{bmatrix} = \begin{bmatrix} [\![\mathbf{x}_1]\!]_{\mathbf{g}} \\ [\![\mathbf{x}_2]\!]_{\mathbf{g}} \\ [\![\mathbf{x}_3]\!]_{\mathbf{g}} \end{bmatrix} = \mathbf{X} \cdot \mathbf{g}$$

$\mathbf{T}$ is invertible over $\mathbb{F}$. Since $\mathbf{A}$ is Vandermonde it is also invertible over $\mathbb{F}$. Therefore $\mathbf{T} \cdot \mathbf{A}$ is invertible over both $\mathbb{F}$ and $\mathbb{Q}$. Setting d to be the least common multiple of the denominators of all entries in $(\mathbf{T} \cdot \mathbf{A})^{-1}$ over $\mathbb{Q}$, there exists an integer matrix $\mathbf{P}$ such that $\mathbf{P} \cdot \mathbf{T} \cdot \mathbf{A} = d \cdot \mathbf{I}$, where $\mathbf{I}$ is the identity matrix. In particular, we obtain $d \cdot y_w = \langle \mathbf{P}_1, \mathbf{X} \cdot \mathbf{g} \rangle$. The extractor sets $\mathbf{x}_w := \langle \mathbf{P}_1, \mathbf{X} \rangle$ and $t_w := d$, which now satisfies $[\![\mathbf{x}_w]\!]_{\mathbf{g}} = \langle \mathbf{x}_w, \mathbf{g} \rangle = t_w \cdot y_w$. $\square$

5.2 Publicly Aggregatable PCS (proof of Theorem 5.2)

The Halo [21] protocol contains a public aggregation protocol for the Bullet-proofs PCS. Inspired by this idea, we show how the HPI protocol of Fig. 3 can be used to compile any homomorphic PCS with opening group $\mathbb{H} = \mathbb{Z}^n$ and commitment group $\mathbb{G}$ into a publicly aggregatable homomorphic PCS with the same commitment group $\mathbb{G}$. Compared with the commitment size and Eval complexity of the original PCS, the commitment size of the transformed PCS is the same, the new Eval communication has an extra $O(\log d)$ elements of $\mathbb{G}$, and the verification overhead is $O(\log d)$ operations in $\mathbb{G}$. Running the public aggregation protocol on k commitments and evaluation points together with an Eval on the aggregate commitment achieves an amortized verification complexity of $O(\log k + \lambda + \frac{V_{\mathsf{Eval}}(\lambda, d)}{k})$ where $V_{\mathsf{Eval}}(\lambda, d)$ is the Eval verifier complexity. Any additive/homomorphic scheme can first be compiled into a homomorphic PCS with opening group $\mathbb{Z}^n$, using the simple compiler described next.

Compiler 1: From Additive to Homomorphic. Given a non-hiding[6] additive PCS (Setup, Commit, Verify, Eval) the new homomorphic non-hiding PCS uses the same Setup, Verify, and Eval protocols, but commits to polynomials using the pre-computed "basis" commitments $(\mathsf{C}_i, \mathsf{open}_i) \leftarrow \mathsf{Commit}(pp, X^{i-1})$ for $i \in [1, d]$. The commitment to $f \in \mathbb{F}^{(<d)}[X]$ with coefficient vector representation $\mathbf{f} = (\hat{f}_0, ..., \hat{f}_{d-1}) \in [0, p)^d$ is the group element $\mathsf{C} := \sum_{i=0}^{d-1} \hat{f}_i \cdot \mathsf{C}_i$. The opening string open for C is the coefficient vector $\mathbf{f}$.

By definition, C is a valid commitment to the polynomial f under the original scheme with opening string open' derived from the "basis" openings open_i using add^* and the coefficients $\mathbf{f}$. The evaluation protocol runs the original Eval using open'. For some schemes (e.g., KZG and Bulletproofs) that are already homomorphic, the linear combination C would be identical to a fresh commitment to f and thus $\mathsf{open}' = \mathsf{open}$. In other words, the transformation described above would have no effect.

The transformed scheme is a homomorphic PCS because $\mathsf{C} = \phi(\mathsf{open})$ where $\phi : \mathbb{Z}^d \to \mathbb{G}$ is the homomorphism that maps $\mathbf{v} \in \mathbb{Z}^d$ to $\sum_{i=1}^{d} v_i \cdot \mathsf{C}_i$ and $\chi(\mathsf{open}) = \mathsf{open} \bmod p$ is the unique coefficient vector of $f \in \mathbb{F}^{(<d)}[X]$. The new scheme is also binding: given a collision $\mathbf{f}' \neq \mathbf{f} \bmod p$ such that $\mathsf{C} = \phi(\mathbf{f}) = \phi(\mathbf{f}')$, the algorithm add^* could be used to derive openings of C to either f or f' from the open_i values, which contradicts the binding property of Commit.

Compiler 2: Homomorphic to publicly aggregatable. Denote the input homomorphic PCS by $\mathcal{PCS} = (\mathsf{Setup}, \mathsf{Commit}, \mathsf{Verify}, \mathsf{Eval})$. The output of the compiler will be a scheme denoted $\mathcal{PCS}^* = (\mathsf{Setup}^*, \mathsf{Commit}^*, \mathsf{Verify}^*, \mathsf{Eval}^*)$ that will support public aggregation. Let $\mathbb{H} = \mathbb{Z}^n$ for some $n > d$. By definition, there are efficiently computable homomorphisms $\phi : \mathbb{Z}^n \to \mathbb{G}$ and $\chi : \mathbb{Z}^n \to \mathbb{F}^{(<d)}[X]$ such that the output $(\mathsf{C}, \mathsf{open}) \leftarrow \mathsf{Commit}(pp, f)$ for any $f \in \mathbb{F}^{(<d)}[X]$ satisfies $\mathsf{C} = \phi(\mathsf{open})$ and $f = \chi(\mathsf{open})$.

For any $\mathbf{v} \in \mathbb{Z}^n$ let $f_{\mathbf{v}} := \chi(\mathbf{v})$. Let $\hat{\mathbb{G}} := \mathbb{G} \times \mathbb{F}$. For a point $x \in \mathbb{F}$, define the homomorphism $\phi_x : \mathbb{Z}^n \to \hat{\mathbb{G}}$ as $\phi_x(\mathbf{v}) := (\phi(\mathbf{v}), f_{\mathbf{v}}(x))$. The new PCS algorithms $(\mathsf{Setup}^*, \mathsf{Commit}^*)$ are identical to $(\mathsf{Setup}, \mathsf{Commit})$. The algorithm Verify^* is the standard "relaxation" of Verify from Sect. 2.1: it accepts tuples $(f, (t, \mathsf{open}))$ such that $\phi(\mathsf{open}) = t \cdot \mathsf{C}$ and $\chi(\mathsf{open}) = t \cdot f$ where $t \neq 0$ is an integer. The protocol Eval^* is transformed as follows:

$\mathsf{Eval}^* \big(\mathcal{P}(f, \mathsf{open}), \mathcal{V}(\mathsf{C}, x, y) \big):$

---

[6] Since the PCS is non-hiding we may assume, without loss of generality, that the commitment algorithm Commit is a deterministic function.

1. The prover/verifier run a modification of the HPI protocol from Fig. 3 with $\mathcal{P}_{\mathsf{HPI}}(n, \mathsf{open}, (\mathsf{C}, y))$ and $\mathcal{V}_{\mathsf{HPI}}(n, (\mathsf{C}, y))$ for the homomorphism $\phi_x : \mathbb{Z}^n \to \hat{\mathbb{G}}$. The verifier stores the output $(x', (\mathsf{C}', y')) \in \mathbb{Z} \times \hat{\mathbb{G}}$ and performs all verification steps *except* for deriving $g' \in \hat{\mathbb{G}}$ or checking $x' \cdot g' = (\mathsf{C}', y')$. The prover derives the coefficient vector $\mathbf{u}$ of the polynomial $u(X) = \prod_{i=1}^{\log n}(\alpha_i + X^{2^{i-1}})$ defined by the verifier challenges, which satisfies $\phi_x(\mathbf{u}) = g'$ and $\phi_x(x' \cdot \mathbf{u}) = x' \cdot g' = (\mathsf{C}', y')$.

2. Run $\mathsf{Eval}\big(\mathcal{P}(f_{x' \cdot \mathbf{u}}, x' \cdot \mathbf{u}), \mathcal{V}(\mathsf{C}', x, y')\big)$, where C' is interpreted as a polynomial commitment to $f_{x' \cdot \mathbf{u}}$ with opening $x' \cdot \mathbf{u}$.

We provide only a sketch of the knowledge soundness analysis. Recall that the extractor in the analysis of Theorem 5.3 succeeds assuming it has *any* labels $(t_v, \mathbf{x}_v, y_v)$ at the leaves of the tree such that $[\![\mathbf{x}_v]\!]_{\mathbf{g}} = t_v \cdot y_v$, i.e. $\phi_s(\mathbf{x}_v) = t_v \cdot y_v$ in this case. The knowledge extractor for Eval^* begins by running the usual extractor for $\mathcal{P}_{\mathsf{HPI}}$, but calls the extractor for Eval to obtain a ϕ_x homomorphism pre-image of (C', y'). This is passed to the extractor for $\mathcal{P}_{\mathsf{HPI}}$, which in turn outputs a witness $(t, \mathbf{v}) \in \mathbb{Z} \times \mathbb{Z}^n$ such that $((\mathbf{v}, t), (\mathsf{C}, y)) \in \mathcal{R}^*_{\mathsf{HPI}}(\phi_x, \mathbb{Z}^n, \hat{\mathbb{G}})$, i.e. $\phi_x(\mathbf{v}) = (t \cdot \mathsf{C}, t \cdot y)$ and $t \neq 0$. Thus, $\phi(\mathbf{v}) = t \cdot \mathsf{C}$ and $f_{\mathbf{v}}(x) = t \cdot y$, so Verify^* accepts $(t^{-1} f_{\mathbf{v}}, (t, \mathbf{v}))$ and $t^{-1} f_{\mathbf{v}}(x) = y$, i.e. $(t^{-1} f_{\mathbf{v}}, (t, \mathbf{v}))$ is an $\mathcal{R}_{\mathsf{Eval}}$ witness for (C, x, y).

The compiled PCS has the same commitment size since the commitment algorithm is unchanged. The overhead in the Eval^* communication is $O(\log d)$ elements of $\hat{\mathbb{G}} = \mathbb{G} \times \mathbb{F}$ and the overhead in verification is $O(\log d)$ operations in $\hat{\mathbb{G}}$ (from Step 1). The prover overhead is $O((\lambda + \log B) \cdot n)$ operations in $\hat{\mathbb{G}}$ assuming $\|\mathsf{open}\|_\infty < B$ (in Step 1) and $O(n)$ integer multiplications to derive $\mathbf{u}$ (also from Step 1). In the case that $|\mathbb{G}| = p$ the integer multiplications become field multiplication modulo p.

If the input PCS Eval protocol is zero-knowledge and the prover/verifier run the zero-knowledge variation of the HPI protocol between $\mathcal{P}_{\mathsf{init}}$ and $\mathcal{V}_{\mathsf{init}}$ then Eval^* is also zero-knowledge. If Eval is already non-interactive (or public-coin and FS compatible) then Eval^* is still public-coin and can be made non-interactive by applying the Fiat-Shamir transform. We conjecture that the transformed protocol is sound, which is true in the random oracle model for constant n [45].:

Conjecture 5.4. If Eval is FS compatible then protocol Eval^* is FS compatible.

Comparison to Halo aggregation. The Halo aggregation protocol for the Bulletproofs PCS uses the fact that the expensive part of verification is deriving $g' = \phi(\mathbf{u})$ and $u(X)$ can be evaluated in time $O(\log d)$. The aggregator proves correctness of g' (interpreted as a commitment to u) by running the Bulletproofs Eval to open it to $u(s)$ at a random point s chosen by the verifier. Multiple instances can be batched using private Eval aggregation. This works only because $\mathbf{u} \in \mathbb{Z}_p$ and $\phi : \mathbb{Z}_p^n \to \mathbb{G}$ is collision-resistant. In a more general homomorphic PCS with $\mathbf{u} \in \mathbb{Z}^n$, ϕ might only be collision-resistant over $\mathbb{Z}^n / \mathrm{ker}(\chi)$ and it may be possible to open g' to $u(X)$ even when $\phi(\mathbf{u}) \neq g'$. The key observation that allows us to generalize the aggregation protocol for any PCS is our novel analysis of the HPI protocol (Theorem 5.3) which shows that the verifier does not need to compute g'; it only needs a proof of knowledge that y' is *some* linear combination of $\mathbf{g}$.

Public aggregation scheme. Each non-interactive proof returned by NI-Eval* has the form $(\pi_{\mathsf{HPI}}, x', y', \pi_{\mathsf{eval}})$ where π_{HPI} is the transcript from the first step, $(x', y') = (x', (C', t')) \in \mathbb{Z} \times (\mathbb{G} \times \mathbb{F})$ is the verifier's intermediate output in the first step, and π_{Eval} is the non-interactive Eval proof from the second step for the commitment C' to the polynomial $f_{x' \cdot \mathbf{u}}$. The vector $x' \cdot \mathbf{u}$ can be computed from the transcript π_{HPI}.

The public aggregation scheme Aggregate takes public inputs $\mathbf{C} = (C_1, ..., C_k) \in \mathbb{G}^k$, $\mathbf{s} \in \mathbb{F}^k$, $\mathbf{t} \in \mathbb{F}^k$, and a vector of NI-Eval* proofs $\boldsymbol{\pi} = (\pi_1, ..., \pi_k)$ where $\pi_i = (\pi_{\mathsf{HPI}}^{(i)}, x'_i, y'_i, \pi_{\mathsf{eval}}^{(i)})$:

$$\mathsf{Aggregate}(\mathcal{P}, \mathcal{V}(pp, \boldsymbol{\pi}, \mathbf{C}, \mathbf{s}, \mathbf{t})) \rightarrow ((\mathsf{open}^*, f^*), (C^*, s^*, t^*, b))$$

The verifier does *not* check $\pi_{\mathsf{Eval}}^{(i)}$ for each $i \in [k]$, and therefore is not yet convinced that $\phi_{s_i}(x'_i \cdot \mathbf{u}_i) = y'_i$. Instead, the aggregation prover/verifier run the private aggregation protocol from Sect. 4.3 where the prover has private inputs $\{f_{x' \cdot \mathbf{u}_i}\}_{i=1}^k$ and opening strings $\{x' \cdot \mathbf{u}_i\}_{i=1}^k$ for each commitment C'_i such that $f_{x' \cdot \mathbf{u}_i}(s_i) = t'_i$. The output of this private aggregation protocol determine the prover's outputs (open^*, f^*) and the verifier's outputs (C^*, s^*, t^*, b).

By the soundness definition of the private aggregation scheme, if the prover can succeed in the Eval protocol on public inputs (C^*, s^*, t^*) with non-negligible probability then there exists a polynomial time knowledge extractor that obtains an $\mathcal{R}_{\mathsf{Eval}}$ witness for each (C'_i, s_i, t'_i), which includes a ϕ_{s_i} pre-image of $y'_i = (C'_i, t'_i)$. These witnesses are then used to extract $\mathcal{R}_{\mathsf{Eval}}$ witnesses for each (C_i, s_i, t_i) as described above in the knowledge-soundness analysis for Eval*.

The public aggregation scheme verification and communication inherits the same complexity as the private aggregation protocol. From Theorem 4.2, the generic scheme from Sect. 4.3 has verifier complexity $O(k \log k)$ operations in $\mathbb{F}$ plus $O(k \cdot \lambda)$ operations in $\mathbb{G}$ and communication of one $\mathbb{G}$ element plus two $\mathbb{F}$ elements. The prover complexity of the private aggregation subprotocol is $O(k \log k)$ operations in $\mathbb{F}$ plus one Commit to a polynomial of degree at most d. In addition, the prover must derive each integer vector $\mathbf{u}_i$, which requires $O(k \cdot n)$ integer multiplications. In the case that $|\mathbb{G}| = p$ the integer multiplications become field multiplication modulo p.

6   SNARKs and IVC from PCS Aggregation

Bünz et al. [26] formally show how a concept they define called PCS accumulation schemes can be used to construct a PCD system, generalizing the Halo protocol [21]. We show that a PCS public aggregation scheme satisfies the definition of a PCS accumulation scheme [26]. Our full version contains a detailed and self-contained exposition of IVC/PCD for path distributed computation directly from PCS aggregation.

A PCS accumulation scheme enables PCD from plain-model "predicate-efficient" SNARKs, defined as a SNARK with a polylogarithmic verifier that is given an oracle for checking PCS Eval proofs. The PCD transformation does not work if the SNARK involves calls to a random oracle, as it would require concretely instantiating the random oracle. Unfortunately, we only know how to construct "predicate-efficient" SNARKs in the random oracle model (e.g., [31,42]). Hence, this result gives a *heuristic* construction of PCD from PCS accumulation.

PCS accumulation scheme. We show that a public aggregation scheme for a PCS (Definition 5.1) satisfies the definition of an accumulation scheme for a non-interactive PCS from [26]. We first review the definition of an accumulation scheme. The definition has small syntactic differences from [26] due to syntactic differences in our PCS definition.

Definition 6.1 (PCS accumulation). *Let* $\mathcal{PCS}$ = (Setup, Commit, Verify, Eval) *denote a PCS with a non-interactive* Eval *protocol given by a prover algorithm* $\mathcal{P}_{\mathsf{Eval}}$ *and verifier algorithm* $\mathcal{V}_{\mathsf{Eval}}$. *An accumulation scheme for* $\mathcal{PCS}$ *has algorithms* (G, I, P, V, D) *with the syntax:*

$$G(\lambda) \to pp_{ac}$$
$$I(pp_{ac}, pp_{pc}) \to (apk, avk, dk) \qquad P(apk, [\{X_i\}_{i=1}^k, \{acc_i\}_{i=1}^\ell) \to (acc, \pi_V)$$
$$D(dk, acc) \to b_D \qquad\qquad V(avk, \{X_i\}_{i=1}^k, \{acc_i\}_{i=1}^\ell, acc, \pi_V) \to b_V$$

The scheme is complete if for any pp_{pc} *and* $(apk, avk, dk) \leftarrow I(pp_{ac}, pp_{pc})$ *and inputs* $(\{X_i\}_{i=1}^k, [acc_i]_{i=1}^\ell)$ *that satisfy* $\mathcal{V}_{\mathsf{Eval}}(pp_{pc}, X_i) = 1$ *for* $i \in [k]$ *and* $D(dk, acc_i) = 1$ *for all* $i \in [\ell]$, *the accumulation scheme prover* $P(apk, \{X_i\}_{i=1}^k, \{acc_i\}_{i=1}^\ell)$ *outputs* (acc, π_V) *such that* $D(dk, acc) = 1$ *and* $V(avk, \{X_i\}_{i=1}^k, \{acc_i\}_{i=1}^\ell, acc, \pi_V) = 1$. *For soundness, the following probability is negligible in* λ:

$$\Pr\left[\begin{array}{l} V(avk, \{X_i\}_{i=1}^k, \{acc_i\}_{i=1}^\ell, acc, \pi_V) = 1 \\ D(dk, acc) = 1 \\ \exists_{i \in [k]} \mathcal{V}_{\mathsf{Eval}}(pp_{pc}, X_i) \neq 1 \vee \exists_{i \in [\ell]} D(dk, acc_i) \neq 1 \end{array} \middle| \begin{array}{l} pp_{pc} \leftarrow \mathsf{Setup}(\lambda, d), pp_{ac} \leftarrow G(\lambda) \\ (apk, avk, dk) \leftarrow I(pp_{ac}, pp_{pc}) \\ \{X_i\}_{i=1}^k, \{acc_i\}_{i=1}^\ell, acc, \pi_V \leftarrow \mathcal{A}(pp_{ac}, pp_{pc}) \end{array}\right]$$

The fact that a non-interactive public aggregation scheme gives an accumulation scheme is an immediate consequence of the definitions. The algorithms G and I are trivial, setting all parameters to pp_{pc}. Each $acc = (\mathsf{C}, x, y, \pi)$ is an Eval tuple. The prover $P(pp_{pc}, \{X_i\}_{i=1}^k, \{acc_i\}_{i=1}^\ell)$ first sets $\mathsf{C} \in \mathbb{G}^{k+\ell}$ so that $\mathsf{C}_i = X_i$ for $i \in [k]$ and $\mathsf{C}_i = acc_{i-k}$ for $i > k$, sets π so that the ith and $(i+k)$th components are the Eval proofs in X_i and acc_i respectively, and sets $(\mathbf{s}, \mathbf{t}) \in \mathbb{F}^{k+\ell} \times \mathbb{F}^{k+\ell}$ so that $(s_i, t_i) = (x_i, y_i)$ from X_i for $i \in [k]$ and from acc_i for $i > k$. It runs $\mathsf{Aggregate}(pp_{pc}, \pi, \mathsf{C}, \mathbf{s}, \mathbf{t})$ to get $(\mathsf{open}^*, f^*, \mathsf{C}^*, s^*, t^*, \pi_{\mathsf{agg}})$ and $\mathsf{Eval}(\mathsf{open}^*, f^*, \mathsf{C}^*, s^*, t^*)$ to get π^*. It returns $\pi_V := \pi_{\mathsf{agg}}$ and $acc := (\mathsf{C}^*, s^*, t^*, \pi^*)$. $D(pp_{pc}, acc)$ calls the Eval verifier. Finally, $V(pp_{pc}, \{X_i\}_{i=1}^k, \{acc_i\}_{i=1}^\ell, acc, \pi_{\mathsf{agg}})$ derives the tuples

$(\boldsymbol{\pi}, \mathbf{C}, \mathbf{s}, \mathbf{t})$, parses $acc = (\mathbf{C}^*, s^*, t^*, \pi^*)$, and runs the aggregation verifier $\mathcal{V}_{\mathsf{Aggregate}}(pp_{\mathsf{pc}}, \boldsymbol{\pi}, \mathbf{C}, \mathbf{s}, \mathbf{t}, \mathbf{C}^*, s^*, t^*, \pi_{\mathsf{agg}})$.

Private accumulation. A small tweak to Definition 6.1 would make it compatible with private aggregation. The accumulation prover is additionally given as inputs a vector of private states $\{st_i\}_{i=1}^{k+\ell}$ and outputs (st, acc, π_V). The other algorithms and the security definition are unchanged. Constructing this from a private aggregation scheme, the state st will contain the prover's private outputs (open^*, f^*) and each st_i contains an (open_i, f_i) pair.

The PCD compiler of [26] can be adapted to work with private aggregation schemes as well. This only affects the proof size which has size $O(N)$ because it includes the "private" states (openings for polynomials of degree N). Intuitively, the construction of PCD from [26] is not materially affected by using *private* accumulation because each prover node in the DAG distributed computation simply passes its private state to its target nodes as "advice". The advice does not impact the size of the recursive statement, which is only dependent on the size of the accumulation verifier. This variation of the compiler was formally proven in follow-up work [25]. To do so they formally define a "split-accumulation" scheme, which coincides with our informal tweak.

Acknowledgments. This work was funded by NSF, DARPA, a grant from ONR, and the Simons Foundation. Opinions, findings and conclusions or recommendations expressed in this material are those of the authors and do not necessarily reflect the views of DARPA.

References

1. Ajtai, M.: Generating hard instances of lattice problems (extended abstract). In: STOC, pp. 99–108 (1996)
2. Attema, T., Cramer, R.: Compressed Σ-protocol theory and practical application to plug & play secure algorithmics. In: Micciancio, D., Ristenpart, T. (eds.) CRYPTO 2020, Part III. LNCS, vol. 12172, pp. 513–543. Springer, Cham (2020). https://doi.org/10.1007/978-3-030-56877-1_18
3. Babai, L.: Local expansion of vertex-transitive graphs and random generation in finite groups. In: 23rd ACM STOC, pp. 164–174 (May 1991)
4. Baum, C., Bootle, J., Cerulli, A., del Pino, R., Groth, J., Lyubashevsky, V.: Sublinear lattice-based zero-knowledge arguments for arithmetic circuits. In: Shacham, H., Boldyreva, A. (eds.) CRYPTO 2018, Part II. LNCS, vol. 10992, pp. 669–699. Springer, Cham (2018). https://doi.org/10.1007/978-3-319-96881-0_23
5. Baum, C., Damgård, I., Larsen, K.G., Nielsen, M.: How to prove knowledge of small secrets. In: Robshaw, M., Katz, J. (eds.) CRYPTO 2016, Part III. LNCS, vol. 9816, pp. 478–498. Springer, Heidelberg (2016). https://doi.org/10.1007/978-3-662-53015-3_17
6. Bellare, M., Goldreich, O.: On defining proofs of knowledge. In: Brickell, E.F. (ed.) CRYPTO 1992. LNCS, vol. 740, pp. 390–420. Springer, Heidelberg (1993). https://doi.org/10.1007/3-540-48071-4_28
7. Ben-Sasson, E., Bentov, I., Horesh, Y., Riabzev, M.: Fast reed-solomon interactive oracle proofs of proximity. In: ICALP 2018, pp. 14:1–14:17 (July 2018)

8. Ben-Sasson, E., Bentov, I., Horesh, Y., Riabzev, M.: Scalable zero knowledge with no trusted setup. In: Boldyreva, A., Micciancio, D. (eds.) CRYPTO 2019, Part III. LNCS, vol. 11694, pp. 701–732. Springer, Cham (2019). https://doi.org/10.1007/978-3-030-26954-8_23

9. Ben-Sasson, E., Chiesa, A., Genkin, D., Tromer, E.: Fast reductions from RAMs to delegatable succinct constraint satisfaction problems: extended abstract. ITCS **2013**, 401–414 (2013)

10. Ben-Sasson, E., Chiesa, A., Riabzev, M., Spooner, N., Virza, M., Ward, N.P.: Aurora: transparent succinct arguments for R1CS. In: Ishai, Y., Rijmen, V. (eds.) EUROCRYPT 2019, Part I. LNCS, vol. 11476, pp. 103–128. Springer, Cham (2019). https://doi.org/10.1007/978-3-030-17653-2_4

11. Ben-Sasson, E., Chiesa, A., Spooner, N.: Interactive oracle proofs. In: Hirt, M., Smith, A. (eds.) TCC 2016, Part II. LNCS, vol. 9986, pp. 31–60. Springer, Heidelberg (2016). https://doi.org/10.1007/978-3-662-53644-5_2

12. Ben-Sasson, E., Chiesa, A., Tromer, E., Virza, M.: Scalable zero knowledge via cycles of elliptic curves. In: Garay, J.A., Gennaro, R. (eds.) CRYPTO 2014, Part II. LNCS, vol. 8617, pp. 276–294. Springer, Heidelberg (2014). https://doi.org/10.1007/978-3-662-44381-1_16

13. Ben-Sasson, E., Goldberg, L., Kopparty, S., Saraf, S.: DEEP-FRI: Sampling outside the box improves soundness. Cryptology ePrint Archive, Report 2019/336 (2019)

14. Bitansky, N., Canetti, R., Chiesa, A., Tromer, E.: From extractable collision resistance to succinct non-interactive arguments of knowledge, and back again. ITCS **2012**, 326–349 (2012)

15. Bitansky, N., Canetti, R., Chiesa, A., Tromer, E.: Recursive composition and bootstrapping for SNARKS and proof-carrying data. In: 45th ACM STOC, pp. 111–120 (June 2013)

16. Bitansky, N., Chiesa, A., Ishai, Y., Ostrovsky, R., Paneth, O.: Succinct non-interactive arguments via linear interactive proofs. TCC **2013**, 315–333 (2013)

17. Blum, M., Evans, W.S., Gemmell, P., Kannan, S., Naor, M.: Checking the correctness of memories. In: 32nd FOCS, pp. 90–99 (October 1991)

18. Bonneau, J., Meckler, I., Rao, V., Shapiro, E.: Coda: Decentralized cryptocurrency at scale. Cryptology ePrint Archive, Report 2020/352 (2020)

19. Bootle, J., Cerulli, A., Chaidos, P., Groth, J., Petit, C.: Efficient zero-knowledge arguments for arithmetic circuits in the discrete log setting. In: Fischlin, M., Coron, J.-S. (eds.) EUROCRYPT 2016, Part II. LNCS, vol. 9666, pp. 327–357. Springer, Heidelberg (2016). https://doi.org/10.1007/978-3-662-49896-5_12

20. Bowe, S., Gabizon, A., Miers, I.: Scalable multi-party computation for zk-SNARK parameters in the random beacon model. Cryptology ePrint Archive, Report 2017/1050 (2017)

21. Bowe, S., Grigg, J., Hopwood, D.: Halo: Recursive proof composition without a trusted setup. Cryptology ePrint Archive, Report 2019/1021 (2019)

22. Bünz, B., Bootle, J., Boneh, D., Poelstra, A., Wuille, P., Maxwell, G.: Bulletproofs: short proofs for confidential transactions and more. In: 2018 IEEE Symposium on Security and Privacy, pp. 315–334 (May 2018)

23. Bünz, B., Fisch, B., Szepieniec, A.: Transparent SNARKs from DARK compilers. In: Canteaut, A., Ishai, Y. (eds.) EUROCRYPT 2020, Part I. LNCS, vol. 12105, pp. 677–706. Springer, Cham (2020). https://doi.org/10.1007/978-3-030-45721-1_24

24. Bünz, B., Maller, M., Vesely, N.: Efficient proofs for pairing-based languages. Cryptology ePrint Archive, Report 2019/1177 (2019)

25. Bünz, B., Chiesa, A., Lin, W., Mishra, P., Spooner, N.: Proof-carrying data without succinct arguments. Cryptology ePrint Archive, Report 2020/1618 (2020)

26. Bünz, B., Chiesa, A., Mishra, P., Spooner, N.: Proof-carrying data from accumulation schemes. Cryptology ePrint Archive, Report 2020/499 (2020)
27. Canetti, R., et al.: Fiat-Shamir: from practice to theory. In: 51st ACM STOC, pp. 1082–1090 (June 2019)
28. Canetti, R., Chen, Y., Reyzin, L., Rothblum, R.D.: Fiat-Shamir and correlation intractability from strong KDM-secure encryption. In: Nielsen, J.B., Rijmen, V. (eds.) EUROCRYPT 2018, Part I. LNCS, vol. 10820, pp. 91–122. Springer, Cham (2018). https://doi.org/10.1007/978-3-319-78381-9_4
29. Chen, Y., Lombardi, A., Ma, F., Quach, W.: Does fiat-shamir require a cryptographic hash function? Cryptology ePrint Archive, Report 2020/915 (2020)
30. Chiesa, A., Forbes, M.A., Spooner, N.: A zero knowledge sumcheck and its applications. Cryptology ePrint Archive, Report 2017/305 (2017)
31. Chiesa, A., Hu, Y., Maller, M., Mishra, P., Vesely, N., Ward, N.: Marlin: Preprocessing zkSNARKs with universal and updatable SRS. Cryptology ePrint Archive, Report 2019/1047 (2019)
32. Chiesa, A., Hu, Y., Maller, M., Mishra, P., Vesely, N., Ward, N.: Marlin: preprocessing zkSNARKs with universal and updatable SRS. In: Canteaut, A., Ishai, Y. (eds.) EUROCRYPT 2020, Part I. LNCS, vol. 12105, pp. 738–768. Springer, Cham (2020). https://doi.org/10.1007/978-3-030-45721-1_26
33. Chiesa, A., Liu, S.: On the impossibility of probabilistic proofs in relativized worlds. In: ITCS 2020, pp. 57:1–57:30 (January 2020)
34. Chiesa, A., Ojha, D., Spooner, N.: FRACTAL: post-quantum and transparent recursive proofs from holography. In: Canteaut, A., Ishai, Y. (eds.) EUROCRYPT 2020, Part I. LNCS, vol. 12105, pp. 769–793. Springer, Cham (2020). https://doi.org/10.1007/978-3-030-45721-1_27
35. Chiesa, A., Tromer, E.: Proof-carrying data and hearsay arguments from signature cards. In: Proceedings of Innovations in Computer Science - ICS 2010, Tsinghua University, Beijing, China, 5–7 January 2010, pp. 310–331 (2010). http://conference.iiis.tsinghua.edu.cn/ICS2010/content/papers/25.html
36. Cooperman, G.: Towards a practical, theoretically sound algorithm for random generation in finite groups (2002)
37. Dixon, J.: Generating random elements in finite groups. Electron. J. Comb. [electronic only] 15 (07 2008). https://doi.org/10.37236/818
38. Drake, J.: https://ethresear.ch/t/slonk-a-simple-universal-snark/6420
39. Fiat, A., Shamir, A.: How to prove yourself: practical solutions to identification and signature problems. In: Odlyzko, A.M. (ed.) CRYPTO 1986. LNCS, vol. 263, pp. 186–194. Springer, Heidelberg (1987). https://doi.org/10.1007/3-540-47721-7_12
40. Fuchsbauer, G., Kiltz, E., Loss, J.: The algebraic group model and its applications. In: Shacham, H., Boldyreva, A. (eds.) CRYPTO 2018, Part II. LNCS, vol. 10992, pp. 33–62. Springer, Cham (2018). https://doi.org/10.1007/978-3-319-96881-0_2
41. Gabizon, A.: AuroraLight: Improved prover efficiency and SRS size in a sonic-like system. Cryptology ePrint Archive, Report 2019/601 (2019)
42. Gabizon, A., Williamson, Z.J., Ciobotaru, O.: PLONK: Permutations over lagrange-bases for oecumenical noninteractive arguments of knowledge. Cryptology ePrint Archive, Report 2019/953 (2019)
43. Gennaro, R., Gentry, C., Parno, B., Raykova, M.: Quadratic span programs and succinct NIZKs without PCPs. In: Johansson, T., Nguyen, P.Q. (eds.) EUROCRYPT 2013. LNCS, vol. 7881, pp. 626–645. Springer, Heidelberg (2013). https://doi.org/10.1007/978-3-642-38348-9_37
44. Goldreich, O., Goldwasser, S., Halevi, S.: Collision-free hashing from lattice problems. IACR Cryptology ePrint Archive (1996). http://eprint.iacr.org/1996/009

45. Goldreich, O., Krawczyk, H.: On the composition of zero-knowledge proof systems. SIAM J. Comput. **9**, 169–192 (1996)
46. Groth, J.: Short pairing-based non-interactive zero-knowledge arguments. In: Abe, M. (ed.) ASIACRYPT 2010. LNCS, vol. 6477, pp. 321–340. Springer, Heidelberg (2010). https://doi.org/10.1007/978-3-642-17373-8_19
47. Groth, J.: On the size of pairing-based non-interactive arguments. In: Fischlin, M., Coron, J.-S. (eds.) EUROCRYPT 2016, Part II. LNCS, vol. 9666, pp. 305–326. Springer, Heidelberg (2016). https://doi.org/10.1007/978-3-662-49896-5_11
48. Groth, J.: On the size of pairing-based non-interactive arguments. Cryptology ePrint Archive, Report 2016/260 (2016)
49. Groth, J., Kohlweiss, M., Maller, M., Meiklejohn, S., Miers, I.: Updatable and universal common reference strings with applications to zk-SNARKs. In: Shacham, H., Boldyreva, A. (eds.) CRYPTO 2018, Part III. LNCS, vol. 10993, pp. 698–728. Springer, Cham (2018). https://doi.org/10.1007/978-3-319-96878-0_24
50. Groth, J., Maller, M.: Snarky signatures: minimal signatures of knowledge from simulation-extractable SNARKs. In: Katz, J., Shacham, H. (eds.) CRYPTO 2017, Part II. LNCS, vol. 10402, pp. 581–612. Springer, Cham (2017). https://doi.org/ 10.1007/978-3-319-63715-0_20
51. Håstad, J., Impagliazzo, R., Levin, L.A., Luby, M.: A pseudorandom generator from any one-way function. SIAM J. Comput. **28**(4), 1364–1396 (1999)
52. Holmgren, J.: On round-by-round soundness and state restoration attacks. Cryptology ePrint Archive, Report 2019/1261 (2019)
53. Kalai, Y.T., Rothblum, G.N., Rothblum, R.D.: From obfuscation to the security of Fiat-Shamir for proofs. In: Katz, J., Shacham, H. (eds.) CRYPTO 2017, Part II. LNCS, vol. 10402, pp. 224–251. Springer, Cham (2017). https://doi.org/10.1007/ 978-3-319-63715-0_8
54. Kate, A., Zaverucha, G.M., Goldberg, I.: Constant-size commitments to polynomials and their applications. In: Abe, M. (ed.) ASIACRYPT 2010. LNCS, vol. 6477, pp. 177–194. Springer, Heidelberg (2010). https://doi.org/10.1007/978-3-642-17373-8_11
55. Kattis, A., Panarin, K., Vlasov, A.: RedShift: Transparent SNARKs from list polynomial commitment IOPs. Cryptology ePrint Archive, Report 2019/1400 (2019)
56. Labs, O.: Coda protocol (2018)
57. Lee, J.: Dory: Efficient, transparent arguments for generalised inner products and polynomial commitments. Cryptology ePrint Archive, Report 2020/1274 (2020)
58. Lipmaa, H.: Progression-free sets and sublinear pairing-based non-interactive zero-knowledge arguments. In: Cramer, R. (ed.) TCC 2012. LNCS, vol. 7194, pp. 169–189. Springer, Heidelberg (2012). https://doi.org/10.1007/978-3-642-28914-9_10
59. Maller, M., Bowe, S., Kohlweiss, M., Meiklejohn, S.: Sonic: Zero-knowledge SNARKs from linear-size universal and updatable structured reference strings. ACM CCS **2019**, 2111–2128 (2019)
60. Parno, B., Howell, J., Gentry, C., Raykova, M.: Pinocchio: nearly practical verifiable computation. In: 2013 IEEE Symposium on Security and Privacy, pp. 238–252 (May 2013)
61. Pippenger, N.: On the evaluation of powers and monomials. SIAM J. Comput. **9**, 230–250 (1980)
62. Pointcheval, D., Stern, J.: Security proofs for signature schemes. In: Maurer, U. (ed.) EUROCRYPT 1996. LNCS, vol. 1070, pp. 387–398. Springer, Heidelberg (1996). https://doi.org/10.1007/3-540-68339-9_33

63. Setty, S.: Spartan: efficient and general-purpose zkSNARKs without trusted setup. In: Micciancio, D., Ristenpart, T. (eds.) CRYPTO 2020, Part III. LNCS, vol. 12172, pp. 704–737. Springer, Cham (2020). https://doi.org/10.1007/978-3-030-56877-1_25

64. Valiant, P.: Incrementally verifiable computation or proofs of knowledge imply time/space efficiency. In: Canetti, R. (ed.) TCC 2008. LNCS, vol. 4948, pp. 1–18. Springer, Heidelberg (2008). https://doi.org/10.1007/978-3-540-78524-8_1

65. Vlasov, A., Panarin, K.: Transparent polynomial commitment scheme with polylogarithmic communication complexity. Cryptology ePrint Archive, Report 2019/1020 (2019)

Proof-Carrying Data Without Succinct Arguments

Benedikt Bünz[1](✉), Alessandro Chiesa[2], William Lin[2], Pratyush Mishra[2], and Nicholas Spooner[3]

[1] Stanford University, Stanford, USA
benedikt@cs.stanford.edu
[2] UC Berkeley, Berkeley, USA
{alexch,will.lin,pratyush}@berkeley.edu
[3] Boston University, Boston, USA
nspooner@bu.edu

Abstract. Proof-carrying data (PCD) is a powerful cryptographic primitive that enables mutually distrustful parties to perform distributed computations that run indefinitely. Known approaches to construct PCD are based on succinct non-interactive arguments of knowledge (SNARKs) that have a succinct verifier or a succinct accumulation scheme.

In this paper we show how to obtain PCD without relying on SNARKs. We construct a PCD scheme given any non-interactive argument of knowledge (e.g., with linear-size arguments) that has a *split accumulation scheme*, which is a weak form of accumulation that we introduce.

Moreover, we construct a transparent non-interactive argument of knowledge for R1CS whose split accumulation is verifiable via a (small) *constant number of group and field operations*. Our construction is proved secure in the random oracle model based on the hardness of discrete logarithms, and it leads, via the random oracle heuristic and our result above, to concrete efficiency improvements for PCD.

Along the way, we construct a split accumulation scheme for Hadamard products under Pedersen commitments and for a simple polynomial commitment scheme based on Pedersen commitments.

Our results are supported by a modular and efficient implementation.

Keywords: Proof-carrying data · Accumulation schemes · Recursive proof composition

1 Introduction

Proof-carrying data (PCD) [CT10] is a powerful cryptographic primitive that enables mutually distrustful parties to perform distributed computations that run indefinitely, while ensuring that the correctness of every intermediate

---

The full version of this paper is available online [BCL+20].

© International Association for Cryptologic Research 2021
T. Malkin and C. Peikert (Eds.): CRYPTO 2021, LNCS 12825, pp. 681–710, 2021.
https://doi.org/10.1007/978-3-030-84242-0_24

state of the computation can be verified efficiently. A special case of PCD is *incrementally-verifiable computation* (IVC) [Val08]. PCD has found applications in enforcing language semantics [CTV13], verifiable MapReduce computations [CTV15], image authentication [NT16], blockchains [Mina; KB20; BMRS20; CCDW20], and others. Given the theoretical and practical relevance of PCD, it is an important research question to build efficient PCD schemes from minimal cryptographic assumptions.

PCD from Succinct Verification. The canonical construction of PCD is via *recursive composition* of succinct non-interactive arguments (SNARGs) [BCCT13; BCTV14; COS20]. Informally, a proof that the computation was executed correctly for t steps consists of a proof of the claim "the t-th step of the computation was executed correctly, and there exists a proof that the computation was executed correctly for $t-1$ steps". The latter part of the claim is expressed using the SNARG verifier itself. This construction yields secure PCD (with IVC as a special case) provided the SNARG satisfies an adaptive knowledge soundness property (i.e., is a SNARK). Efficiency requires the SNARK to have sublinear-time verification, achievable via SNARKs for machine computations [BCCT13] or preprocessing SNARKs for circuit computations [BCTV14; COS20].

Requiring sublinear-time verification, however, significantly restricts the choice of SNARK, which limits what is achievable for PCD. These restrictions have practical implications: the concrete efficiency of recursion is limited by the use of expensive curves for pairing-based SNARKs [BCTV14] or heavy use of cryptographic hash functions for hash-based SNARKs [COS20].

PCD from Accumulation. Recently, [BCMS20] gave an alternative construction of PCD using SNARKs that have succinct *accumulation schemes*; this developed and formalized a novel approach for recursion sketched in [BGH19]. Informally, rather than being required to have sublinear-time verification, the SNARK is required to be accompanied by a cryptographic primitive that enables "postponing" the verification of SNARK proofs by way of an accumulator that is updated at each recursion step. The main efficiency requirement on the accumulation scheme is that the accumulation procedure must be succinctly verifiable, and in particular the accumulator itself must be succinct.

Requiring a SNARK to have a succinct accumulation scheme is a weaker condition than requiring it to have sublinear-time verification. This has enabled constructing PCD from SNARKs that do *not* have sublinear-time verification [BCMS20], which in turn led to PCD constructions from assumptions and with efficiency properties that were not previously achieved. Practitioners have exploited this freedom to design implementations of recursive composition with improved practical efficiency [Halo20; Pickles20].

Our Motivation. The motivation of this paper is twofold. First, can PCD be built from a weaker primitive than SNARKs with succinct accumulation schemes? If so, can we leverage this to obtain PCD constructions with improved *concrete* efficiency?

1.1 Contributions

We make theory and systems contributions that advance the state of the art for PCD: (1) We introduce *split accumulation schemes for relations*, a cryptographic primitive that relaxes prior notions of accumulation. (2) We obtain PCD from any non-interactive argument of knowledge that satisfies this weaker notion of accumulation; surprisingly, this allows for arguments with no succinctness whatsoever. (3) We construct a non-interactive argument of knowledge based on discrete logarithms (and random oracles) whose accumulation verifier has constant size (improving over the logarithmic-size verifier of prior accumulation schemes in this setting). (4) We implement and evaluate constructions from this paper and from [BCMS20].

We elaborate on each of these contributions next.

(1) Split accumulation for relations. Recall from [BCMS20] that an accumulation scheme for a predicate $\Phi \colon X \to \{0,1\}$ enables proving/verifying that each input in an infinite stream $q_1, q_2, \ldots$ satisfies the predicate Φ, by augmenting the stream with *accumulators*. Informally, for each i, the prover produces a new accumulator acc_{i+1} from the input q_i and the old accumulator acc_i; the verifier can check that the triple $(q_i, \mathsf{acc}_i, \mathsf{acc}_{i+1})$ is a valid accumulation step, much more efficiently than running Φ on q_i. At any time, the decider can validate acc_{i+1}, which establishes that for all $j \leq i$ it was the case that $\Phi(q_j) = 1$. The accumulator size (and hence the running time of the three algorithms) cannot grow in the number of accumulation steps.

We extend this notion in two orthogonal ways. First we consider relations $\Phi \colon X \times W \to \{0,1\}$ and now for a stream of instances $\mathsf{qx}_1, \mathsf{qx}_2, \ldots$ the goal is to establish that there exist witnesses $\mathsf{qw}_1, \mathsf{qw}_2, \ldots$ such that $\Phi(\mathsf{qx}_i, \mathsf{qw}_i) = 1$ for each i. Second, we consider accumulators acc_i that are split into an instance part $\mathsf{acc}_i.\mathsf{x}$ and a witness part $\mathsf{acc}_i.\mathsf{w}$ with the restriction that the accumulation verifier only gets to see the instance part (and possibly an auxiliary accumulation proof pf). We refer to this notion as *split accumulation for relations*, and refer to (for contrast) the notion from [BCMS20] as *atomic accumulation for languages*.

The purpose of these extensions is to enable us to consider accumulation schemes in which predicate witnesses and accumulator witnesses are large while still requiring the accumulation verifier to be succinct (it receives short predicate instances and accumulator instances but not large witnesses). We will see that such accumulation schemes are both simpler and cheaper, while still being useful for primitives such as PCD.

See Sect. 2.1 for more on atomic vs. split accumulation, and the full version for formal definitions.

(2) PCD via split accumulation. A non-interactive argument has a split accumulation scheme if the relation corresponding to its verifier has a split accumulation scheme (we make this precise later). We show that any non-interactive argument of knowledge (NARK) having a split accumulation scheme where the *accumulation verifier* is sublinear can be used to build a proof-carrying data (PCD) scheme, *even if the NARK does not have sublinear argument size*. This significantly broadens the class of non-interactive arguments from which PCD can be built, and is the first result to obtain PCD from non-interactive arguments that need not be succinct. Similarly to [BCMS20], if the NARK and accumulation scheme are post-quantum secure, so is the PCD scheme. (It remains an open question whether there are non-trivial post-quantum instantiations of these.)

Theorem 1 (informal). *There is an efficient transformation that compiles any NARK with a split accumulation scheme into a PCD scheme. If the NARK and its split accumulation scheme are zero knowledge, then the PCD scheme is also zero knowledge. Additionally, if the NARK and its accumulation scheme are post-quantum secure then the PCD scheme is also post-quantum secure.*

Similarly to all PCD results known to date, the above theorem holds in a model where all parties have access to a common reference string, *but no oracles.* (The construction makes non-black-box use of the accumulation scheme verifier, and the theorem does not carry over to the random oracle model.)

A corollary of Theorem 1 is that any NARK with a split accumulation scheme can be "bootstrapped" into a SNARK for machine computations. (PCD implies IVC and, further assuming collision-resistant hashing, also efficient SNARKs for machine computations [BCCT13].) This is surprising: an argument with decidedly weak efficiency properties implies an argument with succinct proofs and succinct verification!

See Sect. 2.2 for a summary of the ideas behind Theorem 1, and the full version for technical details.

(3) NARK with split accumulation based on DL. Theorem 1 motivates the question of whether we can leverage the weaker condition on the argument system to improve the efficiency of PCD. Our focus is on minimizing the cost of the accumulation verifier for the argument system, because it is the only component that is not used as a black box, and thus typically determines concrete efficiency. Towards this end, we present a (zero knowledge) NARK with (zero knowledge) split accumulation based on discrete logarithms, with a *constant-size* accumulation verifier; the NARK has a transparent (public-coin) setup.

Theorem 2 (informal). *In the random oracle model and assuming the hardness of the discrete logarithm problem, there exists a transparent (zero knowledge) NARK for R1CS and a corresponding (zero knowledge) split accumulation scheme with the following efficiency:*

NARK			Split accumulation scheme			
Prover time	Verifier time	Argument size	Prover time	Verifier time	Decider time	Accumulator size
$O(M)\,\mathbb{G}$	$O(M)\,\mathbb{G}$	$O(1)\,\mathbb{G}$	$O(M)\,\mathbb{G}$	$O(1)\,\mathbb{G}$	$O(M)\,\mathbb{G}$	$|\text{acc.x}| = O(1)\,\mathbb{G} + O(1)\,\mathbb{F}$
$O(M)\,\mathbb{F}$	$O(M)\,\mathbb{F}$	$O(M)\,\mathbb{F}$	$O(M)\,\mathbb{F}$	$O(1)\,\mathbb{F}$	$O(M)\,\mathbb{F}$	$|\text{acc.w}| = O(M)\,\mathbb{F}$

Above, M *denotes the number of constraints in the R1CS instance,* $\mathbb{G}$ *denotes group scalar multiplications or group elements, and* $\mathbb{F}$ *denotes field operations or field elements.*

The NARK construction from Theorem 2 is particularly simple: it is obtained by applying the Fiat–Shamir transformation to a sigma protocol for R1CS based on Pedersen commitments (and linear argument size). The only "special" feature about the construction is that, as we prove, it has a very efficient split accumulation scheme for the relation corresponding to its verifier. By heuristically instantiating the random oracle, we can apply Theorem 1 (and [BCCT13]) to obtain a SNARK for machines from this modest starting point.

We find it informative to compare Theorem 2 and SNARKs with atomic accumulation based on discrete logarithms [BCMS20]:

- the SNARK's argument size is $O(\log M)$ group elements, *much less* than the NARK's $O(M)$ field elements;
- the SNARK's accumulator verifier uses $O(\log M)$ group scalar multiplications and field operations, *much more* than the NARK's $O(1)$ group scalar multiplications and field operations.

Therefore Theorem 2 offers a tradeoff that minimizes the cost of the accumulator at the expense of argument size. (As we shall see later, this tradeoff has concrete efficiency advantages.)

Our focus on argument systems based on discrete logarithms is motivated by the fact that they can be instantiated based on efficient curves suitable for recursion: the Tweedle [BGH19] or Pasta [Hop20] curve cycles, which follow the curve cycle technique for efficient recursion [BCTV14]. (In fact, as our construction does not rely on any number-theoretic properties of $|\mathbb{G}|$, we could even use the (secp256k1, secq256k1) cycle, where secp256k1 is the curve used in Bitcoin.) This focus on discrete logarithms is a choice made for this paper, and we believe that our ideas can lead to efficiency improvements to recursion in other settings (e.g., pairing-based and hash-based arguments) and leave these to future work.

See Sect. 2.3 for a summary of the ideas behind Theorem 1, and the full version for technical details.

(4) Split accumulation for common predicates. We obtain split accumulation schemes with constant-size accumulation verifiers for common predicates: (i) *Hadamard products (and more generally any bilinear function) under Pedersen commitments* (see Sect. 2.5 for a summary and the full version for details); (ii) *polynomial evaluations under Pedersen commitments* (see Sect. 2.6 for a summary and the full version for technical details). Split accumulation for Hadamard products is a building block that we use to prove Theorem 1.

(5) Implementation and evaluation. We contribute a set of Rust libraries[1] that realize PCD via accumulation via modular combinations of interchangeable components: (a) generic interfaces for atomic and split accumulation; (b) generic construction of PCD from arguments with atomic and split accumulation; (c) split accumulation for our zkNARK for R1CS; (d) split accumulation for Hadamard products under Pedersen commitments; (e) split accumulation

---

[1] https://github.com/arkworks-rs/accumulation.

for polynomial evaluations under Pedersen commitments; (f) atomic accumulation for polynomial commitments based on inner product arguments and pairings from [BCMS20]; (g) constraints for all the foregoing accumulation verifiers. Practitioners interested in PCD will find these libraries useful for prototyping and comparing different types of recursion (and, e.g., may help decide if current systems based on atomic recursion [Halo20; Pickles20] are better off via split recursion or not).

We additionally conduct experiments to evaluate our implementation. Our experiments focus on determining the *recursion threshold*, which informally is the number of constraints that need to be proved at each step of the recursion. Our evaluation demonstrates that, over curves from the popular "Pasta" cycle [Hop20], the recursion threshold for split accumulation of our NARK for R1CS is as low as 52,000 constraints, which is at least 8.5× cheaper than the cost of IVC constructed from atomic accumulation for discrete-logarithm-based protocols [BCMS20]. In fact, the recursion threshold is even lower than that for IVC constructed from prior state-of-the-art pairing-friendly SNARKs [Gro16]. While this comes at the expense of much larger proof sizes, this overhead is attractive for notable applications (e.g., incrementally-verifiable ledgers).

See the full version for more details on our implementation and evaluation, respectively.

Remark 1 (concurrent work). A concurrent work [BDFG20] studies similar questions as this paper. Below we summarize the similarities and the differences between the two papers.

Similarities. Both papers are study by the goal of reducing the cost of recursive arguments. The main object of study in [BDFG20] is additive polynomial commitment schemes (PC schemes), for which [BDFG20] considers different types of *aggregation schemes*: (1) *public* aggregation in [BDFG20] is closely related to atomic accumulation specialized to PC schemes from a prior work [BCMS20]; and (2) *private* aggregation in [BDFG20] is closely related to split accumulation specialized to PC schemes from this paper. Moreover, the private aggregation scheme for additive PC schemes in [BDFG20] is similar to our split accumulation scheme for Pedersen PC schemes (overviewed in Sect. 2.6 and detailed in the full version). The protocols differ in how efficiency depends on the n claims to aggregate/accumulate: the verifier in [BDFG20] uses $n + 1$ group scalar multiplications while ours uses $2n$. (Informally, [BDFG20] first randomly combines claims and then evaluates at a random point, while we first evaluate at a random point and then randomly combine claims.)

Differences. The two papers develop distinct, and complementary, directions.

The focus of [BDFG20] is to design protocols for any additive PC scheme (and, even more generally, any PC scheme with a linear combination scheme), including the aforementioned private aggregation protocol and a compiler that endows a given PC scheme with zero knowledge.

In contrast, our focus is to formulate a definition of split accumulation for general relation predicates that (a) we demonstrate suffices to construct PCD, and (b) in the random oracle model, we can also demonstrably achieve via a split accumulation scheme based on Pedersen commitments. We emphasize that our definitions are materially different from the case of atomic accumulation in [BCMS20], and necessitate careful consideration of technicalities such as the flavor of adaptive knowledge soundness, which algorithms can be allowed to query oracles, and so on. Hence, we cannot simply rely on the existing foundations for atomic accumulation of [BCMS20] in order to infer the correct definitions and security reductions for split accumulation. Overall, our theoretical work enables us to achieve the first construction of PCD without succinct arguments, and also to obtain a novel NARK for R1CS with a constant-size accumulation verifier.

We stress that the treatment of accumulation at a higher level of abstraction than for PC schemes is essential to prove theorems about PCD. In particular, contrary to what is claimed as a theorem in [BDFG20], it is *not* known how to build PCD from a PC scheme with an aggregation/accumulation scheme in any model without making additional heuristic assumptions. This is because obtaining a NARK from a PC scheme using known techniques requires the use of a random oracle, which we do not know how to accumulate. In contrast, we construct PCD in the standard model starting directly from an aggregation/accumulation scheme *for a NARK*, and *no additional assumptions*. Separately, the security of our accumulation scheme for a NARK in the standard model *is* an assumption, which is conjectured based on a security proof in the ROM.

Another major difference is that we additionally contribute a comprehensive and modular implementation of protocols from [BCMS20] and this paper, and conduct an evaluation for the discrete logarithm setting. This supports the asymptotic improvements with measured improvements in concrete efficiency.

2   Techniques

We summarize the main ideas behind our results. In Sect. 2.1 we discuss our new notion of split accumulation for relation predicates, and compare it with the notion of atomic accumulation for language predicates from [BCMS20]. In Sect. 2.2 we discuss the proof of Theorem 1. In Sect. 2.3 we discuss the proof of Theorem 2; for this we rely on a new result about split accumulation for Hadamard products, which we discuss in Sect. 2.5. Then, in Sect. 2.6, we discuss our split accumulation for a Pedersen-based polynomial commitment, which can act as a drop-in replacement for polynomial commitments used in prior SNARKs, such as those of [BGH19]. Finally, in Sect. 2.7 we elaborate on our implementation and evaluation. Figure 1 illustrates the relation between our results. The rest of the paper contains technical details, and we provide pointers to relevant sections along the way.

2.1   Accumulation: Atomic vs Split

We review the notion of accumulation from [BCMS20], which we refer to as *atomic accumulation*, and then describe the weaker notion that we introduce, which we call *split accumulation*.

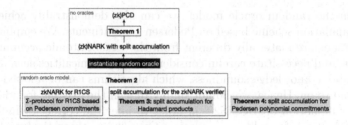

Fig. 1. Diagram showing the relation between our results. Gray boxes within a result are notable subroutines.

Atomic Accumulation for Languages. An *accumulation scheme for a language predicate* $\Phi\colon X \to \{0,1\}$ is a tuple of algorithms (P, V, D), known as the prover, verifier, and decider, that enable proving/verifying statements of the form $\Phi(q_1) \wedge \Phi(q_2) \wedge \cdots$ more efficiently than running the predicate Φ on each input.

This is done as follows. Starting from an initial ("empty") accumulator acc_1, the prover is used to accumulate the first input q_1 to produce a new accumulator $\mathsf{acc}_2 \leftarrow P(q_1, \mathsf{acc}_1)$; then the prover is used again to accumulate the second input q_2 to produce a new accumulator $\mathsf{acc}_3 \leftarrow P(q_2, \mathsf{acc}_2)$; and so on.

Each accumulator produced so far enables efficient verification of the predicate on all inputs that went into the accumulator. For example, to establish that $\Phi(q_1) \wedge \cdots \wedge \Phi(q_T) = 1$ it suffices to check that:

- the verifier accepts each accumulation step: $V(q_1, \mathsf{acc}_1, \mathsf{acc}_2) = 1$, $V(q_2, \mathsf{acc}_2, \mathsf{acc}_3) = 1$, and so on; and
- the decider accepts the final accumulator: $D(\mathsf{acc}_T) = 1$.

Qualitatively, this replaces the naive cost $T \cdot |\Phi|$ with the new cost $T \cdot |V| + |D|$. This is beneficial when the verifier is much cheaper than checking the predicate directly and the decider is not much costlier than checking the predicate directly. Crucially, the verifier and decider costs (and, in particular, the accumulator size) should not grow with the number T of accumulation steps (which need not be known in advance).

The properties of an accumulation scheme are summarized in the following informal definition, which additionally includes an accumulation proof used to check an accumulation step (but is not passed on).

Definition 1 (informal). *An* **accumulation scheme** *for a predicate* $\Phi\colon X \to \{0,1\}$ *consists of a triple of algorithms* (P, V, D)*, known as the prover, verifier, and decider, that satisfies the following properties.*

- Completeness: *For every accumulator* acc *and predicate input* $q \in X$*, if* $D(\mathsf{acc}) = 1$ *and* $\Phi(q) = 1$*, then for* $(\mathsf{acc}^\star, \mathsf{pf}^\star) \leftarrow P(\mathsf{acc}, q)$ *it holds that* $V(q, \mathsf{acc}, \mathsf{acc}^\star, \mathsf{pf}^\star) = 1$ *and* $D(\mathsf{acc}^\star) = 1$*.*
- Soundness: *For every efficiently-generated old accumulator* acc*, predicate input* $q \in X$*, new accumulator* $\mathsf{acc}^\star$*, and accumulation proof* $\mathsf{pf}^\star$*, if* $D(\mathsf{acc}^\star) =$

1 *and* $V(q, acc, acc^*, pf^*) = 1$ *then, with all but negligible probability,* $\Phi(q) = 1$ *and* $D(acc) = 1$.

The above definition omits many details, such as the ability to accumulate multiple accumulators $[acc_j]_{j=1}^m$ and multiple predicate inputs $[q_i]_{i=1}^n$ in one step, the optional property of zero knowledge (enabled by the accumulation proof pf^*), the fact that P, V, D should receive keys apk, avk, dk generated by an indexer algorithm that receives the specification of Φ, and others. We refer the reader to [BCMS20] for more details.

The aspect that we wish to highlight here is the following: in order for the verifier to be much cheaper than the predicate ($|V| \ll |\Phi|$) it must be that the accumulator itself is much smaller than the predicate ($|acc| \ll |\Phi|$) because the verifier receives the accumulator as input. (And if the accumulator is accompanied by a validity proof pf then this proof must also be small.)

We refer to this setting as *atomic accumulation* because the entirety of the accumulator is treated as one short monolithic string. In contrast, in this paper we consider a relaxation where this is not the case, and will enable us to obtain new instantiations that lead to new theoretical and practical results.

Split Accumulation for Relations.   We propose a relaxed notion of accumulation: a *split accumulation scheme for a relation predicate* $\Phi \colon X \times W \to \{0, 1\}$ is again a tuple of algorithms (P, V, D) as before. Split accumulation differs from atomic accumulation in that: (a) an input to Φ consists of a short instance part qx and a (possibly) long witness part qw; (b) an accumulator acc is split into a short instance part $acc.x$ and a (possibly) long witness part $acc.w$; (c) the verifier only needs the short parts of inputs and accumulators to verify an accumulation step, along with a short validity proof instead of the long witness parts.

As before, the prover is used to accumulate a predicate input $q_i = (qx_i, qw_i)$ into a prior accumulator acc_i to obtain a new accumulator and validity proof $(acc_{i+1}, pf_{i+1}) \leftarrow P(q_i, acc_i)$. Different from before, however, we wish to establish that given instances $qx_1, \ldots, qx_T$ there exist (more precisely, a party knows) witnesses $qw_1, \ldots, qw_T$ such that $\Phi(qx_1, qw_1) \wedge \cdots \wedge \Phi(qx_T, qw_T) = 1$. For this it suffices to check that:

- the verifier accepts each accumulation step given only the short instance parts: $V(qx_1, acc_1.x, acc_2.x, pf_2) = 1$, $V(qx_2, acc_2.x, acc_3.x, pf_3) = 1$, and so on; and
- the decider accepts the final accumulator (made of both the instance and witness part): $D(acc_T) = 1$.

Again the naive cost $T \cdot |\Phi|$ is replaced with the new cost $T \cdot |V| + |D|$, but now it could be that an accumulator is, e.g., as large as $|\Phi|$; we only need the *instance part* of the accumulator (and predicate inputs) to be short.

The security property of a split accumulation scheme involves an extractor that outputs a long witness part from a short instance part and proof, and is reminiscent of the knowledge soundness of a succinct non-interactive argument. Turning this high level description into a working definition requires some care,

however, and we view this as a contribution of this paper.[2] Informally the security
definition could be summarized as follows.

Definition 2 (informal). *A* **split accumulation scheme** *for a predicate*
$\Phi\colon X \times W \to \{0,1\}$ *consists of a triple of algorithms* (P, V, D) *that satisfies the
following properties.*

- Completeness: *For every accumulator* acc *and predicate input* $q = (qx, qw) \in
  X \times W$, *if* $D(acc) = 1$ *and* $\Phi(q) = 1$, *then for* $(acc^\star, pf^\star) \leftarrow P(q, acc)$ *it holds
  that* $V(qx, acc.x, acc^\star.x, pf^\star) = 1$ *and* $D(acc^\star) = 1$.
- Knowledge: *For every efficiently-generated old accumulator instance* acc.x,
  old input instance qx, *accumulation proof* $pf^\star$, *and new accumulator* $acc^\star$,
  if $D(acc^\star) = 1$ *and* $V(qx, acc.x, acc^\star.x, pf^\star) = 1$ *then, with all but negligible
  probability, an efficient extractor can find an old accumulator witness* acc.w
  and predicate witness qw *such that* $\Phi(qx, qw) = 1$ *and* $D((acc.x, acc.w)) = 1$.

One can verify that split accumulation is indeed a relaxation of atomic accumulation: any atomic accumulation scheme is (trivially) a split accumulation
scheme with empty witnesses. Crucially, however, a split accumulation scheme
alleviates a major restriction of atomic accumulation, namely, that accumulators
and predicate inputs have to be short.

Next, in Sect. 2.2 we show that split accumulation suffices for recursive composition (which has surprising theoretical consequences) and then in Sect. 2.3 we
present a NARK with split accumulation scheme based on discrete logarithms.

2.2   PCD from Split Accumulation

We summarize the main ideas behind Theorem 1, which obtains proof-carrying
data (PCD) from any NARK that has a split accumulation scheme. To ease
exposition, in this summary we focus on IVC, which can be viewed as the special
case where a circuit F is repeatedly applied. That is, we wish to incrementally
prove a claim of the form "$F^T(z_0) = z_T$" where F^T denotes F composed with
itself T times.

Prior Work: Recursion via Atomic Accumulation.   Our starting point
is a theorem from [BCMS20] that obtains PCD from any SNARK that has an
atomic accumulation scheme. The IVC construction implied by that theorem is
roughly follows.

- The *IVC prover* receives a previous instance z_i, proof π_i, and accumulator
  acc_i; accumulates (z_i, π_i) with acc_i to obtain a new accumulator acc_{i+1} and
  accumulation proof pf_{i+1}; and generates a SNARK proof π_{i+1} of the following
  claim expressed as a circuit R (see Fig. 2, middle box): "$z_{i+1} = F(z_i)$, and

---

[2] By "working definition" we mean a definition that we can provably fulfill under
concrete hardness assumptions in the random oracle model, and, separately, that
provably suffices for recursive composition in the plain model without random
oracles.

there exist a SNARK proof π_i, accumulator acc_i, and accumulation proof pf_{i+1} such that the accumulation verifier accepts $((z_i, \pi_i), \mathsf{acc}_i, \mathsf{acc}_{i+1}, \mathsf{pf}_{i+1})$".
The IVC proof for z_{i+1} is $(\pi_{i+1}, \mathsf{acc}_{i+1})$.
- The *IVC verifier* validates an IVC proof (π_i, acc_i) for z_i by running the SNARK verifier on the instance (z_i, acc_i) and proof π_i, and running the accumulation scheme decider on the accumulator acc_i.

In each iteration we maintain the invariant that if acc_i is a valid accumulator (according to the decider) and π_i is a valid SNARK proof, then the computation is correct up to the i-th step.

Note that while it would suffice to prove that "$z_{i+1} = F(z_i)$, π_i is a valid SNARK proof, and acc_i is a valid accumulator", we cannot afford to do so. Indeed: (i) proving that π_i is a valid proof requires proving a statement about the argument verifier, which may not be sublinear; and (ii) proving that acc_i is a valid accumulator requires proving a statement about the decider, which may not be sublinear. Instead of proving this claim directly, we "defer" it by having the prover accumulate (z_i, π_i) into acc_i to obtain a new accumulator acc_{i+1}. The soundness property of the accumulation scheme ensures that if acc_{i+1} is valid and the accumulation verifier accepts $((z_i, \pi_i), \mathsf{acc}_i, \mathsf{acc}_{i+1}, \mathsf{pf}_{i+1})$, then π_i is a valid SNARK proof and acc_i is a valid accumulator. Thus all that remains to maintain the invariant is for the prover to prove that the accumulation verifier accepts; this is possible provided that the *accumulation verifier* is sublinear.

Our Construction: Recursion via Split Accumulation. Our construction naturally extends the above idea to the setting of NARKs with split accumulation schemes. Indeed, the only difference to the above construction is that the proof π_{i+1} generated by the IVC prover is for the statement "$z_{i+1} = F(z_i)$, and there exist a NARK proof *instance* $\pi_i.\mathbb{x}$, an accumulator *instance* $\mathsf{acc}_i.\mathbb{x}$, and an accumulation proof pf_{i+1} such that the accumulation verifier accepts $((z_i, \pi_i.\mathbb{x}), \mathsf{acc}_i.\mathbb{x}, \mathsf{acc}_{i+1}.\mathbb{x}, \mathsf{pf}_{i+1})$", and accordingly the IVC verifier runs the NARK verifier on $((z_i, \mathsf{acc}_i.\mathbb{x}), \pi_i)$ (in addition to running the accumulation scheme decider on the accumulator acc_i). This is illustrated in Fig. 2 (lower box). Note that the circuit R itself is unchanged from the atomic case; the difference is in whether we pass the *entire* proof and accumulators or just the $\mathbb{x}$ part.

Proving that this relaxation yields a secure construction is more complex. Similar to prior work, the proof of security proceeds via a recursive extraction argument, as we explain next.

For an atomic accumulation scheme ([BCMS20]), one maintains the following extraction invariant: the i-th extractor outputs $(z_i, \pi_i, \mathsf{acc}_i)$ such that π_i is valid according to the SNARK, acc_i is valid according to the decider, and $F^{T-i}(z_i) = z_T$. The T-th "extractor" is simply the malicious prover, and we can obtain the i-th extractor by applying the knowledge guarantee of the SNARK to the $(i+1)$-th extractor. That the invariant is maintained is implied by the soundness guarantee of the atomic accumulation scheme.

For a split accumulation scheme, we want to maintain the same extraction invariant; however, the extractor for the NARK will only yield $(z_i, \pi_i.\mathbb{x}, \mathsf{acc}_i.\mathbb{x})$, and not the corresponding witnesses. This is where we make use of the extraction property of the split accumulation scheme itself. Specifically, we interleave the knowledge guarantees of the NARK and accumulation scheme as follows: the i-th NARK extractor is obtained from the $(i+1)$-th accumulation extractor using the knowledge guarantee of the NARK, and the i-th accumulation extractor is obtained from the i-th NARK extractor using the knowledge guarantee of the accumulation scheme. We take the malicious prover to be the T-th accumulation extractor.

From Sketch to Proof. In the full version we give the formal details of our construction and a proof of correctness. In particular, we show how to construct PCD, a more general primitive than IVC. In the PCD setting, rather than each computation step having a single input z_i, it receives m inputs from different nodes. Proving correctness hence requires proving that *all* of these inputs were computed correctly. For our construction, this entails checking m proofs and m accumulators. To do this, we extend the definition of an accumulation scheme to allow accumulating multiple instance-proof pairs and multiple "old" accumulators.

We also note that the application to PCD leads to other definitional considerations, which are similar to those that have appeared in previous works [COS20;BCMS20]. In particular, the knowledge soundness guarantee for both the NARK *and* the accumulation scheme should be of the stronger "multi-instance witness-extended emulation with auxiliary input and output" type used in previous work. Additionally, the underlying construction of split accumulation achieves only expected polynomial-time extraction (in the ROM), and so the recursive extraction technique requires that we are able to extract from expected-time adversaries.

Remark 2 (knowledge soundness for PCD vs. IVC). The proof of security for PCD extracts a transcript *one full layer at a time*. Since a layer consists of many nodes, each with an *independently-generated* proof and accumulator, a standard "single-instance" extraction guarantee is insufficient in general. However, in the special case of IVC, every layer consists of exactly one node, and so single-instance extraction does suffice.

Remark 3 (flavors of PCD). The recent advances in PCD from accumulation achieve weaker efficiency guarantees than PCD from succinct verification, and formally these results are incomparable. (Starting from weaker assumptions they obtain weaker conclusions.) The essential feature that all these works achieve is that the efficiency of PCD algorithms is independent of the number of nodes in the PCD computation, which is how PCD is defined. That said, prior work on PCD from succinct verification [BCCT13;BCTV14;COS20] additionally guarantees that verifying a PCD proof is sublinear in a node's computation; and prior work on PCD from atomic accumulation [BCMS20] merely ensures that a PCD proof has size (but not necessarily verification time) that is sublinear in a node's computation. The PCD scheme obtained in this paper does not have these additional features: a PCD proof has size that is linear in a node's computation.

recursion circuit via
succinct verification

$R\big((\mathsf{ivk}, z_{i+1}), (z_i, \pi_i)\big)$:
- check that $z_{i+1} = F(z_i)$
- set SNARK instance $\mathbb{x}_i := (\mathsf{ivk}, z_i)$
- check that $\mathsf{SNARK}.\mathcal{V}(\mathsf{ivk}, \mathbb{x}_i, \pi_i) = 1$

recursion circuit via
atomic accumulation

$R\big((\mathsf{avk}, z_{i+1}, \mathsf{acc}_{i+1}), (z_i, \pi_i, \mathsf{acc}_i, \mathsf{pf}_{i+1})\big)$:
- check that $z_{i+1} = F(z_i)$
- set predicate input $\mathsf{q}_i := ((\mathsf{avk}, z_i, \mathsf{acc}_i), \pi_i)$
- check that $\mathsf{ACC.V}(\mathsf{avk}, \mathsf{q}_i, \mathsf{acc}_i, \mathsf{acc}_{i+1}, \mathsf{pf}_{i+1}) = 1$

recursion circuit via
split accumulation

$R\big((\mathsf{avk}, z_{i+1}, \mathsf{acc}_{i+1}.\mathbb{x}), (z_i, \pi_i.\mathbb{x}, \mathsf{acc}_i.\mathbb{x}, \mathsf{pf}_{i+1})\big)$:
- check that $z_{i+1} = F(z_i)$
- set predicate instance $\mathsf{qx}_i := ((\mathsf{avk}, z_i, \mathsf{acc}_i.\mathbb{x}), \pi_i.\mathbb{x})$
- check that $\mathsf{ACC.V}(\mathsf{avk}, \mathsf{qx}_i, \mathsf{acc}_i.\mathbb{x}, \mathsf{acc}_{i+1}.\mathbb{x}, \mathsf{pf}_{i+1}) = 1$

Fig. 2. Comparison of circuits used to realize recursion with different techniques.

2.3 NARK with Split Accumulation Based on DL

We summarize the main ideas behind Theorem 2, which provides, in the discrete logarithm setting with random oracles, a (zero knowledge) NARK for R1CS that has a (zero knowledge) split accumulation scheme whose accumulation verifier has constant size (more precisely, performs a constant number of group scalar multiplications, field operations, and random oracle calls).

Recall that R1CS is a standard generalization of arithmetic circuit satisfiability where the "circuit description" is given by coefficient matrices, as specified below. ("∘" denotes the entry-wise product.)

Definition 3 (R1CS problem). *Given a finite field* $\mathbb{F}$, *coefficient matrices* $A, B, C \in \mathbb{F}^{M \times N}$, *and an instance vector* $x \in \mathbb{F}^n$, *is there a witness vector* $w \in \mathbb{F}^{N-n}$ *such that* $Az \circ Bz = Cz$ *for* $z := (x, w) \in \mathbb{F}^N$?

We explain our construction incrementally. In Sect. 2.3.1 we begin by describing a NARK for R1CS that is *not* zero knowledge, and a "basic" split accumulation scheme for it that is also not zero knowledge. In Sect. 2.3.2 we show how to extend the NARK and its split accumulation scheme to both be zero knowledge. In Sect. 2.3.3 we explain why the accumulation scheme described so far is limited to the special case of 1 old accumulator and 1 predicate input (which suffices for IVC), and sketch how to obtain accumulation for m old accumulators and n predicate inputs (which is required for PCD); this motivates the problem of accumulating Hadamard products, which we subsequently address in Sect. 2.5.

We highlight here that both the NARK and the accumulation scheme are particularly simple compared to other protocols in the SNARK literature (especially with regard to constructions that enable recursion!), and view this as a significant advantage for potential deployments of these ideas in the real world.

2.3.1   Without Zero Knowledge

Let $\mathsf{ck} = (G_1, \ldots, G_M) \in \mathbb{G}^M$ be a commitment key for the Pedersen commitment scheme with message space $\mathbb{F}^M$, and let $\mathsf{Commit}(\mathsf{ck}, a) := \sum_{i \in [M]} a_i \cdot G_i$ denote its commitment function. Consider the following non-interactive argument for R1CS:

$\mathcal{P}(\mathsf{ck}, (A, B, C), x, w)$ $\mathcal{V}(\mathsf{ck}, (A, B, C), x)$

$z := (x, w) \in \mathbb{F}^N$ $z := (x, w)$
$z_A := Az \in \mathbb{F}^M \quad C_A := \mathsf{Commit}(\mathsf{ck}, z_A) \in \mathbb{G}$ $\quad - C_A, C_B, C_C, w \longrightarrow \quad$ $z_A := Az \quad C_A \overset{?}{=} \mathsf{Commit}(\mathsf{ck}, z_A)$
$z_B := Bz \in \mathbb{F}^M \quad C_B := \mathsf{Commit}(\mathsf{ck}, z_B) \in \mathbb{G}$ $z_B := Bz \quad C_B \overset{?}{=} \mathsf{Commit}(\mathsf{ck}, z_B)$
$z_C := Cz \in \mathbb{F}^M \quad C_C := \mathsf{Commit}(\mathsf{ck}, z_C) \in \mathbb{G}$ $z_C := Cz \quad C_C \overset{?}{=} \mathsf{Commit}(\mathsf{ck}, z_C)$
$\qquad\qquad\qquad\qquad\qquad\qquad\qquad\qquad\qquad\qquad C_C \overset{?}{=} \mathsf{Commit}(\mathsf{ck}, z_A \circ z_B)$

The NARK's security follows from the binding property of Pedersen commitments. (At this point we are not using any homomorphic properties, but we will in the accumulation scheme.) Moreover, denoting by $\mathsf{K} = \Omega(\mathsf{M})$ the number of non-zero entries in the coefficient matrices, the NARK's efficiency is as follows:

NARK prover time	NARK verifier time	NARK argument size
$O(\mathsf{M}) \; \mathbb{G}$	$O(\mathsf{M}) \; \mathbb{G}$	$O(1) \; \mathbb{G}$
$O(\mathsf{K}) \; \mathbb{F}$	$O(\mathsf{K}) \; \mathbb{F}$	$O(\mathsf{N}) \; \mathbb{F}$

The NARK may superficially appear useless because it has linear argument size and is not zero knowledge. Nevertheless, we can obtain an efficient split accumulation scheme for it, as we describe next.[3]

The predicate to be accumulated is the NARK verifier with a suitable split between predicate instance and predicate witness: Φ takes as input a predicate instance $\mathsf{qx} = (x, C_A, C_B, C_C)$ and a predicate witness $\mathsf{qw} = w$, and then runs the NARK verifier with R1CS instance x and proof $\pi = (C_A, C_B, C_C, w)$.[4]

An accumulator acc is split into an accumulator instance $\mathsf{acc.x} = (x, C_A, C_B, C_C, C_\circ) \in \mathbb{F}^n \times \mathbb{G}^4$ and an accumulator witness $\mathsf{acc.w} = w \in \mathbb{F}^{N-n}$. The accumulation decider D validates a split accumulator $\mathsf{acc} = (\mathsf{acc.x}, \mathsf{acc.w})$ as follows: set $z := (x, w) \in \mathbb{F}^N$; compute the vectors $z_A := Az$, $z_B := Bz$, and $z_C := Cz$; and check that the following conditions hold:

$$C_A \overset{?}{=} \mathsf{Commit}(\mathsf{ck}, z_A), \; C_B \overset{?}{=} \mathsf{Commit}(\mathsf{ck}, z_B), \; C_C \overset{?}{=} \mathsf{Commit}(\mathsf{ck}, z_C), \; C_\circ \overset{?}{=} \mathsf{Commit}(\mathsf{ck}, z_A \circ z_B) .$$

---

[3] We could even "re-arrange" computation between the NARK and the accumulation scheme, and simplify the NARK further to be the NP decider (the verifier receives just the witness w and checks that the R1CS condition holds). We do not do so because this does not lead to any savings in the accumulation verifier (the main efficiency metric of interest) and also because the current presentation more naturally leads to the zero knowledge variant described in Sect. 2.3.2. (We note that the foregoing rearrangement is a general transformation that does not preserve zero knowledge or succinctness of the given NARK.).

[4] For now we view the commitment key ck and coefficient matrices A, B, C as hardcoded in the accumulation predicate Φ; our definitions later handle this more precisely.

Note that the accumulation decider D is similar, *but not equal*, to the NARK verifier.

We are left to describe the accumulation prover and accumulation verifier. Both have access to a random oracle ρ. For adaptive security, queries to the random oracle should include a hash τ of the coefficient matrices A, B, C and instance size n, which can be precomputed in an offline phase. (Formally, this is done via the *indexer* algorithm of the accumulation scheme, which receives the coefficient matrices and instance size, performs all one-time computations such as deriving τ, and produces an accumulator proving key apk, an accumulator verification key avk, and a decision key dk for P, V, and D respectively.)

The intuition for accumulation is to set the new accumulator to be a random linear combination of the old accumulator and predicate input, and use the accumulation proof to collect cross terms that arise from the Hadamard product (a bilinear, not linear, operation). This naturally leads to the following simple construction.

$P^{\rho_{AS}}(\text{acc}, (\text{qx}, \text{qw}))$:

1. $z_A := A \cdot (\text{qx}.x, \text{qw}.w)$, $z_B := B \cdot (\text{qx}.x, \text{qw}.w)$.
2. $z'_A := A \cdot (\text{acc.x}.x, \text{acc.w}.w)$, $z'_B := B \cdot (\text{acc.x}.x, \text{acc.w}.w)$.
3. $\text{pf} := \text{Commit}(\text{ck}, z_A \circ z'_B + z'_A \circ z_B)$.
4. $\beta := \rho_{AS}(\tau, \text{acc.x}, \text{qx}, \text{pf})$.
5. $\text{acc}^\star.x.x := \text{acc.x}.x + \beta \cdot \text{qx}.x$.
6. $\text{acc}^\star.x.C_A := \text{acc.x}.C_A + \beta \cdot \text{qx}.C_A$.
7. $\text{acc}^\star.x.C_B := \text{acc.x}.C_B + \beta \cdot \text{qx}.C_B$.
8. $\text{acc}^\star.x.C_C := \text{acc.x}.C_C + \beta \cdot \text{qx}.C_C$.
9. $\text{acc}^\star.x.C_\circ := \text{acc.x}.C_\circ + \beta \cdot \text{pf} + \beta^2 \cdot \text{qx}.C_C$.
10. $\text{acc}^\star.w.w := \text{acc.w}.w + \beta \cdot \text{qw}.w$.
11. Output $(\text{acc}^\star, \text{pf})$.

$V^{\rho_{AS}}(\text{acc.x}, \text{qx}, \text{acc}^\star.x, \text{pf})$:

1. $\beta := \rho_{AS}(\tau, \text{acc.x}, \text{qx}, \text{pf})$.
2. $\text{acc}^\star.x.x \overset{?}{=} \text{acc.x}.x + \beta \cdot \text{qx}.x$.
3. $\text{acc}^\star.x.C_A \overset{?}{=} \text{acc.x}.C_A + \beta \cdot \text{qx}.C_A$.
4. $\text{acc}^\star.x.C_B \overset{?}{=} \text{acc.x}.C_B + \beta \cdot \text{qx}.C_B$.
5. $\text{acc}^\star.x.C_C \overset{?}{=} \text{acc.x}.C_C + \beta \cdot \text{qx}.C_C$.
6. $\text{acc}^\star.x.C_\circ \overset{?}{=} \text{acc.x}.C_\circ + \beta \cdot \text{pf} + \beta^2 \cdot \text{qx}.C_C$.

The efficiency of the split accumulation scheme can be summarized by the following table:

Accumulation prover time	Accumulation verifier time	Decider time	Accumulator size
$O(M)$ G	4 G [5]	$O(M)$ G	$|\text{acc.x}| = 4\,\mathbb{G} + n\,\mathbb{F}$
$O(K)$ F	$O(n)$ F	$O(K)$ F	$|\text{acc.w}| = (N - n)\,\mathbb{F}$
1 RO	1 RO	–	–

The key efficiency feature is that the accumulation verifier only performs 1 call to the random oracle, a constant number of group scalar multiplications, and field operations. (More precisely, the verifier makes n field operations, but this does not grow with circuit size and, more fundamentally, is inevitable because the accumulation verifier must receive the R1CS instance $x \in \mathbb{F}^n$ as input.)

---

[5] The verifier performs 4 group scalar multiplication by computing $\beta \cdot \text{qx}.C_C$ and then $\beta \cdot \text{pf} + \beta^2 \cdot \text{qx}.C_C = \beta \cdot (\text{pf} + \beta \cdot \text{qx}.C_C)$ via another group scalar multiplication. Further it is possible to combine C_A and C_B in one commitment in both the NARK and the accumulation scheme. This reduces the group scalar multiplications in the verifier to 3, and the accumulator size to $3\,\mathbb{G} + n\,\mathbb{F}$.

2.3.2   With Zero Knowledge

We explain how to add zero knowledge to the approach described in the previous section.

First, we extend the NARK to additionally achieve zero knowledge. For this we construct a sigma protocol for R1CS based on Pedersen commitments, which is summarized in Fig. 3; then we apply the Fiat–Shamir transformation to it to obtain a corresponding zkNARK for R1CS. Here the commitment key for the Pedersen commitment is $\mathsf{ck} := (G_1, \ldots, G_M, H) \in \mathbb{G}^{M+1}$, as we need a spare group element for the commitment randomness. The blue text in the figure represents the "diff" compared to the non-zero-knowledge version, and indeed if all such text were removed the protocol would collapse to the previous one.

Second, we extend the split accumulation scheme to accumulate the modified protocol for R1CS. Again the predicate being accumulated is the NARK verifier but now since the NARK verifier has changed so does the predicate. A zkNARK proof π now can be viewed as a pair (π_1, π_2) denoting the prover's commitment and response in the sigma protocol. Then the predicate $\varPhi$ takes as input a predicate instance $\mathsf{qx} = (x, \pi_1) \in \mathbb{F}^n \times \mathbb{G}^8$ and a predicate witness $\mathsf{qw} = \pi_2 \in \mathbb{F}^{N-n+4}$, and then runs the NARK verifier with R1CS instance x and proof $\pi = (\pi_1, \pi_2)$.

An accumulator acc is split into an accumulator instance $\mathsf{acc.x} = (x, C_A, C_B, C_C, C_\circ) \in \mathbb{F}^n \times \mathbb{G}^4$ (the same as before) and an accumulator witness $\mathsf{acc.w} = (w, \sigma_A, \sigma_B, \sigma_C, \sigma_\circ) \in \mathbb{F}^{N-n+4}$. The decider is essentially the same as in Sect. 2.3.1, except that now the four commitments are computed using the corresponding randomness in $\mathsf{acc.w}$.

The accumulation prover and accumulation verifier can be extended, in a straightforward way, to support the new zkSNARK protocol; we provide these in Fig. 4, with text in blue to denote the "diff" to accumulate the zero knowledge features of the NARK and with text in red to denote the features to make accumulation itself zero knowledge. There we use ρ_{NARK} to denote the oracle used for the zkNARK for R1CS, which is obtained via the Fiat–Shamir transformation applied to a sigma protocol (as mentioned above); for adaptive security, the Fiat–Shamir query includes, in addition to π_1, a hash $\tau := \rho_{\mathsf{NARK}}(A, B, C, \mathsf{n})$ of the coefficient matrices and the R1CS input $x \in \mathbb{F}^n$ (this means that the Fiat–Shamir query equals $(\tau, \mathsf{qx}) = (\tau, x, \pi_1)$).

Note that now the accumulation prover and accumulation verifier are each making 2 calls to the random oracle, rather than 1 as before, because they have to additionally compute the sigma protocol's challenge.

2.3.3   Towards General Accumulation

The accumulation schemes described in Sects. 2.3.1 and 2.3.2 are limited to a special case, which we could call the "IVC setting", where accumulation involves 1 old accumulator and 1 predicate input. However, the definition of accumulation requires supporting m old accumulators $[\mathsf{acc}_j]_{j=1}^m = [(\mathsf{acc}_j.\mathsf{x}, \mathsf{acc}_j.\mathsf{w})]_{j=1}^m$ and n predicate inputs $[(\mathsf{qx}_i, \mathsf{qw}_i)]_{i=1}^n$, for any m and n. (E.g., to construct PCD we set both m and n equal to the "arity" of the compliance predicate.) How can we extend the ideas described so far to this more general case?

$\mathcal{P}(\mathsf{ck}, (A, B, C), x, w)$ $\mathcal{V}(\mathsf{ck}, (A, B, C), x)$

$z := (x, w) \quad r \leftarrow \mathbb{F}^{N-n}$

$z_A := Az \quad \omega_A \leftarrow \mathbb{F} \quad C_A := \mathsf{Commit}(\mathsf{ck}, z_A; \omega_A)$
$z_B := Bz \quad \omega_B \leftarrow \mathbb{F} \quad C_B := \mathsf{Commit}(\mathsf{ck}, z_B; \omega_B)$
$z_C := Cz \quad \omega_C \leftarrow \mathbb{F} \quad C_C := \mathsf{Commit}(\mathsf{ck}, z_C; \omega_C)$

$r_A := A \cdot (0^n, r) \quad \omega_A' \leftarrow \mathbb{F} \quad C_A' := \mathsf{Commit}(\mathsf{ck}, r_A; \omega_A')$
$r_B := B \cdot (0^n, r) \quad \omega_B' \leftarrow \mathbb{F} \quad C_B' := \mathsf{Commit}(\mathsf{ck}, r_B; \omega_B')$
$r_C := C \cdot (0^n, r) \quad \omega_C' \leftarrow \mathbb{F} \quad C_C' := \mathsf{Commit}(\mathsf{ck}, r_C; \omega_C')$

$\omega_1 \leftarrow \mathbb{F} \quad C_1 := \mathsf{Commit}(\mathsf{ck}, z_A \circ r_B + z_B \circ r_A; \omega_1)$
$\omega_2 \leftarrow \mathbb{F} \quad C_2 := \mathsf{Commit}(\mathsf{ck}, r_A \circ r_B; \omega_2)$

$$\xrightarrow{\begin{array}{c} C_A, C_B, C_C \\ C_A', C_B', C_C', C_1, C_2 \end{array}}$$

$s := w + \gamma r \in \mathbb{F}^{N-n}$ $\xleftarrow{\quad \gamma \in \mathbb{F} \quad}$
$\sigma_A := \omega_A + \gamma \omega_A' \in \mathbb{F}$
$\sigma_B := \omega_B + \gamma \omega_B' \in \mathbb{F}$
$\sigma_C := \omega_C + \gamma \omega_C' \in \mathbb{F}$
$\sigma_0 := \omega_C + \gamma \omega_1 + \gamma^2 \omega_2 \in \mathbb{F}$ $\xrightarrow{\quad s, \sigma_A, \sigma_B, \sigma_C, \sigma_0 \quad}$

$s_A := A \cdot (x, s) \quad C_A + \gamma C_A' \overset{?}{=} \mathsf{Commit}(\mathsf{ck}, s_A; \sigma_A)$
$s_B := B \cdot (x, s) \quad C_B + \gamma C_B' \overset{?}{=} \mathsf{Commit}(\mathsf{ck}, s_B; \sigma_B)$
$s_C := C \cdot (x, s) \quad C_C + \gamma C_C' \overset{?}{=} \mathsf{Commit}(\mathsf{ck}, s_C; \sigma_C)$
$C_C + \gamma C_1 + \gamma^2 C_2 \overset{?}{=} \mathsf{Commit}(\mathsf{ck}, s_A \circ s_B; \sigma_0)$

Fig. 3. The sigma protocol for R1CS that underlies the zkNARK for R1CS.

$\mathsf{P}^{\mathsf{PAS}}((\mathsf{qx}, \mathsf{qw}), \mathsf{acc})$:

1. $z_A := A \cdot (\mathsf{qx}.x, \mathsf{qw}.s), \ z_B := B \cdot (\mathsf{qx}.x, \mathsf{qw}.s)$.
2. $z_A' := A \cdot (\mathsf{acc}.x.x, \mathsf{acc}.w.s), \ z_B' := B \cdot (\mathsf{acc}.x.x, \mathsf{acc}.w.s)$.
3. Sample $x^* \leftarrow \mathbb{F}^n$ and $s^* \leftarrow \mathbb{F}^{N-n}$ and $\omega_2^* \leftarrow \mathbb{F}$.
4. $s_A^* := A \cdot (x^*, s^*), \ s_B^* := B \cdot (x^*, s^*), \ s_C^* := C \cdot (x^*, s^*)$.
5. $C_A^* := \mathsf{Commit}(\mathsf{ck}, s_A^*; \omega_A^*)$ for $\omega_A^* \leftarrow \mathbb{F}$.
6. $C_B^* := \mathsf{Commit}(\mathsf{ck}, s_B^*; \omega_B^*)$ for $\omega_B^* \leftarrow \mathbb{F}$.
7. $C_C^* := \mathsf{Commit}(\mathsf{ck}, s_C^*; \omega_C^*)$ for $\omega_C^* \leftarrow \mathbb{F}$.
8. $\mathsf{pf}_1 := \mathsf{Commit}(\mathsf{ck}, z_A \circ s_B^* + s_A^* \circ z_B; 0)$.
9. $\mathsf{pf}_2 := \mathsf{Commit}(\mathsf{ck}, s_A^* \circ s_B^* + z_A \circ z_B' + z_A' \circ z_B; \omega_2^*)$.
10. $\mathsf{pf}_3 := \mathsf{Commit}(\mathsf{ck}, s_A^* \circ z_B' + z_A' \circ s_B^*; 0)$.
11. $\mathsf{pf} := (x^*, C_A^*, C_B^*, C_C^*, \mathsf{pf}_1, \mathsf{pf}_2, \mathsf{pf}_3)$.
12. Compute $\gamma := \rho_{\mathsf{NARK}}(\tau, \mathsf{qx})$.
13. $\beta := \rho_{\mathsf{AS}}(\tau, \mathsf{acc}.x, \mathsf{qx}, \mathsf{pf})$.
14. $\mathsf{acc}^*.x.x := \mathsf{acc}.x.x + \beta \cdot x^* + \beta^2 \cdot \mathsf{qx}.x$.
15. $\mathsf{acc}^*.x.C_A := \mathsf{acc}.x.C_A + \beta \cdot C_A^* + \beta^2 \cdot (\mathsf{qx}.C_A + \gamma \cdot \mathsf{qx}.C_A')$.
16. $\mathsf{acc}^*.x.C_B := \mathsf{acc}.x.C_B + \beta \cdot C_B^* + \beta^2 \cdot (\mathsf{qx}.C_B + \gamma \cdot \mathsf{qx}.C_B')$.
17. $\mathsf{acc}^*.x.C_C := \mathsf{acc}.x.C_C + \beta \cdot C_C^* + \beta^2 \cdot (\mathsf{qx}.C_C + \gamma \cdot \mathsf{qx}.C_C')$.
18. $\mathsf{acc}^*.x.C_0 := \mathsf{acc}.x.C_0 + \beta \cdot \mathsf{pf}_1 + \beta^2 \cdot \mathsf{pf}_2 + \beta^3 \cdot \mathsf{pf}_3$
        $+ \beta^4 \cdot (\mathsf{qx}.C_C + \gamma \cdot C_1 + \gamma^2 \cdot C_2)$.
19. $\mathsf{acc}^*.w.s := \mathsf{acc}.w.s + \beta \cdot s^* + \beta^2 \cdot \mathsf{qw}.s$.
20. $\mathsf{acc}^*.w.\sigma_A := \mathsf{acc}.w.\sigma_A + \beta \cdot \omega_A^* + \beta^2 \cdot \mathsf{qw}.\sigma_A$.
21. $\mathsf{acc}^*.w.\sigma_B := \mathsf{acc}.w.\sigma_B + \beta \cdot \omega_B^* + \beta^2 \cdot \mathsf{qw}.\sigma_B$.
22. $\mathsf{acc}^*.w.\sigma_C := \mathsf{acc}.w.\sigma_C + \beta \cdot \omega_C^* + \beta^2 \cdot \mathsf{qw}.\sigma_C$.
23. $\mathsf{acc}^*.w.\sigma_0 := \mathsf{acc}.w.\sigma_0 + \beta^2 \cdot \omega_2^* + \beta^4 \cdot \mathsf{qw}.\sigma_0$.
24. Output $(\mathsf{acc}^*, \mathsf{pf})$.

$\mathsf{V}^{\mathsf{PAS}}(\mathsf{qx}, \mathsf{acc}.x, \mathsf{acc}^*.x, \mathsf{pf})$:

1. $\beta := \rho_{\mathsf{AS}}(\tau, \mathsf{acc}.x, \mathsf{qx}, \mathsf{pf})$.
2. $\gamma := \rho_{\mathsf{NARK}}(\tau, \mathsf{qx})$.
3. $\mathsf{acc}^*.x.x \overset{?}{=} \mathsf{acc}.x.x + \beta \cdot x^* + \beta^2 \cdot \mathsf{qx}.x$.
4. $\mathsf{acc}^*.x.C_A \overset{?}{=} \mathsf{acc}.x.C_A + \beta \cdot C_A^* + \beta^2 \cdot (\mathsf{qx}.C_A + \gamma \cdot \mathsf{qx}.C_A')$.
5. $\mathsf{acc}^*.x.C_B \overset{?}{=} \mathsf{acc}.x.C_B + \beta \cdot C_B^* + \beta^2 \cdot (\mathsf{qx}.C_B + \gamma \cdot \mathsf{qx}.C_B')$.
6. $\mathsf{acc}^*.x.C_C \overset{?}{=} \mathsf{acc}.x.C_C + \beta \cdot C_C^* + \beta^2 \cdot (\mathsf{qx}.C_C + \gamma \cdot \mathsf{qx}.C_C')$.
7. $\mathsf{acc}^*.x.C_0 \overset{?}{=} \mathsf{acc}.x.C_0 + \beta \cdot \mathsf{pf}_1 + \beta^2 \cdot \mathsf{pf}_2 + \beta^3 \cdot \mathsf{pf}_3$
        $+ \beta^4 \cdot (\mathsf{qx}.C_C + \gamma \cdot C_1 + \gamma^2 \cdot C_2)$.

Fig. 4. Accumulation prover and accumulation verifier for the zkNARK for R1CS.

The zkNARK verifier performs two types of computations: linear checks and a Hadamard product check. We describe how to accumulate each of these in the general case.

- *Linear checks.* A split accumulator $\mathsf{acc} = (\mathsf{acc}.x, \mathsf{acc}.w)$ in Sect. 2.3.2 included sub-accumulators for different linear checks: x, C_A, C_B, C_C in $\mathsf{acc}.x$ and $w, \sigma_A, \sigma_B, \sigma_C$ in $\mathsf{acc}.w$. We can keep these components and simply use more random coefficients or, as we do, further powers of the element β. For example, in the accumulation prover P a computation such as $\mathsf{acc}^\star.\mathsf{x}.x := \mathsf{acc}.\mathsf{x}.x + \beta \cdot \mathsf{qx}.x$ is replaced by a computation such as $\mathsf{acc}^\star.\mathsf{x}.x := \sum_{j=1}^{m} \beta^{j-1} \cdot \mathsf{acc}_j.\mathsf{x}.x + \sum_{i=1}^{n} \beta^{m+j-1} \cdot \mathsf{qx}_i.x$.

- *Hadamard product check.* A split accumulator $\mathsf{acc} = (\mathsf{acc}.\mathsf{x}, \mathsf{acc}.\mathsf{w})$ in Sect. 2.3.2 also included a sub-accumulator for the Hadamard product check: $C_\circ$ in $\mathsf{acc}.\mathsf{x}$ and $\sigma_\circ$ in $\mathsf{acc}.\mathsf{w}$. Because a Hadamard product is a *bi*linear operation, combining two Hadamard products via a random coefficient led to a quadratic polynomial whose coefficients include the two original Hadamard products and a cross term. This is indeed why we stored the cross term in the accumulation proof pf. However, if we consider the cross terms that arise from combining more than two Hadamard products (i.e., when $m + n > 2$) then the corresponding polynomials do not lend themselves to accumulation because the original Hadamard products appear together with other cross terms. To handle this issue, we introduce in Sect. 2.5 a new subroutine that accumulates Hadamard products via an additional round of interaction.

2.4   On Proving Knowledge Soundness

In order to construct accumulation schemes that fulfill the type of knowledge soundness that we ultimately need for PCD (see Sect. 2.2), we formulate a new *expected-time forking lemma in the random oracle model*, which is informally stated below. In our setting, $(\mathsf{q}, \mathsf{b}, \mathsf{o}) \in L$ if $\mathsf{o} = ([\mathsf{qx}_i]_{i=1}^{n}, \mathsf{acc}, \mathsf{pf})$ is such that $\mathsf{D}(\mathsf{acc}) = 1$ and, given that $\rho(\mathsf{q}) = \mathsf{b}$, the accumulation verifier accepts: $\mathsf{V}^\rho([\mathsf{qx}_i]_{i=1}^{n}, \mathsf{acc}.\mathsf{x}, \mathsf{pf}) = 1$.

Lemma 1 (informal). *Let L be an efficiently recognizable set. There exists an algorithm* Fork *such that for every expected polynomial time algorithm A and integer $N \in \mathbb{N}$ the following holds. With all but negligible probability over the choice of random oracle ρ, randomness r of A, and randomness of* Fork*, if $A^\rho(r)$ outputs a tuple $(\mathsf{q}, \mathsf{b}, \mathsf{o}) \in L$ with $\rho(\mathsf{q}) = \mathsf{b}$, then* $\mathsf{Fork}^{A,\rho}(1^N, \mathsf{q}, \mathsf{b}, \mathsf{o}, r)$ *outputs $[(\mathsf{b}_j, \mathsf{o}_j)]_{j=1}^{N}$ such that $\mathsf{b}_1, \ldots, \mathsf{b}_N$ are pairwise distinct and for each $j \in [N]$ it holds that $(\mathsf{q}, \mathsf{b}_j, \mathsf{o}_j) \in L$.*

This forking lemma differs from prior forking lemmas in three significant ways. First, it is in the random oracle model rather than the interactive setting (unlike [BCC+16]). Second, we can obtain any polynomial number of accepting transcripts in expected polynomial time with only negligible loss in success probability (unlike forking lemmas for signature schemes, which typically extract two transcripts in strict polynomial time [BN06]). Finally, it holds even if the adversary itself runs in expected (as opposed to strict) polynomial time. This is important for our application to PCD where the extractor in one recursive step becomes the adversary in the next. This last feature requires some care, since the running time of the adversary, and in particular the length of its random tape, may not be bounded.

Moreover, in our security proofs we at times additionally rely on an expected-time variant of the *zero-finding game lemma* from [BCMS20] to show that if a particular polynomial equation holds at a point obtained from the random oracle via a "commitment" to the equation, then it must with overwhelming probability be a polynomial identity. For more details, see the full version.

2.5 Split Accumulation for Hadamard Products

We construct a split accumulation scheme for a predicate Φ_{HP} that considers the Hadamard product of committed vectors. For a commitment key ck for messages in $\mathbb{F}^\ell$, the predicate Φ_{HP} takes as input a predicate instance $\mathsf{qx} = (C_1, C_2, C_3) \in \mathbb{G}^3$ consisting of three Pedersen commitments, a predicate witness $\mathsf{qw} = (a, b, \omega_1, \omega_2, \omega_3)$ consisting of two vectors $a, b \in \mathbb{F}^\ell$ and three opening randomness elements $\omega_1, \omega_2, \omega_3 \in \mathbb{F}$, and checks that $C_1 = \mathsf{CM.Commit}(\mathsf{ck}, a; \omega_1)$, $C_2 = \mathsf{CM.Commit}(\mathsf{ck}, b; \omega_2)$, and $C_3 = \mathsf{CM.Commit}(\mathsf{ck}, a \circ b; \omega_3)$. In other words, C_3 is a commitment to the Hadamard product of the vectors committed in C_1 and C_2.

Theorem 3 (informal). *The Hadamard product predicate Φ_{HP} has a split accumulation scheme $\mathsf{AS_{HP}}$ that is secure in the random oracle model (and assuming the hardness of the discrete logarithm problem) where verifying accumulation requires 5 group scalar multiplications and $O(1)$ field operations per claim, and results in an accumulator whose instance part is 3 group elements and witness part is $O(\ell)$ field elements. Moreover, the accumulation scheme can be made zero knowledge at a sub-constant overhead per claim.*

Below we summarize the ideas behind this result. Our construction directly extends to accumulate any bilinear function (see Remark 4).

A Bivariate Identity.   The accumulation scheme is based on a bivariate polynomial identity, and is the result of turning a public-coin two-round reduction into a non-interactive scheme by using the random oracle. Given n pairs of vectors $[(a_i, b_i)]_{i=1}^n$, consider the following two polynomials with coefficients in $\mathbb{F}^\ell$:

$$a(X, Y) := \sum_{i=1}^n X^{i-1} Y^{i-1} a_i \quad \text{and} \quad b(X) := \sum_{i=1}^n X^{n-i} b_i .$$

The Hadamard product of the two polynomials can be written as

$$a(X, Y) \circ b(X) = \sum_{i=1}^{2n-1} X^{i-1} t_i(Y) \quad \text{where} \quad t_n(Y) = \sum_{i=1}^n Y^{i-1} a_i \circ b_i .$$

The expression of the coefficient polynomials $\{t_i(Y)\}_{i \neq n}$ is not important; instead, the important aspect here is that a coefficient polynomial, namely $t_n(Y)$, includes the Hadamard products of all n pairs of vectors as different coefficients. This identity is the starting point of the accumulation scheme, which informally evaluates this expression at random points to reduce the n Hadamard products to 1 Hadamard product. Similar ideas are used to reduce several Hadamard products to a single inner product in [BCC+16; BBB+18].

Batching Hadamard Products.   We describe a public-coin two-round reduction from n Hadamard product claims to 1 Hadamard product claim. The verifier receives n predicate instances $[\mathsf{qx}_i]_{i=1}^n = [(C_{1,i}, C_{2,i}, C_{3,i})]_{i=1}^n$ each consisting of three Pedersen commitments, and the prover receives corresponding predicate witnesses $[\mathsf{qw}_i]_{i=1}^n = [(a_i, b_i, \omega_{1,i}, \omega_{2,i}, \omega_{3,i})]_{i=1}^n$ containing the corresponding openings.

- The verifier sends a first challenge $\mu \in \mathbb{F}$.
- The prover computes the product polynomial $a(X, \mu) \circ b(X) = \sum_{i=1}^{2n-1} X^{i-1} t_i(\mu) \in \mathbb{F}^\ell[X]$; for each $i \in [2n-1] \setminus \{n\}$, computes the commitment $C_{t,i} := \mathsf{CM.Commit}(\mathsf{ck}, t_i; 0) \in \mathbb{G}$; and sends to the verifier an accumulation proof $\mathsf{pf} := [C_{t,i}, C_{t,n+i}]_{i=1}^{n-1}$.
- The verifier sends a second challenge $\nu \in \mathbb{F}$.
- The verifier computes and outputs a new predicate instance $\mathsf{qx} = (C_1, C_2, C_3)$:

$$C_1 = \sum_{i=1}^n \nu^{i-1} \mu^{i-1} C_{1,i} \ ,$$
$$C_2 = \sum_{i=1}^n \nu^{n-i} C_{2,i} \ ,$$
$$C_3 = \sum_{i=1}^{n-1} \nu^{i-1} C_{t,i} + \nu^{n-1} \sum_{i=1}^n \mu^{i-1} C_{3,i} + \sum_{i=1}^{n-1} \nu^{n+i-1} C_{t,n+i} \ .$$

- The prover computes and outputs a corresponding predicate witness $\mathsf{qw} = (a, b, \omega_1, \omega_2, \omega_3)$:

$$a := \sum_{i=1}^n \nu^{i-1} \mu^{i-1} a_i \qquad\qquad \omega_1 := \sum_{i=1}^n \nu^{i-1} \mu^{i-1} \omega_{1,i} \ ,$$
$$b := \sum_{i=1}^n \nu^{n-i} b_i \qquad\qquad\quad \omega_2 := \sum_{i=1}^n \nu^{n-i} \omega_{2,i} \ ,$$
$$\omega_3 := \nu^{n-1} \sum_{i=1}^n \mu^{i-1} \omega_{3,i} \ .$$

Observe that the new predicate instance $\mathsf{qx} = (C_1, C_2, C_3)$ consists of commitments to $a(\nu, \mu), b(\nu), a(\nu, \mu) \circ b(\nu)$ respectively, and the predicate witness $\mathsf{qw} = (a, b, \omega_1, \omega_2, \omega_3)$ consists of corresponding opening information. The properties of low-degree polynomials imply that if any of the n claims is incorrect (there is $i \in [n]$ such that $\Phi_{\mathsf{HP}}(\mathsf{qx}_i, \mathsf{qw}_i) = 0$) then, with high probability, so is the output claim ($\Phi_{\mathsf{HP}}(\mathsf{qx}, \mathsf{qw}) = 0$).

Split Accumulation. The batching protocol described above yields a split accumulation scheme for Φ_{HP} in the random oracle model. An accumulator acc has the same form as a predicate input $(\mathsf{qx}, \mathsf{qw})$: $\mathsf{acc.x}$ has the same form as a predicate instance qx, and $\mathsf{acc.w}$ has the same form as a predicate witness qw. The accumulation decider D simply equals Φ_{HP} (this is well-defined due to the prior sentence). The accumulation prover and accumulation verifier are as follows.

- The accumulation prover P runs the interactive reduction by relying on the random oracle to generate the random verifier messages (i.e., it applies the Fiat–Shamir transformation to the reduction), in order to produce an accumulation proof pf as well as an accumulator $\mathsf{acc} = (\mathsf{qx}, \mathsf{qw})$ whose instance part is computed like the verifier of the reduction and witness part is computed like the prover of the reduction.
- The accumulation verifier V re-derives the challenges using the random oracle, and checks that qx was correctly derived from $[\mathsf{qx}_i]_{i=1}^n$ (also via the help of the accumulation proof pf).

The construction described above is not zero knowledge. One way to achieve zero knowledge is for the accumulation prover to sample a random predicate input that satisfies the predicate, accumulate it, and include it as part of the accumulation proof pf. In our construction we opt for a more efficient solution, leveraging the fact that we are not actually interested in accumulating the random predicate input.

Efficiency. The efficiency claimed in Theorem 3 is evident from the construction. The (short) instance part of an accumulator consists of 3 group elements, while the (long) witness part of an accumulator consists of $O(\ell)$ field elements. The accumulator verifier V performs 2 random oracle calls, 5 group scalar multiplication, and $O(1)$ field operations per accumulated claim.

Security. Given an adversary that produces Hadamard product claims $[\mathsf{qx}_i]_{i=1}^n = [(C_{1,i}, C_{2,i}, C_{3,i})]_{i=1}^n$, a single Hadamard product claim $\mathsf{qx} = (C_1, C_2, C_3)$ and corresponding witness $\mathsf{qw} = (a, b, \omega_1, \omega_2, \omega_3)$, and an accumulation proof pf that makes the accumulation verifier accept, we need to extract witnesses $[\mathsf{qw}_i]_{i=1}^n = [(a_i, b_i, \omega_{1,i}, \omega_{2,i}, \omega_{3,i})]_{i=1}^n$ for the instances $[\mathsf{qx}_i]_{i=1}^n$. Our security proof works in the random oracle model, assuming hardness of the discrete logarithm problem.

In the proof we apply our expected-time forking lemma *twice* (see Sect. 2.4 for a discussion of this lemma and the full version for details including a corollary that summarizes its double invocation). This lets us construct a two-level tree of transcripts with branching factor n on the first challenge μ and branching factor $2n - 1$ on the second challenge ν. Given such a transcript tree, the extractor works as follows:

1. Using the transcripts corresponding to challenges $\{(\mu_1, \nu_{1,k})\}_{k \in [n]}$ we extract ℓ-element vectors $[a_i]_{i=1}^n, [b_i]_{i=1}^n$ and field elements $[\omega_{1,i}]_{i=1}^n, [\omega_{2,i}]_{i=1}^n$ such that $[a_i]_{i=1}^n$ and $[b_i]_{i=1}^n$ are committed in $[C_{1,i}]_{i=1}^n$ and $[C_{2,i}]_{i=1}^n$ under randomness $[\omega_{1,i}]_{i=1}^n$ and $[\omega_{2,i}]_{i=1}^n$, respectively.
2. Define $a(X, Y) := \sum_{i=1}^n X^{i-1} Y^{i-1} a_i \in \mathbb{F}^\ell[X, Y]$ and $b(X) := \sum_{i=1}^n X^{n-i} b_i \in \mathbb{F}^\ell[X]$, using the vectors extracted above; then let $t_i(Y)$ be the coefficient of X^{i-1} in $a(X, Y) \circ b(X)$. For each $j \in [n]$, using the transcripts corresponding to challenges $\{(\mu_j, \nu_{j,k})\}_{k \in [2n-1]}$, we extract field elements $[\tau_i^{(j)}]_{i=1}^{2n-1}$ such that $t_n(\mu_j)$ is committed in $\sum_{i=1}^{n-1} \mu_j^{i-1} C_{3,i}$ under randomness $\tau_n^{(j)}$ and $[t_i(\mu_j), t_{n+i}(\mu_j)]_{i=1}^{n-1}$ are committed in $\mathsf{pf}^{(j)} := [C_{t,i}^{(j)}, C_{t,n+i}^{(j)}]_{i=1}^{n-1}$ under randomness $[\tau_i^{(j)}, \tau_{n+i}^{(j)}]_{i=1}^{n-1}$ respectively.
3. Compute the solution $[\omega_{3,i}]_{i=1}^n$ to the linear system $\{\tau_n^{(j)} = \sum_{i=1}^{n-1} \mu_j^{i-1} \omega_{3,i}\}_{j \in [n]}$. Together with the relation $\{t_n(\mu_j) = \sum_{i=1}^{n-1} \mu_j^{i-1} a_i \circ b_i\}_{j \in [n]}$, we deduce that $C_{3,i}$ is a commitment to $a_i \circ b_i$ under randomness $\omega_{3,i}$ for all $i \in [n]$.
4. For each $i \in [n]$, output $\mathsf{qw}_i := (a_i, b_i, \omega_{1,i}, \omega_{2,i}, \omega_{3,i})$.

Remark 4 (extension to any bilinear operation). The ideas described above extend, in a straightforward way, to accumulating *any bilinear operation* of

702   B. Bünz et al.

committed vectors. Let $f\colon \mathbb{F}^\ell \times \mathbb{F}^\ell \to \mathbb{F}^m$ be a bilinear operation, i.e., such that: (a) $f(a + a', b) = f(a, b) + f(a', b)$; (b) $f(a, b + b') = f(a, b) + f(a, b')$; (c) $\alpha \cdot f(a, b) = f(\alpha a, b) = f(a, \alpha b)$. Let Φ_f be the predicate that takes as input a predicate instance $\mathsf{qx} = (C_1, C_2, C_3) \in \mathbb{G}^3$ consisting of three Pedersen commitments, a predicate witness $\mathsf{qw} = (a, b, \omega_1, \omega_2, \omega_3)$ consisting of two vectors $a, b \in \mathbb{F}^\ell$ and three opening randomness elements $\omega_1, \omega_2, \omega_3 \in \mathbb{F}$, and checks that $C_1 = \mathsf{CM.Commit}(\mathsf{ck}_\ell, a; \omega_1)$, $C_2 = \mathsf{CM.Commit}(\mathsf{ck}_\ell, b; \omega_2)$, and $C_3 = \mathsf{CM.Commit}(\mathsf{ck}_m, f(a, b); \omega_3)$. The Hadamard product $\circ \colon \mathbb{F}^\ell \times \mathbb{F}^\ell \to \mathbb{F}^\ell$ is a bilinear operation, as is the scalar product $\langle \cdot, \cdot \rangle \colon \mathbb{F}^\ell \times \mathbb{F}^\ell \to \mathbb{F}$. Our accumulation scheme for Hadamard products works the same way, mutatis mutandis, for a general bilinear map f.

2.6 Split Accumulation for Pedersen Polynomial Commitments

We construct an efficient split accumulation scheme $\mathsf{AS_{PC}}$ for a predicate Φ_{PC} that checks a polynomial evaluation claim for a "trivial" polynomial commitment scheme $\mathsf{PC_{Ped}}$ based on Pedersen commitments (see Fig. 5). In more detail, for a Pedersen commitment key ck for messages in $\mathbb{F}^{d+1}$, the predicate Φ_{PC} takes as input a predicate instance $\mathsf{qx} = (C, z, v) \in \mathbb{G} \times \mathbb{F} \times \mathbb{F}$ and a predicate witness $\mathsf{qw} = p \in \mathbb{F}^{\leq d}[X]$, and checks that $C = \mathsf{CM.Commit}(\mathsf{ck}, p)$, $p(z) = v$, and $\deg(p) \leq d$. In other words, the predicate Φ_{PC} checks that the polynomial p of degree at most d committed in C evaluates to v at z.

- *Setup:* On input $\lambda, D \in \mathbb{N}$, output $\mathsf{pp}_{\mathsf{CM}} \leftarrow \mathsf{CM.Setup}(1^\lambda, D + 1)$.
- *Trim:* On input $\mathsf{pp}_{\mathsf{CM}}$ and $d \in \mathbb{N}$, check that $d \leq D$, set $\mathsf{ck} := \mathsf{CM.Trim}(\mathsf{pp}_{\mathsf{CM}}, d + 1)$, and output $(\mathsf{ck}, \mathsf{rk} := \mathsf{ck})$.
- *Commit:* On input ck and $p \in \mathbb{F}[X]$ of degree at most $|\mathsf{ck}| - 1$, output $C \leftarrow \mathsf{CM.Commit}(\mathsf{ck}, p)$.
- *Open:* On input (ck, p, C, z), output $\pi := p$.
- *Check:* On input $(\mathsf{rk}, (C, z, v), \pi = p)$, check that $C = \mathsf{CM.Commit}(\mathsf{rk}, p)$, $p(z) = v$, and $\deg(p) < |\mathsf{rk}|$.

Completeness of $\mathsf{PC_{Ped}}$ follows from that of CM, while extractability follows from the binding property of CM.

Fig. 5. $\mathsf{PC_{Ped}}$ is a trivial polynomial commitment scheme based on the Pedersen commitment scheme CM.

Theorem 4 (informal). *The* **(Pedersen) polynomial commitment predicate** Φ_{PC} *has a split accumulation scheme* $\mathsf{AS_{PC}}$ *that is secure in the random oracle model (and assuming the hardness of the discrete logarithm problem). Verifying accumulation requires 2 group scalar multiplications and $O(1)$ field additions/multiplications per claim, and results in an accumulator whose instance part is 1 group element and 2 field elements and whose witness part is d field elements. (See Table 1)*

One can use $\mathsf{AS_{PC}}$ to obtain a split accumulation scheme for a different NARK; see Remark 5 for details.

In Table 1 we compare the efficiency of our split accumulation scheme $\mathsf{AS}_{\mathsf{PC}}$ for the predicate $\varPhi_{\mathsf{PC}}$ with the efficiency of the atomic accumulation scheme $\mathsf{AS}_{\mathsf{IPA}}$ [BCMS20] for the equivalent predicate defined by the check algorithm of the (succinct) PC scheme $\mathsf{PC}_{\mathsf{IPA}}$ based on the inner-product argument on cyclic groups [BCC+16; BBB+18; WTS+18]. The takeaway is that the accumulation verifier for $\mathsf{AS}_{\mathsf{PC}}$ is significantly cheaper than the accumulation verifier for $\mathsf{AS}_{\mathsf{IPA}}$.

Technical details are in the full version; in the rest of this section we sketch the ideas behind Theorem 4.

Table 1. Efficiency comparison between the atomic accumulation scheme $\mathsf{AS}_{\mathsf{IPA}}$ for $\mathsf{PC}_{\mathsf{IPA}}$ in [BCMS20] and the split accumulation scheme $\mathsf{AS}_{\mathsf{PC}}$ for $\mathsf{PC}_{\mathsf{Ped}}$ in this work. Above $\mathbb{G}$ denotes group scalar multiplications or group elements, and $\mathbb{F}$ denotes field operations or field elements.(†: $\mathsf{AS}_{\mathsf{IPA}}$ relies on knowledge soundness of $\mathsf{PC}_{\mathsf{IPA}}$, which results from applying the Fiat–Shamir transformation to a logarithmic-round protocol. The security of this protocol has only been proven via a superpolynomial-time extractor [BMM+19] or in the algebraic group model [GT20].)

Accumulation scheme	Type	Assumption	Accumulation prover (per claim)	Accumulation verifier (per claim)	Accumulation decider	Accumulator size instance	witness
$\mathsf{AS}_{\mathsf{IPA}}$ [BCMS20]	atomic	DLOG + RO †	$O(\log d)\ \mathbb{G}$ $O(d)\ \mathbb{F}$ $[+O(d)\ \mathbb{G}$ per accumulation$]$	$O(\log d)\ \mathbb{G}$ $O(\log d)\ \mathbb{F}$ $O(\log d)\ \mathrm{RO}$	$O(d)\ \mathbb{G}$ $O(d)\ \mathbb{F}$	$1\ \mathbb{G}$ $O(\log d)\ \mathbb{F}$	0
$\mathsf{AS}_{\mathsf{PC}}$ [this work]	split	DLOG + RO	$O(d)\ \mathbb{G}$ $O(d)\ \mathbb{F}$	$2\ \mathbb{G}$ $O(1)\ \mathbb{F}$ $2\ \mathrm{RO}$	$O(d)\ \mathbb{G}$ $O(d)\ \mathbb{F}$	$1\ \mathbb{G}$ $2\ \mathbb{F}$	$d\ \mathbb{F}$

First we describe a simple public-coin interactive reduction for combining two or more evaluation claims into a single evaluation claim, and then explain how this interactive reduction gives rise to the split accumulation scheme. We prove security in the random oracle model, using an expected-time extractor.

Batching Evaluation Claims. First consider two evaluation claims (C_1, z, v_1) and (C_2, z, v_2) for the *same* evaluation point z (and degree d). We can use a random challenge $\alpha \in \mathbb{F}$ to combine these claims into one claim (C', z, v') where $C' := C_1 + \alpha C_2$ and $v' := v_1 + \alpha v_2$. If either of the original claims does not hold then, with high probability over the choice of α, neither does the new claim. This idea extends to any number of claims for the same evaluation point, by taking $C' := \sum_i \alpha^i C_i$ and $v' := \sum_i \alpha^i v_i$.

Next consider two evaluation claims (C_1, z_1, v_1) and (C_2, z_2, v_2) at (possibly) different evaluation points z_1 and z_2. We explain how these can be combined into four claims all at the *same* point. Below we use the fact that $p(z) = v$ if and only if there exists a polynomial $w(X)$ such that $p(X) = w(X) \cdot (X - z) + v$.

Let $p_1(X)$ and $p_2(X)$ be the polynomials "inside" C_1 and C_2, respectively, that are known to the prover.

1. The prover computes the witness polynomials $w_1 := \frac{p_1(X) - v_1}{X - z_1}$ and $w_2 := \frac{p_2(X) - v_2}{X - z_2}$ and sends the commitments $W_1 := \mathsf{Commit}(w_1)$ and $W_2 := \mathsf{Commit}(w_2)$.

2. The verifier sends a random evaluation point $z^* \in \mathbb{F}$.
3. The prover computes and sends the evaluations $y_1 := p_1(z^*), y_2 := p_2(z^*)$, $y_1' := w_1(z^*), y_2' := w_2(z^*)$.
4. The verifier checks the relation between each witness polynomial and the original polynomial at the random evaluation point z^*:

$$y_1 = y_1' \cdot (z^* - z_1) + y_1' \quad \text{and} \quad y_2 = y_2' \cdot (z^* - z_2) + y_2' \ .$$

Next, the verifier outputs four evaluation claims for $p_1(z^*) = y_1, p_2(z^*) = y_2, w_1(z^*) = y_1', w_2(z^*) = y_2'$:

$$(C_1, z^*, y_1) \ , \ (C_2, z^*, y_2) \ , \ (W_1, z^*, y_1') \ , \ (W_2, z^*, y_2') \ .$$

More generally, we can reduce m evaluation claims at m points to $2m$ evaluation claims all at the same point.

By combining the two techniques, one obtains a public-coin interactive reduction from any number of evaluation claims (regardless of evaluation points) to a single evaluation claim.

Split Accumulation. The batching protocol described above yields a split accumulation scheme for Φ_{PC} in the random oracle model. An accumulator acc has the same form as a predicate input: the instance part is an evaluation claim and the witness part is a polynomial. Next we describe the algorithms of the accumulation scheme.

- The accumulation prover P runs the interactive reduction by relying on the random oracle to generate the random verifier messages (i.e., it applies the Fiat–Shamir transformation to the reduction), in order to combine the instance parts of old accumulators and inputs to obtain the instance part of a new accumulator. Then P also combines the committed polynomials using the same linear combinations in order to derive the new committed polynomial, which is the witness part of the new accumulator. The accumulation proof pf consists of the messages to the verifier in the reduction, which includes the commitments to the witness polynomials W_i and the evaluations y_i, y_i' at z^* of p_i, w_i (that is, pf $:= [(W_i, y_i, y_i')]_{i=1}^n$).
- The accumulation verifier V checks that the challenges were correctly computed from the random oracle, and performs the checks of the reduction (the claims were correctly combined and that the proper relation between each y_i, y_i', z_i, z^* holds).
- The accumulation decider D reads the accumulator in its entirety and checks that the polynomial (the witness part) satisfies the evaluation claim (the instance part). (Here the random oracle is not used.)

Efficiency. The efficiency claimed in Theorem 4 (and Table 1) is evident from the construction. The accumulation prover P computes $n + m$ commitments to polynomials when combining n old accumulators and m predicate inputs (all polynomials are for degree at most d). The (short) instance part of an accumulator consists of 1 group element and 2 field elements, while the (long) witness part of an accumulator consists of $O(d)$ field elements. The accumulator decider D computes 1 commitment (and 1 polynomial evaluation at 1 point) in order to validate an accumulator. Finally, the cost of running the accumulator verifier V is dominated by $2(n + m)$ scalar multiplication of the linear commitments.

Security. Given an adversary that produces evaluation claims $[\mathsf{qx}_i]_{i=1}^n = [(C_i, z_i, v_i)]_{i=1}^n$, a single claim $\mathsf{qx} = (C, z, v)$ and polynomial $\mathsf{qw} = s(X)$ with $s(z^*) = v$ to which C is a commitment, and accumulation proof pf that makes the accumulation verifier accept, we need to extract polynomials $[\mathsf{qw}_i]_{i=1}^n = [p_i(X)]_{i=1}^n$ with $p_i(z_i) = v_i$ to which C_i is a commitment. Our security proof (in the full version) works in the random oracle model, assuming hardness of the discrete logarithm problem.

In the proof, we apply our expected-time forking lemma (see Sect. 2.4) to obtain $2n$ polynomials $[s^{(j)}]_{j=1}^{2n}$ for the same evaluation point z^* but distinct challenges α_j, where n is the number of evaluation claims. The checks in the reduction procedure imply that $s^{(j)}(X) = \sum_{i=1}^n \alpha_j^i p_i(X) + \sum_{i=1}^n \alpha_j^{n+i} w_i(X)$, where $w_i(X)$ is the witness corresponding to $p_i(X)$; hence we can recover the $p_i(X), w_i(X)$ by solving a linear system (given by the Vandermonde matrix in the challenges $[\alpha_j]_{j=1}^{2n}$). We then use an expected-time variant of the zero-finding game lemma from [BCMS20] (see the full version) to show that if a particular polynomial equation on $p_i(X), w_i(X)$ holds at the point z^* obtained from the random oracle, it must with overwhelming probability be an identity. Applying this to the equation induced by the reduction shows that, with high probability, each extracted polynomial p_i satisfies the corresponding evaluation claim (C_i, z_i, v_i).

Remark 5 (from $\mathsf{PC_{Ped}}$ *to an accumulatable NARK).* If one replaced the (succinct) polynomial commitment scheme that underlies the preprocessing zkSNARK in [CHM+20] with the aforementioned (non-succinct) trivial Pedersen polynomial commitment scheme then (after some adjustments and using our Theorem 4) one would obtain a zkNARK for R1CS with a split accumulation scheme whose accumulation verifier *is* of constant size but other asymptotics would be worse compared to Theorem 2.

First, the cryptographic costs and the quasilinear costs of the NARK and accumulation scheme would also grow in the number K of non-zero entries in the coefficient matrices, which can be much larger than M and N (asymptotically and concretely). Second, the NARK prover would additionally use a quasilinear number of field operations due to FFTs. Finally, in addition to poorer asymptotics, this approach would lead to a concretely more expensive accumulation verifier and overall a more complex protocol.

Nevertheless, one *can* design a concretely efficient zkNARK for R1CS based on the Pedersen PC scheme and our accumulation scheme for it. This naturally leads to an alternative construction to the one in Sect. 2.3 (which is instead based on accumulation of Hadamard products), and would lead to a slightly more expensive prover (which now would use FFTs) and a slightly cheaper accumulation verifier (a smaller number of group scalar multiplications). We leave this as an exercise for the interested reader.

2.7 Implementation and Evaluation

We elaborate on our implementation and evaluation of accumulation schemes and their application to PCD.

The Case for a PCD Framework. Different PCD constructions offer different trade-offs. The tradeoffs are both about asymptotics (see Remark 3) and about practical concerns, as we review below.

- *PCD from sublinear verification* [BCCT13; BCTV14; COS20] is typically instantiated via preprocessing SNARKs based on pairings.[6] This route offers excellent verifier time (a few milliseconds regardless of the computation at a PCD node), but requires a private-coin setup (which complicates deployment) and cycles of pairing-friendly elliptic curves (which are costly in terms of group arithmetic and size).
- *PCD from atomic accumulation* [BCMS20] can, e.g., be instantiated via SNARKs based on cyclic groups [BGH19]. This route offers a transparent setup (easy to deploy) and logarithmic-size arguments (a few kilobytes even for large computations), using cycles of standard elliptic curves (more efficient than their pairing-friendly counterparts). On the other hand, this route yields linear verification times (expensive for large computations) and logarithmic costs for accumulation (increasing the cost of recursion).
- *PCD from split accumulation* (this work) can, e.g., be instantiated via NARKs based on cyclic groups. This route still offers a transparent setup and allows using cycles of standard elliptic curves. Moreover, it offers constant costs for accumulation, but at the expense of argument size, which is now linear.

It would be desirable to have a *single framework that supports different PCD constructions via a modular composition of simpler building blocks*. Such a framework would enable a number of desirable features: (a) ease of replacing older building blocks with new ones; (b) ease of prototyping different PCD constructions for different applications (which may have different needs), thereby enabling practitioners to make informed choices about which PCD construction is best for them; (c) simpler and more efficient auditing of complex cryptographic systems with many intermixed layers. (Realizing even a single PCD construction is a substantial implementation task.); and (d) separation of "application" logic from the underlying recursion via a common PCD interface. Together, these features would enable further industrial deployment of PCD, as well as making future research and comparisons simpler.

Implementation. The above considerations motivated our implementation efforts for PCD. Our code base has two main parts, one for realizing accumulation schemes and another for realizing PCD from accumulation (the latter is integrated with PCD from succinct verification under a unified PCD interface).

---

[6] Instantiations based on hashes are also possible [COS20] but are (post-quantum and) less efficient.

- *Framework for accumulation.* We designed a modular framework for (atomic and split) accumulation schemes, and use it to implement, under a common interface, several accumulation schemes: (a) the atomic accumulation scheme $\mathsf{AS}_{\mathsf{AGM}}$ in [BCMS20] for the PC scheme $\mathsf{PC}_{\mathsf{AGM}}$; (b) the atomic accumulation scheme $\mathsf{AS}_{\mathsf{IPA}}$ in [BCMS20] for the PC scheme $\mathsf{PC}_{\mathsf{IPA}}$; (c) the split accumulation scheme $\mathsf{AS}_{\mathsf{PC}}$ in this paper for the PC scheme $\mathsf{PC}_{\mathsf{Ped}}$; (d) the split accumulation scheme $\mathsf{AS}_{\mathsf{HP}}$ in this paper for the Hadamard product predicate Φ_{HP}; (e) the split accumulation scheme for our NARK for R1CS. Our framework also provides a generic method for defining R1CS constraints for the verifiers of these accumulation schemes; we leverage this to implement R1CS constraints for all of these accumulation schemes.
- *PCD from accumulation.* We use the foregoing framework to implement a generic construction of PCD from accumulation. We support the PCD construction of [BCMS20] (which uses atomic accumulation) and the PCD construction in this paper (which uses split accumulation). Our code builds on, and extends, an existing PCD library.[7] Our implementation is modular: it takes as ingredients an implementation of any NARK, an implementation of any accumulation scheme for that NARK, and constraints for the accumulation verifier, and produces a concrete PCD construction. This allows us, for example, to obtain a PCD instantiation based on our NARK for R1CS and its split accumulation scheme.

Evaluation for DL Setting. When realizing PCD in practice the main goal is to "minimize the cost of recursion", that is, to minimize the number of constraints that need to be recursively proved in each PCD step (excluding the constraints for the application) without hurting other parameters too much (prover time, argument size, and so on). We evaluate our implementation with respect to this goal, with a focus on understanding the trade-offs between atomic and split accumulation *in the discrete logarithm setting.*

The DL setting is of particular interest to practitioners, as it leads to systems with a transparent (public-coin) setup that can be based on efficient cycles of (standard) elliptic curves [BGH19;Hop20]; indeed, some projects are developing real-world systems that use PCD in the DL setting [Halo20;Pickles20]. The main drawback of the DL setting is that verification time (and sometimes argument size) is linear in a PCD node's computation. This inefficiency is, however, tolerable if a PCD node's computation is not too large, as is the case in the aforementioned projects. (Especially so when taking into account the disadvantages of PCD based on pairings, which involves relying on a private-coin setup and more expensive curve cycles.)

We evaluate our implementation to answer two questions: (a) how efficient is recursion with split accumulation for our simple zkNARK for R1CS? (b) what is the constraint cost of split accumulation for $\mathsf{PC}_{\mathsf{Ped}}$ compared to atomic accumulation for $\mathsf{PC}_{\mathsf{IPA}}$? All our experiments are performed over the 255-bit Pallas curve in the Pasta cycle of curves [Hop20], which is used by real-world deployments.

---

[7] https://github.com/arkworks-rs/pcd.

– *Split accumulation for R1CS.* Our evaluation demonstrates that the cost of
  recursion for IVC with our split accumulation scheme for the simple NARK
  for R1CS is low, both with zero knowledge ($\sim 99 \times 10^3$ constraints) and without ($\sim 52 \times 10^3$ constraints). In fact, this cost is even lower than the cost
  of IVC based on highly efficient pairing-based circuit-specific SNARKs. Furthermore, like in the pairing-based case, this cost does not grow with the size
  of computation being checked. This is much better than prior constructions
  of IVC based on atomic accumulation for $\mathsf{PC}_{\mathsf{IPA}}$ in the DL setting, as we will
  see next.
– *Comparison of accumulation for PC schemes.* Several (S)NARKs are built
  from PC schemes, and the primary cost of recursion for these is determined
  by the cost of accumulation for the PC scheme. In light of this we compare
  the costs of two accumulation schemes:
  - the atomic accumulation scheme for the PC scheme $\mathsf{PC}_{\mathsf{IPA}}$ [BCMS20];
  - the new split accumulation scheme for $\mathsf{PC}_{\mathsf{Ped}}$.
  Our evaluation demonstrates that the constraint cost of the $\mathsf{AS}_{\mathsf{PC}}$ accumulation verifier is 8 to 20 times cheaper than that of the $\mathsf{AS}_{\mathsf{IPA}}$ accumulation
  verifier. In Fig. 6 we report the asymptotic cost of $|V|$ (the constraint cost of
  V) in $\mathsf{AS}_{\mathsf{IPA}}$, $\mathsf{AS}_{\mathsf{PC}}$, and $\mathsf{AS}_{\mathsf{R1CS}}$.[8]

We note that the cost of all the aforementioned accumulation schemes is
dominated by the cost of many common subcomponents, and so improvements

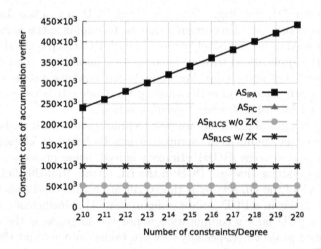

Fig. 6. Comparison of the constraint cost of the accumulation verifier V in $\mathsf{AS}_{\mathsf{IPA}}$, $\mathsf{AS}_{\mathsf{PC}}$,
and $\mathsf{AS}_{\mathsf{R1CS}}$ when varying the number of constraints (for $\mathsf{AS}_{\mathsf{R1CS}}$) or the degree of the
accumulated polynomial (for $\mathsf{AS}_{\mathsf{IPA}}$ and $\mathsf{AS}_{\mathsf{PC}}$) from 2^{10} to 2^{20}. Note that the cost of
accumulating $\mathsf{PC}_{\mathsf{IPA}}$ and $\mathsf{PC}_{\mathsf{Ped}}$ is a lower bound on the cost of accumulating any SNARK
built atop those, and this enables comparing against the cost of $\mathsf{AS}_{\mathsf{R1CS}}$.

---

[8] This comparison is meaningful because the cost of accumulating polynomial com-
    mitments provides a lower bound on the cost accumulating SNARKs that rely on
    these PC schemes.

in these subcomponents will preserve the relative cost. For example, applying existing techniques [Halo20; Pickles20] for optimizing the constraint cost of elliptic curve scalar multiplications should benefit all our schemes in a similar way.

Acknowledgements. This research was supported in part by the Ethereum Foundation, NSF, DARPA, a grant from ONR, and the Simons Foundation. Nicholas Spooner was supported by DARPA under Agreement No. HR00112020023.

References

[BBB+18] Bünz, B., Bootle, J., Boneh, D., Poelstra, A., Wuille, P., Maxwell, G.: Bulletproofs: short proofs for confidential transactions and more. In: S& P 2018 (2018)

[BCC+16] Bootle, J., Cerulli, A., Chaidos, P., Groth, J., Petit, C.: Efficient zero-knowledge arguments for arithmetic circuits in the discrete log setting. In: Fischlin, M., Coron, J.-S. (eds.) EUROCRYPT 2016. LNCS, vol. 9666, pp. 327–357. Springer, Heidelberg (2016). https://doi.org/10.1007/978-3-662-49896-5_12

[BCCT13] Bitansky, N., Canetti, R., Chiesa, A., Tromer, E.: Recursive composition and bootstrapping for SNARKs and proof-carrying data. In: STOC 2013 (2013)

[BCL+20] Bünz, B., Chiesa, A., Lin, W., Mishra, P., Spooner, N.: Proof-carrying data without succinct arguments. In: IACR Cryptol. ePrint Arch. (2020). https://eprint.iacr.org/2020/1618

[BCMS20] Bünz, B., Chiesa, A., Mishra, P., Spooner, N.: Proof-carrying data from accumulation schemes. In: TCC 2020 (2020)

[BCTV14] Ben-Sasson, E., Chiesa, A., Tromer, E., Virza, M.: Scalable zero knowledge via cycles of elliptic curves. Algorithmica **79**(4), 1102–1160 (2016). https://doi.org/10.1007/s00453-016-0221-0

[BDFG20] Boneh, D., Drake, J., Fisch, B., Gabizon, A.: Halo Infinite: Recursive zk-SNARKs from any Additive Polynomial Commitment Scheme. Cryptology ePrint Archive, Report 2020/1536

[BGH19] Bowe, S., Grigg, J., Hopwood, D.: Halo: Recursive Proof Composition without a Trusted Setup. Cryptology ePrint Archive, Report 2019/1021

[BMM+19] Bünz, B., Maller, M., Mishra, P., Tyagi, N., Vesely, P.: Proofs for Inner Pairing Products and Applications. Cryptology ePrint Archive, Report 2019/1177

[BMRS20] Bonneau, J., Meckler, I., Rao, V., Shapiro, E.: Coda: Decentralized Cryptocurrency at Scale. Cryptology ePrint Archive, Report 2020/352

[BN06] Bellare, M., Neven, G.: Multi-signatures in the plain public-Key model and a general forking lemma. In: CCS 2006 (2006)

[CCDW20] Chen, W., Chiesa, A., Dauterman, E., Ward, N.P.: Reducing Participation Costs via Incremental Verification for Ledger Systems. Cryptology ePrint Archive, Report 2020/1522

[CHM+20] Chiesa, A., Hu, Y., Maller, M., Mishra, P., Vesely, N., Ward, N.: Marlin: Preprocessing zkSNARKs with Universal and Updatable SRS. In: EUROCRYPT 2020 (2020)

[COS20] Chiesa, A., Ojha, D., Spooner, N.: Fractal: Post-Quantum and Transparent Recursive Proofs from Holography. In: EUROCRYPT 2020 (2020)

[CT10]   Chiesa, A., Tromer, E.: Proof-Carrying Data and Hearsay Arguments from Signature Cards. In: ICS 2010 (2010)

[CTV13] Chong, S., Tromer, E., Vaughan, J.A.: Enforcing Language Semantics Using Proof-Carrying Data. Cryptology ePrint Archive, Report 2013/513

[CTV15] Chiesa, A., Tromer, E., Virza, M.: Cluster computing in zero knowledge. In: Oswald, E., Fischlin, M. (eds.) EUROCRYPT 2015. LNCS, vol. 9057, pp. 371–403. Springer, Heidelberg (2015). https://doi.org/10.1007/978-3-662-46803-6_13

[Gro16] Groth, J.: On the size of pairing-based non-interactive arguments. In: Fischlin, M., Coron, J.-S. (eds.) EUROCRYPT 2016. LNCS, vol. 9666, pp. 305–326. Springer, Heidelberg (2016). https://doi.org/10.1007/978-3-662-49896-5_11

[GT20]   Ghoshal, A., Tessaro, S.: Tight State-Restoration Soundness in the Algebraic Group Model. Cryptology ePrint Archive, Report 2020/1351

[Halo20] Bowe, S., Grigg, J., Hopwood, D.: Halo2 (2020). https://github.com/zcash/halo2

[Hop20] Hopwood, D.: The Pasta Curves for Halo 2 and Beyond. https://electriccoin.co/blog/the-pasta-curves-for-halo-2-and-beyond/

[KB20]   Kattis, A., Bonneau, J.: Proof of Necessary Work: Succinct State Verification with Fairness Guarantees. Cryptology ePrint Archive, Report 2020/190

[Mina]   O(1) Labs. "Mina Cryptocurrency". https://minaprotocol.com/

[NT16]   Naveh, A., Tromer, E.: PhotoProof: cryptographic image authentication for any set of permissible transformations. In: S& P 2016 (2016)

[Pickles20] O(1) Labs. Pickles. https://github.com/o1-labs/marlin

[Val08] Valiant, P.: Incrementally verifiable computation or proofs of knowledge imply time/space efficiency. In: Canetti, R. (ed.) TCC 2008. LNCS, vol. 4948, pp. 1–18. Springer, Heidelberg (2008). https://doi.org/10.1007/978-3-540-78524-8_1

[WTS+18] Wahby, R.S., Tzialla, I., Shelat, A., Thaler, J., Walfish, M.: Doubly- efficient zkSNARKs without trusted setup. In: S& P 2018 (2018)

Subquadratic SNARGs in the Random Oracle Model

Alessandro Chiesa[1(✉)] and Eylon Yogev[2,3]

[1] UC Berkeley, Berkeley, USA
alexch@berkeley.edu
[2] BU, Boston, USA
[3] TAU, Tel Aviv, Israel

Abstract. In a seminal work, Micali (FOCS 1994) gave the first succinct non-interactive argument (SNARG) in the random oracle model (ROM). The construction combines a PCP and a cryptographic commitment, and has several attractive features: it is plausibly post-quantum; it can be heuristically instantiated via lightweight cryptography; and it has a transparent (public-coin) parameter setup. However, it also has a significant drawback: a large argument size.

In this work, we provide a new construction that achieves a smaller argument size. This is the first progress on the Micali construction since it was introduced over 25 years ago.

A SNARG in the ROM is (t, ϵ)-*secure* if every t-query malicious prover can convince the verifier of a false statement with probability at most ϵ. For (t, ϵ)-security, the argument size of all known SNARGs in the ROM (including Micali's) is $\tilde{O}((\log(t/\epsilon))^2)$ bits, *even* if one were to rely on conjectured probabilistic proofs well beyond current techniques. In practice, these costs lead to SNARGs that are much larger than constructions based on other (pre-quantum and costly) tools. This has led many to believe that SNARGs in the ROM are inherently quadratic.

We show that this is not the case. We present a SNARG in the ROM with a sub-quadratic argument size: $\tilde{O}(\log(t/\epsilon) \cdot \log t)$. Our construction relies on a strong soundness notion for PCPs and a weak binding notion for commitments. We hope that our work paves the way for understanding if a linear argument size, that is $O(\log(t/\epsilon))$, is achievable in the ROM.

Keywords: Succinct arguments · Random oracle · Probabilistically checkable proofs

1 Introduction

A succinct non-interactive argument (SNARG) is a cryptographic proof system for non-deterministic languages whose communication complexity is "succinct" in the sense that it is sublinear in the witness size (or even in the size of the computation that checks the witness). In the last decade, SNARGs have drawn

© International Association for Cryptologic Research 2021
T. Malkin and C. Peikert (Eds.): CRYPTO 2021, LNCS 12825, pp. 711–741, 2021.
https://doi.org/10.1007/978-3-030-84242-0_25

the attention of researchers from multiple communities, being a fundamental cryptographic primitive that has found applications in the real world.

A central goal in the study of SNARGs is improving their efficiency, which may include improving prover time, argument size, or verifier time. For example, achieving small argument size is crucial in real-world applications where SNARGs are broadcast in a peer-to-peer network and redundantly stored at every network node (as in privacy-preserving digital currencies [BCG+14, Ele14]).

SNARGs in the ROM. The goal of this paper is to improve the argument size of SNARGs in the random oracle model (ROM). A SNARG in the ROM is (t, ϵ)-*secure* if every malicious prover that makes at most t queries to the random oracle can convince the verifier of a false statement with probability at most ϵ (over the choice of random oracle). There are two known approaches to construct SNARGs in the ROM: the Micali transformation [Mic00] (building on [Kil92, FS86]), which uses probabilistically checkable proofs (PCPs); and the BCS transformation [BCS16], which uses public-coin interactive oracle proofs (IOPs). Both approaches adopt the same paradigm:

$$\begin{bmatrix} \text{information-theoretic} \\ \text{proof} \end{bmatrix} + \begin{bmatrix} \text{cryptographic commitment} \\ \text{with local opening} \end{bmatrix} \implies \text{SNARG}.$$

Informally, they compile an information-theoretic proof system (PCP or IOP) into a SNARG by relying on a cryptographic commitment scheme that supports local openings. The commitment scheme is a Merkle tree, and each local opening is a path from the desired leaf to the root.

Quadratic Argument Size. In both approaches, the argument size is *quadratic* in the desired security. If the random oracle has output length λ, then compiling a PCP/IOP with proof length l over alphabet Σ and query complexity q leads to an argument of size that is (up to constants):

$$\underbrace{q \cdot \log |\Sigma|}_{\text{information-theoretic proof}} + \underbrace{q \cdot \lambda \cdot \log l}_{\text{cryptographic commitment}} .$$

The term $q \cdot \log |\Sigma|$ is the cost of the information-theoretic proof, and the term $q \cdot \lambda \cdot \log l$ is the cost of the cryptographic commitment (q authentication paths each consisting of $\log l$ digests of size λ). To achieve (t, ϵ) security, the oracle output size is set to $\lambda = O(\log(t/\epsilon))$, and the soundness error of the PCP/IOP must be $O(\epsilon/t)$. For example, a PCP with this soundness error can be obtained by repeating $O(\log(t/\epsilon))$ times the verifier of any constant-query constant-soundness base PCP. This leads to a PCP with query complexity $q = O(\log(t/\epsilon))$, and in turn to a quadratic argument size: $\tilde{O}((\log(t/\epsilon))^2)$. The quadratic complexity is due to the cost of the cryptographic commitment (while, for a small enough alphabet, the cost of the information-theoretic proof is linear).

One might hope to reduce the number of queries of the PCP/IOP to overcome this "quadratic barrier", at the expense of a larger alphabet (even an alphabet of size $2^{O(\lambda)}$ would have a negligible effect on the argument size). However, using state-of-the-art PCPs (e.g., [DHK15]) or even conjectured PCPs (e.g., fulfilling the sliding scale conjecture [BGLR93]) would only shave off a log l factor in the number of queries. Any PCP/IOP that has fewer queries would violate standard complexity-theoretic assumptions, e.g., the exponential-time hypothesis [GH98, CY20].

If one relies on cryptography with "more structure" then better argument sizes are possible. Known SNARGs based on bilinear groups (e.g., [Gro10, GGPR13, BCI+13]) have optimal size: $O(\log(t/\epsilon))$, which translates to a few hundred bytes in practice. Similarly, known SNARGs based on cyclic groups or unknown-order groups (e.g., [BCC+16, BBB+18, BFS20]) are almost as short: $O(\log(t/\epsilon) \cdot \log n)$ (here n is the size of the computation being proved), which translates to just a few kilobytes in practice. This has led to the belief that SNARGs that solely rely on a random function (the random oracle) are fundamentally long.

While the inferior asymptotics of argument sizes of SNARGs in the ROM have not prevented useful applications,[1] they do lead to relatively large concrete sizes (tens to hundreds of kilobytes in practice), which makes them undesirable for many other applications.

This state of affairs is unfortunate because SNARGs in the ROM have several attractive features. First, SNARGs in the ROM are to date the most efficient approach for post-quantum security, and so achieving post-quantum SNARGs with (public verification and) optimal argument size remains an open problem.[2] Moreover, by heuristically instantiating the random oracle with a suitable cryptographic hash function, one obtains SNARGs that are lightweight (no public-key cryptography is used) and easy to deploy (users only need to agree on which hash function to use without having to rely on a trusted party to sample a structured reference string).

1.1   Breaking the Quadratic Barrier

Since it seems implausible to improve the query complexity of the PCP/IOP, how could we reduce the argument size? One way would be to reduce the overhead of the commitment scheme. This would be an amazing achievement on its own but currently seems out of reach (and, in fact, many believe that improving the commitment scheme is impossible). Another way would be to completely deviate from the paradigm of constructing SNARGs from PCPs/IOPs. However, [CY20] tells us that any SNARG in the ROM inherently contains an IOP with closely related parameters. In light of this, the motivating question of our work is: is the quadratic barrier of SNARGs in the ROM inherent or, instead, one can do better by achieving subquadratic, or even linear, argument size?

---

[1] E.g., to increase throughput in peer-to-peer systems such as Ethereum via "roll-up" architectures [Eth].

[2] Known approaches based on lattices achieve privately-verifiable SNARGs with optimal size [BISW17, BISW18] or publicly-verifiable SNARGs with square-root communication complexity [BBC+18].

A New Paradigm. In this work, we show how to go beyond the quadratic barrier by changing the interplay between the information-theoretic proof and the cryptographic compiler. Instead of asking for better soundness with fewer queries, we rely on a *stronger soundness notion* of the PCP with the same number of queries: we compile these strong PCPs into SNARGs *without using a commitment*. The commitment is relaxed with a weak notion of binding that is coupled with our strong soundness notion for the PCP. In particular, the SNARG prover might not be committed to *any* location of a proof string. Informally, our approach can be summarized as follows:

$$\begin{bmatrix} \text{strong information} \\ \text{theoretic proof} \end{bmatrix} + \begin{bmatrix} \text{weak cryptographic} \\ \text{commitment} \end{bmatrix} \implies \begin{matrix} \text{subquadratic} \\ \text{SNARG} \end{matrix} .$$

Results. We use this paradigm to construct the first SNARGs in the ROM of *subquadratic* size.

Theorem 1. *There exists a SNARG for* NP *in the random oracle model that achieves argument size* $\tilde{O}(\log(t/\epsilon) \cdot \log t)$ *with soundness error* ϵ *against t-query adversaries.*

Our construction is the first progress on the Micali construction since it was introduced over 25 years ago. Our construction relies solely on a random oracle and so is plausibly post-quantum secure. Previous SNARGs in the ROM have been proven to be secure in the *quantum* random oracle model [CMS19], and we leave it for future work to adapt these technique to our construction.

The argument size that we achieve, while better than quadratic, is still far from the lower bound of $\Omega(\log(t/\epsilon))$. In particular, our work leaves open the intriguing question:

Are there SNARGs in the ROM that have argument size $O(\log(t/\epsilon))$?

We hope that our work will lead to a better understanding of this fundamental question, where a positive answer is likely to have significant practical benefits.

1.2   Concrete Efficiency

Our new construction achieves argument sizes that are not only asymptotically smaller but also concretely smaller: we obtain up to 2× improvement in argument size over Micali's construction for an illustrative instantiation across different values of t and ϵ. Moreover, the running times of the verifier and the prover of our construction are essentially the same as in Micali's construction.

In more detail, Micali's construction is typically instantiated with a PCP whose verifier is repeated many times to reduce soundness error to $O(\epsilon/t)$. Looking ahead, our construction requires PCPs that satisfy a stronger notion of soundness that (as we will prove) is satisfied by repeated PCPs. Thus, conveniently, we can instantiate both the Micali construction and our construction via the same class (repeated PCPs), and in particular we can directly compare their argument sizes.

For example, in Table 1 we demonstrate the arguments sizes for various values of t and ϵ. We instantiate both constructions with the same repetition of a "base" PCP with soundness error $1/2$, query complexity 3, and proof length 2^{30} over a binary alphabet. By repeating the PCP verifier $\log \frac{1}{2} \frac{t}{\epsilon}$ times, the amplified PCP has soundness error $\varepsilon_{\mathrm{PCP}} \leq \epsilon/t$ and $3 \log \frac{1}{2} \frac{t}{\epsilon}$ queries.

Table 1. Comparison of argument sizes between the Micali construction (in red) and our construction (in blue), for different settings of (t, ϵ). Both constructions are based on the same illustrative PCP.

$\log t$	$-\log \epsilon$			
	64	96	128	160
64	$\dfrac{180\,\mathrm{KB}}{131\,\mathrm{KB}} \approx 1.37\times$	$\dfrac{257\,\mathrm{KB}}{164\,\mathrm{KB}} \approx 1.57\times$	$\dfrac{346\,\mathrm{KB}}{188\,\mathrm{KB}} \approx 1.84\times$	$\dfrac{448\,\mathrm{KB}}{219\,\mathrm{KB}} \approx 2.05\times$
96	$\dfrac{293\,\mathrm{KB}}{237\,\mathrm{KB}} \approx 1.24\times$	$\dfrac{389\,\mathrm{KB}}{272\,\mathrm{KB}} \approx 1.43\times$	$\dfrac{498\,\mathrm{KB}}{317\,\mathrm{KB}} \approx 1.57\times$	$\dfrac{618\,\mathrm{KB}}{361\,\mathrm{KB}} \approx 1.71\times$
128	$\dfrac{432\,\mathrm{KB}}{357\,\mathrm{KB}} \approx 1.21\times$	$\dfrac{547\,\mathrm{KB}}{415\,\mathrm{KB}} \approx 1.32\times$	$\dfrac{674\,\mathrm{KB}}{473\,\mathrm{KB}} \approx 1.42\times$	$\dfrac{814\,\mathrm{KB}}{533\,\mathrm{KB}} \approx 1.53\times$
160	$\dfrac{597\,\mathrm{KB}}{513\,\mathrm{KB}} \approx 1.16\times$	$\dfrac{730\,\mathrm{KB}}{585\,\mathrm{KB}} \approx 1.25\times$	$\dfrac{876\,\mathrm{KB}}{659\,\mathrm{KB}} \approx 1.33\times$	$\dfrac{1032\,\mathrm{KB}}{730\,\mathrm{KB}} \approx 1.41\times$

2   Techniques

We summarize the main ideas behind our main result (Theorem 1).

2.1   The Micali Construction Is Inherently Quadratic

We review the SNARG construction of Micali [Mic00] and explain why its argument size is quadratic.

The Micali Construction. Micali [Mic00] combined ideas from Fiat and Shamir [FS86] and Kilian [Kil92] in order to compile any probabilistically checkable proof (PCP) into a corresponding SNARG. Informally, the SNARG prover uses the random oracle to Merkle hash the PCP to a short root that acts as a short commitment to the PCP string; then, the SNARG prover uses the random oracle to derive randomness for the PCP verifier's queries; finally, the SNARG prover outputs an argument that includes the Merkle root, answers to the PCP verifier's queries, and authentication paths for each of those answers (which act as local openings to the commitment). The SNARG verifier re-derives the PCP verifier's queries from the Merkle root and then runs the PCP verifier with the provided answers, ensuring that those answers are indeed authenticated.

On the Output Length of the Random Oracle. As mentioned in the introduction, the argument size in the Micali construction is $\tilde{O}(\mathsf{q} \cdot \lambda)$, ignoring low-order terms; moreover, under standard complexity assumptions, the number of queries must be $\mathsf{q} = \Omega(\log(t/\epsilon))$ (up to low-order terms) even if using conjectured "best possible" PCPs. What about the oracle output size λ? If we were to set $\lambda = O(\log t)$ then we would obtain the argument size $\tilde{O}(\log(t/\epsilon) \cdot \log t)$ claimed in Theorem 1. However, the Micali construction is *not* secure in this regime, as we now explain.

Consider the following attack. A cheating prover selects an arbitrary Merkle root; uses the random oracle to derive PCP randomness from this Merkle root; finds a PCP string that satisfies the PCP verifier for this choice of PCP randomness; computes the Merkle tree on this PCP string; and hopes that the resulting Merkle root equals the Merkle root that was previously chosen. A success would constitute an "inversion". If this did not work, the cheating prover re-tries until he succeeds (or runs out of queries). If we want the construction to be (t, ϵ)-secure, then any t-query attack can succeed with probability at most ϵ. However, the described attack would succeed with probability roughly $t \cdot 2^{-\lambda}$ which gives us the lower bound $\lambda = \Omega(\log(t/\epsilon))$ (for the Micali scheme to be secure we actually need to set $\lambda = \Omega(\log(t^2/\epsilon))$).

Looking Beyond the Micali Construction. Our goal is to change the construction such that we can set the output length of the random oracle to $\lambda = \tilde{O}(\log t)$. This means that a cheating prover in this regime may find inversions or collisions in the random oracle. In particular, a Merkle tree with this choice of λ is *not* a commitment scheme (e.g., a collision will allow him to open in different ways). Therefore, we will need to find ways to handle this new class of attacks and, in particular, prevent the inversion attack described above.

2.2   Our Construction

Our construction shares features with the Micali construction: the argument prover constructs a PCP string; commits to this PCP string using the random oracle; derives PCP randomness (and thus PCP queries) from the resulting commitment again using the random oracle; and outputs the commitment and certified answers to each PCP query.

At the same time, our construction differs from the Micali construction in several crucial ways. In the sequel, we describe the differences and provide intuition for why these differences are useful towards reducing argument size. In subsequent subsections, we will provide more information about how we establish the security of our construction.

(1) Chopped tree. The argument prover commits to the PCP string via a *chopped* Merkle tree: the Merkle tree is computed layer by layer from the leaves but stops at a specific stop layer i^*. In the Micali construction, the stop layer is $i^* = 0$ (a single vertex called the Merkle root); in our construction, the stop layer is (roughly) $i^* = \log q$ (where q is the query complexity of the PCP), which consists of 2^{i^*} vertices that we collectively call a Merkle *cap*.[3]. The argument prover then uses the Merkle cap similarly to a Merkle root in the Micali construction: it derives PCP randomness from the Merkle cap by using the random oracle (in a single query); and subsequently authenticates answers to PCP queries via paths that are truncated at layer i^*.

As the stop layer i^* increases, argument size increases as well. In the extreme, if $i^* = \log l$ (the stop layer is the leaf layer), then the argument contains the entire PCP string. In our construction, we set (roughly) $i^* = \log q$, in which case the argument size is (almost) the same as when $i^* = 0$ (for the same output size of the random oracle). Intuitively, if the argument prover supplies q authentications paths then, with high probability, most of the vertices in layer $\log q$ would have been already included, so that truncating the paths to layer $\log q$ and including in the argument all the digests in layer $\log q$ does not affect argument size by much. (This is not just asymptotically: our experiments show that this has a negligible effect on the argument size in practice as well.)

Our main observation is that as the stop layer increases, *security increases as well*. In the Micali construction, a single inversion of the Merkle root breaks the scheme: the attacker selects an arbitrary Merkle root, derives corresponding PCP randomness (and thus PCP queries), finds a PCP string that makes the PCP verifier accept with that PCP randomness, computes a (full) Merkle tree on this PCP string, and hopes that the resulting root equals the previously selected root. If the root has output size λ, this takes about 2^λ attempts (which is roughly 2^λ queries). In contrast, in our construction, an inversion of a single vertex in the Merkle cap affects only a $1/q$ fraction of the PCP string, which (in general) is not a winning strategy for a cheating prover. To emulate the prior strategy, the attacker would need to invert all q vertices in the Merkle cap, which is much harder.

(2) Domain separation. The Micali construction involves two random oracles: an oracle for computing the Merkle tree, and another oracle for deriving PCP randomness. (See [Mic00].) In our construction, we use domain separation to "split up" the oracle for the Merkle tree into a separate oracle for each vertex in the (in our case, chopped) Merkle tree. To compute the digest located in position j of layer i in the tree, the argument prover uses the prefix (i, j) in the query to the tree oracle. This does not increase argument size (the indices i and j are known so are not included in the argument) and has essentially no effect on the prover time and verifier time.

This domain separation is crucial for security because, without it, a cheating prover could recycle a single inversion or collision many times. For example, the cheating prover could find a collision in a leaf vertex between the values 0 and 1 and then re-use the same collision for *all* leaves to compute a Merkle tree for

---

[3] Equivalently, the Merkle cap is an ordered list of Merkle roots for smaller sub-trees.

which any location can be opened to 0 or 1. This is insecure, e.g., for any PCP over the binary alphabet.

(3) Permuting the proof. In our construction, the argument prover randomly permutes the PCP string before applying the (chopped) Merkle tree. This requires a random permutation $\mathsf{Perm} \colon [\mathsf{l}] \to [\mathsf{l}]$ that is also known to the argument verifier, and can be derived via the Luby–Rackoff construction from the random oracle (see Sect. 4.1). Thus, if the PCP verifier wishes to read the i-th symbol of the PCP string, the $\mathsf{Perm}(i)$-th leaf should be accessed. This modification also does not increase argument size and has a negligible effect on the time complexity of the argument prover and argument verifier (each permutation call translates to a few calls to the random oracle).

Permuting the PCP string creates the effect of a PCP with *uniform random queries*. This property ensures that there is no "weak" block of symbols in the PCP. Indeed, recall that we chopped the Merkle tree in order to have a Merkle cap instead of a Merkle root, so that if a cheating prover makes a single inversion then this will affect only a small block of the PCP string. However, if all the PCP queries were to this block, then the cheating prover could still win with this single inversion. In contrast, since queries are random (after applying the permutation), we are guaranteed that, with high probability, the queries are (roughly) spread evenly across different blocks.

(4) Robust PCPs. Our construction is designed to work with PCPs that satisfy a stronger soundness notion, which we call *permuted robust soundness*. This notion is similar to the standard property of (strong) robust soundness of PCPs, which captures the probability of being within a particular (block-wise) *distance* from a satisfying proof. To fit our proof, we augment the standard notion to additionally consider a permutation that randomizes the proof locations so that queries are spread across blocks.

While we rely on strong soundness notions of PCPs, we show that *repeated* PCPs satisfy this stronger notion. That is, one can take a base PCP, and repeat it to amplify the soundness. What we show is that not only the soundness is amplified, but the PCP also satisfies the stronger notion of permuted robust soundness (with corresponding parameters). Intuitively, this notion lets us argue the construction's security even when the prover finds a small number of collisions or inversions. The next subsections are dedicated to the precise notion of permuted robust soundness, how to achieve it in repeated PCPs, and how we use it in our proof of security.

2.3 Permuted Robust Soundness

We describe *permuted robust soundness*, the PCP soundness notion that we use for our construction.

Given a block size parameter $\mathsf{b} \in \mathbb{N}$, we view a PCP string $\Pi \in \Sigma^{\mathsf{l}}$ as divided into blocks of size b, that is, as $\Pi \in (\Sigma^{\mathsf{l}/\mathsf{b}})^{\mathsf{b}}$. We denote by $\Delta_{\mathsf{b}}(\Pi, \Pi')$ the block-wise distance between two PCP strings Π and Π' (i.e., the number of blocks of symbols on which they differ); more generally, given a permutation

Perm: $[l] \to [l]$, we denote by $\Delta_b^{\mathrm{Perm}}(\Pi, \Pi')$ this block-wise distance when the two PCP strings are permuted according to Perm (and after are divided into blocks for measuring distance).

The soundness is defined by the following game.

Game 1. The game $\mathcal{G}_{\mathrm{per}}$ receives as input a PCP verifier $\mathbf{V}$, an instance x, a block size parameter $b \in \mathbb{N}$, an allowed distance parameter $d \in \mathbb{N}$, and a cheating prover $\tilde{\mathbf{P}}$. The game $\mathcal{G}_{\mathrm{per}}(\mathbf{V}, x, b, d, \tilde{\mathbf{P}})$ works as follows:

1. Sample a random permutation Perm: $[l] \to [l]$, and give it to $\tilde{\mathbf{P}}$.
2. $\tilde{\mathbf{P}}$ outputs a PCP string $\Pi \in \Sigma^l$.
3. Sample PCP randomness $\rho \in \{0,1\}^r$, and give it to $\tilde{\mathbf{P}}$.
4. $\tilde{\mathbf{P}}$ outputs another PCP string $\Pi' \in \Sigma^l$.
5. The game outputs 1 if and only if $\Delta_b^{\mathrm{Perm}}(\Pi, \Pi') \leq d$ and $\mathbf{V}^{\Pi'}(x; \rho) = 1$.

Definition 1. *A PCP* $(\mathbf{P}, \mathbf{V})$ *for a relation R has* **permuted robust soundness error** $\varepsilon_{\mathrm{per}}(x, b, d)$ *if for every instance* x $\notin L(R)$, *block size* $b \in \mathbb{N}$, *distance bound* $d \in \mathbb{N}$, *and malicious prover* $\tilde{\mathbf{P}}$,

$$\Pr\left[\mathcal{G}_{\mathrm{per}}(\mathbf{V}, x, b, d, \tilde{\mathbf{P}}) = 1\right] \leq \varepsilon_{\mathrm{per}}(x, b, d) \ .$$

Why We Need Permuted Robust Soundness. Before we continue with the security analysis of our construction, we give intuition for how permuted robust soundness is helpful towards security.

Consider the following strategy for a cheating prover, which captures the main ideas in our proof. The prover: selects a PCP string; permutes it according to the random permutation; commits to it via a chopped Merkle tree; and then derives PCP randomness, and thus PCP queries, from the resulting Merkle cap. Each vertex in the Merkle cap is itself a Merkle root for a subtree whose leaves are a block of the PCP string. By inverting a root in the Merkle cap, the cheating prover has complete control on the corresponding block. In particular, the cheating prover can find the minimal set of blocks to modify so to make the PCP verifier accept, and inverts the roots for these blocks. The success probability is (roughly) his probability of successfully inverting all these roots. Thus, it is important that no block has many queries, which is why we use the permutation.

In other words, the cheating prover's success probability depends on the *distance* of the PCP string to an accepting PCP string, where the distance is defined by the block-wise Hamming distance (after the permutation). This is why we need the PCP to have a robust notion of soundness where the probability that a PCP string is close to being accepting is smaller as this distance is smaller. For any constant k, we will bound the probability that the cheating prover can invert k roots, and then compare this with the probability that a proof will be of distance k from an accepting proof.

This is a high-level approach of how to handle this specific attack. However, a cheating prover has a wide range of strategies: find collisions and inversions in arbitrary locations in the chopped Merkle tree; create multiple trees from which to choose from, and derive many different PCP query sets; and try to combine all of the above. The permuted robust soundness is the notion that our proof is built on, however, we will need to somehow address all possible prover strategies.

2.4 Repeated PCPs Satisfy Permuted Robust Soundness

Our main technical lemma regarding permuted robust soundness states that any repeated PCP satisfies the (strong notion of) permuted robust soundness. Note that for constructing SNARGs, the underlying PCP must have an exponentially small soundness error. We know how to build such PCPs only by repeating some base PCP multiple times. Here, we show that in addition to improving the standard soundness, repetition improves the permuted robust soundness of the PCP. Intuitively, for a repeated PCP the distance of a PCP string to an accepting PCP string is proportional to the number of repetitions that reject it, and different repetitions are likely to query different blocks (due to the permutation). This is a simple generic way to construct PCPs suitable for our SNARG construction, which suffices for our asymptotic result and also is useful for concrete efficiency.

In more detail, the κ-*wise repetition* of a PCP system $(\mathbf{P}, \mathbf{V})$, denoted $(\mathbf{P}_\kappa, \mathbf{V}_\kappa)$, is the PCP system obtained by setting $\mathbf{P}_\kappa := \mathbf{P}$ (the PCP string does not change) and setting $\mathbf{V}_\kappa$ to run $\mathbf{V}$ on κ independent choices of randomness. We prove the following lemma.

Lemma 1. *Let $(\mathbf{P}, \mathbf{V})$ be a PCP with soundness error $\varepsilon_{\mathrm{base}}$, proof length l (over any alphabet), and query complexity q; moreover, suppose that each location in the PCP string is queried with probability at most p. For every $\kappa \in \mathbb{N}$ such that $\mathsf{b} \geq \kappa \cdot \mathsf{q} \cdot \varepsilon_{\mathrm{base}}^{-1}$ and $p \leq (8\mathsf{b} \cdot \kappa)^{-1}$, $(\mathbf{P}_\kappa, \mathbf{V}_\kappa)$ has strong permuted robust soundness error*

$$\varepsilon_{\mathrm{per}}(\mathbb{x}, \mathsf{b}, d) \leq \frac{e^{1.2 \cdot d}}{d!} \cdot \mathsf{b}^d \cdot \varepsilon_{\mathrm{base}}(\mathbb{x})^\kappa \ .$$

The formal statement of the lemma and its proof are in Sect. 5. Below we provide an overview of (a simplified version of) this lemma.

Recall that if the base PCP has soundness error $\varepsilon_{\mathrm{base}}$ then its κ-wise repetition has soundness error $\varepsilon_{\mathrm{base}}^\kappa$. This soundness error is for a PCP string that is fixed before the κ samples of PCP randomness are drawn. Here we are instead interested in the probability that the PCP string is d blocks away from convincing the PCP verifier. That is, the cheating prover can arbitrarily change any d blocks after learning the PCP randomness (and, in particular, derive the queried locations).

How much power does this give to the cheating prover? To understand this, we first need to see how the queries are distributed among the blocks. Since we assume that no proof location is queried with too high probability, a typical query set will have all queries distinct (or at least have only a few colliding queries). Then the random permutation will randomize query locations, as if they had been uniform random queries. In sum, queries will be mostly spread out evenly across blocks.

For even further simplicity here, let us assume that no two queries land in the same block. (This is possible as the total number of queries $\kappa \cdot \mathsf{q}$ is less than b.) In this case, the prover can change at most d blocks after seeing the queries and can affect the output of at most d out of the κ repetitions. Without assuming any additional property about the underlying PCP, changing a single query within a repetition might suffice to convince the PCP verifier. Thus we cannot expect soundness better than $\varepsilon_{\text{base}}^{\kappa-d}$. Moreover, the cheating prover chooses which d blocks to change adaptively after seeing all query locations, which grants the cheating prover additional power.

To bound the soundness error we fix in advance a choice of d repetitions among the κ repetitions that the prover controls; the remaining $\kappa - d$ iterations each contribute a multiplicative factor of soundness error $\varepsilon_{\text{base}}$. By a union bound over all choices of the d iterations, we get the expression:

$$\binom{\kappa}{d} \cdot \varepsilon_{\text{base}}^{\kappa-d} \leq \frac{\kappa^d}{d!} \cdot \varepsilon_{\text{base}}^{\kappa-d} = \frac{1}{d!} \cdot \left(\frac{\kappa}{\varepsilon_{\text{base}}}\right)^d \cdot \varepsilon_{\text{base}}^{\kappa} \leq \frac{b^d}{d!} \cdot \varepsilon_{\text{base}}^{\kappa} \ .$$

This expression is better than what we set out to prove. The additional term $e^{1.2d}$ in Lemma 1 comes from removing the simplifying assumptions used above. Without those assumptions, the cheating prover may gain an advantage when a block contains queries from more than one repetition: (i) queries might collide before the permutation is applied, and these queries will be mapped to the same (random) location by the permutation; (ii) even distinct queries might be mapped to the same block after the permutation (and this is likely to happen). The full proof must take these into account, which complicates the expressions above and introduces the additional term $e^{1.2d}$.

Remark 1 (repetition of a robust PCP). Lemma 1 shows that the repetition of *any* PCP satisfies permuted robust soundness. This will let us instantiate our SNARG construction based on the repetition of any PCP, retaining maximal freedom in choosing parameters of the PCP, without worrying about additional properties of the PCP. Nevertheless, we could also consider the repetition of a PCP that is already somewhat robust (in the standard sense), which would improve the soundness expression in the lemma. For example, suppose that in every local view of the PCP string we need to change at least two answers to make the PCP verifier accept. For this case we expect the soundness of the repeated PCP to be close to $\varepsilon_{\text{PCP}}^{\kappa-d/2}$, instead of $\varepsilon_{\text{PCP}}^{\kappa-d}$. We leave it for future work to derive the analogue of Lemma 1 for robust PCPs.

2.5 The Cap Soundness Game

In order to obtain a security analysis of our construction, we introduce an intermediate information-theoretic game, called *cap soundness game*, that enables us to model the effects of attacks against our construction. The intermediate game then leaves us with two tasks: reduce the security of our construction to winning the cap soundness game (see Sect. 2.7); and reduce winning the cap soundness game to breaking the permuted robust soundness of the PCP (see further below).

The Game. The cap soundness game has several inputs: a PCP verifier $\mathbf{V}$; an instance $\mathbb{x}$ (which we will usually omit from the description); an integer λ (modeling the random oracle's output size); a stop layer i^*; a malicious prover

$\tilde{\mathbf{P}}$ to play the game; a query budget $t \in \mathbb{N}$; a collision budget $t_{\mathrm{col}} \in \mathbb{N}$; and a inversion budget $t_{\mathrm{inv}} \in \mathbb{N}$. We denote this game by $\mathcal{G}_{\mathrm{cap}}(\mathbf{V}, \mathbf{x}, \lambda, i^*, \tilde{\mathbf{P}}, t, t_{\mathrm{col}}, t_{\mathrm{inv}})$.

The Graph G. The game is played on a graph $G = (V, E)$ that represents the chopped Merkle trees constructed by the adversary so far. Letting d be the height of a full Merkle tree, vertices in G are the union $V := V_{i^*} \cup V_1 \cup \cdots \cup V_d$ where V_i are the vertices of level i of the tree: for every $i \in \{i^*, \ldots, d-1\}$, $V_i := \{(i, j, h) : j \in [2^i], h \in \{0,1\}^\lambda\}$ is level i; and $V_d := \{(d, j, h) : j \in [2^d], h \in \Sigma\}$ is the leaf level. The indices i and j represent the location in the tree (vertex j in level i) and the string h represents either a symbol of the PCP (if in the leaf level) or an output of the random oracle (if in any other level). Edges in G are *hyper*edges that keep track of which inputs are "hashed" together to create a given output. That is, elements in the edge set E of G are chosen from the collection $\mathcal{E}$ below, which represents an edge between two vertices in level $i + 1$ and their common parent in level i:

$$\mathcal{E} = \left\{ (u, v_0, v_1) : \begin{array}{l} u = (i, j, h) \in V_i \\ v_0 = (i+1, 2j-1, h_0) \in V_{i+1} \\ v_1 = (i+1, 2j, h_1) \in V_{i+1} \end{array} \right\}.$$

The set of valid caps consists of all possible lists of vertices in V_{i^*} that consist a full layer of vertices:

$$C := \left\{ ((i^*, 1, h_1), \ldots, (i^*, 2^{i^*}, h_{2^{i^*}})) : h_1, \ldots, h_{2^{i^*}} \in \{0,1\}^\lambda \right\}.$$

Playing the Game. The game starts with the graph G empty ($E = \emptyset$), and proceeds in rounds; moreover, the game samples a random permutation $\mathsf{Perm} \colon [l] \to [l]$ and gives it to the adversary. After that, in each round, provided there is enough query budget t left, the adversary chooses between two actions: (i) add an edge to E from the set $\mathcal{E}$, provided the edge is allowed; (ii) obtain the PCP randomness for a given Merkle cap. We discuss each in more detail.

- *Adding edges.* When the prover adds to E an edge $(u, v_0, v_1) \in \mathcal{E}$ the query budget is reduced $t \leftarrow t - 1$. Moreover, the collision and inversion budgets may also be reduced if the edge creates a collision or inversion, as described below.
  - **Collisions.** If the edge (u, v_0, v_1) collides with an edge (u, v_0', v_1') that is already in E, the game charges a unit of collision budget by setting $t_{\mathrm{col}} \leftarrow t_{\mathrm{col}} - 1$. Note that the game charges a single unit for each collision edge, and multi-collisions are allowed. Thus, a k-wise collision costs $k - 1$ units of t_{col}. This makes the collision budget versatile in that, for example, a budget of 2 can be used to create two 2-wise collisions or one 3-wise collision.
  - **Inversions.** If the edge (u, v_0, v_1) is added when u is not *free* (defined next), the game charges a unit of inversion budget by setting $t_{\mathrm{inv}} \leftarrow t_{\mathrm{inv}} - 1$. The vertex u is *free* if it is not already connected to a vertex in a level closer to the cap, i.e., if $u \in V_i$ then for every $w \in V_{i-1}$ and $u' \in V_i$ it holds

that $(w, u, u') \notin E$. (Note that the game would not charge an inversion if these edge where added in reverse order, though, as that would not have been an inversion.)

- *Deriving randomness.* The prover submits a cap $(v_1, \ldots, v_{2^{i^*}}) \in C$, and the game samples new PCP randomness ρ. The pair $((v_1, \ldots, v_{2^{i^*}}), \rho)$ is added to a mapping Rand. (The prover is not allowed to submit a cap that already appears in the mapping Rand.) This costs a unit of the query budget, so when this happens the query budget is reduced $t \leftarrow t - 1$.

Winning the Game. When it decides to stop playing, the prover outputs a cap $(v_1, \ldots, v_{2^{i^*}}) \in C$ and a PCP string $\Pi \in \Sigma^l$. The prover wins the game if the following two conditions hold.

- The PCP verifier accepts the PCP string Π when using the randomness associated to $(v_1, \ldots, v_{2^{i^*}})$. That is, $\mathbf{V}^\Pi(\mathbf{x}; \rho) = 1$ for $\rho := \mathsf{Rand}[(v_1, \ldots, v_{2^{i^*}})]$. (If Rand has no randomness for this cap then the prover loses.)
- The PCP string Π is consistent with the cap $(v_1, \ldots, v_{2^{i^*}})$ in the graph G. That is, if the PCP verifier queries location j of Π, then the leaf $u = (d, j, \Pi[\mathsf{Perm}(j)]) \in V_d$ is connected to a vertex in the cap $(v_1, \ldots, v_{2^{i^*}})$ in G. (The collection $\mathcal{E}$ of possible edges ensures that the j-th leaf can be connected to at most one vertex in a cap, the one corresponding to the first i^* bits of the index j.)

We denote by $\varepsilon_{\mathrm{cap}}(i^*, t, t_{\mathrm{col}}, t_{\mathrm{inv}})$ the maximum winning probability in the cap soundness game, with stop layer i^*, by any adversary with query budget t, collision budget t_{col}, and inversion budget t_{inv}.

From Permuted Robust Soundness to Cap Soundness. We reduce the soundness of a cheating prover in the cap soundness game to the soundness in the permuted robust soundness game.

Lemma 2. *Let* $(\mathbf{P}, \mathbf{V})$ *be a PCP for a relation R with permuted robust soundness error* $\varepsilon_{\mathrm{per}}(\mathsf{b}, d)$. *Then,* $(\mathbf{P}, \mathbf{V})$ *has cap soundness error*

$$\varepsilon_{\mathrm{cap}}(i^*, t, t_{\mathrm{col}}, t_{\mathrm{inv}}) \leq t \cdot 2^{t_{\mathrm{col}}} \cdot \varepsilon_{\mathrm{per}}(\mathsf{b} = 2^{i^*}, d = t_{\mathrm{inv}}) \ .$$

The proof of the lemma is somewhat technical and is provided in Sect. 6. Here we provide some intuition on the above expression. The term $\varepsilon_{\mathrm{per}}(\mathsf{b} = 2^{i^*}, d = t_{\mathrm{inv}})$ comes from the fact that if the attacker can make t_{inv} inversions then it suffices for the attacker to commit to a PCP string that is within a block-size distance of t_{inv} from an accepting PCP string (and the blocks have size 2^{i^*} since that is the number of leaves under a vertex in the cap). The multiplicative factor $2^{t_{\mathrm{col}}}$ comes from the fact that if the attacker can find t_{col} collisions then the attacker can open up to $2^{t_{\mathrm{col}}}$ PCP strings for the same cap (as each collision doubles the number of PCP strings that could be consistent with the same cap). The further multiplicative factor t comes from the fact that the attacker can re-try its strategy roughly t times.

2.6 Scoring Oracle Queries

The cap soundness game lets us bound the success probability of an adversary given specific budgets. But what budgets should we use when analyzing a cheating argument prover? For this, we rely on an analysis tool introduced in [anon citation]: a *scoring function* for the query trace of an algorithm in the random oracle model. For convenience and completeness, we review this notion below.

Intuitively, the score of a query trace "counts" the number of collisions and inversions in a way that reflects the probability of that event occurring. The lower the probability, the higher the score. This enables us to translate our claims about cheating argument provers into claims about cheating cap soundness provers, where a high score is translated to a high budget. A strategy that uses a large budget has a higher chance of winning the cap soundness game, but the probability of achieving a corresponding high score is low, and our goal is to balance these two.

The scoring function is separately defined for collisions and for inversions, as motivated below.

- *Scoring collisions.* The score of a k-wise collision is set to be $k - 1$ (assuming k is maximal within the query trace); in particular, a 2-wise collision gets a score of 1. Note that two pairwise collisions and one 3-wise collision both get the same score of 2, even though the latter is less likely to occur. This aligns with our proof since two pairwise collisions yield four possible proof strings, while a 3-wise collision yields only three possible proof strings.
- *Scoring inversions.* Scoring inversions is done by simply counting the number of inversions in the query trace. We now elaborate on what is considered an inversion in the query trace. Recall that queries to the random oracle designated for the (chopped) Merkle tree are compressing: a query is of the form $x = (x_1, x_2) \in \{0,1\}^\lambda \times \{0,1\}^\lambda$ and an answer is $y \in \{0,1\}^\lambda$. Instead, queries to the random oracle designated for deriving PCP randomness are of the form $x \in \{0,1\}^{2^{i^*} \cdot \lambda}$ and an answer is $\rho \in \{0,1\}^r$. For inversions we only consider tree queries, and note that a given tree query may invert one of the two components in a previous tree query or may invert (the one component of) a previous randomness query. Hence, a tree query performed at time j with answer y is an inversion if there exist a previous tree query (at time $j' < j$) of the form $x = (x_1, x_2)$ with $x_1 = y$ or $x_2 = y$, or a previous randomness query x with $x = y$.

The precise definitions of scores and the proof of the following lemma are provided in the full version:

Lemma 3. *For any t-query algorithm that queries the random oracle and every $k \in \mathbb{N}$:*

1. $\Pr\left[collision\ score > k\right] \leq \left(\frac{t^2}{2 \cdot 2^\lambda}\right)^k$;
2. $\Pr\left[inversion\ score > k\right] \leq \frac{1}{k!} \cdot \left(\frac{2t}{2^\lambda}\right)^k$.

2.7 Concluding the Proof of Theorem 1

We are left with putting pieces together to derive the argument size. To this end, we first establish the soundness error of our construction, and then the argument size will follow.

Soundness of Our Construction. We show that our construction is sound given any PCP with permuted robust soundness. Recall that permuted robustness soundness depends on the distance d (Sect. 2.3). In our construction the quantity that matters is an associated worst-case ratio: we say that the PCP has permuted robustness *ratio* $\beta(\mathsf{b})$ if

$$\max_{d \in \{0,1,\ldots,\mathsf{b}\}} \frac{\varepsilon_{\mathrm{per}}(\mathbb{x}, \mathsf{b}, d+1)}{\varepsilon_{\mathrm{per}}(\mathbb{x}, \mathsf{b}, d)} \leq \beta(\mathsf{b}) \ .$$

Then, we show the following lemma.

Lemma 4. *Suppose our construction is instantiated with a random oracle with output size λ, and a PCP with soundness error $\varepsilon_{\mathrm{PCP}}$ and permuted robustness ratio $\beta(\mathsf{b})$ with stop layer i^*. If $\lambda \geq 2\log t + \log \beta(\mathsf{b} = 2^{i^*}) + 3$ then our construction has soundness error $\epsilon(t) \leq t \cdot \varepsilon_{\mathrm{PCP}}$ against t-query adversaries.*

In our soundness analysis we consider *every possible query trace score* and also the probability that the cheating argument prover achieves that score (see Sect. 2.6). For any integer $k \in \mathbb{N}$ we consider the event of the cheating argument prover produces a query trace that has either collision score or inversion score exactly k. We show that, conditioned on the cheating prover producing a query trace of score k, there is a related adversary that wins the cap soundness game with the same probability and budget k (the precise statement is given in Claim 6). Informally,

$$\Pr \left[\begin{array}{c} \text{verifier} \\ \text{accepts} \end{array} \middle| \text{ score } k \right] \leq \varepsilon_{\mathrm{cap}}(i^*, t, k, k) \ .$$

We consider an infinite sum over k, and for each value of k we bound the probability of the adversary getting a score of k multiplied by the maximum winning probability in the cap soundness game given budgets $t_{\mathrm{col}} = k$ and $t_{\mathrm{inv}} = k$. This infinite sum converges to the soundness expression stated in Lemma 4, provided that $\lambda \geq 2\log t + \log \beta + 3$.

In more detail, this approach could be over-simplified via the following equations (for simplicity here we are not careful with constants). First, using Lemma 3 we obtain that the probability that the collision or inversion score equals k is bounded by the sum of the two probabilities:

$$\Pr[\text{score of } k] \leq 2 \cdot \left(\frac{2t^2}{2^{\lambda}} \right)^k \ .$$

This lets us express the success probability of the cheating prover as an infinite sum conditioned on getting a score of k, for any $k \in \mathbb{N}$:

$$\Pr\begin{bmatrix} \text{verifier} \\ \text{accepts} \end{bmatrix} \leq \sum_{k=0}^{\infty} \Pr\begin{bmatrix} \text{verifier} \\ \text{accepts} \end{bmatrix} \text{score of } k \end{bmatrix} \cdot \Pr[\text{score of } k]$$

$$\leq \sum_{k=0}^{\infty} \varepsilon_{\text{cap}}(i^*, t, k, k) \cdot \Pr[\text{score of } k] \leq \sum_{k=0}^{\infty} O\left(t \cdot 2^k \cdot \varepsilon_{\text{per}}(k) \cdot \left(\frac{2t^2}{2^\lambda}\right)^k\right)$$

$$\leq \sum_{k=0}^{\infty} O\left(t \cdot 2^k \cdot \beta^k \cdot \varepsilon_{\text{PCP}} \cdot \left(\frac{2t^2}{2^\lambda}\right)^k\right) = O(t \cdot \varepsilon_{\text{PCP}}) \cdot \sum_{k=0}^{\infty} \left(\frac{4\beta \cdot t^2}{2^\lambda}\right)^k = O\left(t \cdot \varepsilon_{\text{PCP}}\right) .$$

The last equality follows from the fact that $\sum_{k=0}^{\infty} \left(\frac{4\beta \cdot t^2}{2^\lambda}\right)^k = O(1)$ since $\lambda \geq 2\log t + \log \beta + 3$.

Argument Size of our Construction. We choose an appropriate PCP and obtain the argument size claimed in Theorem 1. Recall that Lemma 4 tells us that the soundness error of our construction is $t \cdot \varepsilon_{\text{PCP}}$ provided that the random oracle output size satisfies $\lambda \geq 2\log t + \log \beta + 3$; in particular, to achieve (t, ϵ) security, we need the PCP soundness error to be $\varepsilon_{\text{PCP}} = \epsilon/t$.

Towards this end, we apply Lemma 1 to any constant-query constant-soundness PCP (over a small alphabet), where the probability of querying each proof location is not too high, as required by the lemma (most PCP constructions satisfy this requirement). We get that its κ-wise repetition has permuted robustness ratio $\beta(\mathsf{b}) = O\left(\frac{\mathsf{b}^{d+1} \cdot \varepsilon_{\text{base}}^\kappa}{\mathsf{b}^d \cdot \varepsilon_{\text{base}}^\kappa}\right) = O(\mathsf{b})$ for a block size b. The block size depends on the number of repetitions, the query complexity, and the soundness of the base PCP (where the last two are constant), and thus we have that $\mathsf{b} = O(\kappa)$. To achieve the desired PCP soundness error, we set the number of repetitions to be $\kappa = O(\log(t/\epsilon))$; hence the number of queries is $\mathsf{q} = O(\log(t/\epsilon))$. Finally, we set stop layer according to Lemma 4 to be $i^* = O(\log \mathsf{b})$.

The argument contains the Merkle cap (which has size $2^{i^*} \cdot \lambda$), PCP query answers (which have total size $\mathsf{q} \cdot \log|\Sigma|$), and the authentication paths (which have total size $\mathsf{q} \cdot \lambda \cdot \log(\mathsf{l}/2^{i^*})$). The argument size thus is

$$|\text{argument}| = 2^{i^*} \cdot \lambda + \mathsf{q} \cdot \log|\Sigma| + \mathsf{q} \cdot \lambda \cdot \log(\mathsf{l}/2^{i^*}) = O(\mathsf{q} \cdot \lambda \cdot \log(\mathsf{l}/\mathsf{q}))$$

$$= O\left(\log\frac{t}{\epsilon} \cdot \left(\log t + \log\log\frac{t}{\epsilon}\right) \cdot \log\frac{\mathsf{l}}{\log(t/\epsilon)}\right) = \tilde{O}\left(\log\frac{t}{\epsilon} \cdot \log t\right) ,$$

where the last equality hides $\log\log\frac{t}{\epsilon}$ and $\log\mathsf{l}$ factors (as we assume that $\mathsf{l} = \text{poly}(n)$ where n is the input length).

Achieving Concrete Efficiency. In order to achieve concrete efficiency (e.g., the numbers reported in Table 1), our security analysis improves on the above expression by showing that the hidden constant (in the big-O notation) in the soundness expression can be replaced with the constant 1.

To achieve this, it does not suffice simply to pay attention to the constants in the computations, but we need to separately count the queries performed to a tree oracle and to a PCP randomness oracle. The PCP randomness oracle has a long input length (it maps $2^{i^*} \cdot \lambda$ bits to λ bits). Therefore, we count each query to it as 2^{i^*} queries. This is aligned with how one would implement such an oracle using domain extension ([Mer89, Dam89]). Thus, in the full proof, we introduce two new parameters t_{tree} and t_{rnd} such that it always holds that $t = t_{\text{tree}} + 2^{i^*} \cdot t_{\text{rnd}}$. Hence the full proof contains similar expressions as above, where in some cases, t is replaced with either t_{tree}, t_{rnd}, or their (weighted) sum.

3   Definitions

Relations. A relation R is a set of tuples (x, w) where x is the instance and w the witness. The corresponding language $L = L(R)$ is the set of x for which there exists w such that $(\mathrm{x}, \mathrm{w}) \in R$.

Random Oracles. We denote by $\mathcal{U}(\lambda)$ the uniform distribution over functions $\zeta \colon \{0,1\}^* \to \{0,1\}^\lambda$ (implicitly defined by the probabilistic algorithm that assigns, uniformly and independently at random, a λ-bit string to each new input). If ζ is sampled from $\mathcal{U}(\lambda)$, we call ζ a *random oracle*.

Oracle Algorithms. We restrict our attention to oracle algorithms that are deterministic since, in the random oracle model, an oracle algorithm can obtain randomness from the random oracle. Given an oracle algorithm A and an oracle $\zeta \in \mathcal{U}(\lambda)$, $\mathsf{queries}(A, \zeta)$ is the set of oracle queries that A^ζ makes. We say that A is *t-query* if $|\mathsf{queries}(A, \zeta)| \leq t$ for every $\zeta \in \mathcal{U}(\lambda)$.

3.1   Probabilistically Checkable Proofs

We provide standard notations and definitions for *probabilistically checkable proofs* (PCPs) [BFLS91, FGL+91, AS98, ALM+98]. Let $\mathsf{PCP} = (\mathbf{P}, \mathbf{V})$ be a pair where $\mathbf{P}$, known as the prover, is an algorithm, and $\mathbf{V}$, known as the verifier, is an oracle algorithm. We say that PCP is a PCP for a relation R with soundness error $\varepsilon_{\mathrm{PCP}}$ if the following holds.

- **Completeness.**
  For every $(\mathrm{x}, \mathrm{w}) \in R$, letting $\Pi := \mathbf{P}(\mathrm{x}, \mathrm{w}) \in \Sigma^\mathsf{l}$, $\Pr_{\rho \in \{0,1\}^r}[\mathbf{V}^\Pi(\mathrm{x}; \rho) = 1] = 1$.
- **Soundness.**
  For every $\mathrm{x} \notin L(R)$ and malicious proof $\tilde{\Pi} \in \Sigma^\mathsf{l}$, $\Pr_{\rho \in \{0,1\}^r}[\mathbf{V}^{\tilde{\Pi}}(\mathrm{x}; \rho) = 1] \leq \varepsilon_{\mathrm{PCP}}(\mathrm{x})$.

Above, Σ is a finite set that denotes the proof's alphabet, and l is an integer that denotes the proof's length. We additionally denote by q the number of queries to the proof made by the verifier. All of these complexity measures are implicitly functions of the instance x.

Definition 2. *Let Δ be an absolute distance measure. We say that* PCP *has* **(strong) robustness soundness error** $\varepsilon_{\mathrm{PCP}}$ *with respect to Δ if for every instance* $\mathbf{x} \notin L(R)$, *proof string* $\Pi \in \Sigma^{\mathsf{I}}$, *and (absolute) distance parameter* $d \in [\mathsf{b}]$,

$$\Pr_{\rho \in \{0,1\}^r} \left[\exists \Pi' \ s.t. \ \mathbf{V}^{\Pi'}(\mathbf{x}; \rho) = 1 \ and \ \Delta(\Pi, \Pi') \leq d \right] \leq \varepsilon_{\mathrm{PCP}}(\mathbf{x}, d) \ .$$

Standard soundness corresponds to the case where Δ is the Hamming distance and $\varepsilon_{\mathrm{PCP}}(\mathbf{x}, 0) = \varepsilon_{\mathrm{PCP}}(\mathbf{x})$ for some error function $\varepsilon_{\mathrm{PCP}}(\mathbf{x})$ and $\varepsilon_{\mathrm{PCP}}(\mathbf{x}, d) = 1$ for any $d > 0$. The standard notion of robust soundness is a special case of Definition 2, corresponding to the case where $\varepsilon_{\mathrm{PCP}}(\mathbf{x}, d) = \varepsilon_{\mathrm{PCP}}(\mathbf{x})$ for d in some interval $[0, d^*]$ and $\varepsilon_{\mathrm{PCP}}(\mathbf{x}, d) = 1$ for $d > d^*$.

3.2   Non-interactive Arguments in the Random Oracle Model

We consider non-interactive arguments in the random oracle model (ROM), where security holds against query-bounded, yet possibly computationally-unbounded, adversaries. Recall that a non-interactive argument typically consists of a prover algorithm and a verifier algorithm that prove and validate statements for a binary relation, which represents the valid instance-witness pairs.

Let $\mathsf{ARG} = (P, V)$ be a tuple of (oracle) algorithms. We say that ARG is a non-interactive argument in the ROM for a relation R with (t, ϵ)-*security* if, for a function $\lambda \colon \mathbb{N} \times (0,1) \to \mathbb{N}$, the following holds for every query bound $t \in \mathbb{N}$ and soundness error $\epsilon \in (0,1)$.

– **Completeness.** For every $(\mathbf{x}, \mathbf{w}) \in R$,

$$\Pr \left[V^\varsigma(\mathbf{x}, \pi) = 1 \ \middle| \ \begin{array}{l} \varsigma \leftarrow \mathcal{U}(\lambda(t, \epsilon)) \\ \pi \leftarrow P^\varsigma(\mathbf{x}, \mathbf{w}) \end{array} \right] = 1 \ .$$

– **Soundness.** For every $\mathbf{x} \notin L(R)$ with $|\mathbf{x}| \leq t$ and t-query $\tilde{P}$,

$$\Pr \left[V^\varsigma(\mathbf{x}, \pi) = 1 \ \middle| \ \begin{array}{l} \varsigma \leftarrow \mathcal{U}(\lambda(t, \epsilon)) \\ \pi \leftarrow \tilde{P}^\varsigma \end{array} \right] \leq \epsilon \ .$$

The argument size $\mathsf{s} := |\pi|$ is a function of the desired query bound t and soundness error ϵ. So are the running time pt of the prover P and the running time vt of the verifier V.

4   Our Construction

We describe our construction of a (succinct) non-interactive argument from a PCP. Let $(\mathbf{P}, \mathbf{V})$ be a PCP system for the desired relation, with proof length I over an alphabet Σ and query complexity q; for notational convenience, we set $d := \lceil \log \mathsf{I} \rceil$. The construction is additionally parametrized by a *stop layer*

$i^* \in \{0, 1, \ldots, d-1\}$, which we will set in the analysis (looking ahead, 2^{i^*} will be roughly the number of queries in the PCP).

The Oracles in Our Construction. The algorithms below are granted access to three oracles:

1. a *tree oracle* $\zeta_{\text{tree}} \colon \{0,1\}^{2\lambda} \to \{0,1\}^{\lambda}$, which hashes two elements to one;
2. a *PCP randomness oracle* $\zeta_{\text{rnd}} \colon \{0,1\}^{2^{i^*} \cdot \lambda} \to \{0,1\}^{r}$, which hashes 2^{i^*} elements to r bits, where r is the randomness complexity of the PCP verifier **V**;
3. a random permutation Perm$\colon [\mathsf{l}] \to [\mathsf{l}]$, over the locations of a PCP string.

In our analysis, we assume that these oracle are available; all of them can be derived from a single random oracle $\zeta \colon \{0,1\}^* \to \{0,1\}^*$. First, using domain separation one can create multiple random oracles from a single one. The second oracle has a larger domain, which is derived via domain extension (for example, using the Merkle–Damgård iterated construction [Mer89, Dam89]). The third is derived via Feistel networks, as discussed in Sect. 4.1.

Since the oracles have different input lengths, the cost for querying each oracle differs. We consider a query to the tree oracle as a single query to the random oracle (i.e., reducing a single unit from the cheating prover's query budget). The PCP randomness oracle hashes 2^{i^*} elements and thus its cost will be 2^{i^*} accordingly. We consider queries to the random permutation to be "free". That is, a cheating prover can completely query the permutation oracle with no change to its query budget (this makes our result stronger).

We describe the argument prover P and then the argument verifier V of the tuple $\mathsf{ARG} = (P, V)$.

Argument Prover. The argument prover P takes as input an instance x and a witness w, and computes an argument π as follows.

1. Run the PCP prover **P** on (x, w) to obtain a PCP string $\Pi' \in \Sigma^{\mathsf{l}}$.
2. Use the permutation Perm to permute this PCP string and obtain Π such that $\Pi[i] = \Pi'[\texttt{Perm}(i)]$.
3. Use the random oracle ζ_{tree} to Merkle commit to Π, as follows:
   - For every $j \in [\mathsf{l}]$, set the j-th leaf $h_{d,j} := \Pi_j \in \Sigma$.
   - For $i = d-1, d-2, \ldots, i^*$: for $j \in [2^i]$, compute
     $$h_{i,j} := \zeta_{\text{tree}}(i\|j\|h_{i+1,2j-1}\|h_{i+1,2j}) \in \{0,1\}^{\lambda}.$$
   - Set the Merkle cap $\mathbf{h} := \{h_{i^*,j} \in \{0,1\}^{\lambda}\}_{j \in [2^{i^*}]}$.
4. Derive randomness $\rho := \zeta_{\text{rnd}}(\mathbf{h}) \in \{0,1\}^{r}$ and simulate the PCP verifier **V** on input $(\mathrm{x}; \rho)$ and PCP string Π; this execution induces q query-answer pairs $(j_1, a_1), \ldots, (j_{\mathsf{q}}, a_{\mathsf{q}}) \in [\mathsf{l}] \times \Sigma$.
5. Output
   $$\pi := \Big(\mathbf{h}, (j_1, a_1, p_1), \ldots, (j_d, a_d, p_d)\Big) \tag{1}$$

   where $p_1, \ldots, p_d$ are the authentication paths for the query-answer pairs $(j_1, a_1), \ldots, (j_{\mathsf{q}}, a_{\mathsf{q}})$, truncated at level i^* of the tree.

Argument Verifier. The argument verifier V takes as input an instance $\mathbb{x}$ and a proof π (of the form as in Eq. 1), and computes a decision bit as follows.

1. derive randomness $\rho := \zeta_{\mathrm{rnd}}(\mathbf{h})$ for the PCP verifier from the Merkle cap $\mathbf{h}$;
2. check that the PCP verifier $\mathbf{V}$, on input $(\mathbb{x}; \rho)$ and by answering a query to j_r with a_r, accepts;
3. check that $p_1, \ldots, p_d$ are authentication paths of $(j_1, a_1), \ldots, (j_d, a_d)$ relative to the Merkle cap $\mathbf{h}$.

Argument Size. The argument π contains the Merkle cap $\mathbf{h} \in \{0,1\}^{2^{i^*} \cdot \lambda}$, a $(\log|\Sigma|)$-bit answer for each of q queries, and q authentication paths. This totals to an argument size that is

$$2^{i^*} \cdot \lambda + \mathsf{q} \cdot \log|\Sigma| + \mathsf{q} \cdot \lambda \cdot \log(\mathsf{l}/2^{i^*}) \ . \tag{2}$$

Each of the q queries in $[\mathsf{l}]$ comes with an authentication path containing the $\log(\mathsf{l}/2^{i^*})$ siblings of vertices on the path from the query to the Merkle cap, which amounts to $\lambda \cdot \log(\mathsf{l}/2^{i^*})$ bits. (More precisely, $\log|\Sigma| + \lambda \cdot (\log(\mathsf{l}/2^{i^*}) - 1)$ bits since the first sibling is a symbol in Σ rather than an output of the random oracle.)

As noted in earlier works (e.g., [BBHR19, BCR+19]) parts of the information across the q authentication paths is redundant, and the argument size can be reduced by *pruning*: the prover includes in π the minimal set of siblings to authenticate the q queries as a set. All concrete argument sizes that we report in Table 1 already account for this straightforward optimization.

Remark 2 (salts for zero knowledge and more). The security analysis that we present in this paper (see Sect. 7) works *even* if all the vertices in the tree are "salted", which means that an attacker may include an arbitrary string $\sigma_{i,j} \in \{0,1\}^\lambda$ in the query that obtains the digest $h_{i,j}$, for any $i \in \{0, 1, \ldots, d-1\}$ and $j \in [2^i]$. That is, our results hold against strong attacks (the attacker can obtain multiple random digests $h_{i,j}$ for any given indices i and j). Salts are useful for showing additional properties of SNARGs in the random oracle model, and in particular, to achieve zero-knowledge[BCS16, IMSX15].

4.1 Implementing the Random Permutation

We discuss how to implement the random permutation given the random oracle. We need a pseudorandom permutation over the domain $[\mathsf{l}]$, where l is the length of the PCP. There are multiple ways to do this, and here we use Feistel networks, also known as also known as Luby–Rackoff permutations [HR10, LR88, NR99]. These constructions are parameterized by a number of Feistel rounds r; each round calls the random oracle once, and the more rounds, the better the security. In particular, for any algorithm performing q queries, the advantage in distinguishing it from a truly random permutation is exponentially small. In our case, the "adversary" performing the queries is the PCP verifier, which performs non-adaptive queries. We do not need to fool the cheating prover of the argument scheme. The only goal of the permutation is to spread the PCP queries into evenly divided blocks. We use the following theorem.

Theorem 2 ([HR10, Theorem 3]). *The Feistel permutation over* $[l]$ *with* r *rounds has distinguishing advantage at most* $\frac{q}{r+1}\left(\frac{4q}{l}\right)^r$, *for any non-adaptive* q-*query algorithm.*

In particular, setting r to be large enough (and recalling that q is merely the number of queries in the PCP), we can set the distinguishing probability to be extremely small with negligible effect on our proof, and thus we omit these terms and perm our analysis under the assumption of a truly random permutation. For our theoretical needs, the theorem above suffices. Even setting concrete parameters, the number of rounds needed is relatively small. However, there are several other alternatives with different concrete performance. One example is to use DES (recall that we do not need to hide the key from the cheating prover) or to use other standards such as FFX [BRS10].

5   Permuted Robust Soundness

Definition 3 (Block distance). *Let* $\Pi, \Pi' \in \Sigma^l$ *be two strings, and consider them divided to* b *blocks. That is, we view them as* $\Pi, \Pi' \in (\Sigma^{l/b})^b$. *Define* $\Delta_b(\Pi, \Pi')$ *to be the block-wise distance between* Π *and* Π' *(i.e., the number of blocks of symbols on which they differ).*

Moreover, for any permutation **Perm**, *we define* Δ_b^{Perm} *similarly where we first permute the order according to* **Perm** *and then divide to blocks.*

Game 3. The *permuted robust soundness game* is parametrized by a PCP verifier $\mathbf{V}$, an instance $\mathbb{x}$, a positive integer b, and a non-negative integer d. We denote by $\mathcal{G}_{per}(\mathbf{V}, \mathbb{x}, b, d, \tilde{\mathbf{P}})$ the boolean random variable denoting whether a malicious prover $\tilde{\mathbf{P}}$ wins in this game, according to the description below.

1. **Perm** is sampled as a random permutation over $[l]$.
2. $\tilde{\mathbf{P}}$ outputs a proof string $\Pi \in \Sigma^l$.
3. $\tilde{\mathbf{P}}$ receives a random string $\rho \in \{0,1\}^r$, which represents randomness for the PCP verifier.
4. $\tilde{\mathbf{P}}$ outputs a proof string $\Pi' \in \Sigma^l$.
5. The game outputs 1 if and only if $\mathbf{V}^{\Pi'}(\mathbb{x}; \rho) = 1$, and $\Delta_b^{Perm}(\Pi, \Pi') \leq d$.

Definition 4. *A PCP* $(\mathbf{P}, \mathbf{V})$ *for a relation* R *has* **permuted robust soundness error** $\varepsilon_{per}(\mathbb{x}, b, d)$ *if for every instance* $\mathbb{x} \notin L(R)$, *integers* b, d, *and malicious prover* $\tilde{\mathbf{P}}$,

$$\Pr\left[\mathcal{G}_{per}(\mathbf{V}, \mathbb{x}, b, d, \tilde{\mathbf{P}}) = 1\right] \leq \varepsilon_{per}(\mathbb{x}, b, d) \ .$$

The PCP *has permuted robustness* **ratio** β *(with respect to* b) *if for any* $d \in \{0, 1, \ldots, b\}$ *it holds that:*

$$\varepsilon_{per}(\mathbb{x}, b, d+1) \leq \beta \cdot \varepsilon_{per}(\mathbb{x}, b, d) \ .$$

Lemma 5 (restatement of Lemma 1). *Let* $(\mathbf{P}, \mathbf{V})$ *be a PCP with soundness error* $\varepsilon_{\text{base}}$, *length* I, *and query complexity* q, *and assume each location is queried with probability at most* p. *Let* $\kappa \in \mathbb{N}$ *and let* $(\mathbf{P}, \mathbf{V})_\kappa$ *be the* κ-*repeated version of* $(\mathbf{P}, \mathbf{V})$. *If* $\mathsf{b} \geq \kappa \cdot \mathsf{q} \cdot \varepsilon_{\text{base}}^{-1}$, *and* $p \leq (8\mathsf{b} \cdot \kappa)^{-1}$ *then* $(\mathbf{P}, \mathbf{V})_\kappa$ *has strong permuted robust soundness error*

$$\varepsilon_{\text{per}}(\mathbb{x}, \mathsf{b}, d) \leq \frac{e^{1.2 \cdot d}}{d!} \cdot \mathsf{b}^d \cdot \varepsilon_{\text{base}}^\kappa .$$

Moreover, the robustness ratio is $\beta \leq 2.33 \cdot \mathsf{b}$.

Using the above lemma, we can plug in a PCP with soundness error $1/2$ that uses 3 queries, with proof length I and get the following corollary.

Corollary 1. *For any* $\kappa \in N$, *there is a PCP* $(\mathbf{P}, \mathbf{V})$ *that has query complexity* $\mathsf{q} = 3\kappa$ *and has permuted robust ratio*

$$\beta \leq 2.33 \cdot \kappa \cdot 3 \cdot 2 = 14\kappa .$$

6   Cap Soundness

We define a PCP soundness game that we call *cap soundness game*. The game is played on a graph $G = (V, E)$ that represents the Merkle tree in the Micali construction. The game starts out with the graph being empty ($E = \emptyset$), and the PCP adversary can iteratively choose one of several actions, with some budget limitations that constrain how many collisions and inversions the PCP adversary can create in the Merkle tree. We stress that this game is information-theoretic, and can be viewed as an abstract modeling of the effects of these attacks in the real world. The edges are in fact *hyper*edges in order to keep track of which inputs are "hashed" together to create a specific output. Below we introduce definitions for describing the game, and then relate winning this game to winning the reverse soundness game.

Definition 5. *Let* d, i^*, *and* λ *be positive integers, and* Σ *a finite alphabet. The vertex set* V *is the union* $V_{i^*} \cup \cdots \cup V_d$ *where* $V_d := \{(d, j, h) : j \in [2^d], h \in \Sigma\}$ *and, for every* $i \in \{i^*, \ldots, d - 1\}$, $V_i := \{(i, j, h) : j \in [2^i], h \in \{0, 1\}^\lambda\}$. *We consider graphs of the form* $G = (V, E)$ *where* E *is a set of (hyper)edges chosen from the following collection:*

$$\mathcal{E} = \left\{ (u, v_0, v_1) : \begin{matrix} u = (i, j, h) \in V_i \\ v_0 = (i + 1, 2j - 1, h_0) \in V_{i+1} \\ v_1 = (i + 1, 2j, h_1) \in V_{i+1} \end{matrix} \right\} .$$

For an edge $e = (u, v_0, v_1)$, *we call* u *its base vertex and* v_0, v_1 *its children vertices. We also define:*

- *the* **edges** *of a base vertex* $u = (i, j, h)$ *are* $\mathsf{edges}(u) := \{(u, v_0, v_1) \in E : v_0, v_1 \in V_{i+1}\}$;

– *the* **level** *of an edge* e, *denoted* $\mathsf{level}(e)$, *is* i *if its base vertex has the form* $u = (i, j, h)$.

Each leaf of the graph, namely, a vertex $u = (d, j, h)$ at level d is associated to a symbol, h. A collection of leaves thus determine a string whose location j is the symbol of the j-th leaf.

Definition 6. *Let* $G = (V, E)$ *be a graph over the vertex set* V *as in Definition 5.*

– *A vertex* $u_d \in V_d$ *is* **connected** *in* G *to a vertex* $u_\ell \in V_\ell$ *if there exist vertices* $u_{d-1}, \ldots, u_{\ell+1}$ *such that, for all* $i \in \{d, d-1, \ldots, \ell+1\}$, $u_i \in V_i$ *and there is an edge* $e \in E$ *such that* $u_i, u_{i-1} \in e$.
– *A vertex* $v \in V_i$ *is* **free** *in* G *if for every* $u \in V_{i-1}$ *and* $v' \in V_i$ *it holds that* $(u, v, v') \notin E$.

Notice that the connectivity concerns only paths that begin at any leaf (a vertex at level d) and move directly towards the vertex u_ℓ. That is, at each step on the path, the level decreases by 1. Moreover, a vertex at level i is free if there is no edge that connects it to a vertex at level $i - 1$.

Definition 7. *Let* $G = (V, E)$ *be a graph over the vertex set* V *as in Definition 5, and let* Perm *be a permutation. A string* $s \in (\Sigma \cup \{\bot\})^l$ *is* **consistent with** G *with respect to* Perm *if for every* $j \in [l]$ *such that* $s[j] \neq \bot$ *there exists a vertex* $v_{\mathit{Perm}(j)} = (d, \mathit{Perm}(j), h) \in V_d$ *such that* $h = s[j]$ *and* $v_{\mathit{Perm}(j)}$ *is connected some* $u \in V_{i^*}$ *in* G. *In such a case we write* $\mathsf{Consistent}(G, \mathit{Perm}, s) = 1$.

Game 4. The *cap soundness game* is parametrized by a PCP verifier $\mathbf{V}$, an instance $\mathbf{x}$, and an integer λ. The game receives as input a malicious prover $\tilde{\mathbf{P}}$, a root budget $t_{\mathrm{rnd}} \in \mathbb{N}$, a tree budget $t_{\mathrm{tree}} \in \mathbb{N}$, a collision budget $t_{\mathrm{col}} \in \mathbb{N}$, and an inversion budget $t_{\mathrm{inv}} \in \mathbb{N}$, which we denote $\mathcal{G}_{\mathrm{cap}}(\mathbf{V}, \mathbf{x}, \lambda, \tilde{\mathbf{P}}, i^*, t_{\mathrm{rnd}}, t_{\mathrm{tree}}, t_{\mathrm{col}}, t_{\mathrm{inv}})$. The game works as follows:

– **Initialization:**
  1. Set $E := \emptyset$ to be an empty edge set for the graph $G = (V, E)$.
  2. Set Rand to be an empty mapping from V to verifier randomness.
  3. Perm is a sampled as a uniformly random permutation over $[l]$ and given to the prover $\tilde{\mathbf{P}}$.
– **Round:** $\tilde{\mathbf{P}}$ chooses one of the following options until it decides to exit.
  • **Option** ADD: $\tilde{\mathbf{P}}$ submits a vertex $u = (i, j, h) \in V$ with $i \in \{i^*, \ldots, d-1\}$ and strings h_0, h_1.
    1. Set the (hyper)edge $e := (u, v_0, v_1)$ where $v_0 := (i+1, 2j-1, h_0) \in V_{i+1}$ and $v_1 := (i+1, 2j, h_1) \in V_{i+1}$.
    2. If u is not free then $t_{\mathrm{inv}} \leftarrow t_{\mathrm{inv}} - 1$.
    3. If $|e(u)| \geq 1$ then $t_{\mathrm{col}} \leftarrow t_{\mathrm{col}} - 1$.
    4. Add $e = (u, v_0, v_1)$ to E.
    5. $t_{\mathrm{tree}} \leftarrow t_{\mathrm{tree}} - 1$.
  • **Option** RND: $\tilde{\mathbf{P}}$ submits a cap vertex $v_{\mathrm{h}} \in V_{i^*}$.
    1. If Rand already contains an entry for v_{h} then set $\rho \leftarrow \mathsf{Rand}[v_{\mathrm{h}}]$.
    2. If Rand does not contain an entry for v_{h} then sample $\rho \in \{0,1\}^r$ at random and set $\mathsf{Rand}[v_{\mathrm{h}}] \leftarrow \rho$.

3. $t_{\mathrm{rnd}} \leftarrow t_{\mathrm{rnd}} - 1$.
4. ρ is given to $\tilde{\mathbf{P}}$.

- **Output:** $\tilde{\mathbf{P}}$ outputs a cap $v_1, \ldots, v_{2^{i^*}} \in V_{i^*}$ and leaf vertices $v_1, \ldots, v_{\mathsf{q}} \in V_d$.
- **Decision:** $\tilde{\mathbf{P}}$ wins if all checks below pass.
   1. Construct a PCP string $\Pi \in (\Sigma \cup \{\bot\})^{\mathsf{l}}$: for every $r \in [\mathsf{q}]$, parse the r-th leaf vertex as $v_r = (d, j, h)$ and set $\Pi[\mathrm{Perm}(j)] := h \in \Sigma$; set $\Pi[j] := \bot$ for all other locations.
   2. Retrieve PCP randomness for this root vertex: $\rho^* \leftarrow \mathrm{Rand}[v_h]$.
   3. Check that the PCP verifier accepts: $\mathbf{V}^{\Pi}(\mathbb{x}; \rho^*) = 1$.
   4. Check that Π is consistent in G w.r.t. Perm: $\mathrm{Consistent}(G, \mathrm{Perm}, \Pi) = 1$.
   5. Check that $\tilde{\mathbf{P}}$ is within budget: $t_{\mathrm{col}} \geq 0$, $t_{\mathrm{inv}} \geq 0$, $t_{\mathrm{rnd}} \geq 0$, and $t_{\mathrm{tree}} \geq 0$.

Definition 8. *A PCP* $(\mathbf{P}, \mathbf{V})$ *for a relation R has cap soundness error* $\varepsilon_{\mathrm{cap}}(\mathbb{x}, \lambda, i^*, t_{\mathrm{rnd}}, t_{\mathrm{tree}}, t_{\mathrm{col}}, t_{\mathrm{inv}})$ *if for every* $\mathbb{x} \notin L(R)$*, output size* $\lambda \in \mathbb{N}$*, malicious prover* $\tilde{\mathbf{P}}$*, stop layer i^*, and budgets* $t_{\mathrm{rnd}}, t_{\mathrm{col}}, t_{\mathrm{inv}} \in \mathbb{N}$*,*

$$\Pr\left[\mathcal{G}_{\mathrm{cap}}(\mathbf{V}, \mathbb{x}, \lambda, \tilde{\mathbf{P}}, i^*, t_{\mathrm{rnd}}, t_{\mathrm{tree}}, t_{\mathrm{col}}, t_{\mathrm{inv}}) = 1\right] \leq \varepsilon_{\mathrm{cap}}(\mathbb{x}, \lambda, i^*, t_{\mathrm{rnd}}, t_{\mathrm{tree}}, t_{\mathrm{col}}, t_{\mathrm{inv}}) \ .$$

Lemma 6 (restatement of Lemma 2). *Let* $(\mathbf{P}, \mathbf{V})$ *be a PCP for a relation R with permuted robust soundness error* $\varepsilon_{\mathrm{PCP}}$ *with respect to distance Δ_{b} for parameter b, and suppose it has uniformly random queries. Then, $(\mathbf{P}, \mathbf{V})$ has cap soundness error*

$$\varepsilon_{\mathrm{cap}}(\mathbb{x}, \lambda, i^*, t_{\mathrm{rnd}}, t_{\mathrm{tree}}, t_{\mathrm{col}}, t_{\mathrm{inv}}) \leq t_{\mathrm{rnd}} \cdot 2^{t_{\mathrm{col}}} \cdot \varepsilon_{\mathrm{per}}(\mathbb{x}, \mathsf{b} = 2^{i^*}, d = t_{\mathrm{inv}}) \ .$$

The lemma is proved in the full version.

7   Soundness Based on Permuted Robust Soundness

Theorem 5 (restatement of Lemma 4). *Suppose that our construction (described in Sect. 4) is instantiated with:*

1. *a PCP with soundness $\varepsilon_{\mathrm{PCP}}$ and permuted robustness ratio $\beta(\mathsf{b})$;*
2. *a random oracle with output size λ; and*
3. *stop layer i^*.*

Then, provided that $\lambda \geq 2\log t + \log \beta(2^{i^*}) + 3$, the construction has a soundness error $\epsilon(t)$ against t-query adversaries that is bounded as follows:

$$\epsilon(t) \leq t \cdot \varepsilon_{\mathrm{PCP}} \ .$$

Using this soundness analysis along with concrete PCPs, we get the following corollary:

Corollary 2 (restatement of Theorem 1). *Our construction implies a SNARG for NP in the random oracle model that has (t, ϵ)-security with an argument size of*

$$O\Big(\log(t/\epsilon) \cdot \big(\log t + \log\log(t/\epsilon)\big) \cdot \log(\mathsf{l}/\log(t/\epsilon))\Big) \ . \tag{3}$$

We prove the theorem in Sect. 7.1 and the corollary in Sect. 7.2.

7.1   Proof of Theorem 5

Fix $t \in \mathbb{N}$. Let $\tilde{P}$ be a t-query cheating argument prover. Note that $\tilde{P}$ can make queries to the randomness oracle ζ_{rnd} and tree oracle ζ_{tree} (or the permutation but we are giving these queries to the cheating prover for free). Recall that the randomness oracle t_{rnd} has a larger domain size and thus has cost 2^{i^*}. For any choice of positive integers t_{rnd} and t_{tree} such that $2^{i^*} \cdot t_{\mathrm{rnd}} + t_{\mathrm{tree}} \leq t$, below we condition on the event that $\tilde{P}$ makes t_{rnd} queries to ζ_{rnd} and t_{tree} queries to ζ_{tree}. For any such choice, we obtain the same upper bound (independent of the choice of t_{rnd} and t_{tree}), and hence conclude that the bound holds for the distribution of t_{rnd} and t_{tree} implied by $\tilde{P}$.

We rely on the claim below, which states that a cheating argument prover can be transformed into a cheating PCP prover for the cap soundness game with a small loss, when the budgets for collisions and inversions correspond to the corresponding scores of the trace of the argument prover.

Claim 6. *There is an efficient transformation $\mathbb{T}$ such that, for every cheating argument prover $\tilde{P}$, the cheating PCP prover $\tilde{\mathbf{P}} := \mathbb{T}(\tilde{P})$ satisfies the following condition for every $k \in \mathbb{N}$:*

$$
\Pr \left[V^{\zeta}(\mathbb{x}, \pi) = 1 \;\middle|\; \begin{array}{c} \zeta \leftarrow \mathcal{U}(\lambda) \\ \pi \leftarrow \tilde{P}^{\zeta} \\ \mathrm{tr}_{\mathrm{rnd}} \leftarrow \mathsf{queries}_{\mathrm{rnd}}(\tilde{P}, \zeta) \\ \mathrm{tr}_{\mathrm{tree}} \leftarrow \mathsf{queries}_{\mathrm{tree}}(\tilde{P}, \zeta) \\ |\mathrm{tr}_{\mathrm{rnd}}| = t_{\mathrm{rnd}}, |\mathrm{tr}_{\mathrm{tree}}| = t_{\mathrm{tree}} \\ \mathsf{score}_{\mathrm{col}}(\mathrm{tr}_{\mathrm{tree}}) \leq k \\ \mathsf{score}_{\mathrm{inv}}(\mathrm{tr}_{\mathrm{tree}}) \leq k \end{array} \right] \leq \Pr \left[\mathcal{G}_{\mathrm{cap}}(\mathbf{V}, \mathbb{x}, \lambda, \tilde{\mathbf{P}}, i^*, t_{\mathrm{rnd}}, t_{\mathrm{tree}}, k, k) = 1 \right] .
$$

$$(4)$$

Above $\mathsf{queries}_{\mathrm{rnd}}(\tilde{P}, \zeta)$ *and* $\mathsf{queries}_{\mathrm{tree}}(\tilde{P}, \zeta)$ *respectively denote the queries by $\tilde{P}$ to the oracles ζ_{rnd} and ζ_{tree} obtained from ζ via domain separation.*

The proof of Claim 6 is given at the end of this proof.

We use the oracle scoring lemma to obtain a bound that will be useful in the analysis further below; we also use the assumption that $\lambda \geq 2 \log t + \log \beta + 3$ and the fact that $t \geq t_{\mathrm{tree}}$. The bound holds for any choice of a parameter $k \in \mathbb{N}$.

$$\sum_{k=0}^{\infty} 2^k \cdot \beta^k \cdot \Pr[\text{score}_{\text{inv}}(\text{tr}_{\text{tree}}) = k \vee \text{score}_{\text{col}}(\text{tr}_{\text{tree}}) = k]$$

$$\leq 1 + \sum_{k=1}^{\infty} (2\beta)^k \cdot \left(\frac{1}{k!} \cdot \left(\frac{2t \cdot t_{\text{tree}}}{2^\lambda} \right)^k + \left(\frac{t_{\text{tree}}^2}{2 \cdot 2^\lambda} \right)^k \right)$$

$$= 1 + \sum_{k=1}^{\infty} \frac{1}{k!} \cdot \left(\frac{4t \cdot t_{\text{tree}} \cdot \beta}{2^\lambda} \right)^k + \sum_{k=1}^{\infty} \left(\frac{t_{\text{tree}}^2 \cdot \beta}{2^\lambda} \right)^k$$

$$\leq 1 + \sum_{k=1}^{\infty} \frac{1}{k!} \cdot \left(\frac{4t_{\text{tree}}}{2^3 \cdot t} \right)^k + \sum_{k=1}^{\infty} \left(\frac{t_{\text{tree}}}{2^3 \cdot t} \right)^k \quad (\text{since } \lambda \geq 2 \log t + \log \beta + 3)$$

$$\leq 1 + \frac{t_{\text{tree}}}{t} \cdot \sum_{k=1}^{\infty} \frac{1}{k!} \cdot \left(\frac{4}{2^3} \right)^k + \frac{t_{\text{tree}}}{t} \cdot \sum_{k=1}^{\infty} \left(\frac{1}{2^3} \right)^k$$

$$\leq 1 + 0.65 \cdot \frac{t_{\text{tree}}}{t} + 0.15 \cdot \frac{t_{\text{tree}}}{t}$$

$$\leq 1 + \frac{t_{\text{tree}}}{t} .$$

Using the above bound, we conclude the following:

$$\Pr \left[V^\zeta(\mathbb{x}, \pi) = 1 \, \middle| \, \begin{matrix} \zeta \leftarrow \mathcal{U}(\lambda) \\ \pi \leftarrow \tilde{P}^\zeta \end{matrix} \right]$$

$$\leq \sum_{k=0}^{\infty} \Pr \left[\mathcal{G}_{\text{cap}}(\mathbf{V}, \mathbb{x}, \lambda, \tilde{\mathbf{P}}, i^*, t_{\text{rnd}}, t_{\text{tree}}, k, k) = 1 \right] \cdot$$

$\Pr[\text{score}_{\text{inv}}(\text{tr}_{\text{tree}}, \text{tr}_{\text{rnd}}) = k \vee \text{score}_{\text{col}}(\text{tr}_{\text{tree}}) = k]$ (by Claim 6)

$$\leq \sum_{k=0}^{\infty} \varepsilon_{\text{cap}}(\mathbb{x}, \lambda, i^*, t_{\text{rnd}}, t_{\text{tree}}, k, k) \cdot$$

$\Pr[\text{score}_{\text{inv}}(\text{tr}_{\text{tree}}, \text{tr}_{\text{rnd}}) = k \vee \text{score}_{\text{col}}(\text{tr}_{\text{tree}}) = k]$ (by Definition 8)

$$\leq \sum_{k=0}^{\infty} t_{\text{rnd}} \cdot 2^k \cdot \varepsilon_{\text{per}}(\mathbb{x}, 2^{i^*}, k) \cdot$$

$\Pr[\text{score}_{\text{inv}}(\text{tr}_{\text{tree}}, \text{tr}_{\text{rnd}}) = k \vee \text{score}_{\text{col}}(\text{tr}_{\text{tree}}) = k]$ (by Lemma 6)

$$\leq \sum_{k=0}^{\infty} t_{\text{rnd}} \cdot 2^k \cdot \beta^k \cdot \varepsilon_{\text{per}}(\mathbb{x}, 2^{i^*}, 0) \cdot$$

$\Pr[\text{score}_{\text{inv}}(\text{tr}_{\text{tree}}, \text{tr}_{\text{rnd}}) = k \vee \text{score}_{\text{col}}(\text{tr}_{\text{tree}}) = k]$ (since β is the robustness ratio)

$$\leq \sum_{k=0}^{\infty} t_{\text{rnd}} \cdot 2^k \cdot \beta^k \cdot \varepsilon_{\text{PCP}}(\mathbb{x}) \cdot$$

$\Pr[\text{score}_{\text{inv}}(\text{tr}_{\text{tree}}, \text{tr}_{\text{rnd}}) = k \vee \text{score}_{\text{col}}(\text{tr}_{\text{tree}}) = k]$ (since $\varepsilon_{\text{per}}(\mathbb{x}, 2^{i^*}, 0) = \varepsilon_{\text{PCP}}(\mathbb{x})$)

$$= t_{\text{rnd}} \cdot \varepsilon_{\text{PCP}}(\mathbb{x}) \cdot \sum_{k=0}^{\infty} 2^k \cdot \beta^k \cdot$$

$\Pr[\text{score}_{\text{inv}}(\text{tr}_{\text{tree}}, \text{tr}_{\text{rnd}}) = k \vee \text{score}_{\text{col}}(\text{tr}_{\text{tree}}) = k]$

$$\leq t_{\text{rnd}} \cdot \varepsilon_{\text{PCP}}(\mathbb{x}) \cdot \left(1 + \frac{t_{\text{tree}}}{t} \right) \quad (\text{using the bound proved above})$$

$$= t \cdot \varepsilon_{\text{PCP}}(\mathbb{x}) .$$

This concludes the proof of the theorem, giving an upper bound on the soundness error.

We are left to prove the claim used in the proof above.

Proof (Proof of Claim 6). For the sake of simplicity of the proof, we will assume the following two conditions that are without loss of generality:

- (No duplicate queries): The cheating argument prover $\tilde{P}$ does not make duplicate queries to the random oracle. This can be achieved by having $\tilde{P}$ store the answers to prior queries, and making only new queries to the random oracle, and has no effect on the rest of the proof. Recall that we are considering the Micali construction with salts (see Remark 2), which means that the aforementioned "no duplicate query" condition implies that the prover does not make the same query with the same salt but can make the same query with a different salt (as that results in a different input to the random oracle).
- (Self-verifying): The cheating prover, before submitting his final proof, runs the verify to check that it accepts, and otherwise submits a $\perp$ symbol. This can be achieved by having $\tilde{P}$ run the verifier at the end of its execution. Admittingly, this is not completely without loss of generalization, as this might cost a few additional queries. However, this has a negligible effect on the query complexity and on our results and we omit it.

We use $\tilde{P}$ to construct a PCP prover $\tilde{\mathbf{P}}$ that plays in the cap soundness game $\mathcal{G}_{\text{cap}}$ (Game 4). The PCP prover $\tilde{\mathbf{P}}$ simulates the argument prover $\tilde{P}$ and, whenever $\tilde{P}$ performs a query x to the random oracle, $\tilde{\mathbf{P}}$ performs one of the following actions depending on x.

- *Root query:* x is a query in $\{0,1\}^\lambda$ to the PCP randomness oracle ζ_{rnd}.
  1. Construct the root vertex $v_{\mathbf{h}} := (0, 1, x) \in V_0$.
  2. Submit, via Option RND in $\mathcal{G}_{\text{cap}}$, the root vertex $v_{\mathbf{h}}$.
  3. Receive from $\mathcal{G}_{\text{cap}}$ a random string $\rho \in \{0,1\}^r$ for the PCP verifier.
  4. Send ρ to $\tilde{P}$.
- *Tree query:* x is a query (i, j, h_0, h_1, σ) to the tree oracle ζ_{tree} with indices $i \in \{0, 1, \ldots, d-1\}$ and $j \in [2^i]$, strings h_0, h_1 in $\{0,1\}^\lambda$ or Σ (depending on i) and salt $\sigma \in \{0,1\}^\lambda$.
  1. Sample a random $h \in \{0,1\}^\lambda$ and set $u := (i, j, h) \in V_i$;
  2. Submit u, h_0, h_1 via Option ADD in $\mathcal{G}_{\text{cap}}$;
  3. Send h to $\tilde{P}$.
- *Other query:* x is a query that does not fit either case above.
  1. Sample a random $h \in \{0,1\}^\lambda$ and send h to $\tilde{P}$.

At the end of its simulation, $\tilde{P}$ outputs a proof π that is parsed as in Eq. 1. The cheating prover $\tilde{\mathbf{P}}$ outputs the root vertex $v_{\mathbf{h}} := (0, 1, \mathbf{h})$ where $\mathbf{h}$ is the root contained in π and also outputs the leaf vertices $\{v_r\}_{r \in [q]}$ where $v_r := (d, j_r, a_r)$ specifies the location $j_r \in [l]$ and answer $a_r \in \Sigma$ in π for the r-th query. We now argue that the constructed PCP prover $\tilde{\mathbf{P}}$ satisfies Eq. 4.

Perfect Simulation. We claim that the PCP prover $\tilde{\mathbf{P}}$ performs a perfect simulation of the argument prover $\tilde{P}$, in that $\tilde{\mathbf{P}}$ gives values to $\tilde{P}$ that are identically distributed as the answers from a random oracle ζ. We argue this for (well-formed) queries to ζ_{rnd} and queries to ζ_{tree}; any other types of queries are trivially uniformly random because that is how $\tilde{\mathbf{P}}$ answers in the third bullet.

First, if $\tilde{P}$ issues a query x to the randomness oracle ζ_{rnd}, then $\tilde{P}$ replies with the randomness ρ received from the cap soundness game $\mathcal{G}_{\mathrm{cap}}$, which is uniformly distributed.

Second, suppose that $\tilde{P}$ issues a query x to the tree oracle ζ_{tree}. Since $\tilde{P}$'s queries are distinct, either of i, j, h_0, h_1 are new elements, in which case no value h has been assigned; or the salt σ is new (the salt allows $\tilde{P}$ to get new randomness for the same choice of i, j, h_0, h_1).

When $\tilde{P}$ Wins then $\tilde{\mathbf{P}}$ Wins. We claim that the PCP prover $\tilde{\mathbf{P}}$ wins the cap soundness game whenever the argument prover $\tilde{P}$ convinces the argument verifier V.

Suppose that $V^{\zeta}(\mathrm{x}, \pi) = 1$ for the proof π output by $\tilde{P}$ and the (partial) random oracle ζ implied by the randomness of the simulation and cap soundness game. Let $\rho^* \leftarrow \mathsf{Rand}[v_{\mathbf{h}}]$ where $v_{\mathbf{h}}$ is the root vertex output by $\tilde{\mathbf{P}}$ and Rand is the table maintained by the cap soundness game.

We can deduce the following two items, which mean that $\tilde{\mathbf{P}}$ wins up to budget constraints.

- $\mathbf{V}^{\Pi}(\mathrm{x}; \rho^*) = 1$ where Π is the PCP proof with value $a_r \in \Sigma$ at location $j_r \in [\mathsf{l}]$ for every $r \in [\mathsf{q}]$, and the value $\perp$ at all other locations. This is because if the argument verifier V accepts then the underlying PCP verifier $\mathbf{V}$ also accepts: $\mathbf{V}$ on instance x and randomness ρ^* accepts when, for every $r \in [\mathsf{q}]$, the answer to query j_r is the value a_r.
- For every $r \in [\mathsf{q}]$, the leaf vertex v_r is connected in G to the root vertex $v_{\mathbf{h}}$ (G is the graph maintained by the cap soundness game), provided that $\tilde{P}$ has queried all vertices in the authentication paths in the final proof π (which we assumed is the case). This is because $p_1, \ldots, p_{\mathsf{q}}$ in π are valid authentication paths for the query-answer pairs $(j_1, a_1), \ldots, (j_{\mathsf{q}}, a_{\mathsf{q}})$ with respect to the root $\mathbf{h}$ in π (and the oracle ζ), and thus all the edges between the leaf vertices $\{v_r\}_{r \in [\mathsf{q}]}$ and the root vertex $v_{\mathbf{h}}$ are in the graph.

The Budget of $\tilde{\mathbf{P}}$ Suffices. We left to argue that the budgets given to $\tilde{\mathbf{P}}$ suffices for the cap soundness game to accept. Let ϵ_k be the success probability of the argument prover $\tilde{P}$ conditioned on $\mathsf{score}_{\mathrm{col}}(\mathsf{tr}_{\mathrm{tree}}) \leq k$ and $\mathsf{score}_{\mathrm{inv}}(\mathsf{tr}_{\mathrm{tree}}) \leq k$ where $\mathsf{tr}_{\mathrm{rnd}}$ is $\tilde{P}$'s trace of queries to the randomness oracle ζ_{rnd} and $\mathsf{tr}_{\mathrm{tree}}$ is $\tilde{P}$'s trace of queries to the tree oracle ζ_{tree} (with $|\mathsf{tr}_{\mathrm{rnd}}| = t_{\mathrm{rnd}}$ and $|\mathsf{tr}_{\mathrm{tree}}| = t_{\mathrm{tree}}$).

Consider any fixed oracle ζ that contributes to ϵ_k, i.e., $\tilde{P}$ wins and the scores are at most k. There is a one-to-one mapping of the values of the oracle ζ to the random values in the simulation that make $\tilde{\mathbf{P}}$ win within the required budget of k. The mapping is done in a natural way because $\tilde{\mathbf{P}}$ does a perfect simulation of $\tilde{P}$: the randomness used by the simulation for query x (either tree of root query) corresponds to the value of the random oracle on query x.

Hence, we only need to show that when the scores are bounded by k then the budgets for the cap soundness game suffice to win the game.

- If $\mathsf{score}_{\mathrm{col}}(\mathsf{tr}_{\mathrm{tree}}) \leq k$ then we know that $\tilde{P}$ has found at most k collisions in $\mathsf{tr}_{\mathrm{tree}}$. In this case, $\tilde{\mathbf{P}}$ submits the same number of collisions as $\tilde{P}$ because it imitates its queries. Thus, the collision budget will suffice for the simulation.

- If $\mathsf{score}_{\mathrm{inv}}(\mathsf{tr}_{\mathrm{tree}}) \leq k$ then we know that $\tilde{P}$ has performed at most k "almost inversions" in $\mathsf{tr}_{\mathrm{tree}}$ and $\mathsf{tr}_{\mathrm{rnd}}$ together. In this case, $\tilde{\mathbf{P}}$ simulates the same queries and will use Option INV at most k times. Thus, the inversion budget will suffice for the simulation.
- Since $\tilde{P}$ performs at most t_{rnd} queries to the randomness oracle ζ_{rnd} and at most t_{tree} queries to the tree oracle ζ_{tree}, then $\tilde{\Pi}$ will perform the same amount of queries to Option RND and Option ADD respectively. $\qquad\square$

7.2 The Argument Size

We prove Corollary 2. Fix t and ϵ. As a base PCP, we take any constant query, constant soundness PCP over a binary (or small) alphabet of polynomial length l. We amplify the soundness by repeating $\kappa = O(\log(t/\epsilon))$ times, and get soundness $\varepsilon_{\mathrm{PCP}} = O(\epsilon/t)$, and query complexity $\mathsf{q} = O(\log(t/\epsilon))$. By Corollary 1, we get that the repeated PCP has permuted robustness ratio $\beta = O(\kappa) = O(\log(t/\epsilon))$, with $\mathsf{b} = O(\kappa)$, and $2^{i^*} = O(\mathsf{q})$. Thus, we need to set

$$\lambda = 2\log t + \log \beta + 3 = O(\log t + \log\log(t/\epsilon)) \ .$$

Plugging this in the argument size formula given in Eq. 2, we get that the argument size is:

$$2^{i^*} \cdot \lambda + \mathsf{q} \cdot \log|\Sigma| + \mathsf{q} \cdot \lambda \cdot \log(\mathsf{l}/2^{i^*}) =$$
$$O\left(\log(t/\epsilon) \cdot (\log t + \log\log(t/\epsilon)) \cdot \log(\mathsf{l}/\log(t/\epsilon))\right) \ .$$

Acknowledgments. Alessandro Chiesa is funded by the Ethereum Foundation and Eylon Yogev is funded by the ISF grants 484/18, 1789/19, Len Blavatnik and the Blavatnik Foundation, The Blavatnik Interdisciplinary Cyber Research Center at Tel Aviv University, and The Raymond and Beverly Sackler Post-Doctoral Scholarship. This work was done (in part) while the second author was visiting the Simons Institute for the Theory of Computing.

References

[ALM+98] Arora, S., Lund, C., Motwani, R., Sudan, M., Szegedy, M.: Proof verification and the hardness of approximation problems. J. ACM **45**(3), 501–555 (1998). Preliminary version in FOCS '92

[AS98] Arora, S., Safra, S.: Probabilistic checking of proofs: a new characterization of NP. J. ACM **45**(1), 70–122 (1998). Preliminary version in FOCS '92

[BBB+18] Bünz, B., Bootle, J., Boneh, D., Poelstra, A., Wuille, P., Maxwell, G.: Bulletproofs: short proofs for confidential transactions and more. In: Proceedings of the 39th IEEE Symposium on Security and Privacy, S&P '18, pp. 315–334 (2018)

[BBC+18] Baum, C., Bootle, J., Cerulli, A., del Pino, R., Groth, J., Lyubashevsky, V.: Sub-linear lattice-based zero-knowledge arguments for arithmetic circuits. In: Shacham, H., Boldyreva, A. (eds.) CRYPTO 2018. LNCS, vol. 10992, pp. 669–699. Springer, Cham (2018). https://doi.org/10.1007/978-3-319-96881-0_23

[BBHR19] Ben-Sasson, E., Bentov, I., Horesh, Y., Riabzev, M.: Scalable zero knowledge with no trusted setup. In: Boldyreva, A., Micciancio, D. (eds.) CRYPTO 2019. LNCS, vol. 11694, pp. 701–732. Springer, Cham (2019). https://doi.org/10.1007/978-3-030-26954-8_23

[BCC+16] Bootle, J., Cerulli, A., Chaidos, P., Groth, J., Petit, C.: Efficient zero-knowledge arguments for arithmetic circuits in the discrete log setting. In: Fischlin, M., Coron, J.-S. (eds.) EUROCRYPT 2016. LNCS, vol. 9666, pp. 327–357. Springer, Heidelberg (2016). https://doi.org/10.1007/978-3-662-49896-5_12

[BCG+14] Ben-Sasson, E., et al.: Zerocash: decentralized anonymous payments from Bitcoin. In: Proceedings of the 2014 IEEE Symposium on Security and Privacy, SP '14, pp. 459–474 (2014)

[BCI+13] Bitansky, N., Chiesa, A., Ishai, Y., Paneth, O., Ostrovsky, R.: Succinct non-interactive arguments via linear interactive proofs. In: Sahai, A. (ed.) TCC 2013. LNCS, vol. 7785, pp. 315–333. Springer, Heidelberg (2013). https://doi.org/10.1007/978-3-642-36594-2_18

[BCR+19] Ben-Sasson, E., Chiesa, A., Riabzev, M., Spooner, N., Virza, M., Ward, N.P.: Aurora: transparent succinct arguments for R1CS. In: Ishai, Y., Rijmen, V. (eds.) EUROCRYPT 2019. LNCS, vol. 11476, pp. 103–128. Springer, Cham (2019). https://doi.org/10.1007/978-3-030-17653-2_4

[BCS16] Ben-Sasson, E., Chiesa, A., Spooner, N.: Interactive oracle proofs. In: Hirt, M., Smith, A. (eds.) TCC 2016. LNCS, vol. 9986, pp. 31–60. Springer, Heidelberg (2016). https://doi.org/10.1007/978-3-662-53644-5_2

[BFLS91] Babai, L., Fortnow, L., Levin, L.A., Szegedy, M.: Checking computations in polylogarithmic time. In: Proceedings of the 23rd Annual ACM Symposium on Theory of Computing, STOC '91, pp. 21–32 (1991)

[BFS20] Bünz, B., Fisch, B., Szepieniec, A.: Transparent SNARKs from DARK compilers. In: Canteaut, A., Ishai, Y. (eds.) EUROCRYPT 2020. LNCS, vol. 12105, pp. 677–706. Springer, Cham (2020). https://doi.org/10.1007/978-3-030-45721-1_24

[BGLR93] Bellare, M., Goldwasser, S., Lund, C., Russell, A.: Efficient probabilistically checkable proofs and applications to approximations. In: Proceedings of the 25th Annual ACM Symposium on Theory of Computing, STOC 93, pp. 294–304 (1993)

[BISW17] Boneh, D., Ishai, Y., Sahai, A., Wu, D.J.: Lattice-based SNARGs and their application to more efficient obfuscation. In: Coron, J.-S., Nielsen, J.B. (eds.) EUROCRYPT 2017. LNCS, vol. 10212, pp. 247–277. Springer, Cham (2017). https://doi.org/10.1007/978-3-319-56617-7_9

[BISW18] Boneh, D., Ishai, Y., Sahai, A., Wu, D.J.: Quasi-optimal SNARGs via linear multi-prover interactive proofs. In: Nielsen, J.B., Rijmen, V. (eds.) EUROCRYPT 2018. LNCS, vol. 10822, pp. 222–255. Springer, Cham (2018). https://doi.org/10.1007/978-3-319-78372-7_8

[BRS10] Bellare, M., Rogaway, P., Spies, T.: The FFX mode of operation for format-preserving encryption. NIST Submission 20, 19 (2010)

[CMS19] Chiesa, A., Manohar, P., Spooner, N.: Succinct arguments in the quantum random oracle model. In: Hofheinz, D., Rosen, A. (eds.) TCC 2019. LNCS, vol. 11892, pp. 1–29. Springer, Cham (2019). https://doi.org/10.1007/978-3-030-36033-7_1

[CY20]   Chiesa, A., Yogev, E.: Barriers for succinct arguments in the random oracle model. In: Pass, R., Pietrzak, K. (eds.) TCC 2020. LNCS, vol. 12551, pp. 47–76. Springer, Cham (2020). https://doi.org/10.1007/978-3-030-64378-2_3

[Dam89] Damgård, I.B.: A design principle for hash functions. In: Brassard, G. (ed.) CRYPTO 1989. LNCS, vol. 435, pp. 416–427. Springer, New York (1990). https://doi.org/10.1007/0-387-34805-0_39

[DHK15] Dinur, I., Harsha, P., Kindler, G.: Polynomially low error PCPs with polyloglog n queries via modular composition. In: Proceedings of the 47th Annual ACM Symposium on Theory of Computing, STOC '15, pp. 267–276 (2015)

[FGL+91] Feige, U., Goldwasser, S., Lovász, L., Safra, S., Szegedy, M.: Approximating clique is almost NP-complete (preliminary version). In Proceedings of the 32nd Annual Symposium on Foundations of Computer Science, SFCS '91, pp. 2–12 (1991)

[FS86]   Fiat, A., Shamir, A.: How to prove yourself: practical solutions to identification and signature problems. In: Odlyzko, A.M. (ed.) CRYPTO 1986. LNCS, vol. 263, pp. 186–194. Springer, Heidelberg (1987). https://doi.org/10.1007/3-540-47721-7_12

[GGPR13] Gennaro, R., Gentry, C., Parno, B., Raykova, M.: Quadratic span programs and succinct NIZKs without PCPs. In: Johansson, T., Nguyen, P.Q. (eds.) EUROCRYPT 2013. LNCS, vol. 7881, pp. 626–645. Springer, Heidelberg (2013). https://doi.org/10.1007/978-3-642-38348-9_37

[GH98]   Goldreich, O., Håstad, J.: On the complexity of interactive proofs with bounded communication. Inf. Process. Lett. **67**(4), 205–214 (1998)

[Gro10] Groth, J.: Short pairing-based non-interactive zero-knowledge arguments. In: Abe, M. (ed.) ASIACRYPT 2010. LNCS, vol. 6477, pp. 321–340. Springer, Heidelberg (2010). https://doi.org/10.1007/978-3-642-17373-8_19

[HR10]   Hoang, V.T., Rogaway, P.: On generalized feistel networks. In: Rabin, T. (ed.) CRYPTO 2010. LNCS, vol. 6223, pp. 613–630. Springer, Heidelberg (2010). https://doi.org/10.1007/978-3-642-14623-7_33

[IMSX15] Ishai, Y., Mahmoody, M., Sahai, A., Xiao, D.: On zero-knowledge PCPs: Limitations, simplifications, and applications (2015). http://www.cs.virginia.edu/~mohammad/files/papers/ZKPCPs-Full.pdf

[Kil92] Kilian, J.: A note on efficient zero-knowledge proofs and arguments. In: Proceedings of the 24th Annual ACM Symposium on Theory of Computing, STOC '92, pp. 723–732 (1992)

[LR88]   Luby, M., Rackoff, C.: How to construct pseudorandom permutations from pseudorandom functions. SIAM J. Comput. **17**(2), 373–386 (1988)

[Mer89] Merkle, R.C.: One way hash functions and DES. In: Brassard, G. (ed.) CRYPTO 1989. LNCS, vol. 435, pp. 428–446. Springer, New York (1990). https://doi.org/10.1007/0-387-34805-0_40

[Mic00] Micali, S.: Computationally sound proofs. SIAM J. Comput. **30**(4), 1253–1298 (2000). Preliminary version appeared in FOCS '94

[NR99]   Naor, M., Reingold, O.: On the construction of pseudorandom permutations: Luby-Rackoff revisited. J. Cryptol. **12**(1), 29–66 (1999)

[Ele14] Electric Coin Company. Zcash Cryptocurrency (2014). https://z.cash/

[Eth]   Ethereum. ZK-Rollups. https://docs.ethhub.io/ethereum-roadmap/layer-2-scaling/zk-rollups/

Sumcheck Arguments and Their Applications

Jonathan Bootle[1]([✉]), Alessandro Chiesa[2], and Katerina Sotiraki[2]

[1] IBM Research – Zurich, Zurich, Switzerland
jbt@zurich.ibm.com
[2] UC Berkeley, Berkeley, USA
{alexch,katesot}@berkeley.edu

Abstract. We introduce a class of interactive protocols, which we call *sumcheck arguments*, that establishes a novel connection between the sumcheck protocol (Lund et al. JACM 1992) and folding techniques for Pedersen commitments (Bootle et al. EUROCRYPT 2016).

We define a class of sumcheck-friendly commitment schemes over modules that captures many examples of interest, and show that the sumcheck protocol applied to a polynomial associated with the commitment scheme yields a succinct argument of knowledge for openings of the commitment. Building on this, we additionally obtain succinct arguments for the NP-complete language R1CS over certain rings.

Sumcheck arguments enable us to recover as a special case numerous prior works in disparate cryptographic settings (discrete logarithms, pairings, groups of unknown order, lattices), providing one framework to understand them all. Further, we answer open questions raised in prior works, such as obtaining a lattice-based succinct argument from the SIS assumption for satisfiability problems over rings.

Keywords: Sumcheck protocol · Succinct arguments · Scalar-product protocol

1 Introduction

Sumcheck Protocols. The sumcheck protocol is an interactive proof introduced in [LFKN92] that has played a fundamental role in the theory of probabilistic proofs in complexity theory (e.g., [BFL91, BFLS91, GKR08]) and, more recently, in cryptography. The sumcheck protocol has been used widely in a line of works on *succinct arguments* [CMT12, VSBW13, Wah+17, ZGKPP17, WTSTW18, XZZPS19, Set20]. One of the main benefits of the sumcheck protocol is that, in certain settings, the prover can be implemented in a linear number of operations [Tha13] or as a streaming algorithm [CMT12]; this avoids operations such as the Fast Fourier Transform (common in other succinct arguments) that

---

The full version of this paper is available at https://eprint.iacr.org/2021/333.

T. Malkin and C. Peikert (Eds.): CRYPTO 2021, LNCS 12825, pp. 742–773, 2021.
https://doi.org/10.1007/978-3-030-84242-0_26

are costly in time and in memory. The sumcheck protocol also satisfies strong soundness properties that facilitate arguing the security of the Fiat–Shamir transformation in the plain model [CCHLRR18], which is notoriously hard to analyze for other interactive proofs. Moreover, variants of the sumcheck protocol have spawned lines of research: the univariate sumcheck [BCRSVW19] was used in numerous succinct arguments [BCGGRS19, ZXZS20, CHMMVW20, COS20, CFFQR20, BFHVXZ20]; and the sumcheck protocol for tensor codes [Mei13] was used to obtain probabilistic proofs with linear-size proofs [BCGRS17, RR20] and linear-time provers [BCG20, BCL20].

Folding Techniques. Separately, a line of works starting with [BCCGP16] constructs succinct arguments based on *folding techniques* for Pedersen commitments in the discrete logarithm setting. Informally, to prove knowledge of a long message opening a given Pedersen commitment, the prover engages with the verifier in a reduction that halves the message length by folding the message "around" a verifier challenge. This can be repeatedly applied until the message length is small enough to send the message directly. Beyond commitment openings, [BCCGP16] give protocols for scalar-product relations, which lead to succinct arguments for NP languages such as arithmetic circuit satisfiability. These succinct arguments can be realized via a linear number of group scalar multiplications, or alternatively as streaming algorithms [BHRRS20].

Folding techniques, subsequently improved in [BBBPWM18], have been deployed in cryptocurrencies (Monero [Mon] and PIVX [Piv]) and are widely used thanks to popular open-source libraries [dalek18, Adj]. These practical applications have motivated careful analyses of concrete security [JT20], which facilitates setting security parameters in applications.

Folding techniques have been adapted to work in other cryptographic settings, such as bilinear groups [LMR19], unknown-order groups [BFS20], and lattices [BLNS20]. They have also been formulated in more abstract settings: [BMMTV19] study sufficient properties of commitment schemes that enable folding techniques; and [AC20, ACF20, ACR20, BDFG20] study folding techniques for general group homomorphisms.

Folding techniques for Pedersen (and related) commitments are arguably not fully understood, despite the numerous works and applications mentioned above. For example, they are typically used as non-interactive arguments after the Fiat–Shamir transformation is applied to the (public-coin) interactive argument. Yet the security of this non-interactive argument, even in the random oracle model, has only been proven via a superpolynomial-time extractor [BMMTV19] or in the algebraic group model [GT20]. Moreover, almost all succinct arguments are obtained via some type of probabilistic proof (and there are settings where this is inherent [RV09, CY20]) but no such probabilistic proof is evident in folding techniques.

A Connection? The sumcheck protocol and folding techniques seem rather different protocols but they share several common features. Both protocols have a prover that can be realized via a linear number of operations [Tha13, BCCGP16], or alternatively as a streaming algorithm [CMT12, BHRRS20]; moreover, both protocols satisfy similar notions of strong soundness [CCHLRR18, GT20], which facilitate proving useful security properties. Are these similarities mere coincidences?

1.1 Our Results

We introduce a class of interactive protocols, *sumcheck arguments*, that establishes a novel connection between the sumcheck protocol and folding techniques for Pedersen commitments. This provides a single framework to understand numerous prior works in disparate cryptographic settings (prime-order groups, bilinear groups, unknown-order groups, lattices) and also enables us to answer open questions raised in prior works. We elaborate on these contributions below, and summarize the underlying technical ideas in Sect. 2.

(1) Sumcheck arguments. Recall that the sumcheck protocol is an interactive proof for statements of the form $\sum_{\underline{\omega} \in H^\ell} p(\underline{\omega}) = \tau$ for a given summation domain H, ℓ-variate polynomial p, and claimed sum τ. While typically stated for polynomials over finite fields, the sumcheck protocol works for polynomials over any module M over a ring R (given certain mild conditions). Let $\Sigma[R, M, H, \ell, \tau, \mathcal{C}, p]$ denote the sumcheck protocol for the statement $\sum_{\underline{\omega} \in H^\ell} p(\underline{\omega}) = \tau$ when $H \subseteq R$, $\tau \in M$, and $p \in M[X_1, \ldots, X_\ell]$, and the verifier uses the challenge set $\mathcal{C} \subseteq R$ to sample each round's challenge. (We explain later on in Sect. 2.1 why the sumcheck protocol over modules involves a given challenge set for the verifier.)

A *sumcheck argument* is, informally, a sumcheck protocol used to succinctly prove knowledge of openings for certain commitments (you run the sumcheck reduction followed by a cryptographic analogue of the consistency check). We say that a commitment scheme CM is *sumcheck-friendly* if the statement "I know m of length n such that CM.Commit $(\mathsf{ck}, \mathsf{m}) = \mathsf{cm}$" can be rewritten as the statement "I know m of length n such that $\sum_{\underline{\omega} \in \{-1,1\}^{\log n}} f_{\mathsf{CM}}(p_{\mathsf{m}}(\underline{\omega}), p_{\mathsf{ck}}(\underline{\omega})) = \mathsf{cm}$" where the message polynomial $p_{\mathsf{m}}(\underline{X})$ is over an R-module $\mathbb{M}$, the key polynomial $p_{\mathsf{ck}}(\underline{X})$ is over an R-module $\mathbb{K}$, and the combiner function f_{CM} maps $\mathbb{M} \times \mathbb{K}$ to an R-module $\mathbb{C}$ (and is such that $f_{\mathsf{CM}}(p_{\mathsf{m}}(\underline{X}), p_{\mathsf{ck}}(\underline{X}))$ is a polynomial over $\mathbb{C}$). We observe that commitment schemes of interest are sumcheck-friendly, including various forms of Pedersen commitments (we elaborate on this later). Our main result is to construct a knowledge extractor for the sumcheck protocol applied to such statements, provided CM is *invertible* (a certain property that we discuss later on).

Theorem 1 (informal). *Let* CM *be a sumcheck-friendly commitment scheme that is invertible. Let* cm *be a commitment to a message* m *using a commitment key* ck. *Then (a straightforward extension of)*

$$\Sigma[R, M = \mathbb{C}, H = \{-1, 1\}, \ell = \log n, \tau = \mathsf{cm}, \mathcal{C}, p = f_{\mathsf{CM}}(p_{\mathsf{m}}, p_{\mathsf{ck}})]$$

is an interactive argument of knowledge for an opening to cm *with respect to* ck *with knowledge error* $O(\frac{\log n}{|\mathcal{C}|})$, *where the polynomial in the numerator depends on* CM. *The round complexity is* $O(\log n)$ *and the communication complexity is*

$O(\log n)$ *elements in* $\mathbb{C}$*. Moreover, if* f_{CM} *is a bilinear function, then the prover and verifier complexity is dominated by* $O(n)$ *operations in* $\mathbb{C}$*.*

The above informal statement omits many technical details, such as commitment randomness and relaxed notions of commitment opening necessary to express settings over lattices. Moreover, the informal statement fixes certain choices (such as choosing the summation domain $H = \{-1, 1\}$ and $\ell = \log n$ variables).

As we demonstrate in the full version of this paper, well-known folding techniques from prior works can be viewed, perhaps surprisingly, as special cases of a sumcheck argument. We remark that while the usual security notion of the sumcheck protocol is an unconditional soundness guarantee, the security notion that we establish for a sumcheck argument is a knowledge guarantee, proved from CM's invertibility. In turn invertibility may hold unconditionally or under certain hardness assumptions (we give examples of this in Sect. 2.3.2).[1]

(2) Succinct arguments for R1CS over rings. Building on sumcheck arguments, we obtain zero-knowledge succinct arguments for satisfiability problems defined over *rings*. This is in contrast to most prior succinct arguments, which support satisfiability problems defined over prime-order fields (which are the "scalar fields" associated to underlying cryptographic prime-order groups). This extension is motivated by the fact that certain computations are more efficiently expressed over certain rings (e.g., approximate arithmetic [CCKP19]), and parallels prior lines of work for secret-sharing schemes and multiparty computation protocols [CFIK03, CDESX18, ACDEY19, Abs+20] for supporting computations defined over rings.

We focus on the ring variant of the NP-complete problem known as *rank-1 constraint satisfiability* (R1CS), which is a widely used generalization of arithmetic circuit satisfiability. We obtain a zero-knowledge succinct argument for R1CS over any ring $R_\bullet$ with suitable algebraic properties, assuming the hardness of the *bilinear relation assumption* over a related ring, which is a natural generalization of assumptions such as the DL assumption, the SIS assumption, and others.

Definition 1 (informal). *The R1CS problem asks: given a ring* $R_\bullet$*, coefficient matrices* $A, B, C \in R_\bullet^{n \times n}$ *each containing at most* $m = \Omega(n)$ *non-zero entries, and an instance vector* $\underline{x}$ *over* $R_\bullet$*, is there a witness vector* $\underline{w}$ *over* $R_\bullet$ *such that* $\underline{z} := (\underline{x}, \underline{w}) \in R_\bullet^n$ *and* $A\underline{z} \circ B\underline{z} = C\underline{z}$*? (Here "$\circ$" denotes the entry-wise product of vectors over* $R_\bullet$*.)*

Theorem 2 (informal). *Let* R *be a ring,* M *be an* R*-module,* $\mathcal{C} \subseteq R$ *a challenge space, and* $I \subseteq R$ *an ideal. If pairwise differences in* $\mathcal{C}$ *have suitable pseudoinverses in* $R_\bullet := R/I$ *and the bilinear relation assumption holds over* M*, then there is a zero-knowledge succinct argument of knowledge for the R1CS problem over* $R_\bullet$*. For* $n \times n$ *coefficient matrices with at most* m *non-zero entries, the*

---

[1] Thus sumcheck arguments are distinct from direct algebraic generalizations of the sumcheck protocol to rings [CCKP19].

argument has knowledge error $O(\frac{\log n}{|C|})$, *round complexity* $O(\log n)$, *communication complexity* $O(\log n)$ *elements of* M *and* $O(1)$ *elements of* R, *and prover and verifier complexity dominated by* $O(m)$ *operations in* R *and* $O(n)$ *operations in* M.

One immediate application of our result is to lattice cryptography. Prior work used folding techniques to obtain (zero-knowledge) succinct arguments of knowledge for lattice commitments [BLNS20], but left open the question of obtaining succinct arguments for NP-complete problems relevant to lattices.[2]

Our Theorem 2 directly implies a solution to this open question. This may be surprising because the knowledge extractor for a sumcheck argument over lattices finds only a relaxed opening of a (sumcheck-friendly and invertible) commitment; this relaxed extraction occurs in many other lattice-based arguments of knowledge. This notwithstanding we still derive from it a knowledge extractor for the R1CS problem.

Corollary 1 (informal). *Let* $R := \mathbb{Z}[X]/\langle X^d + 1 \rangle$ *for* d *a power of* 2. *Let* p *and* q *be primes with* q *sufficiently larger than* p. *Assuming hardness of the SIS problem over* R/qR, *there is an argument of knowledge for R1CS over* $R_\bullet := R/pR$ *with knowledge-soundness error* $O(\frac{\log n}{d})$, *round complexity* $O(\log n)$, *communication complexity dominated by* $O(\log n)$ *elements of* R/qR, *and prover and verifier complexity dominated by* $O(m)$ *operations in* $R_\bullet$ *and* $O(n)$ *operations in* R/qR.

Our new lattice-based argument system shows that one can succinctly prove general relations over rings pertinent to lattice cryptography, despite the fact that most lattice-based proofs of knowledge suffer from relaxed soundness properties. This allows users to prove statements about lattice-based encryption and signature schemes directly over their native rings rather than having to convert them into statements tractable for other proof systems, which often leads to computational overheads in practical schemes [BCOS20].

Moreover, Corollary 1 contributes a new succinct argument that is plausibly post-quantum, adding to a surprisingly short list of such candidates. (Prior constructions of post-quantum succinct arguments are from hash functions [CMS19, CMSZ21] or lattice knowledge assumptions [BISW17,BISW18,GMNO18].) An intriguing question left open by our work is whether the *security reduction* of the construction in Corollary 1 can be carried out against an efficient quantum adversary.

Finally, returning to Theorem 2, having a single construction of a zero-knowledge succinct argument over general rings may simplify future practical applications. Our theorem enables having a single abstract implementation that can be debugged and audited once and for all, and can then be instantiated over disparate algebraic settings depending on an application's needs, by simply specifying the desired ring.

---

[2] This differs from using lattices to instantiate the collision-resistant hash function in Kilian's PCP-based protocol [Kil92], because this would not lead to a succinct argument for computations expressed over relevant rings.

(3) On instantiations. By instantiating the sumcheck-friendly commitment CM in Theorem 1 we obtain succinct arguments of knowledge for different relations of interest, as we now explain.

As a simple example, the Pedersen commitment scheme can be formulated in an abstract setting where messages and group generators are replaced by elements of appropriate rings or modules. This *generalized Pedersen commitment scheme* satisfies the conditions in Theorem 1, either unconditionally or under the same assumptions that imply its binding properties. Our sumcheck argument for the generalized Pedersen commitment scheme thus yields succinct protocols for opening Pedersen commitments in different settings, such as prime-order groups, bilinear groups, unknown-order groups, and lattices.

We also study instantiations that capture richer functionalities.

- *Linear-function commitments:* the commitment includes a commitment to the scalar product of a public (query) message and a secret message. This draws inspiration from [AC20] which considers linear-function commitments in the prime-order group setting, bilinear group setting, and strong RSA setting.
- *Scalar-product commitments:* the commitment includes a commitment to the scalar product of two secret parts of the message. This draws inspiration from [BCCGP16,BBBPWM18,BMMTV19] which consider bilinear commitment schemes for prime-order or bilinear groups. Proving knowledge of an opening implies that the commitment was correctly computed, and therefore in this case that a scalar-product relation is satisfied. These scalar-product commitments in fact underlie our proof of Theorem 2 based on Theorem 1.

In Fig. 1 we provide a comparison between succinct arguments with comparable efficiency in prior works, classified by type of relation and algebraic setting. The table demonstrates that our sumcheck arguments recover *all prior types of relations and all algebraic settings* as special cases, and additionally contribute *new combinations that were not achieved before.*

1.2 New Connections and New Opportunities

The novel connection between folding techniques and the sumcheck protocol, captured by our sumcheck arguments, casts many aspects of prior works in a new light. Below we provide several examples.

- [BCCGP16] describes folding techniques for splitting a long vector into more than two pieces before folding, to allow trading argument size for round complexity. This corresponds to running a sumcheck argument using *polynomials of fewer variables and higher individual degree.*
- [BBBPWM18] improves the efficiency of folding techniques via a more complicated use of verifier challenges. This corresponds to running a sumcheck argument using a *different evaluation domain,* and where the sumcheck prover sends polynomials expressed in a *different monomial basis.*
- [CHJKS20] gives weighted inner-product arguments to improve concrete efficiency. This corresponds to a sumcheck argument for *weighted-sums of polynomial evaluations* (see the full version of the paper for details).

	prime-order groups (DL assumption)	bilinear groups (double-pairing assumption)	unknown-order groups (order assumption)	ideal lattices (SIS assumption)
basic commitment				[BLNS20]
linear-function commitment or polynomial commitment	[ACR20; AC20]		[BFS20]	previously open
scalar-product commitment	[BCCGP16]	[LMR19]	previously open	
bilinear commitment	[BMMTV19]		previously open	
sumcheck-friendly commitment	sumcheck arguments from this work			

Fig. 1. Comparison of prior works that use folding techniques to achieve succinct arguments of knowledge, and also our sumcheck arguments. The rows from top to bottom indicate increasingly more general types of commitment (and so a result in a row directly implies a result in all rows above it). The columns indicate different cryptographic settings in which the commitments are constructed (along with corresponding sufficient cryptographic assumptions). Results spanning multiple columns indicate an abstraction that simultaneously captures all those settings. We see that our work captures all prior settings and types of commitments, and also achieves functionalities and settings that were left open by prior works.

- [PLS19] gives a zero-knowledge version of folding techniques that achieves better concrete efficiency by using less prover randomness. This relates to *derandomizing a zero-knowledge sumcheck argument*.
- [BMMTV19, BFS20] consider subprotocols for delegating expensive verifier computation to the prover. This corresponds to *delegating polynomial evaluation*, to help the verifier outsource evaluating the commitment key polynomial. Sumcheck arguments neatly conceptualize the role of polynomials in folding protocols and simplify the task of applying delegation protocols in other settings (see discussed further in the full version).
- Like [BMMTV19, ACF20, BDFG20], sumcheck arguments capture optimizations of folding techniques that compress several target commitment values into one (e.g., the optimization from [BCCGP16] to [BBBPWM18]) as sumcheck arguments applied to alternative commitment schemes.

We expect that other folding techniques such as [ACR20, Lee20] can also be viewed as sumcheck arguments.

Looking ahead, the new perspective offered by sumcheck arguments, with the sumcheck protocol at their core, makes it easier to explore new design options and optimizations for succinct arguments, especially so for those that have already been studied for the (information-theoretic) sumcheck protocol.

Existing analyses of the sumcheck protocol may also inspire analogous ones for sumcheck arguments. For example, the sumcheck protocol can be made non-interactive via the Fiat–Shamir transformation, where the verifier's messages are replaced by the outputs of a hash function. Jawale et al. [JKKZ20] show that the result is a non-interactive argument provided the hash function is *lossy correlation-intractable* (and construct such hash functions based on the LWE assumption). This seems to provide a starting point for studying the security of sumcheck arguments under the Fiat–Shamir transformation.

1.3 Related Work

Folding Techniques. Figure 1 summarizes the main relationship between sumcheck arguments for sumcheck-friendly commitments and prior work that uses folding techniques. Below we additionally discuss the prior works that have studied folding techniques for abstract commitment schemes and homomorphisms.

Bünz et al. [BMMTV19] present folding techniques for doubly-homomorphic commitments over prime-order groups, which are both key-homomorphic and message homomorphic. These can capture non-linear relations such as scalar-product relations under computational assumptions.

Attema, Cramer, and Fehr [ACF20] present folding techniques for pre-images of general group homomorphisms over prime-order groups. These were extended from prime-order groups to $\mathbb{Z}$-modules in [BDFG20], who also noted that a $\mathbb{Z}$-module homomorphism could be phrased as a Pedersen-like function. These techniques give *proofs* for homomorphisms and linear relations, without using computational assumptions.

Both general group homomorphisms and doubly-homomorphic commitment schemes are special cases of sumcheck-friendly commitment schemes. Our work also finds the same distinction between proofs and arguments: our sumcheck argument for "linear" commitment schemes such as the generalized Pedersen commitment scheme (and linear-function commitments) do not require computational assumptions, whereas our sumcheck argument for "quadratic" commitment schemes require computational assumptions.

Reductions from NP-Complete Problems. Attema and Cramer [AC20] construct zero-knowledge succinct arguments for NP-complete relations by (i) using secret-sharing techniques to interactively reduce NP statements to linear relations (under computational assumptions), and then (ii) relying on succinct arguments for linear relations. This "linearization" requires the prover to perform polynomial arithmetic on high-degree polynomials, and hence an efficient realization would likely rely on FFTs. FFTs require linear space-complexity for the prover, and prevent the prover from being implemented in logarithmic space as in the sumcheck protocol [CMT12] or other succinct arguments based on folding protocols [BHRRS20]. In contrast, we reduce NP statements to bilinear relations such as scalar-product relations, and then rely on succinct arguments for scalar products; this reduction can be performed via a linear number of cryptographic operations, and without relying on FFTs.

1.4 Concurrent Work

Attema, Cramer, and Kohl [ACK21] construct zero-knowledge succinct arguments for NP based on the SIS assumption, using folding techniques for lattices. As with [AC20], their construction uses secret-sharing techniques which are likely to rely on FFTs and lead to a prover with large space complexity. Moreover, the techniques in [ACK21] are for lattices, while our techniques based on sumcheck arguments provide a general framework in which lattices are a special case. Additionally, [ACK21] give a detailed analysis of the knowledge error of their lattice-based folding techniques, which was not present in [BLNS20], and establish that the knowledge error can be reduced using parallel repetition.

Albrecht and Lai [AL21] study a variant of the folding techniques in [BLNS20], instantiated in a different choice of ring which offers exact proofs (rather than proofs with relaxed knowledge extraction) and various efficiency advantages. Like [ACK21], they also analyze the knowledge error of their folding techniques, and prove results relating relaxed extraction to ring structure. We are optimistic that their ideas can be incorporated into our sumcheck-based framework.

Ganesh, Nitulescu, and Soria-Vazquez [GNS21] model NP relations over rings and give a generic construction of designated-verifier zero-knowledge SNARKs using techniques related to prior lattice-based SNARK constructions [BISW17, BISW18, GMNO18].

Block et al. [BHRRS21] study a variant of the commitment scheme of [BFS20] in groups of unknown order that is compatible with a streaming formalism, and give space-efficient arguments for NP languages. We are optimistic that their ideas can be incorporated into our sumcheck-based framework.

2   Techniques

We summarize the main ideas behind our results. The first few subsections are dedicated to explaining sumcheck arguments (Theorem 1) in several steps of progressive generality. In Sect. 2.1 we describe the sumcheck protocol for polynomials over modules. Then in Sect. 2.2 we present a succinct zero-knowledge argument for Pedersen commitments based on the sumcheck protocol. In Sect. 2.3 we show how to lift this protocol to any "sumcheck-friendly" commitment, but still in the setting of prime-order groups. Finally in Sect. 2.4 we explain the main considerations in generalizing further to commitments over rings, and in Sect. 2.5 we give an example of how commitments can be formulated in this framework. After that we turn our attention to our other contributions. In Sect. 2.6 we discuss a generic scalar-product protocol built from sumcheck arguments, and then in Sect. 2.7 we explain how it enables us to obtain zero-knowledge succinct arguments for R1CS over rings (Theorem 2 and in particular Corollary 1). In the full version, we also discuss how we obtain polynomial commitment schemes over rings from sumcheck arguments.

2.1   Sumcheck Protocol Over Modules

The sumcheck protocol [LFKN92] directly extends to work with polynomials over *modules*. The prover P_{sc} and verifier V_{sc} receive a sumcheck instance $\mathrm{x}_{\mathrm{sc}} = (R, M, H, \ell, \tau, \mathcal{C})$, where R is a ring, M is a module over R, H is a subset of R, ℓ is a number of variables, $\tau \in M$ is a claimed sum, and $\mathcal{C} \subseteq R$ is a sampling set (more about this below). The prover P_{sc} additionally receives a polynomial

$p \in M[X_1, \ldots, X_\ell]$ such that $\sum_{\underline{\omega} \in H^\ell} p(\underline{\omega}) = \tau$. The protocol has ℓ rounds and works as follows.

1. For $i = 1, \ldots, \ell$:
   (a) P_{SC} sends to V_{SC} the polynomial $q_i(X) := \sum_{\omega_{i+1}, \ldots, \omega_\ell \in H} p(r_1, \ldots,$
       $r_{i-1}, X, \omega_{i+1}, \ldots, \omega_\ell) \in M[X]$;
   (b) V_{SC} sends to P_{SC} a random challenge $r_i \leftarrow \mathcal{C}$.
2. V_{SC} checks that $\sum_{\omega_1 \in H} q_1(\omega_1) = \tau$ and, for $i \in \{2, \ldots, \ell\}$, that $\sum_{\omega_i \in H} q_i(\omega_i) = q_{i-1}(r_{i-1})$.
3. If the checks pass then V_{SC} sets $v := q_\ell(r_\ell) \in M$ and outputs the tuple $((r_1, \ldots, r_\ell), v)$.

The security guarantee of the sumcheck protocol, which requires $\mathcal{C}$ to be a sampling set, is given below.

Definition 2. *We say that $\mathcal{C} \subseteq R$ is a **sampling set** for the R-module M if for every distinct $c_1, c_2 \in \mathcal{C}$ the map that sends $m \in M$ to $(c_1 - c_2) \cdot m \in M$ is injective.*

Lemma 1. *Let $\mathbb{x}_{\text{SC}} = (R, M, H, \ell, \tau, \mathcal{C})$ be a sumcheck instance and a polynomial $p \in M[X_1, \ldots, X_\ell]$ of total degree d. If $\mathcal{C}$ is a sampling set for M then the following holds.*

- Completeness. *If $\sum_{\underline{\omega} \in H^\ell} p(\underline{\omega}) = \tau$ then $\Pr_{\underline{r} \leftarrow \mathcal{C}^\ell}[\langle P_{\text{SC}}(\mathbb{x}_{\text{SC}}, p), V_{\text{SC}}(\mathbb{x}_{\text{SC}}; \underline{r}) \rangle = (\underline{r}, p(\underline{r}))] = 1$.*
- Soundness. *If $\sum_{\underline{\omega} \in H^\ell} p(\underline{\omega}) \neq \tau$ then, for every $\tilde{P}_{\text{SC}}$, $\Pr_{\underline{r} \leftarrow \mathcal{C}^\ell}[\langle \tilde{P}_{\text{SC}}, V_{\text{SC}}(\mathbb{x}_{\text{SC}}; \underline{r}) \rangle = (\underline{r}, p(\underline{r}))] < \frac{\ell d}{|\mathcal{C}|}$.*

Above $\langle A, V_{\text{SC}}(\mathbb{x}_{\text{SC}}; \underline{r}) \rangle$ is the output of $V_{\text{SC}}(\mathbb{x}_{\text{SC}})$ when interacting with algorithm A using randomness $\underline{r}$.

The lemma directly follows from a generalization of the Schwartz–Zippel lemma over modules.

Lemma 2. *Let R be a ring, M an R-module, and $f \in M[X_1, \ldots, X_\ell]$ a non-zero polynomial of total degree D. If $\mathcal{C}$ is a sampling set for M then $\Pr_{\underline{r} \leftarrow \mathcal{C}^\ell}[f(\underline{r}) = 0] \leq \frac{D}{|\mathcal{C}|}$.*

The proof of Lemma 2 follows the same approach as the usual inductive proof of the standard Schwartz–Zippel lemma. The properties of $\mathcal{C}$ are used to establish that a polynomial $f \in M[X]$ of degree D has at most D roots in $\mathcal{C}$, which in turn is used in the base case and in the inductive step.

The sumcheck protocol in the special case when $M = R$ has been used before, e.g., in [CCKP19].

2.2 Sumcheck Argument for Pedersen Commitments

We describe a cryptographic protocol for proving knowledge of an opening of a Pedersen commitment, whose main subroutine is the sumcheck protocol. We refer to such a protocol as a *sumcheck argument*. Note that for now we ignore the goal of zero knowledge, and instead focus on achieving communication complexity that is much smaller than (indeed, logarithmic in) the message whose knowledge is being proved.

Definition 3. *We index the entries of a vector $\underline{v}$ of length $n = 2^\ell$ via binary strings $(i_1, \ldots, i_\ell) \in \{0,1\}^\ell$, and define the corresponding polynomial $p_{\underline{v}}(X_1, \ldots, X_\ell) := \sum_{i_1, \ldots, i_\ell \in \{0,1\}} v_{i_1, \ldots, i_\ell} X_1^{i_1} \cdots X_\ell^{i_\ell}$.*

Protocol 1: sumcheck argument for Pedersen commitments

For $n = 2^\ell$, the prover and verifier receive as input a commitment key $\underline{G} \in \mathbb{G}^n$ and commitment $C \in \mathbb{G}$. The prover also receives as input an opening $\underline{a} \in \mathbb{F}^n$ such that $C = \langle \underline{a}, \underline{G} \rangle$.

The prover and verifier engage in a sumcheck protocol for the instance

$$\mathbb{x}_{\mathrm{sc}} := (R = \mathbb{F}, M = \mathbb{G}, H = \{-1, 1\}, \ell = \log n, \tau = 2^\ell C, \mathcal{C} = \mathbb{F})$$

where the prover uses the polynomial $p(\underline{X}) := p_{\underline{a}}(\underline{X}) \cdot p_{\underline{G}}(\underline{X})$. After the end of the sumcheck protocol, the prover learns $\underline{r} \in \mathbb{F}^\ell$ and the verifier learns $(\underline{r}, v) \in \mathbb{F}^\ell \times \mathbb{G}$. Then the prover computes and sends $p_{\underline{a}}(\underline{r}) \in \mathbb{F}$ to the verifier, and the verifier computes $p_{\underline{G}}(\underline{r}) \in \mathbb{G}$ and checks that $p_{\underline{a}}(\underline{r}) \cdot p_{\underline{G}}(\underline{r}) = v$.

We begin by explaining why Protocol 1 is mathematically well-defined. The "multiplication" operation implicit in the expression $p_{\underline{a}}(\underline{X}) \cdot p_{\underline{G}}(\underline{X})$, which maps $\mathbb{F}[X_1, \ldots, X_\ell] \times \mathbb{G}[X_1, \ldots, X_\ell] \to \mathbb{G}[X_1, \ldots, X_\ell]$, is a natural extension of the scalar multiplication operation $a \cdot G$ which maps $\mathbb{F} \times \mathbb{G} \to \mathbb{G}$. For example, consider the polynomials $p_1(X) = a + a' \cdot X \in \mathbb{F}[X]$ and $p_2(X) = G + X \cdot G' \in \mathbb{G}[X]$, and let $r \in \mathbb{F}$. The product of $p_1(r)$ and $p_2(r)$ can be written as follows:

$$p_1(r) \cdot p_2(r) = (a + a'r) \cdot (G + r \cdot G') = a \cdot (G + r \cdot G') + a'r \cdot (G + r \cdot G')$$
$$= a \cdot G + ar \cdot G' + a'r \cdot G + a'r^2 \cdot G'$$
$$= a \cdot G + r \cdot (a \cdot G' + a' \cdot G) + r^2 \cdot (a' \cdot G') \ ,$$

where the second and third equalities follow from the *bilinear properties* of scalar multiplication.[3] This holds for any $r \in \mathbb{F}$, and so it makes sense to define the "scalar multiplication" of $p_1(X)$ and $p_2(X)$:

$$p_1(X) \cdot p_2(X) = (a + a'X) \cdot (G + X \cdot G') := a \cdot G + X \cdot (a \cdot G' + a' \cdot G) + X^2 \cdot (a' \cdot G') \ .$$

---

[3] For any $a, a' \in \mathbb{F}$ and $G, G' \in \mathbb{G}$ we have $(a + a') \cdot G = a \cdot G + a' \cdot G$ and $a \cdot (G + G') = a \cdot G + a \cdot G'$.

The polynomial $p_{\underline{a}}(\underline{X}) \cdot p_{\underline{\mathsf{G}}}(\underline{X})$, whose coefficients lie in $\mathbb{G}$, is defined this way.

Completeness of Protocol 1 follows from the fact that $\sum_{\underline{\omega} \in \{-1,1\}^n} p_{\underline{a}}(\underline{\omega}) \cdot p_{\underline{\mathsf{G}}}(\underline{\omega}) = 2^{\ell} \langle \underline{a}, \underline{\mathsf{G}} \rangle$. Indeed, each contribution to $\sum_{\underline{\omega} \in \{-1,1\}^{\ell}} p_{\underline{a}}(\underline{\omega}) \cdot p_{\underline{\mathsf{G}}}(\underline{\omega})$ corresponds to the monomials of $p_{\underline{a}}(\underline{X}) \cdot p_{\underline{\mathsf{G}}}(\underline{X})$ of the form $X_1^{2i_1} \cdots X_{\ell}^{2i_{\ell}}$. The coefficient of $X_1^{2i_1} \cdots X_{\ell}^{2i_{\ell}}$ in $p_{\underline{a}}(\underline{X}) \cdot p_{\underline{\mathsf{G}}}(\underline{X})$ arises from a multiplication of the monomials in the terms $a_{i_1,\ldots,i_{\ell}} X_1^{i_1} \cdots X_{\ell}^{i_{\ell}}$ and $\mathsf{G}_{i_1,\ldots,i_{\ell}} X_1^{i_1} \cdots X_{\ell}^{i_{\ell}}$, which multiply to give $a_{i_1,\ldots,i_{\ell}} \cdot \mathsf{G}_{i_1,\ldots,i_{\ell}} \cdot X_1^{2i_1} \cdots X_{\ell}^{2i_{\ell}}$. Thus, $\sum_{\underline{\omega} \in \{-1,1\}^{\ell}} p_{\underline{a}}(\underline{\omega}) \cdot p_{\underline{\mathsf{G}}}(\underline{\omega}) = 2^{\ell} \langle \underline{a}, \underline{\mathsf{G}} \rangle$.

The security guarantee of Protocol 1 is different from that of the sumcheck protocol. The sumcheck protocol has a soundness guarantee: if the polynomial p does not have the claimed sum τ then the verifier accepts with small probability. In contrast, Protocol 1 has a **knowledge soundness** guarantee: there exists an extractor that, given a suitable collection of accepting transcripts for a given commitment key $\underline{\mathsf{G}}$ and commitment C, efficiently finds an opening $\underline{a}$ such that $\mathsf{C} = \langle \underline{a}, \underline{\mathsf{G}} \rangle$.

This difference makes sense: any given Pedersen commitment C can *always* be expressed as a scalar product of some opening $\underline{a}$ and the commitment key generators $\underline{\mathsf{G}}$; in fact, there are many different possible openings $\underline{a}$ for which this is true! Therefore, soundness is not a meaningful notion for Protocol 1.

The security guarantee is summarized by the following lemma, whose proof we sketch in Sect. 2.2.1.

Lemma 3 (informal). *Protocol 1 satisfies the following for every key $\underline{\mathsf{G}} \in \mathbb{G}^n$ and commitment $\mathsf{C} \in \mathbb{G}$.*

- Completeness. *For every $\underline{a} \in \mathbb{F}^n$ such that $\mathsf{C} = \langle \underline{a}, \underline{\mathsf{G}} \rangle$, $\Pr[\langle \mathbf{P}(\underline{\mathsf{G}}, \mathsf{C}, \underline{a}), \mathbf{V}(\underline{\mathsf{G}}, \mathsf{C}) \rangle = 1] = 1$.*
- Knowledge soundness. *Given a suitable tree of accepting transcripts for $\mathbf{V}(\underline{\mathsf{G}}, \mathsf{C})$, one can efficiently extract an opening $\underline{a} \in \mathbb{F}^n$ such that $\mathsf{C} = \langle \underline{a}, \underline{\mathsf{G}} \rangle$.*

Perhaps surprisingly, Protocol 1 is *equivalent* to the "split-and-fold" knowledge protocol for Pedersen commitments introduced in [BCCGP16] (we describe this equivalence in the full version of the paper). Moreover, knowledge soundness can be established without relying on any computational assumptions, a fact that was noted for the "split-and-fold" knowledge protocol in [ACF20, BDFG20].

2.2.1 Proof Sketch of Lemma 3

We discuss knowledge soundness. The extractor takes as input 3^{ℓ} accepting transcripts arranged in a 3-ary tree of depth ℓ, with each path from the root to the leaf identified by a choice of verifier randomness $r_1, \ldots, r_{\ell} \in \mathbb{F}$. For $i \in [\ell]$, the node at layer $i-1$ corresponding to path $r_1, \ldots, r_{i-1} \in \mathbb{F}$ is labeled with the message sent by the prover given challenges $r_1, \ldots, r_{i-1}$ and has three children nodes each corresponding to a distinct challenge $r_i^{(j)} \in \mathbb{F}$. For $i \in [\ell]$, a prover message for the layer $i-1$ is a quadratic polynomial $q_i[r_1, \ldots, r_{i-1}] \in \mathbb{G}[X]$ sent by the prover in the sumcheck protocol given challenges $r_1, \ldots, r_{i-1}$; and a prover message for the layer ℓ is an opening $w[r_1, \ldots, r_{\ell}] \in \mathbb{F}$ sent by the prover after the sumcheck protocol. Since transcripts are accepting, we know that: $\sum_{\omega_1 \in \{-1,1\}} q_1(\omega_1) = 2^{\ell} \mathsf{C}$;

for $i \in \{2, \ldots, \ell\}$, $\sum_{\omega \in \{-1,1\}} q_i[r_1, \ldots, r_{i-1}](\omega) = q_{i-1}[r_1, \ldots, r_{i-2}](r_{i-1})$; and $w[r_1, \ldots, r_\ell] \cdot p_{\underline{G}}(r_1, \ldots, r_\ell) = q_\ell[r_1, \ldots, r_{\ell-1}](r_\ell)$.

The extractor works inductively, processing each layer of the tree starting from the ℓ-th layer and moving upwards towards the root. For $i = \ell, \ldots, 1$ and for every path $(r_1, \ldots, r_{i-1}) \in \mathbb{F}^{i-1}$ in the transcript tree with children $\{r_i^{(j)}\}_{j \in [3]}$, the extractor works as follows.

1. Let $\underline{G}[r_1, \ldots, r_{i-1}] \in \mathbb{G}^{n/2^{i-1}}$ be the coefficients of $p_{\underline{G}}(r_1, \ldots, r_{i-1}, X_i, \ldots, X_\ell)$, and let $\underline{G}_0[r_1, \ldots, r_{i-1}]$ and $\underline{G}_1[r_1, \ldots, r_{i-1}]$ be the coefficients for monomials without X_i and with X_i respectively. For $j \in [3]$, let $\underline{G}'[r_1, \ldots, r_{i-1}, r_i^{(j)}] :=$ $\underline{G}[r_1, \ldots, r_{i-1}] + r_i^{(j)} \cdot \underline{G}_1[r_1, \ldots, r_{i-1}] \in \mathbb{G}^{n/2^i}$ be the coefficients of $p_{\underline{G}}(r_1, \ldots, r_{i-1}, r_i^{(j)}, X_{i+1}, \ldots, X_\ell)$.

2. We inductively know, for each $j \in [3]$, an opening $w[r_1, \ldots, r_{i-1}, r_i^{(j)}] \in \mathbb{F}^{n/2^i}$ to the commitment $q_i[r_1, \ldots, r_{i-1}](r_i^{(j)}) \in \mathbb{G}$ with respect to the key $\underline{G}'[r_1, \ldots, r_{i-1}, r_i^{(j)}]$:

$$\langle w[r_1, \ldots, r_{i-1}, r_i^{(1)}], \underline{G}'[r_1, \ldots, r_{i-1}, r_i^{(1)}] \rangle = q_i[r_1, \ldots, r_{i-1}](r_i^{(1)}) \ ,$$
$$\langle w[r_1, \ldots, r_{i-1}, r_i^{(2)}], \underline{G}'[r_1, \ldots, r_{i-1}, r_i^{(2)}] \rangle = q_i[r_1, \ldots, r_{i-1}](r_i^{(2)}) \ ,$$
$$\langle w[r_1, \ldots, r_{i-1}, r_i^{(3)}], \underline{G}'[r_1, \ldots, r_{i-1}, r_i^{(3)}] \rangle = q_i[r_1, \ldots, r_{i-1}](r_i^{(3)}) \ .$$

3. Since the polynomial $q_i[r_1, \ldots, r_{i-1}]$ is quadratic, we can use linear algebra on the above three equations to compute a quadratic polynomial $\pi[r_1, \ldots, r_{i-1}] \in \mathbb{F}^{n/2^{i-1}}[X]$ such that $\langle \pi[r_1, \ldots, r_{i-1}](X), \underline{G}[r_1, \ldots, r_{i-1}] \rangle = q_i[r_1, \ldots, r_{i-1}](X)$. Then we can obtain an opening $w[r_1, \ldots, r_{i-1}] \in \mathbb{F}^{n/2^{i-1}}$ such that $\langle w[r_1, \ldots, r_{i-1}], \underline{G}[r_1, \ldots, r_{i-1}] \rangle = \sum_{\omega \in \{-1,1\}} q_i[r_1, \ldots, r_{i-1}](\omega)$. Observe that:
   - If $i > 1$, the verifier's checks imply that $\sum_{\omega \in \{-1,1\}} q_i[r_1, \ldots, r_{i-1}](\omega) = q_{i-1}[r_1, \ldots, r_{i-2}](r_{i-1})$, and so $w[r_1, \ldots, r_{i-1}]$ is an opening to the commitment $q_{i-1}[r_1, \ldots, r_{i-2}](r_{i-1})$ under the key $\underline{G}[r_1, \ldots, r_{i-1}]$.
   - If $i = 1$ (this is the last iteration) then the verifier's checks imply that $\sum_{\omega_1 \in \{-1,1\}} q_1(\omega_1) = 2^\ell C$, and so w is an opening to the commitment $2^\ell C$ under the key $\underline{G}$. Dividing by 2^ℓ yields the desired opening.

A key ingredient of the knowledge extractor is the ability to double the length of known openings by manipulating multiple transcripts for a given recursion round. The Pedersen commitment, being a homomorphism into $\mathbb{G}$, allows this unconditionally. Jumping ahead, this property of a commitment scheme, which we call **invertibility**, may require computational assumptions, and is a central component of our sumcheck argument for the general setting of sumcheck-friendly commitments (see Sects. 2.3 and 2.4).

2.3   Sumcheck Argument for Sumcheck-Friendly Commitments

We explain how to formulate a sumcheck argument for proving knowledge of an opening for any commitment scheme that satisfies certain functionality and security properties. We proceed in two steps: in Sect. 2.3.1 we focus on the special case of scalar product protocols under Pedersen commitments to gain intuition, and then in Sect. 2.3.2 we extend this to apply to a *sumcheck-friendly* commitment.

2.3.1 Scalar-Products Under Pedersen Commitments

In Sect. 2.2 we have seen how to construct a sumcheck argument for Pedersen commitments. We now write a sumcheck argument that proves knowledge of openings of *two* Pedersen commitments such that the scalar product of the two openings is a publicly-known value. That is, we obtain a knowledge protocol for the commitment scheme CM that, given a commitment key $(\underline{G}, \underline{H})$, maps a message $(\underline{a}, \underline{b})$ to

$$\mathsf{CM.Commit}\Big((\underline{G}, \underline{H}), (\underline{a}, \underline{b})\Big) := (\langle \underline{a}, \underline{G} \rangle, \langle \underline{b}, \underline{H} \rangle, \langle \underline{a}, \underline{b} \rangle) \ .$$

Protocol 2: sumcheck argument for scalar-products under Pedersen commitments

For $n = 2^\ell$, the prover and verifier receive as input commitment keys $\underline{G}, \underline{H} \in \mathbb{G}^n$, commitments $\mathsf{C}_a, \mathsf{C}_b \in \mathbb{G}$ and target value $t \in \mathbb{F}$. The prover also receives as input openings $\underline{a}, \underline{b} \in \mathbb{F}^n$ such that $\mathsf{C}_a = \langle \underline{a}, \underline{G} \rangle$, $\mathsf{C}_b = \langle \underline{b}, \underline{H} \rangle$ and $t = \langle \underline{a}, \underline{b} \rangle$. (I.e., such that $\mathsf{CM.Commit}((\underline{G}, \underline{H}), (\underline{a}, \underline{b})) = (\mathsf{C}_a, \mathsf{C}_b, t)$.)

The prover and verifier engage in a sumcheck protocol for the instance $\mathbf{x}_{\mathrm{SC}} := (R = \mathbb{F}, M = \mathbb{G} \times \mathbb{G} \times \mathbb{F}, H = \{-1, 1\}, \ell = \log n, \tau = (2^\ell \mathsf{C}_a, 2^\ell \mathsf{C}_b, 2^\ell t), C = \mathbb{F})$ where the prover uses the polynomial $p(\underline{X}) := \Big(p_{\underline{a}}(\underline{X}) \cdot p_{\underline{G}}(\underline{X}), \ p_{\underline{b}}(\underline{X}) \cdot p_{\underline{H}}(\underline{X}), \ p_{\underline{a}}(\underline{X}) \cdot p_{\underline{b}}(\underline{X})\Big) \in (\mathbb{G} \times \mathbb{G} \times \mathbb{F})[X_1, \dots, X_\ell]$.

After the end of the sumcheck protocol, the prover learns $\underline{r} \in \mathbb{F}^\ell$ and the verifier learns $(\underline{r}, v) \in \mathbb{F}^\ell \times (\mathbb{G} \times \mathbb{G} \times \mathbb{F})$. Then the prover computes and sends $p_{\underline{a}}(\underline{r}), p_{\underline{b}}(\underline{r}) \in \mathbb{F}$ to the verifier, and the verifier computes $p_{\underline{G}}(\underline{r}), p_{\underline{H}}(\underline{r}) \in \mathbb{G}$ and checks that $(p_{\underline{a}}(\underline{r}) \cdot p_{\underline{G}}(\underline{r}), \ p_{\underline{b}}(\underline{r}) \cdot p_{\underline{H}}(\underline{r}), \ p_{\underline{a}}(\underline{r}) \cdot p_{\underline{b}}(\underline{r})) = v$.

Similarly to Sect. 2.2, the first and second components of the polynomial $p(\underline{X})$ are well-defined because of the bilinearity of scalar multiplication from $\mathbb{F} \times \mathbb{G}$ to $\mathbb{G}$; moreover, the third component of $p(\underline{X})$ is well-defined because it involves the product of two polynomials over $\mathbb{F}$.

Protocol 2 is complete because

$$\sum_{\underline{\omega} \in \{-1,1\}^\ell} p_{\underline{a}}(\underline{\omega}) p_{\underline{G}}(\underline{\omega}) = 2^\ell \langle \underline{a}, \underline{G} \rangle \ , \qquad \sum_{\underline{\omega} \in \{-1,1\}^\ell} p_{\underline{b}}(\underline{\omega}) p_{\underline{H}}(\underline{\omega}) = 2^\ell \langle \underline{b}, \underline{H} \rangle \ , \qquad \sum_{\underline{\omega} \in \{-1,1\}^\ell} p_{\underline{a}}(\underline{\omega}) p_{\underline{b}}(\underline{\omega}) = 2^\ell \langle \underline{a}, \underline{b} \rangle \ .$$

Moreover, one can show that Protocol 2 satisfies the following knowledge-soundness property: there exists an extractor that, given a suitable collection of accepting transcripts for a given commitment key $(\underline{G}, \underline{H})$ and commitment $\mathsf{C} = (\mathsf{C}_a, \mathsf{C}_b, t)$, efficiently finds an opening $(\underline{a}, \underline{b})$ such that $\mathsf{C} = \mathsf{CM.Commit}((\underline{G}, \underline{H}), (\underline{a}, \underline{b}))$, assuming that the discrete logarithm problem is hard over $\mathbb{G}$. Proving knowledge soundness follows a similar approach to that for Protocol 1 sketched in Sect. 2.2.1. The main difference is that "inverting" from a level to the previous one involves not only solving linear equations to find openings of commitments corresponding to the first two components of the polynomial $p(\underline{X})$, but also arguing that the scalar-product of these openings equals the third component of the polynomial $p(\underline{X})$. This step relies on the hardness of the discrete logarithm problem over $\mathbb{G}$ (which one may have assumed anyway to make the commitment binding). This is different from Protocol 1, where no assumptions were necessary to establish knowledge soundness, and intuitively is because the commitment scheme involves a quadratic, rather than linear, computation on the message.

2.3.2 Extending to Any Sumcheck-Friendly Commitment

The commitments used in Protocols 1 and 2 are examples of a *sumcheck-friendly* commitment scheme. Below we give an informal definition (which omits technicalities such as how commitment randomness is handled).

Definition 4 (informal). *Let $\mathbb{F}$ be a prime-order field and let $\mathbb{M}, \mathbb{K}, \mathbb{C}$ be $\mathbb{F}$-linear spaces. A commitment scheme* CM *is* **sumcheck-friendly** *if there exists an efficient function* $f_{\mathsf{CM}} \colon \mathbb{M} \times \mathbb{K} \to \mathbb{C}$ *such that for every commitment key* ck *and message* m *it holds that* $\mathsf{CM.Commit}(\mathsf{ck}, \mathsf{m}) = \sum_{\underline{\omega} \in H^\ell} f_{\mathsf{CM}}(p_{\mathsf{m}}(\underline{\omega}), p_{\mathsf{ck}}(\underline{\omega}))$ *where: (i) $H \subseteq \mathbb{F}$ is a domain and $\ell \in \mathbb{N}$ a number of variables; (ii) $p_{\mathsf{m}}(\underline{X}) \in \mathbb{M}[\underline{X}]$ can be efficiently obtained from the message m (and, conversely, m can be efficiently obtained from $p_{\mathsf{m}}(\underline{X})$); (iii) $p_{\mathsf{ck}}(\underline{X}) \in \mathbb{K}[\underline{X}]$ can be efficiently obtained from the commitment key ck; (iv) $f_{\mathsf{CM}}(p_{\mathsf{m}}(\underline{X}), p_{\mathsf{ck}}(\underline{X})) \in \mathbb{C}[\underline{X}]$ is a polynomial.*

We can obtain an opening protocol for CM via a sumcheck argument.

Protocol 3: sumcheck argument for sumcheck-friendly commitments

For $n = 2^\ell$, the prover and verifier receive as input commitment key ck and commitment cm. The prover also receives as input an opening m such that $\mathsf{cm} = \mathsf{CM.Commit}(\mathsf{ck}, \mathsf{m})$.

The prover and verifier engage in a sumcheck protocol for the instance

$$\mathbb{x}_{\mathsf{sc}} := (R = \mathbb{F}, M = \mathbb{C}, H, \ell, \tau = \mathsf{cm}, \mathcal{C} = \mathbb{F})$$

where the prover uses the polynomial $p_{\mathsf{m},\mathsf{ck}}(\underline{X}) := f_{\mathsf{CM}}(p_{\mathsf{m}}(\underline{X}), p_{\mathsf{ck}}(\underline{X}))$. At the end of the sumcheck protocol, the prover learns $\underline{r} \in \mathbb{F}^\ell$ and the verifier learns $(\underline{r}, v) \in \mathbb{F}^\ell \times \mathbb{C}$. Then the prover computes and sends $p_{\mathsf{m}}(\underline{r})$ to the verifier, and the verifier computes $p_{\mathsf{ck}}(\underline{r})$ and checks that $f_{\mathsf{CM}}(p_{\mathsf{m}}(\underline{r}), p_{\mathsf{ck}}(\underline{r})) = v$.

The above opening protocol for the sumcheck-friendly commitment scheme CM has perfect completeness, and also has knowledge soundness if CM is *invertible* (a property that we discuss shortly).

Theorem 3 (informal). *Let* CM *be a sumcheck-friendly commitment scheme. If* CM *is invertible then Protocol 3 is an opening protocol for* CM*: there exists an extractor that given a key* ck*, commitment* cm*, and a suitable tree of accepting transcripts for* (ck, cm)*, finds an opening* m *such that* cm = CM.Commit (ck, m)*.*

Completeness. The sumcheck-friendly property tells us that cm $= \sum_{\underline{\omega} \in H^\ell} f_{\mathsf{CM}}(p_{\mathsf{m}}(\underline{\omega}), p_{\mathsf{ck}}(\underline{\omega}))$, so the completeness of Protocol 3 follows from the completeness of the sumcheck protocol.

Knowledge Soundness. Since m can be efficiently obtained from $p_{\mathsf{m}}(\underline{X})$, it suffices for the extractor to recover, from the tree of transcripts, a polynomial $p_{\mathsf{m}}(\underline{X})$ such that cm $= \sum_{\underline{\omega} \in H^\ell} f_{\mathsf{CM}}(p_{\mathsf{m}}(\underline{\omega}), p_{\mathsf{ck}}(\underline{\omega}))$.

The proof strategy is similar to the one described in Sect. 2.2.1: the extractor proceeds layer by layer, starting from the leaf layer of the tree of transcripts and continuing to the root; for each node in a particular layer, the extractor computes a polynomial obtained from the polynomials associated to the node's children. The desired polynomial $p_{\mathsf{m}}(\underline{X})$ is the polynomial associated to the root of the tree.

The invertibility property facilitates progress from children to parents, and states that given enough openings for a commitment of a layer one can find an opening of a commitment of the previous layer.

Definition 5 (informal). CM *is* K*-invertible if there exists an efficient algorithm* $\mathcal{I}$ *satisfying the following. Suppose that* $\mathcal{I}$ *receives* $i \in [\ell]$*, challenge vector* $(r_1, \ldots, r_{i-1}) \in \mathbb{F}^{i-1}$*, distinct challenges* $r_i^{(1)}, \ldots, r_i^{(K)} \in \mathbb{F}$*, opening polynomials* $p_1, \ldots, p_K \in \mathbb{M}[X_{i+1}, \ldots, X_\ell]$*, and commitment polynomial* $q(X) \in \mathbb{C}[X]$ *such that*

$$\forall j \in [K], \ q(r_i^{(j)}) = \sum_{\omega_{i+1}, \ldots, \omega_\ell \in H} f_{\mathsf{CM}}\left(p_j(\omega_{i+1}, \ldots, \omega_\ell), p_{\mathsf{ck}}(r_1, \ldots, r_{i-1}, r_i^{(j)}, \omega_{i+1}, \ldots, \omega_\ell)\right) .$$

(1)

Then $\mathcal{I}$ *outputs an opening polynomial* $p \in \mathbb{M}[X_i, \ldots, X_\ell]$ *such that*

$$\sum_{\omega_i \in H} q(\omega_i) = \sum_{\omega_i, \ldots, \omega_\ell \in H} f_{\mathsf{CM}}\left(p(\omega_i, \ldots, \omega_\ell), p_{\mathsf{ck}}(r_1, \ldots, r_{i-1}, \omega_i, \ldots, \omega_\ell)\right) . \quad (2)$$

The above definition omits technicalities such as the fact that the inputs to the inverter should be restricted to be efficiently generated by an adversary (given the commitment key ck) and the fact that input and output opening polynomials should be restricted to be "admissible" (partial evaluations of p_{m} for some m).

The extractor receives a K-ary tree of accepting transcripts for (ck, cm). In more detail, for every $i \in [\ell]$ and $(r_1, \ldots, r_{i-1}) \in \mathbb{F}^{i-1}$, $q_i[r_1, \ldots, r_{i-1}] \in \mathbb{C}[X]$ is the polynomial corresponding to the path $(r_1, \ldots, r_{i-1})$ in the transcript tree (the prover's polynomial in the i-th round of the sumcheck protocol for these challenges); moreover, for every $(r_1, \ldots, r_\ell) \in \mathbb{F}^\ell$, $w[r_1, \ldots, r_\ell] \in \mathbb{C}$ is the opening corresponding to the path $(r_1, \ldots, r_\ell)$ in the transcript tree (sent by the prover after the sumcheck protocol for these challenges). Every transcript is accepting, so we know that for every $(r_1, \ldots, r_\ell) \in \mathbb{F}^\ell$ it holds that

$$\sum_{\omega_1 \in H} q_1(\omega_1) = \mathsf{cm} \quad , \quad \left\{ \sum_{\omega \in H} q_i[r_1, \ldots, r_{i-1}](\omega) = q_{i-1}[r_1, \ldots, r_{i-2}](r_{i-1}) \right\}_{i \in \{2, \ldots, \ell\}} \quad ,$$

$$\text{and} \quad f_{\mathsf{CM}}(w[r_1, \ldots, r_\ell], p_{\mathsf{ck}}(r_1, \ldots, r_\ell), 1) = q_\ell(r_\ell) \ .$$

The extractor iterates over the whole tree, proceeding with $i = \ell, \ldots, 1$. In the iteration for a path $(r_1, \ldots, r_{i-1}) \in \mathcal{C}^{i-1}$ with children $\{r_i^{(j)}\}_{j \in [K]}$, the extractor uses the inverter $\mathcal{I}$ to transform polynomials $\{p[r_1, \ldots, r_{i-1}, r_i^{(j)}]\}_{j \in [K]}$ in $\mathbb{M}[X_{i+1}, \ldots, X_\ell]$ that satisfy Eq. (1) into a new polynomial $p[r_1, \ldots, r_{i-1}]$ in $\mathbb{M}[X_i, \ldots, X_\ell]$ that satisfies Eq. (2). The initial polynomials $\{p[r_1, \ldots, r_\ell]\}_{(r_1, \ldots, r_\ell) \in \mathcal{C}^\ell}$ are the constant polynomials corresponding to the opening values $\{w[r_1, \ldots, r_\ell]\}_{(r_1, \ldots, r_\ell) \in \mathcal{C}^\ell}$. The fact that transcripts are accepting ensures that the initial polynomials satisfy the required condition, and that each produced polynomial satisfies the invertibility condition for the prior layer.

After all these iterations the extractor has found a polynomial p in $\mathbb{M}[X_1, \ldots, X_\ell]$ such that $\sum_{\omega_1 \in H} q_1(\omega_1) = \sum_{\underline{\omega} \in H^\ell} f_{\mathsf{CM}}(p(\underline{\omega}), p_{\mathsf{ck}}(\underline{\omega}))$; again by the accepting condition we know that $\sum_{\omega_1 \in H} q_1(\omega_1) = \mathsf{cm}$ so we deduce that $\mathsf{cm} = \sum_{\underline{\omega} \in H^\ell} f_{\mathsf{CM}}(p(\underline{\omega}), p_{\mathsf{ck}}(\underline{\omega}))$, and the desired polynomial is p.

Whence Invertibility? Invertibility is incomparable to the commitment's binding property. For example, the Pedersen commitment scheme is unconditionally invertible (see Sect. 2.2.1), whereas invertibility for the scalar-product commitment scheme in Protocol 2 relies on the hardness of the discrete logarithm problem. In Sect. 2.5 we elaborate on how to establish invertibility for different choices of commitment schemes.

Examples. Protocol 3 captures sumcheck arguments for several commitment schemes.

- The Pedersen commitment scheme (used in Protocol 1) is sumcheck-friendly because, for the function $f_{\mathsf{CM}}(a, \mathsf{G}) := 2^{-\ell} a \cdot \mathsf{G}$, for every commitment key $\underline{\mathsf{G}} \in \mathbb{G}^n$ and message $\underline{a} \in \mathbb{F}^n$ it holds that $\mathsf{CM.Commit}(\underline{\mathsf{G}}, \underline{a}) = \sum_{\underline{\omega} \in H^\ell} f_{\mathsf{CM}}(p_{\underline{a}}(\underline{\omega}), p_{\underline{\mathsf{G}}}(\underline{\omega}))$, where $H := \{-1, 1\}$, $\ell := \log n$, and $p_{\underline{a}}(\underline{X}), p_{\underline{\mathsf{G}}}(\underline{X})$ are the multilinear polynomials induced by $\underline{a}, \underline{\mathsf{G}}$ respectively. (See Definition 3.)
- The scalar-product commitment scheme (used in Protocol 2) is sumcheck-friendly because, for the function $f_{\mathsf{CM}}((a, b), (\mathsf{G}, \mathsf{H})) := 2^{-\ell}(a \cdot \mathsf{G}, b \cdot \mathsf{H}, a \cdot b)$, for every commitment key $(\underline{G}, \underline{H}) \in \mathbb{G}^n \times \mathbb{G}^n$ and message $(\underline{a}, \underline{b}) \in \mathbb{F}^n \times \mathbb{F}^n$ it holds that $\mathsf{CM.Commit}((\underline{G}, \underline{H}), (\underline{a}, \underline{b})) = \sum_{\underline{\omega} \in H^\ell} f_{\mathsf{CM}}((p_{\underline{a}}(\underline{\omega}), p_{\underline{b}}(\underline{\omega})), (p_{\underline{G}}(\underline{\omega}), p_{\underline{H}}(\underline{\omega})))$, where $H := \{-1, 1\}$, $\ell := \log n$, and $p_{\underline{a}}(\underline{X}), p_{\underline{b}}(\underline{X}), p_{\underline{G}}(\underline{X}), p_{\underline{H}_0}(\underline{X})$ are the multilinear polynomials induced by $\underline{a}, \underline{b}, \underline{G}, \underline{H}$ respectively. (See Definition 3.)

More generally, all inner-product commitments in [BMMTV19] are sumcheck-friendly; this includes pairing-based commitment schemes appearing in works such as [LMR19]. Below we describe inner-product commitments via the notion of *sum-bilinear* commitments, which is easier to work with in our setting.

Definition 6. *A commitment scheme* CM *is* **sum-bilinear** *over a finite field* $\mathbb{F}$ *if the key, message, and commitment spaces are* $\mathbb{F}$-*linear spaces and the following properties hold for all commitment keys* $\mathsf{ckL}, \mathsf{ckR} \in \mathbb{K}^n$, *and messages* $\mathsf{mL}, \mathsf{mR} \in \mathbb{M}^n$:

$$\mathsf{CM.Commit}\,(\mathsf{ckL} + \mathsf{ckR}, \mathsf{mL} + \mathsf{mR}) = \mathsf{CM.Commit}\,(\mathsf{ckL}, \mathsf{mL}) + \mathsf{CM.Commit}\,(\mathsf{ckR}, \mathsf{mL})$$
$$+\, \mathsf{CM.Commit}\,(\mathsf{ckL}, \mathsf{mR}) + \mathsf{CM.Commit}\,(\mathsf{ckR}, \mathsf{mR}) \quad and$$
$$\mathsf{CM.Commit}\,(\mathsf{ckL}\|\mathsf{ckR}, \mathsf{mL}\|\mathsf{mR}) = \mathsf{CM.Commit}\,(\mathsf{ckL}, \mathsf{mL}) + \mathsf{CM.Commit}\,(\mathsf{ckR}, \mathsf{mR}) \ .$$

Claim (informal). If CM is sum-bilinear then CM is sumcheck-friendly.

Proof sketch. The first property allows us to "lift" the commitment function to a polynomial. For the function $f_{\mathsf{CM}}(\underline{a}, \underline{\mathsf{G}}) = 2^{-\ell}\mathsf{CM.Commit}(\underline{\mathsf{G}}; \underline{a})$, it holds that for every message $\underline{a} \in \mathbb{M}^n$ and commitment key $\underline{\mathsf{G}} \in \mathbb{K}^n$

$$f_{\mathsf{CM}}(p_{\underline{a}}(\underline{X}), p_{\underline{\mathsf{G}}}(\underline{X})) = 2^{-\ell}\mathsf{CM.Commit}\left(p_{\underline{\mathsf{G}}}(\underline{X}), p_{\underline{a}}(\underline{X})\right)$$
$$= 2^{-\ell} \sum_{\underline{i},\underline{j} \in \{0,1\}^\ell} \mathsf{CM.Commit}\left(\underline{\mathsf{G}}_{\underline{j}}, \underline{a}_{\underline{i}}\right) \cdot X_1^{i_1 + j_1} \cdots X_\ell^{i_\ell + j_\ell}$$

where $\ell := \log n$, and $p_{\underline{a}}(\underline{X}), p_{\underline{\mathsf{G}}}(\underline{X})$ are the multilinear polynomials induced by $\underline{a}, \underline{\mathsf{G}}$ via Definition 3. The second property implies that $\sum_{\underline{\omega} \in H^\ell} f_{\mathsf{CM}}(p_{\underline{a}}(\underline{\omega}), p_{\underline{\mathsf{G}}}(\underline{\omega})) = \mathsf{CM.Commit}\,(\mathsf{ck}, \mathsf{m})$ for $H = \{-1, 1\}$.   □

2.4 Extending Sumcheck Arguments to Modules

We have so far discussed sumcheck arguments for sumcheck-friendly commitment schemes involving a prime-order group and its scalar field. Yet sumcheck arguments can be formulated more generally to capture commitments in other settings, such as groups of unknown order [BFS20] and lattices [BLNS20]. We explain the changes for this generalization, and how they affect completeness and knowledge soundness.

Modules, Norms, Slackness. To motivate the considerations that arise, we find it helpful to first recall the Pedersen commitment scheme in other cryptographic settings (ignoring for now randomness for hiding).

– *Pedersen over groups of unknown order.* Let $\mathbb{G}$ be a group of unknown order and let $q, p > 2$ be primes that satisfy certain conditions (determined by the type of instantiation of $\mathbb{G}$). A Pedersen commitment is computed as $\mathsf{CM.Commit}(\underline{\mathsf{G}}, \underline{a}) = \langle \underline{a}, \underline{\mathsf{G}} \rangle \in \mathbb{G}$ where the commitment key $\underline{\mathsf{G}}$ equals $(1 \cdot \mathsf{G}, q \cdot \mathsf{G}, \ldots, q^{n-1} \cdot \mathsf{G})$ for a random group element $\mathsf{G} \in \mathbb{G}$ and the message $\underline{a}$ is a vector in $\left((-\frac{p-1}{2}, \frac{p-1}{2}) \cap \mathbb{Z}\right)^n$.

– *Pedersen over lattices.* Let R be a normed ring and let B_{SIS} be a norm bound of "short" ring elements; a popular choice is $R = \mathbb{Z}_q[X]/\langle X^d + 1 \rangle$ and short ring elements in $R(B_{\mathsf{SIS}})$, i.e. elements of R with norm at most B_{SIS}, for a suitable B_{SIS}. A Pedersen commitment is computed as $\mathsf{CM.Commit}(\underline{G}, \underline{a}) = \langle \underline{a}, \underline{G} \rangle$ where $\underline{G}$ is a matrix of random ring elements and $\underline{a}$ is a vector of short ring elements.

These examples suggest that we need to consider algebraic structures that are not necessarily rings but whose scalars are over a ring, and so we rely on the notion of modules over a ring. Moreover, we need to take into account the norms of openings. Finally, we will only be able to extract a "relaxed" opening for a given commitment, which differs from a regular opening in two ways: (i) the opening might have larger norm than an honestly committed value; (ii) the opening might not satisfy the commitment equation but only a related equation parametrized by a *slackness c*, which we model via an opening algorithm $\mathsf{CM.Open}$ that additionally takes c as input. This is similar to what happens for Schnorr protocols in these settings, as we explain in Sect. 2.5.

Extending the Sumcheck-Friendly Property. We extend the definition of a sumcheck-friendly commitment scheme (Definition 4) as follows: (i) the spaces $\mathbb{M}, \mathbb{K}, \mathbb{C}$ are modules over the same ring R; (ii) the summation domain is a subset H of R; (iii) a message polynomial $p_{\mathsf{m}}(\underline{X})$ is over the module $\mathbb{M}$; (iv) a key polynomial $p_{\mathsf{ck}}(\underline{X})$ is over the module $\mathbb{K}$; (v) the combiner function f_{CM} maps $\mathbb{M} \times \mathbb{K}$ (and a slackness factor) to the module $\mathbb{C}$; (vi) the summation condition now involves an efficient predicate ϕ_{sc} and is as follows:

$$\mathsf{CM.Commit}\,(\mathsf{ck}, \mathsf{m}) = \sum_{\underline{\omega} \in H^\ell} f_{\mathsf{CM}}(p_{\mathsf{m}}(\underline{\omega}), p_{\mathsf{ck}}(\underline{\omega}), 1) \quad \text{and for every slackness } c$$

$$\mathsf{CM.Open}\,(\mathsf{ck}, \mathsf{m}, \mathsf{cm}, c) = 1 \iff \phi_{\mathsf{sc}}\Big(\mathsf{cm}, \sum_{\underline{\omega} \in H^\ell} f_{\mathsf{CM}}(p_{\mathsf{m}}(\underline{\omega}), p_{\mathsf{ck}}(\underline{\omega}), c), c\Big) = 1 \ .$$

(Thus Definition 4 is the special case where $\mathbb{M}, \mathbb{K}, \mathbb{C}$ are $\mathbb{F}$-linear, $R = \mathbb{F}$, ϕ_{sc} checks equality of cm and the sum, and there are no slackness factors.)

Extending Sumcheck Arguments. In the sumcheck argument for a commitment scheme that is sumcheck-friendly according to the extended definition, we must additionally ensure that: (i) we use a challenge set $\mathcal{C} \subseteq R$ for the sumcheck protocol that satisfies certain properties (discussed further below) that facilitate proving knowledge soundness; (ii) we use norm bounds for commitment openings, so the underlying ring R and the module $\mathbb{M}$ must be equipped with a norm. With these in mind, we now rewrite Protocol 3 for the more general setting (differences in blue), which will allow us to capture the different cryptographic settings.

Protocol 4: sumcheck argument for sumcheck-friendly commitments (over modules)

For $n = 2^\ell$, the prover and verifier receive as input commitment key ck and commitment cm. The prover also receives as input an opening m such that $\|p_{\mathsf{m}}(\underline{X})\| \leq B_C$ and $\mathsf{cm} = \mathsf{CM.Commit}\,(\mathsf{ck}, \mathsf{m})$.

The prover and verifier engage in a sumcheck protocol for the instance

$$\mathbb{x}_{\mathsf{sc}} := (R, M = \mathbb{C}, H, \ell, \tau = \mathsf{cm}, \mathcal{C})$$

where the prover uses the polynomial $p_{\mathsf{m},\mathsf{ck}}(\underline{X}) := f_{\mathsf{CM}}(p_{\mathsf{m}}(\underline{X}), p_{\mathsf{ck}}(\underline{X}), 1)$. At the end of the sumcheck protocol, the prover learns $\underline{r} \in R^{\ell}$ and the verifier learns $(\underline{r}, v) \in R^{\ell} \times \mathbb{C}$. Then the prover computes and sends $w := p_{\mathsf{m}}(\underline{r})$ to the verifier. Finally the verifier computes $p_{\mathsf{ck}}(\underline{r})$, checks that $\|w\| \leq B_{\mathsf{SA}}$ (for B_{SA} discussed in the completeness property below), and checks that $f_{\mathsf{CM}}(w, p_{\mathsf{ck}}(\underline{r}), 1) = v$.

Completeness. This follows similarly as in the special case considered in Sect. 2.3.2, with the main difference that the norm bounds must be set so that they hold for any valid execution of the protocol. We need that for any message m (in the message space of the given commitment key ck) such that $\|p_{\mathsf{m}}(\underline{X})\| \leq B_{\mathsf{C}}$ and challenge vector $\underline{r} \in \mathcal{C}^{\ell}$ it holds that $\|p_{\mathsf{m}}(\underline{r})\| \leq B_{\mathsf{SA}}$. An explicit expression for B_{SA} can be computed in a straightforward way from the maximum norm of a challenge in $\mathcal{C}$, the number of variables ℓ of $p_{\mathsf{m}}(\underline{X})$, the degree of $p_{\mathsf{m}}(\underline{X})$, and B_{C} (a bound on the maximum norm of a coefficient in $p_{\mathsf{m}}(\underline{X})$).

Knowledge Soundness. We wish to prove that Protocol 4 is an opening protocol for CM: given a tree of accepting transcripts for the commitment key ck and commitment cm, we can extract a corresponding (relaxed) opening m. Similarly to Sect. 2.3.2, we argue knowledge soundness based on an invertibility property that generalizes the prior one (Definition 5); the challenge set $\mathcal{C}$ is now part of the property.

Definition 7 (informal) CM *is (K, N, ξ)-invertible if there exists an efficient algorithm $\mathcal{I}$ satisfying the following. Suppose that $\mathcal{I}$ receives $i \in [\ell]$, challenge vector $(r_1, \ldots, r_{i-1}) \in \mathcal{C}^{i-1}$, distinct challenges $r_i^{(1)}, \ldots, r_i^{(K)} \in \mathcal{C}$, opening polynomials $p_1, \ldots, p_K \in \mathbb{M}[X_{i+1}, \ldots, X_{\ell}]$, commitment polynomial $q(X) \in \mathbb{C}[X]$, and slackness c such that $\forall j \in [K]$,*

$$\phi_{\mathsf{sc}}\left(q(r_i^{(j)}), \sum_{\omega_{i+1},\ldots,\omega_{\ell} \in H} f_{\mathsf{CM}}\left(p_j(\omega_{i+1}, \ldots, \omega_{\ell}), p_{\mathsf{ck}}(r_1, \ldots, r_{i-1}, r_i^{(j)}, \omega_{i+1}, \ldots, \omega_{\ell}), c\right)\right) = 1 .$$

Then $\mathcal{I}$ outputs an opening polynomial $p \in \mathbb{M}[X_i, \ldots, X_{\ell}]$ of norm at most $N \cdot \max_{j \in [K]} \|p_j\|$ such that

$$\phi_{\mathsf{sc}}\left(\sum_{\omega_i \in H} q(\omega_i), \sum_{\omega_i,\ldots,\omega_{\ell} \in H} f_{\mathsf{CM}}\left(p(\omega_i, \ldots, \omega_{\ell}), p_{\mathsf{ck}}(r_1, \ldots, r_{i-1}, \omega_i, \ldots, \omega_{\ell}), \xi \cdot c\right)\right) = 1 .$$

Theorem 4 *If the sumcheck-friendly commitment scheme CM is (K, N, ξ)-invertible then Protocol 4 is an opening protocol for CM: there exists an extractor that given a commitment key ck, commitment cm for a message with norm bound*

B_C, and a K-ary tree of accepting transcripts for $(\mathsf{ck}, \mathsf{cm})$, finds an opening m with norm $\|p_\mathsf{m}(\underline{X})\| \leq N^\ell B_\mathsf{SA}$ such that $\mathsf{CM.Open}\left(\mathsf{ck}, \mathsf{cm}, \mathsf{m}, \xi^\ell\right) = 1$.

Note that since the extractor works over a tree of depth ℓ, the final loss in norm and slackness involves ℓ factors of N and ξ respectively. Technical details for our sumcheck argument are given in the full version of the paper. The final definition of invertibility that we use (related to Definition 5) has an extra parameter B_INV, which is an absolute upper bound on the norm of a relaxed opening for which invertibility can hold.

The slackness loss ξ depends on the cryptographic setting, and in the settings that we consider, $\xi \neq 1$ in the lattice and in the GUO setting.

2.5   Instantiations of Sumcheck-Friendly Commitments

Our main theorem on sumcheck arguments (Theorem 1) applies to any sumcheck-friendly commitment that is invertible. Below, we summarize how to construct such commitment schemes; details are provided in the full version of the paper.

- In Sect. 2.5.1 we introduce secure bilinear modules.
- In Sect. 2.5.2 we explain how to construct a (generalized) Pedersen commitment scheme from a secure bilinear module, and give intuition for why it is sumcheck-friendly and invertible. In the technical sections, we also discuss other commitment schemes, which capture linear functions and scalar products.
- In the full version of the paper, we outline how to instantiate secure bilinear modules in different cryptographic settings: (i) prime-order groups; (ii) bilinear groups; (iii) unknown-order groups; and (iv) lattices.

2.5.1   Secure Bilinear Modules

A *bilinear module* $\mathcal{M} = (R, M_\mathrm{L}, M_\mathrm{R}, M_\mathrm{T}, e)$ consists of a ring R, three modules $M_\mathrm{L}, M_\mathrm{R}, M_\mathrm{T}$ over R, and a non-degenerate bilinear map $e\colon M_\mathrm{L} \times M_\mathrm{R} \to M_\mathrm{T}$; moreover, R and M_L are equipped with norms. For notational simplicity we denote $e(\underline{a}, \underline{\mathsf{G}})$ as $\langle \underline{a}, \underline{\mathsf{G}} \rangle$ and define $M(B) := \{m \in M \text{ such that } \|m\| \leq B\}$.

A *bilinear-module generator* is a tuple $\mathsf{BM} = (\mathsf{Setup}, \mathsf{KeyGen})$ where: $\mathsf{BM.Setup}$ (given a security parameter and length parameter n) samples a bilinear module $\mathcal{M}$, integer $h \in \mathbb{N}$, and auxiliary string aux; and $\mathsf{BM.KeyGen}$ (given $\mathsf{BM.Setup}$'s output) samples a vector $\underline{\mathsf{G}} = (\underline{\mathsf{G}}_0, \underline{\mathsf{G}}_1)$ in M_R^{n+h}.

A bilinear-module generator BM is *secure* if it satisfies the following.

- It satisfies the *bilinear relation assumption*: for a norm bound B_BRA specified in aux and given $\underline{\mathsf{G}} \leftarrow \mathsf{BM.KeyGen}$, it is hard to find a non-zero $\underline{a} \in M_\mathrm{L}^{n+h}(B_\mathsf{BRA})$ such that $\langle \underline{a}, \underline{\mathsf{G}} \rangle = 0$. (This is a natural generalization of the discrete logarithm assumption, the SIS assumption, and others.)
- The integer h is hiding: there is a distribution $\mathcal{U}_{M_\mathrm{L}}$ on M_L^h such that, for every $\underline{a} \in M_\mathrm{L}^n$, the following two random variables are statistically close:

$$\left\{ (\underline{\mathsf{G}}, \langle \underline{a}, \underline{\mathsf{G}}_0 \rangle + \langle \underline{r}, \underline{\mathsf{G}}_1 \rangle) \,\middle|\, \begin{matrix} \underline{\mathsf{G}} \leftarrow \mathsf{BM.KeyGen} \\ \underline{r} \leftarrow \mathcal{U}_{M_\mathrm{L}} \end{matrix} \right\} \text{ and } \left\{ (\underline{\mathsf{G}}, \langle \underline{r}, \underline{\mathsf{G}}_1 \rangle) \,\middle|\, \begin{matrix} \underline{\mathsf{G}} \leftarrow \mathsf{BM.KeyGen} \\ \underline{r} \leftarrow \mathcal{U}_{M_\mathrm{L}} \end{matrix} \right\} .$$

- The string aux specifies a norm bound B_C such that $B_C \leq B_{BRA}$.
- The string aux specifies pseudoinverse parameters $(\mathcal{C}, \xi, N)$ for (R, M_T): for every $m, m^* \in M_T$, $a \in R$, and distinct $c_1, c_2 \in \mathcal{C}$, if $(c_1 - c_2)m = am^*$ then there exists (and one can efficiently find) $r \in R$ such that $\xi m = rm^*$ and $\|r\| \leq N\|a\|$.

2.5.2   Sumcheck-Friendly Commitments over Bilinear Modules

We use secure bilinear-module generators to construct several sumcheck-friendly commitment schemes that are invertible: a generalized Pedersen commitment scheme , as well as commitment schemes that capture linear functions and scalar products . Below we restrict our technical overview to the Pedersen commitment scheme. Details of the other commitment schemes can be found in the full version of the paper.

Definition 8 (informal)   *Let* BM = (Setup, KeyGen) *be a secure bilinear-module generator and consider an output* $(\mathcal{M}, h, \text{aux})$ *of* BM.Setup *(for a message length n) and an output* $\underline{G} = (\underline{G}_0, \underline{G}_1) \in M_R^n \times M_R^h$ *of* BM.KeyGen. *The* **(generalized) Pedersen commitment scheme** *for messages of length n has messages of the form $\underline{a} \in M_L^n(B_C)$, and a commitment is computed as* $C := \langle \underline{a}, \underline{G}_0 \rangle + \langle \varrho, \underline{G}_1 \rangle$, *where ρ is sampled appropriately from $M_L^h(B_C)$. An opening with slackness $c \in R$ for a commitment $C \in M_T$ under the commitment key $(\underline{G}_0, \underline{G}_1) \in M_R^n \times M_R^h$ is a vector $(\underline{a}, \varrho) \in M_L^n(B_{BRA}) \times M_L^h(B_{BRA})$ such that $c \cdot C = \langle \underline{a}, \underline{G}_0 \rangle + c \cdot \langle \varrho, \underline{G}_1 \rangle$.*

The Pedersen commitment scheme is binding under the bilinear relation assumption (which holds because BM is secure) and is hiding by the property of h (which also holds because BM is secure). Moreover, the Pedersen commitment scheme is (unconditionally) sumcheck-friendly; this can be argued in a similar way as for the usual Pedersen commitment scheme (over prime-order groups).

Establishing invertibility, however, is more challenging. Rather than specifically discussing invertibility of the Pedersen commitment, in this informal overview we describe how the fact that BM is secure enables us to (straightforwardly) obtain an extraction algorithm for the (suitably generalized) Schnorr protocol. This protocol is a simple zero-knowledge argument of knowledge for a commitment opening of a given Pedersen commitment, and the extractor is asked to produce a (possibly relaxed) opening for the commitment given two accepting transcripts sharing the same first message. The considerations that arise when establishing knowledge soundness of the (non-succinct) Schnorr protocol are loosely related to, though technically simpler than, those that arise when establishing invertibility for the Pedersen commitment scheme (which in turns leads to succinct arguments of knowledge via our sumcheck arguments).

Definition 9 (informal)   *In the* **Schnorr protocol** *for the (generalized) Pedersen commitment scheme, the prover and verifier receive a key $\underline{G} = (\underline{G}_0, \underline{G}_1) \in M_R^{n+h}$, commitment $C \in M_T$ and norm bound B_C; and the prover additionally receives as witness a message $\underline{a} \in M_L^n(B_C)$ and randomness $\varrho \in M_L^h(B_C)$ such that $\langle \underline{a}, \underline{G}_0 \rangle + \langle \varrho, \underline{G}_1 \rangle = C$. The prover and verifier interact as follows:*

- the prover samples $\underline{b} \in M_L^{n+h}(\kappa\|\mathcal{C}\|B_C)$, where $\|\mathcal{C}\| := \max_{r \in \mathcal{C}} \|r\|$, and sends $t := \langle \underline{b}, \underline{G} \rangle \in M_T$;
- the verifier sends a random challenge $r \in \mathcal{C}$;
- the prover sends the response $\underline{s} := r \cdot (\underline{a}, \underline{\rho}) + \underline{b} \in M_L^{n+h}$ if $\|\underline{s}\| \leq (\kappa - 1)\|\mathcal{C}\|B_C$ (otherwise aborts);
- the verifier accepts if $\langle \underline{s}, \underline{G} \rangle = r \cdot C + t$ and $\|\underline{s}\| \leq (\kappa - 1)\|\mathcal{C}\|B_C$.

The parameter κ is chosen such that $\underline{b}$ "masks" $(\underline{a}, \underline{\rho})$. We discuss how to choose κ in Sect. 2.6, where similar considerations arise in other protocols; here, instead, we focus on discussing knowledge extraction. The extractor recovers an opening of C from two accepting transcripts $(t, r_1, \underline{s}_1)$ and $(t, r_2, \underline{s}_2)$ sharing the same first message t but with distinct challenges r_1 and r_2. First, subtracting the verification equation for one transcript from that of the other transcript shows that $\langle \underline{s}_1 - \underline{s}_2, \underline{G} \rangle = (r_1 - r_2) \cdot C$. The fact that BM is secure implies that $(\mathcal{C}, \xi, N)$ are pseudoinverse parameters for (R, M_T), so we can compute an $r \in R$ such that $\xi \cdot C = r \langle \underline{s}_1 - \underline{s}_2, \underline{G} \rangle$ with $\|r\| \leq N$. Therefore, the extractor has found a relaxed opening $(\underline{a}', \underline{\rho}') := r(\underline{s}_1 - \underline{s}_2)$ such that $\langle \underline{a}', \underline{G}_0 \rangle + \langle \underline{\rho}', \underline{G}_1 \rangle = \xi \cdot C$ with $\|(\underline{a}', \underline{\rho}')\| \leq N2(\kappa - 1)\|\mathcal{C}\|B_C$. (And we see that the norm B_C must satisfy $N2(\kappa - 1)\|\mathcal{C}\|B_C \leq B_{BRA}$.)

The norm computations above ignore *expansion factors* that appear when computing the norms of expressions that involve the multiplication of ring and module elements (see the full version of the paper for details).

2.6 Succinct Argument for Scalar Products over Rings

We explain how to use sumcheck arguments to obtain zero-knowledge succinct arguments of knowledge for scalar-product relations over rings. This involves choosing a specific sumcheck-friendly commitment to plug in to Theorem 1, and also carefully using randomness to achieve zero knowledge (which is not a guarantee of Theorem 1). Afterwards, in Sect. 2.7 we explain how to build on this to prove Theorem 2.

We first introduce the notion of *protocol-friendly* bilinear-module generator. A bilinear-module generator BM is *protocol-friendly* if it satisfies the following.

- BM is secure (see Sect. 2.5.1).
- M_L is not merely an R-module but also a ring itself (so that scalar products over M_L are defined).[4]
- The string aux specifies $\kappa \in \mathbb{N}$ such that BM is *masking-friendly* (i.e., for every $B \in \mathbb{N}$ with $B_C \leq B \leq B_{BRA}/\kappa$ and $\underline{a} \in M_L^n(B)$, $\{\underline{a} + \underline{b}\}_{\underline{b} \leftarrow M_L^n(\kappa B)}$ is close to uniform).
- The string aux specifies an ideal I such that multiplication by ξ (which is part of the pseudoinverse parameters $(\mathcal{C}, \xi, N)$ also in aux) is invertible modulo I.

The instantiations of bilinear-module generators given in the full version of this paper are also protocol-friendly.

---

[4] In the pairing setting where M_L is not a ring, we define scalar-product commitments differently. See the full version for details.

- *Prime-order groups:* BM.Setup additionally outputs $\kappa := \infty$ and $I := \{0\}$. This means that the argument supports scalar products over $M_{\text{L}}/I = \mathbb{F}_q$, the scalar field of a prime-order group $\mathbb{G}$.
- *Bilinear groups:* BM.Setup additionally outputs $\kappa := \infty$ and $I := \{0\}$. This means that the argument supports scalar products over $M_{\text{L}}/I = \mathbb{G}_1$ (alternatively, $\mathbb{G}_2$), a source group in the bilinear group.
- *GUO setting:* BM.Setup additionally outputs $\kappa := O(2^\lambda)$ and $I := n\mathbb{Z}$ for $n \in \mathbb{Z}$ whose prime factors are greater than or equal to p. This means that the argument supports scalar products over $M_{\text{L}}/I = \mathbb{Z}/n\mathbb{Z}$ for any n satisfying these conditions.
- *Lattice setting:* BM.Setup additionally outputs $\kappa := O(dn)$ and $I := n\mathbb{Z}$ for odd $n \neq -1, 1$. This means that the argument supports scalar products over $M_{\text{L}}/I = \mathbb{Z}/n\mathbb{Z}$ for any n satisfying these conditions.

The commitment scheme that we consider has two-part messages and includes a commitment to their scalar-product; it is the extension of the scalar-product commitment from Sect. 2.3.1 to bilinear modules.

Definition 10 (informal) *Let* BM $=$ (Setup, KeyGen) *be a protocol-friendly bilinear-module generator. The* **(generalized) scalar-product commitment scheme** *for messages of length n has messages of the form $(\underline{a}, \underline{b}) \in M_{\text{L}}^n \times M_{\text{L}}^n$ such that $\|\underline{a}\|, \|\underline{b}\| \leq B_{\text{C}}$, and commitment keys of the form $(\underline{\mathsf{G}}_0, \underline{\mathsf{G}}_1, \underline{\mathsf{H}}_0, \underline{\mathsf{H}}_1, \mathsf{U}_0, \underline{\mathsf{U}}_1) \in M_{\text{R}}^{n+h} \times M_{\text{R}}^{n+h} \times M_{\text{R}}^{1+h}$. A commitment is computed by sampling $\rho_a, \rho_b, \rho_t \in M_{\text{L}}^h(B_{\text{C}})$ and computing*

$$\left(\langle \underline{a}, \underline{\mathsf{G}}_0 \rangle + \langle \rho_a, \underline{\mathsf{G}}_1 \rangle, \ \langle \underline{b}, \underline{\mathsf{H}}_0 \rangle + \langle \rho_b, \underline{\mathsf{H}}_1 \rangle, \ \langle \underline{a}, \underline{b} \rangle \cdot \mathsf{U}_0 + \langle \rho_t, \underline{\mathsf{U}}_1 \rangle \right)$$

In other words, a commitment is the tuple consisting of three generalized Pedersen commitments: for the first part of the message $\underline{a}$, for the second part of the message $\underline{b}$, and for their scalar product $\langle \underline{a}, \underline{b} \rangle \in M_{\text{L}}$.

A valid opening for a commitment $(\mathsf{C}_a, \mathsf{C}_b, \mathsf{C}_t) \in M_{\text{T}}^3$ with keys $(\underline{\mathsf{G}}_0, \underline{\mathsf{G}}_1, \underline{\mathsf{H}}_0, \underline{\mathsf{H}}_1 \mathsf{U}_0, \underline{\mathsf{U}}_1) \in M_{\text{R}}^{n+h} \times M_{\text{R}}^{n+h} \times M_{\text{R}}^{1+h}$ and slackness $c \in R$ is a vector $(\underline{a}, \underline{b}, \rho_a, \rho_b, \rho_t) \in M_{\text{L}}^n(B_{\text{BRA}}) \times M_{\text{L}}^n(B_{\text{BRA}}) \times M_{\text{L}}^{3h}(B_{\text{BRA}})$ such that

$$c^2 \cdot \mathsf{C} = (c \cdot \langle \underline{a}, \underline{\mathsf{G}}_0 \rangle + c^2 \cdot \langle \rho_a, \underline{\mathsf{G}}_1 \rangle, \ c \cdot \langle \underline{b}, \underline{\mathsf{H}}_0 \rangle + c^2 \cdot \langle \rho_b, \underline{\mathsf{H}}_1 \rangle, \ \langle \underline{a}, \underline{b} \rangle \cdot \mathsf{U}_0 + c^2 \langle \rho_t, \underline{\mathsf{U}}_1 \rangle) \ .$$

The generalized scalar-product commitment scheme is binding under the bilinear relation assumption. Moreover, it is sumcheck-friendly (unconditionally). The proof of invertibility follows from algebraic manipulations analogous to the case of generalized Pedersen commitments discussed in Sect. 2.5; though note that establishing invertibility in this case requires computational assumptions (even in the discrete logarithm setting as discussed in Sect. 2.3.1).

We give a zero-knowledge succinct argument of knowledge for the following relation related to the scalar-product of committed messages, which we denote by $\mathcal{R}_{\text{CMSP}}$.

Definition 11 (informal) *The committed scalar-product relation $\mathcal{R}_{\text{CMSP}}(c, B_{\text{C}})$ are the pairs $(\mathbf{x}, \mathbf{w})$ where:*

- *The instance* x *contains*
  - *a protocol-friendly bilinear-module generator* BM;
  - *commitment keys* $(\underline{G}_0, \underline{G}_1, \underline{H}_0, \underline{H}_1, U_0, \underline{U}_1) \in M_R^n \times M_R^h \times M_R^n \times M_R^h \times M_R \times M_R^h$;
  - *commitments* $C_a, C_b, C_t \in M_T$.
- *The witness* w $= (\underline{a}, \rho_a, \underline{b}, \rho_b, t, \rho_t) \in M_L^{2n+1+3h}$ *is such that* $\|\underline{a}\|, \|\rho_a\|, \|\underline{b}\|, \|\rho_b\|, \|t\|, \|\rho\| \leq B_C$ *and*
  - $(\underline{a}, \rho_a)$ *is a valid opening of the Pedersen commitments* C_a *with slackness c;*
  - $(\underline{b}, \rho_b)$ *is a valid opening of the Pedersen commitments* C_b *with slackness c;*
  - (t, ρ_t) *is a valid opening of the Pedersen commitment* C_t *with slackness* c^2 *and* $t = \langle \underline{a}, \underline{b} \rangle \bmod I$.

The relation reasons about scalar-product relations over the quotient ring $R_\bullet = M_L/I$ (M_L modulo I) for the ideal $I \subseteq M_L$ specified in aux. In certain settings, such as the lattice and GUO setting, we only extract openings to commitments with slackness $c \neq 1$, we choose I so that we can "cancel out" the slackness c modulo I as part of knowledge extraction algorithms and prove exact scalar-product relations over $R_\bullet$. We now summarize the scalar-product argument; details can be found in the full version.

The prover begins by computing a commitment $C \in M_T$ to $\langle \underline{a}, \underline{b} \rangle \in M_L$, which may not be equal to $t \in M_L$. Then the prover and verifier engage in the these sub-protocols: (i) an interactive reduction masking the three Pedersen commitments to $\underline{a}, \underline{b}, t$, converting them into a single scalar-product commitment; (ii) a sumcheck argument to prove knowledge of an opening to the scalar-product commitment; and (iii) a consistency check that the committed values $\langle \underline{a}, \underline{b} \rangle$ and t equal modulo I.

Reduction to a Sumcheck Argument. The prover samples masking values $\underline{y}_a$ and $\underline{y}_b$ to rerandomize the commitments to $\underline{a}, \underline{b}, \langle \underline{a}, \underline{b} \rangle$: the prover sends commitments to $\underline{y}_a$ and $\underline{y}_b$, and also to $v_1 := \langle \underline{a}, \underline{y}_b \rangle + \langle \underline{b}, \underline{y}_a \rangle$ and $v_0 := \langle \underline{y}_a, \underline{y}_b \rangle$ (which depend only on $\underline{a}, \underline{b}, \underline{y}_a, \underline{y}_b$). Then the verifier sends to the prover a random challenge $\alpha \in C$. Then the prover computes $\underline{e}_a := \alpha \underline{a} + \underline{y}_a$, $\underline{e}_b := \alpha \underline{b} + \underline{y}_b$, and $\langle \underline{e}_a, \underline{e}_b \rangle = \alpha^2 \langle \underline{a}, \underline{b} \rangle + \alpha v_1 + v_0$. The openings of the rerandomized commitments do not leak any information about $\underline{a}$ or $\underline{b}$, and so the prover can safely send the corresponding commitment randomness to the verifier. Finally, the prover and verifier engage in a sumcheck argument on the scalar-product commitment consisting of the commitments to $\underline{e}_a$, $\underline{e}_b$, and $\langle \underline{e}_a, \underline{e}_b \rangle$. Since the sumcheck argument is invoked on inputs that have been masked, zero knowledge is ensured (i.e., no information about the witness w $= (\underline{a}, \rho_a, \underline{b}, \rho_b, t, \rho_t)$ is revealed) even though the sumcheck argument itself is not zero knowledge.

Checking Consistency Modulo I. The sumcheck argument merely convinces the verifier that the prover knows a witness for the scalar-product commitment (C_a, C_b, C), while the verifier additionally wants to know that the openings of C and C_t are equal modulo I. For this, we rely on a protocol on the commitments to $\langle \underline{a}, \underline{b} \rangle$ and t to check that they are equivalent modulo I. First, before receiving the verifier's challenge α, the prover samples a masking value ζ, and sends to the verifier its Pedersen commitment C_ζ and its reduction $\zeta \bmod I$ (in the clear);

after receiving α the prover sends to the verifier the value $\bar{v} := \alpha \cdot (\langle \underline{a}, \underline{b} \rangle - t) + \zeta$. The verifier then checks that $\bar{v} = \zeta \bmod I$, and that $\bar{v}$ is a valid opening for the commitment to $\alpha \cdot (\langle \underline{a}, \underline{b} \rangle - t) + \zeta$ (for appropriate commitment randomness). Intuitively, if $\bar{v} = \alpha \cdot (\langle \underline{a}, \underline{b} \rangle - t) + \zeta$ for two distinct values of α, then one can solve linear equations to deduce that $\xi \cdot (\langle \underline{a}, \underline{b} \rangle - t) = 0 \bmod I$. Then, since multiplication by the constant ξ from the pseudoinverse parameters $(\mathcal{C}, \xi, N)$ is invertible modulo I (this is required by the protocol-friendly property), we conclude that $\langle \underline{a}, \underline{b} \rangle = t \bmod I$.

2.7   Succinct Argument for R1CS over Rings

We explain the main ideas behind Theorem 2, which provides a zero-knowledge succinct argument of knowledge for R1CS over rings. Recall that the R1CS problem over a ring $R_\bullet$ asks: given coefficient matrices $A, B, C \in R_\bullet^{n \times n}$ and an instance vector $\underline{x}$ over $R_\bullet$, is there a witness vector $\underline{w}$ over $R_\bullet$ such that $\underline{z} := (\underline{x}, \underline{w}) \in R_\bullet^n$ satisfies $A\underline{z} \circ B\underline{z} = C\underline{z}$? To a first order, Theorem 2 is proved by reducing the R1CS problem over $R_\bullet$ to several scalar-product sub-problems over $R_\bullet$, and then relying on the zero-knowledge succinct argument for scalar products in Sect. 2.6. This implies that we support R1CS over the rings supported in that section: $R_\bullet = M_\mathrm{L}/I$, where M_L is the left module of a protocol-friendly bilinear module, and $I \subseteq M_\mathrm{L}$ is an ideal. As with our scalar-product arguments, I is used to cancel out slackness factors and prove exact relations. Below we summarize the reduction from R1CS to scalar products.

The prover $\mathbf{P}$ sends commitments to the full assignment $\underline{z} \in R_\bullet^n$ and to its linear combinations $\underline{z}_A, \underline{z}_B \in R_\bullet^n$. Then $\mathbf{P}$ is left to convince the verifier $\mathbf{V}$ that the committed information satisfies these conditions:

$$\underline{z}_A = A\underline{z} \quad , \quad \underline{z}_B = B\underline{z} \quad , \quad \underline{z}_A \circ \underline{z}_B = C\underline{z} \quad , \quad \underline{x} \text{ is a prefix of } \underline{z} \ .$$

To reduce the first three conditions, the verifier $\mathbf{V}$ sends a structured challenge vector $\underline{r}$. Multiplying on the left by $\underline{r}^\mathsf{T}$ reduces the first three conditions to $\langle \underline{r}, \underline{z}_A \rangle = \langle \underline{r}_A, \underline{z} \rangle$, $\langle \underline{r}, \underline{z}_B \rangle = \langle \underline{r}_B, \underline{z} \rangle$, $\langle \underline{r} \circ \underline{z}_A, \underline{z}_B \rangle = \langle \underline{r}_C, \underline{z} \rangle$; here we defined $\underline{r}_A := \underline{r}^\mathsf{T} A$, $\underline{r}_B := \underline{r}^\mathsf{T} B$, and $\underline{r}_C := \underline{r}^\mathsf{T} C$. Moreover, to reduce the last condition, the verifier $\mathbf{V}$ sends a random challenge vector $\underline{s}$ of the same length as $\underline{x}$; padding $\underline{s}$ with zeroes to get $\underline{s}'$ of the same length as $\underline{z}$, we have $\langle \underline{s}', \underline{z} \rangle = \langle \underline{s}, \underline{x} \rangle$. Note that both parties can each individually compute $\underline{r}_A, \underline{r}_B, \underline{r}_C$ by right-multiplying $\underline{r}$ by A, B, C respectively, and also both parties can each individually compute $\langle \underline{s}, \underline{x} \rangle$.

Next, the prover $\mathbf{P}$ sends a commitment to $\underline{z}'_A := \underline{r} \circ \underline{z}_A$, and also commitments to $\alpha := \langle \underline{r}_A, \underline{z} \rangle$, $\beta := \langle \underline{r}_B, \underline{z} \rangle$, and $\gamma := \langle \underline{r}_C, \underline{z} \rangle$. Then the prover and verifier engage in scalar-product sub-protocols (described in Sect. 2.6) to verify these 7 scalar products (recall each party can compute $\langle \underline{s}, \underline{x} \rangle$):

$$\begin{array}{cccc} \langle \underline{r}, \underline{z}_A \rangle = \alpha & \langle \underline{r}, \underline{z}_B \rangle = \beta & \langle \underline{z}'_A, \underline{z}_B \rangle = \gamma & \\ \langle \underline{r}_A, \underline{z} \rangle = \alpha & , \quad \langle \underline{r}_B, \underline{z} \rangle = \beta & , \quad \langle \underline{r}_C, \underline{z} \rangle = \gamma & , \quad \langle \underline{s}', \underline{z} \rangle = \langle \underline{s}, \underline{x} \rangle \ . \end{array}$$

The prover and verifier use an additional challenge vector $\underline{y}$ and 2 further scalar-product sub-protocols to check that $\langle \underline{z}'_A, \underline{y} \rangle = \langle \underline{z}_A, \underline{r} \circ \underline{y} \rangle$, which shows that $\underline{z}'_A$ was correctly computed from $\underline{z}_A$ and $\underline{r}$.

All commitments in the protocol are hiding, and hence do not leak any information about the witness vector $\underline{w}$. Hence the zero-knowledge property of the above protocol directly reduces to the zero-knowledge property of the scalar-product sub-protocols.

We conclude by noting that if we instantiate the bilinear module with lattices then Theorem 2 gives Corollary 1: a zero-knowledge succinct argument of knowledge for R1CS based on the SIS assumption.

Technical details can be found in the full version of the paper.

Acknowledgments. This research was supported in part by a donation from the Ethereum Foundation. Part of the work was conducted while the first author was employed by UC Berkeley, and part while employed by IBM Research – Zurich, supported by the SNSF ERC Transfer Grant CRETP2-166734 – FELICITY.

References

[AC20]   Attema, T., Cramer, R.: Compressed Σ-protocol theory and practical application to plug & play secure algorithmics. In: Proceedings of the 40th Annual International Cryptology Conference, CRYPTO 2020, pp. 513–543 (2020)

[ACDEY19]   Abspoel, M., Cramer, R., Damgård, I., Escudero, D., Yuan, C.: Efficient information-theoretic secure multiparty computation over $\mathbb{Z}/p^k\mathbb{Z}$ via Galois rings. In: Hofheinz, D., Rosen, A. (eds.) TCC 2019. LNCS, vol. 11891, pp. 471–501. Springer, Cham (2019). https://doi.org/10.1007/978-3-030-36030-6_19

[ACF20]   Attema, T., Cramer, R., Fehr, S.: Compressing proofs of k-out-of-n partial knowledge. IACR Cryptology ePrint Archive, Report 2020/753 (2020)

[ACK21]   Attema, T., Cramer, R., Kohl, L.: A compressed Σ-protocol theory for lattices. Cryptology ePrint Archive, Report 2021/307 (2021)

[ACR20]   Attema, T., Cramer, R., Rambaud, M.: Compressed sigma-protocols for bilinear circuits and applications to logarithmic-sized transparent threshold signature schemes. IACR Cryptology ePrint Archive, Report 2020/1447 (2020)

[AL21]   Albrecht, M.R., Lai, R.W.F.: Subtractive sets over cyclotomic rings: Limits of schnorr-like arguments over lattices. Cryptology ePrint Archive, Report 2021/202 (2021)

[Abs+20]   Abspoel, M., et al.: Asymptotically good multiplicative LSSS over Galois rings and applications to MPC over $\mathbb{Z}/p^k\mathbb{Z}$. In: Moriai, S., Wang, H. (eds.) ASIACRYPT 2020. LNCS, vol. 12493, pp. 151–180. Springer, Cham (2020). https://doi.org/10.1007/978-3-030-64840-4_6

[Adj]   URL: https://github.com/adjoint-io/bulletproofs

[BBBPWM18]   Bünz, B., Bootle, J., Boneh, D., Poelstra, A., Wuille, P., Maxwell, G.: Bulletproofs: Short proofs for confidential transactions and more. In: Proceedings of the 39th IEEE Symposium on Security and Privacy, S&P 2018, pp. 315–334 (2018)

[BCCGP16] Bootle, J., Cerulli, A., Chaidos, P., Groth, J., Petit, C.: Efficient zero-knowledge arguments for arithmetic circuits in the discrete log setting. In: Fischlin, M., Coron, J.-S. (eds.) EUROCRYPT 2016. LNCS, vol. 9666, pp. 327–357. Springer, Heidelberg (2016). https://doi.org/10.1007/978-3-662-49896-5_12

[BCG20] Bootle, J., Chiesa, A., Groth, J.: Linear-time arguments with sublinear verification from tensor codes. In: Pass, R., Pietrzak, K. (eds.) TCC 2020. LNCS, vol. 12551, pp. 19–46. Springer, Cham (2020). https://doi.org/10.1007/978-3-030-64378-2_2

[BCGGRS19] Ben-Sasson, E., Chiesa, A., Goldberg, L., Gur, T., Riabzev, M., Spooner, N.: Linear-size constant-query IOPs for delegating computation. In: Hofheinz, D., Rosen, A. (eds.) TCC 2019. LNCS, vol. 11892, pp. 494–521. Springer, Cham (2019). https://doi.org/10.1007/978-3-030-36033-7_19

[BCGRS17] Ben-Sasson, E., Chiesa, A., Gabizon, A., Riabzev, M., Spooner, N.: Interactive oracle proofs with constant rate and query complexity. In: Proceedings of the 44th International Colloquium on Automata, Languages and Programming, ICALP 2017, pp. 40:1–40:15 (2017)

[BCL20] Bootle, J., Chiesa, A., Liu, S.: Zero-knowledge succinct arguments with a linear-time prover. IACR Cryptology ePrint Archive, Report 2020/1527 (2020)

[BCOS20] Boschini, C., Camenisch, J., Ovsiankin, M., Spooner, N.: Efficient post-quantum snarks for RSIS and RLWE and their applications to privacy. In: Proceedings of the 11th International Conference on Post-Quantum Cryptography, PQCrypto 2020, pp. 247–267 (2020)

[BCRSVW19] Ben-Sasson, E., Chiesa, A., Riabzev, M., Spooner, N., Virza, M., Ward, N.P.: Aurora: Transparent succinct arguments for R1CS. In: Proceedings of the 38th Annual International Conference on the Theory and Applications of Cryptographic Techniques, EUROCRYPT 2019, pp. 103–128 (2019). Full version available at https://eprint.iacr.org/2018/828

[BDFG20] Boneh, D., Drake, J., Fisch, B., Gabizon, A.: Halo Infinite: Recursive zk-SNARKs from any additive polynomial commitment scheme. IACR Cryptology ePrint Archive, Report 2020/1536 (2020)

[BFHVXZ20] Bhadauria, R., Fang, Z., Hazay, C., Venkitasubramaniam, M., Xie, T., Zhang, Y.: Ligero++: a new optimized sublinear IOP. In: Proceedings of the 27th ACM Conference on Computer and Communications Security, CCS 2020, pp. 2025–2038 (2020)

[BFL91] Babai, L., Fortnow, L., Lund, C.: Non-deterministic exponential time has two-prover interactive protocols. Computational Complexity, vol. 1, pp. 3–40 (1991). Preliminary version appeared in FOCS 1990

[BFLS91] Babai, L., Fortnow, L., Levin, L.A., Szegedy, M.: Checking computations in polylogarithmic time. In: Proceedings of the 23rd Annual ACM Symposium on Theory of Computing, STOC 1991, pp. 21–32 (1991)

[BFS20] Bünz, B., Fisch, B., Szepieniec, A.: Transparent SNARKs from DARK compilers. In: Canteaut, A., Ishai, Y. (eds.) EUROCRYPT 2020. LNCS, vol. 12105, pp. 677–706. Springer, Cham (2020). https://doi.org/10.1007/978-3-030-45721-1_24

[BHRRS20] Block, A.R., Holmgren, J., Rosen, A., Rothblum, R.D., Soni, P.: Public-coin zero-knowledge arguments with (almost) minimal time and space overheads. In: Pass, R., Pietrzak, K. (eds.) TCC 2020. LNCS, vol. 12551, pp. 168–197. Springer, Cham (2020). https://doi.org/10.1007/978-3-030-64378-2_7

[BHRRS21] Block, A.R., Holmgren, J., Rosen, A., Rothblum, R.D., Soni, P.: Time- and space-efficient arguments from groups of unknown order. In: Proceedings of the 41st Annual International Cryptology Conference, CRYPTO 2021 (2021)

[BISW17] Boneh, D., Ishai, Y., Sahai, A., Wu, D.J.: Lattice-based SNARGs and their application to more efficient obfuscation. In: Coron, J.-S., Nielsen, J.B. (eds.) EUROCRYPT 2017. LNCS, vol. 10212, pp. 247–277. Springer, Cham (2017). https://doi.org/10.1007/978-3-319-56617-7_9

[BISW18] Boneh, D., Ishai, Y., Sahai, A., Wu, D.J.: Quasi-optimal SNARGs via linear multi-prover interactive proofs. In: Nielsen, J.B., Rijmen, V. (eds.) EUROCRYPT 2018. LNCS, vol. 10822, pp. 222–255. Springer, Cham (2018). https://doi.org/10.1007/978-3-319-78372-7_8

[BLNS20] Bootle, J., Lyubashevsky, V., Nguyen, N.K., Seiler, G.: A non-PCP approach to succinct quantum-safe zero-knowledge. In: Micciancio, D., Ristenpart, T. (eds.) CRYPTO 2020. LNCS, vol. 12171, pp. 441–469. Springer, Cham (2020). https://doi.org/10.1007/978-3-030-56880-1_16

[BMMTV19] Bünz, B., Maller, M., Mishra, P., Tyagi, N., Vesely, P.: Proofs for inner pairing products and applications. Cryptology ePrint Archive, Report 2019/1177 (2019)

[CCHLRR18] Canetti, R., Chen, Y., Holmgren, J., Lombardi, A., Rothblum, G.N., Rothblum, R.D.: Fiat-Shamir from simpler assumptions. Cryptology ePrint Archive, Report 2018/1004 (2018)

[CCKP19] Chen, S., Cheon, J.H., Kim, D., Park, D.: Verifiable computing for approximate computation. IACR Cryptology ePrint Archive, Report 2019/762 (2019)

[CDESX18] Cramer, R., Damgård, I., Escudero, D., Scholl, P., Xing, C.: SPDZ$_{2k}$: efficient MPC mod 2^k for dishonest majority. In: Shacham, H., Boldyreva, A. (eds.) CRYPTO 2018. LNCS, vol. 10992, pp. 769–798. Springer, Cham (2018). https://doi.org/10.1007/978-3-319-96881-0_26

[CFFQR20] Campanelli, M., Faonio, A., Fiore, D., Querol, A., Rodríguez, H.: Lunar: a toolbox for more efficient universal and updatable zkSNARKs and commit-and-prove extensions. Cryptology ePrint Archive, Report 2020/1069 (2020)

[CFIK03] Cramer, R., Fehr, S., Ishai, Y., Kushilevitz, E.: Efficient multi-party computation over rings. In: Proceedings of the 22nd Annual International Conference on Theory and Application of Cryptographic Techniques, EUROCRYPT 2003, pp. 596–613 (2003)

[CHJKS20] Chung, H., Han, K., Ju, C., Kim, M., Seo, J.H.: Bulletproofs+: Shorter proofs for privacy-enhanced distributed ledger. Cryptology ePrint Archive, Report 2020/735 (2020)

[CHMMVW20] Chiesa, A., Hu, Y., Maller, M., Mishra, P., Vesely, N., Ward, N.: Marlin: Preprocessing zkSNARKs with universal and updatable SRS. In: Proceedings of the 39th Annual International Conference on the Theory and Applications of Cryptographic Techniques, EUROCRYPT 2020, pp. 738–768 (2020)

[CMS19] Chiesa, A., Manohar, P., Spooner, N.: Succinct arguments in the quantum random oracle model. In: Hofheinz, D., Rosen, A. (eds.) TCC 2019. LNCS, vol. 11892, pp. 1–29. Springer, Cham (2019). https://doi.org/10.1007/978-3-030-36033-7_1

[CMSZ21] Chiesa, A., Ma, F., Spooner, N., Zhandry, M.: Post-quantum succinct arguments. Cryptology ePrint Archive, Report 2021/334 (2021)

[CMT12] Cormode, G., Mitzenmacher, M., Thaler, J.: Practical verified computation with streaming interactive proofs. In: Proceedings of the 4th Symposium on Innovations in Theoretical Computer Science, ITCS 2012, pp. 90–112 (2012)

[COS20] Chiesa, A., Ojha, D., Spooner, N.: Fractal: post-quantum and transparent recursive proofs from holography. In: Proceedings of the 39th Annual International Conference on the Theory and Applications of Cryptographic Techniques, EUROCRYPT 2020, pp. 769–793 (2020)

[CY20] Chiesa, A., Yogev, E.: Barriers for succinct arguments in the random oracle model. In: Pass, R., Pietrzak, K. (eds.) TCC 2020. LNCS, vol. 12551, pp. 47–76. Springer, Cham (2020). https://doi.org/10.1007/978-3-030-64378-2_3

[GKR08] Goldwasser, S., Kalai, Y.T., Rothblum, G.N.: Delegating computation: interactive proofs for muggles. In: Proceedings of the 40th Annual ACM Symposium on Theory of Computing, STOC 2008, pp. 113–122 (2008)

[GMNO18] Gennaro, R., Minelli, M., Nitulescu, A., Orrù, M.: Lattice-based zkSNARKs from square span programs. In: Proceedings of the 25th ACM Conference on Computer and Communications Security, CCS 2018, pp. 556–573 (2018)

[GNS21] Ganesh, C., Nitulescu, A., Soria-Vazquez, E.: Rinocchio: SNARKs for ring arithmetic. Cryptology ePrint Archive, Report 2021/322 (2021)

[GT20] Ghoshal, A., Tessaro, S.: Tight state-restoration soundness in the algebraic group model. Cryptology ePrint Archive, Report 2020/1351 (2020)

[JKKZ20] Jawale, R., Kalai, Y.T., Khurana, D., Zhang, R.: SNARGs for bounded depth computations and PPAD hardness from sub-exponential LWE. IACR Cryptology ePrint Archive, Report 2020/980 (2020)

[JT20] Jaeger, J., Tessaro, S.: Expected-time cryptography: generic techniques and applications to concrete soundness. In: Pass, R., Pietrzak, K. (eds.) TCC 2020. LNCS, vol. 12552, pp. 414–443. Springer, Cham (2020). https://doi.org/10.1007/978-3-030-64381-2_15

[Kil92] Kilian, J.: A note on efficient zero-knowledge proofs and arguments. In: Proceedings of the 24th Annual ACM Symposium on Theory of Computing, STOC 1992, pp. 723–732 (1992)

[LFKN92] Lund, C., Fortnow, L., Karloff, H.J., Nisan, N.: Algebraic methods for interactive proof systems. J. ACM 39(4), 859–868 (1992)

[LMR19] Lai, R.W.F., Malavolta, G., Ronge, V.: Succinct arguments for bilinear group arithmetic: practical structure-preserving cryptography. In: Proceedings of the 26th ACM Conference on Computer and Communications Security, CCS 2019, pp. 2057–2074 (2019)

[Lee20] Lee, J.: Dory: Efficient, transparent arguments for generalised inner products and polynomial commitments. Cryptology ePrint Archive, Report 2020/1274 (2020)

[Mei13] Meir, O.: IP = PSPACE using error-correcting codes. SIAM J. Comput. **42**(1), 380–403 (2013)

[Mon] URL: https://github.com/monero-project/monero/tree/master/src/ringct

[PLS19] del Pino, R., Lyubashevsky, V., Seiler, G.: Short discrete log proofs for FHE and ring-LWE ciphertexts. In: Proceedings of the 22nd International Conference on Practice and Theory of Public-Key Cryptography, PKC 2019, pp. 344–373 (2019)

[Piv] Pivx implementation of bulletproofs. https://github.com/PIVX-Project/PIVX/tree/Bulletproofs/src/libzerocoin

[RR20] Ron-Zewi, N., Rothblum, R.: Local proofs approaching the witness length. In: Proceedings of the 61st Annual IEEE Symposium on Foundations of Computer Science, FOCS 2020 (2020)

[RV09] Rothblum, G.N., Vadhan, S.: Are PCPs inherent in efficient arguments? In: Proceedings of the 24th IEEE Annual Conference on Computational Complexity, CCC 2009, pp. 81–92 (2009)

[Set20] Setty, S.: Spartan: efficient and general-purpose zksnarks without trusted setup. In: Proceedings of the 40th Annual International Cryptology Conference, CRYPTO 2020, pp. 704–737 (2020)

[Tha13] Thaler, J.: Time-optimal interactive proofs for circuit evaluation. In: Proceedings of the 33rd Annual International Cryptology Conference, CRYPTO 2013, pp. 71–89 (2013)

[VSBW13] Vu, V., Setty, S., Blumberg, A.J., Walfish, M.: A hybrid architecture for interactive verifiable computation. In: Proceedings of the 34th IEEE Symposium on Security and Privacy, Oakland 2013, pp. 223–237 (2013)

[WTSTW18] Wahby, R.S., Tzialla, I., Shelat, A., Thaler, J., Walfish, M.: Doubly-efficient zkSNARKs without trusted setup. In: Proceedings of the 39th IEEE Symposium on Security and Privacy, S&P 2018, pp. 926–943 (2018)

[Wah+17] Wahby, R.S., et al.: Full accounting for verifiable outsourcing. In: Proceedings of the 24th ACM Conference on Computer and Communications Security, CCS 2017, pap. 2071–2086 (2017)

[XZZPS19] Xie, T., Zhang, J., Zhang, Y., Papamanthou, C., Song, D.: Libra: succinct zero-knowledge proofs with optimal prover computation. In: Proceedings of the 39th Annual International Cryptology Conference, CRYPTO 2019, pp. 733–764 (2019)

[ZGKPP17] Zhang, Y., Genkin, D., Katz, J., Papadopoulos, D., Papamanthou, C.: vSQL: verifying arbitrary SQL queries over dynamic outsourced databases. In: Proceedings of the 38th IEEE Symposium on Security and Privacy, S&P 2017, pp. 863–880 (2017)

[ZXZS20] Zhang, J., Xie, T., Zhang, Y., Song, D.: Transparent polynomial delegation and its applications to zero knowledge proof. In: Proceedings of the 41st IEEE Symposium on Security and Privacy, S&P 2020, pp. 859–876 (2020)

[dalek18] Dalek cryptography. A pure-Rust implementation of Bulletproofs using Ristretto (2018)

An Algebraic Framework for Universal and Updatable SNARKs

Carla Ràfols[1,2]($\boxtimes$) and Arantxa Zapico[1]

[1] Universitat Pompeu Fabra, Barcelona, Spain
carla.rafols@upf.edu
[2] Cybercat, Barcelona, Spain

Abstract. We introduce Checkable Subspace Sampling Arguments, a new information theoretic interactive proof system in which the prover shows that a vector has been sampled in a subspace according to the verifier's coins. We show that this primitive provides a unifying view that explains the technical core of most of the constructions of universal and updatable pairing-based (zk)SNARKs. This characterization is extended to a fully algebraic framework for designing such SNARKs in a modular way. We propose new constructions of CSS arguments that lead to SNARKs with different performance trade-offs.

1 Introduction

Zero-Knowledge proofs [23], and in particular, non-interactive ones [7] have played a central role in both the theory and practice of cryptography. A long line of research [22,25,26,32,34] has led to efficient pairing-based zero-knowledge *Succinct Non-interactive ARguments of Knowledge* or SNARKs. These arguments are *succinct*, in fact, they allow to prove that circuits of arbitrary size are satisfied with a constant-size proof. They are also extremely efficient concretely (3 group elements in the best construction for arithmetic circuits [26]).

Despite this impressive performance, some aspects of these constructions of SNARKs are still unsatisfactory. Probably the most problematic and not fully solved issue is their reliance on long trusted, structured, and circuit dependent parameters (a circuit dependent SRS, for *structured reference string*).

Albeit the significant research effort in finding alternatives to bypass the need of a trusted third party by constructing *transparent* arguments, i.e. in the uniform random string model (URS) [2–4,8,11,15,39,40], pairing-based SNARKs

C. Ràfols—This paper is part of a project that has received funding from the European Union's Horizon 2020 research and innovation programme under grant agreement No 856879.

A. Zapico—The project that gave rise to these results received the support of a fellowship from la Caixa Foundation (ID100010434). The fellowship code is LCF/BQ/DI18/11660052. This project has received funding from the European Union's Horizon 2020 research and innovation programme under the Marie Skodowska-Curie grant agreement No.71367.

T. Malkin and C. Peikert (Eds.): CRYPTO 2021, LNCS 12825, pp. 774–804, 2021.
https://doi.org/10.1007/978-3-030-84242-0_27

such as [26] still seem the most practical alternative in many settings due to their very fast verification, which is a must in many blockchain applications. On the other hand, multiparty solutions for the problem are not fully scalable [9,10].

As an alternative to a trusted SRS, Groth et al. [27] define the updatable model, in which the SRS can be updated by any party, non-interactively, and in a verifiable way, resulting in a properly generated structured reference string where the simulation trapdoor is unknown to all parties if at least one is honest. Further, they propose a construction where the SRS is universal and can be used for arbitrary circuits up to a maximum given size.

Arithmetic Circuit Satisfiability can be reduced to a set of quadratic and affine constraints over a finite field. The quadratic ones are universal and can be easily proven in the pairing-based setting with a Hadamard product argument, the basic core of most zkSNARKS constructions starting from [22]. On the other hand, affine constraints are circuit-dependent, and it is a challenging task to efficiently prove them with a universal SRS [13,14,16,19,20,33,37,38].

In Groth et al. [27] they are proven via a very expensive subspace argument that requires a SRS quadratic in the circuit size and a preprocessing step that is cubic. Sonic [33], the first efficient, universal, and updatable SNARK, gives two different ways to prove the affine constraints, a fully succinct one (not so efficient) and another one in the amortized setting (very efficient). Follow-up work (most notably, Marlin [14], Plonk [20], Lunar [13]) has significantly improved the efficiency in the fully succinct mode.

There is an important trend in cryptography, that advocates for constructing protocols in a modular way. One reason for doing so is the fact that, by breaking complicated protocols into simpler steps, they become easier to analyze. Ishai [28] mentions comparability as another fundamental motive. Specially in the area of zero-knowledge, given the surge of interest in practical constructions, it is hard not to lose sight of what each proposal achieves. As Ishai puts it: *"one reason such comparisons are difficult is the multitude of application scenarios, implementation details, efficiency desiderata, cryptographic assumptions, and trust models"*.

Starting from Sonic, all the aforementioned works on universal and updatable zkSNARKs follow this trend. More concretely, they first build an information-theoretic proof system, that is then compiled into a full argument under some computational assumptions in bilinear groups. The main ingredient of the compiler is a polynomial commitment [12,30,31]. However, the information theoretic component is still very complex and comparison among these works remains difficult, for precisely the same reasons stated by Ishai. In particular, it is hard to extract the new ideas in each of them in the complex description of the arguments, that use sophisticated tricks for improving efficiency, as well as advanced properties of multiplicative subgroups of a finite field or bivariate Lagrange interpolation. Further, it is striking that all fully succinct arguments are for restricted types of constraints (sums of permutations in Sonic, sparse matrices in Marlin, and Lunar[1]) or pay a price for additive gates (Plonk). A modular, unified view

---

[1] The number of non-zero entries of the matrices that encode linear constraints cannot exceed the size of some multiplicative group of the field of definition.

of these important works seems essential for a clearer understanding of the techniques. In turn, this should allow for a better comparison, more flexibility in combining the different methods, and give insights on current limitations.

Our Contributions. We propose an algebraic framework that takes a step further in achieving modular constructions of universal and updatable SNARKs. We identify the technical core of previous work as instances of a *Checkable Subspace Sampling* (CSS) Argument. In this information-theoretic proof system, two parties, prover and verifier, on input a field $\mathbb{F}$ and a matrix $\mathbf{M} \in \mathbb{F}^{Q \times m}$, agree on a polynomial $D(X)$ encoding a vector $\boldsymbol{d}$ in the row space of $\mathbf{M}$. The interesting part is that, even though the coefficients of the linear combination that define $\boldsymbol{d}$ are chosen by the verifier's coins, the latter does not need to perform a linear (in Q, the number of rows) number of operations in order to verify that $D(X)$ is correct. Instead, this must be demostrated by the prover.

With this algebraic formulation, it is immediate to see that a CSS argument can be used as a building block for an argument of membership in linear spaces. Basically, given a matrix $\mathbf{M}$, we can prove that some vector $\boldsymbol{y}$ is orthogonal to the rows of $\mathbf{M}$ by sampling, after $\boldsymbol{y}$ is declared, a *sufficiently random* vector $\boldsymbol{d}$ in the row space of $\mathbf{M}$ and checking an inner product relation, namely, whether $\boldsymbol{d} \cdot \boldsymbol{y} = 0$. The purpose of a CSS argument is to guarantee that the sampling process can be checked by the verifier in sublinear time without sacrificing soundness.

Naturally, for building succinct proofs, instead of $\boldsymbol{y}, \boldsymbol{d}$, the argument uses polynomial encodings $Y(X)$ and $D(X)$ (which are group elements after the compilation step). To compute the inner product of this encoded vectors, we introduce a new argument in Sect. 3, which is specific to the case where the polynomials are encoded in the Lagrange polynomial basis, but can be easily generalized to the monomial basis. The argument is a straightforward application of the univariate sumcheck of Aurora [5]. However, we contribute a generalized sumcheck (that works not only for multiplicative subgroups of finite fields), with a completely new proof that relates it with polynomial evaluation at some fixed point v.

These building blocks can be put together as an argument for the language of Rank1 constraint systems. For efficiency, we stick to R1CS-lite, a variant recently proposed by Lunar, which is slightly simpler but still NP-complete. Our final construction can be instantiated with any possible choice of CSS scheme, so in particular it can essentially recover the construction of Marlin and Lunar by isolating the CSS argument implicit in these works, or the amortized construction of Sonic. We hope that this serves to better identify the challenge behind building updatable and universal SNARKs, and allow for new steps in improving efficiency, as well as more easily combining the techniques.

In summary, we reduce R1CS constraint systems to three algebraic relations: an inner product, a Hadamard product and a CSS argument. We think this algebraic formulation is very clear, and also makes it easier to relate advances in universal and updatable SNARKS with other works that have used a similar language, for example, the arguments for inner product of [8], of membership in linear spaces [29], or for linear algebra relations [24].

Finally, we give several constructions of CSS arguments. In Sect. 5.3, we start from the representation of a matrix $\mathbf{W}$ as bivariate polynomial introduced in [14], and present an alternative that comes from applying a linearization step to it. The result is a CSS for sparse matrices, that compared to [13,14], at a minimial increase in communication cost, significantly reduces the SRS. We study several extensions of this argument, for example, to sums of sparse matrices. We also identify a simple building block that allows for a modular construction. In the full version we discuss how these CSS arguments result in zkSNARKs with different performance trade-offs.

1.1 Related Work

Bivariate Polynomial Evaluation Arguments. As mentioned before, the complexity of building updatable and universal zkSNARKs protocols is mainly caused by proving affine constraints. A natural way to encode them is through a bivariate public polynomial $P(X, Y)$; in order to avoid having a quadratic SRS, this polynomial can only be given to the verifier evaluated or partially evaluated in the field. The common approach is to let the verifier chose arbitrary field elements x, y and having the prover evaluate and send $\sigma = P(y, x)$. The challenge is to prove that the evaluation has been performed correctly. In Sonic [33], this last step is called a *signature of correct computation* [36] and can be performed by the prover or by the verifier with some help from an untrusted third party. The drawback of the first construction is that, while still linear, prover's work is considerably costly; also, linear constraints are assumed to be sparse and the protocol works exclusively for a very particular polynomial $P(X, Y)$. The second construction is interesting only in some restricted settings where the same verifier checks a linear amount of proofs for one circuit. Marlin [14] bases its construction on the univariate sum-check protocol of Aurora [5] and presents a novel way to navigate from the naive quadratic representation $P(X, Y)$ to a linear one. This approach results in succinct prover and verifier work, but restricts their protocol to the case where the number of non-zero entries of matrix $\mathbf{W}$ is bounded by the size of some multiplicative subgroup of the field of definition. Lunar [13] uses the same representation as Marlin but improves on it, among other tweaks by introducing a new language (R1CS-lite) that can also represent arithmetic circuit satisfiability, but has a lighter representation than other constraint systems. Plonk [20] does not use bivariate polynomials or require sparse matrices but the SRS size depends on the number of both multiplicative and additive gates. Plonk, Marlin and Lunar use the Lagrange interpolation basis to commit to vectors. Claymore [38] presents a modular construction for zkSNARKs based on similar algebraic building blocks but in the monomial basis: inner product, Hadamard product and matrix-vector product arguments. The latter also uses an implicit CSS argument.

Information Theoretic Proof Systems. These previous works all follow the two step process described in the introduction and build their succinct argument by compiling an information theoretically secure one. Marlin introduces

Algebraic Holographic proofs, that are variation of interactive oracle proofs (IOPs) [6]. Holographic refers to the fact that the verifier never receives the input explicitly (otherwise, succinctness would be impossible), but rather its encoding as an oracle computed by an indexer or encoder. The term algebraic refers to the fact that oracles are low degree polynomials, and malicious provers are also bound to output low degree polynomials. This is similar to the notion of Idealised Low Degree protocols of Plonk. Lunar refines this model by introducing Polynomial Holographic IOPs, which generalize these works mostly by allowing for a fine grained analysis of the zero-knowledge property, including degree checks, and letting prover and verifier send field elements.

Polynomial Commitments. Polynomial commitments allow to commit to a polynomial $p(X) \in \mathbb{F}[X]$, and open it at any point $x \in \mathbb{F}$. As it is common, we will use a polynomial commitment based on the one by Kate et al. [30]. Sonic gave a proof of extractability of the latter in the Algebraic Group Model [18], and Marlin completed the proof to make the commitments usable as a standalone primitive, and also have an alternative construction under knowledge assumptions. Both Marlin and Plonk considered versions of polynomial commitments where queries in the same point can be batched together. For this work, we use the definitions presented in [14].

Work		$|srs_u|$	$|srs_W|$	$|\pi|$	KeyGen	Derive	Prove	Verifier
Sonic [33]	$\mathbb{G}_1$	$4N$	–	20	$4N$	$36n$	$273n$	7P
	$\mathbb{G}_2$	$4N$	3	–	$4N$	–	–	
	$\mathbb{F}$	–	–	16	–	$O(m \log m)$	$O(m \log m)$	$O(l + \log m)$
Plonk [20]	$\mathbb{G}_1$	$3N^*$	8	7	$3N^*$	$8n + 8a$	$11n + 11a$	2P
	$\mathbb{G}_2$	1	1	–	–	–	–	
	$\mathbb{F}$	–	–	7	–	$O((n + a)\log(n + a))$	$O((n + a)\log(n + a))$	$O(l + \log(n + a))$
Marlin [14]	$\mathbb{G}_1$	$3M$	12	13	$3M$	$12m$	$14n + 8m$	2P
	$\mathbb{G}_2$	2	2	–	–	–	–	
	$\mathbb{F}$	–	–	8	–	$O(m \log m)$	$O(m \log m)$	$O(l + \log m)$
Lunar [13]	$\mathbb{G}_1$	M	–	10	M	–	$8n + 3m$	7P
	$\mathbb{G}_2$	M	27	–	M	$24m$	–	
	$\mathbb{F}$	–	–	2	–	$O(m \log m)$	$O(m \log m)$	$O(l + \log m)$
This work	$\mathbb{G}_1$	M	4	11	M	$6m$	$8n + 4m$	2P
	$\mathbb{G}_2$	1	1	–	–	–	–	
	$\mathbb{F}$	–	–	4	–	$O(m \log m)$	$O(m \log m)$	$O(l + \log m)$

Comparison with state of the art universal and updatable zkSNARKs. n: number of multiplicative gates, a: number of additive gates, $m = |\mathbf{F}| + |\mathbf{G}|$, where $\mathbf{F}, \mathbf{G}$ are the matrices that describe the linear relations for the left and right inputs, respectively. N, A, M: maximum supported values for n, a, m. $N^* = M + A$.

Untrusted Setup. The original constructions of pairing-based zkSNARKs crucially depend for soundness on a trusted setup, although, as was shown in [1,17], the zero-knowledge property is still easy to achieve when the setup is subverted. Groth et al. introduced the updatable SRS model in [27] to address the issue of trust in SRS generation. There are several alternatives to achieve transparent setup and constant-size proofs, but all of them have either linear verifier [2,5,8,11], or work only for very structured types of computation [3,39]. An exception is the work of Setty [37]. Concretely, its approach is less efficient in terms of proof size and verification complexity compared to recent constructions of updatable and universal pairing-based SNARKs.

2 Preliminaries

A bilinear group gk is a tuple $gk = (q, \mathbb{G}_1, \mathbb{G}_2, \mathbb{G}_T, e, \mathcal{P}_1, \mathcal{P}_2)$ where $\mathbb{G}_1, \mathbb{G}_2$ and $\mathbb{G}_T$ are groups of prime order q, the elements $\mathcal{P}_1, \mathcal{P}_2$ are generators of $\mathbb{G}_1, \mathbb{G}_2$ respectively, $e : \mathbb{G}_1 \times \mathbb{G}_2 \to \mathbb{G}_T$ is an efficiently computable, non-degenerate bilinear map, and there is an efficiently computable isomorphism between $\mathbb{G}_1$ and $\mathbb{G}_2$. Elements in $\mathbb{G}_\gamma$, are denoted implicitly as $[a]_\gamma = a\mathcal{P}_\gamma$, where $\gamma \in \{1, 2, T\}$ and $\mathcal{P}_T = e(\mathcal{P}_1, \mathcal{P}_2)$. With this notation, $e([a]_1, [b]_2) = [ab]_T$.

For $n \in \mathbb{N}$, $[n]$ is the set of integers $\{1, \ldots, n\}$. Vectors and matrices are denoted in boldface. Given two vectors $\boldsymbol{a}, \boldsymbol{b}$, their Hadamard product is denoted as $\boldsymbol{a} \circ \boldsymbol{b}$, and their inner product as $\boldsymbol{a} \cdot \boldsymbol{b}$. The subspace of polynomials of degree at most d in $\mathbb{F}[X]$ is denoted as $\mathbb{F}_{\leq d}[X]$. Given a matrix $\mathbf{M}$, $|\mathbf{M}|$ refers to the number of its non-zero entries.

2.1 Constraint Systems

Formally, we will construct an argument for the universal relation $\mathcal{R}'_{\text{R1CS-lite}}$, an equivalent of the relation $\mathcal{R}_{\text{R1CS-lite}}$ introduced in Lunar [13]. The latter is a simpler version of Rank 1 Constraint Systems, it is still NP complete and encodes circuit satisfiability in a natural way:

Definition 1. *(R1CS-lite) Let $\mathbb{F}$ be a finite field and $m, l, s \in \mathbb{N}$. We define the universal relation R1CS-lite as:*

$$\mathcal{R}_{\text{R1CS-lite}} = \left\{ \begin{array}{c} (\mathsf{R}, \mathsf{x}, \mathsf{w}) := ((\mathbb{F}, s, m, l, \mathbf{F}, \mathbf{G}), \boldsymbol{x}, \boldsymbol{w}) : \\ \mathbf{F}, \mathbf{G} \in \mathbb{F}^{m \times m}, \boldsymbol{x} \in \mathbb{F}^{l-1}, \boldsymbol{w} \in \mathbb{F}^{m-l}, s = \max\{|\mathbf{F}|, |\mathbf{G}|\}, \\ \text{and for } \boldsymbol{c} := (1, \boldsymbol{x}, \boldsymbol{w}), (\mathbf{F}\boldsymbol{c}) \circ (\mathbf{G}\boldsymbol{c}) = \boldsymbol{c} \end{array} \right\}.$$

As an equivalent formulation of this relation, we use the following:

$$\mathcal{R}'_{\text{R1CS-lite}} = \left\{ \begin{array}{c} (\mathsf{R}, \mathsf{x}, \mathsf{w}) := ((\mathbb{F}, s, m, l, \mathbf{F}, \mathbf{G}), \boldsymbol{x}, (\boldsymbol{a}', \boldsymbol{b}')) : \mathbf{F}, \mathbf{G} \in \mathbb{F}^{m \times m}, \boldsymbol{x} \in \mathbb{F}^{l-1}, \\ \boldsymbol{a}', \boldsymbol{b}' \in \mathbb{F}^{m-l}, s = \max\{|\mathbf{F}|, |\mathbf{G}|\}, \text{ and for } \boldsymbol{a} := (1, \boldsymbol{x}, \boldsymbol{a}'), \boldsymbol{b} := (1, \boldsymbol{b}') \\ \begin{pmatrix} \mathbf{I} & \mathbf{0} & -\mathbf{F} \\ \mathbf{0} & \mathbf{I} & -\mathbf{G} \end{pmatrix} \begin{pmatrix} \boldsymbol{a} \\ \boldsymbol{b} \\ \boldsymbol{a} \circ \boldsymbol{b} \end{pmatrix} = 0 \end{array} \right\}.$$

To see they are equivalent, observe that, if in $\mathcal{R}'_{\text{R1CS-lite}}$ we define the vector $\boldsymbol{c} = \boldsymbol{a} \circ \boldsymbol{b}$, the linear equation reads as $\boldsymbol{a} = \mathbf{F}\boldsymbol{c}$ and $\boldsymbol{b} = \mathbf{G}\boldsymbol{c}$. A formal proof is a direct consequence of the proof that arithmetic circuit satisfiability reduces to R1CS-lite found in Lunar ([13]).

2.2 zkSNARKs

Let $\mathcal{R}$ be a family of universal relations. Given a relation $R \in \mathcal{R}$ and an instance x we call w a *witness* for x if $(x, w) \in R$, $\mathcal{L}(R) = \{x| \ \exists w : (x, w) \in R\}$ is the language of all the x that have a witness w in the relation R, while $\mathcal{L}(\mathcal{R})$is the language of all the pairs (x, R) such that $x \in \mathcal{L}(R)$.

Definition 2. *A Universal Succinct Non-Interactive Argument of Knowledge is a tuple of PPT algorithms* (KeyGen, KeyGenD, Prove, Verify, Simulate) *such that:*

- $(srs_u, \tau) \leftarrow$ KeyGen$(\mathcal{R})$: *On input a family of relations* $\mathcal{R}$, KeyGen *outputs a universal structured common reference string* srs_u *and a trapdoor* τ;
- $srs_R \leftarrow$ KeyGenD(srs_u, R): *On input* $R \in \mathcal{R}$, *this algorithm outputs a relation dependent SRS that includes* srs_u;
- $\pi \leftarrow$ Prove$(R, srs_R, (x, w))$: *On input the relation,* srs_R *and a pair* $(x, w) \in R$, *it outputs a proof* π;
- $1/0 \leftarrow$ Verify(srs_R, x, π): Verify *takes as input* srs_R, *the instance* x *and the proof and produces a bit expressing acceptance* (1), *or rejection* (0);
- $\pi_{sim} \leftarrow$ Simulate(R, τ, x): *The simulator has the relation R, the trapdoor* τ *and the instance* x *as inputs and it generates a simulated proof* π_{sim},

and that satisfies completeness, succinctness and ϵ-knowledge soundness as defined below.

Definition 3. *Completeness holds if an honest prover will always convince an honest verifier. Formally,* $\forall R \in \mathcal{R}, (x, w) \in R$,

$$\Pr \left[\text{Verify}(srs_R, x, \pi) = 1 \ \middle| \ \begin{array}{l} (srs_u, \tau) \leftarrow \text{KeyGen}(\mathcal{R}) \\ srs_R \leftarrow \text{KeyGenD}(srs_u, R) \\ \pi \leftarrow \text{Prove}(R, srs_R, (x, w)) \end{array} \right] = 1.$$

Definition 4. *Succinctness holds if the size of the proof* π *is* $poly(\lambda + \log |w|)$ *and* Verify *runs in time* $poly(\lambda + |x| + \log |w|)$.

Definition 5. *ϵ-knowledge soundness captures the fact that a cheating prover cannot, except with probability at most ϵ, create a proof π accepted by the verification algorithm unless it has a witness w such that* $(x, w) \in R$. *Formally, for all PPT adversaries $\mathcal{A}$, there exists a PPT extractor $\mathcal{E}$ such that:*

$$Pr \left[(x, w) \notin R \wedge \text{Verify}(srs_R, x, \pi) = 1 \ \middle| \ \begin{array}{l} (srs_u, \tau) \leftarrow \text{KeyGen}(\mathcal{R}) \\ R \leftarrow \mathcal{A}(srs_u) \\ srs_R \leftarrow \text{KeyGenD}(srs_u, R) \\ (x, \pi) \leftarrow \mathcal{A}(R, srs_R) \\ w \leftarrow \mathcal{E}(srs_R, x, \pi) \end{array} \right] \leq \epsilon.$$

Definition 6. (KeyGen, KeyGenD, Prove, Verify, Simulate) *is zero-knowledge (a zkSNARK) if for all* $R \in \mathcal{R}$, *instances* x *and PPT adversaries $\mathcal{A}$.*

$$Pr \left[\mathcal{A}(R, srs_R, \pi) = 1 \ \middle| \ \begin{array}{l} (srs_u, \tau) \leftarrow \text{KeyGen}(\mathcal{R}) \\ srs_R \leftarrow \text{KeyGenD}(srs_u, R) \\ \pi \leftarrow \text{Prove}(R, srs_R, (x, w)) \end{array} \right] \approx$$

$$Pr\left[\mathcal{A}(\mathsf{R},\mathsf{srs}_\mathsf{R},\pi_{sim}) = 1 \;\middle|\; \begin{array}{l} (\mathsf{srs}_\mathsf{u},\tau) \leftarrow \mathsf{KeyGen}(\mathcal{R}) \\ \mathsf{srs}_\mathsf{R} \leftarrow \mathsf{KeyGenD}(\mathsf{srs}_\mathsf{u},\mathsf{R}) \\ \pi_{sim} \leftarrow \mathsf{Simulate}(\mathsf{R},\tau,\mathsf{x}) \end{array}\right].$$

Updatability. We will say a universal zkSNARK is *updatable* if srs_u is updatable as defined in [21]. We remark their result states that this is the case if srs_u consists solely of monomials.

2.3 Polynomial Holographic Proofs

In this paper, we use the notion of Polynomial Holographic Interactive Oracle Proofs (PHP), recently introduced by Campanelli et al. [13]. It is a refinement and quite similar to other notions used in the literature to construct SNARKs in a modular way, such as Algebraic Holographic Proofs (AHP) [14] or idealized polynomial protocols [20].

A proof system for a relation R is holographic if the verifier does not read the full description of the relation, but rather has access to an encoding of the statement produced by some holographic relation encoder, also called indexer, that outputs oracle polynomials. In all these models, the prover is restricted to send oracle polynomials or field elements, except that, for additional flexibility, the PHP model of [13] also lets the prover send arbitrary messages. In PHPs, the queries of the verifier are algebraic checks over the polynomials sent by the verifier, as opposed to being limited to polynomial evaluations as in AHPs.

The following definitions are taken almost verbatim from [13].

Definition 7. *A family of polynomial time computable relations $\mathcal{R}$ is field dependent if each relation $\mathsf{R} \in \mathcal{R}$, specifies a unique finite field. More precisely, for any pair $(\mathsf{x},\mathsf{w}) \in \mathsf{R}$, x specifies the same finite field $\mathbb{F}_\mathsf{R}$ (simply denoted as $\mathbb{F}$ if there is no ambiguity).*

Definition 8 (Polynomial Holographic IOPs (PHP)). *A Polynomial Holographic IOP for a family of field-dependent relations $\mathcal{R}$ is a tuple $\mathsf{PHP} = (\mathsf{rnd},\mathsf{n},\mathsf{m},\mathsf{d},\mathsf{n}_e,\mathcal{I},\mathcal{P},\mathcal{V})$, where $\mathsf{rnd},\mathsf{n},\mathsf{m},\mathsf{d},\mathsf{n}_e : \{0,1\}^* \to \mathbb{N}$ are polynomial-time computable functions, and $\mathcal{I},\mathcal{P},\mathcal{V}$ are three algorithms that work as follows:*

- ***Offline phase:*** *The encoder or indexer $\mathcal{I}(\mathsf{R})$ is executed on a relation description R, and it returns $\mathsf{n}(0)$ polynomials $\{p_{0,j}\}_{j=1}^{\mathsf{n}(0)} \in \mathbb{F}[X]$ encoding the relation R and where $\mathbb{F}$ is the field specified by R.*
- ***Online phase:*** *The prover $\mathcal{P}(\mathsf{R},\mathsf{x},\mathsf{w})$ and the verifier $\mathcal{V}^{\mathcal{I}(\mathsf{R})}(\mathsf{x})$ are executed for $\mathsf{rnd}(|\mathsf{R}|)$ rounds, the prover has a tuple $(\mathsf{R},\mathsf{x},\mathsf{w}) \in \mathcal{R}$, and the verifier has an instance x and oracle access to the polynomials encoding R. In the i-th round, $\mathcal{V}$ sends a message $\rho_i \in \mathbb{F}$ to the prover, and $\mathcal{P}$ replies with $\mathsf{m}(i)$ messages $\{\pi_{i,j} \in \mathbb{F}\}_{j=1}^{\mathsf{m}(i)}$, and $\mathsf{n}(i)$ oracle polynomials $\{p_{i,j} \in \mathbb{F}[X]\}_{j=1}^{\mathsf{n}(i)}$, such that $\deg(p_{i,j}) < \mathsf{d}(|\mathsf{R}|,i,j)$.*
- ***Decision phase:*** *After the $\mathsf{rnd}(|\mathsf{R}|)$-th round, the verifier outputs two sets of algebraic checks of the following type:*

- *Degree checks: to check a bound on the degree of the polynomials sent by the prover. More in detail, let* $n_p = \sum_{k=1}^{rnd(|R|)} n(k)$ *and let* $(p_1, \ldots, p_{n_p})$ *be the polynomials sent by* $\mathcal{P}$. *The verifier specifies a vector of integers* $d \in \mathbb{N}^{n_p}$, *which satisfies the following condition*

$$\forall k \in [n_p] : \deg(p_k) \leq d_k.$$

- *Polynomial checks: to verify that certain polynomial identities hold between the oracle polynomials and the messages sent by the prover. Let* $n^* = \sum_{k=0}^{rnd(|R|)} n(k)$ *and* $m^* = \sum_{k=0}^{rnd(|R|)} m(k)$, *and denote by* $(p_1, \ldots, p_{n^*})$ *and* $(\pi_1, \ldots, \pi_{n^*})$ *all the oracle polynomials (including the* $n(0)$ *ones from the encoder) and all the messages sent by the prover. The verifier can specify a list of* n_e *tuples, each of the form* $(G, v_1, \ldots, v_{n^*})$, *where* $G \in \mathbb{F}[X, X_1, \ldots, X_{n^*}, Y_1, \ldots, Y_{m^*}]$ *and every* $v_k \in \mathbb{F}[X]$. *Then a tuple* $(G, v_1, \ldots, v_{n^*})$ *is satisfied if and only if* $F(X) \equiv 0$ *where*

$$F(X) := G\big(X, \{p_k(v_k(X))\}_{k=1,\ldots,n^*}, \{\pi_k\}_{k=1,\ldots,m^*}\big).$$

The verifier accepts if and only if all the checks are satisfied.

Definition 9. *A PHP is complete if for any triple* $(R, x, w) \in \mathcal{R}$, *the checks returned by* $\mathcal{V}^{\mathcal{I}(R)}$ *after interacting with the honest prover* $\mathcal{P}(R, x, w)$, *are satisfied with probability 1.*

Definition 10. *A PHP is ϵ-sound if for every relation-instance tuple* $(R, x) \notin \mathcal{L}(\mathcal{R})$ *and polynomial time prover* $\mathcal{P}^*$ *we have*

$$\Pr\left[\langle \mathcal{P}^*, \mathcal{V}^{\mathcal{I}(R)}(x)\rangle = 1\right] \leq \epsilon.$$

Definition 11. *A PHP is ϵ-knowledge sound if there exists a polynomial time knowledge extractor $\mathcal{E}$ such that for any prover* $\mathcal{P}^*$, *relation* R, *instance* x *and auxiliary input* z *we have*

$$\Pr\left[(R, x, w) \in \mathcal{R} : w \leftarrow \mathcal{E}^{\mathcal{P}^*}(R, x, z)\right] \geq \Pr\left[\langle \mathcal{P}^*(R, x, z), \mathcal{V}^{\mathcal{I}(R)}(x)\rangle = 1\right] - \epsilon,$$

where $\mathcal{E}$ has oracle access to $\mathcal{P}^*$, *it can query the next message function of* $\mathcal{P}^*$ *(and also rewind it) and obtain all the messages and polynomials returned by it.*

Definition 12. *A PHP is ϵ-zero-knowledge if there exists a PPT simulator $\mathcal{S}$ such that for every triple* $(R, x, w) \in \mathcal{R}$, *and every algorithm* $\mathcal{V}^*$, *the following random variables are within ϵ-statistical distance:*

$$\mathsf{View}\left(\mathcal{P}(R, x, w), \mathcal{V}^*\right) \approx_c \mathsf{View}\left(\mathcal{S}^{\mathcal{V}^*}(R, x)\right),$$

where $\mathsf{View}\left(\mathcal{P}(R, x, w), \mathcal{V}^*\right)$ *consists of* $\mathcal{V}^*$'s *randomness,* $\mathcal{P}$'s *messages (which do not include the oracles) and* $\mathcal{V}^*$'s *list of checks, while* $\mathsf{View}(\mathcal{S}^{\mathcal{V}^*}(R, x))$ *consists of* $\mathcal{V}^*$'s *randomness followed by* $\mathcal{S}$'s *output, obtained after having straightline access to* $\mathcal{V}^*$, *and* $\mathcal{V}^*$'s *list of checks.*

We assume that in every PHP scheme there is an implicit maximum degree for all the polynomials used in the scheme. Thus, we include only degree checks that differ from this maximum. In all our PHPs, the verifier is public coin.

The following definition captures de fact that zero-knowledge should hold even when the verifier has access to *a bounded amount* of evaluations of the polynomials that contain information about the witness. Let $\mathcal{Q}$ be a list of queries; we say that $\mathcal{Q}$ is (b, C)-bounded for $b \in \mathbb{N}^{n_p}$ and C a PT algorithm, if for every $i \in [n_p]$, $|\{(i, z) : (i, z) \in \mathcal{Q}\}| \leq b_i$, and for all $(i, z) \in \mathcal{Q}$, $C(i, z) = 1$.

Definition 13. *A PHP is (b, C)-zero-knowledge if for every triple $(R, x, w) \in \mathcal{R}$, and every (b, C)-bounded list $\mathcal{Q}$, the follow random variables are within ϵ statistical distance:*

$$\left(\mathsf{View} \big(\mathcal{P}(\mathbb{F}, R, x, w), \mathcal{V} \big), (p_i(z))_{(i,z) \in \mathcal{Q}} \right) \approx_\epsilon \mathcal{S} \left(\mathbb{F}, R, x, \mathcal{V}(\mathbb{F}, x), \mathcal{Q} \right),$$

where the $p_i(X)$ are the polynomials returned by the prover.

Definition 14. *A PHP is honest-verifier zero-knowledge with query bound b if there exists a PT algorithm C such that PHP is (b, C)-zero-knowledge and for all $i \in \mathbb{N}$, $Pr[C(i, z) = 0]$ is negligible, where z is uniformly sampled over $\mathbb{F}$.*

2.4 Cryptographic Assumptions

Once we compile the PHP through a polynomial commitment into a zkSNARK, the latter will achieve its security properties in the Algebraic Group Model of Fuchsbauer et al. [18]. In this model adversaries are restricted to be *algebraic*, namely, when an adversary $\mathcal{A}$ gets some group elements as input and outputs another group element, it can provide some algebraic representation of the latter in terms of the former.

Definition 15 (Algebraic Adversary). *Let $\mathbb{G}$ be a cyclic group of order p. We say that a PPT adversary $\mathcal{A}$ is algebraic if there exists an efficient extractor $\mathcal{E}_\mathcal{A}$ that, given the inputs $([x_1], \ldots, [x_m])$ of $\mathcal{A}$, outputs a representation $\mathbf{z} = (z_1, \ldots, z_m)^\top \in \mathbb{F}^m$, where $\mathbb{F}$ is the finite field of p elements, for every group element $[y]$ in the output of $\mathcal{A}$ such that:*

$$Adv_{\mathbb{G},\mathcal{A}}^{alg}(\lambda) = \left[\begin{array}{c} [y] \leftarrow \mathcal{A}([x_1], \ldots, [x_m]), \mathbf{z} \leftarrow \mathcal{E}_\mathcal{A}([y], [x_1], \ldots, [x_m]), \\ \text{and } [y] \neq \sum_{j=1}^{m} z_j [x_j] \end{array} \right] = \mathsf{negl}(\lambda).$$

The security of our final argument for R1CS-lite (after compilation) is proven in the algebraic group model under the following assumption:

Definition 16 (q-dlog Asymmetric Assumption). *The $q(\lambda)$-discrete logarithm assumption holds for $gk \leftarrow \mathcal{G}(1^\lambda)$ if for all PPT algorithm $\mathcal{A}$*

$$Adv_{gk,\mathcal{A}}^{q-dlog}(\lambda) = \mathsf{Pr}\left[x \leftarrow \mathcal{A}(gk, [x]_{1,2}, \ldots, [x^q]_{1,2}) \right] = \mathsf{negl}(\lambda).$$

3   Generalized Univariate Sumcheck

In this section, we revisit the sumcheck of Aurora [5]. As presented there, this argument allows to prove that the sum of the evaluations of a polynomial in some multiplicative[2] set $\mathbb{H}$ of a finite field $\mathbb{F}$ sum to 0. We generalize the argument to arbitrary sets $\mathbb{H} \subset \mathbb{F}$, solving an open problem posed there. Additionally, we give a simpler proof of the same result by connecting the sumcheck to polynomial evaluation and other basic properties of polynomials.

Given some finite field $\mathbb{F}$, let $\mathbb{H}$ be an arbitrary set of cardinal m, with some predefined canonical order, and h_i refers to the ith element in this order. The ith Lagrange basis polynomial associated to $\mathbb{H}$ is denoted by $\lambda_i(X)$. The vector $\boldsymbol{\lambda}(X)$ is defined as $\boldsymbol{\lambda}(X)^\top = (\lambda_1(X), \ldots, \lambda_m(X))$. The vanishing polynomial of $\mathbb{H}$ will be denoted by $t(X)$. When $\mathbb{H}$ is a multiplicative subgroup, the following properties are known to hold:

$$t(X) = X^m - 1, \qquad \lambda_i(X) = \frac{h_i}{m} \frac{(X^m - 1)}{(X - h_i)}, \qquad \lambda_i(0) = \frac{1}{m},$$

for any $i = 1, \ldots, m$. This representation makes their computation particularly efficient: both $t(X)$ and $\lambda_i(X)$ can be evaluated in $O(\log m)$ field operations.

We prove a generalized sumcheck theorem below, and derive the sumcheck of Aurora as a corollary for the special case where $\mathbb{H}$ is a multiplicative subgroup. The intuition is simple: let $P_1(X)$ be a polynomial of arbitrary degree in $\mathbb{F}[X]$, and $P_2(X) = \sum_{i=1}^{m} \lambda_i(X) P_1(h_i)$. Note that $P_1(X), P_2(X)$ are congruent modulo $t(X)$, and the degree of $P_2(X)$ is at most $m - 1$. Then, when $P_2(X)$ is evaluated at an arbitrary point $v \in \mathbb{F}$, $v \notin \mathbb{H}$, $P_2(v) = \sum_{i=1}^{m} \lambda_i(v) P_1(h_i)$. Thus, $P_2(v)$ is "almost" (except for the constants $\lambda_i(v)$) the sum of the evaluations of $P_1(h_i)$. Multiplying by a normalizing polynomial, we get rid of the constants and obtain a polynomial that evaluated at v is the sum of any set of evaluations of interest. The sum will be zero if this product polynomial has a root at v.

Theorem 1 (Generalized Sumcheck). *Let $\mathbb{H}$ be an arbitrary subset of some finite field $\mathbb{F}$ and $t(X)$ the vanishing polynomial at $\mathbb{H}$. For any $P(X) \in \mathbb{F}[X]$, $\mathcal{S} \subset \mathbb{H}$, and any $v \in \mathbb{F}, v \notin \mathbb{H}$, $\sum_{s \in \mathcal{S}} P(s) = \sigma$ if and only if there exist polynomials $H(X) \in \mathbb{F}[X]$, $R(X) \in \mathbb{F}_{\leq m-2}[X]$ such that*

$$P(X) N_{\mathcal{S},v}(X) - \sigma = (X - v) R(X) + t(X) H(X),$$

where $N_{\mathcal{S},v}(X) = \sum_{s \in \mathcal{S}} \lambda_s(v)^{-1} \lambda_s(X)$ and $\lambda_s(X)$ is the Lagrange polynomial associated to s and the set $\mathbb{H}$.

---

[2] In fact, the presentation is more general as they also consider additive cosets, but we stick to the multiplicative case which is the one that has been used in other constructions of zkSNARKs.

Proof. Observe that $P(X) = \sum_{h \in \mathbb{H}} P(h)\lambda_h(X) \mod t(X)$. Therefore,

$$
P(X)N_{\mathcal{S},v}(X) - \sigma = \left(\sum_{h \in \mathbb{H}} P(h)\lambda_h(X) \right) \left(\sum_{s \in \mathcal{S}} \lambda_s(v)^{-1}\lambda_s(X) \right) - \sigma
$$

$$
= \left(\sum_{s \in \mathcal{S}} P(s)\lambda_s(v)^{-1}\lambda_s(X) \right) - \sigma \mod t(X).
$$

Let $Q(X) = \left(\sum_{s \in \mathcal{S}} P(s)\lambda_s(v)^{-1}\lambda_s(X) \right) - \sigma$. Note that $Q(v) = \sum_{s \in \mathcal{S}} P(s) - \sigma$. Thus, $\sum_{s \in \mathcal{S}} P(s) = \sigma$ if and only if $Q(X)$ is divisible by $X - v$. The claim follows from this observation together with the fact that $Q(X)$ is the unique polynomial of degree $m - 1$ that is congruent with $P(X)N_{\mathcal{S},v}(X) - \sigma$. $\qquad\square$

Lemma 1. *If $\mathcal{S} = \mathbb{H}$ is a multiplicative subgroup of $\mathbb{F}$, $N_{\mathbb{H},0}(X) = m$.*

Proof. Recall that, as $\mathbb{H}$ is a multiplicative subgroup, $\lambda_i(0) = 1/m$ for all $i = 1, \ldots, m$. Therefore, $N_{\mathbb{H},0}(X) = \sum_{i=1}^{m} \lambda_i(0)^{-1}\lambda_i(X) = m \sum_{i=1}^{m} \lambda_i(X) = m$. $\qquad\square$

As a corollary of Lemma 1 and the Generalized Sumcheck, we recover the univariate sumcheck: if $\mathbb{H}$ is a multiplicative subgroup, $\sum_{h \in \mathbb{H}} P(h) = \sigma$ if and only if there exist polynomials $R(X), H(X)$ with $\deg(R(X)) \leq m - 2$ such that $P(X)m - \sigma = XR(X) + t(X)H(X)$.

3.1 Application to Linear Algebra Arguments

Several works [5,13,14] have observed that R1CS languages can be reduced to proving a Hadamard product relation and a linear relation, where the latter consists on showing that two vectors x, y are such that $y = \mathbf{M}x$, or equivalently, that the inner product of (y, x) with all the rows of $(\mathbf{I}, -\mathbf{M})$ is zero. When matrices and vectors are encoded as polynomials for succinctness, for constructing a PHP it is necessary to express these linear algebra operations as polynomial identities.

For the Hadamard product relation, the basic observation is that, for any polynomials $A(X), B(X), C(X)$, the equation

$$
A(X)B(X) - C(X) = H(X)t(X), \tag{1}
$$

holds for some $H(X)$ if and only if $(A(h_1), \ldots, A(h_m)) \circ (B(h_1), \ldots, B(h_m)) - (C(h_1), \ldots, C(h_m)) = 0$. In particular, $A(X) = a^\top \lambda(X)$, $B(X) = b^\top \lambda(X)$ encode vectors a, b, then $C(X) \mod t(X)$ encodes $a \circ b$. This Hadamard product argument is one of the main ideas behind the zkSNARK of Gentry et al. [22] and follow-up work.

For linear relations, the following Theorem explicitly derives a polynomial identity that encodes the inner product relation from the univariate sumcheck. This connection in a different formulation is implicit in previous works [5,13,14].

Theorem 2 (Inner Product Polynomial Relation). *For some $k \in \mathbb{N}$, let $\boldsymbol{y} = (\boldsymbol{y}_1, \ldots, \boldsymbol{y}_k)$, $\boldsymbol{y}_i = (y_{ij})$, $\boldsymbol{d} = (\boldsymbol{d}_1, \ldots, \boldsymbol{d}_k)$ be two vectors in $\mathbb{F}^{km}$, $\boldsymbol{y}_i, \boldsymbol{d}_i \in \mathbb{F}^m$, and $\mathbb{H}$ a multiplicative subgroup of $\mathbb{F}$ of order m. Then, $\boldsymbol{y} \cdot \boldsymbol{d} = 0$ if and only if there exist $H(X), R(X) \in \mathbb{F}[X]$, $R(X)$ of degree at most $m - 2$ such that the following relation holds:*

$$Y(X) \cdot D(X) = XR(X) + t(X)H(X), \tag{2}$$

where $\boldsymbol{Y}(X) = (Y_1(X), \ldots, Y_k(X))$ is a vector of polynomials of arbitrary degree such that $Y_i(\mathsf{h}_j) = y_{ij}$ for all $i = 1, \ldots, k$, $j = 1, \ldots, m$, and $\boldsymbol{D}(X) = (D_1(X), \ldots, D_k(X))$ is such that $D_i(X) = \boldsymbol{d}_i^\top \boldsymbol{\lambda}(X)$.

Proof. Since $Y_i(\mathsf{h}_j) = y_{ij}$, for all i, j, $Y_i(X) = \boldsymbol{y}_i^\top \boldsymbol{\lambda}(X) \bmod t(X)$. Therefore, $Y_i(X)D_i(X) = (\boldsymbol{y}_i^\top \boldsymbol{\lambda}(X))(\boldsymbol{d}_i^\top \boldsymbol{\lambda}(X)) \bmod t(X)$, and by the aforementioned properties of the Lagrange basis, this is also congruent modulo $t(X)$ to $(\boldsymbol{y}_i \circ \boldsymbol{d}_i)^\top \boldsymbol{\lambda}(X)$. Therefore,

$$Y(X) \cdot D(X) = \sum_{i=1}^{k} Y_i(X)D_i(X) = \sum_{i=1}^{k} (\boldsymbol{y}_i \circ \boldsymbol{d}_i)^\top \boldsymbol{\lambda}(X)$$

$$= \left(\sum_{i=1}^{k} (\boldsymbol{y}_i \circ \boldsymbol{d}_i)^\top \right) \boldsymbol{\lambda}(X) \bmod t(X).$$

By Theorem 1, $\left(\left(\sum_{i=1}^{k} (\boldsymbol{y}_i \circ \boldsymbol{d}_i)^\top \right) \boldsymbol{\lambda}(X) \right) N_{\mathbb{H},0}(X)$ is divisible by X if and only if the sum of the coordinates of $\sum_{i=1}^{k} (\boldsymbol{y}_i \circ \boldsymbol{d}_i)$ is 0. The implication is also true after dividing by $N_{\mathbb{H},0}(X) = m$. The jth coordinate of $\sum_{i=1}^{k} (\boldsymbol{y}_i \circ \boldsymbol{d}_i)$ is $\sum_{i=1}^{k} y_{ij}d_{ij}$, thus the sum of all coordinates is $\sum_{j=1}^{m} \sum_{i=1}^{k} y_{ij}d_{ij} = \boldsymbol{y} \cdot \boldsymbol{d}$, which concludes the proof. □

In the rest of the paper $\mathbb{H}$ will always be a multiplicative subgroup, both for simplicity (as $N_{\mathbb{H},0} = m$), and efficiency (due to the properties that Lagrange and vanishing polynomials associated to multiplicative subgroups have). However, Theorem 2 can be easily generalized to arbitrary sets $\mathbb{H}$ (just multiplying the left side of Eq. (2) by $N_{\mathbb{H},0}$).

4 Checkable Subspace Sampling: Definition and Implications

In a *Checkable Subspace Sampling* (CSS) argument prover and verifier interactively agree on a polynomial $D(X)$ representing a vector $\boldsymbol{d}$ in the row space of a matrix $\mathbf{M}$. The fiber of the protocol is that $D(X)$ is calculated as a linear combination of encoding of the rows of $\mathbf{M}$ with some coefficients determined by the verifier, but the verifier does not need to calculate $D(X)$ itself (this would require the verifier to do linear work in the number of rows of $\mathbf{M}$). Instead, the prover can calculate this polynomial and then convince the verifier that it has been correctly computed.

Below we give the syntactical definition of Checkable Subspace Sampling. Essentially, a CSS scheme is similar to a PHP for a relation R_M, except that the statement $(\mathsf{cns}, D(X))$ is decided interactively, and the verifier has only oracle access to the polynomial $D(X)$. A CSS scheme can be used as a building block in a PHP, and the result is also a PHP.

Definition 17 (Checkable Subspace Sampling, CSS). *A checkable subspace sampling argument over a field $\mathbb{F}$ defines some $Q, m \in \mathbb{N}$, a set of admissible matrices $\mathcal{M}$, a vector of polynomials $\boldsymbol{\beta}(X) \in (\mathbb{F}[X])^m$, a coinspace $\mathcal{C}$, a sampling function $\mathsf{Smp} : \mathcal{C} \to \mathbb{F}^Q$, and a relation:*

$$R_{\mathsf{CSS},\mathbb{F}} = \left\{ \begin{array}{c} (\mathbf{M}, \mathsf{cns}, D(X)) \ : \ \mathbf{M} \in \mathcal{M} \subset \mathbb{F}^{Q \times m}, D(X) \in \mathbb{F}[X], \mathsf{cns} \in \mathcal{C}, \\ \boldsymbol{s} = \mathsf{Smp}(\mathsf{cns}), \text{ and } D(X) = \boldsymbol{s}^\top \mathbf{M} \boldsymbol{\beta}(X) \end{array} \right\}.$$

For any $\mathbf{M} \in \mathcal{M}$, it also defines:

$$R_M = \left\{ (\mathsf{cns}, D(X)) \ : \ (\mathbf{M}, \mathsf{cns}, D(X)) \in R_{\mathsf{CSS},\mathbb{F}} \right\}.$$

It consists of three algorithms:

- *$\mathcal{I}_{\mathsf{CSS}}$ is the indexer: in an offline phase, on input $(\mathbb{F}, \mathbf{M})$ returns a set $\mathcal{W}_{\mathsf{CSS}}$ of $n(0)$ polynomials $\{p_{0,j}(X)\}_{j=1}^{n(0)} \in \mathbb{F}[X]$. This algorithm is run once for each $\mathbf{M}$.*
- *Prover and Verifier proceed as in a PHP, namely, the verifier sends field elements to the prover and has oracle access to the polynomials outputted by both the indexer and the prover; this phase is run in two different stages:*
  - *Sampling: $\mathcal{P}_{\mathsf{CSS}}$ and $\mathcal{V}_{\mathsf{CSS}}$ engage in an interactive protocol. In some round, the verifier sends $\mathsf{cns} \leftarrow \mathcal{C}$, and the prover replies with $D(X) = \boldsymbol{s}^\top \mathbf{M} \boldsymbol{\beta}(X)$, for $\boldsymbol{s} = \mathsf{Smp}(\mathsf{cns})$.*
  - *ProveSampling: $\mathcal{P}_{\mathsf{CSS}}$ and $\mathcal{V}_{\mathsf{CSS}}$ engage in another interactive protocol to prove that $(\mathsf{cns}, D(X)) \in R_M$.*
- *When the proving phase is concluded, the verifier outputs a bit indicating acceptance or rejection.*

The vector $\boldsymbol{\beta}(X) = (\beta_1(X), \ldots, \beta_m(X))$ defines an encoding of vectors as polynomials: vector $\boldsymbol{v}$ is mapped to the polynomial $\boldsymbol{v}^\top \boldsymbol{\beta}(X) = \sum_{i=1}^m v_i \beta_i(X)$. When using a CSS for constructing an argument of membership in linear spaces as in the next section, we choose a characterization of inner product that is compatible with Lagrange polynomials. Thus, in this work, $\beta_i(X)$ is defined as $\lambda_i(X)$, the ith Lagrange polynomial associated to some multiplicative subgroup $\mathbb{H}$ of $\mathbb{F}$. Still, it also makes sense to consider also CSS arguments for other polynomial encodings, e.g. the monomial basis or Laurent polynomials.

We require a CSS argument to satisfy the following security definitions:

Perfect Completeness. If both prover and verifier are honest the output of the protocol is 1:

$$\Pr\left[\langle\mathcal{P}_{\mathsf{CSS}}(\mathbb{F},\mathbf{M},\mathsf{cns}),\mathcal{V}_{\mathsf{CSS}}^{\mathcal{W}_{\mathsf{CSS}}}(\mathbb{F})\rangle=1\right]=1.$$

where the probability is taken over the random coins of prover and verifier.

Soundness. A checkable subspace sampling argument $(\mathcal{I}_{\mathsf{CSS}},\mathcal{P}_{\mathsf{CSS}},\mathcal{V}_{\mathsf{CSS}})$ is ϵ-sound if for all $\mathbf{M}$ and any polynomial time prover $\mathcal{P}_{\mathsf{CSS}}^*$:

$$\Pr\left[D^*(X)\neq s^\top\mathbf{M}\beta(X)\ \middle|\ \begin{array}{l}(\mathsf{cns},D^*(X))\leftarrow\mathsf{Sampling}\langle\mathcal{P}_{\mathsf{CSS}}^*(\mathbb{F},\mathbf{M},\mathsf{cns}),\mathcal{V}^{\mathcal{W}_{\mathsf{CSS}}}(\mathbb{F})\rangle;\\ s=\mathsf{Smp}(\mathsf{cns});\ \langle\mathcal{P}_{\mathsf{CSS}}^*(\mathbb{F},\mathbf{M},\mathsf{cns}),\mathcal{V}_{\mathsf{CSS}}^{\mathcal{W}_{\mathsf{CSS}}}(\mathbb{F})\rangle=1\end{array}\right]\leq\epsilon.$$

The soundness of the CSS argument will ensure that the vector is sampled as specified by the coins of the verifier so the prover cannot influence its distribution. For a CSS argument to be useful, we additionally need that distribution induced by the sampling function is sufficiently "good". This is a geometric property that can be captured in the Elusive Kernel property defined below.

Definition 18. *A CSS argument is ϵ-elusive kernel[3] if*

$$\max_{t\in\mathbb{F}^Q,t\neq0}Pr\left[s\cdot t=0\ \middle|\ s=\mathsf{Smp}(\mathsf{cns});\mathsf{cns}\leftarrow\mathcal{C}\right]\leq\epsilon.$$

In practice, for most schemes, s is a vector of monomials or Lagrange basis polynomials evaluated at some point $x=\mathsf{cns}$, and this property is an immediate application of Schwartz-Zippel lemma, so we will not explicitly prove it for most of our CSS arguments.

4.1   Linear Arguments from Checkable Subspace Sampling

In this section we build a PHP for the universal relation of membership in linear subspaces:

$$\mathcal{R}_{\mathsf{LA}}=\left\{(\mathbb{F},\mathbf{W},\boldsymbol{y}):\mathbf{W}\in\mathbb{F}^{Q\times km},\boldsymbol{y}\in\mathbb{F}^{km}\ \text{s.t.}\ \mathbf{W}\boldsymbol{y}=\mathbf{0}\right\},$$

using a CSS scheme as building block. That is, given a vector $\boldsymbol{y}$, the argument allows to prove membership in the linear space $\mathbf{W}^\perp=\{y\in\mathbb{F}^{km}:\mathbf{W}\boldsymbol{y}=\mathbf{0}\}$. Although relation $\mathcal{R}_{\mathsf{LA}}$ is polynomial-time decidable, it is not trivial to construct a polynomial holographic proof for it, as the verifier has only an encoding of $\mathbf{W}$ and $\boldsymbol{y}$.

A standard way to prove that some vector $\boldsymbol{y}$ is in $\mathbf{W}^\perp$ is to let the verifier sample a *sufficiently random* vector $\boldsymbol{d}$ in the row space of matrix $\mathbf{W}$, and prove $\boldsymbol{y}\cdot\boldsymbol{d}=0$. Naturally, the vector $\boldsymbol{y}$ must be declared before $\boldsymbol{d}$ is chosen. We follow this strategy to construct a PHP for $\mathcal{R}_{\mathsf{LA}}$, except that the vector $\boldsymbol{d}$ is sampled by the prover itself on input the coins of the verifier through a CSS argument.

As we have seen in Sect. 2.1, it is natural in our application to proving R1CS to consider matrices in blocks. Thus, in this section we prove membership in $\mathbf{W}^\perp$ where the matrix is written in k blocks of columns, that is, $\mathbf{W}=(\mathbf{W}_1,\dots,\mathbf{W}_k)$.

---

[3] The name is inspired by the property of t-elusiveness of [35].

The vectors $\boldsymbol{y}, \boldsymbol{d} \in \mathbb{F}^{km}$ are also written in blocks as $\boldsymbol{y}^\top = (\boldsymbol{y}_1^\top, \ldots, \boldsymbol{y}_k^\top)$ and $\boldsymbol{d}^\top = (\boldsymbol{d}_1^\top, \ldots, \boldsymbol{d}_k^\top)$.

Each block of $\mathbf{W}$, as well as the vectors $\boldsymbol{y}, \boldsymbol{d}$ can be naturally encoded, respectively, as a vector of polynomials or a single polynomial multiplying on the right by $\boldsymbol{\lambda}(X)$. However, we allow for additional flexibility in the encoding of $\boldsymbol{y}$: our argument is parameterized by a set of valid witnesses W_Y and a function $\mathcal{E}_Y : W_Y \rightarrow (\mathbb{F}[X])^k$ that determines how $\boldsymbol{y}$ is encoded as a polynomial. Thanks to this generalization we can use the argument as a black-box in our R1CS-lite construction. There, valid witnesses are of the form $(\boldsymbol{a}, \boldsymbol{b}, \boldsymbol{a} \circ \boldsymbol{b})$ and, for efficiency, its encoding will be $(A(X) = \boldsymbol{a}^\top \boldsymbol{\lambda}(X), B(X) = \boldsymbol{b}^\top \boldsymbol{\lambda}(X), A(X)B(X))$, which means that the last element does not need to be sent.

The argument goes as follows. The prover sends a vector of polynomials $\boldsymbol{Y}(X)$ encoding $\boldsymbol{y}$. The CSS argument is used to delegate to the prover the sampling of $\boldsymbol{d}_i^\top$, $i = 1, \ldots, k$ in the row space of $\mathbf{W}_i$. Then, the prover sends $\boldsymbol{D}(X)$ together with a proof that $\boldsymbol{y} \cdot \boldsymbol{d} = 0$. For this inner product argument to work, we resort to Theorem 2 that guarantees that, if $\mathcal{E}_Y$ is an encoding such that if $\mathcal{E}_Y(\boldsymbol{y}) = \boldsymbol{Y}(X)$, then $Y_i(\mathsf{h}_j) = y_{ij}$, the inner product relation holds if and only if the verification equation is satisfied for some $H_t(X), R_t(X)$.

Because of the soundness property of the CSS argument, the prover cannot influence the distribution of $\boldsymbol{d}$, which is sampled according to the verifier's coins. Therefore, if $\boldsymbol{Y}(X)$ passes the test of the verifier, $\boldsymbol{y}$ is orthogonal to $\boldsymbol{d}$. By the Elusive Kernel property of the CSS argument, $\boldsymbol{d}$ will be sufficiently random. As it is sampled after $\boldsymbol{y}$ is declared, this will imply that $\boldsymbol{y}$ is in $\mathbf{W}^\perp$.

Offline Phase: $\mathcal{I}_{\mathsf{LA}}(\mathbb{F}, \mathbf{W})$: For $i = 1, \ldots, k$, run the indexer $\mathcal{I}_{\mathsf{CSS}}$ on input $(\mathbb{F}, \mathbf{W}_i)$ to obtain the set $\mathcal{W}_{\mathsf{CSS}i}$ and output $\mathcal{W}_{\mathsf{LA}} = \bigcup_{i=1}^k \mathcal{W}_{\mathsf{CSS}i}$.

Online Phase: $\mathcal{P}_{\mathsf{LA}}$: On input a witness $\boldsymbol{y} \in W_Y \subset (\mathbb{F}^m)^k$, output $\boldsymbol{Y}(X) = \mathcal{E}_Y(\boldsymbol{y})$.

$\mathcal{P}_{\mathsf{LA}}$ and $\mathcal{V}_{\mathsf{LA}}$ run in parallel k instances of the CSS argument, with inputs $(\mathbb{F}, \mathbf{W}_i)$ and $\mathbb{F}$, respectively, and where the verifier is given oracle access to $\mathcal{W}_{\mathsf{CSS}i}$. The output is a set $\{(\mathsf{cns}, D_i(X))\}_{i=1}^k$, where cns are the same for all k instances. Define $\boldsymbol{D}(X) = (D_1(X), \ldots, D_k(X))$.

$\mathcal{P}_{\mathsf{LA}}$: Outputs $R_t(X) \in \mathbb{F}_{\leq m-2}[X], H_t(X)$ such that

$$\boldsymbol{Y}(X) \cdot \boldsymbol{D}(X) = X R_t(X) + t(X) H_t(X). \tag{3}$$

Decision Phase: Accept if and only if (1) $\deg(R_t) \leq m - 2$, (2) $\mathcal{V}_{\mathsf{CSS}}^i$ accepts $(\mathsf{cns}, D_i(X))$, and (3) the following equation holds:

$$\boldsymbol{Y}(X) \cdot \boldsymbol{D}(X) = X R_t(X) + t(X) H_t(X).$$

Fig. 1. Argument for proving membership in $\mathbf{W}^\perp$, parameterized by the polynomial encoding $\mathcal{E}_Y : W_Y \rightarrow \mathbb{F}[X]^k$, and the set $W_Y \subset \mathbb{F}^{km}$.

Theorem 3. *When instantiated using a CSS scheme with perfect completeness, and when the encoding $\mathcal{E}_Y : W_Y \to \mathbb{F}[X]^k$ satisfies that, if $\mathcal{E}_Y(\boldsymbol{y}) = \boldsymbol{Y}(X)$, then $Y_i(\mathsf{h}_j) = y_{ij}$, the PHP of Fig. 1 has perfect completeness.*

Proof. By definition, $\boldsymbol{D}(X) = (\boldsymbol{s}^\top \mathbf{W}_1 \boldsymbol{\lambda}(X), \dots, \boldsymbol{s}^\top \mathbf{W}_k \boldsymbol{\lambda}(X))$, for $\boldsymbol{s} = \mathsf{Samp(cns)}$. Note that this is because the k instances of the CSS scheme are run in parallel and the same coins are used to sample each of the $\boldsymbol{d}_i$. Thus, $\boldsymbol{D}(X)$ is the polynomial encoding of $\boldsymbol{d} = (\boldsymbol{s}^\top \mathbf{W}_1, \dots, \boldsymbol{s}^\top \mathbf{W}_k) = \boldsymbol{s}^\top \mathbf{W}$. Therefore, if $\boldsymbol{y}$ is in $\mathbf{W}^\perp$, $\boldsymbol{d} \cdot \boldsymbol{y} = \boldsymbol{s}^\top \mathbf{W} \boldsymbol{y} = 0$. By the characterization of inner product, as explained in Sect. 3, this implies that polynomials $H_t(X), R_t(X)$ satisfying the verification equation exist. $\qquad\square$

Theorem 4. *Let CSS be ϵ-sound and ϵ'-Elusive Kernel, and $\mathcal{E}_Y : W_Y \to \mathbb{F}[X]^k$ an encoding such that if $\mathcal{E}_Y(\boldsymbol{y}) = \boldsymbol{Y}(X)$, $Y_i(\mathsf{h}_j) = y_{ij}$. Then, for any polynomial time adversary $\mathcal{A}$ against the soundness of PHP of Fig. 1:*

$$\mathsf{Adv}(\mathcal{A}) \le \epsilon' + k\epsilon.$$

Further, the PHP satisfies 0-knowledge soundness.

Proof. Let $\boldsymbol{Y}^*(X) = (Y_1^*(X), \dots, Y_k^*(X))$ be the output of a cheating $\mathcal{P}_{\mathsf{LA}}^*$ and $\boldsymbol{y}^* = (\boldsymbol{y}_1^*, \dots, \boldsymbol{y}_k^*)$ the vector such that $Y_i^*(\mathsf{h}_j) = y_{ij}^*$. As a direct consequence of Theorem 2, $\boldsymbol{Y}^*(X) \cdot \boldsymbol{D}(X) = X R_t(X) + t(X) H_t(X)$ only if $\boldsymbol{y}^* \cdot \boldsymbol{d} = 0$, where $\boldsymbol{d}$ is the unique vector $\boldsymbol{d}$ such that $\boldsymbol{D}(X) = (\boldsymbol{d}_1^\top \boldsymbol{\lambda}(X), \dots, \boldsymbol{d}_k^\top \boldsymbol{\lambda}(X))$.

On the other hand, the soundness of the CSS scheme guarantees that, for each i, the result of sampling $D_i(X)$ corresponds to the sample coins sent by the verifier, except with probability ϵ. Thus, the chances that the prover can influence the distribution of $\boldsymbol{D}(X)$ so that so that $\boldsymbol{y}^* \cdot \boldsymbol{d} = 0$ are at most $k\epsilon$. Excluding this possibility, a cheating prover can try to craft $\boldsymbol{y}^*$ in the best possible way to maximize the chance that $\boldsymbol{y}^* \cdot \boldsymbol{d} = 0$. Since $\boldsymbol{d}^\top = \boldsymbol{s}^\top \mathbf{W}$, and in a successful attack $\boldsymbol{y}^* \notin \mathbf{W}^\perp$, we can see that this possibility is bounded by the probability:

$$\max_{\boldsymbol{y}^* \notin \mathbf{W}^\perp} \Pr\left[\boldsymbol{d} \cdot \boldsymbol{y}^* = 0 \;\middle|\; \begin{array}{l} \mathsf{cns} \leftarrow \mathcal{C}; \\ \boldsymbol{s} = \mathsf{Smp(cns)}; \\ \boldsymbol{d} = \boldsymbol{s}^\top \mathbf{W} \end{array} \right] = \max_{\boldsymbol{y}^* \notin \mathbf{W}^\perp} \Pr\left[\boldsymbol{s}^\top \mathbf{W} \boldsymbol{y}^* = 0 \;\middle|\; \begin{array}{l} \mathsf{cns} \leftarrow \mathcal{C}; \\ \boldsymbol{s} = \mathsf{Smp(cns)} \end{array} \right]$$

Since $\boldsymbol{s}^\top \mathbf{W} \boldsymbol{y}^* = \boldsymbol{s} \cdot (\mathbf{W} \boldsymbol{y}^*)$, and $\mathbf{W} \boldsymbol{y}^* \neq \boldsymbol{0}$, this can be bounded by ϵ', by the elusive kernel property of the CSS scheme.

For knowledge soundness, define the extractor $\mathcal{E}$ as the algorithm that runs the prover and, by evaluating $Y_i(X)$ in $\{\mathsf{h}_j\}_{j=1}^m$ for all $i \in [k]$, recovers $\boldsymbol{y}$. If the verifier accepts with probability greater than $\epsilon' + k\epsilon$, then $\boldsymbol{y}$ is such that $\mathbf{W} \boldsymbol{y} = \boldsymbol{0}$ with the same probability. $\qquad\square$

Extension to Other Polynomial Encodings. As mentioned, the construction is specific to the polynomial encoding defined by interpolation. However, the only place where this plays a role is in the check of equation (3). Now, if the polynomial encoding $\boldsymbol{\beta}(X)^\top$ associated to the CSS argument for $\mathbf{W}$ was set to be for instance the monomial basis, i.e. $\boldsymbol{\beta}(X)^\top = (1, X, \dots, X^{m-1})$, the argument can be easily modified to still work. It suffices to choose the "reverse" polynomial encoding for $\boldsymbol{y}$, that is define $\boldsymbol{Y}(X) = (\boldsymbol{y}_1^\top \tilde{\beta}(X), \ldots, \boldsymbol{y}_k^\top \tilde{\beta}(X))$, where $\tilde{\beta}(X)^\top = (X^{m-1}, \ldots, X, 1)$, and require the prover to find $R_t(X), H_t(X)$, with $R_t(X)$ of degree at most $m - 2$ such that:

$$\boldsymbol{Y}(X) \cdot \boldsymbol{D}(X) = R_t(X) + X^m H_t(X). \tag{3}$$

Indeed, observe that this check guarantees that $\boldsymbol{Y}(X) \cdot \boldsymbol{D}(X)$ does not have any term of degree exactly $m - 1$, and the term of degree $m - 1$ is exactly $\sum_{i=1}^k \boldsymbol{y}_i \cdot \boldsymbol{d}_i = \boldsymbol{y} \cdot \boldsymbol{d}$.

4.2 R1CS-lite from Linear Arguments

In this section we give a PHP for R1CS-lite by combining our linear argument with other well known techniques. In this section, $\mathbf{W}$ is the block matrix defined in Sect. 2.1.

Offline Phase: $\mathcal{I}_{\text{lite}}(\mathbf{W}, \mathbb{F})$ runs $\mathcal{I}_{\text{LA}}(\mathbf{W}, \mathbb{F})$ to obtain a list of polynomials $\mathcal{W}_{\text{LA}}$ and outputs $\mathcal{W}_{\text{lite}} = \mathcal{W}_{\text{LA}}$.

Online Phase: $\mathcal{P}_{\text{lite}}(\mathbb{F}, \mathbf{W}, \boldsymbol{x}, (\boldsymbol{a}', \boldsymbol{b}'))$ defines $\boldsymbol{a} = (1, \boldsymbol{x}, \boldsymbol{a}'), \boldsymbol{b} = (\mathbf{1}_l, \boldsymbol{b}')$, and computes

$$A'(X) = \left(\sum_{j=l+1}^m a_j \lambda_j(X) \right) / t_l(X), \; B'(X) = \left(\left(\sum_{j=1}^m b_j \lambda_j(X) \right) - 1 \right) / t_l(X),$$

for $t_l(X) = \prod_{i=1}^\ell (X - h_i)$. It outputs $(A'(X), B'(X))$.

$\mathcal{V}_{\text{lite}}$ and $\mathcal{P}_{\text{lite}}$ instantiate $\mathcal{V}_{\text{LA}}^{\mathcal{W}_{\text{LA}}}(\mathbb{F})$ and $\mathcal{P}_{\text{LA}}(\mathbb{F}, \mathbf{W}, (\boldsymbol{a}, \boldsymbol{b}, \boldsymbol{a} \circ \boldsymbol{b}))$. Let $\boldsymbol{Y}(X) = (A(X), B(X), A(X)B(X))$ be the polynomials outputted by $\mathcal{P}_{\text{LA}}$ in the first round.

Decision Phase: Define $C_l(X) = \lambda_1(X) + \sum_{j=1}^{l-1} x_j \lambda_{j+1}(X)$ and accept if and only if (1) $A(X) = A'(X)t_l(X) + C_l(X)$, (2) $B(X) = B'(X)t_l(X) + 1$, and (3) $\mathcal{V}_{\text{LA}}$ accepts.

Fig. 2. PHP for $\mathcal{R}'_{\text{R1CS-lite}}$ from PHP for $\mathcal{R}_{\text{LA}}$. The PHP for $\mathcal{R}_{\text{LA}}$ should be instantiated for $W_Y = \{(\boldsymbol{a}, \boldsymbol{b}, \boldsymbol{a} \circ \boldsymbol{b}) : \boldsymbol{a}, \boldsymbol{b} \in \mathbb{F}^m\}$, $\mathcal{E}(\boldsymbol{a}, \boldsymbol{b}, \boldsymbol{a} \circ \boldsymbol{b}) = (\boldsymbol{a}^\top \boldsymbol{\lambda}(X), \boldsymbol{b}^\top \boldsymbol{\lambda}(X), (\boldsymbol{a}^\top \boldsymbol{\lambda}(X))(\boldsymbol{b}^\top \boldsymbol{\lambda}(X)))$.

Theorem 5. *When instantiated with a complete, sound and knowledge sound linear argument, the PHP of Fig. 2 satisfies completeness, soundness and knowledge-soundness.*

Proof. Completeness follows directly from the definition of $A'(X), B'(X), A(X), B(X)$ and completeness of the linear argument. Soundness and knowledge soundness hold if the linear argument is sound as well, because $\mathcal{V}_{\text{lite}}$ accepts if $\mathcal{V}_{\text{LA}}$ accepts, meaning $\mathbf{W}(\boldsymbol{a}, \boldsymbol{b}, \boldsymbol{a} \circ \boldsymbol{b})^\top = 0$ and $\mathcal{R}'_{\text{R1CS-lite}}$ holds, and for extraction it suffices to use the extractor of the linear argument. $\square$

4.3 Adding Zero Knowledge

To achieve zero-knowledge, it is common to several works on pairing-based zkSNARKS [13,14,22] to randomize the polynomial commitment to the witness with a polynomial that is a multiple of the vanishing polynomial. That is, the commitment to a vector a is $A(X) = \sum a_i \lambda_i(X) + t(X)h(X)$, where $t(X), \lambda_i(X)$ are defined as usual, and the coefficients of $h(X)$ are the randomness. In [22], $h(X)$ can be constant, since the commitment $A(X)$ in the final argument is evaluated at a single point. In other works where the commitment needs to support queries at several point values, $h(X)$ needs to be of higher degree. In Marlin, it is suggested to choose the degree according to the number of oracle queries to maximimize efficiency, and in Lunar this idea is developed into a fine-grained analysis and a vector with query bounds is specified for the compiler. Additionally, for this technique, the prover needs to send a masking polynomial to randomize the polynomial $R(X)$ of the inner product check. The reason is that this polynomial leaks information about $(A(X), B(X), A(X)B(X)) \cdot D(X) \mod t(X)$.

In this section, we show how to add zero-knowledge to the PHP for R1CS-lite of Sect. 4.2 without sending additional polynomials. The approach is natural and a similar technique has also been used in [38]. Let $(b_A, b_B, b_{R_t}, b_{H_t})$ be the tuple of bounds on the number of polynomial evaluations seen by the verifier after compiling for the polynomials $A(X), B(X), R_t(X), H_t(X)$. To commit to a vector $y \in \mathbb{F}^m$, we sample some randomness $r \in \mathbb{F}^n$, where n is a function of $(b_A, b_B, b_{R_t}, b_{H_t})$ to be specified (a small constant when compiling). The cardinal of $\mathbb{H}$ is denoted by $\tilde{m}$ in this section. A commitment is defined in the usual way for the vector (y, r), i.e. $\sum_{i=1}^m y_i \lambda_i(X) + \sum_{i=m+1}^{m+n} r_i \lambda_i(X)$, and, naturally, we require $m + n \leq \tilde{m}$. Our idea is to consider related randomness for $A(X), B(X)$ so that the additional randomness sums to 0 and does not interfere with the inner product argument. The novel approach is to enforce this relation of the randomness by adding one additional constraint to $\mathbf{W}$. The marginal cost of this for the prover is minimal. Starting from the PHP of Fig. 2 we introduce the changes described in Fig. 3.

Offline Phase: For $\tilde{m} = m + n$, the matrix of constraints is:

$$\tilde{\mathbf{W}} = \begin{pmatrix} \mathbf{I}_m & \mathbf{0}_{m \times n} & \mathbf{0}_{m \times m} & \mathbf{0}_{m \times n} & -\mathbf{F} & \mathbf{0}_{m \times n} \\ \mathbf{0}_{m \times m} & \mathbf{0}_{m \times n} & \mathbf{I}_m & \mathbf{0}_{m \times n} & -\mathbf{G} & \mathbf{0}_{m \times n} \\ \mathbf{0}_m^\top & \mathbf{1}_n^\top & \mathbf{0}_m^\top & \mathbf{1}_n^\top & \mathbf{0}_m^\top & \mathbf{0}_n^\top \end{pmatrix}$$

Online Phase: $\mathcal{P}_{\text{lite}}$ samples $r_a \leftarrow \mathbb{F}^n, r_b \leftarrow \mathbb{F}^n$ conditioned on $\sum_{i=1}^n r_{a,i} + r_{b,i} = 0$ and uses $\tilde{a} := (1, x, a', r_a)$, $\tilde{b} := (1_l, b', r_b)$, to construct $\tilde{A}(X)$ and $\tilde{B}(X)$, $\tilde{A}'(X)$ and $\tilde{B}'(X)$ as before.

Fig. 3. Modification of the PHP for $\mathcal{R}'_{\text{R1CS-lite}}$ to achieve zero-knowledge. The omitted parts are identical.

Theorem 6. *With the modification described in Fig. 3 the PHP of Fig. 2 is perfectly complete, sound, knowledge-sound, perfect zero-knowledge and* $(b_A, b_B, b_{R_t}, b_{H_t})$-*bounded honest-verifier zero-knowledge if* $n \geq (b_A + b_B + b_{R_t} + b_{H_t} + 1)/2$, *and* $n \geq \max(b_A, b_B)$.

Proof. The only difference with the previous argument is the fact that the matrix of constraints has changed, which is now $\tilde{\mathbf{W}}$. For completeness, observe that the additional constraint makes sure that $\sum_{i=1}^{n} r_{a,i} + r_{b,i} = 0$, and an honest prover chooses the randomness such that this holds. On the other hand, the sumcheck theorem together with this equation guarantee that the randomness does not affect the divisibility at 0 of $(\tilde{A}(X), \tilde{B}(X), \tilde{A}(X)\tilde{B}(X)) \cdot D(X) \mod t(X)$.

For soundness, note that $\tilde{\mathbf{W}} (\tilde{\boldsymbol{a}}^\top, \tilde{\boldsymbol{b}}^\top, (\tilde{\boldsymbol{a}} \circ \tilde{\boldsymbol{b}})^\top)$, is equivalent to 1) $\boldsymbol{a} = \mathbf{F}(\boldsymbol{a} \circ \boldsymbol{b})$, 2) $\boldsymbol{b} = \mathbf{G}(\boldsymbol{a} \circ \boldsymbol{b})$, and 3) $\sum_{i=1}^{n} r_{a,i} + r_{b,i} = 0$, for $\boldsymbol{a} := (1, \boldsymbol{x}, \boldsymbol{a}')$ $\boldsymbol{b} := (\mathbf{1}_l, \boldsymbol{b}')$. This is because the first two blocks of constraints have 0s in the columns corresponding to $\boldsymbol{r}_a, \boldsymbol{r}_b$, and the other way around for the last constraint. Therefore, by the soundness of the linear argument $\sum_{i=1}^{n} r_{a,i} + r_{b,i} = 0$, and the randomness does not affect divisibility at 0 of $(A(X), B(X), A(X)B(X))^\top \cdot D(X) \mod t(X)$, so the same reasoning used for the argument of Fig. 2 applies.

Perfect zero-knowledge of the PHP is immediate, as all the messages in the CSS procedure contain only public information and the rest of the information exchanged are oracle polynomials.

We now prove honest-verifier bounded zero-knowledge. The simulator is similar to [13] (Th. 4.7), but generalized to the distribution of $D(X)$ induced by the underlying CSS scheme. The simulator gets access to the random tape of the honest verifier and receives x and the coins of the CSS scheme, as well as a list of its checks. It creates honestly all the polynomials of the CSS argument, since these are independent of the witness.

For an oracle query at point γ, the simulator samples uniform random values $A'_\gamma, B'_\gamma, R_{\gamma,t}$ in $\mathbb{F}$ and declares them, respectively, as $A'(\gamma), B'(\gamma), R_t(\gamma)$. It then defines the rest of the values to be consistent with them. More precisely, let $D(X)^\top = \boldsymbol{s}^\top \mathbf{W} \boldsymbol{\lambda}(X) = (D_a(X), D_b(X), D_{ab}(X))$ be the output of the CSS argument, which the simulator can compute with the CSS coins. Then, the simulator sets:

$$A_\gamma = A'_\gamma t_l(\gamma) + \sum_{i=1}^{l} x_i \lambda_i(\gamma), \qquad\qquad B_\gamma = B'_\gamma t_l(\gamma) + 1,$$

$$p_\gamma = D_a(\gamma)A_\gamma + D_b(\gamma)B_\gamma + D_{ab}(\gamma)A_\gamma B_\gamma \qquad H_{t\gamma} = (p_\gamma - \gamma R_{t,\gamma})/t(\gamma),$$

where Q_γ for $Q \in \{A', B', R_t, H_t\}$ is declared as $Q(\gamma)$. The simulator keeps a table of the computed values to answer consistently the oracle queries.

We now argue that the queries have the same distribution as the evaluations of the prover's polynomials if all the queries γ are in $\mathbb{F}\backslash\mathbb{H}$. Since the verifier is honest, and $|\mathbb{H}|$ is assumed to be a negligible fraction of the field elements, we can always assume this is the case. In this case, the polynomial encoding of $\boldsymbol{r}_a, \boldsymbol{r}_b$ acts as a masking polynomial for $A'(X), B'(X), R_t(X), H_t(X)$ and taking into account that $\sum_{i=1}^{n} r_{a,i} + r_{b,i} = 0$ to have the same distribution it is sufficient that $2n - 1 \geq \mathsf{b}_A + \mathsf{b}_B + \mathsf{b}_{R_t} + \mathsf{b}_{H_t}$, and $n \geq \max(\mathsf{b}_A + \mathsf{b}_B)$, as stated in the theorem. Therefore, bounded zero-knowledge is proven.   □

4.4 Combining CSS Schemes

Since a CSS scheme outputs a linear combination of the rows of a matrix $\mathbf{M}$, different instances of a CSS scheme can be easily combined with linear operations. More precisely, given a matrix $\mathbf{M}$ that can be written as $\begin{pmatrix} \mathbf{M}_1 \\ \mathbf{M}_2 \end{pmatrix}$, we can use a different CSS arguments for each $\mathbf{M}_i$.[4] Since all current constructions of CSS arguments have limitations in terms of the types of matrices they apply to, this opens the door to decomposing the matrix of constraints into different blocks that admit efficient CSS arguments. For instance, matrices with a few very dense constraints (i.e. with very few rows with a lot of non-zero entries) and otherwise sparse could be split to use the scheme for sparse matrices of Sect. 3 for one part, and the trivial approach (where one polynomial for each row is computed by the indexer, and the verifier can sample the polynomial $D(X)$ computing the linear combination itself) for the rest. That is, one reason to divide the matrix $\mathbf{M}$ into blocks is to have a broader class of admissible matrices. Another reason is efficiency, since if a block that is either $\mathbf{0}$ or the identity matrix, the verifier can open the polynomial $D(X)$ itself, saving on the number of polynomials that need to be sent. More specifically, for our final construction, we will often split a matrix into two blocks of m rows, $\mathbf{M} = \begin{pmatrix} \mathbf{M}_1 \\ \mathbf{M}_2 \end{pmatrix}$, use the same CSS argument for each matrix with the same coins, and combine them to save on communication. More precisely, if $\boldsymbol{s} = \mathsf{Smp}(\mathsf{cns})$, and $D_1(X) = \boldsymbol{s}^\top \mathbf{M}_1 \boldsymbol{\lambda}(X)$ and $D_2(X) = \boldsymbol{s}^\top \mathbf{M}_2 \boldsymbol{\lambda}(X)$ are the polynomials associated to $\mathbf{M}_1, \mathbf{M}_2$, we will modify the CSS argument so that it sends $D_1(X) + zD_2(X)$ for some challenge z chosen by the verifier, instead of $D_1(X)$ and $D_2(X)$ individually. Note that $D_1(X) + zD_2(X) = (\boldsymbol{s}^\top, z\boldsymbol{s}^\top)\mathbf{M}\boldsymbol{\lambda}(X)$, that is, this corresponds to a CSS argument where the sampling coefficients depend on z also.

This cannot be done generically, it depends on the underlying CSS argument and the type of admissible matrices. Intuitively, this modification corresponds to implicitly constructing a CSS argument for the matrix $\mathbf{M}_1 + z\mathbf{M}_2$, so it is necessary that: a) the polynomials computed by the indexer of the CSS argument for $\mathbf{M}_1, \mathbf{M}_2$ can be combined, upon receiving the challenge z, to the CSS indexer polynomials of $\mathbf{M}_1 + z\mathbf{M}_2$, and b) that $\mathbf{M}_1 + z\mathbf{M}_2$ is an admissible matrix for this CSS argument. For instance, if $\mathbf{M}_1, \mathbf{M}_2$ has K non-zero entries each, and the admissible matrices of a CSS instance must have at most K non-zero entries, then $\mathbf{M}_1 + z\mathbf{M}_2$ is not generally an admissible matrix. We will be using this optimization for our final PHP for sparse matrices, and we will see there that these conditions are met in this case.

---

[4] The naive approach would run both CSS arguments in parallel, but savings might be possible batching the proofs.

5 Constructions of Checkable Subspace Sampling Arguments

Given the results of the previous sections, for our R1CS-lite argument it is sufficient to design a CSS argument for matrices $\mathbf{M} \in \mathbb{F}^{m \times m}$ and then use it on all the blocks of $\mathbf{W}$. In this section, we give several novel CSS arguments for different types of square matrices.

We consider two disjoint sets of roots of unity, $\mathbb{H}, \mathbb{K}$ of degree m and K, respectively. For $\mathbb{H}$ we use the notation defined in Sect. 3. The elements of $\mathbb{K}$ are assumed to have some canonical order, and we use k_ℓ for the ℓth element in $\mathbb{K}$, $\mu_\ell(X)$ for the ℓth Lagrangian interpolation polynomial associated to $\mathbb{K}$, and $u(X)$ for the vanishing polynomial.

Matrices $\mathbf{M} \in \mathbb{F}^{m \times m}$ can be naturally encoded as a bivariate polynomial as $P(X, Y) = \boldsymbol{\alpha}(Y)^\top \mathbf{M} \boldsymbol{\beta}(X)$, for some $\boldsymbol{\alpha}(Y) \in \mathbb{F}[Y]^m, \boldsymbol{\beta}(X) \in \mathbb{F}[X]^m$. Let $\boldsymbol{m}_i^\top$ be the ith row of $\mathbf{M}$, and $P_i(X) = \boldsymbol{m}_i^\top \boldsymbol{\beta}(X)$. Then,

$$P(X, x) = \boldsymbol{\alpha}(x)^\top \mathbf{M} \boldsymbol{\beta}(X) = \sum_{i=1}^{m} \alpha_i(x) P_i(X).$$

That is, the polynomial $P(X, x)$ is a linear combination of the polynomials associated to the rows of $\mathbf{M}$ via the encoding defined by $\boldsymbol{\beta}(X)$, with coefficients $\alpha_i(x)$. This suggests to define a CSS scheme where, in the sampling phase, the verifier sends the challenge x and the prover replies with $D(X) = P(X, x)$, and, in the proving phase, the prover convinces the verifier that $D(X)$ is correctly sampled from coins x. This approach appears, implicitly or explicitly, in Sonic and most follow-up work we are aware of.

In Sonic, $\boldsymbol{\alpha}(Y), \boldsymbol{\beta}(X)$ are vectors of Laurent polynomials. In Marlin, Lunar and in this work, we set $\boldsymbol{\alpha}(Y) = \boldsymbol{\lambda}(Y)$, and $\boldsymbol{\beta}(X) = \boldsymbol{\lambda}(X)$. The choice of $\boldsymbol{\beta}(X)$ is to make the encoding compatible with the inner product defined by the sumcheck, and the choice of $\boldsymbol{\alpha}(Y)$ is necessary for the techniques used in the proving phase of the CSS scheme that will be detailed in this Section.

For the proving phase, the common strategy is to follow the general template introduced in Sonic: the verifier samples a challenge $y \in \mathbb{F}$, checks that $D(y)$ is equal to a value σ sent by the prover, and that $\sigma = P(y, x)$ (through what is called a signature of correct computation, as in [36]). This proves that $D(X) = P(X, x)$. The last one is the challenging step, and is in fact, the main technical novelty of each of the mentioned previous works. In all of them, this is achieved by restricting the sets of matrices $\mathbf{M}$ to have a special structure: in Sonic they need to be sums of permutation matrices, and in Marlin, as later also Lunar, arbitrary matrices with at most K non-zero entries.

This section is organized as follows. We start by giving an overview of our new techniques in Sect. 5.1. In Sect. 5.2, we explain our basic CSS scheme, that works only for matrices with at most one non-zero element per column. In Sect. 5.3, we see how to compose these checks to achieve a CSS argument for arbitrary sparse matrices $\mathbf{M}$. In Sect. 5.4, we give an extension of the basic construction that can be used to generalize the CSS argument from basic matrices to sums of basic matrices without increasing the communication complexity. In the full version we explain how this can be used to extend the CSS argument for sparse matrices to matrices that are sums of sparse matrices without increasing the communication complexity.

5.1   Overview of New Techniques

Our main result of this section is a CSS scheme for any matrix $\mathbf{M} = (m_{i,j}) \in \mathbb{F}^{m \times m}$ of at most K non-zero entries. Assuming the non-zero entries are ordered, this matrix can be represented, as proposed in Marlin, by three functions $\mathsf{v} : \mathbb{K} \to \mathbb{F}$, $\mathsf{r} : \mathbb{K} \to [m]$, $\mathsf{c} : \mathbb{K} \to [m]$ such that $P(X, Y) = \sum_{\ell=1}^{K} \mathsf{v}(\mathsf{k}_\ell) \lambda_{\mathsf{r}(\mathsf{k}_\ell)}(Y) \lambda_{\mathsf{c}(\mathsf{k}_\ell)}(X)$, where the ℓth non-zero entry is $\mathsf{v}(\mathsf{k}_\ell) = m_{\mathsf{r}(\mathsf{k}_\ell), \mathsf{c}(\mathsf{k}_\ell)}$. If the matrix has less than K non-zero entries $\mathsf{v}(\mathsf{k}_\ell) = 0$, for $\ell = |\mathbf{M}| + 1, \ldots, K$, and $\mathsf{r}(\mathsf{k}_\ell), \mathsf{c}(\mathsf{k}_\ell)$ are defined arbitrarily. We borrow this representation but design our own CSS scheme by following a "linearization strategy".

To see that $P(y, x)$ is correctly evaluated, we observe that it can be written as:

$$P(y, x) = \big(\lambda_{\mathsf{r}(\mathsf{k}_1)}(x), \ldots, \lambda_{\mathsf{r}(\mathsf{k}_K)}(x)\big) \cdot \big(\mathsf{v}(\mathsf{k}_1) \lambda_{\mathsf{c}(\mathsf{k}_1)}(y), \ldots, \mathsf{v}(\mathsf{k}_K) \lambda_{\mathsf{c}(\mathsf{k}_K)}(y)\big).$$

We define low degree extensions of each of these vectors respectively as:

$$e_x(X) = \sum_{\ell=1}^{K} \lambda_{\mathsf{r}(\mathsf{k}_\ell)}(x) \mu_\ell(X), \qquad e_y(X) = \sum_{\ell=1}^{K} \mathsf{v}(\mathsf{k}_\ell) \lambda_{\mathsf{c}(\mathsf{k}_\ell)}(y) \mu_\ell(X).$$

If the prover can convince the verifier that $e_x(X), e_y(X)$ are correctly computed, then it can show that $P(y, x) = \sigma$ by using the inner product argument to prove that the sum of $e_x(X) e_y(X) \bmod t(X)$ at $\mathbb{K}$ is σ.

Observe that $e_x(X) = \boldsymbol{\lambda}(x)^\top \mathbf{M}_x \boldsymbol{\mu}(X)$, $e_y(X) = \boldsymbol{\lambda}(y)^\top \mathbf{M}_y \boldsymbol{\mu}(X)$, for some matrices $\mathbf{M}_x, \mathbf{M}_y$ with at most one non-zero element per column. To prove they are correctly computed it suffices to design a CSS argument for these simple matrices. This can be done in a much simpler way than in Marlin (and as in Lunar, that uses a similar technique), who prove directly that a low degree extension of $e_x(X) e_y(X)$ is correctly computed (intuitively, theirs is a quadratic check that requires the indexer to publish more information, as verifiers can only do linear operations in the polynomials output by it). Still, our technique is similar to theirs: given an arbitrary polynomial $e_x(X) = \sum_{\ell=1}^{K} \mathsf{v}(\mathsf{k}_\ell) \lambda_{\mathsf{f}(\mathsf{k}_\ell)}(x) \mu_\ell(X)$, for some function $\mathsf{f} : \mathbb{K} \to [m]$, we can "complete" the Lagrange $\lambda_{\mathsf{f}(\mathsf{k}_\ell)}(x)$ with the missing term $(x - \mathsf{h}_{\mathsf{f}(\mathsf{k}_\ell)})$ to get the vanishing polynomial $t(x)$. The key insight is that the low degree extension of these "completing terms" is $x - v_1(X)$, where $v_1(X) = \sum_{\ell=1}^{K} \mathsf{h}_{\mathsf{f}(\mathsf{k}_\ell)} \mu_\ell(X)$ can be computed by the indexer.

The encoding for sparse matrices requires K to be at least $|\mathbf{M}|$, and generating a field with this large multiplicative subgroup can be a problem. In the full version, we consider a generalization to matrices $\mathbf{M}$ of a special form with sparsity KV, for any $V \in \mathbb{N}$. The interesting point is that communication complexity does not grow with V, and only the number of indexer polynomials grows (as

$2V + 2$). This generalization is constructed from the argument for sums of basic matrices presented in Sect. 5.4.

We stress the importance of the linearization step: it not only allows for a simple explanation of underlying techniques for the proving phase, but also for generalizations such as the one in Sect. 5.4.

5.2 CSS Argument for Simple Matrices

Our basic building block is a CSS argument for matrices $\mathbf{M} = (m_{ij}) \in \mathbb{F}^{m \times K}$ with at most one non-zero value in each column, in particular, $|\mathbf{M}| \leq K$. We define two functions associated to $\mathbf{M}$, $\mathsf{v} : \mathbb{K} \to \mathbb{F}$, $\mathsf{f} : \mathbb{K} \to [m]$. Given an element $\mathsf{k}_\ell \in \mathbb{K}$, $\mathsf{v}(\mathsf{k}_\ell) = m_{\mathsf{f}(\mathsf{k}_\ell),\ell} \neq 0$, i.e., function v outputs the only non zero value of column ℓ and f the corresponding row; if such a value does not exist set $\mathsf{v}(\mathsf{k}_\ell) = 0$ and $\mathsf{f}(\mathsf{k}_\ell)$ arbitrarily. We define the polynomial $P(X,Y)$ such that $D(X) = P(X,x)$ as $P(X,Y) = \boldsymbol{\lambda}(Y)^\top \mathbf{M} \boldsymbol{\mu}(X)$. Observe that, by definition of v and f, $P(X,Y) = \sum_{\ell=1}^{K} \mathsf{v}(\mathsf{k}_\ell) \lambda_{\mathsf{f}(\mathsf{k}_\ell)}(Y) \mu_\ell(X)$.

Offline Phase: $\mathcal{I}_{\mathsf{CSS}}(\mathbb{F}, \mathbf{M})$ outputs $\mathcal{W}_{\mathsf{CSS}} = \{v_1(X), v_2(X)\}$, where

$$v_1(X) = \sum_{\ell=1}^{K} \mathsf{h}_{\mathsf{f}(\mathsf{k}_\ell)} \mu_\ell(X), \qquad v_2(X) = m^{-1} \sum_{\ell=1}^{K} \mathsf{v}(\mathsf{k}_\ell) \mathsf{h}_{\mathsf{f}(\mathsf{k}_\ell)} \mu_\ell(X).$$

Online Phase: **Sampling:** $\mathcal{V}_{\mathsf{CSS}}$ outputs $x \leftarrow \mathbb{F}$ and $\mathcal{P}_{\mathsf{CSS}}$ sends $D(X) = P(X,x)$. **ProveSampling:** $\mathcal{P}_{\mathsf{CSS}}$ finds and outputs $H_u(X)$ such that

$$D(X)(x - v_1(X)) = t(x)v_2(X) + H_u(X)u(X)$$

Decision Phase: Accept if and only if (1) $\deg D(X) \leq K - 1$, and (2) $D(X)(x - v_1(X)) = t(x)v_2(X) + H_u(X)u(X)$.

Fig. 4. A simple CSS scheme for matrices with at most one non-zero element per column.

Theorem 7. *The argument of Fig. 4 satisfies completeness and perfect soundness.*

Proof. When evaluated in any $\mathsf{k}_\ell \in \mathbb{K}$, the right side of the verification equation is $t(x)v_2(\mathsf{k}_\ell) = t(x)\mathsf{v}(\mathsf{k}_\ell)\mathsf{h}_{\mathsf{f}(\mathsf{k}_\ell)}m^{-1}$. Completeness follows from the fact that the left side is:

$$D(\mathsf{k}_\ell)(x - v_1(\mathsf{k}_\ell)) = \big(\mathsf{v}(\mathsf{k}_\ell)\lambda_{\mathsf{f}(\mathsf{k}_\ell)}(x)\big)\big(x - \mathsf{h}_{\mathsf{f}(\mathsf{k}_\ell)}\big) = t(x)\mathsf{v}(\mathsf{k}_\ell)m^{-1}\mathsf{h}_{\mathsf{f}(\mathsf{k}_\ell)}.$$

For soundness, note that the degree of $D(X)$ is at most $K - 1$ and that the left side of the verification is $D(\mathsf{k}_\ell)(x - v_1(\mathsf{k}_\ell))$, so $D(\mathsf{k}_\ell) = t(x)\mathsf{v}(\mathsf{k}_\ell)m^{-1}\mathsf{h}_{\mathsf{f}(\mathsf{k}_\ell)}(x - \mathsf{h}_{\mathsf{f}(\mathsf{k}_\ell)})^{-1} = \mathsf{v}(\mathsf{k}_\ell)\lambda_{\mathsf{f}(\mathsf{k}_\ell)}$, for all $\mathsf{k}_\ell \in \mathbb{K}$. Thus, $D(X) = \sum_{\ell=1}^{K} \mathsf{v}(\mathsf{k}_\ell)\lambda_{\mathsf{f}(\mathsf{k}_\ell)}\mu_\ell(X)$. $\square$

5.3 CSS Argument for Sparse Matrices

In this section, we present a CSS argument for matrices $\mathbf{M}$ that are sparse without any restriction on the non-zero entries per column. We assume a set of roots of unity $\mathbb{K}$ such that $|\mathbf{M}| \leq K$ and define $P(X,Y) = \sum_{\ell=1}^{K} \mathsf{v}(\mathsf{k}_\ell)\lambda_{\mathsf{r}(\mathsf{k}_\ell)}(Y)\lambda_{\mathsf{c}(\mathsf{k}_\ell)}(X)$. As explained in the overview, $P(y,x)$ can be written as the inner product of two vectors that depend only on x and y, and the low degree extensions of these vectors, $e_x(X), e_y(X)$, are nothing but the encodings of new matrices $\mathbf{M}_x$ and $\mathbf{M}_y$ in $\mathbb{F}^{m \times K}$ that have at most one non-zero element per column, so the basic CSS of Sect. 5.2 can be used to prove correctness.

Theorem 8. *The argument of Fig. 5 satisfies completeness and $(2K+1)/|\mathbb{F}|$-soundness.*

Proof. Completeness follows immediately and thus we only prove soundness. Although it does so in a batched form, the prover is showing that the following equations are satisfied,

$$e_x(X)(x - v_\mathsf{r}(X)) = t(x)m^{-1}v_\mathsf{r}(X) + H_{u,x}(X)u(X)$$

$$e_y(X)(y - v_{1,\mathsf{c}}(X)) = t(y)v_{2,\mathsf{c}}(X) + H_{u,y}(X)u(X)$$

$$Ke_x(X)e_y(X) - \sigma = XR_u(X) + u(X)H_{u,x,y}(X),$$

Now, since all the left terms of the equations are defined before the verifier sends z, by the Schwartz-Zippel lemma, with all but probability $3/|\mathbb{F}|$, the verifier accepts if and only such $H_{u,x}(X), H_{u,y}(X), H_{u,x,y}(X), R_u(X)$ exist.

Assuming they do, the rest of the proof is a consequence of (1) soundness of the protocol in Fig. 4, which implies that $e_x(X), e_y(X)$ correspond to the correct polynomials modulo $u(X)$, and (2) Lemma 2 (see below) shows that if the last equation is satisfied, and $e_x(X), e_y(X)$ coincide with the honest polynomials modulo $u(X)$, then $\sigma = P(y,x)$. Because the prover sends $D(X)$ before receiving y and $D(y) = \sigma$, from the Schwartz-Zippel lemma we have that, except with negligible probability, $P(X,x) = D(X)$ and the argument is sound. □

Lemma 2. *Given $e_x(X), e_y(X)$ such that $e_x(X) = \sum_{\ell=1}^{K} \lambda_{\mathsf{r}(\mathsf{k}_\ell)}(x)\mu_\ell(X)$ and $e_y(X) = \sum_{\ell=1}^{K} \mathsf{v}(\mathsf{k}_\ell)\lambda_{\mathsf{c}(\mathsf{k}_\ell)}(y)\mu_\ell(X)$, $P(y,x) = \sum_{\ell=1}^{K} \mathsf{v}(\mathsf{k}_\ell)\lambda_{\mathsf{c}(\mathsf{k}_\ell)}(y)\lambda_{\mathsf{r}(\mathsf{k}_\ell)}(x) = \sigma$ if and only if there exist polynomials $R_u(X) \in \mathbb{F}_{\leq m-2}[X], H_{u,x,y}(X)$ such that:*

$$e_x(X)e_y(X) - \sigma/K = XR_u(X) + H_{u,x,y}(X)u(X).$$

Proof. Note that $e_x(X)e_y(X) = \sum_{\ell=1}^{K} \mathsf{v}(\mathsf{k}_\ell)\lambda_{\mathsf{c}(\mathsf{k}_\ell)}(y)\lambda_{\mathsf{r}(\mathsf{k}_\ell)}(x)\mu_\ell(X) \mod u(X)$. By the univariate sumcheck (Lemma 1), $e_x(X)e_y(X) - \sigma/K$ is divisible by X if and only if $P(y,x) = \sigma$, which concludes the proof. □

Offline Phase: $\mathcal{I}_{\text{CSS}}$ outputs $\mathcal{W}_{\text{CSS}} = \left(v_r(X), v_{1,c}(X), v_{2,c}(X)\right)$, where:

$$v_r(X) = \sum_{\ell=1}^{K} \mathsf{h}_{\mathsf{r}(\mathsf{k}_\ell)}\mu_\ell(X),$$

$$v_{1,c}(X) = \sum_{\ell=1}^{K} \mathsf{h}_{\mathsf{c}(\mathsf{k}_\ell)}\mu_\ell(X), \qquad v_{2,c}(X) = m^{-1}\sum_{\ell=1}^{K} \mathsf{v}(\mathsf{k}_\ell)\mathsf{h}_{\mathsf{c}(\mathsf{k}_\ell)}\mu_\ell(X).$$

Online Phase: Sampling: $\mathcal{V}_{\text{CSS}}$ sends $x \leftarrow \mathbb{F}$, and $\mathcal{P}$ outputs $D(X) = P(X,x)$, for $P(X,Y) = \sum_{\ell=1}^{K} \mathsf{v}(\mathsf{k}_\ell)\lambda_{\mathsf{r}(\mathsf{k}_\ell)}(Y)\lambda_{\mathsf{c}(\mathsf{k}_\ell)}(X)$.

ProveSampling: $\mathcal{V}_{\text{CSS}}$ sends $y \leftarrow \mathbb{F}$ and $\mathcal{P}_{\text{CSS}}$ outputs $\sigma = D(y)$ and $e_x(X), e_y(X)$, where $e_x(X) = \sum_{\ell=1}^{K} \lambda_{\mathsf{r}(\mathsf{k}_\ell)}(x)\mu_\ell(X)$, $e_y(X) = \sum_{\ell=1}^{K} \mathsf{v}(\mathsf{k}_\ell)\lambda_{\mathsf{c}(\mathsf{k}_\ell)}(y)\mu_\ell(X)$, $\mathcal{V}_{\text{CSS}}$ sends $z \leftarrow \mathbb{F}$ and $\mathcal{P}_{\text{CSS}}$ computes $H_{u,x}(X), H_{u,y}(X), R_u(X), H_{u,x,y}(X)$ such that:

$$e_x(X)(x - v_r(X)) = m^{-1}t(x)v_r(X) + H_{u,x}(X)u(X)$$

$$e_y(X)(y - v_{1,c}(X)) = t(y)v_{2,c}(X) + H_{u,y}(X)u(X)$$

$$Ke_x(X)e_y(X) - \sigma = XR_u(X) + u(X)H_{u,x,y}(X),$$

It also defines $H_u(X) = H_{u,x,y}(X) + zH_{u,x}(X) + z^2H_{u,y}(X)$, and outputs $\left(R_u(X), H_u(X)\right)$.

Decision Phase: Accept if and only if (1) $\deg(R_u) \leq K - 2$, (2) $D(y) = \sigma$, and (3) for $i_x(X) = (x - v_r(X))$, $i_y(X) = (y - v_{1,c}(X))$

$$(e_x(X) + z^2 i_y(X))(e_y(X) + zi_x(X)) - z^3 i_x(X)i_y(X)$$
$$- z^2 t(y)v_{2,c}(X) - \sigma/K - zt(x)m^{-1}v_r(X) = XR_u(X) + H_u(X)u(X).$$

Fig. 5. CSS argument for $\mathbf{M}$, with $\mathbb{K}$ such that $|\mathbf{M}| \leq |\mathbb{K}|$.

5.4   CSS Argument for Sums of Basic Matrices

In this section, we use $\mathbf{M}$ for a matrix in $\mathbb{F}^{m \times K}$ that can be written as $\sum_{i=1}^{V} \mathbf{M}_i$, with each $\mathbf{M}_i$ having at most one non-zero element in each column. We define two functions associated to each $\mathbf{M}_i$, $\mathsf{v}_i : \mathbb{K} \to \mathbb{F}$, $\mathsf{f}_i : \mathbb{K} \to [m]$ as in Sect. 5.2. This type of matrices will be used to design a generalization of the CSS argument for sums of sparse matrices in the full version.

Define $P(X,Y) = \lambda(Y)^{\top}\mathbf{M}\mu(X)$, and $D(X) = P(X,x)$. Observe that $P(X,Y) = \sum_{i=1}^{V}\sum_{\ell=1}^{K} \mathsf{v}_i(\mathsf{k}_\ell)\lambda_{\mathsf{f}_i(\mathsf{k}_\ell)}(Y)\mu_\ell(X)$. Let $S_\ell = \{\mathsf{f}_i(\mathsf{k}_\ell) : i \in [V]\}$, and $S_\ell^c = [K] - S_\ell$. The intuition is that, since there are at most V non zero $\mathsf{v}_i(\mathsf{k}_\ell)$ for each ℓ, we can factor as:

$$P(\mathsf{k}_\ell, x) = \sum_{i=1}^{V} \mathsf{v}_i(\mathsf{k}_\ell)\lambda_{\mathsf{f}_i(\mathsf{k}_\ell)}(x) = \prod_{s \in S_\ell^c}(x - \mathsf{h}_s)R_\ell(x),$$

where $R_\ell(X)$ is a polynomial of degree V. So, to "complete" $P(\mathsf{k}_\ell, x)$ to be a multiple of $t(x)$, we need to multiply it by $\prod_{s \in S_\ell}(x - \mathsf{h}_s)$, and the result will be

$t(x)R_\ell(x)$. The trick is that $\hat{I}_\ell(Y) = \prod_{s\in S_\ell}(Y - h_s)$, and $R_\ell(X)$ are polynomials of degrees V, $V-1$, respectively. Thus, if the indexer publishes the coefficients of these polynomials in the monomial basis, they can be reconstructed by the verifier with coefficients $1, x, \ldots, x^V$.

Offline Phase: $\mathcal{I}_{\mathsf{CSS}}(\mathbb{F}, \mathbf{M})$: Define the polynomials $\hat{R}_\ell(Y), \hat{I}_\ell(Y)$, and its coefficients $\hat{R}_{\ell j}, \hat{I}_{\ell j}$:

$$\hat{R}_\ell(Y) = \frac{1}{m} \sum_{i=1}^{V} v_i(k_\ell) h_{f_i(k_\ell)} \prod_{s\in S_\ell - \{f_i(k_\ell)\}} (Y - h_s) = \sum_{j=0}^{V-1} \hat{R}_{\ell j} Y^j,$$

$$\hat{I}_\ell(Y) = \prod_{s\in S_\ell} (Y - h_s) = \sum_{j=0}^{V} \hat{I}_{\ell j} Y^j.$$

Define

$$v_j^{\hat{R}}(X) = \sum_{\ell=1}^{K} \hat{R}_{\ell j} \mu_\ell(X), \qquad v_j^{\hat{I}}(X) = \sum_{\ell=1}^{K} \hat{I}_{\ell j} \mu_\ell(X).$$

Output $\mathcal{W}_{\mathsf{CSS}} = \left\{ \{v_j^{\hat{I}}(X)\}_{j=0}^{V}, \{v_j^{\hat{R}}(X)\}_{j=0}^{V-1} \right\}$.

Online Phase: Sampling: $\mathcal{V}_{\mathsf{CSS}}$ outputs $x \leftarrow \mathbb{F}$ and $\mathcal{P}_{\mathsf{CSS}}$ computes $D(X) = P(X, x)$.

ProveSampling: $\mathcal{P}_{\mathsf{CSS}}$ finds and outputs $H_u(X)$ such that, if $\hat{R}_x(X) = \sum_{j=0}^{V-1} x^j v_j^{\hat{R}}(X)$, and $\hat{I}_x(X) = \sum_{j=0}^{V} x^j v_j^{\hat{I}}(X)$,

$$D(X)\hat{I}_x(X) = t(x)\hat{R}_x(X) + H_u(X)u(X).$$

Decision Phase: Accept if and only if (1) $\deg(D) \le K-1$, and (2) $D(X)\hat{I}_x(X) = t(x)\hat{R}_x(X) + H_u(X)u(X)$.

Fig. 6. A CSS scheme for matrices with at most V non-zero elements per column.

Theorem 9. *The argument of Fig. 6 satisfies completeness and perfect soundness.*

Proof. When evaluated in any $k_\ell \in \mathbb{K}$, the right side of the verification equation is:

$$t(x)\hat{R}_x(x) = \frac{t(x)}{m} \sum_{i=1}^{V} v_i(k_\ell) h_{f_i(k_\ell)} \prod_{s\in S_\ell - \{f_i(k_\ell)\}} (x - h_s)$$

$$= \sum_{i=1}^{V} v_i(k_\ell) \frac{h_{f_i(k_\ell)}}{m} \frac{t(x)}{x - h_{f_i(k_\ell)}} \prod_{s\in S_\ell} (x - h_s) = \prod_{s\in S_\ell} (x - h_s) \sum_{i=1}^{V} v_i(k_\ell) \lambda_{f_i(k_\ell)}(x).$$

The left side of the equation is $D(k_\ell)\hat{I}_x(k_\ell) = \left(\sum_{i=1}^{V} v_i(k_\ell)\lambda_{f_i(k_\ell)}(x) \right)$ $\left(\prod_{s\in S_\ell}(x - h_s) \right)$, so completeness is immediate. For soundness, if the verifier accepts $D(X)$, then $D(k_\ell)\hat{I}_x(k_\ell) = t(x)\hat{R}_x(k_\ell)$ and $\hat{I}_x(k_\ell) = \hat{I}_\ell(x)$, therefore:

$$D(k_\ell) = \hat{I}_\ell(x)^{-1}t(x)\hat{R}_\ell(x) = \big(\prod_{s\in S_\ell^c} (x - h_s)\big)\hat{R}_x(x) = \sum_{i=1}^{V} v_i(k_\ell)\lambda_{f_i(k_\ell)}(x).$$

We conclude that $D(X) = P(X,x) \mod u(X)$. Since both have degree at most $K - 1$, soundness is proven. □

6   A zkSNARK for R1CS-lite

The PHP for R1CS-lite can be compiled to a (zk)SNARK for this relation via standard techniques. Formally, since we have used the model of PHPs, this follows from Theorem 6.1 in [13]. Concretely, when using for compilation the polynomial commitment presented in Marlin (the variant secure in the AGM) and our PHP for R1CS-lite, the theorem states that it is sufficient to prove that the PHP is honest-verifier bounded zero-knowledge, where the bound for each oracle polynomial is the number of oracle queries plus one.

The universal SRS of the zkSNARK will be $\mathsf{srs_u} = \big(\{[\tau^i]_1\}_{i=1}^{\rho}, [\tau]_2\big)$, and the derived one $\mathsf{srs_w}$ consists of the evaluation in x of the polynomials that $\mathcal{I}_{\mathsf{CSS}}$ outputs. Prover and Verifier instantiate $\mathcal{P}_{\mathsf{lite}}$ and $\mathcal{V}_{\mathsf{lite}}$ (for the PHP of Fig. 2 that achieves zero-knowledge through the changes presented in Fig. 3), and all oracle polynomials output by $\mathcal{P}_{\mathsf{lite}}$ are translated into polynomials evaluated (in the source group) at τ. For all degree checks with $\deg(p) < \mathsf{dg}$, $\mathsf{dg} < \rho$, the prover sends a single extra polynomial and field element, while checks for $\mathsf{dg} \geq \rho$ are for free. For each polynomial equation, prover sends extra field elements corresponding to evaluations (or openings) of some of the polynomials involved on it (maximum one per quadratic term, due to the procedure stated in [20] attributed to M. Maller). There are several ways to do this compilation check, but to optimize efficiency the choices are quite standard (for instance, only $A'(X)$ or $B'(X)$, should be opened). All the openings at one point as well as the degrees of the opened polynomials can be proven with one group element and verified with one pairing. Prover's work includes running $\mathcal{P}_{\mathsf{lite}}$ as well as the computation of the polynomial commitment opening procedures. Verifier work is also $\mathcal{V}_{\mathsf{lite}}$ plus the (batched) verification procedure of the polynomial commitments. The vector of queries is $(\mathsf{b}_A, \mathsf{b}_B, \mathsf{b}_{R_t}, \mathsf{b}_{H_t}) = (1, 0, 1, 0)$.

On the other hand, we write the matrix $\mathbf{W}$ that expresses the constraints as:

$$\mathbf{W} = \begin{pmatrix} \mathbf{I}_m & \mathbf{0}_{m\times n} & \mathbf{0}_{m\times m} & \mathbf{0}_{m\times n} & -\mathbf{F} & \mathbf{0}_{m\times n} \\ \mathbf{0}_{m\times m} & \mathbf{0}_{m\times n} & \mathbf{I}_m & \mathbf{0}_{m\times n} & -\mathbf{G} & \mathbf{0}_{m\times n} \\ \mathbf{0}_m^\top & \mathbf{1}_n^\top & \mathbf{0}_m^\top & \mathbf{1}_n^\top & \mathbf{0}_{m\times m}^\top & \mathbf{0}_{m\times n}^\top \end{pmatrix} = \begin{pmatrix} \mathbf{I}' & \mathbf{0} & \mathbf{F}' \\ \mathbf{0} & \mathbf{I}' & \mathbf{G}' \\ w & w & \mathbf{0} \end{pmatrix},$$

where $\mathbf{I}', \mathbf{F}', \mathbf{G}'$ are of size $m \times (m + n)$, w is a row vector of length $m + n$.

Our PHP is built generically for any CSS scheme, but concrete efficiency depends on the specifics of the latter and also how the blocks of rows of $\mathbf{W}$ are combined into it. The last constraint will always be treated separately (to exploit the symmetry of the other blocks), and because of its simple form, the verifier can compute the corresponding $D(X) = (\sum_{i=m+1}^{m+n} \lambda_i(x), \sum_{i=m+1}^{m+n} \lambda_i(x), 0)$ itself, and combine it with the rest by adding (see Sect. 4.4). Below we discuss concrete costs of each of the CSS arguments for the other two blocks.

For the sparse matrice construction of Fig. 5, we assume that $K \geq 2m$, which sets $\rho = K - 1$. This eliminates the degree checks for $e_x(X), e_y(X), R_u(X)$. Assuming $K \geq |\mathbf{F}| + |\mathbf{G}|$, the indexer is run for a matrix $\mathbf{F} + Z\mathbf{G}$, where Z is a variable and thus outputs one polynomial $v_r(X)$, one polynomial $v_{1,c}(X)$ but two polynomials $v_{2,c}^F(X), v_{2,c}^G(X)$ that will let the verifier construct $v_{2,c}(X) = v_{2,c}^F(X) + z v_{2,c}^G(X)$ after choosing challenge z. For $\mathbf{I}'$ it is not necessary to run a CSS argument, as for this block the corresponding polynomial $\mathbf{D}(X)$ is $D_{\mathbf{I}'}(X) = \sum_{i=1}^{m} \lambda_i(x)\lambda_i(X)$ and thus $D_{\mathbf{I}'}(y)$ can be calculated by the verifier in $\log m$ time as $(xt(y) - yt(x))/(x - y) - \sum_{i=m+1}^{m+n} \lambda_i(x)\lambda_i(y)$.

References

1. Abdolmaleki, B., Baghery, K., Lipmaa, H., Zajac, M.: A subversion-resistant SNARK. In: Takagi, T., Peyrin, T. (eds.) ASIACRYPT 2017, Part III. LNCS, vol. 10626, pp. 3–33. Springer, Cham (2017). https://doi.org/10.1007/978-3-319-70700-6_1

2. Ames, S., Hazay, C., Ishai, Y., Venkitasubramaniam, M.: Ligero: lightweight sublinear arguments without a trusted setup. In: Thuraisingham, B.M., Evans, D., Malkin, T., Xu, D. (eds) ACM CCS 2017, Dallas, TX, USA, 31 October–2 November 2017, pp. 2087–2104. ACM Press (2017)

3. Ben-Sasson, E., Bentov, I., Horesh, Y., Riabzev, M.: Scalable, transparent, and post-quantum secure computational integrity. Cryptology ePrint Archive, Report 2018/046 (2018). https://eprint.iacr.org/2018/046

4. Ben-Sasson, E., Bentov, I., Horesh, Y., Riabzev, M.: Scalable zero knowledge with no trusted setup. In: Boldyreva, A., Micciancio, D. (eds.) CRYPTO 2019, Part III. LNCS, vol. 11694, pp. 701–732. Springer, Cham (2019). https://doi.org/10.1007/978-3-030-26954-8_23

5. Ben-Sasson, E., Chiesa, A., Riabzev, M., Spooner, N., Virza, M., Ward, N.P.: Aurora: transparent succinct arguments for R1CS. In: Ishai, Y., Rijmen, V. (eds.) EUROCRYPT 2019, Part I. LNCS, vol. 11476, pp. 103–128. Springer, Cham (2019). https://doi.org/10.1007/978-3-030-17653-2_4

6. Ben-Sasson, E., Chiesa, A., Spooner, N.: Interactive Oracle Proofs. In: Hirt, M., Smith, A. (eds.) TCC 2016-B, Part II. LNCS, vol. 9986, pp. 31–60. Springer, Heidelberg (2016). https://doi.org/10.1007/978-3-662-53644-5_2

7. Blum, M., Feldman, P., Micali, S.: Non-interactive zero-knowledge and its applications (extended abstract). In: 20th ACM STOC, Chicago, IL, USA, 2–4 May 1988, pp. 103–112. ACM Press (19888)

8. Bootle, J., Cerulli, A., Chaidos, P., Groth, J., Petit, C.: Efficient zero-knowledge arguments for arithmetic circuits in the discrete log setting. In: Fischlin, M., Coron, J.-S. (eds.) EUROCRYPT 2016, Part II. LNCS, vol. 9666, pp. 327–357. Springer, Heidelberg (2016). https://doi.org/10.1007/978-3-662-49896-5_12

9. Bowe, S., Gabizon, A., Green, M.D.: A multi-party protocol for constructing the public parameters of the Pinocchio zk-SNARK. In: Zohar, A., Eyal, I., Teague, V., Clark, J., Bracciali, A., Pintore, F., Sala, M. (eds.) FC 2018. LNCS, vol. 10958, pp. 64–77. Springer, Heidelberg (2019). https://doi.org/10.1007/978-3-662-58820-8_5

10. Bowe, S., Gabizon, A., Miers, I.: Scalable multi-party computation for zk-SNARK parameters in the random beacon model. Cryptology ePrint Archive, Report 2017/1050 (2017). http://eprint.iacr.org/2017/1050
11. Bünz, B., Bootle, J., Boneh, D., Poelstra, A., Wuille, P., Maxwell, G.: Bulletproofs: short proofs for confidential transactions and more. In: 2018 IEEE Symposium on Security and Privacy, San Francisco, CA, USA, 21–23 May 2018, pp. 315–334. IEEE Computer Society Press (2018)
12. Bünz, B., Fisch, B., Szepieniec, A.: Transparent SNARKs from DARK compilers. In: Canteaut, A., Ishai, Y. (eds.) EUROCRYPT 2020, Part I. LNCS, vol. 12105, pp. 677–706. Springer, Cham (2020). https://doi.org/10.1007/978-3-030-45721-1_24
13. Campanelli, M., Faonio, A., Fiore, D., Querol, A., Rodríguez, H.: Lunar: a toolbox for more efficient universal and updatable zkSNARKs and commit-and-prove extensions. Cryptology ePrint Archive, Report 2020/1069 (2020). https://eprint.iacr.org/2020/1069
14. Chiesa, A., Hu, Y., Maller, M., Mishra, P., Vesely, N., Ward, N.: Marlin: preprocessing zkSNARKs with universal and updatable SRS. In: Canteaut, A., Ishai, Y. (eds.) EUROCRYPT 2020, Part I. LNCS, vol. 12105, pp. 738–768. Springer, Cham (2020). https://doi.org/10.1007/978-3-030-45721-1_26
15. Chiesa, A., Ojha, D., Spooner, N.: FRACTAL: Post-quantum and Transparent Recursive Proofs from Holography. In: Canteaut, A., Ishai, Y. (eds.) EUROCRYPT 2020, Part I. LNCS, vol. 12105, pp. 769–793. Springer, Cham (2020). https://doi.org/10.1007/978-3-030-45721-1_27
16. Daza, V., Ràfols, C., Zacharakis, A.: Updateable inner product argument with logarithmic verifier and applications. In: Kiayias, A., Kohlweiss, M., Wallden, P., Zikas, V. (eds.) PKC 2020, Part I. LNCS, vol. 12110, pp. 527–557. Springer, Cham (2020). https://doi.org/10.1007/978-3-030-45374-9_18
17. Fuchsbauer, G.: Subversion-zero-knowledge SNARKs. In: Abdalla, M., Dahab, R. (eds.) PKC 2018, Part I. LNCS, vol. 10769, pp. 315–347. Springer, Cham (2018). https://doi.org/10.1007/978-3-319-76578-5_11
18. Fuchsbauer, G., Kiltz, E., Loss, J.: The algebraic group model and its applications. In: Shacham, H., Boldyreva, A. (eds.) CRYPTO 2018, Part II. LNCS, vol. 10992, pp. 33–62. Springer, Cham (2018). https://doi.org/10.1007/978-3-319-96881-0_2
19. Gabizon, A.: AuroraLight: improved prover efficiency and SRS size in a sonic-like system. Cryptology ePrint Archive, Report 2019/601 (2019). https://eprint.iacr.org/2019/601
20. Gabizon, A., Williamson, Z.J., Ciobotaru, O.: PLONK: permutations over lagrange-bases for oecumenical noninteractive arguments of knowledge. Cryptology ePrint Archive, Report 2019/953 (2019). https://eprint.iacr.org/2019/953
21. Garg, S., Mahmoody, M., Masny, D., Meckler, I.: On the round complexity of OT extension. In: Shacham, H., Boldyreva, A. (eds.) CRYPTO 2018, Part III. LNCS, vol. 10993, pp. 545–574. Springer, Cham (2018). https://doi.org/10.1007/978-3-319-96878-0_19
22. Gennaro, R., Gentry, C., Parno, B., Raykova, M.: Quadratic span programs and succinct NIZKs without PCPs. In: Johansson, T., Nguyen, P.Q. (eds.) EUROCRYPT 2013. LNCS, vol. 7881, pp. 626–645. Springer, Heidelberg (2013). https://doi.org/10.1007/978-3-642-38348-9_37
23. Goldwasser, S., Micali, S., Rackoff, C.: The knowledge complexity of interactive proofs. SIAM J. Comput. 18(1), 186–208 (1989)
24. Groth, J.: Linear algebra with sub-linear zero-knowledge arguments. In: Halevi, S. (ed.) CRYPTO 2009. LNCS, vol. 5677, pp. 192–208. Springer, Heidelberg (2009). https://doi.org/10.1007/978-3-642-03356-8_12

25. Groth, J.: Short pairing-based non-interactive zero-knowledge arguments. In: Abe, M. (ed.) ASIACRYPT 2010. LNCS, vol. 6477, pp. 321–340. Springer, Heidelberg (2010). https://doi.org/10.1007/978-3-642-17373-8_19

26. Groth, J.: On the size of pairing-based non-interactive arguments. In: Fischlin, M., Coron, J.-S. (eds.) EUROCRYPT 2016, Part II. LNCS, vol. 9666, pp. 305–326. Springer, Heidelberg (2016). https://doi.org/10.1007/978-3-662-49896-5_11

27. Groth, J., Kohlweiss, M., Maller, M., Meiklejohn, S., Miers, I.: Updatable and universal common reference strings with applications to zk-SNARKs. In: Shacham, H., Boldyreva, A. (eds.) CRYPTO 2018, Part III. LNCS, vol. 10993, pp. 698–728. Springer, Cham (2018). https://doi.org/10.1007/978-3-319-96878-0_24

28. Ishai, Y.: Zero-knowledge proofs from information theoretic proof systems. In Zkproofs Blog (2020). https://zkproof.org/2020/08/12/information-theoretic-proof-systems/

29. Jutla, C.S., Roy, A.: Shorter Quasi-adaptive NIZK proofs for linear subspaces. In: Sako, K., Sarkar, P. (eds.) ASIACRYPT 2013, Part I. LNCS, vol. 8269, pp. 1–20. Springer, Heidelberg (2013). https://doi.org/10.1007/978-3-642-42033-7_1

30. Kate, A., Zaverucha, G.M., Goldberg, I.: Constant-size commitments to polynomials and their applications. In: Abe, M. (ed.) ASIACRYPT 2010. LNCS, vol. 6477, pp. 177–194. Springer, Heidelberg (2010). https://doi.org/10.1007/978-3-642-17373-8_11

31. Kattis, A., Panarin, K., Vlasov, A.: RedShift: transparent SNARKs from list polynomial commitment IOPs. Cryptology ePrint Archive, Report 2019/1400 (2019). https://eprint.iacr.org/2019/1400

32. Kilian, J.: A note on efficient zero-knowledge proofs and arguments (extended abstract). In: 24th ACM STOC, Victoria, BC, Canada, 4–6 May 1992, pp. 723–732. ACM Press (1992)

33. Maller, M., Bowe, S., Kohlweiss, M., Meiklejohn, S.: Sonic: zero-knowledge SNARKs from linear-size universal and updatable structured reference strings. In: Cavallaro, L., Kinder, J., Wang, X., Katz, J. (eds.) ACM CCS 2019, 11–15 November 2019, pp. 2111–2128. ACM Press (2019)

34. Micali, S.: The knowledge complexity of interactive proofs. SIAM J. Comput. **30**(4), 1253–1298 (2000)

35. Morillo, P., Ràfols, C., Villar, J.L.: The Kernel matrix Diffie-Hellman assumption. In: Cheon, J.H., Takagi, T. (eds.) ASIACRYPT 2016, Part I. LNCS, vol. 10031, pp. 729–758. Springer, Heidelberg (2016). https://doi.org/10.1007/978-3-662-53887-6_27

36. Papamanthou, C., Shi, E., Tamassia, R.: Signatures of correct computation. In: Sahai, A. (ed.) TCC 2013. LNCS, vol. 7785, pp. 222–242. Springer, Heidelberg (2013). https://doi.org/10.1007/978-3-642-36594-2_13

37. Setty, S.: Spartan: efficient and general-Purpose zkSNARKs without trusted setup. In: Micciancio, D., Ristenpart, T. (eds.) CRYPTO 2020, Part III. LNCS, vol. 12172, pp. 704–737. Springer, Cham (2020). https://doi.org/10.1007/978-3-030-56877-1_25

38. Szepieniec, A., Zhang, Y.: Polynomial IOPs for linear algebra relations. Cryptology ePrint Archive, Report 2020/1022 (2020). https://eprint.iacr.org/2020/1022

39. Wahby, R.S., Tzialla, I., Shelat, A., Thaler, J., Walfish, M.: Doubly-efficient zkSNARKs without trusted setup. In: 2018 IEEE Symposium on Security and Privacy, San Francisco, CA, USA, 21–23 May 2018, pp 926–943. IEEE Computer Society Press (2018)

40. Xie, T., Zhang, J., Zhang, Y., Papamanthou, C., Song, D.: Libra: succinct zero-knowledge proofs with optimal prover computation. In: Boldyreva, A., Micciancio, D. (eds.) CRYPTO 2019. LNCS, vol. 11694, pp. 733–764. Springer, Cham (2019). https://doi.org/10.1007/978-3-030-26954-8_24

Author Index

Aaronson, Scott 526
Alagic, Gorjan 497
Alon, Bar 436
Ananth, Prabhanjan 346
Au, Man Ho 251

Bartusek, James 406, 467
Beyne, Tim 41
Boneh, Dan 649
Bootle, Jonathan 742
Brakerski, Zvika 497
Bünz, Benedikt 681
Burdges, Jeffrey 157

Chatterjee, Rohit 282
Chia, Nai-Hui 315
Chiesa, Alessandro 681, 711, 742
Chung, Hao 436
Chung, Kai-Min 315, 346, 436
Coladangelo, Andrea 406, 467, 556

Ding, Jintai 70
Ding, Zhimin 251
Drake, Justin 649
Dulek, Yfke 497

Esgin, Muhammed F. 251

Fisch, Ben 649

Gabizon, Ariel 649
Garg, Sanjam 282
Garillot, François 127

Hajiabadi, Mohammad 282
Hosoyamada, Akinori 585, 616
Huang, Mi-Ying 436

Iwata, Tetsu 585

Khurana, Dakshita 282, 406, 467
Kılınç Alper, Handan 157
Kondi, Yashvanth 127

Lee, Yi 436
Liang, Xiao 282

Lin, William 681
Liu, Jiahui 526, 556
Liu, Joseph K. 251
Liu, Qipeng 526, 556
Liu, Yanyi 11

Ma, Fermi 406, 467
Malavolta, Giulio 282
Mishra, Pratyush 681
Mohassel, Payman 127

Nick, Jonas 189
Nikolaenko, Valeria 127

Pandey, Omkant 282
Pass, Rafael 11
Petzoldt, Albrecht 70
Placa, Rolando L. La 346

Ràfols, Carla 774
Rosulek, Mike 94
Rotem, Lior 222
Roy, Lawrence 94
Ruffing, Tim 189

Sasaki, Yu 616
Schaffner, Christian 497
Segev, Gil 222
Seurin, Yannick 189
Shen, Yu-Ching 436
Shiehian, Sina 282
Shmueli, Omri 375
Sotiraki, Katerina 742
Spooner, Nicholas 681

Tao, Chengdong 70
Teague, Vanessa 3

Yamakawa, Takashi 315
Yogev, Eylon 711
Yuen, Tsz Hon 251

Zapico, Arantxa 774
Zhandry, Mark 526, 556
Zhang, Ruizhe 526